DATE DUE

HANDBOOK OF MODERN FINANCE

Editor

DENNIS E. LOGUE

The Amos Tuck School of Business Administration
Dartmouth College

WARREN, GORHAM & LAMONT
Boston • New York

Contributing Authors

Robert Z. Aliber
Professor of International Economics and Finance, Graduate School of Business, The University of Chicago
(Chapter 36)

W. Scott Bauman
Chairman, Finance Department, Northern Illinois University
(Chapter 16)

Stephen A. Berkowitz
Senior Manager, Price Waterhouse
(Chapter 26)

Lloyd Besant
Vice-President, Director of Chicago Board of Trade Education Foundation, Chicago Board of Trade
(Chapter 12)

Colin D. Campbell
Professor of Economics, Dartmouth College
(Chapter 2)

Peter Campisi
Executive Vice-President and Chief Operating Officer, General Foods Credit Corporation
(Chapter 30)

E. Eugene Carter
Professor of Finance, Graduate School of Business Administration, University of Illinois at Chicago
(Chapter 37)

Robert Case
Associate, Morgan Stanley
(Chapter 29)

E. Michael Caulfield
Senior Vice-President, Mellon Bank
(Chapter 32)

T. Daniel Coggin
Vice-President, Manager of Investment Systems Department, Centerre Trust Company of St. Louis
(Chapter 14)

Thomas E. Copeland
Associate Professor of Finance, Graduate School of Management,
University of California, Los Angeles
(Chapter 10)

Mark R. Eaker
Associate Professor of Finance, The University of North Carolina at
Chapel Hill
(Chapter 42)

V. R. Errunza
Associate Professor of Finance and International Business,
McGill University
(Chapter 39)

Donald E. Fischer, CFA
Professor of Finance, Graduate School of Business Administration,
University of Connecticut
(Chapter 9)

Michael A. Goldberg
Economist, Board of Governors, Federal Reserve System
(Chapter 13)

Diana R. Harrington
Associate Professor of Business Administration, Colgate Darden
School, University of Virginia
(Chapter 25)

George H. Hempel
Professor of Finance, Cox School of Business, Southern Methodist
University
(Chapter 3)

Roger G. Ibbotson
Senior Lecturer in Finance and Executive Director of the Center
for Research in Security Prices, Graduate School of Business,
The University of Chicago
(Chapter 18)

Michael M. Janson
Vice-President, Salomon Brothers, Inc.
(Chapter 27)

Alan G. Jirkovsky
Vice-President, Continental Illinois National Bank
(Chapter 5)

Andrew J. Kalotay
Vice-President, Salomon Brothers, Inc.
(Chapter 27)

Donald R. Kendall, Jr.
President, Kendall & Co., Inc.
(Chapter 28)

David S. Kidwell
Blunt National Bank Professor of Finance, University of Tennessee
(Chapter 8)

Timothy W. Koch
Continental National Bank Professor of Bank Management,
Texas Tech University
(Chapter 8)

Jaroslaw Komarynsky
Professor of Finance, Northern Illinois University
(Chapter 16)

Dennis E. Logue
Professor of Business Administration, The Amos Tuck School of
Business Administration, Dartmouth College
(Chapters 27 and 34)

Richard W. McEnally
Meade H. Willis Senior Professor of Investment Banking,
The University of North Carolina at Chapel Hill
(Chapter 7)

A. James Meigs
Senior Vice-President and Chief Economist, First Interstate Bank of
California
(Chapter 1)

George G. C. Parker
Senior Lecturer in Management and Director of Executive Education,
Graduate School of Business, Stanford University
(Chapter 4)

Lee H. Radebaugh
Associate Professor of Accounting and International Business, Brigham
Young University
(Chapter 41)

Peter E. Raskind
Vice-President, First Bank Milwaukee
(Chapter 24)

Donald E. Reed
Treasurer, AMCA International Limited
(Chapter 22)

Rita M. Rodriguez
Director, Export-Import Bank of the United States
(Chapter 37)

Andrew Rudd
Managing Director, BARRA
(Chapter 11)

Dallas L. Salisbury
Executive Director, EBRI—Employee Benefit Research Institute
(Chapter 31)

Thomas Schneeweis
Associate Professor of Finance, School of Management, University of Massachusetts, Amherst
(Chapter 12)

Arthur J. Schomer
Partner, Eisner & Lubin
(Chapter 20)

Laurence B. Siegel
Associate, R. G. Ibbotson Associates, Inc.
(Chapter 18)

Rex A. Sinquefield
Executive Vice-President and Chief Investment Officer, Dimensional Fund Advisors, Inc.
(Chapter 18)

Clyde P. Stickney
Professor of Accounting, The Amos Tuck School of Business Administration, Dartmouth College
(Chapter 15)

Hans R. Stoll
The Anne Marie and Thomas B. Walker, Jr., Professor of Finance, Owen Graduate School of Management, Vanderbilt University
(Chapter 10)

T. Craig Tapley
Assistant Professor of Finance, Graduate School of Business Administration, University of Florida
(Chapter 6)

Roy N. Taub, CFA
Vice-President—Corporate Ratings, Standard & Poor's Corporation
(Chapter 19)

Lee Thomas
Economist, The Chase Manhattan Bank, N.A.
(Chapter 38)

Kerry D. Vandell
Associate Professor of Real Estate and Regional Science, Cox School of Business, Southern Methodist University
(Chapter 33)

James H. Vander Weide
Adjunct Professor, The Fuqua School of Business, Duke University
President, Utility Financial Services
(Chapter 23)

Phillip A. Wellons
Associate Professor of Business Administration, Graduate School of
Business Administration, Harvard University
(Chapter 40)

Michelle J. White
Professor of Economics, University of Michigan
(Chapter 35)

Jarrod W. Wilcox
Senior Vice-President, Batterymarch Financial Management
(Chapter 17)

James D. Willson
Senior Vice-President (Retired), Northrop Corporation
(Chapter 21)

Richard Zecher
Senior Vice-President and Chief Economist, The Chase Manhattan
Bank, N.A.
(Chapter 38)

Preface

Handbook of Modern Finance covers virtually every major issue likely to confront anyone active in business and finance. Corporate financial and business executives, accountants (public and private), attorneys, security analysts, and bankers will find it a useful reference for solving day-to-day business problems, as well as a source of guidance in long-term planning. The book explains institutional arrangements and elaborates on relevant economic and financial theory and its application. In addition, sophisticated quantitative analyses are presented in the context of real-world examples, numerous charts and tables illustrate textual explanations, and end of chapter references direct interested readers to additional technical literature in the field. The intent has been to produce a reference book that would help business professionals do their jobs better and more easily, by providing treatment of every topic of relevance in one volume.

So that the *Handbook* has a continuing usefulness, it will be updated annually to reflect emerging trends, new applications of practical theory, and changes in laws and regulations that affect business operation. The updates will be cross-referenced to the main volume, enabling the user to work with current information at all times.

The book is organized around five major subject areas. Chapters 1 through 12 deal with financial institutions and markets. Not only do these chapters explain how the markets currently operate, but they draw inferences regarding how the markets might evolve. Furthermore, valuation concepts and ways in which these markets (e.g., options and futures) might be used by practitioners are also thoroughly explored.

Chapters 13 through 18 treat a broad spectrum of security analysis and portfolio management issues. These chapters cover interest rate mathematics and determinants, the analysis of financial statements and individual securities, and portfolio management questions.

Chapters 19 through 24 cover short-term internal corporate financial decisions, and Chapters 25 through 35 focus upon financial decisions of long-term consequence. Nearly every chapter in these sections takes the reader from theory to practical application with a minimium of complexity and with strong illustrations.

Chapters 36 through 42 develop concepts and techniques relevant to international financial decision making.

The contributors to this volume are all recognized leaders in their fields. The authors comprise a blend of sophisticated practitioners who understand theory and academics who understand application. Working with these gifted individuals taught me a great deal. I personally found reading the material pleasurably enriching.

When Gene Simonoff of Warren, Gorham & Lamont first approached me about doing this book, I said, "No." I said, "No" the second time, too. He persisted, however, and the third time I agreed. In retrospect, I am glad that he persisted and that I said, "Yes." The book thrust upon me the opportunity to learn much about the many new facets of finance uncovered in the past decade. Indeed, comparing this book to any like it written just ten years ago would be like comparing wide-bodied jets to dirigibles; so much has changed in the way problems are thought about and analysis done.

In addition, the expert authors were fun to work with, and I appreciate and applaud the good grace and professionalism they displayed throughout the process, especially when I had neither.

I also cannot praise enough Annette Gonella and Pamela Goett of Warren, Gorham & Lamont, who showed patience, inventiveness, and persistence in cajoling authors (including me) and handling all the necessary tasks that production of a volume such as this demands. My secretary, Barbara Haskell, deserves thanks, too. She typed letters, manuscripts, and editorial comments, and dealt with written and oral correspondence with great aplomb.

Finally, I want to mention Marcella, my wife, and our sons, Dennis, Jr. and Patrick, for bearing with me when I was preoccupied with work on the book, and because I love them.

DENNIS E. LOGUE

Hanover, New Hampshire
August 1984

Contents

Part IV   Long-Term Financial Management

Part V   International Dimensions of Finance

PART I

The Financial System and Markets

1

The Financial System

A. James Meigs

THE FUNCTIONS OF FINANCIAL MARKETS

Introduction

Financial markets make it possible for people to buy, sell, borrow, lend, give, and exchange claims to future flows of income or wealth in an almost infinite number of ways and with great speed and convenience. These claims ultimately represent property rights over real goods and services, not money, although they are specified customarily in terms of some monetary unit. By trading claims to goods and services in financial markets, people can satisfy far more of their own wants and the wants of others with whatever resources they have than they could if they were limited to moving and bartering physical goods and services directly.

The role of financial markets in liberating the management of wealth from physical constraints of form and location can be seen in, for example, the brokerage offices of Hong Kong, where taxi drivers and manufacturers of computer components, who earn incomes and produce wealth on a tiny island, shift investments among Hong Kong stocks, New York stocks, Chicago commodities, London gold, or any of a half-dozen or more foreign currencies at any hour of the day or night. A generation earlier, many of these people would have kept all of their earnings on their own premises, in land, buildings, materials, tools, and partly finished goods, with perhaps some gold or silver hidden somewhere for emergencies.

This chapter describes and illustrates some of the most important functions of financial markets and financial institutions. This may help the reader to make sense of the technical details in later chapters. Among the functions of financial markets and institutions introduced here are: channeling savings into investments; producing and transmitting information on risks and returns on investments; providing means of payment; shifting the timing in use or consumption of lifetime income; and managing risk. These functions are not distributed among institutions so that one institution specializes in one function. Most financial institutions perform several or all of them in various combinations at the same time, so that the consumer of financial services has many suppliers to choose among. Gains from specialization are to be found in particular departments within each institution.

Among the financial claims used to accomplish these various purposes are: oral agreements; paper certificates of title to real property; leases; bonds; mortgages; commercial paper; acceptances; repurchase agreements; government securities; shares of corporate stock; insurance policies; deposits in banks or other financial intermediaries; futures contracts on commodities exchanges; options; and multiple-page contracts.

Channeling Savings Into Investment

Probably the most important function of financial markets is to channel savings into investment. Financial markets make it possible to separate the act of saving from the act of investing. This may seem too obvious to be worth mentioning, but it does much to explain the differences in living standards between highly developed modern economies and primitive farming or hunting/gathering economies.

The self-sufficient farmer tries to raise his family income by investing family labor and time in terracing a hillside for a rice paddy, by not eating the best hens, and by setting aside part of each crop as seed for the next planting season. Heads of families in more advanced societies, however, may specialize in operating someone else's machinery or in driving trucks. They can invest directly in improving their skills (i.e., their human capital), but they do not have to own or build the machinery or trucks they operate. The key point is that most of us work with capital equipment provided by the savings of others, whom we may never know nor need to know. This has the clear advantage of enabling us to work with more capital than we could have accumulated from our own savings in one lifetime. Our own savings go into machinery or equipment that we may never see and probably would not know how to operate if we did see it. Through time, millions of people use goods markets, labor markets, and financial markets to shift their unique personal skills, their time, and their accumulated wealth from lower-value to higher-value uses.

The convenience of saving in financial forms might increase the share of income saved, thus increasing the rate of capital accumulation; however, this is not always apparent. Some primitive societies may have high savings rates. The more significant gain from using financial markets and institutions for channeling savings into investment probably comes from increasing the efficiency of allocating savings among the many competing uses for capital. The self-sufficient farmer has but a narrow field of investing possibilities (i.e., his own farm), but a factory worker investing through a bank or company pension plan has a much wider range of possibilities. The factory worker does not have to risk everything he owns in one enterprise. Furthermore, he is less vulnerable to the risk of diminishing returns on his investments than is the farmer, whose land may decline in productivity no matter how much investment he lavishes on it.

Producing and Transmitting Information

A major part of the work of financial markets is the production and distribution of information on returns and risks through interest rates and securities prices. Although this market information is not necessarily easy to interpret, it permits the vast majority of savers to make rational choices among competing outlets for investment without requiring them to have the detailed knowledge of expected returns on specific uses of capital that a farmer needs in deciding whether to lay drain tile or to spend more time digging another irrigation ditch. As later chapters explain in more detail, financial-market prices sum up immense quantities of information for the guidance of savers, investors, and borrowers and revise this information minute by minute. In effect, this market-price information tells savers and investors much about how effectively managers of firms employ capital in a wide range of uses. And it tells entrepreneurs where they can acquire capital and on what terms.

Transactions prices on financial markets continually reflect investors' evaluations of investment alternatives. Financial institutions collect and transmit prices and other market information through wires, microwaves, newsprint, and satellites to prospective investors all over the world 24 hours a day. The Hong Kong taxi driver or high-tech manufacturer scanning prices and financial news bulletins in his broker's office at 2:00 A.M. Hong Kong time is able to compare investment opportunities the world over.

Investors and borrowers pay for market information both in fees to security analysts and publishers and in the commissions or spreads between bid and ask prices they pay to financial institutions for executing transactions. This illustrates one of the major advantages of a market system: its ability to economize on costs of information. Market information goes to the people who want it and are willing to pay for it; the rest of the public can ignore it and concentrate on information more relevant to their activities.

Provision of Exchange Media and a Payments System

In any society, something emerges by common consent as a general medium of exchange.[1] In primitive societies the medium of exchange may be a widely used

---

[1] Karl Brunner and Allan M. Meltzer, "The Uses of Money: Money in a Theory of an Exchange Economy," *American Economic Review* (Dec. 1971).

commodity, such as salt or tobacco. In more advanced societies the desire for convenience long ago induced people to accept paper claims on physical goods, rather than commodities, in settling transactions. Today, liabilities of financial institutions and governments serve as money. Economists can, and do, argue endlessly over just which financial claims should be included in a definition of money.[2] Such distinctions may be important in predicting effects of changes in the quantity of a given kind of money on national incomes, prices, and interest rates, but they are not essential to the discussion here. The point is that deposits of banks and some liabilities of other intermediaries, such as savings and loan associations (S&Ls), serve in the traditional functions of money: a store of value; a temporary abode of purchasing power; a medium of exchange; and a unit of account.

A large part of all the work done in financial markets and institutions consists of executing payments transactions for people, in essence transferring titles to property from payers to payees, and in confirming for the people on both sides of each transaction that a given payment has been made. This is now done primarily by transmissions of instructions from computer to computer, rather than by transfer of printed notes or coins. Paper checks are still used as instructions to pay in many transactions, but they are expected to decline in relative importance in terms of value and in number of transactions because of the costs of handling them.

An important part of the payments system consists of foreign-exchange markets, making it possible for people to buy or sell goods and services and financial assets across national boundaries. In the back rooms of banks and other financial institutions all over the world, foreign-exchange traders talk by phone with their counterparts in other countries, buying or selling currencies. A trader may, for example, acquire the Canadian dollars a Japanese public utility uses to pay for Canadian coal. These transactions also serve to provide market information on exchange rates, so that the buyers of leather handbags in Milan can translate their prices from lira to dollars or yen. All of this is done so invisibly that a tourist has only the vaguest idea of why the rates posted in the currency exchanges in railroad stations and airports change from day to day.

Consumers of transaction services performed by financial institutions pay for them in two general ways. One way is through forgoing some interest balances held with the institutions performing the services. This rather cumbersome arrangement has been most prevalent in the United States, where payment of explicit interest on demand deposits has been prohibited by law. It is declining in relative importance as a means of paying for transaction services. The other method is through paying explicit service charges based on some calculation of the amount of work done and the value to the user of the payments service. Competition among the many vendors of payments services and technological improvements in producing payments services have continually reduced real costs of financial transactions in recent years, much as the introduction of jets and the deregulation of air fares have reduced passenger-mile costs of air transportation.

---

[2] For more on the problem of defining money, see Milton Friedman and Anna J. Schwartz, *Monetary Statistics of the United States* (New York: National Bureau of Economic Research, 1970), pp. 89–197.

Shifting the Timing of Consumption Over a Life Cycle

By providing facilities for borrowing and lending, financial markets permit people to shift the timing of their use or consumption of lifetime real incomes and wealth, or to transfer wealth to heirs and other beneficiaries. Young workers, who can reasonably expect to earn higher incomes later in life, are net borrowers who borrow to equip their families with houses, cars, education, television, sound systems, and personal computers. Thus, they can shift future income into current consumption, permitting them to enjoy a higher standard of living than they could if their outlays were limited to their current earnings. Later in life, they become net repayers of debt, or savers, spending less than their current earnings on current consumption. Still later, as their earnings decline when they retire, they draw on financial assets to support consumption outlays greater than their current earnings. Furthermore, through bequests, they can shift current earnings to future generations of heirs or other beneficiaries, such as college students and visitors to art museums.

Financial institutions and markets also enable people to adjust to unanticipated fluctuations in incomes. Thus, in periods of adversity they can draw on savings accounts, sell financial assets, borrow, or delay repayments on debts. When they have windfalls, they can add to savings accounts, buy other financial assets, and repay debts.

Risk-Management Services

Financial markets supply many kinds of risk-management services, such as insurance, portfolio diversification opportunities, and hedging. By purchasing life insurance contracts, a primary wage earner can arrange to replace income that would have been earned in a full working lifetime to support the family in case of untimely death or disability. One can also purchase an annuity contract to protect against the risk of exhausting one's accumulated savings by living longer than expected. These are simply additional examples of the use of financial institutions to manage consumption of expected earnings over a lifetime. Casualty insurance contracts protect against risk of losses of property from theft and accident or any of a vast number of other contingencies.

The importance of insurance services is indicated by the fact that purchases of insurance of all kinds amount to about 34 percent of gross national product in the United States. Because ordinary life contracts also include a savings feature, this figure overstates expenditures for pure insurance services. But even if it were corrected for this, it would still be a very large number. Life, property, and casualty insurance companies alone hold more than 20 percent of the assets of all financial institutions covered in the Federal Reserve System flow of funds accounts.

Diversification through financial institutions and markets permits investors to hold a variety of assets whose prices are not tied to one another. Therefore, as a matter of random chance, losses on some assets should be offset to some degree by gains on others. Diversification is made convenient for investors through opportunities for depositing funds in financial intermediaries, such as banks, that in turn lend to a diversified group of borrowers; through buying shares in mutual funds that hold diversified portfolios of investments; or simply through participating in a company retirement plan whose managers hold a diversified portfolio. Later chapters devoted to the capital asset pricing model explain how investors can elect to accept varying degrees of risk with higher or lower expected returns through selection of assets to be included in a portfolio.

One of the most interesting developments in financial markets in recent years has been the extension of hedging techniques used for many years in commodities markets to financial instruments. Markets in standardized commodities, such as corn and wheat, that are subject to wide price fluctuations long ago developed facilities for trading futures contracts. Farmers or millers, for example, who would like to protect themselves against the risk of large changes in the prices of corn or wheat over some future period can buy or sell contracts in which they promise to take or to deliver fixed quantities of corn or wheat at fixed prices on some future date. If the price of a commodity changes, the farmers' or millers' loss (or gain) on the price of the commodity is largely offset by a gain (or loss) in the price of the futures contracts. In the 1970s, when prices of government securities and other financial assets fluctuated widely, futures contracts in financial instruments, including U.S. Treasury bonds and bills and foreign currencies, were developed and traded, first on the Chicago commodities exchanges and later in New York and London. Trading in financial futures contracts began in Singapore in 1984, which makes it possible for hedgers and speculators to trade financial futures around the clock.

Use of financial futures for hedging was still in its infancy in 1983, although a 20-year Treasury bond contract had become the most widely traded contract on the Chicago Board of Trade. In principle, an institution that wants to be assured of a particular yield, say 10 percent on 20-year Treasury bonds in its portfolio over six months in the future, or that wants to avoid a capital loss on the price of the bonds, can sell an equivalent amount of Treasury bond futures contracts on the Chicago Board of Trade ("go short") to mature at the end of the six months. If market yields on 20-year bonds rise to 11 percent during the life of the contract, the investor would suffer a capital loss on the bonds he bought when they were yielding 10 percent. But the price on the futures contracts should also have fallen by about the same amount, enabling the portfolio manager to buy them back at a gain that would approximately offset the loss on the bonds in the portfolio. If yields fall to 9 percent instead, the hedged portfolio manager will have forgone the opportunity to take a capital gain on the bonds because he will have to close the futures contracts at a loss. In either case he will have kept the market value of his portfolio nearly constant for six months. The transactions costs on such hedging operations are small, so the portfolio manager can in effect buy insurance against unanticipated losses in his portfolio at a small cost.

PRIMARY MARKETS, SECONDARY MARKETS, AND INTERMEDIARIES

Primary Markets

It may help in understanding financial institutions and markets to classify them into primary markets, secondary markets, and financial intermediaries. This merely maps out the main routes through which savings funds flow between the people who generate them and the people who employ them. A given financial institution, incidentally, may operate in any one or all three of these market sectors at various times. Therefore, it may make more sense to classify particular transactions and financial services according to the market sectors in which they are performed than to classify institutions.

An individual or a firm wanting to borrow funds can write a promissory note and sell it directly to a lender or investor. The borrower thus issues a primary security. Such a process is a primary market transaction. In developed primary markets, however, the borrower does not have to find a lender or investor directly; there are many kinds of go-betweens to bring primary issuers and investors together. Here, the borrower benefits from the specialized knowledge of underwriters or dealers who know where investors are and what they may be willing to buy. To put it the other way around, the dealers serve investors by seeking out borrowers for them. The underwriter may buy an entire issue from a corporate borrower or unit of government at an agreed-upon price and then try to sell it to investors. The dealer may just undertake to sell the issue on a "best effort" basis. In the first case, the underwriter is compensated for his services by a spread between the price he pays the issuer and the price at which he sells the issue. If he has misjudged the market, or if conditions change before the whole issue is sold to the final investors, the underwriter may take a loss. Therefore, risk-bearing is another of the services underwriters sell to issuers.

On the best effort arrangement the dealer collects a fee for his services and can return any unsold securities to the issuer. In some cases a go-between collects a finder's fee merely for introducing a lender to a borrower. There are many combinations and permutations of these basic transactions in actual practice, but the principle is simple. In primary markets borrowers sell notes (or shares of stock) to final investors, either directly or through various kinds of agents. Funds flow from investors to issuers.

Secondary Markets

In secondary markets, notes, shares of stock, and other securities that had been issued in primary markets earlier are bought and sold. In these transactions, there is no transfer of funds from investors to borrowers. These markets facilitate the flow of savings into investment in primary markets by making it possible for investors to convert financial claims issued by primary borrowers into cash or other securities on a moment's notice. This frees investors from the need to wait for financial contracts to mature before they can recover their funds, and thus increases their willingness to invest in financial assets.

Secondary markets range from informal groups of traders who deal with each other by telephone, making oral agreements that are later confirmed in writing, to highly organized exchanges, where brokers meet each other face to face at particular trading posts or pits. In either case, an investor places an order to buy or sell a specific security with a broker or a dealer. A broker acts as the investor's agent; he does not take title to the security, but executes the trade with other brokers for a commission. A dealer buys a security from one investor and resells it to another investor or another dealer. He is compensated by the spread between the price he pays and the price at which he sells, and bears the risk of price changes while the security is in his inventory. The primary service of both brokers and dealers is to bring buyers and sellers together.

Financial Intermediaries

The essential function of financial intermediaries, such as commercial banks, S&Ls, and credit unions, is to satisfy simultaneously the portfolio preferences of borrowers, who want to expand their holdings of real assets beyond the limits of their own net worth, and lenders or depositors, who want to hold part of their wealth in assets of stable money value with negligible risk of default.[3] By pooling risks through transactions with many borrowers and many lenders or depositors, intermediaries enable borrowers to be accommodated at lower rates than if they had to borrow directly from individual lenders. Intermediaries also accommodate borrowers who are neither well-known enough nor big enough to issue securities in primary markets or to have their notes or stock traded on secondary markets. A complicated commercial loan to a large or small company is not easily sold, because it may be very difficult for anyone but an expert to evaluate. Intermediaries in effect repackage large loans into small pieces that can be sold to many depositors.

No two commercial loans are exactly alike. Banks and other intermediaries have staffs of experts to evaluate specific loans. Intermediaries thus play crucial roles as filters in the flow of information among lenders and borrowers. They make enough loans to hold the risks of their total loan portfolios to tolerable levels. Even the most skillful lending officers of financial intermediaries, however, can make mistakes or be frustrated by risks beyond their control. That is why banks have stockholders: to bear the residual risks of the banks' loan and investment portfolios.

The pooling of risks in loan and investment portfolios protects depositors by providing them with opportunities to invest in better-diversified portfolios than they could easily achieve by their own efforts. The risks to them are obviously much lower than they would be if people had to lend directly to individual borrowers.

Until recently, it was convenient to classify intermediaries as bank and nonbank intermediaries. Financial regulations adopted in the United States during the 1930s required major types of intermediaries to specialize in particular kinds of intermediary functions. However, financial deregulation legislation in recent years has made this distinction less meaningful by broadening the lending and investing powers of banks and S&Ls so they overlap more. Furthermore, various financial and nonfinancial institutions that were not constrained by the restrictive banking legislation of the 1930s, such as brokerage firms, mutual funds, large retailers, and credit card companies, are now performing functions formerly reserved to the conventionally defined intermedi-

---

[3] This definition is adapted from one by James Tobin and William C. Brainard in their "Financial Intermediaries and the Effectiveness of Monetary Controls," in Donald D. Hester and James Tobin, eds., *Financial Markets and Economic Activity*, Cowles Foundation for Research in Economics at Yale University. Monograph 21 (New York: John Wiley & Sons, 1967), pp. 57–59.

aries. All of the intermediary services previously described probably will be provided in the future by an even wider range of financial and nonfinancial institutions than exist today, and perhaps by some new ones that have not yet appeared on the scene.

It is interesting that the breaking down of enforced specialization among financial intermediaries and other institutions is not confined to the United States. Similar changes are occurring in Japan and the United Kingdom.[4] The difficulties experienced by some of the most specialized institutions, such as S&Ls, in coping with the extreme instability of inflation rates and interest rates in the 1970s have forced governments to allow them more freedom to diversify their operations. Specialization in holding long-term fixed-rate mortgages, in particular, proved to be very risky in the turbulent financial conditions of the 1970s and early 1980s.

GOVERNMENTS AND THE FINANCIAL SYSTEM

The Ultimate Enforcer of Contracts

The most important role of government in financial markets is to act as an enforcer of contracts and an arbiter in case of disagreements. Financial markets are built on millions of implied or specifically stated contracts and complex bundles of property rights. Obviously, markets would be much less efficient if contracts could easily be broken. A lawless society could hardly have a highly developed financial-market system, because savers and borrowers would not be confident that their property rights in financial assets and liabilities were secure. They would be less willing to participate.

The need for an enforcer of contracts is not peculiar to financial markets and so no special large government organization or institutions should be required. The same laws against fraud and coercion that apply in other areas of society apply also to financial markets and transactions. Furthermore, people in financial markets have powerful incentives for complying with agreements and contracts. For example, brokers and dealers make oral agreements involving many millions of dollars in the routine course of business. These usually are for short periods of a day or more each, but they can be very large and they are essential to the speedy execution of transactions. The trading is done within a small community of brokers and dealers who may know one another only as voices on the telephone. If a trader reneged on agreements or attempted to defraud people on the other side of his trades, soon no one would trade with him. It is in everyone's interest, therefore, to trade honestly and to work out adjustments quickly when there are misunderstandings over what a trade really was. Mistakes do happen, as when someone writes down the wrong terms or credits a trade to the wrong party.

The charges of fraud that provide such entertaining material for the press, and so much income for attorneys, arise most often in transactions involving

---

4 Federal Reserve Bank of San Francisco, "Financial Development and Reform in the Pacific Basin," *Economic Review* (Winter 1983).

written agreements and contracts that require complicated definitions of collateral and accounting statements meant to describe the financial condition of the borrower or lender. This is why lending institutions have credit departments to scrutinize loan applications and collections departments to assure that most borrowers will stick to agreed-upon repayment schedules. Resort to the courts is required in only a very small fraction of all financial agreements, but its availability contributes to confidence in the financial system.

Government as Regulator

It is commonly taken for granted that government regulation and supervision of the management of financial institutions improve their functioning. However, this is a highly debatable proposition, if government is already upholding property rights and providing facilities for adjudicating disputes as discussed previously. It is hard to imagine how a bank examiner peering over the shoulder of a bank manager is better able to see to it that the bank is profitably and prudently run than the manager whose career prospects and future wealth depend on the performance and health of the bank. This matter is given more detailed treatment in later chapters.

Securities market regulation, under the Securities and Exchange Commission has the laudable objective of assuring full disclosure of material information concerning the condition and operations of corporations whose securities are offered to the public in primary markets and traded in secondary markets. However, the rules and regulations, particularly those applying to new issues of stocks and other securities, add significantly to the costs of financing in public markets in the United States. They also have diverted a large volume of capital-market financing of both U.S. and foreign corporations away from U.S. capital markets and into the Eurobond markets, where regulatory constraints are less stringent.

Government regulation of financial markets and institutions in many countries, including the United States, is concerned much more with influencing the outcomes of financial decisions than with seeing to it that financial markets carry out the wishes of investors and borrowers efficiently and honestly. Because financial markets allocate capital resources among competing uses, many people are tempted to use the powers of government to direct more capital into some uses than these uses could attract in a free market. Such interventions are: regulation of interest rates on deposits and loans; government-sponsored financial institutions designed to make up for alleged imperfections in financial markets; the use of government guarantees or tax exemptions on the borrowings of preferred kinds of business or consumers; restrictions on entry into particular kinds of financial activities or geographic territories; and requirements that certain institutions confine their lending to particular groups of worthy borrowers. Economists can demonstrate that such interventions as tariffs and other restraints in international trade do not accomplish their declared objectives and impose large costs on the general public.

Although there has been a tendency in recent years to dismantle some of the government interventions in the channeling of savings into investments, they will surely remain as a problem deserving the careful attention of anyone who wants to understand how financial markets and institutions function. Tax considerations in financial transactions, in particular, are an excruciatingly complicated issue deserving far more attention than can be given here. Their effects are so pervasive that they almost suggest another major function of financial institutions and markets is to minimize tax liabilities of owners of wealth.

The Monetary Framework

Because financial claims, although stated in monetary units, ultimately are claims convertible into real goods and services, instability in the purchasing power of money seriously impairs the functioning of financial markets. Unanticipated changes in the purchasing power of money transfer wealth and income from lenders to borrowers and vice versa. Therefore, maintaining a stable monetary framework should be one of the most useful services governments could perform for financial markets, as well as for everyone else. Unfortunately, few, if any, governments have demonstrated the willingness or ability to perform this service well. All of this makes monetary policy, as carried out in most countries today, a major source of risk in financial markets.

Inflation impairs the performance of financial markets by driving some people out of financial assets and into real assets such as gold, real estate, antiques, and works of art, which they believe will protect them against losses of purchasing power. Although these investments may protect against the purchasing-power risk of financial assets, they raise other risks, because selecting them requires a great deal of detailed knowledge and information. Furthermore, if people are surprised by falling inflation rates, as many were in 1981 and 1982, they may find themselves with major purchasing-power losses on their inflation hedges.

If financial markets and intermediaries increase the efficiency of allocating savings among competing capital investments, as argued earlier, the "disintermediation" caused by instability in the purchasing power of money must reduce the long-run growth rate of real income in any economy. Therefore, any improvement in the performance of the monetary authorities that would reduce monetary instability should in time confer significant benefits in terms of real income.

Fiscal Policies

The government is not only an enforcer of contracts, a regulator of financial markets, and manager of the monetary environment; it is also one of the largest transactors in the financial system. Tax collections, government payments for goods and services, and transfer payments account for a large share of all payments flowing through the payments system. Large budget deficits in most industrial countries cause great anxiety in financial circles, because the effects of deficits are difficult to predict. Many people in financial markets look upon the U.S. Treasury's financing operations with all the enthusiasm and confidence of someone sharing a bathtub with an elephant. Nevertheless, trading in government securities and helping various units of government to issue and redeem debt is a very large industry providing employment for thousands of dealers and securities traders. Also, government securities are a convenient medium in which to store funds for short and long periods. Most governments now provide large stocks of such assets for their own citizens and investors in other countries to hold.

The effects of changes in fiscal policies — spending, taxing, and borrowing — on national incomes and interest rates are a conventional concern of macroeconomics. However, changes in fiscal policies also have important microeconomic effects in financial markets. Unanticipated changes in tax rates or expenditure programs, for example, can change ex post returns on particular investments and financial contracts. Therefore, fiscal policies are an important source of financial risk. Uncertainty about future fiscal and monetary policies may be a major reason why real interest rates were so high in the early 1980s.

RECENT DEVELOPMENTS IN FINANCIAL MARKETS

Internationalization

One of the most interesting developments in the evolution of financial markets is their increasing internationalization since the 1960s. Financial markets, of course, have always had an international dimension. European bond buyers, for example, helped to finance the building of railroads across North America during the nineteenth century. North American and European investors financed the building of South American railroads a little later. Chinese bonds issued in 1913 were printed in three or more western languages for the convenience of foreigners. These markets, however, were viewed as primarily national, with some governments willing to let foreign borrowers in and others trying to keep them out.

Perhaps the high point, or low point, in the nationalistic conception of capital markets was in 1961, when the Secretary of the Treasury and other high-ranking U.S. officials attributed part of this country's balance-of-payments difficulties to an alleged lack of a long-term capital market in Europe. European governments and companies borrowed too much in New York, these officials said, and thus aggravated the U.S. capital outflow. This diagnosis may have been just gauche American provincialism, but U.S. efforts to stem the capital outflows with direct controls, and the Interest Equalization Tax, provided a powerful impetus for the development of the first "supranational" financial markets — the Eurodollar market and its offshoots, such as the Eurobond market and the Asian dollar market. The revolution in communications technology that came at the same time made it possible to tie together all of these far-flung operations so they now function 24 hours a day.

First denominated mainly in dollars, these markets now bring lenders and borrowers together in deutsche marks, sterling, French francs, Swiss francs, Swedish kronor, yen, and other currencies. Their most distinctive feature, however, is that no government has found a way to regulate them more than a little bit around the edges. Some governments, such as those of the United Kingdom, Luxembourg, Panama, the Bahamas, Grand Cayman, Hong Kong, and Singapore, have found that they could develop large exports of financial services by being hospitable to people and institutions operating in these supra-national markets. The United Kingdom, in particular, has found it highly advan-tageous to keep hands off the international financial operations of the City of London, even while keeping a firm control over Britain's domestic financial markets. Later chapters supply more detail on the operations of these fascinat-ing, hyperdynamic markets.

Adapting to Inflation

Inflation since the 1960s greatly changed financial markets and practices by increasing instability and uncertainty. Financial markets in the United King-dom and the United States had behaved for a couple of centuries as though both lenders and borrowers expected periods of inflation to be followed by periods of deflation. If an individual holds a bond long enough, therefore, he should be able to get out some day with his principal intact in real terms. Faith in the gold standard, plus the fact that commodity prices in both Britain and the United States were not much higher in 1940, relatively speaking, than they had been at the end of the eighteenth century, contributed to the market confidence that enabled corporations and governments to finance themselves with long-term fixed-rate bonds. That confidence evaporated in the 1960s and 1970s when high, and highly variable, inflation rates came to be recognized as normal rather than abnormal.

Financial markets and institutions responded to the new view of inflation through the 1960s and 1970s by shortening maturities of fixed-rate contracts, shifting to floating interest rates, and developing the markets in financial fu-tures contracts and other hedging devices mentioned earlier.[5] The rise of infla-tion rates also drove many investors away from financial assets and into real assets. A worldwide, permanent reduction of inflation rates would, therefore, greatly increase activity and efficiency in financial markets by reducing risks. Unfortunately, in 1983, there was little evidence that the United States was still on the path toward price stability that was nominally adopted by the Federal Reserve System and the Reagan administration in 1981. If the United States "reflates," most of the rest of the world will reflate as well; consequently, more innovations in financial markets designed to aid people to cope with risk of inflation should be expected.

Financial Innovations and Deregulation

Financial innovations and deregulation induced in part by the uncertainty and instability of the 1970s have financial markets and institutions in a ferment that will produce many changes in the 1980s. Several fears about the forces impel-ling these changes and the expected consequences of the changes should be laid

---

5 For an early analysis of the impact of inflation on corporate finance, see Benjamin Klein, "The Impact of Inflation on the Term Structure of Corporate Financial Instruments: 1900–1972," in William Silber, ed., *Financial Innovation* (Lexington, Mass.: Lexington Books, 1975), pp. 125–149.

to rest by more detailed examination in the rest of this book. However, a few comments can be made here.

One fear is that financial markets and institutions are being driven by mindless, spontaneous technological innovations that are so poorly understood that they could be dangerous. To the contrary, innovations in the financial system, as elsewhere in the economy, are the product of capital investments designed to reduce the costs of producing services and to adapt these services to changes in market demands. In financial institutions, as elsewhere, necessity is the mother of invention. Technological developments in communications and data processing in the general economy have rapidly expanded the possibilities for investments in financial innovation, but they have not been the primary motivating forces.

Some analysts attribute financial innovation mainly to attempts of financial institutions to evade financial regulation. Negotiable certificates of deposit, the Eurodollar market, and the introduction of bank-related commercial paper, for example, are said to have emerged mainly to evade interest-rate ceilings under Regulation Q, promulgated by the Federal Reserve. This charge does have some merit, and it is undoubtedly a source of great annoyance to regulators who are slow to adapt their regulations to evolving financial practices. However, it is too narrow. Regulation is just one of many reasons for financial innovation. If one believes that the costs of most financial regulation exceed the benefits, one should be thankful that the ingenuity of financial managers has mitigated at least some of these costs to the consuming public.

Another fear is that deregulation of financial markets and institutions may lead to chaos and "destructive competition." It is true that much of the financial regulation imposed by the legislation of the 1930s was intended to shield particular institutions and users of credit to some degree from competition with other institutions and credit users. Naturally, people who believe they occupy privileged positions under existing regulations will oppose change. Some of them may be injured by deregulation. Nevertheless, the consumers of financial services will win from any change in the regulations that increases the freedom of financial institutions to offer new services, to reduce production costs, and to adapt to changes in the economic environment.

SUGGESTED READING

Auerbach, Robert. *Financial Markets and Institutions*. New York: Macmillan, 1983.

Baumol, William J. *The Stock Market and Economic Efficiency*. New York: Fordham University Press, 1965.

Bell, Geoffrey. *The Euro-Dollar Market and the International Financial System*. New York: John Wiley & Sons, 1973.

Cargill, Thomas F., and Gillian G. Garcia. *Financial Deregulation and Monetary Control*. Stanford, Calif.: Hoover Institution Press, 1982.

Federal Home Loan Bank of San Francisco. *Savings and Loan Asset Management Under Deregulation*. Proceedings of the Sixth Annual Conference, Dec. 8–9, 1980. San Francisco: Federal Home Loan Bank of San Francisco, 1981.

————. *Managing Interest Rate Risk in the Thrift Industry*. Proceedings of the Seventh Annual Conference, Dec. 10–11, 1981. San Francisco: Federal Home Loan Bank of San Francisco, 1982.

————. *Strategic Planning for Economic and Technological Change in the Financial Services Industry*. Proceedings of the Eighth Annual Conference, Dec. 9–10, 1982.

Federal Reserve Bank of Atlanta. *The Future of the Financial Service Industry*. Proceedings of a Conference, June 3–4, 1981.

Goldsmith, Raymond W. *The Flow of Capital Funds in the Postwar Economy*. New York: National Bureau of Economic Research, 1965.

Gurley, John G., and Edward S. Shaw. *Money in a Theory of Finance*. Washington, D.C.: The Brookings Institutions, 1960.

Hester, Donald D., and James Tobin, eds. *Financial Markets and Economic Activity*. Cowles Foundation for Research in Economics at Yale University. Monograph 21. New York: John Wiley & Sons, 1967.

Kane, Edward J. "Impact of Regulation on Economic Behavior." *Journal of Finance*, Vol. 36, No. 2 (1981), pp. 355–367.

Kuznets, Simon. *Capital in the American Economy: Its Formulation and Financing*. Princeton, N.J.: National Bureau of Economic Research, 1961.

Money and Credit: Their Influence on Jobs, Prices, and Growth. The Report of the Commission on Money and Credit. Englewood Cliffs, N.J.: Prentice-Hall, 1961.

Peltzman, Sam. "Toward a More General Theory of Regulation." *Journal of Law and Economics* (Aug. 1976), pp. 211–240.

Silber, William L., ed. *Financial Innovation*. Lexington, Mass.: Lexington Books, D.C. Heath, 1975.

Stem, Carl H., et al., eds. *Eurocurrencies and the International Monetary System*. Washington, D.C.: American Enterprise Institute for Public Policy Research, 1976.

Yeager, Leland G. *Proposals for Government Credit Allocation*. Washington, D.C.: American Enterprise Institute for Public Policy Research, 1977.

2

The Banking System

Colin D. Campbell

The banking system consists of those financial institutions that both provide people with various types of deposits and make loans. Banks are middlemen between depositors and borrowers. Many depositors want repayment on demand, whereas borrowers usually need time to accumulate funds to repay their loans. Banks accommodate both groups, lending funds on different terms than they accept them. Banks also supply currency and foreign exchange to customers, sell travelers' checks and money orders, sell and redeem U.S. savings bonds, and rent safe-deposit boxes. Some banks also lease equipment and automobiles, operate trust departments, offer computer and bookkeeping services for other banks, deal in marketable U.S. government securities and

TABLE 2.1   Number of Commercial Banks, by Chartering
Authority and Membership in the Federal Reserve System,
Selected Years, 1921–1981

End of Year	All Commercial Banks	National Banks	State Banks	Member Banks	Nonmember Banks
1921 (June)	29,788	8,150	21,638	9,745	20,043
1929	24,026	7,403	16,623	8,522	15,504
1934	15,519	5,462	10,057	6,442	9,077
1941	14,278	5,117	9,161	6,616	7,662
1950	14,121	4,958	9,163	6,870	7,251
1960	13,472	4,530	8,942	6,172	7,300
1970	13,688	4,621	9,067	5,768	7,920
1981	14,882	4,454	10,428	5,474	9,408

Source: U.S. Board of Governors of the Federal Reserve System, Banking and Monetary Statistics (1943), p. 16; Banking and Monetary Statistics 1941–1970 (1976), pp. 40–41; and U.S. Board of Governors of the Federal Reserve System, Annual Report, various years

foreign exchange, service mortgages and other loans, and provide investment advisory services.

Historically, commercial banks were by far the most important type of bank. Since World War II, thrift institutions — savings and loan associations, mutual savings banks, and credit unions — have become an important part of the banking system. Because of recent changes in government regulations, the differences between commercial banks and thrift institutions have diminished. Also, in the 1970s and 1980s, money market mutual funds and cash management accounts established by brokerage firms expanded rapidly and now compete with commercial banks and thrift institutions for deposits.

Several important government agencies that regulate banks are included in the banking system. The most important are the Comptroller of the Currency in the U.S. Department of the Treasury, the Federal Reserve System, the Federal Deposit Insurance Corporation (FDIC), the Federal Home Loan Bank Board (FHLBB) and the International Monetary Fund (IMF).

NUMBER AND SIZE OF COMMERCIAL BANKS

In 1981, there were almost 15,000 commercial banks in the United States. Each of these banks had received a charter authorizing it to engage in banking.

Table 2.1 shows that from 1921 to 1929 many banks went out of business and the number of commercial banks declined from almost 30,000 to 24,000. Most of these were small banks located in declining agricultural areas. During the Great Depression, one-third of the commercial banks ceased operating and, by 1934, the number of banks had dropped to 15,500. Following World War II, the number of banks was reduced further through mergers. This downward

TABLE 2.2   Number and Assets of Insured Commercial Banks, by Asset Size, End of 1980

Asset Size (in millions of dollars)	Number of Banks	Amount of Domestic Assets (in billions of dollars)
Less than $5	658	$ 2.4
5–9	1,911	14.5
10–24	4,651	77.9
25–49	3,546	125.8
50–99	1,969	135.5
100–299	1,158	183.8
300–499	196	75.8
500–999	159	107.8
1,000–4,999	158	332.6
5,000 or more	29	476.8
Total	14,435	$1,533.0

Source: Federal Deposit Insurance Corporation, Annual Report, 1980, p. 234

trend has been reversed since the early 1960s when bank regulators initiated a more liberal chartering policy.

Banks vary greatly in size. Table 2.2 shows that most commercial banks are small and, in 1980, a bank of median size had from $25 million to $50 million in assets. There were, however, 26 commercial banks in the United States in 1982 that each had total assets of more than $10 billion. The two largest (Citicorp in New York and BankAmerica Corporation in California) each had total assets of about $120 billion.[1]

HISTORY OF U.S. BANKING

The first modern commercial bank in the United States was established in Philadelphia in 1781. Before this, there were colonial loan offices or private associations that were similar in some ways to modern banks. They made loans and issued paper money, but did not have deposits on which customers wrote checks. These early loan offices were not incorporated and lasted only for the period of their loans or of the project they were set up to finance.

By 1800, there were just under 30 incorporated banks in the United States; 20 years later there were more than 300. Most of the earliest banks were chartered by state legislatures. However, in the late 1830s, both Michigan and

---

[1] "The Fifty Largest Commercial Banking Companies," Fortune, Vol. 94 (July 12, 1982), pp. 134–135.

New York passed "free banking" acts, making it unnecessary for state legislatures to approve each charter. By 1869, about half of the states had changed to free banking.

Before the Civil War, notes issued by banks were the principal type of money in circulation. The U.S. Constitution had prohibited state governments from issuing paper notes, but a Supreme Court ruling allowed state-chartered banks to issue them. In some states, the required reserves for state bank notes were in the form of specie (gold and silver), but in other states, bonds, other types of interest-earning securities, and interbank deposits in large urban banks were allowed. Before the Civil War, only two states required that banks hold reserves equal to a percentage of their deposits.

The Currency Act of 1863 and the National Bank Act of 1864 set up a system of national banks chartered by the Comptroller. This is unusual since other types of businesses obtain charters from state governments. The objectives of establishing the national banking system were to create a system of banks regulated by the federal government, provide a uniform currency, strengthen the market for federal securities, and be of assistance to the U.S. Treasury in managing the large national debt that was created to finance the Civil War.

A principal feature of the Civil War banking legislation is that national banks were authorized to issue national bank notes. Although these notes, like the state bank notes they were designed to replace, were liabilities of the banks that issued them, they were secured by U.S. government securities and printed by the federal government. The Civil War banking legislation was intended to induce state banks to become national banks by taxing state bank notes; however, many state banks continued to operate successfully because of the growing use of deposits as a substitute for bank notes.

At present, some commercial banks have charters issued by the Comptroller and others have charters from their state governments. The combination of national and state-chartered banks is referred to as a dual system of banking. The term "national" is included in the name of many banks and indicates that they have a federal charter. Table 2.1 shows that in 1981 only 30 percent of the total number of insured commercial banks were national banks. Although relatively small in number, they have almost 55 percent of the total deposits in commercial banks.

After the establishment of the Federal Reserve System in 1914, commercial banks that had applied and been accepted for membership in the Federal Reserve System were known as member banks. By law, all national banks have to be members. State banks may join the system if they desire and if they meet the necessary qualifications. Table 2.1 shows that in 1981 less than 38 percent of insured commercial banks were members; they held about 71 percent of the total deposits in commercial banks. From 1950 to 1980, there had been a steady decline in the number of member banks.

The Depository Institutions Deregulation and Monetary Control Act of 1980 (DIDMCA) reduced the differences between member and nonmember banks and prohibited any further shifting of member banks to nonmember status. All depository institutions are now required to maintain reserves (vault cash or deposits at the Federal Reserve banks) equal to a certain percentage of their checkable deposits and nonpersonal time deposits. The new reserve requirements are in the process of being phased-in and, by 1987, the reserve requirements of all depository institutions will be the same. Before 1980, the reserve requirements of nonmember banks varied from state to state and were usually lower than for member banks.

ORGANIZATION OF BANKS

Most of the very large commercial banks in the United States now operate at many locations within the United States as well as throughout the world. Until recently, the expansion of their activities to areas outside the bank's primary location was usually prohibited by law. Today, large banks in a metropolitan area typically have dozens of branches in the city; in addition, they have branches in other large cities in the state if state laws do not prohibit this. They may have a hundred or more off-site electronic computer terminals. They also have regional offices to service loans located in major U.S. cities such as Los Angeles, Chicago, Dallas, and Atlanta; these offices are not classed as "branches" even though they engage in almost all banking activities except offering regular deposits. In addition, most large banks have several branches located in foreign countries or in foreign subsidiaries.

Intrastate Branches

As shown in Figure 2.1, some states still do not allow branches within the state, although restrictions against branches are gradually breaking down. In 1982, for instance, both Illinois and Pennsylvania relaxed their restrictions against branch banking. Two populous states, California and New York, have extensive branch banking. Some states restrict branches to within the city or county in which the main office is located.

The number of bank branches in the United States has increased from slightly over 4,000 just after World War II to approximately 40,000 in 1981. In spite of this, the most common type of bank in the United States continues to be the unit bank, a separate bank without branches. In contrast, most foreign countries have only a few banks with many branches.

Branch banking had developed in some parts of the United States before the Civil War. Although state banks with branches could become national banks under the Civil War banking legislation, the law did not make clear whether national banks could have branches. Under the national banking system, approval for establishing a branch bank had to be obtained from the Comptroller and, before World War II, few branches were approved. In 1927, the McFadden Act permitted national banks to open branches within the limits of the city, town, or village in which they were located if state laws did not forbid it. However, because of the Great Depression and World War II, few permits to open branches were granted during the 1930s and 1940s.

Interstate Branches

Despite the restrictions against interstate banking, many large banks now have banking offices in other states, and some banks have acquired control of banks

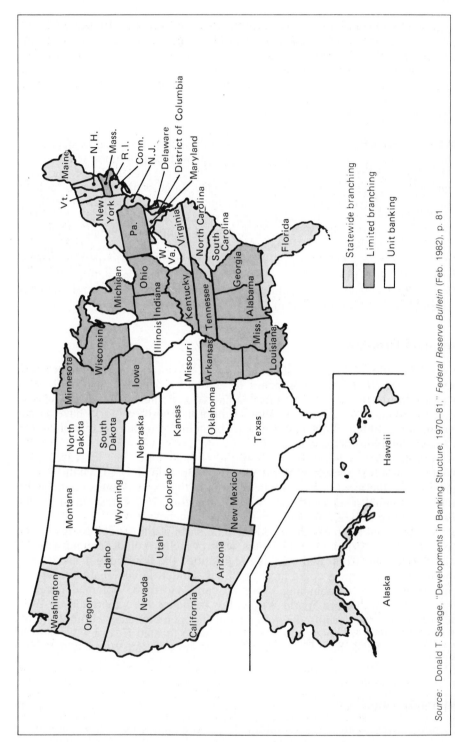

Source: Donald T. Savage, "Developments in Banking Structure, 1970–81," *Federal Reserve Bulletin* (Feb. 1982), p. 81

FIG. 2.1 States with Branch and Unit Banking, 1981

Legend:
- Statewide branching
- Limited branching
- Unit banking

in other states. In addition, the number of Edge Act Corporations has increased from fewer than 40 in 1965 to 130 in 1980. The Edge Act, which was passed by Congress in 1919, allows a bank to set up subsidiaries for conducting foreign business in states other than the location of the home office.[2] Although Edge Act Corporations are not classified as branches, they operate like branches and may accept deposits as well as make loans.

Foreign Branches

In recent years the number of foreign branches of U.S. banks has increased sharply. By 1981, there were approximately 800 branches of 156 member banks in foreign countries and various overseas areas of the United States. The assets of branches of U.S. banks overseas totaled more than $400 billion — almost 25 percent of the amount of their domestic assets. Member banks must obtain the approval of the Board of Governors of the Federal Reserve System to establish a branch in a foreign country. The international operations of national banks are now supervised by the Multinational Banking Division of the Office of the Comptroller of the Currency, although foreign branches continue to operate mainly under the laws of the host country.

Foreign Subsidiaries

The ownership of foreign banks and financial institutions by U.S. banks also increased rapidly in the 1970s.[3] These are called subsidiaries. There are more foreign subsidiaries of U.S. banks than branches, although many of the subsidiaries are very small. In 1981, the total assets of the foreign subsidiaries amounted to approximately $83 billion, and 17 subsidiaries each had total assets exceeding $1 billion. Foreign tax or banking laws sometimes favor operating through subsidiaries rather than through branches, and some foreign governments do not permit foreign banks to have branches in their countries.

United States banks have expanded their overseas operations to circumvent U.S. regulations and to take advantage of opportunities to serve foreign and multinational corporations.[4] When the U.S. government attempted to check growing deficits in its balance of payments with the Interest Equalization Tax (1963–1974) and foreign credit restraint programs (1965–1974), the growth of overseas branches and foreign sources of financing was stimulated.

---

[2] See James V. Houpt, "Performance and Characteristics of Edge Corporations," *Federal Reserve Bulletin* (Jan. 1981), pp. 13–14.

[3] James V. Houpt and Michael G. Martinson, *Foreign Subsidiaries of U.S. Banking Organizations*. Board of Governors of the Federal Reserve System, Staff Study 120 (Washington, D.C.: Oct. 1982).

[4] For data on U.S. bank operations abroad, see Jane D'Arista, "U.S. Banks Abroad," in *FINE: Financial Institutions and the Nation's Economy: Compendium of Papers Prepared for the FINE Study*, U.S. Committee on Banking, Currency and Housing, U.S. House of Representatives, 94th Congress, 2nd session, Committee Print (Washington, D.C.: U.S. Government Printing Office, June 1976), pp. 801–1111; Francis A. Lees, *International Banking and Finance* (New York: John Wiley & Sons, 1974), Chapter 5; and *Federal Reserve Bulletin*, various issues, pp. A56–A57.

Beginning in 1981, the Board of Governors of the Federal Reserve authorized banks in the United States to establish International Banking Facilities that have some of the advantages formerly available only to branches overseas. United States banks are now allowed to engage in certain large financial transactions with foreigners without being subject to reserve requirements or interest-rate ceilings on their international accounts. These operations involve a separate set of books, and the bank's deposits and loans may be denominated in either dollars or other types of currency.[5]

Electronic Computer Terminals

The number of automated teller machines (ATMs) located in such places as supermarkets and shopping centers has expanded rapidly in recent years and made the application of branching regulations more complicated.[6] The Comptroller initially ruled that, for national banks, off-premise terminals did not constitute a branch of the bank. This ruling was later amended to set a limit of 50 miles as the maximum distance a terminal could be from its head office or closest branch. Later, a court decision classified off-premise ATMs and electronic computer terminals as branches that could be prohibited by state law. The U.S. Supreme Court allowed this decision to stand by declining to review it. In recent years, electronic computer terminals have become commonplace in many states. In states where branching is illegal, these devices have afforded a way for banks to offer services at several locations. In 1982, plans were being made by several very large U.S. banks to link together each other's ATMs and allow their customers to withdraw and transfer money (but not to make deposits) in any U.S. locality where the group of banks operates.

Foreign Banks in the United States

In 1982, there were over 350 foreign banks from 50 countries operating some type of banking facility in the United States.[7] Agencies, which accept no deposits from domestic residents, are the dominant form of U.S.-based foreign bank organization both in number of offices and total volume of assets.

Before 1978, the regulation of foreign banks within the United States was largely determined by individual state laws, and many of these state regulations still apply. Some states allow no foreign bank operations of any kind; others allow only limited operations; and some allow foreign banks only from reciprocating countries. New York and California are the principal centers for foreign bank operations.

---

[5] *Federal Reserve Bulletin* (July 1981), pp. 562–563.

[6] See William C. Niblack, "Development of Electronic Funds Transfer Systems," *Review* (Federal Reserve Bank of St. Louis, Sept. 1976), pp. 1–18; and William L. Silber and Kenneth D. Garbade, "Financial Innovation and EFTS: Implications for Regulation," *FINE*, note 4 *op. cit.*, pp. 192–208.

[7] See J. Randall Woolridge and Klaus D. Wiegel, "Foreign Banking Growth in the United States," *Bankers Magazine* (Jan.–Feb. 1981), pp. 30–38; Lees, note 4 *op. cit.*, Chapter 7; and D'Arista, "Foreign Bank Activities in the United States," *FINE*, note 4 *op. cit.*, pp. 731–800.

The federal government extended its control over foreign banks in the United States in the International Banking Act of 1978. While the Act allows foreign banks that had already established out-of-state facilities to continue to operate them, it requires each foreign bank to now select one state as its "home state" of operation. New branches and agencies outside the home state may accept deposits only from nonresidents of that state or from activities related to international trade financing.

The 1978 legislation was intended to equalize the treatment of domestic and foreign banks, and it also provides somewhat more uniform regulation among the states where foreign banks are allowed. Before 1978, domestic banks were not allowed to engage in interstate banking, whereas foreign banks could. In addition, before the 1978 legislation, foreign banks were not subject to the Federal Reserve's reserve requirements for large banks, even though their parent banks were often very large. Since 1978, all branches and agencies of foreign banks with worldwide assets of $1 billion or more have been subject to the same reserve requirements as domestic banks.

Several foreign banks have recently purchased control of U.S. banks in order to establish operations in this country. A foreign bank purchasing control of a U.S. bank must obtain approval from the Board of Governors of the Federal Reserve System, and approval by state government may also be required. A British bank was allowed to purchase the entire stock of the National Bank of North America, the thirty-seventh largest in the country. However, approval is not always granted. In 1979, bank regulators in New York refused to approve an attempt by the Hong Kong and Shanghai Banking Corporation to acquire control of the Marine Midland Bank, the twelfth largest in the country. In that same year, Congress considered legislation that would have ended foreign-bank takeovers for six months.

Bank Holding Companies

Bank holding companies (BHCs) link the management of a group of banks or enterprises engaged in bank-related activities. A BHC is a corporation that owns a sufficient amount of stock in one or more banks or bank-related enterprises to have a controlling interest in them. An example of a very large BHC is First Interstate Bancorp (formerly called Western Bancorporation), which controls banks in most western states.

Although bank holding companies were not common until the mid-1960s, the number of banks controlled by multibank BHCs increased from 723 in 1969 to 2,426 in 1980, and the number of one-bank BHCs increased from 1,352 in 1970 to 2,544 in 1980.[8] By 1980, 70 percent of the deposits in commercial banks in the United States were in banks owned by BHCs. (See Table 2.3.)

Bank holding companies are subject to government regulation because of concern that they might concentrate economic power. Federal legislation starting with the Banking Act of 1933 restricted the combining of bank-related

---

[8] See Carter H. Golembe, "One-Bank Holding Companies," in Herbert V. Prochnow, ed., *The One-Bank Holding Company* (Chicago: Rand McNally, 1969), pp. 66–81; and Gregory E. Boczar, "The Growth of Multibank Holding Companies: 1956–73," *Federal Reserve Bulletin* (Apr. 1976), pp. 300–301.

TABLE 2.3   Number of Registered Bank Holding Companies,
Banks and Branches Controlled, and Deposits, Selected Years,
1957–1980

End of	Number of			Deposits (in billions)	Deposits as a Percentage of Commercial Bank Deposits
	Registered Holding Companies	Banks Controlled	Branches		
1957	50	417	851	$ 15.1	7.5%
1968	80	629	2,262	57.6	13.2
1970	121	895	3,260	78.1	16.2
1972(a)	1,607	2,720	13,441	379.4	61.5
1976	1,912	3,791	19,203	553.6	66.1
1980	3,056	4,954	24,970	840.6	70.4

(a) One-bank holding companies excluded until 1972

Source: Federal Reserve Bulletin, various issues; and Board of Governors of the Federal Reserve System, Annual Statistical Digest, 1973–77 (Washington, D.C., 1978), pp. 277 and 283, and 1980, p. 187

activities with business activities such as investment banking. The Bank Holding Company Act of 1956 provided for registration of companies holding 25 percent or more of the stock of two or more banks, barred new bank acquisitions across state lines, set up regulations covering the acquisition of additional voting stock in banks, and further limited the non-bank-related activities of BHCs. At that time, several banking corporations were required to separate their banking and nonbanking activities.

The growth of multibank bank holding companies resulted from attempts to circumvent the laws prohibiting or restricting branch banking. During the past decade, the formation of BHCs has been concentrated in states that do not allow branch banking or that limit branch banking.

In 1970, new legislation extended government regulations to one-bank BHCs and, since 1972, even they have been required to register. The one-bank BHC allows a bank to conduct nonbank activities. In addition, one-bank BHCs have been organized to take advantage of tax benefits they offer to stockholders. A bank holding company and the bank it owns are allowed to file a consolidated income tax return if 80 percent or more of the stock of the bank is owned by the holding company. The income of the bank is reduced for tax purposes by the BHC's interest payments on its debt.[9]

The Board of Governors of the Federal Reserve administers the 1970 BHC regulations and must approve the nonbank activities of these companies. Although the Federal Reserve Board has approved a large number of applications

9 "Bank Holding Companies," Federal Reserve Bulletin (Feb. 1982), p. 82.

TABLE 2.4   Commercial Bank Loans, June 1982

Type	Seasonally Adjusted Amount (billions of dollars)
Commercial and industrial loans	$ 383.4
Real estate loans	297.3
Loans to individuals	188.3
Agricultural loans	34.5
Loans to nonbank financial institutions	33.6
Security loans	19.5
Lease financing receivables	13.1
All other loans	47.5
Total loans	$1,017.1

Source: *Federal Reserve Bulletin* (Aug. 1982), p. A15

by BHCs to engage in nonbank activities, the assets of nonbank subsidiaries of BHCs are only about 5 percent of the assets of the commercial banking system.

Although in the past federal laws prohibited nonbank corporations from offering banking services, these restrictions have been relaxed. The cash management accounts developed by brokerage firms such as Merrill Lynch offer their customers checkable deposits as well as personal loans. In addition, in 1982, a chain of furniture stores obtained federal approval to offer limited banking services in its stores in four states; the new bank can offer checkable accounts, consumer loans, and financial planning services. Because the new bank is not allowed to make commercial loans, the BHC laws prohibiting nonfinancial institutions from owning banks were said not to apply. This is the first nonfinancial institution to receive such a charter, although there have been a few cases in which nonfinancial institutions have been allowed to take over existing banks.

LENDING ACTIVITIES OF BANKS

Business enterprises typically borrow money from banks to purchase inventory and raw materials, provide for short-term financial needs, and finance plant and equipment. Households borrow from banks to finance the purchase of automobiles, homes, home improvements, and household equipment; to pay for educational expenses and large medical bills; and to cover everyday needs through personal loans. Although banks are not the only source of loanable funds for businesses and households, they are one of the most important.

Table 2.4 shows the principal types of loans made by commercial banks in 1982, classified by the use of the funds borrowed. Commercial and industrial loans are the principal types of commercial bank loans. It is from the importance of these loans that commercial banks got their name. In contrast with commercial and industrial loans, which are usually short-term, the second most important type of loan made by commercial banks is usually long-term — real estate loans.

Commercial Loan Theory of Banking

For many years it was believed that only short-term self-liquidating loans to business firms were appropriate for commercial banks. Commercial loans for inventory are classified as self-liquidating because merchants or manufacturers acquire the funds to repay the loan with interest as they sell their inventory or their output. According to the commercial loan theory of banking, restricting bank loans to short-term self-liquidating loans would not only provide banks with the liquidity they need to operate successfully, but would also protect the banking system from the runs that occurred in periods of bank crises. Instead of relying on the cash flow from commercial loans, most banks in recent years have relied either on borrowing or on the shiftability of assets, usually federal funds sold, certificates of deposit (CDs), or U.S. Treasury bills. At present, it is also generally believed that restricting bank loans to short-term commercial loans is not the best way to assure the stability of a fractional reserve banking system. In a fractional reserve banking system, the volume of bank deposits is much larger than the cash assets held by banks. Although the holding of short-term commercial loans may protect individual banks in periods of crises, it will not protect a fractional reserve banking system from running out of cash whenever people lose confidence in banks and attempt to convert their deposits into currency. To protect the entire banking system from this type of crisis, either a central bank or deposit insurance is necessary.

Characteristics of Bank Loans

When a bank loan is made, the borrower usually signs a written promise to pay the lender a specific amount of money on a fixed date. This promissory note may be signed by cosigners who agree to pay if the borrower fails to do so. In addition, before granting a loan, banks often require that they be assigned legal claim to some of the borrower's assets, such as real estate, automobiles, corporation stock, savings deposits, or life insurance policies. The use of such collateral and the use of cosignatures reduces the banks' risk and enables them to charge lower interest rates than they otherwise would.

Well-established firms that are operating profitably can almost always borrow, but new enterprises seeking financing may have difficulty obtaining loans from commercial banks. Accounting records (such as balance sheets and income statements) summarizing the current financial condition of the borrower are required of commercial and industrial borrowers. Bank lending officers also try to keep informed about the operations of the borrower in order to estimate the prospects for the loan being paid off when due and to enable them to decide whether they would be willing to continue the loan if an extension is requested by the borrower.

Investments in securities are a substitute for bank loans, although banks usually find loans the more profitable of the two. The opportunities to make bank loans depend on business conditions. In periods of recession, when the demand for loans is weak, total bank loans usually drop; funds that might have been lent are then invested in securities. In periods of expansion, banks get additional funds to lend by selling off some of their securities.

The principal source of bank income is the interest that banks receive on their loans and investments in securities. On a single-payment loan of $100 for one year at 10 percent interest, for example, the borrower receives $100 and pays back $110 at the end of the year. On an installment loan, the monthly payments consist partly of interest on the loan and partly of repayment of the principal.

The acceleration and unevenness of the rate of inflation since 1965 have changed the terms of the loans that banks are willing to make. When inflation is anticipated, market interest rates tend to rise so as to discount the higher rate of inflation. In periods of rising interest rates, banks must avoid making loans for much longer periods than the maturity of their deposits so as to assure that the cost of obtaining funds is not higher than the rate of return received on their loans. To avoid the possibility of such losses, banks have shifted to mortgages and business loans with shorter maturities and with variable rates. Banks also attempt to match the maturity of their deposits with assets having a similar maturity. These new terms of bank loans shift the risk caused by changes in interest rates from the banks to the borrowers — the homeowners who have mortgages or the business firms who borrow to finance their ongoing activities. The high risk now borne by those groups is one of the undesirable consequences of the inflationary conditions that have prevailed since the mid-1960s.

Consumer Credit Laws

When making loans, banks must adhere to the procedures that are prescribed by law to protect borrowers. Since 1969, Congress has passed a number of acts to accomplish this: the Truth-in-Lending Act, to inform the customer of the cost of borrowing; the Real Estate Settlement Procedures Act, which sets the procedures for making mortgage loans; the Home Mortgage Disclosure Act, which requires banks to publicize where they have made mortgage loans; the Fair Credit Billing Act, which mandates how complaints about billing errors should be handled; the Equal Credit Opportunity Act, which forbids discrimination on the basis of sex, marital status, age, color, religion, race, or national origin; and the Federal Trade Commission Improvement Act, which forbids the shifting of guarantees to third parties who cannot be held responsible.[10]

Examinations

At present, bank examinations are made primarily by federal government officials, and they are scheduled at regular intervals. Before the Civil War, bank

---

[10] See "Consumer Affairs," *Annual Report of the Board of Governors of the Federal Reserve System, 1975* (Washington, D.C., 1976), pp. 307–346.

examinations were made by state banking commissions, which made examinations only when banks were having difficulty, rather than on a regular basis.

The objective of examinations is to determine whether a bank is being properly managed and whether its loans and investments in securities are listed at reasonable value. If a borrower is behind in its loan payments or if the prospects for repayment appear to be poor, the examiners normally require that the loan be removed from the bank's recorded assets. A bank is not allowed to continue to operate if it has so many bad loans that its total assets are worth less than the total amount of its deposits. Banks with inadequate assets are declared insolvent and are forced to shut down. Policies of this type are not found in all countries, especially not those in which there is considerable government direction of the lending activities of banks. In the United States, also, government bank examiners have recently allowed banks to carry on their books loans to foreign governments that are behind in their payments and are in danger of default.

Economic Allocation of Loanable Funds

In all countries, there is a limit to the amount of loanable funds available to businesses and consumers. To promote the economic growth and prosperity of a country, loans must be made to finance the most productive investments possible. On the other hand, if loans are made to business firms that are unable to pay back the amount borrowed (with interest), loanable funds are wasted. There is a strong inducement for privately owned banks to allocate loanable funds to their most productive uses. Owners of banks receive higher rates of return on their investment in bank stock if banks successfully lend funds at the highest rates of return possible; owners will suffer losses if the bank makes bad loans. Countries with government-owned banks must rely on incentives other than the profit motive of private owners to allocate bank funds to their best uses. Effective alternatives to the profit motive are not easy to devise. In addition, in countries with government-owned banks, bank loans have sometimes been used to subsidize consumers so as to strengthen the political support for the government in power rather than to allocate the country's scarce resources efficiently.

The allocation of credit by banks in the United States is influenced in part by government regulations affecting the kind of loans banks make. A major objective of the federal government since World War II has been to induce banks and thrift institutions to invest in mortgages so as to stimulate home construction. This has been accomplished through guarantees against mortgage default by the Federal Housing Administration and the Veterans Administration and through secondary markets for mortgage loans established by government agencies. The demand for mortgage loans has also been stimulated by setting ceilings on the interest rates charged and by permitting borrowers to deduct the interest on home mortgages in calculating federal income taxes. These policies have been criticized in recent years for reducing the flow of credit to investment in business capital.

Other examples of government influence on the allocation of credit are the Small Business Administration's guarantees of loans to small business enterprises, and the operations of the numerous federal credit agencies designed to direct the flow of credit to agriculture, education, and international trade. Federal agencies involved in influencing the flow of credit include the Federal Land Banks, Banks for Cooperatives, Federal Intermediate Credit Banks, Federal National Mortgage Association, FHLBB, Student Loan Marketing Association, Export-Import Bank of the United States, IMF, and International Bank for Reconstruction and Development.[11]

BANK INVESTMENTS

The investments of commercial banks consist primarily of certificates of deposit in other banks, U.S. Treasury securities (including those issued by agencies of the federal government), and municipal bonds. Banks may also invest in commercial paper and corporate bonds, but usually not in corporate stocks. In addition, many banks sell federal funds (excess reserve deposits at the Federal Reserve banks); federal funds sold are usually classified as interbank loans, but serve purposes similar to a bank's liquid securities.

Secondary Reserves

The liquid investments of banks (federal funds sold, CDs in other banks, and U.S. Treasury bills) are called secondary reserves. The rates of return on these assets are usually less than the rates received by banks on their other earning assets. It is still useful for many banks to own liquid assets because they can be sold immediately to replenish required reserves should deposits decline. When deposits decline, banks experience a shortage of reserves because they hold only a small fraction of their deposits in reserve, whereas a loss of deposits results in an equal decrease in reserves. If a bank has liquid assets that it can sell when its deposits drop, its lending activities will not have to be cut, and there need be no losses from forced sales of long-term securities. Secondary reserves may also be sold to obtain funds to accommodate important depositors who wish to borrow. If a bank is unable to accommodate such borrowers, they may move their deposits to another bank.

A bank's cash in vault and the balances at the Federal Reserve banks are of little use when liquid assets are needed because banks usually hold no more of these reserve assets than is legally required. Banks prefer to hold secondary reserves rather than excess legal reserves because secondary reserves earn interest, whereas balances at the Federal Reserve and cash in vault do not. Correspondent balances at other commercial banks are also not useful as liquid assets because they are relatively small in amount and are expected to be retained at their customary level.

---

11 For information on these federal agencies and the securities they issue, see *Handbook of Securities of the United States Government and Federal Agencies,* 30th ed. (Boston: First Boston Corporation, 1982), pp. 81–123. Also see two volumes issued by the Commission on Money and Credit, *Federal Credit Agencies* and *Federal Credit Programs* (Englewood Cliffs, N.J.: Prentice-Hall, 1963).

Municipal Bonds

Commercial banks invest in substantial amounts of municipal bonds.[12] Holdings of these securities have grown rapidly since World War II and account for a large portion of the total amount of state and local government securities outstanding. Interest on these bonds has the special advantage of being exempt from federal corporate income taxes.

U.S. Government Securities

Since World War II, bank holdings of U.S. government securities have declined in importance compared to bank loans and investments in municipal bonds. During World War II, banks held over half of their total loans and investments in U.S. government securities as a result of the need to assist the Treasury in financing the war.

Banks are legally required to hold an amount of U.S. government securities equal to the federal government's deposit in the bank and, in some states, the state government's deposit. Commercial banks are also induced to own some U.S. government securities because these securities are used as collateral when borrowing from a Federal Reserve bank.

An advantage of owning U.S. government securities is their marketability. Their prices are quoted daily in the newspapers, and the cost of buying and selling them is relatively low. Banks invest in U.S. government securities with maturities of over one year as well as in highly liquid U.S. Treasury bills. If the prices of the issues held by a bank fall, these securities may be sold at a loss, which is then used to minimize corporate income taxes.

BANK DEPOSITS

The deposits offered by banks are divided into two groups: checkable deposits, and savings and time deposits. In 1982, total checkable deposits in all commercial banks amounted to only $300 billion, compared to $800 billion in savings and time deposits.

Checkable Deposits

More than two-thirds of all families in the United States and almost all businesses, nonprofit organizations, and units of government have checking accounts. Customers with checkable deposits may withdraw cash on demand and make payments by writing checks.

From 1933 to 1973, it was illegal for commercial banks to pay interest on demand deposits, even though before 1933 banks had typically paid interest on large accounts. The Federal Reserve's Regulation Q, prohibiting the payment

---

[12] See Robert B. Lamb and Stephen Rappaport, *Municipal Bonds* (New York: McGraw-Hill, 1980); and *Fundamentals of Municipal Bonds* (New York: Public Securities Association, 1982).

of interest on checkable deposits, was part of the banking legislation of the New Deal established as a result of the Great Depression. At that time, many people believed that restricting competition by setting limits on interest rates paid on deposits would contribute to the stability of the banking system by making it unnecessary for banks to invest in excessively risky loans and investments with high rates of return. Many spokesmen for commercial banks initially supported Regulation Q because they believed that it would enable banks to obtain funds at relatively low cost. While they were in effect, these regulations probably benefited borrowers from banks (i.e., businesses and persons with home mortgages) at the expense of depositors.

When market interest rates rose in the 1970s, innovations that circumvented Regulation Q sprang up: Negotiable Order of Withdrawal (NOW) accounts (interest-bearing savings accounts on which checks may be written); automatic transfer from savings (ATS) accounts; phone transfers from savings to demand deposits; the use of savings accounts to pay bills; money market mutual funds; and cash management accounts. Until Congress repealed Regulation Q, the traditional demand deposits offered by commercial banks were in danger of being replaced by these close substitutes, although in 1982 demand deposits were still the predominant type of checkable deposit, amounting to $228 billion compared to $68 billion in NOW and ATS accounts. Business enterprises are still not allowed to own the new interest-earning checkable deposits — NOW, ATS, and Super-NOW accounts. To retain business accounts, however, banks now offer interest-earning "repos" (securities sold under agreement to repurchase).[13] To the business firm, repos are similar to deposits, even though repos are classified as a type of borrowing rather than as deposits. Although checks cannot be written on repos, funds can be immediately transferred to the firm's demand deposits whenever it needs them.

The development of interest-earning checking accounts is the result of the high nominal interest rates caused by the double-digit inflation in the 1970s and early 1980s. When nominal interest rates were low, the convenience of being able to write checks on demand deposits was sufficient to compensate for the low rate of interest that might have been earned on savings or time deposits. When interest rates rose, having a non-interest-bearing checking account became relatively unattractive, and competition among financial institutions led to the development of new types of checkable deposits that outcompeted those that paid no interest.

Use of Checkable Deposits as Money. Presently more than three-fourths of the total amount of money used for making payments in the United States consists of checking accounts in banks. The other types of money in use — coins issued by the U.S. Treasury and Federal Reserve notes issued by the Federal Reserve banks — are much less important than checking accounts.

The use of commercial bank checking accounts as money is an important financial innovation. It has replaced the use of coins and paper money with a vast bookkeeping system in which the amount of money in each checking

---

[13] For a description of this new credit instrument, see Marcia Stigum, *The Money Market: Myth, Reality, and Practice* (Homewood, Ill.: Dow Jones-Irwin, 1978), pp. 86–87, 311–333.

account is recorded on the books of each bank, and depositors transfer funds from their accounts to those of others by writing checks. This method of making payments is superior to the use of coins and paper money because checks can be written for the exact amount of the payment, and they provide a record of the expenditures. Checks are also a safe method of making payment by mail because they are valueless until endorsed.

Checks are more acceptable as a means of payment in the United States than in some other countries partly because of the legal protection offered to those who accept checks. It is a criminal offense to pay for goods by check, knowing that sufficient funds are not available, and then to fail to pay immediately after being notified that the check was not honored by the bank. The offender may be prosecuted in criminal court, and the cost of legal action is borne by the government. In countries in which those who have been defrauded must bear the cost of prosecution, the use of checking accounts is limited.

Savings and Time Deposits

For many people, savings and time deposits are an attractive way of saving because they earn interest and at the same time are less risky than some other investments. Savings or time deposits are very liquid because the dollar amount put in a deposit of this type is fixed and does not fluctuate as do the prices of stocks, bonds, or real estate.

Commercial banks currently offer a wide variety of savings and time deposits: passbook and statement savings deposits; money market deposit accounts; fixed-rate and variable-rate savings certificates; and CDs.

In the past, the most common type of savings and time deposit was the passbook deposit. Even though an advance notice can be legally required before funds are withdrawn from a passbook deposit, in practice banks seldom insist on advance notice. In 1983, the maximum interest rate allowed on passbook deposits in commercial banks was still only 5¼ percent. In recent years, individuals have shifted from passbook deposits to types of savings and time deposits with higher rates of return. The Depository Institutions Deregulation and Monetary Control Act of 1980 (DIDMCA) provided for phasing out the interest-rate ceilings on savings and time deposits over a period of six years.

A new type of savings deposit called money market deposit accounts was authorized in 1982. The authorization to issue this type of savings deposit was a major step in deregulating bank deposits. Although the law requires that these accounts have a minimum balance of $2,500, there is no interest-rate ceiling or specified maturity and they may be held by either individuals or businesses. Although these accounts are not considered checking accounts, individuals can write three checks a month and can have a limited number of authorized automatic transfers. Money market deposit accounts with larger minimum balances typically earn a slightly higher rate of interest than those with the $2,500 legal minimum. The interest rate on these deposits may be changed with market interest rates and is usually paid monthly.

Fixed-rate savings certificates are a type of time deposit available in various maturities. The maximum rates of interest that banks have been allowed to pay on them have seldom changed. In 1983, the maximum rates allowable were graduated from 5¼ percent on maturites from 14 to 89 days to 7¾ percent on maturities of 8 years or more. To withdraw money from savings certificates before maturity, the owner receives a cut in the interest rate and must notify the bank 90 days in advance.

Variable-rate savings certificates were first authorized in 1978. The maximum rate of interest that banks are allowed to pay on variable-rate savings certificates is announced by the U.S. Treasury and varies each week or each quarter. A popular type of variable-rate savings certificate has a maturity of six months, a minimum denomination of $10,000, and a rate of interest that is equal to the average rate at the past four weekly auctions for six-month U.S. Treasury bills plus one-quarter of one percent. Other types have different maturities, minimum denominations, and interest rates.

Negotiable CDs are a type of time deposit purchased primarily by corporations, money market mutual funds, other banks, pension funds, and state and local units of government. The amount of CDs outstanding increased from about $2 billion in 1960 to $260 billion in 1982. The usual denomination is $1 million or more and the minimum denomination is $100,000. The rate of interest paid on CDs is negotiated by the bank with the purchaser. The maturity also may be adjusted for the exact number of months and days desired, but is usually no longer than six months. Since 1973, the rate of interest for large CDs has not been controlled by the federal government. Ceilings were removed in order to enable banks in the United States to compete with Eurodollar banks, which had no ceilings on the rates they paid. Before the interest-rate ceilings on CDs were removed, when market interest rates in international markets rose above the ceilings in the United States, commercial banks in the United States were at a competitive disadvantage.

PROFITABILITY OF BANKS

The profitability of banks depends on the rate of interest received on their loans and investments in relation to both the rate of interest they must pay on their deposits and their operating costs. Their profitability will be higher if they can reduce the legal reserve ratios they are required to hold, the amount of liquid assets they own as a percentage of their deposits, and the amount of their equity as a percentage of their earning assets, and if they can increase the amount of their total assets in relation to their fixed costs. Large banks probably have profit advantages over small banks, and there has been a trend toward larger banking units despite government restrictions on branch banking and interstate banking. An advantage large banks have is that they have been able to provide for their liquidity by managing their liabilities (issuing CDs and borrowing federal funds or Eurodollar deposits) rather than by holding liquid assets. In addition, they typically have lower ratios of equity to their earning assets than smaller banks, and have larger assets relative to their fixed costs. Offsetting these advantages is the disadvantage of having to hold legal reserve ratios for checkable deposits that are larger than those required of small banks.

BANKING INSTABILITY

A major problem of banks is their instability.[14] In the nineteenth century and the early part of this century, there were periodic banking crises in which many banks failed and there were runs on banks. In recent years, an increasing number of banks have failed and many banks on the verge of insolvency have been merged with other banks.

Fractional Reserve Banking

A basic reason for the instability of banks is that they hold reserves equal to only a fraction of their total deposits. At present, banks hold reserves either in cash in vault or deposits at the Federal Reserve banks (which can be immediately converted into Federal Reserve notes). Before the Federal Reserve System was established in 1914, banks held reserves in coin, specie in the form of gold or silver, and paper money issued by the U.S. Treasury or other banks. Normally, fractional reserve banks are able to operate successfully because their daily outflow of "cash" (i.e., coin, paper money issued by the U.S. Treasury and other banks, and specie) is balanced by the daily inflow. In past periods of crisis, however, the outflow was greater than the inflow, many banks ran out of reserves, and they were no longer able to cash checks or convert their notes into cash.

It was widely believed in the nineteenth century that the way to protect the public was to require banks to hold reserves equal to a percentage of their deposits or outstanding notes. Such requirements were enacted in most states. This legislation was based on a misunderstanding of the problem. The purpose of voluntarily holding reserves was to enable a bank to accommodate the public whenever the withdrawals of cash were greater than the inflow. The legislated reserve requirements prohibited banks from using the reserves for the purpose for which they were held. Although the Federal Reserve System still sets minimum reserve requirements for banks, the current purpose of these requirements is to facilitate the regulation of the banking system rather than to try to assure that banks can convert deposits into cash.

Before 1914, a technique that was used to end bank runs was for the governor of the state to proclaim an emergency in which banks did not legally have to convert deposits into cash. In these emergencies, banks would usually remain open and continue to lend money. Also, people could make deposits and pay bills by check, even though they could not obtain cash. These proclamations usually had a desirable psychological effect; as soon as people no longer attempted to convert deposits into cash, cash flowed back to the banks, and the crisis ended. During these crises, however, merchants could not get coin and currency from banks for their cash registers, employers could not get currency to pay their employees, and people were seriously inconvenienced when they needed change for small purchases.

Despite the instability of fractional reserve banking, the development of banks was a major economic innovation. Before the development of banking,

---

[14] See Milton Friedman, *A Program for Monetary Stability* (New York: Fordham University Press, 1960).

money consisted primarily of gold and silver coins. With the development of fractional reserve banking, two more convenient types of money were created: bank notes and bank deposits. In addition, the development of fractional reserve banking made possible a significant expansion in the total supply of money and credit in the United States. In a fractional reserve banking system, however, there was still a limit to the expansion in the amount of notes and deposits that the banks could create. The limit depended on the dollar amount of cash in the economy, the banks' ratio of their cash to their notes and deposits, and the ratio of the amount of cash the public wished to hold in relation to its bank notes and deposits. Assuming that there was $100,000 in cash in the economy, the banks' reserve ratio was 10 percent, and the public's ratio of cash to bank notes and deposits was 15 percent, the following formula shows that the maximum amount of bank notes and deposits that could be issued by the banks is $400,000:

$$\frac{\text{Bank notes}}{\text{and deposits}} = \frac{\text{Dollar amount of cash}}{\substack{\text{Banks' ratio of cash to their deposits and} \\ \text{notes + Public's ratio of cash to their} \\ \text{bank notes and deposits}}} = \frac{\$100,000}{0.10 + 0.15} = \$400,000$$

The banks could not issue more than $400,000 in notes and deposits because if they did their reserve ratio would fall below 10 percent. If there were no creation of bank notes and deposits by the banking system, the total money supply in the economy would have been only $100,000. With fractional reserve banking, the public would have $460,000 in money — $400,000 in bank notes and deposits and $60,000 in cash. Reserves of cash equal to $40,000 would be held by the banks.

Federal Reserve System

The original objective of establishing the Federal Reserve System was to provide a technique for handling the problem of bank runs that would be better than the proclamations suspending specie payments. The National Monetary Commission, established by Congress following the Panic of 1907, concluded that the United States needed a central bank similar to the Bank of England and the other central banks already established in most countries. As stated in the Federal Reserve Act of 1913, the objectives of the Federal Reserve System were to provide both for an expansible amount of currency and for facilities where commercial banks may borrow money in case of need.

After the Federal Reserve System was established, commercial banks in need of currency could always get more Federal Reserve notes by borrowing them from the Federal Reserve banks. Because these notes are liabilities of the Federal Reserve banks, they can be expanded virtually without limit.

Despite the Federal Reserve's borrowing facilities, during the Great Depression from 1929 to 1933, there were runs on banks, a sharp contraction in the total loans and deposits of the banking system, and thousands of bank failures. There was no federal deposit insurance at that time; therefore, when some banks failed, people feared that other banks might fail and, to protect themselves, withdrew their deposits. The troubles spread from bank to bank and eventually threatened the entire banking system. In March 1933, President

Franklin D. Roosevelt issued a proclamation closing all banks for seven days, a period known as the banking holiday.

Although the Federal Reserve System had been designed to solve the problem of runs, during the Great Depression bankers themselves did not initiate enough borrowing from the Federal Reserve to offset the runs. As a result, the runs reduced bank reserves and led to a contraction in the total loans and investments and deposits of the banking system. This contraction worsened conditions because the sale of securities by banks depressed security prices and reduced the market value of the securities owned by banks. The severity of the crisis could have been alleviated if the Federal Reserve authorities had kept bank reserves from declining by purchasing a sufficient quantity of government securities. At that time, however, the Federal Reserve authorities pursued a much more passive monetary policy than they do at present.

Bank Failures

A bank may fail because of bad loans, the decline in the value of the securities it owns, or operating losses. Each of these three contingencies may cut into the shareholders' equity. When the value of a bank's shareholders' equity is below zero, its liabilities are larger than its assets. The bank is then insolvent and is required by government examiners to cease operating.[15]

The most dramatic period of bank failures in the United States was from 1930 to 1933, when more than 9,000 commercial banks suspended operations. The major reason for these failures was the decline in the market value of the bonds owned by the banks. At present, bonds are listed on the balance sheet of a bank at their purchase price, so that a decline in the market price of bonds does not cause a reduction in the bank's assets and thus its shareholders' equity. During the early 1930s, required accounting practices permitted bonds for which continuous price quotations were available to be valued on the balance sheets of banks at their market prices. As a result, when bond prices fell, both the listed value of the bonds that banks had in their portfolios and the value of the shareholders' equity were reduced.

In the period of banking instability since the mid-1970s, the FDIC has typically arranged for the merger of insolvent banks with stronger banks rather than closing down banks by paying off the insured deposits. The number of insolvent banks in this period would have been larger than it had been if their securities had to be valued at their current market price rather than at the price paid for them, or if their mortgages had to be valued at their current market value. A principal reason for the growth of bank failures in this period has been the rise in interest rates. Because some banks had large holdings of long-term mortgages with fixed interest rates, their profits fell because the interest rates paid on their deposits rose above the interest rates earned on their mortgages. In addition, there has been an increase in the number of bad loans. When the rate of inflation declined in 1981 and 1982, many borrowers had difficulty

---

[15] See R. Alton Gilbert, "Bank Failures and Public Policy," *Review* (Federal Reserve Bank of St. Louis, Nov. 1975), pp. 7–15.

paying the high interest rates on the loans they made before the decline in the rate of inflation.

Federal Deposit Insurance Corporation

The FDIC was established in 1934 to protect depositors from bank failures. The FDIC currently insures the deposit of each individual or firm in each bank up to $100,000, basically to prevent runs on banks. Before the FDIC was established, fear that banks might fail caused runs on banks, which contributed to the financial difficulties during serious recessions.

Approximately 30 percent of the deposits of insured banks are not covered because they exceed the $100,000 limit. At present, this limited coverage is of little significance because of the FDIC policy of merging banks that are insolvent with other banks. When an insolvent bank is merged, the entire amount of each deposit is secured. An advantage of merging insolvent banks rather than closing them is that it assures the continuation of normal banking service in the community. Also, FDIC officials believe that in most cases it is less costly to merge an insolvent bank than to go through liquidation, even though the transfer of assets in a merger may be costly to the FDIC.

A disadvantage of deposit insurance is that it has induced banks to hold lower capital/deposit ratios than they had formerly. As a result, banks are now more vulnerable to financial difficulties.[16] Before the FDIC was established, commercial banks had the incentive to have larger capital accounts in order to offer greater protection to depositors. The larger the capital accounts a bank had, the more its assets could fall in value before depositors incurred losses. Because deposits are now protected by deposit insurance, there is little incentive for banks to attempt to be more attractive to depositors by holding higher capital/deposit ratios.

Since the Civil War, government legislation has mandated the amount of shareholders' equity a bank must have. At present, banks classified as "community banks" are required to have a minimum capital/deposit ratio of 7 percent. The ratio required of national and multinational banks is lower than for community banks. Historically, the capital/deposit ratio of banks has declined. For all commercial banks, it was 23 percent in 1900, 14 percent in 1920, 17 percent in 1930, 12 percent in 1940, and less than that since World War II.

A second criticism of the FDIC has arisen in regard to the rapid expansion of CDs. If CDs are insured for 100 percent of their value as a result of the FDIC's merger policy, there is little incentive for investors in CDs to investigate the soundness of a bank, and there is less inducement for banks to assure that depositors are protected. When the FDIC closed the Penn Square Bank in Oklahoma rather than merging it with another bank, the owners of the CDs issued by Penn Square were taken by surprise and suffered large losses because they received only the $100,000 maximum coverage. Critics of the FDIC believe that if the investors in the Penn Square Bank's CDs had expected that

---

[16] Sam Peltzman, "Capital Investment in Commercial Banking and Its Relationship to Portfolio Regulation," *Journal of Political Economy*, Vol. 78 (Jan.–Feb. 1970), pp. 1–26.

their deposits were insured up to only $100,000, they would have investigated the condition of the bank more thoroughly and, as a result, the bank would have been more carefully managed.

MONETARY POLICY

Since its establishment in 1914, the principal function of the Federal Reserve System has shifted from protecting the banking system from instability to controlling the growth of the amount of bank deposits and credit. At the time the Federal Reserve System was established, the United States was on the gold standard, and the growth of the banking system was determined primarily by the inflow and outflow of gold. Under the gold standard, the U.S. Treasury kept the price of gold fixed in terms of the dollar by offering to buy and sell gold at the fixed price. Also, under the gold standard, gold was the principal component of bank reserves; when banks acquired more gold, they were able to expand their loans and deposits, and when they lost gold, they had to contract. The inflow of gold was determined primarily by the international balance of payments of the country. Because gold was the principal type of international money, if the exports of the United States exceeded imports, gold flowed into the United States; and if imports exceeded exports, gold flowed out of the United States.

As the Federal Reserve System developed in the 1920s and 1930s, its open market operations gradually replaced gold as the principal determinant of bank reserves. A major step away from the gold standard occurred in 1933, when the federal government required all persons, business enterprises, and banks in the United States to sell their holdings of gold to the federal government at the then-prevailing legal price of $20.67 per ounce. The U.S. Treasury then raised the price of gold to $35 an ounce, and from then until 1971, bought and sold gold at its official price only from foreign owners and governments. These purchases and sales affected bank reserves just as they did under the gold standard because the Federal Reserve banks held gold certificates based on the gold bullion owned by the U.S. Treasury. When the U.S. Treasury purchased gold, there was an increase in both the amount of gold certificates owned by the Federal Reserve banks and the amount of bank reserves in the Federal Reserve banks; when the U.S. Treasury sold gold, there was the opposite effect. To counter this effect, during this period gold flows were sterilized by open market operations: Federal Reserve authorities usually took actions to offset the effect on bank reserves of purchases and sales of gold. In 1971, the U.S. Treasury ceased purchasing gold from foreign governments. Since then, changes in the quantity of gold in the United States have no longer had any effect on the expansion of bank loans and deposits.

From 1941 to 1951, there was a wartime agreement between the U.S. Treasury and the Federal Reserve System that the Federal Reserve would use its instruments of control to keep market rates at or below $\frac{3}{8}$ percent for 90-day Treasury bills, $\frac{7}{8}$ percent on one-year certificates, and $2\frac{1}{2}$ percent on 10-year Treasury bonds. During this period, the Federal Reserve System was not able to use its instruments of control to follow an easy policy when the economy was slack and a tight policy when the economy needed to be slowed down. Because of the economic expansion during the Korean War, there was strong upward pressure on market interest rates, and the Federal Reserve had to purchase large quantities of government securities in order to keep interest rates on U.S. government securities from rising above their ceilings. This led to an inflationary rate of expansion of bank reserves. The Treasury-Federal Reserve Accord in 1951, ending the agreement to control interest rates in this way, was the start of a new era for monetary policy.

From 1951 to the present time, Federal Reserve authorities have attempted to control the growth of bank loans and deposits so as to influence economic conditions. When Federal Reserve officials have desired reduction in the rate of unemployment, they have taken measures to increase the rate of expansion of bank deposits and bank loans and investments. On the other hand, to combat inflation, they have decreased the rate of expansion of bank deposits and credit.

Tools of Monetary Policy

Open Market Operations. The principal way in which Federal Reserve authorities control the reserves (and thus the loans and deposits) of the banking system is by purchasing and selling U.S. government securities on the open market.[17] When buying securities from government securities dealers, the Federal Reserve Bank of New York pays for the securities with a check drawn on itself. When the dealer deposits the check in a commercial bank, the reserves of that bank are increased. Because there is no offsetting decrease in the reserves of any other bank, the total reserves of the banking system increase, and this makes possible an expansion of the total loans and investments and deposits in the banking system.

The Federal Reserve System can decrease the reserves of banks by selling U.S. government securities. Its holdings of U.S. government securities are then reduced, and the dealer pays for the securities purchased with a check written on a commercial bank. Upon receiving the check, the Federal Reserve bank in that district would reduce the commercial bank's reserve deposit held by the Federal Reserve.

Many factors other than open market operations affect the amount of bank reserves at the Federal Reserve banks, including changes in float; the U.S. Treasury's deposit at the Federal Reserve banks; currency in circulation; loans and acceptances of the Federal Reserve banks; and Treasury currency outstanding. Although Federal Reserve authorities cannot usually control changes in these factors directly, they can offset the effect of such changes through open market operations.

Whether the Federal Reserve buys or sells U.S. government securities on the open market and how much is bought or sold is determined by the Federal Open Market Committee, which meets in Washington, D.C. eight times a year. The committee consists of 12 members: the Federal Reserve System's seven

---

17 For details on the technique of open market operations, see Paul Meek, *U.S. Monetary Policy and Financial Markets* (New York: Federal Reserve Bank of New York, 1982), pp. 114–143.

governors, the president of the Federal Reserve Bank of New York, and four other Federal Reserve bank presidents, who serve on a rotating basis. The chairman of the Board of Governors is also chairman of the Federal Open Market Committee. The members of the Federal Open Market Committee discuss current economic conditions and decide what monetary actions to take. A directive is then issued to guide the Manager of the System Open Market Account, a vice-president of the Federal Reserve Bank of New York, who performs the actual purchases and sales of securities. The transactions are made through U.S. government securities dealers, most of whom are located in New York City.

Changes in the Discount Rate. A second instrument of control of the Federal Reserve System is changes in its discount rate. The discount rate is the rate of interest charged when a bank borrows from a Federal Reserve bank. Depository institutions may borrow from the Federal Reserve banks for the purpose of obtaining the reserves needed to meet their reserve requirements. Also, small banks may arrange in advance to borrow for seasonal needs, and banks with heavy deposit drains are allowed to borrow for longer than usual periods.

The discount rate is not changed more than several times a year. In periods of expansion, when other interest rates are rising, the discount rate is raised; and in periods of recession, when other interest rates are falling, the discount rate is lowered.

Changes in the discount rate may have psychological effects because such changes are widely publicized. Higher discount rates may show that the Federal Reserve System is leaning toward a tighter policy and lower discount rates may show that the Board of Governors is leaning towards an easier policy.

Despite the usual policy of raising the discount rate in periods of expansion and lowering the discount rate in periods of recession, the total amount of loans made by the Federal Reserve banks usually increases in periods of prosperity and decreases in periods of recession. This is because borrowing from the Federal Reserve banks depends on the relationship of the discount rate to other short-term rates rather than to the level of the discount rate. Total loans from the Federal Reserve banks increase in periods of expansion because changes in the discount rate tend to lag behind changes in other short-term rates. In periods of recession, reductions in the discount rate tend to lag behind the decline in other short-term rates. Although a reduction in loans from the Federal Reserve banks reduces bank reserves and an increase in loans increases bank reserves, if such changes in reserves are not desired, Federal Reserve authorities can offset these effects by open market operations.

The availability of discounting at the Federal Reserve banks probably reduces financial instability by increasing the liquidity of banks. Since World War II, there has been a change in the way some banks provide for liquidity. The importance of borrowing (including borrowing from the Federal Reserve banks) has increased, whereas the importance of holding liquid assets has diminished. The loan/deposit ratio of commercial banks has risen from 17 percent in 1945 to more than 90 percent in 1982. This has tended to reduce bank liquidity.

Changes in Reserve Requirements. The Federal Reserve's third major instrument of control is its ability to make changes in the legal reserve requirements of banks. Under the (DIDMCA), the reserve requirements in 1983 for those banks already phased-in are set at 3 percent on net transaction accounts up to $26.3 million and on all nonpersonal time deposits. For net transaction accounts over $26.3 million, 12 percent reserves are required. These reserve requirements established an upper limit to the expansion of the loans and investments and deposits of banks.

Lowering the legal reserve ratios of depository institutions has the same effect on the supply of bank deposits and credit as open market purchases, even though open market purchases increase bank reserves, whereas lower reserve requirements permit banks to make more loans and to hold a larger volume of deposits with the same quantity of reserves. Although this instrument of control is rarely used, reductions in reserve requirements were made in years of business slack: 1953–1954, 1958, 1970, and 1974–1975. An objective of these reductions was to reduce the difference between the reserve requirements of member banks and those of competing nonmember banks and thrift institutions.

Monetary authorities have been reluctant to raise legal reserve requirements. A rise in legal reserve ratios could embarrass banks that are not sufficiently liquid to meet easily the higher reserve requirements. In addition, changes in reserve requirements are a clumsy instrument of control because small changes in the requirements result in large changes in the volume of bank credit and deposits.

An advantage of using this instrument of control is that it affects immediately a very large number of banks. In contrast, the effects of open market operations are felt immediately by only a few banks, although eventually the effects spread throughout the system.

Targets of Monetary Policy

To guide the use of their instruments of control, Federal Reserve authorities have "targets," such as the level of free reserves, the interest rate for federal funds, the rate of expansion of the money supply, and the rate of growth of nonborrowed reserves. They watch the targets in order to tell whether the actions they have taken are easy or tight.

From 1951 until the 1970s, the principal target of monetary policy was the level of "free reserves," the excess reserves held by member banks *less* their borrowings from the Federal Reserve banks.[18] The account manager at the Federal Reserve Bank of New York would purchase or sell just enough securities to hit the target. In order to stimulate the economy, Federal Reserve authorities would raise the level of free reserves; to restrain the economy they would lower the level of free reserves. The concept of free reserves combines in one statistical measure two aspects of Federal Reserve operations that have been closely watched for many years. Increases in the volume of "excess

---

[18] See A. James Meigs, *Free Reserves and the Money Supply* (Chicago: University of Chicago Press, 1962).

reserve" (those held above the legally required amount) allow loans and deposits to be expanded. Changes in the amount of member bank borrowing at the Federal Reserve banks are believed to affect the willingness of commercial banks to borrow in order to expand their loans and deposits.

During the period in which free reserves were used as a target, when free reserves were lowered (excess reserves were relatively low or borrowing was high), market interest rates generally rose; when the level of free reserves was raised, interest rates generally fell. However, from 1964 to 1973, in spite of the drop in the level of free reserves and rising interest rates, the rate of increase in the money supply rose and so did the rate of inflation. This led to the adoption of two new targets: the level of the federal funds rate and the rate of expansion in certain monetary aggregates. In 1975, Congress passed a joint resolution calling for the Federal Reserve to report to them periodically on its plans for the growth of the monetary aggregates. This resolution was later formalized in the Federal Reserve Reform Act of 1977 and the Humphrey-Hawkins Act of 1978.[19]

The use of dual targets resulted in unsatisfactory control over the rate of expansion in the money supply.[20] During the recession of 1973–1975, the rate of expansion of the money supply dropped sharply, probably making the recession more severe than it would otherwise have been. This was followed by a period in which the rate of expansion in the money supply rose very sharply. This led to the shift to a new target in October 1979. Paul Volcker, Chairman of the Board of Governors, announced that there would be more emphasis on the provision of reserves to the banking system than on controlling the money supply by managing the federal funds rate, and the principal target of the Federal Reserve became the growth of nonborrowed reserves.

In using its instruments of control and in attempting to hit its targets, the ultimate goal of the Federal Reserve's monetary policy has been to control such economic variables as price levels, the rate of unemployment, the growth path of nominal gross national product, and the balance of international payments. At the meetings of the Federal Open Market Committee, the members of the committee must decide which is their most important goal. Their policy may be easy, tight, or neutral, and it is often difficult to decide whether they should be combating unemployment or inflation. Their policy has tended to shift back and forth, from combating inflation to combating unemployment.

During the past three decades, monetary policy appears to have had a powerful impact on the growth of nominal national income. When the Federal Reserve has pursued an easy policy, the rate of growth of national income has increased; when it has pursued a tight policy, the rate of growth has decreased. The effects of changes in monetary policy usually occur within a year following such changes. Expansion of bank loans and deposits affects the spending of both borrowers and holders of the additional deposits created, thus altering aggregate demand.

---

[19] For details on the provisions of these acts, see *Federal Reserve Bulletin* (Dec. 1977), pp. 1076–1078; and *1978 Annual Report,* Board of Governors of the Federal Reserve System, pp. 338–340.

[20] See William Poole, "The Making of Monetary Policy, Description and Analysis," *Economic Inquiry,* Vol. 13 (June 1975), pp. 253–265.

When the Federal Reserve increases the amount of bank reserves, the economic impact is magnified because banks can expand both the total amount of their loans and their deposits by several times the amount of the increase in reserves. The ability of the banks to create loans and deposits when they receive additional reserves is a fundamental characteristic of a fractional reserve banking system. When a bank receives additional reserves (as a result of open-market purchases by the Federal Reserve System), the bank will hold only a fraction of the new reserve deposit and lend the rest by increasing the checking account of the borrower. As soon as the borrower uses the funds borrowed, the check written on his checking account will probably be deposited in another bank. When the check is cleared, the second bank's reserves and deposits will be increased, and the first bank will lose most of the reserves it had acquired as a result of the open-market purchase by the Federal Reserve System. The second bank will, like the first bank, hold only a fraction of the new deposit in reserve and lend out the rest. At each bank that is affected, the expansion in loans and deposits is larger than the amount of reserves retained. The expansion in deposits is reduced somewhat because the banks will lose some of the reserves they had acquired when people increase the amount of currency they hold when their deposits increase. In recent years the expansion in total checking accounts and savings and time deposits at commercial banks has been about five times the expansion of reserves.

Major changes in the way in which the Federal Reserve System controls the banking system are expected in the future. Critics of the Federal Reserve's present policies point to its perverse effects on expectations. Although the Federal Reserve can control nominal national income quite well, since 1965 the rate of inflation has accelerated, there have been wide fluctuations in the rate of inflation, and there has been greater instability in real output. The Federal Reserve appears to have only very limited control over either the rate of inflation or real output.

When the Federal Reserve shifts to an easy policy, the initial impact has been an increase in real output, but eventually the easy policy has led to a rise in the rate of inflation. When the Federal Reserve then shifts to a tight policy, the initial effect has been a recession and eventually a decline in the rate of inflation. The decline in real output, however, has tended to persist, and the Federal Reserve has reacted by shifting again to an easy policy, which eventually causes prices to rise, resulting in a long-run upward drift in the rate of inflation.

There are two types of expectation that have adversely affected the results of Federal Reserve policy. The first is expectation based on experience. This type of expectation affects the results of an expansionary monetary policy. When prices rise as a result of an expansionary monetary policy, people soon begin to expect prices to continue to rise at a more rapid rate, and this change in expectation causes the rise in prices to be more rapid than it would otherwise have been. The second concerns what is expected of the Federal Reserve System. This type of expectation affects the results of a tight monetary policy. When unemployment rises and prices fall, people do not expect this fall to last, because they expect the Federal Reserve will soon pursue an expansionary policy due to the rise in unemployment. Because expectations are unchanged, the high rate of unemployment caused by the tight monetary policy persists.

To avoid these perverse effects on expectations, critics advocate that the Federal Reserve be required to pursue a constant long-run goal rather than the present policy of adjusting its instruments of control first to reducing the rate of unemployment and then to lowering the rate of inflation. The principal long-run goals that have been proposed are to stabilize prices, provide for a constant rate of expansion of the money supply, or stabilize the price of gold as was done under the gold standard. If, for example, the long-run goal were to stabilize the level of prices, the Federal Reserve System would not try to reduce the public's expected rate of inflation; and if prices rose, people would not expect the rise in prices to last.

U.S. BANKS IN THE INTERNATIONAL FINANCIAL SYSTEM

Foreign Exchange Operations

Business firms that are engaged in overseas trading usually buy and sell foreign exchange at their commercial banks. Even though most banks do not have a relationship with foreign banks, they can accommodate their own customers by obtaining foreign money from a large commercial bank that does have a relationship with foreign banks. For example, an importer in New Hampshire who needs pounds sterling can exchange dollars for pounds sterling at a local bank. The local bank would purchase the pounds sterling needed from a larger bank with a foreign exchange department. The larger bank owns deposits in pounds sterling in a correspondent bank in Great Britain or in its own branch there, and it can arrange for payment in pounds sterling to the British firm that is owed money by the New Hampshire importer.

The floating of the exchange rate between the dollar and most major currencies in 1973 brought about major changes in the foreign exchange operations of banks. From 1944 to 1973, the exchange rates between the dollar and most other currencies had been fixed in accordance with arrangements established in 1944 by the IMF. In those years, to keep exchange rates fixed, a country such as West Germany would buy dollars with deutsche marks whenever the exchange rate between deutsche marks and dollars fell below the fixed rate, and West German authorities would sell dollars for deutsche marks whenever the exchange rate rose above the fixed rate. To be able to sell dollars, it was necessary for the government of West Germany to own dollar balances large enough to cover any expected needs. When the deutsche mark was floated, the central bank in West Germany announced that it would no longer buy and sell the dollar for the purpose of keeping the exchange rate between the dollar and the deutsche mark fixed. Although exchange rates are no longer fixed, the central banks in countries with floating exchange rates still try to influence exchange rates. This type of regulation is known as a managed float.[21]

The principal advantage of fixed exchange rates was that it eliminated the uncertainties for banks and for importers and exporters resulting from fluctuat-

---

[21] See Dean Taylor, "Official Intervention in the Foreign Exchange Market, or Bet Against the Central Bank," *Journal of Political Economy,* Vol. 90 (Apr. 1982), pp. 356–368.

ing exchange rates. The reason major industrial countries shifted to floating exchange rates was to avoid the periodic foreign exchange crises (primarily in the market for deutsche marks) that had developed under the system of fixed exchange rates. During such crises, West Germany would initially buy dollars to prevent the price of dollars in terms of deutsche marks from falling. Speculation then began that West Germany would soon have to raise its official fixed exchange rate. This caused banks and enterprises engaged in international trade to shift from dollars to deutsche marks and reduced the value of the dollar further. The amount of dollars that the central bank of West Germany had to purchase became so large that it eventually gave up the attempt, and the official price of the deutsche mark in terms of dollars was raised. These crises not only caused serious disruption in foreign exchange markets but also was costly to the West German government. Unless some solution is found for avoiding this type of crisis, the major countries of the world will probably not be willing to return to a system of fixed exchange rates.

After the floating of exchange rates in 1973, the exchange rate for the deutsche mark rose from about 38 cents in 1973 to 55 cents in 1980 and then fell to 41 cents in 1982. The rate for the British pound fell from $2.45 in 1973 to $1.74 in 1977, rose to $2.32 in 1980, and then fell to $1.75 in 1982. The rate for the Canadian dollar fell from $1.00 in 1973 to 81 cents in 1982. Under floating exchange rates, the principal factor causing changes in exchange rates is the different rate of inflation from one country to another. If the rate of inflation is higher in the United States than in West Germany, for example, the effect is an increase in demand for the goods and services of West Germany and reduction in demand by West Germans for goods and services produced in the United States. As a result, in the foreign exchange markets, the demand for deutsche marks increases and the supply of deutsche marks decreases, causing the price of the deutsche mark in terms of dollars to rise. Different movements of interest rates from one country to another also affect exchange rates because exchange rates are affected by changes in capital markets as well as in the markets for goods and services. If real interest rates rise and become higher in the United States than in West Germany, the effect is reduction in the demand for deutsche marks and an increase in the supply of deutsche marks, reducing the price of the deutsche mark in terms of dollars.

Although large industrial countries have floating exchange rates, most small countries have exchange rates that are fixed to the dollar or to another major currency. When exchange rates are fixed, the price level in the smaller country tends to vary directly with the price level in the country to which its currency is tied. When prices rise in the United States, for example, the exports of countries with exchange rates fixed to the dollar tend to increase. This causes them to have surpluses in their balance of payments, an increase in their international reserves in the form of dollars, an expansion in their money supply, and thus a rise in price levels.

Providing International Money

Since World War II, dollar deposits in banks have become the principal type of money used in international trade, even though other currencies, such as the deutsche mark, yen, franc, Swiss franc, and the British pound, are used alongside the dollar. When a Brazilian importer buys goods from Italy, for example, the payment will typically be made by a check in dollars on a U.S. bank. The dollar has become the predominant type of international money for several reasons: It is economical for importers and exporters to use a small number of currencies for international trade, rather than use the currencies of all countries; the United States accounts for a large portion of international trade; there are few restrictions on the convertibility of the dollar into other assets; before 1971 the dollar could be converted into gold; and the value of the dollar was relatively stable before 1965.

World money in the form of dollars in U.S. banks is created when the United States has a deficit in its balance of payments. The excess of imports over exports is paid for by checks in dollars on U.S. banks, and when the foreign enterprises or banks deposit these checks in their deposits in U.S. banks, the total supply of foreign-owned deposits in U.S. banks increases. Almost every year since World War II, the United States has had deficits in its balance of payments. The use of dollar deposits in U.S. banks as a principal type of international money is the major reason for those continuous deficits. In most countries, continuous deficits in the balance of payments is not possible because they would run out of international reserves. In the United States, however, continuous deficits are possible because of the role of banks in the United States as providers of international money.

A major development during the past decade has been the growth of Eurocurrency liabilities, of which approximately 75 percent consist of Eurodollar deposits in banks. Eurodollar deposits are deposits in foreign commercial banks and foreign branches of U.S. commercial banks, denominated in dollars and payable in dollars. London is the center of Eurodollar market activity, even though the market is worldwide. Most Eurodollar liabilities are short-term time deposits and are not held for transactions purposes. The loans and bonds owned by Eurodollar banks are also denominated in dollars, and large corporations and governments are the major borrowers from these banks.

A reason for the growth of Eurodollar banking is that these types of banks can avoid many of the government regulations that have reduced the profitability of banking in the United States. These regulations consist of the relatively high reserve requirements set by the Federal Reserve System; the high cost of federal deposit insurance, the ceilings set on the rates of interest on savings and time deposits; the burdensome costs of complying with the numerous consumer credit laws; and the various restrictions on intrastate and interstate banking. In addition, the remarkable growth of Eurodollar banking is related to the use of the dollar as a type of international money. Dollar deposits in commercial banks now serve not only as the principal type of money used within the United States, but also as the principal type of money used throughout the world for international trade.

SUGGESTED READING

Bagehot, Walter. *Lombard Street: A Description of the Money Market.* New York: C. Scribner's Sons, 1892; first published in 1873.

Campbell, Colin D., and Rosemary G. Campbell. *Introduction to Money and Banking,* 5th ed. Hinsdale, Ill.: Dryden Press, 1983.

Friedman, Milton, and Anna J. Schwartz. *A Monetary History of the United States, 1867 to 1960.* Princeton, N.J.: Princeton University Press, 1963.

Hammond, Bray. *Banks and Politics in America from the Revolution to the Civil War.* Princeton, N.J.: Princeton University Press, 1957.

Klebaner, Benjamin J. *Commercial Banking in the United States: A History.* Hinsdale, Ill.: Dryden Press, 1974.

Mints, Lloyd W. *History of Banking Theory.* Chicago: University of Chicago Press, 1945.

Robertson, Ross M. *History of the American Economy,* 5th ed. New York: Harcourt Brace Jovanovich, 1983.

3

Nonbank Financial Institutions

GEORGE H. HEMPEL

INTRODUCTION

Financial institutions provide the financial products and services needed by savers and borrowers in our economy. Savers' and borrowers' needs are dynamic, and financial institutions must respond to those needs by changing the financial products and services they provide. Furthermore, the regulatory rules under which these financial institutions compete have changed markedly in the late 1970s and early 1980s. The next few years promise more changes than have been witnessed in the past 50 years.

Basic Description and Categories of
Nonbank Intermediaries

Financial institutions supply financial services to the economic community. Most of their assets and liabilities are financial in nature, consisting primarily of money owed to them by nonfinancial units such as households, businesses, and governments; secondarily, of money owed to them by other financial institutions; and corporate stock. The composition of their assets distinguishes them from other productive units of the economy whose assets are composed of tangible assets such as inventory, plant and equipment, and land. Most financial institutions issue contractual obligations, such as deposits or policies, to obtain the funds to purchase these financial assets. The financial institutions' total net worth position, which results from the sale of stock and the accumulation of retained earnings and reserves, represents a relatively minor source of funds. Indeed, it can be argued that financial institutions with the mutual or trusteed forms of organization, as opposed to the corporate form, have only obligations and no net worth.

This chapter discusses major nonbank financial institutions whose primary objectives are (or probably should be) to maximize the wealth of their shareholders. In this way the financial institution's objective function can be analyzed within the same basic framework as the typical nonfinancial firm. The shareholders may be holders of common stock in the corporate form of organization, depositors or policyholders in the mutual form, or beneficiaries in the trusteed form.

Financial institutions whose primary objectives are public policy (even though some are partially privately owned) are not specifically discussed, but some of the management strategies proposed should prove useful in their management. Financial institutions not specifically covered include: Social Security and other federal government pension funds; the Federal Reserve System; the Federal Land Banks; and the federal lending agencies such as the Federal National Mortgage Association, the Government National Mortgage Association, the Export-Import Bank, the Commodity Credit Corporation, the Federal Home Loan Banks, and the Rural Electrification Administration.

For purposes of discussion, nonbank financial institutions are placed in four major categories: thrift intermediaries; contractual institutions; investment companies; and other nonbank financial institutions. Emerging financial service companies and companies whose assets are still primarily nonfinancial are not evaluated, per se. Their impact, however, is evaluated in the final section of this chapter.

Table 3.1 shows the estimated asset size on December 31, 1982, of the covered financial institutions.

Figure 3.1 shows the asset share of the total assets by all financial institutions at the end of 1900, 1929, 1964, 1974, and 1982. The share of the financial institution market held by commercial banks and mutual savings banks fell throughout the period covered. The decline in market share by such banks first appeared to be captured by life insurance companies. However, in recent decades, share of market gains have been dominated by investment companies, pension funds, and S&Ls.

TABLE 3.1   Assets of Financial Institutions, December 31, 1982

Type of Institution	Assets (dollars in billions)	Percentage of Nonbank Assets
Commercial banks	$1,399.9	
Thrift institutions		
Savings and loan associations	$706.0	
Mutual savings banks	174.2	
Credit unions	90.6	
Total thrifts	970.8	31%
Contractual institutions		
Life insurance companies	$563.1	
Property insurance companies	201.5	
Private noninsured pension funds	360.1	
State and local retirement funds	263.8	
Foundations and endowments	79.4	
Total contractuals	1,467.9	47
Investment institutions		
Money market funds	$229.3	
Other investment funds	124.1	
Security dealers and brokers	81.0	
Total investment institutions	434.4	14
Other financial institutions		
Finance companies	$219.1	
Mortgage companies	17.7	
Real estate investment trusts	5.8	
Total other institutions	242.6	8
Total nonbank financial institutions	$3,115.7	
All financial institutions	$4,515.6	

Source: Salomon Brothers, Inc., *1983 Prospects for Financial Markets* (New York: Salomon Brothers, Inc., 1983). Some figures were revised if more recent numbers were available.

The Role of Financial Institutions [1]

The primary economic role of financial institutions can be illustrated by the financial flows over time. Figure 3.2 shows the three primary ways in which the business and household income for a period can be used. First, part of this

[1] This discussion is a summary of the material in George H. Hempel and Jess Yawitz, *Financial Management of Financial Institutions* (Englewood Cliffs, N.J.: Prentice-Hall, 1977).

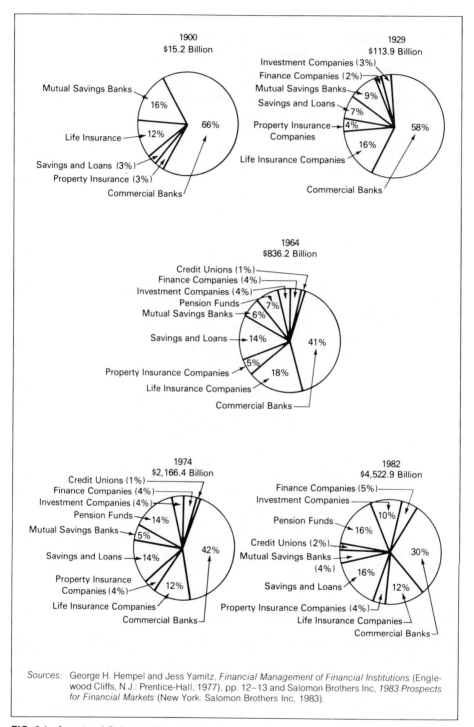

Sources: George H. Hempel and Jess Yamitz, *Financial Management of Financial Institutions* (Englewood Cliffs, N.J.: Prentice-Hall, 1977), pp. 12–13 and Salomon Brothers Inc, *1983 Prospects for Financial Markets* (New York: Salomon Brothers Inc, 1983).

FIG. 3.1 Assets of Selected Financial Institutions, 1900, 1929, 1964, 1974, and 1982

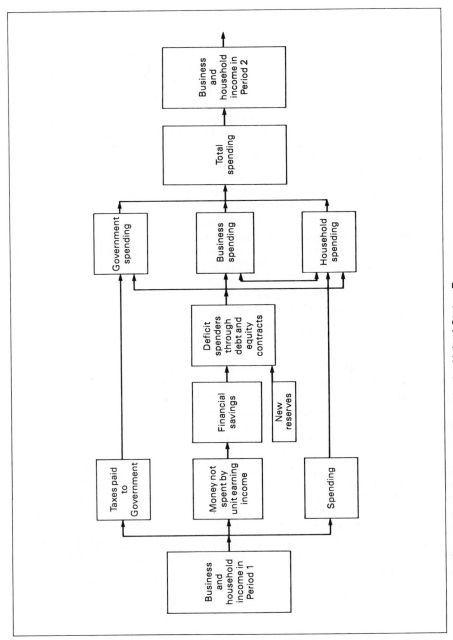

FIG. 3.2 Simplified Graph of Financial Flows in the United States Economy

income is taxed. The remaining "disposable" amount is either spent or not spent by the unit earning the income. What happens to each of these three units of income? Taxes paid to governments are typically spent and constitute a part of total spending and business and household income in the next period. Funds spent by the unit earning them find their way into the spending stream and provide household and business income for the following period. Money not spent by the unit earning the income, plus any new reserves provided from the Federal Reserve (the Fed), are transferred for varying periods to units that want to spend more than they earned in that particular period. These "borrowed" funds are rapidly returned to the spending stream by deficit-spending governments, businesses, and households.

The financial institutions that try to meet the diverse desires of those that save (surplus units) and those that must borrow (deficit units) are often called financial intermediaries.[2] In facilitating the flow of funds between savers and borrowers (see Figure 3.3), financial intermediaries create two separate markets. They purchase primary securities from borrowers and emit secondary, indirect liabilities to savers. In this way, a financial intermediary is able to tailor its assets and liability structure to satisfy the desires of both the ultimate borrowers and the ultimate lenders in the economy. Financial intermediaries simply substitute their own more desirable (to the surplus units) financial liabilities for the financial liabilities of the deficit unit. By holding a diversified portfolio of assets, many intermediaries can reduce risk beyond the reduction available to individual units. They also assist deficit units in finding funds in the desirable amount and form.

In a fully developed financial system, potential surplus units can choose from a wide variety of alternative financial assets, such as primary securities of deficit units and the numerous liability forms offered by financial intermediaries. Deficit units can generally acquire purchasing power in a desirable form, either directly from surplus units or, more commonly, from a financial intermediary. Liquidity and marketability of the securities created in the direct or indirect flows between surplus and deficit units are vastly improved by the existence of a secondary market (e.g., the New York Stock Exchange), where such securities are traded. Such a setting encourages economic efficiency, since the allocation of financing is based on a unit's ability to pay, and profitability, rather than on the form of financing. This greater efficiency would be expected to stimulate both capital accumulation and growth in the economy.

The economic role of financial institutions (and the financing instruments they create) can now be summarized. Some financial institutions aid the saving-investment process by serving as brokers or agents; most aid economic growth much more with their efforts to intermediate the savings-investment function. *Intermediation* affects this process in several ways. (1) It facilitates the separation of the saving decision from the investment decision. Each unit is not required to spend exactly what it earns in each period. In this way the budget constraint is expanded. Spending units can escape the straitjacket of balanced budgets so as to allocate their spending more efficiently. (2) Intermediation

---

[2] Brokers or agents are also institutions that serve as go-betweens and receive commissions for their services. Typically, they do not hold financial assets for long periods themselves, and their services help match surplus and deficit units but do not overcome the differences that may exist between surplus and deficit units.

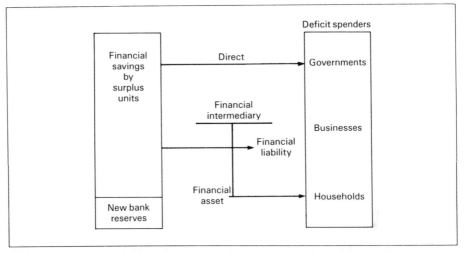

FIG. 3.3   Financial Intermediaries in the Flow Between Surplus and Deficit Units

encourages saving by providing a varied menu of financial assets particularly suited to the needs and/or desires of surplus units. (3) Intermediation encourages investment by providing a variety of available sources of funds to the deficit units. (4) By making borrowing and lending more attractive, it increases the full-employment savings and investment rate and, therefore, the growth rate of capital and income. In addition, intermediation assists in the separation of administration and ownership of wealth. Specialization of activities increases productivity.

Financial institutions also tend to reduce risks to both surplus and deficit units. The uncertainties associated with direct relationships between surplus and deficit units become predictable within reasonable limits when financial institutions work with portfolios of assets and liabilities. By pooling their assets (primarily liabilities of deficit units), financial institutions reduce the risks of default (on the institutions' liabilities) to surplus units. The institutions can also increase liquidity, marketability, and divisibility of their liabilities because the combination of outflow demands of numerous holders is more predictable than the demand by one or a few holders. Deficit units have a greater availability of funds in a form better suited to their payment capability. Thus, financial institutions contribute to the real productivity of the economy and to the overall standard of living, since they are able to satisfy, simultaneously, the needs and preferences of both surplus and deficit units.

Furthermore, specialization of labor and efficiency of size and scale allow financial institutions to act in a cost-reducing role, with surplus units receiving a higher net return and deficit units paying less for their funds than would be possible in the absence of the intermediary role of financial institutions. Also, financial institutions save on the required search cost for both borrowers and lenders. In such a system the task of asset selection for portfolio management is delegated to a professional specialist. Financial institutions with large asset holdings and contiguous operations possess a trading advantage in lower per-unit transaction costs over smaller, nonfinancial units. Deficit units are not required to hire specialists for their generally irregular borrowing (or equity-raising) pattern but can rely on specialists hired by financial institutions.

A Generalized Management Model [3]

The first step in managing a nonbank financial institution is to establish a clear-cut set of objectives; for example, to package assets and liabilities so as to provide desired economic services to surplus and deficit units. The conflicting desires of surplus units for higher returns and of deficit units for lower costs must be balanced. How then does the nonbank financial institution ascertain when it is operating efficiently?

The primary objective of a financial institution is to maximize the share-holders' wealth. Wealth maximization denotes maximizing the benefits (whether cash payments or increases in the value of holdings) to the residual contributors of funds (generally called shareholders) to the financial institution. Contributors with prior claims are paid contractually promised sums; however, shareholders gain from higher actual or potential residual cash benefits. The maximization of these benefits is consistent with the efficient allocation of scarce financial resources. While the social role of nonbank institutions should not be ignored, the quantification of social costs and benefits require the use of individual opinions rather than reliance on market forces. By providing needed financial services in a wealth-maximizing manner, a financial institution will generally perform a needed economic function, and will tend to carry out its social and other obligations over a span of time, provided these obligations are brought to bear on management's decisions.

Wealth maximization is the maximization of the discounted net cash bene-fits to shareholders. This condition can be expressed algebraically as:

$$W = \frac{B_1}{(1 + r)^1} + \frac{B_2}{(1 + r)^2} + \frac{B_3}{(1 + r)^3} + \cdots + \frac{B_n}{(1 + r)^n} \qquad (3.1)$$

where W is the wealth position of its shareholders, B denotes the net cash benefits to the shareholders in periods $1, 2, 3, \cdots$ and n, and r is the appropriate rate of discount that reflects both the timing and the risk associated with the net cash receipts.

The key variables comprising B and r are shown in the following equations:

$$B = R - (C + O + T) \qquad (3.2)$$

$$r = i + p \qquad (3.3)$$

In Equation 3.2, R denotes the gross receipts from the financial institution's assets (A), C represents the costs of its financial liabilities (L), O is the over-head costs associated with R and C, and T is the taxes the institution must pay. Depreciation and other noncash costs are generally a relatively small percent-age of O, so net cash benefits and net income are reasonably similar for most financial institutions. In Equation 3.3, i is an estimated riskless interest rate that reflects the time value of money, and p is the appropriate risk premium

---

[3] This discussion is a summary of the material in Hempel and Yawitz, note 1 *op. cit.*

associated with the assets and liabilities of the institution. By substituting
Equation 3.2 and 3.3 into Equation 3.1, the following is obtained:

$$W = \frac{R_1 - (C_1 + O_1 + T_1)}{1 + (i + p)^1} + \frac{R_2 - (C_2 + O_2 + T_2)}{1 + (i - p)^2} + \cdots + \frac{R_n - (C_n + O_n + T_n)}{1 + (i + p)^n}$$

(3.4)

The interdependent nature of these variables should be evident. R represents
the flow of benefits from the stock of assets and C represents the flow of
negative benefits (costs) from the stock of liabilities, which the financial institution has created in order to obtain funds. O, which has both fixed and variable
components, will depend at least partially on the nature of the asset and liability
positions. For taxable institutions, T can be taken to a variable cost that is a
function of $R - (C + O)$. While the riskless rate (i) is beyond the control of the
financial institution, it will tend to be strongly correlated with both R and C.
Finally, p is a function of the interaction of the risks associated with the portfolios of assets and liabilities. Conceptually, it is useful to think of the required
return $(i + p)$ determined by the markets' perception of the riskiness of the
financial institution's asset, liability, and capital composition.

To make prudent financial management decisions, the manager of a financial institution must consider the combined impact of all relevant variables. For
example, if management considers purchasing liabilities at 8 percent and investing the proceeds in assets earning 10 percent, they must take account of
changes in O, T, and p from the transaction. It may well be that, in spite of the
positive spread between R and C, the total effect, including increases in overhead, taxes, or risks, may actually reduce the wealth of the financial institution.

The wealth-maximization objective, with only modest adjustments, can be
employed for all existing organizational forms of financial institutions: the corporate form, the mutual form, and the trusteed organization.[4] *Corporations* are
controlled by their common stockholders, who elect a board of directors, which
then appoints the management. Common stockholders are entitled to the residual benefits because they supply the risk capital of the corporation. The objective of a corporate-type financial institution should be to maximize the wealth
of its common shareholders relative to these shareholders' investment in the
institution.

Mutual organizations have no common stock and, therefore, no holders of
common stock. For wealth-maximization purposes, the suppliers of funds can
generally be considered as shareholders. Legally, these shareholders (depositors or policyholders) elect the management, which, in practice, tends to be
nearly self-perpetuating. Net benefits are usually either returned to depositors
and policyholders or accumulated for an indefinite time in the enterprise in a
reserve or net worth account. Some mutual institutions, credit unions, in particular, may share their net benefits between borrowers (often with a loan
rebate) and depositors. While the objective of wealth maximization does not

---

4 Finance companies, and some types of investment companies, must be corporations. Savings
and loan associations, casualty insurance companies, and life insurance companies can be corporations or mutual organizations. Mutual savings banks, credit unions, and some forms of investment companies must be mutual organizations. Private and public pension funds generally have
trusteed forms of organization.

indicate how the net benefits should be distributed between these groups, it does seem reasonable that both borrowers and depositors will want the institution to maximize the total wealth available to them.

Trusteed organizations are usually managed by salaried trustees in accordance with the basic documents creating these organizations. The funds accumulated, both principal and net income, accrue to the beneficiary, who usually wants the highest possible return for an acceptable risk level; therefore, the wealth-maximization objective also seems appropriate for this form of organization. Differences in the form of contribution and/or benefit may lead to some complexities in this general objective. For example, the coincidence of risk preferences between beneficiaries and contributors is questionable if fixed benefits are promised to the beneficiary of a trusteed organization. In such a situation, the beneficiary may prefer lower-risk investments, because his return is not affected, while the contributor usually prefers higher-risk and higher-return investments, since the amount he contributes to the trust is more likely to be lowered. In spite of this risk incompatibility, the wealth-maximization objective seems generally appropriate for trusteed forms of organization.

Once wealth maximization has been accepted as the primary objective of the financial institution, one can turn to the implementation of policy decisions consistent with this objective. Conceptually, every management decision should take into account the impact of all variables on the shareholder's wealth position. This can best be demonstrated by the use of a numerical example for a hypothetical financial institution. For simplicity, average returns and costs are assumed to be constant over the perpetual life of the institution.[5] Equations 3.1 and 3.4 can then be restated as follows:

$$W = \frac{B}{r} \tag{3.1a}$$

$$W = \frac{R - (C + O + T)}{(i + p)} \tag{3.4a}$$

The hypothetical nonbank institution, ABC Financial Institution, has $1 billion in assets that can be distributed between lower-risk, lower-return asset A_1 and higher-risk, higher-return asset A_2. These assets are financed by $950 million in liabilities, distributed between lower-cost, higher-risk L_1, and higher-cost, lower-risk L_2, and $50 million in capital or reserves. The returns and costs on these assets and liabilities, the assumed overhead and income tax rate, and the capitalization rates applied to various streams of risky benefits appear in Table 3.2. Given these alternative assets and liabilities, one may consider the allocation decision facing ABC.

Four possible cases are presented in Table 3.3. In Case 1, most (80 percent) of the asset portfolio is invested in relatively safe A_1 while L_1 is the dominant (80 percent) liability source. After net other expenses and taxes are accounted for, the net benefits (called net profits for corporations) of $6.7 million are capitalized at a 13 percent rate, which is assumed to reflect the

---

[5] With constant returns and costs a series of

$$\frac{B_1}{(1 + r)^1} + \frac{B_2}{(1 - r)^2} + \frac{B_3}{(1 + r)^3} + \frac{B_4}{(1 - r)^4} + \cdots + \frac{B_n}{(1 - r)^n} = \frac{B}{r}$$

TABLE 3.2   Assumptions About the ABC Financial Institution

(dollars in millions)

Balance sheet totals	
Assets	$1,000
Liabilities	950
Capital (or reserves)	50
Available asset returns	
A_1 (a low-risk asset)	10%
A_2 (a high-risk asset)	12
Cost of acquiring funds, overhead and taxes	
L_1 (a high-risk source)	7%
L_2 (a low-risk source)	9
O (net other expenses)	$25
t (income tax rate)	30%
$T = t[R - (C + O)]$	
Capitalization rates	
i (riskless rate)	8%
p_1 (low-risk premium)	2
p_2 (medium-risk premium)	5
p_3 (high-risk premium)	8

---

combined risks of the portfolios of assets and liabilities. These returns, capitalized at a risk-adjusted discount rate, produce a wealth position of $52 million for its shareholders.

In Case 2, ABC takes greater risks by dividing its assets equally between A_1 and high-risk A_2. This risk is reflected in the 16 percent capitalization rate demanded by the market. If the other variables remain unchanged, in spite of the higher capitalization rate, the higher net benefit of $10.9 million should lead to a higher wealth of $68 million. In other words, the reward is more than sufficient to justify the additional risk exposure. ABC's capital owners would be better off in Case 2 than in Case 1.

Case 3 illustrates the effects when ABC allocates most (80 percent) of its assets in the lower-risk assets and finances slightly over half of these assets with the high-cost, low-risk liabilities. The wealth level resulting from the lower net benefits of $1.8 million and a capitalization rate of 10 percent is below that in Cases 1 and 2 and would be an unfavorable alternative. The wealth in Case 4, resulting from shifting to the high-earning, high-risk assets while keeping the high-cost, low-risk liabilities, exceeds the wealth obtained in Case 3 but is lower than the wealth in Cases 1 and 2. Using the wealth-maximization objective, ABC shareholders should favor the alternative with the highest wealth, Case 2.

TABLE 3.3   Alternative Decisions by ABC Financial Institution

(dollars in millions)

	Case 1	Case 2	Case 3	Case 4
		BALANCE SHEET		
A_1	$800	$500	$800	$500
A_2	200	500	200	500
L_1	800	800	450	450
L_2	150	150	500	500
C	50	50	50	50
		REVENUES, COST, AND BENEFITS		
R	$104.0	$110.0	$104.0	$110.0
C	69.5	69.5	76.5	76.5
O	25.0	25.0	25.0	25.0
T	2.8	4.6	0.7	2.5
B	6.7	10.9	1.8	6.0
		CAPITALIZATION RATE AND WEALTH		
i	0.08	0.08	0.08	0.08
p	0.05	0.08	0.02	0.05
W	$6.7	$10.9	$1.8	$6.0
	0.13	0.16	0.10	0.13
	or	or	or	or
	$52	$68	$18	$46

Many other cases could be presented for even the very simple decisions facing the ABC Financial Institution. For example, other risk-return possibilities and combinations of assets and liabilities could be considered; net other expenses or taxes could be varied with side effects on asset and liability combinations; and if the company's capital or reserve position were different both net income and risk could be affected. Three basic points seem clear from an analysis of Cases 1 through 4: (1) changes in any one variable can affect any or all of the other relevant variables; (2) since risk affects the capitalization rate, the interactive effect of the portfolio of assets and liabilities must be considered; and (3) this analysis tends to validate the selection of maximizing the net wealth of the shareholders as the primary objective of management decisions by a nonbank financial institution.

Specific Areas for Management Action

While the criterion for every decision should be its effect on the shareholders' net wealth, practical decision making requires emphasis on selected variables for day-to-day nonbank financial institution actions. Most nonbank financial institutions can group the key variables affecting their wealth-maximization objectives into four interrelated categories: spread management; control of net other expenses; liquidity management; and capital (or reserve) management.

Spread management emphasizes the difference between the return on assets (R) and the cost of liabilities (C) over time. While a high positive spread is generally desirable, two limiting aspects need to be emphasized by financial managers. First is that it is a high positive spread over time. A financial institution using short-term liabilities as a source of funds may not want to buy long-term assets, even those with a highly favorable spread, because of the possible adverse movements in the spread over time. Similarly, financial institutions may use long-term assets rather than face the risk that shorter-term assets, even if they provide a higher spread at this time, may yield a low or negative spread later in the life of the liability. Second, the effect or net other expenses (O) and risk (p) of the manner in which R and C are acquired cannot be ignored. For example, the additional overhead and risk may negate the considerably higher gross spread when financial institutions make consumer loans.

Net other expenses is another major area for consideration in proper management of a nonbank financial institution. Statements on control of overhead costs by some security analysts such as ''Whenever I see excavation work start on a new building by a financial institution, I sell their stock short,'' are probably oversimplifications. Nevertheless, two of the major causes of financial stress for any financial institution are being saddled with large fixed overhead costs in periods of stress and ignoring the high overhead cost implications that often accompany seemingly high-profit opportunities. The major recommendation for avoiding the first problem is that the financial institution examine the impact of any increase in overhead costs on net cash flows at varying levels of activity, not just for the most optimistic projections. The second problem is avoided by making rational spread-management decisions that do not ignore the effect of overhead costs. Equally important is the nonbank institution's ability to generate fee and other non-interest income to offset some of the non-interest expenses. Such income sources have been growing rapidly for many institutions and future growth seems essential to wealth maximization.

Liquidity management involves the structuring of the interactive portfolios of assets (A) and liabilities (L) so that funds are available to meet the cash flow demands of both existing liability holders and potential deficit customers. (See Chapter 32 for detailed analysis.) Liquidity management should be applied so as to maximize the spread ($R - C$) at a risk level the financial institution is willing to accept. At an elementary level, liquidity management may emphasize matching the maturity structure [6] of an institution's assets and liabilities. Liquidity management is usually more complex. Factors such as expected fund inflows, access to purchased liabilities, credit risks on assets, and purchasing power risks must be considered. For example, a financial institution that expects its annual cash inflows to exceed matured liabilities over the next several years

---

[6] The term *matching maturity structure* is used to denote a matching of the time profile of cash flows on assets and liabilities.

may attain a higher spread without placing excessive pressure on its liquidity position by structuring its portfolio so that the maturities of its assets exceed the maturities of its liabilities. Some financial institutions can legitimately use liability management (the purchase of funds rather than liquidation of assets to meet liquidity needs) if they can purchase the acquired funds at a positive spread in periods of credit ease and tightness. Firms with lower liquidity pressures may take somewhat greater credit risks in their asset portfolios because they will not be under pressure to sell these assets.

The capital (or reserve) management position is the final major variable involving nonbank financial institution decisions. The capital (or reserve) position is based on the residual from assets minus liabilities. If capital is too high, the return per dollar of capital may be low, and shareholders may not receive sufficient benefits (e.g., dividends, appreciation on common stock, higher interest on savings shares, and lower insurance costs). If capital is too low, higher risk may offset the higher return per dollar of capital. Growth of assets and liabilities may also be constrained by the lack of capital to support that growth. This can be particularly serious for mutual institutions that are unable to raise additional capital from external sources.

THE CHANGING ENVIRONMENT

Nonbank financial institutions, like any business, must adapt to a changing environment. This environment is particularly fragile for financial institutions because it depends not only on normal market forces, such as the economy, competition, and technological changes, but also on enabling legislation and regulation. A single act or regulatory decision can have a significant impact on a financial institution's assets, liabilities, and net benefits. The impact of change on the primary types of nonbank financial institutions from the mid-1970s through the early 1980s is traced in the following section.

The Economic Environment

The economic environment of the late 1970s and early 1980s has significantly changed many nonbank financial institutions. The economic environment of the mid-1980s promises to be equally challenging. The impact of inflation, high interest rates, and fluctuating interest rates has been substantial.

Except for a brief ascent into double-digit inflation in 1974, the annualized rate of inflation using the Consumer Price Index (CPI) fluctuated between 5 and 7 percent throughout most of the 1970s. From 1979 through most of 1982, the annualized rate of inflation ranged from 10 to 14 percent. Inflation reduced the level of financial saving by surplus units and led to much higher interest rates. The liabilities used by financial institutions had to be at higher rates to attract funds from increasingly knowledgeable surplus units. Financial institutions that had large amounts of long-term assets earning at past low-levels (relative to long-term fixed-rate liabilities) suffered large market value declines.

High and fluctuating interest rates are also likely to continue to challenge financial institutions in the next several years. Numerous studies have con-

TABLE 3.4   Changes in the Prime Lending Rate

Years	Number of Changes
1950–1954	6
1955–1959	10
1960–1964	1
1965–1969	15
1970–1974	65
1975–1979	74
1980–1982	98

Source: Federal Reserve Bulletin,
various years

cluded that interest rates on long-term investments tend to exceed the expected rate of inflation by roughly 3 percent (see Chapter 18). Brief periods, such as late 1982 and early 1983, when long-term rates exceeded actual inflation by 6 to 7 percent, occur because people's expectation for inflation probably affected interest rates more than the reported level of inflation. Thus, a prediction of continued high interest rates, although moderated by some improvement in the inflation rate, is consistent with a prediction of continued high inflation.

Wide and rapid fluctuation in interest rates also seem as likely in the 1980s as it was in the late 1970s. The increasing amplitude of interest rate fluctuations can be seen by observing in Table 3.4 the data on changes in the prime lending rate charged by commercial banks. The data in Table 3.4 understate the magnitude of changes in the prime rate because changes were usually one quarter of a percentage point prior to the late 1970s, whereas many prime rate changes in 1980 through 1982 were one half or a full percentage point.

Continued fluctuation in interest rates seems likely if the Fed sticks to its declaration of October 6, 1979. In essence, the Fed said it will place more emphasis on controlling reserves and monetary aggregates and will let interest rates seek levels consistent with its reserve and monetary goals. The prime rate was 12 percent on October 6, 1979, and 20 percent two years later. During these two years, the prime rate had risen to 20 percent, fallen to 11 percent, risen to over 21 percent, fallen to 17 percent, and risen to 20 percent. These rates are fairly representative of the borrowing and lending rates on many nonbank financial institutions' liabilities and assets; thus, balance-sheet management at such institutions is likely to become increasingly challenging.

One paradoxical result of the changing economic environment is that interest rate forecasting has become both more important and more difficult. It is more important because the stakes are higher for nonbank financial institutions exposed to interest rate risks resulting from wider swings in interest rates. It is more challenging because these interest rate swings seem to defy some of the more familiar rules of thumb traditionally used by forecasters to predict interest rates.

Competition

There is some disagreement over the main source of competition for nonbank financial institutions in the late 1980s. Will it be commercial banks, thrift institutions, nondepository institutions (such as money market funds, brokerage firms, or insurance companies), or nonfinancial companies?

Competition of other institutions with commercial banks will probably intensify because of the lack of product differentiation for some financial services; the rapid disappearance of Regulation Q (promulgated by the Federal Reserve), which prohibited banks from rate competition for some categories of deposits; the continuing decline in geographic constraints restricting banking competition; and the greater use of advanced technology by banks. Still, commercial banks suffer from the most repressive regulation.

Competition with and among thrift institutions is also likely to increase. The prediction that nonbank thrift institutions will be unable to compete because of their inferior asset positions and lack of experience in many financial service areas seems overoptimistic. The opposite will probably occur. Some large thrifts will be very competitive in both attracting and employing funds. By the end of 1982, thrifts had acquired permission to do nearly all of the things banks and other institutions can do with the attraction and employment of funds. After some failures, consolidations, and restructuring, the surviving aggressive thrifts may provide even more formidable competition than in the past.

Nondepository financial organizations appear likely to use their competitive edge to offer more diverse financial services. This edge results from the fact that they have fewer restrictions: no reserves, no capital requirements, and less regulation. Some of the nondepository organizations providing financial services are known. For example, much has been written about money market funds and brokerage firms, like Merrill Lynch, which offer cash management accounts. The combination of financial giants, such as Bache with Prudential, and American Express with Shearson in 1981, may be indicative of very competitive financial supermarkets in the near future. In addition, other nondepository financial organizations, such as life insurance companies and private pension funds, are looking carefully at additional segments of financial services they believe would be profitable for themselves.

Finally, more and more companies whose primary business activities are nonfinancial appear to be interested in starting to offer financial assets, liabilities, and services that will compete with many banking products and services. For example, Sears Roebuck and Company has opened a number of financial centers and has announced it will offer consumer savings certificates and a money market mutual fund in the near future. Nonfinancial companies are likely to prove formidable competitors in the coming years.

Technological Change

Technological changes in the 1980s complicate efforts to predict how many nonbank financial institutions will fare in coming years. The pace of technological change for financial institutions has been slower than many predicted in the last few years. On average, the financial service industry is still dominated by a delivery system that requires that people — customers and institution employees — physically handle pieces of paper. Recent developments, however, indicate that substantive movement away from this system is taking place. The technology exists to alter financial institutions' delivery systems rapidly. This technology consists of advances in computer capabilities, which permit easy and inexpensive gathering, storing, analyzing, and retrieving of customer data, and of advances in communication hardware and software, which permit convenient access to customer records at great distances. There is a veritable revolution in the delivery system which has significant implications for decisions in nonbank financial institutions.

By 1983, automated teller machines (ATM) had become widely accepted in most areas of the country. By the mid-1980s, the vast majority of transactions probably will be by electronic impulse made away from the institution's physical location. With existing technology, automated clearing houses, direct payroll crediting, direct bill paying, widespread use of debit cards and point of sales (POS) terminals, and disappearance of float appear very likely. The technology exists and is being implemented by larger firms and their banks. Furthermore, some individuals already can sit at home and pay bills, make deposits, shift among types of deposits, shift from deposits to other financial assets, and so forth, all by electronic impulse. By the late 1980s, such "home banking" may be commonplace. To compete effectively on a cost basis, financial institutions must use the existing technology and find other methods to reduce significantly the cost of most common transactions with all but their very large customers. The task may be literally to keep most customers away from the institution, except for unusual transactions.

In the long run, such technology will increase productivity and reduce costs in nonbank financial institutions. However, the transition period will be difficult. This difficulty is compounded by the trying economic and regulatory environment predicted. Some nonbank financial institutions, particularly very large ones, will be willing and able to take the high costs and risks involved whereas others may still try to drag their feet. The foot-draggers may find themselves rapidly becoming noncompetitive.

Changing Regulatory and Legislative Rules

Financial institutions have been, and likely will continue to be, affected very highly by regulatory and legislative changes. The reason is that the commercial banking system and nonbank financial institutions have a large and direct effect on our economy (see the preceding economic role discussion). A loss of confidence in our payments system, or inefficiency in our financial markets, would be disastrous to U.S. economic prosperity. How to regulate enough and yet promote it through competition has been, and will probably continue to be, a perplexing problem.

A complete history of regulatory and legislative changes is clearly beyond the scope of this chapter.[7] It is worth mentioning that, as a result of the depres-

---

[7] See Chapter 4 of Hempel and Yawitz, note 1 *op cit.,* for a more complete historical background through 1975.

sion starting in 1929, most regulation and legislation in the 1930s tried to compartmentalize financial institutions. Commercial banks had to take in demand and savings deposits, make loans, and buy securities with the funds raised; savings and loan associations (S&Ls) were restricted primarily to savings deposits and real estate mortgages; credit unions were limited primarily to members' deposits and installment loans; brokerage firms were strictly brokers and underwriters; and insurance companies were limited to fixed-return insurance contracts.

The pace of change accelerated in the early 1970s. Bank holding companies (BHCs) received official sanction to provide additional financial services. In order to free the larger banks and thrift institutions from disintermediation (loss of deposits), Regulation Q limits on interest rates were removed from time deposits of over $100,000 in 1973. This action allowed such institutions to compete ratewise for the first time in periods of high market rates. Real estate investment trust became a strong competitive alternative, which faded by the mid-1970s. Selective easing of regulations began to permit thrifts in some regions to offer interest-bearing, negotiable orders of withdrawal (NOW) accounts. Probably the biggest event that shaped things for the coming decade was the deregulation of fixed commission rates for brokerage firms in 1975. Faced with the possibility of debilitating competition, brokerage firms sought new ways (discount brokerage houses) and new competitive products (cash management accounts and money market funds) to obtain adequate returns. In many ways nonbank financial institutions have never needed to take such measures.

In the brokerage industry itself there were numerous consolidations and failures. Less than two thirds of the institutions open in 1975 existed in 1980. The newly created competitive products, such as cash management accounts and money market funds, began to hurt the inflows into banks and thrift institutions unwittingly forced into the competitive fray. Bank and thrift regulators responded in 1978 by allowing the rates on many types of time deposits to be tied to rates on similar maturity Treasury securities. Also, many financial institutions were and are affected by the Bankruptcy Reform Act of 1978. The net effect of this Act has been to increase the cost of lending by financial institutions.

Finally, the passage of H.R. 4986, the Depository Institutions Deregulation and Monetary Control Act of 1980 (DIDMCA), and H.R. 6267, the Garn-St Germain Depository Institution Act of 1982 (DIA) will probably lead to greater changes in nonbank financial institutions than any legislation since the 1930s. H.R. 4986 includes nine titles on far-reaching and diverse subjects, including nationwide authorization of NOW accounts, expanded asset and liability powers for thrift institutions, fees for services provided by the Fed, preemption of state usury laws, and simplification of truth-in-lending regulations.

Longer-run effects of DIDMCA will probably include a more equitable competitive environment and decreased variation of relative growth rates among various types of deposits. The Fed still does not pay interest on reserves left with it; however, the door for this is partially open. The Fed can pay a return up to what its securities portfolio earned during the previous calendar quarter on accounts above required reserves and on supplemental required reserves (up to 4 percent of transaction accounts) that the Fed is permitted to impose under certain situations.

H.R. 4986 also required the Fed to price its services, such as checkclearing and collection, settlement, wire transfer, and float, at their estimated full cost plus a markup so that the resulting prices would be similar to those charged by private businesses. It is too early to know the results of this pricing (services are being priced initially over several years), but it appears certain that financial institutions will have to pay increased explicit cost to the Fed for services. There is some chance that the demand for Federal Reserve services will rise because more bank and thrift institutions may use them, but most banks are investigating other sources that may provide the needed services more efficiently (i.e., at lower cost). The longer-run effects of Federal Reserve pricing will probably include changes in banks' cash management practices, further reduction in float, greater reliance on explicit pricing than on balances, and realistic financial institution pricing of retail transaction deposit services. It is also believed that Federal Reserve pricing will provide additional stimuli to electronic banking, such as debit cards, direct deposits, ATMs, and POS terminals.

Nationwide approval of NOW accounts, which became effective at the beginning of 1981, has led to higher interest expense for transaction-type deposits. These higher interest expenses seem most likely to hurt smaller, retail-oriented financial institutions whose profitability has been more dependent on having substantial amounts in low-cost deposits. In addition, the reserves on savings accounts that are switched to NOW accounts will rise from 3 to 12 percent. Nevertheless, in the longer run, NOW accounts offer positive opportunities to financial institutions. They should bring higher and more stable personal transaction balances and fewer returned checks and overdrafts. Setting the appropriate levels for NOW pricing factors, such as minimum balances and any fee and service charges, will be an important financial institution decision in the 1980s.

The phaseout of Regulation Q ceilings will probably have the most far-reaching effect on financial institutions. A gradual increase in the interest cost of many types of funds and an increase in pressures on interest margins will probably continue. As time passes, the emphasis on funds acquisition is likely to shift from quantity to product design and pricing. Variation in the relative size and growth of various types of deposits will probably decline and more emphasis will be placed on explicit interest rather than on premiums.

Several other parts of H.R. 4986 will also affect financial institutions in the coming years. The increase in insurance coverage on private deposits from $40,000 to $100,000 will mean higher insurance fees but should improve the ability of insured institutions to distinguish their deposit product from competitive, noninsured products. Expanded deposit and lending powers for thrifts should increase competition for obtaining, and profitably using, funds. Finally, the section providing for relaxation of existing usury laws in many states means that lending rates can be more consistent with existing market rates. This relaxation should reduce artificial barriers to funds allocation and should enhance the ability of financial institutions to hold interest margins stable over the business cycle.

H.R. 6267, the DIA was signed by President Reagan on October 15, 1982. H.R. 6267 has eight "titles," or sections. Title 1 enhances the ability of the Federal Savings and Loan Insurance Corporation (FSLIC) and the Federal Deposit Insurance Corporation (FDIC) to merge failing thrift institutions of any size and failing commercial banks with assets of $500 million or higher. Title 2 permits capital infusion through the issuance of capital notes drawn from the assets of the FSLIC or FDIC for qualifying depository institutions. Qualifying rules include capital of less than 3 percent of assets, above 20 percent of the loan portfolio in mortgages or mortgage-backed securities, and losses in the two previous quarters.

Title 3 mandates the phaseout by January 1, 1984 of all interest differentials on maximum rates among depository institutions. Title 3 also mandates the depository institutions deregulation committee (DIDC) to create a new depository instrument "equivalent to and competitive with" money market funds. The instrument has to have the following characteristics: (1) no minimum maturity; (2) no interest rate ceiling; (3) a minimum denomination of $2,500; (4) only three preauthorized or automatic withdrawals and three drafts permitted in any month, reserve requirements of 0 percent for individual accounts, and 3 percent for corporate accounts; (5) all types of depositors eligible; and (6) insurance up to $100,000 by the FSLIC or FDIC. These depository instruments were issued starting December 14, 1982. Title 3 of H.R. 6267 also permits mutual savings banks and S&Ls to have more commercial and consumer loans (up to 10 or 30 percent, respectively, of assets by 1984) and to offer, with restrictions, demand deposits to commercial and agricultural customers.

Title 4 provides relief to national and member banks on provisions of banking laws that are obsolete or restrictive. For example, the legal lending limit is raised to 15 and 25 percent of capital for unsecured and secured borrowers, respectively. Title 5 provides greater operating flexibility to credit unions. Title 6 states that the sale of property, casualty, and life insurance (other than credit life, health, and accident) is not an activity closely related to banking. This wording might discourage BHCs from acquiring insurance agencies; however, acquisitions by small banks are permitted, acquisitions are permitted in sparsely populated areas, and acquisitions prior to May 1, 1982, are grandfathered. Title 7 requires a study of the insurance system for deposits and contains miscellaneous amendments, such as clarification of truth-in-lending, permitting establishment of bank service corporations by one or more banks, and permitting NOWs to be issued to state and local governments. Title 8 requires that all non-federally chartered housing creditors be permitted to offer alternative mortgage transactions in accordance with federal regulations.

The new depository instruments permitted by H.R. 6267, by the DIDC, by money market accounts, and by super-NOW accounts will probably have the most far-reaching effects on financial institutions. These accounts are estimated to have grown to $350 billion for commercial banks, $120 billion for S&Ls, and $50 billion for mutual savings banks during the first six months after they were authorized. Contractual institutions and investment institutions have been struggling to innovate effective competitive products. As the pricing protections of Regulation Q disappear, financial institutions are pricing (some for the first time) new instruments in a very competitive market. While it may be too early to tell the overall impact of these new instruments at this time, it seems likely the shift in most institutions' funding mix to more costly sources will cause interest margins to narrow.

Changes in nonbank financial institutions as more sections of H.R. 4986 and H.R. 6267 become effective should be significant; but the laws have several important deficiencies that may or may not be resolved by future legislation or regulation. For example, there is no provision for removing the remaining constraints on interstate expansion by financial institutions. Restrictions now imposed on depository intermediaries under the Glass-Steagall Act of 1932, such as those aimed at commingled investment accounts, were not addressed. The longer-run implications of the fact that low-yielding, fixed-rate mortgages would remain a significant part of the portfolios of many thrift institutions for some years to come were not explicitly considered. These and similar issues cannot be ignored. The problem is that legislation and regulation tend to be following, not leading, influences on financial institutions. Legislation and regulation tend to validate or legitimize successful innovations in the financial service industry.

ASSETS, LIABILITIES, AND FUND FLOWS
FOR MAJOR NONBANK FINANCIAL INSTITUTIONS

The assets and liabilities at the end of 1975 and 1982 are examined to see the primary types of liabilities used and assets employed for the major institutions, and to explore the shifts in these assets and liabilities due to the changing environment. The fund flows in the last six years and those predicted for 1983 are included to illustrate the changing pattern of funding sources and uses. Tables 3.5 through 3.25 contain the data that support the following summary assessments.

Thrift Institutions

Thrift institutions include S&Ls, mutual savings banks, and credit unions. They are grouped together because they are the three nonbank financial institutions that can now offer a menu of deposit liabilities similar to those offered by commercial banks. In addition, all three are used to emphasize intermediate- and long-term loans to consumers; however, the significant expansion of their asset capabilities in 1980 and 1982 may lead many of the thrift institutions to diversify their asset holdings.

Savings and Loan Associations. At the end of 1982, there were 848 stockholder-owned savings and loan associations under the corporate form and 2,985 mutually owned associations without stockholders. The total number of S&L offices, including branches, was 21,987. Depositors and borrowers ostensibly elect the board of directors of the mutual associations; however, control is easily maintained by the existing directors through proxies obtained at the start of the savings or borrowing relationship. S&Ls can be organized under either federal or state charters. At the end of 1982, there were 1,721 federally chartered associations with assets of $484 billion, and 2,112 state-chartered associations with assets of $222 billion.

TABLE 3.5   Primary Assets and Liabilities of Savings and Loan Associations (as of December 31)

(dollars in billions)

	1975		1982	
	Amount	Percentage of Total	Amount	Percentage of Total
Assets				
Cash and liquid investments	$ 27.3	8.1%	$ 69.9	9.9%
Other investments	3.3	1.0	14.9	2.1
Mortgages	278.7	82.3	482.3	68.3
Mortgage participations and securities	13.9	4.1	63.8	9.0
Nonmortgage consumer loans	2.5	0.7	17.9	2.5
Other assets	12.8	3.8	57.2	8.1
Total	$338.5	100.0%	$706.0	100.0%
Liabilities and net worth				
Deposits				
Earning regular rates	$122.2	36.1%	$111.8	15.8%
Earning above regular rates	162.9	48.1	454.3	64.3
Federal Home Loan Bank advances	17.5	5.2	63.9	9.1
Other borrowed money	4.2	1.3	34.1	4.8
All other liabilities	11.9	3.5	15.7	2.2
Net worth	19.8	5.8	26.2	3.7
Total	$338.5	100.0%	$706.0	100.0%

Source: Federal Home Loan Bank (Washington, D.C., 1983)

Most regulation of savings and loan activities is centralized in the Federal Home Loan Bank System. This system is composed of the Federal Home Loan Bank Board, the 12 regional Federal Home Loan Banks, and member associations. Member associations, which include all federal associations and most state associations, hold approximately 98 percent of the assets of the industry. In addition, the time and savings accounts of all federal and most state associations are insured to $100,000 by the FSLIC. Members of the FSLIC hold slightly over 97 percent of the total assets of the industry. State regulations and state regulatory departments also affect S&L activities within a particular state.

Table 3.5 shows that as of the end of 1975, S&Ls were basically specialized lenders with over 82 percent of these assets in mortgages (nearly all of which paid fixed rates). Another 9 percent of their assets were in cash and generally liquid securities. In 1975, S&Ls had funded these assets primarily through savings deposits (close to 85 percent of their total sources), advances from the Federal Home Loan Banks (another 5.2 percent), and their own reserves and net worth (roughly 5.8 percent). Thus, as late as the mid-1970s, nearly all S&Ls made money by borrowing short term and lending long term at a substantial interest margin.

Economic conditions during the four years from 1979 through 1982 were extremely difficult ones for S&Ls. Interest rates rose dramatically and, instead of the expected upward sloping yield curve (graphic depiction of yield-maturity relationships), there was a downward sloping yield curve. On the margin, new short-term funds were as or more expensive than the yields on long-term mortgages the associations were used to financing. Even worse, the market value of outstanding long-term fixed-rate mortgages plummeted downward so that, by 1981, nearly all associations were insolvent in market value terms. Finally, as shown in Table 3.5, by 1982, most savings deposits were paying in excess of the regular rates to obtain funds. This meant new funds, often costing between 12 and 15 percent, were replacing the old savings deposits costing 5½ percent. The declining funds inflows and net worth (in book value) are shown in Table 3.6.

In 1981 and 1982, there were several outright failures and a large number of consolidations (some forced) among S&Ls. The number of associations declined by roughly 20 percent. There were, however, several positive events that should position S&Ls for a more favorable future. (1) Through the 1980 and 1982 legislation, S&Ls gained much broader asset and liability powers (similar to those of commercial banks). They can issue competitive transaction deposit and money market deposit accounts. They can make nearly the full range of commercial and consumer loans. (2) Many S&Ls use the secondary market for mortgages or alternative mortgage instruments (generally at variable rates) to mitigate the severe interest rate risk the associations faced. (3) Many associations have switched from the mutual to the corporate form of organization and seem capable of raising capital to finance future growth. (4) S&Ls seem to have the full cooperation of their regulators and of most legislators — both groups appear determined to protect and assist associations in the future.

Mutual Savings Banks.   Tables 3.7 and 3.8 show that mutual savings banks are roughly one quarter of the asset size of the S&L industry. In 1975, there were nearly 500 mutual savings banks, but this number had fallen to 424 by the end of 1982. There are no provisions for federal charters; however, state charters can be obtained in 18 states (primarily the New England and mid-Atlantic states). Nearly three fourths of all savings banks in which roughly four fifths of savings bank assets are concentrated are located in Connecticut, New York, and Massachusetts. All savings banks are owned by depositors who receive all earnings after provision for adequate reserves. These depositors elect, usually by proxies obtained at the beginning of their depositor relationship, a board of trustees who appoint management. In practice, the board and management are virtually self-sustaining.

Regulatory departments or agencies in each state have primary regulatory authority over mutual savings banks. Thus, regulation over mutual savings

TABLE 3.6 Sources and Uses of Funds — Savings and Loan Associations

(dollars in billions)

	1977	1978	1979	1980	1981	1982 (estimated)	1983 (projected)
SOURCES OF FUNDS							
Savings capital	$51.0	$44.9	$39.3	$42.1	$13.7	$38.9	$44.0
Repurchase agreements	1.9	2.1	0.5	2.1	7.6	7.7	1.5
Net worth	3.2	3.9	3.6	0.7	(4.9)	(6.0)	1.7
Federal Home Loan Bank advances	4.2	12.0	8.5	6.6	15.7	2.2	2.0
Bonds	1.2	0.7	1.4	0.4	(0.5)	(0.6)	—
Bank loans	1.0	(0.5)	0.4	(0.4)	(0.1)	(0.5)	—
Total	$62.6	$63.1	$53.7	$51.4	$31.5	$41.7	$49.2
USES OF FUNDS							
Investment funds							
State and local securities	—	$ 0.1	($ 0.1)	—	$ 0.1	($ 0.2)	—
Home mortgages	$48.0	49.5	44.0	$33.4	20.4	11.0	$32.0
Multifamily, commercial, and farm mortgages	8.9	6.6	4.8	2.3	2.4	0.5	2.8
Total mortgages	$56.9	$56.1	$48.8	$35.7	$22.8	$11.5	$34.8
Total investment funds	$56.9	$56.2	$48.7	$35.7	$22.9	$11.3	$34.8

Short-term funds

Open market paper	$ 0.2	$ 0.5	$ 0.5	$ 2.0	$ 0.5	$ 0.8	$ 1.3
Consumer credit	1.5	0.3	3.7	2.6	(0.2)	2.7	3.4
Total short-term funds	$ 1.7	$ 0.8	$ 4.2	$ 4.6	$ 0.3	$ 3.5	$ 4.7
U.S. Gov't & Agency Securities	2.7	−.3	−1.4	1.8	.6	3.8	4.5
Total funds	$61.3	$56.7	$51.5	$42.1	$23.8	$18.6	$44.0
Cash and equivalents(a)	0.5	5.4	2.5	7.8	3.7	10.9	2.7
Other — net(b)	0.7	1.0	(0.3)	1.6	4.0	12.2	2.5
Total	$62.6	$63.1	$53.7	$51.4	$31.5	$41.7	$49.2

(a) Includes certificates of deposit, Fed funds, securities purchased on resale agreements, and other short-term paper
(b) 1981 and 1982 data include growth of goodwill accounts in connection with merger activity.

Sources: Federal Savings and Loan Insurance Corporation; Federal Home Loan Bank Board; Board of Governors of the Federal Reserve System, *Flow of Funds Accounts, Assets and Liabilities Outstanding;* Government National Mortgage Association. Estimations and projections are from *Credit and Capital Market, 1983* (New York: Bankers Trust Co., 1983).

**TABLE 3.7   Primary Assets and Liabilities of Mutual Savings Banks
(as of December 31)**

(dollars in billions)

	1975		1982	
	Assets	Percentage of Total	Assets	Percentage of Total
Assets				
Cash	$ 2.3	1.9%	$ 6.9	4.0%
U.S. governments and agencies	7.5	6.2	9.7	5.6
State and local securities	1.5	1.2	2.5	1.4
Corporate and foreign bonds	20.9	17.3	32.6	18.7
Mortgages and mortgage securites	77.2	63.8	108.2	62.1
Stocks	4.4	3.6	3.5	2.0
Other assets	7.3	6.0	10.8	6.2
Total	$121.1	100.0%	$174.2	100.0%
Liabilities and reserves				
Deposits	$109.9	90.8%	$155.2	89.1%
Other liabilities	2.8	2.3	9.8	5.6
General reserves	8.4	6.9	9.2	5.3
Total	$121.1	100.0%	$174.2	100.0%

Source: National Fact Book of Mutual Savings Banking (New York: National Association of Mutual
Savings Banks, 1976, 1983).

banks is as diversified as S&L regulation is centralized. All state regulatory authorities, however, seem firmly committed to the safety of the thrift accounts of bank members and seem to prefer low-risk alternatives among the menu of available risk-return options. Savings account insurance is available from the FDIC (to a maximum of $100,000 per account) or from state funds in some states. There are currently 315 savings banks that are members of the FDIC, and all but one of the remaining banks are affiliated with a state-sponsored insurance fund. In some states, mutual savings banks may belong to the Federal Home Loan Bank System if they so desire. At the present time, 130 savings banks are members of the system.

Table 3.7 shows that in 1975, mutual savings banks emphasized fixed-rate mortgages to a somewhat lesser extent than S&Ls. Because many of their other assets were long-term government or corporate bonds and most of their liabilities were interest sensitive deposits, mutual savings banks suffered the severe profit problems in the 1979–1982 period as did S&Ls. Table 3.8 shows that the situation was so severe that the mutual savings bank industry had reductions in capital (reserves) in 1980, 1981, and 1982 and a decline in total sources of funds in 1981.

There were several forced mergers among larger savings banks in the early

1980s. As with S&Ls, mutual savings banks gained extensive asset and liability powers in the 1980 and 1982 Acts. Their consolidated balance sheet had changed little by the end of 1982; however, there is fragmentary evidence of an evolving deposit mix (emphasizing money market deposit accounts) which may be more effective in attracting funds that can be profitably employed.

Credit Unions. At the end of 1982, there were 20,033 credit unions in the United States. Currently, credit unions can be chartered under both federal and state law. The powers and regulation of credit unions vary widely according to the chartering agency. At the federal level, the National Credit Union Administration examines, supervises, and insures all federally chartered credit unions. At the state level, these powers are generally found in the office of the state bank regulator. At both levels, credit union membership is limited to groups sharing a common bond of occupation, association, or well-defined residential ties. Members elect a board which appoints management. Because of the "common bond" restriction, most credit unions are small in size and many of them are forced to depend on volunteers and part-time employees. For this reason, most credit unions have voluntarily joined the credit union leagues in their state and these leagues have joined together in the Credit Union National Association (CUNA). The state leagues typically provide financial advice, centralized purchasing, and interlending among member unions. Through its various agencies, CUNA provides services such as saver and borrower life insurance, broader interlending and capital market services, computerized accounting services, and the potential for a national electronic monetary transfer system. Accounts in all federal credit unions and any state-chartered institutions that choose the service are insured up to $100,000 by the National Credit Union Share Insurance Fund under the control of the administrator of CUNA.

Tables 3.9 and 3.10 show that close to 90 percent of credit union funds have come from various deposit sources. Actually, many of these deposits are called shares, but resemble savings deposits yielding fixed-interest payments. In addition, in both 1975 and 1982, most credit unions could accept actual time deposits from members. Furthermore, the legislation passed in 1980 and 1982 permitted credit unions even broader deposit powers similar to those of other thrift institutions. The other two potential sources of funds are reserves and borrowings. In most states, credit unions are required to set aside 20 percent of net earnings (before dividends on shares) as reserves until these reserves accumulate to 10 percent of the federally chartered union's risk assets or to 10 percent of shareholders. All federal and most state credit unions are permitted to borrow from other credit unions or other sources up to 50 percent of capital and surplus.

In employing their funds, credit unions usually emphasize loans to members. These tend to produce reasonably high returns and there are political pressures to emphasize such loans; however, these loans are usually restricted as to rate, size, and maturity. For this reason, in recent years (see Tables 3.9 and 3.10) many credit unions have employed a higher portion of their funds in insured bank deposits, other short-term high quality instruments, and U.S. government and agency securities.

TABLE 3.8 **Sources and Uses of Funds — Mutual Savings Banks**

(dollars in billions)

	1977	1978	1979	1980	1981	1982 (estimated)	1983 (projected)
SOURCES OF FUNDS							
Deposits	$11.0	$7.9	$3.0	$7.0	$0.8	$3.8	$8.5
Capital	0.9	0.9	0.8	(0.2)	(1.4)	(0.6)	—
Total	$12.0	$8.8	$3.8	$6.8	($0.6)	$3.2	$8.5
USES OF FUNDS							
Investment funds							
Corporate bonds	$ 1.2	—	($0.8)	$0.7	($1.0)	($0.7)	$0.5
Corporate stocks	0.4	—	—	(0.5)	(0.6)	(0.1)	—
State and local securities	0.4	$0.5	(0.6)	(0.5)	(0.1)	—	—
Total securities	$ 2.0	$0.5	($1.5)	($0.4)	($1.7)	($0.8)	$0.5
Home mortgages	$ 7.2	$6.3	$5.8	$3.4	$0.6	—	$3.5
Multifamily, commercial, and farm mortgages	1.9	1.7	—	(0.8)	(1.4)	($1.5)	(1.0)
Total mortgages	$ 9.1	$8.1	$5.8	$2.6	($0.8)	($1.5)	$2.5
Total investment funds	$11.1	$8.6	$4.3	$2.1	($2.5)	($2.3)	$3.0

Short-term funds							
Open market paper	—	$0.2	$1.1	$1.5	$1.8	$1.0	$1.0
Consumer credit	$ 0.5	0.7	0.1	0.4	(0.3)	0.3	0.4
Total short-term funds	$ 0.5	$0.9	$1.2	$1.9	$1.5	$1.3	$1.4
U.S. government and agency securities							
U.S. government securities (a)	$ 0.1	($1.0)	($0.3)	$0.7	($0.2)	—	$1.0
Federal agency securities	0.1	—	(0.4)	0.6	1.0	$0.5	0.8
Total U.S. government and agency securities	$ 0.1	($1.0)	($0.6)	$1.3	$0.8	$0.5	$1.8
Total funds	$11.7	$8.6	$4.8	$5.3	($0.2)	($0.5)	$6.2
Cash	—	$1.3	($0.5)	$1.2	$1.1	$1.5	$0.9
Other — net	$ 0.2	(1.0)	(0.5)	0.3	(1.6)	2.2	1.4
Total	$12.0	$8.8	$3.8	$6.8	($0.6)	$3.2	$8.5

(a) Does not include securities held under repurchase agreements

Sources: National Association of Mutual Savings Banks; Federal Home Loan Bank Board; Board of Governors of the Federal Reserve System, *Flow of Funds Accounts, Assets and Liabilities Outstanding*; Government National Mortgage Association. Estimates and projections are from *Credit and Capital Markets, 1983* (New York: Bankers Trust Co., 1983).

TABLE 3.9   Primary Assets and Liabilities of Credit Unions
(as of December 31)

(dollars in billions)

	1975		1982	
	Amount	Percentage of Total	Amount	Percentage of Total
Assets				
Cash, deposits, paper, etc.	$ 1.7	4.4%	$18.5	20.5%
Securities	7.9	20.5	20.6	22.8
Loans outstanding	28.9	75.1	51.1	56.7
Total	$38.5	100.0%	$90.2	100.0%
Liabilities				
Deposits	$33.6	87.2%	$80.6	89.3%
Other liabilities	2.9	7.4	5.3	5.9
Reserves	2.1	5.4	4.3	4.8
Total	$38.5	100.0%	$90.2	100.0%

Source: Credit Union National Association (Madison, Wisc.)

Contractual Financial Institutions

The liability holder generally commits to making payments over time. For example, most insurance contracts include commitments on the part of a policyholder over a period of time; pension and retirement funds include commitments on the part of the employer and, sometimes, the employee to contribute toward future benefits. Foundations and endowments can involve the payments of lump sums or payments over time often for the benefit of another party. These are known as contractual institutions.

The primary purpose of insurance is to provide individuals and organizations with a greater degree of certainty with respect to future plans and activities. Purchasers of insurance lower their risk of financial loss from specific hazards. This is usually accomplished by making periodic payments into a fund. If sufficient numbers of individuals or organizations contribute to this fund, the payments should be sufficient to support the loss claims that are presented against the fund. While insurance does not prevent the actual hazard, purchasers of insurance are able to decrease or avoid the uncertainties and consequences of specific types of large financial losses.

The primary functions of an insurance company are to (1) provide a means of reducing important financial uncertainties; (2) provide added protection at the insurance company's risk; and (3) provide other services while administering the collected funds. In order to provide protection and other services, insurance companies hold substantial amounts of assets. With these large asset holdings and cash inflows and outflows, insurance companies are capable of

TABLE 3.10 Sources and Uses of Funds — Credit Unions

(dollars in billions)

	1977	1978	1979	1980	1981	1982 (estimated)	1983 (projected)
Sources of funds							
Share capital and deposits	$7.4	$7.0	$3.9	$3.9	$2.0	$5.3	$7.0
Surplus and reserves	0.3	0.6	0.4	0.2	0.8	0.2	0.6
Total	$7.7	$7.6	$4.4	$4.1	$2.8	$5.5	$7.5
Uses of funds							
Home mortgages	$1.8	$2.1	$0.1	($0.4)	($0.4)	($0.4)	—
Consumer credit	6.4	6.7	2.2	(2.5)	1.9	0.8	$3.5
U.S. government and agency securities							
U.S. government securities	($0.5)	($0.5)	$0.3	$0.7	($0.4)	$0.9	$1.3
Federal agency securities	0.5	—	(0.6)	—	(0.3)	—	0.2
Total U.S. government and agency securities	($0.1)	($0.5)	($0.3)	$0.6	($0.7)	$0.9	$1.5
Total funds	$8.2	$8.3	$2.0	($2.2)	$0.8	$1.2	$5.0
Other — net (a)	(0.4)	(0.7)	2.4	6.3	2.0	4.3	2.6
Total	$7.7	$7.6	$4.4	$4.1	$2.8	$5.5	$7.6

(a) Includes certificates of deposit

Sources: National Credit Union Administration; U.S. Department of Health, Education and Welfare; Federal Reserve Board; Government National Mortgage Association Estimations and projections are from *Credit and Capital Markets, 1983* (New York: Bankers Trust Co., 1983).

transferring funds from one sector of the economy to another. The scope of the services provided by insurance companies is broad enough to encompass nearly every phase of our lives.

Life Insurance Companies. These institutions must be licensed by the state in which they sell insurance and are regulated by state laws that are normally administered by insurance commissions or departments. The number of life insurance companies in the United States has grown rapidly since the end of World War II. At the end of 1945, there were 473 life insurance companies in operation. By the end of 1960, the number had grown to 1,441, and by mid-1982, there were 1,866 (or more than nine tenths) owned by stockholders. The remaining 132 were mutual organizations. These mutual organizations, which are generally older and larger than the stockholder-owned companies, held nearly two thirds of the assets of all United States life insurance companies and accounted for slightly more than one-half of all life insurance in force.

Life insurance companies generally offer protection against three major categories of personal financial risk: (1) premature death with the possible loss of family income; (2) insufficient income when the policyholder passes the prime earning age; (3) accident or sickness which disrupts the earning ability of the policyholder. When large numbers of individuals are involved (e.g., group policies), the insurance company's actuary can accurately predict the number of policyholders likely to suffer these financial risks. The ability to predict accurately the needs of the entire group allows the individual members of the insured group to substitute certainty for uncertainty.

The principal types of contracts sold are term life insurance, whole life insurance, endowment insurance, annuities, and accident and sickness insurance. These contracts can be sold separately to individuals or to groups of individuals who share some common bond. Shifts among the types of contracts can have an influence over the size and form of life insurance assets. For example, a shift from whole life insurance to term life insurance would tend to slow the institution's growth of assets. The three types of regulations most constraining to the financial management of insurance companies are (1) requirements to make policy loans at a relatively low fixed rate of interest; (2) restrictions on the categories of investments and the quality within these categories; and (3) required levels of reserves for the various types of insurance contracts. These regulations, with the exception of some quality standards often based on New York's legal list, vary widely from state to state.

Changes in the asset, liabilities, and cash flows of life insurance companies appear in Tables 3.11 and 3.12. The growth, stability, and predictability of premium receipts and benefit payments are evident in Table 3.12. Few financial institutions can brag of such a stable net cash inflow over a prolonged period. Policy loans represent the major challenge to predictability in fund inflows and outflows. The unpredictable nature of policy loans is illustrated by the fact that net increases in policy loans ranged between $1.7 and $7.3 billion in the last six years (see Table 3.12). Table 3.11 shows that these low-yielding loans had risen to 9.4 percent of life insurance assets by the end of 1982.

In both 1975 and 1982, most of the balance of life insurance company funds

TABLE 3.11   Primary Assets and Liabilities of Life Insurance Companies (as of December 31)

(dollars in billions)

	1975		1982	
	Amount	Percentage of Total	Amount	Percentage of Total
Assets				
Currency and checkables	$ 1.9	0.7%	$ 3.4	0.6%
Open market paper	4.7	1.6	21.0	3.7
Policy loans	24.5	8.5	53.2	9.4
U.S. government securities	4.7	1.6	14.3	2.5
Federal agency securities	1.4	0.5	17.4	3.1
Corporate and foreign bonds	105.3	36.4	197.0	35.0
Mortgages	89.2	30.8	145.4	25.8
State and local securities	4.3	1.5	8.2	1.5
Stock	38.6	13.3	61.7	11.0
Real estate	9.6	3.3	21.3	3.8
Miscellaneous assets	5.2	1.8	20.2	3.6
Total	$289.3	100.0%	$563.1	100.0%
Liabilities and net worth				
Policy reserves	$237.1	82.0%	$459.1	81.5%
Policy dividend accumulations	8.8	3.0	14.3	2.5
Funds for dividends	4.9	1.7	8.5	1.5
Other obligations	17.9	6.2	41.2	7.3
Capital and surplus	20.6	7.1	40.0	7.1
Total	$289.3	100.0%	$563.1	100.0%

Source: *1983 Prospects for Financial Markets* (New York: Salomon Brothers, Inc., 1983)

were invested in long-term fixed-rate securities, such as corporate bonds and mortgages. The dominance of investing predictable inflows to pay predictable benefits in fixed-return securities will probably continue into the future; however, two recent developments are worth noting. One is the rapid growth of assets held in special accounts from nearly $13 billion in 1975 to nearly $55 billion in 1982. A separate account is a fund held separately from all other assets, and allows life insurance companies to offer specialized financial products, such as variable rate life insurance and annuities. The second development is the increasing number of life insurance companies completing acquisitions of, and mergers with, other financial institutions. The life insurance companies bring a variety of financial products and services.

TABLE 3.12 Sources and Uses of Funds — Life Insurance Companies

(dollars in billions)

	1977	1978	1979	1980	1981	1982 (estimated)	1983 (projected)
SOURCES OF FUNDS							
Income							
Premium receipts	$72.3	$ 78.8	$ 84.9	$ 94.2	$107.7	$119.0	$134.0
Net investment income	21.7	25.3	29.6	33.9	39.8	45.8	51.0
Other income	4.0	4.2	4.7	4.3	4.4	4.5	4.6
Total	$98.0	$108.2	$119.1	$132.5	$151.9	$169.3	$189.6
Outgo							
Benefit payments	$46.8	$ 50.5	$ 56.7	$ 64.2	$ 73.7	$ 88.1	$103.8
Operating expenses, taxes and other	18.4	20.9	23.6	27.5	28.2	29.2	30.0
Total	$65.2	$ 71.4	$ 80.2	$ 91.7	$101.8	$117.3	$133.8
Increase in admitted assets	$32.7	$ 36.8	$ 38.9	$ 40.8	$ 50.0	$ 52.0	$ 55.8
USES OF FUNDS							
Investment funds							
Corporate bonds	$16.9	$ 15.9	$ 11.3	$ 8.1	$ 6.3	$ 11.2	$ 15.5
Corporate stocks	1.9	0.7	0.6	0.8	3.4	4.5	5.5
State and local securities	0.5	0.4	—	0.3	0.4	0.8	0.2
Foreign securities	1.7	1.8	0.6	1.0	1.8	1.0	1.2
Total securities	$20.9	$ 18.7	$ 12.5	$ 10.1	$ 12.0	$ 17.5	$ 22.4

Home mortgages	$(1.3)	—	$ 2.7	$ 2.4	$ (0.6)	$ (0.5)	—
Multifamily, commercial, and farm mortgages	6.7	9.7	10.6	11.0	7.4	4.3	$ 5.3
Total mortgages	$ 5.3	$ 9.7	$13.4	$13.4	$ 6.8	$ 3.8	$ 5.3
Total investment funds	$26.3	$28.4	$25.9	$23.5	$18.8	$21.3	$27.7
Short-term funds							
Open market paper	$(0.2)	$ 1.1	$ 1.3	$ 1.9	$ 6.6	$ 7.0	$ 3.8
Policy loans	1.7	2.6	4.7	6.6	7.3	4.8	3.5
Total short-term funds	$ 1.6	$ 3.7	$ 6.0	$ 8.5	$13.9	$11.8	$ 7.3
U.S. government and agency securities							
U.S. government securities	$(0.1)	$ (0.5)	$ 0.1	$ 1.0	$ 2.3	$ 5.0	$ 6.8
Federal agency securities	1.6	2.2	1.7	1.0	3.0	2.7	2.5
Total U.S. government and agency securities	$ 1.6	$ 1.7	$ 1.8	$ 2.0	$ 5.4	$ 7.7	$ 9.3
Total funds	$29.4	$33.7	$33.6	$33.9	$38.0	$40.8	$44.3
Real estate	$ 0.6	$ 0.7	$ 1.2	$ 2.0	$ 3.2	$ 3.2	$ 3.0
Cash	0.1	0.2	0.3	0.5	1.1	0.6	0.8
Other — net	2.6	2.1	3.7	4.3	7.7	7.4	7.7
Total	$32.7	$36.7	$38.9	$40.8	$50.0	$52.0	$55.8
MEMORANDUM							
Separate accounts(a)	$ 2.6	$ 2.6	$ 3.3	$ 6.2	$10.2	$10.2	$10.6

(a) Net of appreciation or depreciation in market value

Sources: American Council of Life Insurance; Federal Home Loan Bank Board; Government National Mortgage Association. Estimations and projections are from *Credit and Capital Markets, 1983* (New York: Bankers Trust Co., 1983).

Property Insurance Companies. These companies protect the insured against losses arising from physical damages to property or loss arising from damages to others for which the insured must be held liable. Property insurance companies are licensed and regulated by state laws administered by state departments or commissions (sometimes the same body that regulates life insurance companies). Most of these companies are organized under either the corporate or mutual (policyholder) form of ownership.[8] At the end of 1982, corporate (stockholder-owned) companies comprised about two thirds of the nearly 3,000 property insurance companies and accounted for roughly three-fourths of industry assets (approximately $201.5 billion). The conditions affecting financial decisions of property insurance are divided into three categories: (1) types of insurance contracts; (2) the nature of reserves; and (3) regulation of rates, reserves, and investments.

Property insurance is typically divided into four broad classifications: (1) fire insurance; (2) marine insurance; (3) surety insurance; and (4) casualty insurance.[9] Most basic fire insurance offers protection against the destruction of physical property as a result of fire, explosion, windstorm, and riot. In addition, contracts can be modified to include protection against losses incurred during the time the insured property is not usable. Marine insurance provides protection for both land and marine transportation of merchandise. Examples of surety insurance include insurance for the construction of a new plant as contracted, or fidelity bonds to insure against loss from dishonest employees. While casualty insurance basically seeks to protect the insured against liability for specified actions, it has been broadened to include all other forms of property insurance not covered by fire, marine, or surety. Examples include automobile liability insurance that auto owners carry as protection against claims resulting from damage to other persons or property; insurance against theft; insurance against excessive bad debt loss; and insurance against claims resulting from occupational accidents. It is worth noting that the events insured under most property contracts are much less predictable than those insured under most life contracts.

The incidence of risk for property insurance is evenly distributed throughout the contract period. Premium income is generally allocated between two types of reserves for payment to policyholders: reserves for losses and reserves for unearned premiums. Reserves for losses represent a liability for claims that have been filed and that are anticipated (a 60 to 65 percent loss ratio is usually assumed). Reserves for unearned premiums equal the amount of collected premiums that would be returned to policyholders for unexpired terms if all policies were canceled. This category of reserves causes net worth to policyholders to be understated, since the acquisition costs have already been incurred and the risks could be reinsured for less than the prepaid premium.

The maximum premium rates charged for the various forms of property

---

[8] The other organizational forms of property insurance are reciprocal exchanges (cooperatives formed to provide coverage for members at cost) and American Lloyds (associations of unincorporated individuals that underwrite unusual risks) represent between 2 and 3 percent of the industry in terms of assets held.

[9] One characteristic of the industry is the existence of multiple line companies offering various types of coverage through affiliated corporations. Some property companies offer life insurance through a subsidiary organization and some life insurance companies have property insurance subsidiaries.

TABLE 3.13 Primary Assets and Liabilities of Property Insurance Companies (as of December 31)

(dollars in billions)

	1975		1982	
	Amount	Percentage of Total	Amount	Percentage of Total
Assets				
Currency, checkables, and miscellaneous	$ 9.7	11.1%	$ 26.2	13.0%
U.S. government securities	4.7	5.4	13.6	6.8
Federal agency securities	3.3	3.8	10.1	5.0
Corporate and foreign bonds	12.2	14.0	26.9	13.3
State and local securities	33.3	38.3	86.4	42.9
Stocks	23.8	27.4	38.3	19.0
Total	$87.0	100.0%	$201.5	100.0%
Total liabilities and reserves	$87.0	100.0%	$201.5	100.0%

Source: 1983 Prospects for Financial Markets (New York: Salomon Brothers, Inc., 1983)

insurance are set by state commissions or regulatory departments in most states. This is particularly true for the better-known types of insurance covering the property of individuals, such as automobile liability insurance. Since applications for rate changes are based on past records, changes in rates tend to lag behind the actual incidence of claims. In some states the insurance commission or department sets lower as well as upper limits on premium rates in order to prevent cut-throat price competition.

State insurance departments or commissions or state law may also regulate the size and form of property insurance companies' reserves and the investment holdings of property insurance companies. Furthermore, the costs of the benefits paid by property insurance companies are less predictable and tend to rise with inflation. Even though property insurance companies are not required to make policy loans, they have greater liquidity needs than do life insurance companies. Property insurance companies tend to have a lower asset accumulation for investment than life insurance companies because property contracts generally cover only one or a few years. There is little possibility of significant accumulation in the early years of a contract when probabilities of occurrence of the insured event may lower. Finally, property insurance companies typically pay more attention to the tax features of investments, since they are subject to relatively high marginal income tax rates.

Table 3.13 shows the dollar and percentage distribution of assets and liabilities of all property insurance companies at the end of 1975 and 1982. Tax-exempt state and local securities were the dominant asset of property insurance companies for both periods. In fact, state and local securities were a higher proportion of total assets in 1982 than 1975, while proportion of assets in corporate stock and bonds declined during this period.

Table 3.14 summarizes the sources and uses of funds for all property insurance companies. The less stable pattern of cash inflows relative to life insurance companies is evident in this table, the primary causes being less predictable insurance benefits and a regulatory lag in setting some premium rates. The uses of funds of property companies depends partially on whether the major source of funds is unearned premium, loss reserves, or surplus. Table 3.14 shows that common stock has been a more popular use of funds in years when surplus increased (i.e., profits from the insurance portion of the business were high), while U.S. government and other more marketable securities grew faster in years when growth in reserves dominated as a source of funds. The major use of funds in the last six years, however, was net increases in tax-free state and local securities.

Private Noninsured Pension Plans. In 1980, there were roughly 190,000 private noninsured pension funds with assets totaling over $360 billion covering approximately 35 million employees (nearly half of all wage and salary workers). (See Chapter 31 for a detailed analysis.) The most common form of noninsured pension plan promises benefits to retired persons based on the level of their wages and their years of service. For an employee who enters the plan at age 30 and plans to retire at 65, the liability of the fund will be to make the appropriate payments after 35 years. Over the 35 years the employee is with the company, contributions to the fund together with their earnings must cumulate to the discounted value of future benefit payments. Since earnings and demographic characteristics are not precisely foreseeable, required contributions must be estimated actuarially.

There are two particularly interesting implications for decisions relative to this form of pension plan. First, higher earnings from aggressive management reduces the required contributions. A lower level of required contributions generally pleases the sponsoring company, since employers contribute an average of 90 percent of total pension contributions. Second, the net growth (contributions exceeding benefits) of the fund as a whole is likely to continue for at least the first generation of employees and often longer. For example, an expanding number of covered employees or liberalization of promised benefit payments (leading to higher current contributions) can delay the time when net growth ceases.

The characteristics of the two other popular forms of private noninsured pension plans, fixed contribution-variable benefit schemes and profit-sharing plans, are somewhat different. The inflow of contributions to the former type vary directly with the number of covered employees rather than with the basis of actuarial estimates. Employees, rather than the employer benefit from better portfolio management. Net growth will occur so long as contributions on behalf of active employees exceed disbursements; therefore, an increasing number of covered employees (but not benefits that are dependent on contributions) can cause net growth to continue. Net growth of deferred-benefit, profit-sharing plans will be the net result of employer or profits and fund earnings. Table 3.15 illustrates the stable and growing nature of net receipts in recent years for all private noninsured pension funds.

TABLE 3.14 Sources and Uses of Funds — Property Insurance Companies
(dollars in billions)

	1977	1978	1979	1980	1981	1982 (estimated)	1983 (projected)
SOURCES OF FUNDS							
Unearned premium reserves	$ 3.5	$ 2.9	$ 3.0	$ 2.1	$ 1.8	$ 1.7	$ 2.7
Loss reserves	10.2	12.4	12.6	11.2	9.5	9.5	11.0
Policy holders surplus(a)	6.2	5.9	5.3	5.5	5.8	5.0	4.5
Total	$19.9	$21.3	$20.9	$18.7	17.1	$16.2	$18.2
USES OF FUNDS							
Investment Funds							
Corporate bonds	$ 3.4	$ 1.4	$ 1.4	($ 1.8)	$ 2.0	$ 2.2	$ 2.2
Corporate stocks	1.9	3.4	5.0	4.1	2.5	0.5	2.5
State and local securities	10.3	13.5	9.6	7.5	4.6	5.0	4.0
Total securities	$15.7	$18.3	$16.1	$ 9.8	$ 9.0	$ 7.7	$ 9.7
Commercial mortgages	0.1	—	0.3	0.3	0.3	0.5	0.3
Total investment funds	$15.8	$18.3	$16.3	$10.2	$ 9.4	$ 8.2	$10.0
Open market paper	—	—	—	2.0	1.0	1.9	1.0
U.S. government securities	$ 3.2	$ 0.9	$ 1.2	$ 1.9	$ 2.3	$ 2.4	$ 3.0
Federal agency securities	0.2	—	—	0.4	—	0.1	—
Total U.S. government and agency securities	$ 3.5	$ 0.9	$ 1.2	$ 2.3	$ 2.3	$ 2.5	$ 3.0
Total funds	$19.3	$19.2	$17.5	$14.4	$12.7	$12.6	$14.0
Cash	$ 0.3	$ 0.4	$ 0.2	$ 0.1	$ 0.2	$ 0.1	$ 0.2
Other — net	0.4	1.6	3.1	4.2	4.2	3.5	4.0
Total	$19.9	$21.3	$20.9	$18.7	$17.1	$16.2	$18.2

(a) Net of appreciation or depreciation in market value

Sources: Alfred M. Best Company, Inc., *Best's Fire and Casualty Aggregates and Averages*, annual editions; and U.S. Treasury Department. Estimations and projections are from *Credit and Capital Markets*, 1983 (New York: Bankers Trust Co., 1983).

TABLE 3.15   Sources and Uses of Funds — Private Noninsured Pension Funds

(dollars in billions)

	1977	1978	1979	1980	1981	1982 (estimated)	1983 (projected)
SOURCES OF FUNDS							
Employer contributions	$26.5	$30.5	$34.0	$38.0	$41.5	$44.2	$48.0
Employee contributions	1.8	1.9	2.0	2.1	2.2	2.2	2.2
Investment income (a)	7.2	7.6	8.0	8.4	9.3	9.6	9.8
Total receipts	$35.5	$40.0	$44.0	$48.5	$53.0	$56.0	$60.0
Benefit payments	16.5	18.2	20.0	22.5	25.0	27.8	30.6
Net receipts	$19.0	$21.8	$24.0	$26.0	$28.0	$28.2	$29.4
USES OF FUNDS							
Investment funds							
Corporate bonds	$ 6.2	$ 7.4	$ 4.7	$ 3.1	$ 2.9	$ 5.0	$ 5.5
Corporate stocks	4.4	5.3	6.1	9.6	7.3	9.0	8.0
Total securities	$10.6	$12.7	$10.9	$12.7	$10.2	$14.0	$13.5

Home mortgages	$ 2.7	$ 2.1	$ 1.3	$ 1.3	$ 1.1	$ 1.2	$ 1.5
Multifamily, commerical, and farm mortgage	0.1	0.4	0.3	1.0	0.4	0.3	0.1
Total mortgages	$ 2.9	$ 2.5	$ 1.6	$ 2.3	$ 1.5	$ 1.5	$ 1.6
Total investment funds	$13.5	$15.2	$12.5	$15.0	$11.7	$15.5	$15.1
Open market paper	$ 0.3	$ 0.8	$ 1.0	$ 1.3	$ 0.7	—	$ 0.5
U.S. government and agency securities							
U.S. government securites	$ 2.1	($ 0.1)	$ 1.4	$ 4.1	$ 7.6	$ 9.0	$10.5
Federal agency securities	0.6	—	1.0	0.4	1.5	0.7	0.5
Total government and agency securities	$ 2.7	($ 0.1)	$ 2.4	$ 4.5	$ 9.1	$ 9.7	$11.0
Total funds	$16.5	$16.0	$15.9	$20.8	$21.5	$25.2	$26.6
Cash	$ 1.5	$ 4.4	$ 0.5	$ 0.7	$ 1.0	—	$ 0.3
Other — net	1.0	1.4	7.6	4.5	5.5	$ 3.0	2.5
Total	$19.0	$21.8	$24.0	$26.0	$28.0	$28.2	$29.4

(a) Includes minor amounts of other income

Sources: Securities and Exchange Commission and Institute of Life Insurance. Estimations and projections are from *Credit and Capital Markets, 1983* (New York Bankers Trust Co., 1983).

TABLE 3.16　Primary Assets and Liabilities of Private Noninsured Pension Funds (as of December 31)

(dollars in billions)

	1975		1982	
	Amount	Percentage of Total	Amount	Percentage of Total
Assets				
Currency, checkables, and miscellaneous	$ 11.2	4.9%	$ 18.2	5.1%
Open market paper	0.6	0.3	3.5	1.0
U.S. government securities	17.6	7.7	44.6	12.4
Federal agency securities	3.3	1.4	15.2	4.2
Corporate and foreign bonds	35.8	15.7	65.5	18.2
Mortgages	2.4	1.1	4.1	1.1
Stocks	156.9	68.9	209.0	58.0
Total	$227.8	100.0%	$360.1	100.0%
Total liabilities	$227.8	100.0%	$360.1	100.0%

Source: 1983 Prospects for Financial Markets (New York: Salomon Brothers, Inc., 1983)

There is intense competition for the business of managing pension funds. The majority of private uninsured pension funds are managed by trust departments of commercial banks. By the early 1980s, such pension funds constituted over 40 percent of the assets of the trust departments of banks. A few investment banking firms and investment management firms also manage pension funds; however, self-administered pension funds are the second most common form of management. This arrangement probably reflects the incentive of some corporate executives to employ their company's pension plan assets aggressively in hopes of lowering retirement costs. These managers of self-administered funds must be careful that they fulfill their fiduciary responsibility. Finally, a few private pension funds are managed by union officials.

The primary assets and liabilities resulting from the minimal liquidity demands and other factors affecting pension funds are shown in Table 3.16. Most private noninsured pension funds chose to emphasize taxable, long-term debt issues in the late 1970s and early 1980s. Their strategy was that, without the hazard of forced liquidation, they could wait until debts mature and be patient about wide changes in market prices. The tax advantages of stocks and state and local bonds are irrelevant to these tax-exempt funds. Types of investments that may have an increased appeal in the future (particularly if their returns exceed those on corporate bonds and common stocks) include mortgages, mortgage-backed federal agency securities, and bonds of foreign governments and countries. The 1982 results also probably reflect the improvements in pension fund performance demanded in the Employment Retirement Income Security Act of 1974.

State and Local Retirement Funds. According to the government's Division of the Bureau of the Census, there are slightly over 2,000 separate state and local government employee retirement funds. The asset funding of future benefits of these funds vary widely, from approximately pay-as-you-go to fully funded, as do the investment policies and restrictions. In recent years these funds tended to have higher funding of future benefits, fewer investment restrictions, and more aggressive investment policies. The investment policies and practices of most state and local government employee retirement funds have tended to move toward those of private pension funds and away from those of the federal retirement funds.

Table 3.17 presents the total and net receipts for all state and local government employee retirement funds for the last six years. Probably the most important characteristic for nearly all of the flows in this exhibit is their remarkable consistency over time. Among the inflows, government contributions have consistently constituted nearly 45 percent, employee contributions have declined from roughly 20 to 15 percent, and earnings on investments have increased slightly from approximately 35 to 40 percent of total receipts over the last decade. The consistency of benefit payments (averaging one-third of total receipts) has meant that net cash receipts have grown at a very consistent rate. These consistencies, if true for individual funds, have the implication that there is little need for liquidity. Investment policies and practices should reflect this condition. As a warning, some individual funds do mature, and those responsible for managing the funds must be careful that their liquidity and investment practices reflect this specific need and not the needs of funds in general.

Table 3.18 discloses the major categories of asset holdings of state and local retirement funds at the end of 1975 and 1982. These funds hold only a limited amount of state and local securities because of their tax-exempt status. Taxable debt securities, particularly U.S. government and agency securities, have grown proportionately the most in recent years. At the end of 1982, corporate bonds and corporate stocks were still the dominant assets of state and local retirement funds.

Foundations and Endowments. Table 3.19 indicates that corporate stocks were by far the dominant asset of foundations and endowments. The proportions in the various asset and liability categories changed very little from 1975 to 1982.

Investment Institutions

Three forms of financial institutions are broadly categorized as investment institutions: money market mutual funds; other investment companies; and security brokers and dealers. The first two forms of financial institutions are typical intermediaries; however, security brokers and dealers are unique. Most security brokers and dealers are primary agents, but some firms both lend to

TABLE 3.17   Sources and Uses of Funds — State and Local Retirement Funds

(dollars in billions)

	1977	1978	1979	1980	1981	1982 (estimated)	1983 (projected)
SOURCES OF FUNDS							
Government contributions	$13.5	$15.0	$16.8	$19.1	$21.8	$23.5	$25.8
Employee contributions	5.8	6.3	6.7	7.1	7.6	7.8	8.2
Investment income	8.8	10.2	12.7	15.7	18.8	21.0	23.0
Total receipts	$28.1	$31.5	$36.3	$41.9	$48.2	$52.3	$57.0
Benefit payments	10.5	12.0	13.3	15.0	17.0	19.0	21.0
Net receipts	$17.6	$19.5	$23.0	$26.9	$31.2	$33.3	$36.0
USES OF FUNDS							
Investment funds							
Corporate bonds	$ 5.3	$ 4.7	$ 6.9	$ 6.3	$ 6.0	$ 8.5	$ 9.0
Corporate stocks	3.7	2.6	4.1	5.3	7.2	7.5	8.0
State and local securities	0.2	0.4	—	0.2	—	0.3	0.4
Total securities	$ 9.2	$ 7.7	$11.0	$11.8	$13.2	$16.3	$17.4

Home mortgages	$ 0.2	$ 0.5	$ 0.2	—	—	$ 0.9	$ 1.2
Multifamily mortgages	0.8	1.2	1.1	$ 1.3	$ 2.3	2.5	2.8
Total mortgages	$ 1.0	$ 1.7	$ 1.3	$ 1.3	$ 2.3	$ 3.4	$ 4.0
Total investment funds	$10.2	$ 9.4	$12.3	$13.1	$15.5	$19.7	$21.4
U.S. government and agency securities							
U.S. government securities	$ 2.3	$ 3.7	$ 4.8	$ 6.9	$ 6.1	$ 8.0	$ 8.7
Federal agency securities	1.4	1.2	2.3	3.4	1.6	1.7	1.4
Total	$ 3.7	$ 4.9	$ 7.1	$10.3	$ 7.7	$ 9.7	$10.1
Total funds	$13.9	$14.3	$19.4	$23.4	$23.2	$29.4	$31.5
Cash	$ 0.3	$ 0.9	$ 1.3	$ 0.6	$ 0.3	$ 0.1	$ 0.2
Other	1.5	2.5	2.8	0.8	2.9	2.0	2.3
Total	$15.7	$17.7	$23.5	$24.8	$26.4	$31.5	$34.0
DISCREPENCY—Sources less uses	$ 1.9	$ 1.8	($ 0.5)	$ 2.1	$ 4.8	$ 1.8	$ 2.0

Sources: U.S. Department of Commerce, *National Income Accounts*; Board of Governors of the Federal Reserve System, *Flow of Funds Accounts, Assets and Liabilities Outstanding*; Bureau of the Census, *Governmental Finance*; U.S. Treasury Department, *Treasury Bulletin*; U.S. Department of Housing and Urban Development, *The Supply of Mortgage Credit*. Estimations and projections are from *Credit and Capital Markets, 1983* (New York: Bankers Trust Co., 1983).

**TABLE 3.18   Primary Assets and Liabilities of State and
Local Retirement Funds (as of December 31)**

(dollars in billions)

	1975		1982	
	Assets	Percentage of Total	Assets	Percentage of Total
Assets				
Currency, checkables, and miscellaneous	$ 3.8	3.3%	$ 0.2	0.1%
Open market paper	0.6	0.5	4.2	1.6
U.S. government securites	2.5	2.2	34.7	13.2
Federal agency securities	5.2	4.5	27.5	10.4
Corporate and foreign bonds	61.6	53.1	112.5	42.6
State and local securities	1.9	1.6	4.0	1.5
Mortgages	7.6	6.6	14.5	5.5
Stocks	32.7	28.2	66.2	25.1
Total	$115.9	100.0%	$263.8	100.0%
Total liabilities	$115.9	100.0%	$263.8	100.0%

Source: *1983 Prospects for Financial Markets* (New York: Salomon Brothers, Inc., 1983)

**TABLE 3.19   Primary Assets and Liabilities of Foundations and
Endowments (as of December 31)**

(dollars in billions)

	1975		1982	
	Amount	Percentage of Total	Amount	Percentage of Total
Assets				
Currency, checkables, and miscellaneous	$ 0.6	1.0%	$ 0.9	1.1%
Open market paper	1.1	1.9	1.4	1.8
U.S. government securities	0.6	1.0	1.5	1.9
Federal agency securities	1.7	2.9	2.1	2.6
Corporate and foreign bonds	11.5	19.7	14.1	17.8
Mortgages	1.0	1.7	1.3	1.6
Stocks	41.8	71.8	58.1	73.2
Total	$58.3	100.0%	$79.4	100.0%
Total net worth	$58.3	100.0%	$79.4	100.0%

Source: *1983 Prospects for Financial Markets* (New York: Salomon Brothers, Inc., 1983).

their customers and invest temporary balances left with the firm, and a few large firms have begun offering intermediary-type liabilities that are invested in various securities.

Money Market Mutual Funds. Two events — the deregulation of the investment banking industry in 1975 and the existence of Regulation Q limits on maximum rates that depository institutions could pay — made money market mutual funds the fastest growing financial institution in the late 1970s and early 1980s. Table 3.20 shows these funds grew from under $4 billion at the end of 1975 to nearly $230 billion at the end of 1982. Basically, money market funds use the proceeds of their "shareholder" inflows to purchase short-term, higher-quality financial instruments. Many individuals and smaller businesses were unable to directly purchase such higher-yielding, short-term market instruments because of the large size required in transactions. By using money market funds, however, these individuals and small businesses participated in yields on short-term instruments considerably above Regulation Q limits on most deposits. Furthermore, most money market mutual funds offered limited checking, wire transfers, mail deposit, and other appealing services.

Table 3.20 illustrates that the dominant investments for money market funds at the end of 1982 were open market paper (such as commercial paper and bankers' acceptances), U.S. government securities, and large certificates of deposit (CDs).

The phenomenal growth of the money market mutual funds ended abruptly in December 1982, when depository financial institutions were permitted to

---

TABLE 3.20   Primary Assets and Liabilities of Money Market Funds (as of December 31)

(dollars in billions)

	1975		1982	
	Amount	Percentage of Total	Amount	Percentage of Total
Assets				
Currency, checkables, and miscellaneous	$0.1	2.8%	$ 24.7	10.8%
Repurchase agreements	0.1	2.8	19.4	8.5
Time deposits	1.9	52.8	52.4	22.9
Open market paper	0.7	19.4	74.0	32.3
U.S. government securities	0.7	19.4	56.8	24.8
Federal agency securities	0.1	2.8	2.0	0.9
Total	$3.6	100.0%	$229.3	100.0%
Total shareholdings	$3.6	100.0%	$229.3	100.0%

Source: 1983 Prospects for Financial Markets (New York: Salomon Brothers, Inc., 1983)

issue insured money market deposit accounts between $2,500 and $100,000 without any rate maximum. Commercial banks, S&Ls, and mutual savings banks began paying interest rates somewhat above what money market mutual funds were able to pay and advertised that their deposit accounts were insured to $100,000. Unable to respond to the rate challenge (since they are limited to paying what their short-term assets earn), money market mutual funds have lost $60 billion in the first half of 1983.

Other Investment Companies. Other investment companies also obtain funds through the sale of their own securities and invest these pooled funds in a portfolio of securities. This portfolio is presumably managed to obtain benefits such as professional selection of securities, skillfull timing of purchases and sales, and diversification that an individual investor may be unable to achieve on his own. Two characteristics are common to all forms of investment companies: (1) their primary function is investment, not investment to meet their financial obligations (as in the case of insurance companies or S&Ls) or to acquire securities for the purpose of control (as in the case of holding companies); (2) income from investments is usually exempt from corporate income taxes (46 percent) if the investment company meets certain qualifications and if it distributes at least 90 percent of its income to its shareholders.

Four types of financial institutions meet these criteria: money market mutual funds; fixed-trust investment companies; closed-end investment companies; and open-end investment companies. Money market mutual funds, which buy short-term financial instruments, were discussed previously. The other three types emphasize the purchase of stocks and bonds with the pool of funds obtained from investors. After briefly describing fixed-trust investment companies and closed-end investment companies, open-end investment companies are analyzed in greater detail.

Fixed-trust investment companies operate with a fixed fund that involves an initial selection of a group of securities deposited in trust for a fixed number of years. Shares that remain outstanding for the duration of the trust are issued for the securities purchased. This type of investment company was popular during the 1920s; however, inflexibility (i.e., inability to grow, inability to switch assets, the fixed maturity, and the poor record of these companies in the early 1930s) caused this form of investment company to decline in popularity. Since the 1970s there has been a resurgence in fixed-asset companies. The aggregate assets of these companies, nearly all of which are invested in state and local securities, totaled close to $20 billion at the end of 1982.

Closed-end investment companies operate as ordinary business corporations. That is, from time to time they offer their own securities at a predetermined price. The securities offered are usually common stock, but the closed-end investment company can also seek financial leverage by issuing preferred stock or debentures. The issued securities are sold on an exchange or in the over-the-counter market in a similar way to the securities of typical nonfinancial corporations. Closed-end investment companies use the funds they have raised to acquire a diversified list of securities, usually emphasizing common stocks. In contrast to the fixed trust, the closed-end company places great emphasis on portfolio management. Large blocks of common stock are bought and sold in accord with management's interpretation of future performance. As with fixed trusts, closed-end investment companies enjoyed their greatest popularity during the 1920s; however, approximately 40 new closed-end companies (generally emphasizing income as a primary objective) were started in the 1970s. New common shares have seldom been offered by existing closed-end companies in the last decade, because most of these shares have market values that are substantially lower than their book values. As of the end of 1982, there were nearly 200 closed-end investment companies with total assets in excess of $12 billion.

Open-end investment companies, or mutual funds as they are popularly called, have three characteristics which differentiate them from the previously discussed types of investment companies. (1) They can only issue one type of liability: ownership shares. They cannot borrow or issue preferred stock. (2) They offer their own shares continuously at current asset value per share plus a selling charge, if any. The selling charge, imposed by a load fund, usually runs 8 to 9 percent for sales of up to about $10,000 (it is gradually reduced for larger sales); however, many mutual funds are no-load funds and have no selling commission, because they rely on advertising or word of mouth publicity to generate publicity. (3) Mutual funds agree to redeem their shares at any time at their current asset value. The per share asset value for selling or redeeming shares is calculated at regular intervals, usually twice daily, and is determined by dividing the market value of all securities (plus any cash or other assets less any liabilities) by the number of shares outstanding.

The other characteristics of most mutual funds are similar to other investment companies. Nearly all mutual funds are qualified as regulated investment companies. So long as all net investment income and capital gains are credited to shareholders (who are taxed on such returns), the fund itself is not taxed. The mutual fund makes no commitment to shareholders apart from a willingness to redeem shares at their asset value and to supervise management of the assets in accordance with the objectives stated in the fund prospectus. Some of the more common investment objectives include: (1) primarily current income; (2) emphasis on capital appreciation; and (3) moderate income and appreciation. While management can be accomplished by the fund itself, most mutual funds have management contracts with organizations that provide all of the necessary administrative services, as well as portfolio management.

The growth of other investment company assets and liabilities is shown in Table 3.21. At the end of 1975, common stocks were clearly the dominant assets, constituting over three-fourths of all other investment company assets. By 1982, state and local securities had joined common stock as the dominant assets of other investment companies.[10] The sources and uses of funds for money market funds and other investment funds from 1977 through 1982 and projections for 1983 appear in Table 3.22.

Security Brokers and Dealers. The primary assets and liabilities of security brokers and dealers at the end of 1975 and 1982 appear in Table 3.23. Short-term deposits and securities, security credits (loans to customers to purchase securities), and corporate stocks were the dominant assets of these institutions for both time periods.

---

[10] The tax exemption of income on state and local securities was allowed to pass through to investment company shareholders starting in the early 1970s.

TABLE 3.21   Primary Assets and Liabilities of Other Investment Funds (as of December 31)

(dollars in billions)

	1975		1982	
	Amount	Percentage of Total	Amount	Percentage of Total
Assets				
Currency, checkables, and miscellaneous	$ 1.2	1.7%	$ 13.7	11.0%
Open market papers	1.9	2.8	4.3	3.5
U.S. government securities	1.1	1.6	3.9	3.1
Corporate and foreign bonds	5.7	8.3	11.5	9.3
State and local securities	6.1	8.8	48.7	39.2
Stocks	53.1	76.8	42.0	33.9
Total	$69.1	100.0%	$124.1	100.0%
Total shareholdings	$69.1	100.0%	$124.1	100.0%

Source: *1983 Prospects for Financial Markets* (New York: Salomon Brothers, Inc., 1983)

Other Financial Institutions

The three final nonbank financial institutions mentioned in this chapter are finance companies, mortgage companies, and real estate investment trusts. Detailed figures are not discussed for the latter two because their combined total assets are less than $25 billion. Generally, mortgage bankers ($17.7 billion in total assets) act as brokers between users of mortgage funds and ultimate lenders such as insurance companies. Many mortgage companies have been acquired by S&Ls and other financial institutions. Several of the remaining mortgage bankers are expanding their line of financial services. Real estate investment trusts ($5.8 billion) grew rapidly in the late 1960s and early 1970s. In 1974, rising rates and real estate credit problems caused many of these trusts to fall from investment favor and they have declined in size in recent years.

Finance Companies. Several trends pertaining to finance companies have important implications for their asset, liability, and fund flows. (1) By the mid-1970s, many of the distinctions between consumer finance companies, sales finance companies (with the exception of captive sales finance companies), and commercial finance companies had disappeared, and the trend was clearly toward finance companies with diversified activities. (2) The number of finance companies has decreased significantly, largely as a result of mergers, but the average size of finance companies has increased significantly over the last decade. (3) While a few small proprietorships or partnerships with individual offices still remain, the corporate form with extensive branching operations has become increasingly important, with advantages including access to the money and capital markets, geographic diversification, and mobility of financial resources. Finally, finance companies are subject to more intensive competition from depository institutions who increasingly seek profitable loans to consumers and smaller businesses, and larger nonfinancial businesses, who seek profits from financing their own sales.

The primary assets and liabilities of all finance companies at the end of 1975 and 1982 are summarized in Table 3.24. This information indicates that loans to consumers are roughly half of all finance company assets. In recent years between 35 and 40 percent of these consumer loans have been cash loans, with nearly all of the remainder being sales installment loans. Loans to businesses have grown to slightly over 40 percent of all finance company assets while other assets, which consist primarily of other loans and investments, have declined to roughly 7 percent.

Table 3.25 indicates there have been some modest changes in the major sources of financing available to finance companies. Short-term liabilities, generally one quarter to one third of which were loans from banks and two thirds to three quarters of which were commercial paper (mostly directly placed), constituted over one half of finance companies' sources of funds. While long-term debt has fluctuated considerably, on the average it has constituted about one sixth of finance companies liabilities over the last decade. Common stock (proceeds from stock issues and retained earnings) totaled close to one third of the funds.

The relative importance of the three main forms of borrowing — borrowing from banks, commercial paper, and long-term debt — varies according to the differentials in interest rates at which the debts can be secured; but it also differs among the three categories of finance companies as a result of their different sizes and needs. The larger size of many sales finance companies (including many captive companies) and many commercial finance companies means they usually have access to lower interest costs in the commercial paper market. Most consumer finance companies and smaller sales and commercial finance companies rely on direct bank borrowing for their short-term financing. Consumer and sales finance companies have, on average, tended to use more long-term debt than commercial finance companies.

Many of the problems faced by finance companies (e.g., high fixed cost of smaller loans, high interest cost, weaker quality loans, and competition from depository institutions and nonfinancial businesses) are likely to continue for the next several years. Further consolidations and mergers with other financial institutions appear likely to continue.

THE FUTURE

Laws and regulations will change. Economic, competitive, and technological forces will have an unpredictable impact. Yet, there are currently in place forces that give some reasonable hints of what financial institutions may be like by, say, 1990. At least four generalizations appear appropriate, unless laws and regulations are extensively changed.

TABLE 3.22 Sources and Uses of Funds — All Investment Companies

(dollars in billions)

	1977	1978	1979	1980	1981	1982 (estimated)	1983 (projected)
SOURCES OF FUNDS							
Unit investment trusts — units issued	$3.5	$3.0	$ 3.4	$ 4.9	$ 5.7	$13.8	$14.5
Money market funds(a) — net assets	0.2	7.0	34.6	30.7	109.7	38.2	(26.0)
Conventional mutual funds							
Sales of capital shares	$6.4	$6.7	$ 6.8	$10.0	$ 9.7	$15.5	$28.0
Less: Redemptions	(6.0)	(7.2)	(8.0)	(8.2)	(7.5)	(7.5)	(7.8)
Net sales of capital shares	$0.4	($0.5)	($ 1.2)	$ 1.8	$ 2.2	$ 8.0	$20.2
Total	$4.1	$9.5	$36.9	$37.3	$117.7	$60.0	$ 8.7
USES OF FUNDS							
Investment funds							
Corporate bonds	$2.0	($0.4)	$ 1.5	$ 1.8	$ 1.8	$ 1.1	$ 2.0
Corporate stocks	(3.7)	(1.6)	(2.8)	(1.8)	(0.6)	2.5	3.5
State and local securities	3.9	3.1	4.0	6.6	8.4	25.7	16.8
Total	$2.2	$1.1	$ 2.7	$ 6.6	$ 9.6	$29.3	$22.3

Open market paper	$1.2	$3.7	$15.5	$13.1	$38.7	$ 2.1	($ 8.0)
U.S. government and agency securities							
U.S. government securities	($0.1)	$0.4	$ 2.6	$ 0.7	$ 18.9	$18.0	$ 1.3
Federal agency securities	—	—	1.6	2.2	5.6	2.3	1.5
Total	($0.1)	$0.4	$ 4.2	$ 2.9	$ 24.6	$20.3	$ 2.8
Total funds	$3.4	$5.2	$22.4	$22.5	$ 72.9	$51.7	$17.1
Certificates of deposit	$0.3	$3.5	$12.8	$ 9.7	$ 34.9	$ 5.8	($ 9.8)
Other — net	0.4	0.8	1.7	5.1	9.8	2.5	1.4
Total	$4.1	$9.5	$36.9	$37.3	$117.7	$60.0	$ 8.7

(a) Includes limited maturity tax-exempt funds

Sources: Investment Company Institute; Board of Governors of the Federal Reserve System, *Flow of Funds Accounts, Assets and Liabilities Outstanding.* Estimations and projections are revised from *Credit and Capital Markets, 1983* (New York: Bankers Trust Co., 1983).

TABLE 3.23   **Primary Assets and Liabilities of Security Brokers and Dealers (as of December 31)**

(dollars in billions)

	1975		1982	
	Amount	Percentage of Total	Amount	Percentage of Total
Assets				
Currency, checkables, and miscellaneous	$22.9	46.0%	$18.2	22.5%
Security credit	8.6	17.3	19.5	24.1
U.S. governments	5.8	11.6	7.3	9.0
Federal agencies	1.2	2.4	8.0	9.9
Corporate and foreign bonds	2.9	5.8	9.6	11.9
State and local securities	0.5	1.0	1.4	1.7
Stocks	7.9	15.9	17.0	21.0
Total	$49.8	100.0%	$81.0	100.0%
Total liabilities and net worth	$49.8	100.0%	$81.0	100.0%

Source: *1983 Prospects for Financial Markets* (New York: Salomon Brothers, Inc., 1983)

TABLE 3.24   **Primary Assets and Liabilities of Finance Companies (as of December 31)**

(dollars in billions)

	1975		1982	
	Amount	Percentage of Total	Amount	Percentage of Total
Assets				
Currency, checkables, and miscellaneous	$ 4.0	4.5%	$ 4.9	2.2%
Corporate business loan	31.8	35.6	91.5	41.8
Noncorporate business loans	8.9	10.0	10.8	4.9
Consumer loans	44.7	50.0	111.9	51.1
Total	$89.4	100.0%	$219.1	100.0%
Liabilities and net worth				
Open market paper	$28.0	31.3%	$ 72.2	33.0%
Bank loans	14.2	15.9	28.8	13.1
Bond issues	30.8	34.5	57.8	26.4
Net worth and other liabilities	16.4	18.3	60.3	27.5
Total	$89.4	100.0%	$219.1	100.0%

Source: *1983 Prospects for Financial Markets* (New York: Salomon Brothers, Inc., 1983)

TABLE 3.25   Sources and Uses Funds — Finance Companies

(dollars in billions)

	1977	1978	1979	1980	1981	1982 (estimated)	1983 (projected)
SOURCES OF FUNDS							
Cash flow							
Retained profits	$ 2.8	$ 3.3	$ 4.1	$ 0.5	$ 3.4	$1.7	$2.0
Reserves	1.6	2.0	3.9	3.0	5.6	2.7	3.2
Total cash flow	$ 4.4	$ 5.3	$ 8.0	$ 3.5	$ 9.0	$4.4	$5.2
Corporate bonds	2.0	2.5	2.5	1.1	1.6	3.7	2.5
Short-term funds							
Open market paper	$ 7.1	$ 6.4	$11.7	$ 0.1	$ 7.8	($3.7)	$0.8
Bank loans	0.6	1.1	1.9	1.0	0.6	—	0.4
Total short-term funds	$ 7.7	$ 7.5	$13.6	$ 1.1	$ 8.4	($3.7)	$1.2
Total	$14.1	$15.3	$24.1	$ 5.7	$19.0	$4.4	$8.9
USES OF FUNDS							
Consumer credit	$ 5.9	$ 9.4	$14.0	$ 8.4	$13.1	$4.0	$6.6
Loans to business							
Retail auto	$ 2.6	$ 2.2	$ 0.4	($ 3.1)	($ 1.4)	$1.1	$1.3
Wholesale auto	3.2	0.8	1.0	(1.6)	0.9	(1.1)	—
Retail paper	2.2	2.3	2.1	4.6	4.5	0.1	0.5
All other	5.5	6.2	6.5	3.5	5.5	(0.3)	0.7
Total loans	$13.5	$11.5	$10.1	$ 3.4	$ 9.5	($0.2)	$2.4
Total funds	$19.4	$20.9	$24.1	$11.8	$22.6	$3.8	$9.1
Other — net	(5.2)	(5.6)	—	(6.1)	(3.6)	0.6	(0.2)
Total	$14.1	$15.3	$24.1	$ 5.7	$19.0	$4.4	$8.9

Sources: Board of Governors of the Federal Reserve System, *Flow of Funds Accounts, Assets and Liabilities Outstanding.* Estimations and projections are from *Credit and Capital Markets, 1983* (New York: Bankers Trust Co., 1983).

First, financial institutions will be considerably less compartmentalized than they were in 1983. Distinctions by product and sometimes by geographic lines will tend to break down. This is not to say that, for example, some S&Ls will not decide to specialize as real estate lenders. However, *all* S&Ls will not be forced to serve the real estate market primarily; indeed, a few will probably choose to offer a wide range of financial services. This general conclusion seems appropriate for many types of financial institutions, such as mutual savings banks, credit unions, insurance companies, and finance companies. The remaining financial institutions (e.g., pension funds, retirement funds, investment funds, and securities dealers) may still be limited as to the range of financial services they sell; however, many of these will probably function as compartmentalized parts of large financial service companies.

Second, dollarwide the bulk of financial intermediation will be handled by a relatively small group (maybe 20 to 30) of firms that are truly financial supermarkets. The term "financial supermarkets" implies offering a wide variety of financial products and services constituting most of the financial needs of the individual or business. Some of these institutions are already large savings banks, S&Ls, and insurance companies. Others will result from combinations of medium to large financial institutions currently in different financial product areas. A few will be large, primarily nonfinancial firms (e.g., Sears Roebuck) that desire to enter the financial sector and have the resources to do so. The surviving financial supermarkets will probably handle at least three-fourths of financial intermediation flows and have the following characteristics: (1) a wide variety of financial products and services; (2) involvement in many financial markets, including international ones; (3) massive resources (say over $50 billion in 1983 terms) to provide products and services, to be in markets, and to afford new technology.

Third, well-managed, smaller financial institutions will survive and compete by offering specialized financial products or services in localized markets. There are many industries in which large and small firms coexist profitably. In fact, capital-intensive, durable-product industries such as automobile production have only a few surviving companies. A parallel example for financial institutions may be department stores. There are several efficient large nationwide department stores, but literally hundreds of successful smaller stores. These small stores offer unique products and services which even the most efficient larger stores are unable to deliver as effectively. Financial institutions that may have a hard time surviving in the coming environment are the middle-sized institutions trying to service broad markets, and poorly managed smaller institutions. To survive, the smaller financial institutions must select products, services, or areas in which they are unique and in which they have management expertise.

Finally, surviving financial institutions will still be relatively safe and will still be heavily regulated. Fearsome comparisons to the 1920s proliferate. The big financial institutions of the 1920s spoke of being department stores of finance, offering not only lending-depository services, but also insurance, brokerage, and real estate services. However, the surviving financial institutions of the 1980s are not likely to be nearly as risky, and regulation is likely to be much more proactive than reactive as in the 1920s. Regulatory bodies such as the FDIC, the Securities and Exchange Commission (SEC), and the Federal

Home Loan Banks did not exist in the 1920s. Other regulatory bodies, such as the Federal Reserve, are more knowledgeable and powerful. Indeed, "deregulation" is a more apt term. Significant changes, such as elimination of ceilings on interest paid by depository institutions, elimination of the fixed commission structure of brokerage firms, and the freedom given a wide range of institutions to compete in a broad mix of financial businesses, have occurred. Nevertheless, the nation and its lawmakers seem mindful of the special economic role financial institutions play and are reluctant to leave them unregulated.

4

Investment Banking

GEORGE G. C. PARKER

ORIGINS OF INVESTMENT BANKING AS A SEPARATE INDUSTRY

The investment banking industry in the United States is unique when compared with those of most other countries. The primary reason for this uniqueness is the Glass-Steagall Act passed by Congress in 1933. Under the Act, the functions of commercial banks and investment banks are largely separated, with commercial banks being prohibited from underwriting and dealing in private debt and equity securities. The intent was to create an industry different from commercial banking, which would provide long-term debt and equity funds for industry and government. The Glass-Steagall Act, however, did *not* prohibit commercial banks from underwriting and selling U.S. government securities or the general obligation securities of state and local government. Thus, in the area of public securities, commercial banks and investment banks often compete as underwriters and dealers.

In countries where there is no legislation prohibiting commercial banks from participating in investment banking activities, the role of investment banking is largely included in the full service of commercial banks. The conspicuous exception to this rule is Japan, which has securities laws that closely resemble those in the United States. Countries where investment banking and commercial banking are combined are said to have a system of "universal banking." Under this system a single financial institution may accept deposits, make loans, purchase securities for investment or resale, and engage in all types of financial transactions as they relate to corporate and individual customers.

It is perhaps understandable that the separation of investment banking from commercial banking occurred in the United States after the collapse of the securities markets in 1929 with the resultant failure of nearly 10,000 banks. While the specific reasons for the passage of the Glass-Steagall Act were not described by Congress, at least four separate reasons for its passage may be suggested, as follows.

Risk

Investment banking is a risky business. Debt and equity markets are inherently subject to large fluctuations in prices with the risk of such fluctuations borne by securities dealers, at least to the extent of their inventory. The Glass-Steagall Act insulated commercial banks from that risk by simply prohibiting them from dealing, underwriting, or investing in private securities. Such insulation seemed particularly appropriate after the failure of nearly 40 percent of all commercial banks during the period between 1929 and 1933, especially since many of those failures were directly attributable to securities speculation by the banks.

Conflict of Interest

It was widely believed at the time of the passage of Glass-Steagall that the quality of the loan portfolios of banks was adversely affected by the relationships that many banks had as investors or as underwriters of the securities of their loan clients. To minimize such potential conflict of interest, it was deemed prudent to separate the deposit-taking, lending, and securities businesses.

Concentration of Power

Some observers have noted that the Glass-Steagall Act was passed in part to break up the large and powerful universal banks, or "investment houses," of New York City, especially J.P. Morgan & Company. Those banks were thought to control an excessively large portion of both the lending and investment business of the nation's largest industrial corporations. Further, this concentration of power was thought at the time to have contributed to the economic collapse of the early 1930s. The fact that there was little actual proof for these assertions did not sway Congress from passing the act to break up these large financial institutions.

Specialization

Finally, there was a desire on the part of Congress to revitalize the securities markets in the early 1930s by creating a new, independent industry that would specialize in the origination and distribution of securities to the public. What resulted was a completely new business that could survive only by promoting the growth of the securities markets. Investment banks had no other way to survive than to sell securities aggressively to institutions and the public. One result of this specialization is that some 50 years after the Act, nearly 15 percent of the U.S. population are direct owners of equity securities. This is a far higher proportion than is found in virtually any other country.

Regardless of the reasons for the passage of the Glass-Steagall Act, the financial system in the United States today is largely an outgrowth of it. The industry that Glass-Steagall created has grown to huge proportions, employing thousands of people and raising $85 billion of new financing for business and government in 1981. See Table 4.1 and Figures 4.1 and 4.2 for some data on the size of the industry.

PRIMARY SERVICES OF AN INVESTMENT BANK

The major activities of an investment bank may be divided into the categories and subcategories described in the following section, and illustrated in Figure 4.3.

Underwriting

Underwriting is among the most basic activities of investment banks, although it is highly cyclical and does not necessarily account for the major portion of profits during all parts of the business cycle. Specifically, underwriting involves the purchase (at a guaranteed price) of securities from corporations and governments for resale to investors. This activity generally takes place in the corporate finance department or the buying department, the latter being descriptive of the process that actually occurs. When the underwriting involves the purchase of newly issued securities, it is referred to as a primary offering. When the investment bank purchases already outstanding securities, the transaction is referred to as a secondary underwriting or offering. It is not uncommon in first public offerings for the new issue to be a combination of primary and secondary offerings, meaning that part of the issue involves new funds for the company and part is the sale of stock by insider shareholders who wish to diversify.

TABLE 4.1   Aggregate New Issues of Securities, 1980–1981

(dollars in millions)

	1980		1981	
	Amount	Number of Issues	Amount	Number of Issues
CORPORATE ISSUES				
Bonds	$56,128	1,455	$63,677	1,390
Public	41,598	522	47,020	488
Negotiated	36,683	441	43,340	435
Competitive	4,915	81	3,681	53
Private placements	14,530	933	16,657	902
Preferred stock	3,697	152	2,649	108
Public	2,242	74	1,676	42
Negotiated	1,812	61	1,356	33
Competitive	430	13	320	9
Private placements	1,455	78	973	66
Common stock	13,536	706	15,342	1,012
Public	13,341	672	15,045	945
Negotiated	12,962	667	14,438	939
Competitive	380	5	607	6
Private placements	195	34	297	67
All issues	73,361	2,313	81,668	2,510
MUNICIPAL ISSUES				
Long-term issues	$48,367	5,589	$47,725	4,734
General obligation	14,102	2,940	12,393	2,221
Revenue	34,265	2,649	35,332	2,513
Short-term issues	27,719	2,344	37,432	3,087
All issues	76,087	7,933	85,157	7,821

INITIAL PUBLIC OFFERINGS
1977–1981

	1977	1978	1979	1980	1981
Share value (dollars in millions)	153	249	506	1,397	3,215
Number of issues	40	45	81	237	448

Source: Securities Industry Yearbook (New York: Securities Industry Association, 1982)

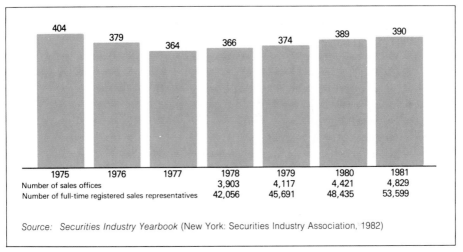

FIG. 4.1 Number of New York Stock Exchange Member Firms Doing Public Business (at year end)

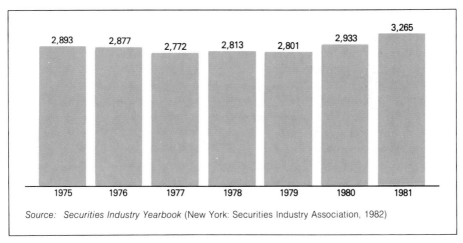

FIG. 4.2 Number of National Association of Securities Dealers Member Firms

Underwriting in the United States may be handled on either a negotiated or competitive bid basis. In a negotiated underwriting, the issuer deals exclusively with a single investment banking firm, which assists in the design, timing, and arrangement of a syndicate to sell the issue. The competitive bidding alternative is largely limited to regulated public utilities and municipal governments, which are required to offer securities under this method. Competitive bidding is discussed in detail in a separate section of this chapter.

Negotiated underwritings may involve a single investment bank, which is called a manager of the deal. Occasionally, however, two or more firms may jointly enter into the management of the underwriting. In such cases the issue is

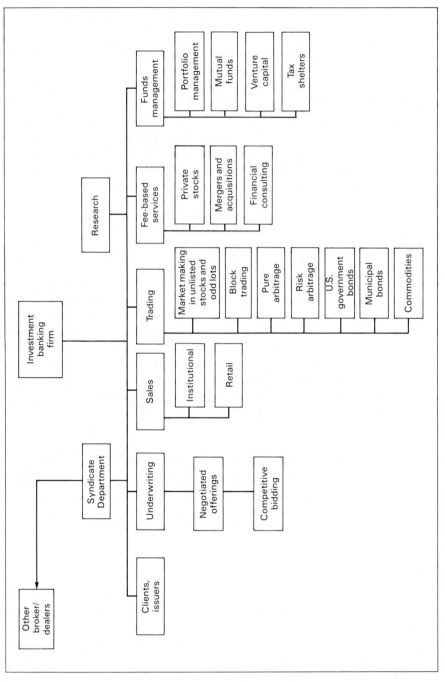

FIG. 4.3 Organization of a Typical Investment Bank

said to be comanaged by more than one firm. In large issues in the 1980s, it is not uncommon for as many as five firms to be involved in comanager status in a single underwriting. Smaller issues tend to have a single firm as manager unless the client firm insists on comanager status due to a special relationship with the investment bankers involved.

To share the underwriting risk, the manager or comanagers generally invite other firms into the offering. The process of risk sharing with other firms is called syndication and may include as few as 5 to as many as 250 firms. Most underwritings involve a syndicate of between 10 and 40 firms. Compensation is paid to the members of the underwriting syndicate according to the size of their underwriting commitment. Firms are usually invited to participate on the principle of reciprocity and their distribution (selling) capabilities. Traditional groupings of firms may also apply, as described later in the syndicate system section.

It must be emphasized that the risk in underwriting involves the risk of being unable to resell the securities at a price that is at least as high as the price paid to the seller. That risk is not trivial, especially during periods of volatility in the debt and equity markets, and the underwriters concession (commission) in the spread is meant to compensate for that risk.

Competition in the underwriting of securities is intense in the economy of the 1980s. This competition has been exacerbated by the inauguration of Rule 415 of the Securities and Exchange Commission (SEC), which went into effect February 24, 1982. The rule has simplified the process for registering securities for resale. Under Rule 415, it is possible for some issuers to preregister a significant amount of securities with the SEC and deal directly with more than one investment banker at the time the issuer wishes to sell the securities into the market. Many observers feel that Rule 415 will significantly alter the industry by moving it away from traditional negotiated deals toward a modified form of competitive bidding.

"Best Efforts" Offering. Occasionally, firms issue securities without a formal underwriting. In those instances the underwriter enters into an agency agreement with the issuer and attempts to sell the securities on a "best efforts" basis. There is no guarantee of amount to the issuer. Best efforts offerings are relatively rare and tend to be used only by similar companies where an underwritten public offering is not feasible.

Sales and Distribution

When securities are purchased by an investment bank, or, more precisely, by a syndicate, they must then be resold. The sales function in most major investment banks is divided into "institutional sales" and "retail sales." Firms that specialize in retail sales are sometimes referred to as wire houses, dating back to the days when the retail offices of such firms were connected to the trading floor of the New York Stock Exchange (NYSE) by telegraph. Although modern communication has long surpassed primitive systems, the term "wire house" endures to describe firms that are active in retail sales to the public. These firms may often be recognized because they frequently have their offices at street level to encourage the walk-in traffic of their retail customers. Among the major national wire houses are the well-known firms of Merrill Lynch, E.F. Hutton, and Prudential-Bache. Most regional firms are also retail-oriented in their market focus.

The counterpart of retail sales is institutional sales, which involves selling large blocks of stock to institutional purchasers such as pension funds, endowment trusts, insurance companies, and other portfolios that are professionally managed. Some firms specialize exclusively in institutional sales and do not sell directly to the public. Institutional firms may be quite large, but they tend to have far fewer offices and far fewer sales personnel than retail firms. Included among the well-known institutional firms are Morgan Stanley, First Boston, Goldman Sachs, and Salomon Brothers.

Many firms have both institutional and retail sales forces to sell securities to all types of buyers. Furthermore, some firms concentrate on national marketing, while others operate only on a regional basis. There are fewer than 30 firms operating nationally, while the number of firms operating on a regional basis is difficult to estimate at any point in time because of the relatively easy entry and exit from the business. The number of both national and regional firms is further subject to modification because of the relatively large number of mergers that take place each year. Nonetheless, fewer than 20 firms across the nation account for the bulk of the underwriting and selling activity of the industry, with the top 10 firms accounting for 86 percent of the new issue managerships in 1982 (see Table 4.2). In this sense, the investment banking business is much more concentrated than the commercial banking business, which has over 13,000 separate competitors.

Trading and Brokerage

In addition to underwriting and selling newly issued securities, investment banks also provide the service of trading securities in the aftermarket, that is, the market for securities after the initial issue. Aftermarket activity may involve simply a brokerage function, whereby the investment bank acts only as an agent for customer's orders; or it may involve a dealer function, whereby the investment bank carries an inventory of the securities traded and trades for its own account as well.

It is noteworthy that the Glass-Steagall Act does not preclude commercial banks from acting as agents or brokers on behalf of customers; instead, the Act merely prohibits commercial banks from acting as dealers. Thus, in the brokerage function, it has always been possible for commercial banks to compete directly with investment banks. Until the 1980s, however, commercial banks did not emphasize their trading capabilities in private debt and equity securities, except for servicing a few large accounts in their trust departments.

Since 1980, it has been increasingly common for commercial banks to offer a trading service to retail customers, usually in the form of discount brokerage. The most conspicuous example of entry into the brokerage business by a bank is the 1982 purchase of Charles Schwab & Company (the nation's largest discount broker) by the Bank of America. Other banks have followed suit throughout the country; today it is estimated that commercial banks will account for as

TABLE 4.2   Largest Underwriting Firms in Investment Banking, by Volume

Top 20 underwriting firms, 1950–1980

(dollars in millions)

Firm	1950	1955	1960	1965	1970	1975	1980
Merrill Lynch	339	203	609	1,342	6,398	14,066	21,298
Salomon Brothers	145	202	144	924	4,589	11,884	17,213
First Boston	556	894	1,340	2,362	7,023	12,198	12,701
Morgan Stanley	645	1,019	970	1,101	4,094	11,226	11,668
Goldman Sachs	—	—	180	707	2,905	8,502	11,058
Lehman Brothers	233	441	610	1,706	5,101	6,450	10,246
Blyth Eastman	265	748	603	1,549	4,019	7,141	9,262
Kidder Peabody	289	301	374	825	2,864	5,768	9,082
Dean Witter	—	101	143	610	1,393	4,256	6,770
E.F. Hutton	—	—	—	—	—	2,596	5,420
Lazard Frères	—	142	143	799	1,327	1,704	4,659
Bache	—	—	—	—	—	—	4,621
Smith Barney	—	321	—	508	2,155	4,333	4,051
Warburg	—	—	—	—	—	—	3,668
Dillon, Read	121	271	230	242	1,270	2,135	3,534
Drexel Burnham	41	—	—	—	899	2,210	2,939
Shearson	—	—	—	—	—	—	2,451
Bear, Stearns	—	—	159	—	—	—	2,413
Rothschild, Unterberg	—	—	—	—	—	—	2,364
Donaldson, Lufkin	—	—	—	—	—	—	1,452

Source: Samuel L. Hayes III, A. Michael Spence, and David Van Praag Marks, *Competition in the Investment Banking Industry* (Cambridge, Mass.: Harvard University Press, 1983), p. 118 (Note: Full credit is given to all managers in comanaged offerings.)

much as 35 percent of the brokerage activity in private debt and equity securities by the end of the 1980s. Again, it is to be stressed that such competition by commercial banks can occur even without a major congressional modification of the Glass-Steagall Act. Should commercial banks capture such a large share of the brokerage business, a profound effect on the profitability of the investment banking industry can be expected.

Listed Securities.   The market-making activities of investment banks in securities listed on the major stock exchanges is highly regulated and must take place on the floor of the respective exchanges, with the exception of certain large blocks (5,000 shares and up) of stock which are partially exempted from strict exchange trading rules. The purpose of requiring "listed" stocks to be traded on the floor of the exchanges dates to the early days of the NYSE, when it was deemed most efficient for all trading in securities to take place at a specific place. These rules, creating a so-called central auction market, were deemed to assure the best price for sellers and buyers alike. Modern communications through the National Association of Securities Dealers Electronic Quotation (NASDEQ) system have made the stock exchange floor trading rules seem anachronistic; yet they persist even in the face of predictions that they would have ended with the advent of the NASDEQ technology.

In spite of the limitations on market making in listed securities, investment banks do compete aggressively for the brokerage of listed securities. The competition takes the form of commissions charged, as well as the quality of the executions obtained for the buyer or seller. Firms may achieve reputations for their executions, which is an important competitive tool. Furthermore, some firms make a market in odd lots (i.e., less than 100 shares of listed securities) because the minimum trading amount on the exchanges is 100 shares.

Over-the-Counter Securities. Unlisted securities, called over-the-counter (OTC) securities, offer the most important market making opportunity for the trading desks of major investment banks. Frequently, the OTC securities in which an investment bank makes a market are from companies or municipalities that are significant underwriting clients for the firm. Firms that make a market in a specific security are listed with the NASDEQ system, although some small, low-volume stocks are traded without being quoted on the NASDEQ system. Prices for these securities are listed on a daily or weekly sheet circulated to broker-dealers.

To be a market maker, a firm must post a bid and asked price and be willing to make limited purchases (100 shares) at that price. Because making markets involves a commitment of the firm's own funds, this activity is generally centralized at a trading desk where the firm has experienced personnel to minimize the risk of the trading positions. Much of the market making in securities is centralized in New York City, the headquarters for most major firms. Regional firms, however, are often significant market makers in regional companies with which they are most familiar. Market making and direct trading is a major profit center for many investment banks as well as an important activity in supporting the securities of their underwriting clients.

Arbitrage. Arbitrage is often closely connected with market making in the trading room of an investment bank. The essential difference between market making and arbitrage is that pure arbitrage involves the simultaneous buying and selling of a security to take advantage of an irrational price differential. An example of pure arbitrage might include a security that, at a particular moment, is trading at different prices on the NYSE and the Pacific Coast Stock Exchange or a convertible bond that is selling below its conversion value. In both instances, the investment bank arbitrage desk would sell the higher-priced securities and cover immediately with the lower-priced security. It is important to note that in pure arbitrage there is no risk. Since investment banks pay no commissions on their own trades, it is the arbitrage desks of investment banks that can usually spot and exploit pure arbitrage opportunities before they are large enough to be profitable to the general public. Arbitrage activities are not only quite profitable to many investment banks, but also provide a public service in keeping the markets rational and efficient.

Risk Arbitrage. The term "risk arbitrage" is something of a misnomer because, by definition, true economic arbitrage is a riskless, simultaneous transaction, as described previously. Nonetheless, the term "risk arbitrage" has crept into the language of investment banking to describe a transaction that includes the purchase and sale of two equity securities on the announcement of a merger. For example, if security A is selling for $40 and security B is selling for $10 and a merger is announced in which company A is offering one share of its stock for three shares of company B stock, the risk arbitrage trader could purchase 300 shares of company B for $3,000 and sell short 100 shares of company A for $4,000. At the consummation of the merger, the exchanged shares would be used to cover the short position and a profit of $1,000 would result. The risk of the transaction is that if the merger does not ultimately occur, for legal or other reasons, the prices of the two securities may decline in value. Risk arbitrage is risky business but, as is so often the case with risky businesses, it can be highly profitable to the astute trader. In the active arena of mergers and acquisitions in recent years, risk arbitrage between merger partners has been a large profit center for numerous investment banks.

"Block Trading" of Debt and Equity. Block trading at investment banks refers to the handling of large blocks of stock, most often purchased and sold by institutions, which are not traded on the floor of the major exchanges. The price at which the blocks trade must generally be reported to the exchange to give information to the investing public, but the trades themselves are effected often using the capital of the investment bank. Block trading is another example of the riskiness of the trading business, because firms often have to take major positions in a security in order to consummate the trade. If mutual fund A, for example, wishes to sell 175,000 shares of security X, the block trader may purchase the shares even though there is a visible buyer for only 150,000 of the shares or even less. The unsold shares must be carried in inventory with all the accompanying price risk until they can be sold. Similarly, an investment bank may make a commitment to sell a large block that it does not own. The price risk in this transaction relates to the ability of the firm to acquire the stock at a price less than it has agreed to sell the shares for. Good block traders are expected to have wide contacts with major customers and a good "feel" for the market. It is a valuable and rare skill with high risks and rich rewards. Finally, it is impossible for an investment bank to be a major factor in block trading unless it has substantial capital to risk in the positioning of securities in inventory, if necessary.

Government Bond Trading. In a modern investment bank, the trading of government bonds, federal, state, and local, is generally done in a separate trading section. This is one activity in which investment banks compete directly with commercial banks; the Glass-Steagall Act specifically exempted government bond underwriting and trading from its provisions. Government bond departments are generally high-volume, low-margin operations subject to many of the same risk-return characteristics of the block trading activity. In major investment banks, the government bond desk is an important business with major income potential.

Research

A large research department often supplements the brokerage and trading operations of an investment bank. These departments generally are not profit centers in the firm; they are cost centers with the value of their services being captured in the profits of brokerage, trading, and corporate finance departments. Research departments prepare reports and opinions about selected securities for customers. Major full-service broker–dealers compete importantly based on the quality of their research reports, which are usually passed on free to customers who execute trades with them. Occasionally, however, research is sold to customers or to other firms on a fee basis.

It is also common for investment banks active in underwriting to prepare research reports on the companies that are their underwriting clients and in which they make a market. These reports are expected to be objective assessments of the stocks and bonds being traded. Finally, investment banks often maintain a research opinion in the securities in which they make a market.

The end of industry-wide fixed commissions on May 1, 1975 significantly changed the research function at many investment banks. Prior to 1975, the commission rates in the brokerage business were nonnegotiable and high enough that elaborate research reports were a primary means of nonprice competition within the industry. Since the mandating of competitive (negotiated) commissions, the amount of free research that firms can profitably provide has been greatly reduced. In fact, in the retail market, discount brokers advertise that their commissions are low, in large part because they offer no research opinions to customers. Even in institutional brokerage there has been a diminution in research services, forcing much of the important securities analysis activity out of the investment banks and into the hands of the buyers of securities, both individual and institutional. This has been a major change in the research function of many firms.

Fee-Based Services

Augmenting the underwriting, sales, brokerage, and trading functions in investment banks is often a series of fee-based services conducted by the corporate finance department or various separate departments of the firm. The most important fee-based services follow.

Private Placements of Debt and Equity. For many firms, the public issuance of securities is neither feasible nor preferable. Reasons may include the small size of the issue, need for speed in issuance, complexity of the securities, or a host of other factors that can make a public underwriting difficult. Capital for these clients is often raised through the mechanism of a private placement sold to institutions or large individual investors. Investment banks provide important fee-based services in designing and marketing private placements. Indeed, a strong private placement capability for an investment bank is an important countercyclical business activity for the firm when the level of public debt and equity offerings is low.

It is noteworthy that, in private placements, commercial banks are increasingly active participants and competitors due to the fact that these placements do not involve underwriting.

Mergers and Acquisitions. Since the 1960s, most major investment banks have been active in the field of representing buyers and sellers in all types of business combinations. This activity is generally managed from a specialized mergers and acquisitions (M&A) department with expert personnel active in both soliciting and negotiating deals. Included in mergers and acquisitions work are both friendly and unfriendly takeovers, with various firms specializing in specific types of mergers. For example, some firms refuse to represent clients in unfriendly tender offers for shares. Other firms have become quite expert in defending companies from unfriendly takeovers by aggressive merger partners.

The level of merger activity in the 1980s has been so extraordinarily large that it has become a significant source of profit for many Wall Street firms. Commissions on a successful purchase or sale can range into several million dollars meaning that M&A work is an expanding function in many full-service firms. Nonetheless, there is a self-correcting mechanism to the current level of M&A work, as many observers have noted, namely, that the pace of merger activity of the early 1980s is not sustainable due to the finite number of companies that can be bought. Also, it is true that mergers tend to take place in larger numbers when equity prices are low and companies can be acquired for what purchasers believe is less than their replacement cost.

Compensation for M&A work may be either on a retainer basis or a percentage of the transaction, or both. Commercial banks compete aggressively with investment banks in M&A work as they do in private placements, although the preponderance of the major mergers currently are still handled by the investment banking community.

Financial Consulting. The expertise available among the personnel of major investment banks, particularly the personnel in the corporate finance or underwriting departments, is also available to assist clients in planning financial strategy. Included may be studies relating to the optimal capital structure of the firm, or the optimal dividend policy. These studies are not unlike those conducted by professional consulting firms and accounting firms, but they rely on the specific expertise of the personnel in the investment bank. Fee-based financial consulting tends to be a business that is accentuated during slow periods in the market, when regular underwriting and trading activities are not as active. The reputation of many major investment banks in the financial consulting field has grown to the point where it is a significant source of income and competitive advantage for those firms that perform it well.

Real Estate Investment and Brokerage. During the 1970s, large institutional investors became increasingly interested in the investment opportunities afforded by real estate. Major investment banks responded to that opportunity by opening real estate departments or real estate subsidiaries to assist investors in their objectives. This frequently involved representing clients in the purchase and sale of large commercial properties, including office buildings, shopping centers, and even agricultural land. While often separated from the more traditional functions of the investment bank, the real estate group has been a source of major profits and client relationships during much of the past decade.

Funds Management. The expertise of investment banks is also available to investors, both institutional and individual, in fee-based fiduciary management of portfolios. This activity closely resembles that of the trust department of a major commercial bank, whereby discretionary investment authority is delegated to the firm and performance is judged against preestablished objectives.

Investment management has taken on an even larger role in many investment banks, with the expansion of mutual funds and money market funds managed through investment management subsidiaries of the large investment banking firms. Especially in the area of money market fund management, such firms as Merrill Lynch have begun to compete aggressively with banks in a service function that closely resembles the deposit taking activities of banks. (Tables 4.3 and 4.4 show the aggregate balance sheets and income statements for investment banks in 1981).

ORIGINS OF THE SYNDICATE SYSTEM

The syndicate system of risk sharing in the underwriting and distribution of securities is integral to the investment banking industry. Understanding the syndicate system requires definitions of the following terms.

Manager

The syndicate manager is the firm that originates the issue and deals directly with the client company. Prior to the formation of a syndicate, the manager is responsible for working with the client in designing the issue, preparing the legal and accounting documents as required by the SEC, and holding due diligence meetings with prospective investors. Most important in the legal requirements for the issue is the preparation of the prospectus for the issue which outlines, in legal form, all the relevant facts about the issuing company. When more than one manager is involved in the origination of the issue, the issue is said to have comanagers. There is an increasing trend in the investment banking business toward comanagerships since the competitiveness of the industry has quickened and more corporations prefer to have a relationship with more than one investment banker. When there are comanagers, however, one firm

**TABLE 4.3   Combined Balance Sheet of New York Stock Exchange
Firms Doing a Public Business, 1981
(as of December 31)**

(dollars in millions, unconsolidated)

Assets	
Cash	$ 2,307
Broker receivables	11,977
Customer receivables	20,785
Securities purchased under agreements to resell	42,436
Long positions	37,262
Fixed assets	909
Other assets	5,284
Total assets	$120,960
Liabilities	
Bank loans payable	$ 10,169
Securities sold under repurchase agreements	51,693
Broker payables	11,141
Customer payables	12,509
Short positions	17,302
Other liabilities	9,978
Subordinated liabilities	1,483
Total liabilities	$114,275
Total ownership equity	6,685
Total liabilities and ownership equity	$120,960

Source: Securities Industry Yearbook (New York: Securities Industry Association, 1982)

generally takes the lead in dealing with the client and in working with the syndicate. That manager is designated as the manager "running the books."

Underwriting Group

This is the group of firms invited by the manager or comanagers to share the risk of underwriting the issue. Members of the underwriting group guarantee to accept securities at a price promised to the seller. The traditional purpose of the underwriting group was to assure that there was enough financial capacity to absorb the issue if the market did not permit its quick resale. It is the underwriting syndicate that appears in the public announcements of the issue that are routinely printed in the financial press. These announcements are most often called tombstones due to the style in which they are printed. Two representative tombstones of actual issues are shown in Figures 4.4 and 4.5.

TABLE 4.4 Combined Revenues and Expenses of New York Stock Exchange Firms Doing a Public Business, 1981

(dollars in millions, unconsolidated)

Revenues

Commissions on:	
Listed equity transactions	$ 3,953
Listed options	610
All other	783
Total	$ 5,346
Gains (losses) on trading accounts from:	
Over-the-counter market making	$ 607
Debt securities	3,082
All other	553
Total	$ 4,242
Gains (losses) on investment accounts	575
Profits (losses) from underwriting and selling groups	1,572
Margin interest	2,890
Mutual fund sales	122
Account supervision	275
Research	16
Commodities	581
Other — securities unrelated	2,958
Other — securities unrelated	1,228
Gross revenues	$19,805

Expenses

Registered representative compensation	$ 3,339
Clerical and administrative	3,102
Salaries for partners, voting stockholder officers	664
Floor brokerage and clearance	726
Communications	1,085
Occupancy and equipment	663
Promotional costs	457
Interest expense	5,683
Error account and bad debt losses	154
Other expenses	1,778
Total expenses	$17,651
Net income before taxes	$ 2,154
Quarterly averages	
Number of firms profitable	289
Number of firms with losses	102

Source: *Securities Industry Yearbook* (New York: Securities Industry Association, 1981)

This announcement is neither an offer to sell nor a solicitation of an offer to buy any of these Securities. The offer is made only by the Prospectus.

350,000 Shares

Equico Lessors, Inc.

(a subsidiary of The Equitable Life Assurance Society of the United States)

$10.625 Cumulative Preferred Stock

(par value $100)

Price $100 a Share

and accrued dividends, if any

Copies of the Prospectus may be obtained in any State from only such of the undersigned as may legally offer these Securities in compliance with the securities laws of such State.

MORGAN STANLEY & CO.
Incorporated

A. G. BECKER PARIBAS Incorporated — THE FIRST BOSTON CORPORATION — GOLDMAN, SACHS & CO.
MERRILL LYNCH WHITE WELD CAPITAL MARKETS GROUP Merrill Lynch, Pierce, Fenner & Smith Incorporated — SALOMON BROTHERS INC
BEAR, STEARNS & CO. — BLYTH EASTMAN PAINE WEBBER Incorporated — DILLON, READ & CO. INC.
DONALDSON, LUFKIN & JENRETTE Securities Corporation — DREXEL BURNHAM LAMBERT Incorporated
E. F. HUTTON & COMPANY INC. — KIDDER, PEABODY & CO. Incorporated — LAZARD FRERES & CO.
PRUDENTIAL-BACHE Securities — L. F. ROTHSCHILD, UNTERBERG, TOWBIN
SHEARSON/AMERICAN EXPRESS INC. — SMITH BARNEY, HARRIS UPHAM & CO. Incorporated
WERTHEIM & CO., INC. — DEAN WITTER REYNOLDS INC.
ALEX. BROWN & SONS — A. G. EDWARDS & SONS, INC.
OPPENHEIMER & CO., INC. — THOMSON McKINNON SECURITIES INC.
ARNHOLD AND S. BLEICHROEDER, INC. — MOSELEY, HALLGARTEN, ESTABROOK & WEEDEN INC.
ROBINSON HUMPHREY/AMERICAN EXPRESS INC — TUCKER, ANTHONY & R. L. DAY, INC.
WHEAT, FIRST SECURITIES, INC.

May 25, 1983

Source: Courtesy of Morgan Stanley & Co. Incorporated

FIG. 4.4 An Underwriting Announcement ("Tombstone") for Preferred Stock

Selling Group

This group represents the firms that actually sell the issue to investors. In issues in which the demand is great, the selling group and the underwriting group are nearly identical, for the major underwriters prefer to sell their portion of the deal rather than give up the commission to rival firms. In other issues, the selling group may be quite different and much larger than the underwriting

3,000,000 Shares

≡✈Lockheed Corporation

Common Stock

Price $95 Per Share

Upon request, a copy of the Prospectus describing these securities and the business of the Company may be obtained within any State from any Underwriter who may legally distribute it within such State. The securities are offered only by means of the Prospectus, and this announcement is neither an offer to sell nor a solicitation of any offer to buy.

Goldman, Sachs & Co.

Bear, Stearns & Co.	The First Boston Corporation	Blyth Eastman Paine Webber	Dillon, Read & Co. Inc.	Donaldson, Lufkin & Jenrette
Drexel Burnham Lambert	E. F. Hutton & Company Inc.	Kidder, Peabody & Co.	Lazard Frères & Co.	Lehman Brothers Kuhn Loeb
Merrill Lynch White Weld Capital Markets Group	Prudential-Bache	L. F. Rothschild, Unterberg, Towbin	Salomon Brothers Inc
Shearson/American Express Inc.	Smith Barney, Harris Upham & Co.	Warburg Paribas Becker	Wertheim & Co., Inc.	Dean Witter Reynolds Inc.

ABD Securities Corporation   Advest, Inc.   Algemene Bank Nederland N.V.   Arnold and S. Bleichroeder, Inc.   Atlantic Capital Corporation

Robert W. Baird & Co.   Banque de Neuflize, Schlumberger, Mallet   Basle Securities Corporation   Bateman Eichler, Hill Richards

William Blair & Company   Blunt Ellis & Loewi   Boettcher & Company   J. C. Bradford & Co.   Alex. Brown & Sons   Cowen & Co.

Crédit Commercial de France   Dain Bosworth   Daiwa Securities America Inc.   F. Eberstadt & Co., Inc.   A. G. Edwards & Sons, Inc.

Eppler, Guerin & Turner, Inc.   EuroPartners Securities Corporation   First Southwest Company   Robert Fleming Incorporated

Hudson Securities, Inc.   Janney Montgomery Scott Inc.   Kleinwort, Benson   Ladenburg, Thalmann & Co. Inc.   McDonald & Company

Montgomery Securities   Morgan Grenfell & Co.   Moseley, Hallgarten, Estabrook & Weeden Inc.   The Nikko Securities Co. International, Inc.

Nomura Securities International, Inc.   The Ohio Company   Oppenheimer & Co., Inc.   Piper, Jaffray & Hopwood   Prescott, Ball & Turben, Inc.

Rauscher Pierce Refsnes, Inc.   Robinson Humphrey/American Express Inc   Rotan Mosle Inc.   Rothschild Inc.   Seidler Amdec Securities Inc.

Sutro & Co.   Tucker, Anthony & R. L. Day, Inc.   Underwood, Neuhaus & Co.   Wheat, First Securities, Inc.   Yamaichi International (America), Inc.

David Allsopp & Associates N.V.   Bacon, Whipple & Co., Inc.   Bank Julius Baer & Co. Ltd.   Sanford C. Bernstein & Co., Inc.

Berliner Handels- und Frankfurter Bank   Brean Murray, Foster Securities Inc.   Cazenove Inc.

Compagnie de Banque et d'Investissements   Crowell, Weedon & Co.   Fahnestock & Co.   Furman Selz Mager Dietz & Birney

Hambros Bank   J. J. B. Hilliard, W. L. Lyons, Inc.   Howard, Weil, Labouisse, Friedrichs   Interstate Securities Corporation

Investment Corporation of Virginia   Johnson, Lane, Space, Smith & Co., Inc.   Johnston, Lemon & Co.   Josephthal & Co.

Kredietbank S.A. Luxembourgeoise   Legg Mason Wood Walker   Moore & Schley Capital Corporation   Neuberger & Berman

Newhard, Cook & Co.   Parker/Hunter   Pictet International   Pierson, Heldring & Pierson N.V.

Rowe & Pitman, Inc.   Scherck, Stein & Franc, Inc.   Schneider, Bernet & Hickman, Inc.   Stifel, Nicolaus & Company

Vereins- und Westbank   Wood Gundy Incorporated   M. M. Warburg-Brinckmann, Wirtz & Co.

Birr, Wilson & Co., Inc.   The Chicago Corporation   Davis, Skaggs & Co., Inc.   R. G. Dickinson & Co.   First Albany Corporation

Gradison & Company   Gruntal & Co.   Herzfeld & Stern   Emmett A. Larkin & Company, Inc.   Cyrus J. Lawrence

Manley, Bennett, McDonald & Co.   A. E. Masten & Co.   Morgan, Keegan & Company, Inc.   Nippon Kangyo Kakumaru International, Inc.

Sanyo Securities America Inc.   Henry F. Swift & Co.   Wedbush, Noble, Cooke, Inc.

March 24, 1983

FIG. 4.5 An Equity "Tombstone" Announcement

group, often including certain retail firms that are not invited to take a major underwriting position.

Compensation in the Underwriting Syndicate

The basis for compensation in an underwriting syndicate is the "spread" in the price of the securities, representing the difference in the price paid to the issuer and the price at which securities are sold to the public. In equity offerings, this spread may range from as low as 2 percent to a maximum of 10 percent. In debt issues, the price spread typically ranges from a low of 0.875 percent to as high as 2 percent with typical spreads in the 1 to 1.5 percent range. If a managing underwriter deems that the normal spread or maximum allowable spread is inadequate to compensate them for the risk of the issue, additional compensation may be taken in the form of options (warrants) on the stock or, in some instances, in direct payment for planning the offering. Such extra payments to the underwriters, however, tend to be rare and to be associated only with highly speculative first public offerings.

The spread, in turn, is divided among the syndicate as follows: the managers (or comanagers) receive 15 to 20 percent; the underwriters receive 10 to 30 percent; and the selling firms receive 50 to 75 percent. Of course, if the managing firm sells all of the securities it has underwritten, that firm will retain the entire spread. In modern investment banking compensation, the major portion of the revenue goes to the managing underwriters and the sellers, with relatively less allocated to the underwriting function than was true many years ago. Of course, since the underwriters and sellers of the issue tend much more to the same firms, this is a less important consideration than it once was.

Underwriting Hierarchy and Reading a "Tombstone"

The announcements of new issues that appear in the financial press, usually after the issue has been sold, contain a great deal of information about the syndication process. These announcements are traditionally called tombstones due to the matter-of-fact format in which they are printed.

A tombstone contains the issuer's name, followed by the size of the issue (number of shares or dollar amount of bonds), followed by the price to the public. Next, the underwriting syndicate is printed, with the name of the manager or comanager appearing on the top line. Should there be more than one manager, the firm appearing on the left-hand side of the first line is usually the firm that is "running the books," meaning that they are keeping track of the selling effort and the underwriting commitment during the underwriting period.

The underwriting syndicate follows the manager's line, usually in alphabetical order. The syndicate is divided into groups representing major participants, submajor participants, second bracket participants, and regional firms. Each separate group in the tombstone is recognizable by a new alphabetical order. It is accepted practice in the syndicate system for each member firm in a given group to participate equally in the underwriting; that is, to accept underwriting responsibility for an equal number of shares to the other firms in that group. Furthermore, the major group typically will underwrite somewhat fewer shares than the managers, and the submajor group will underwrite still fewer shares. Thus, the underwriting income (and risk) for a firm in a given issue is directly correlated to its position in the tombstone announcement. Over long periods of time, reading tombstone announcements can provide an important indicator of the competitive importance and success of a given investment bank in the underwriting business. Observers of tombstone announcements follow the competitive fortunes of firms on Wall Street with great interest.

COMPETITION AMONG INVESTMENT BANKING FIRMS

In recent years there has been a large increase in the degree of competition among investment banking firms. This competition has been heightened by increased activity by commercial banks in areas formerly handled exclusively by investment banks. Of course, commercial banks are still precluded from the primary activities of underwriting and market making in private debt and equity securities. To understand the basis of the new competition, some review of traditional competition in investment banking is in order.

Traditional Competition

Prior to the last decade, the investment banking industry was organized primarily around the negotiated underwriting. In this system, corporations maintained a relationship with their investment banking firm that was similar in many ways to the relationship they had with their accounting firm or law firm. It was a relatively rare event for a corporate client to change investment bankers without good reason. Good reasons might include a change in the personnel handling the account or a major dispute about pricing an issue or its trading in the aftermarket. Occasionally, firms changed investment bankers in a dispute over the research coverage of the firm. By and large, however, an investment banking relationship was considered long term in nature.

Until the last decade or even more recently, the competitive organization of underwriters was typified by a certain degree of specialization in which several major firms, called origination firms, concentrated on originating deals that were then syndicated to large underwriting and selling groups. The originating firms tended to be major institutional firms with strong corporate finance staffs and a long history of relatively stable client relationships. The major distribution firms were often retail oriented firms or wire houses that maintained a large network of salesmen and selling offices.

A major shift in this relatively stable competitive environment occurred during the 1970s, when many of the strong distribution firms openly began to solicit underwriting business from major corporate issuers, with the result that a number of the historical investment banking relationships were the object of intense new competition from nontraditional underwriters. The origin of this new competition was a desire on the part of many of the traditional distribution firms to participate more importantly in the management fees and underwriting fees that accompanied new offerings.

In the early days of the new competition for clients, the major underwriting firms had significant power over the distribution firms because they had the ability to withhold securities (i.e., product) from the distribution firms if they were excessively aggressive in soliciting underwriting clients. Thus, a major distribution firm or wire house needed underwritings to supply its sales force with securities to sell. Furthermore, newly issued securities are particularly important to firms with large sales forces because the selling concessions on new issues are often two to three times larger than they are in transactions in the regular aftermarket. Thus, the complimentary relationship between originating firms and distribution firms had the effect of perpetuating a certain stability in the competitive nature of the industry. Supermajor and major underwriting firms were generally judged to be important competitors according to four basic criteria:[1]

1 *Clients.* The clientele list of a major investment bank was its strongest asset. Given the stability of client relationships, a good clientele list was an assurance of major status in the competitive hierarchy of investment banking firms. The firms that brought many deals to market were the ones invited to participate in other firms' underwritings in a major way.

2 *Capital.* The capital requirements of the NYSE assure that the firms that are to be "major" underwriters must have enough capital to be in compliance with the regulations during the period of an underwriting. Thus, inadequately capitalized firms were automatically precluded from major underwriting participation. As the size of issues has growth in recent years, the importance of the capital requirement has grown proportionately.

3 *Selling power.* Ultimately, underwritings must be sold. The distribution capability of a major underwriter can be in the form of in-house sales capability or the ability to put together a strong syndicate of distribution firms, usually wire houses. In the final analysis, the distribution capability of the major firms is really only tested in the marketplace.

4 *Strong syndicate department.* The effectiveness of syndicate managers within firms is a key variable in maintaining major investment bank position. Since syndicate managers are dealing with other firms on a regular basis, the reputation of these partners for effective and dependable performance is critical in maintaining the position of their firm as a major investment bank.

Increased Emphasis on Distribution

An erosion of many of the previously accepted norms for major status in the investment banking hierarchy of firms has taken place in recent years. The previous emphasis on traditional relationships in the investment banking clientele has been replaced to a significant extent by the ability to place the issue in the hands of investors. Thus, the major distribution firms have been able to demand a more significant role in underwriting, as well as in managing issues. The result is that syndicates have tended to diminish, with fewer firms taking joint responsibility for underwriting and selling new issues. The trend toward comanagerships has also been increased by the greater need for capital in the firms that are to play a major underwriting role.

COMPETITIVE BIDDING

In contrast with the system of negotiated underwriting previously noted, some issuers of securities are required by law to receive competitive bids for their underwritten securities. The competitive bidding practice has as its basis Rule U-50, adopted by the SEC in 1941. The rule requires that regulated public

---

[1] See "Investment Banking: Power Structure in Flux." *Harvard Business Review* (Mar.–Apr. 1971), pp. 136–152.

utilities receive competitive bids from investment bankers when their securities are issued. A similar rule exists for most state and local governments; the U.S. Treasury also follows a system of competitive bidding in the issuance of federal securities.

The premise of competitive bidding requirements is that capital costs can be reduced if more than one firm (or syndicate) is invited into the process of pricing new securities. As might be expected, the procedure is controversial. Many investment bankers maintain that a better price is possible if a single investment banker or syndicate is able to work with the issuer in designing the issue and preselling it into the market. Certainly, in competitive bidding, the amount of preselling possible is considerably reduced, since any single firm is unsure of winning the issue.

Empirical data on the effectiveness of competitive bidding in reducing capital costs are ambiguous in their results. A 1978 study by Parker and Cooperman showed that, while competitive bidding often reduces the size of the underwriting commission, the price received by the company is not significantly different in competitive bidding than it is with negotiated placements. On balance, there is little evidence that capital costs are reduced in competitive bidding; yet, the competitive bidding option may be responsible for keeping capital costs at a minimum.

Public utility firms and state and local governments can request exemptions from the competitive bidding process if they can convince regulatory authorities that a negotiated underwriting will be as advantageous as competitive bidding. The reasons for requesting an exemption may include: (1) an issue too small to attract the interest of multiple bidders; (2) an issue too large to attract more than a single syndicate; or (3) a chaotic market in which the risk of the underwriting is deemed great enough that the preselling is required. In certain extreme cases, where exemptions have not been granted in spite of the aforementioned justifications, bidding has been opened and no bids have been received. This, of course, forces the issuer into a negotiated underwriting.

Rule 415 — A Major Change in Underwriting

A potentially large increase in the extent of competition in the issuance of securities has taken effect with the inauguration of Rule 415 of the SEC, put into effect on a trial basis in February 1982. Under Rule 415, private firms may register securities in advance of their issuance in a process called shelf registration. Securities so registered may then be sold at any time in the coming year by a process closely resembling competitive bidding. Under the rule, the firm simply announces its intention of issuing all or part of the securities allowed under the shelf registration and receives offers from investment bankers for the securities. If the offers are acceptable to the firm, the issue is sold; if they are not, the issue can be delayed temporarily or indefinitely. The clear result of Rule 415 is that firms may have multiple relationships with investment banks and may use different banks in sequence over a short period of time.

Some observers have noted that if Rule 415 becomes a permanent fixture in the industry, it will truly revolutionize the process of issuing securities, with investment bankers becoming wholesalers in every sense of the word. Underwriters will simply "bid" for securities for resale. Traditional relationships will diminish and the "transactional" nature of the business will be vastly increased.

In a Rule 415 transaction, the speed with which announcements and sales are made makes it exceedingly difficult to form a traditional syndicate, or any syndicate at all. Thus, the purchasing firm may take the entire issue for its own account. At most, a limited number of comanagers will be invited into the transaction. Preselling is at a minimum and firms must be willing to position more securities into inventory.

Many traditional major investment banking firms have argued strongly that Rule 415 is not good for either issuers or the investment banking community. On the other hand, some of the large nontraditional underwriters have tended to support Rule 415 in that it gives access to major clients for a number of nontraditional underwriters. Currently, it is too early to know the complete effect that Rule 415 will have on the industry or whether it will be made permanent by the SEC. If it is to become permanent, it may be expected to have as profound an effect on the securities business as the end of negotiated commissions did at the beginning of the 1970s. To date, it is still an unfinished chapter in the evolution of competition.

CHOOSING AN UNDERWRITER

An issuing corporation's choice of an underwriter is a major decision in its financial strategy. Underwriters come in all sizes and styles. There are supermajor and major national firms; there are strong regional firms; and there are small specialty houses that establish a reputation for excellence in certain industries such as high technology, petroleum, transportation, or municipal finance. This reputation is based on an established clientele and a cultivated market for the securities of the industries in which they specialize. Such reputations do not come easily.

The choice among underwriting firms is often not a scientific one. Nonetheless, some guidelines may be important. The services of the firm include assisting the issuer in choosing the type of security to be offered. This includes the choice between debt, equity, or various other more complex securities such as convertible bonds, debt with warrants, or preferred stock. In some instances, the investment banker may even be consulted on the currency in which a security is to be denominated if access to international capital markets is possible.

Increasingly, issuing companies have become expert in designing their own securities issues; thus, the outside expertise of the investment banker in structuring the deal has become, for some companies, relatively less important than in the past. Thus, the advice of the corporate finance professionals in the investment bank may be less important than other factors in choosing an underwriter. Some of these other factors are as follows:

1 Relative importance of the client to the firm. Many corporations must make the imprecise judgment whether it is better to be a major client for a smaller firm or a

relatively less important client to a larger major firm. Smaller, often regional, firms tend to compete in tailor-made service for smaller, regional clients; larger firms (see Table 4.4) tend to concentrate their expertise in Fortune 1000 companies. However, many exceptions to these size groupings are evident.

2 In cases where the issue is to be marketed, regional firms have a particular advantage in marketing stocks that are of interest primarily to regional clientele. Alternatively, many regional issuers wish to sell their securities nationally, which leads them to a national underwriter. It should be noted, however, that many regional firms can support a national selling effort by inviting a national firm to comanage the issue. Some emerging companies find the combination of a regional and a national firm to be the best combination of strength for marketing their securities.

3 Aftermarket attention. The choice of an underwriter also frequently depends on the issuer's assessment of the strength of the underwriter in making an orderly market in the securities after issuance, especially assuming the firm is not listed on a major exchange. If the firm is listed, the underwriter can be expected to follow the securities (particularly equity) by writing appropriate research reports to keep interest in the stock high. Firms develop reputations in the extent to which they support their underwriting clients in the aftermarket. Ultimately, the choice of an underwriter depends on the service the client can expect before and after the issuance. In the competitive world of modern underwriting, clients can be, and frequently are, the object of great attention by more than one investment banker. After the decision is made to proceed with a given firm, however, the competitive activity subsides significantly and the cooperative relationship of a negotiated underwriting commences.

PRICING AN ISSUE

After the underwriter is chosen, pricing the issue is the major remaining factor in a successful deal. To understand the pricing process, it is important to recognize that there are two major constituencies to be represented on a new offering: sellers and buyers. The interests of these two parties are predictably somewhat different. Sellers, representing existing owners, are clearly interested in a high price for their securities; buyers want a low price.

In a debt or equity issue already traded in the market, the pricing problem is significantly reduced, since investment bankers are expected to price the security near the existing market, most often the previous day's closing price. Some deviation from the previous day's price may occur if that price is not considered representative of value due to an unusually small trading volume. Thus, occasionally securities are priced at a small premium or discount from the last close.

For securities that are being publicly offered for the first time, the pricing decision carried considerably more risk. In new issues there is no objective market standard for the correct price. Underwriters in this instance usually attempt to price the issue according to indications of interest, which are received by the syndicate manager from the syndicate members. These indications of interest are not firm, however, until the final pricing is done; thus, the element of risk is never completely eliminated.

To supplement indications of interest, the managing underwriter typically gathers data on similar companies in the industry to estimate intrinsic worth on a comparative basis. Factors included in the intrinsic worth calculation are earnings, growth rates in earnings, capital structure, dividend history, general company visibility and reputation in the industry, and the industry outlook. All of these enter into a final pricing decision on the offering date.

At the time of the pricing recommendation of the underwriter, the issuer has the option of accepting or declining the final price. Should the price not be accepted by the issuer, the offering cannot proceed and the issuer would simply lose the out-of-pocket expenses of preparing the issue. These expenses are not small and are comprised mostly of legal and accounting costs. The underwriter loses the cost of time in preparing the offering, as well as the opportunity cost of the revenue of a successful offering. Since underwriters and clients have a large investment in preparing for the issue, and since they tend to work together closely in the preoffering period, it is rare that they cannot agree on the final offering price at the announced issuance date.

A Successful Offering

In first public offerings of equity, the pricing decision is generally considered successful if the price of the stock rises to a small premium of between 5 and 10 percent in the aftermarket. Should the stock rise more than 15 percent in the immediate aftermarket, there is some small evidence that the security was underpriced, which may leave the issuer less than satisfied with the offering. Should it rise less than 5 percent, purchasers of the stock may be dissatisfied with its performance and may become early sellers, putting severe downward pressure on the price. A security that falls rapidly in the aftermarket is generally not considered good even for the issuer because the market for subsequent issues may be compromised by the poor price performance of the last issue.

Investment bankers must tread a delicate path of satisfying both the sellers and the buyers of the stock. It is the syndicate department that ultimately is responsible for maintaining this sensitive balance. The syndicate manager stands in the middle between the corporate finance department representing the issuer, and the sales department representing the buyer. It is not an easy task to balance the interests of these two constituencies; yet, an investment bank will thrive in the long run only to the extent that its reputation for good pricing decisions is intact. A firm with a reputation for underpricing will lose issuing clients. A firm with a reputation for overpricing will lose purchasers of their issues over time.

CAPITAL REQUIREMENTS

Few issues in investment banking have loomed as large in recent years as the tremendous need for capital to finance growth in the industry. During the last 30 years the partnership form of organization was typical of investment banking firms, with a resulting chronic shortage of capital to finance the activities of the firms. To a major extent, the past decade has brought a revolution in the

TABLE 4.5   Capital Positions of Investment Banks

| | 1981 | | 1980 | | 1981 | | | | | |
	Capital (000)	Rank	Capital (000)	Rank	Offices No.	Rank	Employees No.	Rank	Registered Representatives No.	Rank
All Firms										
Merrill Lynch & Co.	$1,263,907	1	$969,481	1	526	1	32,000	1	9,400	1
Salomon Brothers Inc.	719,100	2	330,700	4	10	88	2,338	18	626	13
The E.F. Hutton Group Inc.	534,492	3	448,038	3	318	5	11,300	3	4,532	2
Shearson/American Express Inc.	526,982	4	469,883	2	350	3	10,702	4	3,859	4
Goldman, Sachs & Co.	389,000	5	219,000	8	15	68	2,873	15	335	29
Bache Group Inc.	388,967	6	251,893	6	226	7	8,994	6	3,428	6
Dean Witter Reynolds Organization Inc.	305,600	7	274,067	5	348	4	11,700	2	4,500	3
Paine Webber Inc.	240,295	8	243,228	7	240	6	9,857	5	3,497	5
First Boston, Inc.	220,898	9	153,234	10	15	68	1,650	20	410	19
Morgan Stanley Inc.	204,000	10	135,000	12	8	—	2,108	19	294	33
Stephens Inc.	195,968	11	167,243	9	1	234	139	—	87	82
The Drexel Burnham Lambert Group, Inc.	173,327	12	134,251	13	46	18	4,077	9	779	12
Donaldson, Lufkin & Jenrette, Inc.	166,134	13	98,110	18	57	15	3,850	10	211	44
Lehman Brothers Kuhn Loeb Inc.	161,865	14	136,995	11	10	88	2,341	17	441	17
Bear, Stearns & Co.	142,500	15	112,000	16	12	78	2,800	16	800	11

Warburg Paribas Becker — A.G. Becker	16	142,052	14	119,089	17	62	3,000	14	140	63
Kidder, Peabody & Co.	17	128,467	15	112,390	64	12	4,376	8	1,150	10
A.G. Edwards & Sons, Inc.	18	123,571	17	99,902	202	8	3,193	13	1,566	8
Thomson McKinnon Inc.	19	109,401	21	79,403	135	9	3,685	11	1,675	7
Smith Barney, Harris Upham & Co.	20	107,131	19	94,676	92	10	4,553	7	1,500	9
Spear, Leeds & Kellogg & Subsidiaries	21	93,951	22	56,231	12	78	702	43	60	—
L.F. Rothschild, Unterberg, Towbin	22	88,357	20	79,688	9	—	1,544	21	451	15
Oppenheimer & Co.	23	67,429	24	50,626	6	—	1,525	22	371	26
Neuberger & Berman	24	66,216	23	55,700	1	—	330	72	40	—
Kemper Financial Services, Inc.	25	60,550	—	—	1	—	550	48	13	—
Alex. Brown & Sons	26	53,985	28	45,677	20	52	873	35	292	34
John Nuveen & Co.	27	53,755	26	46,100	14	71	343	69	135	65
Stern Brothers & Co.	28	52,935	25	47,880	4	—	79	—	26	—
Brown Brothers Harriman & Co.	29	51,182	27	46,098	12	78	886	34	140	63
Discount Corporation of New York	30	43,343	33	35,490	2	—	152	—	54	—
Wertheim & Co.	31	42,701	32	38,038	4	—	439	55	173	52
Prescott, Ball & Turben	32	41,504	—	—	34	27	936	30	307	31
The Ziegler Company	33	41,458	31	38,423	28	33	320	75	45	—
Moseley, Hallgarten, Estabrook & Weeden Inc.	34	40,800	29	42,900	36	26	1,290	23	350	27
McMahan, Bratman, Morgan & Co.	35	40,679	—	—	2	—	100	—	—	—
Cowen & Co.	36	39,037	34	35,302	14	71	803	37	340	28

Source: Securities *Industry Yearbook* (New York: Securities Industry Association, 1982)

financing of investment banking firms and a trend toward the corporate form of organization as a means of increasing the permanent capital available for growth.

To understand the need for capital in a modern investment bank, Table 4.5 shows the balance sheet of all NYSE firms for 1979 and 1980. Capital is needed primarily to finance customer receivables (credit extended for customer purchases) and trading account inventories. While some of the funds for these activities are available through bank borrowings and other liabilities, ultimately the ability of a firm to grow or to do major business in underwriting, block trading, and retail services depends on the amount of equity capital at its disposal. Firms that do not have that capital run out of borrowing capacity and are simply not able to compete as effectively.

The Partnership Form

The partnership form of organization in the industry dated back to the 1700s when there were few formal contracts between firms, and the full personal liability of partners was essential to the confidence of other firms in executing transactions. Until 1970, for example, the NYSE refused membership to firms that were not partnerships, the rationale being that liability without limit for traders on the floor was integral to the functioning of the Exchange. In 1970, however, the investment banking firm of Donaldson, Lufkin & Jenrette pioneered the concept of the public corporation as a form of organization for an investment bank. It issued $12 million of new equity and started a trend that has influenced the subsequent organization of many prominent firms.

The advantages of the corporate form in capital accumulation and retention are great. In partnerships, when the partners resign or retire, most wish to take their capital with them. Some partnerships have managed to overcome this problem by agreement that partners can withdraw their capital only over a period of years after leaving the firm. This agreement allows other partners to replenish the capital with their own funds. With the corporate form of organization, however, capital is permanent for the firm (excluding reductions from losses or dividends), and the firm may expand its capital when necessary by issuing new equity to the public. Furthermore, as owners wish to withdraw capital, they may do so by selling their shares in the public market, leaving the capital of the firm intact. The capital positions of the major national investment banks are shown in Table 4.5.

Mergers for Added Strength

An extension of the corporate form of organization in investment banking firms has been the sale of these firms to financial and nonfinancial holding companies. Most conspicuous among these sales or mergers has been the purchase of Dean Witter Reynolds by Sears Roebuck, and the purchase of Salomon Brothers by the Phibro Company. In the event of a slow-moving issue, distribution capability can be all-important in maintaining a firm's reputation as an effective underwriter. The impact of these mergers, and others of a similar nature, has yet to be completely felt, but it is generally agreed that the capital strength of these new firms gives them some important competitive advantages in coping with the large capital requirements of a modern trading and underwriting function.

SUMMARY

The investment banking industry in the United States is critical to the viability of our financial system. Since the passage of the Banking Act of 1933 (Glass-Steagall Act of 1933), commercial banking and investment banking have operated as separate industries. This is in contrast with the system of "universal banking," where commercial banks perform most investment banking activities, including underwriting, market making, and securities brokerage.

In the 1980s, commercial banks began to compete directly with investment banks in virtually all services except underwriting and trading in private securities. Unless the Glass-Steagall Act is repealed, however, investment banking will continue to be a freestanding industry in the United States and will be at the heart of the formation of new capital for industry. Furthermore, it is at the center of the viability of an active secondary market for securities. It is the secondary market for securities that ultimately makes a primary market possible, because it is only when the secondary market functions well that investors are interested in participating in primary capital formation activities.

As in the past, investment banking competition is keen, although the form of competition undergoes continual change. Competition in the 1980s has tended to focus on maintenance of adequate capital, ability to handle transactions effectively, strong selling ability, and specialized expertise to generate fee income.

Should the Glass-Steagall Act be modified in the 1980s, investment banks can be expected to enter the commercial banking business (i.e., deposit taking) and commercial banks will predictably enter the traditional investment banking arenas of underwriting and dealing in securities. The implications of modifying our financial system, should Congress decide to do so, will be wide-ranging for both the suppliers and users of investment banking services.

SUGGESTED READING

Birmingham, S. *Our Crowd*. New York: Harper & Row, 1969.

Block, E. *Pricing a Corporate Bond Issue: A Look Behind the Scenes*. New York: Federal Reserve Bank of New York, 1964.

Brooks, John. *Once in Golconda*. New York: Harper & Row, 1969.

Caroso, Vincent P. *Investment Banking in America: A History*. Cambridge, Mass.: Harvard University Press, 1970.

Friend, Irwin, et al. *Investment Banking and the New Issues Market*. New York: World Publishing Co., 1967.

Hayes, Samuel L. III. "Investment Banking, Power Structure in Flux." *Harvard Business Review,* Mar.–Apr. 1971, pp. 136–152.

———. "The Transformation of Investment Banking." *Harvard Business Review,* Jan.–Feb. 1979, pp. 153–170.

———, et al. *Competition in Investment Banking.* Cambridge, Mass.: Harvard University Press, 1983.

Logue, D., and J. Lindvall. "The Behavior of Investment Bankers: An Econometric Investigation." *Journal of Finance,* Vol. 29, Mar. 1974, pp. 203–215.

Parker, George G.C., and Daniel Cooperman. "Competitive Bidding in the Underwriting of Public Utility Securities." *Journal of Financial and Quantitative Analysis,* Dec. 1978, pp. 885–902.

Securities Industry Association Handbook. New York: Securities Industry Association, 1982.

Van Horne, Jas. C. *Financial Management and Policy,* 5th ed. Englewood Cliffs, N.J.: Prentice-Hall, 1980, Chapter 20.

Wechsberg, Joseph. *The Merchant Bankers.* Boston: Little Brown, 1966.

5

The Money Markets and Money Market Instruments

ALAN G. JIRKOVSKY

DEFINITION OF THE MONEY MARKET

The money market represents one part of the overall U.S. and international capital markets, which also include the stock and the bond markets. It is distinct from the bond market in that its focus is on short-term financial instruments, typically with original maturities of less than one year. The money market has a primary and a secondary component. The primary market provides a mechanism for quickly raising short-term financing to meet seasonal or more permanent cash needs. The secondary market is characterized by a high degree of liquidity; participants can readily buy and sell these short-term financial assets as their cash needs or positions change.

Actually, the money market itself is a collection of markets involving activity in each of the various money market instruments. These instruments include short-term obligations of the federal government and federal agencies, commercial banks' certificates of deposit (CDs), federal funds, bankers' acceptances (BAs), repurchase agreements (RPs), and commercial paper. The price or rate of these instruments is determined by supply in the market, credit conditions, and the overall state of the economy.

The money market has no centralized location. It is a system of telephone communications that link all parts of the country and many foreign financial centers. Although there are many participants, activity is centralized among commercial banks with active trading desks; 35 primary government security dealers that include some banks; commercial paper dealers; BA dealers; money market brokers; and the New York Federal Reserve. The Federal Reserve (Fed) makes use of the money market to implement monetary policy.

Participants in the Money Market

Money market securities characteristically are associated with a relatively high degree of safety, presenting minimum risk of default and capital loss, although events in various financial markets may alter this view from time to time. The customers issuing securities are characterized by their high credit standing, and thus have the highest probability of paying their obligation. The short-term aspect of the market allows for minimum time exposure on the part of the lender and less price volatility due to rate fluctuations. The standing of the customer and the short maturity are the chief factors that contribute to the high degree of liquidity in the market.

Borrowers in the money market are made up of the U.S. Treasury, government agencies, commercial banks, security dealers, large finance companies, and well-known nonfinancial companies. While all borrowers exhibit a high degree of credit quality, price differentiation does exist. This differentiation is influenced by the market's relative perception of each borrower, the supply of a particular customer's debt instruments already in the market, and how a customer approaches the market. Because of its credit rating, the U.S. Treasury provides the base (or lowest) rates in the market on which other rates are quoted. The Treasury makes use of the money market because the ready demand for its securities provides an easy selling program. Banks use the money market for funding through CD and BA issuance and for managing cash positions through Fed funds borrowings. Financial and nonfinancial companies will fund working capital needs through the issuance of commercial paper.

Suppliers of funds in the market include commercial banks, state and local governments, large nonfinancial companies, nonbank financial institutions, foreign banks, and individuals participating either directly or, for the most part, through money market mutual funds. The Federal Reserve acts as both a supplier and borrower of funds in its implementation of monetary policy. Banks will use the market to invest short-term excess funds, knowing that securities

securities is reaffirmed. The manager then instructs the traders on the desk accordingly.

Traders start a process called the go-around. The signal is flashed to the primary dealers that a buy or sell is about to happen, and traders ask cash dealers for their bid or offer prices on the securities. After comparing the various bids or offers, the Fed selects the best set of prices and calls back those dealers selected to complete the deal. The Fed tends to enter the market at a consistent time, usually 11:40 A.M. to 11:50 A.M. Eastern time.

In adding reserves, the open market desk will either buy securities or do RPs. The Fed will do RPs for its own account, which are system RPs, or for customers, known as customer RPs. RPs are agreements to buy securities on the condition that they are bought back sometime in the future. These instruments are discussed in detail later in the chapter. The Fed's distinction between buying securities or doing repos is according to whether it is seeking to increase reserves permanently or attempting to offset some uncontrollable fluctuation caused by float, the U.S. Treasury, or some other operating factor. Thus, when the cry is heard from trading desks across the country, "Fed's doing system RPs," the traders know that the Fed is temporarily increasing reserves. While system RPs have a direct impact on reserves, customer RPs may or may not, depending on the flow of funds.

To decrease reserves, or drain, the Fed will sell securities or do reverse RPs, simply called reverses. Selling securities drains reserves out of the banking system in order to make payment. Again, the distinction between sales and reverses is the degree of permanence sought. "Matched sales" signifies that the desk is doing reverses to temporarily drain reserves. When the desk enters the market, it does so in size. Typical Treasury bill transactions may range from $1 billion to $1.25 billion. Bonds may go from $800 to $1 billion, and the RP activity may be in the $1 billion to $4 billion range. These numbers represent a single day's activity.

Fed Watching

In the money market, the name of the game is interest rate forecasting and expectations. Participants in the market do what they do because of some feel for the direction of short-term interest rates. For example, banks will structure their liability books on the basis of their outlook, shortening maturities if a drop is expected, or lengthening in view of an upturn in rates. Security dealers and portfolio managers will position securities or sell short, depending on their expectations.

The outlook for interest rates is influenced by the level of economic activity, inflation, Federal Reserve policy, and credit demands. However, the market also forms its expectations for interest rates from the growth of the money supply. If high growth is seen, the market looks for a possible tightening by the Fed, which leads potentially to higher short-term rates. From another perspective, high money growth triggers expectations for higher levels of inflation, which in turn drive up rates, including long rates. Although a trend of continuing high money growth signals a possible inflationary uptick, short-term fluctuations do not translate into long-term inflation. Therefore, it is important for the market to distinguish trends from short-term occurrences. In fact, recent discussions on the part of the Fed and market participants have centered on reducing emphasis on weekly M1 changes. Suggestions have been made that only monthly changes to the aggregates should be released.

A change in the Fed funds rate affects all short-term rates almost directly. Why this happens will be explained later. The point now is that what the Fed does to affect the Fed funds rate has an impact on all participants in the market. Therefore, it is in almost everyone's interest to try to determine the Federal Reserve's plan of action in order to guess the direction of rates. What the Fed is doing or is going to do is arrived at through a sophisticated (or at least strangely complex) surveillance activity known simply as Fed watching. Fed watching is the sifting through of any information and the scanning of any market activity that is felt to signal the Fed's intentions for the money supply and the Fed funds rate. It has often been said that the secret to success in Fed watching is to watch what the Fed watches. That sounds easy, except that the Fed doesn't always concentrate on the same thing, and it usually doesn't tell, until much later, what that is.

Nevertheless, the Fed watchers do follow a systematic procedure. Each month the Fed releases the minutes of the previous month's FOMC meetings. These can provide a wealth of information. However, they tell what the FOMC was thinking then, not now. As a start, the minutes do provide information on money supply targets and the funds rate. Watchers then will track actual money supply growth against the targets. If actual M1 or M2 has been exceeding the stated targets, a Federal Reserve tightening might be expected. Of course, the Fed also could have shifted its targets, but that would not be known until the next month.

This is when the watchers pretend that they are the FOMC and review economic trends and capital markets, trying to anticipate whether target changes will occur. If the guess is that the targets will be raised, then a present increase in the aggregates may not signal a tightening. Watching the money supply figures is tricky, because in the short term the Fed is looking at two aggregates, M1 and M2, and they often do not react in the same ways. Also, the Fed must determine whether any off-target growth is the result of temporary technical factors or is part of a trend. Consequently, the Fed sometimes lags in its reaction to money supply changes.

This has described the longer view of Fed activity. Because of today's degree of interest rate volatility, profits can be made, or losses can be incurred, from day to day or even from hour to hour. Thus, Fed watching tends also to have a very short-term focus, shorter than the monthly growth patterns.

In short-term watching, the market focuses on any minute clue that could signify a policy shift, and reacts accordingly. Every move the open market desk makes is second-guessed for its meaning. If the desk does reverses, is this a technical adjustment, or is the Fed unveiling a new round of tightening? Some watchers even attach significance to the fact that the desk sometimes enters the market five minutes late or early. Any statements that Federal Reserve officials may make to the public are also closely monitored, because they might provide that important tip.

Because the stakes are high, banks, dealers, and others invest much in terms of personnel and other resources in Fed watching, although how successful these efforts are remains questionable. Experienced Fed watchers learn not to rely solely on forecasts of what the Fed may do. The market often perceives motives behind the Fed's actions that the FOMC may never have intended. There may be many practical operational reasons why the Fed was late doing its RPs, or an official might have voiced his own opinion rather than the consensus policy of the FOMC. The subtleties of such uncertainties and the fine tuning they call for keep the markets active and interesting.

INSTRUMENTS IN THE MONEY MARKET

Treasury Bills

Treasury bills are short-term debt obligations of the U.S. Treasury and make up the largest dollar volume of any instrument in the money markets. They represent the highest form of liquidity of all instruments in the money market because of their lack of credit risk, variety of maturities, and the constant supply of new instruments in the market. Treasury bills have played an ever-increasing role in the government's debt-management program since their inception in 1929. Prior to the mid-1940s, the amount of bills outstanding at any given time was usually less than $2.5 billion. Current outstanding volume is about $325 billion. Recent growth in Treasury bill volume is illustrated in Figure 5.1.

Treasury bills are sold on a discount basis, the difference between the price paid and par, reflecting the interest earned over the period to maturity. Various maturities have been used over time, but now bills are issued in 91-day, 182-day, and 364-day, maturities. These correspond to what are commonly called three-month, six-month, and year, bills. Prior to 1970, bills were issued in minimum denominations of $1,000. The minimum denomination today is $10,000 par value.

Treasury Bill Auction. Every week the Treasury offers new three-month and six-month bills through its regular auction. On Tuesday of each week the amount of the Treasury offering is set. At this time, when issued (WI) trading is allowed. That is, bills can be bought and sold between dealers before the actual auction occurs. Settlement in these transactions takes place after the auction. The auction itself is held on Monday, with delivery and payment taking place on Thursday.

Bids appear in two forms: competitive and noncompetitive. Noncompetitive bids, made by individuals and other small investors, specify the dollar amount of bills to be purchased, with a price determined by the average of all competitive bids accepted. Noncompetitive bids, which are awarded up to $1 million, assure that a buyer will not miss an opportunity by bidding too low, nor pay too much by bidding on the high side.

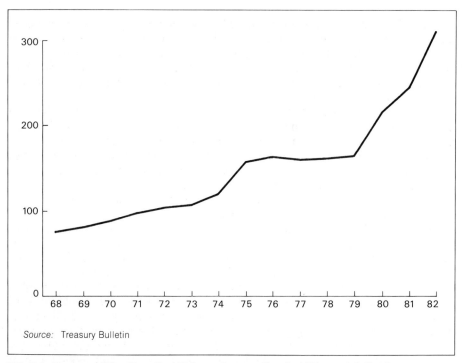

FIG. 5.1 Treasury Bills: Year-End Volume Outstanding (in billions of dollars)

Competitive bids are placed by large investors and dealers. A competitive bid specifies both an amount and a price that the investor is willing to pay. Each subscriber in the auction may enter multiple competitive bids specifying quantities he is willing to buy at different prices.

Bids are submitted to the various Federal Reserve banks until the bidding is closed at 1:30 P.M. New York time each Monday. At that time all bids are tabulated and submitted to the Treasury for allocation. The Treasury first sets aside an amount sufficient to fill all noncompetitive bids. The competitive bids then are allocated, starting with the highest bid and moving down the list until the remaining bills have been sold. The term "stop-out price" refers to the last bid, or the lowest price at which securities are awarded. Those who have bid below the stop-out price receive no bills. The noncompetitive bids are charged the average price derived from the total of the competitive bids awarded. Noncompetitive bids usually are less than 15 percent of the total auction, although occasionally they rise above this level.

The volume of bills issued each week is quite large. The typical three-month bill auction is currently in the $6 billion range, with the weekly six-month bill issue about the same in size. In addition, every fourth Thursday the Treasury sells year bills. The average issue size recently has been in excess of $7 billion.

An an example of the size of the Treasury's auction, look at the week of April 25, 1983. On that day the Treasury auctioned $6.2 billion in three-month bills and $6.2 billion in six-month bills. The average discount rates for the three- and six-month bills were 8.15 and 8.22 percent respectively. For the three-month bill, tenders totaled $15.8 billion out of the $6.2 billion actually issued. Noncompetitive bids totaled $941 million, or 15.2 percent of the total awarded. The six-month bill received $15.1 billion in bids and $835 million of noncompetitive bids, or 13.4 percent.

As can be seen from these tender numbers, the market demonstrates the ability to absorb large volumes of Treasury securities. Therefore, the Treasury has great flexibility in its debt management program through varying the volume of bills issued. The auction process also keeps the Treasury from having to second-guess the market on rates. The rates are determined by the auction, and the Treasury merely picks the volume it will issue.

Because of their liquidity and minimum credit risk, Treasury bills appeal to a wide range of money market investors. The minimum denomination of $10,000 and the fairly easy procedures the Fed has set up for noncompetitive bids make bills an attractive investment for individuals. However, two developments have cut into individuals' demands. The first was the change in the Federal Reserve's Regulation Q that allowed financial institutions to issue six-month money market certificates with rates tied to six-month Treasury bills. Many individuals found it more convenient to make deposits at their banks rather than purchase bills through the auction. Recent changes to Regulation Q have eliminated rate ceilings on all time deposits with maturities over 31 days. The second development has been the growth in money market mutual accounts. These accounts allow individuals to invest in pools of money market securities and receive professional management of their funds for nominal fees. Both these activities have given individual investors the ability to invest small amounts at competitive market rates in something other than Treasury bills.

Another group of investors is made up of commercial banks. Banks will hold bills in their own portfolios as investments during periods of slack loan demand, primarily for liquidity management purposes. Banks also will buy bills for their trading accounts for the purpose of generating trading profits when resold. Another class of investors is foreign investors. Their holdings increased rapidly as many of the oil-exporting countries found Treasury bills to be a good investment. Also, the Fed is a major holder through its FOMC operations. Other investors include state and local governments, which use the bill market to invest tax receipts and proceeds from bond issues before they are needed. Another big participant has been added to the market through the rapid growth of money market mutual funds.

Treasury Bill Yield Calculations. Treasury bills are a discount instrument, as opposed to an interest-bearing or coupon security. This means that the security is purchased at a discount from its par value, which is paid at maturity. The difference between par and the discount value is the interest earned. Another distinguishing feature of Treasury bills is that the discount value and rate are calculated as if there were 360 days in a year. Thus, bills are calculated on an ''actual over 360'' basis, meaning the actual number of days against a 360-day year. These conventions and those used for other instruments make direct comparisons of quoted yields among various instruments misleading unless all yields are recomputed on a common ground.

EXHIBIT 5.1   Computing Yield

EXAMPLE 1

Compute the amount of discount on a 91-day $1 million bill sold at an 8.00 percent discount rate.

Step 1.   Compute Discount

$$\text{Amount of discount} = \$1,000,000 \times 8.00\% \times \frac{91 \text{ days}}{360 \text{ days}} = \$20,222.22$$

Step 2.   Compute Price

$$\text{Price} = \text{Par} - \text{Discount} = \$1,000,000 - 20,222.22 = \$979,777.78$$

If the price were given, the discount rate could be calculated using this formula:

$$\text{Discount rate} = \frac{360}{91} \times \frac{\$1,000,000 - \$979,777.78}{\$1,000,000} = 8.00\%$$

The discount rate differs from the true yield, however. In this example, the investor is putting up $979,777.78 for 91 days and will receive $20,222.22 in interest. Therefore, the true yield is the amount of interest divided by the principal invested, adjusted for the number of days. Because this is an actual yield calculation, 365 days in a year are used rather than 360 days. If a leap year is involved, 366 days will be used.

Step 3.   Compute Yield

$$\text{Yield} = \frac{\text{Discount (or interest)}}{\text{Price}} \times \frac{365}{\text{Number of days}}$$

$$= \frac{\$20,222.22}{\$979,777.78} \times \frac{365}{91} = 8.28\%$$

Note that the actual yield is higher than the discount rate, which was 8.00 percent in this example. An alternative way of stating the previous formula, using the discount rate rather than the discount price, is:

$$\text{Yield} = \frac{365 \times \text{Discount rate}}{360 - (\text{Discount rate} \times \text{number of days})}$$

EXAMPLE 2

An 8.00 percent Treasury note of $1 million would pay $80,000 in interest over the year in two equal installments of $40,000 after six months and $40,000 again after one year. The first payment is assumed to be reinvested at 8.00 percent [1] for the remaining half of the year, and the total interest received would be:

$$\$40,000 + (\$40,000 \times 8.00\% \times \tfrac{1}{2} \text{ year}) + \$40,000 = \$81,600$$

The second term represents the extra interest from investing the first coupon payment, a result of compounding of interest.

On a simple interest basis, the yield would be:

$$\frac{\$81,600}{\$1,000,000} = 8.16\%$$

However, the bond equivalent yield, which assumes semiannual compounding with interest reinvested at the same rate as the yield, would be 8.00 percent.

Take a $1 million year bill at 8.00 percent and go through the steps from computing the discount to the bond equivalent yield. Remember, a year bill is 52 weeks or 364 days.

$$\text{Discount} = \$1,000,000 \times 8.00\% \times \frac{364}{360}$$

$$= \$80,888.89$$

$$\text{Price} = \$1,000,000 - \$80,888.89 = \$919,111.11$$

$$\text{Simple interest yield} = \frac{\$80,888.89}{\$919,111.11} \times \frac{365}{364} = 8.82\%$$

Now, the formula for the bond equivalent yield for a bill with one year to maturity can be expressed as:

$$\text{Yield} = 200 \times \frac{\text{Par}}{\text{Price}} - 1$$

$$= 200 \times \frac{\$1,000,000}{919,111.11} - 1$$

$$= 8.62\%$$

These formulas are good for computing yield for Treasury bills with maturities of less than six months. They are also good for bills with maturities over six months if the yield comparison is to be made on a simple interest basis. Simple interest merely takes the amount of interest earned divided by the principal on an annualized basis. Compounding of interest is not considered. In other words, if an investor lent $1 million for a year and received $80,000 in interest, the simple interest yield would be 8.00 percent.

Yields can be computed in various ways, each having a different meaning to those investing funds. The key is to place investment alternatives on a comparable basis. In the money market, discount securities and coupon securi-

---

[1] In bond equivalent yield calculations, the coupon payments are assumed to be reinvested at a rate equal to the bond equivalent yield. The bond equivalent yield is solved for as an internal rate of return problem.

ties are made comparable by calculating their equivalent bond yield, which is based on an assumption of semiannual coupon payments with compounding of interest. To clarify this point, look at Treasury notes, a coupon instrument with maturity of one year or longer (see Example 2 of Exhibit 5.1).

As can be seen from Exhibit 5.1, the coupon instrument sells at a yield of 8.00 percent and has a bond equivalent yield of 8.00 percent, while the year bill sells at an 8.00 percent discount rate and has a bond equivalent yield of 8.62 percent.

For Treasury bills with maturities of over six months and less than one year, the calculation of bond equivalent yield is quite complex. It involves computing a partial period compounding of interest. Therefore, bond equivalent yields for various instruments are usually provided on bond dealers' quote sheets. These quote sheets provide amounts outstanding, bid and asked prices, and maturity and coupon information, along with an equivalent yield and other data for the various securities that a dealer is trading. Computer programs and calculators also have been developed to compute these yields.

Trading of Treasury Bills. The Treasury markets typically open around 9:00 A.M. Eastern time each day and close around 3:30 P.M. Eastern time. At the opening the market is very active, as the direction of the market, up or down, is being determined. At Federal Reserve time the market quits, and the pace often picks up just before the market closes.

Treasury bills usually trade at very narrow spreads between the bid (buy) price and the asked (sell) price. The newer the bill, the narrower the spreads. For example, a new three-month bill may have a bid–ask spread of 2 to 4 basis points. One basis point on a 90-day bill of $1 million is worth $25.[2] As the bills age, the spread becomes wider. The spread on a bill that is four weeks old may be as high as 10 basis points. The volume of trading in Treasury bills is very large. A normal day may run around $5 billion.

Federal Agency Securities

One of the fastest-growing components in the credit markets over recent years has been the debt of federal agencies. The role of the federal agencies is that of financial intermediaries with the purpose of administering selected lending programs of the U.S. Government. Over time Congress has targeted specific economic sectors for credit assistance, most notably agriculture and housing. Federal agencies were formed to provide this assistance by developing consistent flows of economic funding to those sectors. Agencies perform their function by issuing debt in both the money markets and the capital markets and then channeling the proceeds to lending institutions through direct loans or the purchase of loans originated by the institutions.

---

[2] The value of a basis point, 0.01 percent for a Treasury bill, is worth 27.7777 cents per day remaining per million dollars.

$(0.01 = 360 \text{ days}) \times \$1,000,000 = \$0.277777$

$\$0.277777 \times 0.90 \text{ days} = \$25.00$

There are basically two major categories of federal agencies: federally sponsored agencies and government-owned agencies; that is, government-owned agencies that have the full financial backing of the U.S. Government. Many of these agencies provide credit to small businesses, students, and communities financing development projects, among others. These agencies typically raise funds through the Federal Financing Bank, a centralized financing authority supervised by the Treasury. Federally sponsored agencies are not really agencies of the government, but are privately owned by the financial institutions and borrowers they support and have only limited backing by the government. In some cases this support is in the form of an ability to borrow from the Treasury or, by authorization of the Treasury, to buy securities. These agencies originally were started with government capital but have since paid back these funds, becoming private. There are five federally sponsored agencies that are exclusively involved in lending to the housing and agriculture sectors. Three of the agencies are the Federal Land Banks (FLBs), the Federal Intermediate Credit Banks (FICBs), and the Banks for Cooperatives (BFCs), which together make up the Farm Credit System (FCS). The other two are the Federal Home Loan Banks (FHLBs) and the Federal National Mortgage Association (FNMA), or Fannie Mae, which support the housing market.

The FCS agencies are the oldest of the federally sponsored agencies. The FCS is made up of a nationwide family of banks and local associations completely owned by those farmers and their cooperatives that use them. There are twelve FLBs, which make long-term loans to farmers and rural residents for purchasing farm land, homes, equipment, livestock, and for construction and repair. The FICBs make short-term and intermediate-term loans to farmers. The twelve FICBs are entirely owned by the local Production Credit Associations, which in turn are owned by their farmer-members. The twelve district BFCs provide credit to cooperatives owned by farmers. The credit may be for working capital or to finance buildings and equipment. In addition, there exists the Central Bank for Cooperatives, owned by the district banks, which participates with the district banks in financing larger loans.

The FHLBs through their 12 regional districts, provide funds to member institutions, which include all federally chartered savings and loan associations (S&Ls), and other mortgage lending institutions, such as state-chartered S&Ls and mutual savings banks. The FHLBs provide liquidity to its members when cyclical loan growth and disintermediation have caused demand for funds. Longer funds also are provided in order to stimulate the housing industry on a continuing basis. The FNMA's responsibility is to provide assistance to the secondary market when money is tight and funds are difficult to get in the market. This is accomplished by purchasing Federal Housing Administration loans, Veterans Administration loans, and conventional loans from banks, S&Ls, and mortgage bankers.

Growth of Agency Debt. As noted earlier, the debt from federal agencies has grown extremely fast. In 1965, securities outstanding from the federally sponsored agencies totaled $13.8 billion. By 1970, that amount had grown to $38.9 billion and then to $78.8 billion in 1975. At the end of 1982, the combined debt of these agencies stood at $241.4 billion. Figure 5.2 provides a recent history of the growth in the volume of federal agency debt outstanding.

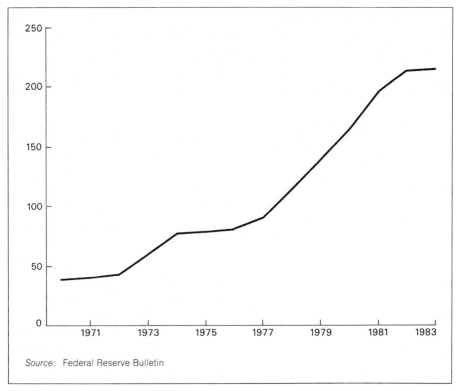

Source: Federal Reserve Bulletin

FIG. 5.2   Federally Sponsored Agencies: Combined Debt Outstanding (in billions of dollars)

Federally sponsored agencies issue two types of short-term debt. One is coupon securities similar to Treasury notes, and the other is discount securities similar to Treasury bills. Bonds are sold on a periodic basis, while discount notes are sold on a continuous basis, with a range of maturities being offered. While bonds are sold through a selling group that is assembled by the agency's fiscal agent, discount notes typically are sold through a small group of dealers associated with the agency.

The FLBs, the FICBs, and the BFCs sell their debt jointly through Farm Credit "consolidated systemwide" bonds and notes. Each month the system offers six- and nine-month bonds with minimum denominations of $5,000. The issuing takes place in book-entry form only, meaning that an actual paper certificate is not provided to the issuer. Instead, a computer record is kept at the Fed in the account of the purchasing institution. The institution itself keeps the records of individual investors for whom it holds the securities. Discount notes are issued by the system on a daily basis, with maturities ranging from 5 to 270 days. These securities come in certificate form only.

The FHLBs sell bonds with maturities over one year and short-term discount notes. These discount notes also are sold daily at maturities of 30 to 270 days. The minimum denomination has been set high at $100,000 to deter small savers from withdrawing deposits from the agencies' members in order to buy securities.

FNMA also sells discount securities in the 30- to 270-day range. The minimum denomination is $5,000. However, a minimum purchase of $50,000 is required, also to help prevent disintermediation.

Federal agencies use the same price and maturity conventions as Treasury securities. Therefore, the discount price, discount rate, and bond equivalent yield calculations are found using the same formulas as for Treasury securities.

Primary and Secondary Markets. The agencies follow a similar method for marketing their coupon certificates. Each agency has a fiscal agent located in New York who assembles a selling group whenever an issue is to come to market. These selling groups are nationwide and are made up of security dealers, dealer banks, and brokerage houses. These participants in turn distribute securities to individual investors. Because securities are issued under an act of Congress, they are exempt from Securities and Exchange Commission (SEC) registration. Discount notes are offered continuously through a small number of dealers.

Most issues follow a typical procedure. The first step is for the fiscal agent to announce to the selling group the size of a particular issue. The selling group, as many as 140 dealers in the case of the FHLBs, is polled for the level of interest in the issue. Dealers bid for the securities with no rate specified, or provide subject bids that specify a minimum rate at which they will take the issue. Dealers are then allocated specific shares of the total to be sold. The next step is to determine pricing, with the objective being to sell close to or at par. The fiscal agent may receive input on pricing from the Treasury and a large group of its dealers. Members of the selling group receive a fee for the distribution.

The selling group usually also maintains an active secondary market. The growth in the secondary market has paralleled the growth in agency securities (agencies) outstanding. This market is more developed than that for any private asset. The volume of secondary market transactions in short-term agencies typically exceeds that of short-term government coupon issues (Treasury bills excluded). Dealer transactions in agencies due within one year averaged $1.1 billion daily in 1980, compared with $400 million daily for U.S. government coupons with one year or less remaining.

Most dealers are in the market every day trading agencies, although not to the same extent as Treasury securities when bills are included. The bid-asked spreads in agencies are wider than in governments, and liquidity is less than in governments. One factor that has increased the attractiveness of agencies has been the development of RPs in these securities. Agencies are now part of the Federal Reserve repurchase operation. Also, the Fed purchases agencies for direct investment as part of its open market operations. These factors have increased the willingness of dealers to position larger amounts of agencies and, in turn, have improved the market.

Advantages of Agency Securities for Investors. Agency securities provide investors with certain benefits that may not be found in other money market securities. First, the risk perception compares favorably to that of the Treasury. Some agencies are backed up by a limited authority to borrow from the Treasury. There is a spread over governments, so the yield is higher for roughly the same perceived level of risk. Agencies, except for FNMAs, are exempt from state and local taxes. The liquidity, although less than governments because of the smaller size, is greater than for most other money market instruments. Also, there are some specific advantages for banks. Agencies are eligible collateral for borrowing at the Fed and qualify for collateral for Treasury tax and loan accounts. They also are public securities that can be held without limit by national banks.

Federal Funds

Federal funds are short-term loans made between financial institutions in immediately available funds. Fed funds can be considered the most liquid of money market instruments for two reasons: the great majority of the transactions have a maturity of one day; and, because of the mechanism by which these funds flow through the Fed, they are, in most cases, instantaneously transferred from seller to buyer. Because the reserves that banks are required to hold against their deposits pay no interest, there is a great incentive to keep these balances at a minimum. The Fed funds market provides this opportunity. Also, Fed funds can provide an economical funding source to large banks, as these funds often are cheaper than other alternatives for bank financing. Not all participants in the money market can buy or sell Fed funds. Federal Reserve regulations restricts access to the market to certain financial institutions.

History of Fed Funds. In the early 1920s, some banks that had to borrow periodically from the Fed to meet their reserve requirements began to realize that there were other banks that often had surplus reserves that were not invested. With the dawn of this awareness, banks began to trade Fed funds with each other. In the 1930s and 1940s, trading in Fed funds became stagnant as most banks experienced excess reserves. During World War II, banks used the large supply of Treasury bills as a trading vehicle to settle reserve positions. As banks discovered that trading bills was not the easiest way to exchange reserves, Fed funds transactions picked up again.

Today the Fed funds market provides an attractive investment alternative to retail banks that may have short-term surplus funds. Virtually all banks have access to the market. Because of its size, a small bank may not be able to place its surplus funds with a money center bank, but it might be able to place as little as $50,000 overnight with a regional bank at a rate just slightly off the market. The regional bank, in turn, might be able to place much larger amounts with a money center bank. In fact, large banks have realized the value of cultivating a network of correspondents and other banks that are willing to sell them funds on a daily basis. The money center banks, therefore, will provide their network banks with competitive market prices for even small amounts and also will back the small banks with offers to sell them funds when necessary. Most trades are done directly among banks, but the market has been enhanced also by the development of Fed funds brokers. These brokers will put together the vast array of participants, respecting the anonymity of whoever stands behind the various bids and offers until a deal is closed. This function is especially helpful when a bank is attempting to do a large job without disclosing its intention to the entire market. Brokers typically deal in large amounts, handling few transactions under $5 million.

Before the early 1960s, banks were using Fed funds strictly for reserve settlements. Banks can normally borrow from the Fed for settlement purposes through the use of the Federal Reserve's discount window. During the period, Fed funds would sell below the discount rate, because if a bank was willing to pay more than the Fed funds rate, it was signaling to the market that it could not borrow from the Fed, a sign of trouble. The Fed funds rate was held down by the level of the discount rate. As a result, many smaller banks began borrowing Fed funds from their larger correspondents and investing the proceeds in Treasury bills at a positive spread. The large banks often ended up paying more on the margin for funds to support these sales. It was necessary for some bank to break the implied ceiling on the discount rate. In late 1964, Morgan led the way by being the first to bid over the discount rate for Fed funds. This started a new era, as funds began trading at rates reflecting true supply and demand. Today many large banks rely on Fed funds as a major component of their overall funding mix and not merely as a means of adjusting reserve balances.

Transactions in the Market. Fed funds are immediately available funds because of how the transaction takes place. One case involves correspondents or customers who maintain demand deposits with their bank to support various services. When the correspondent wants to sell funds to the bank, it calls with instructions to move funds from its demand deposit account. The next day the bank moves the funds back, with interest, into the correspondent's account. Although the borrowing bank has to pay interest on the Fed funds, it does not incur any reserves as it does for demand deposits. A second case involves banks selling to each other through their reserve accounts at the Fed. When a transaction is completed, the banks instruct the Fed to move funds from the sellers' reserve account to the buyers' reserve account. The next day the Fed is instructed to reverse the transaction, including any payment of interest. When different Federal Reserve districts are involved, the transaction takes place through the Fed wire.

Activity in the Fed funds market usually varies by the day of the week. All banks are required to settle their reserve position at the Fed on Wednesdays. Since reserve requirements are based on a daily average balance over a one-week period, shortfalls that might have existed throughout the week have to be made up by Wednesday. However, a bank that finds itself with excess reserves on Wednesday will forego profit opportunities for carrying uninvested funds, since the Fed pays no interest. Therefore, a wild scramble might take place as all the banks attempt to adjust their reserve accounts at the same time. If reserves are tight in the market due to the FOMC's activity, it is not unheard of to see the Fed funds rate jump 10 percent or more above the normal trading range. If reserves are large, the rate may drop to as low as 1 to 2 percent, still a better deal than the Fed's zero percent.

Besides overnight Fed funds, a limited amount of term Fed funds is sold. These funds may go anywhere from two days to over one month, priced at a fixed rate. Small banks buying funds may have to provide collateral in the form of government securities. These are known as secured Fed funds transactions.

The rate quoted on Fed funds is an add-on rate, using a 360-day basis. Therefore, the interest on a $50-million overnight transaction quoted at 8½ percent is:

$$\$50,000,000 \times 0.085 \times \frac{1}{360} = \$11,805.56$$

If the deal is done through a broker, an additional cost of about $0.50 per $1 million per day is paid by both the buyer and the seller. This transaction thus would cost each participant $25.

If the above rate is to be calculated on an annual-equivalent basis, it is necessary to adjust for actual days. On a simple interest basis, the 8½ percent quoted rate would be:

$$8.50\% \times \frac{365}{360} = 8.62\%$$

It should be noted that the simple interest calculation provides an annualized rate for one day. It does not take into account compounding of interest, which is daily on overnight Fed funds. The aggregate volume of Fed funds traded daily is impossible to determine, because funds may be bought and sold several times during a day. However, the Federal Reserve's bulletin reports the volume of Fed funds and RPs recently in excess of $60 billion for commercial banks with assets of over $1 billion as of December 31,1977.

Any institution with an excess reserve position at the Fed makes up the lending side of the market. This would include commercial banks, federal agencies, S&Ls, mutual savings banks, agencies and branches of foreign banks, and government security dealers.

Repurchase Agreements

Repurchase agreements at first appear to be a fairly complex type of money market instrument. RPs represent a means of borrowing money by selling securities to the lender and simultaneously entering into an agreement to repurchase those same securities at a later date. In effect, the transaction is a secured form of lending in which the securities that are sold are the collateral for the loan. In most cases the term of the RP is overnight, but it may be several days, weeks, or longer. A continuous-contract RP is a series of overnight loans that are automatically renewed each day unless terminated by either party.

The RP market provides short-term investment opportunities to corporations, state and local governments, and other nonbank investors who can't sell directly into the Fed funds market and find that other investments have maturities too long for their needs. The secured nature adds an extra dimension of attractiveness to investors. Banks find the RP market to be a useful source of short-term funding and an economical one, since the rate tends to trade below Fed funds. Banks have large volumes of securities in their investment portfolios and their trading accounts, both of which provide the collateral. The rate on RPs is one of the lowest in the money markets. Additionally, there are no reserve requirements for banks on RP funds, as long as the securities used are either U.S. government or federal agencies. Besides banks, government security dealers use the RP market for extensive funding of their security positions and for arbitrage gains through RPs and reverse RPs.

One of the factors that has helped develop the RP market into one of the largest and most active sectors of the money market has been the increased sophistication of cash management techniques. Years ago when rates were not as high or as volatile as in recent times, firms would pay little attention to excess balances in their demand deposit accounts. Opportunity costs were not that big a consideration. However, as rates rose, so did the incentive to seek higher yields. The secured nature of RPs and the settlement in immediately available funds effectively make an interest-bearing demand deposit available to businesses.

The terminology contributes to the confusion about RPs among the uninitiated. One cannot talk about RPs without discussing reverses. A reverse RP is the same transaction, but seen from the viewpoint of the lender of funds. The lender provides funds while receiving a security. This is known as reversing in. The lender then will resell the security at maturity and receive back his funds. Banks and security dealers will often reverse in a security, thus lending funds. Subsequently, they may repurchase that very same security to borrow funds. Of course, when the original reverse matures and the security must be returned to the customer, the bank must purchase a like security in the market to be returned. Reversing in and repurchasing out the same security is done because large banks and dealers can usually achieve a positive, although small, spread with this transaction. When the maturities of the RP and the reverse are the same, this is called a matched book. However, dealers will often mismatch the maturities of the RPs and reverses to increase their spread.

Interest on RPs is negotiated at the time of the transaction, and the rate is usually influenced by the current Fed funds rate. The rate is not at all determined by the securities bought or sold. They serve solely as collateral for the loan. Overnight RPs usually are slightly less than the overnight Fed funds rate, approximately 25 basis points, with the lower rate due to the collateral.

The rate on RPs is an add-on rate using a 360-day basis, similar to Fed funds. Therefore, the amount of interest is:

$$\text{Interest} = \text{Principal amount} \times \text{Repo rate} \times \frac{\text{Days}}{360}$$

The simple effective interest rate is computed the same as on Fed funds, multiplying the quoted rate by 365/360.

A lender of funds wants the collateral to serve its intended purpose. He therefore wants the value of the securities he purchases to be at least equal to the funds he provides. Therefore, RPs are priced using the market value of the security, not the par value. The normal practice in the market used to be to price "flat"; that is, any interest on coupon securities that accrued over the term of the RP was ignored. In term RPs, considerable risk is involved with this practice. A borrower who repurchases out a security expects to obtain the full value of that security at the time of repurchase, including any interest accrued over the period. While the borrower has received funds reflecting the value of the security, he has received nothing representative of this interest. If the lender should go bankrupt or fail to return the securities, the borrower may lose this accrued interest. The convention now is to price with accrued interest, adjusting the value at both the initiation of the transaction and at maturity.

The failure of Drysdale Government Securities in May of 1982 has caused much turmoil in the RP market that still remains to be settled. Pricing with accrued interest is new since Drysdale. At issue and in litigation is the distinction of who owns what, and what is collateral in an RP transaction.

Another risk in a term RP is that as rates change, the market value of the securities will change. A lender who entered a transaction 100 percent collateralized may find himself something less than that at some point in the future if the market should drop. Therefore, most term RPs are done with the lender of funds (i.e., the party reversing in securities) reserving the right to reprice the value of the collateral, adjusting for any drop in security prices. Repricing can be done anytime during the agreement; however, there are usually no set time periods. Often, repricing is a formal part of the RP. This reduces some of the risk to the lender.

As part of its FOMC activities, the Fed plays an active role in the RP market. Permanent changes to the reserve position are accomplished through outright purchases of securities. However, any temporary adjustments are carried out through RPs, if adding reserves, or reverses, if draining.

Negotiable Commercial Certificates of Deposit

Negotiable CDs are one of the principal sources of bank funding. They also represent a major liquid asset with attractive yields for investors. Negotiable CDs are fairly new instruments, having originated in 1961.

A negotiable CD is an instrument that represents a large time deposit liability of a bank. The certificate specifies the dollar amount of the deposit, the rate of interest to be paid (usually fixed), and the final maturity of the deposit. The minimum size of a negotiable CD is $100,000, although normally they are issued in pieces of $1 million or larger to facilitate trading in the secondary market. The minimum legal maturity for CDs is 14 days. More typical maturities are in the one- to three-month range and six months. Some issuance takes place at one year and beyond, but there is very sporadic activity at these maturities.

History and Regulation of Negotiable CDs. The early CDs were in the form of time deposits. Time deposits, however, provided no liquidity to investors. They were not negotiable, and ownership of the deposit could not be sold or transferred. As corporations and individuals became more sophisticated in their cash management techniques, the instruments in the money market became more attractive than regular bank time deposits or demand deposits, which paid no interest. Banks were growing and many were finding that their need for funds could not be met through their traditional funding sources, such as demand and consumer time deposits. In February 1961, First National City Bank (Citibank) began offering negotiable CDs as a response to the need for funds. At the same time, Discount Corporation of New York announced that it would make a secondary market for the negotiable CDs of money center banks. Soon other banks began issuing their CDs.

Regulation on CDs has changed considerably over the years in response to the money market. When first developed, CDs were subject to the Federal Reserve's Regulation Q which governs the maximum interest rate that can be paid on various deposits. Although the Regulation Q rate ceiling was increased from time to time, the change to a new level usually lagged prevailing rate increases on other money market instruments. Therefore, banks often were forced out of the CD market because they couldn't pay investors competitive rates. In 1969, the rate ceiling so constrained banks that they massively shifted to the Euromarkets to generate deposits. In 1973, the Fed dropped Regulation Q on CDs of $100,000 and larger, making them directly comparable to all other money market instruments. Another regulation affecting CDs has been Regulation D, which specifies what amount of reserves have to be held against these deposits. The effect of this regulation has been an effective cost to the banks that is higher than the quoted rate. Over time Regulation D has changed, with the amount of reserves on CDs decreasing. The latest change occurred in October 1980, when a phase-in lower reserve requirement was implemented. This phase-in will result in a 3 percent reserve requirement on CDs by February 1984.

The Primary Market. Most banks attempt to place their new CD issues directly with investors rather than selling through CD dealers. One immediate advantage to a bank is that it thereby avoids the dealer's commission, making the CDs a little cheaper. More fundamental is the objective of having more control over where the CDs are ending up. Banks would prefer to place CDs only with investors who would hold their securities until final maturity. Large issuers of CDs tend to be in the primary market on a continuous basis and do not wish to see their efforts unduly influenced by secondary trading in their name. If a dealer took a large position in a bank's CDs with the idea of selling as soon as a profit could be made, the price of a bank's primary issue could be severely hampered if the bank was "writing into the market," or issuing its paper, at the same time that the dealer was selling. Too much supply of a bank's CDs drives the rate up, costing the bank more. That is not to say that dealers cannot provide a benefit to the banks. If a dealer is offering a competitive rate or an issuer has a big job to do, CDs will be placed directly to the dealer. There is some irony in that banks heavily use a funding instrument that was designed to provide liquidity but would prefer that no one trade this instrument.

One of the benefits to banks' funding is that CDs offer some flexibility in the maturities in which they can be issued. Banks may seek different maturities for liquidity reasons, interest rate risk reasons, or simply price. Of course, the market has something to say about how much can be issued for what time frames. Banks indicate their desires for various maturities by their posted rates. An aggressive three-month rate says a bank is actively seeking that pricing tenor, while a weak six-month rate shows no interest in that maturity. Rates are set by communicating with other banks and dealers over the phone to determine what is trading in the market. Each participant quotes his "CD run," or the list of rates across the maturity scale at which he is prepared to do business. Loyal customers, who may regularly be large buyers of a bank's CDs, may be given a preferential rate different from the run. This is considered to be part of grooming stable and regular sources of funds. Also, size is an issue: A bank may be willing to pay a little more for $25 million than for $100,000.

Negotiable CDs are settled in immediately available funds. Interest is paid at maturity for issues up to one year and on a semiannual basis, like a coupon, for longer-term securities. Rates are quoted on an interest-bearing basis, not a discount basis. The calculation of interest is based on actual days to maturity with a 360-day year. To contrast an interest-bearing instrument with interest due at maturity with a discount instrument, look at a Treasury bill and a CD, both quoted at 8.00 percent with a 91-day maturity, for $1 million.

$$\text{Yield on } 8.00\% \text{ T-bill} = \frac{365 \times 8.00\%}{360 - (8.00\% \times 91)} = 8.28\%$$

$$\text{Yield on } 8.00\% \text{ CD} = 8.00\% \times \frac{365}{360} = 8.11\%$$

This yield calculation applies to any fixed-rate CD with a maturity of one year or less. Interest on the 91-day CD is computed by the following:

$$\$1,000,000 \times 8.00\% \times \frac{91}{360} = \$20,222.22$$

Because the instrument is not discounted, interest is computed on the entire par value.

The all-in cost, or total cost, of a CD to a bank also includes the cost of reserves and FDIC insurance.[3] Reserves mean that the entire proceeds of the CD is not available for funding purposes. Effectively, a higher cost to the bank is created for the remaining funds that can be used. If a bank issued a $1 million CD at 8.50 percent, and the reserve rate is 3.00 percent,[4] the amount of funds available would be:

$$\$1,000,000 \times (1 - 0.0300) = \$970,000$$

If the term of the CD were 90 days, the amount of interest paid would be $21,250, 8.50 percent on the total $1 million. The rate paid on the available funds is:

$$\frac{\$21,250}{\$970,000} \times \frac{360}{90} = 8.76\%$$

An easier way to state the effective rate is:

$$\frac{\text{Nominal rate}}{1 - \text{Reserve rate}} = \frac{8.50}{1 - 0.0300} = 8.76\%$$

---

[3] Banks who are insured by the FDIC are required to pay a fee equal to $\frac{1}{12}$ percent of their deposits on an annualized basis.

[4] The phase-in of charges to Fed Regulation D governing requirements will make the reserve percentage a flat 3 percent, regardless of maturity on all CDs. This change is scheduled to be completed by Spring 1984.

BA, the bank guarantees payment to the seller by accepting a time draft drawn on it by the buyer. The buyer is obligated to make payment to the bank.

In a typical transaction, after a bank agrees to provide its guarantee, a letter of credit is issued on behalf of the buyer. The letter of credit authorizes the buyer to draw a draft on the bank for an indicated amount. The draft specifies the time from presentation at which the funds are payable. The letter of credit also specifies terms the seller must meet before the bank will accept the draft. These terms may include documentation proving that the goods have been shipped. After the goods are shipped, the seller forwards any required documents, along with the time draft, to the buyer's bank. At this time the bank indicates its guarantee to pay the draft by stamping it "Accepted," which is accompanied by the signature of a bank officer.

At this point the acceptance, guaranteed by the bank, belongs to the seller. If the seller wants cash immediately, he will sell or discount the acceptance with the accepting bank. The value is determined by the going discount rate in the market for acceptances. The bank now could keep the acceptance or rediscount it into the money market. If it is rediscounted, the final investor will present the acceptance to the bank at maturity and collect the face amount. Figure 5.4 illustrates the transaction.

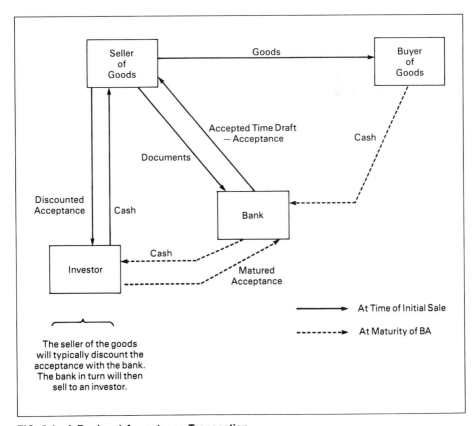

FIG. 5.4 A Bankers' Acceptance Transaction

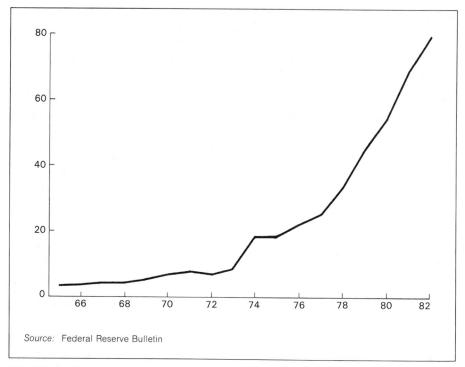

Source: Federal Reserve Bulletin

FIG. 5.5 Bankers' Acceptances: Volume Outstanding (in billions of dollars)

History. The passage of the Federal Reserve Act in 1913 gave national banks permission to accept time drafts. Before that, major acceptance activity had been taking place in Europe in sterling-denominated acceptances. The Fed, as part of its monetary policy in the early years, offered to buy BAs at quoted rates at any time. This did much to foster the development of the market. The market continued to grow until the Depression resulted in a decline in international trade, which led to a decline in acceptances. After World War II, the market began to grow again as international trade picked up.

Federal Reserve banks were authorized to buy and sell acceptances for their own accounts in 1955. This gradually promoted the market even more, and banks tended to stimulate the growth in acceptances for various reasons. In 1969–1970, with the high level of rates and Regulation Q ceilings preventing them from issuing CDs at competitive levels, banks turned toward acceptances as a form of lending and raising funds. Growth became rapid in the 1970s; in 1977, the Fed decided not to purchase acceptances outright for its own account through open market operations. It did, however, decide to continue to do RPs in acceptances and to buy for the accounts the Fed manages on behalf of foreign central banks. Figure 5.5 shows the growth in acceptances outstanding since 1965.

Bankers' acceptances have several advantages for banks. By rediscounting the acceptance in the market, banks can finance their customers' credit needs without tying up any of their own funds. Thus, acceptances are a good financing alternative when credit is tight. BAs that meet certain Federal Reserve criteria for eligibility do not incur reserve requirements when rediscounted. Finally, acceptances can be very profitable to banks. A commission is paid to the bank, often one percent per annum or higher, upon creation of the acceptance. A bank also has an opportunity to make a spread between what it initially discounts the acceptance at and what it can rediscount it at at a later time. The process itself is no more difficult than issuing CDs.

The borrower also has advantages. Bankers' acceptances fall under a separate limit from the legal lending limit, allowing for additional extensions of credit if necessary. Often, the cost of the acceptance, including the commission, may be less than the all-in cost of a traditional credit transaction. For small- and intermediate-sized firms, it is often cheaper than issuing commercial paper, which may not even be possible for some. However, the fixed commission causes borrowing costs to be much higher, should the acceptance be prepaid.

Investors have a high degree of liquidity and safety in acceptances. Yields on 90-day acceptances are closely in line with rates on 90-day CDs. The instrument is a liability of the accepting bank and also an obligation of the drawer of the draft. An active dealer market exists, providing good liquidity to the investor. Investors include state and local governments, savings institutions, foreign central banks, insurance companies, investment funds, banks, and individuals.

The Market. Yields on BAs as with Treasury bills are quoted on a discount basis. Most BAs have three-month maturities, although they also exist in a variety of other maturities up to six months for eligible acceptances. Banks attempt to create acceptances in sizes that will facilitate secondary trading. Thus, a large deal may be broken up into several smaller BAs, or a series of small deals may be packaged. Typical trading sizes are usually in multiples of $500,000. Anything less than $500,000 is considered an odd lot. A round lot today in the dealer market is $5 million.

There is a wide diversity of credit quality in the market. Dealers will quote a series of banks on the run. However, investors' perceptions of the various issuers influence what dealers will hold. Because of the range of credit quality and the variety of maturities that BAs are created at, dealers do not hold short positions. Instead, they hold fairly large inventories. The secondary market in BAs is much like the secondary market in CDs.

Commercial Paper

This is a short-term, unsecured promissory note. Payment of the paper is backed by the issuing firm's financial health, liquidity, and earnings power. Issuers of commercial paper include both financial and nonfinancial firms, usually large corporations that tend to have the highest credit ratings. Commercial paper is sold on a discount basis, with rates quoted as a discount rate. It also may be sold on an interest-bearing basis similar to a CD.

Commercial paper dates back to the early nineteenth century, when it evolved from bills of exchange. Firms began raising funds for working capital by selling open market paper as an alternative to sometimes scarce bank loans.

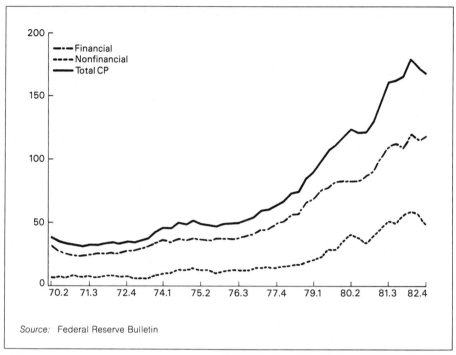

FIG. 5.6 **Commercial Paper: Volume Outstanding (in billions of dollars)**

In contrast to the situation today, the early issuers usually were the inferior credit risks. Increasing consumer demand for short-term credit in the 1920s led to the rapid growth of consumer finance companies, followed by rapid growth in the commercial paper market as these firms turned toward the market for financing. From the 1930s through World War II, however, the market steadily declined in size.

After the war, as the financing of consumer durables picked up again, the paper market grew, bolstered also by the commercial banks' response to Federal Reserve regulation. In 1966, when market rates went above Regulation Q rate ceilings, banks could not obtain sufficient funds to meet their customers' loan demand. Therefore, banks introduced their customers to the commercial paper market and, at the same time, sold them the required back-up lines of credit. This allowed them to support their customers and earn fees off the lines without committing any funds. In 1969, when rates hit the Regulation Q ceiling again, banks formed holding companies. These holding companies were used in turn to issue commercial paper, again not subject to rate ceilings, the proceeds of which were used to buy up some of the loan portfolios from their subsidiary banks. The market continues to grow, as more customers continue to find paper an economical alternative to short-term bank loans. Today's volume is about $170 billion, as shown in Figure 5.6.

Commercial paper is a very flexible funding instrument. For public issue, it requires no registration with the SEC, provided that it meets certain requirements; for example, the original maturity may be no longer than 270 days, and the proceeds must be used to finance current transactions. Typical size is $100,000 or larger, although smaller denomination paper is sometimes issued. Most paper issued today falls in the 20- to 45-day maturity range.

Issuers of commercial paper include finance companies on a continuous basis, nonfinancial companies issuing for short-term or seasonal needs, and bank holding companies that finance their nonbank-related activities with paper. To successfully issue paper, an issuer must have a backup line of credit with a bank, and a credit rating. Even with the very short maturities, because of the large volumes any one firm might have out in the market, there can be a substantial risk that a firm cannot pay at maturity nor roll over its paper. For that reason, firms maintain lines of credit from banks equal to roughly 100 percent of their outstandings. These lines act as insurance and cost the issuer a fee.

Also, most commercial paper is rated by at least one of three rating agencies: Moody's Investor Service, Standard & Poor's Corporation, and Fitch Investor Service. Their ratings are based on a firm's financial strength and are an indicator of its ability to meet its obligation. These ratings strongly influence the rate paid in the market. There has been considerably greater concern over credit quality since 1970, when the Penn Central went under, defaulting on $82 million in paper. Immediately after the default, many companies found it difficult to roll over their own paper and were forced to rely on their backup lines and other means of raising funds. Firms pay a fee to the agencies to get rated.

Another cost, along with interest, fees for lines, and rating agency fees, is the operational cost of issuing. Of the almost 1,000 firms that issue paper, a relative handful (fewer than 80), issue directly into the market. All the others issue through dealers. The standard dealer commission for issuing paper is ⅛ percent. Direct issuers, such as the large finance companies, are in the market every day. Some may be issuing several hundred million dollars at a time and have total outstandings in the billions. They can justify their own sales forces. Smaller and less frequent issuers go through dealers, paying the ⅛ percent commission. For $100 million in paper outstanding, this cost amounts to $125,000 annually.

Rates on commercial paper tend to track at a spread above Treasury bills of comparable maturity. The spread widens when money is tight. One reason for the spread is the credit risk associated with paper. The other relates to the fact that there is virtually no secondary market in paper, at least nothing close to Treasury bills.

The lack of a secondary market of any magnitude may be due to a combination of factors, foremost of which is that the paper market is even more heterogeneous than the CD market. There is a wide range of issuers with various credit ratings and a variety of maturities. Paper of different issuers, even with the same quality rating, is not readily substitutable. Another reason is that many investors tend to hold to maturity, perhaps because the maturities tend to be very short.

Dealers who sell paper, and direct issuers, will redeem paper before maturity, usually at ⅛ percent over the market, but this is expensive and therefore seldom done. One dealer estimates its redemption rate at less than 2 percent.

THE EURODOLLAR MARKET

Definition and History

The term "Eurodollars" refers to dollars on deposit in a bank or branch of a bank located outside the United States. Although the majority of Eurodollar deposits are held in Europe, the term refers to dollar deposits in other locations as well, such as Singapore, Tokyo, and Hong Kong. When a deposit is moved from a U.S. bank to a foreign bank, a Eurodollar deposit is created. Eurodollars, regardless of where they are deposited, never really leave the United States. The ownership of those dollars is what is transferred. Refer to Chapter 37 for a detailed discussion of the mechanics of creating a Eurodollar deposit.

The Euromarkets developed as substitutes to their domestic counterparts, providing certain advantages. The term "Euromarkets," more precisely, means external markets that operate outside of the traditional financial markets. Thus, the Eurodollar market is not a part of the domestic U.S. dollar market, although it is closely linked through international transactions. The term "Euro," used instead of "external," reflects the geography of its origins rather than the scope of its function.

In foreign lending and borrowing involving the traditional domestic markets, all transactions are subject directly to the rules and institutional arrangements of the respective markets. These jurisdictions are circumvented by locating the market for credit in a particular currency outside the country of that currency. Differences in rates and terms in the Euromarkets exist because of the inapplicability of various regulatory constraints in the domestic markets.

For example, no reserve requirements are incurred on Eurodollar deposits. Also, there are no interest rate restrictions on Eurodollar deposits as there are on domestic CDs under Regulation Q. This absence of regulations and other hindrances enables the Eurodollar market to operate more efficiently, economically, and competitively.

The origins of the Eurodollar market date back to the 1950s, when eastern European governments decided to transfer their dollar deposits from the United States to Europe to avoid possible attachment of the accounts by U.S. claimants and also to help establish lines of credit in Europe. Other events continued to contribute to the further growth of the market, such as Regulation Q rate ceilings on domestic CDs in the 1960s and the recycling of OPEC dollars during the oil crisis of the 1970s.

The main issuers of Eurodollar deposits are foreign branches of U.S. banks, although other foreign banks are major issuers, including British, Canadian, Swiss, German, French, and Japanese banks. Investors or depositors are large corporations, central banks and other government bodies, supranational institutions such as the Bank for International Settlements, and wealthy individuals. The locations of Eurodollar activity are centered primarily in London and New York. Singapore and Hong Kong also have developed into Eurodollar centers, but to a much less degree due to a lack of natural supply of dollar activity. To avoid taxes, many exotic booking centers have developed in such places as Bahrain, Nassau, and the Cayman Islands.

Eurodollar Time Deposits

Investors in the Eurodollar market have the choice between two major instruments: Eurodollar time deposits and Eurodollar CDs. The Eurodollar time deposit (TD) makes up the bulk of the deposits. Time deposits are for fixed periods; once deposited they remain with the bank until maturity. They are also nonnegotiable. An initial investor cannot sell his TD to another investor. In rare cases, a bank and its customer may agree to "break" a deposit.

The maturities of TDs can range from one day to several years, with the majority of transactions taking place in the seven-day to six-month range. Rates are negotiated between the bank and the depositor and are based on market conditions and the bank's need for funds. Rates on deposits in the Eurodollar market are higher than in the domestic market. The higher rates can be justified because of the higher competitive framework and the lack of statutory regulation in the Euromarket, such as reserves requirements.

The Interbank Market. The majority of Eurodollar TD activity takes place in the interbank market. The interbank market is made up of Eurobanks from all over the world that are actively lending and borrowing money back and forth with other participants. Banks that do not have a deep access to funds from third-party depositors are willing to pay slightly more to obtain funds from other banks in the interbank market. A bank that has just received a Eurodollar deposit will have a use for those funds. If funding a loan is not required, that bank will place the funds with another bank. It makes a placement, an asset on its books, which is a deposit with another bank. That deposit may be lent to a third party or placed again in another bank. Several levels of interbank placements often may be made before funds deposited in the market find their way to an ultimate borrower. In determining how much one bank may be willing to deposit in another bank, each bank draws up lines or limits with other banks that are felt to be creditworthy. This process is intended to limit risk. Lines are often reciprocal between banks. Therefore, if a bank wishes to receive deposits from another bank, it must be prepared to place funds with that bank from time to time. Banks sometimes will be active in placement activity only to foster relationships in order to develop a form of insurance should they need funds in the future. The normal bid/asked spread in the interbank markets is about ⅛ percent. Thus, running a matched book in placements and deposits is usually not done strictly for return. Banks, in fact, will often mismatch the maturities of their placements and deposits to achieve a higher spread over their deposits.

What banks pay for funds in the interbank market is a function of tiering. Tiering refers to the classification of banks according to their creditworthiness. The top tier banks, the four or five top U.S. banks, pay the best rates, and others are scaled off from this. The credit differentiation varies from time to time and becomes more pronounced in those periods when the financial community perceives potential banking problems.

Eurodollar CDs. These are much like domestic dollar CDs, except that they are issued offshore in Eurodollars by the foreign branch of a U.S. bank or by a foreign bank. Eurodollar CDs are dollar-denominated negotiable instruments which evidence a deposit in a Eurobank for a specific rate and a specific period. The first Eurodollar CD was issued by Citibank in 1966. Today virtually all Eurobanks issue Eurodollar CDs. The market is primarily in London, and so the term "London dollar CDs" is often used.

Eurodollar CDs are issued in denominations ranging from as low as $10,000 up to several million. The most common denominations are $1 million and $5 million. Maturities can range from overnight to five years, with the majority of activity concentrated in the short maturities, such as three and six months. Euro CDs are quoted on an interest-bearing basis with a 360-day year, like domestic CDs. Interest is paid at maturity, or usually on an annual basis if the term is greater than one year.

Euro CD rates run higher than domestic CD rates, and are a little lower than interbank rates, usually about ⅛ percent less for comparable maturities, primarily because CDs have liquidity. An active secondary market exists where spreads on bid and offer rates are about ¼ percent. The secondary market is not as well defined as the domestic CD market.

The major issuers of Euro CDs are the top 10 U.S. banks, British banks, Canadian bank branches, Japanese branches, and branches of regional U.S. banks. Tiering in price takes place along the same lines as Euro TDs, with the top banks paying the best rates. Some CDs are sold in several portions to appeal to smaller investors. These are known as tranche CDs and are offered for sale in a fashion analogous to a security issue.

Risk. The higher rates in the Eurodollar market are explained in part by the perceived higher level of risk, as compared with the domestic markets. Since there should be no credit risk differential between a U.S. bank and its London branch, the difference in perceived risk is one of geographic jurisdiction.

As shown before, any Eurodollar transaction must clear through a bank in the United States, regardless of where the deposit or loan originates. Therefore, at least two governments are involved, the United States and the government of the nation where the branch is located. The risk is that either government could intervene in the payment of funds. A depositor outside the United States runs the risk that the United States might restrict the disposition and transfer of foreign-held funds, known as nonresident convertibility. This is a remote possibility. The second risk is that the government of the country in which the Eurobank operates may seize the assets. This is country risk, or sovereign risk, and varies by country. These risks contribute to the rate differential between the domestic and Euromarkets.

INTEREST RATE BEHAVIOR AND RELATIONSHIPS

As would be expected, movements in interest rates for the various money market instruments are very highly correlated. This is due in part to the high degree of substitutability among instruments. Banks, for example, are able to use a variety of instruments at different maturities to meet their funding needs.

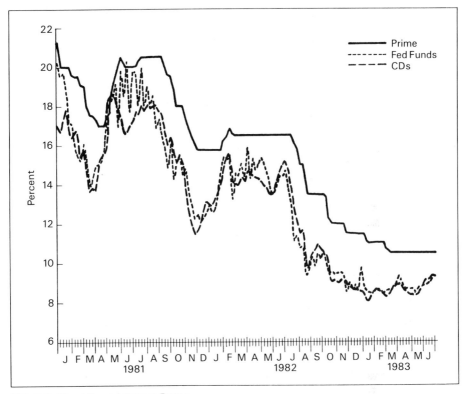

FIG. 5.7 Short-Term Interest Rates

Funding shifts can take place between Fed funds, domestic CDs, Eurodollar deposits, bankers' acceptances, etc. At the same time, investors are able to choose among instruments according to their perceptions of credit quality, rate forecasts, and other factors. This substitutability of both issuers and investors causes changes in rates in one sector of the money market to be transmitted almost immediately to other sectors. The volatility of some recent money market rates is shown in Figure 5.7.

The most volatile rate, and the key to all other rate movements, is the Fed funds rate. It is directly responsive to changes in the level of nonborrowed reserves in the banking system, which is a function of the Federal Reserve's strategy toward controlling money supply. Also, a change to the discount rate will cause an immediate change in the Fed funds rate.

The rates on Treasury bills are a kind of benchmark for the remaining term instruments in the market. Changes in the Fed funds rate have an immediate impact on the 90-day bill rate. Treasury bills are the major instrument in the money market and have a very broad and sensitive market of their own. Most open market purchases by the Fed, and practically all sales, are done in Treasury bills. This explains part of the tie to the Fed funds rate. Another important factor in this linkage is dealers' cost of financing their positions. Most positions are financed with RPs, whose rates move directly with Fed funds. If 90-day bill

TABLE 5.3 Spreads Between Various Money Market Rates Weekly Rates from 1981 Through June 1983

	Average Spread %	High %	Low %	% Variability[a]
90-day BAs to 90-day T-bills	1.18	3.12	0.13	0.68
90-day CDs to 90-day T-bills	1.16	3.10	0.09	0.68
90-day Euro CDs to 90-Day T-bills	1.78	4.06	−0.21	0.80
90-day commercial paper to 90-day T-bills	1.18	3.01	0.06	0.68
Prime to 90-day CDs	2.41	4.37	0.39	0.74

(a) Standard Deviation

rates are significantly above Fed funds, dealers can carry their positions at positive spreads. They would then be inclined to buy more bills, driving the price up. Thus, the rate will decline until it is more in line with Fed funds. If the bill rate was significantly under the Fed funds rate, the positions would be at a negative carry and would prompt dealers to sell. The selling would force price down and yield up until they came closer in line. Thus, the cost of financing has a major influence on the bill rates.

Other maturities of government securities are affected by the 90-day bill rate almost as rapidly. For example, the six-month bill is viewed by dealers as an extension of the 90-day bill, and its rate moves accordingly. In investing, the dealer weighs a decision of whether to buy a six-month bill or a 90-day bill that can be rolled over at its maturity. The decision is a function of the relative yields between 90 days and 6 months and the dealer's forecast of the movement in interest rates. The actions of dealers in the market influence the yield on the six-month bill.

Movements in the government rates in turn influence all the other instruments. Spreads between each money market security and Treasury bills of like maturity are influenced by a variety of factors. Perceived credit quality is one. This explains why agency securities are a bit higher than bills, even though they track very close. CDs track still a little higher because of the credit risk involved with them. These spreads, however, are not cast in cement and do change from time to time. The liquidity of an instrument also influences the relative spread. This explains part of the price differential between domestic CDs and Euro CDs, which tend to have a less liquid secondary market. The supply of a particular instrument in the market influences its relative price or yield. A scarce supply will drive up the price and cause the rate to drop. A final factor is whether the markets are tight or whether money is easy. For most instruments, the spreads are much narrower off governments when money is easy. For example, BAs may normally trade 15 to 25 basis ponts off of bills, but when money is easy, this spread may be only a few points. Some of these spreads for a recent period of time are illustrated in Table 5.3.

Because today's participants in the money market have reached new levels of sophistication, the interrelationship of rate movements among instruments is almost instantaneous. Many dealers and traders use computers and sophisticated statistical techniques to monitor various spread and yield relationships. When a price or yield moves out of line, it is flagged immediately, and market forces tend to drive it back in line.

Volatility in Rate Levels

Before fall of 1979, volatility in the Fed funds rate and other money market rates existed but tended not to be very pronounced. The Fed's policy was to control monetary growth by controlling the Fed funds rate. Target levels for the rate were set, and a narrow range of variability was allowed. On October 6, 1979, the Fed shifted its policy to one of controlling the level of reserves. The result has dramatically increased volatility in the Fed funds rate, as shown in Figure 5.8. This tends to remain the case today, and, of course, it means much higher levels of variability in all other money market rates. The range of rate variability is now more dramatic, as shown in Table 5.4.

Within this rate variability are certain somewhat regular patterns, some being seasonal or cyclical. For example, the business cycle influences the pattern of short-term rates. When the economy slows and the demand for credit falls, rates tend to fall. Then as the recovery begins and credit demands increase, rates rise. The short-term patterns in rates are impacted by the fundamentals of Fed policy, supply and types of securities being issued by the Treasury, loan demands at banks, and other factors.

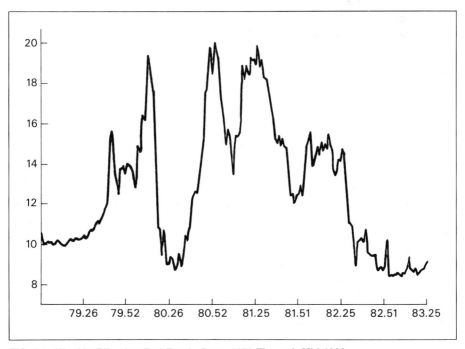

FIG. 5.8 Weekly Effective Fed Funds Rate, 1979 Through Mid-1983

TABLE 5.4   Interest Rate Variability Average Weekly Rates

1970–OCTOBER 1979

	High	Low	Average	Standard Deviation
Fed funds	13.55%	3.18%	6.94%	2.35%
90-day CDs	12.66	3.54	7.11	2.19
Prime rate	13.50	4.63	7.90	2.09

OCTOBER 1979–1982

	High	Low	Average	Standard Deviation
Fed funds	20.06%	8.42%	13.27%	3.44%
90-day CDs	20.58	8.15	13.07	3.27
Prime rate	21.50	10.50	15.48	3.26

TABLE 5.5   Prime Rate Changes

Year	Number of Prime Rate Changes
1970	5
1971	13
1972	7
1973	17
1974	23
1975	21
1976	8
1977	6
1978	15
1979	15
1980	39
1981	25
1982	11

Source: Federal Reserve Bulletin

The Prime Rate

The prime rate is unique in that, although influenced by changes in short-term money market rates, it is an administered rate. The prime changes when banks decide to change it, not necessarily when the market dictates it should change. Bank loans are not a part of the money market, but there is a direct relationship. First of all, to many corporate borrowers, short-term bank loans are only one alternative; others include commercial paper or the Eurodollar market. A second factor is that the prime rate is a short-term rate and thus an indicator of supply and demand forces in the short-term market. Participants in the money markets place great emphasis on changes to the prime rate.

Over time the prime rate has been recognized as the rate announced by banks as being what they charged to their most creditworthy customers. Rates for other customers are pegged at some spread over prime. The prime rate was first established in the 1930s. First set at 1½ percent, it did not change until 1947. From then through the 1960s, the prime changed very infrequently, generally in response to changes in market rates. Prior to 1970, the greatest number of prime rate changes took place in 1968, when the prime changed five times. Since 1970, changes in the prime have been much more frequent and pronounced in response to the generally higher level of rates and increased volatility. Table 5.5 shows the number of prime rate changes since 1970.

In the late 1960s and early 1970s, extreme public and political pressure was applied to banks to keep them from increasing the prime, even though banks' cost of funds had been increasing. In response, some banks went to a formula prime, based on some function of market-determined rates. Some tied the prime to a moving average of commercial paper rates, with the rational that commercial paper was an alternative borrowing rate. Another formula was based on a spread over commercial CDs. Thus, changes to prime rate appeared to be less an arbitrary move by banks to raise rates, and more a market-determined development. This worked, except when political pressure was put on banks to hold the prime.

Today, prime is more reflective of a bank's cost of purchased funds and therefore tied more closely to money market conditions, which is why, in recent years, it has changed more frequently and reached higher levels. At the end of 1980, the prime reached its all-time high of 21½ percent. Now, prime is probably a less significant rate than before. Competition from other sources of funds, like the Euromarket, has forced banks to make loans available to their customers, using other pricing formulas. Many new loans are priced off of various banks' costs of funds. Thus, fewer and fewer corporations are borrowing from banks at prime rate. The prime is still influenced, however, by what banks pay for their CDs, Eurodeposits, and Fed funds. Figure 5.9 shows the last decade's pattern of prime rate behavior.

FINANCIAL FUTURES

A relatively recent development in the money markets has been the rapid growth in financial futures contracts. As interest rates have continued their trend toward higher levels and increased variability, financial futures have

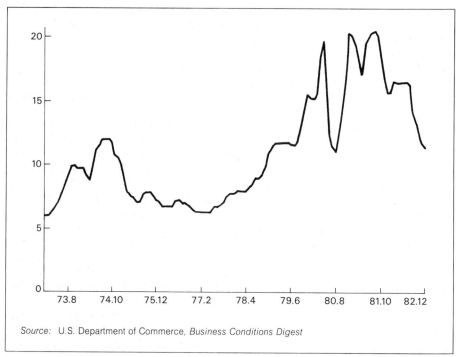

Source: U.S. Department of Commerce, Business Conditions Digest

FIG. 5.9 Bank Prime Lending Rate

grown in popularity as a means of protecting investors from price fluctuations and has given traders and speculators in financial markets new ways of taking risk for a profit.

A financial futures contract is a contract to buy or sell a particular financial instrument at a specific date in the future for a specific price. It can be used to lock in a price today for a financial instrument that will not be bought or sold until some future time. The buyer or seller thus transfers the risk of a change in price to another party. This hedging of risk has been the single most important factor contributing to the growth in the financial futures market. (See Chapter 12 for further discussion.)

The first financial futures contract was traded in October 1975, when a market was opened for Government National Mortgage Association (GNMA) certificates. This was followed in January 1976 by a futures contract in 90-day U.S. Treasury bills, the most popular trading contract. Today, besides GNMA certificates and Treasury bills, financial futures contracts exist in Treasury bonds and Treasury notes, 90-day bank CDs, and 90-day Eurodollars. An earlier contract in 90-day commercial paper is no longer traded because of lack of interest. Financial futures markets also exist in various foreign currencies. Financial futures have shown such growth and popularity that it is not unusual for daily volume and total positions in the Treasury bond and Treasury bill markets to exceed the volume and positions in the underlying Treasury cash securities markets. Recent average trading volume in Treasury bill futures has been in the 10,000 to 15,000 contract range. In terms of dollars, this represents $10 billion to $15 billion in underlying bills.

Financial futures are used by investors and institutions to lock in (i.e., guarantee) a specific interest rate for investing or borrowing sometime in the future. This is referred to as hedging interest rate exposure. Hedging a future investment rate is known as a long hedge. In such a case, the investor buys a futures contract that guarantees delivery of a security sometime in the future at a price determined today. Say, for example, the investor anticipated buying Treasury bills three months from now because of a scheduled cash inflow. The investor would buy the appropriate bill contract that would guarantee a price on the bills to be delivered in three months. The standard bill contract is for $1 million. The value of the contract moves with interest rates. If, three months from now, Treasury bill rates drop, the value of the contract will have increased, offsetting lost interest from investing at the lower rate.

In a similar manner, institutions can hedge their borrowing costs. Hedging the costs of borrowing involves selling a futures contract, which is called a short hedge. If rates should go up, the cost of borrowing would increase. However, the value of the futures contract decreases and the sale can be covered at a lower cost, resulting in a gain to the seller. This gain should offset the increase in borrowing cost caused by the higher rates.

Financial futures prices do parallel movements in prices in the underlying cash instruments. But these fluctuations in prices are not always equal to changes in the cash markets. Thus, the hedger really is exchanging the risk of absolute price movement in a security for the risk of volatility in the relationship between cash and futures. This risk in the price relationship is known as basis risk. The amount of basis risk incurred is a function of the cash instrument. An investor hedging the purchase of a Treasury bill incurs one level of basis risk by using the Treasury bill contract. An institution trying to hedge the cost of its prime rate loan through shorting a CD contract will incur a much greater basis risk, since there is volatility not only between the cash market and the futures market but also between the prime rate and the CD rate.

Arbitrage transactions between cash and futures minimize the basis risk, that is, they ensure somewhat of a stable relationship between the two. For example, the current yield in the cash market of three-month Treasury bills and six-month Treasury bills implies a projection of what three-month bills will be three months into the future. This is known as the cash forward rate. The current futures contract, given the proper time period, also implies the three-month bill rate three months into the future. Normally, these implied rates in the two markets should be close. Say they were not. Assume an investor held a six-month bill with an implied three-month forward rate of 9.00 percent and that the futures contract three months from now is priced at 9.25 percent. The investor would be likely to sell his cash security and buy the futures contract (provided that the difference between the extra 0.25 percent yield three months from now makes up any lost yield in the current period). Selling the cash drives the yield up, and buying the futures pushes the yield down, closing the gap between the two rates. Likewise, if the cash yield were higher than the futures, the investor would buy the cash and sell the futures. Such activity tends to keep the cash and futures prices in a steady relationship.

SUGGESTED READING

Coats, Warren L., Jr. "How to Improve Control of the Money Supply." *The AEI Economist* (Mar. 1981).

Dufey, Gunter, and Ian H. Giddy. *The International Money Market*. Engelwood Cliffs, N.J.: Prentice-Hall, 1978.

Henning, Charles L., et ai. *Financial Markets and the Economy*. Engelwood Cliffs, N.J.: Prentice-Hall, 1981.

Homer, Sidney, and Martin L. Leibowitz. *Inside the Yield Book*. Engelwood Cliffs, N.J.: Prentice-Hall, 1972.

Instruments of the Money Market. Federal Reserve Bank of Richmond. Richmond, Va.: 1981.

The Market for Federal Funds and Repurchase Agreements. Board of Governors of the Federal Reserve System, Staff Studies. Washington, D.C.: July, 1979.

Melton, William C., and Jean M. Mahr. "Bankers' Acceptances." *Federal Reserve Bank of New York Quarterly Review* (Summer 1981), pp. 39–55.

Ritter, Lawrence S., and William L. Silber. *Money*. New York: Basic Books, 1981.

Stigum, Marcia. *The Money Market: Myth, Reality, and Practice*. Homewood, Ill.: Dow Jones-Irwin, 1978.

6

Mathematics of Finance: Money and Time

T. Craig Tapley

The areas covered in this chapter include: (1) time value of money, (2) bank loans, (3) bond analysis, and (4) futures contracts. It is assumed that the reader has some understanding of the problem that needs to be solved. If not, other chapters in this book discuss the relevant underlying economic and financial theory.

TIME VALUE OF MONEY

The time value of money is a generic term which encompasses all aspects of converting cash flows at one time to their equivalent values at another time. The starting point is that a dollar today is worth more than a dollar one year from today. Depending on the problem to be analyzed, the interest rate may be referred to as a discount rate, compounding rate, opportunity cost, cost of capital, yield to maturity, or a growth rate. Whichever name is used, if the problem is one of converting a value at one time to its equivalent value at another time, the basic calculations remain the same.

Definition of Variables

i = interest or discount rate on an annual basis

A = periodic annuity payment

M = number of compounding or discounting periods within a year

N = number of years

FV = future or compounded value

PV = present or discounted value

$FVIF(i\%,N)$ = compound value interest factor at i percent for N periods

$PVIF(i\%,N)$ = present value interest factor at i percent for N periods

In addition, the subscript a refers to a regular annuity, the subscript ad refers to an annuity due, and the subscript p refers to a perpetuity. All other variables are defined within the text.

Compounding of a Single Sum

The compounding of a single sum is the conversion of an earlier (present) value into an equivalent later (future) value. The use of the terms "earlier" and "later" makes clear that the reference point need not be real time. The future value depends on the present value, the applicable interest rate, and the number of compounding periods.

Calculation of a Future Value. The future value of a single sum, compounded at an interest rate of i percent for N periods, is calculated as:

$$FV = [\ PV\ ][(1 + i)^N]$$
$$= [\ PV\ ][FVIF(i\%,N)]$$

The value $(1 + i)^N$ is called the future value interest factor of a single sum. Future value interest factors for various values of i and N have been precalculated and are contained in Table 6.1.

EXAMPLE 1. Assume that $100 is deposited in a savings accout, paying interest at an annual rate of 5 percent. This $100 and any interest earned is left on deposit for five years. What is the value of this account at the end of five years?

$$FV = [\$100][(1.05)^5]$$
$$= [\$100][FVIF(5\%,5)]$$
$$= [\$100][1.2763] = \$127.63$$

This savings account has a value of $127.63 at the end of five years. The value is comprised of the initial deposit of $100 (principal) plus accumulated interest. The year-by-year accumulation of interest is as follows:

Year	Beginning Balance	Interest for Year	Ending Balance
1	$100.00	$5.00	$105.00
2	105.00	5.25	110.25
3	110.25	5.51	115.76
4	115.76	5.79	121.55
5	121.55	6.08	127.63

TABLE 6.1 Future Value of a Single Sum: $FVIF(i\%,N) = (1 + i)^N$

Period	1%	2%	3%	4%	5%	6%	7%	8%	9%	10%	12%	14%	15%	16%	18%	20%	24%	28%	32%	36%
1	1.0100	1.0200	1.0300	1.0400	1.0500	1.0600	1.0700	1.0800	1.0900	1.1000	1.1200	1.1400	1.1500	1.1600	1.1800	1.2000	1.2400	1.2800	1.3200	1.3600
2	1.0201	1.0404	1.0609	1.0816	1.1025	1.1236	1.1449	1.1664	1.1881	1.2100	1.2544	1.2996	1.3225	1.3456	1.3924	1.4400	1.5376	1.6384	1.7424	1.8496
3	1.0303	1.0612	1.0927	1.1249	1.1576	1.1910	1.2250	1.2597	1.2950	1.3310	1.4049	1.4815	1.5209	1.5609	1.6430	1.7280	1.9066	2.0972	2.3000	2.5155
4	1.0406	1.0824	1.1255	1.1699	1.2155	1.2625	1.3108	1.3605	1.4116	1.4641	1.5735	1.6890	1.7490	1.8106	1.9388	2.0736	2.3642	2.6844	3.0360	3.4210
5	1.0510	1.1041	1.1593	1.2167	1.2763	1.3382	1.4026	1.4693	1.5386	1.6105	1.7623	1.9254	2.0114	2.1003	2.2878	2.4883	2.9316	3.4360	4.0075	4.6526
6	1.0615	1.1262	1.1941	1.2653	1.3401	1.4185	1.5007	1.5869	1.6771	1.7716	1.9738	2.1950	2.3131	2.4364	2.6996	2.9860	3.6352	4.3980	5.2899	6.3275
7	1.0721	1.1487	1.2299	1.3159	1.4071	1.5036	1.6058	1.7138	1.8280	1.9487	2.2107	2.5023	2.6600	2.8262	3.1855	3.5832	4.5077	5.6295	6.9826	8.6054
8	1.0829	1.1717	1.2668	1.3686	1.4775	1.5938	1.7182	1.8509	1.9926	2.1436	2.4760	2.8526	3.0590	3.2784	3.7589	4.2998	5.5895	7.2058	9.2170	11.703
9	1.0937	1.1951	1.3048	1.4233	1.5513	1.6895	1.8385	1.9990	2.1719	2.3579	2.7731	3.2519	3.5179	3.8030	4.4355	5.1598	6.9310	9.2234	12.166	15.916
10	1.1046	1.2190	1.3439	1.4802	1.6289	1.7908	1.9672	2.1589	2.3674	2.5937	3.1058	3.7072	4.0456	4.4114	5.2338	6.1917	8.5944	11.805	16.059	21.646
11	1.1157	1.2434	1.3842	1.5395	1.7103	1.8983	2.1049	2.3316	2.5804	2.8531	3.4785	4.2262	4.6524	5.1173	6.1759	7.4301	10.657	15.111	21.198	29.439
12	1.1268	1.2682	1.4258	1.6010	1.7959	2.0122	2.2522	2.5182	2.8127	3.1384	3.8960	4.8179	5.3502	5.9360	7.2876	8.9161	13.214	19.342	27.982	40.037
13	1.1381	1.2936	1.4685	1.6651	1.8856	2.1329	2.4098	2.7196	3.0658	3.4523	4.3635	5.4924	6.1528	6.8858	8.5994	10.699	16.386	24.758	36.937	54.451
14	1.1495	1.3195	1.5126	1.7317	1.9799	2.2609	2.5785	2.9372	3.3417	3.7975	4.8871	6.2613	7.0757	7.9875	10.147	12.839	20.319	31.691	48.756	74.053
15	1.1610	1.3459	1.5580	1.8009	2.0789	2.3966	2.7590	3.1722	3.6425	4.1772	5.4736	7.1379	8.1371	9.2655	11.973	15.407	25.195	40.564	64.358	100.71
16	1.1726	1.3728	1.6047	1.8730	2.1829	2.5404	2.9522	3.4259	3.9703	4.5950	6.1304	8.1372	9.3576	10.748	14.129	18.488	31.242	51.923	84.953	136.96
17	1.1843	1.4002	1.6528	1.9479	2.2920	2.6928	3.1588	3.7000	4.3276	5.0545	6.8660	9.2765	10.761	12.467	16.672	22.186	38.740	66.461	112.13	186.26
18	1.1961	1.4282	1.7024	2.0258	2.4066	2.8543	3.3799	3.9960	4.7171	5.5599	7.6900	10.575	12.375	14.462	19.673	26.623	48.038	85.070	148.02	253.33
19	1.2081	1.4568	1.7535	2.1068	2.5270	3.0256	3.6165	4.3157	5.1417	6.1159	8.6128	12.055	14.231	16.776	23.214	31.948	59.567	108.89	195.39	344.53
20	1.2202	1.4859	1.8061	2.1911	2.6533	3.2071	3.8697	4.6610	5.6044	6.7275	9.6463	13.743	16.366	19.460	27.393	38.337	73.864	139.37	257.91	468.57
21	1.2324	1.5157	1.8603	2.2788	2.7860	3.3996	4.1406	5.0338	6.1088	7.4002	10.803	15.667	18.821	22.574	32.323	46.005	91.591	178.40	340.44	637.26
22	1.2447	1.5460	1.9161	2.3699	2.9253	3.6035	4.4304	5.4365	6.6586	8.1403	12.100	17.861	21.644	26.186	38.142	55.206	113.57	228.35	449.39	866.67
23	1.2572	1.5769	1.9736	2.4647	3.0715	3.8197	4.7405	5.8715	7.2579	8.9543	13.552	20.361	24.891	30.376	45.007	66.247	140.83	292.30	593.19	1178.6
24	1.2697	1.6084	2.0328	2.5633	3.2251	4.0489	5.0724	6.3412	7.9111	9.8497	15.178	23.212	28.625	35.236	53.108	79.496	174.63	374.14	783.02	1602.9
25	1.2824	1.6406	2.0938	2.6658	3.3864	4.2919	5.4274	6.8485	8.6231	10.834	17.000	26.461	32.918	40.874	62.668	95.396	216.54	478.90	1033.6	2180.0
26	1.2953	1.6734	2.1566	2.7725	3.5557	4.5494	5.8074	7.3964	9.3992	11.918	19.040	30.166	37.856	47.414	73.948	114.47	268.51	612.99	1364.3	2964.9
27	1.3082	1.7069	2.2213	2.8834	3.7335	4.8223	6.2139	7.9881	10.245	13.110	21.324	34.389	43.535	55.000	87.259	137.37	332.95	784.63	1800.9	4032.2
28	1.3213	1.7410	2.2879	2.9987	3.9201	5.1117	6.6488	8.6271	11.167	14.421	23.883	39.204	50.065	63.800	102.96	164.84	412.86	1004.3	2377.2	5483.8
29	1.3345	1.7758	2.3566	3.1187	4.1161	5.4184	7.1143	9.3173	12.172	15.863	26.749	44.693	57.575	74.008	121.50	197.81	511.95	1285.5	3137.9	7458.0
30	1.3478	1.8114	2.4273	3.2434	4.3219	5.7435	7.6123	10.062	13.267	17.449	29.959	50.950	66.211	85.849	143.37	237.37	634.81	1645.5	4142.0	10143
40	1.4889	2.2080	3.2620	4.8010	7.0400	10.285	14.974	21.724	31.409	45.259	93.050	188.88	267.86	378.72	750.37	1469.7	5455.9	19426.	66520.	*
50	1.6446	2.6916	4.3839	7.1067	11.467	18.420	29.457	46.901	74.357	117.39	289.00	700.23	1083.6	1670.7	3927.3	9100.4	46890.	*	*	*
60	1.8167	3.2810	5.8916	10.519	18.679	32.987	57.946	101.25	176.03	304.48	897.59	2595.9	4383.9	7370.1	20555.	56347.	*	*	*	*

*FVIF>99,999

If the earned interest had been withdrawn at the end of each year, then the interest calculated for the subsequent period would always be based on a beginning balance of $100. This would give total interest earned for the five-year period of $25. The difference between this value and the actual interest earned of $27.63 arises because the interest is left on deposit to earn interest itself. This interest-on-interest is the basis for all compounding.

EXAMPLE 2. In 1950, the earnings per share of XYZ Corporation were $2.34. These earnings grew at an annual rate of 7 percent over the next 10 years. What were the earnings per share in 1960?

$$FV = [\$2.34][(1.07)^{10}]$$
$$= [\$2.34][FVIF(7\%,10)]$$
$$= [\$2.34][1.9672] = \$4.60$$

Discounting of a Single Sum

The conversion of a later value into an earlier value is called discounting and is the inverse process of compounding. Intuitively, the question is what present value, when it is compounded, will be equal to the future value.

Calculation of a Present Value. As already shown, the general equation for a future value may be written as:

$$FV = [PV][(1 + i)^N]$$

If this equation is solved for present value, the resulting equation is:

$$PV = [FV][(1/1 + i)^N]$$
$$= [FV][PVIF(i\%,N)]$$

The value $(1/1 + i)^N$ is called the present value interest factor of a single sum. Present value interest factors for various values of i and N have been precalculated and are contained in Table 6.2.

It should be clear that compounding and discounting are inversely related, since

$$PVIF(i\%,N) = [1/FVIF(i\%,N)]$$

EXAMPLE 1. X is currently renting his home, but has an option to purchase the house in two years at a price of $80,000. If X can earn an annual interest rate of 6 percent on his savings, how much does he have to deposit today in order to have the total purchase price in two years?

$$PV = [\$80,000][(1/1.06)^2]$$
$$= [\$80,000][PVIF(6\%,2)]$$
$$= [\$80,000][0.8900] = \$71,200$$

EXAMPLE 2. In 1980, Y's stock portfolio had a value of $25,469.68. Y had held this portfolio for 10 years and earned an annual rate of return of 9.8 percent. How much did Y invest originally?

TABLE 6.2   Present Value of a Single Sum: $PVIF(i\%,N) = (1/1 + i)^N$

Period	1%	2%	3%	4%	5%	6%	7%	8%	9%	10%	12%	14%	15%	16%	18%	20%	24%	28%	32%	36%
1	.9901	.9804	.9709	.9615	.9524	.9434	.9346	.9259	.9174	.9091	.8929	.8772	.8696	.8621	.8475	.8333	.8065	.7813	.7576	.7353
2	.9803	.9612	.9426	.9246	.9070	.8900	.8734	.8573	.8417	.8264	.7972	.7695	.7561	.7432	.7182	.6944	.6504	.6104	.5739	.5407
3	.9706	.9423	.9151	.8890	.8638	.8396	.8163	.7938	.7722	.7513	.7118	.6750	.6575	.6407	.6086	.5787	.5245	.4768	.4348	.3975
4	.9610	.9238	.8885	.8548	.8227	.7921	.7629	.7350	.7084	.6830	.6355	.5921	.5718	.5523	.5158	.4823	.4230	.3725	.3294	.2923
5	.9515	.9057	.8626	.8219	.7835	.7473	.7130	.6806	.6499	.6209	.5674	.5194	.4972	.4761	.4371	.4019	.3411	.2910	.2495	.2149
6	.9420	.8880	.8375	.7903	.7462	.7050	.6663	.6302	.5963	.5645	.5066	.4556	.4323	.4104	.3704	.3349	.2751	.2274	.1890	.1580
7	.9327	.8706	.8131	.7599	.7107	.6651	.6227	.5835	.5470	.5132	.4523	.3996	.3759	.3538	.3139	.2791	.2218	.1776	.1432	.1162
8	.9235	.8535	.7894	.7307	.6768	.6274	.5820	.5403	.5019	.4665	.4039	.3506	.3269	.3050	.2660	.2326	.1789	.1388	.1085	.0854
9	.9143	.8368	.7664	.7026	.6446	.5919	.5439	.5002	.4604	.4241	.3606	.3075	.2843	.2630	.2255	.1938	.1443	.1084	.0822	.0628
10	.9053	.8203	.7441	.6756	.6139	.5584	.5083	.4632	.4224	.3855	.3220	.2697	.2472	.2267	.1911	.1615	.1164	.0847	.0623	.0462
11	.8963	.8043	.7224	.6496	.5847	.5268	.4751	.4289	.3875	.3505	.2875	.2366	.2149	.1954	.1619	.1346	.0938	.0662	.0472	.0340
12	.8874	.7885	.7014	.6246	.5568	.4970	.4440	.3971	.3555	.3186	.2567	.2076	.1869	.1685	.1372	.1122	.0757	.0517	.0357	.0250
13	.8787	.7730	.6810	.6006	.5303	.4688	.4150	.3677	.3262	.2897	.2292	.1821	.1625	.1452	.1163	.0935	.0610	.0404	.0271	.0184
14	.8700	.7579	.6611	.5775	.5051	.4423	.3878	.3405	.2992	.2633	.2046	.1597	.1413	.1252	.0985	.0779	.0492	.0316	.0205	.0135
15	.8613	.7430	.6419	.5553	.4810	.4173	.3624	.3152	.2745	.2394	.1827	.1401	.1229	.1079	.0835	.0649	.0397	.0247	.0155	.0099
16	.8528	.7284	.6232	.5339	.4581	.3936	.3387	.2919	.2519	.2176	.1631	.1229	.1069	.0930	.0708	.0541	.0320	.0193	.0118	.0073
17	.8444	.7142	.6050	.5134	.4363	.3714	.3166	.2703	.2311	.1978	.1456	.1078	.0929	.0802	.0600	.0451	.0258	.0150	.0089	.0054
18	.8360	.7002	.5874	.4936	.4155	.3503	.2959	.2502	.2120	.1799	.1300	.0946	.0808	.0691	.0508	.0376	.0208	.0118	.0068	.0039
19	.8277	.6864	.5703	.4746	.3957	.3305	.2765	.2317	.1945	.1635	.1161	.0829	.0703	.0596	.0431	.0313	.0168	.0092	.0051	.0029
20	.8195	.6730	.5537	.4564	.3769	.3118	.2584	.2145	.1784	.1486	.1037	.0728	.0611	.0514	.0365	.0261	.0135	.0072	.0039	.0021
25	.7798	.6095	.4776	.3751	.2953	.2330	.1842	.1460	.1160	.0923	.0588	.0378	.0304	.0245	.0160	.0105	.0046	.0021	.0010	.0005
30	.7419	.5521	.4120	.3083	.2314	.1741	.1314	.0994	.0754	.0573	.0334	.0196	.0151	.0116	.0070	.0042	.0016	.0006	.0002	.0001
40	.6717	.4529	.3066	.2083	.1420	.0972	.0668	.0460	.0318	.0221	.0107	.0053	.0037	.0026	.0013	.0007	.0002	.0001	*	*
50	.6080	.3715	.2281	.1407	.0872	.0543	.0339	.0213	.0134	.0085	.0035	.0014	.0009	.0006	.0003	.0001	*	*	*	*
60	.5504	.3048	.1697	.0951	.0535	.0303	.0173	.0099	.0057	.0033	.0011	.0004	.0002	.0001	*					

* The factor is zero to four decimal places.

Table 6.2 does not contain interest factors for 9.8 percent, but the present value may be easily calculated with any calculator:

$$PV = [\$25,469.68][(1/1.098)^{10}]$$
$$= [\$25,469.68][0.3926238] = \$10,000.00$$

Regular Annuity

An annuity is a series of periodic payments with the size of each payment the same for each period. In a regular annuity the payments occur at the end of each period. An example is an installment loan where the first repayment takes place at the end of the first installment period, not when the loan is originally made. It is possible to convert this series of payments into either a future value or a present value.

Future Value: Time-Line Analysis. The future value of an annuity can be evaluated as the sum of the future value of the individual cash flows comprising the annuity. This is easily seen diagrammatically through a time-line analysis.

EXAMPLE. Assume that $100 is deposited at the end of each year for five years, and that each deposit earns an annual interest rate of 5 percent. What is the total value of the deposits at the end of five years?

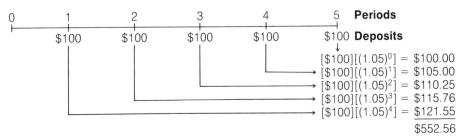

The future value of this five-year annuity is $552.56. Since this is a regular annuity, all deposits occur at the end of the period. This means that the last deposit is compounded forward zero years. Note that the value of any number raised to the zero power is one.

Future Value: Calculations. The future value of a regular annuity may be calculated as follows:

$$FV_a = [A][(1 + i)^0] + [A][(1 + i)^1] + \cdots + [A][(1 + i)^{N-1}]$$
$$= [A][(1 + i)^0 + (1 + i)^1 + \cdots + (1 + i)^{N-1}]$$
$$= [A]\left[\sum_{t=0}^{N-1} (1 + i)^t\right]$$

TABLE 6.3 Future Value of an Annuity: $FVIF_a(i\%,N) = \dfrac{(1+i)^N - 1}{i}$

Periods	1%	2%	3%	4%	5%	6%	7%	8%	9%	10%	12%	14%	15%	16%	18%	20%	24%	28%	32%	36%
1	1.0000	1.0000	1.0000	1.0000	1.0000	1.0000	1.0000	1.0000	1.0000	1.0000	1.0000	1.0000	1.0000	1.0000	1.0000	1.0000	1.0000	1.0000	1.0000	1.0000
2	2.0100	2.0200	2.0300	2.0400	2.0500	2.0600	2.0700	2.0800	2.0900	2.1000	2.1200	2.1400	2.1500	2.1600	2.1800	2.2000	2.2400	2.2800	2.3200	2.3600
3	3.0301	3.0604	3.0909	3.1216	3.1525	3.1836	3.2149	3.2464	3.2781	3.3100	3.3744	3.4396	3.4725	3.5056	3.5724	3.6400	3.7776	3.9184	4.0624	4.2096
4	4.0604	4.1216	4.1836	4.2465	4.3101	4.3746	4.4399	4.5061	4.5731	4.6410	4.7793	4.9211	4.9934	5.0665	5.2154	5.3680	5.6842	6.0156	6.3624	6.7251
5	5.1010	5.2040	5.3091	5.4163	5.5256	5.6371	5.7507	5.8666	5.9847	6.1051	6.3528	6.6101	6.7424	6.8771	7.1542	7.4416	8.0484	8.6999	9.3983	10.146
6	6.1520	6.3081	6.4684	6.6330	6.8019	6.9753	7.1533	7.3359	7.5233	7.7156	8.1152	8.5355	8.7537	8.9775	9.4420	9.9299	10.980	12.135	13.405	14.798
7	7.2135	7.4343	7.6625	7.8983	8.1420	8.3938	8.6540	8.9228	9.2004	9.4872	10.089	10.730	11.066	11.413	12.141	12.915	14.615	16.533	18.695	21.126
8	8.2857	8.5830	8.8923	9.2142	9.5491	9.8975	10.259	10.636	11.028	11.435	12.299	13.232	13.726	14.240	15.327	16.499	19.122	22.163	25.678	29.731
9	9.3685	9.7546	10.159	10.582	11.026	11.491	11.978	12.487	13.021	13.579	14.775	16.085	16.785	17.518	19.085	20.798	24.712	29.369	34.895	41.435
10	10.462	10.949	11.463	12.006	12.577	13.180	13.816	14.486	15.192	15.937	17.548	19.337	20.303	21.321	23.521	25.958	31.643	38.592	47.061	57.351
11	11.566	12.168	12.807	13.486	14.206	14.971	15.783	16.645	17.560	18.531	20.654	23.044	24.349	25.732	28.755	32.150	40.237	50.398	63.121	78.998
12	12.682	13.412	14.192	15.025	15.917	16.869	17.888	18.977	20.140	21.384	24.133	27.270	29.001	30.850	34.931	39.580	50.894	65.510	84.320	108.43
13	13.809	14.680	15.617	16.626	17.713	18.882	20.140	21.495	22.953	24.522	28.029	32.088	34.351	36.786	42.218	48.496	64.109	84.852	112.30	148.47
14	14.947	15.973	17.086	18.291	19.598	21.015	22.550	24.214	26.019	27.975	32.392	37.581	40.504	43.672	50.818	59.195	80.496	109.61	149.23	202.92
15	16.096	17.293	18.598	20.023	21.578	23.276	25.129	27.152	29.360	31.772	37.279	43.842	47.950	51.659	60.965	72.035	100.81	141.30	197.99	276.97
16	17.257	18.639	20.156	21.824	23.657	25.672	27.888	30.324	33.003	35.949	42.753	50.980	55.717	60.925	72.939	87.442	126.01	181.86	262.35	377.69
17	18.430	20.012	21.761	23.697	25.840	28.212	30.840	33.750	36.973	40.544	48.883	59.117	65.075	71.673	87.068	105.93	157.25	233.79	347.30	514.66
18	19.614	21.412	23.414	25.645	28.132	30.905	33.999	37.450	41.301	45.599	55.749	68.394	75.836	84.140	103.74	128.11	195.99	300.25	459.44	700.93
19	20.810	22.840	25.116	27.671	30.539	33.760	37.379	41.446	46.018	51.159	63.439	78.969	88.211	98.603	123.41	154.74	244.03	385.32	607.47	954.27
20	22.019	24.297	26.870	29.778	33.066	36.785	40.995	45.762	51.160	57.275	72.052	91.024	102.44	115.37	146.62	186.68	303.60	494.21	802.86	1298.8
21	23.239	25.783	28.676	31.969	35.719	39.992	44.865	50.422	56.764	64.002	81.698	104.76	118.81	134.84	174.02	225.02	377.46	633.59	1060.7	1767.3
22	24.471	27.299	30.536	34.248	38.505	43.392	49.005	55.456	62.873	71.402	92.502	120.43	137.63	157.41	206.34	271.03	469.05	811.99	1401.2	2404.6
23	25.716	28.845	32.452	36.617	41.430	46.995	53.436	60.893	69.531	79.543	104.60	138.29	159.27	183.60	244.48	326.23	582.62	1040.3	1850.6	3271.3
24	26.973	30.421	34.426	39.082	44.502	50.815	58.176	66.764	76.789	88.497	118.15	158.65	184.16	213.97	289.49	392.48	723.46	1332.6	2443.8	4449.9
25	28.243	32.030	36.459	41.645	47.727	54.864	63.249	73.105	84.700	98.347	133.33	181.87	212.79	249.21	342.60	471.98	898.09	1706.8	3226.8	6052.9
26	29.525	33.670	38.553	44.311	51.113	59.156	68.676	79.954	93.323	109.18	150.33	208.33	245.71	290.08	405.27	567.37	1114.6	2185.7	4260.4	8233.0
27	30.820	35.344	40.709	47.084	54.669	63.705	74.483	87.350	102.72	121.09	169.37	238.49	283.56	337.50	479.22	681.85	1383.1	2798.7	5624.7	11197.9
28	32.129	37.051	42.930	49.967	58.402	68.528	80.697	95.338	112.96	134.20	190.69	272.88	327.10	392.50	566.48	819.22	1716.0	3583.3	7425.6	15230.2
29	33.450	38.792	45.218	52.966	62.322	73.639	87.346	103.96	124.13	148.63	214.58	312.09	377.46	456.30	669.44	984.06	2128.9	4587.6	9802.9	20714.1
30	34.784	40.568	47.575	56.084	66.438	79.058	94.460	113.28	136.30	164.49	241.33	356.78	434.74	530.31	790.94	1181.8	2640.9	5873.2	12940.8	28172.2
40	48.886	60.402	75.401	95.025	120.79	154.76	199.63	259.05	337.88	442.59	767.09	1342.0	1779.0	2360.7	4163.2	7343.8	22728	69377	*	*
50	64.463	84.579	112.79	152.66	209.84	290.33	406.52	573.76	815.08	1163.9	2400.0	4994.5	7217.7	10435	21813	45497	*	*	*	*
60	81.669	114.05	163.05	237.99	353.58	533.12	813.52	1253.2	1944.7	3034.8	7471.6	18535	29219	46057	*	*	*	*	*	*

* FVIF > 99,999

$$= [\,A\,]\left[\frac{(1+i)^N}{i} - \frac{1}{i}\right]$$

$$= [\,A\,][FVIF_a(i\%,N)] = [\,A\,]\left[\sum_{t=0}^{N-1} FVIF(i\%,t)\right]$$

Future value interest factors for a regular annuity, for various values of i and N, have been precalculated and are contained in Table 6.3.

EXAMPLE. X has just had a child and has decided that starting on the child's first birthday, X will deposit \$1,000 each year for the child's college education. If X makes 18 deposits and each earns a 6 percent annual rate of return, then how much will the child have for college when she turns 18?

$$FV_a = [\$1,000]\left[\frac{(1.06)^{18}}{0.06} - \frac{1}{0.06}\right]$$

$$= [\$1,000][FVIF_a(6\%,18)]$$

$$= [\$1,000][30.905] = \$30,905.00$$

Present Value: Time-Line Analysis. The present value of an annuity can be calculated using a time-line analysis and the same example that was used for future value: \$100 is deposited each year for five years and the annual interest rate is 5 percent. The present value of this regular annuity is then equal to:

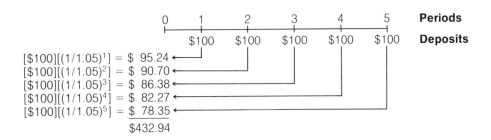

The present value of this regular annuity is \$432.94. It may be found by discounting the individual cash flows that comprise the annuity.

Present Value: Calculations. The present value of a regular annuity may be calculated as follows:

$$PV_a = [\,A\,]\left[\left(\frac{1}{1+i}\right)^1\right] + [\,A\,]\left[\left(\frac{1}{1+i}\right)^2\right] + \cdots + [\,A\,]\left[\left(\frac{1}{1+i}\right)^N\right]$$

$$= [\,A\,]\left[\left(\frac{1}{1+i}\right)^1 + \left(\frac{1}{1+i}\right)^2 + \cdots + \left(\frac{1}{1+i}\right)^N\right]$$

$$= [\,A\,]\left[\sum_{t=1}^{N}\left(\frac{1}{1+i}\right)^t\right]$$

TABLE 6.4 Present Value of an Annuity: $PVIF_a(i\%, N) = \dfrac{1}{i} - \dfrac{1}{(i)(1+i)^N}$

No. of Payments	1%	2%	3%	4%	5%	6%	7%	8%	9%	10%	12%	14%	15%	16%	18%	20%	24%	28%	32%
1	0.9901	0.9804	0.9709	0.9615	0.9524	0.9434	0.9346	0.9259	0.9174	0.9091	0.8929	0.8772	0.8696	0.8621	0.8475	0.8333	0.8065	0.7813	0.7576
2	1.9704	1.9416	1.9135	1.8861	1.8594	1.8334	1.8080	1.7833	1.7591	1.7355	1.6901	1.6467	1.6257	1.6052	1.5656	1.5278	1.4568	1.3916	1.3315
3	2.9410	2.8839	2.8286	2.7751	2.7232	2.6730	2.6243	2.5771	2.5313	2.4869	2.4018	2.3216	2.2832	2.2459	2.1743	2.1065	1.9813	1.8684	1.7663
4	3.9020	3.8077	3.7171	3.6299	3.5460	3.4651	3.3872	3.3121	3.2397	3.1699	3.0373	2.9137	2.8550	2.7982	2.6901	2.5887	2.4043	2.2410	2.0957
5	4.8534	4.7135	4.5797	4.4518	4.3295	4.2124	4.1002	3.9927	3.8897	3.7908	3.6048	3.4331	3.3522	3.2743	3.1272	2.9906	2.7454	2.5320	2.3452
6	5.7955	5.6014	5.4172	5.2421	5.0757	4.9173	4.7665	4.6229	4.4859	4.3553	4.1114	3.8887	3.7845	3.6847	3.4976	3.3255	3.0205	2.7594	2.5342
7	6.7282	6.4720	6.2303	6.0021	5.7864	5.5824	5.3893	5.2064	5.0330	4.8684	4.5638	4.2883	4.1604	4.0386	3.8115	3.6046	3.2423	2.9370	2.6775
8	7.6517	7.3255	7.0197	6.7327	6.4632	6.2098	5.9713	5.7466	5.5348	5.3349	4.9676	4.6389	4.4873	4.3436	4.0776	3.8372	3.4212	3.0758	2.7860
9	8.5660	8.1622	7.7861	7.4353	7.1078	6.8017	6.5152	6.2469	5.9952	5.7590	5.3282	4.9464	4.7716	4.6065	4.3030	4.0310	3.5655	3.1842	2.8681
10	9.4713	8.9825	8.5302	8.1109	7.7217	7.3601	7.0236	6.7101	6.4177	6.1446	5.6502	5.2161	5.0188	4.8332	4.4941	4.1925	3.6819	3.2689	2.9304
11	10.3676	9.7868	9.2526	8.7605	8.3064	7.8869	7.4987	7.1390	6.8052	6.4951	5.9377	5.4527	5.2337	5.0286	4.6560	4.3271	3.7757	3.3351	2.9776
12	11.2551	10.5753	9.9540	9.3851	8.8633	8.3838	7.9427	7.5361	7.1607	6.8137	6.1944	5.6603	5.4206	5.1971	4.7932	4.4392	3.8514	3.3868	3.0133
13	12.1337	11.3484	10.6350	9.9856	9.3936	8.8527	8.3577	7.9038	7.4869	7.1034	6.4235	5.8424	5.5831	5.3423	4.9095	4.5327	3.9124	3.4272	3.0404
14	13.0037	12.1062	11.2961	10.5631	9.8986	9.2950	8.7455	8.2442	7.7862	7.3667	6.6282	6.0021	5.7245	5.4675	5.0081	4.6106	3.9616	3.4587	3.0609
15	13.8651	12.8493	11.9379	11.1184	10.3797	9.7122	9.1079	8.5595	8.0607	7.6061	6.8109	6.1422	5.8474	5.5755	5.0916	4.6755	4.0013	3.4834	3.0764
16	14.7179	13.5777	12.5611	11.6523	10.8378	10.1059	9.4466	8.8514	8.3126	7.8237	6.9740	6.2651	5.9542	5.6685	5.1624	4.7296	4.0333	3.5026	3.0882
17	15.5623	14.2919	13.1661	12.1657	11.2741	10.4773	9.7632	9.1216	8.5436	8.0216	7.1196	6.3729	6.0472	5.7487	5.2223	4.7746	4.0591	3.5177	3.0971
18	16.3983	14.9920	13.7535	12.6593	11.6896	10.8276	10.0591	9.3719	8.7556	8.2014	7.2497	6.4674	6.1280	5.8178	5.2732	4.8122	4.0799	3.5294	3.1039
19	17.2260	15.6785	14.3238	13.1339	12.0853	11.1581	10.3356	9.6036	8.9501	8.3649	7.3658	6.5504	6.1982	5.8775	5.3162	4.8435	4.0967	3.5386	3.1090
20	18.0456	16.3514	14.8775	13.5903	12.4622	11.4699	10.5940	9.8181	9.1285	8.5136	7.4694	6.6231	6.2593	5.9288	5.3527	4.8696	4.1103	3.5458	3.1129
25	22.0232	19.5235	17.4131	15.6221	14.0939	12.7834	11.6536	10.6748	9.8226	9.0770	7.8431	6.8729	6.4641	6.0971	5.4669	4.9476	4.1474	3.5640	3.1220
30	25.8077	22.3965	19.6004	17.2920	15.3725	13.7648	12.4090	11.2578	10.2737	9.4269	8.0552	7.0027	6.5660	6.1772	5.5168	4.9789	4.1601	3.5693	3.1242
40	32.8347	27.3555	23.1148	19.7928	17.1591	15.0463	13.3317	11.9246	10.7574	9.7791	8.2438	7.1050	6.6418	6.2335	5.5482	4.9966	4.1659	3.5712	3.1250
50	39.1961	31.4236	25.7298	21.4822	18.2559	15.7619	13.8007	12.2335	10.9617	9.9148	8.3045	7.1327	6.6605	6.2463	5.5541	4.9995	4.1666	3.5714	3.1250
60	44.9550	34.7609	27.6756	22.6235	18.9293	16.1614	14.0392	12.3766	11.0480	9.9672	8.3240	7.1401	6.6651	6.2402	5.5653	4.9999	4.1667	3.5714	3.1250

$$= [\,A\,]\left[\frac{1}{i} - \frac{1}{(i)(1 + i)^N}\right]$$

$$= [\,A\,]\,[PVIF_a(i\%,N)] = [\,A\,]\left[\sum_{t=1}^{N} PVIF(i\%,t)\right]$$

Present value interest factors for a regular annuity, for various values of i and N, have been precalculated and are contained in Table 6.4.

EXAMPLE. X has agreed to make a three-year loan at an annual interest rate of 8 percent. If the annual repayments are $1,746.15, then what is the original amount of this loan?

$$PV_a = [\$1,746.15]\left[\frac{1}{0.08} - \frac{1}{(0.08)(1.08)^3}\right]$$

$$= [\$1,746.15][PVIF_a(8\%,3)]$$

$$= [\$1,746.15][2.5771] = \$4,500.00$$

Relationship Between Future Value and Present Value. There is a relationship between the future value and the present value of an annuity, although it is not an inverse relationship. In the prior time-line examples, where $100 was deposited each year for five years at an annual interest rate of 5 percent, the values found were:

$$FV_a = \$552.56$$
$$PV_a = \$432.94$$

Time value of money calculations convert a value at one point in time to its equivalent value at another point in time. Thus these values are equivalent:

$$PV_a = [\,FV_a\,][PVIF(i\%,N)]$$
$$= [\$552.56][PVIF(5\%,5)]$$
$$= [\$552.56][0.7835] = \$432.94$$
$$FV_a = [\,PV_a\,][FVIF(i\%,N)]$$
$$= [\$432.94][FVIF(5\%,5)]$$
$$= [\$432.94][1.2763] = \$552.56$$

Another way of looking at PV_a is that it is the amount one would have to deposit today to create an annuity. Given this example, if $432.94 is deposited at an annual interest rate of 5 percent, then $100 can be withdrawn each year for five years. After the fifth withdrawal, the balance should be zero:

Year	Beginning Balance	Interest	Withdrawal	Ending Balance
1	$432.94	$21.65	$100.00	$354.59
2	354.59	17.73	100.00	272.32
3	272.32	13.62	100.00	185.94
4	185.94	9.30	100.00	95.24
5	95.24	4.76	100.00	0.00

This ability to convert a value at one time to its equivalent value at another time is the basis and primary function of time value of money calculations.

Annuity Due

The only difference between a regular annuity and an annuity due is that the cash flows associated with an annuity due occur at the beginning of the period. An example is life insurance, where the first payment is made when the contract is signed.

Future Value: Time-Line Analysis. The calculation of future value for an annuity due can be demonstrated using the same values already applied to a regular annuity: $100 is deposited each year for five years at an annual interest rate of 5 percent. Now, however, the payments occur at the beginning of each period. The future value is then equal to:

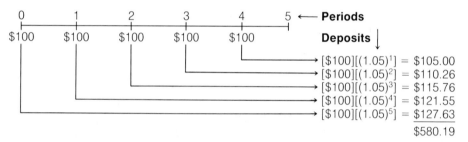

The future value of this five-period annuity due is $580.19. Since deposits are now made at the beginning of the period, the last deposit is compounded forward one period.

Future Value: Calculations. The future value of an annuity due may be calculated as follows:

$$FV_{ad} = [\,A\,][(1 + i)^1] + [\,A\,][(1 + i)^2] + \cdots + [\,A\,][(1 + i)^N]$$

$$= [\,A\,][(1 + i)^1 + (1 + i)^2 + \cdots + (1 + i)^N]$$

$$= [\,A\,]\left[\sum_{t=1}^{N} (1 + i)^t\right]$$

$$= [\,A\,]\left[\sum_{t=1}^{N} FVIF(i\%, t)\right]$$

$$= [\,A\,][FVIF_{ad}(i\%, N)]$$

The tables do not contain future value interest factors for annuities due. However, there is a direct relationship between the interest factor for a regular annuity and the interest factor for an annuity due.

If a final payment had been made in period N, then an N-period annuity due could be evaluated as an $(N + 1)$-period regular annuity. The compounding factor associated with this last payment is $(1 + i)^0 = 1.0$. Therefore, the interest factor associated with an N-period annuity due is equal to the interest factor for an $(N + 1)$-period regular annuity minus 1.0:

$$FV_{ad} = [A] \left[\sum_{t=0}^{N} (1 + i)^t - 1.0 \right]$$

$$= [A] \left[\frac{(1 + i)^{N+1}}{i} - \frac{1}{i} - 1.0 \right]$$

$$= [A][FVIF_a(i\%, N + 1) - 1.0]$$

EXAMPLE. The annual premium on X's insurance policy is \$445. If the insurance company invests the premiums to earn 7 percent after all fees to the company, then what is the cash value of this policy after 29 years?

$$FV_{ad} = [\$445] \left[\frac{(1.07)^{30}}{0.07} - \frac{1}{0.07} - 1.0 \right]$$

$$= [\$445] [FVIF_a(7\%, 30) - 1.0]$$

$$= [\$445][93.460] = \$41{,}589.70$$

The future value of this 29-year annuity due is \$41,589.70. Its value is calculated by first finding the interest factor for a 30-year regular annuity and then subtracting 1.0 from this value. This new interest factor is then multiplied by the annuity payment.

Present Value: Time-Line Analysis. To demonstrate the calculation of present value for an annuity due, use the same example. Deposits of \$100 are made each year for five years at an annual interest rate of 5 percent. Each deposit is made at the beginning of the period. The present value of this annuity due is then equal to:

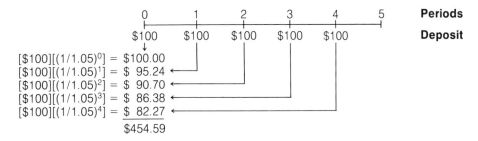

The present value of this five-period annuity due is \$454.59. If a payment had not been made at time period 0, then this would have been equal to a four-period regular annuity.

Present Value: Calculations. The present value of an annuity due may be calculated as follows:

$$PV_{ad} = [\,A\,][(1/1 + i)^0] + [\,A\,][(1/1 + i)^1] + \cdots + [\,A\,][(1/1 + i)^{N-1}]$$

$$= [\,A\,][(1/1 + i)^0 + (1/1 + i)^1 + \cdots + (1/1 + i)^{N-1}]$$

$$= [\,A\,]\left[\sum_{t=0}^{N-1} (1/1 + i)^t\right]$$

$$= [\,A\,]\left[\sum_{t=0}^{N-1} PVIF(i\%,t)\right]$$

$$= [\,A\,][PVIF_{ad}(i\%,N)]$$

The tables do not contain present value interest factors for annuities due. However, once again there is a direct relationship between the interest factor for a regular annuity and the interest factor for an annuity due.

If an initial payment had not been made at time period 0 then an N-period annuity due could be evaluated as an $(N - 1)$-period regular annuity. The discounting factor associated with this initial payment is $(1/1 + i)^0 = 1.0$. Therefore, the interest factor associated with an N-period annuity due is equal to the interest factor for an $(N - 1)$-period regular annuity plus 1.0:

$$PV_{ad} = [\,A\,]\left[\sum_{t=1}^{N-1} \left(\frac{1}{1 + i}\right)^t + 1.0\right]$$

$$= [\,A\,]\left[\frac{1}{i} - \frac{1}{(i)(1 + i)^{N-1}} + 1.0\right]$$

$$= [\,A\,][PVIF_a(i\%,N - 1) + 1.0]$$

EXAMPLE. X has an opportunity to purchase a whole life insurance policy. X may either make annual payments of \$375, starting today, for the next 19 years (20 payments) or make a single payment today. If the applicable annual interest rate is 6 percent, then what is the value of the single payment that would be required today?

$$PV_{ad} = [\$375]\left[\frac{1}{0.06} - \frac{1}{(0.06)(1.06)^{19}} + 1.0\right]$$

$$= [\$375][PVIF_a(6\%,19) + 1.0]$$

$$= [\$375][12.1581] = \$4,559.29$$

The present value of this 20-payment (years 0–19) annuity due is \$4,559.29. Its value is calculated by first finding the interest factor for a 19-year regular annuity and then adding 1.0 to this value. This new interest factor is then multiplied by the annuity payment.

Perpetuities

A perpetuity is an annuity that has an infinite life or time to maturity. One example of a perpetuity is the British Consol Bond, so called because it consolidated the debt incurred during the Napoleonic Wars. These bonds will never mature, but promise to pay a constant amount in interest each year. Another example of a perpetuity is preferred stock which has an infinite maturity, but (for most types of issues) has a fixed payment each year (i.e., the dividend).

Calculations. The future value of a perpetuity is a trivial solution. Since it will provide an infinite number of cash payments with an infinite total dollar value, its compounded value must also be infinite. The same is not true for the present value of a perpetuity. The present value of a perpetuity may be written as:

$$PV_p = [\,A\,]\left[\sum_{t=1}^{\infty}\left(\frac{1}{1+i}\right)^t\right]$$

Because of the infinite life of the annuity and because the cash flow is the same in each period, this equation reduces to a simpler form:

$$PV_p = [\,A\,][(1/i)]$$

EXAMPLE. The preferred stock of XYZ Corporation pays an annual preferred dividend of $10 per share. If X requires a 16 percent annual rate of return, then how much should X pay for this preferred stock?

$$PV_p = [\$10][1/0.16)] = \$62.50$$

If X pays $62.50 for this preferred stock, then he would receive a 16 percent rate of return by receiving a $10 dividend each year:

$$\$10 = [\$62.50][0.16]$$

Annuities as Differences of Perpetuities. The present value and future value interest factors for regular annuities may be calculated as:

$$FVIF_a(\,i\%,N\,) = \left[\frac{(1+i)^N}{i} - \frac{1}{i}\right]$$

$$PVIF_a(i\%,N) = \left[\frac{1}{i} - \frac{1}{(i)(1+i)^N}\right]$$

These equations may be obtained by considering an annuity as the difference between two perpetuities.

The cash flows associated with an N-period annuity are equal to the cash flows associated with a perpetuity starting at time period 0, minus the cash flows associated with a perpetuity starting at period N. This may be represented by the following time-line analysis:

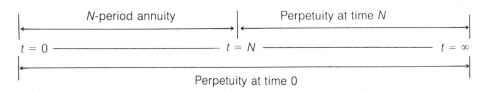

The future value of an N-period annuity — its value at time period N — requires that both of the perpetuities also be evaluated at time period N. The value of the perpetuity starting at time period 0 evaluated at period 0 is:

$$PV_p = [\ A\ ][(1/i)]$$

To transform this value into its equivalent value at time N, it must be compounded forward N periods:

$$FV_p = [\ A\ ][(1/i)][(1 + i)^N]$$

The value of the perpetuity starting at time period N evaluated at time period N is:

$$PV_p = [\ A\ ][(1/i)]$$

The future value of the N-period annuity is the difference between these two perpetuities:

$$FV_a = [\ A\ ][(1/i)][(1 + i)^N] - [\ A\ ][(1/i)]$$

$$= [\ A\ ]\left[\frac{(1 + i)^N}{i} - \frac{1}{i}\right]$$

The present value of an N-period annuity — its value at time period 0 — also requires that both of the perpetuities be evaluated as of time period 0. The value of the perpetuity starting at time period 0 evaluated at period 0 is:

$$PV_p = [\ A\ ]\left[\left(\frac{1}{i}\right)\right]$$

The value of the perpetuity starting at time period N evaluated at time N is:

$$PV_p = [\ A\ ]\left[\left(\frac{1}{i}\right)\right]$$

To transform this value into its equivalent value at time 0, it must be discounted back N periods:

$$PV_p = [\ A\ ]\left[\left(\frac{1}{i}\right)\right]\left[\left(\frac{1}{1 + i}\right)^N\right]$$

The present value of this N-period annuity is the difference between the two perpetuities:

$$PV_a = [\ A\ ]\left[\left(\frac{1}{i}\right)\right] - [\ A\ ]\left[\left(\frac{1}{i}\right)\right]\left[\left(\frac{1}{1 + i}\right)^N\right]$$

$$= [\ A\ ]\left[\frac{1}{i} - \frac{1}{(i)(1 + i)^N}\right]$$

Nonannual Periods

The previous examples all used annual compounding and discounting periods. However, the general equations that have been presented are also applicable to nonannual periods. If there are M periods per year, then the procedure is to divide the annual interest rate by M and to multiply the number of years by M.

Future Value: Calculations. The future value of a single sum with M compounding periods per year is equal to:

$$FV = [PV]\left[\left(1 + \frac{i}{M}\right)^{N*M}\right]$$

$$= [PV]\left[FVIF\left(\frac{i}{M}\%, N*M\right)\right]$$

EXAMPLE 1. X deposits $100 for a period of five years at an annual interest rate of 12 percent. What is the future value if compounding occurs semiannually?

$$FV = [\$100]\left[\left(1 + \frac{0.12}{2}\right)^{5*2}\right]$$

$$= [\$100][FVIF(6\%, 10)]$$

$$= [\$100][1.7908] = 179.08$$

EXAMPLE 2. Y deposits $500 for a period of one year at an annual interest rate of 6 percent. If compounding occurs daily, then what is the value of this amount at the end of one year?

$$FV = [\$500]\left[\left(1 + \frac{0.06}{365}\right)^{1*365}\right]$$

$$= [\$500][1.0618313] = \$530.92$$

Interest in this example was calculated using a 365-day year (366 days during a leap year). This is referred to as exact interest and is the basis that most banks use to calculate daily interest. However, there are other securities, such as commercial paper, Treasury bills (T-bills), and repurchase agreements (RPs), where quotations are based on a 360-day commercial year. Regardless of whether a 360-day or a 365-day year is used, the general procedure remains the same.

A special case of nonannual periods is continuous compounding. The future value of a single sum under continuous compounding is equal to:

$$FV = [PV][e^{(i)(N)}]$$

where e has an approximate value of 2.7182818.

EXAMPLE 3. Z deposits $1,000 for a period of 10 years at an annual interest rate of 5 percent, but interest is compounded continuously. What is the future value of this amount at the end of 10 years?

$$FV = [\$1,000][e^{(0.05)(10)}]$$

$$= [\$1,000][1.64872] = \$1,648.72$$

Present Value: Calculations. The present value of a single sum with M compounding (discounting) periods per year is equal to:

$$PV = [FV]\left[1 \Big/ \left(1 + \frac{i}{M}\right)^{N*M}\right]$$

$$= [FV]\left[PVIF\left(\frac{i}{M}\%, N*M\right)\right]$$

EXAMPLE 1. If the annual interest rate is 12 percent, but interest is compounded on a semiannual basis, what is the value of $100 to be received at the end of five years?

$$PV = [\$100] \left[1 \Big/ \left(1 + \frac{0.12}{2} \right)^{5*2} \right]$$

$$= [\$100][PVIF(6\%,10)]$$

$$= [\$100][0.5584] = \$55.84$$

EXAMPLE 2. If the annual interest rate is 8 percent, but interest is compounded quarterly, then what is the present value of $5,000 to be received in 10 years?

$$PV = [\$5,000] \left[1 \Big/ \left(1 + \frac{0.08}{4} \right)^{10*4} \right]$$

$$= [\$5,000][PVIF(2\%,40)]$$

$$= [\$5,000][0.4529] = \$2,264.50$$

Continuous discounting is once again a special case. The present value of a single sum under continuous discounting is equal to:

$$PV = [\ FV\ ][(1/e^{(i)(N)})]$$

$$= [\ FV\ ][e^{-(i)(N)}]$$

EXAMPLE 3. If the annual interest rate is 5 percent, but discounting is on a continuous basis, then what is the present value of $1,000 to be received at the end of 10 years?

$$PV = [\$1,000][(1/e^{(0.05)(10)})]$$

$$= [\$1,000][e^{-(0.05)(10)}]$$

$$= [\$1,000][0.6065307] = \$606.53$$

Annuities: Calculations. The interest factors associated with annuities are equal to the sum of the interest factors associated with the individual cash flows comprising the annuities. Therefore the same rules that were applied to compounding and discounting individual cash flows, with nonannual periods, also apply to annuities.

$$FV_a = [\ A\ ] \left[FVIF_a \left(\frac{i}{M}\%, N*M \right) \right]$$

$$PV_a = [\ A\ ] \left[PVIF_a \left(\frac{i}{M}\%, N*M \right) \right]$$

The timing of the annuity payment each period must be considered. It is possible to calculate the present value and the future value of an annuity where the payment periods do not equal the compounding periods. For simplicity, assume that the payment periods match the compounding periods.

EXAMPLE. The annual interest rate is 16 percent and an annuity consists of a \$25 cash flow to be received every three months (quarterly) for five years. This means that X receives, or pays out, 20 quarterly cash flows of \$25 each. The future value and present value are calculated as:

$$FV_a = [\$25]\left[\sum_{t=0}^{19}\left(1 + \frac{0.16}{4}\right)^t\right]$$

$$= [\$25]\left[\frac{(1 + 0.16/4)^{5*4}}{0.16/4} - \frac{1}{0.16/4}\right]$$

$$= [\$25][FVIF_a(4\%,20)]$$

$$= [\$25][29.778] = \$744.45$$

$$PV_a = [\$25]\left\{\sum_{t=1}^{20}\left[1\Big/\left(1 + \frac{0.16}{4}\right)^t\right]\right\}$$

$$= [\$25]\left[\frac{1}{0.16/4} - \frac{1}{(0.16/4)(1 + 0.16/4)^{5*4}}\right]$$

$$= [\$25][PVIF_a(4\%,20)]$$

$$= [\$25][13.5903] = \$339.76$$

Continuous compounding and discounting are once again a special case. For annuities, however, the special case either assumes a stream of receipts received continuously over time or requires the use of integral calculas. Therefore, this special case is not discussed here.

Annual and Effective Rates. For nonannual periods, it is also possible to use something that is referred to as the effective annual rate. For instance, if the stated annual interest rate is 5 percent, but compounding is on a semiannual basis, then interest is earned at the rate of 2.5 percent per six-month period. Over one year, the effective annual interest rate is:

$$[1.025][1.025] - 1.0 = 0.050625$$

This effective annual interest rate is greater than the stated annual interest rate. This is because interest on interest is being earned at a faster rate. Once this effective annual interest rate has been found, it may be used to compound or discount a cash flow on an annual basis.

EXAMPLE. Find the present value of \$100 to be received in five years if the stated annual interest rate is 8 percent, but discounting is performed on a quarterly basis.

Step 1. The effective annual interest rate is equal to:

$$\left[\left(1 + \frac{0.08}{4}\right)^4\right] - 1.0 = 0.0824322$$

Step 2. The present value, using the effective annual interest rate is:

$$PV = [\$100][1/1.0824322^5]$$

$$[\$100][0.6729713] = \$67.30$$

This is the same value that would be found using a quarterly rate of 2 percent:

$$PV = [\$100] \left[\left(1/1 + \frac{0.08}{4}\right)^{5*4}\right]$$

$$= [\$100][PVIF(2\%,20)]$$

$$= [\$100][0.6730] = \$67.30$$

It is necessary to know whether a quoted annual rate is a stated annual rate that implicitly assumes nonannual periods or an effective annual rate that already incorporates the nonannual periods. Usually the answer is found by the context in which it is used. For instance, yields on corporate bonds are a stated annual rate and one-half of the stated rate applies to each six-month period. On the other hand, bankers are required to specify the effective annual rate, in addition to the stated rate, on loans.

Solving for N, A, or i, and Linear Interpolation

The equations that have been developed for the time value of money calculations imply that, given all other variables, it should be possible to solve for the number of periods, N, the value of the annuity payment, A, or the interest rate i.

Solving for N. For simple cash flows, N is an easy variable to solve for, especially if one has access to a financial calculator. The solution procedure is demonstrated by the following example:

EXAMPLE. At an annual interest rate of 6 percent, how long will it take for $100 to double in value?

METHOD 1

This problem may be set up as either a future value or a present value problem. The general form is:

$$\$200 = [\$100][FVIF(6\%,N)]$$

or

$$\$100 = [\$200][PVIF(6\%,N)]$$

If a financial calculator is used, the following values are supplied:

Future value = $200

Present value = $100

Interest rate =   6%

Solving for N gives a value of 11.895661. This solution may be verified by the following calculations:

$$FV = [\$100][(1.06)^{11.895661}] \quad = \$200$$

$$PV = [\$200][(1/1.06)^{11.895661}] = \$100$$

Method 2

This problem may also be solved using interest factor tables and linear interpolation to arrive at an approximation for N. Here present value interest factors are used.

$$\$100 = [\$200][PVIF(6\%,N)]$$
$$=> PVIF(6\%,N)] = [\$100/\$200] = 0.50$$

According to Table 6.2, when the interest rate is 6 percent, the interest factor takes on a value of 0.50 somewhere between $N = 11$ ($IF = 0.5268$) and $N = 12$ ($IF = 0.4970$). Now, imagine the following set of lines:

$N = 11$	$N = ?$	$N = 12$
$IF = 0.5268$	$IF = 0.50$	$IF = 0.4970$

These two lines are exactly the same length. The top line is labeled in units of discounting periods, while the bottom line is labeled in units of interest factor values. The length of the top line is one period, whereas the length of the bottom line is 0.0298 interest factor units.

Since the two lines are exactly the same length, the length of the top line from $N = 11$ to $N = ?$ is equivalent to the length of the bottom line from $IF = 0.5268$ to IF $= 0.50$, or 0.0268 interest factor units. The portion of the bottom line represented by 0.0268 interest factor units is:

$$[0.0268/0.0298] = 0.8993$$

or 89.93 percent of its length. Therefore, the distance from $N = 11$ to $N = ?$ must be 89.93 percent of the length of the top line. Since the total length of the top line is 1 period, the distance from $N = 11$ to $N = ?$ must be equal to:

$$[1 \text{ period}][0.8993] = 0.8993 \text{ periods}$$

This implies that $N = ?$ is equal to:

$$11 + 0.8993 = 11.8993 \text{ periods}$$

This compares to the exact answer of 11.895661 periods. Some difference between the two is expected, since interpolation attempts to represent a complex polynomial relationship as a linear function.

The general procedure for interpolation may be expressed as follows:

$$N = N_1 + \left[\frac{FVIF(i\%,N_1) - FVIF(i\%,N)}{FVIF(i\%,N_1) - FVIF(i\%,N_2)}\right] [N_2 - N_1]$$

Using the values from the prior example results in:

$$N = 11 + \left[\frac{0.5268 - 0.5000}{0.5268 - 0.4970}\right] [12 - 11] = 11.8993 \text{ periods}$$

Solving for A. The following example outlines the procedures to calculate the amount of a periodic annuity payment.

EXAMPLE. X's child will enter college in five years and X would like to have $10,000 saved by that time. The annual interest rate on X's savings is 12 percent, but interest is compounded monthly. How much should X deposit each month, starting one month from today, so he will have $10,000 at the end of five years?

The $10,000 is now a future value and the annuity payment may be calculated as:

$10,000 = [A][FVIF_a(1\%,60)]$
$= [A][81.669]$
$A = [$10,000/81.669] = 122.45

Solving for i. For simple cash flows (single sums or annuities), i may be calculated in a manner similar to the way the value of N was calculated. Either a financial calculator or interpolation of interest factor tables may be used. In addition, the interest rate associated with the future value and present value of single sums may be calculated using any calculator that has a power function key (y^x).

EXAMPLE 1. What is the annual interest rate that will allow $35 to grow to $100 over a period of 10 years?

METHOD 1

This problem may be solved as either a present value or a future value problem. Using future value interest factors, this problem is represented by the following equation:

$$100 = [$35][(1 + i)^{10}]$$
$$=> (1 + i)^{10} = [$100/$35] = 2.8571429$$

Taking the tenth root of both sides of this equation yields the following:

$(1 + i) = [(2.857149)^{1/10}] = 1.1106909$
$=> i = 1.1106909 - 1.0 = 0.1106909$

METHOD 2

Linear interpolation may be used to determine an approximation for i. Table 6.1 shows that a future value interest factor of 2.8571 lies between an interest rate of 10 percent ($IF = 2.5937$) and an interest rate of 12 percent ($IF = 3.1058$). The interpolated value then is equal to:

$$i = 0.10 + \left[\frac{2.5937 - 2.8571}{2.5937 - 3.1058} \right] [0.12 - 0.10] = 0.110287053$$

EXAMPLE 2. A regular annuity pays $25 every three months for five years. If the present value of this annuity is $347.41, then what is the stated annual interest rate and what is the effective annual interest rate?

Step 1. Letting i' equal the interest rate per quarter, the problem may be represented by the following equation:

$$\$347.41 = [\$25][PVIF_a(i',20)]$$
$$=> PVIF_a(i',20) = [\$347.41/\$25] = 13.8964$$

In Table 6.4 an interest factor of 13.8964 is found to lie between an interest rate of 3 percent ($IF = 14.8775$) and an interest rate of 4 percent ($IF = 13.5903$). The interpolated value then is equal to:

$$i' = 0.03 + \left[\frac{14.8775 - 13.8964}{14.8775 - 13.5903}\right][0.04 - 0.03] = 0.0376$$

Step 2. The interest rate 0.0376 is a quarterly interest rate. The stated annual interest rate equals:

$$i = [0.0376][4] = 0.1504$$

The effective annual interest rate is:

$$i = [(1.0376)^4] - 1.0 = 0.1591$$

Newton's Approximation Technique

It is impossible to use interest factor tables and linear interpolation to determine the interest rate when dealing with complex cash flows. As an example of a complex cash flow, consider a loan of $4,800 with repayments of $1,000 each year for five years and a $2,200 balloon payment in the sixth year. The cash flows associated with this loan may be presented as follows:

Year	Cash Flow
0	$4,800
1	−1,000
2	−1,000
3	−1,000
4	−1,000
5	−1,000
6	−$2,200

The interest rate on this loan must be such that the present value of the cash repayments in years 1–6 must be exactly equal to the amount borrowed in year 0. This also means that the present value of all cash flows, in years 0–6, when added together, must equal zero.

Calculation of the Interest Rate. If X equals $(1/1 + i)$, then the functional form for the present value of these cash flows may be written as:

$$f(X) = 0.0 = [\$4,800][X^0] - [\$1,000][X^1] - [\$1,000][X^2] - [\$1,000][X^3]$$
$$- [\$1,000][X^4] - [\$1,000][X^5] - [\$2,200][X^6]$$

The value for i that solves this equation is the interest rate on this loan. However, since the equation is a sixth-degree polynomial, it must be solved by an iterative process, which is too complex to be dealt with here. (See Chapter 13 for an evaluation of this technique.)

BANKS LOANS AND EFFECTIVE INTEREST RATES

When money is borrowed from a bank, the stated interest rate, also referred to at times as the simple or regular interest rate, may be much lower than the effective interest rate on the loan. Because of this, the Truth-in-Lending Act now requires all financial institutions to state the effective interest rate or annual percentage rate (APR) on the loan. The APR depends on the specific type of loan that is taken out.

Definition of Variables

i = stated or simple interest rate

P = principal amount borrowed

CB = percentage of the loan that must be kept on deposit as a compensating balance

APR = annual percentage rate or effective interest rate

Straight Loan

A straight loan, also called a term loan, is one where both the principal and interest are repaid at the end of the borrowing period. Interest expense is equal to the stated interest rate times the principal amount borrowed.

Calculations. The APR on a straight loan is equal to the stated rate on an annual basis. To illustrate this, assume that $1,200 is borrowed for a term of one year at a stated rate of 10 percent. The interest expense is equal to:

[$1,200][0.10] = $120

At the end of one year, the principal amount of $1,200 and interest of $120 must be repaid. The APR is then equal to:

$$APR = \frac{[P][i]}{[P]}$$

$$= \frac{[\$1,200][0.10]}{[\$1,200]}$$

$$= 0.10$$

The reason that the APR and the stated rate are the same is that the borrower has the use of the entire $1,200 for the whole year. It is the early repayment, or nonuse, of the principal borrowed that increases the APR.

Discounted Loan

In a discounted loan the interest is prepaid at the time of borrowing. The usual procedure is for the financial institution to deduct the interest expense from the proceeds that the borrower receives.

Calculations. If $1,200 is borrowed on a discounted basis for one year at a stated interest rate of 10 percent, then the amount that the borrower actually receives is equal to:

[$1,200] − [$1,200][0.10] = $1,080

This is equal to the principal amount borrowed minus the interest expense. At the end of the year, the borrower makes a total repayment (of principal) of $1,200. This is equivalent to borrowing $1,080 for one year and paying total interest of $120. The *APR* can be calculated as the interest expense divided by the amount of funds which the borrower actually has the use of:

APR = [$120/$1,080]

= 0.1111

The general formula for the effective rate on a discount basis is:

APR = [i]/[1 − i]

= [0.10/0.90]

= 0.1111

Compensating Balance

There are times when a financial institution will agree to a loan only if some percentage of the loan, called the compensating balance, is kept on deposit with the institution. If the borrower's balances are already sufficient to cover the required compensating balance, then this requirement will not affect that borrower's effective rate. However, if the borrower must keep some portion of the loan proceeds on deposit with the institution, then this will reduce the total funds available for the borrower's use, thus increasing the effective rate.

Calculations. The specific calculation of *APR* will depend on the type of loan and the actual amount of the loan required as a compensating balance.

EXAMPLE 1. A loan of $1,200 is made for a term of one year at a stated interest rate of 10 percent. The compensating balance requirement is 15 percent of the amount of the loan. What is the *APR* on this loan?

The amount that must be kept on deposit as a compensating balance is equal to:

[$1,200][0.15] = $180

This means that the borrower has the use of,

$1,200 − $180 = $1,020

for the year. At the end of the year the borrower will repay the $1,200 of principal plus $120 in interest. The effective rate is equal to:

$APR = [\$120]/[\$1,200 - \$180] = 0.1176$

The general equation for the effective rate may be written as:

$APR = [i]/[1 - CB]$
$= [0.10/0.85] = 0.1176$

EXAMPLE 2. The sum of $1,200 is borrowed on a discounted basis for one year at a stated interest rate of 10 percent. In addition, a compensating balance equal to 20 percent of the amount of the loan is required. What is the *APR*?

The amount of prepaid interest on this loan is equal to:

$[\$1,200][0.10] = \$120$

The amount of the compensating balance is equal to:

$[\$1,200][0.20] = \$240$

Therefore, the borrower has the use of

$\$1,200 - \$120 - \$240 = \$840$

for the year. At the end of the year, the borrower will repay $1,200 of principal. The effective interest rate is equal to:

$APR = [\$120]/[\$1,200 - \$120 - \$240] = 0.1429$

The general equation for the effective rate may be written as:

$APR = [i]/[1 - i - CB]$
$= [0.10/0.70]$
$= 0.1429$

Installment Loan

An installment loan is one that requires periodic payments of principal and interest during each installment period. For bank loans, the installment period is usually each month or each quarter. The installment payment is the same for each period and is therefore equivalent to an annuity.

Calculations. An approximation to the effective rate may be found as follows: If $1,200 is borrowed on a 12-month installment basis at a stated interest rate of 10 percent, then the principal owed is reduced to zero by the end of the year. Therefore, on average, the borrower has the use of

$[\$1,200 + \$0]/[2] = \$600$

for the entire year. At a stated interest rate of 10 percent, the total interest expense is still $120. An approximation to the effective rate would then be:

$[\$120/\$600] = 0.20$

The true effective rate may be found in the following manner. The total amount to be repaid over the year is $1,200 in principal and $120 in interest, or a total of $1,320. If this amount is repaid on a monthly basis, then the monthly payments are equal to:

$[\$1,320/12] = \$110$

These monthly payments consist of a principal repayment plus interest on the unpaid balance of the loan.

The effective rate can be analyzed in terms of present value concepts. The financial institution has agreed to loan the borrower $1,200 today (the present value) in return for an annuity stream of $110 each month for 12 months. The true effective interest rate is simply the discount rate that equates the present value of the $110 annuity stream with the beginning value of $1,200:

$$\$1,200 = [\$110]\left[\sum_{t=1}^{12}\left(\frac{1}{1+i}\right)^t\right]$$

$$=> i = 0.014976663$$

However, this is the interest rate per month. On an annual basis, the interest rate is:

$$APR = [(1.014976663)^{12}] - 1.0 = 0.1952883$$

Discounted Installment Loan

Like a regular discounted loan, interest on a discounted installment loan is prepaid. The principal is then repaid in equal periodic payments.

Calculations. The effective interest rate for a discounted installment loan is found in much the same manner as for a regular installment loan. If $1,200 is borrowed on a 12-month installment basis with prepaid interest at a stated rate of 10 percent, then the borrower prepays $120 in interest. This gives the borrower usable funds, initially, of $1,080. The monthly payments consist only of a repayment of principal, since interest has been prepaid. The monthly payments are equal to:

$[\$1,200/12] = \$100$

The effective interest rate is then equal to:

$$\$1,080 = [\$100]\left[\sum_{t=1}^{12}\left(\frac{1}{1+i}\right)^t\right]$$

$$=> i = 0.016593678$$

$$=> APR = [(1.016593678)^{12}] - 1.0 = 0.218341$$

Amortization Schedule

An amortization schedule specifies the principal and interest repayments for each period of an installment loan. As such, it also specifies the ending principal balance after each periodic repayment.

Calculations. It has previously been determined that a one-year, $1,200 installment loan at a stated interest rate of 10 percent has an effective monthly interest rate of 1.4976663 percent. It has also been shown that the monthly payment for this loan is $110, comprised of a principal repayment and interest on the remaining balance. To derive an amortization schedule, the following calculations must be made for each period:

Interest Payment = [Beginning Balance][0.014976663]

Principal Repayment = $110 − Interest Payment

Ending Balance = Beginning Balance − Principal Repayment

An amortization schedule for the $1,200 installment loan would look as follows:

Month	Beginning Balance	Interest Payment	Principal Payment	Ending Balance
1	$1,200.00	$ 17.97	$ 92.03	$1,107.97
2	1,107.97	16.59	93.41	1,014.56
3	1,014.56	15.19	94.81	919.75
4	919.75	13.77	96.23	823.52
5	823.52	12.33	97.67	725.85
6	725.85	10.87	99.13	626.72
7	626.72	9.39	100.61	526.11
8	526.11	7.88	102.12	423.99
9	423.99	6.35	103.65	320.24
10	320.34	4.80	105.20	215.14
11	215.14	3.22	106.78	108.36
12	i08.36	1.64	108.36	0.00
		$120.00	$1,200.00	

BOND ANALYSIS: NON-INTEREST-BEARING SECURITIES

Non-interest-bearing securities are also referred to as discounted securities. Unlike regular corporate bonds which pay periodic interest (i.e., pay a coupon), interest is earned on these bonds by their appreciation in price over time. That is, these securities originally sell for less than their maturity or face value. All other factors constant, the price approaches the face value as the time to maturity approaches zero. Note, this is not the same thing as a coupon bond that is selling at a discount.

Definition of Variables

d = discount rate as a percent of the face value
D = dollar value of the discount
F = face or maturity value of the security
P = current price of the security
Y = equivalent bond yield of the security
i_J = simple interest rate using a J-day year
P' = price per dollar of face value
t_M = time remaining until maturity
t_H = time held by the original investor

Discount Rates and Pricing

The discount rate determines the dollar value of the discount or the difference between the price and the maturity value. At times, this is also referred to as the quoted yield of the security. For most securities, such as Treasury bills and commercial paper, the discount rate is stated as a 360-day year annual rate. All subsequent calculations must take into account the actual number of days until maturity.

Calculation of the Dollar Discount. As stated previously, the discount rate is based on a 360-day year. The dollar discount will be determined by the discount rate, the face value of the security, and the number of days until maturity. The general equation for the dollar discount is:

$D = [F][d][t_M/360]$

EXAMPLE. An investor has just purchased a six-month (180-day) T-bill. The face value of this security is $10,000 and the discount rate is 9.75 percent. What is the dollar value of the discount for this security?

$D = [\$10,000][0.0975][180/360] = \$487.50$

Intuitively, this security promises to pay a discount of 9.75 percent or $975 if held for one year. Since the investor will hold this security for one-half year, he is entitled to half of the discount or $487.50.

Calculation of Price. The price of a discounted security is equal to the face value minus the dollar discount. It may be calculated by either of the following two formulas:

$P = [F] - [D]$

$$P = [F]\left[1 - \frac{(d)(t_M)}{360}\right]$$

EXAMPLE. What is the price of a 180-day, $10,000 face value T-bill if the discount rate is 9.75 percent?

METHOD 1

The dollar discount associated with this security, calculated in the previous section, is $487.50. Therefore, the price is equal to:

$P = \$10,000 - \$487.50 = \$9,512.50$

METHOD 2

The price may also be calculated as follows:

$$P = [\$10,000] \left[1 - \frac{(0.0975)(180)}{360} \right] = \$9,512.50$$

Calculation of the Discount Rate. Given the face value of the security, the time to maturity, and either the dollar discount or the price, the annual discount rate may be calculated using the following equations:

$$d = \left[\frac{D}{F}\right]\left[\frac{360}{t_M}\right]$$

$$d = \left[\frac{F - P}{F}\right]\left[\frac{360}{t_M}\right]$$

EXAMPLE. What is the annual discount rate for a 180-day T-bill with a face value of $10,000 and a current price of $9,512.50?

METHOD 1

The dollar discount is equal to:

$D = \$10,000 - \$9,512.50 = \$487.50$

This implies that the discount rate is equal to:

$d = [\$487.50/\$10,000][360/180] = 0.0975$

METHOD 2

The discount rate may also be calculated as:

$$d = \left[\frac{\$10,000 - \$9,512.50}{\$10,000}\right]\left[\frac{360}{180}\right] = 0.0975$$

Equivalent Simple Interest Rate

Since the investor pays less than the face value of the discounted security, the interest rate earned, which is based on price, must be greater than the discount rate, which is based on the face value. The usual procedure is to state this simple interest rate on the basis of a 365-day year.

Calculations. The simple interest rate is a function of the original price paid and the amount of price appreciation earned over the investment horizon. Allowing the subscripts b and s to represent the buying price and the selling price, the simple interest rate may be calculated as:

$$i_{365} = \left[\frac{P_s - P_b}{P_b}\right]\left[\frac{365}{t_H}\right]$$

If the investor holds the security until it matures, then the price appreciation will be equal to the dollar discount at time of purchase — no return is earned from changes in the general level of market interest rates. The simple interest rate may then be calculated as:

$$i_{365} = \frac{[(365)(d)]}{[360 - (d)(t_M)]}$$

EXAMPLE 1. If an investor purchases a 90-day T-bill for $9,500 and sells it in 45 days for $9,750, then what is the simple interest rate, or the rate of return, that he earns on this investment?

$$i_{365} = \left[\frac{\$9,750 - \$9,500}{\$9,500}\right]\left[\frac{365}{45}\right] = 0.21345$$

EXAMPLE 2. An investor purchases a 180-day T-bill at a price of $9,512.50. This T-bill has a face value of $10,000 and a discount rate of 9.75 percent. If the investor holds this security until it matures, then what is his simple interest rate on this investment?

METHOD 1

The simple interest rate may be calculated as:

$$i_{365} = \left[\frac{\$10,000 - \$9,512.50}{\$9,512.50}\right]\left[\frac{365}{180}\right] = 0.1039$$

METHOD 2

The simple interest rate may also be calculated as follows:

$$i_{365} = [(365)(0.0975)]/[360 - (0.0975)(180)] = 0.1039$$

Effective Return

The simple interest rate that was calculated in the previous section assumed an add-on type of interest. The distinction between add-on interest and compound interest is not really important except for the direct comparison securities with different maturities. In other words, the investor must be concerned with the actual investment horizon.

Calculations. Assume that an investor has an investment horizon of 120 days. Also assume that 120-day T-bills have a discount rate of 10 percent and

30-day T-bills have a discount rate of 10.25 percent. The equivalent simple interest rate for these two securities would be:

120-day: $i_{365} = [(365)(0.10)]/[360 - (0.10)(120)] = 0.1049$

30-day: $i_{365} = [(365)(0.1025)]/[360 - (0.1025)(30)] = 0.1048$

For the 120-day T-bill, the simple interest rate of 10.49 percent assumes that the investor could earn

$$[0.1049] \left[\frac{120}{365}\right] = 0.0345$$

every 120-days. For the 30-day security, the simple interest rate of 0.1048 assumes that the investor could earn

$$[0.1048] \left[\frac{30}{365}\right] = 0.0086$$

every 30 days.

From the simple interest rates of 10.49 percent and 10.48 percent, it might appear that the investor would be better off purchasing the 120-day security. However, assume that over the 120-day investment horizon the investor believes that he could purchase either the 120-day security at a discount rate of 10 percent or four consecutive 30-day securities each at a discount rate of 10.25 percent. In the second case, one security matures every 30 days and the proceeds are reinvested in a new 30-day security, so the investor actually earns compound interest. The effective rate of return for the 30-day T-bills is equal to:

$$30\text{-day: } i_{365} = \left[\left(1 + \left(\frac{0.1048}{365}\right)(30)\right)^{(120/30)} - 1.0\right]\left[\frac{365}{120}\right] = 0.1062$$

Because of compounding, the investor is better off, in terms of his effective return, if he is able to invest in four consecutive 30-day T-bills, each with a discount rate of 10.25 percent.

If the investment horizon were 360 days and each of these securities could be rolled over at their stated discount rate, then the effective rates of return would be:

$$120\text{-day: } i_{365} = \left[\left(1 + \left(\frac{0.1049}{365}\right)(120)\right)^{(360/120)} - 1.0\right]\left[\frac{365}{360}\right] = 0.1086$$

$$30\text{-day: } i_{365} = \left[\left(1 + \left(\frac{0.1048}{365}\right)(30)\right)^{(360/30)} - 1.0\right]\left[\frac{365}{360}\right] = 0.1099$$

Equivalent Bond Yield

The equivalent bond yield is also referred to as the coupon yield equivalent and is reported on most bond dealer's quote sheets. Its purpose is to make possible direct comparisons between the interest earned on discount securities and the yield to maturity on coupon paying bonds. Since most coupon securities pay interest on a semiannual basis, the time to maturity for the discount security is important in determining its equivalent bond yield.

Calculations: Fewer Than 182 Days. A coupon bond with fewer than 182 days to maturity will make no coupon payments until it matures. As such, it is equivalent to a discounted security. Its yield to maturity is already on an equivalent basis to the simple interest rate of the discounted security.

EXAMPLE. What is the equivalent bond yield for a 95-day T-bill with a quoted discount rate of 11.5 percent?

Since the time to maturity for this security is less than 182 days, the equivalent bond yield is equal to the simple interest rate, which is equal to:

$$Y = [(365)(0.115)]/[360 - (0.115)(95)] = 0.1202$$

Calculations: More Than 182 Days. A coupon bond with more than 182 days to maturity will make a coupon payment before it matures. To calculate the equivalent bond yield for a discounted security, it must be treated as if it too paid interest on a semiannual basis. The formula for the equivalent bond yield is:

$$Y = \frac{-\dfrac{(2)(t_M)}{365} + (2)\left[\left(\dfrac{t_M}{365}\right)^2 - \left(\dfrac{(2)(t_M)}{365} - 1.0\right)\left(1 - \dfrac{1}{P'}\right)\right]^{(1/2)}}{\left[\dfrac{(2)(t_M)}{365} - 1.0\right]}$$

EXAMPLE. A 225-day T-bill has a quoted discount rate of 12 percent. What is the equivalent bond yield on this security?

Step 1. $P' = \left[1 - \dfrac{(0.12)(225)}{360}\right] = 0.925$

Step 2. The equivalent bond yield is then equal to:

$$Y = \frac{-\dfrac{(2)(225)}{365} + (2)\left[\left(\dfrac{225}{365}\right)^2 - \left(\dfrac{(2)(225)}{365} - 1.0\right)\left(1 - \dfrac{1}{0.925}\right)\right]^{(1/2)}}{\left[\dfrac{(2)(225)}{365} - 1.0\right]}$$

$$= 0.1299$$

This says that there would be no difference, all factors held constant, between holding a 225-day T-bill with a discount rate of 12 percent, and a 225-day coupon bond with a yield to maturity of 12.99 percent.

BOND ANALYSIS: INTEREST-BEARING SECURITIES

Most corporate bonds, as well as municipals and Treasury notes and bonds, pay interest on a semiannual basis. To find the interest paid during the year, multiply the par value (face or maturity value) of the bond by the annual coupon rate. This amount is then divided by two to determine the amount of interest paid every six months. It is important to know that corporate securities use a 180-day coupon period — a commercial year of 360 days or 30 days per month, whereas government securities use an exact year of 365 days (366 days for a leap year). In addition, corporate securities are delivered five business days after the sale, whereas government securities are delivered the same day or the day after the sale. Prices for these securities are calculated as of the delivery date. Finally, if a bond is sold between coupon dates, it will have accrued interest since the last coupon date. This accrued interest must be added to the quoted price to determine the actual amount that the investor is required to pay.

Definition of Variables

C = annual coupon rate

F = face, par, or maturity value of the bond

P = quoted price for the bond

N = number of coupon periods remaining

Y = yield to maturity or the discount rate used in present value calculations

AI = amount of accrued interest

AY = approximation for the actual yield

CY = approximation for the yield to call

RY = approximation for the actual realized yield

t_{PM} = time from purchase until maturity in days

t_{PS} = time from purchase until settlement of maturity in days

t_H = time held by the original investor since the last coupon date

t_C = time remaining until call in years

t_M = time remaining until maturity in years

t_{IH} = investor's time horizon

t_{CD} = actual number of days between coupon periods

PV = present value of future cash flows

$PVIF(Y\%,N)$ = present value interest factor for a single sum at a yield of Y percent for N periods

$PVIF_a(Y\%,N)$ = present value interest factor for an annuity at a yield of Y percent for N periods

Accrued Interest

When a bond is sold between coupon dates, the price actually paid by an investor is equal to the present value of all future cash flows to be received. This value is greater than the quoted price by the amount of accrued interest, where the accrued interest is equal to that portion of the next coupon to be received that is owed to the original owner of the bond. The actual calculation of accrued interest depends on whether the security is a corporate security or a government security.

Calculations: Corporate Securities. Accrued interest on corporate securities is calculated using a 180-day coupon period. All months within the coupon period are assumed to have 30 days. The accrued interest may be calculated as follows:

$$AI = [F]\left[\frac{C}{2}\right]\left[\frac{t_H}{180}\right]$$

EXAMPLE. Assume that a 9 percent coupon bond with a face value of $1,000 has just been purchased. Interest on this bond is paid semiannually, and it has been 45 days since the last coupon payment. What is the accrued interest on this bond?

$$AI = [\$1,000]\left[\frac{0.09}{2}\right]\left[\frac{45}{180}\right] = \$11.25$$

This amount is added to the bond's quoted price to determine the amount actually paid by the purchaser.

Calculations: Government Securities. Unlike corporate securities, government securities use the actual number of days within the coupon period to determine the amount of accrued interest. This period may range from 181 days to 184 days. The accrued interest may be calculated as follows:

$$AI = [F]\left[\frac{C}{2}\right]\left[\frac{t_H}{t_{CD}}\right]$$

EXAMPLE. A Treasury bond with a face value of $100,000 is issued with a coupon rate of 8.75 percent. Coupon payment dates for this bond are November 15 and May 15. If this bond is purchased on January 5, what is the value of accrued interest?

There are 181 days between November 15 and May 15, and 184 days between May 15 and November 15. If the date of sale is included, then there are 51 days between November 15 and January 5. The amount of accrued interest may be calculated as:

$$AI = [\$100,000]\left[\frac{0.0875}{2}\right]\left[\frac{51}{181}\right] = \$1,232.73$$

Yield to Maturity

The yield to maturity is the discount rate that is used to determine the present value of all future cash flows to be received. The yield is reported on an annual basis but is an add-on interest rate. That is, one-half of the reported yield is the correct rate to use per six-month period for coupon bonds with semiannual payments of interest.

Calculation of Yield. For interest-bearing securities, the calculation of yield to maturity is the same as finding the internal rate of return (discount rate) for a complex cash flow. For instance, assume that a five-year, 9 percent coupon bond is purchased for $961.39. If this bond pays interest on a semiannual basis, then what is its annual yield?

METHOD 1

A 9 percent coupon rate implies that this bond will pay

[$1,000][0.09/2] = $45

every six months for five years (10 six-month periods). In addition it will pay a maturity value of $1,000. The pricing equation for this bond is then equal to:

$$\$961.39 = [\$45]\left[\sum_{t=1}^{10}\left(\frac{1}{1 + \dfrac{Y}{2}}\right)^t\right] + [\$1,000]\left[\left(\frac{1}{1 + \dfrac{Y}{2}}\right)^{10}\right]$$

$$= [\$45]\left[PVIF_a\left(\frac{Y}{2}\%,10\right)\right] + [\$1,000]\left[PVIF\left(\frac{Y}{2}\%,10\right)\right]$$

This equation may be solved for Y using either a financial calculator or an iterative solution process such as Newton's Approximation Technique.

METHOD 2

The yield to maturity for this bond may also be solved using bond tables. (A portion of a bond table is presented in Table 6.5.) The first step in using bond tables is to refer to that portion of the table that lists yields for the particular coupon rate of interest; in this problem that would be the 9 percent coupon table. The next step is to convert the current price of the bond to its percentage of par value — this is how bond prices are reported in the financial press. In this example the price would be reported as 96.14. Scan across the columns until reaching a time to maturity of five years, then scan down the rows until the price closest to 96.14 is found. This corresponds to a yield of 10 percent.

Approximation of Yield. The yield to maturity is the solution to a complex polynomial function. However, there are several formulas used by the industry which are quite simple and provide a close approximation to the true yield. For instance, if an investor plans to hold a bond until it matures, than an approximation for the true yield may be calculated as:

$$AY = \frac{[(F)(C) + (P_M - P_P)/(t_M)]}{[(P_M + P_P)/(2)]}$$

where the subscripts M and P refer to the maturity price and purchase price of the security, respectively.

EXAMPLE 1. A 9 percent coupon bond has five years to maturity. If an investor paid $961.39 for this bond and it will mature for $1,000, then what is the approximate yield to maturity for this bond?

$$AY = [(\$1,000)(0.09) + (\$1,000 - \$961.39)/(5)]/[(\$1,000 + \$961.39)/(2)]$$

$$= 0.0996457$$

This result is very close to the true yield of 10 percent.

Today, many bonds issued by corporations are callable. This means that the corporation may force the early retirement of the bonds. The usual proce-

TABLE 6.5   Yield to Maturity

Yield	1 yr	2 yr	3 yr	4 yr	5 yr	6 yr	7 yr	8 yr	9 yr	10 yr
7.00	101.90	103.67	105.33	106.87	108.32	109.66	110.92	112.09	113.19	114.21
7.25	101.66	103.20	104.64	105.98	107.23	108.39	109.48	110.48	111.42	112.30
7.50	101.42	102.74	103.96	105.10	106.16	107.14	108.05	108.90	109.69	110.42
7.75	101.18	102.28	103.29	104.23	105.10	105.91	106.66	107.35	107.99	108.59
8.00	100.94	101.81	102.62	103.37	104.06	104.69	105.28	105.83	106.33	106.80
8.25	100.71	101.36	101.96	102.51	103.02	103.49	103.93	104.33	104.70	105.04
8.50	100.47	100.90	101.30	101.67	102.00	102.31	102.60	102.86	103.10	103.32
8.75	100.23	100.45	100.65	100.83	101.00	101.15	101.29	101.42	101.54	101.64
9.00	100.00	100.00	100.00	100.00	100.00	100.00	100.00	100.00	100.00	100.00
9.25	99.77	99.55	99.36	99.18	99.02	98.87	98.73	98.61	98.50	98.39
9.50	99.53	99.11	98.72	98.37	98.05	97.75	97.49	97.24	97.02	96.82
9.75	99.30	98.67	98.09	97.56	97.09	96.65	96.26	95.90	95.57	95.28
10.00	99.07	98.23	97.46	96.77	96.14	95.57	95.05	94.58	94.16	93.77
10.25	98.84	97.79	96.84	95.98	95.20	94.50	93.86	93.29	92.76	92.29
10.50	98.61	97.36	96.22	95.20	94.28	93.45	92.69	92.01	91.40	90.85
10.75	98.38	96.92	95.61	94.43	93.36	92.41	91.54	90.77	90.06	89.43
11.00	98.15	96.49	95.00	93.67	92.46	91.38	90.41	89.54	88.75	88.05
11.25	97.93	96.07	94.40	92.91	91.57	90.37	89.30	88.33	87.47	86.69
11.50	97.70	95.64	93.80	92.16	90.69	89.38	88.20	87.15	86.21	85.37
11.75	97.47	95.22	93.21	91.42	89.82	88.39	87.12	85.98	84.97	84.07
12.00	97.25	94.80	92.62	90.69	88.96	87.42	86.06	84.84	83.76	82.80
12.25	97.03	94.39	92.04	89.96	88.11	86.47	85.01	83.72	82.57	81.55
12.50	96.80	93.97	91.46	89.24	87.27	85.53	83.98	82.61	81.40	80.33
12.75	96.58	93.56	90.89	88.53	86.44	84.60	82.97	81.53	80.26	79.13

dure is to defer the first call date for a period of time after the initial issue of the bond (e.g., five years). After this period, the bonds may be called by the corporation. If the bond is called, then the investor will receive the bond's maturity value plus a call premium — usually a maximum of one year's interest. However, the bondholder then forgoes the right to any other coupons on the bond.

If the bond is selling for more than its maturity value plus one year's interest, then there is a very good chance that the bond will be called at the first call date. The yield to call will usually be less than the corresponding yield to maturity. If it is, the financial press will usually report the yield to call as the bond's yield. An approximation for the yield to call may be calculated as:

$$CY = [(F)(C) + (P_C - P_P)/(t_C)]/[(P_C + P_P)/(2)]$$

where the subscripts C and P refer to the call price and the purchase price, respectively.

EXAMPLE 2. A 9 percent coupon bond is purchased for $1,213.55. The time to maturity for this bond is 20 years, but it is callable in three years at a call price of $1,090. What are the approximate yields to maturity and to call?

$$AY = \frac{[(\$1,000)(0.09) + (\$1,000 - \$1,213.55)/(20)]}{[(\$1,000 + \$1,213.55)/(2)]}$$

$$= 0.0717$$

$$CY = \frac{[(\$1,000)(0.09) + (\$1,090 - \$1,213.55)/(3)]}{[(\$1,090 + \$1,213.55)/(2)]}$$

$$= 0.0424$$

Finally, an investor who sells a bond before maturity may be interested in the actual realized yield on this bond. An approximation for this realized yield may be calculated as:

$$RY = \frac{[(F)(C) + (P_S - P_P)/(t_{IH})]}{[(P_S + P_P)/(2)]}$$

EXAMPLE 3. A 9 percent coupon bond is purchased for $865. It is sold for $950 after being held for four years. What is the approximate realized yield for this bond?

$$RY = [(\$1,000)(0.09) + (\$950 - \$865)/(4)]/[(\$950 + \$865)/(2)]$$

$$= 0.1226$$

Government Securities During the Final Coupon Period. The yield on government securities during the final coupon period may be calculated as:

$$Y^* = \left[\frac{\left(1 + \dfrac{C}{2}\right)}{(P' + AI') - 1.0} \right] \left[\frac{(2)(t_{CD})}{(t_{PM})} \right]$$

This is the value that will be quoted as the bond's yield, but it is only an approximation for the true yield. To obtain the true yield, two corrections may have to be made:

1. Since $(2)(t_{CD})$ will never be exactly equal to 365 days, the approximate yield must be adjusted by the factor $[(365)/(2)(t_{CD})]$.

2. It is possible that the bond will not mature on a business day (this is true for most securities). Therefore, the time from purchase to settlement will not be equal to the time from purchase to maturity. If this is the case, then the approximate yield must be adjusted by the factor $[t_{PM}/t_{PS}]$.

This implies that the true yield is equal to:

$$Y = [\; Y^* \;] \left[\frac{(365)}{(2)(t_{CD})} \right] \left[\frac{t_{PM}}{t_{PS}} \right]$$

EXAMPLE. An investor settles on an 8 percent Treasury bond on March 17, 1983. This bond pays coupons November 15 and May 15, and matures on May 15, 1983. The maturity value of this bond is \$100,000, the current quoted price is \$99,960.48, and the amount of accrued interest is \$2,696.13. What is the approximate yield and the true yield on this security?

Step 1. There are 181 days between November 15 and May 15. There are 122 days between November 15 and March 17, and 59 days between March 17 and May 15. However, May 15, 1983 is a Sunday. Therefore, the settlement of maturity will not occur until the following day, which is 60 days from the date of purchase.

Step 2. The amount of accrued interest (given in this example) can be calculated as:

$$AI = [\$100,000] \left[\frac{0.08}{2} \right] \left[\frac{122}{181} \right] = \$2,696.13$$

The accrued interest per dollar of face value is then equal to:

$$AI' = [\$2,696.13/\$100,000] = 0.0269613$$

Step 3. The quoted price, which does not include accrued interest, is \$99,960.48. The price per dollar of face value is then equal to:

$$P' = [\$99,960.48/\$100,000] = 0.9996048$$

Step 4. The approximate yield on this security may now be calculated as follows:

$$Y^* = \left[\left(1 + \frac{0.08}{2} \right) / (0.9996048 + 0.0269613) - 1 \right] [(2)(181)/(59)]$$

$$= 0.0802919$$

Step 5. The true yield, which is nothing more then a simple interest rate, may then be calculated as:

$$Y = [0.0802919][(365)/(2)(181)][59/60]$$

$$= 0.079608$$

It can be shown that this value is the true yield, expressed as a simple interest rate, for this security:

Step 1. The interest rate earned over the 60 days from purchase to the settlement of maturity is equal to:

[0.079608][60/365] = 0.0130862

Step 2. If a simple interest rate of 0.0130862 is earned on an initial investment of:

$99,960.48 + $2,696.13 = $102,656.61

then, after 60 days, the investment should have an ending value equal to:

[$102,656.61][1.0130862] = $104,000

which is exactly equal to the maturity value and the final coupon which will be received on May 16.

Bond Pricing

The quoted price of a bond is equal to the present value of the future cash flows to be received minus the accrued interest. Bonds are priced as of the delivery date. Corporate bonds assume a 180-day coupon period, whereas government securities use the exact number of days within the coupon period. Thus, for bonds not selling at a coupon date, a distinction must be made between corporate and government securities.

Calculation of a Price at a Coupon Date. If a bond is purchased for delivery at a coupon date, then accrued interest will be zero. If the bond pays interest on a semiannual basis, then all future cash flows to be received will be discounted over full periods at one-half of the quoted yield to maturity.

EXAMPLE. A 10 percent coupon bond has a quoted yield of 9.8 percent. If interest on this bond is paid semiannually and the bond has 10 years to maturity, then what is its current price?

Step 1. Since this bond is being priced at a coupon date, its accrued interest is zero.

Step 2. This bond will make 20 semiannual payments of $50, starting six months from today, and a final maturity payment of $1,000.

Step 3. The appropriate discount rate is equal to one-half of the quoted yield, or 4.9 percent per six-month period.

Step 4. The current price is equal to the present value of all future cash flows to be received discounted at the six-month rate:

$$P = [\$50] \left[\sum_{t=1}^{20} \left(\frac{1}{1.049} \right)^t \right] + [\$1,000] \left[\left(\frac{1}{1.049} \right)^{20} \right]$$

$$= \$1,012.57$$

Calculation of a Price Between Coupon Dates: Corporate Securities.
When a corporate bond is sold between coupon dates, accrued interest is
calculated using a 180-day coupon period. The price that the investor must pay
is equal to the quoted price plus the accrued interest, which is simply the
present value of all future cash flows to be received. This section demonstrates
straightforward present value calculations and two additional pricing methods
used by the industry.

EXAMPLE. On June 8, 1983, a 10 percent coupon bond with a quoted yield
of 12 percent is purchased. This bond makes interest payments on March 15
and September 15, and matures on September 15, 1984. What is the quoted
price (add-interest price) and the actual price (flat price) for this bond?

This bond will be delivered for settlement after five business days (one
week) or on June 15, 1983. All calculations are made as of the delivery date.
The cash flows and timing for this bond may be represented as follows:

Date	Cash Flow
June 8, 1983 — Sale	
June 15, 1983 — Delivery	
September 15, 1983	$ 50
March 15, 1984	50
September 15, 1984	1,050

The delivery date of June 15, 1983 falls halfway between the last coupon payment and the next coupon payment (90 days). Accrued interest on this bond
may be calculated as:

$$AI = [\$1,000] \left[\frac{0.10}{2}\right]\left[\frac{90}{180}\right] = \$25.00$$

METHOD 1

To find the present value of the cash flows, the following steps may be
used:

Step 1. Calculate the price of the bond as of the next coupon payment
date. This price will not include the next coupon to be received:

$$PV = [\$50][(1/1.06)^1] + [\$1,050][(1/1.06)^2]$$
$$= \$981.67$$

Step 2. Add to the calculated price the next coupon to be received:

$$PV = \$981.67 + \$50$$
$$= \$1,031.67$$

This is the present value of all future cash flows to be received, evaluated as of
the next coupon date.

Step 3. Discount this new value back to the actual delivery date:

$$PV = [\$1,031.67] \left[\left(\frac{1}{1.06} \right)^{(90/180)} \right]$$

$$= \$1,002.05$$

This is the flat price or the price that the investor actually has to pay.

Step 4. To calculate the quoted price or add-interest price, subtract the accumulated interest:

$$P = \$1,002.05 - \$25.00$$

$$= \$977.05$$

METHOD 2

The flat price may also be calculated as a one-step process:

$$PV = [\$50] \left[\left(\frac{1}{1.06} \right)^{(90/180)} \right] + [\$50] \left[\left(\frac{1}{1.06} \right)^{(270/180)} \right] + [\$1,050] \left[\left(\frac{1}{1.06} \right)^{(450/180)} \right]$$

$$= \$1,002.04$$

This is the same price as calculated under Method 1 except for a slight rounding error. For this particular problem, there is also a slight rounding error when the two industry methods are used.

METHOD 3

The first industry method demonstrated here calculates the quoted or add-interest price. The calculation follows.

Step 1. Using the current yield, calculate the price as of the last coupon payment date. This would be as of March 15, 1983 and would be equal to:

$$P_{M83} = [\$50][PVIF_a(6\%,3)] + [\$1,000][PVIF(6\%,3)]$$

$$= \$973.27$$

Step 2. Using the current yield, calculate the price as of the next coupon payment date. This would be as of September 15, 1983 and would be equal to:

$$P_{S83} = [\$50][PVIF_a(6\%,2)] + [\$1,000][PVIF(6\%,2)]$$

$$= \$981.67$$

Step 3. Determine the price appreciation or depreciation over the coupon period:

$$\$981.67 - \$973.27 = \$8.40 \text{ of appreciation}$$

Step 4. Determine the proportion of the total price appreciation or depreciation that is applicable to the time period from the last coupon date to the delivery date:

$$[\$8.40] \left[\frac{90}{180} \right] = \$4.20$$

Step 5. The quoted or add-interest price is equal to the price at the last coupon date plus the applicable price appreciation or depreciation since the last coupon date:

$P = \$973.27 + \$4.20$

$\quad = \$977.47$

Step 6. The flat price, or actual payment required at delivery, is equal to the quoted price plus accrued interest:

$PV = \$977.47 + \$25.00$

$\quad = \$1,002.47$

METHOD 4

This industry method calculates the flat price of the bond. The steps are as follows:

Step 1. Using the current yield, calculate the price as of the last coupon date. This would be as of March 15, 1983 and would be equal to:

$P_{M83} = [\$50][PVIF_a(6\%,3)] + [\$1,000][PVIF(6\%,3)]$

$\quad = \$973.27$

Step 2. Using a 180-day coupon period, find the amount of interest that would result in a 12 percent annual yield if this bond had been bought at the last coupon date and held until the delivery or settlement date:

$\text{Interest} = [\$973.27]\left[\dfrac{0.12}{2}\right]\left[\dfrac{90}{180}\right] = \$29.20$

Step 3. The flat price is equal to the price at the last coupon date plus the applicable interest which results in the current yield of 12 percent:

$PV = \$973.27 + \$29.20$

$\quad = \$1,002.47$

Step 4. The quoted price is equal to the flat price minus the amount of accrued interest:

$P = \$1,002.47 - \$25.00$

$\quad = \$977.47$

Calculation of a Price Between Coupon Dates: Government Securities. The price of a government note or bond may also be calculated as the present value of all future cash flows to be received. However, as was true for accrued interest, the exact number of days between coupon payment dates, as well as the exact number of days between the last coupon payment date and the date of delivery, must be determined.

EXAMPLE. A 9⅜ government bond is purchased for delivery on June 22, 1983. The face value of this bond is $100,000, the current yield is 8 percent, and it pays interest semiannually on May 15 and November 15. If this bond matures on May 15, 1985, then what is the quoted price of this bond and what price is actually paid?

Step 1. There are 184 days between May 15 and November 15. There are 38 days between the last coupon date and the date of delivery, and 146 days between the date of delivery and the next coupon date.

Step 2. Accrued interest on this bond is equal to:

$$AI = [\$100,000] \left[\frac{0.09375}{2} \right] \left[\frac{38}{184} \right]$$

$$= \$968.07$$

Step 3. The applicable discount rate is one-half of the quoted yield, or 4 percent per six-month period. However, the purchaser has to wait $146/184$ of a period before receiving his first coupon. The timing and the amount of all cash flows to be received is presented below.

Date of Payment	Amount	Periods Until Receipt
November 15, 1983	$ 4,687.50	146/184
May 15, 1984	4,687.50	1 + 146/184
November 15, 1984	4,687.50	2 + 146/184
May 15, 1984	104,687.50	3 + 146/184

Step 4. The present value of the cash flows to be received is equal to:

$$PV = [\$4,687.50][(1/1.04)^{(146/184)}] + [\$4,687.50][(1/1.04)^{(1+146/184)}]$$
$$+ [\$4,687.50][(1/1.04)^{(2+146/184)}] + [\$104,687.50][(1/1.04)^{(3+146/184)}]$$
$$= \$103,329.13$$

This is the amount that is actually paid on delivery for this bond.

Step 5. The quoted price is equal to the flat price minus the amount of accrued interest:

$$P = \$103,329.13 - \$968.07 = \$102,361.06$$

Government Securities During the Final Coupon Period. Remember from an earlier discussion that the yields on government securities during their final coupon period are expressed as a simple interest rate. Given the quoted yield, which may not be equal to the true yield, the actual price of a government security may be calculated as follows:

$$P' = \left[1 + \left(\frac{C}{2} \right) \right] / [1 + (Y^*)(t_{PM})/(2)(t_{CD})] - AI'$$

EXAMPLE. On June 30, 1983, an investor settles on a 9.75 percent government coupon bond with a quoted yield of 10.25 percent. This bond has a face value of $100,000 and matures on September 15, 1983. What is the quoted price for this bond and what price is actually paid?

Step 1. There are 184 days from the last coupon payment (March 15) to the date the bond matures. There are 107 days from the last coupon payment to the delivery or settlement date, and 77 days from the settlement date to the maturity date.

Step 2. The accrued interest on this bond is equal to:

$$AI = [\$100,000] \left[\frac{0.0975}{2} \right] \left[\frac{107}{184} \right]$$

$$= \$2,834.92$$

Since the face value of this bond is $100,000, the accrued interest per dollar of face value is equal to:

$$AI' = [\$2,834.92/\$100,000] = 0.0283492$$

Step 3. The quoted price on this bond, per dollar of face value, is equal to:

$$P' = \left[1 + \left(\frac{0.0975}{2} \right) \right] \bigg/ [1 + (0.1025)(77)/(2)(184)] - 0.0283492$$

$$= 0.9983805$$

which, since the face value of this bond is equal to $100,000, implies that

$$P = [\$100,000][0.9983805] = \$99,838.05$$

Step 4. The actual price that the investor is required to pay is equal to:

$$PV = \$99,838.05 + \$2,834.92 = \$102,672.97$$

It can be shown that this price results in the quoted yield of 10.25 percent. If the yield is 10.25 percent, then this implies that the yield per six-month period is equal to:

$$[0.1025/2] = 0.05125$$

However, for the last coupon period this is the simple interest rate for a 184-day period. Since the investor holds the bond for only 77 days, the applicable simple interest rate for his holding period is:

$$[0.05125][77/184] = 0.021447$$

If the investor purchases the security for a total price of $102,672.97 and earns a simple interest rate of 2.1447 percent, then the ending value of his investment should be equal to:

$$[\$102,672.97][1.021447] = \$104,875$$

which is exactly equal to the maturity value of this security plus the final coupon to be received.

Premiums and Discounts on Coupon Bonds

If a bond's price is greater than par (yield less than the coupon rate), then the bond is selling at a premium. If a bond's price is less than par (yield greater than the coupon rate), then the bond is selling at a discount. The calculation of a bond's current price is discussed in a prior section. Once the current price is known, the premium or discount on the bond is simply the difference between this price and the par or maturity value of the bond. However, there is another method which uses the difference between the coupon rate and the quoted yield to determine the amount of premium or discount for the bond.

Calculation of a Discount. The amount of discount for a bond is equal to the present value of an annuity stream which represents the difference between the coupon rate and the quoted yield.

EXAMPLE. On April 1, 1983, an investor takes delivery of a 12 percent coupon bond. This bond has a face or par value of $1,000 and pays interest on April 1 and October 1. This bond matures on October 1, 1986, and the current yield to maturity is 14 percent. What is the amount of discount for this bond?

METHOD 1

Calculate the current price for this bond. It is equal to:

$$P = [\$60][PVIF_a(7\%,7)] + [\$1,000][PVIF(7\%,7)]$$
$$= \$946.11$$

The discount for this bond is then equal to:

$$\text{Discount} = [\$10][PVIF_a(7\%,7)]$$
$$= \$53.89$$

METHOD 2

Any discount on this bond will be due to the difference between the coupon rate of 12 percent and the current yield of 14 percent. For this security to sell at par with a yield of 14 percent, it would have to pay interest of $70 every six months. Since it actually pays only $60 every six months, this is a difference of $10. This difference of $10, which will occur at each coupon date, is what lowers the price of the bond below its par value. However, this difference can be evaluated as an annuity and its present value determined by discounting it at the current yield to maturity:

$$\text{Discount} = [\$10][PVIF_a(7\%,7)]$$
$$= \$53.89$$

The current price of this bond is therefore equal to:

$$P = \$1,000.00 - \$53.89$$
$$= \$946.11$$

Calculation of a Premium. The same logic that was used to calculate the amount of the discount may also be used to calculate the amount of the premium.

EXAMPLE. On April 1, 1983, an investor takes delivery of a 12 percent coupon bond. This bond has a face or par value of $1,000 and pays interest on April 1 and October 1. This bond matures on October 1, 1986, and the current yield to maturity is 10 percent. What is the amount of the premium for this bond?

METHOD 1

The current price for this bond may be calculated in a straightforward manner. The price is equal to:

$$P = [\$60][PVIF_a(5\%,7)] + [\$1,000][PVIF(5\%,7)]$$
$$= \$1,057.86$$

The amount of the premium is therefore equal to:

Premium $= \$1,057.86 - \$1,000.00$
$= \$57.86$

METHOD 2

Since the current yield on this bond is 10 percent, it would have to pay $50 in interest every six months for it to sell at par. It actually pays $60 in interest every six months. This difference of $10, which will occur at each coupon date, is what increases the price of this bond above its par value. This difference may be evaluated as an annuity and its present value determined by discounting it at the current yield to maturity:

Premium $= [\$10][PVIF_a(5\%,7)]$
$= \$57.86$

The current price of this bond is equal to:

$$P = \$1,000.00 + \$57.86$$
$$= \$1,057.86$$

Amortization and Accumulation Schedules

Although a coupon bond may be selling at either a premium or a discount, if it is held until maturity, then its final payment must be equal to its par or face value. This decrease in the amount of the premium or discount occurs because of a roll-down in the bond's maturity. Discounts are said to be accumulated over time, while premiums are said to be amortized over time.

Another way of phrasing this is that when a bond is selling at a premium (yield less than the coupon rate), then the realized yield will be equal to the coupon income less the decrease in the market price of the bond. If a bond is selling at a discount (yield greater than the coupon rate), then the realized yield will be equal to the coupon income plus the increase in the market price of the bond.

EXAMPLE 1. On April 1, 1983, an investor takes delivery of a 12 percent coupon bond. This bond has a face value of $1,000 and pays interest on April 1 and October 1. The bond matures on October 1, 1986, and the current yield is 14 percent. Construct an accumulation schedule for this bond.

The price of this bond at each coupon date may be calculated using the following formula:

$$P = [\$60][PVIF_d(7\%,N)] + [\$1,000][PVIF(7\%,N)]$$

where N is the number of six-month periods until maturity. The amount of accumulation will be the change in the market price over each coupon period. The required dollar return, so as to earn the quoted yield, will be equal to the yield on a six-month basis times the market price of the bond at the beginning of the coupon period. This will also be equal to the coupon income received plus the accumulation of discount. This may be presented as shown below:

Evaluation Date	Coupon Income	Accumulation	Required Return	Market Value
April 1, 1983	—	—	—	$ 946.11
October 1, 1983	$60	$6.23	$66.23	952.34
April 1, 1984	60	6.66	66.66	959.00
October 1, 1984	60	7.13	67.13	966.13
April 1, 1985	60	7.63	67.63	973.76
October 1, 1985	60	8.16	68.16	981.92
April 1, 1986	60	8.73	68.73	990.65
October 1, 1986	60	9.35	69.35	1,000.00

To illustrate, on April 1, 1983, the market price of this bond was $946.11. To earn a 7 percent yield over the next six months, an investor must earn a total dollar return of:

[$946.11][0.07] = $66.23

This required return of $66.23 will be comprised of $60.00 in coupon income plus an increase in the market price of $6.23.

EXAMPLE 2. On April 1, 1983, an investor takes delivery of a 12 percent coupon bond. This bond has a face value of $1,000 and pays interest on April 1 and October 1. This bond matures on October 1, 1986, and the current yield is 10 percent. Construct an amortization schedule for this bond.

The price of this bond at each coupon date may be calculated using the following formula:

$$P = [\$60][PVIF_d(5\%,N)] + [\$1,000][PVIF(5\%,N)]$$

where N is equal to the number of six-month periods until maturity. The amount of amortization will be the change in the market price over each coupon period. The required dollar return, so as to earn the quoted yield, will be equal to the yield on a six-month basis times the market price of the bond at the beginning of the coupon period. This will also be equal to the coupon income minus the amortization of the premium. This may be presented as follows:

Evaluation Date	Coupon Income	Amortization	Required Return	Market Value
April 1, 1983	—	—	—	$1,057.86
October 1, 1983	$60	$7.11	$52.89	1,050.75
April 1, 1984	60	7.46	52.54	1,043.29
October 1, 1984	60	7.84	52.16	1,035.45
April 1, 1985	60	8.23	51.77	1,027.22
October 1, 1985	60	8.64	51.36	1,018.58
April 1, 1986	60	9.07	50.93	1,009.51
October 1, 1986	60	9.51	50.49	1,000.00

To illustrate, on April 1, 1983, the price of this bond was $1,057.86. To earn a 5 percent yield over the next six months, the investor must earn a total dollar return of:

[$1,057.86][0.05] = $52.89

This required return of $52.89 will be comprised of $60.00 in coupon income less the decrease in the market price of $7.11.

Sinking Funds

A bond with a sinking fund provision requires the corporation to make periodic deposits, usually with the bond's trustee, whose sum will be sufficient to redeem the bond in full at maturity. This is done either by investment of the periodic payments until maturity or by the periodic repurchase of outstanding bonds. This section concentrates on the former method.

Calculations: Size of the Sinking Fund Payment. Once the size and maturity of a bond issue are known, a corporation needs to determine the size of the sinking fund payment that is required. The solution to this is nothing more than the solution to a future value of an annuity problem.

EXAMPLE 1. A corporation issues $1 million worth of bonds on September 1, 1983 with a maturity date of September 1, 1988. The indenture agreement specifies that the corporation must make semiannual payments to a sinking fund administered by the bond's trustee. Assume that the corporation will make its first payment to the sinking fund on March 1, 1984 and its last payment on September 1, 1988. If the deposits will earn an effective rate of 8.16 percent (4 percent per semiannual period), then what is the size of the sinking fund payment?

This is nothing more than a 10-period annuity problem, whose future value must be equal to the maturity value of the bond:

$$\$1,000,000 = [\ SF\ ][FVIF_a(4\%,10)]$$
$$= [\ SF\ ][12.006]$$
$$=> SF = [\$1,000,000/12.006]$$
$$= \$83,291.69$$

EXAMPLE 2. Consider the prior example, but now assume that the first payment takes place on September 1, 1983 and the last payment takes place on March 1, 1988. What is the size of the sinking fund payments?

This is now an annuity due problem, whose solution is represented by the following equation:

$$\$1,000,000 = [\ SF\ ][FVIF_{ad}(4\%,10)]$$
$$= [\ SF\ ][FVIF_{a}(4\%,11) - 1.0]$$
$$= [\ SF\ ][12.486]$$
$$=> SF = [\$1,000,000/12.486]$$
$$= \$80,089.70$$

Calculations: Number of Sinking Fund Payments. When a corporation issues a bond with a sinking fund provision, it must be sure that it will be able to meet both the sinking fund and interest payments on the bond each period. This fact may act to restrict the number of sinking fund payments (maturity of the bond) that are possible.

EXAMPLE. Assume that a firm wishes to issue $1 million of 10 percent coupon bonds. These bonds will pay interest on a semiannual basis, but the firm can guarantee only $125,000 for each six-month period toward the interest and sinking fund payments. What is the minimum number of sinking fund payments possible?

Since interest is paid each six months, the possible contribution to the sinking fund is as follows:

Total semiannual payment	$125,000
Less: Interest	50,000
Sinking fund contribution	$ 75,000

The number of sinking fund payments required now depends on the rate of return that the firm is able to earn on its deposits. If it can earn 3 percent each six months and the first payment is made six months from the date of issue, then the number of payments needed to accumulate the maturity value of $1 million may be found as a regular annuity problem:

$$\$1,000,000 = [\$75,000][FVIF_{a}(3\%,N)]$$
$$=> FVIF_{a}(3\%,N) = [\$1,000,000/\$75,000]$$
$$= 13.333$$

The value for N may then be found either by linear interpolation or by the use of a financial calculator:

$$N = 11.38 \text{ six-month periods}$$
$$= 5.69 \text{ years}$$

Since firms do not issue bonds with maturities of 5.69 years, it should extend the period and issue a bond with a maturity of six years. The actual sinking fund payment required may then be calculated as:

$$\$1,000,000 = [\ SF\ ][FVIF_a(3\%,12)]$$
$$= [\ SF\ ][14.192]$$
$$=> SF = [\$1,000,000/14.192]$$
$$= \$70,462.23$$

BOND ANALYSIS: ADDITIONAL ISSUES

This section discusses some additional issues for fixed-income securities. These issues include measures of risk, measures of return, and duration.

Definition of Variables

N = number of discounting periods

P = current price

Y = yield to maturity or discount rate

D_1 = duration of a fixed-income security

HV = horizon volatility

CF_t = cash flow received at the end of period t

$PVIF(i\%,N)$ = present value interest factor of a single sum at a discount rate of i percent for N periods

$PVIF_a(i\%,N)$ = present value interest factor of an annuity at a discount rate of i percent for N periods

Measures of Risk

Traditional measures of risk for fixed-income securities are the yield value of a thirty-second, the price value of one basis point, and the percent price volatility. A new measure that is being advocated is the horizon volatility. It specifies the basis point change in return that will result from a one basis point change in yield. However, let us first discuss the traditional measures of risk or volatility.

Yield Value of a Thirty-Second. Price quotes for bonds are reported in values of percentage points and thirty-seconds of par. The yield value of a thirty-second gives the change in yield that will result from a change in price of one-thirty-second ($0.03125).

For instance, assume that a five-year, 8 percent coupon bond is currently selling for 102⁵⁄₃₂ to yield 7.4752 percent. If its price goes up to 102⁶⁄₃₂, its new yield will be 7.4677 percent. Therefore, a price increase of ⅟₃₂ results in a 0.0075 percent (0.75 basis points) decrease in yield. The value 0.75 is the yield value of a thirty-second for this bond. Given this value, it is possible to obtain a close approximation to the exact yield change for any given change in price.

Price Value of One Basis Point. If the yield value of a thirty-second for a security is known, then it is easy to obtain the price value of one basis point for that security. The price value of one basis point indicates how much the price will increase (or decrease), in terms of percent of par, for every basis point decrease (or increase) in yield.

In the previous example, the yield value of a thirty-second was 0.75 basis points. This implies that the price value of one basis point is equal to:

$$[-0.03125]/[\pm 0.75] = \pm 0.04167$$

This says that if the yield on the bond in the example goes from 7.4752 percent up to 7.4852 percent (one basis point), then the price will drop by approximately \$0.04167, expressed as a percent of par.

Percent Price Volatility. The percent price volatility is the price value of one basis point as a percentage of the bond's current price. In the prior example the percent price volatility is equal to:

$$[\$.04167/\$102.15625] = 0.04079\%$$

Horizon Volatility. The total return for a bond incorporates the percentage change in price over the investment horizon. Although price may vary during this investment period, it is only the change at the horizon that is important in determining the bond's actual return. This concept of price change at the horizon is incorporated into a measure called the horizon volatility. It measures the basis point change in return, given the basis point change in yield over the investment horizon.

EXAMPLE. A six-year, 8 percent coupon bond is selling at par (8 percent yield). Over a one-year investment horizon, this bond rolls down to a five-year, 8 percent coupon bond with a yield of 7.4752 percent. What is the horizon volatility of this bond?

The horizon volatility may be calculated as follows:

Step 1. Look at the bond at the end of the investment horizon. It has previously been shown that the yield value of a thirty-second for a five-year, 8 percent coupon bond with a yield of 7.4572 percent is 0.75 basis points. Therefore, the percent price volatility at the horizon may be calculated as follows:

Decimal value of a thirty-second	0.03125
Yield value of a thirty-second	÷ 0.75
Price value of one basis point	0.04167
Horizon price	÷ 102.15625
Percent price volatility	0.04079%

Step 2. Now consider the bond at the beginning of the investment period. The horizon volatility may be calculated as follows:

Percent price volatility at the horizon	0.04079%
Current price horizon price (\$100.00/\$102.15625)	÷ 0.97889
Percent price change at the horizon, expressed as a ratio of current and horizon price	0.04167
Translation factor to convert to basis points	× 100.00000
Horizon volatility	4.167

This says that the investment period return should increase by 4.167 basis points for every one basis point decrease in yield. Note that the horizon volatility is very similar to the price value of one basis point. This occurs because it has been assumed that the bond is originally selling at par.

The use of the horizon volatility may be illustrated by the prior example. Over the one-year investment horizon the yield went from 8 percent down to 7.4572 percent. This is a decrease of 52.48 basis points. Using the concept of horizon volatility, this implies a return from price appreciation of:

$$[0.5248\%][4.167] = 2.18684\%$$

The actual return from price appreciation would be:

$$[\$102.15625 - \$100.00]/[\$100.00] = 2.15625\%$$

The advantage of horizon volatility is that it allows for the rapid calculation of returns under differing scenarios of yield changes. It may also be used to determine an approximation for a bond's rolling-yield.

Measures of Return: Rolling-Yield

The yield curve specifies how much additional yield may be obtained from an increase or decrease in the maturity of a fixed-income security. A basic problem with this yield, is that it assumes that the security is held until it matures. Therefore, it is difficult to directly compare securities with different maturities. One way around this problem is to calculate a rolling-yield, which specifies the holding period return for all maturities over some predefined investment horizon.

The rolling-yield acts as a benchmark return. It assumes that the yield curve will remain constant over the investment period. Each security will then have positive (or negative) price appreciation as the security rolls down (or up) the yield curve over time. This is somewhat unrealistic in that some changes in the "shape" and the level of the yield curve over time would be expected. However, the rolling-yield at least gives us a starting point for further scenario analyses of return.

Calculations. The rolling-yield consists of three items:

1 Coupon income

2 Reinvestment income

3 Price appreciation

EXAMPLE. A five-year, 10 percent coupon bond is currently selling at par. The investment horizon is one year, and the current yield on a four-year security with equivalent risk is 9 percent. What is the rolling-yield for this security?

1 *Coupon income.* Over the investment period, $100 ($50 every six months) in coupon income is paid out. Since this bond is selling at par, the return from this coupon income will be equal to:

$$[\$100/\$1,000] = 0.10$$

2 *Reinvestment income.* There is also a return associated with the first $50 of coupon income that is paid, since it may be reinvested for a six-month period. Although the exact reinvestment rate may vary, assume that an appropriate reinvestment rate would be 5 percent for the six-month period. This implies that the reinvestment income is equal to:

$$[\$50][0.05] = \$2.50$$

which implies a return from reinvestment income of:

$$[\$2.50/\$1,000] = 0.0025$$

3 *Price appreciation.* If the yield curve remains constant, then at the end of the investment horizon the purchaser will hold a four-year, 10 percent coupon bond with a yield to maturity of 9 percent. The price of this bond would be:

$$P = [\$50][PVIF_a(4.5\%,8)] + [\$1,000][PVIF(4.5\%,8)]$$
$$= \$1,032.98$$

Thus, the total price appreciation is:

$$\$1,032.98 - \$1,000.00 = \$32.98$$

which implies a return from price appreciation of:

$$[\$32.98/\$1,000.00] = 0.03298$$

The rolling-yield is then equal to:

$$0.10 + 0.0025 + 0.03298 = 0.13548$$

The rolling-yield of 13.548 percent is greater than the current yield for the five-year security of 10 percent. This is always true given an upward sloping yield curve, and the reverse is true given a downward sloping yield curve.

The advantage of the rolling-yield is that it acts as a benchmark return for marking further comparisons. It may also be combined with the concept of horizon volatility to perform scenario analysis. For example, if the yield curve remains constant for this investment period, then the five-year security will have a realized return of 13.548 percent. The yield curve is not actually expected to remain constant across time. However, assume the horizon volatility for the five-year bond has been calculated. If the yield of this bond at the end of the investment horizon is expected to differ from 9 percent, then this difference would be multiplied by the horizon volatility. This amount would then be added to or subtracted from the rolling-yield to obtain an approximation of the realized return under the new scenario of a change in the yield curve. Since this process may be computerized, scenario analysis becomes quite easy to do.

Duration and Immunization

Reinvestment rate risk (i.e., changes in market yields) is a major concern to those investors who have purchased fixed-income securities. Increases (or decreases) in the reinvestment rate will increase (or decrease) reinvestment income from the coupons received. At the same time, they will decrease (or increase) the applicable market price of the security if it must be sold. A concept that is now being used to "immunize" against reinvestment rate risk is duration.

Duration may be considered to be the weighted average maturity for a fixed-income security. As such, it takes into consideration that some of the cash flows associated with a bond (the coupons) will be received before maturity. There are many different ways to calculate this average maturity, including some that consider the stochastic process driving changes in the yield curve. However, this discussion concentrates on the traditional measure of duration, also referred to as D_1.

Calculation of Duration. Duration is a weighted average measure of maturity with the cash flows weighted by the time remaining until they are received. The formula for the duration of an N-period bond is as follows:

$$D_1 = \sum_{t=1}^{N} \frac{(t)(CF_t)/(1 + Y/2)^t}{P}$$

where the weighted cash flows are discounted at the bond's current yield and the sum is divided by the current price of the bond.

EXAMPLE 1. What is the duration of a two-year, 8 percent coupon bond that pays interest semiannually and is selling at par?

Periods Until Receipt of Cash Flow		Cash Flow	Weighted Cash Flow	Present Value at 4%
1	×	$ 40 =	$ 40	$ 38.46
2		40	80	73.96
3		40	120	106.68
4		1,040	4,160	3,555.99
				$3,775.09

The duration of this bond is then equal to:

$D_1 = [\$3,775.09/\$1,000.00] = 3.77509$ six-month periods

EXAMPLE 2. What is the duration of a three-year, 8 percent coupon bond that pays interest semiannually and is also selling at par?

Periods Until Receipt of Cash Flow		Cash Flow	Weighted Cash Flow	Present Value at 4%
1	×	$ 40 =	$ 40	$ 38.46
2		40	80	73.96
3		40	120	106.68
4		40	160	136.77
5		40	200	164.39
6		1,040	6,240	4,931.56
				$5,451.82

The duration of this bond is equal to:

$D_1 = [\$5,451.82/\$1,000.00] = 5.45182$ six-month periods

Duration of Portfolios. The duration of a portfolio is considered to be equal to the weighted average duration of the securities comprising the portfolio.

EXAMPLE. Consider the two securities in the examples in the previous section. If an investor invests 86.6 percent of his funds in the two-year security and 13.4 percent of his funds in the three-year security, then what will be the duration of the resulting portfolio?

$D_1 = [3.77509][0.866] + [5.45182][0.134] = 4.00$ six-month periods

Immunization of a Portfolio. Duration is said to immunize against reinvestment rate risk if the duration of the portfolio (security) is equal to the time remaining in the investment horizon.

EXAMPLE. Consider the portfolio in the prior example. It has a duration of two years and its weighted yield is:

$[0.08][0.866] + [0.08][0.134] = 0.08$

If the investment horizon is two years and the investor holds this portfolio, then a one-time change in the reinvestment rate should still allow him to earn an 8 percent realized yield. To illustrate this, assume that right after this portfolio is purchased the reinvestment rate will either remain at 8 percent, or there will be a one-time change to either 7 or 9 percent.

Reinvestment Rate	Weight	Security	Coupon Income	Capital Gains	Interest on Interest	Total Dollar Return	Realized Compounded Yield
7%	0.866	2 year	$138.56	$0.00	$ 7.45	$146.01	7.94%
7	0.134	3 year	21.44	1.27	1.15	23.86	8.36
7	1.000	Portfolio	$160.00	$1.27	$ 8.60	$169.87	8.00
8	0.866	2 year	$138.56	$0.00	$ 8.54	$147.10	8.00%
8	0.134	3 year	21.44	0.00	1.32	22.76	8.00
8	1.000	Portfolio	$160.00	$0.00	$ 9.36	$169.86	8.00%
9	0.866	2 year	$138.56	$0.00	$ 9.64	$148.20	8.06%
9	0.134	3 year	21.44	− 1.25	1.49	21.68	7.64
9	1.000	Portfolio	$160.00	−$1.25	$11.13	$169.88	8.00%

No matter what happens to the reinvestment rate, the realized compounded yield will remain 8 percent. Increases (or decreases) in reinvestment income are exactly offset by decreases (or increases) in capital gains at the time of sale.

However, there are some serious problems with duration. It was no accident that both of the securities in this examples had current yields of 8 percent, and that they both had shifts of the reinvestment rate to either 7 or 9 percent. For duration to immunize a portfolio effectively, parallel shifts of a flat yield curve are required. Another problem is the assumption that the reinvestment rate would change immediately after the purchase of the securities and would remain at that rate until the end of the investment period. This assumption is unrealistic, and the portfolio must be reimmunized every time a coupon is received or there is a change in the market rate of interest (almost continuously). As a practical matter, most investors will reimmunize only periodically, say every six months to a year. Even with all its faults, using duration to immunize a portfolio, if it is done with some thought, will greatly reduce the amount of reinvestment rate risk.

FUTURES AND FORWARDS

A forward contract is an agreement between a buyer and a seller of a commodity which specifies the price that will be paid for the commodity when it is delivered at some future date. It has been said that futures contracts are simply marketable forward contracts that are traded on regulated exchanges. However, profit and loss on futures contracts is calculated each day (i.e., value is marked-to-market) and is debited or credited against the margin account. Forward contracts are not marked-to-market.

Futures contracts are traded on many different commodities, including grains, metals, lumber, and financial securities. Recently trading has started on stock index futures. This section concentrates on one particular contract, a 90-day T-bill futures contract.

Definition of Variables

D = dollar value of discount

P = current price

d_J = discount rate or yield for security J

t_J = time from delivery or settlement until maturity for security J

RP = implied term repo rate

SY = strip yield rate

IFR = implied forward rate

$_J i_M$ = simple interest rate or equivalent bond yield for security J based on an M-day year

The subscripts c and f refer to a cash security and a futures security, respectively.

Pricing Relationships

T-bill futures contracts on the International Monetary Market (IMM) are quoted in terms of an index value, where the index is equal to 100 minus the discount rate. The basic contract is for $1 million of 90-day T-bills. The contracts are deliverable in the third week of March, June, September, and December. T-bill futures contracts use the same equations for price, dollar discount, discount rate, simple interest rate, and equivalent bond yield that were developed previously for non-interest-bearing securities.

Calculations. The only difference between the pricing of a cash T-bill and a T-bill futures contract is that the number of days used in the calculations for the futures contracts are measured from the day of settlement (delivery) until maturity. In pricing cash T-bills, this number is measured from the date of the purchase of the security until maturity.

EXAMPLE. Assume that the IMM quote for a 90-day T-bill futures contract, for delivery in 11 days, is 87.76. This gives a discount rate of:

$$d = 100.00 - 87.76$$
$$= 12.24 = 0.1224$$

This discount rate is stated on the basis of a 360-day year. If this futures contract is purchased and held for delivery, then in 11 days the purchaser will receive a 90-day cash T-bill and will be guaranteed a price of:

$$P = [\$1,000,000] \left[1 - \frac{(0.1224)(90)}{360} \right]$$
$$= \$969,400$$

This implies that the amount of the dollar discount is equal to:

$$D = \$1,000,000 - \$969,400$$
$$= \$30,600$$

The simple interest rate, or the equivalent bond yield since this contract is less than 182 days, is equal to:

$$i_{365} = [(365)(0.1224)]/[360 - (0.1224)(90)]$$
$$= 0.1280$$

Another value that is often useful in calculating profit and loss is the value of an "01." For a 90-day T-bill futures contract this is equal to $25. It says that the price of the contract will increase (or decrease) by $25 for each basis point decrease (or increase) in the discount rate.

Hedging. T-bill futures contracts may be used to hedge against price level risk, but they cannot be used to hedge against spread variation risk.

EXAMPLE 1. X plans to invest in $1 million worth of 90-day cash T-bills in June. It is now March, and June T-bill futures contracts have a yield (discount rate) of 8 percent. X is concerned about the rate that he will actually be able to earn in June. If X would be satisfied with an 8 percent rate, then he can lock this rate in by purchasing a 90-day T-bill futures contract in March; he will have created a long hedge. In June, when X takes delivery of the futures contract, he will receive 90-day cash T-bills at a guaranteed price of:

$$P = [\$1,000,000] \left[1 - \frac{(0.08)(90)}{360} \right]$$

$$= \$980,000$$

No matter what the actual rate is on cash T-bills in June, X will have guaranteed himself an 8 percent rate. By the use of this long hedge, X has gotten rid of downside price level risk (changes in the level of interest rate) as well as upside potential. Although this is often cited as an example of a perfect hedge, the requirements of margin money and marking-to-market actually makes this hedge less than perfect.

EXAMPLE 2. To illustrate spread variation risk, assume now that Y plans to purchase 90-day cash T-bills in May instead of June. Y would also use the June futures contracts to hedge, since there are no May contracts, but Y is now exposed to spread variation risk. Assume that in May, when Y takes off the hedge and purchases the cash T-bills, Y faces an upward sloping yield curve. The yield on 90-day cash T-bills is 9 percent, while the yield on June T-bills futures contracts is 9.5 percent (approximately equal to the yield on 120-day cash T-bills). Y would then have obtained the following effective yield from his hedged position:

Futures:	
Value at sale (9.5%)	$976,250
Value at purchase (8.0%)	980,000
Loss on futures position	$ 3,750
Cash T-bills:	
Value at purchase (9.0%)	$977,500
Loss on futures position	3,750
Effective price of cash T-bills	$981,250

Y's effective discount rate is then equal to:

$$d = \left[\frac{\$1,000,000 - \$981,250}{\$1,000,000} \right] \left[\frac{360}{90} \right] = 0.075$$

The effective discount rate is 50 basis points less than the original yield of 8.0 percent on the futures contract when Y initiated the hedge. This is eactly equal to the spread between the cash security (9.0 percent) and the futures contract (9.5 percent) when the hedge was lifted. If the yields had been reversed — cash 9.5 percent and futures 9.0 percent — then the effective discount rate would have been 8.5 percent or 50 basis points higher than the original yield on the futures contract. This is the basis of spread variation risk — it is not known what the spread will actually be when the hedge is taken off.

Also note that the effective price has increased from $980,000 to $981,250. This difference of $1,250 is exactly equal to the value of an "01" times the ending spread of 50 basis points:

[$25][50 basis points] = $1,250

Interest Rate Parity

If the pure expectations theory of the term structure is correct (see Chapter 13) and if markets are efficient, then rates on futures contracts should be equal to the implied forward rates on equivalent cash securities. In practice, these rates are usually not the same. Therefore, wise investors must know how to calculate implied forward rates from cash securities and strip yields from futures securities, if they are to make correct investment decisions.

Implied Forward Rates. Assume that an investor has a 180-day investment horizon and only two possible investment strategies: (1) He can invest in a 180-day cash T-bill (security 1) with a discount rate of 9 pecent or (2) he can invest in two consecutive 90-day cash T-bills (securities 2 and 3), where the first cash T-bill (security 2) has a discount rate of 8 percent.

If the pure expectations theory of the term structure is correct, then there should be no difference between the two strategies. This means that the two discount rates which are known must imply the value of the third. There are two methods to determine this implied forward rate.

METHOD 1

The first step is to convert the known discount rates to simple interest rates over their maturity life:

$$_1i_{365} = [(365)(0.09)]/[360 - (0.09)(180)]$$
$$= 0.0955497$$
$$_1i_{180} = [0.0955497][180/365]$$
$$= 0.0471204$$
$$_2i_{365} = [(365)(0.08)]/[360 - (0.08)(90)]$$
$$= 0.0827664$$
$$_2i_{90} = [0.0827664][90/365]$$
$$= 0.0204082$$

Given the simple interest rates for the 90-day and the 180-day securities, the implied simple interest rate for a 90-day cash security, starting in 90 days, must be equal to:

$$_3i_{90} = [1.0471204/1.0204082] - 1.0$$
$$= 0.0261779$$
$$_3i_{365} = [0.0261779][365/90]$$
$$= 0.1061663$$

Given the simple interest rate on the basis of a 365-day year, the corresponding discount rate is equal to:

$$d = [(360)(i_{365})]/[365 + (t)(i_{365})]$$

Using our data gives us the following implied forward discount rate for security 3:

$$IFR = [(360)(0.1061663)]/[365 + (90)(0.1061663)]$$
$$= 0.102$$

METHOD 2

The implied forward discount rate may also be calculated directly from the following equation:

$$IFR = \left\{1 - \frac{[1 - d_1t_1/360]}{[1 - d_2t_2/360]}\right\}\left\{\frac{360}{t_3}\right\}$$

Using the data in this example yields the following:

$$IFR = \left\{1 - \frac{[1 - (0.09)(180)/360]}{[1 - (0.08)(90)/360]}\right\}\left\{\frac{360}{90}\right\}$$

$$= 0.102$$

Futures Rates and Implied Forward Rates. The rate just calculated of 10.2 percent is the implicit rate for the 180-day cash T-bill over the last 90 days of its life. Another way of saying this is that the discount rate of 9.0 percent for 180 days is equal to 8.0 percent for the first 90 days, and 10.2 percent for the last 90 days. This rate of 10.2 percent should be compared to the discount rate for a 90-day T-bill futures contract for delivery in 90 days. If the futures rate is greater than 10.2 percent, then it is better to purchase a 90-day cash T-bill and, at the same time, a 90-day T-bill futures contract for delivery in 90 days. If the futures rate is less than 10.2 percent, then it is better to purchase the 180-day cash T-bill.

EXAMPLE. Using data from the previous example, assume that the implied forward rate is 10.2 percent but the futures rate is 11.0 percent. If $1 million is invested in the 180-day cash T-bill with a simple interest of 9.55497 percent, as already calculated, then the ending value of the investment after 180 days would be equal to:

$$[\$1,000,000] \left[1 + (0.0955497)\left(\frac{180}{365}\right)\right] = \$1,047,120.40$$

The alternative strategy is to invest in a 90-day cash T-bill and a 90-day T-bill futures contract for delivery in 90 days. The simple interest rate for the 90-day cash T-bill (already calculated) is equal to 0.0827664. The simple interest rate for the futures contract, given a discount rate of 11.0 percent, is equal to:

$$i_{365} = \frac{(365)(0.11)}{360 - (0.11)(90)}$$

$$= 0.1146815$$

This means that the ending value of the $1 million investment under this strategy is equal to:

$$[\$1,000,000] \left[1 + (0.0827664)\left(\frac{90}{365}\right)\right]\left[1 + (0.1146815)\left(\frac{90}{365}\right)\right] = \$1,049,262.90$$

Strip Yields. Just as the discount rates on cash securities may be used to derive an implied forward rate, the discount rates on futures contracts may be used to derive something called the strip yield. For instance, the strip yield for a 180-day cash T-bill is the rate implied by the discount rates on a 90-day cash T-bill and a 90-day T-bill futures contract for delivery in 90 days. The strip yield may be calculated using the following formula:

$$SY = \left\{\left[1 - \frac{d_c t_c}{360}\right]\left[(d_f)\left(\frac{t_f}{360}\right) - 1\right] + 1\right\}\left\{\frac{360}{t_c + t_f}\right\}$$

EXAMPLE. Assume that the yield on a 155-day cash T-bill is 10.0 percent, while the yield on a 90-day T-bill futures contract, to be delivered in 155 days, is 9.0 percent. The strip yield, or the implied discount rate for a 245-day cash T-bill, is then equal to:

$$SY = \left\{\left[1 - \frac{(0.10)(155)}{360}\right]\left[(0.09)\left(\frac{90}{360}\right) - 1\right] + 1\right\}\left\{\frac{360}{155 + 90}\right\}$$

$$= 0.0949$$

If the actual yield for the 245-day cash T-bill is greater than 9.49 percent, then it is better to purchase the 245-day security. If the actual yield is less than 9.49 percent, then it is better to purchase the 155-day cash T-bill and, at the same time, the 90-day T-bill futures contract for delivery in 155 days.

Repurchase Agreements

Many T-bill dealers finance their inventories or purchases with repurchase agreements (repos or RPs). With a repo, the dealer "borrows" the money to finance the purchase by simultaneously selling the security to a repo investor. (This description is somewhat simplified.) At the same time, the dealer agrees to repurchase the security at some designated time in the future. The total amount that the dealer must pay at this future time will be equal to the original price of the security (the amount borrowed) plus interest on the amount borrowed. The stated interest rate on a repo, the term RP rate, is stated on the basis of a 360-day year.

Implied RP Rates. If a dealer finances a T-bill with a repo for only part of the T-bill's life, then the dealer is said to have created a tail. For instance, if the dealer finances a 180-day T-bill for the first 90 days using a term RP, then he has created a 90-day tail at the end of the repo period. The dealer's ultimate objective is, of course, to purchase the 180-day T-bill at one price and to sell the 90-day tail at a higher price. However, the actual price that he will be able to obtain for the 90-day tail depends on the current discount rates at the time of sale. One way for the dealer to insure against unfavorable rate level changes would be to sell a 90-day T-bill futures contract, for delivery in 90 days, when he originally purchases the 180-day cash T-bill.

The actual profit on this deal depends not only on the cash and futures prices, but also on the term RP rate. It should be clear that there will be some term RP rate whereby the dealer would just break even. This rate is called the implied repo rate. It may be calculated as follows:

$$RP = \left[\frac{d_c t_c - d_f t_f}{360 - d_c t_c}\right]\left[\frac{360}{t_{RP}}\right]$$

EXAMPLE. Assume that the discount rate on a 180-day cash T-bill is 10 percent, and that the discount rate on a 90-day T-bill futures contract, to be delivered in 90 days, is 9 percent. The implied repo rate is then equal to:

$$RP = \left[\frac{(0.10)(180) - (0.09)(90)}{360 - (0.10)(180)}\right]\left[\frac{360}{90}\right]$$

$$= 0.1157895$$

If the actual term RP rate is equal to the implied repo rate, then the dealer will just break even. This can be demonstrated with a cash-in, cash-out analysis.

Assume that an investor has purchased $1 million (face value) of 180-day cash T-bills at a discount rate of 10 percent. He intends to finance this T-bill for the first 90 days using a repo, where the term RP rate is 0.1157895. In addition, the investor has sold a 90-day T-bill futures contract for delivery in 90-days at a yield of 9 percent. Over the 90-day period his cash-in, cash-out positions are as follows:

Transaction	Cash-In	Cash-Out
Purchase 180-day cash T-bills @ 10%		$ 950,000
Borrow purchase price using 90-day term RP	$ 950,000	
Deliver 90-day tail against the futures contract @ 9.0%	977,500	
Repay term RP borrowings		950,000
Pay term RP interest @ $[0.1157895]\left[\frac{90}{360}\right]$ or 2.89474%		27,500
Total cash positions	$1,927,500	$1,927,500

If the actual term RP rate is less than the implied RP rate, then the investor will make a profit. If the rate is greater, then the investor will have a loss.

SUGGESTED READING

Many sources were used as references while writing this chapter. The following is a partial listing of further interest to the reader. In addition to explanations and examples of the mathematics of finance, these books include discussions of security types, markets for securities, and theory.

Garbade, Kenneth D. *Securities Markets*. New York: McGraw-Hill, 1982.

Gould, Bruce G. *The Dow Jones-Irwin Guide to Commodities Trading*. Homewood, Ill.: Dow Jones-Irwin, 1973.

Kaufman, George G. *The U.S. Financial System: Money, Markets and Institutions*, 2nd ed. Englewood Cliffs, N.J.: Prentice-Hall, 1983.

Leibowitz, Martin L. *Total Return Management: A Goal-Oriented Framework for Bond Portfolio Analysis.* New York: Salomon Brothers, 1979.

Levine, Sumner N. *Investment Manager's Handbook.* Homewood, Ill.: Dow Jones-Irwin, 1980.

Loll, Leo M., Jr., and Julian G. Buckley. *The Over-the-Counter Securities Markets,* 4th ed. Englewood Cliffs, N.J.: Prentice-Hall, 1981.

Loosigian, Allan M. *Interest Rate Futures.* Homewood, Ill.: Dow Jones-Irwin, 1980.

Maginn, John L., and Donald L. Tuttle. *Managing Investment Portfolios: A Dynamic Process.* Sponsored by The Institute of Chartered Financial Analysts. New York: Warren, Gorham & Lamont, 1983.

Powers, Mark J., and David J. Vogel. *Inside the Financial Futures Markets.* New York: John Wiley & Sons, 1981.

Radcliffe, Robert C. *Investment: Concepts, Analysis, and Strategy.* Glenview, Ill.: Scott, Foresman, 1982.

Reilly, Fran K. *Investment Analysis & Portfolio Management.* Hinsdale, Ill.: Dryden Press, 1979.

Schwarz, Edward W. *How To Use Interest Rate Futures Contracts.* Homewood, Ill.: Dow Jones-Irwin, 1979.

Sharpe, William F. *Investments,* 2nd ed. Englewood Cliffs, N.J.: Prentice-Hall, 1981.

Stigum, Marcia. *Money Market Calculations: Yields, Break-Evens, and Arbitrage.* Homewood, Ill.: Dow Jones-Irwin, 1981.

———. *The Money Market: Myth, Reality, and Practice.* Homewood, Ill.: Dow Jones-Irwin, 1978.

Van Horne, James C. *Financial Market Rates and Flows.* Englewood Cliffs, N.J.: Prentice-Hall, 1978.

7

The Long-Term Bond Market

RICHARD W. MCENALLY

The long-term bond market provides a major channel for the flow of capital to corporations and government bodies. It is also a significant outlet for the investment funds of individuals and institutions. This chapter reviews this market from both these sides. The emphasis is on the decisions these participants must make in issuing or investing in bonds and, in particular, on the risk/return consequences of these decisions. The first section discusses some basic features on bond instruments. Next is a brief review of the characteristics of the bonds issued by some major types of investors. Then, after an examination of the mechanics of bond price/yield relationships, the effects that bond instrument and bond issuer characteristics have on the value of bonds and, hence, on their costs to the issuer and their return to the investor are explored. The final section deals with the investment management of bond portfolios, including some new techniques and instruments that have come to play a role in fixed-income investment management.

BASIC SECURITY ATTRIBUTES

The classic long-term bond essentially consists of a package of two promises: a promise to make a series of equal payments at semiannual intervals over the life of the bond, called the coupons or coupon payments, and a promise to make a significantly larger lump-sum payment at the end of the life of the bond, called the payoff at maturity, maturity value, or par value. By convention, the dimensions of long-term bonds are usually discussed on a per hundred dollars of par value basis. Thus, the size of the coupon stream is specified by reference to the coupon rate, or dollar coupons per hundred dollars of par value per year, with it being understood that each semiannual coupon payment consists of half this number of dollars. The coupon rate, name of issuer, and year in which the bond pays off are usually sufficient to identify a bond. Therefore, a bond market price quotation for the "LTV 5s of '88" refers to an issue of the LTV corporation that makes semiannual payments of $2.50 per hundred dollars of par value until some time in 1988, at which time it makes a final semiannual coupon payment of $2.50 plus a payment of $100 per hundred dollars of par value. (From standard sources, such as *Moody's Bond Record* or *Standard & Poor's Bond Guide,* it can further be determined that the end of the life of the bond, or maturity date, is July 15, 1988; the implication is that the semiannual payments will be made every January 15 and July 15 through this date.)

The price quotation on this particular bond might be given as "76⅜." Following the "per hundred" convention, this means a price of $76.375 per hundred dollars of par value. It is also understood that the bond is priced "with interest" unless otherwise stated, meaning that the purchaser must pay the seller the proportion of a coupon that has been earned since the last coupon payment, the accrued coupon. (If a bond does not trade "with interest," it is said to trade "flat.") For example, if this bond were purchased on a February 15 at 76⅜, the invoice price would be $76.375 + [$2.50 × (⅙)] = $76.375 +

$.417 = $76.792 per hundred dollars of par value purchased.[1] Actually, most bonds are denominated in units of one thousand dollars of par value. Therefore, the LTV 5s of 1988 would actually be priced at $763.75 per bond, and each bond would provide semiannual coupons of $25 and would pay off at $1,000 at maturity.

Individual bond issues have a number of important attributes aside from issuer, coupon rate, maturity date, and price. Some of these arise from specific provisions in the contract between the issuer and purchasers, called the indenture, while others are due to external influences, such as the tax code and the markets in which the bonds trade.

Features Contained in the Indenture

Security Status. Some bonds are secured by claims on specific assets of the issuer so that, in the event of an act of default (a failure to make a cash payment as contractually scheduled), the bondholders have a claim on the assets or the proceeds from their liquidation. Such bonds are frequently referred to as mortgage bonds. Others simply represent a general obligation of the issuer; they are often called debentures. The claims represented by some bonds, subordinated debentures, rank behind the claims of mortgage-bond holders, general obligation-bond holders, or other unsecured creditors.

Call Provisions. Borrowers frequently reserve the right to pay off a bond issue prior to maturity. Call provisions permit them to do this. A typical call provision will specify that, under certain conditions, the issuer can retire bonds by paying the holder a call price, their par value plus a call premium. Thus, calling a bond is akin to prepaying a home mortgage, and the call premium is analogous to a prepayment penalty.

There are actually three types of call provisions, with rather different motivations underlying each. The most critical from the viewpoint of both the borrower and lender, frequently referred to as a refunding provision or refunding restriction, is intended to permit the issuer to take advantage of a reduction in borrowing costs subsequent to issuance of the bonds. Such a provision will typically include a deferred call period, during which the bond issue cannot be called for the purpose of refinancing at lower interest rates. For example, the issue might be noncallable during the first 5 or 10 years of its life. At the end of the deferred call period, the bond becomes callable for refunding purposes at a schedule of prices set out in the indenture. These call prices generally decline over the life of the issue and are frequently equal to par in the last few years of the issue's life. A common initial call premium is one year's coupons.

---

[1] This example assumes that exactly one month, representing one sixth of a coupon period, has elapsed since the last coupon payment and that five sixths of a coupon period remains. Therefore, it is consistent with the "day count" convention for corporate bonds, where it is assumed that a year consists of twelve months of equal length with thirty days in each. For some fixed-income securities, such as U.S. government bonds, actual days are counted. Full details on day count conventions are given by Bruce M. Spense et al., *Standard Securities Calculation Methods* (New York: Security Industry Association, 1973).

Bond issuers also normally reserve the right to call a bond issue for business purposes unrelated to refunding, such as financial reorganization. Moreover, if the issue has a sinking fund provision, as subsequently discussed, it will usually be callable for purposes of permitting the issuer to meet the sinking fund requirements. A separate schedule of call prices will be provided in the indenture for each of these types of call. Business purpose and sinking fund call provisions are considered noncontroversial by most bond issuers and buyers.

Sinking Fund. Occasionally, provision is made for the repayment of a bond issue gradually over its life rather than in one lump sum at maturity. Sinking fund clauses accomplish this objective. The term "sinking fund" tends to conjure up a process in which the borrower sets aside a sum of money each year so that, at the maturity date of the bond issue, there is a large pool of cash to pay off the bond issue. In fact, sinking funds now rarely operate in this way; rather, they provide for the actual retirement of a portion of the bond issue at periodic intervals. For example, the indenture might specify that, for a bond issue with an initial term to maturity of 25 years, the issuer must retire 5 percent of the bond issue annually beginning at the end of the sixth year of the bond's life. Such a sinking fund, which will retire 95 percent of the issue prior to the final maturity date, would be regarded as a "strong" sinking fund. A "weak" sinking fund might retire only 40 or 50 percent of the issue prior to maturity.

The indenture usually specifies that sinking fund requirements can be met by calling the necessary bonds, after which they are retired. Sometimes the indenture will contain a "doubler," a provision that gives the issuer the option of retiring additional bonds via sinking fund call if it so chooses. If the bond issue is sold to the general public, the issuer will typically have the option of meeting sinking fund requirements by acquiring bonds in the open market, an option that can be very valuable if the bonds are priced below the call price.

Features Not Contained in the Indenture

Marketability. Marketability or liquidity refers loosely to the degree to which bonds can be bought or sold quickly and with minimum price concessions. One extreme in marketability is represented by directly or privately placed bonds, which are sold initially to one or a very few institutional investors rather than to the general investment public. Such direct or private placements have *no* marketability, except perhaps in an occasional especially negotiated transaction.

Quality of Promise. A bond places an obligation on the issuer to do things in the future — frequently in the far distant future, sometimes 40 years or more. Unfortunately, bond issuers do not always keep their promises. Bond quality refers to the likelihood that the borrower will be willing and able to discharge its obligations fully and in a timely manner.

A common guide to bond quality is the rating assigned to a specific bond

TABLE 7.1 Descriptions of Bond Ratings

	Moody's	Standard & Poor's	Characteristics
Investment Grade	Aaa	AAA	Highest quality available; "gilt edge"; ability to repay is extremely strong
	Aa	AA	High quality, with only slightly less ability to pay than highest grade
	A	A	Upper medium grade, with strong ability to repay, possibly with some susceptibility to adverse economic conditions or changing circumstances
	Baa	BBB	Medium grade, with adequate ability to pay at the present time
	Ba	BB	Has speculative elements, with only moderate ability to pay
	B	B	Speculative issues, currently making contractual payments
Speculative	Caa	CCC	Issues of poor quality which may be in default on contractual payments
	Ca	CC	Highly speculative issues, characterized by major uncertainties, often in default
	C	C	In default, with poor prospects
	C	D	In default, with interest and/or principal payments in arrears

issue by one of the rating agencies, such as Moody's, Standard & Poor's, and Duff and Phelps. (See Chapter 19 for details on credit analysis.) Table 7.1 summarizes the rating scheme of the first two of the above-mentioned agencies. Although the ratings are probably influenced by many specific, measurable attributes of the issuer or by the specific bond issue, in the final analysis they are judgmental calls by the agencies. It is noteworthy that the ratings appear to incorporate assessments of bond marketability in addition to pure default risk considerations, although there is dispute as to the extent to which this is so.

Sometimes the quality of the promise of specific debt issues is enhanced by guarantees given by third parties. For example, the U.S. Government guarantees the payment of coupons and principal on some bonds issued by U.S. shipping companies for the construction of vessels that meet specified criteria. Obviously, such guarantees can increase the creditworthiness of the bonds, but it should be equally obvious that the guarantee is at best only as good as the guarantor, and that its value may be reduced by potential problems in forcing the guarantee to be made good.

Tax Status. Bonds vary considerably in the tax treatment of the coupon income they provide and in any capital gain or loss that results from owning them. Moreover, the tax treatment of these components of return is frequently different at the federal and state levels. Such tax considerations are obviously of the utmost importance to the investor and, hence, to the issuer.

Eligibility. Frequently, a body that is in a position to do so will specify that only certain types of debt issues can be used to fulfill some objective. Such debt is then said to be eligible for that purpose. For example, many municipalities specify that any of their funds placed with a depository institution must be backed by an especially segregated pool of federal government securities, and the insurance commissioners in some states restrict investment by insurors doing business in that state to an approved list of securities. Such eligibility may well have a bearing upon the approved securities' values, other characteristics being equal.

MAJOR BOND ISSUER CHARACTERISTICS

Bonds are essentially nothing more than contracts, and, as such, they can and do have almost infinite variations. This section describes typical attributes of bonds issued by some of the major borrowers in the long-term bond market. However, it should be noted that in the bond area, as in other fields of business and finance, there is no substitute for reading the contract and acquiring immediately relevant information.[2]

---

[2] A standard source of information on debt issues of the United States and its agencies is *Handbook of Securities of the United States Government and Federal Agencies*, published biannually by The First Boston Corporation. Information on other types of debt issues may be found in various *Moody's Manuals*, including the *Industrial Manual, OTC Industrial Manual, Public Utilities Manual, Transportation Manual, Bank and Finance Manual*, or *Municipal and Gov... ...nt Manual*, as appropriate. The last of these also covers U.S. government and agency debt.

U.S. Treasury Issues

The federal government is a major borrower in the long-term bond market, one whose relative importance has increased over the years and whose securities have come to represent a point of departure in bond design, pricing, and the like.

Long-term debt issued by the U.S. Treasury is conventional with respect to coupon and maturity payment patterns, with initial term to maturity varying widely, up to about 30 years. Such debt represents an unsecured general obligation of the U.S. Government. It has no sinking fund features. A limited number of U.S. Treasury issues are callable in the last five years of their life only. Specific issues are formally denoted as "bonds" or "notes," but this is a distinction without a difference. Notes initially are limited to maturities of 10 years or less and tend to be issued in larger amounts; thus, they have more marketability than bonds. However, for a given term to maturity, coupon and quantity outstanding, the two types of issues are interchangeable.

Due to the taxing and money creation powers of the U.S. Government, U.S. Treasury debt is regarded as free of default risk. For this reason, and because of its large quantity outstanding, both in total and with respect to specific issues, it is much more marketable than other forms of long-term debt. Marketability does vary considerably among issues, however, with the longer term to maturity and smaller issues exhibiting considerably less marketability than large issues of short term.

U.S. Treasury debt is subject to federal income taxes, with coupon receipts being taxed as ordinary income, and realized capital gain or loss being subjected to the usual capital gain or loss treatment, including favored treatment for long-term capital gains. However, Treasury securities are exempt from taxation at the state and local levels.

Agency Issues

An increasing fraction of U.S. government borrowing operations over the years has been conducted by the federal agencies, bodies created by the government to discharge specific tasks, such as to finance housing, rural electrification, or farmland acquisition. The agencies perform their financing function by borrowing in the public markets and then relending to the constituents they serve. Agency debt is conventional with respect to coupon and maturity, and normally does not have special features such as call or sinking fund provisions. Its credit quality varies. Issues of some agencies, such as the Government National Mortgage Association (GNMA), are guaranteed by the full faith and credit of the U.S. Government, while other issues, such as Federal National Mortgage Association (FNMA) debt, are only backed by the strength of the agency itself plus a strong implication that in the event of financial difficulty, the agency would be assisted by the federal government. Agency debt tends to be quite marketable, although less marketable than direct debt of the U.S. Treasury itself, in part because individual issues are of considerably smaller size.

At the federal level, the taxation of agency debt parallels that of U.S. Treasury debt; it is fully taxable. However, the tax status of agency debt at the state and local levels varies according to the issuing agency; some is taxed and some is tax-exempt. For this reason, and because of the differing nature of the federal guarantee, there is no substitute for knowing the characteristics of the individual issue under consideration.

Corporate Debt

Corporate debt is a term usually reserved for reference to the debt issued by for-profit business enterprises. Because of the power of the contract, and because patterns of funds needs by corporations vary widely, there is considerably more variety in the characteristics of corporate bonds outstanding than in issues of the federal government and its agencies. Nevertheless, some generalizations are possible. The typical corporate bond is conventional in its pattern of coupon flows and payoff at maturity, and is callable following a deferred call period, usually 5 or 10 years. Coupon income and capital gain or loss are subject to taxation in the usual manner at the federal level and are taxed as well at the state and local levels in whatever way other forms of ordinary income and capital gain or loss are taxed. Except for occasional issues guaranteed by the federal government, all corporate debt is formally subjected to default risk. Obviously, credit quality varies widely; however, bonds issued by some large, stable corporations are regarded virtually as safe as U.S. Treasury debt, while debt of companies in poor financial straits may be viewed as having so much default risk that it trades virtually as common stock. Corporate bonds also vary widely in marketability, although, even under the best of conditions, marketability is nowhere close to that of Treasury or agency debt. (See Chapter 10 for a further discussion of liquidity and marketability.)

It is typical and useful to subdivide corporate bonds according to the issuer, with common subdivisions being industrial bonds (i.e., those issued by an unregulated enterprise), utility bonds, transportation bonds, and financial bonds, depending upon the nature of the business and its regulation. Finer subdivisions are also possible; for example, the market appears to make a clear distinction among the bonds issued by a telephone company versus an electric utility versus a gas pipeline, and, indeed, it even appears to distinguish among bonds of electric utilities according to the primary fuel source.

With respect to the four major categories of issuer, industrial bonds typically provide more generous call protection to the investor than utility bonds; a deferred call period of 10 years is common. The majority of industrial bonds are unsecured, and most have some sort of sinking fund provision. Utility bonds typically offer no more than five years of call protection (this is frequently mandated by the regulatory authority), and are secured by mortgages on specific property. While many utility bonds appear to have sinking fund provisions, the indentures in such cases usually provide that the utility can satisfy the sinking fund by pledging additional property, and, indeed, this is the common practice, so normally there is no effective sinking fund. With the exception of the fact that transportation company bonds are frequently secured, it is not possible to generalize about features for transportation and financial bonds.

In addition to long-term bonds, corporations also frequently issue so-called notes with initial maturities of 10 or fewer years. In their essence, notes are nothing more than short-term bonds. They are typically noncallable over their life, have no sinking fund provision, and are unsecured.

Long-term corporate debt, as observed previously, is sometimes placed directly with investors rather than sold to the general investment public. By restricting the number of investors to whom an issue is marketed and sold, the issuer can avoid registration of the issue with the Securities and Exchange Commission and the associated disclosures and expenses. The traditional investors in direct placements (i.e., the larger life insurance companies and some pension funds), maintain professional staffs to analyze credit risk and negotiate direct placement loans. Since the issuer negotiates directly with the lender, it is possible to tailor a directly placed bond issue to accommodate the special needs of the issuer, whereas a publicly placed bond issue must be rather standard in its terms and conditions. For these reasons, two broad types of corporate bond issues tend to be dominant in the direct placement market. The prototypical direct placement is issued by smaller companies that wish to raise amounts of money that would be below the threshold for public issues (i.e., $10 million), that do not have established financial records, or that have specialized financing needs. The direct placement market is also used by large, financially strong corporate borrowers that wish to raise money for specialized projects, or that otherwise have constraints that are not easily explained within the strictures of a prospectus. For example, much of the debt issued to finance the North Slope petroleum pipeline was privately placed, presumably because of the temporary strain this financing put on the borrowers' balance sheets and because of the necessity to present plans and forecasts in marketing the debt.

Except for specialized indenture covenants designed to accommodate specific borrower or lender requirements, privately placed corporate debt is usually similar to publicly placed debt, with one exception: the issuer does not have the option of acquiring bonds in the marketplace in order to meet sinking fund requirements.

Other Relevant Instruments

In addition to the securities previously described, some other long-term bond-like security forms are relevant to borrowers, lenders, or both.

Municipal bonds are debt securities issued by states, localities, and special state-chartered government bodies. As is well-known, the coupon income (but not capital gain or loss) on municipal debt is exempt from federal income taxes, and specific issues may enjoy favorable tax status at the state and local levels as well. It is perhaps less well-known that municipal bonds, because of the large number of small issues, as a group tend to be much less marketable than conventional Treasury and corporate bonds. Municipal bonds are fully discussed in Chapter 8. However, it is important to remember that they represent a viable alternative for investors to long-term conventionally taxed debt. It is also important to recognize that an increasing portion of corporate borrowing takes place through the medium of industrial revenue bonds, bonds issued by a municipal body to construct a facility leased to an industrial user, with the lease payments pledged by the municipal body to pay off the debt.

Preferred stocks are corporate equities with a promised, fixed dividend that must be paid prior to payment of dividends on common stocks. Most preferreds are cumulative, meaning any dividends passed cumulate and must be paid prior to paying common dividends. Most are also perpetual, meaning there is no provision for their scheduled retirement at a specific point in time. Preferred shareholders also have a preference over common shareholders in receiving the proceeds from liquidating the firm up to the stated par or liquidating value of the preferred. For these reasons, preferred stocks are regarded somewhat like low grade corporate bonds in the marketplace. While the dividends on preferred stocks do not represent a tax-deductible expense to the corporation, they are 85 percent tax-exempt when received by a corporate taxpayer, a feature that makes them especially attractive to taxpaying corporations, such as property-liability insurance companies and, increasingly, life insurance companies. In recent years sinking fund preferreds, which do have explicit provision for retirement via sinking funds, have become popular. They are liked by insurance companies because they can be carried on statutory financial statements at acquisition cost, whereas ordinary preferreds must be carried at market value.

Residential and commercial mortgages have long been a popular investment medium with some types of institutional investors, such as thrift institutions and life insurance companies. However, their popularity has been limited by a number of factors, including the need for specialized skills in the lending process and the comparative lack of marketability of the resulting instrument. While circumstances remain much the same for commercial mortgages, they are now much different for residential mortgages. Over the past decade or so, arrangements have evolved that permit investors to place funds into home mortgages without any direct connection with the lending process. Several federal agencies and large private lenders have also issued mortgage-backed bonds, which in essence are nothing more than bonds secured by mortgages. Under one arrangement, involving mortgage pools, participations, or pass-throughs, shares in packages of mortgages assembled by lenders are sold to investors who then receive a pro rata share of monthly mortgage payments less a fee for the administration of the pool. The prototype of this type of arrangement, and by far the largest, is the GNMA program. GNMA pass-throughs, as they are called, are packages of Veterans Administration and Federal Housing Administration mortgages that have full faith and credit guarantees of the U.S. Government, and they have a reasonably active aftermarket. A number of participations packaged by other federal agencies and by private lenders are similar in form but usually incorporate some sort of private mortgage insurance. Such instruments have become a popular alternative to corporate bonds in institutional investment portfolios because of their safety, marketability, and yield characteristics. Their popularity has been hampered, however, by the uncertainty regarding the pattern of cash flows arising from the wide flexibility accorded the homeowner for mortgage prepayment, and possibly by their lack of familiarity as well.

INVESTMENT CONSIDERATIONS — YIELD, PRICE, AND RISK

Price and Yield Calculations

The yield on a bond is the basic measure of its cost to the issuer and the investment return it provides to the investor. It is also a proxy for bond price, for once the coupon and term to maturity of a bond is known, its price is determined by its promised yield, and conversely.

The "yield" of a security is essentially nothing more than the dollars of return per hundred dollars of initial investment it provides the investor per year. "Dollars of return" is synonymous with "enhancement of value." For example, a bond with a coupon rate of 12 percent and a term to maturity of 20 years, purchased initially at par, will generate $12 of additional value for the investor for each $100 initially invested in it; provided it is held to maturity, there is no gain or loss on its retirement. Each year, the investor's initial investment has been enhanced by 12 percent, so this is the yield on the bond.

While the concept of yield is not complicated, computations of it and with it can become quite complex. A number of these computational issues are explored in Chapter 6. However, two issues merit some attention here.

The first has to do with a semiannual compounding convention, which is the standard in the long-term bond area. In the immediately preceding example of the 12 percent coupon bond, the annual coupon will be received by the investor in two semiannual payments of $6 per hundred dollars of par value. Therefore, if the investor reinvests the coupon receipt paid at the end of the first half of the year, actual portfolio enhancement over the year should be a little more than 12 percent, due to the interest earned on the reinvested coupon. In fact, the rate of growth of the investment over the year, with semiannual compounding, is $[(1.06)^2 - 1] \times 100\% = 12.36\%$. However, by convention, the annual yield on bonds is expressed as twice the semiannual rate of return to the investor. For this reason, conventional yield numbers understate the rate of growth of fixed-income portfolios. For the same reason, care should be exercised in comparing yields on alternative investments, such as thrift institution time deposits, with yields on bonds, because yields quoted on the non-bond alternatives usually reflect the gains of compounding within a year, while the bond yields do not.

The second complication arises because fixed-income securities are not normally purchased at par. Therefore, over the life of the instrument, the investor or investors who hold it must realize a capital gain or loss in addition to receiving the semiannual coupons. This capital gain or loss is reflected in a basic representation of the bond pricing equation,

$$P = \sum_{t=1}^{2n} (C/2)/(1 + y/2)^t + M/(1 + y/2)^{2n} \tag{7.1}$$

where: P = price of the bond

n = life of the bond in whole years

C = annual coupon

y = the annual yield

M = maturity value

This equation has the effect of incorporating algebraically what was said previously in words: a bond is the sum of two promises, one to pay an annuity or fixed sum at regular intervals over the life of the bond, and another to pay a single, much larger amount at the end of the bond's life. The first term in the expression measures the present value of the annuity of coupons, while the second reflects the present value of the single payment at maturity. The equa-

TABLE 7.2   Price Determination for a 6 Percent Coupon, Three-Year Bond at a Yield to Maturity of 12 Percent

(1) Years From Present	(2) Coupon Periods From Present	(3) Cash Flow	(4) Discount Factor	=	(5) Present Value Factor	(6) Present Value (3) × (5)
0.5	1	$ 3	$1/(1.06)$		0.94339	$ 2.830
1.0	2	3	$1/(1.06)^2$		0.88999	2.670
1.5	3	3	$1/(1.06)^3$		0.83961	2.519
2.0	4	3	$1/(1.06)^4$		0.79209	2.376
2.5	5	3	$1/(1.06)^5$		0.74725	2.242
3.0	6	103	$1/(1.06)^6$		0.70496	72.611
Sum = Price						$85.248

tion does take account of the facts that coupons are received semiannually and the basic interval of time is the half year, but it also incorporates the convention that the annual yield is double the semiannual yield, which actually drives the computations.[3]

Table 7.2 shows the application of this equation to a bond with a coupon rate of 6 percent and a remaining term to maturity of three years when the yield is 12 percent. Under these conditions, the bond is worth less than par, $85.248 versus $100, or, in the terminology of the market, it sells at a discount, because the coupon rate is below the yield demanded by the market. Had the coupon rate been above the market yield, the bond would sell above par, or at a premium. What is going on is that if the coupon is below the yield, the investor pays less than par initially, with two effects: the size of the coupons relative to the initial investment is increased, and, in addition, there is a capital gain over the life of the investment, both of which increase the dollars of return per dollar of initial investment. The converse occurs when the coupon rate is above the yield. The resulting yield is customarily referred to as the yield to maturity, perhaps because it incorporates the capital gain, which cannot be finally realized until maturity.

The equation is written in a form in which price is a function of yield, even though, in many cases, the price is known and the yield is sought. This is done because the equation for yield as a function of price is very difficult to write, due to the many power terms of yield. The practical implication is that yields cannot be computed directly from the equation; instead, it is in effect necessary to solve Equation 7.1 for many yields and, in that way, to infer what yield is associated with a given price. In practice this is done by reference to yield books, which show a variety of coupon-term-yield price combinations or, more

---

[3] This is not the actual equation used in fixed-income analysis; that equation, which provides for fractional coupon payments and incorporates some complications arising from the fact that bonds normally sell "with interest," is an order of magnitude more complex.

TABLE 7.3   Funds Flow From $85.248 Invested at 6 Percent
Semiannually for Three Years

End of Half Year	End of Coupon Period	Interest Added	Balance	Withdrawal	Ending Balance
—	0	—	—	—	$85.248
0.5	1	$5.115	$ 90.363	$ 3	87.363
1.0	2	5.242	92.605	3	89.605
1.5	3	5.376	94.980	3	91.980
2.0	4	5.519	97.499	3	94.499
2.5	5	5.679	100.169	3	97.169
3.0	6	5.830	103.000	103	—

recently, by specialized calculators or computer programs, which take advantage of techniques for rapidly converging on a solution to such a problem.

Table 7.3 shows the results of a set of calculations based on the bond evaluated in Table 7.2 to make an important point. In these calculations it is assumed that the price of the bond obtained in Table 7.2, $85.248, is placed in an investment such as a passbook account into which the thrift institution every six months adds interest at 6 percent on the principal in the account over the entire preceding six months. Immediately after this interest is added, a sum equal to a semiannual coupon on the bond is withdrawn. As the calculations show, at the end of a run of periods equal to the life of the bond, the account will contain just enough money to enable payment of a final semiannual coupon plus $100, the par value of the bond. The point is that the money invested in a bond at its purchase price does indeed earn at a rate equal to the yield to maturity.

The Effect of Tax Considerations

Investors are frequently interested in the yield an investment will provide after allowance for the burden of taxes. Such a yield can be obtained by modifying Equation 7.1 and obtaining a solution, again using trial-and-error methods. It is necessary to reduce each coupon-related cash flow, $C/2$, by the taxes that would be due on that flow; multiplying by $(1 - t_0)$, where t_0 is the tax rate on ordinary income, does this. If the bond is purchased at a discount or premium, then tax effect of the capital gain or loss must also be taken into account. The Internal Revenue Code allows investors to either amortize the premium or discount on a straight-line basis over the life of the bond or to recognize the gain or loss at maturity. Such premium or discount amortization is treated as an adjustment to the coupon. The usual practice is to defer the gain on a bond purchased at a discount until maturity, thereby both deferring the taxes on the gain and making it a favorably taxed long-term gain under most circumstances, but to amortize the loss on a bond purchased at a premium, so as to reduce taxes on the coupon income.

When these adjustments are made to Equation 7.1, the result for bonds purchased at a discount is:

$$P = \sum_{t=1}^{2n} (C/2)(1 - t_0)/(1 + y/2)^t + [M - (M - P)t_g]/(1 + y/2)^{2n} \qquad (7.1a)$$

where t_g is the tax rate on capital gains and for bonds purchased at a premium

$$P = \sum_{t=1}^{2n} [C/2 + (P - M)/2n][1 - t_0]/(1 + y/2)^t + M/(1 + y/2)^{2n} \qquad (7.1b)$$

where terms are as defined before.

Promised vs. Expected Yields

The cash payments from investing in some bonds, such as those issued by the U.S. Treasury, are certain. In most situations, however, the possibility of default exists. In such circumstances the conventional yield to maturity probably overstates the rewards that the marketplace is expecting to obtain from the investment. Thus, in the mind of the investment community, the promised or nominal yield is adjusted downward by the probability of default to something more like an expected yield. It is customary in discussions of the bond market, whether they occur in a day-to-day, or in a more formal, context, to treat nominal yields as though they are certain. However, it is well to keep in mind that these are high-side proxy measures for the anticipated investment rewards on which the market is actually operating.

Yield Changes and Price Changes

Common sense and the previous equations both suggest that bond prices must change as interest rates change. A grasp of the relationships between yield and price changes is essential to understanding the determinants of yields on bonds of different characteristics, and it is also critically important in fixed-income portfolio management. This is the sort of thing managers must know if they are to structure bond portfolios to take advantage of anticipated changes in yields, or if they wish to assess the interest rate-induced price risk of an investment situation.

Table 7.4 shows the results of pricing out four bonds under three interest rate scenarios. Three of the bonds have coupons of 10 percent and terms to maturity of 10, 20, and 30 years; the fourth has a coupon of 5 percent and a term to maturity of 20 years. In the first line of the table, the yield to maturity at which the bonds are priced is 10 percent; in the second line it is 12 percent, and in the third line it is 8 percent. By analyzing the pattern of price change which these bonds display as they are repriced, some fundamental conclusions can be reached regarding price/yield relationships.

The most consistent and obvious result of this repricing exercise is that the bond prices move in opposite direction to the yield change; an increase in the yield decreases the price, and conversely, in all cases.

**TABLE 7.4   Bond Prices at Alternative Yields
(Change From Price at 10 Percent)**

Yield	10% Coupon, 10-Year Maturity	10% Coupon, 20-Year Maturity	10% Coupon, 30-Year Maturity	5% Coupon, 20-Year Maturity
10%	$100.00	$100.00	$100.00	$57.10
12	$ 88.53	$ 84.95	$ 83.84	$47.34
	(−11.5%)	(−15.0%)	(−16.2%)	(−17.1%)
8	$113.59	$119.79	$122.62	$70.31
	(13.6%)	(19.8%)	(22.6%)	(23.1%)

A second observation that can be made is that the sensitivity of bond prices to yield changes increases with term to maturity. The first three bonds have the same coupon and the same price, $100, when priced out at a yield initially equal to their coupon, on the first line. However, as the yield moves upward or downward by two percentage points, the longer the term the greater the departure of the price from par.

A third conclusion, which can also be observed by examining the price change of these three bonds closely, is that the sensitivity of prices to yield changes increases at a decreasing rate with term to maturity. This is an elaboration of the second conclusion. Each additional 10 years of maturity results in a larger movement in price upward when yields decrease, or downward when they increase, but the incremental movement gets smaller and smaller. For example, the decrease in yields from 10 to 8 percent increases the price of the 10-year bond by 13.6 percent; the same move increases the price of the 20-year bond by 19.8 percent, or 6.2 percentage points more; but for the 30-year bond, the price increase is only 2.8 percentage points greater, or 22.6 percent.

A final conclusion of interest deals with the effect of coupon level on the relationship between price change and yield change. For this purpose, it is useful to compare the price behavior of the 5 and 10 percent coupon bonds with 20 years to maturity. Since the 5 percent coupon bond is not initially priced at par, the percentage price changes from the first line are more useful than absolute price changes: such changes are given under the prices of the repriced bonds. What is seen from these percentage changes is that the smaller the coupon the larger the relative price change induced by a given change in yield. In other words, the price responsiveness of bonds to yield changes varies inversely with the coupon.

These conclusions are familiar to most who work with fixed-income securities, and they have stood them in good stead. However, in application, they suffer from two drawbacks: One is that they do not tell how price responsive bonds are. For example, knowing that one bond has a specified number of years longer term than another does not tell how much more price response to yield change the longer bond will display. A somewhat more serious drawback is that these conclusions do not give much insight into the relative effects of coupon and term to maturity. For example, between two bonds, one with both a smaller coupon and a shorter term to maturity than the other (a frequent comparison that arises in fixed-income management), it is not possible to say which will be more responsive to yield changes. The basic problem is that these conclusions do not provide any quantitative guidelines to price-yield sensitivity. It is always possible to make "what if" calculations as in Table 7.4, but this can be cumbersome.

An approach to this question that has recently become quite popular utilizes the measure duration, developed originally by Frederick Macaulay in 1938, but was relatively unknown until the last decade or so.[4]

The duration of a bond is a weighted-average measure of its life, in which the time a cash flow occurs is weighted by the proportionate contribution of that flow to the present value (price) of the bond. Algebraically, duration, D, is given as

$$D = \sum_{t=1}^{2n} (t/2)(C/2)/(1 + y/2)^t/P + [(2n/2)M/(1 + y/2)^{2n}]/P \tag{7.2}$$

which looks much like the basic bond-pricing equation, Equation 7.1, except that each cash flow term is divided by price to give its proportionate contribution to price, and premultiplied by $t/2$ or $2n/2$, the time into the future in years at which that cash flow occurs. Thus, duration incorporates consideration of the bond's coupon, term to maturity, and yield to maturity in a single number. Table 7.5 shows the arithmetic that goes into the calculation for the 6 percent coupon three-year bond priced to yield 12 percent considered previously, and may make the process more understandable.

The percentage change in a bond's price relative to the percentage change in one plus its yield is equal to the negative of its duration,

$$[\Delta P/P]/[\Delta(1 + y)/(1 + y)] = -D \tag{7.3}$$

which is to say that duration is an elasticity measure relating changes in price to changes in the discount factor. With a bit of rearrangement of Equation 7.3, a more useful (and certainly more popular) form of this relationship can be obtained:

$$(\Delta P/P)100\% = (\Delta y\ 100\%)(-D^*) \tag{7.4}$$

where D^*, adjusted duration, is equal to $D/(1 + y)$. Equation 7.4 simply says that the percentage change in the price of a bond is equal to the percentage *point* change in its yield multiplied by the negative of its adjusted duration. Its adjusted duration in turn is nothing more than its duration divided by one plus its initial yield. For example, the bond in Table 7.5 has a duration of 2.769 years, and, since its initial yield is 12 percent, its adjusted duration is 2.472 years, or $2.769/(1 + 0.12)$; if its yield should increase from 12 to 14 percent, a two percentage point change, its price would decrease by 4.94 percent; if its initial yield should decrease by one percentage point, its price would increase by 2.47 percent.

---

[4] Frederick R. Macaulay, *The Movement of Interest Rates, Bond Yields, and Stock Prices in the United States Since 1865* (New York: Columbia University Press, 1938.)

TABLE 7.5 Duration Computation for a 6 Percent Coupon Three-Year Bond Priced to Yield 12 Percent

(1) Years From Present	(2) Coupon Periods From Present	(3) Cash Flow	(4) Present Value Factor	(5) Present Value (3) × (5)	(6) Present Value as Proportion of Price (5)/Price	(7) Time of Receipt Weighted by Proportion (1) × (6)
0.5	1	$ 3	0.94339	$ 2.830	0.0332	0.0166
1.0	2	3	0.88999	2.670	0.0313	0.0313
1.5	3	3	0.83961	2.519	0.0295	0.0442
2.0	4	3	0.79209	2.376	0.0279	0.0558
2.5	5	3	0.74725	2.242	0.0263	0.0658
3.0	6	103	0.70496	72.611	0.8518	2.5554
Sum = Price				$85.248		
Sum = 1.0					1.0000	
Sum = Duration						2.7961

Duration has the property of additivity, which in this context means that the value-weighted-average duration of a bond portfolio has the same property as the duration of an individual bond in terms of evaluating price response to yield change. This feature accounts for much of the usefulness of duration in fixed-income investment management.

Figure 7.1 shows the effects of bond characteristics and bond market conditions on duration. Figure 7.1(a) shows that duration does increase with term to maturity, coupon held constant, but does so at a decreasing rate until a point is reached at which additional life produces no further increases in duration. Figure 7.1(b) shows that duration decreases as bond coupon increases, term to maturity held constant. Both these patterns are consistent with earlier observations regarding term to maturity or coupon and bond price change in response to yield change; that is, longer term and lower coupon mean more price volatil-

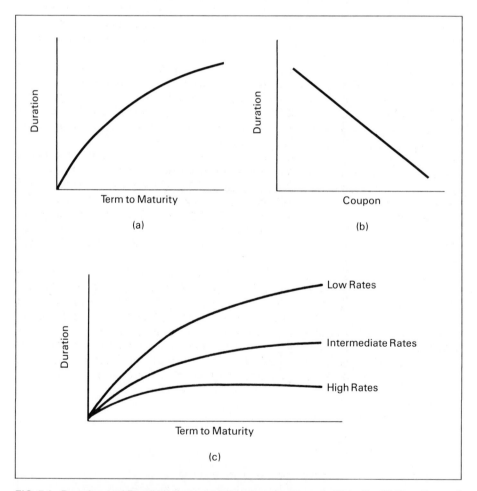

FIG. 7.1   Duration and Bond Attributes. (a) Duration and Term to Maturity; (b) Duration and Coupon; (c) Duration and Interest Rate Level

ity, just as longer duration implies greater price volatility. Finally, Figure 7.1(c) shows the effects of the level of interest rates on the relationship between duration and term to maturity. It can be seen that the higher the interest rates the smaller the durations, and the more quickly the duration/term to maturity relationship flattens out. This pattern means that, at higher interest rates, bonds of different maturities are more alike in terms of price responsiveness to yield change, and it also means that, at higher rates, bond prices show less response to a given change in yields.

Reinvestment Rates and Realized Compound Yields

It is sometimes asserted that the yield to maturity measure assumes that intermediate flows over the life of a bond are reinvested at the yield to maturity. As Table 7.3 and the related discussion indicates, this assertion is not correct, for yield to maturity is a purely internal rate. However, it is true that the average rate of return realized on a bond investment over its life can be quite different from its yield to maturity, provided intermediate flows are reinvested at yields which differ from the yield to maturity.

Table 7.6 illustrates the problem. Here a 20-year bond with a 10 percent coupon is priced at par. The middle column shows what happens when it is possible to reinvest all the intermediate coupon flows at a yield of 10 percent. At the end of 20 years, the terminal value of the investment is $704, and the terminal value ratio, or dollars of terminal value per dollar of initial investment, is 7.04. The annual rate at which the investment grows over the 20 years, the realized compound yield, is indeed 10 percent in this case.[5] However, this is not so if intermediate flows must be reinvested at some other rate. For example, in the first column, where it is assumed that the reinvestment rate is only 8 percent, the terminal value drops to $575.13, the terminal value ratio to 5.75, and the realized compound yield is only 8.94 percent. On the other hand, an increase in reinvestment rates, such as to 12 percent in the third column, raises the terminal value to $873.81, the terminal value ratio to 8.73, and the realized compound yield to 11.14 percent.

In the Table 7.6 example, only intermediate coupon flows must be reinvested. The reinvestment rate effect becomes considerably more spectacular when principal value or principal plus a call premium must be reinvested. Table 7.7 shows these circumstances. Here the investment horizon is still 20 years, but after 10 years the entire principal must be reinvested, a situation analogous to that which would arise if only a 10-year bond was purchased initially, or if the initial bond investment was called without a premium after 10 years. As long as the reinvestment rate remains at 10 percent, there is no problem; the

---

[5] Formulas used for these calculations are as follows:

$$\text{Terminal value} = \sum_{t=1}^{2n} C/2(1 + R/2)^t + M$$

Terminal value ration = Terminal value/price

Realized compound yield = $[(\text{Terminal value ratio})^{1/2n} \times 2] - 2$

where R = annual reinvestment rate and other terms are as used before.

TABLE 7.6   Investment Results From a 10 Percent Coupon, 20-Year Bond, Priced at Par, With Reinvestment

	Reinvestment Rate		
	8 Percent	10 Percent	12 Percent
Total coupons	$200.00	$200.00	$200.00
Earnings from coupon reinvestment	275.10	404.00	573.80
Total value of coupons at maturity	$475.10	$604.00	$773.80
Payoff at maturity	100.00	100.00	100.00
Total terminal value	$575.10	$704.00	$873.80
Initial price	$100.00	$100.00	$100.00
Terminal value ratio	5.751	7.040	8.738
Realized compound yield	8.94%	10.00%	11.14%

realized compound yield is still 10 percent. However, the larger amount to be reinvested has the effect of accentuating the impact of a diminution or increase in the reinvestment rate. For example, at an 8 percent reinvestment rate, the realized compound yield is only 8.66 percent, versus 8.94 percent previously, while at a 12 percent reinvestment rate, the realized compound yield is 11.47 percent, versus the 11.14 percent previously.

These examples have several messages; the most obvious is that in reinvesting, the rate of return that will be obtained from conventional coupon bonds is uncertain. There is no guarantee that a rate of return equal to the yield to maturity will be achieved, even if the bonds are free of default risk (i.e., they

TABLE 7.7   Investment Results From a 10 Percent Coupon, 10-Year Bond, Priced at Par, Over a 20-Year Horizon, With Reinvestment

	Reinvestment Rate		
	8 Percent	10 Percent	12 Percent
Total coupons	$100.00	$100.00	$100.00
Earnings from coupon reinvestment	48.90	65.30	83.90
Total value of coupons at maturity	$148.90	$165.30	$183.90
Payoff at maturity	100.00	100.00	100.00
Total terminal value	$248.90	$265.30	$283.90
Value at end of horizon	$545.40	$704.00	$929.80
Initial price	$100.00	$100.00	$100.00
Terminal value ratio	5.454	7.040	9.298
Realized compound yield	8.66%	10.00%	11.47%

are subject to reinvestment rate risk). Should interest rates subsequently rise, the investment may do better than anticipated, but a decline in rates will reduce rewards below those suggested by the yield to maturity. Therefore, the yield to maturity may be an irrelevant, or even a misleading, number in some circumstances. To make good decisions, it may be necessary to think in terms of realized compound yields, despite the fact that reinvestment rates will have to be forecasted. A subsequent section deals with ways of minimizing exposure to the reinvestment rate in the event the investor should choose to do so.

THE PRICING OF LONG-TERM BONDS

Thus far, the chapter has reviewed the features of long-term bonds, identified features associated with the bonds of different types of issuers, and examined some mechanics of bond price and yield. This section in effect puts all this material together by looking at the price determinants of specific bond issues. In other words, the question of how the marketplace values the various features of bonds is addressed. As a framework for discussion, the numbers contained in Table 7.8 are used, which show yields at selected points in time for a representative selection of securities.[6] (See Chapter 13 for a discussion of interest rate determinants.)

Term to Maturity

In Table 7.8, the first seven rows contain yields on U.S. Treasury bonds of varying maturity. Such bonds are ideal for appraising the effects of term on yield, because in other respects they are about as "pure" or homogeneous as can be hoped for; they are free of default risk, and their prices or yields are unaffected by many special features, such as call provisions or sinking funds.

These yields do not display a consistent pattern across the different maturities at each time point. Sometimes yield increases with term to maturity, and sometimes it decreases; and the incremental yield between bonds of different maturities is not constant in either direction. However, there is some tendency for the yields to increase with term to maturity, especially in the shorter maturities. This pattern is consistent with the generally accepted conception of the yield/maturity relationship, as shown in Figure 7.2; the ideal yield curve, or the plot of yields on default-free securities against term to maturity, rises with term to maturity, rapidly at first, then at a decreasing rate, until it is almost horizonal at the longest maturities.

The usual explanation for this shape of the ideal yield curve is based on the effect of term to maturity on the price change/yield change relationship. As seen in a preceding section, the longer the maturity of a bond the greater the percentage change in its price for a given change in yields. Therefore, if investors are adverse to fluctuations in the value of their bond investments, as seems

---

6 While these numbers are indeed promised yields to maturity rather than prices, they can be treated as inverse representations of price that are standardized for coupon rate.

TABLE 7.8   Yields of Selected Long-Term Bonds

	June 1980	December 1980	June 1981	December 1981	June 1982	December 1982	June 1983
U.S. government bonds[a]							
1. 1-year	8.16%	14.88%	14.86%	12.85%	14.07%	8.91%	9.66%
2. 2-year	8.73	14.08	14.51	13.29	14.47	9.66	10.18
3. 3-year	8.91	13.65	14.29	13.66	14.48	9.88	10.32
4. 5-year	9.21	13.25	13.95	13.60	14.43	10.22	10.63
5. 10-year	9.78	12.84	13.47	13.72	14.30	10.54	10.85
6. 20-year	9.89	12.49	13.20	13.73	14.18	10.62	11.12
7. 30-year	9.81	12.40	12.96	13.45	13.92	10.54	10.93
8. Federal agencies — 10 years[b]	10.45	12.35	13.20	13.85	14.10	11.20	11.05
9. Municipals — 20 years[a][c]	7.63	10.11	10.67	12.91	12.45	9.96	9.52
10. Aaa corporates[a][d]	10.58	13.21	13.75	14.23	14.81	11.83	11.74
11. Baa corporates[a][d]	12.71	15.14	15.80	16.55	16.92	14.14	13.37
12. Aa industrials[b][e]	11.20	13.38	14.25	14.50	15.00	12.13	12.25
13. Aa utilities[b][e]	11.88	14.38	15.38	15.50	15.88	12.50	12.25
14. Preferred stocks[a]	9.78	11.94	12.23	12.83	12.96	11.20	10.81

(a) From *Federal Reserve Bulletin*, various issues. Monthly averages
(b) From Salomon Brothers, Inc. As of first of month
(c) *Bond Buyer* series
(d) Seasoned, long term
(e) New issue, 20-year maturity

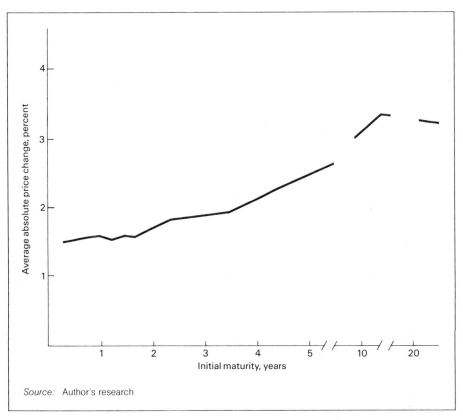

FIG. 7.2 **Return Volatility and Term to Maturity, U.S. Government Bonds, Quarterly, 1965–1977**

likely, and if interest rates vary by approximately the same amount across bonds of different term, then the additional price fluctuation of longer-term bonds should cause them to be viewed as more risky, and investors should demand higher yields to compensate them for bearing this risk. A careful analysis of the data in Table 7.8 reveals that, in fact, yields vary less for longer-term bonds, a phenomenon discussed later. (The average changes in yields from year-end to year-end in the table are 2.65 percentage points for 1-year bonds, 2.14 percentage points for 2-year bonds, 1.76 percentage points for 5-year bonds, 1.43 percentage points for 10-year bonds, 1.39 percentage points for 20-year bonds, and 1.30 percentage points for 30-year bonds.) Even so, longer-term bonds do tend to have greater price fluctuation, as shown in Figure 7.3. Apparently, the increasing responsiveness of longer-term bond price to changes in yield overpowers, at least in part, the dampening in yield variation of longer-term bonds. It is also evident from Figure 7.3 that the actual price fluctuation of longer-term bonds increases at a decreasing rate. Thus, the pattern of price change versus maturity provides a plausible explanation for the shape of the conventional or normal yield curve. This explanation is frequently

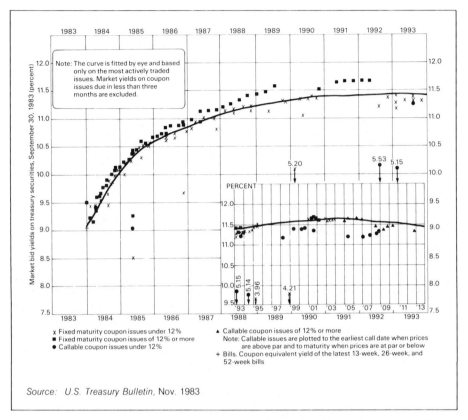

FIG. 7.3   Yield Curve Based on Yields of Treasury Securities, September 30, 1983, Based on Closing Bid Quotations

referred to as the liquidity premium hypothesis for the term structure of interest rates, as the yield/term relationship is often dubbed.

What about the situations in which the yield curve departs from this normal shape? The term structure literature offers two major competing explanations for this phenomenon. One is the segmentation hypothesis, which is based on the notion that investors in bonds, at least U.S. Treasury bonds, are self-divided into two groups. One of these, typified by commercial banks, has a propensity to invest in short-term securities; the other, of whom the life insurance companies are representative, prefer to invest long. The shape of the yield curve will then reflect the relative portfolio positions of these two groups. It is normally asserted as well that the portfolio position of the shorts is much more volatile than that of the longs. For example, in slack economic times the commercial banks may find themselves with excess funds, due to a lack of loan demand with which they flood the bond market, driving down yields on the short-term securities. In the meantime the long investors are going about their business as usual, so long yields are relatively less affected. The result will be a steeply upward-sloping yield curve. On the other hand, in periods of strong economic activity the banks will tend to liquidate their bond portfolio in order to make more profitable loans, thereby depressing prices and raising yields on short-term securities relative to those of longer term, and producing a downward-sloping yield curve. These scenarios are consistent with the observed yield curves at different parts of the economic cycle; that is, yield curves do in fact tend to be steeply upward sloping in periods of economic depression and downward sloping in times of especially tight money.

The major competitor to the segmentation hypothesis as an explanation for the shape of the term structure is the expectations hypothesis. According to this hypothesis, observable yields on longer-term securities reflect existing yields on short-term securities plus anticipated future short-term yields; when future short-term yields are expected to be below present short-term yields, present long-term yields should be below the short-term yields, and conversely.

To see why this pattern might prevail, two investors are considered. One has a relatively long-term horizon and is attempting to keep investment funds at work. Reinvestment rates are of considerable interest to him. If he anticipates that yields will drop in the future, he will prefer to lock his funds up now in long-term securities, and in attempting to do so, he will drive long-term prices up and yields down relative to those of short term. His alternative to investing for the long run is to invest short, with the anticipation of rolling over his funds into new short-term investments, but he will do so only if he can earn a high rate on his funds initially invested short in order to compensate for the lower anticipated reinvestment rate. The other investor is strictly interested in short-term capital gains, but she also anticipates a decline in interest rates. She will prefer to buy long in order to obtain the larger price increases long-term securities will provide if interest rates do indeed decline, thereby raising prices and reducing yields on long bonds. She will buy short-term issues only if short yields are high enough to compensate for the capital gains she will forego. The result in either event is a downward-sloping yield curve.

These stories can be told in a somewhat different manner to justify an upward-sloping yield curve should yields be anticipated to increase by the two investors. It is noteworthy that the expectations hypothesis, by asserting that long rates are an average of present and expected future short rates, provides a direct explanation for the tendency for long rates to fluctuate less than short rates.

It is difficult to appeal to observation in order to determine whether the segmentation hypothesis or the expectations hypothesis is the more valid. Both tend to be consistent with observed term structures, as times when bank-lending resources are strained tend to be just the times at which interest rates are expected to decline in the future, and conversely. In combination with the liquidity premium hypothesis, with which both are compatible, either of these theories can explain extremes in the slope of yield curves, as in Figure 7.4, which shows several typical yield curves and the explanations provided by each theory.

Marketability

The eighth row of Table 7.8 shows yields on long-term bonds issued by the federal agencies. These yields are always above those on U.S. Treasury securi-

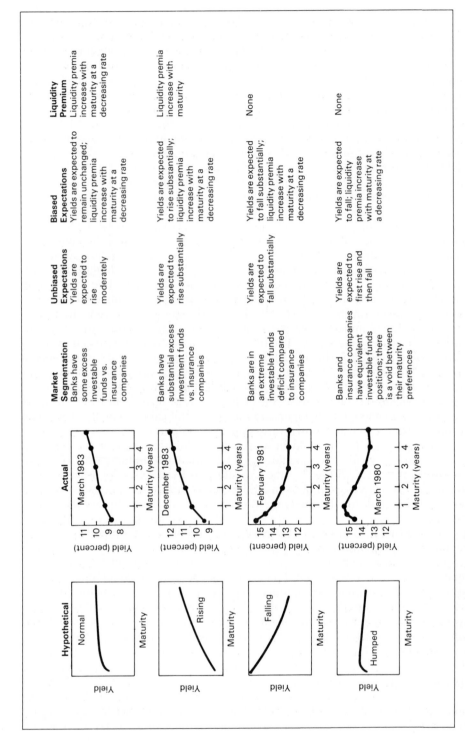

FIG. 7.4 Yield Curves and Their Explanations

ties of comparable maturity, 10 years. Several factors may account for this yield difference, including possible differences in perceived credit quality and institutional considerations such as eligibility. However, it is likely that a major factor is the lower marketability of the agency issues in comparison with the Treasuries. In any event, it is generally accepted that more marketable bond issues command higher prices and thus carry lower yields. Possibly the clearest example of this proposition, though it is difficult to document, is in the pricing of privately placed versus publicly placed corporate debt, where, it is frequently asserted, a yield increment of 25 to 50 basis points (a quarter to a half of a percentage point) on the direct placements is demanded by the marketplace.

Quality of the Promise

Rows ten and eleven of Table 7.8 show the yields on long-term publicly placed corporate debt rated Aaa and Baa. In both cases these yields are above those on comparable maturity federal agency and Treasury bonds. It is not possible to assign the yield differential between the Aaa bonds and the two types of government issues exclusively to differences in the quality of the promise (marketability considerations, tax considerations, and more subtle variations such as differences in sinking fund features probably play a role as well), but differences in default risk almost surely account for much of the yield differential between the two grades of corporate bonds.

In a preceding section a distinction was drawn between promised or nominal yields, of which the yields in Table 7.8 are representative, and yields expected by the marketplace after adjustment downward for anticipated acts of default. An obvious question, and one that is extremely important for fixed-income investment, is whether expected yields are also greater for bonds of lower quality, that is, whether a pure risk premium is built into the yield structure in addition to the more obvious actuarial adjustment for defaults. If indeed there is such a risk premium, then a strategy of investing in lower quality bonds should generate superior investment return over time. This is the strategy underlying the "junk bond" funds that have become popular in recent years.

Many believe there is such a risk premium, basing their argument either on the theoretical ground that the marketplace should extract a reward for bearing default risk, or on the empirical observation that in postwar years, lower grade bonds have generated higher returns than higher grade bonds. Others are not sure. They observe that there are a large group of investors, life insurance companies are frequently mentioned, who have widely diversified portfolios, considerable expertise in evaluating risk, and long investment horizons. Such investors may well be able to tolerate default risk and will happily do so if the expected returns for such a strategy should exceed those of a lower risk strategy. They also point out that the postwar experience may reflect nothing more than overestimates of the frequency and severity of corporate bond defaults, perhaps due to an underestimate of the continuing strength of the U.S. economy; in order for realized returns to provide a correct guide to expected returns, it is necessary that the incident of defaults be approximately as expected before the fact.

While it may now be dated to the point of being irrelevant, there is an interesting study bearing on this issue. In a monumental investigation underwritten initially by the Works Progress Administration to generate work for unemployed economists and statisticians during the Depression, a team of investigators headed by W. G. Hickman examined the investment experience of all straight corporate bonds issued in an initial amount of $5 million or more between 1900 and a period that was eventually carried up through 1943.[7] This period has the advantage of spanning a great variety of economic conditions in the U.S. economy, including the years of the Depression. Among other things, they looked both at the promised yields on these securities at the time of issue and the actual returns provided to investors, taking account of acts of default and events in which the bonds were called. They found that, while on average there were positive risk premia built into the yields at which the bonds were initially issued, these premia were almost completely neutralized by acts of default, which tended to lower yields on the lower grade bonds, and by events of call, which tended to raise yields on the higher grade bonds.

However, the story does not end at this point. Some years later the Hickman data were reanalyzed by Fraine and Mills.[8] These investigators claimed that the Hickman conclusions were distorted in two ways. First, at the end of the study period in 1943, bonds outstanding at that time were valued at market in order to determine their realized returns, but this was a time in which interest rates were held artificially low in connection with financing the war effort, and thus, bond prices were artificially high. Second, including the effects of bonds being called at premia over par tended to overstate expected returns. Therefore, they repeated the analysis valuing all bonds outstanding in 1943 at prices of par or at market, whichever was lower, and by treating all bonds called as paid off at par. The result was then a positive incremental return realized on average by the purchasers of the lower grade bonds.

Hickman had a further finding that was essentially undisputed by Fraine and Mills, which is probably the more important for practical bond issuance or investment decisions. The yield differentials between bonds of different quality are anything but constant over time; this is readily evident in Table 7.8. Hickman found that lower grade bonds issued at times when the before-the-fact yield premia on such bonds were extremely large tended to provide significantly higher investment returns than higher grade bonds, even after defaults, presumably because the market overestimated the risks of default and extracted large risk premia. On the other hand, lower grade bonds issued at times when the yield premia were small tended to underperform high grade bonds. The message, which is no doubt valid today, is that the swings in the market's assessment of default risk, and hence in the premia it extracts for bearing default risk, tend to exceed actual variation in default risk, so that lower grade bonds can be quite rewarding investments in some markets, yet be relatively overpriced in others.

---

[7] W. Braddock Hickman, *Corporate Bond Quality and Investor Experience* (Princeton, N.J.: Princeton University Press and National Bureau of Economic Research, 1958).

[8] Harold G. Fraine and Robert H. Mills, "Effects of Default and Credit Deterioration on Yields of Corporate Bonds," *Journal of Finance,* Vol. 16 (Sept., 1961), pp. 423–434.

Tax Considerations

Rows nine and fourteen of Table 7.8 show respectively the yields on municipal bonds and preferred stocks. While municipals are the subject of another chapter, they are useful here to illustrate a more general point about taxation and bond prices. It is hardly surprising that the municipal bond yields are uniformly below those on corporate bonds of equivalent quality, since the coupon income from the municipals is exempt from federal taxation. Taxpaying investors therefore find it attractive to purchase these bonds despite their comparatively low yields because, after taxes, the yields are at least as high as those they can obtain on fully taxed securities. In effect, what is happening is that investors are focusing on after-tax yields and pricing bonds accordingly, while yields which are customarily quoted are pretax yields. Therefore, the lower pretax yields reflect the value of the special tax feature. Other subtle effects of such tax-adjusted yield pricing are seen in a later discussion of coupon considerations.

The yields on preferred stocks also reflect such tax considerations, but less obviously. It is evident from Table 7.8 that this particular series of preferred stock yields is uniformly lower than the yields on Aaa corporate bonds, a phenomenon which may, at first blush, seem very peculiar, as the corporate bonds represent a senior claim and the preferred stocks represent a very junior claim on essentially the same assets and income stream. However, tax considerations make this phenomenon very rational. Dividend income is 85 percent tax-exempt when received by a corporate taxpayer. Therefore, to taxpaying corporate investors in fixed-income securities, the preferred stock dividends are essentially tax-free. Considering yield only, they can purchase preferred stocks, bidding their prices up and forcing their yields down, until the point at which the yields after taxes to them are just equal to those of fully taxed securities. The result is lower yields, pretax, on these partially tax-sheltered securities than on fully taxed fixed-income securities. Obviously, this same consideration tends to reduce the attractiveness of preferred stocks to investors who are not taxpaying corporations.

Refunding Call Features

Most longer-term corporate issues become refundable at the option of the issuer sometime during their life. Such call features unequivocally reduce the attractiveness of the bonds to investors and therefore increase the yields on the bonds in the marketplace. The prospect of call is unappealing to investors for two reasons.

First, it tends to result in a price ceiling on the bond. If interest rates decline and prices approach the call price, the knowledge that the bond is subject to being called at that price causes prospective investors to become disenchanted with the bond and unwilling to pay much more for it. Even if the bond is not currently callable but might soon become callable, then the knowledge of that possibility will have a similar impact. This effective price ceiling puts a lid on the capital gains that can be realized from the bond should interest rates drop, and the rare opportunity to make large capital gains on bonds is not something fixed-income portfolio managers pass up lightly! [9]

The second reason investors do not like refunding call is the reinvestment problem it poses. If interest rates have declined to the point that the issuer finds it attractive to replace the bonds with funds borrowed at a lower rate, then it virtually follows that the long-run investor is going to be forced to roll over funds at a lower interest rate and therefore will suffer a loss. This is so even when the bond carries a substantial call premium. For example, consider a hypothetical 10 percent coupon bond with 20 years remaining to maturity and callable at 110. It is assumed that yields on bonds of similar quality and term to maturity, but not threatened by call, dropped to 8 percent. At this yield the example bond should sell for approximately $120 in the absence of the call feature. If the issuer called the bond, the investor would be able to acquire 1.1 bonds carrying an 8 percent coupon and priced at par. The annual coupon income on these bonds would be only $8.80 (1.1 × $8), a loss of coupon income of $1.20 per year. Over the remaining 20 years this loss would aggregate to $24, considerably in excess of the extra $10 of par value the investor would receive at maturity. Therefore, the investor comes out behind over the long run even though in the short run he has done quite well, selling his bond above par and probably making a nice capital gain in the process.

The same considerations that make a refunding call unattractive to the investor make it very rewarding to the issuer. Even though the issuer must often pay more than par for the bond in order to effect its call, the reduced interest expense over the life of the original issue can more than compensate. A message here for both issuers and purchasers of bonds with call provisions is that the apparent level of yields on such issues is overstated. The increased probability of subsequent call for bonds issued under such conditions means that, over the original maturity horizon of bonds issued under such conditions, the issuer will likely not pay as much nor will the investor earn as much as the initial yield on the bonds implies. The effect, then, is to shave down the apparent peaks in interest rates.[10]

Sinking Fund Provisions

As noted previously, most corporate bonds issued by industrial firms carry sinking funds of varying intensity. The presence of such sinking funds tends to reduce the yield demanded by the marketplace. This yield effect is sometimes attributed to risk considerations, the idea being that the sinking fund results in

---

[9] It should be noted that because of this effective price ceiling, bonds whose prices are artificially held down by it, or "cushion bonds," can sometimes be bought at yields that are abnormally high in the prevailing interest rate environment. These bonds are cushioned against price declines if interest rates should rise, at least to a point, because their prices are artificially low. However, the change in effective maturity that can occur when the marketplace's horizon shifts from the point at which call is expected to the maturity date of the issue can produce substantial price declines if rates do rise enough to make call unlikely.

[10] For evidence on the effect of call in reducing yields at local peaks over the years 1956–1964, see Frank C. Jen and James E. Wert, "The Effect of Call Risk on Corporate Bond Yields," *Journal of Finance*, Vol. 22 (Dec. 1967), pp. 637–651.

gradual paydown of the issue and avoids any crisis at maturity that might occur if a large balloon of debt becomes due at one time. Such an explanation probably has some validity, especially for bonds of less creditworthy issuers. The fact that a sinking fund reduces the effective term to maturity of a bond is probably also important in reducing yields.

However, another, more subtle, influence is possibly more significant in explaining the reduced yield. Sinking fund provisions of publicly placed bonds normally give the issuer the option of calling the bonds or acquiring them in the marketplace in order to satisfy the debt reduction requirement. If the bonds are selling at a discount, which has been the experience on bonds in many of the postwar years, then the issuer can save money by acquiring them below par rather than calling them at or above par. Indeed, under these circumstances the issuer can bid very aggressively for the bonds and still come out ahead. This possibility is not lost on the more sophisticated fixed-income investors, and in recent years they have routinely attempted to "collect" bonds with strong sinking funds and a limited floating supply in the hopes of subsequently reselling them to the issuer. The result, of course, is lower yields than the bonds would otherwise carry.

It should be evident, however, that the sinking fund provision can be a two-edged sword. For bonds selling at a premium, the sinking fund call can serve very much as a refunding call even when the bonds are not currently refundable or are callable for refunding only at a higher price. This adverse effect of the sinking fund provision can be especially pronounced when the issue has a doubler provision allowing the issuer to increase the size of the sinking fund call at its option.

From the issuer viewpoint, the option to acquire the bonds in the aftermarket rather than pay them off at par or above is a valuable one; it means that if interest rates should rise over the life of the issue, then the effective interest expense may be considerably less than suggested by its initial price and coupon. The fact that directly placed bonds do not carry this option therefore reduces their attractiveness as a means of raising capital.[11]

Security Status

Despite what one's intuition might suggest, debt indenture covenants, which give bondholders a claim on some assets of the issuer, do not usually appear to have much effect on bond yields. Indeed, casual observation suggests that the opposite may be so. It is almost as though issuers secure bonds only if their intrinsic creditworthiness is such that they must do so in order to obtain financing, and the market, recognizing this, demands a higher yield from such issuers. The worth of claims on specific assets probably lies more in the power they give bondholders over the operations of the issuer than on the realizeable value of the assets in question, many of which have low marketability. A possible exception may be found in the transportation industries, where some types of equipment, by virtue of being highly mobile and reasonably marketable, do

---

[11] See Andrew J. Kalotay, "Sinking Funds and the Realized Cost of Debt," *Financial Management*, Vol. 12 (Spring, 1982), pp. 43–54.

constitute good enough security to actually reduce the risk exposure of the investors.

Rows twelve and thirteen of Table 7.8 break out two types of corporate bond yields: the yields on newly issued Industrial bonds and Utility bonds rated Aa. It is readily apparent that the industrials have lower yields than the equivalent utilities. It is not totally evident why this is so. Professional bond portfolio managers frequently attribute it to supply/demand considerations, pointing out that there is a rather steady flow of new utility bonds due to their financing programs, while the new supply of industrial bonds, especially those of high quality, is rather limited. The result may be something of a "scarcity factor" at work. It is not conceivable to think that the market would pay more than a rational price for any security, including an industrial bond, simply because it is rare, but it may be that utility bonds are not perfect substitutes for industrial bonds because of some consideration, such as portfolio diversification.

Another possibility is that utility and industrial bonds are not actually equivalent securities. As noted previously, the industrials usually carry sinking fund provisions, while the utilities do not, and they usually are issued with more initial call protection than the utilities; both these differences may increase the value of the industrials relative to the utilities. The perceived credit quality of industrial bonds may also be higher than equivalently rated utility bonds. For example, the market may be responding to the greater flexibility of the industrials than of the regulated utilities to enter or leave markets and to raise or lower prices. In any event, the higher yield on utility than on industrial bonds is a quite noticeable characteristic of bond pricing that is probably representative of other yield differences among various sectors of the long-term bond market.

Coupon Level or Price Discount

All of the features reviewed previously in this section are built into the specification of the bond: its term to maturity, sinking fund status, and the like. However, one of the most important attributes in determining yields of bonds is the coupon rate or something that is closely akin to it, the discount of the price from par. Since most bonds are initially issued with coupons approximately equal to prevailing yields to maturity and, hence, with prices approximately equal to par, this coupon level or price discount phenomenon is confined to bonds that have been outstanding for some time in a rising interest rate environment. The nature of the relationship, which is a quite pronounced one, is that the yield to maturity tends to be lower as the coupon is lower and as the price discount from par is higher. This relationship appears to hold for all types of conventionally taxed bonds, including government and corporate issues.

Two factors seem to be responsible. The first is tax considerations and, in particular, the capital gains treatment accorded the appreciation on a bond bought at a discount and held to maturity. To illustrate how this influence might operate, the three hypothetical bonds appearing in Table 7.9 are considered. Each has years to maturity and no sinking fund, but the coupon rates are 10, 8, and 6 percent. Assuming for a moment that the prevailing yield on bonds of this quality and maturity is 10 percent, then the first row of the table shows the

TABLE 7.9   Prices and Yields of 10-Year Bonds

	Coupon		
	6 Percent	8 Percent	10 Percent
Price at 10 percent yield to maturity	$78.08	$87.54	$100.00
After-tax yield at ordinary rate of 30 percent, capital gains rate of 12 percent	7.50%	7.27%	7.00%
Price to yield 7 percent after tax	$78.82	$89.41	$100.00
Pretax yield at this price	9.30%	9.67%	10.00%

prices the bonds would command in the marketplace, with the 10 percent coupon bond selling for par and the 8 and 6 percent coupon bonds selling for progressively larger price discounts. Now it is assumed each of these bonds are purchased by an investor in a 30 percent tax bracket on ordinary income and in a 12 percent bracket on capital gains. As the second row of the table shows, this investor would realize progressively higher yields to maturity on the bonds with the larger price discounts after taking into account the taxes that would have to be paid. However, this situation would not prevail very long in an efficient market in which the typical investor was in the 30 percent tax bracket. What would happen is that the market would bid up the price and drive down the yield of the discount bonds compared to the par bond. The third row of the table contains a set of prices that would make the after-tax yield on each of the discount bonds equal to the after-tax yield of 7 percent of the par bond to this typical investor. Finally, the fourth row of the table shows the pretax yields associated with these tax-neutral prices, and indeed they are lower if the coupon is lower or the discount higher.

There is a rather obvious investment implication in this demonstration. Investors in low or zero tax brackets would rationally prefer the current coupon bond because of its higher yield to them. Investors in tax brackets higher than 30 percent would still prefer the discount bonds. This general implication is well understood by professional fixed-income portfolio managers even though there is considerable uncertainty as to the equilibrating rate in the marketplace. It has been suggested that this rate is around 30 percent in the U.S. government bond market, but it has traditionally been viewed as little higher than zero in the corporate bond market. These figures are probably dated, and the currently relevant government rate is probably below 30 percent, while the corporate rate is meaningfully above zero.

The primary difficulty in estimating the equilibrating rate for corporate bonds is that it overlaps with the second consideration that accounts for the lower yields to maturity on lower coupon, higher discount bonds, the implicit call protection provided by the coupon or discount. It should be readily evident that the risk of call on a callable bond with a 10 percent coupon exceeds the risk of call on an 8 percent coupon bond, and its risk of call in turn exceeds that on a

6 percent bond, as interest rates would have to fall progressively further before it would pay the issuer to call the lower coupon bonds to replace them with even lower cost debt capital. Indeed, a low coupon is the best protection against call that is available; bonds with deferred call periods will one day become callable, and call premia will decline over time, but a bond with a low coupon will always retain that characteristic. In order to obtain this call protection, investors will sacrifice some yield to maturity on bonds where call is a possibility, such as corporate bonds.

Seasoning

It is frequently alleged by professional bond managers that a process of "seasoning" operates in the bond market, whereby newly issued bonds yield more than similar bonds which have been outstanding for some time. This seems rather unlikely, and, in fact, the priors are that the yield differences would be in the opposite direction, as it is generally agreed that the marketability of newly issued bonds exceeds that of seasoned issues. Indeed, evidence has recently been produced that tends to the conclusion that the seasoning effect is actually due to the tendency of the seasoned bonds to carry coupons below those on the new issues, with the effects noted in the prior section.[12]

Recapitulation and Interpretation

The bottom line, then, is that the yield of a bond, or its mechanically derived price, depends on many things. Term to maturity is important, as are coupon level and marketability considerations, for both government-issued and corporate bonds. Moreover, for corporate bonds, features of the indenture, including sinking fund and call provisions, are important, as is the identity of the issuer itself and the credit quality of the instrument. These considerations are significant in designing a bond issue or structuring a bond portfolio because of their influence on the yield or cost of the issue.

It is noteworthy that while the prices and yields of bonds with different features tend to rise and fall together, the relative prices of these features change over time. For example, in Table 7.8 it can be seen that the yield spreads between the different lines, representing different sectors of the bond market, do not remain constant. Therefore, in designing an issue or structuring a portfolio, the concern is not only with the typical price of some characteristic or sector, but also with the current price relative to other alternatives. In one environment a company may issue intermediate rather than long-term bonds, or currently callable rather than deferred call bonds, because the structure of bond market prices or yields suggests that it is relatively cheap to do so. In a similar manner, portfolio managers, who obviously have more flexibility than bond issuers, may frequently shift among different bond market sectors, depending on their assessment of the risks and rewards from doing so.

---

[12] John D. Martin and R. Malcolm Richards, "The Seasoning Process for Corporate Bonds," *Financial Management,* Vol. 11 (Summer, 1981), pp. 41–48.

INVESTMENT MANAGEMENT OF FIXED-INCOME PORTFOLIOS

Professional investment managers customarily separate the management of fixed-income securities from the management of other assets, such as equities, and refer to this package of securities as the fixed-income portfolio. Presumably, this practice is a reflection of characteristics, objectives, and concerns of fixed-income portfolios and portfolio management which differentiate them from other types of investment problems. Moreover, fixed-income portfolios differ among themselves in terms of their objectives and concerns, and, for this reason, quite different management techniques are appropriate when dealing with the various kinds of portfolios.

Portfolio Objectives and Concerns

Fixed-income portfolios appear to self-group into three categories. A common type of portfolio, one that is probably representative of traditional fixed-income investment management, is intended to provide a steady and reliable flow of spendable income over time, where "income" is equated with coupon payments by the security issuer. Portfolios created for the benefit of foundations, educational institutions, charities, and other eleemosynary institutions are prototypes; many portfolios managed for the benefit of individuals (such as the "income beneficiary" in an income beneficiary-remainderman trust) are also representative of this type. Mature pension funds in the liquidation phase are also essentially income portfolios even though they draw on both principal and the income stream to provide benefits. The portfolio and beneficiary are frequently tax-exempt or in modest tax brackets. Primary concerns in the management of such portfolios are things that could impair the income stream, such as acts of default, widespread exercise of call options by issuers, and the possibility of having to reinvest maturing bonds at low interest rates. These income portfolios tend to be managed conservatively, and they have traditionally stressed a passive, buy-and-hold investment posture, although there has been some trend toward more active management in the last two decades.

A second type of fixed-income portfolio, at the opposite end of the spectrum from the income-oriented portfolio, is the one in which total returns, considering both coupon income and capital gain or loss, are the investment objective. The fixed-income component of balanced mutual funds, the portfolios of aggressive individual investors, and occasionally the fixed-income holdings of pension funds in the growth phase typify such total return-oriented investment. In portfolios of this type, fixed-income securities are effectively no more than another type of investment medium, albeit one with somewhat distinctive features that have some affect on management practices. Tax considerations can be critical, as in the case of portfolios managed aggressively for individual accounts. In the management of such portfolios, changes in value and the things that affect value, such as changes in the level of interest rates and in the relative prices or yields in the various fixed-income sectors, are the name of the game. The objective is to structure the portfolio to best exploit these kinds of market changes. Total return investment tends to be active rather than passive, and may involve frequent trading. In recent years this type of fixed-income security investment has become quite popular.

A third type of fixed-income portfolio is managed with an eye to accumulation of value. Such portfolios typically have a long time horizon and a continuing commitment to fixed-income securities; cash income flows, as well as other cash flows, such as those which result from maturing bonds, are reinvested in the portfolio. The portfolio is frequently tax-exempt. Bond funds representing pooled individual retirement accounts typify this type of investment, and many pension funds in the growth or accumulation stage are managed in this manner. The overall objective is to generate the maximum amount of value at some point or series of points in the future, subject to keeping risk levels within tolerable limits. Therefore, the major task is profitable initial investment or reinvestment of portfolio flows, and reinvestment risk is the primary concern. The style of management of such portfolios is in a stage of flux. Traditionally, they were managed in a very passive manner. Over time this passive investment has tended to give way to a more active style, but recently there has been a considerable move backward to passive techniques, especially some comparatively new passive investment management techniques.

Portfolio Management Practices and Techniques

An Overview. Fixed-income portfolio management has not traditionally been among the more dynamic areas of investment management, to say the least. The image of the investor who buys newly issued bonds and locks them away until they mature has a substantial base in reality. However, since the mid-1960s, fixed-income investment managers have become much more aggressive, or "active," as they describe it. This increased activity is probably attributable to two specific developments, in addition to a general rethinking of investment practices that has had an impact on all areas of investments. First, the heightened volatility of interest rates and bond prices has made it prospectively more rewarding to seek out opportunities for gain and to avoid losses if possible. Second, increased marketability in the bond market and the greater relative importance of the more liquid government bond market together have made active management more feasible than formerly. It is interesting, though, that since 1979, there has been something of a swing back to passive investment management. The difference is that the new passive investment management has its basis in caution rather than in indolence, and much of it incorporates new theoretically suggested responses to reinvestment rate risk.

Credit Analysis and Management. Regardless of the portfolio objective, the matter of bond quality must always be addressed. Fixed-income investment management has traditionally been described as a negative art, one in which the manager identifies a universe of bonds that meet specified portfolio criteria, and then proceeds to eliminate those that pose unacceptable risk in terms of characteristics such as credit quality. However, actual portfolio management practices with respect to credit analysis and the assessment of default risk vary widely. Many managers implicitly accept the proposition that the agency ratings of credit quality provide reasonably satisfactory representations of default risk, especially when the costs of additional analysis are considered, and they do little or no further credit analysis. Others also seem to accept this proposition but routinely go through rather standardized credit analysis for the purpose of providing checks on the rating agencies and possibly satisfying regulatory bodies to whom they are subject, some of whom require independent credit analysis.

At the other extreme, some fixed-income investment managers feel that enough situations exist in which specific bonds are improperly rated by the agencies and then traded according to these improper ratings to make it worthwhile to seek them out through detailed, extensive credit analysis. For obvious reasons, these managers tend to be associated with large fixed-income portfolios. Their objective is to identify, for purchase, bonds with higher credit quality than is consistent with the bonds' market yields, and to avoid bonds whose yields are excessively low compared to their true default risk. Sometimes they also seek to identify bonds that will be rerated by the agencies before this rerating is reflected in the bonds' prices so that they can profitably trade in the bonds in advance of the market adjustment.

Practices with respect to default risk levels that are tolerated in the portfolio also vary widely. Some portfolios adhere to a policy of high quality holdings only. This stance is consistent with the notion that high yield alone cannot compensate for low quality, since it may take many years of earning a percentage point or two higher yield to compensate for the loss of principal value that may occur in the event of default.[13] However, it may also be motivated by more subtle considerations. Low quality bonds are much more susceptible to breaks in price simply because of heightened concern in the marketplace about the prospect of default. A high quality strategy avoids exposure to such market risk. It also simplifies the problem when a portfolio manager is trying to accomplish a pure play on some other bond-pricing element, such as attempting to exploit an anticipated change in interest rates. In addition, because the returns of lower grade bonds are more highly correlated with returns on common stocks, presumably because the level of concern about the prospect of default varies with the same things that drive the stock market, high quality bonds can provide more diversification to a portfolio containing common stocks.[14]

An alternative view, which has become quite popular in recent years, tolerates low grade bonds if the yields are satisfactory. The underlying rationale is that actual events of default are comparatively rare, and, when they do occur, they tend to be due to issuer-specific events, which can be diversified away, rather than to economy-wide conditions, which are nondiversifiable. Fixed-income portfolios are usually widely diversified (i.e., lists of holdings may range from a hundred or two names to over a thousand) so the effects of

---

[13] Such a stance is typified by the observation of Graham, Dodd, and Cottle in their classic work *Security Analysis,* where they observe (page 310): "Deficient safety cannot be compensated by an abnormally high coupon rate alone." Since they are talking about new issue bonds, "coupon rate" is analogous to yield to maturity, Benjamin Graham et al., *Security Analysis: Principles and Techniques* (New York: McGraw-Hill, 1962).

[14] See Richard W. McEnally, "Some Portfolio-Relevant Risk Characteristics of Long Term Marketable Securities," *Journal of Financial and Quantitative Analysis,* Vol. 8 (Sept., 1973), pp. 565–585.

default risk should be largely diversified away. If the return/risk ratio is favorable, then over time the low grade portfolios should dominate other portfolios. A clear example of this strategy is provided by bond funds that specialize in extremely low grade bonds, or so-called junk bonds. Some of the junk bond funds have obtained prominence because of comparatively long records of superior performance. Indeed, there are those who argue that the success of junk bond funds has attracted so many investors to this strategy that good, high yielding junk bonds are no longer readily available.

High quality and low quality investment strategies are consistent with almost all bond portfolio objectives. An intermediate posture toward bond quality, one popular with active, total return-oriented investment managers, is driven by a feeling that sometimes the price of quality in terms of foregone yield is very cheap and sometimes it is very dear. Therefore, these managers monitor the yield spreads among bonds of different quality, and structure their portfolios according to the size of this spread and their anticipations of the way in which it will change. This approach toward bond portfolio management is representative of a more general approach to portfolio management that is addressed later.

Maturity Management. Clearly, the maturities within a bond portfolio represent a significant dimension of the portfolio. Although this is another area of fixed-income investment management in which there has been changes in recent years, three types of portfolios representing different approaches or strategies toward maturity management have traditionally been identified.

The most obvious of these strategies results in laddered or spaced-maturity portfolios. With laddering, the maturities in the portfolio are scheduled in such a way that a reasonably stable proportion of the portfolio matures at regular time intervals. The funds received from maturing bonds might be paid out to beneficiaries of the portfolio or they might be reinvested, depending on the investment objective and time horizon of the portfolio. If the portfolio is in a distribution phase, then the laddering strategy effectively avoids the risk of having to sell bonds in an unfavorable interest rate environment. If the portfolio is oriented toward the production of income or the accumulation of value, the laddering strategy avoids the risk of having a large proportion of the portfolio exposed to reinvestment at the yields available at any given point in time. In effect, reinvestment risk is effectively managed by diversifying reinvestment over time. Therefore, this strategy is essentially passive rather than active in nature, and it is more appropriate for income-oriented or accumulating portfolios than for total return-oriented portfolios.

At the opposite extreme is the strategy that results in bullet portfolios, portfolios concentrated around a single maturity date. Bullet portfolios can be consistent with both passive and active management. For example, if a portfolio, either an income-oriented portfolio or an accumulating portfolio, has a specific liquidation date, then the strategy of investing in bonds maturing at or shortly before that date is an obvious and frequently advocated one. (As shall be seen, however, there may be better strategies in the case of accumulating portfolios.) However, bullet portfolios are more frequently associated with actively managed total return-oriented portfolios, where the target of the bullet may be a distant maturity date, a near one, or some position in between, depending on the portfolio manager's expectations of the pattern of change in interest rates and the conviction with which these expectations are held.

Another maturity strategy that is occasionally encountered results in dumbbell portfolios, portfolios that are concentrated approximately equally in short-maturity securities and long-maturity securities. The result, therefore, is to structure the portfolio into a very defensive segment and a very aggressive segment, with the hope that the aggressive segment will provide returns and the defensive segment will reduce risk in a way that will beat alternative maturity patterns. This strategy appears to owe some of its popularity to "what if" experiments conducted with historical bond price and yield data. In such experiments the dumbbell strategy does frequently appear to produce more returns than laddered or bullet strategies with the same average portfolio maturity. However, it has recently been suggested that such experiments are flawed. Since duration increases at a decreasing rate with term to maturity, a dumbbell portfolio should have a shorter duration and lower price volatility than any other equivalent-maturity portfolio; thus, it is asserted, these experiments do not actually hold risk constant among the portfolios.[15]

Sector Management. A sector is any identifiable segment of the bond market within which securities share a similar characteristic. Obviously, bonds of different quality or different maturity ranges represent segments of the bond market. Other segments might be defined by reference to the coupon level of bonds, the identity of their issuer, the extent of their call protection, or their sinking fund features, to give just a few examples. Even in passive investment it is desirable to formulate guidelines regarding the sectoral composition of the portfolio. These guidelines presumably reflect the situation of the portfolio with respect to its objectives, risk tolerance, tax status, and the like, and also reflect the portfolio manager's perceptions of the reward/risk trade-offs in the various sectors.

Sectoral considerations also play a role in active portfolio management. As previously emphasized, yield spreads among the various segments of the bond market are anything but constant over time. Many bond portfolio managers routinely monitor the yield spread relationships among sectors of the bond market very closely, and move funds from sectors that appear to be relatively overvalued (excessively low relative yields) to those that seem relatively undervalued (excessively high relative yields), based on historical relationships, supply/demand analysis, or their intuition. In this way they hope to pick up value by participating in favorably relative price movements even when the general direction of bond prices is neutral or unfavorable. Movement among bonds of varying quality or maturity simply represents two types of sector management.

---

[15] G. O. Bierwag and George C. Kaufman, "Bond Portfolio Strategy Simulations: A Critique," *Journal of Financial and Quantitative Analysis,* Vol. 13 (Sept., 1978), pp. 519–528.

Bond Swapping. Most professional bond managers are of the opinion that temporary price disparities occasionally develop among bonds that are substantially identical, differing only in the identity of the issuer within a rating grade, or only having slight differences in coupon or term to maturity. They frequently attempt to profit from these disparities by swapping relatively overpriced bonds in their portfolios for relatively underpriced bonds offered them by dealers. This activity within sectors resembles movement among bond sectors, but it is both less risky and not as prospectively rewarding due to the high similarity of the bonds involved. However, the difference is one of degree, and many bond swaps do have an element of sector management about them. The transactions usually are actual swaps; that is, one package of bonds is traded for another, usually with some boot (called the take-out or give-up) going along with one package. In order to encourage dealers to bring them prospective trades, portfolio managers who actively trade bonds routinely provide dealers with inventories of their portfolio holdings and keep the dealers informed of their preferences for trades. Active traders may well turn over their portfolios several times a year in this manner. Such bond swapping is compatible with passive styles of portfolio management, but many managers also view it as a profitable supplement to more agressive bond portfolio management.

Active Management via Scenario Analysis. Scenario analysis is in essence nothing more than a systematic, integrated approach to sector management. It was suggested previously that a common technique in active total return portfolio management involves varying the portfolio maturity to exploit anticipated changes in interest rates. As has been seen, the responsiveness of a fixed-income security's price (or the value of a portfolio of fixed-income securities) to changes in the interest rate tends to increase with term to maturity, or alternatively, longer duration securities or portfolios display more price responsiveness to changes in their yield. Knowing these relationships, the portfolio manager might extend maturities when interest rates are expected to decline, hoping to maximize the increase in value, or alternatively, maturities might be decreased when interest rates are expected to rise, in order to minimize price erosion. A similar strategy might be adopted with respect to coupon level; since smaller coupons tend to accentuate responsiveness of price to interest rate changes, or increase duration, the portfolio manager might reduce portfolio coupon levels in the first instance and increase them in the second. Equivalent strategies might also be formulated with respect to other bond characteristics, such as quality, call provisions, or identity of issuer.

Provided the expected changes in interest rates or yields in fact occur and the changes are large, then these strategies should work fairly well. However, they might not be so effective for smaller changes, especially those that are generally expected. For example, as seen in the review of the expectations hypothesis for the term structure of interest rates, when interest rates are generally anticipated to decline, this expectation will become built into the structure of prices and yields on securities of different maturities in a way that negates easy gains from a maturity-based portfolio strategy. Similarly, it has also been shown that there is a tendency for the prices of low coupon bonds to be bid up prior to large decreases in yields to the extent that actually holding a portfolio of low coupon bonds during such a period often is not so rewarding as a portfolio of intermediate or current coupon bonds.[16] No doubt the market also prices out the potential gains from other bond features, such as call protection, in a similar manner. The point is that effective bond strategies cannot operate simply on the basis of mechanical effects of bond characteristics on the bond yield change-price change relationship. Attention must also be given to the way these characteristics are priced in the marketplace. (Strategies based on the mechanical relationships should work when yield changes are substantial, however, because large changes are almost always, at least in part, unanticipated; presumably, the market only prices out the effects of anticipated changes.)

Over the years bond portfolio managers have learned to deal with the effects of market anticipations on active portfolio strategies by working with "what if" or scenario analysis. For example, in attempting to structure the maturity dimensions of a portfolio, a manager with a one-year horizon might forecast what the yield curve would look like in one year. The manager would then take the observable beginning-of-year yield curve and work out the total returns, considering both coupon yield and changes in value, that would occur with bonds of different initial maturity if the yield curve changed over the year in the manner forecasted.[17] In this way an optimum maturity strategy could be determined, taking into account both the initial market pricing of maturity and anticipated changes in yields. Similar analyses could be conducted for bonds of different coupon level, call protection, and the like.

This general approach has served portfolio managers well, but it has also been limited by difficulties arising from dealing with only one bond characteristic at a time and concentrating on a single "best" future forecast. Recently a number of computer-based proprietary systems have been developed for conducting such scenario analysis in a more extensive and systematic fashion. These systems usually require forecasts of the yield curve and prices of other major bond attributes. Frequently they permit multiple forecasts with probabilities attached to each. The systems then take the existing structure of yields and work out the total return outcomes from portfolios of different configuration. Many of them can be applied to specific existing portfolios of securities in order to identify issues that are particularly desirable or undesirable. Those that permit multiple forecasts with associated probabilities can also be used to quantify the risk as well as the statistically expected return of alternative portfolio configurations. Unfortunately, the major impediment to the use of such techniques remains the difficulty of forecasting future prices with enough accuracy to make the exercise worthwhile.

Managing Reinvestment Rate Risk in Accumulating Portfolios. For a number of reasons, most notably historically high levels of interest rates and

---

[16] Michael D. Joenk et al., "The Price Elasticity of Discounted Bonds: Some Empirical Evidence," *Journal of Financial and Quantitative Analysis,* Vol. 13 (Sept., 1978), pp. 559–566.

[17] Mechanically, the manager would assume a bond with a coupon equal to the yield read off the initial yield curve at the initial maturity of interest, and compute its price at the yield on the forecasted yield curve at the new term to maturity, equal to the initial maturity reduced by one year in this case; the total return for this initial maturity would then be equal to the initial yield, adjusted for the length of the holding period, plus the computed price change.

the increasing importance of pension fund investment in fixed-income portfolio management, the problem of controlling reinvestment rate risk has received considerable attention in recent years. At least three approaches to this problem have evolved.

Dedicated Portfolios. The reinvestment rate problem exists only when there are portfolio proceeds to be reinvested; when there is no reinvestment, there is no problem. Occasionally, investment situations arise, or can be created, when it is possible to structure a portfolio of bonds whose pattern of cash flows, including both coupon payments and principal repayments, exactly duplicates the pattern of cash demands placed upon the portfolio. A classic example is provided in the pension context by a mature, fully funded pension fund that must simply pay off a stream of defined benefits, which at least actuarially can be predicted with a high degree of accuracy. Such a set of circumstances can also be created by segregating the retired portion of the beneficiaries of a more general pension plan. It is then a fairly straightforward mathematical programming problem to construct a portfolio that not only exactly duplicates this pattern of benefits, but also does it with the lowest possible initial investment. While the use of dedicated portfolios is basically a passive form of investment management, it is possible to inject an element of active management into the process by engaging in simple like-for-like swaps that do not alter the portfolio's cash flow pattern. In the pension area a number of consultants and investment managers are prepared to help specify the pattern of cash flow needs, identify and construct the minimum cost portfolio, and administer the actual liquidation of the portfolio.

Immunization. Many portfolios face patterns of funds flow needs that simply cannot be addressed by dedicated portfolios. For example, using conventional bonds only, it is not possible to construct a portfolio that will have all its cash flows occurring in six and one-half years, but such targeted funds needs do arise in practice. Using a technique called immunization, it is possible, at least conceptually, to provide any specified pattern of funds flows while fully protecting the portfolio against uncertainties due to changing reinvestment rates. This technique has become quite popular in the United States in the past five years or so, especially in pension fund applications. Immunization involves the second use of duration referred to earlier. The technique is attributable to the English actuary E. M. Redington;[18] however, an article published in 1971 by Fisher and Weil generated the awareness of, and interest in, the technique on which its current popularity is based.[19]

The basic point of immunization is quite simple. If the weighted-average duration of a portfolio is kept always equal to the time remaining until the end of the investment horizon, then that portfolio is immune to the effects of chang-

---

[18] F. M. Redington, "Review of the Principles of Life-Office Valuation," *Journal of the Institute of Actuaries,* Vol. 78 (1952), pp. 286–315.

[19] Lawrence Fisher and Roman L. Weil, "Coping with the Risk of Interest Rate Fluctuation: Returns to Bondholders from Naive and Optimal Strategies," *Journal of Business,* Vol. 44 (Oct. 1971), pp. 408–431.

ing interest rates. The realized rate of return on the portfolio will at worst be equal to its yield to maturity, and it may exceed this yield. The appropriate weighted-average duration is one in which durations of the individual securities are weighted by their proportionate contributions to the total market value of the portfolio. If the portfolio must provide funds flows at more than one horizon point, then the portfolio can be broken down into a series of subportfolios, one for each flow.

Unfortunately, understanding why duration works is not so simple. The proof that it works is algebraic and complex, but basically what happens is that an immunized portfolio will have a life in years which exceeds the time remaining until the end of the investment horizon. (Recall that the duration of a conventional coupon-paying bond is always less than its term to maturity.) Therefore, at the end of the horizon, the portfolio must be liquidated via sale rather than through the securities in the portfolio maturing. This implication, of course, is quite contrary to the conventional wisdom to the effect that the prudent, minimum risk strategy is to invest the portfolio in securities that mature at the end of the investment horizon. With immunization, an increase in market yields, which reduces the value of the portfolio when it is liquidated at the end of the investment horizon, is just offset by the added income that results from investing intermediate coupons at the higher yields. Conversely, with a decrease in market yields, the value of the portfolio at the end of the investment horizon increases, but this capital gain is just offset by the loss of terminal portfolio value that occurs due to the necessity to reinvest intermediate portfolio flows at the lower yields.

Table 7.10 shows the point. It is based on a 10 percent coupon bond with 10 years remaining to maturity. Priced at par to yield 10 percent, such a bond has a duration of almost exactly six and one-half years (actually, 6.545 years). Therefore, over an investment horizon of 6.5 years, the terminal value, terminal value ratio, and realized compound yield from this bond should be essentially unaffected by changes in yields. The table shows these numbers and their

TABLE 7.10   Reinvestment Rate Immunization With a 10 Percent Coupon 10-Year Bond, Priced at Par, Over a 6½-Year Horizon

	Subsequent Interest Rate		
	8 Percent	10 Percent	12 Percent
Total coupons	$ 65.00	$ 65.00	$ 65.00
Earnings from coupon reinvestment	18.10	23.60	29.40
Total value of coupons	$ 83.10	$ 88.60	$ 94.40
Ending price of bond	106.00	100.00	94.40
Total terminal value	$189.10	$188.60	$188.80
Initial price	$100.00	$100.00	$100.00
Terminal value ratio	1.892	1.886	1.888
Realized compound yield	10.04%	10.00%	10.02%

derivation assuming that yields remain at 10 percent over the life of the bond, drop immediately after purchase to 8 percent, or rise immediately after purchase to 12 percent. In each case all coupon income is reinvested after receipt at the prevailing rate, and, after six and one-half years, the bond is sold at a price that will provide the purchaser with a 10, 8, or 12 percent yield to the remaining three and one-half years to maturity. As the table shows, the terminal value of the total investment over this horizon is essentially unaffected by subsequent yields; the capital gain does compensate for lost accumulation from coupon reinvestment if rates drop, while the capital loss is just offset by additional reinvestment accumulation if rates rise.

It can be seen in the table that the actual terminal value of the investment is slightly higher at a subsequent yield of 8 or 12 percent than at 10 percent, and likewise, the realized compound yield is marginally higher than 10 percent at the two alternative reinvestment rates. This result is *not* due to any mistake or rounding error in the computations; rather, it reflects a point made previously: Under immunization the initial yield, or immunized yield, is the worst possible outcome, and it is obtained only if yields remain constant; any change in yields can only increase the rewards from the immunized investment.

Reality is never quite as kind as the assumptions in hypothetical examples. The calculations underlying Table 7.10 are based on some rather unrealistic assumptions, but many of the complications of reality turn out not to be insurmountable in practice. The table is based on a single bond, but the point which is made is valid for a portfolio of bonds as well; it is only necessary to substitute the weighted-average portfolio duration for the individual bond's duration. The table also assumes that the yield changes once only, and that this change occurs immediately after purchase of the bond. In practice, of course, yields are not so well behaved. However, immunization formally requires that the portfolio be rebalanced after each coupon receipt, and such rebalancing largely overcomes the problem of changing yield levels. (In practice, portfolios probably do not need to be rebalanced so frequently in order to obtain satisfactory levels of immunization.) Probably the most troublesome assumption underlying Table 7.10, although not an obvious one, is that the yield curve is initially flat and moves upward and downward but does not change its shape. This assumption is implied by the use of Macaulay's duration in the immunization. It turns out that a number of other forms of duration have been developed, which in theory are compatible with other patterns of change in the yield curve. They are considerably more complex than Macaulay's duration. However, in tests of the various duration alternatives, Macaulay's duration has not been shown to be inferior to the more complex forms in actually immunizing portfolios.[20]

The most substantial problem in implementing immunization strategies is the lack of sufficiently long durations. As indicated in the earlier discussion of duration, for conventional coupon bonds, Macaulay's duration increases with term to maturity only to a point. Under present interest rate conditions, this point is approximately eight years; no matter how long the term to maturity, conventional coupon-paying bonds will not have a duration much in excess of

---

[20] Gerald O. Bierwag et al., "The Art of Risk Management in Bond Portfolios," *Journal of Portfolio Management*, Vol. 7 (Spring 1981), pp. 27–36.

eight years. Unfortunately, eight years is not very long in comparison with many fixed-income investment horizons (e.g., the 40 years or more that might be associated with a pension fund portfolio or life insurance company portfolio.) Some effort has been made to respond to this problem by expanding the universe of securities considered for inclusion in the immunizing portfolio to include common stocks and interest rate futures. As shall be seen subsequently, the market has also responded by providing unconventional fixed-income instruments with durations in excess of those on coupon bonds.[21]

Immunization is a passive investment strategy in the sense that the portfolio is not managed aggressively to take advantage of anticipated changes in interest rates, but portfolio trading and swapping, which does not alter the duration of the portfolio, is not inconsistent with immunization and may add value. As with dedicated portfolios, a number of consultants and investment managers are prepared to design and implement immunization programs to meet specific investment needs.

Contingent Immunization. A variation on immunization, which permits active portfolio management, labeled contingent immunization by its developer, Martin Leibowitz of Salomon Brothers, Inc., has recently attracted considerable attention in the fixed-income investment community.[22] Basically, under contingent immunization, the portfolio is actively managed as long as doing so is rewarding; immunization is only implemented if it appears necessary in order to achieve a predetermined target return or target value for the portfolio over some investment horizon. At each periodic review point, a portfolio "trigger value" is determined: the minimum value the portfolio must have at that point in order to reach the target value if it is then immunized at prevailing interest rates. If the actual portfolio value is above this trigger, active management continues; if not, the portfolio is immediately immunized. Therefore, in a very real sense, contingent immunization is not, and may not become, immunization at all. Immunization is simply a fallback position to which the portfolio sponsors or managers have made a commitment if they are unsuccessful with active management. However, contingent immunization does respond to a frequent criticism of conventional immunization; that is, while it limits the losses that can occur from adverse reinvestment, it also eliminates the possibility of reaping the gains that active portfolio management may bring.

PORTFOLIO PERFORMANCE EVALUATION

Evaluation of investment performance is important as an aid to identifying superior or inferior managers and as a means of improving subsequent investment performance. The state of the performance evaluation art is not as ad-

---

[21] For more information on immunization, see Richard W. McEnally, "How to Neutralize Reinvestment Rate Risk," *Journal of Portfolio Management,* Vol. 6 (Spring 1980), pp. 59–63.

[22] Martin L. Leibowitz and Alfred Weinberger, "The Uses of Contingent Immunization," *Journal of Portfolio Management,* Vol. 8 (Fall 1981), pp. 51–55.

vanced in the fixed-income area as in equity investment, but a number of consultants have begun to market performance evaluation products for fixed-income portfolios. Most of these products are oriented toward portfolios managed for total returns, and most have two goals: to compare the performance of the actual portfolio with some external benchmark, and to decompose the performance into its major elements.

Two types of performance benchmarks are typically employed. As in the equity investment area, portfolio performance is often compared to indexes designed to reflect general market returns, and several organizations maintain indexes for this purpose. However, this approach may be inappropriate if a bond portfolio is circumscribed from investment in some sectors of the bond market because of policy or other considerations. In these circumstances, performance evaluation is usually driven by comparison with the results of a guideline or baseline portfolio representing an agreed-upon ideal or neutral composition for the portfolio in question. By reference to indexes of bond market returns by sector, also maintained by several organizations, it is a fairly easy matter to determine what the performance of the unmanaged baseline portfolio would have been.

Regardless of the standard of comparison, performance evaluation then normally proceeds by analyzing the differences in the returns of the managed portfolio and the benchmark according to the elements that generate these differences. Typical decomposition schemes will usually isolate the effects of differential returns of (1) a maturity (or duration) strategy that represents a departure from the benchmark; (2) a sectoral balance that is different from the benchmark; and (3) a superior selection of securities from within a sector. Some performance evaluation approaches also isolate the contribution of bond-swapping activity separately.

RECENT BOND MARKET DEVELOPMENTS

The observation was made at the beginning of this chapter to the effect that the typical long-term bond is a quite standardized instrument. However, in recent times a number of innovative forms of long-term bonds have been marketed. Regardless of the nature of the innovation, this process represents an effort to "complete" markets, as economists put it, and thereby make both parties better off by providing some combination of features that did not previously exist or could not be readily created by market participants. The number of innovations is legion. Some of the more significant include the following.

Original Issue Discount Bonds

The objective of completing markets is typified by original issue discount (OID) bonds which, as the term implies, are bonds whose coupon rate at the time of issuance is below current coupon equivalent yields. The extreme form of the OID bond is a bond with a zero coupon. Zero coupon bonds are therefore single payment obligations, bonds with no associated stream of annuity payments.

The first OID bond to attract wide attention, the Martin Marietta 7s of 2011, was marketed in March 1981, and for the next several years, a large number of low or zero coupon bonds were issued by other corporate borrowers. Maturities on the low coupon issues have ranged from 3 to 20 years, while maturities on the zero coupon bonds have been confined to 10 or fewer years.[23]

Some of the attractions of these bonds to the investor should be evident from the preceding sections. Original issue discount bonds are essentially free of call risk, and they carry much less reinvestment rate risk than current coupon issues, due to the smaller stream of cash flows to be reinvested. In the extreme case of the zero coupon issues, there is no reinvestment rate risk, of course, as there is no coupon flow to be reinvested. Moreover, since the duration of a zero coupon bond is obviously equal to its term maturity, such bonds provide a convenient mechanism for lengthening the duration of immunizing portfolios beyond the range that is possible with coupon issues.

In the Unites States, investors must recognize ordinary taxable income on the straight-line amortization of the discount on bonds issued initially at a discount. The associated tax on OIDs would tend to be burdensome to taxpaying investors, especially in the case of the zero coupon issues where there is no cash flow from the bond to pay the tax. For this reason, the purchase of OIDs in this country have largely been for tax-exempt accounts, including pension funds and Individual Retirement Accounts. Initially, the OIDs were quite popular with individual taxpaying investors in Japan because that country does not tax capital gains. In effect, the OIDs gave Japanese partially or fully tax-exempt income at rates competitive with fully taxed bonds of comparable quality. However, the Japanese Government soon indicated its displeasure over the purchase of such issues by Japanese nationals, and this effectively stopped the further sale of the bonds in Japan. Original issue discount bonds were also attractive to corporate issuers. Initial yields were somewhat below those on current coupon bonds of comparable maturity, but this might have been somewhat misleading: it is possible that the lower yield might have been offset or more offset by the absence of the call option, differences in effective maturity, and the fact that OIDs shift reinvestment rate risk to the issuer. However, OIDs had an attraction to the issuer beyond low yield. The tax treatment of interest expense to the issuer was the mirror image of the tax treatment to the investor; they were allowed to deduct interest expense equal to the straight-line amortization of the discount in addition to any coupon interest. This has the effect of making the after-tax cost of the OIDs to the issuer quite modest, especially at double-digit interest rates. Therefore, such bonds offered something to both issuer and investor, with the taxpayer making up the difference. However, the Internal Revenue Service soon began to require "scientific" amortization of the discount, in which the allowable interest expense was only equal to the yield to maturity on the bond times the accumulated value of the initial sales proceeds invested at this yield. Since this ruling, the issuance of OIDs by corporations has essentially come to a stop.

---

[23] A good review of OIDs is provided by Andrew Silver, "Original Issue Deep Discount Bonds," *Federal Reserve Bank of New York Quarterly Review*, Vol. 6 (Winter 1981–1982), pp. 18–28.

Stripped Bonds

The rise in popularity of OIDs was accompanied by recognition of a fact that should have been evident in any event; the conventional coupon bond, combining an annuity stream and a single-payment loan due at the bond's maturity, represents something of a compromise for both income-oriented investors and accumulating investors. Therefore, a number of large brokerage firms and investment bankers began to unpackage conventional bonds by selling claims on the coupon stream and the maturity payment separately. The usual practice is to acquire a block of U.S. government bonds, place them in trust, and market claims on the two streams at prices that in the aggregate exceed the cost of the underlying block. Unlike the OIDs, such "stripped" bonds, as the maturity payment claims are called, have continued to be quite popular, with new issues appearing frequently and with active secondary markets for the more popular issues.

Bonds With New Options Features

Options features on bonds, even on bonds without equity features, are not new. The call option, for example, has been a common feature of corporate bonds for many years. However, in recent years a broader range of options have become available. There are many variations, but most options features give to either the issuer or the investor the right to terminate the bond early or to extend its life beyond its initial maturity date. In effect, then, such options have the effect of shifting the exposure to interest rate changes between borrower and lender. Some issues have also been marketed that give the investor the option of increasing the size of the investment at some point after the initial issue date. The spirit of this option is similar to those that shift maturities; in particular, it acts as a partial shield to the investor against declining interest rates.

Bonds With Floating Rates

Short-term interest rates tend to move closely with the rate of inflation, and thus a series of short-term investments can at least partially insulate the investor against inflation. Moreover, short term-investments are relatively immune to price erosion from increasing rates. A series of short-term loans can also be attractive to borrowers whose asset returns tend to be tied to interest rates, such as commercial banks. However, some lenders prefer to commit their funds for lengthy periods, just as some borrowers like to lock up sources of funds for protracted intervals. As a response to these considerations, some borrowers have issued long-term bonds whose coupons are periodically adjusted according to the level of some short-term interest rate series. Such floating rate issues vary in many details, including the rapidity of the adjustment and the rate series to which they are tied. A number of them have limitations on the size of the adjustment that can take place at any time or on the bands within which the rates can fluctuate. Some also have options permitting either the borrower or the lender to convert them to fixed-rate issues. The success of floating-rate issues in the marketplace is possibly best described as "moderate," suggesting

TABLE 8.1   State and Local Debt Outstanding, 1945–1983

(dollars in billions)

Year	Public Purpose		Private Purpose Industrial Development Bonds	Total
	Short-Term	Long-Term		
1945	$ 0.3	$ 14.5	—	$ 14.8
1950	1.3	23.1	—	24.4
1955	2.1	43.8	—	45.9
1960	3.5	67.3	—	70.8
1965	5.5	94.8	—	100.3
1970	13.3	131.1	—	144.4
1975	18.6	198.6	$ 6.7	223.8
1980	14.9	291.1	45.9	351.9
1982	21.4	328.4	74.5	424.3
1983 (a)	17.8	354.9	79.9	452.6

(a) Through June 1983

Source: Board of Governors of the Federal Reserve System, *Flow of Funds Accounts, Assets and Liabilities Outstanding*, August 1983

TABLE 8.2   State and Local Government Long-Term Financing by Purpose, 1982

(dollars in billions)

Purpose	Amount	Percentage of Total
Housing finance	$15.6	20.8%
Gas and electric	9.4	12.6
Hospital	9.2	12.2
Schools	6.4	8.5
Pollution control	6.1	8.1
Water and sewer	4.5	6.0
Industrial aid	2.8	3.7
Highways and bridges	1.1	1.5
Other	19.8	26.6
Total	$74.9	100.0%

Source: The Bond Buyer

municipal interest on bonds issued in-state, and most local governments do not tax their own bonds. In contrast, several states levy personal property taxes on municipals, and capital gains are *not* tax-exempt. Currently, the maximum capital gains rate for individuals is 20 percent. The only exception to this rule is that when the municipal security is originally issued at a discount (below par), the original discount is considered interest income by the Internal Revenue Service (IRS) and is tax-exempt. However, if the security increases in price after it is issued, that portion of the gain above par is subject to taxation if the investor sells the security and realizes the gain.

Yield Comparisons

The relevant return to investors is the income earned after taxes. The investment decision whether to purchase a taxable or tax-exempt security thus depends upon the relative yields between the two securities and the marginal income tax rate of the investor. In the following example it is assumed that the current pretax yield to maturity on a taxable corporate bond sold at par is 10 percent, while the current tax-exempt yield on a par municipal bond of comparable maturity and rating is 6 percent. The after-tax yield (R_{at}) on the corporate bond is calculated as:

$$R_{at} = R_t(1 - T) \qquad\qquad (8.1)$$

where: R_t = pretax yield

           T = investor's marginal tax rate

R_{at} is then compared with the tax-exempt yield on a municipal. The after-tax yields on the two bonds are shown below for investors in a variety of tax brackets:

Investor's Marginal Tax Rate	Municipal Yield	After-Tax Corporate Yield
20%	6%	10(1 − 0.20) = 8.0%
30	6	10(1 − 0.30) = 7.0
40	6	10(1 − 0.40) = 6.0
46	6	10(1 − 0.46) = 5.4
50	6	10(1 − 0.50) = 5.0

An investor in the 20 percent tax bracket, for example, would receive an 8 percent after-tax return by purchasing a 10 percent taxable corporate bond. As the investor's marginal tax rate increases, the after-tax yield on the 10 percent corporate bond declines. At the 40 percent tax bracket, the investor would be indifferent between buying a taxable or tax-exempt municipal security. Finally, an investor in a marginal tax bracket above 40 percent would prefer a tax-exempt security to a taxable one, other factors equal.

TABLE 8.3   Marginal Tax Rate (T^*) at Which Investors Are Indifferent Between Long-Term Municipal and Taxable Securities (a)

Year	Moody's Yearly Averages, 20-Year Aa-Rated Bonds		T^*
	Municipal Yield	Corporate Yield	
1970	6.28%	8.32%	25%
1971	5.36	7.78	31
1972	5.19	7.48	31
1973	5.09	7.66	34
1974	6.04	8.84	32
1975	6.77	9.17	26
1976	6.12	8.75	30
1977	5.39	8.24	35
1978	5.68	8.92	37
1979	6.12	9.94	38
1980	8.06	12.50	36
1981	10.89	14.75	26
1982	11.31	14.41	22
	Average value (1970–1982)		31%

(a) The marginal tax rate (T^*) that clears the tax-exempt and taxable market is computed as $T^* = 1 -$ (Municipal yield/Corporate yield)

Source: Moody's Bond Service

Given T and R_t, Equation 8.1 determines the minimum municipal yield to induce an investor in tax bracket T to buy municipals rather than taxable bonds. Thus, if the investor's marginal tax rate is sufficiently high, municipal securities will yield relatively higher yields than taxables. If the investor's tax rate is sufficiently low, the opposite will hold. At the margin, tax-exempt and taxable yields will adjust so that the last investor who views these securities as substitutes will be indifferent; the after-tax yields between the two alternatives are equal. Thus, it is the marginal tax rate of the last investor that determines the relative rate relationship between comparable tax-exempt and taxable securities.

The tax-exempt feature of municipal bonds largely limits the investment to commercial banks and insurance companies subject to the full corporate income tax rate, or to individuals in high personal income tax brackets. Table 8.3 shows the marginal tax rate (T^*) on a yearly basis above which investors found municipal bonds attractive relative to taxable securities of comparable risk. Over the last decade, T^* has averaged 32 percent and has ranged between 25 and 40 percent. Thus, in recent years, investors whose marginal tax rate exceeds 40 percent have always found that municipal securities yield more.

NEW ISSUE

In the opinion of Bond Counsel, interest on the Series 1983 Bonds is exempt from income taxation by the United States of America under existing laws and regulations, except under certain conditions as explained under the caption "Tax Exemption" herein, and the Series 1983 Bonds and the income therefrom are exempt from all taxation in the State of Hawaii, except inheritance, transfer and estate taxes.

OFFICIAL STATEMENT

$97,050,000

STATE OF HAWAII

AIRPORTS SYSTEM REVENUE BONDS, REFUNDING SERIES OF 1983

(Payable solely from the receipts of the aviation fuel
tax and the revenues of the State of Hawaii airports system)

Dated: May 1, 1983   Due: July 1, as shown below

Principal and interest (January 1 and July 1, commencing January 1, 1984) is payable at the office of the Director of Finance of the State of Hawaii, Honolulu, Hawaii, or, at the option of the holder, at the principal office of Bankers Trust Company, New York, New York. The Series 1983 Bonds will be initially issued as coupon bonds in the denomination of $5,000, registrable as to principal only, and exchangeable for fully registered bonds in the denomination of $5,000 or any integral multiple thereof. Coupon bonds and fully registered bonds are interchangeable as provided in the Certificate, as supplemented.

The Series 1983 Bonds are subject to redemption prior to maturity, as more fully described herein.

The Series 1983 Bonds are being issued for the purpose of providing funds to redeem the State's Series 1981 Bonds on July 1, 1991 and to pay the principal of and interest on the Series 1981 Bonds as the same shall be due prior to such redemption date. The Series 1983 Bonds are special limited obligations of the State. The Series 1983 Bonds shall be payable solely from and secured solely by the Revenues derived by the State from the ownership or operation of the statewide system of airports and receipts from the aviation fuel tax.

The Series 1983 Bonds do not constitute a general or moral obligation of the State nor a charge upon the general fund of the State. The full faith and credit of neither the State nor any political subdivision thereof are pledged to the payment of or as security for the Series 1983 Bonds.

Payment of the principal of and interest on the Series 1983 Bonds will be insured under a municipal bond insurance policy to be issued by the Municipal Bond Insurance Association simultaneously with the delivery of the Series 1983 Bonds, as described herein.

$30,645,000 SERIAL BONDS

Amount	Due July 1	Coupon	Price	Amount	Due July 1	Coupon	Price
$ 415,000	1984	4.75%	100%	$2,105,000	1991	7.60%	100%
1,765,000	1985	5.25	100	2,195,000	1992	7.80	100
1,790,000	1986	6.00	100	2,340,000	1993	8.00	100
1,840,000	1987	6.50	100	2,450,000	1994	8.20	100
1,900,000	1988	6.75	100	3,020,000	1995	8.40	100
1,955,000	1989	7.00	100	3,280,000	1996	8.50	100
2,030,000	1990	7.30	100	3,560,000	1997	8.50	100

$22,995,000 8⅞% TERM BONDS DUE JULY 1, 2002—NR
$43,410,000 8⅞% TERM BONDS DUE JULY 1, 2008—PRICE 99%

(accrued interest from May 1, 1983, to be added)

The Series 1983 Bonds are offered when, as and if issued, subject to the approval of legality by Wood & Dawson, New York, New York. Certain legal matters will be passed on for the Underwriters by O'Melveny & Myers. It is expected that the Series 1983 Bonds in definitive form will be available for delivery in New York City on or about June 7, 1983.

BLYTH EASTMAN PAINE WEBBER
INCORPORATED

May 6, 1983

FIG. 8.1 Cover Page of a Revenue Bond Official Statement

Taxable Yield Equivalents

An investor considering the purchase of a municipal or taxable bond can similarly compare the yield on a municipal bond (R_{te}) with that of a comparable taxable by analyzing the municipal's taxable yield equivalent. Equation 8.1 suggests that an investor is indifferent between securities when $R_{te} = R_{at}$. Substituting in Equation 8.1, the equivalent taxable yield on a municipal bond for an investor in marginal tax bracket T is:

$$\text{Equivalent taxable yield} \; = \; \frac{R_{te}}{(1 - T)} \qquad\qquad (8.2)$$

An investor in the 46 percent tax bracket realizes an equivalent taxable yield of 22.22 percent when investing in a municipal that pays 12 percent interest. Thus, an investor would have to earn at least 22.22 percent on a comparable taxable security before that security's after-tax yield would exceed that of a comparable tax-exempt municipal.

DESCRIPTION OF A MUNICIPAL BOND

Municipal bonds are generally issued in denominations of $5,000. Prior to 1960, the conventional denomination was $1,000. Some municipal governments have recently tried to issue bonds with denominations as low as $100 or $500 in an attempt to tap the small investor market. This practice has not become popular with investors because small denomination bonds have no secondary market.

Like corporate bonds, municipals are identified by four characteristics. First, is the name of the issuer. Municipals are issued by any state or local government entity or their political subdivisions. Second, each bond has a stated maturity date on which the entire face amount (par value) must be repaid. The third feature, the coupon rate, specifies the percentage of par value indicating how much interest is paid periodically. The rate and the dollar amount of the coupon payment is fixed over the life of the bond, with most bonds carrying semiannual coupon payments. The last characteristic is the bond's yield (or price), which varies with credit market conditions; that is, because the coupon interest is fixed at the time the bond is issued, the price of the bond must vary in order to keep the yield in line with newly issued bonds. Bond prices are quoted as a percentage of the par value equal to 100. A discount bond trades at a price below 100, about 98 percent or $980 per 1,000 par value; a premium bond sells at a price above 100, about 102 percent or $1,020.

Unlike most other fixed-income securities, municipal bonds are generally serial bonds. A typical bond issue is made up of maturities beginning with one year and increasing annually until the bond issue's final maturity. Thus, it is not uncommon for a serial bond issue to be comprised of 20 to 30 different maturities. The serialization of the issue helps the municipality spread out its debt service payments and stay within operating budget requirements. Also, the periodic repayment of bonds provides some assurance to bondholders that the municipality is properly managing its financial affairs and will be able to make future interest and principal payments. Figure 8.1 shows the front page of a municipal bond issue's official statement which, among other things, shows the issue's serial maturity structure and each issue's coupon rate and proposed reoffering (market) yield.

Municipal bond issues may also be term bonds, which come due on a single maturity date or may be structured to have both serial and term principal maturities. Each term maturity in a serial bond issue is labeled a bullet according to market terminology. The proportion and combination of serial and term maturities depends on the demand from particular market segments. For example, if casualty insurance companies express a strong pre-offering demand for term bonds of particular maturity, term maturity bonds may be included in the issue.

Term bonds, with rare exception, are subject to a sinking fund payment schedule. Sinking funds are reserves set aside yearly by the issuer to redeem term bonds over the life of the issue. As such, they help issuers spread their payments evenly. Term bonds are most often selected for mandatory redemption prior to maturity by lot and are redeemable at par.

Many municipals also contain a call provision. A call provision gives the bond issuer the option to buy back the bonds at a predetermined price in advance of the maturity date. The purchase price is known as the call price and is usually set at the bond's par value or slightly above par, usually by one year's coupon payment. When bonds are called, bondholders are informed through a notice in a paper of general circulation, such as *The Bond Buyer*. A callable bond may initially contain a deferment period, which is a period of time in which the bond cannot be called. After the deferment period, which is typically 10 years, the bonds are callable. Call provisions benefit issuers by allowing them to retire bonds in an orderly manner for refunding or for other reasons, such as debt restructuring. They also enable issuers to refund outstanding debt at lower interest costs when market rates decrease. Call provisions penalize investors in that potential for capital gains is limited, and, if called for refunding, the investor is left with the principal to be invested at a lower interest rate. As such, callable bonds usually sell for penalty yields as compared to similar noncallable bonds.

Until recently, almost all municipal bonds were bearer bonds. As the name implies, bearer bonds are negotiable for any person who holds them. Coupons are physically attached to the bond and to receive payment, the bondholder clips the coupon from the bond and submits them to the issuer's paying agent. Whoever submits the coupons receives the payment.

With registered bonds, the holder's name is registered with the issuer. Coupon payments and/or principal payments are automatically sent to the bondholder; there is no need to clip coupons. Before an investor sells a registered bond, it must be properly endorsed and the issuer notified of the change of ownership. Thus, the investor is protected from possible losses.

Effective July 1, 1983, all new municipal bond issues must be registered bonds. Congress passed this controversial provision to help the IRS maintain better control over the collection of certain taxes owed on municipal bonds. Specifically, it was believed that few investors were paying taxes on capital gains resulting from the sale of bearer bonds. Also, some felt that, in estate planning, investors purchased cheap discount bearer bonds to avoid inheritance taxes. Most corporate bonds are registered bonds.

TYPES OF MUNICIPAL SECURITIES

State and local government securities are generally classified as either general obligation bonds or revenue bonds. Until the mid-1970s, general obligation bonds dominated the municipal market. Since 1976, however, the majority of new municipals have been revenue issues, so now revenue bonds account for 70 percent of the market.

General Obligation Bonds

General obligation bonds are backed by the municipality's power to tax and, if needed, to foreclose upon taxable real and personal property. This security pledge is commonly called a full faith and credit obligation and is the strongest promise a municipality can make to investors to repay its debt obligations. The quality or level of risk of general obligation debt, therefore, depends upon the economic base (income and property values) of the local community and the total amount of debt outstanding. General obligation debt is generally issued to finance essential public services (e.g., education, health care, and police and fire protection); and public improvements (e.g., sewers and drains). If the municipal authority's tax power is restricted, such as to a maximum tax rate, the bonds are still considered general obligation bonds, but are referred to as limited tax bonds. In addition, municipalities can issue general obligation bonds that are secured not only by the taxing powers of the issuer, but also from certain identifiable fees which provide additional revenues from outside the general funds. Such bonds are known as double barrel bonds because of the dual nature of the revenue sources. Finally, general obligation bonds usually require voter approval and, as a result, have been the slowest growing portion of municipal debt markets in recent years. This trend can be seen in Figure 8.2, which shows the composition of securities issued by municipal governments over time.

Revenue Bonds

Revenue bonds are sold to finance a particular revenue-producing project, and, in the event of default, the bonds are backed by the revenues generated by the project. Typical revenue projects are toll roads and bridges, water and sewer treatment plants, university dormitories, municipal arenas, power plants, convention centers, and port facilities. Depending upon the project, revenue bonds may be more risky then general obligation bonds. For example, Chesapeake Bridge and Tunnel Authority bonds went into default when a section of the bridge was destroyed. However, municipal bonds as a class, both general obligation and revenue bonds have had a repayment record second only to U.S. government securities. Their relative default risk compared to other bonds has thus been low historically.

Several recent events have, however, changed the public's perception of municipal default risk. First, many state and local governments experienced severe budget problems in the early 1980s. This resulted from a combination of declining tax revenues and increased expenditures with the recession, reduced

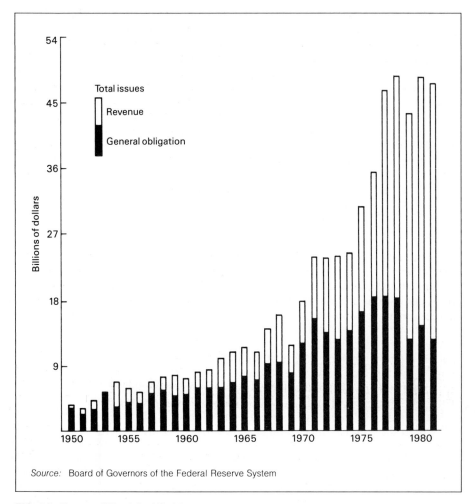

FIG. 8.2 Types of Municipal Debt

federal aid, and high borrowing costs associated with increased interest rates. At the same time, it is generally agreed that state and local governments' borrowing needs will remain high due to the decaying infrastructure in many areas. Second, two major municipal borrowers recently defaulted on their outstanding debt. In early 1983, the San Jose (California) School District declared bankruptcy, and deferred debt service payments until the courts resolve the difficulties. Shortly thereafter, the Washington Public Power Supply System (WPPSS) defaulted on $2.25 billion of bonds sold to finance the construction of two nuclear power plants. With regard to WPPSS' bonds, the Washington Supreme Court voided contracts that required ratepayers to pay off the outstanding bonds. Thus, the loss was shifted to WPPSS bondholders. Such legal uncertainties have increased default risk premiums on many other, non-related municipal bonds.

Revenue bonds are authorized for issuance in a manner similar to that of general obligation bonds, except that the amount of revenue bonds outstanding is not subject to statutory or constitutional debt limitations. Voter approval is similarly not necessary. As can be seen in Figure 8.2, there has been a virtual explosion of revenue bonds within the last decade. The reasons for this growth are varied. Much of the growth has come about as state and local governments attempted to finance a variety of social welfare programs, such as housing for low-income groups, improved medical facilities, and student loan programs. As voters became resistant to tax hikes in the 1970s, revenue bond financing became popular because voter approval was not required. Also, the passage of Proposition 13 (Jarvis-Gann Initiative) in California during the summer of 1978 and the enactment of similar laws by other states has encouraged municipalities to issue revenue bonds rather than general obligation bonds.

Though new uses for revenue bonds seem to abound, there are four basic classes of revenue bonds in wide use today.

Enterprise or User Fee Bonds.   These bonds are the most commonly issued by municipal governments. The bonds are used to finance projects where the fees or revenues generated are the source of payment for the debt service and principal. Examples include water, sewer, electric power, airport, and convention center revenue bonds.

Mortgage-Backed Bonds.   These bonds are issued to provide low-cost loans to finance single-family and low-income multifamily housing. The amortization of these loans is used to pay the interest and principal on these bonds. For example, housing revenue bonds are issued for multifamily housing projects for the low-income families and senior citizens under Section 8 of the Federal Housing Act. Though these bonds are not guaranteed by the federal government, their credit risk is low because the U.S. Department of Housing and Urban Development (HUD) accumulates cash reserves for each housing project. These funds are available in the event that project residents fail to pay rent. Similarly, a variety of single-family mortgage revenue bonds have been issued, which are secured by mortgage loan repayments on single-family homes. Security features vary but often include guarantees from government agencies, such as the Federal Housing Administration, and private mortgage insurers.

It is frequently argued that the tax-exempt privilege of municipal bonds has been abused in the issuance of mortgage-backed bonds by some municipalities. The reason is that not all of the low-interest funds have gone to the low- and moderate-income families they were designed to benefit. Because of this abuse, Congress has banned these bonds beginning December 31, 1983.

Lease Rental Bonds.   The state or local government creates a nonprofit authority to issue revenue bonds to finance the construction of a facility, such as a school. The local government using the authority then leases the project from the authority and pays the lease payments out of tax revenues. Leaseback authorities are often created to allow local governments to circumvent constitutional or statutory aggregate debt ceilings. A wide variety of projects are financed by lease rental bonds, such as school buildings, private university buildings, park and recreational facilities, and nonprofit hospital and health-care facilities.

Industrial Use Bonds. These are bonds that allow the private sector access to the tax-exempt market and are used to finance a variety of industrial and commercial activities that range from manufacturing plants to shopping centers. The most common type is IDBs, whose purpose is to help local governments attract industry to the area and to increase the number of jobs available as well as local tax revenues. In 1968, Congress enacted legislation that limits each small-issue IDB to a maximum of $10 million. Another common type is pollution control bonds, which are used to finance equipment for industrial plants to reduce or eliminate air and water pollution. Outstanding industrial use bonds equaled $74.5 billion in 1982, almost 18 percent of total municipal debt outstanding (Table 8.1).

Short-Term Debt

Short-term debt is issued by state and local governments to provide operating funds or to temporarily finance capital projects. Municipal notes are issued for periods as short as 30 days to about one year and usually are available in $25,000 denominations, with interest payable to maturity. Most municipalities are prohibited by statute from permanently financing capital projects with short-term funds. The use of short-term debt by state and local governments grew astronomically beginning in the 1960s. New issues amounted to only $4 billion in 1960, or 35 percent of total new issues. This percentage held constant until the 1970s, when municipal operating expenditures increased substantially. The following types of short-term debt are frequently issued by state and local governments.

Tax, Revenue, and Bond Anticipation Notes. Tax and Revenue Anticipation Notes, also called TANs and RANs, respectively, are issued in anticipation of tax collections or other expected revenues. Bond Anticipation Notes (BANs) are issued to provide temporary financing until the time is right to issue long-term bonds. For example, a school district may need to start construction on a school, but interest rates are too high to permit the issuance of bonds. BANs can be sold to finance the project until interest rates decline. When this happens, the BANs are then retired and the long-term debt issued. Most notes are typically issued for periods between six months and one year, with BANs occasionally issued for periods as long as three years. Most of these short-term securities are purchased by commerical banks.

Project Notes. These notes are issued by local housing authorities under an agreement with HUD to finance federal programs for urban renewal, neigh-borhood development, and low-income housing. The notes are backed by the revenue from the particular project and by the full faith and credit of HUD, which is widely viewed to be equivalent to a federal guarantee.

**TABLE 8.4   Major Investors in State and Local Government
Bonds as a Percentage of Total Municipals Outstanding**

(dollars in billions)

Year	Total Debt Outstanding	Commercial Banks	Property and Casualty Insurance Companies	Individuals	Other
1955	$ 45.9	28.2%	9.1%	42.2%	20.5%
1960	70.8	25.0	11.4	43.5	20.1
1965	100.3	38.7	11.3	36.3	13.7
1970	144.4	48.6	11.8	31.9	7.7
1975	223.8	46.0	14.9	30.4	8.7
1980	351.9	42.4	22.9	25.5	9.2
1981	373.7	41.3	22.5	26.7	9.5
1982	424.3	37.4	20.5	30.4	11.7

Source: Board of Governors of the Federal Reserve System, *Flow of Fund Accounts, Assets and
Liabilities Outstanding,* August 1983

Tax-Exempt Commercial Paper. Municipal commercial paper was first issued in the early 1970s and became an important financing vehicle in the 1980s. This is a market for large issuers only. The minimum denominations are usually $100,000, and the average transaction size is $1 million or more. Because of the size requirements, relatively few government entities can participate in this market. Currently, about 50 municipalities sell commercial paper. For those who can meet the transaction size requirement and issue paper on a regular basis. commercial paper typically sells for as much as a one percentage point below comparable one-year offerings.

INVESTOR DEMAND FOR MUNICIPAL BONDS

The tax-exempt feature is the main attraction of municipal bonds for investors. As a result, the demand for municipals has traditionally been concentrated almost entirely in investor groups with high marginal tax rates: commercial banks, property and casualty insurance companies (PCIs), and individuals. Other investors have better alternative tax shelters, so municipal securities are not attractive. Table 8.4 shows the total amount of municipal securities outstanding and the percentage held by different investors for selected years from 1955 to 1982. As can be seen, the relative importance of each of the three major investor groups has shifted over the years. At year-end 1982, these three groups held almost 90 percent of the outstanding municipal securities.

The Market Clearing Process

An examination of the investment motives of each of the three major investor groups will illustrate how the municipal market clears with respect to the available supply of municipal securities. The decision to purchase municipal securities by commercial banks and PCIs is largely insensitive to movements in municipal yields relative to taxable yields. The reason for this is that these institutions pay taxes at the full corporate rate and, during the last 30 years, have almost always found that tax-exempt securities yield more after-tax than comparable taxable investments. Thus, the fundamental determinant of fully taxed firm holdings of tax-exempt securities is their expected profits, and not the relative yield between tax-exempt and taxable yields.

Specifically, profit-maximizing financial institutions make taxable investments until taxable income earned is sufficient to cover expenses and generate $70,000 in profits, the level at which their marginal tax rate jumps to 40 percent. After this point, all remaining funds are invested in tax-exempt securities or alternative tax-sheltered investments. These institutions structure their holdings of tax-exempts so as to reduce their expected taxable income to zero. The wisdom of this proposition is illustrated by considering the consequence of alternative investing. To purchase tax-exempts before covering all expenses sacrifices income, because before-tax yields on taxable securities exceed the yield on tax exempts. Purchases of taxable securities by institutions in the 46 percent tax bracket also sacrifice income because exempt yields almost always exceed 54 percent of comparable taxable yields.

Individuals are subject to marginal tax rates that vary between 14 and 50 percent and, as a group, are extremely sensitive to changes in relative interest rates when making investment decisions. This has the effect of making individuals the marginal investors in tax-exempt securities. Thus, any tax-exempt securities issued in excess of the desired holdings of fully taxed firms must be purchased by lower tax-bracketed individuals. The greater the excess, the higher tax-exempt yields must rise relative to taxable yields to induce households in successively lower tax brackets to buy tax-exempts. On the other hand, an increase in profits of banks or PCIs will lower tax-exempt yields, because fewer municipal securities must be placed with lower tax-bracketed individuals.

Commercial Bank Demand

Since the 1970s, commercial banks have been the largest holder of municipal securities, owning roughly 40 percent of all outstanding municipals (Table 8.4). However, this has not always been the case. Prior to 1960, their participation was limited and erratic, and in 1960, their percentage of the total market reached a low point of 25 percent. Beginning in 1961, bank holdings of municipal securities grew steadily, reaching a record high in 1972 when they owned 50.5 percent of total municipals outstanding. Since that time, there has been a gradual decline in bank holdings of municipal securities and many experts believe this may be a long-term trend.

A number of factors have contributed to this withdrawal from the market. First, commercial banks have increasingly relied on other tax-sheltered investments to shield income. Large commercial banks have offset domestic tax liabilities with taxes paid to foreign governments on income generated from international banking activities. Banks of all sizes have engaged in tax-sheltered leasing operations, which generate substantial depreciation allowances and tax credits. More recently, the Economic Recovery Act of 1981 expanded the definition of a lease, and liberalized depreciation methods, which further increased the attractiveness of alternative tax shelters. Second, bank profits have declined substantially in recent years as a result of the economic recession and the general deregulation of interest rates paid on bank liabilities. The recession seriously harmed banks with heavy energy-related loan portfolios by forcing them to recognize substantial loan losses. Similarly, many banks with large loans to lower developed countries have been unable to collect the obligated debt service payments. Again, the loss potential is enormous. Deregulation has further lowered profits by increasing the cost of bank funds without a corresponding increase in asset yields. Since October 1983, banks can pay unregulated rates on all liabilities with original maturities beyond 31 days. Deposits have subsequently shifted to these higher yielding accounts. Finally, the rapid increase in the volume of tax-exempt IDBs held by banks as part of their loan portfolios further reduces the need to purchase conventional municipal securities. In sum, the increase in the use of foreign tax credits, tax-sheltered leases, interest rate deregulation, and private placement of industrial development suggests a continued decline in bank holdings of traditional municipal securities.

Commercial banks have shown a strong preference for certain types of municipals. Specifically, banks prefer (1) high quality bonds (low default risk) to low quality bonds; (2) short-term bonds to long-term bonds; and (3) general obligations bonds to revenue bonds. Banks prefer high quality bonds for two basic reasons. First and most important, banks are restricted by regulation to purchase primarily investment grade securities (bonds rated Baa and above). This mandate stems from the desire on the part of bank regulators to promote bank safety. Second, bank needs for liquidity favor high grade securities, which are generally more marketable than noninvestment grade securities (bonds rated below Baa and nonrated bonds). A survey by the American Banker's Association in 1980 showed that nearly 84 percent of bank holdings of municipals were rated in the three highest credit rating categories, and nearly 90 percent were investment grade securities.

Commercial banks also have a well-defined preference for short-term securities. This preference is attributed to the short-term average maturity and high-rate sensitivity of bank liabilities. Deregulation has not only increased the cost of bank deposits but also has increased the volatility of rates paid. Banks have attempted to reduce this interest rate risk with matching short-term asset maturities. Much like Treasury bills, short-term municipal securities provide banks with liquidity when needed. Municipals however, have the advantage of generating tax-sheltered income. This maturity preference was illustrated in a survey by the American Banker's Association, which showed that, in 1980, 42 percent of all bank holdings of municipal securities matured within 5 years or less, 31 percent matured within 6 to 10 years, and only 27 percent had maturities beyond 10 years.

Finally, banks also prefer general obligation bonds over revenue bonds. General obligation bonds are less risky and a higher proportion are investment grade. Because depository agreements often favor general obligation securities, these bonds can be used as collateral against public deposits and provide greater coverage. Moreover, general obligations are more typically directed at perceived community needs. Revenue bonds, in contrast, tend to benefit private industry or a narrow segment of the population. In addition, most states and localities require that public deposits of banks be collateralized by marketable securities. More general obligation bonds apply against pledging requirements. The survey conducted by the American Banker's Association indicated that, in 1980, nearly 70 percent of all municipal bonds held by commercial banks were general obligation bonds.

Property and Casualty Insurance Companies

At year-end 1982, PCIs were the third largest investors in municipal securities. Their demand has been rather unstable, ranging from a low of 9.1 percent during 1955 to a high of almost 23 percent in 1980. However, the general trend since 1960 has been an increase in their proportionate holdings of municipal securities.

There are several reasons for the gradual shift into tax-exempts. First, PCIs held far more U.S. government securities in their investment portfolios during the 1950s than was probably necessary for adequate liquidity. Rather than liquidating these assets and suffering capital losses during years of rising interest rates, PCIs simply replaced maturing U.S. government securities with tax-exempts. Second, because of the improved secondary market for tax-exempt securities, municipal securities yields exhibit increased liquidity relative to Treasury securities. Finally, increasing tax burdens on corporations during the last fifteen years have forced PCIs to be more conscious of their tax position. For example, during this period, corporations experienced the imposition of a tax surcharge on profits, the removal and subsequent reinstatement of the investment tax credit, and the continuous adjustment of depreciation allowance.

Property and casualty insurance companies buy municipals to shelter expected profits from taxes. PCIs, like banks, pay taxes at the full corporate rate, and municipal securities represent their best tax shelter. Life insurance companies, in contrast, have a relatively low effective tax rate and consequently buy few municipal securities. The reason PCI municipal investment is so unstable is the cyclical nature of the underwriting business and the unpredictability of insurance claim payments. During the upswing in business activity, PCIs normally increase their purchases of municipal securities with increased premium income and reduced claims. These periods are usually followed by low rate increases by state insurance commissions and intense price competition among similar firms. With the downswing in economic activity, underwriting losses on insurance policies mount as premium and investment income fail to keep pace with the cost of settling claims. As underwriting losses increase, PCIs reduce their investment in municipal securities because they expect to have less to shield for taxes.

Besides tax exemption, municipal bonds possess some regulatory advantages for PCIs. Property and casualty insurance companies are regulated by state insurance departments, which utilize various tests to assess financial solvency. The amount of statutory surplus is one of the principal tests to determine the amount of insurance a particular PCI may underwrite. When computing statutory surplus, a company's assets must be valued. In most states, regulations require that common and preferred stocks be valued at market prices, while bonds are valued at acquisition cost. Hence, changes in stock prices will affect an insurance company's statutory surplus, while changes in bond prices will not. Thus, investment in tax-exempt and taxable bonds by PCIs is even more attractive. Further, even though long-term bonds experience greater price volatility than other securities of shorter maturity, a significant decline in bond prices does not affect the ability to write new business.

Property and casualty insurance company investment strategy has been to seek the highest expected return from relatively low-risk investments. Because the municipal bond yield curve is almost always upward-sloping, PCIs tend to purchase long-term municipal securities. Similarly, PCIs prefer revenue bonds over general obligation securities because they tend to provide higher returns. It is estimated that PCIs currently hold nearly 60 percent of all outstanding revenue bonds.

Individual Investors

Retail investor participation in the municipal bond market has fluctuated widely since 1955 (Table 8.4). Individual investors accounted for as much as 45 percent of all outstanding municipals in 1957 and as few as 26 percent of the market in 1980. Since 1980, their participation in the market has increased dramatically to where they have purchased an estimated 75 percent of net new issues in 1983. Mutual funds representing indirect individual investment have recently been important investors acquiring 20 percent of new issues in 1982.

The demand for municipal securities by individuals has been characterized as a residual element in the demand equation for municipal bonds in that they are the group that clears the market after banks and PCIs acquire their share. As a group, individual investor demand is extremely sensitive to variations in municipal yields relative to yields on similar taxable securities. As expected, individuals acquire more municipals when municipal interest rates are high, relative to rates on taxable securities. This has been the case since 1980, with individuals buying 60 percent of new issues and tax-exempt yields at relative peaks compared with both Treasury yields and corporate yields.

Though individuals' investment has increased since 1980, it is difficult to project future trends. Any reduction in personal income tax rates, the maximum tax rate, and the long-term capital gains rate will reduce household demand for municipal securities. Two recent developments will affect individuals' demand. Beginning in 1985, the personal income tax rate will be indexed to inflation. This will eliminate "bracket creep," which creates an artificial demand for municipal securities. Beginning in the mid-1960s, bracket creep became a serious problem for households when inflation increased individuals' taxable nominal income, forcing them into progressively higher tax brackets. In addition, beginning January 1, 1985, individual taxpayers will be entitled to a 15 percent exclusion of "qualified interest income" over "qualified interest expense." Taxable interest will be substituted for tax-exempt interest to the extent that investors have not already covered this exclusion.

The Municipal Market Outlook

Where the municipal market is headed during the latter part of the 1980s depends on changes in the volume of tax-exempt securities that will be issued relative to changes in demand for tax-sheltered income sought by commercial banks, PCIs, and individual investors. With respect to supply, the amount of tax-exempt financing potentially facing the municipal market is immense. Gross new issues of long-term bonds exceeded $78 billion in 1982. If this pace continues, the municipal bond market faces the prospect of underwriting three fourths of a trillion dollars of securities during the upcoming decade. State and local governments face a tremendous rehabilitation of the infrastructure, including roads, bridges, transit systems, and water and sewer lines. Unless new financing alternatives arise, these projects will be funded in the municipal bond market where issues must compete with less traditional tax-exempt financings on behalf of private borrowers.

Who will purchase these municipals? Property and casualty insurance companies are not likely candidates, at least not during the early 1980s, with their large underwriting losses. Commercial banks with declining profits and other tax shelters will likely not add substantially to their holdings. The only viable investor is the individual. But the incentive to seek tax-exempt income on the part of the individual investor recently has been dampened. The reduction and indexation of personal income taxes as well as decreases in the long-term capital gains rate will have an adverse impact upon the marginal demand for municipal securities. Additionally, the individual investor now has other investment alternatives available to shelter income, such as lower estate taxes and expanded individual retirement account (IRA) and KEOGH account plans.

In sum, the 1980s may prove to be a difficult period for state and local government financing. The municipal bond market faces a large forward calendar of financing, while two major purchasing sectors, commercial banks and PCIs, may have reduced demand for tax-exempt securities. Thus, for the market to clear, households will need to be compensated with a significant increase in yield. Thus, barring any major favorable change in the tax laws, municipal interest rates will probably increase permanently, relative to similar taxable interest rates.

MUNICIPAL MARKET CHARACTERISTICS

Credit Ratings

Investors typically do not formulate the probabilty of default themselves, but use credit ratings and written reports provided by rating services or investment bankers. A borrower defaults anytime it fails on the promise to pay coupon interest and/or principal at the agreed time. The degree of default risk inherent in a security can be measured as the difference between the rate paid on a risky security less the rate on a default-free security, with all other factors being held constant. That difference is called the default risk premium, and it varies systematically over the business cycle. Default risk premiums widen

TABLE 8.5 Municipal Bond Credit Ratings

Explanation	Moody's	Standard & Poor's	Default Risk Premium
Best quality, smallest degree of risk	Aaa	AAA	Lowest
High quality, slightly more long-term risk than top rating	Aa1 Aa2 Aa3	AA+ AA AA−	
Upper medium grade, possible impairment in the future	A1 A2 A3	A+ A A−	
Medium grade, lack outstanding investment characteristics	Baa1 Baa2 Baa3	BBB+ BBB− BBB−	
Speculative issues, protection may be very moderate	Ba1 Ba2 Ba3	BB+ BB BB−	
Very speculative, may have small assurance of interest and principal payments	B1 B2 B3	B+ B B−	
Issues in poor standing, may be in default	Caa	CCC	
Speculative in a high degree, with marked shortcomings	Ca	CC	
Lowest quality, poor prospects of attaining real investment standing	C	C D	Highest

during periods of economic decline, and narrow during periods of economic expansion.

Credit Rating Agencies. The two major credit rating agencies are Moody's Investor Service and Standard & Poor's. Both of them rank securities in order of the perceived probability of default, and publish ratings as letter grades. The rating scheme they use for municipal bonds is shown in Table 8.5. The highest credit-quality bonds, those with the lowest default risk, are rated triple A. As the perceived default risk of a bond increases, the bond rating declines, and the lower a bond's credit rating, the higher is the yield it carries.

Bonds rated in the top four rating categories, Aaa to Baa for Moody's and AAA to BBB for Standard & Poor's, are called investment grade bonds. State and federal laws frequently require commercial banks, insurance companies, pension funds, and other financial institutions to purchase securities rated as investment grade quality. Moody's may also assign a bond a prefix "Con.," which means a rating is conditional; that is, the credit rating is conditional upon

TABLE 8.6   Municipal Note and Commercial Paper Credit Ratings

		Moody's	Standard & Poor's
Explanation	Note	Commercial Paper	Commercial Paper
Highest degree of safety	MIG 1	P-1 (a)	A-1+
Very strong degree of safety	MIG 2	P-1 (a)	A-1
Strong degree of safety	MIG 3	P-2	A-2
Satisfactory degree of safety	MIG 4	P-3	A-3

(a) Moody's assigns a single credit rating to securities in the top two categories.

(1) completion of a project; (2) demonstrated earnings for projects with little operating experience; (3) rental income beginning once the project is completed; or (4) some other limiting factor. Likewise, Standard & Poor's uses the letter "P" to indicate a provisional rating that is intended to be removed after completion of a project or at the start of earning income.

Moody's and Standard & Poor's also rate short-term municipal paper: Moody's rates municipal notes and commercial paper, and Standard & Poor's rates only commercial paper. Table 8.6 shows the rating schemes used by the two agencies. As with bond ratings, the higher the quality rating, the lower the security's default risk and the lower the yield on the security. All the rating categories shown in Table 8.6 are considered to be of investment grade quality by both Moody's and Standard & Poor's, and the agencies will also produce written reports for investors on the issues that they rate.

The rating agencies consider a number of factors when assigning a bond a credit rating. For general obligation bonds, among the most important areas are (1) the issuer's debt structure so that the overall debt burden can be determined; (2) the issuer's ability and political discipline for maintaining a balanced budget; (3) the quality and viability of the issuer's tax base; and (4) an assessment of the issuer's overall socioeconomic environment: population growth, employment distribution, diversification of industry, real estate property valuation, and trends for future growth. For revenue bonds, many of the same factors are considered, but an emphasis is placed upon the quality and stability of the project's expected cash flow, and the quality of the project's management. Once a bond rating is assigned to a particular issue, the rating is periodically reviewed by the rating agency and is subject to change. A lower rating increases the future borrowing cost of the issuer and may limit the issuer's access to money and capital markets. Finally, there is evidence that bond-rating agencies do a reasonable job of classifying bonds according to their probability of default. Empirical studies report a high correlation between credit ratings assigned by agencies and actual default experience.

Recent Credit Quality Problems. Until the 1970s, state and local government securities had experienced few defaults. No major defaults had occurred since the Great Depression of the 1930s. However, the 1970s and early 1980s were periods marked with high inflation and economic instability. As a result of these turbulent economic times, many municipalities, especially large cities, suffered serious financial difficulties, which caused investors to reassess the credit standings of municipal securities in general. The most dramatic of these financial difficulties was the default of New York City on its debt obligations in the summer of 1975. The default was the largest in our nation's history. The default was of particular interest because it brought to light the legal and political difficulties involved in a large-scale municipal default. In the wake of New York City's default, other large northeastern cities (e.g., Boston, Buffalo, Cleveland, Detroit, Philadelphia, and Newark) suffered degrees of financial difficulty and found their credit costs soaring. Most noteworthy of the previously mentioned cities was the default of Cleveland in December 1978. The widely publicized 1983 default is that of the Washington Public Power Supply System (called WHOOPS), which defaulted on $2.25 billion worth of bonds used to finance two nuclear power plants. Interestingly, in 1981 these bonds carried credit ratings of A1 (Moody's) and A+ (S&P). Though defaults have not been widespread, investors remain highly sensitive to the quality of new issues.

The Primary Market

The primary market for municipal bonds average about 100 new bond issues per week. A state or local government can sell its new issues by offering them publicly to the investment community or by placing them privately with small groups of investors, usually financial institutions. When a public offering is selected, the issue is underwritten by an investment banking house or by the municipal bond department of a commercial bank. Public offerings can be brought to market by either competitive sale or by negotiation. Competitive sales are sealed bids in which the bond issue is sold to the bidder submitting the lowest bid according to stipulated criteria. Negotiated sales are contractual arrangements between the issuer and the underwriter, in which the underwriter assists in preparing the bond for sale in return for the exclusive right to underwrite and distribute the issue.

The method of sale a particular issuer uses is determined by legal, traditional, and economic factors. Most states have laws that require general obligation issues to be offered by public bid. In general, the public sale of general obligation bond issues is legally governed by the rules that apply to the letting of other types of revenue bonds do not require that bond issues be sold by competitive bidding. One reason for this legal difference is the source of the interest and principal payments. Revenue bond interest and principal payments are primarily payable from the cash flows generated by the project and are not payable from general tax revenues. Since the greatest amount of revenue bond issues impose no claim upon the taxing authority of the municipality, the courts have held that revenue bonds can be sold without advertising for bids.

There is a good deal of controversy over which method of sale results in the lowest borrowing cost to the issuer. In general, it is believed that competitive sales provide issuers with the lowest new issue borrowing cost because of the competitive aspects of the bidding process. Specifically, bond issues that receive only one competitive bid sell at the same interest cost as negotiated sales; competitive issues that receive two competitive bids sell for about 20 basis points less than comparable negotiated issues, and as the number of bids increases, the interest cost differential between competitive and negotiated sales becomes even larger. For bond issues with lower bond ratings, the impact of the lack of competition is even larger. Besides the potential interest cost savings favoring competitive bidding, it is believed that competitive sales act as a deterrent against fraud or other dishonest manipulation.

Underwriting a New Bond Issue

The Underwriting Syndicate. The underwriting of municipal securities is usually carried out through a syndicate of banks and security dealers. Syndicates underwrite municipal securities by purchasing them from the issuing government and reselling the securities in the open market, hopefully for a large price. When a new bond issue is purchased by an underwriter, the municipality is discharging two responsibilities: (1) the distribution of the bonds to investors; and (2) the risk that investors might fail to buy all other bonds at the expected prices. Thus, the risk of marketing failure is shifted to the underwriting syndicate. The risk accepted by the syndicate is the chance that they may not be able to sell the bonds during the planned time period and at the planned reoffering yields. If they cannot sell all the bonds at these prices, the underwriter may earn less than expected or suffer a loss on the deal. The number of underwriters involved in a particular issue depends upon the size and nature of the municipality and the geographic region. It also depends upon the syndicate relationship between underwriters. In total, there are over 14,500 potential commercial bank underwriters, as well as 530 investment bankers. Of this total, the 100 most active underwrite 90 percent of the total dollar volume. Additionally, hundreds of smaller regional investment bankers compete in the underwriting of small bond issues within their locality. Many regional firms specialize in underwriting only certain types of bond issues, such as sewer or water authority bonds, and usually do not underwrite other types of issues of which they have no experience.

The size and purpose of the issue as well as the relationships among firms determine the size and composition of commercial and/or investment banks in the underwriting syndicate. As many as several hundred firms can be included. A syndicate is organized and directed by one or more managing underwriters. When there is more than one manager, one firm is designated the lead underwriter. Certain firms specialize in managing underwriting syndicates. Commercial banks are dominant in managing the sale of general obligation bonds, while investment banks dominate the management of revenue bond sales. In 1980, commercial banks accounted for 8 of the 15 most active managing underwriters of general obligation issues. Only two commercial banks ranked in the leading 25 revenue issue managers. Commercial banks underwrite fewer revenue issues because they are prohibited from underwriting most types of revenue bonds by the Glass-Steagall Act of 1933.

Bringing a Competitively Sold Bond Issue to Market. When a municipality sells bonds by competitive bid, it solicits bids through an Official Notice of

Sale published in newspapers. These notices usually contain the following information: (1) date, time, and place to submit bids; (2) amount of the serial maturities; (3) type and purpose of the bonds, including a statement about security of interest and principal payments; (4) the basis of award; (5) miscellaneous bidding restrictions; and (6) miscellaneous bond features such as callability. At the time that bids are invited, the identifying aspects of the bond package, except for the coupon specifications, are already determined. This pre-sale planning and bond design is called the origination phase of the issue, and includes decisions about the dollar amount of bonds to be sold, the sale date, the serial maturity structure, and the call provisions. Origination also almost always includes preparation of the prospectus. The prospectus, called the Official Statement, contains information regarding the financial, economic, and social characteristics of the issuer. It also contains a description of how the funds acquired by the bond sale will be used. During the origination phase, issuers secure in-house and/or external financial advice. Approximately one half of all general obligation issuers and two thirds of all revenue bond issuers utilize the services of an external financial advisor prior to the sale.

The bidders in the typical bond issue are investment banking firms or commercial banks.[2] An underwriter's bid constitutes a statement of the coupon rates assigned to each of the maturities plus the price the bidder is willing to pay for the bonds. A bidder seeks to win the bid by submitting a coupon structure and a bid amount that results in the best bid according to the criterion stipulated in the Official Notice of Sale.

If the winning bidder is an underwriter, the underwriter resells the bonds to ultimate investors. This usually involves dividing the serial package into constituent maturities. The planned reoffering price of each bond is determined by the proposed yield to maturity, the coupon rate, and the number of semiannual periods to maturity. It is the intent of the bidding underwriters to sell the bonds at an average reoffering price that exceeds the average bid price by an amount that will compensate them for costs involved and that generates a competitive return on capital. The total revenue generated by selling the bonds at their planned reoffering yields is called production. Planned production minus the bid amount is gross underwriter spread. The underwriter can increase planned spread by either increasing the average reoffering price or by lowering the bid amount.

The lowest interest cost (or highest dollar amount paid for the bonds) is the basis for award. The most commonly used measure of interest cost is net interest cost (NIC). NIC is the sum of the dollar amount of coupon interest paid multiplied by the number of years to maturity less any premium, divided by the number of bond years.[3] Because this method of award does not consider

---

[2] Commercial banks are restricted from underwriting virtually all revenue bonds.

[3] $NIC = \left[\sum_{n=s}^{m} n \cdot A_n C_n - P\right] \Big/ \sum_{n=s}^{m} n \cdot A_n$

where: P = premium bid over aggregate par value for all securities
C_n = coupon rate on bonds maturing in n periods
A_n = total par value of bonds maturing in n periods
n = number of years bond outstanding
s = years to first maturity
m = years to last maturity

the time value of money, the system can lead to inefficient bid awards that increase state and local government borrowing costs. In the last several years, some municipal issuers have used a bid procedure that considers the time value of coupon interest payments. This method is called true interest cost (TIC). TIC calculation can be performed by an algorithm easily programmed on a computer. Even if NIC is used, there are now simple program and bidding rules that minimize inefficient bid awards.

Where measured in terms of yield, the average reoffering yield and planned spread add up to NIC. Thus, the higher the underwriter spread and/or the higher the reoffering yield, the higher the municipalities borrowing cost (i.e., NIC). For underwriters, a higher reoffering yield or a higher spread means less risk of an unsuccessful reoffering and, in the case of spread, a higher profit. For investors, the higher the reoffering yield relative to similar bonds, the more attractive the issue.

The syndicate procedures for bid preparation are generally uniform among firms within the industry. Larger syndicates (e.g., 25 members or more) tend to have more formal procedures than smaller syndicates (e.g., five or more members). All member firms have a strong interest in the bid variables because at the time of bid submission each firm is assigned a portion of the bonds they will be responsible for distributing in the event of a winning bid. This portion is called the participation. If the yields are set too low, the bid might be won, but it will be more difficult to accomplish the distribution, and the syndicate might have to revise the reoffering yields upward, which reduces the actual spread below the anticipated spread. If the reoffering yields are set too high, the syndicate will not realize any direct monetary gain for the bidding effort because it will fail to win the bid.

Prior to the bidding date, each member firm analyzes the market for the new issue. Firms attempt to identify the equilibrium supply and demand conditions for the specific issue. A comparison is often made between the new issue and the yields on comparable outstanding issues being traded in the secondary market. Firms also solicit demand information from potential bond buyers. However, the sales force's conversations with investors may not give the underwriter perfect information about minimum market clearing yields because larger customers are often contacted by more than one member firm and/or more than one syndicate. Also, because they desire the highest possible yields, larger customers are reluctant to reveal their minimum required yields or even the exact extent of their interest in the new issue.

The syndicate arrives at a final bid through one or more price meetings. During these meetings, member firms compare their expectations about issue demand, market conditions, and competing bids. The larger or the more important the issue, the more time and resources are allocated to the price meetings and bid preparation. An issue about which price discussion is deemed to be of lesser importance by the manager will sometimes minimize the necessity for a face-to-face meeting of the members. In these cases the "meeting" is conducted by telephone. The manager(s) and other participating underwriters, who have relatively large participations, usually have more authority over the pricing decisions than do other syndicate members. Since the latest market information may indicate an alteration of the bid, syndicate members usually confer as short a time before the bidding deadline as practical.

After the bonds have been awarded, the manager allocates the bonds to syndicate members. Member firms have a designated order period during which to subscribe to bonds (order bonds for resale). At the end of this period, allotments are made. In reoffering, each member must adhere to the predetermined price unless the manager and the majority of the members agree to make a change in yields. If the bonds are not immediately sold, the syndicate members continue to be liable for unsold bonds.

The Secondary Market

The role of brokers and dealers in the municipal market is similar to that in the corporate bond market; that is, brokers provide a search service in that they act as a "matchmaker" and bring buyers and sellers together; dealers provide search services but also make markets for securities by maintaining an inventory from which they buy or sell for profit. Most dealers operate as brokers, and many also act as underwriters. Together, dealers and brokers help provide a liquid and a continuous market to investors. However, the secondary market for municipal securities is not as liquid as that of the corporate or government security market.

The secondary market for municipal securities is primarily a negotiated over-the-counter market. Small local issues are traded infrequently with commercial banks and local brokerage houses making up the market. The bonds of some large well-known municipalities do have active secondary markets. Dealers employ traders who buy and sell bonds for the account of the firm through other dealers, brokers, individuals, and financial institutions. Brokers who want bonds for their clients contact one or more of the dozen or so major municipal bond brokers, requesting bids on the desired security. Larger brokers often send out bid-wanted notices on private communication wires and receive bid quotations from interested dealers. The broker then selects the best bid (lowest price) for his client.

Dealers quote a bid price — the price at which they are willing to buy, and an ask price — the price at which they are willing to sell, on securities they are willing to trade from their inventories. The difference between the bid and ask price is the dealer's markup or spread. Because of the relatively inactive secondary markets for most municipal bonds, the dealer spreads are usually larger for municipals than for other types of bonds. Dealer spreads can range from as low as $2.50 per $1,000 of par value on a large block of actively traded bonds to as high as $40 per $1,000 on little traded or odd lot bonds. The average spread is around $20.00 per $1,000 for transactions by individual investors. For institutional investors, the dealer spread rarely exceeds $5.00 per $1,000. An odd lot in the municipal bond market is technically a block worth $25,000 (five bonds) or less in par value. For practical purposes, most dealers trade in blocks of $100,000.

In addition to telephone and wire communications, dealers also advertise their municipal bond offerings for the retail market in a publication known as the *Blue List*. This is a 100-page-plus booklet published every week by Standard & Poor's, and lists issues alphabetically, first by state and then by city or issuing authority. Issues advertised in the *Blue List* are often cited as a kind of inventory figure for the municipal market. It is generally believed, however, that dealers do not advertise all the issues they own, so the figure understates market inventories. The *Blue List* is not generally available to the public and is used primarily by professional traders and institutional investors. A page from the December 19, 1983 *Blue List* is shown in Figure 8.3.

Regulation of the Municipal Market

Following the great crash of 1929, Congress enacted a series of laws intended to curb abusive stock market practices that had accrued and to return stability to security markets. The most important of these are (1) the Securities Act of 1933, which deals primarily with full and truthful disclosure about securities sold in the primary market; and (2) the Security and Exchange Act of 1934, concerned with seeing that adequate information is provided about securities traded in secondary markets and established the Security and Exchange Commission (SEC). Surprisingly, Congress specifically exempted municipal securities from both the registration requirements of the 1933 Act and the periodic reporting requirements of the 1934 Act. However, antifraud and misleading information requirements did apply to sales and distribution of municipal securities. The exact reasons for the exemption are difficult to ascertain. Probably the most important are (1) political courtesy between federal and municipal governments (states rights); (2) the lack of widespread fradulent practices in the municipal market; and (3) sophisticated institutional investors who do not need the same safeguards as do individual investors dominate the market.

   In response to the financial difficulties of several municipalities and evidence of fraud in the sale of municipal securities, Congress passed the first major regulation of the municipal securities market, the Security Act Amendment of 1975. The Act brought the major participants involved in selling securities (i.e., dealers, brokers and underwriters) under the regulatory authority of the Security and Exchange Act of 1934. Furthermore, the legislation established a 15-member Municipal Securities Rule Making Board (MSRB) as an independent, self-regulatory agency. The MSRB's primary responsibility is the development of rules governing the activities of brokers and dealers (including dealer banks). The Board has no enforcement powers or inspection powers, and all the rules adopted must be approved by the SEC. Once adopted, the enforcement of rules is vested with the SEC, the National Association of Securities Dealers, and selected bank regulatory agencies, such as the Board of Governors of the Federal Reserve System. Finally, the Securities Act Amendment of 1975 does not require that municipal issuers comply with the registration requirement or the periodic reporting requirement of the 1934 Act. Thus, municipal issuers are not under the same disclosure and reporting standard as are corporate issuers. However, even in the absence of federal legislation, underwriters are beginning to insist upon greater financial disclosure by municipal issuers because of the SEC's stricter enforcement of the antifraud provisions.

State Bond Banks

High interest rates caused by inflation during the 1970s forced state and local governments to examine alternatives that would allow them to sell their new

The Blue List
of Current Municipal Offerings
(A Division of Standard & Poor's Corporation)

Published every weekday except Saturdays and Holidays by
The Blue List Publishing Company, 25 Broadway, New York, N. Y. 10004
Telephone 212 208-8200
Reg U S Patent Office • Printed in U S A

The bonds set forth in this list were offered at the close of business on the day before the date of this issue by the houses mentioned, subject to prior sale and change in price. Every effort is made by The Blue List Publishing Company and the houses whose offerings are shown in The Blue List to avoid mistakes and inaccuracies, but due to the fact that many offerings come in by wire and that the list is published after the offering houses have closed for the day, occasional errors are unavoidable. Neither The Blue List Publishing Company nor the offering houses take responsibility for the accuracy of offerings listed herein.

ANNUAL SUBSCRIPTION RATE (approximately 250 issues): Hand Delivery (Wall Street Area) $360.00; First Class Mail $475.00

AMT. M	SECURITY	PURPOSE	RATE	MATURITY	YIELD OR OFFERED PRICE	BY
	ALABAMA					
50	ALABAMA		6.90	9/ 1/90	8.25	PRUBANY
25	ALABAMA		7.70	3/ 1/93	8.75	STEPPAF
25	ALABAMA		7.90	9/ 1/94	8.75	PRUBANY
10	ALABAMA		8	9/ 1/95	9.00	CHEMICBK
500	ALABAMA	SER.A	8.10	9/ 1/96	9.30	SMITHB
500	ALABAMA		8.20	9/ 1/97	9.50	PRUBANY
50	ALABAMA		8.25	9/ 1/98	9.30	FIRSTCHI
865	ALABAMA		8.25	9/ 1/98	9.40	MANUFHAN
1250	ALABAMA		8.25	9/ 1/98	9.50	SHAWMUTB
470	ALABAMA		8.25	9/ 1/98	9.40	SMITHB
250	ALABAMA		8.375	3/ 1/01	90	CITIBANK
100	ALABAMA		8.375	3/ 1/01	91 3/4	CFNBHBM
100	ALABAMA		8.375	3/ 1/01	89 3/4	IRVTRUST

· Items so marked did not appear in the previous issue of The Blue List.
· Prices so marked are changed from previous issue.
c Items so marked are reported to have call or option features. Consult offering house for full details.

AMT. M	SECURITY	PURPOSE	RATE	MATURITY	YIELD OR OFFERED PRICE	BY
	ALABAMA-CONTINUED					
250	ALABAMA		8.375	3/ 1/01	89 1/2	LBKLNY
500	ALABAMA		8.375	3/ 1/01	90	MANUFHAN
100	ALABAMA		8.375	3/ 1/01	90 1/2	MEEHAN
50	ALABAMA	P/R @ 103	11.875	3/ 1/01 C92	8.40	HEARSTER
25	ALABAMA	P/R @ 103	11.875	3/ 1/01 C92	8.40	LBKLNY
250	ALABAMA		8.375	9/ 1/01	90	CITIBANK
100	ALABAMA		8.375	9/ 1/01	90	HAWKBUST
500	ALABAMA		8.375	9/ 1/01	89 3/4	IRVTRUST
50	ALABAMA		8.375	9/ 1/01	90	MANUFHAN
50	ALABAMA		8.375	9/ 1/01	93	STANLETC
50	ALABAMA		8.375	9/ 1/01	95	ZUCKERAM
195	ALABAMA	P/R @ 103	11.875	9/ 1/01 C92	8.40	BEARSTEM
100	ALABAMA	P/R @ 103	11.875	9/ 1/01 C92	8.70	KIDDERNY
850	ALABAMA HIGHWAY AUTH.		7.25	8/ 1/89	8.00	SALOMON
55	ALA.HSG.FIN.AU.	FSLIC	8.50	4/ 1/95	98	HUUGHMMF

THE BLUE LIST
OF CURRENT MUNICIPAL OFFERINGS

December 19 1983 Monday

Volume 193 Number 55

INDEX

New Housing Authority Bonds......184A
Local Housing Authority Bonds......——
Industrial Development and
  Pollution Control Bonds......190A
Notes......197A
Tax-Exempt Investment Trusts......——
New Issue Delivery Dates......203A
Pre-refunded Bonds......204A
Federally Sponsored Bonds......214A
Corporate Bonds......215A
Preferred Stocks......230
Offerings Wanted......231
Swaps Follow Page......
Late CUSIP's Follow......
List of Advertisers......N/A

FIG. 8.3 The Municipal Bond Blue List

bond issues at the lowest possible borrowing cost. One alternative is the formation of a state bond bank. A state bond bank is an arrangement whereby towns, counties, and other municipal entities pool their long-term debt to form a larger bond issue. Bond banks may reduce the borrowing costs of participants because the large bond issues may attract more bidders, have lower underwriting cost per bond, and be more marketable. In addition, the existence of a reserve fund and a state's moral obligation of financial support if financial difficulties arise may decrease the issue's perceived default risk. To date, five states and Puerto Rico have established bond banks. The first state was Vermont (1970), followed by Maine (1972), Puerto Rico (1973), Alaska (1975), North Dakota (1975), and New Hampshire (1979).

A bond bank is created with the passage of a law by a state legislature authorizing its formation. States typically lend or appropriate funds to get the bond bank started. Alaska, for example, appropriated $3 million to start its bond bank. A bond bank begins operation by accepting applications from local governments that wish to sell their bonds through the bond bank. Participation in the bond bank is optional. The government unit provides financial data so that bond bank officials can judge the issues' credit quality in order to decide whether or not to admit the applicant to the bond bank pool. Generally, applicants with a large amount of debt outstanding or ill-conceived projects are rejected because they might damage the credit standing and/or marketability of the issue. When the approved applicants have met their normal necessary constitutional requirements to issue debt, and the bond bank pool has reached a minimum size (usually $6 to $10 million), the bond bank prepares to issue bonds under its name for an amount equal to the sum of the individual issues plus an amount for a reserve fund. The reserve fund is available to meet interest and/or principal payments in the event that any of the participating municipalities fail to meet their debt service payments; the reserve fund is usually the maximum debt service for one year. The bond bank then purchases a credit rating from Moody's and/or Standard & Poor's. Finally, the bond bank officials decide whether to offer the bonds to underwriters on a negotiated or competitive basis. Most bond bank issues are sold through negotiation.

After the sale of the issue, bond bank officials distribute the funds to the bond bank participants and invest the reserve funds in U.S. Treasury securities or in federal agency securities. The spread between the return on taxable government securities and the tax-exempt rate on the bond bank is an arbitrage profit for the bond bank. The arbitrage profit usually covers all the expenses of the bond bank operation. If this amount proves insufficient, the bond bank participants pay the remaining expenses on a pro rata basis. The state itself does not bear any of the direct costs of the bond bank operation. However, states do have a moral obligation to provide funds to cover any deficiencies to the bond issue's reserve fund. Over the life of the bonds, participants send their interest and principal payments directly to the bond bank's trustee until their individual financial obligation is met and the participants' cumulative payments retire the bond issue. For individual municipalities, the critical question is whether they should sell their new bond issues directly to an underwriter or participate in a state bond bank. To make this decision, state and local governments need to know the interest cost difference between a bond bank issue and a direct sale, given the municipality's financial circumstances and the characteristics of the proposed bond issue. Three factors most critical to this decision are: (1) the dollar size of the issue; (2) the issuer credit rating; and (3) whether the issue can be sold competitively or must be a negotiated deal. Empirical evidence by Kidwell and Rogowski (Mar.–Apr. 1983) suggests that: (1) all municipalities who must sell the bonds by negotiated sale will reduce their borrowing costs by joining a bond bank; and (2) all issuers who can sell their bonds competitively and are rated A or below by the credit rating agencies can achieve interest cost savings in a bond bank. Typical interest cost savings range between 10 to 150 basis points (one percent = 100 basis points). Also, the smaller the dollar size of the bond issue, the greater the interest saving from participating bond bank issues.

Where viewed in dollar terms, the interest cost difference for even a small bond issue can be quite large. For example, using Kidwell and Rogowski's empirical estimates, a small municipality that plans to sell a $500,000 negotiated issue could achieve the following dollar interest cost savings. Assuming that the bond issue is a serial issue with 20 equal $25,000 payments and has an average maturity of 10 years (final maturity of 20 years), then a one basis point change in NIC is equivalent to about $380 in the present value of interest over the life of the bond issue. Thus, for different bond ratings, the interest cost savings achieved would be:

Bond Rating	Present Value of Interest Cost Savings
Aaa	$23,940
Aa	30,020
A	38,000
Baa	58,520

Municipal Bond Insurance

A relatively new phenomenon in the tax-exempt marketplace is municipal bond insurance. Municipal bond insurance is an unconditional contractual guarantee by a PCI to pay the bondholder coupon interest and principal in the event of default by the issuer, for whatever the reason. Bond insurance is purchased at the time the bonds are issued; the entire premium is prepaid and the policy is nonrefundable. Once issued, the default insurance is in effect for the life of the bond issue, and it cannot be canceled by the insurance company. Municipal bond insurance is purchased by municipalities who believe that the insurance will lower their new issue borrowing cost by improving their credit standing (lower default risk) and/or improving the marketability of their bonds.

Although municipal bond insurance has been available since 1971, only two groups of PCIs have entered the market: the American Municipal Bond Assurance Corporation (AMBAC) established in 1971, and the Municipal Bond Insurance Association (MBIA) established in 1974. In 1982, the Industrial Development Bond Insurance (IDBI Managers, Inc.) began insuring small tax-exempt industrial development bond issuers. The above insurance companies are located in New York State and therefore are subject to the reserves and capital requirements imposed by the New York State Insurance Commission.

AMBAC and MBIA insure only new issues. However, even if an investor acquires the bonds in the secondary market, the bonds are fully insured. Thus, even though the financial strength of the issuer may vary over the life of the bond, the credit quality remains relatively unchanged, and insured bonds are less volatile in price. AMBAC insures all types of municipal securities, while MBIA does not insure IDBs.

Advantages of Insurance

Bond insurance benefits both municipalities who pay less in interest and investors who accept less risk. All insured bonds are rated AAA by Standard & Poor's. Moody's does not consider insurance in its evaluation of an issuer's credit quality. Municipalities should purchase insurance only when the present value of the interest savings exceeds the insurance premium. Thus, without the insurance, the credit quality of qualifying municipalities is relatively low. Both AMBAC and MBIA reject applications for insurance when their own credit analysis of the issuer indicates excessive default risk.

Even though insured bonds are AAA rated by Standard & Poor's, they trade at yields above Aaa rated bonds. Sylvan Feldstein (1983) recently reported that the average yield spread between 20-year MBIA-insured bonds and Aaa general obligations varied between 68 and 79 basis points from 1980–1982. Thus, investors who purchase insured bonds obtain a higher yield than pure prime-rated securities. Through 1981, none of the approximately 1,000 MBIA insured bonds defaulted and only 11 out of over 2,100 AMBAC-insured bonds defaulted. When an issuer defaults, bondholders notify AMBAC, which then makes the promised interest and principal payments. The increased liquidity of insured bonds is derived from their improved credit standing and the increased demand due to the fact that the bonds qualify as investment grade securities. Banks and other financial institutions with fiduciary responsibilities are effectively restricted to investment grade securities.

Insurance will likely become more popular in future years. The variety of unknown issuers and the complexity in determining the security behind new issues virtually mandates that many borrowers purchase insurance. With a volatile economic and interest rate environment, insurance also protects the bondholder from extreme declines in value due to rating changes or interest rate increases. Finally, given the recent uncertainties in the municipal market, individual investors who now dominate the market may look more closely at securities whose interest and principal is guaranteed.

INDUSTRIAL DEVELOPMENT BONDS

Much of the recent growth in tax-exempt financing can be attributed to private purpose IDBs. Since 1980, almost 50 percent of net long-term issues have been for private purposes, with outstanding issues equal to $80 billion at mid-year 1983 (see Table 8.1). While local governments issue the securities, they essentially loan the tax-exemption to private corporations. As such, corporations borrow at subsidized rates to finance their facilities.

TABLE 8.7   Qualifying Exempt Industrial Development Bond Facilities and Purposes

- Sewage or solid waste disposal facilities
- Electric energy and gas facilities
- Airports, docks, and wharves
- Water supply facilities

- Sports and convention or trade-show facilities
- Certain hydroelectric generating facilities
- Industrial parks
- Mass transit systems
- Residential mortgage programs*

* Authority to issue mortgage subsidy bonds expired on December 31, 1983.

The extraordinary growth in IDBs has focused considerable attention on their usage. Critics contend that this tax-exempt financing misallocates resources, reduces federal tax revenues, and raises municipal borrowing costs for traditional purposes. Supporters argue that IDBs create jobs locally, thereby adding to the state and local government tax base and increasing federal income tax revenues. The U.S. Congress recently restricted the use of IDBs for selected purposes, and set a state-by-state cap on annual issues beginning in 1984. The cap limits gross IDB issues in each state to the greater of $200 million or $150 per state resident. Not surprisingly, states and municipalities are protesting vigorously.

Forty-seven states have passed legislation authorizing IDBs. Municipalities or their political subdivisions issue the bonds to finance land and depreciable assets for nonexempt businesses. These assets are then leased or sold to corporations under installment contracts with periodic payments sufficient to meet debt service requirements on the IDBs.

Bonds are classified as IDBs if they satisfy two criteria. First, a majority of the proceeds must be used by nonexempt business. Second, a majority of the debt service payments must be secured by revenues or property of the nonexempt business and not by local governments. Recent IDBs have been revenue bonds exclusively, as businesses provide the *only* potential source of repayment. Municipalities neither pledge their tax or credit powers nor bear any financial liability for the debt, but simply loan their tax-exempt borrowing capability to private businesses. Thus, IDBs are not subject to voter approval, and new issue volume is determined solely by municipal officers.

Current Restrictions on IDB Usage

Prior to 1968, all bonds issued by state and local governments were considered tax-exempt. In response to an increase in IDB financings, Congress passed the Revenue and Expenditure Control Act of 1968, which limited IDB usage to two classes of bonds: exempt issues and small issues. Exempt issues finance facilities that presumably provide considerable social benefits and where no private individual benefits financially. There are no size limits on the issue or capital expenditure restrictions if "substantially all" of the proceeds are used to purchase land or depreciable property. Designated purposes and qualifying facilities are shown in Table 8.7. Small issues, in contrast, are issued for the primary benefit of nonexempt corporations. States and localities do not share in the revenues of the projects financed.

With a small issue IDB, the borrower has the choice of issuing the bonds under a $1 million or $10 million limit. In the first case, the sum of the new IDB issue and all outstanding IDBs related to the project financed and principal user cannot exceed $1 million, In the second case, total capital expenditures by the principal user of the facility financed cannot exceed $10 million during a six-year period centered on the date of the IDB issue. If the limits are exceeded, the bonds lose their small issue tax exemption. Regardless of the limit selected, "substantially all" of the issue proceeds must be used for land and depreciable assets.

The Tax Equity and Fiscal Responsibility Act of 1982 clarified two concerns related to IDB issues. First, it established guidelines for determining when pooled issues of IDBs should be treated as separate tax-exempt issues under the limitations previously discussed. Formerly, many firms were able to easily circumvent small issue restrictions by dividing large projects into segments each supported by different development groups. Now bonds lose their small issue exemption if they finance two or more facilities in more than one state and if the same groups are the principal user. Second, it established reporting requirements whereby prior public approval of IDB financing must be obtained and new issues must be reported quarterly to the IRS.

Benefits of Industrial Development Bonds

Local government officials typically argue that IDBs benefit local communities by attracting new industry that otherwise would not have undertaken such projects. Communities presumably benefit from increased employment due to new jobs, increased personal income, and an expanded local tax base. At the same time, there is little explicit cost to a locality as the incentive is reduced private sector borrowing costs. Whether these benefits accrue in the aggregate is another issue. If, for example, a firm relocates a plant in response to IDB financing, the community losing the firm suffers unemployment, lower income, and a declining tax base.

Without question, private corporations realize most of the benefits from small issue IDB financing. The primary benefit is reduced borrowing costs. Consider, for example, a 10-year, $5 million IDB financing with equal annual principal repayment at a 7.5 percent coupon rate where the corporation's taxable alternative is 11.5 percent. In the first year alone, the firm would save $200,000 in interest or $108,000 after taxes at 46 percent. Over the life of the bond issue, the firm would save $594,000 after taxes. This lowers the firm's cost of capital and may make new projects financially feasible.

There are, however, many other advantages to the business. First, the IRS recognizes the business as the owner of the project for federal tax purposes even though the local government issues the debt and leases the facility. This enables the business to (1) claim any investment tax credit; (2) take accelerated depreciation allowances on the facility; (3) deduct normal operating expenses; and (4) deduct part of each lease payment as interest. Because many state and local governments, in contrast, view the municipality as the owner, the firm

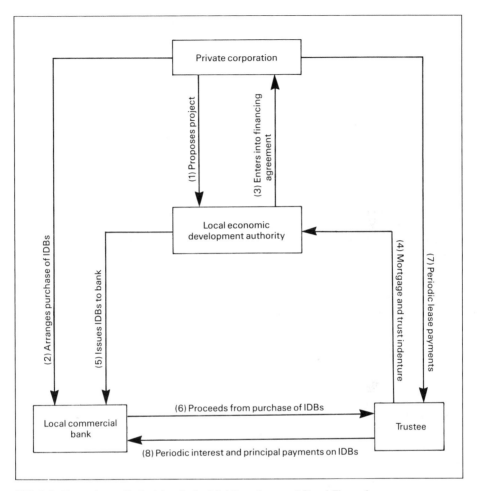

FIG. 8.4 Procedures Underlying Industrial Development Bond Financing

can sometimes avoid sales taxes on materials used in construction and avoid local property taxes. Some governments, however, impose assessments against IDB facilities equal to their reduced local taxes from the exemption.

The Underlying Structure of IDB Financing

The procedures followed in an IDB financing vary between different municipalities. The general format, however, is outlined in Figure 8.4. In most instances, corporations approach local governments with a proposed project. Frequently, the firm has prepared a package of materials demonstrating the financial strength of the firm and viability of the project. It may provide the legal expertise and supporting documents. The firm then negotiates with local commercial banks to buy the prospective IDBs specifying maturities, pricing, and collateral that are acceptable to both parties. If the local economic development authority accepts the proposal, it issues a resolution that authorizes a financial agreement between the authority and the private corporation. This agreement formally stipulates the terms under which IDBs are issued.

Typically, the authority retains title to all facilities purchased or built and leases them back to the business. The periodic lease payments are set equal to the principal and interest payments on the IDBs over the life of the bonds. At the end of the lease, the firm buys the facility at a nominal price.

The parties to the transaction establish a mortgage and trust indenture, which provides for a trustee to administer the payments. The trustee, which may be the local commercial bank, ensures that all transactions are handled at arm's length. After the bonds are issued, the trustee collects the lease payments from the business and makes the interest and principal payments to the bondholder.

There are several potential pitfalls for the private corporation. First, it must convince the local development authority to authorize the IDBs. Local government officials are often unaware of the procedures involved and the steps required to avoid liability. Thus, businesses frequently provide their own legal staff to clarify the issues. Second, the firm must find a buyer for the IDBs before the financing is effected. Most IDB financings are for long-term capital projects. Banks are hesitant to accept 20-year bonds because it is difficult to assess the economic viability of a firm or project over such a long period. IDBs are generally not rated and thus are relatively illiquid. Most IDBs are priced on a floating-rate basis, with 65 to 75 percent of the bank prime rate a common method. This at least removes some of the interest rate risk to the bank. Similarly, it is often written into the bond indenture that the IDBs will be immediately callable at a significant premium, or that the coupon rate will be raised to a taxable yield equivalent if they lose their tax exemption.

The last major difficulty is retaining the tax exemption on the bond issues by meeting all the legal requirements under the Internal Revenue Code. While the different characteristics of IDBs present a variety of problems, the two fundamental concerns are the capital expenditure limit and the application of the bond proceeds. The expenditure limit restricts the project user from making capital outlays in excess of $10 million for six years surrounding the IDB issue. The user should stipulate in the financing agreement that it will not deliberately exceed the limit and thus eliminate the bonds' tax-exempt status. The use of bond proceeds relates to a "substantially all" test. The regulation stipulates that no less than 90 percent of the total bond proceeds minus issue costs and a reserve fund must be spent on land and depreciable assets. Unfortunately, IRS rulings are somewhat vague on what costs qualify for deduction. Issuers should obtain a legal opinion from outside bond counsel or the local county attorney which indicates that the terms of the indenture meet the requirements for tax exemption.

A HYPOTHETICAL IDB ISSUE

The characteristics of a hypothetical IDB issue are shown in Figure 8.5. This particular $2 million issue is to be used to finance the construction of a supermarket

BOND PROCEEDS: $2,000,000

CENTER CITY, TENNESSEE

INDUSTRIAL DEVELOPMENT REVENUE BONDS, 1983
(Discount Supermarket)

Estimated project costs

1. Land		$ 160,000
2. Fixtures		425,000
3. Building costs; new construction and remodeling		1,150,000
4. Financing charges		
a. State industrial commission application fee	$ 1,500	
b. Financial advisor fee (1 percent)	20,000	
c. Bond counsel fee (1 percent)	20,000	
d. Friendly Supermarket	5,500	
e. Industrial development corporation counsel fee	2,000	
f. Trustee fee	2,000	
Total		$ 51,000
5. Engineering and architectural fees		45,000
6. Interest paid during project construction		44,000
7. Miscellaneous expenses and contingencies		125,000
Total project cost		$2,000,000

IDB issue data

Amount of issue: $2,000,000

Interest rate: 75 percent of City National Bank's prime rate* (currently 8.25 percent)

Term: 15 years, equal annual principal payments

* The prime rate is defined as the base rate used to price City National Bank's commercial loans.

FIG. 8.5 A Hypothetical Industrial Development Bond Issue

in Center City, Tennessee. The user of the bond proceeds, Discount Supermarket, applied for project financing through the Center County Industrial Development Corporation. The development corporation, in turn, obtained aproval from the state industrial commission, which by law must evaluate every IDB issue.

As part of the application, the corporation estimates that approximately 50 jobs will be created with an annual payroll of $500,000. The new jobs include a store manager, shift managers, checkout personnel, shelf stockers, and carryout personnel. The project will consist of 28,000 square feet of supermarket space to be divided into meat, fruit and vegetable, and sundry departments. The user owns the site free of all liens or encumbranches.

The estimated component costs of the new venture are shown in Figure 8.5. Specifically, the proceeds of the issue will be used to buy land and fixtures; to pay for construction; to pay $5,000 in finance charges including filing fees with the state commission, trustee fees, and legal fees; and over $200,000 more for engineering and design fees, interest during construction, and miscellaneous expenses. The legal fees are paid to obtain opinions that interest on the bonds will be tax-exempt. Of the $2 million total, almost 87 percent covers capital outlays. This percentage varies directly with issue size over different IDB issues.

The terms of the IDB issue are listed at the bottom of the exhibit. These bonds were purchased by City National Bank in a direct placement as part of the bank's loan/investment portfolio. The serial bond issue will be repaid in 15 years with equal annual principal payments. Interest to the bank floats at 25 percent of the bank's prime rate. Debt service during the first year will equal approximately $300,000.

CRITICISMS OF INDUSTRIAL DEVELOPMENT BONDS

The recent growth in IDB financing has spurred efforts to restrict IDB usage even further. Critics contend that the tax exemption has been abused and that the costs to the U.S. Treasury exceed the benefits to local communities. The abuses are well-documented. A 1981 Congressional Budget Office Study reported that 7 percent of a sample of small IDBs issued from 1978–1979 were used by the top Forture 50 nonindustrial companies or the top Fortune 1000 industrial firms. From 1975 to 1980, K-Mart Stores used almost $221 million of IDBs to finance stores in 19 states. More recently, IDBs have been issued to finance a Howard Johnson Hotel and numerous medical complexes and offices for doctors, dentists, and lawyers. These are not the types of firms that most taxpayers appreciate subsidizing with low-interest loans. In 1982, Congress did restrict the usage for massage parlors and fast-food establishments, which were large users.

The dollar cost to the U.S. Treasury is difficult to assess. Investors in IDBs avoid paying federal income taxes on coupon interest; thus, federal tax revenues are reduced. Some groups have estimated these lost federal revenues in excess of $1 billion annually. Others argue that tax revenues at all levels of government actually increase with the new business and employment generated by IDBs. The true effect depends on whether IDBs add to business activity. With many local governments in all jurisdictions issuing IDBs, it seems plausible that governments largely compete against each other to retain business. Thus, the regional benefits from attracting business are offset by the losses in communities from which firms relocate. Industrial development bonds thus serve simply to pass the tax exemption and lower borrowing costs to non-exempt businesses.

Other criticisms are equally important. With a normal demand curve for municipals, IDB issues increase borrowing costs for all traditional tax-exempt purposes by increasing the supply of municipal securities. It is thus more expensive to finance outlays for schools and roads. Industrial development bonds are inequitable in that firms that do not use them operate at a cost disadvantage. Similarly, many of the firms that do use IDBs do not need financial assistance and already have access to taxable debt alternatives. Studies further indicate that the availability of raw materials, low-cost labor, and utilities are more important than borrowing costs for most firms when selecting a plant location. In short, small issue IDBs appear to be both inequitable and neutral in attracting new business. Thus, their continued usage and future growth may slow markedly.

SUGGESTED READING

Allardice, David R. "Small-Issue Industrial Revenue Bonds in the Seventh Federal Reserve District." *Economic Perspectives*. Federal Reserve Bank of Chicago. Chicago: Winter 1982.

Aronson, Richard J., and Eli Schwartz, eds. *Management Policies in Local Government Finance*. Washington, D.C.: International City Management Association, 1975.

Fabozzi, Frank, et al., eds. *The Municipal Bond Handbook*, Vols. 1 and 2. Homewood, Ill.: Dow Jones-Irwin, 1983.

Feldstein, Sylvan G. "Municipal Bond Insurance and Pricing," *The Municipal Bond Handbook*, eds. Frank Fabozzi, et al. Homewood, Ill.: Dow Jones-Irwin, 1983.

Gray, Gary, and Randall Woolridge. "Industrial Development Bonds — Opportunities and Challenges." *The Bankers Magazine* (July-Aug. 1981).

Kidwell, David S., and Robert J. Rogowski. "Bond Banks: A State Assistance Program that Helps Reduce New Issue Borrowing Costs." *Public Administration Review* (Mar.–Apr. 1983).

——— "State Bond Bank Issues: Method of Sale and Market Acceptance Over Time." *Financial Management* (Summer 1983).

Lamb, Robert, and Stephen P. Rapport. *Municipal Bonds: The Comprehensive Review of Tax-Exempt Securities and Public Finance*. New York: McGraw-Hill, 1980.

Laufenberg, Daniel E. "Industrial Development Bonds: Some Aspects of the Current Controversy." *Federal Reserve Bulletin* (Mar. 1982).

McMullen, J. S. "Industrial Revenue Bond Financing: What's It All About?." *The Journal of Commercial Bank Lending* (Dec. 1980).

Moak, Lennox L. *Municipal Bonds: Planning, Sale, and Administration*. Municipal Finance Officers Association. Chicago, Ill.: 1982.

Moody's Investors Service. *Pitfalls in Issuing Municipal Securities*. New York: 1982.

Peterson, John E., and Wesley C. Hough. *Creative Capital Financing for State and Local Governments*. Chicago, Ill.: Municipal Finance Officers Association. Chicago, Ill.: 1983.

Public Securities Association. *Fundamentals of Municipal Bonds*. New York: 1981.

Scheinberg, Steven E. "Small-Issue Industrial Development Revenue Bonds," *The Municipal Bond Handbook*, eds. Frank Fabozzi, et al. Homewood, Ill.: Dow Jones-Irwin, 1983.

9

Corporate Equities

DONALD E. FISCHER

This chapter presents an overview of the various types of corporate equities, the ways in which they are issued and traded, and the widely accepted methods of determining their value.

OVERVIEW OF CORPORATE EQUITIES

The Nature of Equity Capital

Equity capital differs from debt capital in a number of key ways. These differences are considered by firms in contemplating the use of equity as opposed to debt capital for raising funds. The basic differences concern the ownership of the firm, the claims of stockholders on its income and assets, and the maturity of the two types of stock.

Rights of Ownership. Unlike creditors, holders of equity capital money (preferred and common stockholders) are owners of the business firm. The money invested by equity holders does not have to be repaid. These dollars represent permanent capital that is expected to remain on the firm's books indefinitely. Holders of equity capital often receive voting rights which permit them to select the firm's directors and to vote on other issues. Creditors get voting privileges only when the firm has defaulted or violated the terms of a loan agreement or bond contract. As long as the firm meets all the requirements of a loan agreement, only certain equity holders are given voting rights. It is only when the firm is approaching or in financial difficulty that creditors may receive some voice in management.

Claims on Income and Assets. Holders of equity capital receive a claim on both income and assets that is secondary to the claims of the firm's creditors.
The claims of equity holders on income cannot be paid until the claims of all creditors have been satisfied. These claims include both interest and principal. Once these claims have been satisfied, the firm's board of directors can decide whether to distribute any of the remaining funds to the firm's owners. Certain owners may have preference over other owners with respect to the distribution of the firm's earnings. It is important to recognize that a firm's ability to make these payments may be constrained due to its cash position or certain loan covenants. The firm may have sufficient earnings, but no cash; it is the availability of cash that permits the firm to distribute earnings to owners.
The claim of equity holders on the firm's assets is secondary to the claims of its creditors. The stockholder's claim on assets is relevant primarily when the firm becomes bankrupt. When this happens, the assets are liquidated and the proceeds are distributed first to the government, then to secured creditors, then to general creditors, and finally to equity holders. The last rarely receive the book value of their equity in the event of liquidation, so they expect greater compensation in the form of dividends and/or rising market prices on their holdings.

Maturity. Equity capital does not mature, but equity holders are often able to liquidate their holdings through the various security exchanges. Since equity will be liquidated only during bankruptcy proceedings, holders recognize that the price realized on a sale may fluctuate with the firm's current and expected earnings.

Preferred Stock

Preferred stock gives its holders certain privileges that make them senior to the common stockholders. Preferred stockholders are promised a fixed periodic return, which is stated either as a percentage or in dollars. In other words, either 10 percent preferred stock or $10 preferred stock can be issued. The way the dividend is stated depends on whether the preferred stock has a par value. The par value of a stock is the face amount of the stock specified in the corporate charter; it is important for certain legal purposes. The annual dividend is stated as a percentage on par value preferred stock and in dollars on no par preferred stock. A 10 percent preferred stock with a $100 par value is expected to pay $10 (10 percent of $100) in dividends per year. In recent years we have also seen the advent of preferred stocks whose dividend is adjustable ("floating") in accordance with some bench mark rate.

Basic Rights of Preferred Stockholders

The basic rights of preferred stockholders with respect to voting, the distribution of earnings, and the distribution of assets are somewhat more favorable than the rights of common stockholders. Since preferred stock is a form of ownership and has no maturity date, its claims on income and assets rank behind those of the firm's creditors.

Voting Rights. Preferred stockholders have many of the characteristics of both creditors and owners. They are promised a fixed periodic return, similar to the interest paid creditors, but do not expect to have invested capital repaid by the firm at maturity. Thus preferred stock can be thought of as quasi-debt. The fixed return characteristic of debt coupled with the permanent nature of the preferred stock investment suggests a hybrid type of security. Since the preferred stock investment is permanent, it does represent ownership; but because the preferred stockholders' claim on the firm's income is fixed and takes precedence over the claim of common shareholders, they do not expose themselves to the same degree of risk as common stockholders. Preferred stockholders are therefore *not* normally given the right to vote. In certain instances, they may receive voting rights.

Distribution of Earnings. Preferred stockholders are given preference over common stockholders with respect to the distribution of earnings. If the stated preferred stock dividend is not declared by the board of directors, the payment of dividends to common stockholders is prohibited. Thus without dividend payments to preferred stockholders the market price of common stock may be damaged.

Distribution of Assets. When assets are liquidated as a result of bankruptcy, preferred stockholders are normally given preference over common stockholders, although preferred stockholders must wait until the claims of all creditors have been satisfied. The amount of the claim of preferred stockholders in liquidation proceedings is normally equal to the par or stated book value of the preferred stock. Preferred stockholders may be given a slight premium above the stock's book value, depending on the initial agreement under which the stock was issued.

Special Features of Preferred Stock. A number of features are generally included as part of a preferred stock issue. These features, along with a statement of the stock's par value, the amount of dividend payments, and the dividend payment dates, are specified in an agreement. Certain protective covenants may also be included in this agreement.

There may be a provision stating that if preferred stock dividends are passed for a specified number of periods, the preferred stockholders are entitled to elect a certain number of directors.

A preferred stock issue can prohibit the issuance of any additional securities senior to the preferred stock. Constraints also may be placed on additional preferred stock issues. The issuance of additional common stock is not viewed negatively by preferred stockholders, since added funds are raised without impairing the preferred stockholders' claims on earnings and assets. If a clause does not prohibit new issues of debt and preferred stock, there may be a constraint on the amount of new funds that can be raised with senior securities.

Often, preferred stock issues prohibit the firm from merging with any other firm. The sale of all or a portion of the firm's assets may be specifically prohibited. Mergers, or sales of assets, could change the firm's capital and asset structures in a fashion detrimental to the interests of preferred stockholders.

In order to prevent the firm from using a large portion of its cash, thus impairing future preferred dividends, preferred stock issues may prohibit or limit the amount of cash dividends or common stock repurchases the firm can make in any year.

Cumulation. Most preferred stock is cumulative with respect to any dividends omitted. That is, all dividends in arrears must be paid prior to the payment of dividends to common stockholders. Since the only way the common stockholders, who are the firm's true owners, can receive dividends is by first satisfying the claims of preferred stockholders on dividends, it is in their best interests to pay preferred stock dividends when they are due.

Participation. Most issues of preferred stock state that the preferred stockholders receive only required dividend payments. On rare occasions participating preferred stock is issued. Dividend payments based on certain formulas allow the preferred stockholder to participate with common stockholders in the receipt of dividends beyond the specified amount.

The Call Feature. Preferred stock is generally callable, which means that the issuer can retire outstanding stock within a certain period of time at a specified price. The call option generally cannot be exercised until a period of years has elapsed since the issuance of the preferred stock. The call price is normally set above the initial issuance price (e.g., par plus one year's dividend as a penalty). Making preferred stock subject to call provides the issuer with a method of bringing the fixed payment commitment of the preferred stock issue to an end.

The Conversion Feature. Preferred stock often contains a feature that permits its conversion into a specified number of shares of common stock. Sometimes the number of shares of common stock received or the time period for conversion changes according to a prescribed formula. A more in-depth discussion of conversion is presented later in this chapter.

Retirement and Refinancing. There are a number of ways of providing for the retirement of preferred stock.

One uncommon method of retiring preferred stock is to provide a sinking fund to retire shares at a specified rate over a given period of time. This type of planned retirement makes the preferred stock quite similar to long-term debt except that if the firm were unable to make a sinking fund payment for preferred stock, bankruptcy would not result.

By including a call feature in preferred stock, the issuer can replace an outstanding issue with some less expensive form of financing. Whether refinancing is justified depends on the cost of maintaining the preferred stock as opposed to the cost of an alternate source of financing.

A company can also purchase its own preferred stock on the open market at prevailing market prices.

Common Stock

The true owners of the business firm are the common stockholders. A common stockholder is sometimes referred to as a residual owner, since in essence he receives what is left after all other claims on the firm's income and assets have been satisfied. Since the common stockholder accepts what is left after all other claims have been satisfied, he is placed in a quite uncertain or risky position with respect to returns on his invested capital. As a result of this generally uncertain position, he expects to be compensated by adequate dividends and capital gains.

Characteristics of Common Stock. An understanding of the basic characteristics of common stock provides a grasp of the nature of common stock financing. This section discusses par values, authorized and outstanding stock, voting rights, stock splits, dividends, and the distribution of earnings and assets.

Par Value. Common stock may be sold either with or without a par value. A par value is a relatively useless value arbitrarily placed on the stock in the corporate charter. It is generally quite low, since in many states the firm's owners can be held legally liable for an amount equal to the difference between the par value and the price paid for the stock if the price paid for the stock is less than the par value. Setting the par value quite low, in the range of $1, reduces the possibility that the stock will sell for less than the par value. Firms often issue no par stock, in which case they may assign it a value or place it on the books at the price at which it is sold.

A low par value may also be advantageous in states where certain corporate taxes are based on the par value of stock; if a stock has no par value, the tax may be based on an arbitrarily determined per share figure.

Authorized and Outstanding Stock. A corporate charter must state the number of shares of common stock the firm is authorized to issue. Not all authorized shares will necessarily be outstanding. Extra shares are frequently reserved for potential mergers and acquisitions, conversion of other securities, and employee option programs. Since it is often difficult to amend the corporate charter to authorize the issuance of additional shares, firms generally attempt to authorize more shares than they plan to issue. A possible disadvantage of this approach is the fact that in some states certain corporate taxes are based on the number of shares authorized. It is possible for the corporation to have issued more shares of common stock than are currently outstanding if it has repurchased stock. Repurchased stock is referred to as treasury stock.

Voting Rights. Generally each share of common stock entitles the holder to one vote in the election of directors or in other special elections. Votes are generally assignable and must be cast at the annual shareholders' meeting. Occasionally nonvoting common stock is issued when the firm's present owners wish to raise capital through the sale of common stock but do not want to give up any voting power. Three aspects of voting require special attention: proxies, majority voting, and cumulative voting.

Since most small stockholders often cannot attend the annual meeting in order to vote their shares, they may sign a proxy statement giving their votes to another party. The existing management generally receives the stockholders' proxies, since it is able to solicit them at company expense. Occasionally, when the ownership of the firm is widely dispersed, outsiders may attempt to gain control by waging a proxy battle. This requires soliciting a sufficient number of votes to unseat the existing management. In order to win a corporate election, a majority of the shares voted, not those outstanding, is required. Proxy battles generally occur when the existing management is performing poorly; however, the odds on a nonmanagement group winning a proxy battle are generally slim.

In the majority voting system, each stockholder is entitled to one vote for each share of stock owned. The stockholders vote for each position on the board of directors separately, and each stockholder is permitted to vote his shares for *each* director he favors. The directors receiving the majority of the votes are elected. It is impossible for minority interests to select a director, since each shareholder can vote his shares for as many of the candidates as he wishes. As long as management controls a majority of the votes, it can elect all the directors.

Some states require and others permit the use of a cumulative voting system to elect corporate directors. This system gives a number of votes equal to the number of directors to be elected to each share of common stock. The votes can be given to any director(s) the shareholder desires. The advantage of this system is that it provides the minority shareholders with an opportunity to elect at least some directors.

Stock Splits. Stock splits are commonly used to lower the market price of a firm's stock. Quite often the firm believes that the price of its stock is too high and that lowering the market price will enhance trading activity. Stock splits are often made prior to new issues of a stock in order to enhance the market-ability of the stock and stimulate market activity. A stock split has no effect on the firm's financial structure. It only increases the number of shares outstanding and reduces the stock's par value.

Stock can be split in any way desired, for example, five for four or six for five. Sometimes reverse stock splits are made; that is, a certain number of outstanding shares are exchanged for a new share. This is done when a stock is selling at too low a price to appear respectable. It is not unusual for a stock split to cause a slight increase in the market value of the firm's stock. This is attributable to both the informational content of stock splits and the fact that total dividends usually increase slightly after a stock split. Reverse stock splits can be employed as a maneuver to "freeze out" minority interests intent upon unfriendly takeover attempts.

Dividends. The payment of corporate dividends is at the discretion of the board of directors. Most corporations pay these dividends quarterly as a result of the quarterly dividend meeting of the board of directors. Dividends may be paid in cash, stock, or merchandise. Cash dividends are most common and merchandise dividends are least common. The common stockholder is not promised a dividend, but he grows to expect certain dividend payments from the historical dividend pattern of the firm. Before dividends are paid to the common stockholders, the claims of all creditors, the government, and preferred stockholders must be satisfied.

The Distribution of Earnings and Assets. As mentioned earlier, the holder of common stock has no guarantee of receiving any periodic distribution of earnings in the form of dividends, nor is he guaranteed anything in the event of liquidation. Bankruptcy proceedings are unlikely to bring anything to the common stockholder. However, as long as he pays more than the par value for the stock, he is assured of not losing any more than he has invested in the firm. Moreover, the common stockholder can receive unlimited returns both through the distribution of earnings and through appreciation in the value of his holdings. Nothing is guaranteed to him, but the possible rewards for providing risk capital can be great. The common stockholder must view the firm as a going concern; and if his feelings change, opportunities to sell or divest himself of his holdings do exist.

Convertible Securities and Warrants

We now focus on optional features of security issues: conversion options, warrants, and stock rights.

Both conversion features and warrants allow the firm to shift its future capital structure automatically. The conversion feature, which may be attached to either a bond or preferred stock, permits the firm's capital structure to be changed without increasing the total financing. Stock warrants may be attached to a long-term debt or preferred stock. They permit the firm to raise additional funds in the future by selling common stock. The use of warrants shifts the firm's capital structure toward a less highly leveraged position, since new equity capital is obtained.

Both conversion features and warrants are used commonly today. Bonds that can be converted into common stock are the most common type of convertible security; warrants attached to corporate bond issues are the most common type of warrants. Both convertible securities and warrants may be listed and traded on organized security exchanges.

Stock rights provide for the maintenance of pro rata ownership by existing common shareholders. They are similar to short-lived warrants (with a life of one to two months) but allow for the purchase of shares for less than the prevailing market price.

Characteristics of Convertible Securities. A conversion feature is an option included as part of either a bond or preferred stock issue which permits the holder of the bond or stock to convert his security into a different type of security. Bonds can be convertible into preferred or common stock, but preferred stock can be convertible only into common stock. A conversion feature often adds to the marketability of an issue. This section discusses the types of convertible securities, the general features of convertibles, motives for convertible financing, and certain other considerations.

Types of Convertible Securities. Either corporate bonds or preferred stocks may be convertible. These securities are most commonly convertible into common stock. The most common type of convertible security is the bond. Both convertible bonds and convertible preferred stock normally have a call feature as well as the conversion feature. The call feature permits the issuer to force conversion if it so desires. Convertible preferred stocks are usually convertible over an unlimited time; convertible bonds normally are convertible only for a specified period of years.

General Features of Convertibles. The general features of convertible securities include the conversion ratio, the conversion period, the conversion value, and the conversion premium.

The Conversion Ratio. The conversion ratio is the ratio in which the convertible security can be exchanged for common stock. The conversion ratio can be stated in two ways.

1. The conversion ratio may be stated by indicating that the security is convertible into *x* shares of common stock. In this situation the conversion ratio is given; to find the conversion price, the face value (not the market value) of the convertible security must be divided by the conversion ratio. For example, company *A* has outstanding a convertible preferred stock with a par value of $100 convertible into four shares of common stock. The conversion ratio for the preferred stock is 4. The conversion price for the preferred stock is $25 ($100 ÷ 4).

2. Instead of the conversion ratio, the conversion price may be given. The conversion ratio can then be obtained by dividing the face value of the convertible security by the conversion price. Often the conversion price is not constant but changes in response to the length of time the issue has been outstanding or to the proportion of the issue that has been converted. A convertible security could have a conversion price of $25 for the first 10 years and $30 after 10 years. These types of acceleration features are often included in a bond indenture or preferred stock covenants in order to give the issuer the power to force conversion. For example, company *B* has outstanding a convertible 25-year bond with a face value of $1,000. The bond is convertible at $25 per share into common stock for the next three years and at $30 for the remainder of its life. The conversion ratio for the first five years is 40 ($1,000 ÷ $25); for the remainder of the bond's life, it is 33.33 ($1,000 ÷ $30).

The issuer of a convertible security normally establishes a conversion price or conversion ratio that makes the conversion price per share at the point of issuance of the security between 10 and 20 percent above the current market price of the firm's stock.

The Conversion Period. Convertible securities are often convertible only before or after a certain date. Sometimes conversion is not permitted until two to five years have passed. In other instances conversion is permitted only for a limited number of years, say for five or ten years after its issuance. Other issues are convertible at any time during the life of the security. Convertible preferred stocks are generally convertible for an unlimited time. Time limitations on conversion are imposed by the issuer to suit the firm's forecast long-run financial needs.

The Conversion Value. The conversion value of a convertible security is the value of the security measured in terms of the market value of the security into which it may be converted. Since most convertible securities are convertible into common stock, the conversion value can generally be found simply by multiplying the conversion ratio by the current market price of the firm's common stock. For example, company *C* has outstanding a $1,000 bond, which is convertible into common stock at $62.50 a share. The conversion ratio is therefore 16 ($1,000 ÷ $62.50). Since the current market price of the common stock is $65 per share, the conversion value is $1,040 (16 × $65). Since the conversion value is above the bond value of $1,000, conversion is a viable option for the owner of the convertible security. Of course, the security holder may anticipate a still greater conversion value; in that case, he would maintain his present position unless the issuer forces conversion by using its call privilege.

The Conversion Premium. The conversion premium is the percentage difference between the conversion price and the issuance price of a security. As pointed out previously, the conversion premium is normally set initially in the 10 to 20 percent range. The actual size of the premium depends largely on the nature of the company. If the company's stock is not expected to appreciate greatly over the coming years, a low premium will be used; if considerable appreciation in the price of the stock is expected, the conversion premium may be in the 15 to 20 percent range. The conversion premium given to a convertible security can greatly affect the future success of the security. For example, company *D* has just issued a $1,000 convertible bond. The bond is convertible into 20 shares of the firm's common stock at a price of $50 per share. Since the firm's common stock is currently selling at $42 per share, the conversion premium is $8 per share ($50 − $42) or $160 ($8/share × 20 shares). The conversion premium can be stated as a percentage by dividing the difference between the conversion price and the market price per share by the market price per share. The conversion premium is approximately 19 percent ($8 ÷ $42).

Warrants

A warrant provides the investor with an option to purchase a fixed number of shares of common stock at a predetermined price during a specified time period. In the past warrants have been used primarily by weaker firms as "sweetener" attachments to bonds or preferred stock to improve their marketability.

While warrants are similar to convertibles in that both provide investors with a chance to participate in capital gains, the mechanics of the two instruments differ greatly. From the standpoint of the issuing firm there are two major differences: (1) When convertibles are exchanged for common stock there is an elimination of debt and a reduction in fixed financing charges, whereas when warrants are exchanged there is no reduction in fixed charges. (2) When convertibles are exchanged there is no cash inflow into the firm — one type of security is merely exchanged for another; but with warrants, since they are merely an option to buy the stock at a set price, a cash inflow accompanies the exchange.

Characteristics and Features of Warrants. The exercise price is that at which the warrant allows its holder to purchase the firm's common stock. The investor trades a warrant plus the exercise price for common stock. Typically, when warrants are issued the exercise price is set above the current market price of the stock. Thus, if the stock price does not rise above the exercise price, the warrant will never be converted. In addition there is also a step-up exercise price; that is, a warrant with which the exercise price changes over time.

While some warrants are issued with no expiration date, most warrants expire after a number of years. In issuing warrants as opposed to convertibles, the firm gives up some control over when the warrants will be exercised. With convertibles, the issuing company can force conversion by calling the issue or using step-up conversion prices; with warrants, only the approach of the expiration date or the use of step-up exercise prices can encourage conversion.

Most warrants are detachable in that they can be sold separately from the bond or preferred stock to which they were originally attached. Thus if an investor purchases a primary issuance of a corporate bond with a warrant attached, he has the option of selling the bond alone, selling the warrant alone, or selling the combination intact. Nondetachable warrants cannot be sold separately from the bond or preferred stock to which they were originally attached. Such a warrant can be separated from the senior security only by being exercised.

The exercise ratio states the number of shares that can be obtained at the exercise price with one warrant. If the exercise ratio on a warrant were 1.5, one warrant would entitle its owner to purchase one and one-half shares of common stock at its exercise price.

Stock Rights

Stock rights, which provide certain common stock purchase privileges to existing shareholders, are an important tool of common stock financing. Without them, the shareholders run the risk of losing their proportionate control of the corporation. Certain aspects of rights financing are discussed below.

Preemptive Rights. Most issues of common stock provide shareholders with preemptive rights which allow the stockholders to maintain their proportionate ownership in the corporation when new issues are made. Most states require that shareholders be extended this privilege unless it is explicitly prohibited by the corporate charter. Preemptive rights permit existing shareholders to maintain their voting control and prevent the dilution of their ownership and earnings. From the firm's viewpoint, the use of preemptive rights offerings to raise new equity capital may be cheaper than a public issue of stock. For example, company E currently has 100,000 shares of common stock outstanding and is contemplating issuing an additional 10,000 shares through a rights offering. Each existing shareholder will receive one right per share, and each right will entitle the shareholder to purchase 1/10 of a share of new common stock (10,000 ÷ 100,000). Therefore 10 rights will be required to purchase one share of the stock. The holder of 1,000 shares of existing common stock will receive 1,000 rights, each permitting the purchase of 1/10 of a share of new common stock. This enables him to purchase 100 shares of new common stock. If he exercises his rights, he will end up with 1,100 shares of common stock, or one percent of the total number of shares outstanding. This is the same proportion he had prior to the rights offering.

The Mechanics of Rights Offerings. When a company makes a rights offering the board of directors must set a date of record. This is the last date on which the recipient of a right must be the legal owner indicated in the company's stock ledger. Due to the lag in bookkeeping procedures, stocks are usually sold ex rights (i.e., without rights) four business days prior to the date of record. Prior to this point, the stock is sold cum rights or rights on, which means that purchasers of the stock will receive the rights.

The issuing firm sends rights to holders of record, who are free to exercise them, sell them, or let them expire. Rights are transferable, and many are traded actively enough to be listed on the various stock exchanges. They are exercisable for a specified period of time, generally not more than a few months, at a price somewhat below the prevailing market price. Since fractions of shares are not always issued, it is sometimes necessary to either purchase additional rights or sell extra rights. The value of a right depends largely on the number of rights needed to purchase a share of stock and the amount by which the right exercise price is below the current market price.

Management Decisions. A firm must make two basic decisions when preparing for a rights offering. The first is the price at which the right holders can purchase a new share of common stock. The subscription price must be set below the current market price. How far below depends on management's evaluation of the sensitivity of the market to a price change, the degree of dilution in ownership and earnings expected, and the size of the rights offering.

Once management has determined the subscription price, it must determine the number of rights required to purchase a share of stock. Since the amount of funds to be raised is known in advance, the subscription price can be divided into this figure to get the total number of shares that must be sold. Dividing the total number of shares outstanding by the total number of shares to be sold will give management the number of rights required to purchase a share of stock.

The Value of a Right. Theoretically the value of a right should be the same if the stock is selling with rights on (cum rights) or ex rights. However, the market value of a right may differ from its theoretical value.

Once a rights offering has been declared, shares will trade for only a few days with rights on. An equation can be used to find the value of a right when the stock is trading with rights on.

$$R = \frac{M_0 - S}{N + 1} \qquad (9.1)$$

where: R = theoretical value of a right
M_0 = market value of the stock with rights on
S = subscription price of the stock
N = number of rights needed to purchase a share of stock

It is assumed that company F stock is currently selling with rights on at a price of \$54.50 per share, the subscription price is \$50 per share, and eight rights are required to purchase a new share of stock. The value of a right is 50 cents ((\$54.50 − \$50.00) ÷ (8 + 1)). A right should therefore be worth 50 cents in the marketplace.

When a share of stock is traded ex rights, meaning that the value of the right is no longer included in the stock's market price, the share price is expected to drop by the value of a right. The market value of the stock trading ex rights, M_e should be

$$M_e = M_0 - R$$

The value of a right when the stock is trading ex rights is given as:

$$R = \frac{M_0 - S}{N}$$

The use of these equations can be illustrated by returning to the company F example. According to the equation, the market price of company F stock selling ex rights is \$54 (\$54.50 − \$0.50). Substituting this value gives us the value of a right when the stock is selling ex rights, which is 50 cents ((\$54.00 − \$50.00) ÷ 8). The theoretical value of the right is the same whether the stock is selling with rights on or ex rights.

The Market Behavior of Rights. Stock rights are negotiable instruments that are traded on security exchanges. The market price of a right will generally differ from its theoretical value. The extent to which it will differ will depend on how the firm's stock price is expected to behave during the period when the right is exercisable. By buying rights instead of the stock itself, investors can achieve much higher returns on their money when stock prices advance.

A Comparison of Warrants and Rights. The similarity between a warrant and a right should be clear. Both result in new equity capital, although the warrant provides for deferred equity financing. The right provides for the maintenance of pro rata ownership by existing owners, while the warrant has no such feature; rather, the warrant is generally used to make other forms of financing more attractive. The life of a right is typically only one or two months, whereas a warrant is generally exercisable for a period of years. Also, rights are issued at an exercise price below the prevailing market price of the stock, while warrants are generally issued at an exercise price 10 to 20 percent above the prevailing market price.

OWNERSHIP OF EQUITY SECURITIES

Distribution of Ownership

The distribution of ownership of outstanding equity securities for 1975–1979 is shown in Table 9.1. Households constitute the largest holders of equity securities. Holdings by institutions, particularly by pension funds, have become much more important in recent years. Private pension funds are the largest institutional holders of common stocks, followed by insurance companies (all types) and mutual funds. Increased holdings by both life and property insurance companies are largely the result of relaxation of restrictions on the scope of their investments that began in the 1960s.

TABLE 9.1   Total Holdings of Corporate Equity Securities by Sector and Selected Institutions, 1975–1979

(end of calendar year)

(dollars in billions)

	1975	1976	1977	1978	1979
Households	660	827	777	808	907
Foreign	35	43	40	42	50
Mutual savings banks	4	4	5	5	6
Life insurance companies	28	34	33	36	40
Other insurance companies	14	17	17	19	26
Private pension funds	89	110	102	108	136
State and local government retirement funds	24	30	30	33	44
Mutual funds	34	37	32	31	34
Brokers and dealers	3	4	4	3	3

Source: Board of Governors of the Federal Reserve System, *Flow of Funds Accounts, Assets and Liabilities Outstanding,* 1969–1979.

The Primary Market for Equity Securities

New issues of corporate stock may be sold directly by the issuing firm or indirectly through investment banking institutions and dealers. Four significant means of direct issue of equity securities are as follows:

1 Sale of a new issue of common stock to current stockholders;

2 Sale of new shares of stock to current stockholders as part of a "dividend reinvestment" plan;

3 Direct placement of a new stock issue with institutional investors; and

4 Sale of new shares to employees via a company saving or incentive plan of stock purchase.

The initial offering of new common shares of stock to current stockholders (the preemptive right of shareholders to maintain their proportionate share of ownership) may be required by the law of the state of incorporation or by the corporate charter. Even if not required, such a rights offering may be advantageous to the issuing corporation.

Dividend reinvestment plans as a means of issuing new equity shares are of relatively recent vintage. These plans simply require agreement by a current stockholder that the dividends declared by the firm will be applied to the purchase of new securities instead of being distributed in cash. The advantage to the shareholder is the avoidance of the reinvestment costs that might otherwise be incurred.

TABLE 9.2   New Security Issues of Corporations, 1975–1981

(dollars in billions)

	1975	1976	1977	1978	1979	1980	1981
Bonds	$42.7	$42.4	$42.0	$36.9	$40.2	$53.2	$44.6
Preferred stocks	3.4	2.8	3.9	2.8	3.6	3.6	1.8
Common stocks	7.4	8.3	7.9	7.5	7.7	16.8	23.5
Total	$53.5	$53.5	$53.8	$47.2	$51.5	$73.6	$69.9

Source: Securities and Exchange Commission and Federal Reserve System

Neither private placement nor employee purchase plans account for large sales of new equity shares. Private placement is generally limited to issues of high-grade preferred stocks of public utility firms and to issues of small, financially sound firms for which use of an investment banker is either infeasible or unattractive because of the relatively small size of the new issue. Overall, direct issue by all these various means accounts for less than 15 percent of new common stock issues and less than 5 percent of new preferred stock issues.

Most new equity issues are distributed to investors through investment bankers via underwriting or agency selling arrangements. The role of investment bankers in the issue of new equity securities parallels their role in the issue of new corporate bonds (see Chapter 4). New public issues of equity securities are subject to the regulations and disclosure requirements of the Securities Act of 1933, as administered by the Securities and Exchange Commission (SEC).

The SEC also regulates the secondary markets for securities under the statutory authority of the Securities Act of 1934. In addition to imposing disclosure requirements on publicly owned corporations, this statute charges the SEC with regulatory purview over the organized security exchanges, the over-the-counter market, investment banking firms, brokers, dealers, and investment companies. Security trading is also subject to state regulation and to private sector regulation by the organized security exchanges and the National Association of Security Dealers.

Table 9.2 illustrates the growth in importance of bond and stock financing over recent years, and Table 9.3 illustrates stock financing by major industry groups.

The Secondary Markets for Equity Securities

Secondary markets exist for many financial instruments, but the secondary market for corporate stocks is the largest in dollar volume and number of trades. Trading in the organized exchanges is dominated by equities in both dollar volume and number of trades. In the over-the-counter market, the total

TABLE 9.3   Common and Preferred Stock Offerings by Industry Group, 1975–1981

(dollars in millions)

	1975	1976	1977	1978	1979	1980	1981
Manufacturing	$ 1,670	$ 2,237	$ 1,189	$ 1,241	$ 1,679	$ 4,839	$ 5,037
Commercial	1,470	1,183	1,834	1,816	2,623	5,245	7,557
Transportation	1	24	456	263	255	549	779
Public utility	6,235	6,121	5,865	5,140	5,171	6,230	5,577
Communication	1,002	776	1,379	264	303	567	1,778
Real estate and financial	448	771	1,049	1,631	1,293	3,059	4,585
Total	$10,826	$11,112	$11,772	$10,355	$11,324	$20,489	$25,313

Source: Securities and Exchange Commission and Federal Reserve System

dollar volume of bond trading exceeds that of equities, but more trades involve equities than bonds. Such secondary market dominance is not surprising in view of the fact that the estimated market value of outstanding equities exceeds $1 trillion.

The Security Exchanges. There are two national organized security exchanges, the New York Stock Exchange (NYSE) and the American Stock Exchange (AMEX), accounting for about 80 percent and 10 percent, respectively, of all organized exchange trading (in terms of number of shares traded). The other 10 percent is accounted for by regional organized exchanges, with the bulk of the trading occurring on the Midwest, Pacific, and Philadelphia-Baltimore-Washington exchanges.

To have its securities listed on an organized exchange, a firm must meet the trading volume and disclosure requirements of that particular exchange. The most stringent requirements are those of the NYSE, followed by the AMEX. The largest corporations are listed on the "Big Board" (the NYSE), while smaller (but national) firms are generally listed on the AMEX. The regional exchanges usually list securities of regional firms, but they also list some NYSE and AMEX stocks (multiple listing cases). Trading volume in the latter category generally exceeds that in the former.

Organized security exchanges have the following characteristics:

1 Trading of securities takes place at a particular physical site — the floor of the exchange.
2 Trading is conducted among members of the exchange.
3 Trading is conducted according to the rules of the exchange, which dictate the manner in which trades are to be carried out by the exchange members and govern the conduct of the members, forbidding practices relating to manipulation of security prices.

Particular securities are traded at a designated post, a location on the floor of the exchange. At each post all trades are orally voiced (loudly) and recorded. Exchange members trade in a variety of capacities. Some act as specialists in a particular security or securities. (The specialist is charged with the responsibility for making a market in a security, that is, selling when others will not sell and buying when others will not buy.) Some members trade for their own accounts, and some trade for the accounts of other members. Most members, however, trade for commission brokerage firms and thus perform a pure broker function.

The Over-the-Counter Market. The trading of securities not listed on organized exchanges is conducted in the over-the-counter (OTC) market (which is mostly an "over-the-telephone" market). The OTC market is essentially a network of dealers who make the market in the various OTC securities. Dealers stand ready to buy any reasonable quantity of the security (or securities) in which they deal at the bid price, and to sell at the asked price. The dealer's gross profit margin stems from the spread between the bid and asked prices.

It is estimated that more than 14,000 various stock issues are actively traded in the OTC market. Such broad activity is made possible by an extensive and sophisticated communications network. Telephone and teletype facilities connect dealer trading rooms throughout the country. The National Association of Security Dealers Automatic Quotation system provides current bid and asked prices on a continuous basis for more than 3,000 stocks. These quotations are made possible by having dealers in regularly quoted securities record any change in bid and asked prices in a central computer. Dealers seeking current quotations on these stocks have ready access to the computer memory, and all bids and offers (and names of dealers) for a given stock can be displayed instantly on a video device.

The principal equity securities traded in the OTC market include bank stocks, insurance company stocks, and stocks of small, regional, and closely held corporations. There is also a great deal of OTC trading in stocks listed on organized exchanges. The trading of stocks listed on exchanges is referred to as the "third market" (organized exchange and OTC trading being the other two) and, indeed, the dollar volume of such trading is about 10 percent of NYSE volume. There is also a "fourth market" in which institutions exchange securities directly without involving brokers or dealers, but it is of minor importance at present.

Trading in equity securities in the secondary market is dominated by financial institutions, especially on the NYSE. It is estimated that institutions currently account for about two-thirds of total trading (in dollar volume) on the NYSE. The growth in institutional dominance of the equities secondary market is a consequence of increased institutional ownership of equities, more frequent trading, and the fact that trades generally involve large blocks of stock. It is likely that the ability of the institutions to employ considerable analytical and information resources for purposes of security analysis has contributed to secondary market efficiency — the pricing of securities in accordance with informed perceptions of risk and expected return.

VALUATION OF EQUITIES AND THEIR DERIVATIVES

Valuing Preferred Stock

The principles underlying the valuation of a nonparticipating preferred stock are summarized by the following simple formula:

$$P_0 = \frac{d}{r} \tag{9.2}$$

where: P_0 = price of the nonparticipating preferred

   d = stated annual dividend rate

   r = appropriate discount rate

In effect, Equation 9.2 says that the preferred's price is equal to the present value of its infinite stream of promised dividend payments. To illustrate, assume a preferred stock pays an annual dividend of $10 per share. The value of a share to an investor requiring a 10 percent rate of return would be $100 ($10/0.10).

In the case of a participating preferred stock, we must modify Equation 9.2 to incorporate a term that accounts for the value of any expected extra dividends that may be paid over the life of the security. Because these extra returns are a function of the earnings of the issuer, they need not be constant over time. Thus, the algebraic expression for the price of a participating preferred stock P_p is as follows:

$$P_p = \frac{d}{r} + \sum_{t=1}^{\infty} \frac{d^*}{(Hr)^t}$$
(9.3)

where: d^* = expected value of the participating portion of the dividend paid in period t

In both equations the discount rate, r, incorporates not only the pure rate of interest but also premiums for the decline in the purchasing power of the dollar and the risk that the promised (or expected) dividends will not be paid.

Preferred Stock Yields vs. Bond Yields. When they purchase a corporation's preferred stock, investors expose themselves to more risk than they would assume by owning the firm's bonds and less risk than would come with holding its stock. This being the case, we might expect to find that the promised yields on the preferred stocks of companies having a given level of risk were higher than the yields on these firms' bonds. Table 9.4 presents bond and preferred stock yields for the period from 1965 through 1980. Yields on preferred stocks are below yields on bonds. On the surface, this may appear somewhat anomalous. Why should the market pay more for securities that carry greater risk? Presumably, in a risk-averse world, investors should demand greater promised return in the face of greater risk.

Before concluding that we have come upon an exception, we should quickly mention that the data in Table 9.4 do not tell the whole story. In particular, they do not indicate that only 15 percent of the dividends earned by corporate holders of preferred stocks were subject to federal income taxation. In other words, preferred stocks carried a significant tax advantage over bonds for corporate investors. This advantage encourages corporations to purchase preferred shares with the result that their yields are below the yields on bonds.

Table 9.5 presents a comparison of the after-tax promised yields on high-grade preferred stocks and corporate bonds for a corporate investor in the 40 percent marginal federal income tax bracket and an individual who is also taxed at the 40 percent rate. As expected, the after-tax yields on the preferred stocks are substantially higher than the after-tax yields on the bonds for the corporate investor. The difference between the two — almost 3 percent — represents an important inducement for taxable corporate investors. Indeed, for them this difference makes preferred stocks a most attractive investment medium.

For individual investors, however, high-grade preferred shares are not particularly attractive. Whether measured before or after taxes, their returns are lower than the yields on corporate bonds that expose the investor to less risk of default. Not surprisingly, then, few individuals show a strong preference for investing in high-grade, nonparticipating, nonconvertible preferred stocks.

TABLE 9.4   Yields on High-Grade Bonds and Preferred Stocks, 1965–1980

Year	(1) Aaa Corporate Bonds	(2) Preferred Stocks	(3) Spread (2) − (1)
1965	4.49%	4.33%	−0.16
1966	5.13	4.97	−0.16
1967	5.51	5.34	−0.17
1968	6.18	5.78	−0.40
1969	7.03	6.41	−0.62
1970	8.04	7.22	−0.82
1971	7.39	6.75	−0.64
1972	7.21	7.27	+0.06
1973	7.44	7.23	−0.21
1974	8.57	8.23	−0.34
1975	8.83	8.38	−0.45
1976	8.43	7.97	−0.46
1977	8.04	7.65	−0.39
1978	8.73	8.25	−0.48
1979	9.63	9.07	−0.56
1980	11.94	10.57	−1.37

Source: *Federal Reserve Bulletin*, various issues

Common Stock Valuation

Some companies' liquidation value — the amount that would remain after selling their assets and paying off their debts — is greater than the price at which their shares trade in the open market. Corporate raiders are always on the lookout for such companies and are willing to pay a premium over market price to buy up their shares, as long as the liquidating value is high enough to make the effort worthwhile. At a minimum, a share of stock is worth its estimated liquidating value (net liquidating value of the company divided by number of shares outstanding). Of course, the liquidating value of a company's net assets often is not apparent from a simple look at its published balance sheets. Even when the liquidating value can be determined, however, in most cases companies are worth more as going concerns and their stocks sell at higher prices than liquidating value. Therefore, most stock valuation methods are aimed at determining going-concern values.

Investment theorists argue that the best measure of going-concern value is the present value of expected future dividends. By this method of valuation, estimates first are made of the future earnings of a company. Next a judgment

TABLE 9.5 Comparison of After-Tax Yields of Bonds and Preferred Stocks for Investors in Different Tax Brackets

CORPORATE INVESTORS

	Bond	Preferred Stock
Before-tax yield	8.63%	8.36%
Taxable yield	8.63	1.25
Taxes at 40 percent rate	3.45	0.50
After-tax yield	5.18%	7.86%

INDIVIDUAL INVESTORS

	Bond	Preferred Stock
Before-tax yield	8.63%	8.36%
Taxable yield	8.63	8.36
Taxes at 40 percent rate	3.45	3.34
After-tax yield	5.18%	5.02%

is made about the proportion of earnings likely to be paid as dividends. Finally the present value of the projected dividend stream is calculated by discounting the estimated dividends at a required rate of return which reflects the degree of uncertainty about the accuracy of the estimates.

While the same general principles apply to the valuation of common stocks as to bonds or preferred stocks, two features make the analysis of common stocks more difficult. The first complicating feature is the degree of certainty with which receipts can be forecast. For bonds and preferred stocks, this presents little difficulty, since the interest payments or preferred dividends are known with relative certainty. In the case of common stocks, however, forecasting future earnings, dividends, and stock prices can be difficult. The second complicating feature is that, unlike interest and preferred dividends, common stock earnings and dividends are generally expected to grow, not remain constant.

Estimating the Value of a Stock for Period One. The price today of a share of common stock, P_0, depends on the return investors expect to receive if they buy the stock and the riskiness of these expected cash flows. The expected returns consist of two elements: (1) the dividend expected in each year t, defined as d_t, and (2) the price investors expect to receive when they sell the stock at the end of year n, defined as P_n. The price includes the return of the original investment plus a capital gain (or minus a capital loss). If investors expect to hold the stock for one year and the stock price is expected to grow at the rate g, the valuation equation is:

$$P_0 = \frac{\text{Expected dividend} + \text{Expected price (both at end of year 1)}}{1.0 + \text{Required rate of return}} \quad (9.4)$$

$$= \frac{d_1 + P_1}{(1 + r)} = \frac{d_1 + P_0(1 + g)}{(1 + r)}$$

which results in Equation 9.5 after simplification.

$$P_0 = \frac{d_1}{r - g} \quad (9.5)$$

Equation 9.5 represents the present value of the expected dividends and the year-end stock price, discounted at the required rate of return. Solving Equation 9.5 gives the expected price for the stock. For example, suppose you are thinking of buying a share of common stock and holding it for one year. You note that the company earned $3 per share last year and paid a dividend of $1.90. Earnings, dividends, and the stock price have been rising at about 5 percent a year, on the average, and you expect this growth to continue.

The next step is to determine the required rate of return on the stock. The current rate of interest on U.S. Treasury securities is about 8 percent, say, but the stock is clearly more risky than government securities. For example, competitors can erode the company's market or labor problems can disrupt operations. Further, even if earnings and dividends meet projections, the stock price can still fall as a result of a generally weak market.

Given all these risk factors, you conclude that a 15 percent required rate of return, r, on the stock is appropriate. The estimated dividend for the coming year, d_1 is:

$$d_1 = d_0(1 + g) = \$1.90(1.05) = \$2$$

The necessary information to estimate the value of the stock is now in hand:

$$P_0 = \frac{d_1}{r - g} \quad (9.6)$$

$$= \frac{\$2}{0.15 - 0.05} = \$20$$

To you, $20 represents a reasonable price for the stock. If the actual market price is less, you will buy it; if the actual price is higher, you will not buy it or you will sell if you own it.

Valuation Under Growth Patterns. To this point we have used a one-period model of stock valuation in which investors hold the stock for one year, receive one dividend, and then sell the stock at the end of the year. We now take up multiperiod stock valuation.

Using the stream-of-dividends approach, a share of common stock is regarded as similar to a share of preferred stock, and its value is established as the present value of its stream of dividends:

Value of stock $= P_0 = PV$ of expected future dividends

$$= \frac{d_1}{(1 + r)^1} + \frac{d_2}{(1 + r)^2} + \cdots$$

$$= \sum_{t=1}^{\infty} \frac{d_1}{(1 + r)^t} \tag{9.7}$$

Unlike preferred dividends, common stock dividends are not generally expected to remain constant in the future. This fact makes common stock valuation a more complex task than bond or preferred stock valuation.

Equation 9.7 is a general model in the sense that the time pattern of d, can be anything. For many purposes, however, it is useful to estimate a particular time pattern for d, and then develop a simplified version of the stock valuation model expressed in Equation 9.7.

Constant Growth. Year after year, the earnings and dividends of most companies have been increasing. In general, this growth is expected to continue in the foreseeable future at about the same rate as the gross national product. Thus, if such a company's current dividend is d_0, its dividend in any future year t will be $d_1 = d_0(1 + g)^1$, where $g =$ the expected rate of growth. For example, if a company just paid a dividend of \$2.00 ($d_0 = \$2.00$) and its investors expect an 8 percent growth rate, the estimated dividend one year hence is $d_1 = (\$2.00)(1.08) = \$2.16$; two years hence it is \$2.33; and five years hence it is:

$$d_1 = d_0(1 + g)^t$$
$$= \$2.00(1.08)^5$$
$$= \$2.94$$

Using this method of estimating future dividends, the current price, P_0, is determined as follows:

$$P_0 = \frac{d_1}{(1 + r)^1} + \frac{d_2}{(1 + r)^2} + \frac{d_3}{(1 + r)^3} + \cdots$$

$$= \frac{d_0(1 + g)^1}{(1 + r)^1} + \frac{d_0(1 + g)^2}{(1 + r)^2} + \frac{d_0(1 + g)^3}{(1 + r)^3} + \cdots$$

$$= \sum_{t=1}^{\infty} \frac{d_0(1 + g)^t}{(1 + r)^t} \tag{9.8}$$

If g is constant, Equation 9.8 can be simplified as follows:

$$P_0 = \frac{d_1}{r - g} \tag{9.9}$$

Notice that the constant growth model expressed in Equation 9.9 is identical to the single-period model, Equation 9.6, developed in an earlier section.

A necessary condition for the constant growth model is that r be greater than g; otherwise, Equation 9.9 gives nonsense answers. If r equals g, the equation yields an infinite price; if r is less than g, a negative price results. Since neither infinite nor negative stock prices make sense, it is clear that in equilibrium r must be greater than g.

Variable Growth. While continuous growth in excess of the discount rate $(g > k)$ is an unreasonable assumption because it produces infinite present values, many companies do exhibit very rapid growth for 5, 10, or more years. Ultimately, usually as a result of product obsolescence or competition, the growth slows. Indeed, if it did not, the company would eventually swallow up the entire economy. Analysts deal with such cases by assuming that growth will pass through one or more stages of deceleration until finally settling down at a constant growth rate equal to that of the average company. The constant-growth formula is applied to determine the value of the stock at that point, and the assumed terminal price is discounted to the present and added to the present value of the dividends paid during the rapid-growth period. That is:

P_0 = Present value of dividends prior to constant-growth period +
   Present value of assumed terminal price of stock

As a simple illustration, suppose that the initial dividend (d_0) is \$1 and that growth is assumed to pass through only two stages:

g_1 = 20%, lasts for 10 years $(n = 10)$

g_2 = 10%, the growth rate of the average company, lasts forever (year 11 forward).

Further, suppose we assume that an appropriate discount rate for this stock is 14 percent, except that the uncertainty of the forecast of an extra-rapid growth rate for the first 10 years suggests a larger discount rate during that period, perhaps 18 percent. Thus,

r_1 = 18%, r_2 = 14%

The valuation equation in this example would be as follows (see Table 9.6 for the arithmetic):

$$P_0 = \left[\sum_{t=1}^{n} \frac{d_0(1 + g_1)^t}{(1 + r_1)^t}\right] + \left[\frac{d_n + 1}{(r_2 - g_2)} \times \frac{1}{(1 + r_2)^n}\right]$$

$$= \left[\sum_{t=1}^{10} \frac{d_0(1.20)^t}{(1.18)^t}\right] + \left[\frac{d_{11}}{(0.14 - 0.10)} \times \frac{1}{(1.14)^{10}}\right]$$

$$= \$10.98 + \$45.92$$

$$= \$56.90$$

The Role of Asset Values. During most of the postwar period, stock valuation has focused on the relationships between stock prices and earnings and dividends. In recent years, however, as inflation became rampant, investors began increasingly to question whether normal accounting measurements

---

TABLE 9.6 Two-Stage Growth Valuation

PRESENT VALUE OF DIVIDENDS DURING INITIAL GROWTH PERIOD
(20 percent annual growth for 10 years, discounted at 18 percent annual rate)

Period (n)	(1) Value of Dividends (d_t)	(2) Present Value Factor	(3) Present Value of Dividends (Columns 1 × 2)
0	$1.00	—	—
1	1.20	0.847	$ 1.08
2	1.44	0.718	1.03
3	1.73	0.608	1.05
4	2.07	0.515	1.07
5	2.49	0.437	1.09
6	2.99	0.370	1.11
7	3.58	0.313	1.12
8	4.30	0.266	1.14
9	5.16	0.225	1.16
10	6.19	0.191	1.18
			$10.98

$$\sum_{t=1}^{10} \frac{d_0(1.20)^t}{(1.18)^t} = \$10.98$$

PRESENT VALUE OF ASSUMED TERMINAL PRICE

$$\frac{d_{11}}{r_2 - g_2} = \frac{\$6.19 \times 1.10}{0.14 - 0.10} = \frac{\$6.81}{0.04} = \$170.27$$

$$\frac{1}{(1 + r_2)^{10}} = \frac{1}{(1.14)^{10}} = \frac{1}{3.7072} = 0.2697$$

$$\$170.27 \times 0.2697 = \$45.92$$

---

of earnings were meaningful and, consequently, whether dividends were being paid from true earnings or were simply a return of capital — a disguised liquidation of the business. Reflecting these concerns, a growing number of discussions of stock valuation have included references to the relationships between stock prices and asset values. It is recognized that assets have no real value except to the extent that they are a source of future earnings and dividends, but there is a growing feeling that if the assets are there, the earnings ultimately will follow.

The SEC now requires large companies to publish annual estimates of current-dollar values of inventories and fixed assets. These data can serve as a bench mark for determining whether the market value of a company's common stock is high or low in relation to asset values. The corporate takeover explosion of recent years was prompted by analyses which revealed that if a company wanted to get into a new business, it was much cheaper to tender for the stock of a company already in that business — even if the tender price had to be at a 40 to 60 percent premium over market to be successful — than to build a new business from scratch.

Determining the Value of Convertibles

The key characteristic of convertible securities that greatly enhances their marketability is their ability to minimize the possibility of a loss while providing a possibility of capital gains. Closely related to this characteristic is the fixed pattern of interest or dividend income from convertible securities. In order to understand these characteristics, an understanding of the basic values of convertible securities is needed. This section discusses the three values of a convertible security — the bond or preferred stock value, the stock or conversion value, and the market value. Also discussed are a few special considerations.

Bond or Preferred Stock Values. The bond, or preferred stock, value of a convertible security is the price at which it would sell in the market without the conversion feature. It is found by determining the value of a straight bond or preferred stock issued by a firm having the same operating and financial risk. As indicated earlier, a convertible security's value will normally be greater than that of a straight bond or preferred stock. The bond or preferred stock value is typically the floor, or minimum, price at which a convertible bond or preferred stock will be traded.

Calculating Bond Values. The straight value of a convertible bond can be found by discounting the bond interest payments and maturity value at the rate of interest that would have to be charged on a straight bond issued by the company. In other words, the bond value of a convertible bond is equal to the present value of the interest and principal payments discounted at the straight bond interest rate. The Black Company has just sold a $1,000, 20-year convertible bond with an 8 percent coupon. The bond interest will be paid at the end of each year and the principal will be repaid at maturity. A straight bond could have been sold with a 10 percent coupon, but the addition of the conversion feature compensates for the lower rate on the convertible. The bond value of the convertible is calculated as shown in Table 9.7. This value, $830.12, is the minimum price at which the convertible bond is expected to sell if interest rates do not change. Only when the stock price is below the conversion price will the bond be expected to sell at this level.

Calculating the Preferred Stock Value. The minimum price at which a convertible preferred stock can be expected to sell can be found in a similar manner. Since the preferred stock is a form of ownership, its life is assumed to be infinite and therefore the present value factor used to find its value is not

TABLE 9.7   Calculating Bond Values

Years	(1) Payment	(2) Present Value Factor at 10%	(3) Present Value (1) × (2)
1–20	$ 80 (a)	8.514 (b)	$681.12
20	1,000	0.149 (c)	149.00
		Bond value	$830.12

(a) $1,000 at 8% = $80
(b) Present value factor for a 20-year annuity at 10%
(c) Present value factor for $1 in year 20 at 10%

readily available. The preferred stock value of a convertible preferred stock is assumed to equal the present value of preferred dividends over an infinite life discounted at the yield on a straight preferred stock. The present value factor for an infinite-lived annuity is given by:

$$k = \frac{1}{r} \tag{9.10}$$

where: k = present value factor for an infinite-lived annuity
              r = appropriate discount rate

An example will clarify the calculations required to find the value of preferred stock. The Black Company has just issued a 9 percent convertible preferred stock with a $100 par value. If the firm had issued a nonconvertible preferred stock, the annual dividend would probably have been 11 percent. Dividends are paid annually at the end of each year. Multiplying the annual dividend of $9 (9 percent of $100) by the factor for the present value of an infinite-lived annuity at 11 percent, which is 9.09 (1 ÷ 0.11), yields a value for the preferred stock of $81.81. If the market price of common stock fell below the conversion price, the preferred stock would be expected to sell for no less than $81.81.

Stock or Conversion Values. The stock, or conversion, value of a convertible security was defined earlier as the value of the convertible measured in terms of the market price of the common stock into which the security can be converted. When the market price of the common stock exceeds the conversion price, the stock or conversion value is expected to exceed the straight bond or preferred stock value of the convertible. An example will clarify the nature of the stock or conversion value. The Black Company convertible bond described earlier is convertible at $50 per share. This means that it can be converted into 20 shares, since it has a $1,000 face value. The conversion value

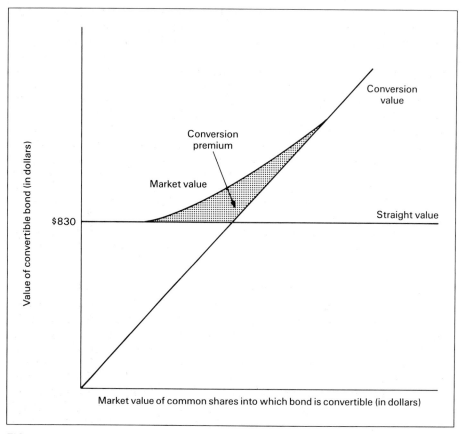

FIG. 9.1 Value of a Convertible Bond

of the bond when the stock is selling at $40, $50, $60, $70, and $80 per share is
shown below.

Market Price of Stock	Conversion Value
$40	$ 800
50	1,000
60	1,200
70	1,400
80	1,600

Since the straight value of this bond is $830.12, it should not sell for less than
this amount, regardless of how low its conversion value is. If the market price
per share was $40, the bond would still sell for $830.12, not $800.

Market Values. The market value of a convertible is likely to be greater than either its straight value or its conversion value. The amount by which the market price exceeds the straight or conversion value is often designated the market premium. The closer the straight value is to the conversion value, the larger the market premium. Even when the conversion value is below the straight value, a premium based on expected stock price movements exists. The same type of premium exists when the conversion value is above the straight value; this premium is attributed to the convertible security purchaser's expectations also. The general relationship between the straight value, the conversion value, the market value, and the market premium of the company's convertible bond, described in the preceding examples, is shown in Figure 9.1. As Figure 9.1 shows, the straight bond value acts as a floor for the security's value. When the market price of the stock exceeds a certain value, the conversion value of the bond exceeds the straight bond value. Also, due to the expectations of investors about movements in the price of the firm's common stock, the market value of the convertible often exceeds both the straight and the conversion value of the security, resulting in a market premium of the security.

Special Considerations. Unfortunately, the behavior of convertible security values — specifically the straight value of a convertible — is not precisely as described. The straight value of a bond or preferred stock is not necessarily fixed over a long period of time. It can be affected by a number of company and capital market factors. If the firm runs into operating or financial difficulties, it is quite possible that its creditworthiness will deteriorate and the risk associated with its securities will increase. Due to this increase in risk, the rate at which the payments associated with its bonds or preferred stock are discounted will rise, thereby lowering their straight value. It is also possible for the firm's credit rating to rise, so that the straight value of its convertible securities rises also.

10

Trading Markets

THOMAS E. COPELAND

HANS R. STOLL

In this chapter, trading markets in equity securities, debt securities, futures contracts, and options are examined in detail. Because all trading markets have certain common characteristics, the first section and the last two sections of the chapter are concerned with questions and issues that apply to all trading markets.

A trading market is a secondary market, that is, one in which a financial instrument, such as a share of stock or an option, can be sold and resold. Trading markets are distinguished from negotiated markets or private placement markets (such as the venture capital market) in which resale of a financial instrument usually is difficult. Trading markets are also distinguished from new issues markets, the purpose of which is to raise new capital rather than to trade existing securities.

ECONOMICS OF TRADING MARKETS

The Function of Trading Markets

From the perspective of an investor, the function of a trading market is to provide liquidity at fair prices. Investors seek liquidity for three reasons: (1) because they have new information about a particular security, (2) because they wish to save out of current consumption (buy securities) or dissave (sell securities), and (3) because a change in their attitude toward risk warrants a change in the composition of their portfolios. Liquidity is achieved if investors can trade large amounts of securities without affecting price. Prices are fair if they reflect the underlying value of the security correctly.

From the perspective of society, the function of trading markets is to summarize correctly the information that investors have about securities and to set prices so as to allocate resources to their proper uses. While trading in outstanding securities involves no allocation of new resources, prices in trading markets are essential for determining how savings will be allocated among competing uses. For example, in the stock market, the ability of a company to sell additional shares as well as its decision about paying out earnings depends on the stock price. In the commodities markets, farmers' planting decisions and storage decisions depend on the futures price.

Allocation Efficiency

A market is said to be allocationally efficient if the prices of securities in that market are "right" in the sense that they give the correct signals for the allocation of resources. Allocational efficiency has two aspects: First, it requires informational efficiency — the market for gathering information is efficient in that the marginal benefit to society of gathering more information is equal to the marginal cost to society of gathering that information. When this occurs, securities analysts are doing their job. Second, allocational efficiency requires pricing efficiency — the available information is quickly and correctly reflected in securities prices. Pricing efficiency means that traders react quickly to new information and cause it to be reflected correctly in security prices. It also means that no market participant is so large as to be able to affect prices in the absence of new information.

If a trading market is allocationally efficient in the sense described, certain propositions about that market follow. First, investing in that market is said to be a "fair game." This means that investors can expect to earn a normal return that is commensurate with the risk assumed, but they cannot expect to earn more. This normal return is available whether or not the investor carries out research. Indeed, research based on publicly available information, whether technical or fundamental, has no benefit, because by the definition of allocational efficiency, public information is already reflected in securities prices. Profits can be made only by predicting information that will cause prices to change.

The second proposition that follows from our definition of allocational efficiency is that new information, with which one might make a superior forecast of security price changes, is hard to get. If a market is informationally efficient, many security analysts compete for new information, with the result that none has consistent access to superior information. While a security analyst may occasionally discover new information and make superior predictions, those superior investment results tend to be offset by the costs of acquiring information. Note that informational efficiency does not rule out the possibility of acquiring nonpublic information. It implies only that such information is costly to acquire.

For the most part, academic investigators have found that the major U.S. trading markets are allocationally efficient, both in the pricing and informational aspects. A discussion of some of the empirical findings is contained in the last section of this chapter.

Operational Efficiency

A market is said to be operationally efficient if the commissions of brokers and the bid-ask spreads of dealers are as low as possible for the level of services rendered by these intermediaries. Trading markets provide various services which may be grouped into three categories: (1) communication and execution; (2) clearing, settlement, and recordkeeping; and (3) market making. There must be a mechanism by which investors that desire to trade find each other, establish mutually satisfactory prices, and execute transactions. This is done through the services of a broker, who is an agent, and through various communication devices that range from face-to-face communication on the floor of an exchange, to telephones, to sophisticated computer communication systems. After a transaction has been agreed upon, title and money must change hands and records of the transaction must be established on the account of the customer, on the account of the issuer, and by various intermediaries. This service is generally performed by the broker and ranges from physical transfer of certificates of ownership to transfers via book entries in a computer system. Finally, since investors are not always able (through their brokers) to find the other side of a transaction immediately, the services of a dealer, who stands ready to buy or sell for his own account as principal, may be required. The dealer must be compensated for his costs, which include the risk associated with keeping an inventory of securities. The dealer's compensation comes from the fact that he purchases securities at a bid price and resells them at a higher ask price.

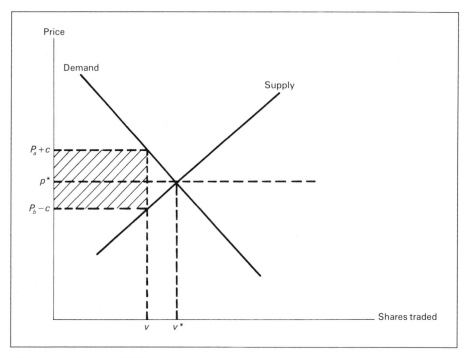

FIG. 10.1 Operational Efficiency

Figure 10.1 illustrates the concept of operational efficiency. The demand curve represents the shares that securities buyers would like to buy at alternative prices, and the supply curve represents the shares that securities sellers would like to sell at alternative prices. The intersection of demand and supply gives the equilibrium price, p^*, and the volume of trading, v^*, in the absence of transaction costs. In an allocationally efficient market, the equilibrium price reflects "all that is knowable" in the sense described previously. Trading volume arises because investors disagree about what they know and because portfolio adjustments and liquidity needs necessitate trading even in the absence of information.

Investors are not generally able to trade at p^* because of the cost of maintaining trading markets. Buyers buy at the ask price of the dealer, p_a, and pay a commision, c, to the broker. Sellers sell at the bid price of the dealer, p_b, and pay a commission, c. The difference between the buyer's price and the seller's price is

$$(p_a + c) - (p_b - c) = p_a - p_b + 2c$$

which is the bid-ask spread of the dealer plus two commissions. Transaction costs cause investors to reduce their volume of trading from v^* to v. The amount of the reduction depends on the slope of the demand and supply schedules. A trading market is operationally efficient if the bid-ask spread and commission charges are as low as possible for a given level of services.

The revenues of the securities industry are then given by $(p_a - p_b + 2c)v$, the shaded rectangle; that is, the amount earned per share traded multiplied by the number of shares traded. The welfare of the securities industry depends critically on the size of this rectangle and on the cost to the industry of rendering its transaction services. The size of the rectangle depends on the charge per transaction (the vertical distance) and the volume of trading (the horizontal distance).

Types of Markets

Trading markets may be classified by security type or by organizational form of the trading market. The major security types are equity (common and preferred stock) and debt. Debt instruments range from short-term money market instruments such as Treasury bills and banker's acceptances to long-term bonds issued by the U.S. government, by corporations, or by state and local governments. In recent years, futures contracts and option contracts have increased in importance. The markets for these four financial instruments are examined in greater detail later in this chapter.

Trading markets may differ in their organizational structures. Financial instruments may be traded in a dealer or in an auction market, in a continuous market or in a call market, in an over-the-counter (OTC) market or on an exchange. In a pure dealer market, investors, represented by their brokers, always trade with a dealer at the dealer's bid or ask price. In a pure auction market, investors, represented by their brokers, trade directly with each other. If a satisfactory price cannot be arrived at, the investor must wait to trade. In a continuous market, trading in the security takes place at all times. In a call market, trading takes place at specific times of the day, when the security is "called" for trading. A continuous market requires the participation of a dealer who is willing to trade immediately, while a call market can operate without dealers.

An exchange is a physical location where trading takes place. An OTC market is not a physical location; rather it is a communications network using telephones and computers. Most exchange markets in the United States are continuous auction markets. A continuous auction market combines features of a dealer market and an auction market. Investors, represented by their brokers, have the opportunity to trade directly with each other to the extent they are present at the same time at the same physical location on the floor of such an exchange, but they can also trade with a dealer (e.g., the specialist on the New York Stock Exchange (NYSE), the scalper on the commodities exchange) who is willing to provide liquidity at a price that is reflected in his bid-ask spread. OTC markets are dealer markets in which investors, or brokers representing investors, trade with dealers, not directly with each other. In the United States, most debt instruments are traded in an OTC dealer market, as are certain equity securities. No major U.S. securities market is a pure call auction market, since all U.S. markets are aimed at maintaining continuous trading. This has not always been so. The NYSE, for example, began as a call auction market in which particular securities were traded at particular times during the day. The Paris Bourse and the Tel Aviv Stock Exchange operate today according to the principles of a call auction market.

Types of Orders

In all trading markets, investors may give their brokers a range of instructions. A *market order* instructs the broker to trade at the best price available under current market conditions. A *limit order* instructs the broker to trade at a specified price or better. A limit buy order specifies a price below the current market price. A limit sell order specifies a price above the current market price. Limit orders also specify how long the order is to remain outstanding. Frequently the decision to use a market order or limit order depends on the trading activity in the security. In an inactive market, it may be advisable to use a limit order because market prices deviate from their "correct" value and because the bid-ask spread may be large. In an active market, market prices deviate less from their "correct" value and spreads are smaller. Thus, a market order is satisfactory. A *stop order* instructs the broker to trade when the market reaches a specified price. Once the price is reached, a stop order becomes a market order. A stop buy order specifies a price above the current market and would be used to limit losses on a short position. A stop sell order specifies a price below the current market and would be used to limit losses on a long position.

Trading markets differ in the frequency with which market orders and limit orders are utilized. In call auction markets (such as the Paris Bourse or Tel Aviv Stock Exchange), all orders are limit orders, and the final price is determined so that buyers match sellers at a price at least as good as the limit price specified by each side. In continuous markets with active trading, a large fraction of orders are market orders.

Since a limit order specifies prices away from the current market price, it must be held until the market price hits the limit price. Trading markets differ in their procedure for holding limit orders. In some markets, all limit orders in a particular security are centrally held. For example, on the Chicago Board Options Exchange (CBOE), all limit orders are held by a "board broker," who has no duties other than to handle limit orders and who is compensated by a portion of the broker's commission when limit orders are executed. On the NYSE, limit orders are held by the specialist, who receives floor brokerage when he executes limit orders on behalf of other brokers. In other markets, such as the OTC market and futures markets, limit orders are held by individual market makers. There appear to be significant benefits to centralizing limit orders: when limit orders are dispersed, each broker must check the market price continuously to see if it is approaching the limit prices of his customers; when they are centralized, considerable duplication of effort is avoided.

Regulation of Trading Markets

Several government agencies regulate trading markets. The Securities and Exchange Commission (SEC), established in 1934, oversees trading in equities, corporate bonds, options, and municipal bonds. The Commodities Futures Trading Commission (CFTC) regulates trading in futures contracts. The U.S. Department of the Treasury oversees trading in government securities.

Federal regulation of the securities markets rose out of the stock market crash of 1929 and the investigation of pools and other manipulative devices that was carried out by the Senate Committee on Banking and Currency. The

Securities Act of 1933 (1933 Act) applies to new issues of securities. It requires registration by the issuer, the underwriter, and control persons, as well as requiring the provision of a prospectus to all potential purchasers. Antifraud provisions are contained in Section 17(A) of the Act. The Securities Exchange Act of 1934 (1934 Act) applies primarily to trading in already issued securities, that is, to trading markets. Major sections of the 1934 Act are concerned with full disclosure, antifraud, and antimanipulation provisions. Periodic reporting requirements of the 1934 Act provide for disclosure by listed corporations. The 1934 Act also regulates the business conduct of brokers and dealers that are members of exchanges. Under the principle of self-regulation, the SEC has, with certain exceptions, only indirect oversight responsibility over exchanges and their members and leaves to the exchanges the responsibility for enforcing the explicit provisions of the 1934 Act. The Maloney Act of 1938 extends the authority of the SEC to include the supervision of the OTC market. The Maloney Act provides for the registration of any qualified association of brokers and dealers, and the National Association of Security Dealers (NASD) is registered pursuant to this Act.

The CFTC was established in its present form by an act of Congress in 1974. The CFTC is responsible for overseeing trading in all futures contracts. Prior to 1974, only trading in the agricultural commodities was formally regulated, and that authority rested with the Commodity Exchange Authority housed within the Department of Agriculture.

Although the Treasury has no formal authority to regulate government securities markets, it maintains oversight over these markets and, with the help of the Federal Reserve Board, conducts periodic studies of the structure and functioning of the government securities market.

EQUITY TRADING MARKETS

Major Trading Markets

Exchange Markets. The NYSE, which traces its beginning to an agreement among 24 brokers signed in 1792, is the principal market for trading equities in the United States. At the end of 1982, the NYSE listed the common stocks of 1,499 companies with a total market value of $1,271 billion. The annual dollar volume of trading was $488 billion in 1982 (See Table 10.1).

The right to trade on the floor of the NYSE is conferred by ownership of one of 1,366 "seats." Seats may be purchased and sold, and the price of a seat reflects the value to a broker of having access to the floor. In the last 20 years, seat prices reached a high of $515,000 in 1969 and a low of $35,000 in 1977. As of September 1983, seat prices were approximately $425,000. Recently, access to the NYSE floor has been broadened by allowing brokerage firms to rent the right to electronic access to the floor, that is, the right to channel orders through existing computer communications equipment. Electronic access does not confer the right to physical access by an individual.

The majority of seats on the NYSE are owned by commission house brokers, who are partners in brokerage firms that execute orders for the public. At the end of 1982, 387 member firms, each with one or more seats, dealt

TABLE 10.1   Equity Trading Markets in the U.S., 1982

	NYSE	AMSE	Regionals	NASDAQ
Number common stocks	1,499	884	256	2,960
Dollar volume of trading in 1982	488 billion	19 billion	68 billion [a]	84 billion
Market value of listings	1,271 billion	75 billion	4.8 billion [b]	153 billion

(a) Includes volume of dually listed stocks
(b) Dually listed not included

Source: Security and Exchange Commission *Statistical Bulletin*, New York Stock Exchange *Fact Book*, NASDAQ *Fact Book*

directly with the public. Approximately 400 seats are owned by specialists, who do not deal directly with the public. (Specialists are discussed in a subsequent section of this chapter.) The remaining seats are held by floor brokers, who execute orders on the floor on behalf of other brokers, or by floor traders, who trade for their own account. At the end of 1982, approximately 230 member firms, each with one or more seats, did not deal directly with the public.

The American Stock Exchange (AMEX) lists the shares of smaller companies not listed on the NYSE. At the end of 1982, 884 companies were listed on the AMEX. The market value of these firms was $75 billion at the end of 1982, and 1982 dollar volume was $19 billion. Equities are also traded on regional exchanges: the Philadelphia, Midwest, Pacific Coast, Boston, Cincinnati, Inter-Mountain, and Spokane Exchanges. Most of the volume on these exchanges is in stocks that are also listed on the NYSE or AMEX. The number of companies listed solely on regional exchanges is small.

Trading activity in NYSE- or AMEX-listed stocks is reported on a consolidated tape no matter where the transaction is executed. In addition to the regional exchanges, a certain amount of trading in listed securities is carried out on the National Association of Securities Dealers Automated Quotation (NASDAQ) system of the OTC market described subsequently. The tape reports information on the number of shares and the price of each transaction.

The Over-the-Counter Market. Whereas an exchange market is a physical location, an OTC market is a communications network connecting customers to the physically dispersed dealers that make the market. One of the most dramatic developments in the securities industry in the last 10 years has been the development and growth of NASDAQ — an automated quotation (AQ) system for facilitating trading in stocks that was developed by the NASD in 1971. Prior to the introduction of NASDAQ, dealer quotations in OTC securities were supplied daily on printed "pink sheets" and reflected closing quotations for the previous day. At the end of 1982, approximately 3,000 common stocks having a market value of $153 billion were listed solely on NASDAQ. In addition,

one who does not hold customer securities. An introducing broker may act on a "fully disclosed basis," in which case customers know the name of the clearing broker, and the clearing broker settles the individual customer accounts of the introducing broker. Alternatively, the introducing broker may act on an "omnibus basis," in which case the clearing broker only settles accounts vis-à-vis the introducing broker, leaving to the introducing broker the task of maintaining the accounts of his individual customers. Today most clearing brokers have direct customer links, but there is a tendency for some clearing brokers to specialize in providing wholesale clearing services for other brokers.

The final ring in the clearing process depicted in Figure 10.3 is the customer. Customer-side settlement (as opposed to street-side settlement, as just discussed) varies according to whether the customer wishes delivery of securities or is willing to hold securities in street name. If securities are kept in street name, the only record of the transaction is the confirmation and the customer's monthly statement. If the customer seeks delivery, the broker must send certificates to the transfer agent who records a change of ownership on the books of the issuer and mails certificates to the customer. In the past the desire of large institutional investors, such as bank trust departments, to receive delivery of certificates slowed the clearing process substantially. Today major custodian banks are members of DTC and are willing to accept book entry transfer.

Cost of Trading

The services of a trading market are not provided without cost. The information, execution, and clearing systems just described are costly to establish and to maintain. Brokers and dealers recover these costs and make a profit by charging a commission (when acting as an agent) or buying at the bid price and selling at the ask price (when acting as a dealer).

Commissions. Commission charges must cover the costs of the registered representative (about 40 percent of the commission) and all the other costs in the execution process, including any floor brokerage paid to other brokers.

Prior to May 1, 1975 (May Day), commissions on the NYSE were fixed at a minimum. As a result of the Securities Acts Amendments of 1975, commissions are determined competitively, as are most other prices in the U.S. economy. Since May Day, average commission rates have declined, and the decline has been particularly dramatic in the case of large institutional orders. According to the SEC, commissions on institutional orders dropped from 0.84 percent of the price in 1975 to 0.36 percent of the price in 1980. Commissions on smaller orders have not declined as much — from 1.73 percent of the price in 1975 to 1.39 percent of the price in 1980. Commissions vary by type of stock and type of service provided. Commission rates tend to be higher for small, less actively traded stocks than for large, actively traded stocks. Discount brokerage firms charge lower commissions than full service firms which offer more counseling and advice.

Bid-Ask Spread. While not appearing on a customer's confirmation, the bid-ask spread is a real cost of trading in securities markets. The cost is reflected in a higher price paid by the buyer and a lower price received by the seller. On the typical NYSE stock the spread is about 1.4 percent of the price. This spread combined with two commissions (each about 1.4 percent of the price) means that the round-trip transactions cost of a trade on the NYSE — the vertical height of the shaded rectangle in Figure 10.1 — is about 4.2 percent of the price of the stock. There is considerable variation in the spread of different stocks according to the volume of trading in the stock, the price of the stock, the volatility of the stock, and other factors.

Margin Trading

Investors may borrow funds to help finance the purchase of securities. The initial margin requirement, set by the Federal Reserve Board, determines the fraction of the purchase price that the customer must finance out of his own funds. Since January 3, 1974, the margin requirement has been 50 percent, which means that an investor who wishes to purchase $1,000 worth of common stock must supply $500 of his own money and may borrow the rest. All listed stocks and a large number of NASDAQ stocks are eligible for margining.

Investors who borrow from their broker must keep shares in street name as collateral for the broker's loan. An interest rate ranging from 0.5 percent to 3 percent above the broker's call money rate is charged. An account that falls below the initial margin requirement is restricted, and the equity of the account must be increased before additional securities can be purchased. The minimum maintenance margin requirement at which the customer must supply additional funds or face liquidation of his position is established by self-regulatory organizations such as the NYSE, where it is currently 25 percent. The exchanges sometimes establish special margin requirements for individual issues that exhibit unusual volume or price volatility. Individual brokers also have the option of setting higher minimum maintenance margins for their customers.

Short Selling

Short selling is the sale of a security that the investor does not own. In order to make delivery within the five-day settlement period, the security must be borrowed from another investor. There are three parties involved in a short sale: the short seller, the buyer of the shares sold short, and the lender of the shares.

A lender will not lend shares unless he is at least as well off as he would be by keeping his shares. This means that he must receive any dividends paid on the stock (which must be paid by the short seller) and he must be guaranteed that the shares can be returned to him upon demand. This requirement is met by the establishment of an escrow account, which is marked to market daily so that it always contains sufficient funds to buy back the shares in the market should the lender wish them to be returned. Frequently the lender demands an additional premium for the time and trouble involved in lending his shares.

The buyer receives shares as if he were involved in an ordinary transaction. He owns the shares and receives dividends from the company. The lender does not own the shares, although he is in the same economic position as if he did. His dividend is paid not by the company but by the short seller.

The short seller must supply margin equal to 50 percent of the current market price of the shares. However, he requires no loan. Indeed, he (or his broker) receives the proceeds of the short sale, which can be invested to earn interest (for him or his broker). According to SEC regulations, short selling is permissible only on an uptick (i.e., only after the price has increased by at least an eighth of a point).

Short selling is used in a variety of ways. Investors who believe the stock price will fall sell short in the hope of buying back the shares at a later date at a lower price. Short selling also is used frequently in arbitrage situations, such as a merger. If company *A*, currently selling at $40 per share, is taking over company *B*, currently selling at $30 per share, and if the takeover offer is a one-for-one exchange of shares, arbitragers might sell *A* short and buy *B*. If the merger goes through, the arbitragers can cover their short position with the shares of *A* received in the merger. A variety of other arbitrage or semiarbitrage opportunities can arise with respect to the same security traded in different markets or with respect to related securities such as options.

Financial Integrity of Securities Firms

Customers are concerned about the financial integrity of their brokerage firms because they leave securities in street name or because they temporarily leave idle funds with their broker (free credit balances). Even customers who pay fully for securities and demand delivery bear some risk in the period between the trade date and the final delivery date of the certificates. Risks exist because securities left in street name and margined by the customer may be pledged as collateral for bank loans to the broker or may be lent out, and free credit balances may be used by the brokerage firm for the firm's activities. Should a brokerage firm fail, the customer is in the position of any other creditor seeking redress in bankruptcy court.

Society is concerned with the financial integrity of brokerage firms because failure of a brokerage firm may precipitate a lack of confidence in other brokerage firms and produce a cumulative run on brokerage firms not unlike the bank runs of the 1930s.

Two types of safeguards protect customers: insurance and regulatory constraints on the brokerage firm. As a result of the paper work crisis of 1969–1970, a decline in the market shortly thereafter, and the resulting failure of a number of brokerage firms, Congress created the Securities Investor Protection Corporation (SIPC), which insures customer accounts in amounts up to $100,000. SIPC is financed by assessments on brokerage firms.

Regulatory constraints take two forms: a net capital requirement and segregation requirements. These requirements are administered directly by the SEC or by self-regulatory organizations such as the NYSE or NASD. The net capital requirement limits the amount by which a brokerage firm's indebtedness may exceed its net capital. (Net capital is assets minus liabilities.) For the purpose of the net capital rule, assets are subject to a reduction in value, or "haircut," the amount of which depends upon the liquidity of the asset, and liabilities exclude certain subordinated loans that are included in equity. At present, a net capital ratio in excess of 10 (i.e., liabilities divided by net capital in excess of 10) subjects the brokerage firm to examination and a restriction on its activities.

Under segregation requirements, customers' securities that have been paid for in full must be segregated. Segregation is in bulk, not by individual customer name. Cash received as the proceeds of short sales on behalf of customers is also segregated.

The Changing Structure of the Stock Market

In the past 10 years the stock market has experienced rapid change that has led to increased competition among securities firms and between securities firms and other financial intermediaries. The factors responsible for these changes are threefold. First, the computer and improved communications technology have reduced the cost of serving many customers in different locations desiring different services. In effect, reduced costs of communication and recordkeeping have increased the extent of the market and thereby promoted competition among more financial institutions across a broader geographical area.

Second, these technological developments and the growth of pension funds and other forms of institutionalized saving have produced a new class of large investors. With respect to securities markets, these institutional investors have substantial bargaining power, and they have been an important force in stimulating competition and improved service in the provision of brokerage services.

Third, regulatory changes in the securities industry have removed impediments to competition. Pressure from the Antitrust Division of the Justice Department as well as other pressures produced a change in regulatory philosophy at the SEC and in the Congress that culminated in the passage of the Securities Acts Amendments of 1975. These amendments abolished fixed commission rates on the NYSE and called for increased competition in all aspects of the securities industry.

The National Market System. Among other things, the Securities Acts Amendments of 1975 called for a reduction in direct government regulation of securities exchanges and a greater reliance on competition within the framework of a single national market system (NMS). This system would not be restricted to a specific physical location, and communication and trading through a computer could replace face-to-face communication and trading on an exchange floor. Access to an NMS system would be available to any qualified broker or dealer.

To satisfy congressional criteria, an NMS would need three key elements: (1) A computerized national transaction reporting system that records and reports all transactions wherever they take place. (2) A computerized national central limit order book (CLOB) that lists limit order prices of investors as well as bids and offers of dealers. (3) A mechanism to "lock in" a transaction on the computer when an acceptable price is observed in CLOB.

A national transaction reporting system — the consolidated tape — is in place for listed securities. However, the remaining two elements of NMS are not operational on a national basis. While there are no technological obstacles, NMS has been hindered by the cost of implementing these features. In addition, many brokers who benefit from the current trading procedures oppose the speedy establishment of NMS and the greater competition that NMS would imply. The SEC has also decided to let NMS "evolve" rather than to impose a specific blueprint.

Some evolution is occurring toward linking various physical markets to produce an NMS. The various regional exchanges and NASDAQ are linked to each other and to the NYSE through the intermarket trading system (ITS), which allows an order received in one market to be executed at a better price in another market. ITS does not allow automatic execution; however, it is an efficient communications link between markets.

Rule 390. NYSE Rule 390 requires that all NYSE member firms' transactions as principal be brought to the floor of the NYSE. A major debate revolves around the status of Rule 390. Those in favor of its complete abolition argue that abolition would remove restrictions on the market to which orders are sent and would therefore remove the remaining obstacles to the implementation of NMS. Those opposed to the abolition of Rule 390 are concerned about market fragmentation and the loss of order flow. In particular, floor members of the NYSE are concerned that markets for all transactions will be made "upstairs," directly between investors and brokers without the need to bring such orders to the floor of the exchange. Opponents also argue that Rule 390 should not be relaxed before procedures for protecting limit orders in different markets are established. On June 11, 1980, the SEC, in its Rule 19C-3, prohibited the application of NYSE Rule 390 to securities listed after April 26, 1979. This experiment in the relaxation of Rule 390 has not changed trading procedures materially because the use of ITS has been cumbersome and order-routing procedures automatically channel orders to the NYSE floor.

Alternative Routes to a National Market System. While the debate is continuing with respect to exchanges and securities listed on exchanges, substantial progress toward a national market system for OTC securities is being made. NASDAQ is being upgraded to provide data on transactions as well as dealer quotations. Furthermore, since all dealer quotations are displayed simultaneously, it is a small step to the automatic execution of orders against the best bid or ask, and such an automatic execution system is currently being planned for small orders.

Thus, forces leading to an NMS appear to have been set in motion. An NMS is likely to arise as a result of the further development of the ITS link, or, if this link proves unworkable, other markets such as NASDAQ may grow in importance. In future years stock trading, like bond trading, may be conducted over communication links connecting physically dispersed locations, at least for institutional size transactions. The role of exchanges may be greatly diminished.

DEBT MARKETS

Although less familiar to the public, debt markets are as large and as liquid as stock markets. Debt markets may be categorized by maturity: *Money markets* trade short-term, highly liquid debt instruments such as U.S. Treasury bills, banker's acceptances, and federal funds. *Capital markets for debt* trade longer-term securities such as U.S. government bonds, municipal government bonds, and corporate bonds. In this discussion debt markets are categorized by issuer.

U.S. Government Debt Markets

The large deficits of the U.S. government through the 1970s and 1980s have resulted in huge primary and secondary markets for Treasury bills, notes, and bonds as well as for the debt of U.S. government agencies such as the Government National Mortgage Association (GNMA), Federal Intermediate Credit Banks (FICBs), Federal Home Loan Banks (FHLBs), Federal Land Banks, (FLBs), and Federal Farm Credit Banks (FFCBs). By far the largest primary market is for Treasury securities. For example, in October 1983 the Treasury proposed to issue a record $16 billion of new Treasury notes in a single auction. Auctions of $5 billion are not infrequent.

The form of Treasury debt with the shortest term is called a Treasury bill. It is a promise to pay a stipulated amount (called the face value of the bill) on a stated maturity date. There are no intermediate payments such as coupons. Most bills are issued with original maturities of either 91, 182, or 364 days. Original issue Treasury bills may be purchased either by submitting a competitive tender stating the price the bidder is willing to pay and the quantity to be purchased, or by submitting a noncompetitive tender wherein the buyer agrees to purchase a stated quantity at the average of the accepted competitive prices. Competitive bidders are uncertain whether they will get any bills, but know exactly the price they will pay if their bid is accepted. Noncompetitive tenders will always be accepted, but the amount is limited to $500,000 per bidder. The Treasury acts as a perfectly discriminating monopolist in Treasury bill auctions. It first totals all noncompetitive bids, then accepts competitive bids starting with the highest. The fraction of noncompetitive bids has ranged from a low of 6.3 percent to a high of 30 percent.

The secondary market for Treasury bills is extremely competitive and highly efficient. More than 30 dealers continuously provide bid and ask quotations and will purchase and sell bills for their own inventory and at their own risk. The bid-ask spreads are quite small, frequently no more than one or two basis points (a basis point is one hundredth of one percent) and standard size transactions range from $5 million to $25 million. There is a large interdealer market (sometimes called the "Garban market") which is fully computerized. The best quotes of the dealer community appear continuously on computer screens, thereby eliminating the need to make a large number of phone calls to uncover the best price. This automation and the size of transactions makes the Treasury bill market perhaps the most efficient and liquid in the world.

Treasury notes and Treasury bonds are coupon bonds with original issue maturities of one year or more. Notes usually have maturities ranging from 1 to 10 years; bonds may have any maturity, but typically mature in 25 to 30 years from their issue date. All Treasury coupon bonds are exchanged in secondary markets on an accrued interest basis. In addition to the transaction price of the bond, buyers must compensate sellers for all interest accrued since the last coupon. Original issue Treasury notes and bonds are sold via either a price auction or a yield auction. In a price auction the coupon rate and maturity are specified in advance. Both competitive and noncompetitive offers are accepted. In a yield auction only the maturity date is specified. Investors submit competitive tenders stating the yield to maturity they are willing to accept on the quantity they are bidding for. The Treasury accepts bids of increasing yield until all bonds have been purchased, and it then sets a coupon for the issue.

Federal agency debt is issued in large blocks. The proceeds are re-lent through local financial intermediaries to ultimately benefit smaller borrowers such as home owners and farmers. There is a fairly active secondary market for federal agency debt. The short-maturity coupon issues of FFCBs and FHLBs trade in very liquid markets.

Commercial Bank Liabilities

One of the most liquid of all debt markets is the Federal funds market. Fed funds are not a security at all, but rather the purchase or sale of unsecured reserve balances of commercial banks. Those banks that have funds in excess of Federal Reserve Bank reserve requirements will lend, usually overnight, to another bank which is short of its reserve requirement. Fed funds conventionally trade in $5 million blocks in a brokered market. Garvin-Guy Butler, Mabon, Nugent, and Lasser Brothers are among the principal brokers. About 100 large commercial banks participate in the national market on a daily basis. In addition to overnight loans, Fed funds are occasionally lent on a term basis for several weeks or months.

Repurchase agreements (RPs) are collateralized loan contracts. A borrower will sell securities (usually U.S. government or agency securities or certificates of deposit) to a lender and simultaneously agree to buy back the same securities at a later date for the same price plus interest. Rates on RPs are usually very close to the rates on Fed funds of the same maturity. Although commercial banks are frequent participants in RPs the major borrowers are government securities dealers. Corporations and municipal governments with money to invest for short periods are major suppliers (lenders) in the RP market. Many of the transactions are made via direct contract between the borrower (a dealer in Treasury securities) and the lender (a corporation or municipal government).

A certificate of deposit (CD) is a negotiable deposit liability of the issuing commercial bank. Because CDs are negotiable, they can be bought or sold in a secondary market. CDs are interest-bearing securities and may sell for a price above or below their face value depending on the market rates of interest at the time. Original issue CDs are usually sold on a tap basis, which means that commercial banks offer them continuously rather than having a periodic offering of large quantities. Maturities of new CDs are at the option of the buyer but must be for at least 14 days from the original issue. Nonbank broker-dealers also help to sell CDs. In return for a commission fee, the broker locates investors interested in the issue. When an investor is found, the broker then buys the CD from the issuing bank and sells it to the investor on a "bought as sold" basis. This procedure exposes the broker to no risk because no inventory is held. The secondary market for CDs is operated by nonbank firms such as Salomon Brothers, First Boston Corporation, and Merrill Lynch. The standard block size is $5 million. Yields on outstanding CDs are usually slightly above new issues from the same bank because an investor can tailor a new issue maturity to his needs; this is not possible for issues traded in the secondary market.

Corporate Debt Markets

Commercial paper is unsecured short-term corporate debt that pays no coupons. It promises to pay a stated face value upon maturity. Investors receive a return because commercial paper is sold at a discount from its face value. Almost all commercial paper has a maturity of nine months or less when it is originally issued. New issues of commercial paper may be placed directly on a tap basis in denominations of $100,000 with the maturity at the discretion of the buyer, or they may be placed by dealers such as The First Boston Corporation, A.G. Becker, or Goldman, Sachs. Dealer-placed paper is typically sold in $250,000 lots and may be underwritten or brokered. If it is underwritten, the dealer buys the entire issue for its own inventory and takes the risk of reselling it. The issuing corporation pays an underwriting fee in order to avoid the risk. Alternately the issue may be placed on a bought-as-sold brokered basis. In this case the corporation receives a higher price, but bears more risk. Although there is no secondary market for directly placed commercial paper, some liquidity is provided because corporations usually stand ready to buy back their own paper, if the need arises. In addition, dealers will occasionally bid to buy back paper at a premium of roughly 25 basis points. Thus, the effective bid-ask spread on commercial paper is substantially wider than the spread of one or two basis points in the more liquid Treasury bill market.

Corporate bonds are interest-bearing corporate debt which usually have original issue maturities of 5 to 30 years. Bonds are issued infrequently in large blocks either via a private placement on a brokered basis with a life insurance company or via an underwritten public offering. If the new issue is a public offering, an underwriting syndicate of dealers will form to buy the new bonds from the firm and then resell them to the public. About six weeks before the offering date the issuer files a registration statement with the SEC, although a recent innovation called "shelf registration" allows the issuer to file as much as a year before the offering and to choose the best time for the offering. The day before a public offering, the members of the underwriting syndicate meet with the issuing firm to decide on the coupon rate and offering price for the bonds. If the yield is too high, the issuer might withdraw; if it is too low, the syndicate may break up because the bonds will be too hard to sell. After the price, coupon rate, and terms of the bond are established, a final prospectus is filed with the SEC. The offering is then sold at a common price to the public on a subscription basis. If the issue is sold out, the members of the underwriting syndicate divide their profits, but if the issue is not sold, then the syndicate may break up and the members will try to sell the bonds for whatever price they can.

Secondary trading of registered corporate bonds occurs in a nonbank dealer market because the Glass-Steagall Act expressly prohibits commercial banks from acting as dealers in corporate securities. Investors who wish to transact in corporate bonds will contact their broker, who will then contact a dealer who will offer bid and ask quotes. Trading in corporate debt is relatively infrequent and, as a result, the market is very thin. Weeks may pass between transactions in a particular security.

Municipal Government Debt

Municipal bonds are the interest-bearing debt of municipal governments or their agencies. Their most important feature is that their coupon interest income is not subjected to federal income taxes. Note, however, that capital gains on municipal debt are taxable. Municipal debt is usually classified by the type of security underlying it. General obligation bonds are secured only by the general revenues of the municipality. Revenue and authority bonds for the construction of all highways, ports, parking facilities, utilities, or public housing are secured by the revenue streams that they bring in.

Municipal securities are issued via a process which is a hybrid of the unrestricted competition of Treasury auctions and the negotiated underwriting of corporate debt. Although the bonds are advertised for sale to the public, they are offered on an all-or-nothing basis. In practice, this restricts bidding to syndicates of broker-dealers which buy a new issue and then reissue it to the public. The Glass-Steagall Act does not prohibit commercial banks from participating in municipal bond syndicates. Competition among syndicates may affect the interest paid by municipalities. Richard West (1966) found that municipalities that received only a single bid had to pay an average premium of 23 basis points above prevailing market rates.

The secondary market in municipal securities has several tiers. Recent offerings with large outstanding volumes are traded actively through the dealer activities of large banks and nonbank broker-dealers. Next, there is a dealer market which trades a large variety of smaller issues. Finally, there is an extremely thin market for the small issues of local school districts and local governments. The bid-ask spread on a municipal bond may be as low as 0.25 percent on an actively traded issue or as high as 5 percent on inactive issues.

FUTURES MARKETS

Futures markets are the most rapidly growing of all trading markets. While futures contracts in agricultural commodities have been traded since before the turn of the century, rapid expansion in the number of contracts has occurred only recently with the advent of futures on financial instruments. Futures exchanges in the United States and their more actively traded contracts are shown in Table 10.3.

Nature of a Futures Contract

A futures contract is just that, a contract. In a futures contract, the buyer (the long) agrees to buy an asset (such as wheat, a foreign currency, gold, a Treasury bill) at a later date at a price established today. The seller (the short) agrees to sell the underlying asset at maturity at the price specified. Neither the underlying asset nor the purchase price specified in the contract changes hands today. Both parties to the contract must, however, deposit margin, usually about 10 percent of the contract value. This margin is different from margin in the stock

TABLE 10.3   U.S. Futures Markets and Active Futures Contracts

Exchange	Grains and Oilseeds	Livestock and Meat	Food, Fiber, Wood	Metals, Oil	Debt Instruments	Currencies	Equity Instruments
Chicago Board of Trade	Corn Soybeans Wheat Soybean meal Soybean oil Oats	Iced broilers	Western plywood	Silver Gold Unleaded gas Crude oil Heating oil	GNMA mortgages Treasury bonds Treasury notes		
Chicago Mercantile Exchange and International Money Market		Live cattle Pork bellies Live hogs Feeder cattle Iced broilers Fresh eggs	Lumber Potatoes Stud lumber	Gold	Treasury bills Treasury notes Bank CDs Eurodollar	U.K. pound Deutsche mark Swiss franc Canadian dollar Japanese yen Mexican peso French franc	S&P 500 stock index S&P 100 stock index
New York Commodity Exchange Inc.				Gold Copper Silver			
New York Futures Exchange							NYSE composite index
New York Cotton Exchange			Orange juice Cotton	Propane			
Kansas City Board of Trade	Wheat						Value Line stock index
Minneapolis Grain Exchange	Wheat						
Mid-American Commodity Exchange and Monetary Market	Wheat Corn Oats Soybeans Rough rice	Live cattle Live hogs	Refined sugar	Silver Gold	Treasury bonds Treasury bills	Deutsche mark British pound Japanese yen Canadian dollar Swiss franc	
New York Mercantile Exchange			Round white potatoes	Platinum Palladium Heating oil Leaded gasoline Crude oil			
Coffee, Sugar and Cocoa Exchange			Coffee Sugar #11 Sugar #12 Cocoa				

market or bond market, in which payment and delivery are made at the trade date. Margin in futures markets is a performance guarantee and is required from both the buyer and seller. Interest-earning assets may be pledged to meet the margin requirement.

While most futures contracts call for delivery of the underlying asset at maturity, delivery can be avoided by taking an offsetting position before maturity. Thus, a long in March wheat futures can avoid receiving delivery of wheat in March by selling March wheat futures prior to the maturity month. Delivery is rare in futures markets because participants who wish to possess the underlying asset usually prefer to purchase the asset in the cash market where the grade and delivery point of the asset can be more precisely specified; they prefer to use the futures markets as a temporary hedge while the cash market transaction is being arranged. Certain new contracts, such as stock index futures, do not call for delivery but call for cash settlement. In cash settlement traders make a gain or loss measured as the difference between the contract price and the cash price of the underlying asset at maturity.

An active and liquid futures market is possible only for standardized assets. Standardization is necessary so that each participant knows precisely what he is buying and selling. However, even an asset like wheat is not inherently perfectly standard: Different grades of wheat are grown. As a result, futures contracts are written in terms of a standard grade but permit delivery of other grades at a premium or discount from the standard contract price. Broadening the delivery terms limits the ability of anyone to control the available supply so as to engineer a corner or short squeeze in the delivery month. While broadening the definition of the assets acceptable for delivery limits the danger of price manipulation in the delivery month, too broad a definition limits the hedging usefulness of a futures contract because the relationship between the futures price and the cash price is no longer very precise. This conflict between precise standardization and a broad definition to avoid manipulation in the delivery month is inherent in the design of most commodity contracts.

Another important feature of futures contracts is the number of delivery months. Agricultural commodities have approximately six delivery months at any moment of time, extending approximately 15 months into the future (e.g., in October the delivery months for wheat are December of the current year and March, May, July, September, and December of the next year). Other futures contracts, such as silver and some of the financial futures, have delivery months extending more than two years into the future. Again, the contract design involves a balancing of objectives. Having too many contract months reduces the liquidity in any one of the contract months, while having too few contract months limits the usefulness of the contract.

Trading Mechanics

As in the stock market, anyone interested in trading futures contracts establishes an account at a brokerage firm and deals with an account executive who has passed an examination on commodity futures markets and is registered with the CFTC. Customers are also required to sign a "risk disclosure statement" which describes the risks involved in trading futures contracts.

As in the stock market, market orders, limit orders, or stop orders may

TABLE 10.4   Illustration of Trading and Settling in Futures Markets

Time	Buyer	Seller	Cumulative Contract Volume	Open Interest	Price	Cumulative Profit			
						A	B	C	D
1	A	B	1	1	4.00	0	0	0	0
2	C	A	2	1	4.01	0.01	−0.01	0	0
3	C	D	3	2	3.98	0.01	0.02	−0.03	0

Note: (1) Long positions = Short positions = Open interest
      (2) Total profits of all traders at any point in time are zero.

be used (with variations). There is no limit order book in futures markets. Instead, each broker holds his own "deck" of orders, including limit orders. In futures markets, spread orders are also possible. A spread order calls for the simultaneous purchase and sale of futures contracts of different delivery months in the same underlying asset.

As in the stock market, orders are first routed to a firm's back office and then to the trading floor of the appropriate exchange. The trading floor is quite different from the trading floor of a stock exchange because there is no single specialist making a market at a particular location. Instead, there is a large "trading pit" filled with brokers and traders dealing directly with each other via hand signals and voice contact. Many traders are acting as brokers on behalf of their customers. Others, scalpers, are very short-term traders who perform the same function as dealers in the stock market. Scalpers trade for their own account; they buy at a bid price when there is excessive public selling and sell at an ask price when there is excessive public buying. Others, day traders and position traders, take speculative positions for their own account.

A price reporter enters price information into a computer next to the trading pit. The information is displayed on the floor and disseminated worldwide. Information on transaction size is not reported. Volume and open interest are reported only on the following day by the clearing house of the commodities exchange. Volume is the number of contracts traded in a day; open interest is the number of contracts outstanding at the end of the day.

The clearing house is central to the proper functioning of a futures exchange. It compares and settles transactions carried out on the floor of the exchange. Not all brokerage firms are members of the clearing house, and those that are not clear through a clearing house member. The clearing house facilitates trading by interposing itself between the buyer and seller after a transaction has been agreed upon. This makes possible an active secondary market for buyers and sellers, since positions can now be reversed by dealing with the clearing house without having to deal with the original parties to the contract.

The illustration in Table 10.4 may clarify the process. Assume that we are concerned with December wheat and that all transactions are for one contract (5,000 bushels). At time 1 the contract is opened for trading, and A and B agree to trade at a price of $4 per bushel. Volume is one contract and open interest is one contract. The clearing house becomes the buyer to B and the seller to A. When A becomes a seller at time 2, the clearing house is the buyer to A. Since A is now a buyer and seller of the same contract on the books of the clearing house, his position is closed out by the clearing house (and he makes a profit of 1 cent). In effect, C replaces A as the offsetting long to B's short position, without B's knowledge. At time 2, cumulative volume has increased by one to two contracts, while open interest remains at one. When C buys a second contract from D at time 3, cumulative volume and open interest each increase by one contract.

A feature of futures markets is that accounts are settled daily with respect to the clearing house. Thus, at time 3, C has lost 3 cents a bushel even though C has not closed out his long position. C must therefore post additional margin, whereas B has excess margin (of 2 cents), which may be withdrawn. Note that long positions always equal short positions and that total profits of all traders are zero.

Purposes of Futures Markets

Futures markets serve two economic functions: (1) They allow price risk to be shifted from the less able or less willing to the more able or more willing and (2) they provide information that is useful to processors and other users of the underlying asset.

In futures markets, risk is shifted from hedgers to speculators. A hedger is someone who holds, processes, or has an obligation to deliver the underlying asset. To limit his risk, a hedger establishes a futures market position that is opposite to his cash market position. For example, a storer of a commodity such as wheat (an asset) would sell futures (a liability) to protect himself against adverse price fluctuations in wheat. Speculators take a position in futures markets opposite to that of hedgers in hopes of making a profit. Evidence suggests that, on average, speculators do not make profits; this, in turn, implies that hedgers receive insurance against price risk at zero cost.

Even in the absence of hedging uses, futures markets can be beneficial because speculators, acting on the best information available to them, cause futures prices to reflect all that is knowable. Thus the futures market is allocationally efficient in the sense described previously, and futures prices act as useful signals to processors, storers, and farmers. In the absence of futures markets, such information would not be generally available, and producers, storers, and farmers might make decisions based on less complete information.

Neither the risk-shifting nor the information function needs to be performed in markets in which prices are certain. Futures markets arise when there is price instability. For example, currency futures only became popular after the advent of flexible exchange rates. The fact that futures markets arise in volatile markets sometimes leads to the incorrect inference that futures markets cause volatile markets.

OPTION MARKETS

In the last decade options contracts have become more and more important, because of both the rapid growth of trading on organized options exchanges and the rapid development of option pricing theory. This part of the chapter first describes the nature of various types of options contracts (e.g., puts and calls on various underlying assets such as stocks, bonds, and indices); then discusses the development of major options exchanges and the mechanics of trading in them.

Types of Option Contracts

A call option gives its owner the right to purchase an underlying security, usually a share of stock, at a predetermined price for a fixed interval of time. For example, at the close of the CBOE on Thursday, September 21, 1983, there were 12 call options on shares of AT&T common stock. Their prices as well as the closing price of AT&T stock are given in the following chart.

CALL OPTIONS ON AT&T, SEPTEMBER 21, 1983

Striking or Exercise Price	Maturity Month			AT&T Closing Price
	October	January	April	
60	7	8	9	67½
65	2 7/16	4	5 5/8	67½
70	1 1/16	1 7/8	2 5/8	67½
75	1/16	—	—	67½

If an investor purchases an April option with a $70 exercise (or striking) price, he is betting 2 5/8 that AT&T's stock price, which closed at $67.50, will rise above $70 before the third Friday in April 1984. All option contracts mature on the third Friday of the stated month unless it is a holiday. Most options may be exercised any time up to and including their maturity date. When options have this early exercise feature, they are called American options. If they cannot be exercised until maturity, they are called European options.

The other major type of option contract is a put. It gives its owner the right to sell a share of stock at the stated exercise price either any time up to its maturity date (if it is an American put) or at the maturity date (if it is a European put). Shown below are the put options written on AT&T.

PUT OPTIONS ON AT&T, SEPTEMBER 21, 1983

Striking or Exercise Price	Maturity Month			AT&T Closing Price
	October	January	April	
60	1/16	7/16	1 1/8	67½
65	1 1/16	1 7/8	2 5/8	67½
70	4	4 7/8	5 3/4	67½

For example, if an investor buys an April put with a $65 exercise price, he bets $2 5/8 that AT&T's stock price will fall from its current level of $67.50 to below $65 sometime before the third Friday in April 1984.

Major Exchanges and Option Instruments

By Autumn 1983 options were being traded on the CBOE, the AMEX, NYSE, and several regional exchanges including the Pacific, the Philadelphia, and the Midwest Exchanges. In addition to puts and calls on common stock, options are also written on stock indices (the NYSE index, the Value Line index, the Standard and Poor's (S&P) 100 index, the S&P 500 index, the AMEX market value index, a computer technology index, and an oil and gas index), on foreign currencies, and on U.S. government notes and bonds (Treasury notes, 13-week Treasury bills, and Treasury bonds). Options on certain agricultural commodities are planned. The growth in popularity of options contracts is amazing when one recalls that the first standardized option contracts were listed on the CBOE on April 26, 1973.

Contract Standardization and Liquidity

A major reason for the rapid growth of options markets is that they have provided standardization and liquidity in order to facilitate trading. Prior to 1973, all options were traded on the OTC market where put and call dealers and brokers brought would-be buyers and sellers together, arranged terms, helped with paper work, and charged substantial fees required for the work involved. There was little standardization of contracts, low volume, and virtually no secondary market. A buyer wishing to close out a position prior to expiration could exercise an option, but it was usually too costly to try to find another buyer so that the option could be sold prior to expiration. The obvious advantage of CBOE options is that they have a common exercise price, a common maturity, and are all written on 100 shares of stock. Standardization makes it easy to buy and sell option contracts in the secondary market and avoids the necessity of waiting until maturity to exercise the option.

Mechanics of Trading

The Options Clearing Corporation greatly facilitates trading in listed options because it severs direct links between buyers and sellers in the manner described for futures markets. If a buyer chooses to exercise an option, the Options Clearing Corporation computer will randomly choose a seller who has not closed his position and assign the exercise notice accordingly. The Corporation also guarantees delivery of the underlying security if a seller defaults. In addition, the Options Clearing Corporation makes it possible for a buyer to "sell out" of a position and a seller to "buy in" a position at any time. If a trader has offsetting positions, the computer simply eliminates both positions. The Options Clearing Corporation is capitalized with funds provided by clearing members of the Options Exchange.

Listed option contracts are protected against stock splits and stock dividends by adjusting the exercise price and the number of shares underlying the contract. For example, if a firm declares a 50 percent stock dividend, a call option would be adjusted to cover one-and-a-half as many shares at two-thirds of the original exercise price per share. Listed options are not, however, protected against cash distributions to shareholders, such as dividends or spinoffs. In this case, the option holder must resort to early exercise in order to be protected. For example, in December 1976, General Motors stock was selling for around $75 per share. Call options were outstanding with an exercise price of $60 per share. On the next day the company was scheduled to go ex dividend with a dividend of $3 per share. This implied that the stock would fall to approximately $72 per share. Before the ex dividend date the value of the option could not fall below the stock price minus the exercise price, that is, $15 per share. But the very next day the stock price would fall to around $72 per share and the option price would also fall (it fell to 12 5/8). On one day the option was worth $15 and on the next day everyone knew it would fall in value because the call option was not dividend protected. The only rational thing to do was to exercise the option just before the stock went ex dividend.

Margin requirements are much more complicated for options transactions than for common stock. Investors who purchase or sell options contracts without hedging their position by purchasing the underlying security are said to have naked options positions. No margin is allowed for buyers of naked options. On the other hand, writers (sellers) of naked options must deposit a margin of at least 30 percent of the price of the underlying security plus or minus the amount the call is in-the-money or out-of-the-money. For example, if AT&T is selling for $67.50, the writer of an April contract for 100 call options at an exercise price of $60 must deposit 30 percent of $67.50 times 100 (i.e., $2,025) plus the in-the-money amount of $750 (i.e., $7.50 per share times 100), for a total of $2,775. The proceeds from the option sale (i.e., $900) may be applied to the margin requirement.

There are further complications to the margin requirements when an investor takes a complex position (e.g., a straddle) using options on the same stock. Since the actual margin requirement will vary across brokers, it is necessary to consult the brokerage house for exact requirements.

Options commissions are established on a competitive, negotiable basis. There is no fixed commission schedule. Table 10.5 gives representative commissions charged by full-service brokerage houses (as opposed to discount houses). The numbers in parentheses show the transactions costs as a percentage of the value of the contract being traded. Although options commissions are a high percentage of the value of the contract, it is important to remember that the alternative is buying or selling the stock itself. Options give the investor more "action" per dollar of commissions costs than stock investments can.

The tax treatment of options trading is often complicated and may require expert legal opinion. The discussion given here is only a summary of common situations. When previously purchased options are sold in the secondary market prior to their maturity date, any gains or losses will be considered short-term capital gains or losses if the option is held for less than one year. Otherwise they are long-term capital gains or losses. The tax treatment for an option seller (writer) who closes out his position is not symmetric. The difference between

TABLE 10.5   Commission Fees for Option Trading

Option Price	Number of Contracts (100 shares each)		
	1	5	10
$ 0.50	$10(20.0%)	$ 30(12.0%)	$ 50(10.0%)
1.00	25(25.0%)	66(11.0%)	90 (9.0%)
2.00	25(12.5%)	70 (7.0%)	105 (5.3%)
5.00	25 (5.0%)	87 (3.5%)	145 (2.9%)
10.00	25 (2.5%)	110 (2.2%)	190 (1.9%)

the sale price initially received and the price paid for the closing purchase is always considered a short-term gain or loss (except for options dealers who must pay ordinary taxes on the gain or loss).

When a call option is exercised, the buyer is considered to have bought the stock for a total cost equal to the exercise price plus the price originally paid for the option plus any commissions or other costs involved in the purchase of the option and its exercise. The period between the initial purchase of the option and its exercise is irrelevant for tax purposes. All profits or losses are attributed to holding the security itself, which begins on the exercise date for the option buyer and ends on that date for the seller.

If a call option expires unexercised, the buyer's loss is considered to be a short- or long-term capital loss, depending on the interval from purchase to expiration. The seller's gain is always considered a short-term capital gain.

A wash sale occurs if an investor sells one security and within a 61-day period, beginning 30 days before and ending 31 days after the sale, buys another security that is substantially identical to the security sold. Any loss from a wash sale is not deductible. Call options are regarded as being substantially identical to the underlying stock. Thus, if stock is sold at a loss and then an option is bought during the 61-day wash sale period, the loss on the stock is not tax deductible. If these transactions occur in reverse order (i.e., if the call is sold at a loss before the stock is purchased), the wash sale rule does not apply.

Benefits of Options

The standardization of options contracts has facilitated the rapid growth in their popularity. However, the growth could not have occurred unless options provided some fundamental benefits. Those benefits can be found by studying the wide variety of investment strategies that options make possible.

Most obviously, options can be used for sheer speculation. In many cases, a naked option position is much more sensitive to changes in stock prices than is a highly margined position in the same stock.

Another use of options is hedging. For example, if the owner of a share of stock wishes to limit his downside risk, he can hedge by either writing call options or buying put options in the correct hedge ratio. Thus, options may be used as a type of portfolio insurance.

There are an almost unlimited number of combinations of options and the underlying securities which allow investors to tailor the risk and return characteristics to their desired specifications. This variety is, perhaps, the major benefit of options contracts.

FACTORS AFFECTING TRANSACTION COSTS IN TRADING MARKETS

Each of the trading markets that have been examined here imposes transaction costs on investors in the form of commissions and the bid-ask spread. These costs are necessary to compensate brokers and dealers for the services they render in providing information, speedy execution, and clearing services. This section summarizes the key factors that have been found to determine these costs, particularly the costs incurred by the dealer.

The Bid-Ask Spread

A dealer provides immediacy to investors who do not want to enter limit orders and wait to trade. The dealer is prepared to purchase at the bid price securities he may not want, or to sell at the ask price securities he may not have (and needs to borrow).

Breakdown of Dealer Costs. The dealer's costs of providing immediacy can be broken down into three elements: holding costs, order costs, and information costs. (See Stoll, 1978a.) Holding costs represent the costs of holding an inventory of securities that the dealer would prefer not to hold because of the price risk and potential for losses. The possibility of loss is a function of the price variability of the security and the size of the dealer's position. The compensation the dealer demands also depends on his willingness to take risk and on the amount of capital he has at his disposal.

Order costs represent the clerical costs of carrying out a transaction, the cost of the dealer's time, and the cost of the physical communications and office equipment necessary to carry out the transaction. To a considerable degree, order costs are fixed with respect to any particular transaction.

Information costs arise if some investors trade with the dealer because they have superior information. Since the dealer quotes a two-sided market based on information available to him, any investor with information not available to the dealer can trade with the dealer at a favorable price. Suppose the dealer quotes 30 to 30½ and an investor has information that the stock will decline below 30. That investor will sell at 30 to the dealer and reap a benefit when (and if) the stock price falls. As Bagehot (1971) first showed, since the dealer cannot identify information traders in advance, he must charge a spread large enough to be compensated for the average losses he incurs with respect to information traders. Since the spread is charged to all traders, traders without information, in effect, pay the dealer's cost of trading with those that have information.

A related information cost arises if the dealer does not adjust his bid-ask price continuously. In that case even new public information, which justifies a price different from the dealer's current bid and ask, allows speedy traders to benefit at the dealer's expense. Copeland and Galai (1983) show that speedy traders benefit because they are able to trade at a bid or ask price based on old information before the dealer has time to change his spread to reflect the new information.

Empirical Evidence. Although all the factors that affect the bid-ask spread cannot be measured, empirical evidence of Demsetz (1968), Stoll (1978b), Tinic (1972), and others (see Cohen, et al., 1979) indicates that the following factors are important empirical determinants of the spread:

1 *The volume of trading in a security.* The greater the volume of trading, the easier it is for the dealer to dispose of an unwanted inventory position and the easier it is to cover his fixed costs of handling orders. Securities with high volume therefore tend to have lower spreads than those with low volume.

2 *Price volatility.* The greater the variability of return of a security, the greater the risk to the dealer and therefore the larger the spread he tends to charge.

3 *Price.* Empirical evidence for the stock market indicates that the higher the price of a stock, the lower the *proportional* spread. The explanation for this relationship is not totally clear. It appears that price is a proxy for risk and that low price stocks tend to have greater risk and therefore larger proportional spreads. Low price stocks also have larger proportional spreads because the minimum quoted spread (one-eighth dollar) is a relatively large fraction for stocks selling at low prices.

4 *Extent of information trading.* The amount of informational trading measured by turnover (where turnover is defined as the ratio of volume of trading to shares outstanding) is positively related to the spread.

5 *Degree of competition.* Empirical evidence also indicates that the spread is lower when several dealers are making markets in the same stock. Competition limits the ability of a dealer to charge more than his costs of providing immediacy.

Behavior of the Spread Over Time. After a purchase by the dealer, the dealer tends to lower his bid price because he is less anxious to buy more shares of the same security. Simultaneously, he tends to lower the ask price because he wishes to sell the securities he has acquired. Thus, the spread is frequently unchanged over time even though both the bid and ask price are changed so as to create an incentive for public investors to trade in a way that moves the dealer's inventory back to the desired level.

Commissions

A commission is charged by a broker who acts as an agent and does not assume any price risk, as does a dealer. The commission reflects the costs of executing and clearing an order as well as the costs of advising customers. Large orders tend to be more difficult to execute and clear, thus they require a higher dollar commission. However, the increase in costs is not proportional to the order size and therefore the proportional commission tends to decline as the size of the order increases.

Empirical studies of commission charges on stock transactions support the view that there are economies of scale in handling larger transactions (Edmister, 1978; Stoll, 1979, p. 61). The commission as a fraction of the value of the transaction declines with the number of shares traded. Holding constant the number of shares traded, the percentage commission also declines with the price per share.

FACTORS AFFECTING THE PRICE OF SECURITIES: ALLOCATIONAL EFFICIENCY

One of the major structural differences between the U.S. economy and the economies of other developed nations in Europe and Asia is that the dollar volume of trading in trading markets here is a much larger percentage of gross national product than anywhere else. Given this fact, one would hope that our securities markets operate efficiently. The previous section discussed factors affecting operational efficiency. Here allocational efficiency is examined. What is it? What empirical evidence supports or refutes it?

Framework for Examining Allocational Efficiency

Earlier in this chapter allocational efficiency was defined to include two aspects: informational efficiency and pricing efficiency. In an informationally efficient market, society gathers relevant information about securities so long as its marginal benefit exceeds its marginal cost. What type of information is relevant? The speculative equilibrium hypothesis, best described by Keynes (1936), is that investors base their investment decisions entirely on their anticipation of other individuals' behavior without any necessary relationship to the actual payoffs that the assets are expected to provide. An alternative viewpoint, called the rational expectations hypothesis, predicts that prices are formed on the basis of the expected future payouts of assets, including their resale value to third parties. Although it is impossible to test these alternative hypotheses empirically, an interesting experimental study using human subjects was conducted by Forsythe, Paltrey, and Plott (1982). They concluded that investors' behavior is better described by rational expectations.

Pricing efficiency is concerned with speed of price adjustment to the arrival of new information in the market place. Empirical evidence indicates that market prices react very rapidly, although not instantaneously.

Fama (1970) has provided a framework for analyzing allocational efficiency by partitioning the relevant information set. A market is said to be weak-form efficient if securities prices today fully reflect all historic price information. The implication is that no pattern in past prices can be used to forecast changes in future prices. In other words, technical analysis of price patterns is useless for making systematic capital gains. The next section discusses the empirical evidence that has validated this proposition of weak-form efficiency. The semistrong form of market efficiency arises when prices fully reflect all publicly available information. The implication for investors is that it is impossible to use annual reports of corporations, newspaper articles, or brokerage house newsletters to form trading rules to outperform the market. Again, the next section discusses evidence that supports this hypothesis. Finally, strong-form market efficiency implies that no investor can earn excess returns using any information whether it is publicly available or not. If strong-form efficiency were true, then even insiders who have information not available to the marketplace could not earn excess returns. Empirical evidence rejects the strong-form hypothesis.

The Empirical Evidence — Are Markets Allocationally Efficient?

Hundreds of academic studies have tested market efficiency; there is not enough space here to report them all. Consequently, a few have been selected as representative.

The weak form of market efficiency has been tested by using various trading rules based on filters. Alexander (1961) and Fama and Blume (1966) used a filter rule according to which stock is purchased when it rises x percent from its previous low, then held until the price falls x percent from its high. At that time the stock is sold and a short position maintained until the price goes up x percent. The objective of such a filter rule is to make profits from runs in stock prices. The filter rule tests have two important results. First, filters greater than 1.5 percent could not beat a simple buy and hold strategy. Therefore, the weak form of the efficient market hypothesis is confirmed. Second, although filters smaller than 1.5 percent did beat the market before transaction costs, the profits were completely eliminated by transaction costs as low as 0.1 percent, a rate paid by even a floor trader on the NYSE. This illustrates the relationship between allocational and operational efficiency. If transaction costs are high, then there will be a greater illusion of market inefficiency because trading rule profits, before transaction costs, will be high.

The performance of managed portfolios provided a test of the semistrong form of market efficiency. A partial list of studies of the risk-adjusted performance of mutual funds includes work by Friend and Vickers (1965), Sharpe (1966), Treynor (1965), Friend, Blume, and Crockett (1970), Jensen (1968), and Mains (1977). Most studies found that mutual fund performance was neutral on average. The most recent study, by Mains (1977), reported that the gross (risk-adjusted) rates of return for 80 percent of the mutual funds were higher than the market but that their net performance, after subtracting out management fees and brokerage commissions, was neutral. The implication is that mutual funds can beat the market by just enough to cover their costs of gathering and processing information and the cost of transactions. Hence, the evidence from mutual funds is consistent with market efficiency.

Semistrong-form market efficiency can be tested directly by using the recommendations of the Value Line Investor Survey, which are based on publicly available information. Value Line uses a complex computerized filter rule to predict future performance. Stocks are rated 1 through 5, with 1 being the best performance predicted during the next 12 months. Copeland and Mayers (1982) found statistically significant performance only for Value Line Portfolio 5. However, the measured abnormal performance was small (only 3.05 per six months) and would have been eliminated by the transaction costs of an active trading strategy based on Value Line recommendations. Hence, the empirical results, once again, are consistent with the semistrong form of market efficiency.

A particularly interesting series of studies by Scholes (1972), Kraus and Stoll (1972), and Dann, Mayers, and Raab (1977) has focused on the phenomenon of block trading. As mentioned previously, large blocks of securities are typically not handled by the NYSE specialist; rather, they are placed by the floor trader with customers of his brokerage firm. Once the block has been sold, usually at a discount from its equilibrium price level, it is announced on the NYSE ticker. Semistrong-form market efficiency can be tested by observing the length of time it takes for the stock price to adjust upward to a new equilibrium level. Dann, Mayers, and Raab (1977) report that for a sample of large blocks, traders must react within five minutes of the block announcement on the ticker tape in order to earn a positive rate of return after transaction costs. Not only is this evidence consistent with semistrong market efficiency, it also tells us that market prices react very quickly to news events. Kraus and Stoll (1972) and Dann, Mayers, and Raab (1977) also reported that if a trader can purchase at the block price, then it is possible to earn positive risk-adjusted returns, even after certain transaction costs. This may be interpreted as evidence contrary to the strong form of market efficiency because certain traders can use information that is not publicly available to earn abnormal returns.

A better case for rejecting strong-form efficiency is made by the empirical evidence on insider trading provided by Jaffe (1974) and Finnerty (1976). They formed portfolios that mimicked the trading behavior of corporate insiders. In both studies the results indicate that insiders can beat the market on a risk-adjusted return basis both when buying and selling securities of their own firms.

The weight of empirical evidence indicates that securities markets (at least in the United States) are allocationally efficient in the weak and semistrong forms but not in the strong form. Individuals possessing information that is not publicly available can and do earn abnormal returns.

SUGGESTED READING

Books

Block, E., and R. A. Schwartz, eds. *Impending Changes for Securities Markets: What Role for the Exchanges?* Greenwich, Conn.: JAI Press, 1979.

Bookstaber, R.M. *Option Pricing and Strategies in Investing*. Reading, Mass.: Addison-Wesley, 1980.

Commodity Trading Manual. Board of Trade of City of Chicago. Chicago: 1982.

Copeland, T.E., and J.F. Weston. *Financial Theory and Corporate Policy*, 2nd ed., Chapters 9 and 10. Reading, Mass.: Addison-Wesley, 1983.

Eiteman, W., et al. *The Stock Market*. New York: McGraw-Hill, 1966.

Friend, I., et al. *Mutual Funds and Other Institutional Investors*. New York: McGraw-Hill, 1970.

Garbade, K. *Securities Markets*. New York: McGraw-Hill, 1982.

Hieronymus, T. *Economics of Futures Trading*. Commodity Research Bureau. New York: 1971.

Keynes, J.M. *The General Theory of Employment, Interest and Money*. New York: Harcourt Brace, 1936.

The New York Stock Exchange Market. New York Stock Exchange. June 1979.

Peck, A.E., ed. *Selected Writings on Futures Markets: Basic Research in Commodity Markets*. Board of Trade of the City of Chicago. Chicago: 1983.

Robbins, S. *The Securities Markets*. New York: Free Press, 1966.

Sharpe, W. *Investments*. Englewood Cliffs, N.J.: Prentice-Hall, 1981.

West, R., and S. Tinic. *The Economics of the Stock Market*. New York: Praeger, 1971.

Articles

Alexander, S.S. "Price Movements in Speculative Markets: Trends or Random Walks." *Industrial Management Review* (May 1961).

Bagehot, Walter [pseud.]. "The Only Game in Town." *Financial Analysts Journal*, Vol. 27 (Mar.-Apr. 1971).

Cohen, K., et al. "Market Makers and the Market Spread: A Review of Recent Literature." *Journal of Financial and Quantitative Analysis*, Vol. 14 (Nov. 1979).

Copeland, T., and D. Galai. "Information Effects on the Bid-Ask Spread." *Journal of Finance* (1983).

Copeland, T., and D. Mayers. "The Value Line Enigma (1965–1978): A Case Study of Performance Evaluation Issues." *Journal of Financial Economics*, Vol. 10 (Nov. 1982), pp. 289–321.

Dann, L., et al. "Trading Rules, Large Blocks and the Speed of Adjustment." *The Journal of Financial Economics* (Jan. 1977), pp. 3–22.

Demsetz, H. "The Cost of Transacting." *Quarterly Journal of Economics*, Vol. 82 (Feb. 1968).

Edmister, R. "Commission Cost Structure: Shifts and Scale Economies." *Journal of Finance*, Vol. 33 (May 1978), pp. 477–485.

Fama, E. "Efficient Capital Markets: A Review of Theory and Empirical Work." *The Journal of Finance* (May 1970), pp. 383–417.

———, and M. Blume. "Filter Rules and Stock Market Trading Profits." *The Journal of Business* (Jan. 1966, spec. supp.), pp. 226–241.

Finnerty, J.E. "Insiders and Market Efficiency." *Journal of Finance* (Sept. 1976), pp. 1141–1148.

Forsythe, R., et al. "Asset Valuation in an Experimental Market." *Econometrica* (May 1982), pp. 537–567.

Friend, I. "The Economic Consequences of the Stock Market." *American Economic Review*, Vol. 52, May 1972, pp. 212–219.

———, and D. Vickers. "Portfolio Selection and Investment Performance." *Journal of Finance* (Sept. 1965), pp. 391–415.

Garbade, K. "Electronic Quotation Systems and the Market for Government Securities." *Quarterly Review*. Federal Reserve Bank of New York, Vol. 3 (Summer 1978), pp. 13–20.

Hurley, E. "The Commercial Paper Market." *Federal Reserve Bulletin*, Vol. 63 (June 1977), pp. 525–536.

Jaffe, J. "The Effect of Regulation Changes on Insider Trading." *The Bell Journal of Economics and Management Science* (Spring 1974), pp. 93–121.

Jensen, M. "The Performance of Mutual Funds in the Period 1945–64." *The Journal of Finance* (May 1968), pp. 389–416.

Kraus, A., and H. Stoll. "Price Impacts of Block Trading on the New York Stock Exchange." *The Journal of Finance* (June 1972), pp. 569–588.

Logue, D. "Market Making and the Assessment of Market Efficiency." *Journal of Finance*, Vol. 30 (Mar. 1975).

Mains, N.E. "Risk, the Pricing of Capital Assets, and the Evaluation of Investment Portfolios: Comment." *Journal of Business* (July 1977), pp. 371–384.

Peake, J. "The National Market System." *Financial Analysts Journal*, Vol. 34 (July-Aug. 1978).

Scholes, M. "The Market for Securities: Substitution Versus Price Pressure and the Effects of Information on Share Prices." *Journal of Business* (Apr. 1972), pp. 179–211.

Sharpe, W.F. "Mutual Fund Performance." *Journal of Business* (Jan. 1966).

Smidt, S. "Which Road to An Efficient Stock Market? Implications of the SEC Institutional Investor Study." *Financial Analysts Journal*, Vol. 27 (Sept.-Oct. 1971).

Stoll, H. "The Pricing of Security Dealer Services: An Empirical Study of NASDAQ Stocks." *Journal of Finance* (Sept. 1978(b)).

———. "Regulation of Securities Markets: An Examination of the Effects of Increased Competition." *Monograph Series in Finance and Economics*. New York University, Salomon Brothers Center, Monograph 1979-2. New York: 1979.

———. "The Supply of Dealer Services in Securities Markets." *Journal of Finance* (Sept. 1978(a)).

Tinic, S. "The Economics of Liquidity Services." *Quarterly Journal of Economics*, Vol. 86 (Feb. 1972).

Treynor, J.L. "How to Rate Mutual Fund Performance." *Harvard Business Review* (Jan.-Feb. 1965), pp. 63–75.

West, R. "More on the Effects of Municipal Bond Monopsony." *Journal of Business*, Vol. 39 (Apr. 1966), pp. 305–308.

Zwick, B. "The Market for Corporate Bonds," *Quarterly Review* (Autumn 1977), pp. 27–36. New York: Federal Reserve Bank of New York, 1977.

11

Option Markets

ANDREW RUDD

INTRODUCTION

The widespread acceptance of exchange-traded options is commonly regarded as one of the more significant and successful investment innovations of the 1970s. It is easy to understand this viewpoint. The first organized exchange for option trading, the Chicago Board Options Exchange (CBOE), opened its doors for business in April 1973 with a roster of call options on only 16 common stocks. From this inconspicuous beginning, options trading grew in less than 10 years to a point where in excess of 10,000 stock option contracts on over 350 different common stocks were listed on four U.S. exchanges. In fact, the total number of shares involved in options trading on organized exchanges in the United States has frequently exceeded the number of shares traded on the

New York Stock Exchange (NYSE), even though there are in excess of 1,500 common stocks listed on the NYSE.

Options are also traded on a wide variety of financial instruments other than common stocks, including Treasury bonds, Treasury bond futures, and stock indexes. More remarkable, the acceptance of options has not been restricted to the U.S. investment community; options on various financial instruments trade on exchanges in Toronto, Amsterdam, Sydney, London, and many other places throughout the world. Finally, the development of a robust options theory by academicians and investment analysts had kept pace with, if not surpassed, the growth in options trading itself; it is now virtually impossible to pick up an investment handbook, academic journal, or professional publication without seeing one or more articles on option pricing or option trading strategies.

Although the acceptance of options by both individual and institutional investors has been spectacular, options have implications that go far beyond just being a novel financial contract. Many financial securities either have options associated with them or can be valued in an options theoretic framework. For example, it is not uncommon to use option theory to value the default premium or sinking fund feature associated with risky corporate debt. Fortunately, many of these financial instruments can be analyzed using exactly the same tools as are required for the analysis of listed stock options.

Definition of Option Contracts

Ownership of an option contract simply conveys the *right* (not the obligation) to undertake either the purchase or sale of an underlying asset at or before some specified date. The distinction between right and obligation is important since it differentiates the option contract from other similar instruments, such as forward or future contracts, which legally require the owner to fulfill certain obligations. Of course, the owner of the option contract may wish to complete the transaction if it is economically beneficial, but there is no legal duty to do so.

For example, an option to buy an apartment building in San Francisco conveys the right to purchase a specific piece of real estate (the underlying asset) at a certain price at or before a fixed time. If real estate prices fall, the holder of the option may not wish to complete the transaction, in which case the option expires and becomes worthless. Alternatively, the option holder may think it is beneficial to proceed with the transaction, in which case the holder exercises the option and the seller of the option is obligated to fulfill the requirement of the contract to sell the apartment building.[1] Finally, it is conceivable that the option holder, prior to the fixed ending date of the contract, may find another investor or broker willing to purchase the option contract (i.e., purchase the right to purchase the apartment building at a fixed price at or before a fixed time). One of the innovations of the CBOE was the standardization of listed stock option contracts to promote the secondary trading of options.

---

[1] Notice that there is no requirement that the seller of the option initially own the underlying asset. In this example, however, the ability of the seller to complete the transaction may be questioned if the building is not already owned. On organized exchanges, collateral is collected from sellers of options to prevent default.

The purchase price of the option is frequently called the option premium. The fixed price at which the transaction is completed is called the exercise price or the strike price, and the fixed time is called the expiration date or option maturity. There are two types of option contract: If the option conveys the right to purchase the underlying asset, it is called a call; if the option conveys the right to sell the underlying asset, it is called a put.

An investor who purchases an option is called the buyer or holder and is said to hold the option long. Conversely, an investor who sells an option is called the writer and is said to have sold the option short. One of the innovations of the options market is that it is particularly easy for an investor to go long or short as desired; an investor may wish to purchase options at one time, write options at another time, or buy and write options simultaneously at a third time.

Another important characteristic of the option contract is whether the option can be exercised at any time prior to the expiration date or only at the expiration date. If the option can be exercised at any point during its lifetime, it is called an American option. If the option can be exercised only at maturity, it is called a European option. In fact, all options that trade on organized exchanges, both in the United States and abroad, are American options. Hence, for practical purposes the distinction can be ignored. However, as discussed later in this chapter, theoretical considerations require that the distinction be maintained.

The two types of options are defined as follows:

- An American call is an option to buy a fixed quantity of a given underlying asset at a fixed price until a fixed date.
- An American put is an option to sell a fixed quantity of a given underlying asset at a fixed price until a fixed date.

The underlying asset for the listed stock options traded on the organized exchanges is the common stock of a major corporation. As noted earlier, however, options on other underlying assets are becoming increasingly common. In this chapter the underlying asset is a common stock, unless specifically noted otherwise.

The fixed quantity of the underlying asset referred to in the contract definition is usually 100 shares, although sometimes after the underlying asset undergoes a share split or stock dividend the number of shares optioned may change. Notice the contract specifications do not change after a cash dividend; options traded on the organized exchanges are said to be payout unprotected in that there is no adjustment for cash payouts on the underlying asset.

The complete specification of a general option contract includes seven items:

1 The option type: put or call

2 The name of the underlying asset (common stock)

3 The expiration date

4 The exercise price

5 The number of shares of the underlying asset (common stock) optioned

TABLE 11.1   IBM Calls

| | Expiration Date | | |
Exercise Price	April	July	October
65	35	*	*
70	29⅝	*	*
75	24¾	26	*
80	20½	20½	*
85	15⅛	16¾	*
90	10¾	12⅞	15¼
95	6½	10	12
100	3¼	7⅛	9⅝
110	½	3⅛	5⅜

* No option is offered.

6 The exercise policy: European or American

7 The degree of payout protection

Unless otherwise noted, the organized exchanges set the number of shares at 100, permit exercise prior to maturity (American options), and do not adjust for dividends (payout unprotected).[2] Hence, for listed stock options, investors really need consider only four important items: the option type, the name of the stock, the expiration date, and the exercise price.

Elementary Pricing Relationships

Option exchanges normally establish for each stock six or more standard call and put options that differ only by maturity and exercise price. For example, on a recent date 20 different IBM calls were traded on the CBOE. The exercise prices, expiration dates, and reported closing prices are given in Table 11.1.

The first IBM call has an exercise price of $65, was last traded at $35, and expires in April.[3] It is referred to as the IBM/April/65 call. To purchase this call on 100 shares would cost a total of $3,500 plus commissions; a writer of this call of 100 shares would receive $3,500 less commissions and less any collateral the broker may require to ensure performance of the contract.[4] To purchase the IBM/April/110 call on 100 shares would cost only $50 plus com-

---

[2] Some options do not trade on one of the organized exchanges, but in the so-called over-the-counter (OTC) market. These options are usually payout-protected and European.

[3] Trading in options continues up to 3 P.M. Eastern time on the third Friday in its expiration month.

[4] The collateral is called margin. See A. Rudd and M. Schroeder, "The Calculation of Minimum Margin," *Management Science* (Dec. 1982), pp. 1368–1379, for further details.

missions. In fact, on this day the closing price of IBM was $99 7/8, so the purchase cost of 100 shares was $9,987.50 plus commission. How can one explain these price differences?

The holder of the IBM/April/65 call could exercise it immediately, by paying $65 per share to the writer. For the 100-share contract this would cost $6,500, for which he would receive stock worth $9,987.50, yielding a profit (before commissions) of $3,487.50. Notice that this amount is less than would be obtained by selling the contract in the market; the difference of $12.50 being the value the market places on the right to hold on to the option until expiration. Between the current time and expiration the stock may rise in price, causing an increase in the value of the option contract. The amount of $3,487.50 is called the intrinsic value of the option and the amount of $12.50 the time value of the option.

The IBM/April/110 call will now be examined. The holder would clearly not exercise the option since this action would result in the loss of $110 minus $99 7/8 per share, or $1,012.50 for the 100-share contract. Hence, the intrinsic value of the option is zero, and its time value is the total price of 50 cents. In other words, by market consensus the value of holding the option to expiration in the hope that IBM may trade at one stage above $110 is $50 per contract. Writers are willing to accept $50 now, and purchasers are willing to spend $50 now in a "bet" on the price of IBM on (or before) the expiration of the option. If the IBM price ever rises above $110, the purchaser wins and the writer loses to the tune of the difference between the stock price and the exercise price. By comparison, if the IBM price remains below $110, the call expires worthless and the purchaser loses the original call contract premium of $50, which the writer gains.

Notice that the smallest intrinsic value is zero and occurs when the exercise price is greater than the stock price; in this situation the option is said to be out-of-the-money. When the intrinsic value is positive (i.e., the exercise price is less than the stock price), the option is said to be in-the-money. When the stock price is in the region of the exercise price, the option is said to be at-the-money. Also, the smallest time value is zero and occurs when there is "no life left in the option," that is, at the expiration date when the option premium is equal to its intrinsic value.

The situation for puts is similar. Table 11.2 shows the puts on IBM that traded on the CBOE on a recent date. Only one put with an exercise price of $65 is offered; it is the IBM/April/65 put, but it did not trade during the day. The IBM/April/70 traded, and its last price was 1/16. Hence for a 100-share contract, the put would cost only $6.25. Why such a small price for this put? The answer, of course, is that the exercise of the put would require the holder to deliver the underlying IBM stock to the writer in exchange for the $70 (per share) exercise price. Since the stock closed at almost $100, no investor would immediately exercise the put. In fact, the contract value of $6.25 represents the value of a form of insurance against the possibility that IBM closes beneath $70 prior to the maturity of the option.

The IBM/April/110 put last traded at 10 1/4, or $1,025 for the 100-share contract. Immediate exercise of this put would entail the delivery of IBM stock worth $9,987.50 in return for an aggregate exercise price of $11,000, for a net profit of $1,012.50 per 100-share contract. The holder of the put would there-

TABLE 11.2   IBM Puts

	Expiration Date		
Exercise Price	April	July	October
65	+	*	*
70	1/16	*	*
75	+	1/8	*
80	+	7/16	*
85	1/16	3/4	*
90	1/4	1 13/16	2 15/16
95	15/16	3 1/4	4 3/4
100	2 13/16	5 1/2	7
110	10 1/4	+	12 3/4

⁺ The option did not trade.
* No option is offered.

fore be wealthier by $12.50 (before commissions) if the contract were to be sold on the exchange rather than exercised.

As before, the value of the contract if exercised (zero for the IBM/April/75 and $1,012.50 for the IBM/April/110) is called the intrinsic value of the option, and the difference between the option price and the intrinsic value is called the time value. Puts are in-the-money when they have positive intrinsic value and out-of-the-money when their intrinsic value is zero. They are said to be at-the-money whenever the exercise price is very close to the underlying asset price.

These relationships are shown graphically in Figure 11.1 The top panel plots the IBM calls with $65 and $110 exercise prices. The lower panel plots the puts with $70 and $110 exercise prices. Several important points are evident from the figure. First, the time value for different April calls (or puts) need not be the same. For example, investors are only willing to pay (for the 100-share contract) $6.25 time value for the April/70 put, but $12.50 for the April/110 put.[5]

Next, the longer the time to maturity, the greater the time value of both the puts and calls. This follows directly from the fact that the longer the time to maturity, the more likely the underlying asset will move to a price where exercise is (more) beneficial. For example, the IBM calls with exercise prices of $100 are all just out-of-the-money. The July options have three months more than the April options during which the IBM price can increase, driving the call in-the-money. The additional $3 7/8 ($7 1/8 − $3 1/4) per share represents the consensus value that market participants place on this three-month period. Notice also that the value of the additional three-month period from July to

---

[5] The largest time value for the April puts is associated with the April/100 put. For a 100-share contract on this option, investors are willing to pay 100 times [$2 13/16 − (100 − 99 7/8) = $2.6875] or $268.75.

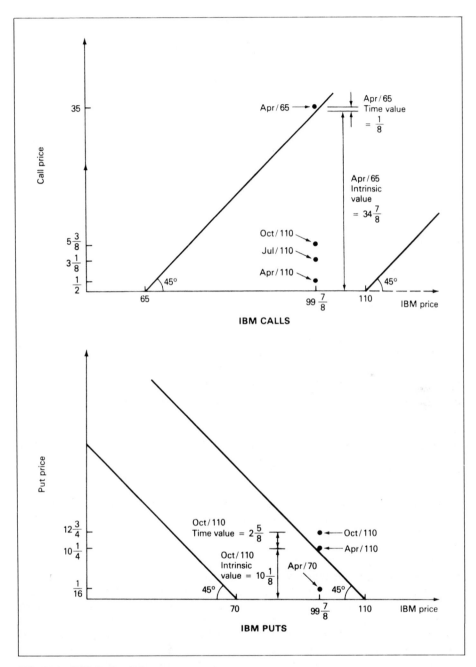

FIG. 11.1 IBM Option Prices

October is only valued at $2 1/2 per share, hence for the $100 exercise price options, the market places greater value on the first three months rather than the second. For the calls with $90 exercise prices, however, the reverse is true; purchasing the July rather than April maturity option costs only an incremental $2 1/8 per obtained share, but purchasing the October rather than July maturity option costs $2 3/8 incremental per optioned share.

Finally, a curious anomaly shows up with the $80 exercise price calls, where both the April and July options cost $20 1/2. If this is really true,[6] why would anybody purchase the April option or anybody write the July option? Purchasers would prefer the July call and writers the April call, leading to an imbalance of supply and demand.

A large part of understanding options has to do with isolating the important factors that influence option prices and evaluating an option's time value. One particular method for pricing options is described in detail in the second part of this chapter; however, even at this stage a series of important relationships governing option prices can be enumerated:

1 Both put and call prices are the sum of two components: intrinsic value and time value.

2 A call's (or put's) intrinsic value is the amount by which the stock price exceeds the exercise price (or exercise price exceeds the stock price).

3 Time value for options with some life prior to maturity is always positive; at the expiration date, it is zero. Time value increases with time to maturity, and for any given maturity it tends to be largest for the at-the-money options.

Simple Strategies and Their Profitability

The easiest way to understand the impact of options is to examine various strategies when the options are held to expiration. This analysis is more straight-forward than permitting the closing of the option position prior to expiration because, as noted in the previous section, at expiration call prices are simply the amount by which the stock price exceeds the exercise price.

Figure 11.2 shows the profits that accrue to purchasers of the IBM/April/100 call option. The minimum price line shows the minimum price of the call as a function of the IBM price at expiration; it is zero up to the point where IBM trades at $100, and increases $1 for each $1 increase in the stock price beyond $100. As indicated above, it is the potential for profitable investment (occurring for the call when the stock price exceeds the exercise price) that forms the basis for option valuation. In order to gain this potential, the buyer pays the call price to the writer, who thereby places himself in the position for a potential loss or contingent obligation. The obligation is the delivery of the stock to the option purchaser at the fixed exercise price, contingent on the stock trading at a greater price.

This analysis indicates that the profits to the call writer are just the mirror image about the horizontal of the call purchaser's profit. The writer's profit as

---

[6] The likely explanations for these prices are that (a) one is more timely than the other or (b) there was an error in reporting the correct closing prices.

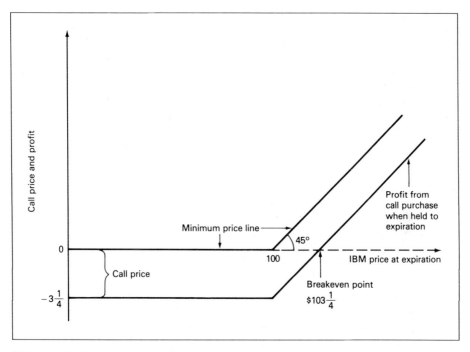

FIG. 11.2 Profits From Purchasing the Apr/100 Call

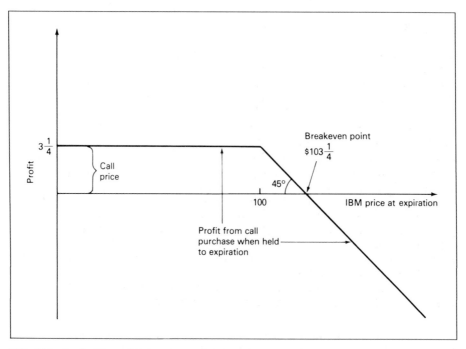

FIG. 11.3 Profits From Writing the Apr/100 Call

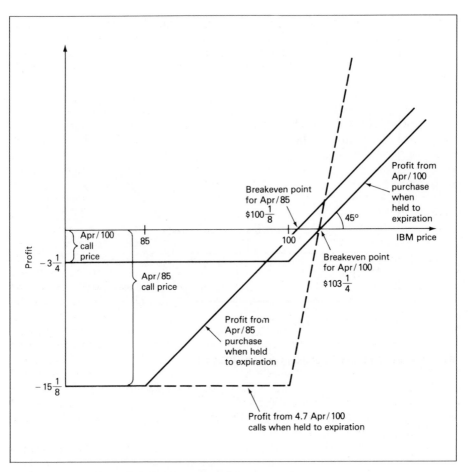

FIG. 11.4 Profits From Call Purchase Strategies

a function of the stock price is given in Figure 11.3. Notice that the positions net each other out; a long and short position in the same call has neither risk nor profit potential. For this reason investment in options is a zero sum game; option purchasers profit at the expense of option writers, and vice versa.

Figure 11.4 shows two variants on the simple strategy of purchasing calls. First, notice the effect of changing the exercise price. The lower the exercise price, the greater the minimum price line for every stock price at expiration. In other words, the lower the exercise price, the larger the potential payoff for every stock price. However, the increased payoff potential comes with a higher initial call price, hence the profits for low stock prices are reduced while the profits for large stock prices are increased. This is made clear in the figure where the profit line for the April/85 call is superimposed over the profit line for the April/100 call, shown previously in Figure 11.2.

The second variant of the simple strategy is the impact of purchasing more than one call contract. Of course, if the call expires out-of-the-money, the

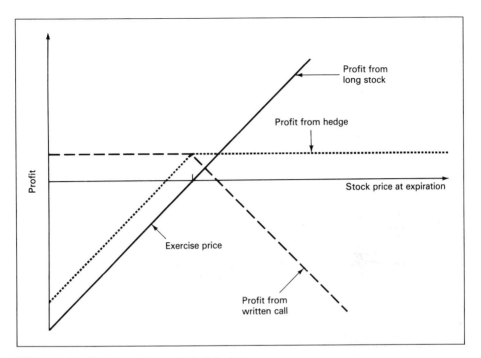

FIG. 11.7 Profits From a Covered Call Hedge

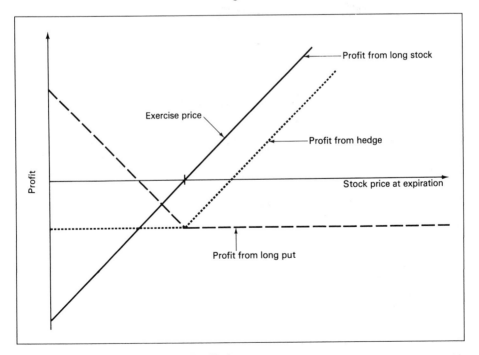

FIG. 11.8 Profits From a Covered Put Hedge

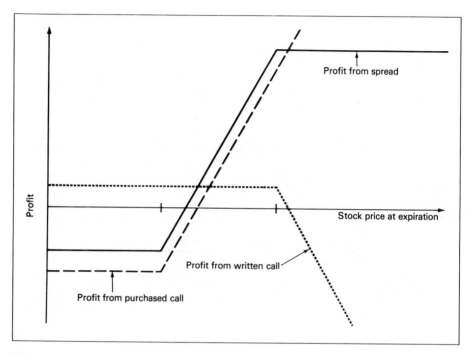

FIG. 11.9 Profits From a Call Spread

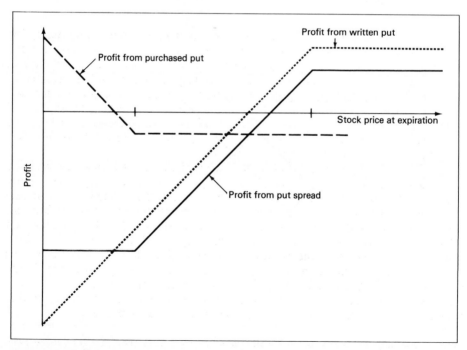

FIG. 11.10 Profits From a Put Spread

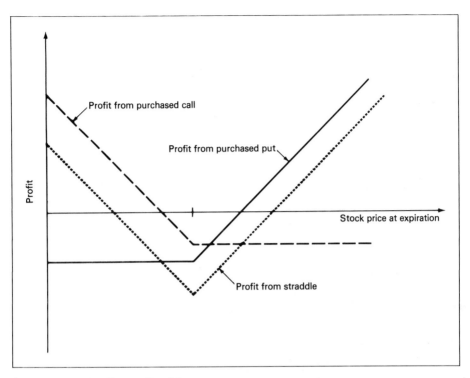

FIG. 11.11   Profits From a Straddle

Figures 11.9 and 11.10 show two representative versions of another option strategy known as a spread. An option spread is a portfolio of calls (or puts) on the same underlying asset where profits on one or more calls (or puts) offset losses on the other calls (or puts). There are an almost endless variety of spreads, each seemingly with a graphic name, designed to capture some part of the stock return distribution.[7] Figure 11.9 shows a spread where calls of identical maturity are held; the call with the larger exercise price is written and the call with the smaller exercise price is purchased. Figure 11.10 shows a similar spread, but now using put options.

The final strategies introduced here are called combinations. A combination is a portfolio containing puts and calls on the same underlying asset, where the options are either all purchased or all written. The most common combination is called a straddle, which contains a purchased put and a purchased call where both options have the same exercise price and same maturity. The profit diagram for a straddle is shown in Figure 11.11, and appears like a letter V. If the stock price remains close to the common exercise price, then the investor shows losses, with the maximum loss equal to the sum of the option prices. If the stock price jumps considerably from the exercise price in either direction, however, then the investor can make a profit when one option ends up in-the-money and the other ends up out-of-the-money (and worthless).

---

[7] See, e.g., R. Jarrow and A. Rudd, *Option Pricing* (Homewood, Ill.: Dow Jones-Irwin, 1983), for further details.

TABLE 11.3   Cash Flows to the Arbitrage Portfolio

		Cash Flow at Maturity			
		$S_T \leq K$ ($S_T = \$50$)		$S_T > K$ ($S_T = \$150$)	
Portfolio	Initial Cash Flow				
1. Long call	$-C_0$ ($-\$3\frac{1}{2}$)	0	($\$0$)	$S_T - K$	($\$50$)
2. Long stock	$-S_0$ ($-\$100$)	S_T	($\$0$)	S_T	($\$150$)
Long put	$-P_0$ ($-\$2\frac{1}{2}$)	$K - S_T$	($\$50$)	0	($\$0$)
Loan of KB_0	$+KB_0$ ($+\$99$)	$-K$	($-\$100$)	$-K$	($-\$100$)
Total	$KB_0 - P_0 - S_0$ ($-\$3\frac{1}{2}$)	0	($\$0$)	$S_T - K$	($+\$50$)

These simple strategies show some of the virtuosity of the option contract. The dominant characteristic by far of an option is that the payoff can be molded to suit the preferences of the investor. The strategies in this section show that highly nonlinear payoff diagrams, which are quite unlike the payoff diagrams for other assets, can be constructed.

Put/Call Parity

In this section the relationship between put and call prices is explored in more detail. For the sake of simplicity, assume that the options are European (i.e., they cannot be exercised prior to maturity) and the underlying asset pays no cash dividends prior to the expiration date of the options.[8] The technique used to prove the result is called arbitrage: If two portfolios have exactly the same payoffs for all future states of the world, then they must have the same price now. If not, then the act of arbitrage would force the two prices to be identical, as investors purchase one portfolio (the "cheap" portfolio) while simultaneously selling the other (the "expensive" portfolio).

First, C_0, P_0, and S_0 are defined to be the initial (time zero) prices of a call, put, and underlying stock, respectively. Similarly, C_T, P_T, and S_T are the three prices at the maturity of the options (time T). Let K be the common exercise price of the options and let B_0 be the initial price of a zero-coupon, riskless bond that delivers $1 at time T.

For example, let $S_0 = \$100$, $K = \$100$, $P_0 = \$2\ 1/2$, and $C_0 = \$3\ 1/2$. If the maturity of the option is exactly one month away and the interest rate is one percent per month, then the initial price of the zero-coupon, riskless bond is $B_0 = \$0.99$.

Consider two portfolios. The first is a long call, and the second is composed of a long stock, a long put, and a loan of KB_0 (i.e., the present value of the exercise price payable at option maturity). Table 11.3 shows the cash flow to these two portfolios. There are two cases at possible maturity: (1) The stock

---

[8] These assumptions can easily be eliminated at the cost of more complex algebra. See Jarrow and Rudd, note 7 *op. cit.*, for further details.

price ends up below the exercise price (i.e., the call is out-of-the-money and the put is in-the-money); and (2) the stock price ends up above the exercise price (i.e., the call is in-the-money and the put is out-of-the-money).

Table 11.3 shows the values of the two portfolios in these two situations. For the numerical example, the two values are $S_T = \$50$ and $S_T = \$150$. As is obvious from the table, the dollar payoffs from the portfolios are the same, as, indeed, are the payoffs when written in symbols. Arbitrage, therefore, ensures that the protfolios must have the same initial price, which is $3 1/2 = \$100 + 2 1/2 - 99$. In symbols, this put/call parity equation is given by

$$C_0 = S_0 + P_0 - KB_0$$

In words, the call price is equal to the stock price plus the put price less the present value of the exercise price. If this relationship did not hold, say $C_O > S_O + P_O - KB_O$, then, at least under these assumptions, the call could be written and portfolio 2 purchased (obtain loan then purchase stock and put) to gain risk-free profits.

This put/call parity theorem justifies the intuitive feeling that the call is a "levered stock position, with insurance." The stock holding and loan combine to give the levered stock position, and the put provides the insurance since it eliminates losses should the stock price fall. Moreover the theorem shows that the put and call prices cannot get too far "out of line." If they do, then arbitrage may be possible to force them back into their natural relationship.[9] This observation underlies the strategies of conversion, which are described in detail later in the chapter.

Exchange-Traded Options

In the future, when historians analyze the securities markets over the last quarter of this century, one recurring theme is bound to be the rapid proliferation of new financial instruments. Exchange-traded options are certainly a major part of this proliferation. To complete this introduction on options markets, the major option contracts which are traded on options markets in the United States are listed following. To some extent this is a thankless task, since the list will surely be outdated by the time this manuscript is published. Nevertheless, even this "dated" listing of the wide variety of option contracts provides a useful perspective on the growth of options trading.

The following categories of underlying assets on which the important options are traded can be isolated:

1 Common stocks

2 Stock indexes

3 Fixed income securities

4 Foreign currencies

5 Futures contracts (both commodity and financial)

---

[9] Beware that certain assumptions which are not true in the real world have been made. Without these assumptions the put/call parity theorem becomes more complex, and there is not necessarily any unique relationship between puts and calls.

The characteristics of the options within these five asset categories are discussed in turn. Later in this chapter the trading strategies associated with these options are discussed.

Common Stocks. Options on common stocks were originally listed on the CBOE, which was formed for the purpose of trading stock options. In addition to the CBOE, stock options are now traded on the American Stock Exchange (AMEX), the Philadelphia Stock Exchange, and the Pacific Stock Exchange. The relative importance of the four exchanges is as follows:

	Optionable Stocks (Approx.)	*Approximate Percentage*			
		Call Volume	*Put Volume*	*Call Open Interest* [10]	*Put Open Interest*
CBOE	140	50	50.0	50.0	55
AMEX	100	25	30.0	30.0	30
Philadelphia	80	10	12.5	12.5	10
Pacific	60	10	7.5	7.5	5

In total, average daily option volume is in the region of 100,000 to 600,000 contracts, which represents approximately 40 to 70 percent of the daily volume of trading on the NYSE.

Stock Indexes. Options on two stock indexes are currently traded. The indexes are the CBOE 100, which is traded on the CBOE, and the Major Market Index (MMI), which is traded on the AMEX. Both option contracts are of comparatively recent origin; the CBOE 100 contract first traded on March 11, 1983 and the MMI contract on April 29, 1983.

The CBOE 100 index is a market capitalization weighted index formed from 100 stocks on which options are traded on the CBOE. Because of its construction, it resembles quite closely the S&P 500 and the NYSE composite indexes, and it is not dissimilar to many institutional portfolios. For this reason, options on the CBOE 100 may potentially be very useful for hedging market risk in institutional portfolios.

The MMI, on the other hand, is constructed to perform like the Dow Jones Industrial Average (DJIA). It is composed of an equal number of shares in 20 stocks (15 of which also appear in the DJIA); effectively, this construction method causes the stocks to be weighted by their price. Since the DJIA is the index which many individual investors pay most attention to, it is thought that the MMI will become a vehicle for hedging by individuals of market moves as measured by the DJIA.

Fixed-Income Securities. Both the AMEX and the CBOE trade options on U.S. government fixed-income securities. These options are usually referred

---

[10] The open interest represents the number of option contracts outstanding at any particular time.

to as interest rate options, since trading in these options represents a strategy with respect to interest rates.

The AMEX has two forms of contracts: one on U.S. Treasury notes with a $20,000 principal value and one on 13-week U.S. Treasury bills with $200,000 principal value. The Treasury note options have a specific Treasury note as the underlying asset; in May 1983, the underlying notes for the three option contracts trading were the 13 3/4 percent of 1992, the 10 1/2 percent of 1992, and the 10 1/2 percent of 1993.

The CBOE also has two different forms of interest rate options; both have specific U.S. Treasury bonds as specific underlying assets, but one is for $100,000 principal value and the other for $20,000 principal value. In May 1983, the specific underlying assets for the contracts were the 14 percent of 2011 and the 10 3/8 percent of 2012.

There is a general feeling that all the interest rate options contracts have been something of a disappointment. Daily volume is low, as is the contract open interest. There appears little doubt that the major location of option trading to hedge interest rate risk is on the Chicago Board of Trade where the Treasury bond futures options are traded.

Foreign Currencies. In December 1982, the Philadelphia Stock Exchange started trading options on the British pound sterling. In only five months, demand was such that the exchange could list five contracts; British pounds, Swiss francs, deutsche marks, Canadian dollars, and Japanese yen.

The contracts appear to be valuable for some financial institutions and corporations. However, volume, and hence liquidity, is still comparatively small, so the effectiveness of the option contracts for hedging currency risk is still not proven.

Futures Contracts. The Chicago Board of Trade, the Chicago Mercantile Exchange, the New York Futures Exchange, the Commodity Exchange Inc. (COMEX), and the Coffee, Sugar and Cocoa Exchange all trade options. The most important option contracts appear to be the Treasury bond futures options contract (traded on the Chicago Board of Trade) and the two stock index futures options contracts (traded on the New York Futures Exchange and the Chicago Mercantile Exchange). The COMEX trades a gold option, while the Coffee, Sugar and Cocoa Exchange has a sugar option. Neither of these two options has a particularly large volume.

An option on a future is conceptually the same as an option on any other asset. The only thing to remember is that the exercise of an option on a future causes a futures contract to be delivered, rather than, for example, a share of common stock. Having the future as the underlying asset rather than the actual asset is a significant advantage when there is no (public) market in the actual asset. This is the case with stock indexes and assets. For example, stock indexes are a composite of their constituent securities, hence to buy or sell the index one has to buy or sell the constituents, since there is no market for the indexes themselves. There is a market for Treasury bonds, but it is a telephone or over-the-counter market between large dealers and the value of a single Treasury bond is not easy to find. For these assets where no (public) market exists, a

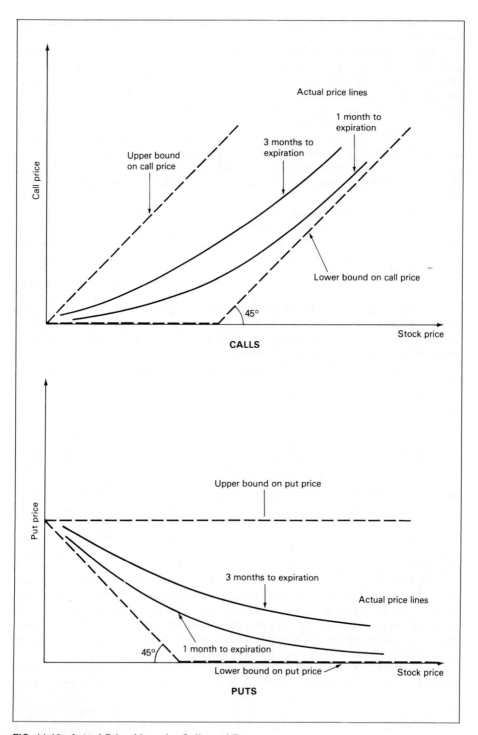

FIG. 11.12 Actual Price Lines for Calls and Puts

futures market occasionally thrives. This is certainly true for the stock indexes and Treasury bonds.

Hence, pricing and trading the underlying asset future is easier than pricing and trading the actual underlying asset. This makes certain strategies (such as hedging where the underlying asset is traded in conjunction with the option) far more effective with the futures option than the actuals option.

OPTION VALUATION

When options are held to expiration, it is fairly easy to perform simple analyses of option strategies. Options, however, have different expiration dates, hence it is not always realistic to invoke the assumption of holding to expiration. This leads to the need to develop a pricing model for options at every point in time prior to maturity. Several models have been developed for option pricing, but all are fairly complex mathematically.

This section describes the first important approach to option pricing. It was developed in 1973 by Professors Fischer Black and Myron Scholes of Stanford University.[11] Although other models have been developed since that attempt either to correct perceived deficiences or to increase applicability, the Black-Scholes formula retains a substantial following among fund managers, brokers, and option market makers. Before examining the model in detail, it is helpful first to review briefly how option prices should behave prior to maturity and then to enumerate the factors which influence option prices.

The Actual Price Line

The price of a call (put) at expiration should equal its intrinsic value, namely the excess of the stock price over the exercise price (the exercise price over the stock price). In fact, an American option must be priced at all times no less than its intrinsic value, which forms a lower bound on the option's price since it can be exercised for this amount at any time. In addition, prior to maturity the option will be priced above this lower bound by an amount equal to the time value. How large can the time value get?

Certainly, one upper bound on the option value is the stock price for the call and the exercise price for the put, since in both cases these prices represent the maximum possible payoffs. Hence, option prices must lie within this region at all times. Figure 11.12 shows the regions for both puts and calls together with typical actual price lines for an option at two dates prior to maturity. The actual price line indicates how the price of the option will behave as a function of the stock price at one point prior to maturity. As time to maturity decreases, the actual price line moves down, until at maturity it "collapses" into the lower bound on the option price, its intrinsic value.

An interesting implication of the actual price line is the computation of the change in option prices for a small change in the underlying asset price. If the

---

[11] The formula was originally published in Fischer Black and Myron Scholes, "The Pricing of Options and Corporate Liabilities," *Journal of Political Economics* (May 1973), pp. 637–659.

stock moves a small amount over a very short time interval (so the actual price line does not move toward the option lower price bound), then the option price will move along the actual price line. The crucial measurement showing the effect of the stock on the option is the slope of the actual price line; for deep out-of-the-money calls the slope is almost zero (indicating little option price change for a given stock movement), while for deep in-the-money calls, the slope is almost one (indicating the option price changes almost a dollar for a dollar with the stock).

The slope of the actual price line is frequently called the riskless hedge ratio or the option delta. Its application to hedging is clear: If a number of shares of the underlying asset equal to the slope of the actual price line are purchased for every call written (or every put purchased), then the hedge will be riskless over small intervals of time and for small stock price changes. To see this, consider a call hedge set up in the specified manner. There are two interesting cases to consider. First, suppose the stock price increases. Then the stock component of the hedge will increase by the slope of the actual price line times the stock price increase, which is exactly the loss on the written call. Similarly, if the stock price declines, the loss on the stock component of the hedge is offset by the gain on the call component. In short, the hedge is riskless! Notice that a riskless hedge requires a holding of a greater number of options than shares of stock since the slope of the actual price line is less than one in absolute magnitude.

A related concept to the option delta is the option elasticity, which measures the rate of return on the option for a given rate of return on the stock. The formula for the elasticity is $(\Delta O/O)/(\Delta S/S)$ where ΔO is the small change in the option price resulting from a small change, ΔS, in the stock price, and O and S are the option and stock prices, respectively. Hence $\Delta O/O$ is the rate of return on the option and $\Delta S/S$ is the rate of return on the stock. The elasticity can be rewritten $(\Delta O/\Delta S)(S/O)$, where $\Delta O/\Delta S$ is the slope of the actual price line, or option delta, and S/O is the ratio of stock and option prices. It can be shown that the option elasticity is greater than one in absolute magnitude (positive for calls, negative for puts). Hence, although the absolute price change for options will be less than the price change for the stock, the absolute rate of return for options will be greater than for stocks.

Factors Influencing Option Prices

Several characteristics of an option contract are listed in the first section of this chapter. Many of these characteristics influence the option's value, however, there are several other factors that also influence option value. The important factors can be separated into three groups by the element they depend on:

1 The underlying asset
2 The option contract
3 The economy in general

Factors That Depend on the Underlying Asset. Included within this group are the price, the volatility, and the dividend policy of the underlying asset.

Clearly the larger the price, the larger the call value and the smaller the put value, since there is a larger potential payoff from the call and a smaller payoff from the put.

The impact of the volatility of the underlying asset is a little more complex. In general, the payoff from the option depends on the distribution of the underlying asset at the expiration of the option. The greater the range of underlying asset prices at expiration, the greater the probability and extent to which the option will be in-the-money and the greater the potential payoff from the option. Notice that, although a greater range of prices will also increase the likelihood that the option ends up out-of-the-money, this is not of such great importance; if the option ends up a little out-of-the-money or a lot out-of-the-money, its value will still be zero. The concept of the "range of prices" can be made more precise with statistical theory, but it is sufficient here to think of the important measure as being the variability or volatility in the evolution of the stock price between the current date and expiration.

The final factor in this group is the dividend policy of the underlying asset. If the option is European and payout protected, the dividend policy has no effect. For other options, however, there are two distinct effects from the dividend policy: First, cash dividends cause the stock price to fall, which increases put prices and decreases call prices. Second, cash payouts can effect the exercise policy of American options. This latter effect is more complicated to analyze and requires some advanced techniques. Current research seems to indicate, however, that the effect is not of major importance.

Factors That Depend on the Option Contract. The principal factors in this category are the expiration date and the exercise price of the contract; however, all the characteristics mentioned earlier are relevant. For American options, a longer time to maturity implies greater flexibility of the contract and thus increases its value. Increasing the exercise price decreases the potential payoff from the call and increases the potential payoff from the put. Hence, an increase in the exercise price will increase put prices and decrease call prices.

Factors That Depend on the Economy in General. The most important of these factors is the risk-free interest rate. The interest rate enters from the need for discounting future cash flows, in particular the exercise price of the option. Since an increase in the interest rate decreases the present value of the exercise price, there is a tendency for call prices to increase and for put prices to decrease. However, the effect can be more complicated in certain situations; without further assumptions, a definitive conclusion as to the effects of interest rates cannot be reached.

The Black-Scholes Formula

The idea of the riskless hedge introduced earlier was used by Black and Scholes to develop a formula for valuing European options on non-dividend paying underlying assets. Their insight was to use the hedge, instantaneously rebalanced, so that it was riskless over the entire period until maturity of the option. Since the hedge was riskless it should earn the riskless rate on the funds invested.

This fact together with some high-powered mathematics describing the movement of stocks in continuous time were sufficient to derive their formula.

The Black-Scholes call valuation formula is:[12]

$$C_0 = S_0 N(d_1) - K B_0 N(d_2)$$

where:
$\quad\quad C_0 =$ current call value
$\quad\quad S_0 =$ current call price
$\quad\quad K =$ exercise price
$\quad\quad B_0 =$ price of a riskless zero coupon bond that matures at the expiration of the option with value \$1
$\quad\quad N(d) =$ value of the cumulative standard normal distribution function. This value represents the probability that the value of d or less will be drawn from the distribution
$\quad\quad d_1 = [\log(S_0/KB_0) + \tfrac{1}{2}\,\sigma^2 T]/\sigma\sqrt{T}$
$\quad\quad d_2 = d_1 - \sigma\sqrt{T}$
$\quad\quad \log(\ ) =$ natural logarithm of $(\ )$
$\quad\quad T =$ maturity of the option
$\quad\quad \sigma =$ volatility of the underlying asset

The formula looks undeniably complex. Fortunately, its interpretation is rather straightforward. The first term, $S_0 N(d_1)$, is the expected value of the stock price given that it exceeds the exercise price (i.e., given that the option ends up in-the-money) times the probability of the stock price exceeding the exercise price. Figure 11.13 shows the probability distribution of the stock price at the expiration date. The shaded area represents that part of the probability distribution which exceeds the exercise price. Hence, the first term is the expected value of the shaded area times the probability of being in the shaded area. The second term subtracts off the cost of exercising the option, namely the present value of the exercise price times the probability that the option ends up in-the-money.

With the exception of the two terms involving the normal distribution, $N(d_1)$ and $N(d_2)$, the remainder of the formula is quite simple. In fact, even the two terms from the normal distribution can be approximated very easily so that the formula can be computed on a hand-held calculator.[13] Notice that all the expected variables appear in the formula: the current stock price, S_0; the volatility of the underlying asset, σ; the exercise price, K (in fact, the relevant term is the present value of the exercise price, KB_0); the time to maturity, T; and the riskless interest rate, which is expressed here as the price of a riskless zero coupon bond, B_0.

It is possible to take derivatives of the formula with respect to these variables to discover their impact on option prices. The exact formulas are not repeated here,[14] although it is comforting to report the signs of the derivatives:

---

[12] For a straightforward derivation see Jarrow and Rudd, note 7 *op. cit.*, Chapter 7.

[13] For a listing of the code for the HP67, see Rubinstein & Cox, *Option Markets* (Manuscript dated December 1978, to be published by Prentice-Hall).

[14] See, e.g., Jarrow and Rudd, note 7 *op. cit.*, Chapter 9.

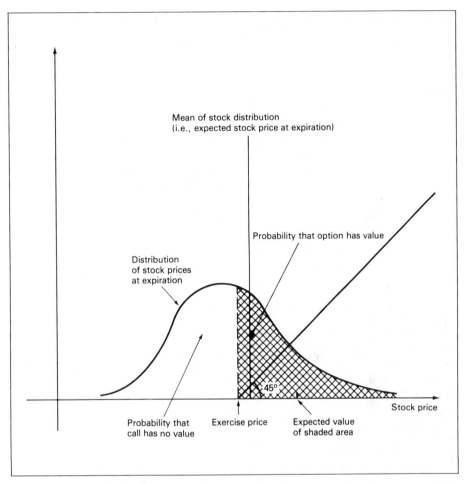

FIG. 11.13 Distribution of Stock Prices at Expiration and the Value of a Call

Effect of stock price	$\partial C_0/\partial S_0 > 0$
Effect of exercise price	$\partial C_0/\partial K < 0$
Effect of time to maturity	$\partial C_0/\partial T > 0$
Effect of volatility	$\partial C_0/\partial \sigma > 0$
Effect of interest rates	$\partial C_0/\partial r > 0$

These results are exactly as anticipated, including the effect of interest rates, about which there is some ambiguity without resorting to a model such as the Black-Scholes formula.

An Illustration of Black-Scholes Usage

As an illustration of the formula's usage, reexamine the IBM/April/100 call listed in Table 11.1. A word of warning is in order: The formula applies exactly only to European payout protected calls, but listed options are American payout unprotected. In fact, IBM did not pay a cash dividend between the date of the prices listed in Table 11.1 and the expiration of the April options, hence the issue of dividend payments and payout protection does not arise; therefore, the formula can be applied without fear of bias from this source. However, the pricing of an American option as if it were a European option is far more controversial. This point is discussed in more detail in the next section, but for now it is worth pointing out that in this case distinction is not important.

As indicated above, five inputs are needed. These are:

$$S_0 = \$99.875$$
$$K = 100$$
$$T = 0.08 \text{ years}$$
$$r = 0.085$$
$$\sigma = 0.255$$

The first two of these inputs require no further explanation. The call had exactly four weeks of its life remaining, which has been converted to years. The interest rate on large certificates of deposit was approximately 8 1/2 percent, which has been taken as a proxy for the interest rate. The last input, the volatility for IBM, is the most problematic since it is not directly observable in the market.

There are a number of ways that the volatility can be obtained. The most common method is to compute the standard deviation of a history of (frequently 180 daily) logarithmic stock returns. Another method is to use the implicit volatility from a prior day; this is the volatility which "solves" the formula, given that it is the only unknown. There are several good analyses of these different methods in the literature.[15] Finally, several option services supply estimates of volatility for the various underlying stocks; the estimate from one of these is used here.

It follows from these inputs that (under continuous compounding) the price of the zero coupon bond is:

$$B_0 = e^{-rt} = e^{-0.0068} = \$0.99$$

Further:

$$KB_0 = 99$$
$$T = 0.28$$
$$\sigma\sqrt{T} = 0.07$$

---

[15] *Ibid.*

$$\sigma^2 T = 0.005$$
$$S_0/KB_0 = 1.009$$
$$\log(S_0/KB_0) = 0.009$$

Now d_1 and d_2 can be computed as:

$$d_1 = 0.16$$
$$d_2 = 0.088$$

From a table of the cumulative standard normal distribution, it is easy to find that:

$$N(d_1) = 0.5636$$
$$N(d_2) = 0.5351$$

Hence, the Black-Scholes call price is:

$$C_0 = (99.875)(0.5636) - (99)(0.5351)$$
$$= 56.29 - 52.97$$
$$= \$3.32$$

This compares with the reported price of $3.25. If the inputs are to be believed, then the option is slightly undervalued. It probably does not represent a purchase opportunity, however, since commissions and other transactions costs (in particular, the bid-ask spread) are frequently much greater than the mispricing.

Limitations of the Black-Scholes Model

Such an elegant formula as that derived by Black-Scholes is not obtained without making some fairly stringent assumptions. The most important of these are as follows:

1 The markets for options and common stock are frictionless.
2 The risk-free rate is constant over the life of the option.
3 The underlying stock pays no dividends.
4 The distribution of stock prices at the end of any finite time interval is lognormal with constant variance.

Assumption 1 is a standard assumption in finance theory. Essentially, it guarantees that every investor can construct his desired portfolio without cost. In reality, of course, it is not true for all investors, but it may not be so far in error for brokers and large dealers that prices may be set *as if* the assumption held.

Assumption 2 is a convenience which can be removed at the expense of greater mathematical sophistication.[16] In fact, the call price is not too sensitive to interest rates, and since rates over the maximum nine-month holding period of listed stock options are not too variable (at least not as variable as the stock price), it is questionable whether the generalized formulas are worth the incremental effort.

Assumption 3 is invoked for two reasons: First, the payment of cash dividends causes the stock price to change and (at least for the theoretical analysis) some model is required to explain the change. Second, there is a strong interaction between the early exercise of American options and dividend payments.[17] For example, for sufficiently large dividends (causing a large price drop in the stock on the ex dividend date), it may pay call holders to exercise their options early to capture the dividend. For practical purposes, what is required is a formula for American options on dividend paying stocks. Unfortunately, general models to value such options are quite complex, hence for simplicity a number of approximations are frequently made which are based on the Black-Scholes formula. The most common approximation is to apply the formula as it stands, but using as input the stock price less the present value of any dividends anticipated prior to the maturity of the option. It can be shown that this approximation is reasonable under many circumstances, but that it does not capture the entire dividend/early exercise effect.[18]

Assumption 4 comes in two parts. First, the distribution of stock prices has to be lognormal; and, second, it has a constant variance. As may be expected, there have been a number of option pricing formulas developed since 1973 that have been based on alternative (and usually more complex) specifications of the underlying stock distribution.[19] None of these formulas has achieved widespread acceptance in the investment community, and it is doubtful if they provide much benefit when applied to listed stock options. In contrast, however, there is good reason to believe that interest rate options and foreign currency options could be more accurately analyzed with the generalized models than with the Black-Scholes formula.

Put Option Valuation

The pricing of European puts on non-dividend paying stocks is no more difficult than pricing calls. Both the put/call parity theorem and the Black-Scholes formula apply in this situation, so it is trivial to solve for the put value. For example,

$$P_0 = C_0 - S_0 + KB_0$$

---

[16] Professor Robert Merton has derived a formula with stochastic interest rates; see his article, "Theory of Rational Option Pricing," *Bell Journal of Economics and Management Science* (Spring 1973), pp. 141–183.

[17] A detailed theoretical analysis is provided in Jarrow and Rudd, note 7 *op. cit.*

[18] *Ibid.*

[19] For details on several of these models, see Jarrow and Rudd, note 7 *op. cit.*

and

$$C_0 = S_0 N(d_1) - K B_0 N(d_2)$$

so

$$\begin{aligned} P_0 &= S_0(N(d_1) - 1) - K B_0(N(d_2) - 1) \\ &= S_0 N(-d_1) - K B_0 N(-d_2) \end{aligned}$$

where the last step follows from the well-known relationship that $N(d_1) + N(-d_1) = 1$ and $N(d_2) + N(-d_2) = 1$.

As with the call formula, the derivatives of the put formula can be evaluated with respect to the inputs. These are:

Effect of stock price	$\partial P_0/\partial S_0 < 0$
Effect of exercise price	$\partial P_0/\partial K > 0$
Effect of time to maturity	$\partial P_0/\partial T \geqslant 0$
Effect of volatility	$\partial P_0/\partial \sigma > 0$
Effect of interest rates	$\partial P_0/\partial r < 0$

The only surprise among these derivatives is the effect of increasing the time to maturity. For the Black-Scholes European put formula, increasing the time to maturity has no single effect on the put price. This is slightly disconcerting since it was argued previously that for an American put increasing the time to maturity unambiguously increases the put price.

This difference illustrates one of the shortcomings of the European put formula: In many circumstances it is not a very good approximation to the American put price. Certainly it is a worse approximation than the European call formula is for American call prices. One reason for this is that there are more occasions when the American put should be exercised early. One extreme example is when the stock price drops to zero before the expiration of the put. There is no point in waiting until expiration to exercise, since the maximum possible payoff from the put (namely the exercise price) can be gained immediately.

As with the call formula, there are several approximations that can be used to adjust the formula for cash dividends. However, a more satisfactory approach, which accounts for both cash dividend payments and the biases caused by early exercise, is to use a *numerical* method for evaluating the American put price. The standard numerical procedure is based on an article by Professors Cox, Ross, and Rubinstein and called the binomial method.[20] It is easily programmed on a computer and is widely used.

---

[20] J. Cox et al., "Option Pricing: A Simplified Approach," *Journal of Financial Economics* (Sept. 1979), pp. 229–263. See also Jarrow and Rudd, note 7 *op. cit.*, Chapter 13.

How Well Does the Option Pricing Model Work?

Much effort has been expended testing the Black-Scholes call pricing formula and its generalizations. However, there has been far less work than one would suspect given the wide usage of the models. (There has been much less effort directed toward testing the option formulas than, for example, the Capital Asset Pricing Model.) Further, there has been virtually no empirical research on the pricing of puts.

In general, the empirical work has suggested two major findings:

1 Overall, the option pricing models work exceedingly well. The *average* difference between the market and the model prices over all options has tended to be a few cents. Moreover, when the model has indicated that the option was overvalued (or undervalued), then writing (or buying) the option has tended to be profitable.

2 There appear to be a number of systematic biases between the market and model prices. For example, out-of-the-money calls tend to have market prices somewhat higher than predicted by the model. However, the exact nature of the biases and their magnitude is still the matter of some debate.

OPTION TRADING STRATEGIES

In this last part, the uses of options in trading strategies are discussed. As with any asset class, a great deal of information about the return characteristics of options can be found by examining the historical performance of a representative index. However, since options have only short lives and may change considerably over very short time intervals (e.g., from in-the-money to out-of-the-money), the construction of a representative option index is not easy. Not only is such an index desirable for learning about the nature of option returns, it is required for the systematic analysis of an option portfolio manager.

The next topic in this part is a more detailed description of how options impact an equity portfolio. This is currently an area of increasing academic interest and the subject of a number of recent articles. Finally, some of the most common listed stock option strategies used by institutional investors, and the strategies now being employed for index options and debt options, are reviewed.

Option Indexes

There are a number of possible uses of asset indexes. For example, the level of a call option index could usefully indicate whether call prices are currently overvalued or undervalued relative to some historical norm. In investment management, two of the most useful applications of a representative index are (1) to develop some intuition about the asset's return characteristics for use in asset allocation decisions and (2) to provide a benchmark for analyzing the performance of option managers. The first use requires a long series of periodic returns from which descriptive characteristics such as the average return, standard deviation, skewness, and, perhaps, beta (systematic risk exposure) are computed. The requirements for the second usage are more subtle. Certainly, the construction of the index should be such that an option manager could replicate the performance of the index (not taking into account transactions costs). In other words, the index should represent a "do-able" strategy. A second requirement is that the index, if used as a benchmark, must be representative of the option manager's style. For example, there is no point in measuring the performance of a manager who buys calls against an index which attempts to capture the returns of a covered call strategy.

There have been a number of attempts over the past few years to compute option indexes.[21] With very few exceptions, they have been designed to capture the relative valuation of calls (or puts). For example, the CBOE publishes a call and a put index, the CBOE Time Premium Indexes, which measure, respectively, the time values of a hypothetical six-month at-the-money call and put. These indexes suggest whether calls or puts as a whole are currently cheap or expensive relative to the historical record. They provide no indication as to the valuation of individual options or the returns likely to be obtained in the option markets.

Some return indexes are published. These are usually computed by investment consultants or brokers and as such are not as widely disseminated as the value indexes. One of the most comprehensive sets of indexes is that made available by BARRA.[22] They compute 60 indexes, each of which reports the "buy-and-hold" return of one aspect of the call or put market. For example, two indexes track the overall performance of the call option market and the put option market, respectively, and two others track the returns on covered call option and covered put option strategies.

The indexes are constructed from a representative stratified sample of about 2,000 options which changes from month to month as options are issued and expire. Each underlying stock is typically represented by four calls and three puts. The addition of new options is reflected by stratified random sampling, so as to keep the total sample as typical as possible of the entire option market. Once an option enters the index, it remains until the end of the month prior to its expiration. The value of the index at any time is the open interest, weighted sum of the prices of the options comprising the index. This unusual weighting scheme is the theoretically correct procedure to ensure that the index truly represents the relative importance of the various option investment opportunities. Since the composition of the index changes monthly, continuity from month to month is assured by means of a series of monthly adjustment factors.

From the two overall indexes, subindexes may be monitored, such as an index of "middle maturity at-the-money calls." The subindexes are identified as follows: (1) by the type of option (call or put), (2) by the option maturity, and (3) by the strike price. The option maturity and strike price are both divided into three ranges:

Option Maturity: ● Short (less than three months)
                     ● Middle (three to six months)
                     ● Long (over six months)

[21] See, for example, D. Galai, "Option Indices," *Journal of Finance* (May 1979), on which the CBOE Time Premium index is based; and G. Gastineau, *The Stock Options Manual* (New York: McGraw-Hill, 1979). *Barrons* publishes the CBOE Time Premium index in its weekly issues.

[22] BARRA is an investment consulting firm based in Berkeley, California.

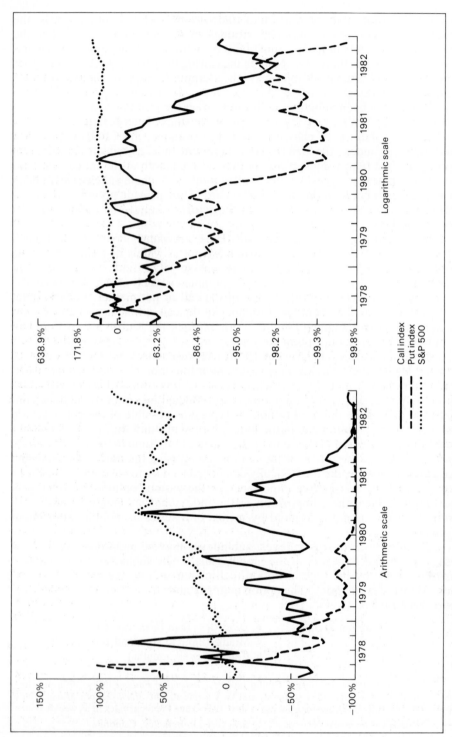

FIG. 11.14 Returns on Option Indexes (Cumulative Rates of Return)

Strike Price: • Out-of-the-money
                       • At-the-money
                       • In-the-money

There are 15 subindexes for puts and 15 for calls, or 30 subindexes in total. It is also possible to construct from these 30 subindexes a number of indexes that describe the performance of hedge strategies.

Figure 11.14 shows two versions of the cumulative performance of the call and put indexes (computed monthly) over the five-year period ending December 31, 1982. The left-hand diagram shows proportional rates of return while the right-hand diagram shows the rates of return plotted on a logarithmic scale. The graphs indicate the performance of long call and long put (monthly buy-and-hold) strategies over the five years ending December 31, 1982. For comparison, the performance of the S&P 500 is also shown. The solid line shows the return on the call index. (The mirror image about a line drawn through the origin gives the representative performance of a written call strategy.) The wide swings of the call index indicate the extreme risk of the call strategy and, when properly enacted, the significant benefit of using calls as a market-timing instrument.

Largely because of the bear market starting at the beginning of 1981, the cumulative rate of return on the call index is approximately -90 percent. The effect of the market upswing starting in mid-1982 is hardly shown in the left-hand diagram because the level of the index had fallen so low. In fact, from the middle to the end of 1982, the index almost quadrupled. This can be seen from the graph plotted with the logarithmic scale, which makes comparable each monthly return for the level of the index. The put index fares worse than the call index, dropping sharply during the bull market in 1980, and then dropping further still during the last six months in 1982.

The beta of the overall call option index, with respect to the S&P 500 stock index, is 8.9. The beta of the overall put option index, with respect to the S&P 500, is -7.8. These are the average betas for the five-year history. The investor in options should note that a small market value commitment to an option portfolio has a magnified effect upon the equity risk of the overall portfolio.

Figure 11.15 shows the performance of the covered call (each share of the underlying security held long has one call written against it) and covered put (each share of the underlying security is covered with one put held long) indices (again juxtaposed with the S&P 500 for comparison). Overall the covered call index outperformed the S&P 500, while the covered put index underperformed. The covered call index, which is representative of the average covered call writing strategy, displayed almost a 150 percent rate of return cumulatively over the five years, compared with the just over 40 percent rate of return on the S&P 500. The beta of the covered call index with respect to the S&P 500 is 0.8 and the beta of the covered put index is 0.6.

The index returns show that the typical call and put options were both overvalued on average in this five-year period. The representative call (or put) option writing strategy showed abnormal performance in this period. Conversely, a strategy to buy calls or puts would have provided inadequate return to compensate for their exposure to equity market risk. Investors who participated in call writing strategies are likely to have experienced abnormal positive returns over the five years ending December 1982.

linked to the option manager or not, since the use of this base will give results that are accurate in representing the contribution of the option portfolio to the utility of the client.[23]

The logic behind the use of incremental return to the client's total asset base is straightforward. In the absence of the option manager, the client's return can be easily identified. When the option strategy is added, the client experiences an incremental return. Is the increment beneficial or not? Clearly this is a natural measure of the productivity of the option manager. Indeed, it is natural to study the usefulness of any kind of manager by comparing the performance of the total portfolio that would be held in the absence of his activities to the total portfolio including the manager's contribution.

Frequently, however, use of the client's total asset portfolio as the base is rejected because of data collection difficulties, and a smaller base is substituted. There are two obvious candidates for this smaller base: (1) the total value of the assets nominally under the option manager's control, provided that this is a positive and relatively constant number; (2) the total value of the cash and equity portfolios that are directly related to the option manager, by virtue of the contributions to the cash portfolio and writing options against the equity portfolio. It is important to note that in both these cases the risk/reward trade-off applied to performance analysis must be adjusted.

Performance analysis can be used retrospectively to determine the apparent skill shown by the manager during some historical period, as well as prospectively to predict the likely superior performance of the manager. In either case, the measure of performance should be fair and not "gameable." Fairness requires that when money managers are doing their best to improve the circumstances of the client, then the money managers who have greater skill should be expected to rank higher on the performance measure than less skillful managers. Further, the manager should not be able to benefit by gaming against the performance method, so as to improve the performance ranking without making any contribution to the client.

Both criteria strongly argue for the use of a normal portfolio or normal bogie for each option manager.[24] The normal portfolio represents the typical or neutral position of the manager and serves as a benchmark for active management. The option manager performs active management by making active "bets" relative to the neutral position. The difference between the managed portfolio return and the normal portfolio return is the active return, which represents the value added by the manager's skill. Notice, the active return is independent of the return that arises from the manager's permanent style or strategy.

The use of normal portfolios permits accurate performance comparisons across managers. If comparisons between managers are made without neutralizing

---

[23] It can be shown that under some circumstances the use of a smaller base is biased against the skillful option manager. For details see B. Rosenberg and A. Rudd, "Option Performance Analysis," *Proceedings of the Seminar on the Analysis of Security Prices* (Chicago: University of Chicago Press, 1981), pp. 37–74.

[24] For further discussion on the use of normal portfolios in option performance measurement see A. Rudd, "Performance Measurement of Option Portfolios," (Talk at the American Stock Exchange Options Colloquium, March 31, 1981). Published in *Transcripts of the 1981 Amex Options Colloquium*, Day Two (Mar. 31, 1981), pp. 24–30.

the influence of the performance of each manager's long-term orientation or preferred "habitat," then, most likely, managers who have concentrated on the sector that has performed best most recently will be erroneously deemed the most skillful. This indicates that performance analysis is solely concerned with the manager's active return.

The manager and client should jointly define the normal options portfolio to reflect the manager's typical investment strategy. The normal portfolio may contain call and put options, the underlying equities and short-term Treasury bills, each with dollar investment values that correspond to the typical dollar values invested in each category. Within the options component of the normal portfolio, weights should be assigned to long, medium, and short maturity and in-the-money, at-the-money, and out-of-the money options so as to best represent the managers' typical strategy and style.

Once the active portfolio returns have been computed, the next step is the analysis of performance. Although some limited implications can be drawn directly from the return series, the more useful results require the adjustment of the active returns for the risk. This analysis requires the use of a risk model for options, which must be integrated with a similar risk model for the underlying securities, to describe the important factors influencing option returns and relate them to the factors in the equity market.

Option risk models are discussed in detail in the next section. For the purposes here, it is sufficient to note that the option risk model provides the mechanism for the adjustment for risk and the decomposition of option return to the important factors influencing the option market. Since one of these factors is the underlying stock itself, the option return is related to factors impacting only the option market together with factors that impact the equity market as well. Moreover, because interest rates affect option returns, one can also argue that bond market factors (e.g., the term structure of interest rates) should also be part of this attribution of option performance. This latter specification is crucial when managers justify an option strategy in terms of factors external to the options market; for example, when deep in-the-money covered call writing is pursued as a surrogate for a fixed income strategy.

There are several levels of performance analysis. At the least detailed level of analysis, investment returns are attributed to category timing (as among cash (or bonds), equities, and call and put options) and to within-category selectivity. The former reflects the managers' wisdom in devoting funds among the available investment vehicles, while the latter reflects the manager's superior performance, if any, in asset selection within each category.

The next level of analysis, which is exceedingly important for understanding the role of option management in the overall portfolio, reflects a distinction between timing the important factors which influence the equity and option markets (market factor timing) and performance that arises independently of the factors (residual performance). The former reflects the manager's skill in timing the equity market and the options market, relative to the cash market.

Under this approach, the manager's actions in the option market and (if there are any) in the equity market, affect the equity portfolio beta, and thereby contribute to equity market timing. Option transactions contribute to equity market timing because of the option's linkage to its underlying security. Moreover option actions also contribute to option market timing. Those elements of performance that are not related to active timing of these two markets are attributed to residual performance within each of the investment categories. This analysis underscores the strong effect of option investment upon the equity market exposure of the total portfolio. For example, much of the performance contribution of option management relates to deliberate or inadvertent changes in the equity beta.

At the most detailed level of analysis, the performance contributions of individual factors within the markets and of specific returns of individual assets are studied. This framework provides a complete attribution of return and presents the most intricate performance monitor. For example, an option investment is viewed as partial equity and bond positions. Abnormal option return arises from mispricing of the underlying security (i.e., the stock specific return) in addition to the specific return of the option itself, net of any linked effect from the other markets.

Option Risk Models

As indicated previously, option risk models [25] decompose the option return into the important factors influencing the option market. From the discussion in the second part of this chapter, it follows that the underlying stock must be one of the important factors. In particular, over short intervals of time it may be expected that the return on the option in excess of the risk-free rate should approximate the underlying stock excess return times the option elasticity. In symbols,

$$r_0 - r = \eta(r_s - r) + \ldots$$

where: r_0 = return on the option
          r_s = return on the stock
          r = risk-free rate
          η = option elasticity

The term $\eta(r_s - r)$ is therefore the fraction of the option return that can be associated with the underlying security.

The ellipsis dots at the end of the equation indicate that there may be other factors influencing the option return. What are these other factors? Certainly the same factors that influenced option prices will be important. Note that here the option return rather than price is being modeled, hence the relevant term in the decomposition is the return on the factor rather than the factor value itself. Since some of the factors (such as exercise price) do not change, they will not be relevant in the model of option returns.

A simple model for call return may include the following terms:

Excess call return = return due to underlying stock
                     + return due to change in interest rates
                     + return due to change in variance

---

[25] For further information see J. Evnine and A. Rudd, "A Multiplier Factor Risk Model for Options," (Paper presented at the Joint National ORSA/TIMS Meeting, Chicago, Ill., Apr. 25–27, 1983).

+ return due to autonomous changes in the call market
  as a whole
+ specific return

The next step is to estimate the correlations between the various factors. The end result is a risk model for options. In concept, this is very similar to the market model for common stocks which is used quite extensively by investment managers. The option risk model has a number of interesting uses. First, it is possible to determine the risk exposure of an option portfolio and hence to determine the risk levels of a combined option-stock portfolio. For example, it is possible to determine the degree of systematic risk and total risk that is reduced by writing options against the underlying equities. Second, performance analysis of option portfolio returns is made more meaningful with a risk model once it is possible to estimate the degree of risk associated with each component of return. Third, it is possible to identify the style of the manager with fair precision and to provide feedback on the manager's judgments. For example, are the active "bets" that are being made consistent with the level of risk which is being borne? Fourth, there are a number of sophisticated applications where the risk model can be used in conjunction with an optimization program to produce maximally efficient portfolios subject to certain prespecified criteria.

Institutional Listed Stock Option Strategies

The most important listed stock option strategies include the following.[26]

Long Calls and Treasury Bills. This strategy is a surrogate for holding long common stocks. The long call holding, which usually comprises approximately 10 percent of the portfolio, provides exposure to the equity market, while the Treasury bill holding provides "stability." From the previous discussion, the long call holding has a beta of approximately 9, hence the beta of the combined call and Treasury bill portfolio is close to 1. The strategy has the advantage that the maximum loss is predefined (the 10 percent call holding), while the potential for the strategy is comparable with the stock-only portfolio.

Cash Secured Put Writing. Here the strategy is to deposit the put exercise price in escrow (to provide collateral) while writing the put. When held to expiration, the payoff from the written put is similar to the covered call (see Figures 11.6 and 11.7), hence many investors view cash secured put writing as covered call writing. One important difference between the strategies is the greater likelihood of the put rather than the call being exercised prior to expiration.

Covered Call Writing. This is by far the most common institutional strategy. The common justifications are that writing calls against an existing equity

---

[26] A more detailed listing of strategies can be found in Jarrow and Rudd, note 7 *op. cit.*, Chapter 3.

position (1) provides increased return from receiving the call premiums and (2) reduces the risk of the portfolio. To some extent, there are fallacies in these arguments. First, the additional income from the call premiums is in return for taking the obligation to receive the stock at the exercise price at the option of the call holder. This obligation effectively eliminates the upside potential of the stock (see Figure 11.7). Second, there are many ways of reducing the risk of the portfolio (e.g., placing funds in riskless assets). Writing calls is only beneficial if the calls are overvalued (hence providing incremental return) or the use of the calls is less costly than other assets in reducing risk.

Conversion. This is an arbitrage strategy, based on perceived mispricing between the put and call markets. If the investor believes that put prices are too expensive relative to calls, then the put can be written and the call purchased. If the put/call parity theorem discussed previously held, then this strategy would produce riskless profits before transaction costs. Unfortunately, the existence of early exercise causes the conversion strategy to be risky, although if the option prices get too far out of line it can still be a profitable strategy.

Portfolio Insurance. The strategy of portfolio insurance,[27] as currently practiced, is not in fact a "listed stock option" strategy. However, since it could be implemented using listed options and is important in fund management, it should be described here.

The assets that every portfolio manager would like to have available are call or put options on his portfolios. In other words, if there were listed options (or the options could be fabricated) on every managed portfolio, then managers and/or clients could decide whether or not to hedge the portfolio (by writing calls or purchasing puts). Obviously listed options on all managed portfolios do not exist, but they can be fabricated.

One method follows directly from the discussion of option valuation presented previously. It was shown that over short intervals of time a portfolio containing the correct number (defined as the option delta) of shares of the underlying stock held long and one written call was equivalent to a holding in a riskless bond. This being the case, it is simple to see that the call can be duplicated (over a short period of time) by a portfolio containing the correct proportions of the underlying stock and the riskless bond. Of course, these correct proportions must be adjusted through time, so the portfolio can replicate the instantaneous return on the call option.

This simple idea is the basis for developing portfolio insurance strategies. For example, a put on any managed portfolio can be fabricated by "continuously" trading in a particular manner between a riskless bond portfolio and the managed portfolio. Although the idea is very straightforward, its implementation is complex, since methods for dealing with changes in the volatility of the portfolio and minimizing transaction costs, for example, have to be worked out. Currently, several organizations have produced software packages that generate the re-

---

[27] The original article in this area is by Hayne Leland, "Who Buys Portfolio Insurance?" *Journal of Finance* (May 1980), pp. 581–594. See also R. Ferguson, "Two Approaches to Asset Allocation," *Pensions and Investment Age* (Sept. 19, 1983), p. 38.

balancing transactions to insure portfolios using this form of dynamic trading strategy.

The other method for constructing an option on a portfolio is to select a portfolio of options that behaves like the desired option by means of the use of an option risk model. Basically, the approach is to compute the exposures of the managed equity portfolio to the factors of return. From these exposures, it is possible to compute the exposures of the hypothetical option on the managed portfolio to the factors of return influencing the option market. The final step requires the use of an optimization program, in conjunction with the risk model, to construct a portfolio of listed stock options and stock index options that behaves as nearly as possible like the hypothetical option.[28]

Both approaches have advantages and disadvantages. The dynamic trading strategy is elegant but somewhat difficult to implement efficiently and inexpensively. The second approach requires more sophisticated technology, but the trading requirements are typically less severe than the first approach.

Uses of Stock Index Options

Stock index options have been introduced comparatively recently, so much of the usage is by brokers rather than institutions. The two major uses by the brokers are in block positioning (i.e., hedging large positions before they are sold) and taking direct "bets" on market moves. This latter usage seems to have captured the imagination of individual investors, who have made considerable use of the market. The institutional usage, such as it is, appears to be concentrated in hedging market risk and using the option as a market timing device. This latter strategy is interesting, since the market "bet" can be enacted quickly and for low cost.[29]

Uses of Debt Options

Debt options are used in much the same way as stock index options (namely, block positioning by brokers and hedging out interest rate moves), but because of the large number of different debt instruments, there are interesting possibilities for cross-hedges. A cross-hedge occurs when the option is hedged against an asset that is highly correlated with (but not the same as) the underlying asset. One interesting example is the cross-hedge between municipal bonds and Treasury bond options, which arises to reduce the price risk from the municipal bond while still retaining its tax-free coupon income.

The development of the market is such that the majority of trades originate with short-term arbitrageurs rather than longer-term investors who hold positions for strategic considerations. As the market grows, so too will the acceptance and usage of debt options by institutions rather than short-term investors.

---

[28] This approach is developed further in J. Evnine and A. Rudd, "Option Portfolio Risk Analysis," *Journal of Portfolio Management* (Winter 1983).

[29] See also J. Evnine and A. Rudd, "Stock Index Option: Preliminary Evidence," (Paper presented at the Berkeley Program in Finance, Silverado, Cal., Sept. 11–14, 1983).

12

Financial Futures Markets

LLOYD BESANT

THOMAS SCHNEEWEIS

WHAT IS A FINANCIAL FUTURES CONTRACT?

Description

The creation and development of the fixed-income foreign currency and stock index futures markets in the 1970s and 1980s resulted from the need to reduce uncertainty regarding prices of financial assets and foreign earnings.[1] Individ-

---

[1] The views expressed in this article are solely those of the authors and do not necessarily reflect the views of the institutions they represent.

uals who plan to make investments face the risk of an unexpected decrease in interest rates (or an increase in security prices). Individuals who plan to borrow in the future and those who plan to sell securities face the risk of unexpected increases in interest rates or decreases in the price of the securities they plan to sell. Futures markets permit the creation of a futures position to offset the risk of a position held (or anticipated) in the cash market. A financial futures contract represents a commitment to buy (take delivery) or to sell (deliver) an amount of a financial instrument (or in certain futures markets the cash equivalent of the specified financial instrument) based on specified delivery conditions. Individuals facing the risk of unexpected decreases in cash prices (rise in yields) may sell futures to lock in present prices (yields). Those facing the risk of unexpected increases in cash prices (fall in yields) may buy futures to ensure present prices (yields).

The major exchanges trading financial futures include the Chicago Mercantile Exchange (CME), the Chicago Board of Trade (CBT), the New York Futures Exchange (NYFE), and the Kansas City Board of Trade (KCBT).[2] A summary of the commodity exchanges trading financial futures on foreign currencies equity indexes and long-term fixed-income securities is given in Table 12.1. While price uncertainty can also be reduced through forward contracts, financial futures permit unique opportunities not available in forward and cash markets (see Table 12.2). In contrast to forward contracts, futures are standardized in contract size and delivery date. Futures contracts offer a price established in an open auction market in a regulated marketplace with established clearinghouses ensuring the integrity of the transactions. In contrast to the cash market, the futures market permits individuals to secure delivery of a cash security through a regulated market. In addition, futures markets permit positions in the futures contract in lieu of a transaction in the cash market.

In fact, the futures position is normally only a temporary substitute for the sale or purchase of the financial security in the cash market. While futures contracts call for delivery, the principal purpose of the futures markets is not the delivery (marketing) of the deliverable security. Only about 2 to 5 percent of the contracts traded on futures exchanges result in delivery. The futures position is often closed out when the spot market transaction occurs by selling (buying) the contract in the futures market rather than taking (making) delivery.

Margin. It is important to note that an individual's gain and/or loss in the futures contract is not determined when the position is closed out but is settled daily. To ensure that an individual will meet any daily losses on futures positions, a customer must post margin before he is allowed to trade. Margins on futures transactions can be thought of as security deposits or performance bonds. Futures margin requirements are set by the exchange at a level high enough to ensure the financial integrity of the clearing members and the market. Because either buyer or seller could lose money on any given day, both sides post margin. As the price changes, each side's account is "marked to the market," that is, debited or credited to reflect the most recent settlement price.

---

[2] Detailed information on the various futures markets is available in information booklets provided by the exchanges as well as the Commodity Futures Trading Commission.

When the account goes below a prescribed maintenance level, additional margin must be deposited to maintain the position.

Additional margin (variation margin) can also be called for when the price volatility of a commodity warrants it. If gains on the spot position are costly to liquidate or if the value of the position being hedged is not highly correlated with the future, the need to mark to market will be considered an important component of hedge management. Also, when an anticipated spot position is being hedged, the profits on the spot will not be available for margin requirements during the hedge period.[3] In these circumstances, a "hedging reserve" is needed to cover losses that may or may not be accompanied by realized gains on the spot portfolio or asset. The size of this hedging reserve depends on the size of the futures position (which should be based on the correlations between the spot and futures prices), on the volatility of daily futures prices, and on the amount of liquid assets available to the hedgers as part of their normal operations.

Hedging. In hedging financial instruments, both direct and cross hedges may be constructed. When a futures contract is available in the financial instrument in which the spot position is held, a direct hedge is used. When a futures contract is not available in the financial instrument in which the spot position is held, a cross hedge is used: a futures contract is sold calling for the delivery of another security. Risk is reduced to the extent that the gain (loss) in the futures position offsets the loss (gain) on the spot position. Thus, futures markets permit the exchange of the risk of possible price changes in the cash market for the risk of a change in the relationship between the cash and futures prices.

Basis Risk. The benefits of using financial futures to hedge the price movement of a present or anticipated cash position depend on how well the cash price follows the futures price.[4] The difference between the cash and futures prices is called the basis.

The basis can be positive or negative. For fixed-income futures, the basis is normally positive when yield curves are positively sloped and negative when

(text continues on page 12-10)

---

[3] Hill, Joanne, et al. "An Analysis of the Impact of Variation Margin in Hedging Fixed Income Securities." *Review of Research in Futures Markets*, Vol. 2, No. 1 (1983), pp. 136–159, using daily futures price data observed over three-month periods in 1978 through 1980, studied the mark-to-market experience of short positions in Treasury-bond futures. Overall profits from the investment of interim profits, and losses from the financing of interim losses, amounted to less than 5 percent of total profits and losses. There were, however, large differences in mark-to-market account levels over the time of each hedging period and across sample hedging periods. On the average, a short hedge was profitable during the sample periods that were dominated by rising interest rates. Thus, the inclusion of interest on variation margin balances increased this profit as interest was accrued at increasing interest rate levels. It can be said, therefore, that the ex ante returns and risks of short or long positions in financial futures are usually higher when variation margin investment and financial results are taken into account.

[4] For interest rate futures, futures prices are generally based on the instrument that is cheapest to deliver. Because a number of bonds can be deliverable against Treasury bills, Treasury bonds, GNMAs, Treasury notes, and certificates of deposit the individual will deliver the "cheapest" instrument that fulfills contract obligations. It is not necessary, however, that individuals accepting delivery will receive the cheapest to deliver. Various market conditions (e.g., the availability of the cheapest-to-deliver security) may result in alternative instruments being delivered.

TABLE 12.1 Commodities for Which Markets Are Designated to Trade / Designated Contract Markets, Fiscal Year 1982

Commodity / Exchange (a)	Date of Designation (b)	Trading Began (c)	Contract Size
	CURRENCIES		
Belgian franc/NYME	7/18/75	9/12/74	2,000,000
British pound			
CME	7/18/75	5/16/72	25,000
NYFE	5/28/80	8/07/80	25,000
NYME	7/18/75	9/12/74	25,000
Canadian dollar			
CME	7/18/75	5/16/72	100,000
NYFE	5/28/80	8/07/80	100,000
NYME	7/18/75	9/12/74	100,000
Deutsche mark			
CME	7/18/75	5/16/72	125,000
NYFE	5/28/80	8/07/80	125,000
NYME	7/18/75	9/12/74	125,000
Dutch guilder			
CME	7/18/75	5/16/73	125,000
NYME	7/18/75	9/12/74	125,000
French franc/CME	7/18/75	9/23/74	250,000
Italian lire			
CME	9/30/81	—	25,000,000
NYME	7/18/75	—	25,000,000
Japanese yen			
CME	7/18/75	5/16/72	12,500,000
NYFE	5/28/80	8/07/80	12,500,000
NYME	7/18/75	9/12/74	12,500,000

Mexican peso			
CME	7/18/75	5/16/72	1,000,000
NYME	7/18/75	9/12/74	1,000,000
Swiss franc			
CME	7/18/75	5/16/72	125,000
NYFE	5/28/80	8/07/80	125,000
NYME	7/18/75	9/12/74	125,000

FINANCIAL INSTRUMENTS

Certificates of deposit (Domestic/90-Day)			
CBT	7/21/81	7/22/81	$1,000,000
NYFE	6/30/81	7/9/81	1,000,000
CME	7/28/81	7/29/81	1,000,000
Commercial paper			
90-day/CBT	7/12/77	9/26/77	1,000,000
30-day/CBT	9/11/78	5/14/79	3,000,000
Eurodollars			
CME	12/08/81	12/9/81	1,000,000
CBT	12/15/81	—	1,000,000
NYFE	12/15/81	—	1,000,000
GNMA (d)			
ACE (e)	8/22/78	9/12/78	100,000
CBT	9/11/75	10/20/75	100,000
CMX	10/16/79	11/13/79	100,000
CD/CBT	9/11/78	9/12/78	100,000
CD/NYFE	9/23/81	—	100,000

(continued)

TABLE 12.1   Commodities for Which Markets Are Designated to Trade / Designated Contract Markets, Fiscal Year 1982 (continued)

Commodity / Exchange (a)	Date of Designation (b)	Trading Began (c)	Contract Size
Stock index			
Stock index average/CBT	—	—	Spot market value of the contract grade portfolio
Standard & Poor's	4/20/82	4/21/82	$500 × Index
Value Line average/KCBT	2/16/82	2/24/82	500 × Index
Comex 500 stock index/CMX	4/28/82	—	500 × Index
NYSE composite index/NYFE	5/4/82	5/6/82	500 × Index
U.S. Treasury bills			
90 days/ACE (e)	6/19/79	6/26/79	$1,000,000
1 year/CME	8/25/78	9/11/78	250,000
90 days/CME	11/26/75	1/6/76	1,000,000
6 months/CME	9/21/82	—	500,000
90 days/CMX	6/19/79	10/2/79	1,000,000
90 days/MACE	3/29/82	4/2/82	1,000,000
90 days/NYFE	7/15/80	8/14/80	1,000,000
U.S. Treasury bonds			
20 years/ACE (e)	10/16/79	11/14/79	100,000
15 years/CBT	8/2/77	8/22/77	100,000
20 years/NYFE	7/15/80	8/7/80	100,000
15 years/MACE	9/9/81	9/18/81	50,000
U.S. Treasury notes			
4–6 years/CBT	6/19/79	6/25/79	100,000
4 years/CME	6/19/79	7/10/79	100,000
2 years/CMX	9/30/80	12/2/80	100,000
6½–10 years/CBT	9/23/81	5/3/82	100,000
21–24 months/CBT	9/30/81	—	100,000

— = Not available

(a) Includes only the 11 exchanges designated as contract markets by the Commodity Futures Trading Commission (CFTC) with active trading as well as one inactive exchange. Initials used in the table are shown here:

ACE	Amex Commodity Exchange	MACE	MidAmerica Commodity Exchange
CBT	Chicago Board of Trade	MGE	Minneapolis Grain Exchange
CME	Chicago Mercantile Exchange	NOCE	New Orleans Commodity Exchange
CMX	Commodity Exchange, Inc.	NYCE	New York Cotton Exchange
CSCE	Coffee, Sugar & Cocoa Exchange	NYFE	New York Futures Exchange
KCBT	Kansas City Board of Trade	NYME	New York Mercantile Exchange

(b) The term "effective date of designation" is the date upon which the exchange was authorized to begin trading in the contract, not the date of issuance of the designation order.

If an exchange was previously designated by the Secretary of Agriculture as a contract market in a commodity and that designation was in effect on July 18, 1975, the CFTC did not specifically designate the exchange as such on July 18, 1975. Those designations continued in full force and effect by virtue of Section 411 of the Commodity Futures Trading Commission Act of 1974. Prior to July 18, 1975, the commodities for which designation was granted by the Secretary of Agriculture were among the list of commodities explicitly set forth in Section 2(a)(1) of the Commodity Exchange Act, as amended ("Act"). (This listing was limited to the agricultural and animal product commodities.)

On July 18, 1975, the CFTC gave contract market designation to many of the exchanges which traded in previously unregulated commodities. The CFTC had given provisional contract market designations to these exchanges on April 18, 1975, and had extended such designations on May 5. The effect of the July 18, 1975 designations was to bring under federal regulation all commodities for which a futures contract was actively traded. Previously unregulated commodities, such as Comex's mercury and rubber contract, for which no contract market designation was granted on that date were not permitted to continue futures trading after July 18.

(c) The "trading began" column indicates, according to data supplied by the exchange, when trading began in a commodity. It is the date of the first recorded futures trading in the commodity, though the contract terms may have changed since. Dates of some contract term changes, especially those that have originated since the establishment of CFTC, are shown if the change affects the contract size or the deliverable supply.

In the case of copper, silver, and zinc traded on Comex, trading was suspended for periods of time and then later resumed.

It should be noted that MACE was called the Chicago Open Board of Trade until its name change, which took effect November 22, 1972. On January 8, 1973, the Commodity Exchange Authority (CEA) amended its previous designation orders to show the name MACE instead of Chicago Open Board of Trade. The effective date of the amended order was November 22, 1972.

KCBT was an unincorporated association until it incorporated in 1973, and CEA designated KCBT as a contract market in those commodities for which the association was previously designated, the effective date of designation being July 1, 1973.

(d) GNMA II contracts began trading in early 1984. For information on contract specifications, contact the CBT.

(e) Contracts vacated July 3 and February 2, 1981, respectively.

Source: Commodity Futures Trading Commission Annual Report

TABLE 12.2   Comparison of Futures Market and Forward/Cash Markets

Characteristic	Forward	Futures	Cash
Size of contract	Nonstandardized	Standardized	Nonstandardized
Delivery date	Nonstandardized	Standardized	Nonstandardized (usually immediate)
Method of transaction	Bank or broker system (e.g., phone contact)	Open auction among buyers and sellers on central exchange floor	Broker
Participants	Banks, brokers, etc.	Banks, brokers, etc.	Individuals
Commissions	Set by spread between bank's buy and call prices	Published small brokerage fee and negotiated rates on block trades	Set by broker spread
Security deposit	Compensating bank balances usually required	Small security deposit required	Payment on delivery
Clearing operation (financial integrity)	No separate clearinghouse function	Handled by exchange clearinghouse; daily settlements to the market	No separate clearinghouse

Marketplace	Worldwide (broker connected)	Central exchange floor with worldwide communications	Worldwide (broker connected)
Economic justification	■ Price discovery ■ Risk reduction	■ Price discovery ■ Risk reduction	Immediate wealth transfer and price discovery
Accessibility	Limited to large customers who deal in foreign trade	Open to anyone who meets exchange conditions	Dependent on security size and amount
Regulation	Self-regulating	Commodity Futures Trading Commission	Generally self-regulating
Frequency of delivery	90 percent settled by actual delivery	No less than 1 percent settled by delivery	Immediate
Price fluctuations	No daily limit	Daily limit imposed by the exchange with a rule provision for expanded daily price limits	No limit
Market liquidity	Offsetting with other banks	■ Public offset ■ Arbitrage offset	Issue dependent

yield curves are negatively sloped. Since money may be borrowed to purchase a futures contract, the price of the futures contract (FC) should equal the price of today's deliverable cash security (S) plus any difference between the cost of borrowing (CB) and accrued interest (AI) on the bond purchased.

$$FC = S + (CB - AI)$$

The difference between CB and AI is called the cost of carry. When short-term rates are below long-term rates, dealers and others for whom the cost of carry is positive (yield on deliverable security exceeds financing cost) can quote lower prices on futures contracts (deferred sales).[5] In contrast, when long-term rates are below short-term rates, dealers and others who have a negative cost of carry (financing costs greater than yield on deliverable security) may quote higher prices on futures contracts (deferred sale) to compensate for holding inventory.[6] As delivery approaches, cash and futures prices should tend to converge as cost of carry effects become insignificant and arbitrage keeps prices of like financial assets in line.[7]

Understanding the basis is important because the purpose of hedging is the creation of a futures position that offsets a cash market position so that the dollar price change is identical on each side of the hedge. If a hedger sells the futures short to protect against an unexpected decrease in prices, the hedge is referred to as a "short" hedge. If a hedger buys the futures to protect against an unexpected increase in prices, the hedge is referred to as a "long" hedge. The effect of basis changes on profitability can be seen more easily when the basis is viewed as either "strengthening" or "weakening."

When the basis is increasingly positive (or decreasingly negative), the basis is said to be strengthening. The futures price is falling more (rising less) than the cash price. As illustrated in Table 12.3, a short hedge is profitable if the basis strengthens. When the basis is increasingly negative (or decreasingly positive), the basis is said to be weakening. The futures price rises more (falls less) than the cash price. As illustrated in Table 12.3, a long hedge is profitable if the basis weakens.

Changes in basis, therefore, can have either a desirable or an undesirable impact on a hedge. If the fluctuation in the basis is less than the price movement of cash, however, the variability of the change in value of the hedged position will be less than the variability of the unhedged cash position. The fluctuation in the basis is known as basis risk: the risk that the futures and cash

---

[5] This article does not present various pricing models for financial futures. For a discussion of cash future relationships see *Financial Instrument Markets: Cash Future Relationships* (Chicago Board of Trade 1982). For examples of pricing models for financial futures see Edward Schwartz, et al., *Financial Futures: Fundamentals, Strategy, and Applications* (Richard Irwin, forthcoming); Bradford Cornell and Kenneth R. French, "The Pricing of Stock Index Futures," *Journal of Futures Markets* (Spring 1983), pp. 1–14; and Fisher Black, "The Pricing of Commodity Contracts," *Journal of Financial Economics* (Jan.–Feb. 1975), pp. 167–179.

[6] For stock index futures, the difference between the cash and futures price is equal to the difference between the interest earned on investments equal to the market value of the index and the dividends received if the index is held. When the interest earned is greater than dividends received, individuals quote higher prices for the deferred futures contracts.

[7] Basis relationships may vary due to conditions other than changes in the cost of carry. Various market conditions (e.g., changing the cheapest-to-delivery security) may result in basis variations.

TABLE 12.3   Hedge Positions

SHORT HEDGE

Cash		Futures		Basis	
Buy:	100	Sell:	97	+3	
Sell:	93	Buy:	89	+4 (basis gets more positive)	
	−7		+8	change:	+1
Net: +1					

LONG HEDGE

Cash		Futures		Basis	
Market Price:	100	Buy:	97	+3	
Buy:	105	Sell:	103	+2 (basis gets less positive)	
	−5		+6	change:	−1
Net: +1					

markets will not move in the same direction or magnitude. For an example of basis relationships in the U.S. Treasury bond (T-bond) market over 1980 and 1981, see Figure 12.1.

For hedging purposes, variation in the basis should be less than the price variation of the cash instrument. A hedge should reduce risk by substituting the smaller basis risk for the larger security price variation. Thus, for a hedge to be successful, the characteristics of the cash and futures instruments must be sufficiently similar to result in a high degree of positive correlation in their respective price changes during the hedge period.

Uses of Financial Futures

The main roles of financial futures are price discovery and risk transfer. Futures prices provide a means by which a security's value in the future is estimated today. Since the futures markets permit an individual to buy or sell assets at a price set today for delivery in the future, financial futures contracts also provide a convenient way to hedge the risk of unexpected price changes. For instance, a foreign currency, equity, or fixed-income hedge is usually caused by buying (selling) a futures contract to initiate a futures position and closing out (offsetting) the position at a later date by selling (buying) the contract in the futures market rather than taking delivery.[8] The hedger benefits to the extent that a gain in the futures position offsets a loss in the spot position.

---

[8] Numerous examples of various hedges exist. Both the CBT and the CME provide information booklets describing various hedging strategies. For a review of the effectiveness of financial futures hedging see Bruce Wardrep and James F. Buck, "The Efficiency of Hedging With Financial Futures: A Historical Perspective," *Journal of Futures Markets* (Fall 1982), pp. 243–254.

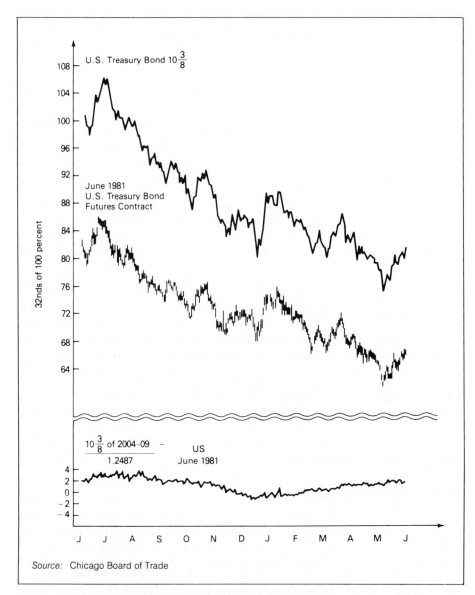

Fig. 12.1 Basis Relationships in the U.S. Treasury Bond Market, June 1980–June 1981 (U.S. Treasury bond 10 3/8, with June 1981 basis)

An investor purchasing long-term bonds in March may wish to reduce the risk of interest rate variability by simultaneously selling a June GNMA or T-bond futures contract. As shown in Table 12.4, if interest rates rise during the holding period, the losses in the spot market are reduced by gains in the futures market.

Likewise as shown in Table 12.4, the foreign currency futures market offers similar protection against unanticipated currency price changes. An exporter selling goods to a German customer on March 1 but not expecting delivery (payment) until June may wish to sell a June deutsche mark futures contract. If the value of the mark falls in the interim, the loss in the spot market is balanced by the gain in the futures position. It is important to note that opposite price movements result in similar final values. A fall in interest rates results spot gains but losses in the futures market. A rise in foreign currency values results in gains in the spot market but losses in the futures market. Table 12.4 also shows that the stock futures market offers protection against anticipated equity portfolio price changes. In March a portfolio manager expecting to liquidate his portfolio later in the year may wish to reduce his risk of equity price variability by selling a specified number of June equity futures contracts. As illustrated in Table 12.4, if equity prices fall during the holding period, the losses in the spot market are reduced by the gains in the futures market.

There is, of course, no guarantee that the cash market gain or loss will be offset by the futures trade. Hedging does not ensure against losses or assure gains. Anticipated cash price changes are built into the structure of future prices; therefore only unanticipated price changes may be hedged. However, hedging may reduce the variability of changes in portfolio values over time. The actual reduction in value change variability depends on the number of futures contracts purchased relative to the size of the cash position.

Hedge Uses. The uses of financial futures for hedging purposes are unlimited. Banks, for instance, normally have an imbalance between the maturity of their assets and their liabilities. When assets are of longer maturity than liabilities, banks are exposed to a rise in rates on their liabilities to be issued in the future. In the event that their assets are shorter in maturity than their liabilities, banks are exposed to a decline in earnings on assets acquired in the future. Financial futures enable bank managers to hedge their interest-rate exposure by bringing the maturities of assets and liabilities into closer balance. In determining futures strategy, banks must determine if they wish to hedge individual issues or the net exposure (interest-rate sensitivity). It is important to note that a hedge on an individual issue may result in a greater net interest-rate sensitivity for the total asset/liability structure of the bank.

Investment bankers may use financial futures to separate the price of their security transactions from their actual underwriting and trading. Investment bankers are at risk due to the possibility of a decrease in interest rates (rise in price) on investments they plan to make and increase in interest rates (fall in price) on securities they plan to sell. Investment bankers can also use futures to hedge their inventory of assets against market yield risks. Due to market constraints, investment bankers may be unable to sell bonds and may wish to liquidate their positions over a period of time. Instead of selling the cash bonds,

TABLE 12.4   Sample Futures Transactions

Date	Cash	Futures
	BOND FUTURES	
March 1	Hold $5 million (face value) of GNMA 8.00%	Sell 50 June GNMA futures
		Face value of deliverable: 50 × $100,000 = $5 million
	Yield: 13.00%	Yield: 13.25%
	Market value: 70-12	Selling Price: 69-10
	Total market value: $3.519 million	Total market value: $3.465 million
June 1	Hold same GNMA	Buy 50 June GNMA futures
	Yield: 14.00%	Yield: 13.85%
	Market value: 66-01	Market value: 66-14
	Total market value: $3.302 million	Total market value: $3.322 million
	Loss in value: $207,000	Gain: $143,000
		Net loss: $64,000
	CURRENCY FUTURES	
March 1	Hold commitment to receive in June $5 million in deutsche marks at exchange rate 0.4200 DM/$ (DM11,904,761)	Sell 95 June deutsche mark futures (contract size DM125,000) at price 0.4210 DM/$
		Total value: $4,999,375

June 1   Receive deutsche marks per commitment
Convert to dollars at exchange rate 0.4160 DM/$
Total receipts: $4,952,380

Buy 95 June deutsche mark futures at price 0.4164 DM/$
Total value: $4,944,750

Currency loss: $47,619   Gain: $54,625

Net gain: $7,006

STOCK FUTURES

March 1   Hold $10 million in equity portfolio

Sell 178 June Standard & Poor's (S&P) contracts
Face value of futures position:
$178 \times \$56,000 = \$9,968,000$ (S&P index value = 112)
Total market value: $9,968,000

Total market value: $10 million

June 1   Sell equity portfolio for $9 million

Buy 178 June S&P futures contracts at $50,000
(S&P index value = 100)
Total market value: $8,900,000

Total market value: $9 million

Loss in value: $1 million   Gain: $1,068,000

Net gain: $68,000

investment bankers can sell bond futures contracts as a substitute for the actual sale of those bonds. If interest rates increase, the profits on the futures will offset declines in the value of the cash bonds.

As sources of capital, investment bankers and mortgage bankers provide private placements as well as assured forward commitments at fixed rates. With this kind of commitment, investment bankers face the risk that bond or stock prices will fall significantly before the securities can be retailed. The forward commitment can be hedged by selling futures contracts until the bonds or stocks are obtained. Investment bankers or mortgage bankers who make forward commitments on a continuous basis and can assume successful sale may wish to lock in today's rates. Futures markets provide a way to capture today's market rates in advance of the time when proceeds of sale are available.

While corporations and municipalities are often suppliers of capital in the short run, they are, in general, net borrowers of funds. As suppliers of capital, corporate and municipal treasurers may hedge against unexpected interest rate declines on future investment or set interest income on available proceeds of bond sales or revenue. As demanders of credit, corporate and municipal officers may wish to hedge against increasing interest-rate costs on future borrowings. For instance, corporations or municipalities wishing to finance a future project by issuing commercial paper are at risk that short-term rates will rise and increase the cost of borrowing. As an alternative, they may sell a short-term future (e.g., a Treasury bill, or T-bill) before the actual sale of commercial paper. After the commercial paper is issued, the futures contract is bought back. If rates rise (prices fall), the profit on the futures contract will offset the increase in the cost of the short-term financing. If rates fall (prices rise), the loss on the futures contract will be offset by the fall in the capital costs of financing.

In addition to short-term financings, corporations and municipalities often require long-term financings. The risk of unexpected changes in long-term rates can be reduced by selling futures to hedge an unexpected rise in yields. If yields fall, the loss on repurchasing the futures will be offset by the gain from lower capital costs in the spot market.

Non-Hedge Uses. Efficient pricing in the futures market is enhanced through the competitive trading activities of the different buyers and sellers in the market.[9] Futures market participants are usually classified into three categories: (1) hedgers, (2) speculators, and (3) arbitragers. Speculators are motivated by the potential profit from their correct forecasts of unanticipated price changes. Hedgers desire to avoid the potential loss from unexpected price changes. Arbitragers are motivated by the profit potential resulting from immediate price distortions existing between the cash and futures markets as well as within the futures market.

---

[9] For a critical review of efficiency studies in financial futures markets as well as a study of arbitrage possibilities in T-bond futures, see James Hoag and Karin Peterson L. Barge, *Quasiarbitrage Opportunities in the Treasury Bond Futures Market,* paper presented at Eastern Finance Association Meetings (New York: 1983).

The activities of all three groups — hedgers, speculators, and arbitragers — are necessary for the orderly functioning of the market. Investors and corporate managers who use the futures markets to transfer risk require individuals capable of taking risk. Speculators are willing to buy and/or sell futures based on their forecast of future spot prices. Speculation can be achieved by taking open positions or spreading. Spreading in financial futures relates to purchasing the same financial futures in different contract months, or different financial futures in the same or different contract months. Arbitrage involves the simultaneous buying and selling of the same asset or types of assets at different prices to assure a profit. Therefore, pure arbitrage is defined as a riskless position that requires zero net investment and generates positive profits. Arbitrage should ensure that similar assets in competing markets (e.g., cash-futures, cash-cash, or futures-futures) produce similar returns. Investors must be aware that, like a perfect hedge, pure arbitrage opportunities are very rare. In pure arbitrage, prices must be available simultaneously in the two markets. In practice, arbitrage often refers to a low risk trade rather than a riskless position. Given the zero net investment available to some market participants, arbitrage possibilities are quickly removed.

TYPES OF FUTURES CONTRACTS

In May 1972 currency futures began trading on the CME's International Monetary Market (IMM). In October 1975, the CBT introduced GNMA collateralized depository receipt (CDR) contracts. Financial futures contracts have since grown to include short- and long-term government securities, bank paper, and stock index futures. A summary of actively traded currency, fixed-income, and equity contracts is presented in Table 12.5. The following sections discuss the contract characteristics of the principal financial instrument futures as well as the markets in which they are traded.

Fixed-Income Futures: Short-Term Instruments

Ninety-Day Treasury Bill Futures Contract. The 90-day T-bill futures contract opened on January 2, 1976 on the IMM. Any individual who is exposed to short-term interest-rate risk or who wishes to profit from correct forecasts of short-term rates may participate in the T-bill market.[10]

The T-bill market comprises institutions or individuals that are experienced in short-term lending or borrowing, such as banks, brokerage houses, and securities dealers with positions in short-term securities. In addition, large corporations that have positions in cash equivalent securities or are issuers of commercial paper have use for short-term futures instruments. The T-bill futures contract calls for delivery of $1 million in face value of 90-day T-bills.

---

[10] For an example of the use of short-term financial futures, see George McCabe and James M. Blackwell, "The Hedging Strategy: A New Approach to Spread Management: Banking and Commercial Lending," *Journal of Bank Research* (Summer 1981).

TABLE 12.5   Summary of Actively Traded Futures Contracts

Commodity	Size	Exchange	Ticker Symbol	Minimum Price Fluctuations
Financials				
U.S. T-bond	$ 100,000	—	US	1/32
GNMA CDR contract	100,000	—	GM	1/32
10-year note	100,000	—	TY	1/32
90-day U.S. T-bill	1,000,000	—	TB	0.01(a)
90-day domestic CD	1,000,000	—	DC	0.01
90-day Eurodollar time deposit	1,000,000	—	ED	0.01
Stock indexes				
S&P 500 Stock index		CME	SP	0.05
NYSE Composite index	$500 times value of index	NYFE	YX	0.05
Value Line index		KCBT	KV	0.05
Foreign currencies				
Pound sterling	$ 25,000	—	BP	$2.50
Canadian dollar	100,000	—	CD	$10.00
Dutch guilder	125,000	—	DG	$12.50
Deutsche mark	125,000	—	DM	1 point
Japanese yen	12,500,000	—	JY	1 point
Mexican peso	1,000,000	—	MP	1 point
Swiss franc	125,000	—	SF	1 point
French franc	250,000	—	FR	5 points

(a) One basis point

Dollar Value of Minimum Fluctuation	Limit Move	Last Day of Trading	Original Margin	Maintenance Margin
$31.25	2 points ⎫	Business day prior to	$3,000	$2,000
31.25	2 points ⎬	last 7 business days	3,000	2,000
31.25	2 points ⎭	of delivery month	3,000	2,000
25.00	0.60 points	Second day following third weekly T-bill auction in contract month	2,500	2,000
25.00	0.60 points	Day prior to last business day of month	2,500	2,000
25.00	0.60 points	Second London business day before third week	2,500	2,000
$25.00	5.00 points, except during delivery month	Third Thursday of delivery month	$6,000	$3,000
25.00	None	Business day prior to last business day in delivery month	3,500	1,500
25.00	None	Last business day of delivery month	6,500	2,500
$ 2.50	500 points	Second day before third Wednesday	$1,500	$1,000
10.00	75 points	Day before third Wednesday	1,500	1,000
12.50	100 points	Second day before third Wednesday	1,500	1,000
12.50	100 points	Second day before third Wednesday	1,500	1,000
12.50	100 points	Second day before third Wednesday	1,500	1,000
10.00	150 points	Day before third Wednesday	4,000	3,000
12.50	150 points	Second day before third Wednesday	2,500	2,000
2.50	500 points	Second day before third Wednesday	1,500	1,000

Delivery months for up to two years in the future are March, June, September, and December. The last day of trading is the second business day (usually a Wednesday) following the T-bill auction in the third week of the delivery month. A sample of futures price quotations is shown in Table 12.6. For each delivery date the opening, high, low, and settle prices are listed, as well as the price change during that day. The closing annualized discount rate (yield) and change are also given, as well as open interest (number of contracts outstanding) and daily volume figures.

While yields are the basic unit of the T-bill cash market, T-bill futures trading is done in terms of prices. The use of prices for T-bill futures allows the bill future to be put on the same price basis as futures on other deliverable instruments. The minimum price index change (or discount rate change) is 0.01. This corresponds to a $25 change in the actual value of the futures contract.

On the business day following the last day of trading, individuals who have long or short positions in the contract have delivery obligations. The buyer informs the exchange clearinghouse that a commitment exists to deliver the securities by noon of the last trading day. On the next trading day, the buyer must have provided a wire transfer of Federal funds in the amount of the price to the seller's account. The clearinghouse ensures that the commitments are matched and that the delivery occurs as specified.

Certificate of Deposit. The certificate of deposit (CD) contract on the IMM was introduced in July 1981. The denomination and contract months for the CD future are identical to those for the T-bill future. Prices for CD futures are quoted in a similar fashion to T-bill futures, as shown in Table 12.6. The prices are simply indexes calculated by subtracting the annual interest rate from 100. A price move of 0.01 represents $25 of contract value. The maximum or limit move is 0.80 or $2,000 (80 × $25). Delivery calls for "no name CDs" that mature between the sixteenth day and last day of the month that follows three months after the delivery month. The identity of the particular bank CDs that will be accepted is not announced until two business days before the first day they can be delivered into the contract.

Eurodollar Futures. Eurodollar deposit contracts began trading on the IMM in December 1981. Contracts call for delivery in March, June, September, and December of each year. Prices are quoted on an index basis as 100 minus the annualized Eurodollar futures rate. The delivery value of the Eurodollar future, like the CD and T-bill futures, is $1 million.

The final settlement is made in cash directly through the IMM Clearinghouse based on the London Interbank Offer Rate (LIBOR) on the last trading day. The LIBOR rate on which settlement for the IMM contract is based is the average three-month time deposit rate quote on a random selection of 12 banks from the top 20 banks in the London Eurodollar market. Quotes at the termination of trading on this day and a quote collected at a randomly selected time in the last 80 minutes of trading are averaged to determine the settlement rate.

TABLE 12.6 Financial Instruments Futures Prices

```
GNMA 8% (CBT)-$100,000 prncpl; pts. 32nds. of 100%
June    67-18 67-19 67-10 67-16  -  3 13.720 + .022 19,253
Sept    66-19 66-20 66-13 66-17  -  5 13.951 + .038 10,327
Dec     65-25 65-25 65-16 65-20  -  7 14.172 + .054  3,498
Mar85   65-02 65-02 64-28 64-28  -  8 14.358 + .063  1,078
June    .... .... .... 64-09     -  8 14.507 + .063    206
Sept    63-27 63-27 63-26 63-26  -  7 14.627 + .056    111
Dec     63-13 63-14 63-13 63-13  -  7 14.731 + .056    262
Mar86   63-01 63-03 63-00 63-03  -  6 14.813 + .049    204
   Est vol 3,000; vol Fri 3,398; open int 34,939, +228
TREASURY BONDS (CBT)-$100,000; pts. 32nds of 100%
June    64-24 64-27 64-17 64-22  -  9 12.990 + .057 127,541
Sept    64-06 64-10 63-30 64-04  -  9 13.104 + .057  20,201
Dec     63-23 63-26 63-18 63-22  -  9 13.195 + .057   7,451
Mar85   63-11 63-14 63-08 63-10  -  9 13.273 + .059   5,716
June    62-29 63-03 62-29 62-31  -  9 13.346 + .060   4,179
Sept    62-20 62-25 62-20 62-22  -  9 13.405 + .053   1,473
Dec     62-14 62-17 62-12 62-14  -  9 13.457 + .054   1,128
Mar86   .... .... .... 62-07     -  9 13.506 + .054   1,231
June    61-30 62-05 61-30 62-01  -  9 13.547 + .054   1,927
Sept    61-28 61-31 61-27 61-27  -  9 13.588 + .055     340
Dec     61-23 61-23 61-22 61-22  -  9 13.622 + .055      52
   Est vol 85,000; vol Fri 102,635; open int 171,239, +2,187
TREASURY NOTES (CBT)-$100,000; pts. 32nds of 100%
June    75-03 75-03 74-29 75-03  -  4 12.417 + .027  26,018
Sept    74-12 74-14 74-09 74-14  -  4 12.559 + .027   1,975
Dec     73-24 73-28 73-24 73-28  -  4 12.682 + .027      87
Mar85   .... .... .... 73-11     -  4 12.800 + .028       1
   Est vol 3,800; vol Fri 3,600; open int 28,081, +20.
TREASURY BILLS (IMM) -$1 mil.; pts. of 100%
                                      Discount     Open
        Open  High  Low Settle Chg Settle Chg Interest
June    89.92 89.96 89.88 89.94  -  .04 10.06 +  .04 30,245
Sept    89.42 89.50 89.40 89.47  -  .01 10.53 +  .01 16,799
Dec     89.06 89.12 89.02 89.11  +  .03 10.89    .03  4,433
Mar85   88.72 88.81 88.72 88.79  +  .01 11.21  -  .01  1,938
June    88.48 88.53 88.46 88.52     .... 11.48  ....    656
Sept    88.26 88.30 88.25 88.30     .... 11.70  ....    333
Dec     88.10 88.10 88.06 88.09  -  .02 11.91 +  .02    160
Mar86   87.90 87.90 87.90 87.90  -  .02 12.10 +  .02    103
   Est vol 16,862; vol Fri 14,563; open int 54,667, +577.
BANK CDs (IMM)-$1 million; pts. of 100%
June    88.99 89.02 88.91 88.96  -  .03 11.04 +  .03 17,109
Sept    88.41 88.42 88.32 88.38  -  .03 11.62 +  .03  8,875
Dec     87.88 87.94 87.87 87.93  -  .02 12.07 +  .02  4,973
Mar85   87.48 87.55 87.47 87.55     .... 12.45  ....  1,795
June    87.14 87.22 87.14 87.21     .... 12.79  ....  2,047
Sept    86.83 86.92 86.83 86.91     .... 13.09  ....    467
   Est vol 6,326; vol Fri 5,327; open int 35,266, +276.
```

Long-Term Instruments: GNMAs, Treasury Bonds, Treasury Notes

Individuals exposed to the risk of short-term fluctuations in interest rates who look to profit from shifts in long-term rates may use long-term futures contracts. These contracts may be used to hedge exposure to government bond auctions, government and corporate bond portfolios, and mortgage commitments.[11]

Quotations for T-bond, Treasury note (T-note), and GNMA CDR futures are shown in Table 12.6. The opening, high, low, and closing or settle prices are given for each delivery month. All price quotes are in thirty-seconds. The

---

[11] For the use of financial futures in the management of long-term corporate debt, see Richard W. McEnally and Michael L. Rice, ''Hedging Possibilities in the Flotation of Debt Securities,'' *Financial Management* (Winter 1979), pp. 12–18.

TABLE 12.7   GNMA Collateralized Depositary Receipt Principal Factors

GNMA Certificate Interest Rate	Amount Equivalent to $100,000 Principal Balance of GNMA 8 Percent Certificates	GNMA Certificate Interest Rate	Amount Equivalent to $100,000 Principal Balance of GNMA 8 Percent Certificates
6½	$112,123.30	16	$62,208.40
7	107,816.70	16½	60,744.10
7½	103,806.20	17	59,347.20
8	100,000.00	17½	58,013.10
8½	96,501.80	18	56,737.60
9	93,167.70	18½	55,517.00
9½	90,032.20	19	54,347.80
10	87,146.00	19½	53,226.90
10½	84,328.90	20	52,151.20
11	81,743.90	20½	51,118.20
11½	79,302.10	21	50,125.30
12	76,972.40	21½	49,170.30
12½	74,766.40	22	48,250.90
13	72,674.40	22½	47,365.30
13½	70,721.40	23	46,511.60
14	68,823.10	23½	45,714.30
14½	67,057.80	24	44,918.60
15	65,359.50	24½	44,150.10
15½	63,745.00	25	43,407.50

Source: Chicago Board of Trade

settle, yield to maturity, and yield change are also reported, followed by the open interest.

The GNMA futures traded at the CBT were first offered in October 1975. The prices quoted are based on $100,000 of principal balance with an 8 percent coupon. GNMA pools can be delivered at other coupon rates via adjustment of the principal balance by a conversion factor as shown in Table 12.7. The actual delivery instrument in the GNMA futures is the collateralized depositary receipt or CDR. This is a document prepared and signed by a bank certifying that it has received on deposit the equivalent of $100,000 principal balance of GNMA 8 percent certificates. CDRs can be acquired by those wishing to deliver into a GNMA futures contract by originating a new CDR or by taking from another originator.

T-bond futures call for delivery of T-bonds with $100,000 face value during the delivery period. Deliverable bonds must have a maturity date and a call date no sooner than 15 years from the delivery date. T-note futures are also based on $100,000 face value per contract. Deliverable notes are those maturing no less than 6½ years and no more than 10 years from the delivery date.

TABLE 12.8 Bond and Note Conversion Factors

DELIVERABLE TREASURY BONDS

Coupon	Maturity	Dec 83	Mar 84	Jun 84	Sep 84	Dec 84	Mar 85	Jun 85
8¼	May 15, 2000–2005	1.0223	1.0223	1.0220	1.0220	1.0216	1.0216	—
7⅝	Feb. 15, 2002–2007	0.9645	0.9646	0.9650	0.9651	0.9655	0.9655	0.9660
7⅞	Nov. 15, 2002–2007	0.9878	0.9880	0.9879	0.9882	0.9881	0.9883	0.9882
8⅜	Aug. 15, 2003–2008	1.0367	1.0363	1.0363	1.0359	1.0359	1.0355	1.0355
8¾	Nov. 15, 2003–2008	1.0736	1.0734	1.0728	1.0726	1.0720	1.0718	1.0711
9⅛	May 15, 2004–2009	1.1117	1.1113	1.1105	1.1102	1.1093	1.1089	1.1081
10⅜	Nov. 15, 2004–2009	1.2383	1.2374	1.2360	1.2350	1.2336	1.2326	1.2310
11¾	Feb. 15, 2005–2010	1.3785	1.3764	1.3749	1.3727	1.3711	1.3689	1.3672
10	May 15, 2005–2010	1.2025	1.2019	1.2007	1.1999	1.1987	1.1979	1.1967
12¾	Nov. 15, 2005–2010	1.4856	1.4838	1.4813	1.4794	1.4768	1.4748	1.4722
11¾	Feb. 15, 2001	1.3452	1.3425	1.3403	1.3374	1.3351	1.3322	1.3298

(continued)

TABLE 12.8   Bond and Note Conversion Factors (continued)

DELIVERABLE TREASURY BONDS

Coupon	Maturity	Dec 83	Mar 84	Jun 84	Sep 84	Dec 84	Mar 85	Jun 85
13⅛	May 15, 2001	1.4747	1.4718	1.4681	1.4650	1.4612	1.4580	1.4541
13⅞	May 15, 2006–2011	1.6058	1.6036	1.6007	1.5984	1.5954	1.5930	1.5898
13⅜	Aug. 15, 2001	1.5016	1.4979	1.4948	1.4910	1.4877	1.4837	1.4804
15¾	Nov. 15, 2001	1.7276	1.7233	1.7180	1.7134	1.7080	1.7032	1.6976
14	Nov. 15, 2006–2011	1.6238	1.6216	1.6187	1.6165	1.6135	1.6111	1.6080
14¼	Feb. 15, 2002	1.5909	1.5868	1.5833	1.5790	1.5753	1.5709	1.5671
11⅝	Nov. 15, 2002	1.3487	1.3470	1.3446	1.3427	1.3402	1.3383	1.3357
10⅜	Nov. 15, 2007–2012	1.2505	1.2499	1.2487	1.2480	1.2468	1.2461	1.2448
10¾	Feb. 15, 2003	1.2663	1.2645	1.2632	1.2614	1.2600	1.2581	1.2566
10¾	May 15, 2003	1.2675	1.2663	1.2645	1.2632	1.2614	1.2600	1.2581
12	Aug. 15, 2008–2013	1.4268	1.4251	1.4234	1.4221	1.4209	1.4190	1.4177
11⅛	Aug. 15, 2003	1.3060	1.3041	1.3026	1.3006	1.2991	1.2970	1.2954
11⅞	Nov. 15, 2003	1.3812	1.3794	1.3771	1.3753	1.3728	1.3709	1.3683

DELIVERABLE TREASURY NOTES

Coupon	Maturity	Dec 83	Mar 84	Jun 84	Sep 84	Dec 84	Mar 85
10¾	Aug. 15, 1990	1.1373					
13	Nov. 15, 1990	1.2566	1.2496				
14½	May 15, 1991	1.3521	1.3433	1.3337	1.3245		
14⅞	Aug. 15, 1991	1.3822	1.3724	1.3631	1.3529	1.3433	
14¼	Nov. 15, 1991	1.3555	1.3474	1.3385	1.3301	1.3208	1.3121
14⅝	Feb. 15, 1992	1.3860	1.3769	1.3683	1.3588	1.3499	1.3401
13¾	May 15, 1992	1.3421	1.3350	1.3271	1.3197	1.3114	1.3037
10½	Nov. 15, 1992	1.1549	1.1521	1.1486	1.1457	1.1421	1.1390
10⅞	Feb. 15, 1993	1.1820	1.1782	1.1749	1.1710	1.1675	1.1634
10⅛	May 15, 1993	1.1368	1.1345	1.1317	1.1293	1.1263	1.1238
11⅞	Aug. 15, 1993	1.2545	1.2496	1.2453	1.2402	1.2357	1.2305
10¾	July 15, 1990	1.1373					
11½	Oct. 15, 1990	1.1796	1.1747				
11¾	Nov. 15, 1993	1.2503	1.2463	1.2416	1.2374	1.2325	1.2281

Note: This table shows the Treasury bonds and notes eligible for delivery against CBT bond and note contracts along with the conversion factors for the listed delivery months. Additional coupons may become eligible as the U.S. Government issues new debt, and traders should be aware of these new issues as they become available.

Source: Chicago Board of Trade

Price quotations in the T-bond (T-note) futures market are based on a bond (note) with an 8 percent coupon rate and a 15-year (10-year) maturity. However, various bonds (notes) may be delivered. As of December 1983, any of the long-term U.S. Treasury bonds (notes) listed in Table 12.8, which starts on page 12-23, may be delivered against expiring bond (notes) futures contracts. However, each eligible coupon and maturity has a different value and, for delivery, this value must be adjusted to reflect the contract standard at the established settlement price.

The CBT relates the futures price to coupons other than 8 percent via a set of conversion factors that represent the relative values of these deliverable bonds. For any delivery month, all deliverable issues have a specific conversion factor reflecting their value and maturity at that particular time. (Conversion factors are available from Financial Publishing Co., Boston, MA 02215, Pub. #765)

As new issues come into supply before or during the delivery month, they are added to the list. As a bond's time to maturity decreases below the eligible limit, it is dropped from the deliverable supply. A seller delivering any one of the eligible bonds calculates the invoice amount for a particular issue by multiplying the futures settlement price by the appropriate conversion factor and adding the accrued interest. The buyer then holds an investment with a yield equal to the yield he would have received had he paid the settlement price and received an 8 percent coupon. For example, if a seller delivers 12¾ percent bonds against one bond futures contract in December 1983 at a settlement price of 65-00, he invoices the buyer $0.6500 \times 1.4856 \times \$100,000 = \$92,200$ plus accrued interest. The same procedure is used for invoicing T-note contracts, with an 8 percent, 10-year note used as the standard note.

All active financial futures contracts traded on the CBT (T-bond, T-note, and GNMA futures) have similar delivery sequences. Timing and quality of delivery are at the option of the seller of futures (the "short") during the delivery month. This includes the possibility of delivery after the futures cease trading seven business days prior to the end of the month. Buyers (or "longs") holding these futures contracts over the delivery period face the risk of untimely delivery of the securities either by selling in the cash market or by redelivering them in the futures market. There is risk, however, associated with changes in the value of the cash securities over the period the buyer must hold them before they are sold or redelivered.

The delivery process takes three days. This allows the buyer, seller, and clearinghouse sufficient time to notify the appropriate parties, deliver the bonds, and transfer the funds. The activities that take place on each of the three days are covered in Figure 12.2.

Stock Index Futures Contracts

In addition to interest rate futures, the CME and the NYFE have futures contracts based on the Standard & Poor's (S&P) 500 and New York Stock Exchange (NYSE) indexes, respectively. The Kansas City Futures Exchange opened the first stock index futures on the Value Line index in February 1982. Stock index futures provide a means of adjusting spot exposure to the overall

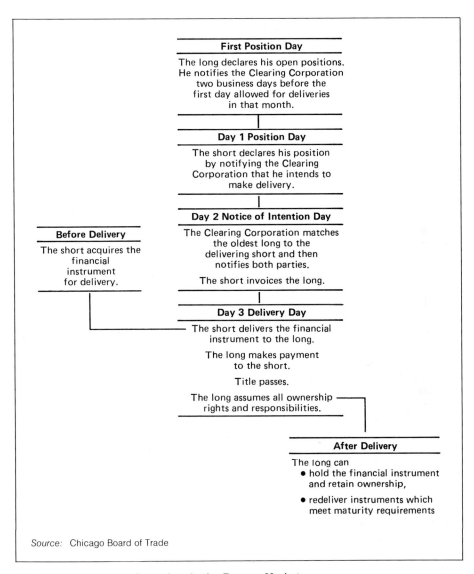

First Position Day

The long declares his open positions. He notifies the Clearing Corporation two business days before the first day allowed for deliveries in that month.

Day 1 Position Day

The short declares his position by notifying the Clearing Corporation that he intends to make delivery.

Day 2 Notice of Intention Day

The Clearing Corporation matches the oldest long to the delivering short and then notifies both parties.

The short invoices the long.

Before Delivery

The short acquires the financial instrument for delivery.

Day 3 Delivery Day

The short delivers the financial instrument to the long.

The long makes payment to the short.

Title passes.

The long assumes all ownership rights and responsibilities.

After Delivery

The long can
- hold the financial instrument and retain ownership,
- redeliver instruments which meet maturity requirements

Source: Chicago Board of Trade

FIG. 12.2 The Delivery Procedure in the Futures Market

stock market.[12] These futures permit an individual to increase risk (reduce risk) exposure in anticipation of a bull (bear) market. Stock index futures can also serve as substitutes for spot positions in the stock index. Futures on stock indexes represent a contract to buy or sell in the index at a predetermined price. This price is the price or value of the futures contract at the time of initiation. The value of the futures contract is $500 times the stocks' quoted

---

[12] For the use of stock index futures in risk management, see Stephen Figlewski and Stanley J. Kon, "Portfolio Management with Stock Index Futures," *Financial Analysts Journal* (Jan.–Feb. 1980), pp. 52–60.

TABLE 12.9   Stock Indexes

S&P 500 FUTURES INDEX (CME) 500 Times Index

June	160.70	161.65	160.20	161.40	+	.50	177.10 155.00	29,420
Sept	163.10	164.00	162.55	163.75	+	.45	178.15 156.80	1,906
Dec	166.20	166.20	164.90	166.00	+	.70	179.20 158.60	186
Mar85	168.20	168.20	166.90	167.80	+	.70	180.25 160.50	19
June	170.30	170.30	168.80	169.80	+	.80	180.70 161.75	6
Sept	172.05	172.05	170.50	171.55	+	.85	172.05 165.70	5

Est vol 38,498; vol Fri 37,207; open int 31,542, - 848.

S&P 500 STOCK INDEX (Prelim)
160.08 160.43 159.30 160.04 + .15

S&P 100 FUTURES INDEX (CME) 200 Times Index

May	158.10	158.90	157.95	158.90	+	.60	158.90 153.10	6
June	158.50	159.80	158.20	159.55	+	.65	177.80 152.20	2,828
July	.....	.....	.....	160.15	+	.65	157.90 154.05	1
Sept	161.75	161.75	160.75	161.90	+	.60	162.00 154.30	6

Est vol 475; vol Fri 893; open int 2,841, + 10.

S&P 100 STOCK INDEX (Prelim)
158.84 159.15 157.61 158.68 + .39 ....

NYSE COMPOSITE FUTURES (NYFE) 500 Times Index

June	92.40	93.10	92.20	92.95	+	.40	103.00 82.30	6,498
Sept	93.60	94.20	93.40	94.15	+	.40	103.10 89.25	1,097
Dec	94.90	95.40	94.80	95.35	+	.40	103.55 91.35	610
Mar85	96.10	96.60	96.10	96.55	+	.40	103.80 93.00	200
June	97.30	97.30	97.10	97.75	+	.40	105.00 94.25	73
Sept	98.50	98.80	98.50	98.95	+	.40	99.00 96.00	22

Est vol 14,844; vol Fri 11,621; open int 8,500, 43.

NYSE COMPOSITE STOCK INDEX
91.89 92.21 91.65 91.98 + .04

KC VALUE LINE FUTURES (KC) 500 Times Index

June	180.50	181.70	180.20	181.45	+	.70	212.00 176.15	3,292
Sept	183.20	183.95	182.60	183.85	+	.50	213.50 178.45	113
Dec	.....	.....	.....	186.25	+	.50	210.00 182.20	3

Est vol 2,850; vol Fri 2,883; open int 3,413, + 109.

KC VALUE LINE COMPOSITE STOCK INDEX
180.17 180.43 179.68 179.91 .25

price. A sample of price quotations for stock index futures and their underlying indexes is shown in Table 12.9. The minimum trading increment is 0.05 or $25 (0.05 × $500). S&P 500 futures have a daily limit of 5.00 points or $2,500 in price changes, except in the delivery month.

Unlike most other futures contracts, stock index futures settle in cash rather than in delivery of the stock in the index underlying the futures contract. Cash settlement is used because of the cost and logistical problems of buying the stocks in the right amounts to carry out physical delivery. Futures have a specific termination time and data at which the final settlement price is set and the futures cease trading. For all stock futures contracts the time is 4 P.M., Eastern Standard Time, of the last trading day of the contract. Thus the final settlement price is tied to the closing value of the index on the last trading day. Cash settlement is carried out after adjustment for losses or gains marked-to-market daily. If the settlement price is above the price at which the futures contract was established, funds that have been marked to market by the futures sellers are credited to those with long futures positions.

Currency Futures

With the change from fixed to floating rates in the early 1970s, variability in foreign currency values increased dramatically. The possibilities of the cur-

TABLE 12.10   Foreign Currencies

```
BRITISH POUND (IMM)  25,000 pounds, $ per pound
June   1.4020 1.4640 1.3990 1.4040 ...  .0010 1.5520 1.3950 17,376
Sept   1.4100 1.4115 1.4065 1.4115      .0010 1.5240 1.3975  2,541
Dec    1.4155 1.4185 1.4140 1.4190      .0010 1.5100 1.3990     96
Mar85                      1.4265       .0010 1.5170 1.4000     76
   Est vol 5,058; vol Fri 3,377; open int 20,089,  395.
CANADIAN DOLLAR (IMM)  100,000 dlrs.; $ per Can $
June    .7806 .7807 .7763 .7769   .0040 .8168 .7763 7,314
Sept    .7805 .7805 .7767 .7772   .0038 .8147 .7767   611
Dec     .7801 .7801 .7769 .7774   .0040 .8048 .7769 1,740
Mar85   .7800 .7800 .7776 .7776   .0040 .8050 .7776 1,433
June    .7820 .7820 .7820 .7780   .0040 .7835 .7820     3
   Est vol 4,248; vol Fri 1,362; open int 11,101, +241.
JAPANESE YEN (IMM)  12.5 million yen; $ per yen (.00)
June    .4441 .4443 .4429 .4440 + .0004 .4565 .4180 29,650
Sept    .4492 .4496 .4485 .4494 + .0005 .4615 .4351  1,932
Dec     .4554 .4558 .4545 .4557 + .0004 .4663 .4395    814
Mar85                     .4619 + .0004 .4695 .4615     17
   Est vol 8,075; vol Fri 12,664; open int 32,413, -1,178.
SWISS FRANC (IMM)  125,000 francs-$ per franc
June    .4502 .4510 .4490 .4495 - .5045 .4490 23,373
Sept    .4586 .4590 .4572 .4575   .0014 .5020 .4572  1,629
Dec     .4663 .4663 .4655 .4655   .0015 .5000 .4655    314
Mar85   .4745 .4760 .4735 .4735   .0018 .5035 .4735     27
June                      .4820 - .0015 .4900 .4835      6
   Est vol 11,629; vol Fri 13,512; open int 25,349, +307.
W. GERMAN MARK (IMM)  125,000 marks; $ per mark
June    .3708 .3710 .3693 .3703 -- .0011 .4002 .3568 32,688
Sept    .3761 .3761 .3742 .3753 -  .0011 .4037 .3602  1,720
Dec     .3810 .3810 .3796 .3805 -  .0011 .4080 .3640    491
Mar85                      .3855 - .0011 .4110 .3699     19
   Est vol 12,874; vol Fri 22,387; open int 34,918,  357.
```

rency futures markets for hedging, speculation, and arbitrage are endless. Companies borrowing or investing abroad, manufacturers exporting or importing goods or raw materials, and investors selling or purchasing foreign securities are some currency futures market users. In short, for any condition under which the uncertainty of the future value of the currency is of concern, the currency markets provide a means of hedging the risk.[13] Foreign currency futures were established at the IMM in 1972. The IMM quotes currencies in terms of the U.S. dollar. A sample of price quotations for currency futures is shown in Table 12.10. All quotations, therefore, are prices per unit of the foreign currency. Delivery procedures follow those prescribed for other financial futures traded on the IMM.

MARKET ORGANIZATION

A general knowledge of the regulations, trading rules, terminology, and risks is important for an understanding of financial futures markets. As shown in Table

---

[13] For the effectiveness of foreign currency futures, see Joanne Hill and Thomas Schneeweis, "The Hedging Effectiveness of Foreign Currency Futures," *Journal of Financial Research* (Spring 1982), pp. 95–104; and Joanne Hill, et al. "An Analysis of the Impact of Variation Margin in Hedging Fixed-Income Securities," *Review of Research in Futures Markets*, No. 1 (1983), pp. 136–159.

12.1, a number of exchanges trade financial futures. Financial futures contracts traded on U.S. commodity exchanges are regulated by exchange rules that have been approved by the Commodity Futures Trading Commission (CFTC). The rules and regulations clearly define the size of a contract, what is eligible for delivery, where delivery must take place, how a contract is priced and invoiced, and when trading begins and stops.

The Exchange

As of January 1983, there were six actively traded interest rate futures contracts in the United States. The CBT conducts trading in U.S. T-bond, GNMA, and 10-year T-note contracts. The IMM trades shorter maturities contracts (e.g., 90-day T-bill, 90-day CD, and 90-day Eurodollar contracts). Foreign currency futures are traded principally on the CME. In addition to these contracts, stock index futures are traded on a number of exchanges. The S&P Composite index is traded on the CME, the NYSE Composite index is traded on the NYFE, and the Value Line index is traded on the Kansas City Futures Exchange. While each of these exchanges may have minor differences in organizational structure, their similarities outweigh their differences.

Exchange Members

Members who trade on the floor of an exchange can be classified into two major categories: (1) commission brokers and (2) locals. Commission brokers, or floor brokers, make trades on an independent basis as well as for commission firms or other dealers holding seats on the exchange. When not trading for his own account, a floor broker receives his instructions through the firm with which he is associated or for which is acting. Orders are normally received by telephone and recorded and time stamped before they are executed. The floor broker might be instructed to execute the order at the current market price, at a specific price or price range, or at a specific time. If the floor broker trades for his personal account, he must ensure that customer orders are filled before executing his personal order at an equal or better price.

    In contrast to commission brokers, locals trade for themselves. Locals can be position traders, day traders, scalpers, or spreaders. The scalper provides instant market liquidity for orders by buying from or selling to a broker wishing to execute a public order. During the day he trades off the minimum fluctuations that occur during trading. At the end of the day, the scalper hopes to have a zero net position. The day trader is similar to the scalper in that he holds market positions only during the day and wishes to have a zero (flat) position at market close. The day trader holds his position longer than the scalper. The position trader generally initiates and holds a position longer than one day. In contrast to the day trader or scalper, he has open positions at market close. The spreader trades futures across contract months or various futures within a single contract month. The spreader may hold his position over a day or close it at day's end.

The Clearing Corporation

The integrity of futures is maintained through the clearing corporation. Clearing corporation membership is determined by financial and professional criteria established by the board of directors of an exchange. The clearinghouses have daily responsibilities to reconcile, clear, and issue all trades. In addition to determining margin requirements for all marking-to-market contracts, the corporation also adjusts open positions to settlement prices. Daily margin calls are made to clearing members whose balances reflect a debit. If a member fails to meet a margin call by 9:15 A.M. the following day, all open positions of the firm are assigned to other clearing members in a predetermined manner. If a member's position reflects a net gain, the additional credit balance is available for withdrawal that morning.

By acting as the intermediary for all trades and providing daily collection of profit and losses, the corporation ensures that a buyer (seller) who wishes to sell (purchase) his futures contract after purchasing (selling) it does not have to worry if the original seller (buyer) wishes to purchase it back. If a seller of a contract wishes to make delivery, the clearing corporation notifies the member with the oldest outstanding long position in that particular commodity. The selling member is then notified of the name of the buying member. The final invoicing and payment procedures are conducted between the buyer and seller under the rules of the clearing corporation.

Orders Frequently Used

For most individuals, trades are conducted through their representative futures commission merchants (FCMs). FCMs are individuals or entities engaged in soliciting and accepting orders from customers for the purchase or sale of futures contracts, and accepting money or property to purchase the contracts. An associated person (AP) is an FCM or his agent who acts in the capacity of soliciting and accepting customer orders.

A commodity trading advisor (CTA) is a person who advises (for profit) as to the value and trading of financial futures. Commodity pool operators (CPOs) are persons engaged in a business, such as an investment trust, that receives funds for the purpose of trading financial futures. For a futures order to be executed, the order must be processed through a floor broker or his offices.

Market Order. The most frequently used order is a market order, which instructs a floor broker to promptly execute an order at the most favorable price available.

Limit Order. A buy limit order stipulates that the floor broker execute the order within the limit set by the customer. If it is a sell limit order, the broker cannot sell for an amount less than that stipulated. If the price is touched, it is not guaranteed that the order is executed. Commodity trading price moves are rapid and numerous brokers may have orders to fill at an identical level. The limit order, however, assures a client that he will not pay more or sell for less than a specified price.

TABLE 12.11   Average Month-End Open Interest, Estimated Number of Contracts Traded, and Number of Contracts Settled by Delivery by Major Groups, All Markets Combined

Fiscal Year	Financial Instruments	Currencies
AVERAGE MONTH-END OPEN INTEREST		
(in contracts)		
1977	17,909	10,204
1978	57,221	22,578
1979	186,410	34,257
1980	190,966	52,262
1981	408,813	55,028
1982	359,038	73,550
NUMBER OF CONTRACTS TRADED (a)		
1977	604,522	393,234
1978	1,595,383	1,345,527
1979	4,570,694	2,003,746
1980	10,212,968	3,718,635
1981	20,091,322	5,397,939
1982	31,251,497	8,284,391
NUMBER OF CONTRACTS SETTLED BY DELIVERY		
1977	2,267	4,060
1978	5,315	8,830
1979	21,350	6,861
1980	32,854	22,544
1981	47,728	49,471
1982	50,082	47,817

(a) Based on a standard 5,000 bushel contract

Source: Commodity Futures Trading Commission Annual Report

Stop Orders. Stop orders are executed differently than limit orders. A buy stop order is placed above the current market price and becomes a market order if the price is touched. A sell stop order is placed below the current market price.

Straight Cancel Order. A straight cancel order cancels out an order in the pit. If a client forgets to cancel or replace an order before entering a new one, both the old and new order may be executed.

Open Orders — Good Until Cancelled. These orders will continue to be placed in the pit until the order is executed or is cancelled by the customer.

Order Fulfillment. Once a commodity futures order is entered by a customer, the broker must get the order to the trading floor of the appropriate exchange. In some cases a customer may be allowed to call directly to an order desk to ensure expeditious executions. When an order is received on the floor of an exchange, it is recorded and time stamped. A copy of the order is rushed into the pit and given to a floor broker for execution. A market order is filled immediately. Other orders are held by the pit broker for the appropriate execution. Until an order is cancelled, the broker assumes responsibility for its proper execution. When the order has a price limit, the phone clerk or floor broker files it in his deck. Limit orders are filed by price, with the transaction being completed as the market moves to the unit price. If the broker holds more than one order at the same price, the orders must be executed in the sequence received.

Trading Activity

Efficient pricing in the futures markets is enhanced through the trading activities and competition of different buyers and sellers. Two principal measures of the ability of a market to accept orders are trading volume and open interest. Trading volume is the number of unit contract transactions during a period of time. The trading volume is given for only one side of the trade: A volume of 20,000 translates to 20,000 contracts bought and 20,000 contracts sold. Since for every buyer there must be a seller, the number of contracts bought must always equal the number of contracts sold. Open interest is the number of open contracts at a point in time. Average month-end open interest, estimated number of contracts traded, and number of contracts settled by delivery for financial instruments and currencies are given in Table 12.11. Estimated average month-end open interest, 12-month total volume of trading, and deliveries by financial futures contract for fiscal years ending September 30, 1981 and September 30, 1982 are given in Table 12.12.

The principal trading activity in most futures markets is by the hedger. Trading activity is of value to the hedger only if the financial futures market reduces the overall riskiness of the cash position. The futures position was determined assuming a naive hedge and a commonly used method for determining a minimum risk hedge ratio (historical ratio of the covariance between price

TABLE 12.12 Contract Market Review: Estimated Average Month-End Open Interest, 12-Month Total Volume of Trading, and Deliveries by Commodity, Fiscal Years Ending September 30, 1981 and September 30, 1982

Exchange/Commodity	Contract Unit	Month-End Open Interest (in Contracts)		Volume of Trading (in Contracts)		Settled by Delivery	
		1980–1981	1981–1982	1980–1981	1981–1982	1980–1981	1981–1982
Chicago Board of Trade							
U.S. T-bond	$ 100,000	242,966	194,486	11,973,459	16,556,569	24,911	25,554
Commercial paper loan, 90-day	1,000,000	24	—	2,590	—	—	—
Commercial paper loan, 30-day	3,000,000	—	—	1	—	—	—
U.S. T-note, 4–6 years	100,000	—	2	2,771	—	38	—
GNMA mortgage (CDR)	100,000	64,249	64,249	2,392,076	2,198,646	9,806	2,644
GNMA mortgage (CD)	100,000	64	476	476	15	239	105
Domestic CD, 90-day	1,000,000	2,481	2,481	90,531	213,715	93	192
U.S. T-note, 6.5–10 years	100,000	14,706	14,706	—	655,895	—	7,080
MidAmerica Commodity Exchange							
U.S. T-bond	$ 50,000	10,373	1,384	10,373	406,069	—	152
U.S. T-bill	500,000	—	382	—	70,540	—	9
Kansas City Board of Trade							
Value Line index	$500 × index	—	3,836	—	352,248	—	938
Chicago Mercantile Exchange and International Monetary Market Index and Option Market							
Canadian dollar	$ 100,000	8,492	12,809	458,592	948,139	8,836	9,210
French franc	250,000	96	317	1,598	9,131	140	802
Swiss franc	125,000	9,496	13,589	1,210,039	2,475,614	8,795	6,654

	Contract size						
Dutch guilder	125,000	—	—	—	4	—	—
Deutsche mark	125,000	11,598	13,164	1,485,124	1,806,012	9,969	6,444
Mexican peso	1,000,000	1,985	4,045	18,005	61,125	760	2,225
British pound sterling	25,000	13,892	15,297	1,377,716	1,434,415	12,835	12,333
Japanese yen	12,500,000	9,330	14,320	832,665	1,549,951	7,361	10,249
U.S. T-bill, 90-day	1,000,000	37,904	42,537	5,072,432	6,782,275	5,613	4,214
U.S. T-bill, 1-year	250,000	1	—	8	—	4	—
U.S. Note, 4-year	100,000						
Domestic CD, 90-day	1,000,000	2,277	9,207	104,474	1,610,017	330	2,732
Eurodollar, 3-month	1,000,000	—	9,020	—	217,492	—	2,256
S&P 500 index	$500 × index	—	10,036	—	1,430,479	—	1,711
Commodity Exchange							
U.S. T-bill, 90-day	$ 1,000,000	122	—	21,645	—	853	—
GNMA mortgage (CD)	100,000	—	—	—	—	—	—
U.S. T-note, 2-year	100,000	799	4	47,624	217	2,769	—
New York Futures Exchange							
U.S. T-bill, 90-day	$ 1,000,000	358	—	26,480	—	1,328	—
U.S. T-bond	100,000	5,445	1,880	225,527	7,882	1,899	1,939
Domestic CD, 90-day	1,000,000	817	71	90,855	27,084	45	60
British pound sterling	25,000	74	—	3,829	—	426	—
Canadian dollar	100,000	7	—	230	—	35	—
Deutsche mark	125,000	4	—	147	—	15	—
Japanese yen	12,500,000	6	—	91	—	27	—
Swiss franc	125,000	48	—	903	—	272	—
NYSE composite index	$500 × index	—	4,693	—	722,354	—	459

Source: Commodity Futures Trading Commission Annual Report

TABLE 12.13   The New Options Markets

Instrument	Options on Physicals	Options of Futures Contracts
Stock indexes	Chicago Board Options Exchange (S&P 100 (formerly CBOE 100), S&P 500)	Chicago Mercantile Exchange (S&P 500)
	American Stock Exchange (Amex Major Market index, Amex Market Value index)	New York Futures Exchange (NYSE Composite index)
	New York Stock Exchange (NYSE Composite index)	
U.S. Government debt	American Stock Exchange (T-bills, T-notes)	Chicago Board of Trade (T-bonds)
	Chicago Board Options Exchange (T-bonds)	
Foreign currencies	Philadelphia Stock Exchange (Various currencies (a))	

(a) Canadian dollar, deutsche mark, Japanese yen, Swiss franc, and pound sterling

Source: *FRBNY Quarterly Review* (Autumn 1983)

changes in the cash and futures markets and the variance of the futures price changes).[14] For the period of analysis, the results show the relative effectiveness of financial futures trading. Studies have shown that for T-bonds, GNMA certificates, currency, and stock, variance in the monthly spot price changes is reduced when approximately 50 percent of a naive hedge or a minimum risk hedge ratio is used.[15] Futures trading therefore provides individuals a means to decrease (or increase) their equity, interest-rate risk, or currency exposure.

USING OPTIONS IN AN INVESTMENT STRATEGY

In addition to financial futures, security options have also experienced rapid market growth. Options currently exist on individual stock issues, government debt (T-bills, T-notes, T-bonds), stock indexes, and foreign currencies.[16] In addition, options are being traded on an experimental basis on T-bond futures and stock index futures.[17] Table 12.13 lists currently traded options and their markets. (See Chapter 11 for an elaboration of option valuation models.)

In contrast to futures, which require the purchase or sale of the underlying instrument (unless the futures position is offset prior to delivery), the holder of an option may decide to let the option expire at delivery.[18] The option represents a *right* rather than an *obligation* to buy or sell a specific quantity of an underlying asset at a given price on or before a specified delivery date. The option is therefore a type of price insurance. Whereas gains and losses on

[14] Alternative methods of hedge ratio determination include OLS regression (Joanne Hill and Thomas Schneeweis, "The Use of Interest Rate Futures in Corporate Financing and Security Investment," *Proceedings: International Futures Trading Seminar* (Chicago Board of Trade, 1981)), duration (Robert Kolb and R. Chiang, "Improving Hedging Performance Using Interest Rate Futures," *Financial Management* (Autumn 1981), pp. 72–79), and basis analysis (Joanne Hill, et al., "Hedge Ratio Determination Based on Bond Yield Forecasts," *Review of Research in Futures Markets,* No. 3 (Chicago Board of Trade, 1983), pp. 338–349.

[15] For examples of the effectiveness of naive and historically derived minimum risk hedge ratios for government and corporate bonds, GNMA certificates, and foreign currency, see Joanne Hill and Thomas Schneeweis, "The Use of Interest Rate Futures in Corporate Financing and Security Investment," *Proceedings: International Futures Trading Seminar* (Chicago Board of Trade, 1981), and Joanne Hill and Thomas Schneeweis, "A Note on the Hedging Effectiveness of Foreign Currency Futures," *Journal of Futures Markets* (Winter, 1981), pp. 659–664.

[16] For excellent discussion of the new option markets, see L. Goodman, "New Option Markets," *Quarterly Review of the Federal Reserve Bank of New York* (Autumn 1983). Recent books on option pricing and strategy include Robert A. Jarrow and Andrew Rudd, *Option Pricing* (Homewood, Ill.: 1983), and Richard M. Bookstaber, *Option Pricing and Strategies in Investing* (Reading, Mass.: Addison-Wesley, 1981).

[17] For a comparison of options and futures, see Eugene Moriarty, et al., "A Comparison of Options and Futures in the Management of Portfolio Risk," *Financial Analysts Journal* (Jan.–Feb. 1981), pp. 61–67, and Richard Bookstaber, "Interest Rate Hedging for the Mortgage Banker: The Effect of Interest Rate Futures and Loan Commitments on Portfolio Return Distributions," *Review of Research in Futures Markets,* No. 1 (1982), pp. 22–51.

[18] The terms of delivery for the new option contracts include cash settlement, and physical delivery options on futures contracts require delivery of the futures contract. Foreign currency options require delivery of a specified amount of foreign currency. Options on stock indexes stipulate cash settlement. Options on debt require either fixed delivery (debt instruments with fixed characteristics) or variable (an existing debt issue).

futures contracts are limited only by the price of the underlying asset, the option market separates and limits the buyer's upside and downside risk.

Options are divided into two categories: calls, a holder's option to buy, and puts, a holder's option to sell. For options on financial futures, the buyer of a call option acquires the right to purchase (go long on) the future at the strike price any time before the expiration date (the date on which the option becomes void). On the other side, the seller, or writer, undertakes the obligation of assuming a short futures position if the option is exercised. With a put option, the buyer acquires the right to sell the future before the expiration date, while the seller undertakes the obligation of delivery.

Since buyers may or may not exercise their right, they have no obligation to perform after paying the premium, and there is no additional margin requirement. Conversely, the writer undertakes a firm commitment and is required to deposit margin when a position is opened. Margin is marked to market daily. As with futures, exercise is assured by clearing corporations, and the needs of original buyers and sellers are matched. The purchase of a call (put) retains upside (downside) profit opportunities. The net profit of a call (put) equals the underlying asset's increase above (decrease below) the option exercise price minus the option's premium.

Despite the differences in guaranteed delivery contracts, options and futures are close substitutes. In fact, the prices of puts, calls, and futures on the same underlying asset and the risk-free rate are related in such a way that, in equilibrium, the prices of any three of the instruments determine the price of the fourth. For example, a long position in a call option and a short position in a put option result in a payoff equal to that of a long position in a futures contract at expiration. Institutional constraints and transaction costs may make strategies such as this impractical. Options, like futures, are used for their own hedging and speculation purposes.

Hedging With Options

If one owns an underlying asset, to maintain a fully hedged position any change in the asset's price should be offset by an equivalent but opposite value change in the short position. Thus if a $1 change in an asset caused a 50-cent change in the call price, one could construct a fully hedged position by writing calls on twice as many assets as are bought. For example, if the investor is short two equity calls, a $1 increase (decrease) in a stock price is matched by a $1 decrease (increase) in the call position's value. Any change in the stock's price then will be precisely offset by a change in the option position's value. The hedge may be maintained by adjusting the ratio of stocks to calls whenever necessary.[19]

---

[19] Assuming that an investment in the combined riskless position should earn the riskless interest rate (approximately the rate on short-term government securities), Black-Scholes developed a call valuation formula which is a function of five variables. Call values increase with time to maturity, interest rates, the underlying stock's price, and volatility; they decrease as the striking price increases. For a given measure of return variability, exercise price, time to expiration, risk-free rate, and stock price, the Black-Scholes model also estimates the riskless hedge ratio (the number of shares held long for each one-share option written to invest in a neutral hedge).

Speculation

Options on a large number of units of an underlying asset can be bought for relatively small sums. Such an option position greatly magnifies the upside effect of price moves in that security. For example, the largest rise among NYSE issues in 1982 was Chrysler, which went from just above 3 to slightly above 18 (about a six-fold increase). Because of this upside leverage and downside loss limitation, in-the-money options are typically priced above their intrinsic values. Far out-of-the-money options and any out-of-the-money options near their expirations are, in contrast, usually almost worthless.

Risk

Since the option is exercised only at the buyer's desire, a purchased option can be considered a limited risk. The maximum loss is the premium paid to purchase the option. In contrast there is no comparable constraint on the risk in writing an option. While the option writer's maximum profit is the premium received from the option buyer, his potential loss equals the adverse movement of the underlying asset's price from the option's exercise price minus the option premium. In effect, the option writer is guaranteed a gross receipt equal to the option premium, but his net return may be considerably less, since he may suffer unlimited net loss.

Selling calls on stock that is owned (covered option writing) is considered conservative. In contrast, naked writers do not own any of the underlying stock. Such writers hope that the optioned stock will not rise above the striking price while the option remains in force. If the call is exercised, the naked writer is forced to buy the required shares at the market price and immediately sell them to the option holder. The naked writer takes a loss on the difference. Naked writing is similar to selling short. Both the naked writer and the short seller profit from a price decline and have potentially unlimited exposure to price rises. Like selling short, naked writing requires a margin deposit sufficient to guarantee the stock's purchase, if required. For example, in early 1981, near-expiration calls on Amax 50s (traded on the CBOE) were trading for 50 cents. Since the Amax stock was then under 40, the likelihood of exercise seemed remote. Just before the options were about to expire, however, SOCAL offered to acquire Amax for a price in the 70s. The market value of the Amax 50s rose to over $10. Option traders who had written Amax 50s for 50 cents were forced to cover at $10 or more.

Options vs. Futures

The risk/return rewards of options contrast with those for futures. In evaluating any given investment portfolio, it is important to consider both the expected return and the expected risk. For example, Figure 12.3(a) compares the hypothetical return distributions of a bond portfolio in a stable and volatile environment. While the expected return is higher in a volatile environment, the standard deviation of return (i.e., the risk) is also greater.

Bond futures make it possible to take advantage of the high level of interest rates and at the same time reduce the risk of interest-rate fluctuations. This is

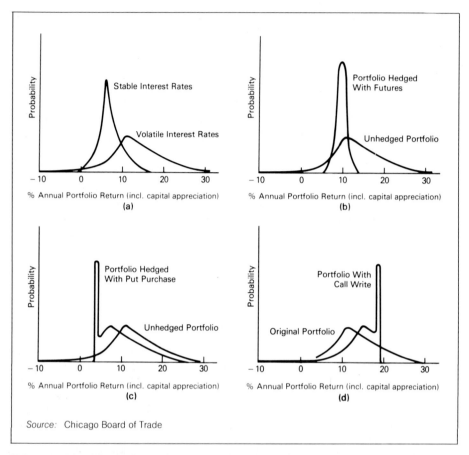

FIG. 12.3 **Hypothetical Return Distribution for a Bond Portfolio: (a) Not Hedged; (b) Hedged by Selling Futures; (c) Hedged by Purchasing Put Options; (d) Enhanced by Writing Call Options**

shown in Figure 12.3(b). But what bond futures do is change the fundamental nature of the portfolio's return distribution. As shown in Figure 12.3(c), with options on bond futures, a manager can actually modify the portfolio's risk/ reward structure and reduce the risk.

Options are especially designed to hedge the risks of a potential transaction that is not certain to take place. For instance, a U.S. firm may not be certain that a foreign sale may occur. If the firm purchases a put on the foreign exchange and the sale is not completed, the firm simply will not exercise the put. If the firm had sold a future, the firm would have to obtain currency for delivery or offset the futures position.

Tax Implications

Congress, reacting to perceived abuses of futures and options markets for tax purposes, enacted major revisions in the tax treatment of cash, futures, and options transactions into the Economic Recovery Tax Act of 1981.[20] At present, individual investors in futures are taxed on the 60/40 rule (long-term/short-term) with year-end mark to market. In contrast, for the individual investor all option trades are taxed as capital gains. Any trade closed in less than one year is considered a short-term capital gain. Since all listed options are under a one-year maturity, all option trades are treated as short-term capital gains. More specifically, if a put or call is bought and is later sold or expires unexercised, the resulting gain or loss from that transaction is a short-term capital gain or loss. If a combination of options is traded, each option is treated separately for income tax purposes.

While various Internal Revenue Service pronouncements are still being considered, for the individual investor options on futures are generally viewed as taxed in accordance with futures tax law, while options on debt are taxed in accordance with option tax policy. It is important to note that the tax rules for the corporation, investment company, tax-exempt organization, nonresident alien, and investors who are considered to be dealers or traders for their own account may differ. In more complex situations a professional tax advisor should be consulted.

REGULATION OF FUTURES TRADING

Regulation of commodity futures was originally based upon self-policing by the exchanges. The first federal oversight of commodity futures trading was initiated in 1922 with the Grain Futures Act. In 1936 the Commodity Exchange Act replaced the Grain Futures Act. The Commodity Exchange Act was subsequently amended as newly discovered needs arose. The increasing use of commodity markets and the problems surfacing in the 1972 Russian grain purchase led Congress in 1974 to drastically amend the 1936 Commodity Exchange Act. The 1974 amendments authorized the CFTC.[21] The CFTC is responsible to Congress for the functions previously assigned to the Department of Agriculture in the Commodity Exchange Act.[22]

The CFTC has regulatory authority over almost anything that is or can be the subject of a futures contract. As new product areas (e.g., options on futures) developed, a further distinction was necessary between the Securities and Exchange Commission (SEC) and CFTC on areas of regulation. Under a 1981 agreement the CFTC regulates (1) all futures contracts, (2) broadly based stock and bond index futures, (3) options on futures contracts (including financial futures), and (4) options on foreign currencies trading on commodity markets. The SEC regulates (1) all options directly on securities (stock as well as

---

[20] Tax policy on financial futures and options is under continual review. Investors are advised to consult officials for details on the appropriate financial accounting for interest rate futures.

[21] As required by law, the CFTC was reauthorized in 1978 and 1982.

[22] For a detailed discussion of regulation of futures trading see Howard Schneider, "Regulation of Futures Trading," *Handbook of Financial Markets*, Frank J. Fabozzi and Frank C. Zarb, eds. (New York: 1981). The CFTC Annual Report also reviews current and anticipated regulatory procedures.

bonds, bills, and stock indexes) and (2) options on foreign currencies trading on stock exchanges.

The principal concerns of the CFTC are the safeguarding of funds, the control of monopoly, and the prevention of price manipulation. A cursory view of the structure of the CFTC permits a better view of its regulatory directions and remedies. CFTC's organizational chart is shown in Figure 12.4. The principal regulatory divisions of the CFTC include the Division of Enforcement, the Division of Economics and Education, the Division of Trading and Marketing, and the Office of the General Counsel.

The CFTC's Division of Enforcement is responsible for investigation and prosecution of violations of the Commodity Exchange Act and CFTC regulations. This division is divided into two sections, customer protection and market integrity. The customer protection section investigates and litigates alleged violations of the sale of regulated instruments to the investing public. The market integrity section investigates possible violations directly in the exchanges.

The Division of Economics and Education is responsible for the daily analysis of market conditions to ensure against price manipulation and/or exchange disruptions. This division is also in charge of review of new futures contracts as well as the periodic review of current contracts. In addition to the CFTC's own surveillance programs, the exchanges themselves are responsible for self-monitoring. The CFTC's Division of Trading and Markets determines how the exchanges themselves are meeting their market surveillance and enforcement responsibilities. In addition, this division is in charge of screening applicants and reviewing exchange applications for contract market designation. Also, the Division of Trading and Markets considers exchange requests to implement new or revised rules and drafts regulations governing the operations of contract months and the registration, surveillance, and auditing entities regulated by the CFTC.

Lastly, the Office of the General Counsel is the CFTC's chief legal advisor and litigation counsel. The Counsel's office acts as reviewer of all major regulatory, legislative, and administrative matters. The Counsel also acts as advocate for the CFTC with the cooperation of the Solicitor General before the U.S. Supreme Court and the U.S. Court of Appeals, and defends the CFTC against actions brought against it.

Among the CFTC's principal regulatory responsibilities are the following:

1 Designation of (licensing) exchanges as "contract markets"

2 Conduct of periodic rule enforcement reviews of exchanges

3 Review and approval of all significant exchange rules except those related to the level of futures margins

4 Surveillance of all contracts to prevent price manipulation and market congestion

5 Registration and regulation of commodity professionals (e.g., FCMs)

6 Enforcement of statuatory prohibitions in administrative and civil judicial forums and referral of criminal violations to Department of Justice

7 Anti-fraud initiatives

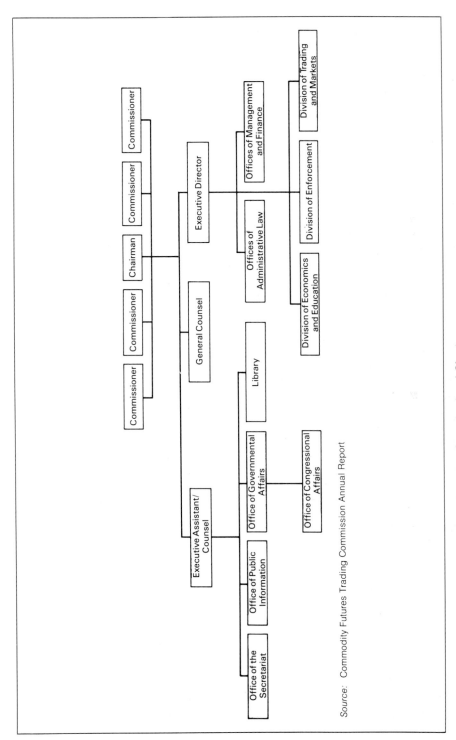

Source: Commodity Futures Trading Commission Annual Report

FIG. 12.4 Commodity Futures Trading Commission — Organizational Chart

This description of division directives covers only a few of the CFTC's major responsibilities. In addition to monitoring and correcting past grievances, the CFTC acts in concert with exchanges to prevent future problems from occurring. The CFTC is a regulator only in the last resort. The CFTC avoids direct government intervention as long as the exchanges themselves are attempting to deal effectively with a problem. Only when self-regulatory activities are incapable of solving the problem does the CFTC use its various powers such as suspending trading, imposing margins, or forcing a contract's liquidation.

To further enhance self-regulatory efforts, in September 1981 the CFTC registered the National Futures Association (NFA) as a self-regulatory organization. NFA activities should complement the CFTC's efforts to protect market participants with specific responsibility for registration, testing programs, and financial auditing. While the CFTC and the self-regulatory actions of the exchanges have proven successful in preventing severe breakdowns in the futures markets, areas of future stress are evident. In the near future the CFTC faces a number of critical decisions. These include (1) the degree of self-regulation, (2) the correct mission and size of the agency, (3) jurisdiction, (4) inside information, (5) cash settlement, (6) hedging, (7) off-exchange instruments, and (8) international exchange links. The success of the futures market depends ultimately on consumer confidence that the industry and additional regulatory boards have the consumer's interests in mind.

SUGGESTED READING

Books

Kolb, Robert. *Interest Rate Futures: A Comprehensive Introduction.* Richmond, Va.: Robert F. Dame, 1982.

Powers, Mark, and David Vogel. *Inside the Financial Futures Markets.* New York: John Wiley & Sons, 1981.

Schwartz, E., et al. *Financial Futures: Fundamentals, Strategy, and Applications.* Homewood, Ill.: Richard D. Irwin (forthcoming).

Introduction of Futures Markets

Arak, Marcell, and Christopher McCurdy. "Interest Rate Futures." *Quarterly Review of the Federal Reserve Bank of New York* (Winter 1979–1980), pp. 33–46.

———. "Interest Rate Futures." *Interest Rate Futures: A Comprehensive Anthology,* eds. G. Gay and R. W. Kolb. Richmond, Va.: Robert F. Dame, 1983, pp. 55–80.

Chicago Board of Trade. *Financial Instruments Markets: Cash-Futures Relationships* (1980).

Stevens, S. A. "A Mortgage Futures Market: Its Development, Uses, Benefits and Costs." *Federal Reserve Bank of St. Louis Review* (Apr. 1976), pp. 20–27.

Theory of Futures Markets

Arrow, Kenneth. "Futures Markets: Some Theoretical Perspectives." *Journal of Futures Markets* (Summer 1981), pp. 107–115.

Cornell, Bradford. "Spot Rates, Forward Rates and Exchange Market Efficiency." *Journal of Financial Economics* (Aug. 1977), pp. 55–60.

Cox, John, et al. *The Relationship Between Forward Prices and Futures Prices*. Columbia University, Center for the Study of Futures Markets, Working Paper No. 9. May 1981.

Fama, Eugene. "Forward Rates as Predictors of Future Spot Rates." *Journal of Financial Economics* (Oct. 1976), pp. 361–378.

Figlewski, Steven. "Futures Trading and Volatility in the GNMA Market." *Journal of Finance* (May 1981), pp. 445–456.

Simonoff, Jeffrey. "Application of Statistical Methodology to the Evaluation of Timing Devices in Commodities Trading." *Journal of Futures Markets* (Winter 1981), pp. 649–656.

Stein, Jerome. "The Simultaneous Determination of Spot and Futures Prices." *American Economic Review* (Dec. 1961), pp. 1012–1025.

Stoll, Hans. "Commodity Futures and Spot Price Determination and Hedging in Capital Market Equilibrium." *Journal of Financial and Quantitative Analysis* (Nov. 1979), pp. 873–894.

Telser, L., and H. N. Higinbotham. "Organized Futures Markets: Costs and Benefits." *Journal of Political Economy* (Oct. 1977), pp. 969–1000.

Concepts, Basic Strategies, and the Pricing of Futures

Emory, John, and Robert Scott. "Evidence of Expected Yields Implied From Term Structure and the Futures Market." *Business Economics* (May 1979), pp. 22–27.

Fisher, Black. "The Pricing of Commodity Contracts." *Journal of Financial Economics* (Jan.–Feb. 1976), pp. 167–179.

Froewiss, Kenneth. "GNMA Futures: Stabilizing or Destabilizing." *San Francisco Federal Reserve Bank Economic Review* (Spring 1978), pp. 20–29.

Jones, Frank. "The Integration of the Cash and Futures Markets for Treasury Securities." *Journal of Futures Markets* (Spring 1981), pp. 33–58.

Leibowitz, M. "Yield Basis for Financial Futures." *Financial Analysts Journal* (Jan.–Feb. 1981), pp. 43–51.

Sandor, Richard. "Trading Financial Instruments." *Industry Research Seminar: Proceedings,* Vol. 1 (1980) pp. 20–30.

Applications of Hedging to Financial Institutions and Corporations

Arditti, Fred. "Interest Rate Futures: An Intermediate State Toward Efficient Risk Reallocation." *Journal of Bank Research* (Autumn 1978), pp. 146–150.

Dew, Kurt. "Bank Regulations for Futures Accounting." *Interest Rate Futures: A Comprehensive Anthology,* eds. G. Gay and R. W. Kolb. Richmond, Va.: Robert F. Dame, 1983, pp. 413–420.

——. "Bank Regulations for Futures Accounting." *Issues in Bank Regulation* (Spring 1981), pp. 16–23.

——, and Terrance Martell. "T-Bill Futures, Commercial Lending, and The Synthetic Fixed Rate Loan." *Journal of Commercial Bank Lending* (June 1981), pp. 27–38.

Ederington, Louis. "The Hedging Performance of the New Futures Market." *Journal of Finance* (Mar. 1979), pp. 157–170.

Hill, Joanne, and Thomas Schneeweis. "Reducing Volatility with Financial Futures." *Financial Analysts Journal* (Mar.–Apr. 1984).

———. "Risk Reduction Potential of Financial Futures for Corporate Bond Positions." *Interest Rate Futures: A Comprehensive Anthology*, eds. G. Gay and R. W. Kolb. Richmond, Va.: Robert F. Dame, 1983.

Hill, Joanne, et al. "An Analysis of the Impact of Variation Margin in Hedging Fixed Income Securities." *Review of Research in Futures Markets*, Vol. 2, No. 1 (1983), pp. 136–159.

Schneeweis, Thomas, et al. "Hedge Ratio Determination Based on Bond Yield Forecasts." *Review of Research in Futures Markets*, Vol. 2, No. 3 (1983), pp. 338–349.

Arbitrage and Unbiased Expectations

Branch, Ben. "Testing the Unbiased Expectations Theory of Interest Rates." *Financial Review* (Fall 1978), pp. 51–66.

———. "Testing the Unbiased Expectations Theory of Interest Rates." *Interest Rate Futures: A Comprehensive Anthology*, eds. G. Gay and R. W. Kolb. Richmond, Va.: 1983, pp. 143–158.

Lang, Richard, and Robert Rasche. "A Comparison of Yields on Futures Contracts and Implied Forward Rates." *Federal Reserve Bank of St. Louis Review* (Dec. 1978), pp. 12–30.

Option Theory and Strategy

Black, F., and M. Scholes. "The Pricing of Options and Corporate Liabilities." *Journal of Political Economy* (May–June 1973), pp. 637–654.

Bookstaber, Richard M. *Option Pricing and Strategies in Investment*. Reading, Mass.: Addison-Wesley, 1981.

Moriarty, Eugene, et al. "A Comparison of Options and Futures in the Management of Portfolio Risk." *Financial Analysts Journal* (Jan.–Feb. 1981), pp. 61–67.

Regulation

"Conference on Regulation in Futures Markets." *Journal of Futures Markets* (Winter 1981).

Houthaker, H. "The Regulation of Financial and Other Future Markets." *Journal of Finance* (May 1982), pp. 481–491.

PART II

Security Analysis, Pricing, and Portfolio Management

13

The Determinants of Interest Rates

Michael A. Goldberg

THE RATE OF INTEREST

Introduction

Interest is the amount of money that the lender demands and the borrower agrees to pay at some later date as compensation for money exchanged today between these parties. Expressed in terms of the amount of money exchanged, this cost to the borrower (or revenue to the lender) becomes a proportion or rate. The interest rate is the price of credit. It represents what the lender needs as

Michael A. Goldberg, Economist, Federal Reserve Board. The views presented in this chapter are those solely of the author and do not represent the views of the Board of Governors of the Federal Reserve System or its staff.

compensation for forgoing the opportunity of using its money to increase present consumption, and what the borrower is willing to pay in terms of forgone consumption tomorrow in order to increase money holdings and expenditures today. Borrowing costs need not be expressed in terms of money alone. They can be expressed in terms of real commodities; for example, if 1 bushel of wheat is borrowed today, 1.05 bushels of wheat must be repaid one year from today. However, direct exchange of present real goods for future real goods is rare because of the inconvenience of trading through barter. Thus, as a practical matter, all exchanges of present and future consumption are in the form of money and at a price quoted in terms of an interest rate.

The Importance of the Rate of Interest

All commodities have a price; even noncommodities such as money and credit have a price.[1] What makes the interest rate such an important price — one that almost always generates substantial discussion in the financial press and one that is of serious concern to the monetary authorities that attempt to monitor and regulate the volume of money outstanding — is the fact that it serves as the linkage, or bridge, between the real and financial sectors. That is, when a firm wishes to expand by purchasing new capital equipment and hiring and training new workers, it must go to the financial markets to get the money to pay for these expenditures. Before doing this, it analyzes the cash flow stream associated with these real investments and determines whether this stream is sufficiently large to cover the borrowing costs and provide a return to equity owners commensurate with the risk of investment. Methodologically this analysis takes the form of discounting the stream of cash flows by some weighted average of the firm's costs of capital; those projects with a nonnegative net present value are accepted. This procedure bridges the real and financial sectors. The rate of interest on the firm's borrowed funds (e.g., new bond issues, bank loans) are incorporated into this computation as the firm's cost of debt capital. Furthermore, because bonds and stocks are to some degree substitutable, the influence of the interest rate on the firm's overall cost of capital is not limited to the debt capital component but should also be incorporated into all the other cost components. In the aggregate, the rate of interest is such that the total amount of real resources demanded by the public and private sectors just equals the aggregate level of savings in the economy.

The objective of this chapter is to study this nominal, or money, rate of interest. This task is somewhat more complicated than the study of other prices due largely to (1) the closeness and complexity of the relationship between money and credit; (2) the various different possible lengths of time, or maturities, over which individuals or firms may wish to borrow and lend; and (3) differences in the creditworthiness of borrowers. Each of these complications is discussed in turn.

---

[1] As the price of a commodity can be expressed in number of dollars and cents required to purchase that commodity, it must necessarily be true that the reciprocal of that price is the price of money denominated in terms of the units of goods necessary to purchase one dollar.

EXHIBIT 13.1   An Illustration of Money and Credit

Consider a bank that has just received a deposit inflow (possibly generated by a Federal Reserve System purchase of government bonds) in the form of cash or cash equivalent (e.g., a draft drawn against a Federal Reserve bank) in the amount of $100. The initial change in the bank's balance sheet from this deposit is illustrated in stage 1 below. If the reserve requirement on this deposit is 12 percent, the bank will lend out $88 at the interest rate of x percent, where x must be sufficient to generate a demand for bank credit equal to $88. If customer A requests this loan, then the granting of the loan will have an incremental effect on the bank's balance sheet as that indicated in stage 2 below. The T-account entry in stage 2 shows clearly that the bank has written up a loan asset of $88 and created a deposit liability against itself of $88, which customer A has access to draw against. At the end of stage 2 the bank's total incremental change in deposit liabilities is $188, which is $88 greater than its initial inflow. Because this $88 is withdrawable by customer A to be used for any purpose, it represents an increment to the money supply.

   In stage 3 customer A withdraws this $88 by writing a check against it. This reduces the bank's cash assets by $88 and its deposit liability to customer A by the same amount. The *net change* in the bank's balance sheet from all these transactions is depicted below as of the end of stage 3.

Stage 1		*Stage 2*		*Stage 3*	
Assets	Liabilities	Assets	Liabilities	Assets	Liabilities
ΔCash +$100	ΔDeposits +$100	ΔLoans +$88	ΔDeposits +$88 (Due *A*)	Cash $12 Loans $88	Deposits $100

From this last T-account it can be seen that the bank has retained its $88 loan credit, but that the money created when this loan was written up is circulating through the economy.

The Determination of the Rate of Interest

What determines the rate of interest or, more appropriately, the level of interest rates? Is it the demand and supply of loanable funds, or credit, or is it the demand and supply of money?

   The confusion surrounding interest rates is tied to the closeness of the relationship between money and credit. When a bank issues a loan it "creates" money, that is, a demand deposit liability (see Exhibit 13.1). In other words, the bank writes up a loan asset in the amount of the agreed upon credit and issues a liability against itself which its customer can draw drafts against. It is only natural, therefore, to view any increase in bank reserve assets (as would occur through purchases of government securities by the Federal Reserve System (Fed)) as an increase in the supply of loanable funds which should result in lower interest rates.[2] However, this effect must be reconciled with the empirical findings that higher rates of money growth are associated with higher rates of interest. The confusion surrounding interest rates may be resolved by recognizing that money serves as the medium through which credit is granted and repaid (upon maturity of the loan the customer must either deposit cash, a bank check, or be able to debit balances from his own deposit account to repay the loan), but that the interest rate is the price of the credit. More specifically, the interest rate is the price of the bank's loan asset and not the price of its liability. Thus, while the loan stays on the bank's books, the money created through the granting of the credit can turn over repeatedly in the purchase of goods and services. The uses to which money is put ultimately has an impact on the price level and the nominal interest rate. In accordance with the views of Milton Friedman of the University of Chicago, there are three basic effects of an increase in the supply of money: the liquidity effect, the income and price level effect, and the price anticipation effect.[3]

The Liquidity Effect. The initial effect of a change in the money supply that is not fully anticipated by investors is the alteration of the individual's preferred investment portfolio. In the case of an unanticipated increase (or decrease) in the supply of money, individuals will be holding relatively too much (or too few) of their assets in the form of money balances. As these investors attempt to rebalance their preferred portfolio holdings they affect the prices of investment securities thereby altering the rate of interest and causing it to adjust to the new equilibrium supply of money. For example, if an increase in the supply of money results in individuals holding more money balances than they like, then their initial response is to replace these money balances with interest-yielding securities. The increased demand for these securities has the effect of driving up securities prices and lowering the rate of interest. The lower interest rate results in individuals demanding relatively more cash balances in their portfolio (the demand for money increases as the opportunity cost of money declines). Hence, a new equilibrium is reached when the decline in the interest rate increases the demand for money balances so as to offset the increase in the supply of money.[4] The liquidity effect therefore results in the negative relationship between interest rates and the demand for money balances depicted in Figure 13.1.

---

[2] From a different perspective, any increase in money should lead to an imbalance in individuals' preferred portfolio compositions. To lead to a new equilibrium, interest rates must decline to induce individuals to demand more money balances. See John M. Keynes, *The General Theory of Employment, Interest, and Money* (London, Macmillan, 1936).

[3] For an excellent nontechnical discussion of these issues, the reader is referred to Milton Friedman, "Factors Affecting the Level of Interest Rates," *Proceedings of the 1968 Conference on Savings and Residential Financing* (Chicago: U.S. Savings and Loan League, 1969), reprinted in Thomas M. Havrilesky and Robert Schweitzer, *Contemporary Developments in Financial Institutions and Markets* (Arlington Heights, Ill.: Harlan Davison, 1983). For a more technical presentation of Friedman's views and those of his critics, see Robert J. Gordon, ed., *Milton Friedman's Monetary Framework* (Chicago: The University of Chicago Press, 1974).

[4] This equilibrium condition is easily recognizable as that of Keynes, found in John M. Keynes, *op. cit.* The mechanism for transmitting these money supply changes into prices is consistent with the Yale school of thought associated with James Tobin.

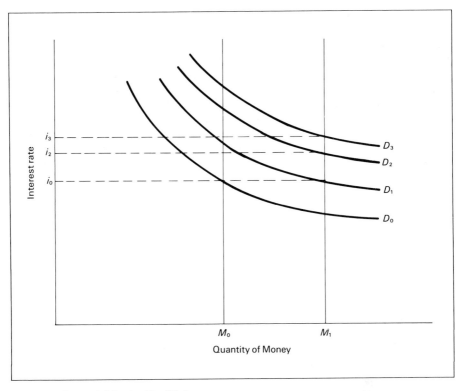

FIG. 13.1　Financial Sector Equilibrium

The liquidity effect is common to both the Keynesian and monetarist views; however, monetarists argue that the liquidity effect is just the initial phase of the process by which money supply determines the interest rate level. In this phase interest rates are the only prices assumed to react to money supply changes. The latter two effects determine the impact of money on commodities prices and feed back into the price of credit.

The Income and Price Level Effect. The reduction in interest rates resulting from the liquidity effect leads to increased business borrowing. Corporate management or entrepreneurs interpret the lower borrowing costs as equivalent to a reduction in their marginal cost of operations (or equivalently a reduction in the firm's overall cost of capital). Since thus far the money supply increase has not affected the firm's marginal revenues, management expands operations by borrowing and investing until once again the firm reaches the profit-maximizing output where the marginal revenue and marginal cost of operations are equal.[5] This expansion takes on real proportions when there are unemployed resources in the economy that now become employed due to this interest rate reduction.

_____

[5] This condition is necessary for profit maximization, as can be found in any good text on the principles of microeconomics.

On the other hand, if the economy is originally at full employment, then the reduction in interest rates results in employers increasing their borrowings in order to bid workers away from their existing positions. This bidding war merely causes the wages of these factors of production to be bid up (by the amount of the relative change in money) without any real increase in output. In the first scenario real income increases, while in the second situation real income is unchanged. In both cases nominal income rises (where nominal income is real income measured in current dollars) and the increased demand for credit by business generate a pressure on interest rates that tends to counteract the initial liquidity effect.

In terms of Figure 13.1, if the increase in the quantity of money from M_0 to M_1 of, for example, 5 percent is matched exactly by an increase in real income of 5 percent, then there is no price effect of the change in money supply and the demand for money balances shifts outwards from D_0 to D_1 as more money balances are necessary in the economy because of the increase in real trans-actions associated with this growth spurt. Assuming the firm's gross (before interest) profit margin per unit produced was unaffected by this increase in the scale of firm operations, the equilibrium interest rate remains at i_0, where once again the marginal costs of firm operations equal marginal revenues, and plant expansion ceases.

Suppose now that the increase in the supply of money is greater than the increase in real income (because the factors of production are not readily available for hire at existing prices); for example, the money supply increases by 8 percent and real income increases by 5 percent. In this case the demand for money balances attributable to the increase in real income again increases to D_1. But there is a further increase in the demand for money balances because of the increase in the price level. If prices respond quickly to this increase in the quantity of money, and the turnover rate of money is assumed to be unchanged, then the demand for nominal money balances shifts out beyond D_1 to D_2.[6] This causes the interest rate to increase from i_0 to i_2; this increase should be 3 percent (nominal change in money minus real growth) at which point the marginal revenue of production (grossed up by the 3 percent increase in the price of goods sold) again equals the marginal costs.

The Price Anticipation Effect. The final effect of a change in the quantity of money is on the turnover rate, or velocity, of money. If people believe that prices will increase, then money becomes less valuable and individuals prefer to hold fewer cash balances at every level of interest rates. As individuals reduce their demand for cash balances in favor of interest-earning assets, their money holdings must turn over more frequently in order to purchase the same real volume of goods. Consequently, the velocity of money (measured as $V = Py/M$ where V = velocity, P = price level, y = real income, and M = quantity of money) is a function of individuals' expectations of price movements. The consequences of a change in the velocity of money are identical to the conse-

---

[6] Equivalently, if the horizontal axis in Figure 13.1 had been the real quantity of money, M/P where P = price level, the supply of real money balances would be unchanged at M_1 but the demand for such balances would be greater than that associated with D_1 because nominal income would be greater.

quences of a change in the money supply when velocity is constant; that is, for $MV = Py$ the impact on nominal income, Py, is the same if the quantity of money increases by 5 percent or velocity increases by 5 percent. Therefore, if the money supply grows more rapidly than the anticipated rate of growth of real income, and this differential (3 percent in the previous illustration) is expected to persist, then the anticipated impact of this differential on prices causes an increase in the velocity of money. The higher nominal income associated with this increase in V leads to an equilibrium interest rate that exceeds i_2 in Figure 13.1. For example, if the velocity of money increased one percent, in addition to the 3 percent differential between money supply and real income growths, then i_3 would be 4 percent higher than i_0 and one percent higher than i_2.

Milton Friedman succinctly described the total impact of the just described effects of money on interest rates in the following passage:[7]

> Empirically, there is a tendency for a rapid rate of monetary growth to be followed by a decline in interest rates and, after a lag, by a rise and then a final ultimate movement to a level higher than the starting point. . . . It turns out that the initial decline in interest rates after an acceleration of monetary growth lasts about six months. Clearly there is a variation but the average period is about six months. The time it takes to get back to the initial level is something like 18 months. The period it takes to get to the final equilibrium level is very long.[8]

Interest Rates — Real and Nominal

The preceding discussion illustrates the complex, and oftentimes confusing, interdependencies of the interest rate, the quantity of money, and the price level. One of the conclusions of that discussion is that a monetary expansion which results in anticipated price level changes has an effect that is impounded in the current interest rate. Of course, prices may be somewhat sticky and not react immediately to fiscal and monetary changes, but when prices are anticipated to change, they cause shifts in the individual's liquidity preference schedule (the curved line in Figure 13.1) and possible movements along it, thereby affecting the interest rate.

Irving Fisher is generally credited with being the first economist to note the distinction between the nominal rate of interest, which has been shown to depend on what happens to the value of money (as measured by the quantity of goods that can be purchased for a fixed sum of money), and the real rate of interest, which more accurately reflects the terms of the credit defined with reference to goods (or barter) without the associated transactions costs.[9] If the value of money is stable in terms of goods, that is, no price inflation or deflation, then the rate of interest in terms of money is the same as in terms of goods. However, when the value of money changes, these rates of interest differ.

Fisher recognized that distinguishing between the rate of interest on money and "goods" is complicated by the fact that there are "theoretically just as many

---

[7] Milton Friedman, *op. cit.*, p. 21.

[8] Friedman's own research with Anna J. Schwartz indicates that "very long" may be between 20 and 30 years.

[9] Irving Fisher, *The Theory of Interest* (New York: Macmillan, 1930).

rates of interest expressed in terms of goods as there are kinds of goods diverging from one another in value."[10] He considered that a rate of interest defined in terms of real income (a composite of consumption goods and services) would be the best standard because "income is the most fundamental factor in our lives."[11] Therefore the real rate of interest can be obtained by deducting the change in a cost of living index number (P) from the nominal, or money, rate of interest. In theory the nominal interest rate, i_n, is expected to equal the real rate, i_r, plus the anticipated change in the purchasing power of money. That is,

$$i_n = i_r + E\left(\frac{\Delta P}{P}\right) \tag{13.1}$$

In practice, the realized change in prices may not equal the expected change because there is some unanticipated component to the actual price change or there is "a universal lack of foresight" (Fisher, 1930, p. 44) in forming these expectations of purchasing power changes. Figure 13.2 illustrates the relationship between the short-term (three-month) nominal rate of interest on U.S. government securities and the three-month change in the consumer price index over the period January 1970 through December 1982. Despite the fact that the interest rate series embodies expected price changes, and other factors affecting i_r, while the consumer price series represents actual observed changes in prices, Figure 13.2 illustrates that these series move closely together over time.[12]

Other Factors Influencing Interest Rate Levels

Still abstracting from the question of how assets of different maturities are priced, the short-term interest rate (or, more generally, the level of interest rates) is a function of several factors in addition to monetary policy which influence the real component of the rate of interest. Some of the more important of these factors include aggregate savings, business and consumer investment, government deficits or surpluses, income taxes, and the risk of borrower default.

The primary source of the supply of credit in the marketplace is the aggregate amount of savings. As savings increase (or decrease) there is an increase (or decrease) in the supply of credit and downward (or upward) pressure on interest rates. The individual's savings decision is a function of several factors. One very important factor is the saver's subjective preference of present consumption over future consumption. Fisher preferred to refer to this time preference as "human impatience" because individuals generally prefer a bird in the hand to two in the bush. The impact of these subjective preferences and the time shape of the individual's stream of real income (adjusted for any uncertainty in this stream) is easily depicted in the standard two-period paradigm. Figure 13.3 illustrates an individual's optimal consumption decision when that person has a certain real income of y_0 in the current period and a certainty-equivalent income of y_1 in the second period. The present value (in real terms) of the individual's

---

[10]*Ibid.*, p. 42.

[11]*Ibid.*

[12]The correlation coefficient between the yield on the three-month Treasury bill and the three-month change in the seasonally adjusted Consumer Price Index (CPI) over this time interval is 45 percent. For the unadjusted CPI, this correlation is 44 percent.

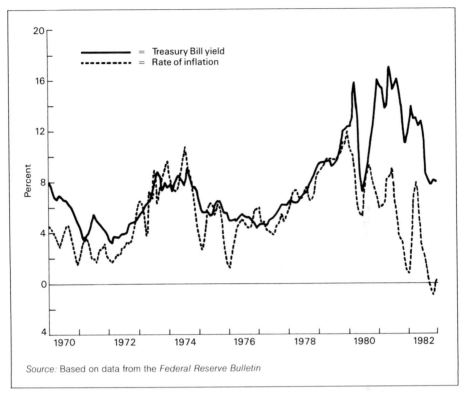

FIG. 13.2   Inflation and the Short-Term Rate of Interest

income stream is

$$y_0 + \frac{y_1}{1 + i_r}$$

(Alternatively, y_0 and y_1 can be expressed in nominal terms with i_n being the appropriate rate of interest.) From this figure it can be seen that the individual receives greatest utility (U) at the point K, where he saves an amount GC and uses this savings in the second period to consume in excess of that period's income endowment by the amount of HF. This ability to trade off present income for future income has resulted in a greater utility $(U^* - U_0)$ for this individual than if he had consumed all of his income when it was earned. If the savings of all individuals are summed, the supply of real savings at the real interest rate i_r is found.

Just as individuals are the principal suppliers of credit through savings, business firms (and the U.S. Treasury) are the principal demanders of credit. Firms are willing to borrow at some positive real rate of interest when they can employ the debt proceeds to increase real productivity and future cash flows by more than the cost of the debt.

The U.S. Government can either supply credit by running a budget surplus or demand credit by running a budget deficit. Since operating expenses have

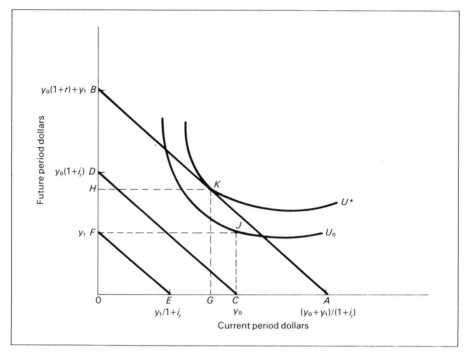

FIG. 13.3 The Individual's Consumption-Savings Decision

exceeded operating revenues since 1969, the U.S. Treasury has become a large demander of credit.

Income tax considerations also should influence the level of nominal interest rates. Because lenders must report interest income as taxable, unless it comes from the obligations of tax-exempt institutions, income tax considerations are expected to be impounded in interest rates. In particular, the interest rate on taxable securities is expected to be in excess of that on comparably risky tax-exempt securities thereby ensuring comparable after-tax returns to the investor.[13]

Finally the creditworthiness of the borrower (i.e., the probability of borrower default) influences the interest rate to that borrower. The previous discussion assumed implicitly that the rate of interest was risk-free or, equivalently, that certainty-equivalent rates of interest were being considered. Since lenders bear the risk of borrower default, they are expected to demand some interest-rate premium as compensation for bearing this risk (this is discussed further later in this chapter). As a result U.S. Treasury securities should always yield a rate of

---

[13]Clearly, not all investors will be indifferent between taxable and tax-exempt bonds because individuals have different marginal tax brackets. In a classic finance paper, Merton H. Miller, "Debt and Taxes," *Journal of Finance*, Vol. 32, No. 2 (May 1977), pp. 261–275, it was shown that a bond market equilibrium will prevail when the interest rate on taxable bonds is such that the after-tax return to an individual with a personal tax rate equal to the corporate tax rate exactly equals the rate of interest on the tax-exempt bond.

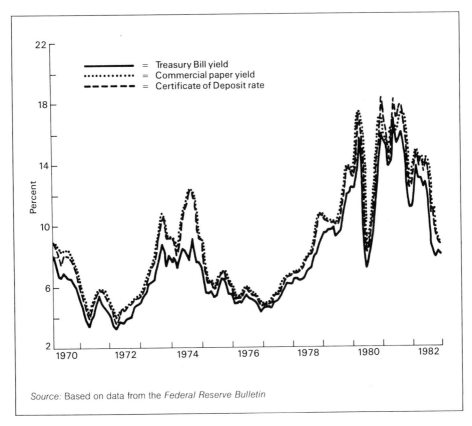

FIG. 13.4 Short-Term Interest Rates

return to the lender that is less than other securities with the same maturity because of the capability of the government to either print money or raise taxes to ensure the retirement of its debt. Figure 13.4 illustrates the rates of interest on three-month Treasury bill securities (T-bills), three-month prime bank large-denomination negotiable certificates of deposit (CDs), and four- to six-month dealer-placed prime quality commercial paper over the period January 1970 through December 1982.[14] This figure indicates that interest rates on bank CDs and dealer-placed commercial paper are nearly identical most of the time and that both are in excess of the T-bill rate. In addition, the spreads between these rates and the T-bill rate varied over this time interval. The collapse of the U.S. National Bank of San Diego in October 1973, and of Germany's I.D. Herstatt and the Franklin National Bank of New York in 1974 created somewhat of a "flight to quality," which noticeably increased the interest rate spread between these private sector and government securities during 1973 and 1974.

---

[14] Because Treasury bills and commercial paper are quoted on a discount basis, they were first converted to a yield to maturity basis before being plotted in order to make them comparable with the bank CD rate.

THE TERM STRUCTURE OF INTEREST RATES

Introduction

In the preceding sections the rate of interest is discussed as if all bonds have the same maturity date and the only thing that differentiates between them is the default risk of the borrower. In fact, bonds can differ because of different maturity horizons and different repayment schemes as well. The following sections analyze how these factors affect the nominal rates of interest (or yields) on bonds.

The Mathematics of Bond Pricing

Although bonds that the individual purchases at face value F and receives $F(1 + r)$ at maturity one period later (where r represents the market rate of interest) do exist, they are more the exception than the rule. Many of the short-term money market instruments, such as T-bills, banker's acceptances, and commercial paper, sell on a discount basis; that is, they sell at a price P that is less than their maturity value, with the difference between these values, $F-P$, being their accumulated interest. For example, if a three-month T-bill selling at an annual discount rate, d, of 6.4 percent has a face value of \$100 at maturity, the price of the bond is:

$$P = F \left(1 - \frac{d}{4}\right)$$
$$= \$100(1 - 0.016) \tag{13.2}$$
$$= \$98.40$$

The accumulated interest on this bond is \$1.60, and the rate of interest (r) is the accumulated interest divided by the purchase price:

$$P \left(1 + \frac{r}{4}\right) = F \tag{13.3}$$

or

$$\frac{r}{4} = \frac{(F - P)}{P}$$

therefore,

$$r = \$1.60/\$98.40 \times 4 = 6.50\% \text{ per annum}$$

The difference between this discount bond and the one issued at face value with the market interest rate of r is simply that the initial outlays differ. Therefore the accumulated interest in one (the discount bond) must be divided by a purchase price less than face value, while in the other case (the bond with $P = F$) the accumulated interest is divided by the bond's face value. For more on this subject, see Chapter 6.

In the case of a coupon (c) bond, the rate of interest or yield to maturity (used interchangeably here) is still the price the lender charges for giving up the current amount of P. Consider the case of an individual who is willing to lend \$1,000 to a corporation at an interest rate of 10 percent for 10 years. Assume further that the firm pays off this credit by making semiannual interest payments of $50 (the equivalent of 10 percent per year) and then paying the principal upon maturity. Therefore the constant coupon payment, C, is $50, r is 10 percent, the compounding frequency or number of payments per year, m, is 2, the number of years to maturity, n, is 10, and the value of the interest payment annuity is:

$$\sum_{t=1}^{mn} \frac{C}{\left(1 + \dfrac{r}{m}\right)^t} = \sum_{t=1}^{20} \frac{\$50}{(1 + 0.05)^t} = \$50(12.4622) = \$623.11$$

The present value of the principal repayment is:

$$\frac{F}{\left(1 + \dfrac{r}{m}\right)^{mn}} = \frac{\$1,000}{(1.05)^{20}} = \$1,000(0.37689) = \$376.89$$

Therefore,

$$P = \$623.11 + \$376.89 = \$1,000$$

Equivalently, the lender is willing to give up $1,000 today in exchange for a stream of coupon payments and a principal repayment that when discounted at 10 percent equal the amount of the loan. Since the coupon rate is exactly equal to the discount rate, the market value of the bond is equal to its face value.

A bond is composed of two distinct components: The first is an annuity equal to the value of the coupon payment over the life of the bond; the second is the value of the bond repayment upon maturity. To calculate the bond price, a set of present value tables with the discount factor of 10 percent per year is used. Since the reciprocal of the present value is the cumulative value (e.g., $P = F / (1 + r)$ implies that $F = P(1 + r)$), it should be clear that the rate at which future cash flows are discounted to get a price today is the same rate at which a loan being made today will accumulate interest and take on a final value tomorrow. This two-part valuation has been simplified by the publication of books of bond tables (for an expanded discussion, see Chapter 6).

In the context of multiperiod bonds, the rate of interest is generally referred to as the yield to maturity (YTM). The following section compares how the YTM varies with the term to maturity (TTM, or length of time to maturity) of a bond.

The Yield Curve

The relationship between a bond's YTM and its TTM at a given moment in time can be plotted on a two-dimensional diagram. The curve drawn through these points is called the yield curve. Yield curves are typically drawn on the basis of data for U.S. Treasury securities because these obligations are default-free. This property of Treasury securities allows one to isolate the effects of the maturity period on the YTM that are common to all fixed-income fixed-maturity securities. Yield curves drawn for securities with positive probabilities of default differ from the curve constructed for Treasury securities by the default-risk premium implicit in the YTM of these securities and the manner in which this premium varies with the TTM.

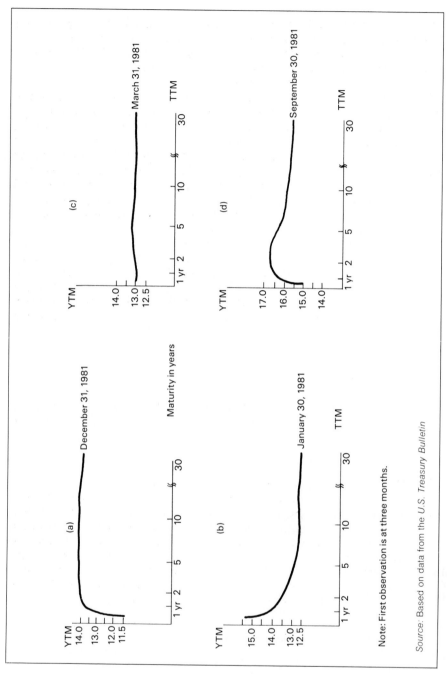

FIG. 13.5   Yield Curves

Figure 13.5 illustrates four yield curves, each with a different shape. Figure 13.5(a) is the upward sloping yield curve that prevailed on December 31, 1981; Figure 13.5(b) is the downward sloping yield curve of January 30, 1981; Figure 13.5(c) is a relatively flat yield curve of March 31, 1981; and Figure 13.5(d) is the slightly humped yield curve of September 30, 1981.

An upward sloping (or ascending) yield curve indicates that longer-term securities are selling to yield a higher rate of return to the investor than near-term securities. For example, Figure 13.5(a) indicates that on December 31, 1981, an investor could have purchased a T-bill with three months to maturity with a yield of approximately 11.5 percent or a Treasury bond to mature after the end of 1984 (maturity of five years or longer) at a yield of 14.0 percent. With a downward sloping yield curve the converse holds; that is, a short-term bond sells to yield more to the investor than a bond with a longer TTM. When the yield curve is flat — a rather uncommon event in recent years — a bond's yield to maturity is independent of its term to maturity. Finally, for a "humped" yield curve, the very short- and long-term securities are selling to yield the investor a return that is less than the intermediate-term bonds. For example, in the yield curve drawn for September 30, 1981, the three-month T-bill is selling to yield 15.0 percent and the bond with maturity of three years or longer has a computed yield of no more than 16.5 percent; however, the Treasury securities with maturities between nine months and three years have a computed annual yield of no less than 16.5 percent.

Explanations of the Term Structure of Interest Rates

What makes a yield curve take the particular shape it does? Several conflicting theories attempt to explain the term structure. In the following sections, three of these theories are described.

The Expectations Theory. According to the expectations theory, in the ideal world of no transaction costs and taxes, where everyone has the same expectation of future short-term interest rates, the rate of return on a particular bond of n periods is the geometric average of the current, or spot, single-period bond rate and the expected values of the $(n-1)$ single-period rates of interest that are expected to prevail in the marketplace in the future. The investor is indifferent between holding long-term bonds or holding short-term bonds and rolling over his investments because he anticipates each strategy to result in the same accumulated values at the end of his investment horizon.

$$_{t+n}R_t = \text{YTM (expressed on a per period basis) of an } n\text{-period bond available in period } t$$

$$_{t+1}r_t = \text{single-period spot interest rate (on a per period basis) on a bond available in period } t$$

$$_{t+k+1}r_{t+k} = expected \text{ future interest rate on a single-period bond to be available } k \text{ periods in the future}$$

If the investor is to obtain the same return on a two-period bond that he expects to receive from two single-period bonds, then

$$(1 + {}_{t+2}R_t)^2 = (1 + {}_{t+1}r_t)(1 + {}_{t+2}r_{t+1}) \tag{13.4}$$

Similarly for indifference between a three-period bond and three single-period bonds,

$$(1 + {}_{t+3}R_t)^3 = (1 + {}_{t+1}r_t)(1 + {}_{t+2}r_{t+1})(1 + {}_{t+3}r_{t+2}) \tag{13.5}$$

Equations 13.5 and 13.6 imply that

$$(1 + {}_{t+3}R_t)^3 = (1 + {}_{t+2}R_t)^2(1 + {}_{t+3}r_{t+2}) \tag{13.6}$$

or that the investor can accumulate the same return over a three-period planning horizon by investing in a three-period bond or any combination of two-period bonds and/or single-period bonds. For an n-period bond,

$$(1 + {}_{t+n}R_t)^n = (1 + {}_{t+1}r_t)(1 + {}_{t+2}r_{t+1}) \cdots (1 + {}_{t+n}r_{t+n-1}) \tag{13.7}$$

therefore,

$$_{t+n}R_t = \sqrt[n]{(1 + {}_{t+1}r_t)(1 + {}_{t+2}r_{t+1}) \cdots (1 + {}_{t+n}r_{t+n-1})} - 1 \tag{13.8}$$

and $_{t+n}R_t$ is the geometric average of the current and $(n-1)$ anticipated future short-term rates of interest.

For this theory of the term structure to hold, both borrowers and lenders must be risk-neutral, that is, they make their investment and borrowing decisions based solely on their expectations of future interest rates and not on the uncertainty surrounding their expectation estimates. For the investors, long-term bonds must generate a cumulative return over the individual's investment horizon that is at least as great as what that investor *expects* to receive from any combination of shorter-term bonds over the same investment period. Similarly risk-neutral borrowers are unwilling to pay long-term interest rates in excess of what they anticipate to be their cost of debt by borrowing for a shorter period of time and rolling over these liabilities. Therefore, if all borrowers and lenders have homogeneous assessments of the future rates of interest, then the equilibrium long-term bond rate is the one given by Equation 13.8. This is illustrated in Figure 13.6. In the figure $_{t+n}R_t^*$ represents the n-period rate consistent with Equation 13.8. At the yield of $_{t+n}R_t^*$ demanders and suppliers are indifferent between long-term and short-term bonds, hence the thickened line. At rates $_{t+1}R_t$ in excess of $_{t+n}R_t^*$, investors (lenders) substitute out of shorter-term bonds into long-term bonds (this substitution may result in a discrete jump rather than the smooth curve depicted in the figure), thus the demand for bonds, $r_D(B)$, is increasing in $_{t+n}R_t$. However, suppliers of bonds, $r_S(B)$, would never offer bonds at this rate because they can issue shorter-term bonds at a cheaper expected cost. Thus the supply curve is increasing for $_{t+n}R_t$ less than $_{t+n}R_t^*$, but it is perfectly flat at $_{t+n}R_t^*$. The result is an infinite set of possible market equilibria along the darkened segment in Figure 13.6 at the price $_{t+n}R_t^*$. No unique market equilibrium exists because there is no unique optimal quantity of long-term bonds, since these bonds are functionally equivalent to a combination of short-term bonds.

The implications of this theory on the shape of the yield curve can be readily ascertained. Assume a three-period bond has each period defined to be one year. If the current single-period short-term rate of interest is 6.0 percent and the

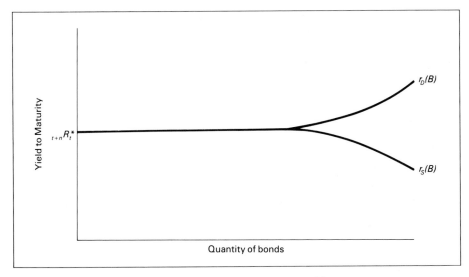

FIG. 13.6 Bond Market Equilibrium Under the Expectations Theory

single-period rates expected to prevail in the future are all 6.0 percent, then Equation 13.8 implies that the annual YTM on this three-year bond must also be 6.0 percent; that is, when investors anticipate no change in short-term rates, the yield curve is flat. Consider next the case where the current short-term rate is 6.0 percent, but the single-period future rate expected to prevail one year hence is 7.0 percent and two years hence is 8.0 percent (i.e., $_{t+2}r_{t+1} = 7.0\%$, $_{t+3}r_{t+2} = 8.0\%$). The yield on the three-period bond computed from Equation 13.8 is approximately 7.0 percent (actually 6.997 percent).[15] The yield on the two-year bond available at this time would be

$$_{t+2}R_t = \sqrt{(1.06)(1.07)} - 1 \cong 6.50\%$$

Therefore, the yield to maturity increases with term to maturity when investors believe that future interest rates will increase.

If investors believe that short-term rates will decline, as when the current rate is 8.0 percent and the single-period short rates expected to prevail in the two subsequent years are 7.0 percent and 6.0 percent, respectively, then $_{t+1}R_t = {_{t+1}}r_t = 8.0\%$, $_{t+2}R_t = 7.5\%$, $_{t+3}R_t = 7.0\%$. In this case the yield curve is descending.

Finally, consider the case when the current short-term rate is 6.0 percent, but this rate is anticipated to increase to 6.5 percent for one year and then decrease back to 6.0 percent. In this situation $_{t+1}R_t = 6.0\%$, $_{t+2}R_t = 6.25\%$, $_{t+3}R_t = 6.17\%$, and the yield curve has a hump in it. Hence, to obtain the kind of yield curve that prevailed on September 30, 1981 (Figure 13.5(d)), the expectations theory requires that investors expect short-term rates to first increase and then decline.

---

[15] The actual bond yield is slightly less than the simple arithmetic average of the current and forward rates because the arithmetic average does not take into account the reinvestment of accrued interest whereas the geometric average does.

The Liquidity Preference Theory. The liquidity preference theory of the term structure is generally associated with John Hicks, although the concept of liquidity preference was first introduced by John Maynard Keynes.[16] Keynes employed the term "liquidity preference" to describe a preference by individuals to hold assets whose values have little or no sensitivity to changes in interest rates over bonds on which capital losses would occur in the event of an interest rate increase. The asset with minimum liquidity risk is money. Hence, when individuals anticipate an increase in interest rates, they increase their preference for money balances and reduce their demands for bonds. In terms of the interrelationship between short- and long-term bonds, liquidity preference is evidenced by a preference of investors for shorter-term bonds (or bills) because, as is shown subsequently, their values are less sensitive to change when there is an unanticipated, but permanent, change in interest rate levels.[17]

In this theory of the term structure, speculators cannot have long and short securities positions with each long-term bond selling to yield its anticipated accumulated value. Market imperfections that do not allow risk-neutral investors to borrow at the same rate as the government, even if they collateralize their debt with U.S. Treasury securities, may be responsible. Alternatively, perhaps there are no risk-neutral individuals.

Hicks viewed the market for long-term bonds as being composed of hedgers and speculators.[18] He viewed the hedgers to be the bond issuers who "want to hedge their future supplies of loan capital, just as they want to hedge their future supplies of raw materials" (Hicks, 1946, p. 146). The same cannot be said of the lenders:

> If no extra return is offered for long lending, most people (and institutions) would prefer to lend short, at least in the sense that they would prefer to hold money on deposit in some way or other. But this situation would leave a large excess of demands to borrow long which would not be met. Borrowers would thus tend to offer better terms in order to persuade lenders to switch over into the long market. . . . A lender who did this would be in a position exactly analogous to that of a speculator in a commodity market. He would only come into the long market because he expected to gain by so doing, and to gain sufficiently to offset the risk incurred. (Hicks, 1946, pp. 146–147)[19]

The risk faced by the lender can be attributed to the larger price fluctuations inherent in longer-term, as opposed to shorter-term, bonds. For example, consider two discount bonds with face value of $100, one with a TTM of one year, the other with a TTM of 10 years. If both bonds are selling to yield the investor a

---

[16] John Hicks, *Theory of Value*, 2nd ed. (London: Oxford University Press, 1946); and John M. Keynes, *op. cit.*

[17] Another way of viewing liquidity preference as applied to the yield curve is to relate each *k*-period bond to money with the resulting interest rate on that bond reflecting that rate which just balances out the individual's demand for money with his demand for *k*-period bonds. See David W. Lusher, "The Structure of Interest Rates and the Keynesian Theory of Interest." *Journal of Political Economy*, Vol. 50, No. 2 (Apr. 1942), p. 274. The differential yields between bonds will therefore reflect the differentials in the investor's trade-off between these assets and money.

[18] John Hicks, *op. cit.*, p. 146.

[19] This is equivalent to Keynes's concept of "normal backwardation."

return of 7 percent, then the price of the one-year bond, P_1, would be

$$P_1 = \frac{\$100}{(1.07)} = \$93.46$$

while the price of the ten-year bond, P_{10}, would be

$$P_{10} = \frac{\$100}{(1.07)^{10}} = \$50.83$$

If interest rates suddenly change so that both bonds are now selling to yield 8 percent (as when there is a parallel upward shift of a flat yield curve), then $P_1 = \$92.59$ and $P_{10} = \$46.32$. Thus the holder of the short-term bond incurs a loss of \$0.87 or, 0.9 percent of his initial investment, compared to a loss of \$4.51, or 8.8 percent, for the holder of the 10-year bond.

If, at the time of their bond purchases, investors anticipate that all forward rates of interest will be 7 percent, then risk-averse investors will not be willing to purchase the 10-year bond without fair compensation for the risk of its price variability; that is, all things being equal, investors will pay a price premium for the liquidity of the short-term asset relative to its long-term counterpart or equivalently they will demand an interest-rate premium for the illiquidity of the long-term bond.

Since in the preceding illustration the only thing that differentiates the 1-year from the 10-year bond is the period for which funds are committed to the 7 percent investment, the length of this commitment must explain the differential price variability. The 10-year bond has more price variability because \$50.83 is tied up for 10 years. If interest rates change immediately after the investment, then the bond purchaser will have forgone the opportunity of having used these funds to purchase a higher-yielding bond. The longer the TTM, the greater this opportunity cost. Since the purchasers of the 7 percent one-year bond can rollover their principal plus accumulated interest in a nine-year 8 percent bond, they incur an opportunity cost on their investment only for one year. Hence the latter strategy is less risky to those individuals who have greater disutility for the capital losses associated with rising interest rates than the enhanced utility of the capital gains associated with interest rate declines.

The liquidity preference theory says that investors will add an interest-rate premium, equal to $_{t+k}L_{t+k-1}$, to each anticipated short-term rate $_{t+k}r_{t+k-1}$ (where $1 < k \leqslant n$), so that the accumulated return on an n-period bond would be

$$(1 + {}_{t+n}R_t)^n = (1 + {}_{t+1}r_t)(1 + {}_{t+2}r_{t+1} + {}_{t+2}L_{t+1}) \cdots$$
$$(1 + {}_{t+n}r_{t+n-1} + {}_{t+n}L_{t+n-1}) \qquad (13.9)$$

and

$$_{t+n}R_t = \sqrt[n]{(1 + {}_{t+1}r_t)(1 + {}_{t+2}r_{t+1} + {}_{t+2}L_{t+1}) \cdots (1 + {}_{t+n}r_{t+n-1} + {}_{t+n}L_{t+n-1})} - 1$$
$$(13.10)$$

Each expression of the form $_{t+k}r_{t+k-1} + {}_{t+k}L_{t+k-1}$ is referred to as the *forward* short rate for period k. The long-term bond yield is therefore the geometric average of unity plus the current and forward short-term rates of interest. In the expectations theory of the term structure, the forward rate

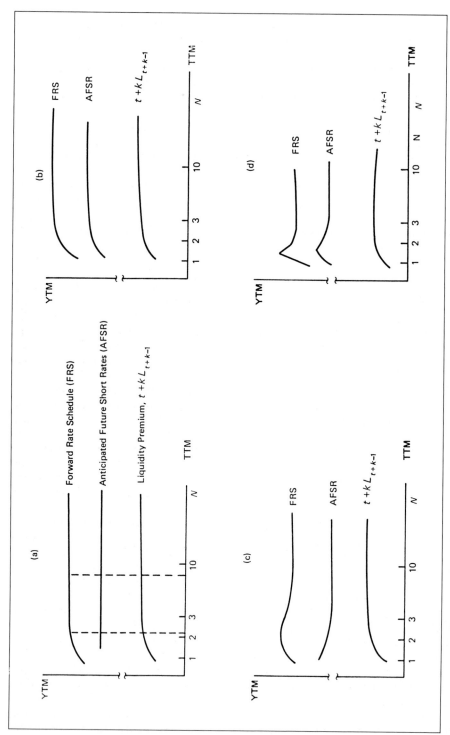

FIG. 13.7   Forward Rate Schedules Under the Liquidity Preference Theory

exactly equals the expected future short-term rate of interest. In the liquidity preference theory, the forward rate always exceeds the anticipated future short-term rate.

The implications of the liquidity preference explanation on the shape of the yield curve can be derived from Figure 13.7. In this figure several schedules of forward market rates are constructed; from these schedules implications regarding the yield curve can be drawn. In each figure the liquidity premium schedule is drawn as a nonlinear function which is increasing, but at a decreasing rate in the bond's TTM. This assumption implies that average yields ought to rise with TTM at a decreasing rate, which is consistent with the empirical evidence.[20] Figure 13.7(a) shows a schedule of forward interest rates constructed under the assumption that investors' expect future short-term interest rates to be constant. The sum of the interest-rate premium for each period and the single-period short-term rate expected to prevail in that period yields the forward rate schedule. In Figure 13.7(a), the forward rate schedule is ascending in TTM. This shape is due entirely to the shape of the liquidity preference schedule. Since (as observed in the discussion of the expectations theory) the yield curve is ascending when the schedule of forward rates is ascending, it can be concluded from Figure 13.7(a) that when individuals are risk averse and demand an interest-rate premium for holding longer-term bonds, then the yield curve will be upward sloping when investors anticipate short-term interest rates to be unchanged.

Figure 13.7(b) illustrates the situation where investors expect future short-term rates to be increasing. Clearly the yield curve is ascending in this case.

Figure 13.7(c) depicts the interesting case where investors have decreasing expectations of future short-term interest rates and a liquidity premium schedule that is increasing. The combination of these schedules can produce a somewhat humped forward rate schedule, as shown in this illustration. A schedule of expected future short-term rates which first rises and then declines will produce a similarly humped (although with a somewhat accentuated hump) forward rate schedule, as shown in Figure 13.7(d). Therefore, since humped forward rate schedules imply humped yield curves, this explanation of interest rates can explain humped yield curves as occurring either when individuals expect short-term rates to be strictly declining or when investors simultaneously anticipate these rates to increase and then decrease.

The liquidity preference theory of the term structure would appear to result in relatively few perfectly flat and strictly declining yield curves. This accords well with empirical observations. The preponderance of yield curves observed in recent years are either increasing (when individuals either expect short rates to remain unchanged or to increase) or somewhat humped (when individuals expect rates to either decline or first increase and then decline).

Figure 13.8 depicts the bond market equilibrium under this explanation of the term structure. Whereas a risk-neutral investor would be willing to purchase an n-period bond to yield $_nR_I^*$ (derived from Equation 13.8), the demand for bonds schedule in Figure 13.8 indicates that risk-averse investors need higher yields to stimulate their increased demand for long-term bonds. On the supply side, although risk-neutral bond issuers would prefer to pay no more than

---

[20] See Reuben A. Kessel, *The Cyclical Behavior of the Term Structure of Interest Rates*, Occasional Paper No. 91 (New York: National Bureau of Economic Research, 1965), pp. 49–50.

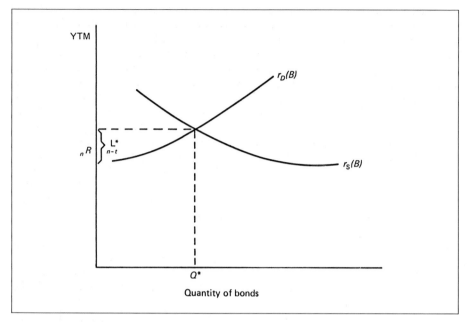

FIG. 13.8   Bond Market Equilibrium Under the Liquidity Preference Theory

$_nR_t^*$, risk-averse borrowers may be willing to pay an interest-rate premium in excess of $_nR_t^*$ in order to lock up funds for n periods. This results in a downward sloping supply of bonds schedule, as shown in Figure 13.8; only extremely risk-averse borrowers would be willing to issue long-term bonds at very high rates, while at lower rates more risk-tolerant borrowers would also issue bonds.

The demand and supply of bond schedules in Figure 13.8 result in a unique bond market equilibrium characterized by Q^*, $_nR_t^L$, and risk premium $_nL_t^*$. This premium is analogous to an insurance premium. In equilibrium the bond issuer is willing to pay the amount $_nL_t^*$ to insure against having to pay in excess of $_nR_t^*$ for his funds; that is, for a "fee" of $_nL_t^*$ the bond issuer pays only the future interest expenses that were anticipated as of period t and the bond purchaser pays all (in terms of changes in the value of his asset holdings) the deviations of the actual interest expenses from their expected future short-term values.[21]

The Institutional Hedging or Habitat Theory.   Grouped together in the third category of term structure explanations are those theories with the basic property that yields to maturity for a bond with a specific maturity are explained in part by borrower and lender preferences for holding and issuing, respectively, claims with that maturity.

---

[21] The insurer, in this example, also receives all the benefits when the actual rates are less than anticipated ex ante.

In its extreme form, the preference by borrowers and lenders for a particular period's bond may be independent of the rates of return on bonds of all other maturities; that is, there is no substitutability by either party between bonds of different maturities. This hypothesis, labeled the *market segmentation hypothesis,* implies that if bonds are available with a maturity up to *n* periods, then the rate of return on each bond will be determined as if there were *n* different bond markets with independent supply and demand schedules. The implication of this theory is that YTMs can vary widely between bonds of different maturities.

The proponents of this view, and less extreme variations which allow for limited substitutability between bonds of different maturities, argue that there are institutional restrictions on the asset side and hedging pressures on the liability side that result in these "maturity habitats."[22] While speculators and life insurance companies may make their investment decisions with the liquidity aspects of their assets as only a minor consideration, most other lenders do have distinct preferences for liquid assets: Commercial banks and other depository institutions whose liabilities are principally of a short-term nature prefer shorter-term assets to hedge their liability costs (note the prevalence of intermediate-term bank business loans that are made on a variable-rate basis); many lenders are restricted by legal and customary requirements intended to ensure that they hold assets of a certain degree of liquidity; and firms may have particular foreseeable cash disbursements they must make (e.g., taxes, capital expenditures) which they can hedge by investing current excess working capital in assets to mature in time to meet their cash disbursements. On the borrowing side, bond issuers are tailoring their offerings to the period of time necessary to fund the particular project or investment that gave rise to the debt offering, so the maturity of the debt is related to the purpose of the borrowing. Thus changes in the proportion of short- to long-term private debt depend upon whether the debt is issued to fund working capital or long-term fixed plant and equipment.

The above-mentioned hedging pressures are a key factor in explaining the yield curve in the habitat theory as different traders are likely to have different habitats. Furthermore, borrowers and lenders in their "preferred habitat" may have positive or negative risk premiums from that implied by the expectations theory reflecting the extent to which there is an excess demand or supply of funds within their preferred habitats at the yield of $_{t+n}R_t^*$.[23] In the Hicksian model, all investors are assumed to prefer the short-period habitat so longer-term instruments have to offer an interest-rate premium to attract investors to these securities. However, if a trader in fact preferred an *n*-period habitat, then he would have to be offered an interest-rate premium on the single-period bond in order to attract him out of the *n*-period asset and into *n* single-period assets.

In summary, the hedging or habitat model says that the spread between long- and short-term rates of interest depends largely on the relative supply and demand for these instruments by transactors in their preferred habitats. Although rates on different U.S. Treasury securities move simultaneously in the same direction, this may result more from changes in business conditions and

---

[22] In particular see John M. Culbertson, "The Term Structure of Interest Rates," *Quarterly Journal of Economics*, Vol. 71, No. 4 (Nov. 1957), pp. 485–517.

[23] See Franco Modigliani and Richard Sutch, "Innovations in Interest Rate Policy," *American Economic Review*, Vol. 56, No. 2 (May 1966), pp. 178–197.

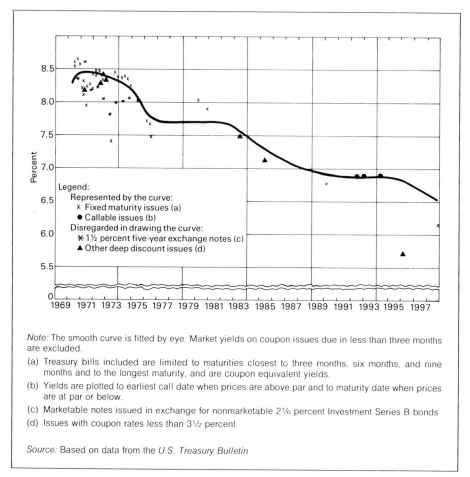

FIG. 13.9 Yields of Treasury Securities, December 31, 1969 (based on closing bid quotations)

Note: The smooth curve is fitted by eye. Market yields on coupon issues due in less than three months are excluded.

(a) Treasury bills included are limited to maturities closest to three months, six months, and nine months and to the longest maturity, and are coupon equivalent yields.

(b) Yields are plotted to earliest call date when prices are above par and to maturity date when prices are at par or below.

(c) Marketable notes issued in exchange for nonmarketable 2⅜ percent Investment Series B bonds

(d) Issues with coupon rates less than 3½ percent

Source: Based on data from the *U.S. Treasury Bulletin*

monetary policy rather than unlimited substitutability between bonds of different maturities.

If risk-neutral "arbitrageurs" can borrow in the maturity range where the expected return is low and invest in those particular maturity categories anticipated to yield a high rate of return, then the yield structure would conform to that of the expectations theory. This is an empirical question. Figure 13.9 presents the yield curve constructed from the bid prices of market quotes on U.S. Treasury securities for December 31, 1969. This yield curve does not fit the data in a smooth manner. While its initial hump can be consistent with the Hicksian theory when investors anticipate short-term rates to decline, the remainder of the yield curve does not appear to lend itself to a simple, and convincing, explanation from either the expectations or liquidity preference theories. Beyond some intermediate-term period, individuals generally have insufficient information to anticipate cyclical interest rate movements and generally assume the short-term rate to be constant thereafter. This implies that the long-term yield should flatten out beyond this intermediate stage as it reaches what might be thought of as its long-run normal level. Figure 13.9 indicates that during the tight money period of 1969–1970, when rates as of year-end 1969 were clearly expected to decline, the actual long-term yields did not revert to a long-run normal level. The deviations of the actual yield from this normal level are consistent with the existence of maturity habitats.

One interesting aspect of the maturity habitat theory is that because there is limited substitutability between short- and long-term bonds on the part of borrowers and lenders, a substantial change in the maturity structure of debt should be reflected in the term structure of interest rates. Therefore, in accordance with this theory, the U.S. Treasury could alter the shape of the yield curve by either shortening or lengthening the average maturity of its liabilities. This, in fact, became the policy of the Kennedy Administration in the beginning of 1961. Operation Twist was an attempt by the administration to raise the yields on short-term securities by shortening the average maturity of the Treasury's obligations. This policy was initiated in an attempt to curb the outflow of short-term capital and improve the U.S. balance of payments position while simultaneously encouraging long-term investment. An increase in the relative supply of short-term securities was expected to drive up the rates on these particular securities while a decrease in long-term bonds was expected to lower these rates so that the yield curve would "twist" in the desired direction. Although short-term rates actually did rise substantially relative to long-term rates in subsequent periods, it remains unclear as to whether this change in the term structure should be attributed to the success of Operation Twist or to the typical movement in the yield curve over the business cycle.[24]

The Cyclical Behavior of the Term Structure

Figure 13.10 plots the yield to maturity of a three-month T-bill, a 20-year Treasury bond, and the spread between these securities over the time interval 1970 through 1982. There have been substantial interest rate movements over this period as depicted by this chart, most notably since the latter part of 1979.[25] As business conditions change, both long- and short-term rates are expected to change, but because short-term rates are only influenced by current developments while long-term rates are an average of current and forward yields, the shorter-term rates are expected to be more sensitive to movements in the business cycle. In particular, the spread between long-term rates and short-term rates is expected to diminish and turn negative during interest cycle peaks and become more positive when there is a contraction in the business cycle.

Figure 13.10 confirms that the spread between long- and short-term rates has varied substantially over the 1970–1982 period and that the short-term rates were the more volatile (the standard deviation of the short-term rates around

---

[24] The reader is referred to Modigliani and Sutch, *ibid.* for an empirical analysis of the success of Operation Twist.

[25] Short-term interest rate variability since October 1979 can be attributed in part to a monetary policy change on the part of the Federal Reserve System to give priority to monetary targets instead of interest rate targets.

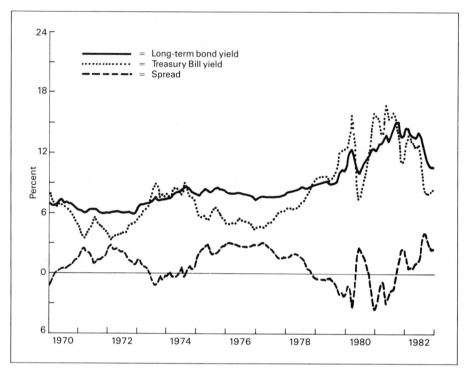

FIG. 13.10   Movement of Long-Term and Short-Term Rates of Interest, 1970–1982

their mean value was 37 percent higher than that of the long-term rates). The average spread between these rates over this interval was 0.96 percent, resulting from more instances of positive than negative spreads, which is consistent with the liquidity preference theory.

OTHER FACTORS AFFECTING BOND YIELDS

The Effect of the Coupon Rate on Yield to Maturity

The coupon rate has two distinct effects on the term structure. The first is a tax effect, because interest income is taxable at the ordinary income tax rate whereas capital gains are taxed at a more favorable rate. The second is a TTM effect: because bonds with higher coupon rates have a lower average maturity, investors get cash back, in some sense, sooner, hence those bonds have less price variability.

The Tax Effect. Because a bond's coupon payments are taxed at a higher rate than its capital gains, if two bonds are selling to yield the same before-tax return to the investor, but one is a low coupon-rate, high ("deep") discount bond while the other is a high coupon-rate bond selling at par or a premium above par, the deep discount bond will have a higher after-tax yield.[26] To compensate taxable investors for the greater tax burden of high-coupon bonds, these bonds should be selling at a slightly higher before-tax YTM than the deep discount bonds. On the other hand, investors' preference for the high cash flow associated with periodic coupon payments may lead them to sacrifice some after-tax yield and result in their valuing high-coupon bonds more than discount bonds at the same before-tax yield. Figure 13.9 indicates that U.S. Treasury securities, which were selling on a deep discount basis with coupon rates of less than 3.5 percent, had before-tax YTMs that were lower than those of high-coupon bonds. Thus it appears, at least for December 31, 1969, that high-coupon bonds sold at a yield to compensate investors for their adverse tax treatment.

Because of any tax effects resulting from coupon structure, yield curves should be drawn only through bonds with comparable coupon rates.

The Average Maturity Effect. The coupon payment's second effect is attributable to the fact that these payments represent a cash inflow to the investor which tends to reduce the overall period for which his investment is outstanding. The computation of a bond's average maturity is complicated by the fact that its cash flows in each period must be adjusted for any differences owing to the time value of money. However, a measure of average maturity can be computed by weighting each period's cash flow (coupon or principal repayment) by the present value of that payment to the total present value of the bond, that is,

$$D = \frac{\sum\limits_{t=1}^{N} [PV(CF_t)]t}{\sum\limits_{t=1}^{N} PV(CF_t)} \tag{13.11}$$

where $PV(CF_t)$ is the present value of the cash flow in period t. The statistic D is referred to as "duration." The higher the coupon rate, the lower the bond's duration and the less liquidity risk associated with the bond.

The interrelationships between coupon rate, duration, and liquidity risk, can be illustrated by comparing these properties for three different five-year bonds all with maturity value of $1,000 and selling to yield a return (ignoring taxes) of 8 percent. Bond 1 has an annual coupon rate of 8 percent and an initial price of $1,000. Bond 2 has an annual coupon rate of 12 percent and an initial price of $1,160.16. Bond 3 is a pure discount bond with no coupon payments, selling at a price of $681. The cash flows associated with each of these bonds and the appropriate value factors are given in Table 13.1. Each bond's duration

---

[26] For an original issue deep-discount bond, the investor must claim a part of the discount in each period as accrued interest income which is taxed as ordinary income. However, if an investor purchases an already existing (seasoned) bond at a price below par, he receives capital gains treatment on the difference.

TABLE 13.1   Duration and Liquidity Risk

		Cash Flows		
	PV Factor	Bond 1	Bond 2	Bond 3
Year 1	0.926	$ 80	$ 120	—
Year 2	0.857	80	120	—
Year 3	0.794	80	120	—
Year 4	0.735	80	120	—
Year 5	0.681	80	120	—
Maturity	0.681	1,000	1,000	$1,000

	Bond 1	Bond 2	Bond 3
Bond price: YTM = 8%	$1,000.00	$1,160.16	$681.00
Duration (in years)	4.31	4.11	5.00
Bond price: YTM = 10%	$924.28	$1,075.92	$621.00
Change in bond price	−$75.72	−$84.24	−$60.00
Change in bond price/ initial price	−7.57%	−7.26%	−8.81%

is also presented in this table. To illustrate this duration calculation, the computation for bond 1 is shown here:

$$D_1 = \frac{[0.926(\$80)]1}{\$1,000} + \frac{[0.857(\$80)]2}{\$1,000} + \frac{[0.794(\$80)]3}{\$1,000}$$
$$+ \frac{[0.735(\$80)]4}{\$1,000} + \frac{[0.681(\$80 + 1,000)]5}{\$1,000}$$
$$= 4.31 \text{ years}$$

The results in Table 13.1 indicated that the bonds' durations were inversely proportional to their coupon rate, that is, the highest coupon rate had the lowest measure of duration while the zero-coupon bond had the highest duration statistic.

To illustrate the impact of this average-maturity effect on the bond's relative price variability, assume the YTMs on all three bonds increase unexpectedly to 10 percent. The market prices on bonds 1, 2, and 3 now are $924.28, $1,075.92, and $621.00, respectively. As indicated in the table, the capital loss expressed as a rate of return on initial investment is smallest for the high-coupon bond and greatest for the discount bond. This result derives from the mathematical property of the duration measure that for a given change in the structure of forward rates, the relative changes in bond prices is a direct function of the security's duration. Hence, high-coupon bonds effectively have a shorter average maturity than low-coupon bonds and require less of an interest-rate premium to compensate for liquidity risk.

The Effect of Callability on Bond Yield

A call provision on a bond gives the issuer the right to buy back the bond at a specified price (the call price) and a specified time, or period of time, prior to the maturity of the bond issue. The call price is generally in excess of the par value of the bond.

The call feature always works to the benefit of the bond issuer and to the detriment of the investor. If interest rates decline with a commensurate increase in the market value of noncallable bonds, an issuer will call the bond when its market value is above the call price and issue a new bond at the lower rate of interest. For example, if the call price of a bond is $105 but its market value equivalent (an uncallable bond with all other considerations the same) is $108, the issuer can exercise its repurchase option at the call date and issue a new bond with identical coupon payment and remaining term to maturity as the original.[27] Since the new bond sells for $108 and has the identical cash flow stream as the bond that was called, the call option netted the issuer a certain profit of $3. On the other hand, if interest rates increase and the market value of the bond declines, then the issuer does not call the bond and the investor is left with a capital loss on his bond, which is now characterized by a coupon-rate below the market yield to maturity.

The possible outcomes associated with the call feature make it the equivalent of a call option with the bond issuer being the holder of the option and the bond investor being the writer. The issuer exercises the option when interest rates decline and lets the option expire unexercised when rates go up. The bond investor bears the risk that interest rates will decline. As with all call options, this investor demands a premium for insuring the issuer against any adverse outcomes. This premium takes the form of a higher YTM on a callable bond. For example, if a noncallable bond is selling at a price of $78, and the value of the option on a callable bond is $3, then the investor in the callable option pays the "net" price of $75 (the noncallable bond price minus the investor's premium for writing a call option)[28] and receives a somewhat higher *YTM* than the investor in the noncallable bond.[29]

The value of the call feature naturally is higher when the probability of exercise is greater. Since most bonds are callable at a price in excess of par, this implies, all things being equal, that the higher the coupon rate on the bond, the more likely it is to be called. Also, other things equal, an option with a longer life is worth more than a shorter-lived option. Thus the option component of a 20-year bond which is immediately callable has a higher value than an option allowing the bond to be called only after a deferred period of five years. As a result the YTM on a bond with a deferred call provision should not be as high as that on a bond which is immediately callable.

In Figure 13.9 the callable bonds of the U.S. Treasury are depicted by circles. These bonds appear to lie on the yield curve and not, as would be

---

[27]Clearly no one would pay more than $105 for this bond if they expected the issuer to redeem it.

[28]For an excellent discussion of options pricing, the reader is referred to William F. Sharpe, *Investments*, 2nd ed., Chapter 16 (Englewood Cliffs, N.J.: Prentice-Hall, 1981).

[29]These figures would have to be adjusted for any "call penalty" paid by the issuer, such as one year of coupon payments.

expected, above it. This may be a spurious result due to a scarcity of observations in the 1990–1999 maturity range, but is more probably due to the call feature having negligible value. This is because these bonds have an initial maturity of 30 years and are callable only after 25 years. Therefore they have a 25-year deferral privilege and a relatively short time for the option to run before expiration (five years). As a result the present value of any expected gains to the Treasury by exercising this option is negligible, however the value of these gains will increase as the bond draws nearer to its call date. It should also be noted that when the Treasury plots the YTM on its callable bonds, it does so on a yield-to-first-call basis, that is, it is assumed that the bond will be called at its first call date and the yield is computed to that date. This effectively converts the 30-year bond into a 25-year bond. Most analysts also use this measure, despite its crudeness, in order to have some notion of what the worst possible yield would be if they planned on holding the security until, at least, its first call date. However, one should not reject outright a callable bond with a yield-to-first-call which is slightly below the yield of a noncallable bond which matures as of the first call date. If interest rates decline, but not by enough to justify exercise of the call option (both because the exercise price is in excess of the bond's face value and because of the transaction costs associated with a new bond issue), the investor will be better off with the callable bond than buying the noncallable to mature at first-call and then reinvesting the proceeds in a second bond with a lower YTM.

Unlike Treasury securities, where most bonds are not callable—and where callability may be deferred for 25 years when they are—virtually all corporate bonds are callable, with industrial bonds typically having deferred callability of 10 years and utility bonds five years. Also, a majority of municipal bonds are callable; typically with a deferral privilege of 10 years.[30] Therefore when one compares the spread between these securities and U.S. government securities, one must recognize that changes in this spread may, in part, be attributable to changes in the value of the call option.

Default Risk and Yield Differences

Thus far, this discussion of the term structure of interest rates has considered only one element of risk that influences a security's yield, that is, the asset's sensitivity to capital losses in the event of an increase in interest rates. Questions of default on the promised coupon payments or principal repayment have been circumvented by considering only U.S. government securities. This section considers corporate and municipal bonds with positive probabilities of default and defines the "default premium" of a security to be the differential between the YTM of that security and the yield on a comparable Treasury security. Comparability here implies the same call provision. In the absence of comparable securities, the observed yield difference is the result of both the call provision and the default premium.

Default risk is simply the risk that the borrower will not be able to meet his contractual interest payments or principal repayment. A bond is technically in default when any contractual commitment is violated. However, there are

---

[30]Serial-issue bonds are generally not callable, while term bonds are.

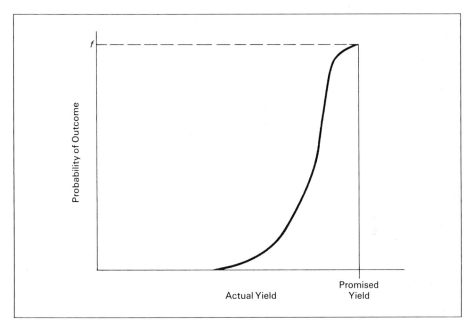

FIG. 13.11 Possible Investment Outcomes

degrees of default: The borrower and its creditors may agree to a slightly modified repayment schedule, perhaps merely delaying the interest payment for a period, or no agreement may be forthcoming and the borrwer will be forced into bankruptcy. When a lender purchases a bond, the best possible outcome it can obtain is what is promised in the bond contract. Any deviation in actual or realized return from this promised rate is directly attributable to default. Since the investor can conceivably (although quite improbably) lose the full value of its bond investment but is more likely to recover the principal and some interest, the highly skewed distribution in Figure 13.11 may reasonably represent the investor's probability distribution over returns, where $1-f$ is the probability of bond default.

The relatively high probabilities of outcomes somewhat less than the promised yield represent the yield outcomes when a rescheduling of the bond's repayment is necessary but lenders are reasonably confident of the borrower's ability to repay and no incremental infusions of cash are necessary. For example, bond 1 in Table 13.1 is promising to yield a rate of return of 8.0 percent. If, however, the issuer cannot make the $80 interest payment in year 4 but makes up for this by a $160 coupon payment in year 5, then this would lower the investor's realized YTM from 8.0 to 7.9 percent. The more adverse outcomes represent those situations where the borrower does not have the means to repay its debt and legal proceedings are necessary to liquidate the firm's assets.

If noncallable corporate bonds and Treasury securities with the same TTM were priced to yield the same rate of return, then no rational investor would buy the corporate bond because of the positive probability that the issuer would

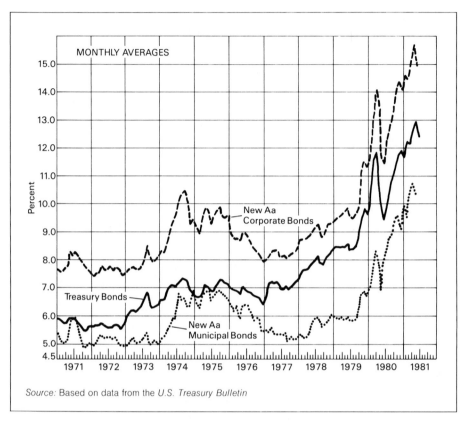

FIG. 13.12   **Average Yields of Long-Term Treasury, Corporate, and Municipal Bonds**

default on the obligation. The investor would demand a default premium that would be at least as great as the expected default loss (expressed as a rate of loss on invested capital); the default premium would be equal to this rate for the risk-neutral investor and greater than it for the risk-averse investor. In Figure 13.4 the impact of default risk on the YTMs of prime commercial paper and large negotiable bank certificates of deposit is shown. Figure 13.12 illustrates the impact of this risk on long-term (newly issued, 20-year), high grade (but not best quality) corporate and municipal bonds for the period beginning 1971 through mid-year 1981.[31] This figure shows that the spread between the yields on corporate and municipal bonds relative to Treasury bonds has varied substantially over this time interval. In general, Aa municipal bonds have yielded less than Treasury bonds. This is because the interest income on these obligations is tax

---

[31] The Treasury bond series is a composite which does not include any bonds which are due or callable before 10 years. The corporate bonds have an original maturity of at least 20 years. Prior to June 1973, the series reflected bonds without call protection. From June 1973 to July 1976, the series was adjusted to reflect 5 years of call protection. Since that time the series reflects bond yields regardless of call protection.

TABLE 13.2 Bond Ratings

MOODY'S RATINGS OF CORPORATE AND MUNICIPAL BONDS[a]

Rating	Quality
Aaa	Best
Aa	High grade
A	Upper-medium grade
Baa	Medium grade
Ba	Speculative elements
B	Unattractive
Caa	Poor standing
Ca	Highly speculative; may be in default or have other shortcomings
C	Lowest grade; extremely poor prospects

STANDARD & POOR'S RATINGS OF CORPORATE DEBT[b]

Rating	Quality
AAA	Highest
AA	Slightly below highest
A	Strong capacity to pay interest and repay principal but not as good as AA
BBB	Adequate customer protection
BB B CCC CC	Predominantly speculative with respect to interest and principal payments; BB indicates the lowest degree of speculation and CC the highest
C	Income bonds for which no interest is paid
D	Debt is in default with interest and/or principal repayment in arrears

(a) Within each rating classification between Aa and B, Moody's employs numerical quotations of 1, 2, and 3. Grade 1 represents the best third, Grade 2 the midrange, and Grade 3 the lowest third of the securities within each classification.

(b) The ratings from AA to B may be modified by the addition of a plus or minus to show gradations within these classifications. Standard & Poor's ratings of municipal bonds differs somewhat from the above ratings of its corporate issues.

---

exempt while the interest income on Treasury bonds is taxable. Even with this tax advantage, however, Aa municipals were selling to yield a before-tax return greater than that available on Treasury securities during the first half of 1975. This higher yield on municipal bonds was in large part due to the highly publicized problems with New York City debt which raised default premiums substantially as investors were reevaluating the risk of these securities in light of New York's inability to pay off its maturing obligations. The increase in the spread between Treasury and municipal securities since 1977 probably reflects both a reduction in the default premium of the municipals relative to 1975 and an increase in the value of their tax advantage. In contrast the spread between corporate and Treasury securities narrowed beginning in 1976. The differences in the movements of these spreads may indicate the increased importance of the tax advantage, however, Aa municipals were selling to yield a before-tax return beginning in 1976 (see Figure 13.2).

The perception of the default risk on a municipal or corporate bond is apparently determined largely by investment agencies such as Moody's Investors Service and Standard & Poor's. These agencies evaluate the quality of a bond and give their evaluations in terms of a letter grade. Table 13.2 presents a key to the ratings of these agencies. In general, the empirical evidence indicates that the rating agencies do a remarkably good job of evaluating the default risk of these securities.[32]

SUMMARY

The objective of this chapter is to further the reader's understanding of what the rate of interest is and how it is affected by such factors as time preference, taxes, the anticipated rate of inflation, fiscal and monetary policy, default risk, callability, and term to maturity. The study of the rate of interest is further complicated by the fact that the field of economics is governed by the ever-changing economic behavior of individuals and institutions. Unlike the natural sciences which are governed by deterministic physical laws, the evolutionary manner in which people change their expectations of the impact of monetary and fiscal policy on price inflation and alter their propensities to save or consume are key determinants of interest rate levels and the speed at which the effects of public policies are transmitted to the credit markets. The stochastic nature of economic man has resulted in heated debates among economists (witness the ever-continuing dialogue between "monetarists" and "Keynesians") as to the short- and long-run implications of economic policy decisions and the explanation of why the term structure of interests rates looks the way it does.

SUGGESTED READING

Bowsher, Norman N. "Rise and Fall of Interest Rates." Federal Reserve Bank of St. Louis *Review*, Vol. 62, No. 7 (Aug.–Sept. 1980), pp. 16–23.

Cook, Timothy J. "Some Factors Affecting Long-Term Yield Spreads in Recent Years." Federal Reserve Bank of Richmond *Monthly Review*, Vol. 59, No. 9 (Sept. 1973), pp. 2–14.

Cox, John C., et al. "A Reexamination of Traditional Hypotheses About the Term Structure of Interest Rates." *Journal of Finance*, Vol. 36, No. 4 (Sept. 1981), pp. 769–799.

---

[32] W. Braddock Hickman, *Corporate Bond Quality and Investor Experience* (New York: National Bureau of Economic Research, 1958); and Thomas F. Pogue and Robert M. Soldofsky, "What's in a Bond Rating?," *Journal of Financial and Quantitative Analysis*, Vol. 4, No. 2 (June 1969), pp. 201–228.

Culbertson, John M. "The Term Structure of Interst Rates." *Quarterly Journal of Economics*, Vol. 71, No. 4 (Nov. 1957), pp. 485–517.

Fisher, Irving. *The Theory of Interest*. New York: Macmillan, 1930.

Fisher, Lawrence. "Determinants of Risk Premiums on Corporate Bonds." *Journal of Political Economy*, Vol. 67, No. 3 (June 1959), pp. 217–257.

Friedman, Milton. "Factors Affecting the Level of Interest Rates." *Proceedings of the 1968 Conference on Savings and Residential Financing*. Chicago: U.S. Savings and Loan League, 1969.

Gordon, Robert J., ed. *Milton Friedman's Monetary Framework*. Chicago: The University of Chicago Press, 1974.

Havrilesky, Thomas M., and Robert Schweitzer. *Contemporary Developments in Financial Institutions and Markets*. Arlington Heights, Ill.: Harlan Davidson, 1983.

Hickman, W. Braddock. *Corporate Bond Quality and Investor Experience*. New York: National Bureau of Economic Research, 1958.

Hicks, John. *Theory of Value*, 2nd ed. London: Oxford University Press, 1946.

Keynes, John M. *The General Theory of Employment, Interest, and Money*. London: Macmillan, 1936.

Kessel, Reuben A. *The Cyclical Behavior of the Term Structure of Interest Rates*. Occasional Paper No. 91. New York-National Bureau of Economic Research, 1965.

Lusher, David W. "The Structure of Interest Rates and the Keynesian Theory of Interest." *Journal of Political Economy*, Vol. 50, No. 2 (Apr. 1942), pp.272–279.

Lutz, Friedrich A. "The Structure of Interest Rates." *Quarterly Journal of Economics*, Vol. 55, No. 1 (Nov. 1940), pp. 36–63.

Malkiel, Burton. *The Term Structure of Interest Rates: Expectations and Behavior Patterns*. Princeton: Princeton University Press, 1966.

———. *The Term Structure of Interest Rates: Theory, Empirical Evidence, and Applications*. New York: McCaleb-Sieler Publishing, 1970.

McCulloch, J. Huston. "An Estimate of the Liquidity Premium." *Journal of Political Economy*, Vol. 83, No. 1 (Feb. 1975), pp. 95–119.

Meiselman, David. *The Term Structure of Interest Rates*. Englewood Cliffs, N.J.: Prentice-Hall, 1962.

Miller, Merton H. "Debt and Taxes." *Journal of Finance*, Vol. 32, No. 2 (May 1977), pp. 261–275.

Modigliani, Franco, and Richard Sutch. "Innovations in Interest Rate Policy." *American Economic Review*, Vol. 56, No. 2 (May 1966), pp. 178–197.

Nobay, A. Robert, and Harry G. Johnson. "Monetarism: A Historic–Theoretic Perspective." *Journal of Economic Literature*, Vol. 15, No. 2 (June 1977), pp. 470–485.

Pogue, Thomas F., and Robert M. Soldofsky. "What's in a Bond Rating?" *Journal of Financial and Quantitative Analysis*, Vol. 4, No. 2 (June 1969), pp. 201–228.

Sharpe, William F. *Investments*, 2nd ed. Englewood Cliffs, N.J.: Prentice-Hall, 1981.

Van Horne, James C. *Financial Market Rates and Flows*. Englewood Cliffs, N.J.: Prentice-Hall, 1978.

14

Modern Portfolio Analysis

T. DANIEL COGGIN

INTRODUCTION

This chapter presents a summary of some of the major results of quantitative investment analysis that have been gathered under the heading modern portfolio analysis or, as it is often called, modern portfolio theory (MPT). While the general findings discussed in the following pages are applicable to stocks, bonds, and real estate, the primary focus is on common stocks. To date, this is where the bulk of the theory has been derived and tested.[1] It should also be noted that the terms asset and security are used interchangeably in this chapter.

　　Modern portfolio analysis was once the province of academics, with financial practitioners largely unaware of or unwilling to become interested in the subject. However, as more MPT-trained MBAs began to enter the world of financial analysis and portfolio management, the situation changed. Now, practitioners are very receptive to new developments in modern portfolio analysis and often contribute new ideas themselves. Modern portfolio analysis has revolutionized the world of financial management, contributing important new methods for quantifying investment risk and return and for measuring investment performance. Increasingly, financial analysts and portfolio managers must be aware and make use of the tools of modern portfolio analysis in order to stay on top of their respective jobs. This chapter presents an overview of the methodology of modern portfolio analysis, its uses, and some of the new directions it is taking.

THE CONSUMPTION-INVESTMENT DECISION

The Basic Problem of Investment Analysis

In order to understand the process of investment management using modern portfolio analysis, one must understand the quantitative foundation upon which it is based. It is best to begin with the consumption-investment decision, which is at the heart of all investment analysis.

　　The potential investor is faced with a decision which, in its simplest form, asks: Should I consume all of my income today, or should I take some portion and invest it in an asset that will yield a return at some future date that is greater than the amount initially invested? Thus, this decision implies a trade-off between consumption now (period 1) and consumption later (period 2). Trading some of this year's consumption for an incrementally larger amount of consumption next year is sometimes called lending, while the converse is sometimes called borrowing. In this section, the focus is on lending and it is called investing.

---

[1] For a discussion of the recent work that has been done applying the principles of modern portfolio analysis to other specific asset types, see H. Gifford Fong, "Portfolio Construction: Fixed Income," *Managing Investment Portfolios*, eds. J. L. Maginn and D. L. Tuttle (Boston: Warren, Gorham & Lamont, 1983) for fixed income securities; Jeffrey D. Fisher, "Portfolio Construction: Real Estate," *Managing Investment Portfolios*, eds. J. L. Maginn and D. L. Tuttle (Boston: Warren, Gorham & Lamont, 1983) for real estate; and Robert F. Stambaugh, "On the Exclusion of Assets From Tests of the Two-Parameter Model," *Journal of Financial Economics*, Vol. 10 (Summer 1982) for combinations of these assets.

A graph is used to depict the opportunity set for period 1 consumption (this year) and period 2 consumption (next year) for an investor, I. It is assumed that I can trade as much or as little as he wants of his consumption in period 1 for consumption in period 2. This implies that the investment available to I is perfectly divisible into large or small parts. It is further assumed that I can obtain this set of consumption outcomes for periods 1 and 2 with no risk (i.e., with certainty). Figure 14.1 presents I's two-period consumption set.

Choosing a Consumption Combination. I can, in the extreme, consume his entire $100 of income in period 1; or, he can consume $0 in period 1 and invest it all in an asset returning $110 in period 2. All the combinations between these two extremes are also available and lie on the line segment YX in Figure 14.1. Which one will I choose? The answer is that he will choose the point on line YX that maximizes his personal tastes, preferences, or utility. In order to deal with the notion of personal utility, we introduce another concept, the indifference curve. Figure 14.2 reveals I's indifference curve for the two-period consumption problem.

The curved line marked I_0 in Figure 14.2 is I's indifference curve. It represents the loci of all combinations of period 1 and period 2 consumption with which I is equally happy or indifferent. The logic of indifference curves holds that, at equal levels of risk, more return is preferred to less. Hence, there are imaginary curves above and below I_0. I will choose the combination of period 1 and period 2 consumption on line YX, which is tangent to I_0. This is represented by point T in Figure 14.2 and corresponds to a combination of $30 consumption in period 1 and $77 consumption in period 2. Point T offers the maximum satisfaction (utility) for I, given the combinations of period 1 and period 2 consumption available on line YX.

Calculating Rate of Return

It is not enough merely to know that I chose to trade $70 (i.e., $100 − $30) worth of consumption in period 1 for $77 worth of consumption in period 2. It is also important to know what rate of return I earned on this investment. The mechanics of this calculation are quite straightforward. I started with $100 of period 1 income. He consumed $30 and invested $70. His return on the $70 period 1 investment was $77 in period 2. The rate of return (ROR), in percentage, is:

$$\text{ROR} = \frac{\text{Return} - \text{Investment}}{\text{Investment}} \times 100 \qquad (14.1)$$

For I, there is

$$\text{ROR} = \frac{\$77 - \$70}{70} \times 100 = 10\% \qquad (14.2)$$

I earned $7 on his $70 investment, which translated into a 10 percent ROR. Since YX is a straight line, the ROR on *any* combination of period 1 and period 2 consumption in Figure 14.2 is 10 percent. If we assume no transaction costs, this number would correspond to the market rate of interest. Thus, the distin-

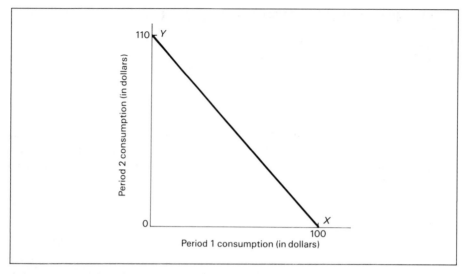

FIG. 14.1 Investor I's Two-Period Consumption Set

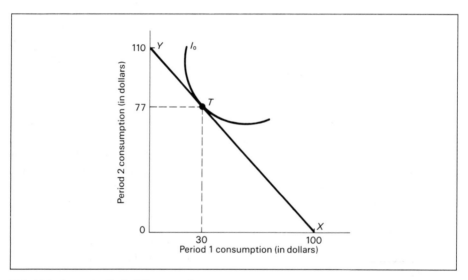

FIG. 14.2 Investor I's Indifference Curve

guishing factor with respect to various combinations of period 1 and period 2 consumption is I's preference for a particular combination (i.e., point T).

In the preceding discussion, it has been shown how an individual makes a single investment decision and how he calculates his rate of return under conditions of certainty. However, individuals are faced with choices among investment assets that have uncertain or risky returns. These investment decisions are facilitated by the existence of capital markets, which transfer funds between lenders and borrowers.

CHOOSING A PORTFOLIO OF RISKY ASSETS

Measuring Portfolio Return

The return on a portfolio of risky assets is also straightforward to calculate.[2]

$$R_p = \sum_{i}^{n} w_i(R_i) \tag{14.3}$$

This equation states that the return on a portfolio of n assets (R_p) is equal to the sum of the individual asset weights in the portfolio times its return, for each asset i. Thus, if portfolio P has three assets, each having a return of 10 percent and each comprising 33.3 percent of the portfolio, then:

$$R_p = 0.333(10\%) + 0.333(10\%) + 0.333(10\%) \tag{14.4}$$
$$= 10\%$$

R_p is sometimes called the holding period return, or the ex post return, and is the actual portfolio return measured over some specific time period. If an individual is dealing with expected (or anticipated) returns, then a little different mathematical notation is used.

$$E(R_p) = \sum_{i}^{n} w_i E(R_i) \tag{14.5}$$

The $E(\ )$ signifies expectations. This is sometimes called ex ante return and is the expected portfolio return over some specific time period. It should be noted that some writers designate $E(R_p)$ with a bar $(^-)$, i.e., $\bar{R}_p$.

Measuring Portfolio Risk

Before the work of Harry Markowitz, investors were counseled to pick the highest quality stocks with the highest expected returns, or advice to that effect. Markowitz (1952, 1959) revolutionized the investment world by quantifying the concept of investment *risk*. The dictionary defines risk as "hazard, peril, exposure to loss or injury," and Sharpe (1970) calls it the "fuzziness" or uncertainty associated with a prediction. Markowitz quantified investment risk as the variance about an asset's expected return.

Assume that an individual is considering an investment, stock XYZ, which has the period 1 expected return distribution probabilities shown at the top of page 14-6.

Substituting probabilities (p_i) for weights (w_i) in Equation 14.3, we have:

$$E(R_{XYZ}) = 0.50(15\%) + 0.30(10\%) + \cdots + 0.02(-5\%) \tag{14.6}$$
$$= 11\%$$

Thus, 11 percent is the mean or expected value of the probability distribution for the returns on stock XYZ. Some writers denote expected asset return as a random variable with a tilde $(^-)$, that is, $E(\tilde{R})$.

---

[2] Details behind the mathematics here may be found in Chapter 6.

STOCK XYZ

Return	Probability or Likelihood of Occurrence
15%	0.50
10	0.30
5	0.13
0	0.05
−5	0.02
	1.00

Variance, Covariance, and Correlation of Returns. The variance of the expected return for XYZ, Var(XYZ), is a measure of the dispersion of possible outcomes. If an asset is riskless, it has an expected return dispersion of zero. The equation for the variance of the expected return for stock XYZ is:

$$\text{Var}(XYZ) = \sum_i p_i [\, R_i - E(R_{XYZ})\,]^2 \tag{14.7}$$

In our example, this translates into:

$$\text{Var}(XYZ) = 0.50(15\% - 11\%)^2 + \cdots + 0.02(-5\% - 11\%)^2 \tag{14.8}$$
$$= 24\%$$

The variance associated with a distribution of returns measures the tightness with which the distribution is clustered around the mean or expected return. Markowitz argued that this tightness or variance is equivalent to the uncertainty or riskiness of the investment. Since the variance is in squared units, it is common to see the variance converted to the standard deviation or square root of the variance:

$$\text{SD}(XYZ) = \sqrt{\text{Var}(XYZ)} \tag{14.9}$$

The two are conceptually equivalent; that is, the larger the variance or standard deviation of $E(R)$, the greater the implied investment risk. See Chapter 16 for details about variance analysis.

The variance of a portfolio of n assets (where $n > 2$), Var(p), is a little more difficult to calculate. It depends not only on the variance of each asset, but also upon how closely each asset tracks each other asset. The formula is:

$$\text{Var}(p) = \sum_i^n w_i^2 \text{Var}(i) + \sum_i^n \sum_j^n w_i w_j \text{SD}(ij) \qquad \text{for } i \neq j \tag{14.10}$$

In words, this formula states that the variance of the portfolio expected return is the sum of the weighted variances of the individual assets plus the sum of the weighted covariances of the assets. The covariance is a new term in this discussion and has a precise mathematical translation; however, its practical meaning is the degree to which the returns on two assets vary or change together. A positive covariance means the returns on two assets tend to move or change in the same direction, while a negative covariance means the returns tend to

TABLE 14.1   Hypothetical Illustration of Correlation Between
Asset Returns

		Asset Returns by Period				
	Stock	1	2	3	4	5
Case I: Cor(AB) = +1.0	A	2%	4%	6%	8%	10%
	B	4	8	12	16	20
Case II: Cor(AB) ≅ 0.0	A	12	8	20	4	16
	B	8	0	4	6	2
Case III: Cor(AB) = −1.0	A	2	4	6	8	10
	B	20	16	12	8	4

change in opposite directions. Hence, the variance of the portfolio expected return is the weighted sum of the individual variances of the assets in the portfolio plus the weighted sum of the degree to which the assets vary together.

The covariance is analogous to the correlation between the expected returns for two assets. Specifically, the correlation between the returns for assets A and B, written Cor(AB), is defined as the covariance of the two assets, written Cov(AB), divided by the product of their standard deviations:

$$\text{Cor}(AB) = \frac{\text{Cov}(AB)}{\text{SD}(A)\text{SD}(B)} \tag{14.11}$$

The correlation and the covariance are conceptually equivalent terms. Dividing the covariance by the product of the standard deviations simply makes the correlation a number that is comparable across different assets. The correlation coefficient can have values ranging from +1.0, denoting perfect comovement in the same direction, to −1.0, denoting perfect comovement in opposite directions. As an illustration of the correlation between asset returns, consider the following three hypothetical cases for common stocks A and B in Table 14.1.

Case I illustrates perfect positive correlation or comovement, both A and B move up together in respectively equal increments. Case II illustrates near zero correlation, both stocks move in a largely random fashion. Case III illustrates perfect negative correlation, stock A goes up in equal increments while stock B moves down in equal increments. In reality, there are few examples that exactly fit these three cases. Most common stocks have a small but positive correlation of returns with each other over time. However, the three illustrations do demonstrate the basic concept of the correlation or covariance of asset returns.

Portfolio Diversification. The idea of portfolio diversification has a precise mathematical definition. Intuitively, however, diversification embodies the idea of spreading investment risk among several different assets in a portfolio, in an effort to lower total portfolio risk. A portfolio may contain assets that are diversified within an asset class (i.e., a well-diversified portfolio of common stocks), or it may contain assets that are diversified across asset types (i.e., a

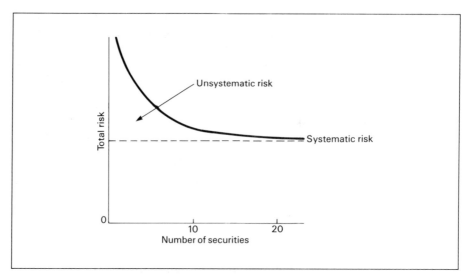

FIG. 14.3 Systematic and Unsystematic Portfolio Risk

well-diversified portfolio of stocks, bonds, and real estate). Chapter 39, International Portfolio Diversification, discusses investing in the capital markets of other countries. Investment risk can be classified into two general types: systematic and unsystematic.

Systematic and Unsystematic Risk. William Sharpe named the portion of an asset's variability that can be attributed to the common factor as systematic risk. It is also sometimes called undiversifiable or market risk. Systematic risk is the minimum level of risk that can obtain for a portfolio by means of diversification across a large number of randomly selected assets. As such, systematic risk is that which results from general market and economic conditions that *cannot* be diversified away. Sharpe named the portion of an asset's variability that can be diversified away as unsystematic risk. It is also sometimes called diversifiable risk, residual variance, or company specific risk. The manner in which diversification reduces unsystematic risk for portfolios can be illustrated with a simple graph.

Figure 14.3 shows that at a portfolio size of about 20 randomly selected assets (in this case, common stocks), the level of unsystematic risk is almost completely diversified away. Essentially, all that is left is systematic or market risk. Total asset risk is defined as the sum of the systematic and unsystematic risk components. There are essentially two diversification strategies that attempt to remove unsystematic risk from investment portfolios: naive and Markowitz.

Naive Diversification. This strategy is achieved when an investor simply invests in a number of different stocks or asset types and hopes that the variance of the expected return on the portfolio is lowered. For example, a well-known rule of equity investing for professional managers holds that equity portfolios should be diversified across several different industries. Naive diversification is closely related to a practice Francis and Archer (1979) have termed financial interior decorating. According to this approach, an investment counselor seeks to design portfolios to match the personality of the investor. As Francis and Archer note, the assumption of the financial interior decorator is that certain types of investors have certain investment return requirements that can be fulfilled by artfully designing a portfolio to suit them.

For example, widows have high current income needs, thus they should invest in so-called low risk-high dividend assets (such as bonds or electric utility stocks). Little or no attention is paid to the degree of correlation between the returns on the assets within these categories. Concentrating one's investments in any one asset category is an invitation to the greater risk implied by the usually high covariance of asset returns within such categories. They usually go *up* together, but they also tend to come *down* together! There is a better way to approach the diversification problem.

Markowitz Diversification. This strategy is primarily concerned with the degree of covariance between asset returns in a portfolio. Indeed, the great contribution of Markowitz diversification is the formulation of an asset's risk in terms of a portfolio of assets, rather than as an isolated asset. Markowitz diversification seeks to combine assets in a portfolio with returns that are less than perfectly correlated, in an effort to lower portfolio risk (variance) without sacrificing portfolio return. It is this concern for maintaining portfolio return, while lowering risk through an analysis of the covariance between asset returns, that separates Markowitz diversification from the naive approach and makes it more effective. The Markowitz diversification and the importance of asset correlations can be illustrated with a simple two-asset portfolio example.

Assume that common stock C and common stock D are available, where $E(R_C) = 10\%$, $SD(C) = 30\%$ and $E(R_D) = 25\%$, $SD(D) = 60\%$. Further assume that the correlation between the returns for the two stocks are $Cor(CD) = +1.0$ (Case I), 0.0 (Case II), and -1.0 (Case III). If an equal 50 percent weighting to both stocks C and D is assigned, the expected portfolio return can be calculated as:

$$E(R_p) = 0.50(10\%) + 0.50(25\%) \tag{14.12}$$
$$= 17.5\%$$

Then, the following can be substituted into the equation for the standard deviation of the expected return on the simple two-stock portfolio, $SD(p)$:

$$SD(p) = \sqrt{w_C^2 Var(C) + w_D^2 Var(D) + 2w_C w_D Cor(CD) SD(C) SD(D)} \tag{14.13}$$
$$= \sqrt{(0.50)^2 (30\%)^2 + (0.50)^2 (60\%)^2 + 2(0.50)(0.50) Cor(CD)(30\%)(60\%)}$$
$$= \sqrt{0.1125 + 0.09[Cor(CD)]}$$

For the three cases of $Cor(CD)$ there are:

Case	Cor(CD)	E(R_p)	SD(p)
I	+1.0	17.5%	45.0%
II	0.0	17.5	33.5
III	−1.0	17.5	15.0

This example clearly illustrates the effect of Markowitz diversification. As the correlation between the expected returns on stocks C and D decreases from $+1.0$ to 0.0 to -1.0, the standard deviation (i.e., the expected uncertainty) of the expected portfolio return also decreases from 45 percent to 15 percent. However, the expected portfolio return remains 17.5 percent for each case. This phenomenon is sometimes called the magic of diversification. The magic should be no secret to the reader now. The principle of Markowitz diversification states that as the correlation (covariance) between the returns for assets that are combined in a portfolio decreases, so does the variance (hence the standard deviation) of the return for that portfolio. The magic is thus the degree of correlation between the expected asset returns. Thus, the good news is that investors can maintain expected portfolio return and lower portfolio risk by combining assets with low to negative correlations. However, the bad news is that there are very few assets that have small to negative correlations with other assets! The problem of Markowitz diversification then becomes one of searching among large numbers of assets in an effort to discover the optimum portfolio, the portfolio with the minimum risk at a given level of expected return or, equivalently, the highest expected return at a given level of risk. The stage is now set for a discussion of Markowitz efficient portfolios and their construction.

Constructing Markowitz Efficient Portfolios

Markowitz diversification leads to the construction of Markowitz efficient portfolios of assets. By "efficient," Markowitz meant portfolios that have the highest expected return at a given level of risk. In order to construct an efficient portfolio, some basic assumptions about asset selection behavior must be discussed.

1 All investors prefer the highest expected return at a given level of risk.

2 All investors choose portfolios based upon expected asset returns, variances, and covariances. These expectations are usually derived from historical averages, mathematical projections, or analysts' estimates.

3 All investors have a common period 1 investment horizon.

The technique of constructing Markowitz efficient portfolios from large groups of stocks requires a massive number of calculations. In a portfolio of n securities, there are $(n^2 - n)/2$ unique covariances to calculate. Hence, for a portfolio of just 50 securities, there are 1,225 covariances that must be calculated. For 100 securities, there are 4,950! Furthermore, in order to solve for the portfolio that minimizes risk for each level of return, a mathematical technique called quadratic programming (and a computer) must be used. A discussion of this technique is beyond the scope of this chapter.[3] However, it is possible to illustrate the general idea of the construction of efficient portfolios by referring again to a simple two-asset portfolio.

---

[3] The interested reader can consult Harry M. Markowitz, *Portfolio Selection* (New Haven, Conn.: Yale University Press, 1959) or Andrew Rudd and Henry K. Clasing, Jr., *Modern Portfolio Theory* (Homewood, Ill.: Dow Jones-Irwin, 1982) for a good introduction to the topic.

TABLE 14.2 Portfolio Expected Returns and Standard Deviations for Varying Proportions of Stocks C and D

Portfolio	Proportion of C	Proportion of D	$E(R_p)$	$SD(p)$
1	100%	—	10.0%	30.0%
2	75	25%	13.8	3.9
3	50	50	17.5	6.8
4	25	75	21.2	17.4
5	—	100	25.0	60.0

One should recall that there are two assets, common stocks C and D; where $E(R_C) = 10\%$, $SD(C) = 30\%$ and $E(R_D) = 25\%$, $SD(D) = 60\%$. We now further assume that $Cor(CD) = -0.5$. Using Equation 14.5 for $E(R_p)$ and Equation 14.13 for $SD(p)$, the expected portfolio return and standard deviation are calculated for different proportions of C and D in the portfolio in Table 14.2. Given these available combinations of stocks C and D, it is now possible to introduce the notion of feasible and efficient sets of portfolios.

Feasible and Efficient Sets. With only two assets, the feasible set of portfolios is graphed as a curved line in risk-return space that represents those combinations of risk and expected return that are attainable by constructing portfolios from the available combinations of the two assets. In Figure 14.4, the

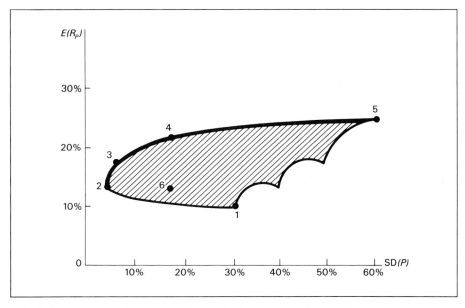

FIG. 14.4 Feasible and Efficient Sets for Portfolios of Stocks C and D

portfolio B is greater than that for portfolios L and M, but so is its risk. The *CML* represents the linear efficient set for all investors.

The capital market line implies that all investors should hold the same portfolio (the market portfolio) and differ only in the means of financing it (by lending or borrowing). This is diametrically opposed to the previously described financial interior decorator school of portfolio management. One should recall that this technique is characterized by the investment manager choosing portfolios to match the client's investment personality. As will be shown, the tools of modern portfolio analysis allow the portfolio manager to decompose risk more rigorously and explicitly into its systematic and unsystematic components. To do this, the characteristic line is introduced.

The Characteristic Line. This line relates on an individual asset i to return on the market M by the following equation:

$$R_{it} = \alpha_i + \beta_i R_{Mt} + \varepsilon_{it} \tag{14.16}$$

The equation for the characteristic line is identical to Equation 14.14 for the market model. The percentage of systematic risk is often measured by R^2, the coefficient of determination from the regression estimation of the characteristic line for asset i. Hence, unsystematic risk is $1 - R^2$. As we noted earlier, total investment risk for an asset is the sum of the systematic and the unsystematic risk components. The beta coefficient, β_i, is the slope of the characteristic line for asset i, and measures the degree to which the returns on asset i change systematically with changes in the market return in historical data. Hence, beta is referred to as an index of that systematic risk, due to general market conditions that cannot be diversified away. For example, if stock i has a beta of 1.5, it means that in historical data stock i had a return equal to 1.5 times that of the market return on average. The beta for the market portfolio is, of course, 1.0.

Table 14.3 gives estimates of historical beta plus systematic and unsystematic risk for each of the Dow Jones 30 industrial stocks, estimated from 60 months of return data prior to December 31, 1981. Studies have shown that for the average New York Stock Exchange (NYSE) common stock, systematic risk is about 30 percent, while unsystematic risk is about 70 percent of return variance. To estimate the characteristic line for a portfolio of stocks, one would estimate Equation 14.16 for portfolio returns, R_{pt}. The statistics derived are directly analogous to those derived for individual stocks. The R^2 for a well-diversified portfolio of stocks will typically exceed 0.90, indicating that unsystematic risk is less than 10 percent of total portfolio return variance.

The Security Market Line

The capital market line represents an equilibrium condition in which the expected return on a portfolio of assets is a linear function of the expected return on the market portfolio. A directly analogous relationship holds for individual security expected returns:

$$E(R_i) = R_F + \frac{E(R_M) - R_F}{\text{Var}(M)} \text{Cov}(iM) \tag{14.17}$$

This is the equation for the security market line (SML).

TABLE 14.3   Market Model Statistics for the Dow Jones 30 Industrials, December 31, 1981

	Beta	Systematic Risk	Unsystematic Risk
Allied Corp.	1.05	0.43	0.57
Aluminum Co. of America	0.92	0.39	0.61
American Brands	0.73	0.39	0.61
American Can	0.76	0.28	0.72
American Express	0.89	0.35	0.65
American Telephone	0.27	0.14	0.86
Bethlehem Steel	1.07	0.39	0.61
DuPont	0.91	0.41	0.59
Eastman Kodak	0.74	0.23	0.77
Exxon	0.55	0.27	0.73
General Electric	0.74	0.55	0.45
General Foods	0.59	0.22	0.78
General Motors	0.62	0.27	0.73
Goodyear	0.65	0.27	0.73
Inco	1.14	0.34	0.66
IBM	0.63	0.38	0.62
International Harvester	1.41	0.50	0.50
International Paper	1.05	0.48	0.52
Merck	0.65	0.28	0.72
Minnesota Mining	0.69	0.33	0.67
Owens-Illinois	0.75	0.29	0.71
Proctor & Gamble	0.45	0.20	0.80
Sears Roebuck	0.68	0.32	0.68
Standard Oil of California	0.39	0.07	0.93
Texaco	0.29	0.07	0.93
Union Carbide	0.85	0.50	0.50
U.S. Steel	0.88	0.27	0.73
United Technologies	1.12	0.48	0.52
Westinghouse	1.11	0.48	0.52
Woolworth	0.84	0.29	0.71

Note: Values estimated from 60 months of return data prior to December 31, 1981

This equation states that, given the assumptions of the CAPM, the expected (or required) return on an individual asset is a positive linear function of its covariance with the market portfolio. That is, the expected return on asset i is equal to the risk-free rate plus a risk premium equal to the price of risk times the quantity risk. Since $\mathrm{Cov}(iM)/\mathrm{Var}(M) = \beta_i$, we can rewrite the equation for

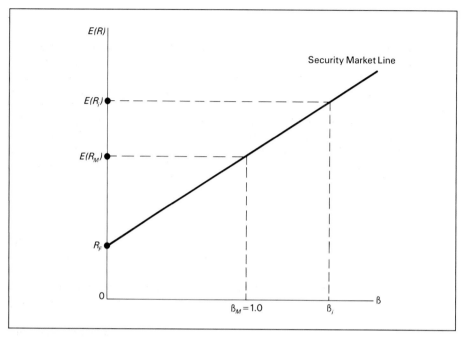

FIG. 14.7 The Security Market Line

the SML as:

$$E(R_i) = R_F + \beta_i[\, E(R_M) - R_F \,]$$ (14.18)

which is also the most common equation for the CAPM. The $E(R_i)$ from Equation 14.18 is sometimes called the risk-adjusted required rate of return on asset *i*. A graph of the SML is presented in Figure 14.7.

In equilibrium, individual security expected returns will lie on the SML and off the CML. This is true because of the high degree of unsystematic risk that remains in individual securities that can be diversified out of portfolios of securities. It follows that the only risk investors will pay a premium to avoid is market risk. Hence, two assets with the same amount of systematic risk will have the same expected return. In equilibrium, only efficient portfolios will lie on both the CML and the SML. This underscores the fact that the systematic risk measure, beta, is most correctly considered as an index of the contribution of an individual security to the systematic risk of a well diversified portfolio of securities. Research has shown that when investors do not hold large, well-diversified portfolios, the CAPM and beta become inaccurate formulations.

The CAPM as a Predictive Model. The equations for the CML and the SML represent an ex ante model for expected returns. This is an important difference between the CML and SML, and the market model. The market model is an ex post or descriptive model used to describe historical data and is not derived from an explicit theoretical framework. Hence, the market model makes no prediction of what expected returns should be.

Beta

Estimating Historical Beta. The beta estimate is an index of systematic risk for an individual asset or a portfolio of assets. It measures the sensitivity of asset returns to the return on the market portfolio. Hence, betas for individual assets or portfolios can be directly compared to betas for other assets or portfolios. The theoretical (ex ante) beta from the CAPM has been defined as essentially a measure of the expected covariance of an asset with the market portfolio, in the context of a well-diversified portfolio of assets. How historical (ex post) beta is estimated in practice has not been discussed. The historical beta for a portfolio of n assets (β_p) is simply a weighted average of the observed historical betas for the individual assets (β_i) in the portfolio:

$$\beta_p = \sum_i^n w_i \beta_i \qquad (14.19)$$

This is a very handy result because it means that one need not use quadratic programming to measure the systematic risk of a portfolio if the individual asset betas are known.

For individual assets, the historical beta is estimated from a time series regression of the returns on the asset onto the returns on the market portfolio (i.e., estimation of Equation 14.16).

Figure 14.8 presents a scattergram for the returns on the market portfolio and stock XYZ for a number of time periods. The usual procedure is to compile

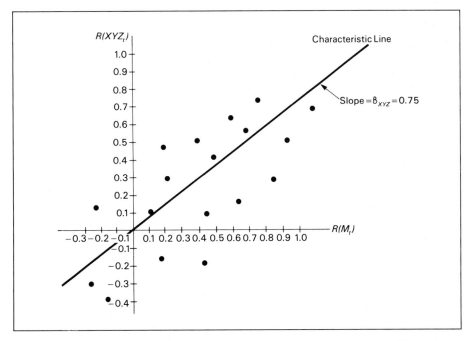

FIG. 14.8 Characteristic Line for Stock *XYZ* (returns in percentage per month)

60 months of actual return data on the stock and the market portfolio. To this data, Equation 14.16 is fit by means of linear regression. This is represented by the straight line in Figure 14.8. The beta from this estimation is equal to the slope of the fitted regression line. For stock XYZ, the beta is 0.75. This means that, for the historical data plotted in Figure 14.8, the return on stock XYZ was 0.75 times the return on the market portfolio on average. Some of the empirical findings regarding this measure are summarized below.

Beta Stability. The most serious problem for the estimation of common stock betas is the fact that they are not stable; that is, beta coefficients change over time. Some authors suggest that historical betas for individual common stocks may even be random coefficients. There are at least two sources of beta instability. The first is statistical estimation error, having to do with such things as the length of the time interval over which returns are measured (e.g., daily, monthly, or quarterly). Research has shown that stock returns vary in the speed at which they react to changes in the market return, with large capitalization stocks reacting more quickly. Hence, there can be an interval bias in beta estimation relating to the time interval over which betas are estimated. While betas estimated for individual stocks are characteristically unstable, betas estimated for portfolios of stocks tend to be relatively more stable over time.

Another source of apparent beta instability has to do with the use of beta as a single index of systematic risk. As evidenced in the section on Multiindex Models, common stocks have been shown to have multiple sources of systematic risk. Hence, any single risk measure that attempts to aggregate all sources of systematic risk can appear to be unstable, when it is one or more of the macroeconomic or microeconomic sources of systematic risk that are changing. For example, assume oil prices were a macroeconomic source of systematic risk. When the level of oil price expectations changes, ceteris paribus, stocks that are more sensitive to oil price expectations would react, while other stocks with the same single index beta would not. If beta were used as the systematic risk measure, those stocks that reacted to changes in oil price expectations would appear to be unstable, when they were actually reacting to but one of the systematic risk factors included in the traditional single index beta. In this example, the stocks that did not react to changes in oil price expectations would appear stable.

Thus, if betas are to be useful in a predictive sense, they must be updated frequently.

Adjustments to Historical Beta. Marshall Blume found that portfolio betas tend to regress toward 1.0 over time. The economic logic is that the underlying riskiness of a firm tends to move toward the riskiness of the average firm. His research indicates that the following adjustment may produce a more accurate forecast beta:

$$\beta_2 = a + b\beta_1 \qquad\qquad (14.20)$$

where β_1 and β_2 are historical betas for periods seven years apart. The parameters a and b are estimated by regression analysis and used to calculate $\beta_3 = a + b\beta_2$, where β_3 is the *forecast* beta. Merrill Lynch and Value Line currently use this method to estimate forecast betas. Vasicek (1973) has proposed a Bayesian adjustment procedure based upon the sampling error (uncertainty) for each common stock beta estimate. While Vasicek's adjustment slightly outperforms Blume's in terms of forecast accuracy, both methods outperform the unadjusted historical beta. Some investment organizations allow investment analysts to adjust historical betas subjectively based upon their outlook for the individual firms in question. Several other scholars have suggested modifications to the beta estimation procedure that are applicable to stocks that are infrequently traded. Recent work has shown that, on average, the predictive ability of beta is inversely related to the length of the investment horizon and directly related to portfolio size, adjustments notwithstanding.

Fundamental Beta. A great deal of recent attention has been given to the development of a beta that takes explicit account of the fundamental characteristics of the firm as well as its covariance with the market portfolio. A number of researchers have dealt with this topic. However, the best-known example of a fundamental beta was developed by Barr Rosenberg and his colleagues at the University of California at Berkeley (1976).

The basic idea of the fundamental beta is that, in addition to the single measure of the historical covariance of an asset with the market, there are other sources of systematic risk related to the fundamental characterstics of the firm. Rosenberg has made some changes to the variables in his original equation. A recent version includes 58 variables grouped into 13 groups, or risk indices, as Rosenberg calls them. These include variability in markets, success, size, trading activity, growth, earnings/price ratio, book/price ratio, earnings variation, financial leverage, foreign income, labor intensity, yield, and low capitalization. The details of the most recent estimation of Rosenberg's fundamental beta system are proprietary. However, Rosenberg does claim that his system produces a better estimate of future beta than historical beta alone. Several other firms offer such estimates on a commercial basis.

Semivariance Beta. This beta estimation technique is a recent entrant into the competition for a better beta. It is a highly mathematical technique, which shows that a stock can have one beta as the market portfolio increases in value, and another beta as the market portfolio decreases in value, a sort of bull and bear market beta concept. Levkoff (1983) claims a significant increase in the predictive capability of the semivariance beta over the historical beta estimate.

Tests of the CAPM

Estimating the Model. The number of articles found under the general heading "tests of the CAPM" is impressive. One bibliographic compilation lists almost 1,000 papers on the topic. Consequently, only the basic results are given here.

In general, a two-pass regression technique is used to test the CAPM. The first pass involves the estimation of beta for each security by means of the time series regression described by Equation 14.16. The betas from the first-pass regression are then used to form portfolios of securities ranked by portfolio beta. The portfolio returns, the return on the risk-free asset, and the portfolio betas are then used to estimate the second-pass, cross-sectional regression:

$$R_p - R_F = \gamma_0 + \gamma_1 \beta_p + \varepsilon_p \tag{14.21}$$

The return data are frequently aggregated into five-year periods for this regression.

The actual process of testing the CAPM using the two-pass regression methodology involves the consideration of some econometric problems (e.g., measurement error, correlated error terms, and beta instability) that are beyond the scope of this chapter.[4]

Assuming that the capital market can be described as fair game (that is, there is no opportunity for investors to use information from previous periods to earn abnormal returns), several testable hypotheses for Equation 14.21 implied by the CAPM can be listed.

1 The relationship between beta and return should be linear.

2 The intercept term, γ_0, should not differ significantly from zero.

3 The coefficient for beta, γ_1, should equal $R_M - R_F$.

4 Beta should be the only systematic risk factor that is priced by the market. That is, other factors such as P/E ratio, dividend yield, and firm size should not add explanatory power to the equation.

5 Over long periods of time, the rate of return on the market portfolio should be greater than the return on the risk-free asset. This is because the market portfolio has more risk than the risk-free asset. Hence, risk-adverse investors would price it so as to generate a greater return.

Results. The general results of the empirical tests of the CAPM are as follows:

1 The relationship between beta and return is linear, hence the functional form of Equation 14.21 is correct.

2 The intercept term, γ_0, is significantly different from zero.

3 The coefficient for beta, γ_1, is less than $R_M - R_F$. The combination of results 2 and 3 implies that low beta stocks have higher returns than the CAPM predicts and high beta stocks have lower returns than the CAPM predicts.

4 Beta is not the only systematic risk factor priced by the market. Several studies have discovered other factors that explain stock returns (e.g., a price/earnings factor [Basu, 1977, 1983], a dividend factor [Litzenberger and Ramaswamy, 1979], and a firm size factor [Banz, 1981]).

---

[4] The interested reader should consult Merton H. Miller and Myron S. Scholes, "Rates of Return in Relation to Risk," *Studies in the Theory of Capital Markets,* ed. M. C. Jensen (New York: Praeger, 1972); Eugene F. Fama, *Foundations of Finance* (New York: Basic Books, 1976); Richard Roll, "Performance Evaluation and Benchmark Errors II," *Journal of Portfolio Management,* Vol. 7 (Winter 1981); and Richard Roll, "A Critique of the Asset Pricing Theory's Tests," *Journal of Financial Economics,* Vol. 4 (Mar. 1977) for a discussion of these issues.

5 Over long periods of time (usually 20–30 years), the return on the market portfolio is greater than the risk-free rate. (However, even though the ex ante CAPM always predicts a higher return for the market portfolio, historical data have revealed a market return less than the risk-free asset over shorter periods.)

New Sources of Predictive Data. A basic problem in evaluating the CAPM is the fact that it is an ex ante model relating expectations for returns on an asset to expectations for returns on the market portfolio, but has been tested in ex post (historical) data. This is because good data on market expectations have been traditionally scarce. However, there are commercial investor information services that compile expectational data from research departments on Wall Street and from large- to medium-sized institutional investment organizations. These data bases make possible more meaningful tests of the ex ante version of the CAPM.

The mixed results from the empirical tests on the CAPM have prompted some researchers to reexamine the rather restrictive simplifying assumptions of the pure CAPM in order to see what effect relaxing some of these assumptions might have on the ability to extend the model to better fit real data.

Extensions of the CAPM

Black's Zero Beta Model. Black (1972) examined the results for the original CAPM when the assumption of a single borrowing and lending rate for all investors was relaxed. Hence, Black's model does not require the existence of a pure risk-free asset. However, his model does assume unrestricted short selling. Short selling involves borrowing stock from a broker and selling it at the current price, anticipating that the stock price will subsequently go down with a net profit realized on the repayment to the broker. This implies the existence of a portfolio that is uncorrelated with the market portfolio; that is, it implies a portfolio with a zero beta. In fact, since returns on almost all assets are positively correlated to some degree, the use of short selling is practically required in order to construct a zero beta portfolio. The equation for Black's zero beta model is:

$$E(R_p) = E(R_Z) + \beta_p[E(R_M) - E(R_Z)] \tag{14.22}$$

where $E(R_Z)$ is the expected return on the zero beta portfolio. This model is sometimes called the two-factor model. Portfolio returns are specified to be a function of two factors: the return on the zero beta portfolio and the return on the market portfolio.

The work of Black, Jensen, and Scholes (1972) indicates that the two-factor model gives a better description of actual return data than the original CAPM. Both models imply a linear relationship between returns on assets and returns on the market, with beta as the appropriate measure of systematic risk. While removing the requirement of a pure riskless asset makes the two-factor model more realistic in one sense, the requirement of unrestricted short selling is not valid for many investors (e.g., pension funds).

Dividends and Taxes. A frictionless capital market implies that investors pay no taxes on gains or income from their investments. While this is true of some investments (e.g., pension funds, endowments) it is not the general rule. Black and Scholes (1974) have tested a version of the CAPM that includes a term for dividend yield and found that the general equilibrium relationship predicted by the original CAPM still holds. However, Litzenberger and Ramaswamy (1979, 1982) proposed a model that includes a dividend yield factor and found a strong positive effect on equilibrium security returns. The upshot of their model is that the market requires a higher return on stocks with high dividend yields (due to the tax effect). This result is consistent with the findings of other researchers. Miller and Scholes (1982), however, argue that the existence of a true dividend effect (as opposed to a spurious effect due to problems of measurement) is still an open question. At least one professional fund manager currently offers a yield tilt fund to take advantage of the higher expected returns on high dividend paying stocks. The jury is still out on the utility of this approach.

Heterogeneous Expectations. The assumption that all investors have identical expectations for asset returns, variances, and covariances (homogeneous expectations) is a particularly strong one. The basic problem created by allowing heterogeneous expectations is that expected asset returns variances and covariances become complex weighted averages of individual expectations. Lintner (1969) has examined the consequences of allowing heterogeneous expectations and has concluded that the general form of the original CAPM would still hold. However, there would exist a market portfolio that is *not* necessarily efficient. The existence of heterogeneous expectations makes the CML and the SML more fuzzy. The more investor expectations differ, the more uncertain predictions concerning expected asset returns become.

P/E Ratio and Firm Size. The work of Basu (1977, 1983) and Banz (1981) has indicated that systematic risk factors exist that are priced by the market relating to the magnitude of the price to earnings ratio and the market capitalization of the firm. Basu has presented strong evidence to support the hypothesis that low P/E firms have higher risk-adjusted returns than high P/E firms, and Banz has presented equally strong evidence that small firms have higher risk-adjusted returns than large capitalization firms. Dreman (1983) has also published a study supporting the low P/E effect. A debate is now underway in the financial literature concerning the validity of these two findings, with new studies appearing all the time. Several commercial portfolio managers offer investment funds that invest in very small capitalization firms. By investing in such a fund, investors can further diversify their portfolios and capture any persistence of the higher returns that have been documented historically.

A Critique of Tests of the CAPM

One of the most controversial papers written on the CAPM is Richard Roll's (1977), "A Critique of the Asset Pricing Theory's Tests." A full presentation of Roll's argument cannot be given here; however, his major points are discussed.

Following Roll's argument, the CAPM is a general equilibrium model based upon the existence of a market portfolio that is defined as the value-weighted portfolio of all investment assets. Furthermore, the market portfolio is defined to be ex ante mean-variance efficient (i.e., lie on the ex ante efficient frontier for all investors). Roll shows that the only true test of the CAPM is whether the market portfolio is in fact ex ante mean-variance efficient. However, the true market portfolio has not, or at least has not yet, been observed since it includes all investment assets (e.g., stocks, bonds, real estate, art objects, and human capital).

The consequences of this "nonobservability" are these.

1 Tests of the CAPM are extremely sensitive to which market proxy is used, even though returns on most market proxies (e.g., the S&P 500 and the NYSE index) are highly correlated.

2 A researcher cannot unambiguously discern whether the CAPM failed his test because the true market portfolio was ex ante mean-variance inefficient, or because the market proxy was inefficient. Alternatively, the researcher cannot unambiguously discern whether his test supported the CAPM because the true market portfolio was ex ante mean-variance efficient or because the market proxy was efficient.

3 The effectiveness of variables such as dividend yield in explaining risk-adjusted asset returns is evidence that the market proxies used to test the CAPM are not ex ante mean-variance efficient.

Hence, Roll submits that the CAPM is not testable until the exact composition of the true market portfolio is known, and the only way to test the CAPM using ex post data is to observe whether the ex post true market portfolio is mean-variance efficient. As a result of his findings, Roll states that he does not believe there ever will be an unambiguous test of the CAPM. He does not say that the CAPM is invalid. Rather, Roll says that there is likely to be no unambiguous way to test the CAPM and its implications due to the nonobservability of the true market portfolio and its characteristics.

Does this mean that the CAPM is useless to the financial practitioner? The answer is no, it is not. What it means is that the implications of the CAPM should be viewed with caution. Moreover, a basic prediction of the CAPM, the linearity of the relationship between beta and return, has been supported by empirical studies and can be used to aid financial practitioners in making investment decisions.

MULTIINDEX MODELS

Early Multiindex Models

There are three basic portfolio selection models: Markowitz, Sharpe single index, and multiindex. Before discussing the multiindex model, however, the early work on industry index models is described.

King's Industry Index Model. King's was the first major study (1966) to examine the effect of industry factors as well as the market factor in explaining common stock price behavior. King selected a sample of 63 common stocks with good data over the period 1927–1960 and classified them into six industries by Standard Industry Classification (SIC) code. King used a statistical technique called factor analysis to examine the covariance structure of these stocks over the period. His analysis indicated that the market factor accounted for about 50 percent of the variation in price, while industry effects accounted for about 10 percent of the variation. The remaining 40 percent was attributed to individual security effects. Moreover, King found that the strength of the market factor appeared to decline over time. Thus, King was able to provide evidence that industry factors exist in addition to the market factor of the single index model. This finding weakens the validity of the assumption of uncorrelated error terms in the market model.

Cohen and Pogue's Multiindex Model. One of the first attempts to test a multiindex model against the single index model, with respect to the formation of efficient portfolios, was that of Cohen and Pogue (1967). The general form of the diagonal multiindex model they tested was:

$$R_i = a_i + b_i I_M + b_{i1} I_1 + \cdots + b_{iN} I_N + \varepsilon_i \qquad (14.23)$$

where: I_M = market index

I_N = N industry indices

and each firm is loaded on the market index and one other industry index (i.e., the industry to which the firm belongs, with the market component removed). The firm's loadings (b_i's) on all other indices are zero.

Cohen and Pogue tested this model against the standard Markowitz and single index models and found that, in general, the index models were not dominated by the Markowitz model in terms of ex post performances, while the single index model dominated the multiindex model in terms of both ex ante efficiency and ex post performance.

Farrell's Cluster-Analytic Model. Farrell (1974, 1975, 1976) conducted a similar test between the single index and multiindex models, using the period 1961–1969 as a base period and the period 1970–1974 as a forecast period. A significant difference between his research and that of Cohen and Pogue was the method used of classifying stocks into industry groups. Cohen and Pogue used SIC codes; Farrell used cluster analysis (a statistical technique similar to factor analysis). By using cluster analysis, Farrell was able to select his 100 stocks into four clusters (growth, cyclical, stable, and oil), which were highly correlated within clusters and which had small correlations between clusters. Farrell called these clusters homogeneous groups. Thus, Farrell's method was an improvement over the mechanical use of SIC codes.

Using this technique, Farrell (1974) found that his multiindex model (with the four clusters plus the market index) was able to account for 45 percent of the variance in returns for the 100 stocks in the sample. The market factor accounted for 31 percent of the variance and the four clusters accounted for an incremental 14 percent of the variance. The remaining 55 percent was attributable to other industry and specific company effects. In addition, Farrell (1976) found that portfolio selection via the multiindex model yielded portfolios that were generally better diversified and more efficient (i.e., lower risk at the same level of return) than those formed using the single index model. Farrell's work indicates that the multiindex model may be a promising candidate to replace the single index model for portfolio selection.

Rosenberg's Mixed Model. Rosenberg (1974) has shown that a combination of the single index with the multiindex model may be useful. Rosenberg first showed how to remove the effect of the market and estimate the extramarket covariance using a single index model. In later work, he regressed the extramarket covariance on a number of accounting and market-based variables (including industry classification and firm variables, such as debt/equity ratio and dividend payout). The goal is to provide a much more complete and detailed decomposition of stock return variance.

The Problem With Multiindex Models. A nagging problem for the practical application of multiindex models of stock selection is the stability of the indexes over time. That is, how long do these index effects persist? If they are not stable, then portfolio results based on the formation of portfolio by an outdated multiindex model may actually be inferior to those based on the application of the simpler single index model.

The Arbitrage Pricing Theory

The recent work of Ross (1976, 1977) derives an alternative to the single index CAPM, which allows multiple factors of risk that systematically affect return. In his arbitrage pricing theory (APT), Ross assumes that asset returns are governed by a "K-factor return generating model" of the form:

$$R_i = E_i + b_{i1}F_1 + \cdots + b_{iK}F_K + \varepsilon_i \tag{14.24}$$

where: R_i = actual return on asset i

   E_i = expected return on asset i

   b_{iK} = sensitivity of return on asset i to the Kth systematic risk factor (estimated from historical data)

   F_K = zero mean Kth factor common to all assets under consideration

   ε_i = zero mean random error term

A full development of the APT cannot be given here. However, the essence of the theory is the linear return generating model for expected asset returns:

$$E_i - E_0 = \lambda_1 b_{i1} + \cdots + \lambda_K b_{iK} \tag{14.25}$$

where: E_i = expected return on asset i

   E_0 = return on the risk-free asset (if it exists)

   λ_K = risk premium for the Kth systematic risk factor

   b_K = sensitivity of returns on asset i to the Kth systematic risk factor

The test of the APT essentially involves testing for the existence of nonzero constants: $E_0, \lambda_1, \ldots, \lambda_K$ (see Roll & Ross, 1980, for details).

The theory is called an arbitrage theory because Ross (1977) is able to show that if, in equilibrium, expected asset returns were not a linear function of the K factors, an investor could construct a portfolio using short selling that requires zero net investment and has greater than zero expected return. This result would violate the "no free lunch" law of financial theory.

As Roll and Ross note, the APT is particularly appealing "because it agrees perfectly with what appears to be the intuition behind the CAPM." The popularity of the CAPM (at least for practitioners) lies not in its elegant basis on mathematical utility theory. Rather, the CAPM has endured because of its dependence upon a widely observed phenomenon — the common variability of security returns — and its ability to decompose investment risk into diversifiable and nondiversifiable components. These results are based upon a linear return generating process, which is a derivative of the CAPM. As Roll and Ross emphasize, the idea of a linear return generating process is a first principle of the APT, and is clearly illustrated by Equation 14.24.

Ross has proposed that the APT offers a testable alternative to the CAPM. The APT makes no assumptions about the market portfolio. The other assumptions about APT correspond to those of the CAPM.

Copeland and Weston (1983) have summarized the advantages of the APT over the CAPM to be:

1 The APT makes no assumption about the empirical distribution of asset returns.

2 The APT makes no assumption about individual utility functions other than risk aversion.

3 The APT is an equilibrium model based on several systematic risk factors, not just beta.

4 The APT is a model of relative asset pricing and hence does not require information about the entire market portfolio to price any subset.

5 The APT does not require a mean-variance efficient market portfolio.

6 The APT is easily extended to the multiperiod case.

Tests of the APT. The APT is a relatively new theory, and hence the financial literature contains only a few tests of its accuracy. The research to date seems to indicate that the APT is a promising alternative to the single index CAPM in explaining asset returns. This research indicates that the APT may explain a significantly greater amount of the variance in common stock returns than the CAPM. However, there are some unresolved questions concerning the practical application of the APT.

Problems With the APT. There remains the question of how many or what factors explain security prices. Roll and Ross indicate that there are at least three but give few clues as to what they are. Several good candidates exist (e.g., microeconomic factors, such as P/E ratio, dividend yield, and firm size), but, to date, this question is very much up in the air. Tony Estep and his colleagues at Salomon Brothers investment banking firm (New York) have built a model similar to the general APT formulation, which posits four macroeconomic factors systematically affecting common stock returns: defense spending, oil prices, real economic growth, and inflation. Sharpe (1982) has called into question the "naive application" of the original single index CAPM (of which he was the father) and has noted the existence of 13 market and industry factors in the pricing of the NYSE index since 1931. Sharpe also mentions another problem that was noted earlier, the stability of the factors over time.

The key intuition of the general multiindex model is that there are multiple factors of investment risk that systematically affect asset returns (i.e., macroeconomic and microeconomic factors more specific than the general market factor). This intuition is likely to endure and become more relevant to practitioners who can use multiindex models (like the APT) to make factor bets on stocks that have favorable sensitivities to major macroeconomic factors, such as oil prices and inflation, or to microeconomic factors, such as dividend yield and firm size. Even though the original single index CAPM has been shown to be deficient in some important respects and the multiindex alternative clearly offers hope of improvement, there remain some significant practical uses of the basic CAPM insights regarding the relationship between investment risk and return.

USES OF MODERN PORTFOLIO ANALYSIS

Common Stock Selection

Fouse (1976, 1977) outlined a technique by which the fundamental insights of the CAPM can be combined with classic valuation theory to produce a model of investment value that can be used by investors to select common stocks. The basic model has been adopted by a number of investment organizations. Fouse argued that "the expected rate of total return that equilibrates current price with a forecast dividend stream is the single most important piece of information to have about a common stock." This number is called the implied discount rate and is calculated by using the dividend discount model (DDM) with general form:

$$P_0 = \frac{D_1}{(1 + K)} + \frac{D_2}{(1 + K)^2} + \cdots + \frac{D_n}{(1 + K)^n} \tag{14.26}$$

where: P_0 = current price of the stock

D_n = dividend at time $1, \ldots, n$

K = implied discount rate, sometimes called the expected return on the stock

Risk and Reward. In the institutional context, the inputs to the DDM (e.g., forecasts for earnings, dividends, and rates of growth/decay for earnings and dividends) are supplied by investment analysts who are assigned groups of companies to follow. The analysts also play an important role in the assignment of companies to risk sectors. This is where the integration of the CAPM with the classic valuation model takes place.

We have noted that the linearity of the relationship between systematic risk (beta) and return has been generally supported in the financial literature. We have also noted that portfolio betas are more stable and hence more useful in a predictive sense. The historical betas (or the fundamental betas) for the stocks on the list of companies followed by the investment organization can be aggregated into portfolios called risk sectors. This procedure allows investment analysts to adjust subjectively individual betas to better fit expectations for a company.

The risk sectors are constructed by taking the stocks on the list followed by the analysts and combining them into five groups based upon the general beta distribution of the S&P 500. When the relationship between the five risk sectors and the actual (price) return for various subperiods between December 31, 1974 and September 30, 1976 was examined, the predicted relationship was observed. That is, the higher the average systematic risk, the higher the actual portfolio return.

Liquidity and Reward. A similar procedure was followed for a ranking of the stocks by the amount of dollar trading required to produce a one percent change in price. These ranks were called liquidity sectors. An inverse relationship was observed between liquidity and return; that is, the more liquid portfolios had lower actual returns. This was due, in part, to the fact that less liquid stocks tend to be smaller and more risky. Hence, the greater risk is rewarded by higher returns. However, there might also have been a reward for bearing liquidity risk alone.

An Example. This methodology can be used in a passive mode (i.e., purchase those stocks, by risk or liquidity sector, which have the highest expected return from the DDM), or in an active mode (i.e., use analysts' forecasts for changes in the risk and liquidity profiles of the market to make stock purchase selections). An example of the results obtained by one investment organization using a modified version of Fouse's approach in the active mode is presented in Table 14.4.

The recommendation quintiles (RQs) in Table 14.3 were formed by combining the risk quintiles (by beta) with the expected return quintiles from a DDM. Specifically, a staff of professional investment analysts provided the DDM with forecasts for short- and long-term growth rates for earnings and dividends for each of the 240 companies. These forecasts were updated on a monthly basis. Each month the expected returns were ranked into five quintiles, by beta, of 48 stocks each. Each beta quintile was then subdivided into five quintiles, by expected return from the DDM, of about nine stocks each. RQ 1 was formed by aggregating the five top-ranked expected return quintiles from the beta quintiles. RQ 2 was formed by aggregating the five second-ranked expected return quintiles from the beta quintiles. RQs 3, 4, and 5 were similarly formed. The RQs were rebalanced each month, with stocks that fell out of a particular quintile being replaced by those that moved into that quintile. The results of this strategy are seen in Table 14.3. The strategy rankordered stocks

---

TABLE 14.4 Total Return by Recommendation Quintile for 1981

($N = 240$ stocks)

Recommendation Quintile	December 31, 1980 to June 30, 1981	June 30, 1981 to December 31, 1981	December 31, 1980 to December 31, 1981
1 (strong purchase)	7.01%	4.77%	12.12%
2	14.11	−2.81	10.89
3	6.82	−5.11	1.36
4	3.70	−8.,95	−5.59
5 (strong sale)	1.95	−10.27	−8.51
S&P 500 (market weighted)	−1.02	−3.92	−4.91

Source: Investment Systems Department, Centerre Trust Company of St. Louis

---

by RQ code quite nicely for 1981. Hence, an investor would clearly have done well to have invested in the RQ 1 stocks and stayed away from the RQ 3, 4, and 5 stocks in 1981.

A number of investment organizations have adopted this strategy or a variation of it. For example, in some applications the size of the RQs is adjusted to reflect a belief that most stocks are fairly valued. Hence, RQ 1 (the most undervalued stocks) and RQ 5 (the most overvalued stocks), would contain fewer stocks than RQs 2, 3, and 4.

Portfolio Performance Evaluation

The early work on the evaluation of investment performance concentrated on mutual funds. As Hagin (1979) notes, this is largely due to the fact that for some time only mutual funds were required to disclose their performance figures. Performance data are now available on a variety of investment institutions. We have seen that risk adverse investors will hold portfolios of assets in order to maximize their expected return at a given level of risk. An important aspect of this process is the evaluation of the performance of the portfolio, given this goal.

The Treynor Index. Treynor (1965) developed an index that evaluates the performance of a portfolio based upon the level of systematic risk, beta. The equation for Treynor's index, T_p, is:

$$T_p = \frac{R_p - R_F}{\beta_p} \tag{14.27}$$

where: R_p = average return on portfolio p

R_F = risk-free rate

β = beta for portfolio p

These numbers are taken from Treynor's equation for the portfolio characteristic line.

The logic behind Treynor's index is simply stated. Well-diversified portfolios have average unsystematic risk levels near zero. Hence, investors will only pay a premium to avoid systematic or market risk. The appropriate measure of market risk is the systematic risk index beta. Thus, Treynor posited that the appropriate measure of portfolio performance is the portfolio risk premium, $(R_p - R_F)$, divided by the portfolio risk index, β_p.

The Sharpe Index. Sharpe (1966) developed a reward to variability index, which evaluates portfolio performance based upon the level of total risk, $SD(p)$. The equation for Sharpe's index (corrected for bias as a function of the number of return observations T [Korkie, 1983]), S_p, is:

$$S_p = \frac{R_p - R_F}{SD(p)} \times \frac{T}{T + 0.75} \tag{14.28}$$

where R_p and R_F are defined as before, and $SD(p)$ is the standard deviation of the T portfolio return observations.

The Sharpe index implies that the investor is concerned with the ratio of the portfolio risk premium to the total risk of the portfolio. This measure is particularly appropriate for the investor who puts all (or nearly all) of his investment in a single portfolio. Hence, this investor is likely to be interested with the total risk of the portfolio, measured by $SD(p)$.

The Jensen Index. Jensen (1969) proposed a measure of investment performance that relates the actual return on a portfolio to that return which would have been expected had the portfolio manager invested in the market portfolio and the risk-free asset at the same beta level as the actual portfolio. That is, the Jensen differential performance index is defined as the actual portfolio return minus the risk-adjusted expected portfolio return from the CAPM.

A Comparison of the Measures. The Treynor, Sharpe, and Jensen measures are single index measures that are typically used to rank-order portfolio investment performance. Table 14.5 presents the results of an analysis of the returns on 123 mutual funds over the period 1960–1969. Two basic findings emerge. First, all three performance measures tend to increase with the aggressiveness of the fund objective (i.e., from income to maximum capital gain). Second, the more aggressive the fund, the higher the average fund beta and the higher the mean monthly (risk-adjusted) excess return. There is, therefore, clear evidence of a reward for bearing higher risk in these data.

A discussion of measures used to decompose portfolio performance into its contributing components (e.g., stock selection and market timing) may be found in Chapter 17, Managing Security Portfolios.

Problems With Performance Evaluation. The performance indices mentioned above are not without problems. The assumption of a single riskless

TABLE 14.5 Objectives and Performance

	Risk		Mean Monthly Excess Return	Performance Measures		
Objective of Fund	Systematic Risk (Beta)	Total Variability (Standard Deviation)		Sharpe[a] Measure	Treynor[b] Measure	Jensen[c] Measure
Maximum capital gain	1.22	5.90	0.693%	0.117	0.568	0.122
Growth	1.01	4.57	0.565	0.124	0.560	0.099
Growth-income	0.90	3.93	0.476	0.121	0.529	0.058
Income-growth	0.86	3.80	0.398	0.105	0.463	0.004
Balanced	0.68	3.05	0.214	0.070	0.314	-0.099
Income	0.55	2.67	0.252	0.094	0.458	-0.002
Sample means	0.92	4.17	0.477	0.112	0.518	0.051
Market-based portfolios	—	—	—	0.133	0.510	—
Stock market index	1.00	3.83	0.510	0.133	0.510	—
Bond market index[d]	0.18	1.42	0.093	0.065	0.516	N/A

(a) Reward-to-variability ratio: mean excess return divided by the standard deviation of fund return

(b) Reward-to-volatility ratio: mean excess return divided by beta

(c) Alpha: estimated constant from least-squares regression of fund excess returns on market excess returns (Jensen's delta)

(d) Proxy measure based on arithmetic means of results for Keystone B-1 and B-4 funds, with returns adjusted for 0.042 percent per month average management fee.

Source: John G. McDonald, "Objectives and Performance of Mutual Funds, 1960–1969," *Journal of Financial and Quantitative Analysis* (June 1974)

borrowing and lending rate is generally false and hence makes the calculation of required returns on portfolios more complicated than commonly used performance measures allow. The instability of beta, even for portfolios, renders the results of performance measures, which assume a stable portfolio beta over the measurement interval, less than completely accurate. Finally, there is the research of Roll (1978, 1980, 1981), which indicates that the use of a non ex ante mean variance efficient market index in performance evaluation creates ex ante benchmark errors. These benchmark errors are different from the usual sampling error of statistical estimation and can invalidate the measurement of α_p, the (ex post) risk-adjusted excess portfolio return defined by the equation:

$$\alpha_p = (R_p - R_F) - \beta_p(R_M - R_F) \tag{14.29}$$

A full presentation of the problem is beyond the scope of this chapter. Peterson and Rice (1980) have argued that the Treynor and Sharpe measures can withstand Roll's criticisms.

Asset Allocation

An important question in the world of practical investment management concerns the optimal allocation of investments among various assets in an effort to achieve a desired investment goal. This is the classic investment problem of asset allocation.

The Asset Allocation Process. A member of the academic community was once heard to say:

> In asset allocation questions you must start from scratch and decide what portfolio you should be holding. There is a definite position that you start with. The default position is you hold everything, absolutely everything, in market proportions, including international investments and real estate. If you hold anything else, the burden of proof is on you.

Of course, in the ideal investment world, this academic friend is perfectly correct. The optimum investment portfolio is the pure market portfolio. However, since no one has ever observed this portfolio and all of its components, investors must consider a more realistic alternative to meeting their investment objectives. Thus, one of the first questions to be answered in solving the asset allocation problem is: What is the investment objective of the investor? See Chapter 17 for an elaboration on this topic.

Today's investor can choose among many investment opportunities: common stocks, corporate and U.S. government bonds, municipal bonds, real estate, options, international securities and, most recently, financial futures. Realistically speaking, institutional investors (e.g., banks, insurance companies, and investment counseling firms) are usually the only investors with enough funds available to diversify across the broad spectrum of investment opportunities listed in the preceding sentence. The process of choosing between these alternative assets involves two steps. First, the investor must

TABLE 14.6   Five Sample Optimal Asset Allocation Alternatives Over a Five-Year Investment Horizon

Asset Type	Economic Scenarios				
	1	2	3	4	5
Stocks	25%	35%	45%	55%	65%
Bonds	55	35	45	40	30
Real estate	10	10	5	—	—
Cash	10	20	5	5	5
Portfolio expected return	13	14	15	17	19
Standard deviation	4	5	6	9	12

define the set of permissible assets. This means all assets that are not permitted by legal restriction or by investment policy must be eliminated from consideration. Second, the investor must decide which assets are most desirable, given the overall investment goal.

This latter step usually involves forming expectations about the general economic outlook for the next 5–10 years (e.g., inflation factors and economic growth expectations). Once these expectations are formalized, the investor can decide which investments are most attractive, given the predicted economic scenario or scenarios. Often, the institutional investor will consult an advisor or commercial service that offers an asset allocation product to help with this decision. There are a number of commercial services that offer such a product. This process involves supplying forecasts for expected returns, volatilities, and covariances for selected asset types to a portfolio optimization routine, which calculates efficient portfolios for the given economic scenario(s). The output of such a routine is generally in the form shown in Table 14.6. The investor then chooses the most likely economic scenario, in his judgment, and structures his portfolio accordingly.

The Value of the Asset Allocation Process. In the opinion of many investment managers, the real value of going through the asset allocation process is not so much the seemingly precise numbers that come out of the portfolio optimization routine, although these asset weightings are useful and important. For a critique of the use of asset allocation simulation models, see Sharpe (1982) and Tepper (1982). The real value of the asset allocation process is the communication and cooperation between the manager and the investor that are so much a part of the process. Both the manager and the investor are forced to talk through and work out the establishment of investment goals, the attractiveness of various asset types, and the choice of an economic scenario. By working through the answers to these questions together, the manager and the investor learn valuable information about each other's style, outlook, and information requirements.

Dynamic Asset Allocation. The notion of dynamic asset allocation, developed by Rubinstein and Leland (1981), is a very recent entrant into the world of asset allocation products. Sometimes called portfolio insurance, this idea is having a revolutionary impact upon the way managers and clients perceive the asset allocation problem. Prior to the work of Leland and Rubinstein, asset allocation was viewed as a static process. That is, an optimum investment strategy was chosen and maintained until such time as overall economic and market conditions changed to the extent that the asset allocation strategy had to be reworked. The dynamic asset allocation strategy of Rubinstein and Leland is structured to adjust continually to moves in the value of the portfolio so as constantly to assure a (prespecified) required minimum return, while allowing the value of the portfolio to appreciate when market conditions permit. The dynamic asset allocation strategy sets an assured minimum return below which the return on the portfolio will not drop, while placing no limit on the amount by which the portfolio can appreciate. However, the "no free lunch" law of finance requires that a premium be paid for this insurance. The price of the assurance of a minimum return is some loss of total capture of upward moves in the value of the fully invested portfolio.

The mechanics of how the dynamic asset allocation strategy works are based on options pricing theory and involve the creation of a single synthetic put on the entire portfolio in question. This strategy is more fully explained in Rubinstein and Leland (1981) and in Chapter 11.

SUGGESTED READING

The reader is urged to consult the original sources cited here for more information on specific topics of interest. This chapter has not included a discussion of options as an investment vehicle, although options enjoy a prominent position in more advanced treatments of portfolio analysis. A very good introduction to this topic is found in Gastineau (1979) and in Chapter 11.

There are a number of books currently available that deal with the topic of modern portfolio analysis. Several of the more complete treatments are (ranked in ascending order of mathematical rigor): Hagin (1979), Farrell (1983), Francis (1980), Elton and Gruber (1981), Rudd and Clasing (1982), Francis and Archer (1979), and Copeland and Weston (1983). With regard to monographs and periodicals, the Financial Analysts Reseach Foundation (Charlottesville, Va.) continues to publish very readable papers on topics in this area. Articles on modern portfolio analysis regularly appear in the following journals (ranked in ascending order of mathematical rigor): the *Financial Analysts Journal, The Journal of Portfolio Management, Financial Management,* the *Journal of Financial and Quantitative Analysis, The Journal of Business, The Journal of Finance,* and the *Journal of Financial Economics. Pensions and Investment Age* (a newspaper) and the *Institutional Investor* (a magazine) also carry short articles on current topics in modern portfolio analysis.

Modern Portfolio Analysis for Other Asset Types

Fisher, Jeffrey D. "Portfolio Construction: Real Estate." *Managing Investment Portfolios,* eds. J. L. Maggin and D. L. Tuttle. Boston: Warren, Gorham & Lamont, 1983.

Fong, H. Gifford. "Portfolio Construction: Fixed Income." *Managing Investment Portfolios,* eds. J. L. Maginn and D. L. Tuttle. Boston: Warren, Gorham & Lamont, 1983.

Stambaugh, Robert F. "On the Exclusion of Assets From Tests of the Two-Parameter Model." *Journal of Financial Economics,* Vol. 10 (Summer 1982).

Weinstein, Mark. "The Systematic Risk of Corporate Bonds." *Journal of Financial and Quantitative Analysis,* Vol. 16 (Sept. 1981).

Choosing a Portfolio of Risky Assets

Fisher, Irving. *The Nature of Capital and Income* (1906). Reprinted New York: Augustus M. Kelley, 1965.

———. *The Theory of Interest* (1930). Reprinted New York: Augustus M. Kelley, 1965.

Markowitz, Harry M. *Portfolio Selection.* New Haven, Conn.: Yale University Press, 1959.

———. "Portfolio Selection." *Journal of Finance,* Vol. 7 (Mar. 1952).

Rudd, Andrew, and Henry K. Clasing, Jr. *Modern Portfolio Theory.* Homewood, Ill.: Dow Jones-Irwin, 1982.

Sharpe, William. *Portfolio Theory and Capital Markets.* New York: McGraw-Hill, 1970.

Tobin, James. "Liquidity Preference as Behavior Towards Risk." *Review of Economic Studies,* Vol. 25 (Feb. 1958).

The Capital Asset Pricing Model

Beja, Avraham. "On Systematic and Unsystematic Components of Financial Risk." *Journal of Finance,* Vol. 27 (Mar. 1972).

Black, Fischer. "Capital Market Equilibrium with Restricted Borrowing." *Journal of Business,* Vol. 45 (July 1972).

Copeland, Thomas E., and J. Fred Weston. *Financial Theory and Corporate Policy,* 2nd ed. Reading, Mass.: Addison-Wesley, 1983.

Elton, Edwin J., and Martin J. Gruber. *Modern Portfolio Theory and Investment Analysis.* New York: John Wiley & Sons, 1981.

Fama, Eugene F. "Efficient Capital Markets." *Journal of Finance,* Vol. 25 (May 1970).

———. *Foundations of Finance.* New York: Basic Books, 1976.

———. "Risk Return and Equilibrium," *Journal of Finance,* Vol. 23 (Mar. 1968).

———, and Merton H. Miller. *The Theory of Finance.* Hinsdale, Ill.: Dryden Press, 1972.

Francis, Jack C. *Investments,* 3rd ed. New York: McGraw-Hill, 1980.

———, and Stephen H. Archer. *Portfolio Analysis,* 2nd ed. Englewood Cliffs, N.J.: Prentice-Hall, 1979.

Fuller, Russell J. "Capital Asset Pricing Theories." The Financial Analysts Research Foundation, Monograph No. 12. Charlottesville, Va.: 1981.

Lintner, John. "The Aggregation of Investor's Diverse Judgements in Purely Competitive Security Markets." *Journal of Financial and Quantitative Analysis*, Vol. 4 (Dec. 1969).

———. "The Valuation of Risk Assets and the Selection of Risky Investments in Stock Portfolios and Capital Budgets." *Review of Economics and Statistics*, Vol. 47 (Feb. 1965).

Mossin, Jan. "Equilibrium in a Capital Asset Market." *Econometrica*, Vol. 34 (Oct. 1966).

Ross, Stephen A. "The Current Status of the Capital Asset Pricing Model (CAPM)." *Journal of Finance*, Vol. 23 June 1978.

Sharpe, William F. "Capital Asset Prices." *Journal of Finance*, Vol. 14 (Sept. 1964).

———. "A Simplified Model for Portfolio Analysis." *Management Science*, Vol. 9 (Jan. 1963).

Treynor, Jack L. "How to Rate Management of Investment Funds." *Harvard Business Review*, Vol. 43 (Jan.-Feb. 1965).

———. "Toward a Theory of Market Value of Risky Assets." Unpublished Paper. Arthur D. Little, 1961.

Beta

Alexander, Gordon J., and Norman L. Chervany, "On the Estimation and Stability of Beta." *Journal of Financial and Quantitative Analysis*, Vol. 15 Mar. 1980.

Blume, Marshall E. "Betas and Their Regression Tendencies." *Journal of Finance*, Vol. 30 (June 1975).

———. "On the Assessment of Risk." *Journal of Finance*, Vol. 26 (Mar. 1971).

Cohen, Kalman J., et al. "Estimating and Adjusting for the Intervalling-Effect Bias in Beta." *Management Science*, Vol. 29 (Jan. 1983).

Dimson, Elroy. "Risk Measurement When Shares Are Subject to Infrequent Trading." *Journal of Financial Economics*, Vol. 7 (June 1979).

Fabbozi, Frank J., and Jack C. Francis. "Beta As a Random Coefficient." *Journal of Financial and Quantitative Analysis*, Vol. 13 (Mar. 1978).

Hawawini, Gabriel, A., and Ashok Vora. "Investment Horizon Diversification and the Efficiency of Alternative Beta Forecasts." *Journal of Financial Research*, Vol. 5 (Spring 1982).

Klemosky, Robert C., and John D. Martin. "The Adjustment of Beta Forecasts." *Journal of Finance*, Vol. 30 (Sept. 1975).

Levkoff, J. Stephen. "Rethinking Risk and Return." Paper Presented at the Annual Meeting of the Southeast American Institute for Decision Sciences. Williamsburg, Va.: 1983.

Levy, Haim. "The CAPM and Beta in an Imperfect Market." *Journal of Portfolio Management*, Vol. 6 (Winter 1980).

Rosenberg, Barr, and James Guy. "Prediction of Systematic Risk From Investment Fundamentals, Part I." *Financial Analysts Journal*, Vol. 32 (May-June 1976).

————. "Prediction of Systematic Risk From Investment Fundamentals, Part II." *Financial Analysts Journal*, Vol. 32 (July-Aug. 1976).

Rosenberg, Barr, and Walt McKibben. "The Prediction of Systematic Risk in Common Stocks." *Journal of Financial and Quantitative Analysis*, Vol. 8 (Mar. 1973).

Scholes, Myron, and Joseph Williams. "Estimating Betas From Nonsynchronous Data." *Journal of Financial Economics* (Dec. 1977).

Scott, Elton, and Stewart Brown. "Biased Estimators and Unstable Betas." *Journal of Finance*, Vol. 35 (Mar. 1980).

Sunder, Shyam. "Stationarity of Market Risk." *Journal of Finance*, Vol. 35 (Sept. 1980).

Vasicek, Oldrich A. "A Note on Using Cross-Sectional Information in Bayesian Estimation of Security Betas." *Journal of Finance*, Vol. 28 (Dec. 1973).

Tests of the Capital Asset Pricing Model

Banz, Rolf W. "The Relationship Between Return and Market Value of Common Stocks." *Journal of Financial Economics*. Vol. 9 (Mar. 1981).

Basu, S. "Investment Performance of Common Stocks in Relation to Their Price-Earnings Ratios." *Journal of Finance*, Vol. 32 (June 1977).

————. "The Relationship Between Earnings' Yield, Market Value and Return for NYSE Common Stocks." *Journal of Financial Economics*, Vol. 12 (June 1983).

Black, Fischer, et al. "The Capital Asset Pricing Model." *Studies in the Theory of Capital Markets*, ed. M. C. Jensen. New York: Praeger, 1972.

Black, Fischer, and Myron Scholes. "The Effects of Dividend Yield and Dividend on Common Stock Prices and Returns." *Journal of Financial Economics*, Vol. 1 (May 1974).

Brennan, Michael J. "Taxes, Market Valuation and Corporation Financial Policy." *National Tax Journal* (Dec. 1970).

Dreman, David. *The New Contrarian Investment Strategy*. New York: Random House, 1983.

Jensen, Michael C. "Risk, the Pricing of Capital Assets and the Evaluation of Investment Portfolio." *Journal of Business*, Vol. 42 (Apr. 1969).

————. "Tests of Capital Market Theory and Implications of the Evidence." *Handbook of Financial Economics*, ed. J. L. Bicksler. Amsterdam: North Holland, 1979.

Litzenberger, Robert H., and Krishna Ramaswamy. "The Effect of Personal Taxes and Dividends on Capital Asset Prices." *Journal of Financial Economics*, Vol. 7 (June 1979).

————. "The Effects of Dividends on Common Stock Prices." *Journal of Finance*, Vol. 37 (May 1982).

Merton, Robert C. "An Intertemporal Capital Asset Pricing Model." *Econometrica*, Vol. 41 (Sept. 1973).

Miller, Merton H., and Myron S. Scholes. "Dividends and Taxes." *Journal of Political Economy*, Vol. 90 (Dec. 1982).

————. "Rates of Return in Relation to Risk." *Studies in the Theory of Capital Markets*, ed. M. C. Jensen. New York: Praeger, 1972.

Roll, Richard. "A Critique of the Asset Pricing Theory's Tests." *Journal of Financial Economics,* Vol. 4 (Mar. 1977).

Multiindex Models

Cohen, Kalman J., and Jerry A. Pogue. "An Empirical Evaluation of Some Alternative Portfolio Selection Models." *Journal of Business,* Vol. 40 (Apr. 1967).

Farrell, James L., Jr. "Analyzing Co-Variation of Returns to Determine Homogeneous Stock Groupings." *Journal of Business,* Vol. 47 (Apr. 1974).

———. *Guide to Portfolio Management.* New York: McGraw-Hill, 1983.

———. "Homogeneous Stock Groupings." *Financial Analysts Journal,* Vol. 31 (May-June 1975).

———. "The Multi-Index Model and Practical Portfolio Analysis." Occasional Paper No. 4, Charlottesville, Va.: The Financial Analysts Research Foundation, 1976.

King, Benjamin F. "Market and Industry Factors in Stock Price Behavior." *Journal of Business,* Vol. 39, Part 2 (Jan. 1966).

Rosenberg, Barr. "Extra-Market Components of Covariance Among Security Prices." *Journal of Financial and Quantitative Analysis,* Vol. 9 (Mar. 1974).

Sharpe, William F. "Factors in New York Stock Exchange Security Returns, 1931–1979." *Journal of Portfolio Management,* Vol. 8 (Summer 1982).

The Arbitrage Pricing Theory

Chen, Nai-Fu. "Some Empirical Tests of the Theory of Arbitrage Pricing." CRSP Working Paper No. 69, University of Chicago, 1982.

Fogler, H. Russell. "Common Sense On CAPM, APT and Correlated Residuals." *The Journal of Portfolio Management,* Vol. 8 Summer 1982.

Gehr, Adam, Jr. "Risk-Adjusted Capital Budgeting Using Arbitrage." *Financial Management,* Vol. 10 (Winter 1981).

———. "Some Tests of the Arbitrage Pricing Theory." *Journal of the Midwest Finance Association,* Vol. 7 (1978).

Kryzanowski, Lawrence, and Minh Chan To. "General Factor Models and the Structure of Security Returns." *Journal of Financial and Quantitative Analysis,* Vol. 18 (Mar. 1983).

Reinganum, Marc R. "The Arbitrage Pricing Theory." *Journal of Finance,* Vol. 36 (May 1981).

Roll, Richard, and Stephen A. Ross. "An Empirical Investigation of the Arbitrage Pricing Theory." *Journal of Finance,* Vol. 35 (Dec. 1980).

Ross, Stephen A. "The Arbitrage Theory of Capital Asset Pricing." *Journal of Economic Theory,* Vol. 13 (Dec. 1976).

———. "Return, Risk, and Arbitrage." *Risk and Return in Finance,* Vol. 1, eds. I. Friend and J. L. Bicksler. Cambridge, Mass.: Ballinger, 1977.

Shanken, Jay. "The Arbitrage Pricing Theory." *Journal of Finance,* Vol. 37 (Dec. 1982).

Uses of Modern Portfolio Analysis

Bethke, William M., and Susan E. Boyd, "Should Dividend Discount Models Be Yield-Tilted?" *The Journal of Portfolio Management,* Vol. 9 Spring 1983.

Brigham, Eugene F. *Financial Management, Theory and Practice,* 3rd ed. Chicago: Dryden Press, 1982.

Condon, Kathleen A. "Portfolio Construction: Asset Allocation." *Managing Investment Portfolios,* eds. J. L. Maginn and D. L. Tuttle. Boston: Warren, Gorham & Lamont, 1983.

Dietz, Peter O., and Jeannette R. Kirschman. "Evaluation Portfolio Performance." *Managing Investment Portfolios,* eds. J. L. Maginn and D. L. Tuttle. Boston: Warren, Gorham & Lamont, 1983.

Figlewski, Stephen, and Stanley J. Kon, "Portfolio Management With Stock Index Futures." *Financial Analysts Journal,* Vol. 38 Jan.-Feb. 1982.

Fouse, William L. "Risk and Liquidity." *Financial Analysts Journal,* Vol. 32 (May-June 1976).

————. "Risk and Liquidity Revisited." *Financial Analysts Journal,* Vol. 33 (Jan.-Feb. 1977).

Frankfurter, George M., and Herbert E. Phillips. "MPT Plus Security Analysis for Better Performance." *Journal of Portfolio Management,* Vol. 8 (Summer 1982).

Friend, Irwin, and Marshall Blume. "Measurement of Portfolio Performance Under Uncertainty." *American Economic Review,* Vol. 60 (Sept. 1970).

Gastineau, Gary. *The Stock Options Manual,* 2nd ed. New York: McGraw-Hill, 1979.

Hagin, Robert L. *Modern Portfolio Theory.* Homewood, Ill.: Dow Jones-Irwin, 1979.

Korkie, Bob. "External vs. Internal Performance Evaluation." *Journal of Portfolio Management,* Vol. 9 (Spring 1983).

Leland, Hayne E. "Who Should Buy Portfolio Insurance." *Journal of Finance,* Vol. 35 (May 1980).

McDonald, John G. "Objectives and Performance of Mutual Funds, 1960–1969." *Journal of Financial and Quantitative Analysis,* Vol. 9 (June 1974).

Peterson, David, and Michael L. Rice. "A Note on Ambiguity in Portfolio Performance Measures." *Journal of Finance,* Vol. 35 (Dec. 1980).

Roll, Richard. "Ambiguity When Performance Is Measured by the Securities Market Line." *Journal of Finance,* Vol. 33 (Sept. 1978).

————. "Performance Evaluation and Benchmark Errors I." *Journal of Portfolio Management,* Vol. 6 (Summer 1980).

————. "Performance Evaluation and Benchmark Errors II." *Journal of Portfolio Management,* Vol. 7 (Winter 1981).

Rubinstein, Mark, and Hayne E. Leland. "Replicating Options With Positions in Stock and Cash." *Financial Analysts Journal,* Vol. 37 (July–Aug. 1981).

Sahgal, Pavan. "Beta Used in Assessing Corporate Allocation." *Pensions and Investment Age* (Mar. 7 1983).

Sharpe, William F. "Discussion." *Journal of Finance,* Vol. 37 (May 1982).

————. "Mutual Fund Performance." *Journal of Business,* Vol. 39 (Jan. 1966).

Tepper, Irwin. "Discussion." *Journal of Finance,* Vol. 37 (May 1982).

15

Financial Statement Analysis

CLYDE P. STICKNEY

Investment, financing, and operating decisions are made in terms of the expected return (or cost) of various alternatives relative to the risk involved. One useful source of information for assessing returns and risks is the financial statements prepared periodically by business firms. This chapter provides an overview of the principal financial statements included in corporate annual reports and describes tools, or techniques, for analyzing them.

OVERVIEW OF FINANCIAL STATEMENTS

Three financial statements are typically included in corporate annual reports:

1 Balance sheet
2 Income statement
3 Statement of changes in financial position

An understanding of the purpose and content of each of these financial statements requires an understanding of the business activities each statement attempts to portray.

Summary of Business Activities

A firm's business activities may be viewed as comprising three components:

1 Investing activities
2 Financing activities
3 Operating activities

Investing activities involve decisions as to whether resources should be invested in receivables, inventories, plant and equipment, research and development, employee training, or other alternatives. Procedures for making investment decisions are discussed in Chapters 22 and 25.

Financing activities involve decisions as to the source of capital that will be tapped to obtain the funds necessary to carry out investing activities. Capital might be acquired from short- or long-term creditors or from owners. Chapter 26 discusses important considerations in making financing decisions.

Firms invest resources in anticipation of generating a return or profit. The process of manufacturing and selling goods and services in anticipation of profit comprises the operating activities of a firm. Figure 15.1 depicts these three activities graphically.

Balance Sheet — Measuring Financing Position

The balance sheet, or statement of financial position, presents a snapshot of the resources of a firm (assets) and the claims on those resources (liabilities and owners' equity) as of a specific time. Table 15.1 presents a balance sheet for General Products Company as of December 31, 1984 and December 31, 1985.

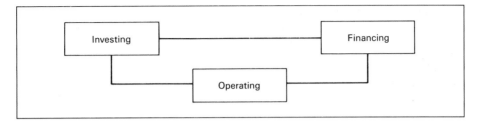

FIG. 15.1 Types of Business Activities

The assets portion of the balance sheet reports as of a specific time the effects of all of a firm's past investment decisions. The liabilities and owners' equity portion of the balance sheet reports as of a specific time the effects of all of a firm's past financing decisions. Capital has been obtained from both short- and long-term creditors and from owners.

The balance sheet derives its name from the fact that it shows the following balance or equality:

Assets = Liabilities + Owners' Equity

That is, a firm's assets or resources are in balance with, or equal to, the claims on those assets by creditors and owners. The balance sheet views resources from two perspectives: a listing of the specific forms in which they are held (e.g., cash, inventory, equipment) and a listing of the persons or entities that provided the funds to obtain the assets and therefore have claims on them (e.g., suppliers, employees, governments, stockholders). Thus, the balance sheet portrays the equality of investing (assets) and financing (liabilities plus owners' equity) activities.

Assets — Recognition, Valuation, and Classification

Which resources of a firm are recognized as assets? At what amount are they stated? How are assets classified within the asset portion of the balance sheet? The responses to these questions are determined by generally accepted accounting principles (GAAP). These principles are set forth by official rule-making bodies within the accounting profession. Since 1973, the rule-making body has been the Financial Accounting Standards Board (FASB). The specification of acceptable accounting principles is made by the FASB only after receiving extensive comments from various preparers and users of financial statements.

Assets are resources that have the potential for providing a firm with future economic benefits; for example, the ability to generate future cash inflows or to reduce future cash outflows. The resources that are recognized as assets are those (1) for which a firm has acquired rights to their future use as a result of a past transaction or exchange and (2) for which the future benefits can be measured, or quantified, with a reasonable degree of precision.[1] Resources

---

[1] *Elements of Financial Statements of Business Enterprises,* Financial Accounting Standards Board, Statement of Financial Accounting Concepts No. 3 (1980), para. 19.

**TABLE 15.1   General Products Company Balance Sheet
(as of December 31 — in millions of dollars)**

	1985	1984
Assets		
Cash	$ 1,601	$ 1,904
Marketable securities	600	672
Current receivables	4,339	3,647
Inventories	3,343	3,161
Current assets	$ 9,883	$ 9,384
Property, plant, and equipment — net	5,780	4,613
Investments	1,820	1,691
Other assets	1,028	956
Total assets	$18,511	$16,644
Liabilities and Owners' Equity		
Short-term borrowings	$ 1,093	$ 871
Accounts payable	1,671	1,477
Progress collections	2,084	1,957
Dividends payable	170	159
Taxes payable	628	655
Other payables	1,946	1,753
Current liabilities	$ 7,592	$ 6,872
Long-term borrowings	1,000	947
Other liabilities	1,565	1,311
Total liabilities	$10,157	$ 9,130
Minority interest in equity of consolidated affiliates	154	152
Common stock ($2.50 par value; 251,500,000 shares authorized; 231,436,949 shares issued 1985 and 1984	579	579
Amounts received for stock in excess of par value	659	656
Retained earnings	7,151	6,307
	8,389	7,542
Deduct common stock held in treasury	(189)	(180)
Total share owners' equity	8,200	7,362
Total liabilities and equity	$18,511	$16,644

of a firm that are normally not recognized as assets because of failing to meet one or both of the above criteria include purchase orders received from customers, employment contracts with corporate officers, and a quality reputation with employees, customers, or citizens of the community.

Assets on the balance sheet are either *monetary* or *nonmonetary*. Monetary assets include cash and claims to a fixed amount of cash receivable in the future. The latter includes accounts and notes receivable and investments in bonds. Monetary assets are stated as the amount of cash expected to be received in the future. If the date or dates of receipt extends beyond one year, the monetary asset is stated as the present value of the future cash flows (using a discount rate appropriate to the claim at the time it initially arose). Nonmonetary assets include inventories, plant, equipment, and other assets that do not represent a claim to a fixed amount of cash. Nonmonetary assets could be stated as the amount initially paid to acquire them (historical cost), the amounts required currently to acquire them (current replacement cost), the amount for which the asset could currently be sold (current realizable value), or the present value of the amount expected to be received in the future from selling or using the asset (present value of future cash flows). GAAP require that nonmonetary assets on the balance sheet be stated at their historical cost amounts because this valuation is more objective and verifiable than other possible valuation bases. Supplemental disclosures must be made in the notes, however, as to the current replacement cost of inventory, plant, and equipment.

The classification of assets within the balance sheet varies widely in published annual reports. The principal asset categories are as follows:

Current Assets. These include cash and other assets that are expected to be sold or consumed during the normal operating cycle of a business, usually within one year. Cash, accounts receivable, inventories, and prepayments are the most common current assets.

Property, Plant, and Equipment. These are the tangible, long-lived assets used in a firm's operations over a period of years and generally not acquired for resale. This category includes land, buildings, machinery, automobiles, furniture, fixtures, computers, and other equipment.

Investments. Included in this category are long-term investments in the debt or equity securities of other entities. If such investments are made for short-term purposes, they are classified under current assets.

Intangibles. These include rights established by law or contract to the future use of property. Patents, trademarks, and franchises are classified among intangibles. Most troublesome asset recognition questions revolve around which rights satisfy the criteria for an asset.

Liabilities — Recognition, Valuation, and Classification

A liability represents a firm's obligation to make payment of cash, goods, or services in a reasonably definite amount at a reasonably definite future time for benefits or services received in the past.[2] Obligations to financial institutions,

---

2 *Ibid.*, para 28.

suppliers, employees, and governments are recognized as liabilities. Most troublesome questions regarding liability recognition relate to unexecuted contracts. Labor union agreements, purchase order commitments, and some lease and pension agreements are not recognized as liabilities because benefits will be received in the future rather than having been received in the past. Unexecuted contracts and other contingent claims, if material, are disclosed in notes to the financial statements.

Most liabilities are monetary, requiring payments of fixed amounts of cash. Those due within one year are stated as the amount of cash expected to be paid to discharge the obligation. If the payment dates extend beyond one year, the liability is stated as the present value of the required future cash flows (discounted at an interest rate appropriate to the obligation when it initially arose). Some liabilities, such as warranties, require the delivery of goods or services instead of the payment of cash. These liabilities are stated as the expected future cost of these goods or services.

Liabilities are classified in various ways on published balance sheets. Virtually all firms use a current liabilities category, which includes obligations expected to be settled within one year. The remaining liabilities are included in a section that may be labeled noncurrent liabilities, long-term debt, or another title.

Owners' Equity Valuation and Disclosure. The owners' equity or stockholders' equity in a firm is a residual interest or claim. That is, the owners have a claim on all assets not required to meet the claims of creditors. The valuation of assets and liabilities in the balance sheet therefore determines the valuation of total owners' equity.

The total owners' equity is separated into amounts initially contributed by stockholders for an interest in a firm (i.e., preferred stock, common stock) and the amount of net income subsequently realized by a firm in excess of dividends declared (i.e., retained earnings).

Income Statement — Measuring Operating Performance

The total assets of a firm may change over time because of investing and financing activities. For example, common stock may be issued for cash, a building may be acquired and a mortgage assumed for part of the purchase price, and holders of convertible bonds may exchange them for shares of common stock. These investing and financing activities affect the amount and structure of a firm's assets and equities.

The total assets of a firm may also change over time because of operating activities. Goods or services are sold to customers for an amount that, it is hoped, is larger than the cost to the firm of acquiring or producing the goods and services. Capital is provided to a firm by creditors and owners with the expectation that the capital will be used to generate a profit and provide an adequate return to the suppliers of capital. The second principal financial statement, the income statement, provides information about the operating performance of a firm for some particular period of time.

Table 15.2 presents an income statement for General Products Company

**TABLE 15.2 General Products Company Income Statement
(for the years ended December 31 — in millions of dollars)**

	1985	1984	1983
Revenues			
Sales of products and services to customers	$24,959	$22,461	$19,654
Expenses			
Cost of goods sold	$17,751	$15,991	$13,915
Selling, general, and administrative expense	4,258	3,716	3,205
Depreciation, depletion, and amortization	707	624	576
Operating expenses	$22,716	$20,331	$17,696
Operating margin	2,243	2,130	1,958
Other income	564	519	419
Interest and other financial charges	(314)	(258)	(224)
Earnings			
Earning before income taxes and minority interest	$ 2,493	$ 2,391	$ 2,153
Provision for income taxes	(958)	(953)	(894)
Minority interest in earnings of consolidated affiliates	(21)	(29)	(29)
Net income applicable to common stock	$ 1,514	$ 1,409	$ 1,230
Earnings per common share (in dollars)	$6.65	$6.20	$5.39

for 1983, 1984, and 1985. Net income is equal to revenues and gains minus expenses and losses. Revenues measure the inflows of net assets (i.e., assets less liabilities) from selling goods and providing services. Expenses measure the outflows of net assets that are used up, or consumed, in the process of generating revenues. As a measure of operating performance, revenues reflect the services rendered by a firm and expenses indicate the efforts required or expended. Gains and losses arise from sales of assets or settlements of liabilities that are only peripherally related to a firm's primary operating activities (e.g., sale of a building, early extinguishment of long-term debt). These gains and losses arise when the amount received or paid differs from the amount at which the asset or liability is stated on the books.

Accrual Basis of Accounting. The operating, or earnings, process for a manufacturing firm might be depicted as shown in Figure 15.2. Net income from the series of activities is equal to the amount of cash received from customers minus the amount of cash paid for raw materials, labor, and the services of production facilities.

If the entire operating process occurred within one accounting period, there would be few difficulties in measuring operating performance. Net in-

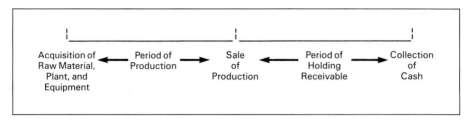

FIG. 15.2 Operating Process for a Manufacturing Firm

come would be equal to cash in minus cash out. However, raw materials are acquired in one accounting period and used in several future accounting periods. Plant and equipment are acquired in one accounting period and used over many accounting periods. Goods or services are often sold in an earlier period than when cash is received from customers.

Under a cash basis of accounting, revenue is recognized when cash is received from customers and expenses are recognized when cash is paid to suppliers, employees, and other providers of goods and services. The cash basis of accounting provides a poor matching of revenues and expenses when a firm's operating process extends over several accounting periods, and therefore is a poor measure of operating performance for specific periods of time. To overcome these deficiencies of the cash basis, GAAP require that the accrual basis of accounting be followed in measuring operating performance.

Under the accrual basis of accounting, revenue is recognized when the earnings process is substantially complete and cash or a receivable subject to reasonably objective measure has been received. For most firms, revenue is recognized at the time goods are sold or services are rendered. Expenses are then matched with their associated revenues. For example, the cost of manufacturing a product remains on the balance sheet as an asset until the time of sale. At the time of sale, revenue in the amount of the cash expected to be collected is recognized. The cost of manufacturing the product is recognized as a matching expense. When costs cannot be easily linked with a particular revenue, they are recognized in the period when their services have been consumed in operations (e.g., the corporate president's salary). The accrual basis of accounting focuses on the acquisition and use of economic resources in operations and not necessarily on their associated cash flows. The accrual basis provides a better measure of operating performance because inputs are more accurately matched with outputs.

Classification Within Income Statement. Investment valuation models are often based on the future earnings stream of an asset or collection of assets. Predictions of the future earnings, or net income, of a firm are often based on the past trend of earnings. Such projections from past data will not be appropriate if unusual or nonrecurring amounts are included in net income. To provide more useful information for prediction, GAAP require that the income statement include some or all of the following sections or categories, depending on the nature of the firm's income for the period.

1 Income from continuing operations;

2 Income, gains, and losses from discontinued operations;

3 Adjustments for changes in accounting principles;

4 Extraordinary gains and losses.

The great majority of income statements include only the first section. The other sections are added if necessary.

Statement of Changes in Financial Position — Measuring Funds Flows

The third principal financial statement is the statement of changes in financial position. This reports the inflows, or sources, and outflows, or uses, of funds during a period of time. Table 15.3 presents a statement of changes in financial position for General Products Company for 1983, 1984, and 1985. In this statement, funds are defined as cash plus marketable securities.

Rationale for the Statement of Changes in Financial Position. W.T. Grant Co. filed for bankruptcy in 1975. For virtually all years prior to 1975, Grant had operated profitably. It had a positive balance in retained earnings at the time of bankruptcy. Despite generating net income each year, Grant continually found itself strapped for cash and unable to pay suppliers, employees, and other creditors.

The experience of Grant is not unusual. Many firms, particularly those experiencing rapid growth, discover that their cash position is deteriorating, despite an excellent earnings record. This occurs for two principal reasons:

1 The timing of cash receipts from customers does not necessarily coincide with the recognition of revenue, and the timing of cash expenditures to suppliers, employees, and other creditors does not necessarily coincide with the recognition of expenses under the accrual basis of accounting. In the usual case, cash expenditures precede the recognition of expenses, and cash receipts occur after the recognition of revenue. Thus, net income for a period might be positive but more cash is used in operations than is provided by operations.

2 The firm may be obligated to retire outstanding debt or need to acquire new plant and equipment at a time when there is insufficient cash available.

In many cases, a profitable firm finding itself short of cash is able to obtain the funds required from either short- or long-term creditors or from owners. Amounts borrowed from creditors must be repaid with interest. Owners may require that periodic dividends be paid in cash. Eventually, cash must be generated internally from operations if a firm is to survive. Cash flows are the connecting link between investing, financing, and operating activities. They permit each of these three principal business activities to continue functioning smoothly and effectively. As demonstrated later in this chapter, information from the statement of changes in financial position is useful in assessing the liquidity risk of a firm.

TABLE 15.3   General Products Company Statement of Changes in Financial Position
(for the years ended December 31 — in millions of dollars)

	1985	1984	1983
Sources of Funds			
Operations:			
Net income	$1,514	$1,409	$1,230
Items of income not requiring (or producing) cash from operating activities:			
Depreciation, depletion, and amortization	707	624	576
Minority interest in earnings	21	29	29
Earnings retained by nonconsolidated finance affiliate	(22)	(18)	(15)
Other	119	8	57
Changes in working capital accounts other than cash, marketable securities, and short-term borrowings:			
Increase in accounts payable and other current liabilities	276	314	245
Increase in accounts receivable	(692)	(358)	(306)
Increase in inventories	(182)	(158)	(399)
Total from operations	$1,741	$1,850	$1,417
New financing:			
Increase in short-term borrowing	222	472	325
Increase in long-term borrowing	122	50	96
Issue of common stock	—	—	3
Sale of treasury shares	136	148	190
Sale of noncurrent assets:			
Sale of property, plant, and equipment	143	102	149
Sale of investments	—	—	24
Total sources	$2,364	$2,622	$2,204
Uses of Funds			
Dividends	$ 670	$ 624	$ 570
Increase in old financing:			
Reduction in long-term borrowing	69	97	386
Purchase of treasury shares	145	156	196
Investment in noncurrent assets:			
Increase in property, plant, and equipment	1,948	1,262	1,055
Increase in investments	129	281	—
Total uses	$2,961	$2,420	$2,207
Changes in cash and marketable securities	$(597)	$ 202	$(3)

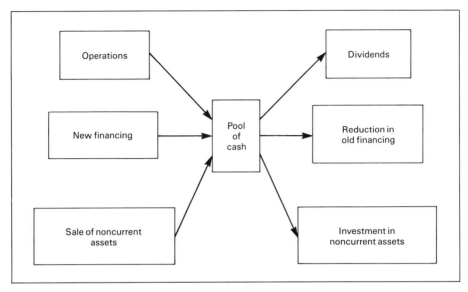

FIG. 15.3 Sources and Uses of Cash

Classification of Cash Flows. Figure 15.3 depicts the various sources and uses of cash. These are described as follows:

1 *Sources — Operations.* The excess of cash received from customers over the cash paid to suppliers, employees, and others is the most important source of cash. When assessed over several years, cash flow from operations indicates the extent to which the operating or earnings activities have generated more cash than is used up. The excess can be used to finance receivables, inventories, or plant and equipment; to pay dividends; or to repay debt. As shown in Table 15.3, cash flow provided by operations is often computed by beginning with net income. Expenses not using cash are then added and revenues not providing cash are then subtracted. Also, changes in working capital accounts other than cash and short-term borrowing are added or subtracted to obtain cash flow from operations.

2 *Sources — New Financing.* Additional cash may be obtained from short-term bank borrowing or from issuance of long-term debt or capital stock.

3 *Sources — Sale of Noncurrent Assets.* The sale of buildings, equipment, and other noncurrent assets results in an increase in cash. These sales generally cannot be viewed as a major source of cash because the amounts received from the sales are not likely to be sufficient to replace the assets sold.

4 *Uses — Dividends.* Dividends are generally a recurring use of cash because most publicly held firms are reluctant to reduce or omit the payment of dividends, even during a year of poor operating performance.

5 *Uses — Reduction in Old Financing.* In most instances, publicly held firms redeem or pay long-term debt at maturity with the proceeds of another bond issue. Thus, these redemptions often have little effect on the net change in cash. Some firms also reacquire their own capital stock for various reasons.

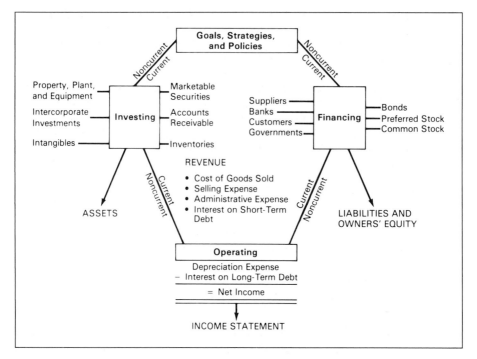

FIG. 15.4 Relationship of Business Activities to Financial Statements

6 *Uses — Investment in Noncurrent Assets.* The acquisition of noncurrent assets, such as buildings and equipment, usually represents the major use of cash.
These assets must be replaced as they wear out and additional noncurrent assets
must be acquired if a firm is to grow.

Summary of Principal Financial Statements

Figure 15.4 summarizes the relationship between the activities discussed previously and the three principal financial statements. The inner portion of the
diamond reflects the current assets and current liabilities that are used principally in carrying out the operating activities of a firm. The outer portion reflects
the noncurrent assets that provide a firm with productive capacity, the noncurrent or long-term sources of financing, and the associated cost of these long-
term investment (depreciation) and financing (interest) activities. The statement of changes in financial position reports the inflows and outflows of cash
from these three principal business activities.

ANALYSIS OF FINANCIAL STATEMENTS

Objectives of Financial Statement Analysis

Financial statements report the results of past performance and the current
financial position of a firm. A creditor or an investor in a firm's bonds or stock

is interested in the expected future performance and financial position of the firm. Data from the financial statements are useful to the extent that they aid the user in assessing or predicting variables of interest in the investment decision. Most financial statement analysis is directed at some aspect of a firm's *profitability* or a firm's *risk*.

Before examining analytic tools for assessing profitability and risk, it may be useful to first question the benefits to be derived from analyzing financial statements. Theoretical and empirical work during the past two decades has shown that the stock market is efficient in reacting to published information about a firm. That is, market participants react intelligently and quickly to information they receive, so market prices continually reflect underlying economic values.

Two questions regarding the role of financial statement analysis in an efficient market might be raised:

1 Do market participants have the necessary technical knowledge of financial accounting and reporting to react intelligently to financial statement information?

2 If the market reacts quickly to information contained in the financial statements, what benefit is derived from analyzing such statements?

Sophistication of Market Participants. There are two schools of thought regarding the level of accounting sophistication of market participants. One school argues that market participants are primarily small individual investors. Such participants have neither the time nor the expertise to interpret and analyze financial statements and detect the subtleties of financial reports. Therefore, they make incorrect investment decisions on the basis of differences that are illusory. Extrapolating the behavior of these individuals, the market is believed to react naively to the release of new information and thus to be inefficient.

A second school of thought argues that market participants lacking the necessary accounting expertise use the services of information and decision intermediaries to aid in their investment decisions. Professional financial analysts are an example of the former, and mutual funds and pension funds are examples of the latter. These intermediaries possess the necessary accounting expertise to react intelligently to reported information. By following the advice or accepting the decisions of these intermediaries, individual investors effectively behave as if they had considerable accounting sophistication. Thus, the market reacts intelligently to new information.

Based on a comprehensive survey of theoretical and empirical work on efficient capital markets, Basu [3] concludes:

[O]ur survey of previous research on the association between stock prices and accounting information reveals that the market's reaction to financial statement data is, indeed, quite sophisticated. Stock prices seem to adjust both rapidly and

---

[3] S. Basu, *Inflation Accounting, Capital Market Efficiency and Security Prices,* Society of Management Accountants of Canada (1978), p. 25.

unbiasedly to the release of financial statement data. In addition to reported "face of the statement" accounting numbers, information in the notes to the financial statements, as well as that in other forms of disclosure, seem to be impounded in stock market prices. To the extent financial statement data *per se* are not timely, the market seems to have turned to alternate sources of information. More important, the market reaction to accounting numbers does not seem to be mechanistic or naive. On the contrary, the evidence is consistent with the view that the market does look behind financial statement numbers to the underlying economic phenomena. For example, the market does not seem to be tricked by accounting changes that increase reported earnings but have no economic consequences on the entity, nor does it seem fooled by an arbitrary choice of alternative accounting methods. In short, the reaction to financial statements and other data is consistent with what one would expect in an efficient capital market.

Benefit of Financial Statement Analysis. One implication of an efficient capital market is that financial statements cannot be routinely analyzed to find undervalued or overvalued securities. Any new information reported in the financial statements is quickly embedded in security prices. What then is the value of financial statement analysis?

One response is that such analysis must be done by someone, presumably by sophisticated financial analysts, if the market is to react appropriately to new information. Such analysis, however, is done soon after the information is released and quickly embedded in market prices.

A second response is that much financial statement analysis must be done outside of a capital market setting. Banks grant credit to business firms and are interested in the liquidity of these enterprises. Investment bankers must set offering prices for the shares of firms initially going public. Government antitrust agencies must compare the relative profitability of various firms and industries in deciding antitrust actions.

Usefulness of Ratios

The various items in the financial statements may be difficult to interpret in the form in which they are presented. For example, the profitability of a firm may be difficult to assess by looking at the amount of net income alone. It is helpful to compare earnings with the assets or capital required to generate those earnings. Relationships between various items in the financial statements can be expressed in the form of ratios to enhance understanding and interpretation.

Ratios are, by themselves, difficult to interpret. For example, does a rate of return on common stock of 8.6 percent reflect good performance? Once calculated, the ratios must be compared with some standard. Several possible standards might be used.

1 The corresponding ratio during the preceding period for the same firm;

2 The corresponding ratio for a similar firm in the same industry;

3 The average ratio for other firms in the same industry.

Difficulties encountered in using these bases for comparison are discussed subsequently.

In the sections that follow, several ratios and other analytical tools for assessing profitability and risk are discussed. The analysis compares amounts for General Products Company for 1985 with the corresponding amounts for 1983 and 1984. Such an analysis is referred to as time-series analysis. Comparison of a given firm's ratios with those of other firms is referred to as cross-section analysis. Cross-section analysis is discussed more fully later.

Analysis of Profitability

Table 15.4 summarizes the most meaningful profitability ratios.

Rate of Return on Assets. This is the most important profitability ratio for assessing management's performance in using assets to generate earnings. This ratio is often called the return on investment or the all-capital earnings rate. It is calculated as follows:

$$\text{Rate of return on assets} = \frac{\begin{array}{c}\text{Net income} \\ + \\ \text{Interest expense} \\ \text{net of income} \\ \text{tax savings} \\ + \\ \text{Minority interest} \\ \text{in earnings}\end{array}}{\begin{array}{c}\text{Average total} \\ \text{assets}\end{array}}$$

Management's performance in using assets is independent of how the acquisition of those assets has been financed. Thus, the earnings figure in the numerator of the rate of return on assets is income before deducting any payments or distributions to the providers of capital. Because interest is a payment to a capital provider, interest expense should not be deducted in measuring the return on total assets. To derive income before interest charges, it is usually easier to start with net income and add to that figure. The amount added to net income is not, however, the interest expense shown on the income statement. Because interest expense is deductible in calculating taxable income, interest expense does not reduce after tax net income by the full amount of interest expense. The amount added back to net income is interest expense reduced by income tax savings. If a consolidated subsidiary is not wholly owned by the parent company, the minority interest's share of earnings must also be added back to net income. In a consolidated balance sheet, all of the assets of a subsidiary are combined with those of the parent company (i.e., the parent's share plus the minority interest's share in the assets). Because the denominator includes all of the assets of the consolidated entity, the numerator should include all of the income, not just the parent's share.

Because the earnings rate during the year is being computed, the measure of investment should reflect the average amount of assets during the year. A crude but usually satisfactory figure for average total assets is one-half the sum of total assets at the beginning and at the end of the year.

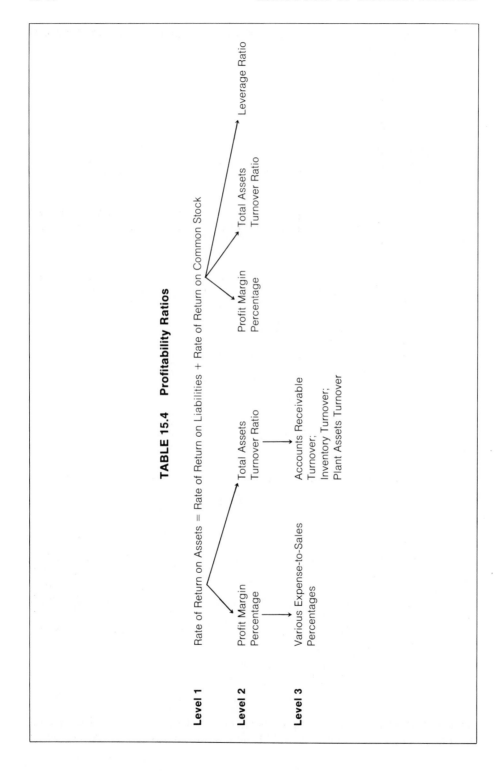

TABLE 15.4   Profitability Ratios

Level 1   Rate of Return on Assets = Rate of Return on Liabilities + Rate of Return on Common Stock

Level 2   Profit Margin Percentage → Total Assets Turnover Ratio;   Profit Margin Percentage → Total Assets Turnover Ratio → Leverage Ratio

Level 3   Various Expense-to-Sales Percentages;   Accounts Receivable Turnover; Inventory Turnover; Plant Assets Turnover

The calculation of rate of return on assets for General Products Company for 1985 is as follows:

$$\frac{\begin{array}{c}\text{Net income}\\+\\\text{Interest expense}\\\text{net of income}\\\text{tax savings}\\+\\\text{Minority interest}\\\text{in earnings}\end{array}}{\begin{array}{c}\text{Average total}\\\text{assets}\end{array}} = \frac{\$1,514 + (1 - 0.46)(\$314) + \$21}{(0.5)(\$16,644 + \$18,511)} = 9.7\%$$

The rate of return on assets was 8.2 percent in 1983 and 8.9 percent in 1984. Thus, the rate of return on assets increased steadily during this three-year period.

Disaggregating the Rate of Return on Assets. One means of studying changes in the rate of return on assets is to disaggregate the ratio into two other ratios as follows:

$$\begin{array}{ccc}\begin{array}{c}\text{Rate of}\\\text{return}\\\text{on assets}\end{array} = & \begin{array}{c}\text{Profit margin percentage}\\\text{(before interest expense}\\\text{and related income tax}\\\text{savings and minority}\\\text{interest in earnings)}\end{array} \times & \begin{array}{c}\text{Total assets}\\\text{turnover}\\\text{ratio}\end{array}\end{array}$$

$$\frac{\begin{array}{c}\text{Net income}\\+\\\text{Interest expense}\\\text{net of income}\\\text{tax savings}\\+\\\text{Minority interest}\\\text{in earnings}\end{array}}{\begin{array}{c}\text{Average total}\\\text{assets}\end{array}} = \frac{\begin{array}{c}\text{Net income}\\+\\\text{Interest expense}\\\text{net of income}\\\text{tax savings}\\+\\\text{Minority interest}\\\text{in earnings}\end{array}}{\text{Revenue}} \times \frac{\text{Revenue}}{\begin{array}{c}\text{Average total}\\\text{assets}\end{array}}$$

The profit margin percentage is a measure of a firm's ability to control the level of operating costs, or expenses, relative to revenues generated. By holding down costs, a firm will be able to increase the profits from a given amount of revenue and thereby improve its profit margin percentage. The total assets turnover ratio is a measure of a firm's ability to generate revenues from a particular level of investment in assets.

The disaggregation of the rate of return on assets for General Products Company for 1985 is as follows:

$$\frac{\$1,704.6}{\$17,577.5} = \frac{\$1,704.6}{\$24,959 + \$564} \times \frac{\$24,959 + \$564}{\$17,577.5}$$

$$9.7\% \quad = \quad 6.7\% \quad \times \quad 1.45$$

The corresponding amounts are 8.2 percent (6.9 percent × 1.2) for 1983 and 8.9 percent (6.8 percent × 1.3) for 1984. Thus, the improvement in the rate of

TABLE 15.5   Net Income and Various Expenses as a Percentage of Revenues

	1985	1984	1983
Revenues	100.0%	100.0%	100.0%
Expenses:			
Cost of goods sold	69.5%	69.6%	69.3%
Selling, general, and administration	16.7	16.2	16.0
Depreciation, depletion, and amortization	2.8	2.7	2.8
Income taxes excluding amount relating to interest	4.3	4.7	5.0
Total	93.3%	93.2%	93.1%
Income before interest and related tax savings and before minority interest in earnings	6.7%	6.8%	6.9%
Interest (net of tax savings)	(0.7)	(0.6)	(0.6)
Minority interest in earnings	(0.1)	(0.1)	(0.2)
Net income	5.9%	6.1%	6.1%

return on assets over the three years is due to an increasing total assets turnover. The profit margin percentage has decreased slightly over three years.

Improving the rate of return on assets can be accomplished by increasing the profit margin percentage, the rate of asset turnover, or both. Some firms, however, may have little flexibility in altering one of these components. For example, a firm committed under a three-year labor union contract may have little control over wage rates paid. Or a firm operating under market- or government-imposed price controls may not be able to increase the prices of its products. In these cases, the opportunities for improving the profit margin percentage may be limited. In order to increase the rate of return on assets, the level of investment in assets such as inventory, plant, and equipment must be reduced, or, to put it another way, revenues per dollar of assets must be increased.

Analyzing Changes in the Profit Margin Percentage.   Profit, or net income, is measured by subtracting various expenses from revenues. To identify the reasons for any changes in the profit margin percentage, changes in a firm's expenses relative to sales can be examined. One approach is to express individual expenses and net income as a percentage of revenues. Such an analysis is presented in Table 15.5 for General Products Company. Note that the conventional income statement format has been altered somewhat in this analysis by subtracting interest expense (net of its related income tax savings) and minority interest in earnings as the last expense items. The percentage on the line labeled "Income before interest and related income tax savings and before minority interest in earnings" corresponds to the profit margin percentage (before interest and related tax savings and minority interest in earnings) presented in the preceding section.

Although the profit margin percentage has been relatively stable over the three-year period, the percentage of selling, general, and administrative expenses to revenue has increased while the percentage of income taxes to revenues has decreased. The reasons for these changing percentages, although small, might be explored further. For example, advertising expenditures might be increasing without a corresponding effect on sales.

Analyzing Changes in the Total Assets Turnover Ratio. The total assets turnover ratio depends on the turnover ratios for its individual asset components. Three turnover ratios are commonly calculated: accounts receivable turnover, inventory turnover, and plant asset turnover.

Accounts Receivable Turnover. The rate at which accounts receivable turn over gives an indication of their nearness to being converted into cash. The accounts receivable turnover is calculated by dividing net sales on account by average accounts receivable. For General Products Company, the accounts receivable turnover for 1985, assuming that all sales are on account (i.e., none is for immediate cash), is calculated as follows:

$$\frac{\text{Net sales on account}}{\text{Average accounts receivable}} = \frac{\$24,959}{(0.5)(\$3,647 + \$4,339)}$$

$$= \quad 6.3 \text{ times per year}$$

The concept of accounts receivable turnover is often expressed in terms of the average number of days receivables are outstanding before cash is collected. The calculation is to divide the accounts receivable turnover ratio into 365 days. The average number of days that accounts receivable are outstanding for General Products Company for 1985 is 57.9 days (365 days/6.3 times per year). Thus, on average, accounts receivable are collected two months after the date of sale. The accounts receivable turnover for 1984 was 6.1; for 1983, it was 5.8. Thus, the average number of days receivables are outstanding was reduced over the three years.

The interpretation of the average collection period depends on the terms of sale. If the terms of sale for General Products Company are net 30 days, the accounts receivable turnover indicates that collections are not being made in accordance with the stated terms. Such a ratio would warrant a review of the credit and collection activity for an explanation and for possible corrective action. If the firm offers terms of net 90 days, then the results indicate that accounts receivable are being handled well.

Inventory Turnover. The inventory turnover ratio is considered to be a significant indicator of the efficiency of operations for many businesses. It is calculated by dividing cost of goods sold by the average inventory during the period. The inventory turnover for General Products Company for 1985 is calculated as follows:

$$\frac{\text{Cost of goods sold}}{\text{Average inventory}} = \frac{\$17,751}{(0.5)(\$3,161 + \$3,343)}$$

$$= \quad 5.5 \text{ times per year}$$

Thus, inventory is typically on hand an average of 66.4 days (365/5.5) before it is sold. For 1984, the inventory turnover was 5.3, and for 1983, it was 5.2.

The interpretation of the inventory turnover figure involves two opposing considerations. Management would like to sell as many goods as possible with a minimum of capital tied up in inventories. An increase in the rate of inventory turnover between periods would seem to indicate more profitable use of the investment in inventory. On the other hand, management does not want to have so little inventory on hand that shortages result and customers are turned away. An increase in the rate of inventory turnover in this case may mean a loss of customers and thereby offset any advantage gained by decreased investment in inventory. Some trade-offs are therefore required in deciding the optimum level of inventory for each firm and thus the desirable rate of inventory turnover.

The inventory turnover ratio is sometimes calculated by dividing sales, rather than cost of goods sold, by the average inventory. As long as there is a relatively constant relationship between selling prices and cost of goods sold, changes in the *trend* of the inventory turnover can usually be identified with either measure. It is inappropriate to use sales in the numerator if the inventory turnover ratio is to be used to calculate the average number of days inventory is on hand until sale.

Plant Asset Turnover. The plant asset turnover ratio is a measure of the relationship between sales and the investment in property, plant, and equipment. It is calculated by dividing sales by average plant assets during the year. The plant assets turnover ratio for General Products Company for 1985 is

$$\frac{\text{Sales}}{\text{Average plant assets}} = \frac{\$24,959}{(0.5)(\$4,613 + \$5,780)}$$

$$= \quad 4.8 \text{ times per year}$$

Thus, for each dollar invested in fixed assets during 1985, $4.80 was generated in sales. The plant asset turnover for 1984 was 4.78; for 1983, if was 4.83.

Changes in the plant asset turnover ratio must be interpreted carefully. Investments in plant assets (e.g., production facilities) are often made several periods before the time when sales are generated from products manufactured in the plant. Thus a low or decreasing rate of plant asset turnover may be indicative of an expanding firm preparing for future growth. On the other hand, a firm may cut back its capital expenditures if the near-term outlook for its products is poor. Such action could lead to an increase in the plant asset turnover ratio.

It was noted earlier that the total assets turnover ratio of General Products Company increased form 1.2 to 1.45 between 1983 and 1985. Most of the increase was due to increases in the turnover of receivables and inventories.

Summary of the Analysis of the Rate of Return on Assets. This section began by stating that the rate of return on assets is a useful measure for assessing management's performance. The rate of return on assets was then disaggregated into profit margin and total assets turnover components. The profit margin percentage was in turn disaggregated by relating various expenses and net income to sales. The total assets turnover was further analyzed by calculating turnover ratios for accounts receivable, inventory, and plant assets. The depth of analysis in a particular case depends on the significance of observed changes in the ratios across time or differences in the ratios across firms.

Rate of Return on Common Shareholders' Equity. The investor in a firm's common stock is probably more interested in the rate of return on common shareholders' equity than the rate of return on assets. To compute the amount of earnings assignable to common stock equity, the earnings allocable to any preferred stock equity (usually the dividends on preferred stock declared during the period) must be deducted from net income. The capital provided during the period by common shareholders can be determined by averaging the aggregate par value of common stock, capital contributed in excess of par value on common stock, and retained earnings (or by deducting the equity of preferred shareholders from total shareholders' equity) at the beginning and end of the period.

The rate of return on common shareholders' equity of General Products Company for 1985 is calculated as follows:

$$\frac{\text{Net income} - \text{Dividends on preferred stock}}{\text{Average common shareholders' equity}} = \frac{\$1,514 - 0}{(0.5)(\$7,362 + \$8,200)} = 19.5\%$$

The rate of return on common shareholders' equity of General Products Company (19.5 percent) is larger in this case than the rate of return on assets (9.7 percent). The return to the common shareholders' equity is larger than the rate of return on assets because the aggregate payments to the other suppliers of capital (e.g., creditors and bondholders) are less than the overall 9.7 percent rate of return generated from capital that they provided. Because common shareholders have a residual claim on the assets and earnings of a firm, they have a claim on all earnings in excess of the cost (including interest on borrowed funds) of generating those earnings.

The common shareholders earned a higher rate of return only because they undertook more risk in their investment. These shareholders were placed in a riskier position because General Products Company incurred debt obligations with fixed payment dates. Failure to make these fixed interest payments could result in the firm being declared insolvent. The phenomenon of common shareholders trading extra risk for a potentially higher return is referred to as financial leverage.

Disaggregating the Rate of Return on Common Shareholders' Equity. The rate of return on common shareholders' equity can be disaggregated into several components in a manner similar to the disaggregation of the rate of return on assets. The rate of return on common shareholders' equity might be disaggregated as follows:

| Rate of return on common shareholders' equity | = | Profit margin percentage (after interest and minority interest in earnings, and after preferred dividends) | × | Total assets turnover ratio | × | Leverage ratio |

or, in terms of items seen in the financial statements:

$$
\begin{array}{ccccc}
\text{Net income} - & & \text{Net income} - & & \text{Average} \\
\text{Dividends on} & & \text{Dividends on} & & \text{total assets} \\
\dfrac{\text{preferred shares}}{\begin{array}{c}\text{Average common}\\ \text{shareholders'}\\ \text{equity}\end{array}} & = & \dfrac{\text{preferred shares}}{\text{Revenues}} & \times \dfrac{\text{Revenues}}{\begin{array}{c}\text{Average}\\ \text{total assets}\end{array}} \times & \dfrac{\text{or equities}}{\begin{array}{c}\text{Average common}\\ \text{shareholders'}\\ \text{equity}\end{array}}
\end{array}
$$

The profit margin percentage indicates the portion of the revenue dollar left over for the common shareholders after all operating costs have been covered and all claims of creditors, minority shareholders, and preferred shareholders have been subtracted. The total assets turnover, as discussed previously, indicates the revenues generated from each dollar of assets. The leverage ratio indicates the extent to which capital (assets or total equities) has been provided by common shareholders. The larger the leverage ratio, the smaller the portion of capital provided by common shareholders and the larger the proportion provided by creditors and preferred shareholders. Thus, the larger the leverage ratio, the greater will be the extent of leverage.

The disaggregation of the rate of return on common shareholders' equity ratio for General Products Company for 1985 is as follows:

$$
\frac{\$1,514}{(0.5)(\$7,362 + \$8,200)}
$$

$$
= \frac{\$1,514}{\$24,959 + \$564} \times \frac{\$24,959 + \$564}{(0.5)(\$16,644 + \$18,511)} \times \frac{(0.5)(\$16,644 + \$18,511)}{(0.5)(\$7,362 + \$8,200)}
$$

$$
19.5\% = \quad 5.9\% \quad \times \quad 1.45 \quad \times \quad 2.26
$$

Table 15.6 shows the changes in the rate of return on common shareholders' equity between 1983 and 1985 and the leading contributing factors. The combination of an increasing total assets turnover and increasing financial leverage has led to a significant increase in the rate of return to common shareholders.

Earnings Per Share of Common Stock. Another frequently encountered measure of profitability is earnings per share of common stock. This ratio is computed by dividing net income attributable to common stock by the average number of common shares outstanding. If a firm has outstanding securities that can be converted into or exchanged for shares of common stock (e.g., stock options, convertible bonds), then a fully diluted earnings per share amount may have to be disclosed.

Earnings per share has been criticized as a measure of profitability because it does not consider the amount of assets or capital required to generate that level of earnings. Two firms with the same earnings per share will not be

TABLE 15.6   Analysis of Changes in Rate of Return on Common Shareholders' Equity

	Rate of Return on Common Shareholders' Equity	Profit Margin = Percentage ×	Total Assets Turnover Ratio ×	Leverage Ratio
1985	19.5%	5.9%	1.4	2.3
1984	17.4	6.1	1.3	2.2
1983	15.4	6.1	1.2	2.1

equally profitable if one of the firms requires twice the amount of assets or capital to generate those earnings than does the other firm.

Earnings per share amounts are also difficult to interpret when comparing firms. For example, assume that two firms have identical earnings, common shareholders' equity, and rates of return on common shareholders' equity. One firm may have a lower earnings per share simply because it has a larger number of shares outstanding (due perhaps to the use of a lower par value for its shares).

Earnings per share amounts are often compared with the market price of the stock. This is usually expressed as a price/earnings (P/E) ratio (market price per share/earnings per share). For example, the common stock of General Products Company is selling for $75 per share at the end of 1985. The P/E ratio is 11.3 : 1 ($75/$6.65). This ratio is often presented in tables of stock market prices and in financial periodicals. The relationship is sometimes expressed by saying that "the stock is selling at 11.3 times earnings."

Analysis of Risk

The second parameter in investment decisions is risk. Portfolio theory makes a distinction between systematic and nonsystematic risk. (See the discussion in Chapter 14.)

Systematic risk relates to the covariability of a firm's stock price with changes in the prices of all securities; it is measured by market beta. Because stock market prices ultimately reflect the underlying cash flows of a firm, systematic risk is a function of the covariability of a firm's cash flows with the cash flows of all firms in the economy. Because the latter is difficult to ascertain, systematic risk is generally measured using stock price data. Systematic risk is nondiversifiable. The investor must select a level of systematic risk considered tolerable, build a portfolio with the desired level of systematic risk, and accept the level of return commensurate with that risk level.

Nonsystematic risk is firm-specific risk. It reflects the particular combination of risk factors faced by a specific firm given its operating, financing, and investing decisions. Portfolio theory posits that firm-specific risk can be eliminated by building a diversified portfolio of securities. If the portfolio contains securities of firms with varying degrees of labor versus capital intensity, varying degrees of financial leverage, and varying degrees of other firm-specific dimensions of risk, then these risk dimensions can be essentially diversified away.

While the theory of risk assessment in a portfolio setting is well developed in the literature (see the discussion in Chapter 14), the role of financial statement analysis in these risk assessments is less clear. Some initial empirical work has been done attempting to relate accounting measures of risk with market beta, but the results have been inconclusive. Virtually no work has been done at either a theoretical or an empirical level regarding the role financial statement analysis might play in forming diversified portfolios of securities in which nonsystematic risk has been eliminated.

The discussion of risk analysis in the sections that follow is based largely on analytical tools conventionally used for assessing firm-specific risk. Readers interested in empirical work demonstrating the usefulness of these conventional analytical tools in predicting credit ratings, bond ratings, bankruptcies, and similar events are referred to the books and articles by Altman, Foster, and Kaplan that are listed in the bibliography.

Measures of Short-Term Liquidity Risk

Investors or creditors whose claims will become payable in the near future are interested in the short-term liquidity or ''nearness to cash'' of a firm's assets. One tool for predicting whether or not cash will be available when the claims become due is a budget of cash receipts and disbursements for several months or quarters in the future. Such budgets are often prepared for management and used internally for planning cash requirements. Budgets of cash receipts and disbursements are not generally available for use by persons outside a firm. Investors must therefore use other tools in assessing short-term liquidity.

Funds Flow From Operations. The statement of changes in financial position is one published source of information for assessing liquidity. The amount of funds provided by operations indicates the extent to which the operating activities have generated sufficient cash for the payment of dividends and the acquisition of fixed assets. The statement also indicates the extent to which additional financing has been used for those purposes. Table 15.3 indicates that the operations for General Products Company have consistently provided about 70 percent of the funds required by the firm.

In some instances, firms define funds as working capital (i.e., current assets minus current liabilities) instead of cash. This broader definition of funds may mask short-term liquidity problems. For example, operations may be a net provider of working capital but most of the increase in funds might be associated with a buildup of receivables and inventory. In this case, operations could be a net user, rather than provider, of cash. Additional insights into the impact of operations on liquidity can be obtained by converting working capital provided by operations to cash flow provided by operations. To convert working

TABLE 15.7   General Products Company Short-Term Liquidity Ratios

Ratio		Dec. 31, 1984	Dec. 31, 1985
Current ratio	$= \dfrac{\text{Current assets}}{\text{Current liabilities}}$	$\dfrac{\$9,384}{\$6,872} = 1.4:1$	$\dfrac{\$9,883}{\$7,592} = 1.3:1$
Quick ratio	$= \dfrac{\text{Cash, marketable securities, accounts receivable}}{\text{Current liabilities}}$	$\dfrac{\$6,223}{\$6,872} = 9:1$	$\dfrac{\$6,540}{\$7,592} = 9:1$
Working capital ratio	$= \dfrac{\text{Current assets}}{\text{Total assets}}$	$\dfrac{\$\ 9,384}{\$16,644} = 56.4\%$	$\dfrac{\$\ 9,883}{\$18,511} = 53.4\%$

capital from operations to cash flow from operations involves the following steps:

1 Begin with the amount of working capital provided by operations.
2 Add the amount of the change in current operating accounts (other than cash) that experienced a net credit change during the period. These are decreases in receivables, inventories, and prepayments, and increases in current operating liability accounts.
3 Subtract the amount of the change in current operating accounts that experienced a net debit change during the period. These are increases in receivables, inventories, and prepayments, and decreases in current operating liability accounts.
4 The result is cash flow provided by operations.

Figure 15.5, overleaf, graphically shows the importance of this conversion. Shown there is a plot of net income, working capital provided by operations, and cash flow provided by operations for W.T. Grant Co. for the 10 years preceding bankruptcy. Net income and working capital provided by operations moved in parallel and did not signal Grant's liquidity problems. With two minor exceptions, however, Grant's cash flows from operations were negative for the 10 years preceding its bankruptcy. Because of buildups of receivables and inventories, operations were consistently unable to generate cash. External funding sources were tapped for several years, but ultimately the firm lost its ability to obtain needed capital and went bankrupt. Cash flow from operations is shown here to be a useful source of information for assessing short-term liquidity risk.

Liquidity Ratios. Several ratios are also commonly used in assessing short-term liquidity. The most popular ones are the current ratio, quick ratio, and working capital ratio. Their calculation using data for General Products Company is shown in Table 15.7.

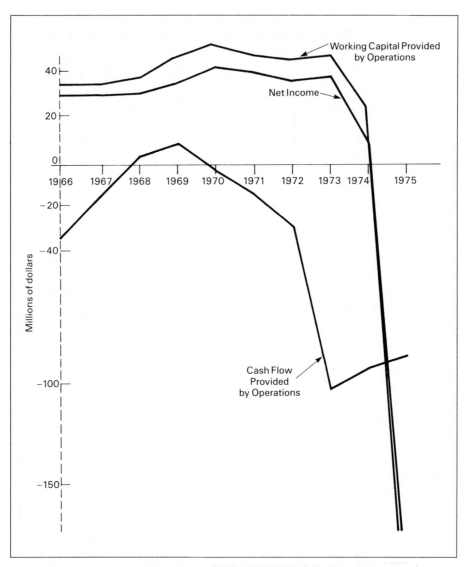

**Fig. 15.5   W.T. Grant Company Net Income, Working Capital, and Cash Flow From
          Operations for Fiscal Years Ending January 31, 1966–1975**

In general, changes in these liquidity ratios are highly correlated with each other. An analyst need not calculate all the ratios in studying a firm's liquidity.

These and other balance sheet ratios have been criticized because they are susceptible to "window dressing;" that is, management can take deliberate steps to produce a financial statement that presents a better ratio at the balance sheet date than the average or normal ratio during the year. For example, toward the close of the year normal purchases on account may be delayed or loans to officers, classified as noncurrent assets, may be collected and the proceeds used to reduce current liabilities.

To overcome these criticisms of balance sheet ratios, other liquidity ratios that use flow data have been suggested in the literature. One ratio relates cash inflow from operations to the average amount of current liabilities during a period. This ratio is intended to provide information similar to the current ratio but is not as susceptible to year-end window dressing. Another ratio sometimes encountered is the defensive interval.[4] It is calculated by dividing the average daily cash expenditures for operating expenses into a firm's most liquid assets — generally cash, marketable securities, and accounts receivable. The defensive interval is the number of days the firm could theoretically remain in business without additional sales or new financing. In studies of bond default and bankruptcy, this ratio has been found to be a good predictor.

Measures of Long-Term Solvency Risk

Measures of long-term solvency are used in assessing the firm's ability to meet interest and principal payments on long-term debt and similar obligations as they become due. If the payments cannot be made on time, the firm becomes insolvent and may have to be reorganized or liquidated.

Perhaps the best indicator of long-term solvency is a firm's ability to generate profits over a period of years. If a firm is profitable, it will either generate sufficient funds from operations or be able to obtain needed funds from creditors and owners. The measures of profitability discussed previously are therefore applicable for this purpose as well. Two other commonly used measures of long-term solvency are debt ratios and the number of times that interest charges are earned.

Debt Ratios. There are several variations of the debt ratio, but the one most commonly encountered in financial analysis is the long-term debt ratio. It reports the portion of the firm's long-term capital that is furnished by debt holders. To calculate this ratio, total noncurrent liabilities are divided by the sum of total noncurrent liabilities, minority interest in consolidated subsidiaries, and total shareholders' equity.

Another form of the debt ratio is the debt/equity ratio. To calculate the debt/equity ratio, total liabilities (current and noncurrent) are divided by total equities (liabilities + shareholders' equity = total assets).

The two forms of the debt ratio for General Products Company on December 31, 1984 and 1985 are shown in Table 15.8. In general, the higher these ratios, the higher the likelihood that the firm may be unable to meet fixed interest and principal payments in the future. The decision for most firms is how much financial leverage, with its attendant risk, they can afford to assume. Funds obtained from issuing bonds or borrowing from a bank have a relatively low interest cost but require fixed, periodic payments that increase the likelihood of bankruptcy. In assessing the debt ratios, analysts customarily vary the standard in direct relation to the stability of the firm's earnings. The more stable the earnings, the higher the debt ratio that is considered acceptable or safe. The debt ratios of public utilities are customarily high, on the order of 60

---

[4] George H. Sorter and George Benston, "Appraising the Defensive Position of a Firm: The Interval Measure," *The Accounting Review*, Vol. 35 (Oct. 1960), pp. 633–640.

TABLE 15.8   General Products Company Long-Term Solvency Ratios

Ratio		Dec. 31, 1984	Dec. 31, 1985
Long-term debt ratio	= $\dfrac{\text{Noncurrent liabilities}}{\begin{array}{l}\text{Noncurrent liabilities,}\\ \text{minority interest,}\\ \text{shareholders' equity}\end{array}}$	$\dfrac{\$\ 2{,}258}{\$\ 9{,}772} = 23.1\%$	$\dfrac{\$\ 2{,}565}{\$10{,}919} = 23.5\%$
Debt/equity ratio	= $\dfrac{\text{Total liabilities}}{\text{Total assets}}$	$\dfrac{\$\ 9{,}130}{\$16{,}644} = 54.9\%$	$\dfrac{\$10{,}157}{\$18{,}511} = 58.9\%$

to 70 percent. The stability of public utility earnings makes these ratios acceptable to many investors who would be dissatisfied with such large leverage for firms with less stable earnings.

Because several variations of the debt ratio appear in corporate annual reports, care is necessary in making comparisons of debt ratios among firms. These long-term solvency ratios are likewise highly correlated, so it is generally unnecessary to calculate more than one of them. Being balance sheet ratios, they too are subject to year-end window dressing, but to a lesser extent than the short-term liquidity ratios.

Interest Coverage: Times Interest Charges Earned. Another measure of long-term solvency is the number of times that interest charges are earned or covered. This ratio is calculated by dividing net income before interest expense, minority interest, and income tax expenses by interest expense. For General Products Company, the times interest charges earned ratios for 1983, 1984, and 1985 are

$$\text{Times interest charges earned} = \frac{\text{Net income before interest, minority interest, and income taxes}}{\text{Interest expense}}$$

$$1983 \qquad \frac{\$2{,}153 + \$224}{\$224} = 10.6 \text{ times}$$

$$1984 \qquad \frac{\$2{,}391 + \$258}{\$258} = 10.3 \text{ times}$$

$$1985 \qquad \frac{\$2{,}493 + \$314}{\$314} = 8.9 \text{ times}$$

The purpose of this ratio is to indicate the relative protection of bondholders and to assess the probability that the firm will be forced into bankruptcy by a failure to meet required interest payments. If periodic repayments of principal on long-term liabilities are also required, the repayments might be included in the denominator of the ratio. Fixed lease and pension payments might also be included in the calculations. If so, the ratio would be described as the number of times that fixed charges were earned or covered.

The times interest or fixed charges earned ratios can be criticized as measures for assessing long-term solvency because the ratios use earnings rather than cash flows in the numerator. Interest and other fixed payment obligations are paid with cash and not with earnings. When the value of the ratio is relatively low (for example, two to three times), some measure of cash flows, such as cash flows from operations, may be preferable in the numerator.

Interpreting the Results of Financial Statement Analysis

The results of financial statement analysis are difficult to interpret without some standard or base for comparison. Several common standards for comparison are discussed in the following sections.

Time-Series Analysis. One approach is to compare various ratio amounts with the corresponding amounts for the same firm from earlier periods. This is the approach followed throughout this chapter in interpreting the ratios for General Products Company. The principal advantage of this approach is that it permits the analyst to focus on *changes* in the profitability, liquidity, and solvency of a firm, given its particular set of operating strategies and policies, product lines, production techniques, accounting methods, and so forth. The principal weakness of this approach is that economy-wide and industry factors are not explicitly taken into consideration in interpreting the ratios. For example, a decrease in the rate of return on assets from 8 percent to 6 percent for a particular firm might be viewed as an unhealthy sign. However, if it is recognized that the economy was in a recession during the period and most other firms found their rates of return cut in half, then the 25 percent decrease in rate of return would be interpreted differently.

The Securities and Exchange Commission (SEC) requires that the annual report to shareholders and the 10-K report submitted to the SEC include a discussion by management of the reasons for important changes in a firm's profitability, liquidity, and capital structure.[5] These explanations are helpful in interpreting the results of a time-series analysis.

Cross-Section Analysis. A second approach is to compare various ratio amounts with similar amounts for the same time period for other firms in the industry. There are several sources of standard, or average, industry ratios, including those published by Dun & Bradstreet, Robert Morris Associates, Prentice-Hall, and the Federal Trade Commission. The major strength of using standard industry ratios is that a firm is compared with its competitors operating in similar input and output markets. Thus, economy-wide and industry factors affecting all firms will impact the ratios of each of the firms. The concern in interpreting the performance of a particular firm is whether it did better, about the same, or worse than its competitors.

---

[5] *Accounting Series Release No. 279*, Securities and Exchange Commission (Sept. 1980).

There are two major weaknesses of using standard industry ratios. First, firms seldom do business in only one industry. Most large firms are diversified. General Products Company, for example, does business in power systems, industry products, and broadcasting. The rates of return and risk from these activities differ. The amount of capital required for these activities also differs. Yet General Products Company is classified in only one industry category in calculating average industry ratios. If other firms classified in that industry are also diversified but diversified into different product lines, then the average ratios lose meaning.

A second weakness of average industry ratios is that no adjustments are made for differences in the accounting principles used by various firms. The choice of inventory cost-flow assumption (first in, first out (FIFO) versus last in, first out (LIFO)) and depreciation method, the treatment of pensions, and the accounting for other transactions and events can have a significant impact on the financial statements. Unless these and other differences in accounting methods are filtered out, comparisons of financial statement ratios may be misleading.

Adjustments for Accounting Principles

Published financial statements and notes in recent years have increasingly included information that permits the analyst to adjust the reported amounts for differences between firms in the accounting principles used. This section discusses adjustments for the cost-flow assumption (FIFO vs. LIFO), the depreciation method, and the recognition of pensions.

FIFO vs. LIFO Cost-Flow Assumption. No accounting method for inventories based on historical cost can simultaneously report current cost data in both the income statement and the balance sheet. If a firm reports current costs in the income statement under LIFO, then its balance sheet amount for ending inventory contains very old data. The SEC is concerned that readers of financial statements not by misled by out-of-date information. It requires firms using LIFO to disclose in notes to the financial statements the amounts by which LIFO inventories would have increased if they had been recorded at current cost, or FIFO. From this disclosure and the inventory equation, an analyst can compute what a LIFO firm's income would have been had it been using FIFO instead. In this way, the financial statements of firms using LIFO can be made more comparable with the financial statements of firms using FIFO.

A note to the financial statements of General Products Company states:

> The cost of the inventories of the consolidated companies is calculated principally by the LIFO method. . . . The FIFO cost of these inventories was approximately $4,763 million at December 31, 1985, and $4,391 million at December 31, 1984.

General Products Company's beginning inventories under LIFO (see Table 15.1) amounted to $3,161 million, its ending inventory amount to $3,343 million, and its cost of goods sold totaled $17,751 million. Table 15.9 demonstrates

TABLE 15.9   General Products Company Inventory Data From Financial Statements and Footnotes (in millions of dollars)

	LIFO Cost-Flow Assumption (Actually Used)	Excess of FIFO Over LIFO Amount	FIFO Cost-Flow Assumption (Hypothetical)
Beginning inventory	$ 3,161	$1,230	$ 4,391
Purchases	17,933[a]	0	17,933[a]
Cost of goods available for sale	$21,094	$1,230	$22,324
Less ending inventory	3,343	1,420	4,763
Cost of goods sold	$17,751	$ 190	$17,561

(a) Purchases = Cost of Goods Sold + Ending Inventory − Beginning Inventory
      $17,933 = $17,751   + $3,343   − $3,161

Note: Amounts shown in boldface are given in General Products Company's financial statements. Other amounts are computed as indicated.

the calculation of cost of goods sold on a FIFO basis. Recall from the inventory equation,

$$\frac{\text{Beginning}}{\text{inventory}} + \text{Purchases} - \frac{\text{Ending}}{\text{inventory}} = \frac{\text{Cost of}}{\text{goods sold}}$$

FIFO's higher beginning inventory increases reported cost of goods available for sale and the cost of goods sold by $1,230 million, relative to LIFO. FIFO's higher ending inventory decreases cost of goods sold by $1,420 million, relative to LIFO. Hence, the cost of goods sold is $1,420 million minus $1,230 million, or $190 million, less under FIFO than it was under LIFO. General Products Company's pretax income would be $190 million more under FIFO than under the LIFO flow assumption actually used. Assuming FIFO's use for tax purposes and a 46 percent tax rate, income taxes would have been $87.4 million higher under FIFO and net income would have been $102.6 million ($190 − $87.4) higher. Table 15.10 shows the calculations of rate of return on assets and rate of return on shareholders' equity using both LIFO and FIFO cost-flow assumptions. As expected during a period of rising prices, the rates of return are higher on a FIFO basis because older costs are used in computing cost of goods sold.

Depreciation Methods. Most firms calculate depreciation using the accelerated cost recovery system (ACRS) for tax purposes in order to minimize the present value of income tax payments. For financial reporting, most firms use the straight-line depreciation method. However, some firms use the double declining balance or sum-of-the-year's-digits depreciation method for financial reporting. Thus, published financial statements are based on accelerated depre-

TABLE 15.10   Rates of Return for General Products Company for 1985 Using LIFO and Using FIFO

Rate	LIFO Cost-Flow Assumption (Actually Used)	FIFO Cost-Flow Assumption (Hypothetical)
Rate of return on assets	$\dfrac{\$1,705^{(a)}}{\$17,577.5^{(a)}} = 9.7\%$	$\dfrac{\$1,705 + 190 - \$87.4}{\$17,577.5 + (0.5)(\$1,230 + \$1,420) - (0.5)(\$565.8^{(b)} + \$653.2^{(c)})} = 9.8\%$
Rate of return on common shareholders' equity	$\dfrac{\$1,514^{(a)}}{\$7,781^{(a)}} = 19.5\%$	$\dfrac{\$1,705 + \$190 - \$87.4}{\$7,781 + (0.5)(\$664.2^{(d)} + \$766.8^{(e)})} = 21.3\%$

(a) See calculations earlier in chapter.
(b) 0.46 × $1,230
(c) 0.46 × $1,420
(d) (1.0 − 0.46)($1,230)
(e) (1.0 − 0.46)($1,420)

ciation methods for some firms and the straight-line method for other firms. For capital-intensive firms with large investments in depreciable assets, these differences in depreciation methods can have a significant impact on the analysis of these firms' profitability.

Because most firms take the maximum depreciation deductions allowed by law on their returns, the analyst can achieve comparability of income statements across firms by converting the depreciation charges reported in the financial statements to the amounts claimed on the tax return. The resulting amounts of depreciation may not be "right" in the sense of measuring the disappearance of the future benefits of long-term assets, but they will be comparable from one firm to another.

Firms that use an ACRS depreciation method for tax purposes and some other method for financial reporting are required to recognize deferred taxes for the timing difference between taxable income and pretax book income. The notes to the financial statements will usually indicate the amount of deferred taxes that relate to depreciation timing differences. For example, the notes to the financial statements of General Products Company indicate that during 1985 there were deferred taxes of $55.2 million which related to depreciation timing differences. With this information, it is possible to estimate the amount of the excess of depreciation claimed on the tax return over the amount reported in the financial statements. The $55.2 million deferred tax amount is equal to the timing difference for depreciation multiplied by the marginal tax rate. Because the marginal tax rate for most corporations is 46 percent, the excess of tax over book depreciation is estimated to be $120 million ($55.2 million/0.46). Multiplying this amount by the complement of the tax rate indicates the decrease in net income from using ACRS depreciation rather than straight-line depreciation for financial reporting: $64.8 million = $120 million × (1 − 0.46). Net income for 1985 for General Products Company would have been $1,449.2 million ($1,514 million − $64.8 million) if ACRS depreciation had been used for financial reporting, as compared to $1,514 million using the straight-line method.

Computing the effect of using ACRS depreciation on the balance sheet is more difficult. To do so an analyst must know the proportion of the deferred income taxes account on the balance sheet that relates to depreciation timing differences. Such information is seldom disclosed. As a consequence, the adjustments to reported amounts for differences between firms in the depreciation method used must generally focus on the income statement only.

Recognition of Supplemental Actuarial Value for Pension Plan. GAAP do not currently require the recognition as a liability of the supplemental actuarial value, or prior service obligation, of a pension plan. Because the notes to the financial statements disclose the amount of the supplemental actuarial value, the analyst can treat the obligation as a liability.

A note to the financial statements of General Products Company states, in part:

Unrecognized supplemental actuarial value at December 31, 1985, was estimated at $587 million. . . . Based on the the latest actuarial valuation, which recognizes the increased pension liabilities resulting from wage and salary improvements and increases for retirees effective July 1, 1985, unrecognized supplemental actuarial value approximates $616 million . . . at December 31, 1985.

The recognition of a liability of $616 million at December 31, 1985 requires either that an asset be increased or that shareholders' equity be decreased in order to keep the balance sheet in balance. Theoretical arguments can be made for both treatments. Recognition of an asset is justified if the benefits of granting credit for prior employee service are expected to increase future productivity of employees. A decrease in shareholders' equity is appropriate if the failure to recognize supplemental actuarial value in the past is viewed as a mistake that is now being corrected.

Summary of Adjustments. The adjustments discussed previously for the cost flow assumption, depreciation method, and pension liability recognition are illustrative of the transformations that can be made to reported data.[6] Similar adjustments might be made for leases, deferred taxes, and other items. Empirical work on the efficiency of capital markets suggests that investors do filter out the effects of differences in accounting principles when using financial statement data.[7]

Limitations of Financial Statement Analysis

The analytical computations discussed in this chapter have a number of limitations that should be kept in mind by anyone using them. Several of the more important limitations are the following:

1 The ratios and other analytical tools are based on financial statement data and are therefore subject to the same criticisms as the financial statements (e.g., use of acquisition cost rather than current replacement costs or net realizable value, the latitude permitted firms in selecting from among various GAAP).

2 Changes in many ratios are highly associated, or correlated, with each other. For example, the changes in the current ratio and quick ratio between two different times are often in the same direction and approximately proportional. It is therefore not necessary to compute all the ratios to assess a particular factor.

3 When comparing the size of a ratio between periods for the same firm, one must recognize conditions that have changed between the periods being compared

---

6 More adjustments of this sort are illustrated for the 30 companies in the Dow-Jones Industrials in Daniel A. Lasman and Roman L. Weil, "Adjusting the Debt-Equity Ratio," *Financial Analysts Journal,* Vol. 34 (Sept.-Oct. 1978), pp. 49–58. An analysis of the effects of alternative accounting principles on various financial statement ratios is presented in James P. Dawson et al., "Restating Financial Statements for Alternative GAAP's: Is It Worth the Effort?" *Financial Analysts Journal,* Vol. 36 (Nov.-Dec. 1980), pp. 38–46.

7 For a review of the theory of efficient markets and its implications for accounting, see Nicholas J. Gonedes and Nicholas Dopuch, "Capital Market Equilibrium, Information-Production, and Selected Accounting Techniques: Theoretical Framework and Review of Empirical Work," *Studies on Financial Accounting Objectives: 1974* (Supplement to Vol. 12, *Journal of Accounting Research*), pp. 48–129.

(e.g., different product lines or geographical markets served, changes in economic conditions, changes in prices).

4 When comparing ratios of a particular firm with those of similar firms, one must recognize differences between the firms (e.g., use of different methods of accounting, differences in the method of operations, different types of financing).

SUGGESTED READING

Altman, Edward I. *Corporate Financial Distress*. New York: John Wiley & Sons, 1983.

Beaver, William. *Financial Reporting: An Accounting Revolution*. Englewood Cliffs, N.J.: Prentice-Hall, 1981.

Bernstein, Leopold. *Financial Statement Analysis: Theory, Application and Interpretation*. Homewood, Ill.: Richard D. Irwin, 1983

Davidson, Sidney, et al. *Intermediate Accounting: Concepts, Methods and Uses*. Hinsdale, Ill.: Dryden Press, 1982.

Foster, George. *Financial Statement Analysis*. Englewood Cliffs, N.J.: Prentice-Hall, 1978.

Kaplan, Robert. "The Information Content of Financial Accounting Numbers: A Survey of Empirical Evidence." In *Symposium of Impact of Accounting Research in Financial Accounting and Disclosure on Current Practice*, pp. 134–173. Chapel Hill, N.C.: Duke University Press, 1978.

Lev, Baruch. *Financial Statement Analysis: A New Approach*. Englewood Cliffs, N.J.: Prentice-Hall, 1974.

16

Security Analysis

W. Scott Bauman

Jaroslaw Komarynsky

OVERVIEW AND PURPOSES OF SECURITY ANALYSIS

Security analysis is the task of researching securities of corporations, such as stocks and bonds, for the purpose of making investment decisions. This research is conducted by professional security analysts, institutional investors, and individual investors. In analyzing securities, the analyst considers the appraisal of investment risks and expected returns. The results of this analysis are used by individual investors, investment advisors, and portfolio managers to decide which securities should be purchased, held, and sold in investment accounts.

When a specific stock or bond is analyzed, the depth and breadth of research conducted depends on the audience for whom the work is being done. The diversity of investors that use security research can be appreciated by noting the different types of organizations that conduct security research, as listed in Table 16.1.

A great deal of security research is done by investment banking and brokerage firms. These organizations are described as being on the "sell side of the street" because their research is done as a service for customers who are expected to buy and sell securities through these brokerage firms (and pay commissions). In the case of a public offering of a new stock or bond issue, a very detailed prospectus document, describing the company and the issue, is prepared and distributed to investors by the investment banker.

In the case of securities already trading in the open market, research departments of brokerage firms prepare a wide variety of reports. A distinction is made between research done for the *retail* clientele and for the *institutional* clientele. Retail type research is directed to small and individual investors, while institutional type research is directed to larger professional investors. Although the research departments of some brokerage firms cater to both types of clientele, some deal with only the retail market and others serve only institutional customers. While most of the security analysis reports for a particular stock may contain the same summary conclusions in respect to investment risks and return expectations, institutional reports (as compared to retail reports) disclose much more detailed analysis and supported factual information.

Organizations that are compensated for the management of portfolio accounts are referred to as being on the "buy side of the street." These organizations, as listed in Table 16.1, make extensive use of the external institutional research of brokerage firms. In addition, these organizations (particularly the larger ones) have their own security research departments that conduct investment analysis. The analysts in these departments make reports that are designed to address the specific objectives and financial requirements of portfolios and investment accounts managed by the organization. These reports tend to be summary in nature because they rely in part on information in the external reports prepared by brokerage firms and investment publishing services.

A third category of security analysis research is performed by organizations that publish the results for their subscribers. Publications range from bound and looseleaf services containing factual financial data about corporations and industries to periodicals containing specific investment opinions and advice. The subscribers include libraries, individuals, and institutions. Consequently, the nature of these security analysis reports varies widely depending

---

Table 16.1   Organizations Conducting Professional Security Analyses

Sell side research
  Investment brokerage firms
    Institutional sales
    Retail sales
  Investment banking firms
Buy side research
  Investment management organizations
    Bank trust investment division
    Investment counsel firms
    Insurance companies
    Mutual funds
    Pension funds
    Others
Investment publishing services

---

on the backgrounds of the subscribers and the purposes of the publication service.

The Components of Security Analysis

Because security analysis research is conducted by different organizations for a variety of users, the elements employed likewise vary depending on the circumstances. To understand the task of security analysis, visualize how it fits into the total decision-making process of investors. The individual or professional investor must make decisions about individual securities to construct a portfolio of securities best suited (optimal) to the investor's objectives and needs. Three separate though closely related tasks must be integrated to build an optimal portfolio.

One task is matching the investment features of the securities available to the investment return goals and financial risk constraints of particular investors. Because the return and risk requirements of investors vary, some research reports describe the features of an investment within the context of these requirements. The return feature for a security, for example, may be described as possessing "a maximum capital appreciation potential" or as offering "a reasonable, stable income." The risk features may be described as "high investment quality" or as "a speculative businessman's risk." Many reports provide basic recommendations to buy, hold, or sell. Some reports provide time horizon guidance such as "a long-term buy" or "a short-term sell."

A second task is analyzing the external environment that is researched by comparing the relative attractiveness of securities in different categories. To do this, the outlook for the economy and the investment market environment is evaluated. The various economic and security market sectors are studied in order to appraise relative risks and return opportunities. For example, how attractive are bonds vs. stock, long-term bonds vs. short-term bonds, the durable goods sector vs. the technological growth sector, and the computer industry vs. the telecommunication industry? This task is important because external trends in economic activity, interest rates, inflation, industry competition, stock market sentiment, and so forth have a major impact on the performance of an individual company's securities.

The third task is the analysis of securities of individual companies. The security analysts in most investment research departments are organized along industry lines; hence, they are sometimes referred to as industry analysts. In a large department several analysts may be assigned to one industry, while, one analyst may follow several different industries. Based on this type of organizational structure, many research reports comprise the analysis of selected securities in a single industry or sector. These reports provide an appraisal of the risks, return prospects, and valuations of securities in a particular industry group or sector.

The final step in the investment decision-making process is for the investor or investment manager to integrate (1) the requirements of the account, (2) the external environment, and (3) the features of available securities into an appropriately diversified and balanced portfolio. This chapter deals with the tasks of security research pertaining to the analysis of the external environment and the analysis of stocks and bonds of corporate issuers.

The Approaches to Security Research

The judgments of particular security analysts and investors determine what information is researched about a given security as well as how a security is researched. In addition, the format used to communicate the research results to investors varies depending on how the results are to be used by the investor or account manager. Perhaps one of the best ways to illustrate the diversity of security research is to describe two contrasting approaches.

The Top-Down Approach. The traditional approach to security analysis begins with the analysis of broad external factors of the economy and financial markets, then proceeds to the more specific sectors, and finally ends with an individual issuer and security. This top-down approach starts with a broad perspective and ends with a narrow analysis of specific stock and bond issues.

Figure 16.1 illustrates the analytic steps as an inverted pyramid.

Two purposes are achieved by this approach. First is the determination of the outlook for major economic forces, such as aggregate demand and inflation, that will impact simultaneously all the bonds or stocks in large segments of the money and capital markets. Determining the trend of broad forces, such as corporate profitability, short- and long-term interest rates, and the money supply, puts the analyst in a better position to evaluate the relative impact of these external forces on the future performance of individual securities.

Second, the top-down approach permits comparisons between financial markets and between business sectors with respect to the outlook for investment profitability and risks. For example, this comparative analysis indicates

I. Outlook for economic and business conditions in the United States and the world

II. Corporate sector
   Demand for goods and services
   Aggregate cash flow, liquidity
   Profitability

Inflation and other economic forces

III. Money and capital market conditions

IV. A. Outlook in credit markets — short-term and long-term interest rates

   B. Outlook in the equity market

V. Outlook in industrial sectors
   Capital goods producers
   Consumer durable goods producers
   Consumer nondurable goods producers
   Merchandising
   Growth and technology
   Services
   Mining and minerals
   Transportation
   Regulated utilities

VI. Specific industries

VII. Specific companies

VIII. Specific bond or stock

FIG. 16.1 The Top-Down Approach

how investors should allocate their funds within portfolios between short-term and long-term bonds, between bonds and stocks, and among securities in different industrial sectors. (See Chapters 14 and 17.) Once this major allocation is determined, then a comparative analysis is made of the various industries and companies in those sectors that have been chosen for investment. Industries and corporate issuers in the less attractive sectors are not studied. A drawback to the top-down approach is that certain industries or stocks that offer outstanding profit opportunities may be overlooked. Because of this potential drawback, some analysts and investors select their investments by using the bottom-up approach either alone or in conjunction with the top-down approach.

The Bottom-Up Approach. In the bottom-up approach, several statistically based criteria are used as screens or filters to select securities for possible purchase from a large universe of securities. One screen or several may be used to select stocks from a universe of several thousand stocks. A security research organization may maintain and update its own computerized financial data

bank of a universe of securities or it may subscribe to an outside service that
furnishes computer magnetic tape files, such as the Standard & Poor's Com-
pustat Service or the Value Line Investment Survey. These data banks contain
annual, quarterly, and monthly financial statement items, market prices, volume of shares traded, and so forth for up to 20 years for each company. The
typical data that can be used to establish company screens include:

- The current price-earnings (P/E) ratio as compared to the past five-year average
  P/E ratio (relative P/E ratio);
- The annual growth rate in earnings per share in the latest four quarters as
  compared to the average growth rate in the previous five years (earnings mo-
  mentum);
- The total market value of the common stock outstanding (size of company);
- The percent change in the stock price in the latest 12 months as compared to the
  percentage change in the previous 12 months (relative price strength);
- Stock beta over the past five years;
- The standard deviation of the stock's monthly rate of return over the past five
  years;
- Stock alpha (described in Chapter 14).

The purpose of these screens is to identify stocks having specific risk
characteristics and the potential for above average rates of return that may
meet the portfolio requirements of the accounts under management. For example, if an analyst is selecting stocks for an aggressive growth account when the
outlook for the stock market appears favorable, he establishes criteria screens
so stocks selected have a relatively low P/E ratio, increasing earnings momen-
tum, small company size, strong relative price strength, high beta, positive
alpha, and high standard deviation. The computer then searches through the
data file for stocks that meet the specific threshold levels of these criteria. The
number of stocks identified depends on the stringency of the criteria threshold
levels and the number of stocks in the data bank universe. Once the stocks have
been identified, a fundamental analysis of the companies is conducted to determine whether their outlook is favorable. The final selection of stocks that are to
be purchased or retained in the investment accounts is based on this analysis.
The process of using computer runs may be repeated weekly, monthly, or
quarterly, depending on the time interval used to screen securities in the portfolio accounts.

Security Coding System. Investors that use either the top-down approach
or the bottom-up approach may be accomodated by a security analysis reporting system that uses summary statistics and codes to report on each security. A
security coding system can provide guidance to investors with different objectives and different approaches to security analysis. A typical report lists the
securities being continually monitored, disclosing summary statistics similar to
the screens described previously together with codes that reveal the expected
investment return potential and a risk quality rating for each security. The

investor or account manager then relies on the coding system to make security decisions.

ANALYSIS OF THE EXTERNAL ENVIRONMENT

Because one-third or more of the investment returns from the typical stock or bond is affected by broad economic and industrial forces, the investor or security analyst needs to identify these relevant forces and make projections into the future. An analyst employing the top-down approach begins the analysis of the external environment by examining first the outlook for broad economic forces and second the outlook for various industries. By making projections of these relevant forces — their direction, probable magnitude, and possible effects on corporations and on the returns of their securities — the analyst is in a better position to make investment decisions. Based on the outlook for these external forces, the investor or analyst is better able to determine the extent to which portfolios should allocate funds to the bond market, the stock market, major submarket sectors, and various industries.

Analysis of Economic Forces

Only those broad economic forces that affect corporate financial performance and investment returns, particularly forces that may affect the industries in which there is a probable investment interest, are important. Broad forces that will materially affect future corporate earnings and future payments of interest and dividends to corporate investors should be studied. Consequently, the analyst is interested in the forces that affect demand for corporate products and services, product prices, costs and availability of labor, energy, materials, capital expenditures, corporate taxes, the cost and availability of external funds, and so on, are all of interest.

Because the health, growth, and fluctuations of the economy have a major, direct influence as well as a ripple effect on corporate performance, a complete analysis examines the forces that affect the economy. Some of the major forces affecting investment risk and return opportunities are as follows:

1 The growth and the age composition of the population provide indications regarding both consumers and labor. For example, growth in the young population produces a less skilled labor force, growth in the elderly population entails attrition in the labor force through retirement, while growth in the middle-aged, educated population results in more skilled and productive labor. Likewise, on the consumer demand side, growth in family formations and in the birth rate foreshadows a future demand for durable consumer goods, such as home appliances, cars, housing, and public schools; growth in the elderly population is manifested in a demand for health-care services, leisure-time entertainment, and retirement funding.

2 Resources spent on training, education, research, technological developments, and other innovations lead to

a New and better products and services, and, as such, induce or create their own demand for corporate services; and

b More efficient (lower cost) production of goods and services.

Examples of the first type of innovations are the development of computer games, color television, cable television, and life-saving drugs, which create their own consumer demand. But this demand also displaces other products, such as simpler games, monochrome television, theaters, and hospital care. The second type of innovations includes robotics, microcomputers, and telecommunication systems which reduce corporate operating expenses and increase labor productivity, but also create technological obsolescence of assets and structural unemployment. The United States is spending about $100 billion in various types of research and development. Expenditures on education and training help people to become more skilled and economically productive.

3 An economy that allocates adequate new capital at reasonable financial costs to the private sector fosters growth in corporate output and profits. New capital is needed to invest in plant, equipment, inventory, and to modernize and replace obsolete assets, to reduce operating costs and increase productivity, and to finance the purchase of consumer durable goods and housing. A depressed stock market and high inflation rates, interest rates, taxes, and government deficits tend to crowd out private capital formation and impede growth in the corporate sector, and vice versa.

4 The discovery of and access to raw materials, natural resources, and energy sources are essential to fuel the economic engine and provide the substances needed to fabricate capital and consumer goods. Technological discoveries of new synthetics, new sources of energy, desalting of water, recycling of materials, and purification of coal are some examples of potential exploitations of untapped resources that can encourage industrial growth.

5 International acceptance of the law of comparative advantage, which provides for the free flow of capital and goods across national borders, fosters investment opportunities and the discipline of healthy international competition. If the world continues to become more economically integrated, the geographic horizons of security analysis will broaden.

6 A capstone factor is a society's commitment to growth in economic productivity and to a strong free market system. Behavioral scientists argue that people are the most valuable resource in a society or in a corporation. If so, an economy will prosper if those associated with it are informed, educated, and possess the desire, discipline, and spirit to support high standards of performance. The public commitment of a society can change over time with societies flourishing, maturing, and sometimes stagnating. The great empires of Egypt, Athens, China, Rome, Spain, France, and England declined in greatness because of a deterioration in moral commitment, misdirected leadership, or an inability to adapt to new competitive forces. The U.S. society has thus far adjusted to and exploited new economic opportunities reasonably well. However, the past is no guarantee of the future inasmuch as a society continually arrives at crossroads. The public can commit itself to creating a better society through honest work, freedom of choice, initiative, and creation of wealth; or it can become preoccupied with demanding more from government and from employers than it is willing to pay for in taxes and hard work; or it can become preoccupied with the socialistic redistribution of wealth and with excessive intervention of government in our private lives. Consequently, the analyst needs to be alert to social trends, such as changes in government policies, labor productivity, inflation, unemployment, and social discontent, in each country in which he invests.

The relationships between the performance of aggregate economic activity and the performance of corporate activity also must be examined. Based on empirical evidence, a general positive relationship exists in the trends of economic activity, aggregate corporate sales, corporate earnings, and stock prices. After taking into account short-term lead-lag relationships, these four variables tend to rise and fall together. With occasional exceptions, stock prices and corporate earnings tend to decline in advance of or quite early in the downturn in the business cycle; stock prices tend to recover in the late stages of the recession, with earnings beginning to rise in the latter part of the recession or in the early part of the business recovery. The stock market and corporate earnings are so sensitive to economic activity that they sometimes decline when economic growth merely slows or levels off. Therefore, in projecting corporate performance, the *rate of change* in economic activity must be considered as well as whether the economic trend will be up or down.

The stock prices and earnings of some companies are more sensitive to changes in aggregate activity than those of other companies. At one end of the continuum, the sales and earnings of steel and automobile manufacturers are closely tied to the business cycle; at the other end, the earnings of tobacco, beer, and cosmetic companies are much more closely tied to the cost of raw materials or advertising expenses. Therefore, projecting the sales and earnings of individual industries and companies requires an understanding of the nature of their relation to aggregate business activity in order to determine how much weight to place on forecasts of external aggregate forces.

Investors buy and sell securities on the basis of their expectations of future changes in economic activity because they realize that changes in economic trends affect corporate sales, earnings, and dividend payments. Consequently, stock price changes tend to lead changes in business activity by several months. Therefore, the trends in gross national product, aggregate corporate profits, monetary conditions, government fiscal policy, and inflation should be forecast sufficiently in advance to anticipate turning points in stock prices and corporate earnings and thereby allow investment decisions to be made in a timely fashion. Broad external forces must be projected at least four months ahead, but preferably one to several years ahead.

Forecasting Techniques. A variety of methods are used to forecast the cyclical and long-term trends of business conditions, but none of them are perfect. In fact, a high degree of accuracy cannot be expected from business forecasts whether they represent the work of one analyst or a consensus of economists. Nevertheless, as inaccurate as business forecasts (particularly those made at economic turning points) may be, investment decisions are likely to be better when they are based on a careful analysis of full and current information regarding changing business conditions.

Leading Economic Indicators. The leading economic indicator approach was developed by the National Bureau of Economic Research. Economic time series are chosen as leading indicators, coincident indicators, or lagging indicators, depending on whether the indicator *tends* to change direction before (lead), at the same time (coincident), or after (lag) general economic activity changes direction. These series are reported monthly by the U.S. Bureau of the Census in *Business Conditions Digest*. The Standard & Poor's Composite Stock Index and corporate profits are two relatively reliable lead indicators; they tend to turn 4 to 12 months in advance of turns in the business cycle.

If the purpose of forecasting the business cycle is to take advantage of the stock market cycle, then other indicators that provide a longer lead time than the stock market must be observed. The new housing building permits series tends to turn up slightly earlier than the stock market with respect to business expansions. Indicators that tend to turn down earlier with respect to business expansions are the average workweek, initial claims for unemployment insurance, housing building permits, corporate profits, and the ratio of product prices to labor costs.

Two difficulties in using lead indicators are that the lead time can vary considerably from one cycle to another and that indicators can sometimes give false signals by changing direction for a few months without a subsequent change in the business or stock market cycle. If more investors follow an indicator, its lead time could become very short relative to the stock market cycle.

Correlation Method. To predict the trends of corporate sales and earnings performance, causal factors or variables that help to explain these trends are sought. Based on research, some analysts consider trends in the following data as indicative of corporate performance: changes in gross national product, business inventories, bond interest rates, the money supply, inflation rate, durable goods orders, plant utilization rate, and federal fiscal policies. An analyst forecasts the performance of corporations by observing and projecting those variables that are considered to be causal in nature. This correlation of causal and dependent variables can be made by the analyst in a subjective judgmental fashion or by a formal econometric or statistical regression model.

Survey Method. Whether analysts admit it or not, one of the most common ways an analyst develops expectations regarding the future is by studying the forecasts of other informed analysts. There are many forecasts of economic and corporate activity. Projections are made and reported by economic analysts employed in the government, banks, universities, brokerage firms, financial publishing firms, trade associations, and business firms. An analyst or investor may rely on forecasters because they are intelligent, have more professional training and experience in using forecasting techniques, or spend more time on this task than he does. A limitation to this survey method is that some forecasters are more talented than others, forecasters can disagree with one another, and the majority of forecasters are sometimes quite wrong at critical turning points in the economy.

Forecasters on Wall Street are sometimes infected by crowd psychology. It is obviously preferable to follow contrary opinions on those occasions when the majority are wrong. The survey method can be used intelligently by checking the reliability of past projections made by forecasters and studying the facts with a critical eye (including assumptions, steps of analysis, underlying reasons, and techniques employed by a forecaster to support his conclusions). In this fashion, insight into the depth and quality of analysis is gained, and the reasonableness of the assumptions and the soundness of the reasoning can be considered. Finally, the critical surveyor is free to disagree with the assumptions on the basis of the facts and to draw his own conclusions.

Industry Analysis

Once projections regarding the broad external forces have been made to determine how investment funds should be allocated to bonds, stocks, and their major submarket sectors, the next step in the top-down approach is to analyze the specific forces that affect the financial performance of individual industries in order to select suitable industries for investment.

The analysis of industries is important for several reasons. For the purpose of portfolio risk diversification, it is necessary to determine the degree to which the financial performance of a particular industry correlates over time both with aggregate corporate performance and with other industries. For example, if the economy is expected to expand strongly, then the analyst considers selecting industries, such as the building industry, that are expected to produce a financial performance that correlates with the economic expansion, that is, industries that participate in the economic expansion. Conversely, if the economy is expected to contract, then the analyst considers industries, such as the drug industry, that are expected to perform on the basis of favorable special developments that are unique to those industries, that is, industries in which the industry performance has a low correlation or interrelationship with aggregate business activity. (This tactic, in effect, diversifies against aggregate business risk.)

An understanding of how the performance of each industry correlates over time with other industries is also needed to control or limit the concentration of risks in portfolios. If, for example, the financial performances of the construction, steel, and automobile industries are significantly correlated over time, then these relationships must be considered when deciding what proportion of a portfolio's funds are to be allocated to this particular economic sector. If the correlation between the food and electronic industries is low, then investment in these two industries reduces a portfolio's total risk.

Another major reason for industry analysis is that companies that are attractive investments tend to be found in industries with favorable investment characteristics. Consequently an efficient way to find attractive investments is to identify industries with a favorable outlook. It was found, for example, that a very significant portion of the earnings performance of individual oil companies and department stores are correlated with the earnings performance of their respective industries. On the other hand, to overlook companies that have an attractive outlook in industries where a company's earnings have a low correlation with industry earnings. Also, multi-industry companies and companies that have no apparent industry classification should not be overlooked.

Several methods used to determine the outlook for an industry's sales, profits, and investment security returns are described in the following sections. It should be kept in mind that the basic approach to the analysis of an industry needs to be adapted to any unique or peculiar characteristics that exist in a particular industry. Research and development and patent protection, for example, are very important in high technology industries; the regulatory climate concerning pricing or rate-making decisions are important in regulated industries; interest rate levels are important in capital-intensive industries; sales promotion and distribution is important in consumer products industries; repair services are important in the durable goods industries; labor relations are important in labor intensive industries; and environmental pollution control is important in waste producing industries.

Correlation Method. To use the correlation method, it is necessary to find and forecast independent variables that influence, explain, or are associated with an industry's sales, earnings, and investment returns. In making projections for an industry's sales, an analyst searches for variables that provide a logical explanation, such as these obvious examples:

Independent Variable	Industry Sales
Temperatures during the winter	Heating oil and gas
Birth rate	Baby food and toys
High temperatures and humidity during the summer	Beer
Growth in the population of teenagers and young adults	Soft drinks
Improvements in the interstate highway and urban expressway systems	Gasoline and diesel fuel

In the case of multiple correlations, two or more independent variables should be identified. To project drug industry sales and profits, for example, an analyst might hypothesize that they are influenced by these variables:

1 Growth in the segments of the population prone to illness and accidents and in need of medication, such as the elderly and the young.

2 Growth in research expenditures for the discovery of more effective drugs.

3 The average time interval taken by the Food and Drug Administration to license new drugs for distribution.

4 Severity of the winter season and viral epidemics.

5 Government expenditure for health-care programs such as Medicare and Medicaid.

$$\text{Net profit margin} = \frac{\text{Net income}}{\text{Net sales}} = \frac{\$104,000}{\$900,000} = 0.1156 \text{ or } 11.56\%$$

This ratio measures the company's operating efficiency after all operating expenses and income taxes are subtracted from gross profit.

Rate of Return on Common Equity. The rate of return on common equity is calculated by dividing net income available for common stock (net income after taxes minus preferred dividends) by average common equity.

$$\text{Return on common equity} = \frac{\text{Net income for common stock}}{\text{Average common equity}}$$

$$= \frac{\$94,000}{\$500,000} = 0.188 \text{ or } 18.8\%$$

This ratio is very important to common stockholders because it measures the return earned on their invested capital.

Rate of Return on Operating Assets. Operating assets are total assets minus intangible assets. In this equation operating assets are divided into net income after taxes.

$$\text{Return on operating assets} = \frac{\text{Net income}}{\text{Average operating assets}}$$

$$= \frac{\$104,000}{\$1,000,000} = 0.104 \text{ or } 10.4\%$$

The rate of return on operating assets indicates the overall operating efficiency of a company.

In addition to the preceding profitability ratios, analysts sometime calculate the rate of return on net worth and the rate of return on the capital structure. The main purpose of calculating these ratios is to show the impact of financial leverage on the rate of return and risk. The changes to the earnings before interest and taxes (EBIT) for Husky Company, as shown in Table 16.5, illustrate that financial leverage can magnify gains and losses. For example, in the first case, when EBIT increased 50 percent from the original $230,000, the rate of return on common equity increased more than 50 percent. On the other hand, when EBIT decreased 50 percent, the rate of return on common equity decreased from 18.8 to 6.8 percent, which is more than a 50 percent decrease. The magnification of gains and losses is also reflected in the earnings per share for common stockholders. Therefore, the analysis of securities for investment purposes is not complete without a study of the impact of financial leverage on the risk and return on capital invested in a business enterprise.

After all necessary financial ratios have been calculated for a particular company, the next important task is to make comparisons. First, the trend and stability of those ratios over long time periods should be examined because ratios for only one period may be misleading. Trend comparisons add depth to the analysis because they look at several years, thus helping to determine the

TABLE 16.5   Return on Common Equity as Affected by Leverage

	No Changes in EBIT	50% Increase in EBIT	50% Decrease in EBIT
Earnings before interest and taxes	$230,000	$345,000	$115,000
Interest paid on bonds	(30,000)	(30,000)	(30,000)
Earnings before taxes	$200,000	$315,000	$ 85,000
Income taxes (48%)	(96,000)	(151,200)	(40,800)
Net income after taxes	$104,000	$163,800	$ 44,200
Preferred dividends	(10,000)	(10,000)	(10,000)
Net income for common stock	$ 94,000	$153,800	$ 34,200
Return on common equity	18.8%	30.8%	6.8%
Earnings per share	$4.70	$7.69	$1.71

degree of stability in the operating performance of the company. Next, the ratios of the company under study should be compared with the ratios of similar companies in the same industry. Finally, the overall performance of the studied company should be compared with the performance of the industry and, where appropriate, with the performance of the economy.

Per Share Statistics — Analysis and Forecasting

Once the financial condition and operating efficiency of a company have been analyzed, the next tasks are to analyze the trends and stability of the per share statistics and to forecast future trends. The major per share statistics for analyzing common stocks are (1) earnings per share, (2) cash flow per share, (3) dividends per share, (4) dividend payout ratio, (5) P/E ratio, (6) book value per share, and (7) the ratio of market price to book value per share. These values are calculated here for Husky Company. (It is assumed that the market price per share of Husky Company is $35.)

$$\text{Earnings per share} = \frac{\text{Net income for common stock}}{\text{Average number of shares outstanding}} = \frac{\$94,000}{20,000} = \$4.70$$

$$\text{Cash flow per share} = \frac{\text{Net income for common stock plus depreciation}}{\text{Average number of shares outstanding}}$$

$$= \frac{\$94,000 + \$20,000}{20,000} = \$5.70$$

$$\text{Dividend per share} = \frac{\text{Dividends paid}}{\text{Average number of shares outstanding}} = \frac{\$40,000}{20,000} = \$2.00$$

$$\text{Dividend pay-out ratio} = \frac{\text{Dividend per share}}{\text{Earnings per share}} = \frac{\$2.00}{\$4.70} = 0.426 \text{ or } 42.6\%$$

$$\text{P/E ratio} = \frac{\text{Market price per share}}{\text{Earnings per share}} = \frac{\$35.00}{\$4.70} = 7.4$$

$$\text{Book value per share} = \frac{\text{Total common equity}}{\text{Average number of shares outstanding}}$$

$$= \frac{\$500,000}{20,000} = \$25.00$$

$$\text{Ratio of market price to book value} = \frac{\text{Market price per share}}{\text{Book value per share}}$$

$$= \frac{\$35.00}{\$25.00} = 1.4 \text{ or } 140\%$$

The trend and stability of the earnings per share must be determined. If the earnings per share fluctuates very widely, this may have a negative impact on the trend in the market price and, therefore on the returns for the investor. The higher the volatility in earnings per share, the higher the risk. In the case of cash flow per share, a more complete picture of the company's profitability is desirable. Cash flow per share includes not only earnings per share, but also such arbitrary items as depreciation, depletion, and other noncash expenses.

The trends, stability, and growth in dividend payments, as well as the payout ratio, must be considered. Some investors prefer a high payout ratio and great stability in dividend payment because of their need for income. On the other hand, some investors prefer smaller dividends, with the company reinvesting more earnings for future growth.

The P/E ratio, sometimes called the earnings multiplier, is a function of the quality and expected future growth in earnings. Usually, investors pay more for a common stock if earnings are expected to increase substantially.

The final important per share statistic is the book value per share, and particularly its relationship to the market price. In the case of Husky Company, the ratio of market price to book value per share is 1.4. This indicates that investors are willing to pay a 40 percent premium over the book value. In some cases, book value per share may be misleading because of different accounting methods used to value inventory and compute depreciation. On the other hand, the book value per share of some firms, such as commercial banks, may be a more reliable measure of value because of the nature of their assets. In the case of commercial banks, the ratio of market price to book value normally is close to 1.0.

A very important task in stock analysis is estimating or forecasting the future benefits of owning a security. The choice of any security for an investment portfolio is influenced largely by expectations about the company's potential. Several methods used to determine the outlook for a company's future sales, earnings, and investment return are discussed briefly here.

The forecasting of the future potential for a company usually starts with forecasting its sales. The sales forecast generally relies on the relationship of a company's sales to various external and internal variables. Major external factors are: (1) general economic condition; (2) disposable personal income; (3) level of interest rates, particularly if the company sells durable goods; (4) competitive position of the company in its industry; (5) product or services substitution; and (6) other economic and industry factors that influence demand for a company's products and/or services. The following internal factors are usually important: (1) the nature and quality of product and/or services; (2) innovation and improvements of products; (3) activities in promotion of sales; (4) services provided to customers, in the case of durable goods; (5) productive capacity and efficiency; and (6) availability of the product at the right time and the right place.

The next step is forecasting earnings and dividends of a company. Estimating earnings requires thorough examination of such factors as (1) rate of change of the company's sales; (2) cost of raw material and energy; (3) cost of labor, including fringe benefits; (4) other operating and administrative expenses; (5) extraordinary income and expenses; (6) depreciation; (7) interest payments; and (8) income taxes. In addition, future capital investment, financing methods, and their impact on the company's operating performance should be considered. Finally, the kind of accounting policies and practices being followed by the company should be examined, because different accounting practices may significantly affect the quality of reported earnings.

In estimating dividends, the following factors should be examined: (1) outlook for and stability of the company's earnings; (2) outlook for liquidity; (3) need for future financing; (4) legal restrictions on a company's dividend policies, such as capital impairment rules and maintenance of retained earnings and working capital; and (5) attitude of management with regard to dividend policies.

Methods of forecasting the future potential of a company vary from a simple, naive projection type to sophisticated econometric models. For example, some analysts perform their forecasts by calculating the annual percentage changes for each year over some past time period (such as 5 to 10 years), then making a forecast on the expectation that the future trend will be similar to the past one. Graphically, the trend analysis may be made by drawing a freehand line through past periodic observations. Here the analyst plots company's sales or earnings on semilog paper in order to get a picture of how these observations have been changing proportionally over time. The slope of the freehand line is equivalent to the compounded growth rate over the period being investigated. These trend lines may be used to estimate future sales or earnings.

Regression and correlation analysis also may be used to forecast a company's sales and earnings. In performing a regression analysis, the analyst uses a company's sales or earnings as a dependent variable and selects external or internal variables (listed previously) as independent or explanatory variables. This method is used to estimate a regression equation showing the structural relationship that existed in the past between explanatory variables and a dependent variable. For example, disposable personal income and the level of interest rate can be used as the explanatory variables for a company's sales of durable goods, the dependent variable. Once the regression model has been estimated with past data and the level of statistical significance has been determined, the model can then be used to estimate future sales or earnings for the company.

Usually the closer the relationship between two variables, the greater the confidence that may be placed on the estimate. For example, if it is found that the correlation between a company's sales and disposable personal income is very close to one, then the degree of the relationship is very strong. Thus more confidence can be placed on a sales estimate that is based on disposable personal income. If the correlation between sales and another variable is close to zero, this indicates no relationship, and this variable cannot be used to estimate sales. On the other hand, if the correlation between sales and some other variable is close to minus one, then an inverse relationship exists; if this variable is moving up, then sales are expected to go down, and vice versa.

In utilizing these forecasting techniques, it is assumed that past relationships will be similar in the future. Frequently, however, the past may not be a good predictor of the future. Therefore, in making any prediction of a company's sales, earnings, and investment return the process of forecasting just described (which is based on historical information) should be modified by subjective forecasting based on seasoned judgment.

Several methods that can be used to forecast the future performance of companies are described here. Other analytical forecasting techniques, such as time series analysis and probabilistic forecasting, are discussed in books on business forecasting and econometric statistics.

VALUATION OF COMMON STOCKS

The purpose of owning common stocks as investments is to receive a return in the form of cash dividend payments and market price appreciation. To enjoy the opportunity of a return, investment risks must be assumed by the investor. Therefore, the objectives of investors are to seek a return from stocks and to limit risk of loss. At the very heart of the investment selection process is the task of estimating the rate of return expected from individual investments within some planning time horizon and estimating the level of risks or probabilities of receiving this return. The two parameters — expected return and risk — are vitally linked to determine the value of a stock, as shown in Figure 16.2. Within the context of security analysis, this value is variously referred to as the estimated investment value, intrinsic value, true value, or present value.

The position of the traditional or fundamental analytical school of thought is that the market fluctuates widely around the true value, so that the price is sometimes above and at other times below its value. According to this view, the task of the security analyst is to estimate the value of a security through an independent analysis of the corporate issuer, its industry, and the external environment. The results of this analysis enable the analyst to recommend the possible purchase of a stock that is undervalued (i.e., the market price is below the estimated value), because the security offers a high expected return, or to recommend the possible sale of a stock that is overvalued, because the security offers a low or negative expected return.

The position of the efficient market hypothesis (EMH) school is that the current market price is the best available estimate of a stock's true value. The argument used to support this position is that many investors and analysts analyze all relevant information regarding investments as soon as it becomes available and act promptly on the information, so stock prices adjust quickly to the value estimated by these intelligent and fully informed market participants.

The EMH comprises three different versions. The weak form asserts that

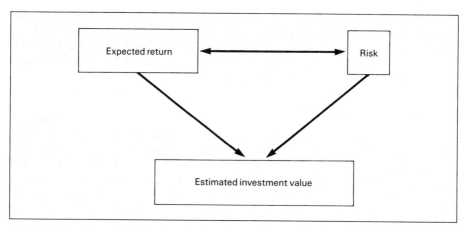

FIG. 16.2 The Three Major Variables in the Analysis of a Security

the information conveyed by past market price fluctuations in a stock are fully reflected in the stock's current market price. The weak form of the EMH contradicts the technical market analysis approach, which claims that future price changes in a stock can be predicted by reading and interpreting the graph charts of past stock price cycles. Considerable empirical statistical evidence amassed in support of the weak form tends to refute the ability to make investment profits (after the payment of brokerage commissions) on the basis of predictions that rely on commonly used technical market analysis decision rules.

The semistrong form of the EMH asserts that all publicly disclosed information is promptly reflected in stock prices at the time it is announced. This challenges the usefulness of fundamental research analysis. The approach of fundamental analysis is to gather and analyze information about the economy, industries, companies, and securities; to interpret this data; to apply judgments about the future; and to identify stocks that are undervalued or overvalued. Many studies have tested the semistrong form; however, the research findings have mixed conclusions. Many studies have shown that fundamental security recommendations do not produce superior returns, while some other more recent studies have revealed that selected research organizations and fundamental methods have produced superior stock returns.

The strong form of the EMH asserts that professional portfolio managers are unable to produce consistently superior portfolio returns after the deduction of management fees and security transaction costs. To test this hypothesis, studies analyze the performance over many years of large numbers of professionally managed portfolios, such as mutual funds. These studies observe that some portfolios do appear to produce superior returns consistently over time, but their number out of the total sample of portfolios is not large enough to reject the statistical test of significance that these outliers occurred by chance alone. On the other hand, it could be argued that there are some superior managers, but formal statistical tests cannot disprove it.

Based on the tests of the various versions of the EMH, a widely held view is that the prices in the stock market do not always reflect true values, but that security analysts have to engage in careful, thorough, and timely research in order to uncover undervalued stocks. This is to say that the market is highly efficient, but it is not always perfectly efficient.

Estimated Investment Value

The most widely recognized theory explaining investment value is the present value theory. This theory is used routinely by bond investors through the application of bond value tables, by lenders through present value tables, and by insurers through annuity tables. Professional investors in common stocks are increasingly recognizing the relevance of this theory and are applying it by the use of dividend discount models. Accordingly, the value placed on a stock is determined by the expected size and timing of future cash payments, and by the level of risk or uncertainty associated with such payments. At the fulcrum of each fundamental investment decision to buy, hold, or sell are three parameters: the present value (estimated investment value), the estimated future cash payments, and the expected rate of return or discount rate. Using a dividend discount model, the estimated worth of a stock to an investor is equal to the sum of the discounted future cash payments expected. Mathematically, this may be expressed as:

$$V_0 = \frac{D_1}{(1 + r)^1} + \frac{D_2}{(1 + r)^2} + \cdots + \frac{D_n}{(1 + r)^n} + \frac{V_n}{(1 + r)^n} \qquad (16.1)$$

where: V_0 = estimated present value *or* current market price

D = expected future dividend payments in years 1, 2, and so on through year n

r = expected or assumed rate of return or discount rate in years 1, 2, and so on through year n, which is determined by the degree of uncertainty of future cash payments

n = final year of the investment holding period or of the planning time horizon

V_n = expected present value or stock price at the end of year n

This equation may be illustrated by a simple example. Assume that the Husky Company paid an annual divided of $1.00 last year; that the company and its dividends are growing at 8 percent per year; and that the investor expects a rate of return of 13 percent and plans to hold the stock for two years then sell it at a price level to provide a dividend yield of 5 percent. Therefore, the dividend rate is expected to be $1.08 in the first year ($1.00 × 1.08) and $1.17 in the second year ($1.08 × 1.08). The stock price at the end of the second year is expected to be $25.20. (Values are rounded to the nearest cent to simplify the example.)

$$\frac{D_3}{V_2} = 0.05$$

$$\frac{\$1.17(1.08)}{V_2} = 0.05$$

$$V_2 = \frac{\$1.26}{0.05}$$

$$V_2 = \$25.20$$

The estimated investment value or present value of Husky Company is:

$$V_0 = \frac{\$1.08}{(1.13)^1} + \frac{\$1.17}{(1.13)^2} + \frac{\$25.20}{(1.13)^2}$$

$$V_0 = \$0.96 + \$0.92 + \$19.74$$

$$V_0 = \$21.62$$

If the investor purchases the stock at $21.62, receives dividends of $1.08 and $1.17 in each of the next two years, and sells the stock at the end of that time at $25.20, he will earn an average annual rate of return of 13 percent.

This discount rate of 13 percent is equal to the expected rate of return only if the stock is purchased at $21.62. Investors who believe that market prices tend to be efficient accept the current market price of a stock as being a correct reflection of the market consensus and assume that it is equal to the estimated present value. The discount rate r then becomes the unknown variable in the equation. If the Husky Company stock sells at $21.92, the investor finds through trial and error, that the discount rate is 12 percent.

$$\$21.92 = \frac{\$1.08}{(1 + r)^1} + \frac{\$1.17}{(1 + r)^2} + \frac{\$25.20}{(1 + r)^3}$$

$$r = 0.12$$

On the other hand, fundamental analysts, who believe that the market is not efficient and that market prices fluctuate above and below the true values, seek to purchase undervalued stocks. Under these circumstances, the analyst selects a discount rate for a stock that is considered to be appropriate. The appropriate discount rate is frequently considered to be composed of three components:

i = real or riskless interest rate, which is adjusted for and free from inflation and other investment risks.

f = inflation premium, which is the inflation rate in the general price level for goods and services.

k = risk premium, which is the additional return required by investors for assuming the risks inherent in the particular investment.

Therefore, the discount rate r for a stock is:

$$r = i + f + k$$

The analyst estimates the three components to find r. There are different ways to find r; the following simple illustration demonstrates one method. Assume that the current short-term U.S. Treasury bill interest rate reflects the real interest rate plus the expected inflation rate. The Treasury bill rate is 8 percent, but is expected to drop to 7 percent and stay around that level over the next several years. The expected inflation rate is 4 percent. Therefore, the real rate of interest is assumed to be 3 percent. An analysis of the risks of the Husky Company and its stock leads to the conclusion that it requires a risk premium of 6 percent. Therefore, the stock's discount rate should be 13 percent:

$$r = 0.03 + 0.04 + 0.06$$

$$r = 0.013 \text{ or } 13\%$$

Under these circumstances, Husky Company stock should be purchased at a price of $21.62, or less, so as to provide a discount rate of 13 percent or more. If the price of the stock is $21.24, the stock is considered undervalued and the expected return is 14 percent:

$$\$21.24 = \frac{\$1.08}{(1 + r)^1} + \frac{\$1.17}{(1 + r)^2} + \frac{\$25.20}{(1 + r)^2}$$

$$r = 0.14 \text{ or } 14\%$$

In this instance, the expected rate of return is equal to the three components of the discount rate plus a fourth component (denoted as a), variously referred to as a stock's alpha, abnormal return, or risk-adjusted return:

$$r = i + f + k + a$$

$$r = 0.03 + 0.04 + 0.06 + 0.01$$

$$r = 0.14 \text{ or } 14\%$$

In the case of Husky Company, the alpha of 1 percent is an additional return expected to occur when the stock price rises to the estimated sale price of $25.20 during the investor's planning time horizon of two years.

The estimated sale price or terminal value of $25.20 for Husky Company stock is an important figure in determining investment values. This terminal value is nothing more than the present value of the stock two years from now based on the discounted level of dividends that are expected to be paid in the third and subsequent years.

Constant Growth Model. Equation 16.1 can be greatly simplified for companies whose cash dividend rates are expected to grow at a constant rate, which tends to be true for stable or mature companies. The estimated investment value or present value of such a stock is:

$$V_0 = \frac{D_1}{r - g} \tag{16.2}$$

where: g = expected average annual rate of growth in dividends per share

   D_1 = dividends per share expected during the next four quarters

If the dividends of Husky Company are expected to grow at a stable rate of 8 percent, its estimated present value is $21.60:

$$V_0 = \frac{\$1.08}{0.13 - 0.08}$$

$$V_0 = \$21.60$$

The dividend growth rate for a company is forecast by estimating the company's future internal rate of return on equity capital and the company's dividend payout ratio or its complement, the earnings retention ratio. The growth rate is equal to the internal rate of return multiplied by the retention ratio:

$$g = RB$$

where: R = net income of the company as a percentage of the company's net worth equity capital

B = percentage of net income retained and reinvested in the company (and not paid out as dividends)

If Husky Company's expected internal rate of return is 20 percent and its retention ratio is 40 percent, then its growth rate is 8 percent.

$$g = (0.20)(0.40)$$

$$g = 0.08$$

Earnings Multiplier Model.   Because corporate earnings are the primary source of funds with which a going concern pays dividends over the long run, many analysts estimate the investment value of stocks by relating earnings per share to stock prices in the form of P/E ratios. The P/E ratio (*PER*) as calculated for a stock is equal to the current market price (P_0) divided by the expected earnings per share (E_1):

$$PER = \frac{P_0}{E_1} \tag{16.3}$$

If the market price of Husky Company stock is $19 3/4 and its expected earnings are $1.80, then its P/E ratio is 11.0:

$$PER = \frac{\$19.75}{\$\ 1.80}$$

$$PER = 11.0$$

Closely related to the P/E ratio is the earnings multiplier that is used to estimate a stock's true value. The investment value for a stock is equal to the *normalized* annual earnings per share expected in the next four quarters (E_1) multiplied by a selected earnings multiplier (M):

$$V_0 = (E_1)(M) \tag{16.4}$$

The normalized earnings per share is the expected reported earnings corrected for nonrecurring accounting type distortions and abnormal business cycle aberrations. A multiplier is selected based on two variables: (1) the expected future growth rate of earnings per share and (2) the riskiness of earnings per share. The relations of both these variables in the valuation process may be seen by a derivation of the equation for the constant growth model (Equation 16.2):

$$V_0 = \frac{D_1}{r - g}$$

If both sides of this equation are divided by E_1, the result is the earnings multiplier M:

$$\frac{V_0}{E_1} = \frac{D_1/E_1}{r - g} \tag{16.5}$$

It was noted in Equation 16.4 that

$$V_0 = (E_1)(M)$$

So,

$$\frac{V_0}{E_1} = M$$

Therefore,

$$M = \frac{D_1/E_1}{r - g} = \frac{p}{r - g}$$

Consequently, the earnings multiplier (within the simplified context of constant growth) is equal to the dividend payout ratio (p) divided by the discount factor ($r - g$). The multiplier is, therefore, positively correlated to both the earnings growth rate and the payout ratio; that is, the higher the payout ratio or the higher the growth, then the higher the multiplier should be. Likewise, the multiplier is negatively correlated with the discount rate; that is, the greater the riskiness of the stock or the higher the rate of return required, then the lower the multiplier should be.

If, for example, Husky Company stock has a dividend rate of $1.08, normalized earnings per share of $1.80, a discount rate of 13 percent, and a growth rate of 8 percent, then its multiplier is 12.0:

$$M = \frac{\$1.08/\$1.80}{0.13 - 0.08} = \frac{0.60}{0.05}$$

$$M = 12.0$$

The estimated value of Husky Company stock is $21.60:

$$V_0 = (\$1.80)(12.0)$$

$$V_0 = \$21.60$$

If the price of Husky Company stock is $19 3/4 and sells at a P/E ratio of 11 times earnings, the stock is undervalued because its earnings multiplier (the expected P/E ratio) is 12 times earnings.

Investment Risk

An important task of security analysis is the classification of stocks on the basis of risk measures. The expected rate of return and the probability distribution of returns for a stock are subject to several different risks. These risks need to be identified so investors may select stocks to diversify their portfolios and protect against excessive risks. Modern portfolio theory has contributed a methodology by which the various risks of common stocks may be controlled within the context of constructing portfolios. To construct a suitably diversified portfolio, the investor needs to rely on several inputs that are generated from the security analysis process. Within the context of modern portfolio theory, risk is measured as the volatility, variability, or standard deviation of expected rates of returns of stocks over a relevant time period. The standard deviation (S) is a convenient statistic used to measure the dispersion or deviations of individual values from the average or mean of their values. For example, the average annual (geometric) mean return on common stocks, as measured by the Standard & Poor's Composite Stock Index, during 1926–1981, was 9.1 percent with a market risk (S_m) of 21.9 percent. Because the distribution of these returns approximates a normal distribution, about two-thirds of the annual returns fell within a range of 9.1 percent ± 21.9 percent, or between 31.0 percent and minus 12.8 percent. This risk measure of approximately 22 percent for the stock market has remained surprisingly constant over the years, so this figure is often used in projecting the risk of the stock market into the future.

Total Risk of a Stock. In like fashion, the total risk of an individual stock (designated as stock i) can be measured as the standard deviation (S_i) of its (monthly, quarterly, or annual) expected rate of return over a particular time period, such as five years. It has been observed that some stocks have higher total risks (higher S_i) than others for a variety of reasons, such as greater volatility of corporate sales, product prices, and earnings or greater operating leverage or financial leverage. Based on modern portfolio theory, stocks with higher risk are expected to have higher expected returns because investors have an aversion to risk and therefore require a higher return or risk premium. This relationship is portrayed in Figure 16.3, which shows rates of return expected by the analyst on the vertical axis and total risk as determined by the analyst on the horizontal axis. A straight line, the security market line (SML), is drawn from the vertical intercept for R_f, the risk-free rate (the U.S. Treasury bill interest rate is frequently used to represent this rate), and the expected return of the stock market index (m). The line slopes upward to reflect the positive risk-return trade-off. Stocks are plotted on the SML if their market prices equal the analyst's estimated investment values. The stocks plotted *on* the SML to the right of the stock market index are riskier than the market, while the stocks *on* the SML to the left of *m* are less risky. Stocks plotted above the SML are estimated to be undervalued and have a positive alpha (positive risk-adjusted return), while those stocks plotted below the SML are overvalued and have a negative alpha. It has been found that this total risk can be dissected into two major risk components: systematic risk and residual risk.

Systematic Risk. Systematic risk measures the sensitivity of the return of a stock (R_i) to the return of a stock market index (R_m) over a period of time. To measure this risk relationship more precisely, the return attributable to a stock's riskiness is frequently adjusted by taking out (subtracting) the risk-free

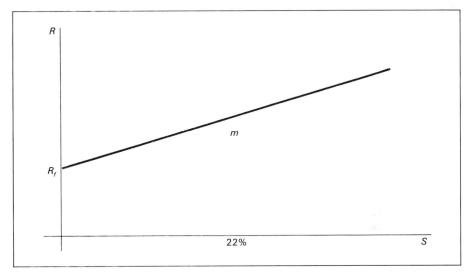

FIG. 16.3 Security Market Line

rate (the Treasury bill interest rate is frequently used for this purpose) in order to compare the excess return of a stock $(R_i - R_f)$ with the excess return of the market $(R_m - R_f)$. This risk relationship for stock i during a time period is shown in Figure 16.4. The periodic excess returns of stock i are plotted on the vertical axis against the same periodic excess returns of the stock market on the horizontal axis. A least square regression line is superimposed on the plot points, which is called the characteristic line. The slope of the characteristic line measures how responsive the return of stock i is to the return of the stock market. This measure of responsiveness or sensitivity is called a stock's beta (B). While the average stock has a beta of 1.00, some stocks have high betas, or very volatile returns, while others have betas less than 1.00, or relatively more stable returns. This systematic risk when coupled with the stock market risk is called a stock's future market risk:

$(B_i)(S_m)$

A stock's future market risk is estimated by analyzing the relationship of the company's underlying financial performance to the broad forces at work in the aggregate business cycle. The beta of each company differs depending on the relationship between: aggregate fluctuations in the economy and a company's product demand, product prices, leverage, and so on. Approximately a third of the average stock's total risk is attributable to the stock's market risk.

Residual Risk. The remaining risk of a stock is the residual risk, that part of the total risk that is not explained by market risk. The residual risk is variously called nonmarket risk, nonsystematic risk, or diversifiable risk. This risk is easier for the investor to control because he can remove as much of it as

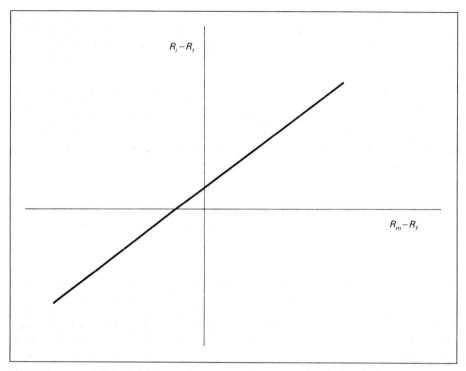

FIG. 16.4 Characteristic Line

he wants from his portfolio by diversifying. Some sources of residual risk for a given stock are:

1 Extramarket covariance
   • Common factors
   • Industry risk
2 Specific risk

Extramarket covariance pertains to those sources of volatility that simultaneously impact the returns of two or more stocks. Industry risk includes those sources that tend to impact all the stocks in the same industry. For example, if the Organization of Petroleum Exporting Countries (OPEC) unexpectedly raised the price of crude oil or if the government decided to raise the import tax on oil, this development would be expected to impact the returns of the stocks of just about all the international crude oil producers. Consequently, it is necessary to be fully aware of industrywide risks and their possible effects on stock returns. Common factors are more subtle in nature because their effects tend to cut across traditional industry lines. Groups of stocks that tend to share different common factors include growth stocks, stable income type stocks, and cyclical stocks. The returns of the stocks within each of these groups tend to move together over time. Cyclical stocks of durable goods companies tend to fluctuate with the outlook of the business cycle, growth stocks tend to fluctuate with the outlook for business growth in the economy, while higher yielding income type stocks may be sensitive to fluctuations in bond interest rates. The outlook for such common factors must be analyzed to determine the risks and expected returns of individual stocks.

The final type of residual risk is specific risk, which is a source of volatility that impacts the return of only one stock. Notable examples include the specific management problems encountered by Penn Central, Lockheed, Chrysler, Equity Funding, and Penn Square Bank. The specific risks associated with each company that is researched must be analyzed to estimate the future return and risk for each stock.

Summary. Modern portfolio theory combines these various sources of risk and return mathematically in a regression model. The expected excess return of stock i is:

$$R_i - R_f = a_i + B_i(R_m - R_f) + e_i$$

The alpha, a_i, is the expected abnormal return estimated for a stock that is undervalued; alpha is zero for a stock that is efficiently priced. The error term, e_i, is expected to have an average value of zero in the long run; but it is expected to fluctuate over short time intervals. These short-term fluctuations are caused by residual risk and are statistically measured as the standard error of residual (U_i). Because the magnitude of residual risk varies widely among individual stocks and groups of stocks, its size must be estimated for each security researched.

The total risk (S_i) for each stock is:

$$S_i = \sqrt{(B_i S_m)^2 + U_i^2}$$

This is to say that the total risk of a stock is a function of the stock's beta, the risk of the market, and the stock's residual risk.

VALUATION OF PREFERRED STOCKS

Major Features of Preferred Stocks

Preferred stocks are hybrid securities, combining some of the features of common stocks and most of the characteristics of bonds. In evaluating a preferred stock for investment purposes, the factors usually considered are (1) contractual provisions and (2) an analysis of the stock's behavior in the market and the trade-off between return and risk.

When a specific preferred stock is being considered, the contractual provisions that must be examined are the kind of preferences offered and the extent of the impact of those preferences upon the investment quality of the stock. The exact nature of these preferences are described as provisions in the certificate of incorporation. There are several important provisions.

In general, preferred stock has preferential treatment over common stock with regard to the payment of cash dividends; that is, owners of common stocks may not receive any cash dividends until dividends on preferred stocks have been paid in full. However, the payment of preferred dividends is contingent on the company's earnings and is not legally mandatory, as is the case for interest payments on bonds. Therefore, interest on bonds must be paid before any dividends can be paid on preferred or common stocks. Most preferred stock issues have a cumulative dividend provision: If dividends are not paid in any designated time period, they are cumulated and the company must pay these dividends before any cash dividends may be declared and paid on common stock. If dividends are noncumulative and they are passed (not paid), they are lost forever. Some preferred stocks carry a participation provision. This means that the holders may receive additional cash dividends if payments to the owners of common stock exceed a predetermined amount as specified in the preferred stock agreement.

Another important feature of a preferred stock agreement is whether preferred stock owners have preference over owners of common stock with regard to liquidation of assets. In the event of reorganization or liquidation of the company, the owners of preferred stock with such a preference have the right to receive the par value or stated value of their shares before any money is distributed to the owners of common stocks, but not before the owners of bonds, or any other creditors, are paid.

Some preferred stocks, like bonds, have a convertible feature that allows the owners to convert the preferred stock into common stock at a stipulated conversion ratio within a specified time period. The owners of these preferred stocks may participate in the future growth in corporate earnings, which may result in a higher market price for convertible preferred stocks as compared to nonconvertible preferreds. Other features, such as call provisions and sinking fund provisions, also should be considered in the analysis of preferred stock for investment purposes.

The owners of preferred stock usually have the right to vote to approve the issuance of additional preferred stock, to merge the company, and to amend the corporate charter. If the preferred dividends are not paid for a certain period of time, preferred owners may have a right to elect members to the board of directors.

Estimation of Investment Value

In a prior section the concept of present value was used to determine the investment value of common stocks. This concept, with some modifications, is used here to estimate the investment value of preferred stocks. It is easier to estimate the investment value of preferred stocks than common stocks. In the case of common stocks, the future cash flow (dividends and changes in market price) and the required rate of return or discount rate are more volatile and uncertain. With preferred stocks, the cash dividend rate is fixed, the market price fluctuates less, and the required rate of return or discount rate is more stable. In estimating the investment value for a preferred stock, two important variables are usually considered: (1) the fixed preferred dividend rate that the

investors in bonds are fully informed about the amount and the timing of payments promised by the issuing company. A major unknown variable is the discount rate. The discount rate is the minimum acceptable rate of return that the investor in the bond would be able to receive by investing in comparable bonds with the same degree of risk. Once the discount rate is determined, the investment value of a bond can be estimated by applying a present value equation. For further analysis of bonds, see Chapters 7, 13, 18, and 25.

A SECURITY ANALYSIS OUTLINE

Many items of information are gathered, analyzed, and interpreted in order to formulate decisions as to what securities should be purchased, held, and sold for investment purposes. To summarize the relevant information that is researched by security analysts, a checklist containing most of the data that is considered in the security investment decision-making process is provided here.

This checklist is not necessarily applicable in its entirety to all security analysis research assignments, but includes suggested points that may be of value.

I ANALYSIS OF THE EXTERNAL ENVIRONMENT

1 *Economic and Market Factors:*
  a The long-term record of aggregate economic growth
  b Leading, lagging, coincident, and other economic indicators
  c Growth in aggregate corporate profit
  d Monetary variables (e.g., money supply)
  e Long-term record, trend, and return from different types of securities
  f Short-term and long-term outlook for the economy, capital market, and money market
  g International economy — current conditions and future outlook

2 *Social and Political Environment:*
  a Governmental regulatory attitudes toward the economy, industries, and business organizations
  b Stability and permanence of sociopolitical conditions

3 *Analysis of an Industry:*
  a Permanence and stability in growth of the industry
  b The product market(s), product demand, type of customers, and competitive conditions
  c Innovations in product and/or services and other new developments
  d Availability of raw material, labor, and external financing
  e Geographic decentralization
  f Long-term trend in industry's profitability
  g Short-term and long-term outlook for the demand of products and/or services and for the industry's profitability

II ANALYSIS OF A COMPANY

1 *Market Position of the Company* — Nature and long-term record of growth and stability in demand for products and/or services, market share, dominance and leadership in competitive position, and marketing strategies

2 *Economic Environment* — Sensitivity to business cycles, reserves of raw material, labor relations, and availability of external financing

3 *Operating Characteristics* — Nature and stability of the production process, cost structure, research and developments, innovations, patent protection, and overall operating efficiency

4 *Quality of Management* — Management ability to set out the major goals in regard to overall expansion to meet and to deal with changes in the economic and sociopolitical environments; to maintain competitive position for its product and/ or services; to maintain harmonious relations with stockholders, employees, and customers; and to carry out its policies so that its expectations are fulfilled

5 *Assets and Financial Structure* — Critical evaluation of composition of working capital and capital investment, and evaluation of soundness in financial and capital structure

6 *Operating Results* — Growth and stability of sales and/or revenues, cost controls, profit margins and the rates of return on owners' equity, total capital structure, and total operating assets

7 *Accounting Policies* — Critical evaluation of accounting policies in regard to inventory valuation, depreciation policies, reported operating and nonoperating earnings, and so on

8 *Per Share Statistics* — Growth and stability in earnings per share, cash flow per share, dividends per share, P/E ratio, book value per share, and market price per share

9 *Outlook for the Company:*
    a Demand for products and/or services
    b Growth rate in sales and/or revenue
    c Innovation and new developments
    d New financing and investment strategies
    e Profitability as measured by profit margins, and rates of returns on common equity, net worth, capital structure, and operating assets
    f Earnings and dividends per share
    g Dividend yield and payout ratio
    h P/E ratio
    i Market price per share
    j Changes in management
    k Other important developments

III VALUATION OF SECURITIES

1 *Common Stocks:*
    a Expected stream of dividends

   b Expected P/E ratio
   c Time horizon
   d Required rate of return
   e Risk — systematic and nonsystematic

2 *Bonds:*
   a Expected interest rates
   b Maturity and call dates
   c Required rate of return
   d Yield to maturity
   e Risk — business risk, interest rate risk, and inflation risk

3 *Preferred Stocks:*
   a Expected stream of dividends
   b Call dates
   c Required rate of return
   d Risk — business risk, interest rate risk, and inflation risk

SUGGESTED READING

Amling, Frederick. *Investments: An Introduction to Analysis and Management.* Englewood Cliffs, N.J.: Prentice-Hall, 1978.

Bernstein, Leopold A. *Financial Statement Analysis: Theory, Application and Interpretation.* Homewood, Ill.: Richard D. Irwin, 1974.

Cohen, Jerome B., et al. *Investment Analysis and Portfolio Management,* 4th ed. Homewood, Ill.: Richard D. Irwin, 1982.

D'Ambrosio, Charles A. *Principles of Modern Investments.* Palo Alto, Cal.: Science Research Associates, Inc., 1976.

Darst, David M. *The Complete Bond Book: A Guide to All Types of Fixed-Income Securities.* New York: McGraw-Hill, 1975.

Fischer, Donald E., and Ronald J. Jordan. *Security Analysis and Portfolio Management,* 3rd ed. Englewood Cliffs, N.J.: Prentice-Hall, 1983.

Foster, George. *Financial Statement Analysis.* Englewood Cliffs, N.J.: Prentice-Hall, 1978.

Francis, Jack Clark. *Management of Investments.* New York: McGraw-Hill, 1983.

Gitman, Lawrence J., and Michael D. Joehnk. *Fundamentals of Investing.* New York: Harper and Row, 1981.

Graham, Benjamin, et al. *Security Analysis: Principles and Techniques,* 4th ed. New York: McGraw-Hill, 1962.

Hayes, Douglas A., and W. Scott Bauman. *Investments: Analysis and Management,* 3rd ed. New York: Macmillan, Inc., 1976.

Helfert, Erich A. *Techniques of Financial Analysis,* 5th ed. Homewood, Ill.: Richard D. Irwin, 1982.

Homer, Sidney, and Martin L. Leibowitz. *Inside the Yield Book: New Tools for Bond Market Strategy.* Englewood Cliffs, N.J.: Prentice-Hall, 1976.

Huang, Stanley S.C. *Investment Analysis and Management.* Cambridge, Mass.: Winthrop, Inc., 1981.

Ibbotson, Roger G., and Rex A. Sinquefield. *Stocks, Bonds, Bills and Inflation: The Past and the Future.* Charlottesville, Va.: Financial Analysts Research Foundation, 1982.

Institute of Chartered Financial Analysts. *C.F.A. Readings in Financial Analysis.* Homewood, Ill.: Richard D. Irwin, 1981.

Khoury, Sarkins J. *Investment Management: Theory and Application.* New York: Macmillan, Inc., 1983.

Latane, Henry A., et al. *Security Analysis and Portfolio Management.* New York: The Ronald Press Co., 1975.

"Major Institutional Investors, The Fourth Survey Summary." New York: Louis Harris & Associates, Nov. 1975.

Mittra, Sid, and Chris Gassen. *Investments Analysis and Portfolio Management.* New York: Harcourt Brace Jovanovich, Inc., 1981.

Phillips, Herbert E., and John C. Ritchie, Jr. *Investment Analysis & Portfolio Selection.* Cincinnati, Ohio: South-Western Publishing Co., 1983.

Porter, Michael E. *Competitive Strategy: Techniques for Analyzing Industries and Competitors.* New York: The Free Press, 1980.

Radcliffe, Robert C. *Investment: Concepts, Analysis, and Strategy.* Glenview, Ill.: Scott, Foresman and Company, 1982.

Reilly, Frank K. *Investments.* Hinsdale, Ill.: Dryden Press, 1982.

Sharpe, William F. *Investments,* 2nd ed. Englewood Cliffs, N.J.: Prentice-Hall, 1981.

Standard & Poor's Analysts Handbook. New York: Standard & Poor's Corporation (annually).

Standard & Poor's Industry Surveys. New York: Standard & Poor's Corporation (quarterly).

Thorndike Encyclopedia of Banking and Financial Tables, rev. ed., Boston: Warren, Gorham & Lamont, 1983.

Tinic, Seha M., and Richard R. West. *Investing in Securities: An Efficient Market Approach.* Reading, Mass.: Addison-Wesley Publishing Co., 1979.

Value Line Investment Survey. New York: Value Line, Inc. (weekly).

17

Managing Security Portfolios

JARROD W. WILCOX

INTRODUCTION

This chapter deals with some of the attitudes and tools needed to manage security portfolios effectively. Although the examples will be taken from the stock market, the underlying principles are common to all investments. The ideas are based on personal intuition and experience as well as on scientific rigor. Good portfolio management requires both.

As investors, most of us act as if the lessons learned from operating businesses are valid in the Alice-in-Wonderland world of the stock market. Here are four examples of the results.

1 We buy and sell securities too frequently. These trades are usually based on what is believed to be new information about the company's future. However, too often the data discovered have already been reflected in the price. Unfortunately, the costs of trading are significant; frequent trading often has an adverse effect on portfolio performance.

2 We underestimate the essential randomness in price changes introduced by many intelligent people buying and selling, trying to outguess each other as to what will next increase in popularity. Consequently, we leap to conclusions based on good or poor results over time periods that are too short. We decide on the merit of a security, of an investment philosophy, or even of an investment manager without first understanding the role played by chance. Assuming our results to be more controllable than they truly are, we overmanage. We are whipsawed from one ill-timed decision to another. If bonds go down, we move to stocks just in time for bond prices to rally, then back to bonds, and so on. If we ourselves have mediocre results, we may still ascribe great skill to the performance results of the luckiest investment managers.

3 We fall in love with favorite stocks or a favorite stock group. Consequently, our portfolio may be poorly diversified and unnecessarily risky for a given degree of expected return. We ignore whole classes of less familiar investments, which could help us diversify away risk or increase return at the same risk. A current example is foreign equities. In the past, small-company stocks, gold, and real estate have been underutilized. We are usually attracted to these less familiar investments only after they have enjoyed especially good returns, which are unlikely to continue.

4 We tend to view our investments as isolated from our other activities. In so doing, we ignore opportunities for diversifying away risk imposed by noninvestment sources. For example, it is not unusual for a company's pension fund to invest heavily in the company's own stock, or perhaps in the same industry, because the trustees are familiar with the opportunities there. But any decline in industry profitability would lessen the fund's market value at the same time that more employees would be collecting termination benefits, and the company would be less able to make contributions.

These mistakes are so pervasive and deeply rooted that it is worthwhile first trying to dislodge the assumptions on which they rest. Only then will it make sense to proceed in top-down fashion from setting objectives to choice of investments.

IMPORTANT CONCEPTS FOR INVESTMENT MANAGERS

Subjective Stock Values

Financial market prices are set, based on buying and selling generated by the interplay of differing subjective viewpoints. For example, there is no one true value for a share of common stock. There is one price at a given point in time, together with many different views of value.

Stocks mainly represent the right to receive potential dividends from potential earnings. Investing in these equities would be much more sensible and straightforward if market participants had an objective means of determining whether a stock was priced too high or too low relative to the value of these rights. But even if all investors had the same preferences, which is far from the case, value would often be very uncertain. While stock price ought to be equal to the present value of all future dividends, naturally there are differences of opinion among market participants as to what the future will hold, how best to predict it, and even what is the appropriate time-discount rate to use in establishing present value.

For example, many investors shortcut such a dividend discount valuation, which may be so complex as to be unmanageable, by relating price/earnings (P/E) ratios to a base ratio for existing earnings, plus a premium for expected future earnings growth. Even these growth expectations do not seem to arise objectively. Evidence indicates that past growth in earnings per se has little ability to predict future growth in earnings (Paynor & Little (1966)). Consequently, P/E ratios, which reflect growth expectations, are poorly correlated with objectively available historical growth in earnings, and primarily seem to reflect a variety of subjective judgments and forecasts.

This phenomenon is illustrated by Figure 17.1, which examines a large sample of companies covered by *The Value Line Survey*. The horizontal axis shows ten-year average annual growth rate in earnings per share through 1981. The vertical axis shows average 1981 normalized P/E multiples. The overall relationship between P/E ratios and past growth is low.

Anecdotal evidence suggests that large numbers of market participants do rely on past growth in earnings as a primary input to judging stock value. It is clear from Figure 17.1 that other investors offset these participants, relying on more indirect indicators of future earnings growth, such as changes in market share and new product introduction. The choice of weights given to possible indicators of future growth, and thus value, is subjective and is a source of controversy between buyers and sellers.

Financial Markets vs. Ordinary Experience

Ordinary experience has provided us with the wrong intuitions about the stock market. Stock market mechanisms include the following unusual features:

1 The dividend and price appreciation benefits of stock purchases continue into the future without further effort. These benefits, and thus value, need only be judged relative to the initial price paid. An unprofitable company bought at a low price often makes a good investment, and vice versa.

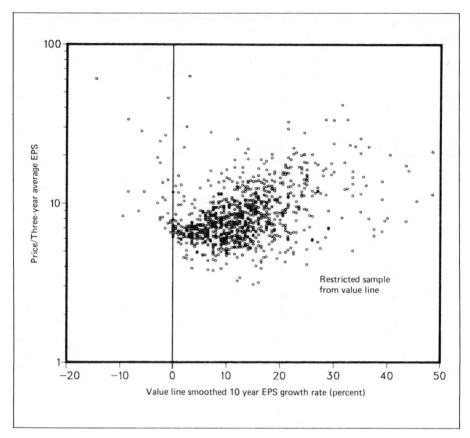

FIG. 17.1 1981 Price-Earnings Ratio and Ten-Year Earnings Growth

2 There may be hundreds of active buyers and sellers for any given stock on any given day. No single market participant, often including the company's management, has as much information as has already been expressed in the stock price resulting from the transactions among other participants. The delay time in changing effective supply or demand in reaction to price changes or any other news is usually no more than a few hours or days as compared to months or years for many real products and services.

These mechanisms cause new data and ideas about the future to be absorbed into the price of a given stock quickly and on little volume. It is often frustrating to attempt to put business information to use in predicting stock market price changes because it has already been put to use by others.

On the one hand, there may be no above-average payoff to the investor unless his data or ideas surpass those of nearly all other participants. Investment research duplicating that used by quicker participants has no payoff. This is very unlike ordinary experience, where more effort, higher motivation, and a little better idea will usually be rewarded, even if within a limited sphere.

On the other hand, the saving grace of this quick incorporation of new information into current prices means that stock purchase decisions based on wrong data or wrong ideas, so long as they allow diversification and do not run up brokerage costs, do about as well as random choice. Again, this is very unlike industrial product and service markets, where investments based on wrong assumptions end up as disasters.

The Efficient Market

This is a market that is extremely competitive and free of the various frictions that prevent price from fully reflecting new information.

In one form, the "weak form," the stock market may be efficient enough that price changes for a given stock cannot be predicted based on past price history. This means that successive price changes must undergo a kind of "random walk." In the 1960s, a variety of academic studies showed that U.S. stock prices for well-followed securities were indeed unpredictable (Cootner (1964)).

In the "semistrong form," the efficient market property suggests that any public information, not just past price, will be absorbed so quickly that it will be useless for predicting further stock price changes after it has been disseminated. Again, a variety of studies suggest this to be true for popular types of information, such as earnings reports (Ball & Brown (1968)). Obviously, this semistrong form of efficiency may extend to one form of predictive information, which is well followed, but not to another, which may be newly emergent. By the time an indicator is tested by academic studies, the market seems to have become rather efficient with respect to it. It is this kind of efficiency that most confuses the novice investor, who frequently observes that prices fall on the date that good news is announced, not realizing the news had already been absorbed before the public announcement.

In the most extreme form, the "strong form," the market is so efficient that no market participant has any ability to predict price changes. Therefore, differences in return among investors reflect only differences in risk taken and in luck. Here, the evidence is mixed.

Various academic studies show that the average institutional equity manager does not do any better than large unmanaged portfolios of the same risk and asset class (Sharpe (1978); Malkiel (1981)). Many in the financial community still refuse to accept this finding, but it is compelling.

However, there is fairly good evidence that some investment advisors have published recommendations whose results could not have been expected by chance. Also, some investment managers have impressive long-term records. Consequently, an agnostic position is taken here on what has for some become almost a religious issue. It is the goal of each ambitious investor to make the market less efficient. The result of their combined efforts make it ever more so.

Investment Portfolios

Specific Examples. Figure 17.2 shows the distribution of average annual returns over the decade ending in 1981 provided by investments in about 800 stocks from Value Line. (The same sample is used for Figures 17.2 through 17.5.) These companies have complete records and fourth quarter fiscal year-ends.

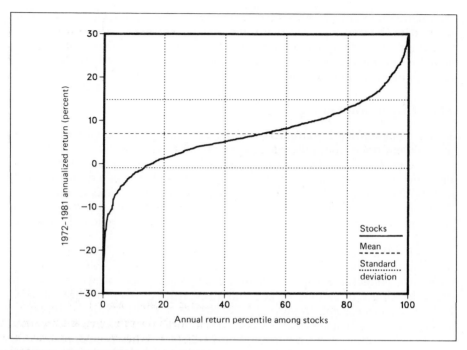

FIG. 17.2 Annualized Returns for Stocks

The mean of the distribution is 6.9 percent, with a standard deviation of 7.9 percent around the mean. Note that this fairly wide dispersion is already much less than would be seen for single-year returns. We are looking at ten-year averages, with extra good performance in some years offset by poor results in other years.

We might be tempted to extrapolate differences in annual return into the future. This would be a mistake. The efficient market hypothesis leads us to expect that past returns for particular stocks will not be much help in predicting their future returns. Figure 17.3 shows the average return in the first five years versus the second five years for each stock. We do not see much tendency for the leaders of one period to be leaders later.

Figure 17.4 should be compared with Figure 17.2. It shows the reduced dispersion in return obtained by diversifying through a portfolio of 10 randomly chosen stocks. Standard deviation in 10-year average return is reduced from 7.9 to 2.3 percent. This reduction is close to the value predicted for independent risks:

$$\frac{2.3}{7.9} \approx \frac{1}{\sqrt{\text{number of observations}}} = \frac{1}{\sqrt{10}}$$

Figure 17.5 indicates that past stock return volatility does carry over into the future. The stocks at the right, with higher past standard deviation in returns, shown on the horizontal scale, have a greater dispersion in 1982 returns, as shown on the vertical scale.

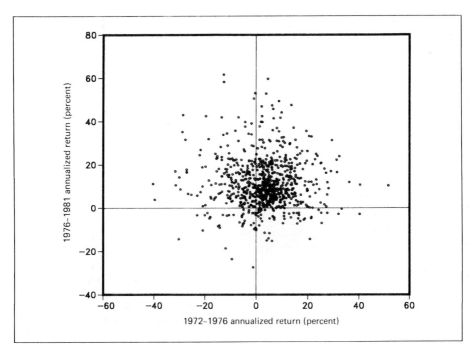

FIG. 17.3 Stock Returns Have No Memory

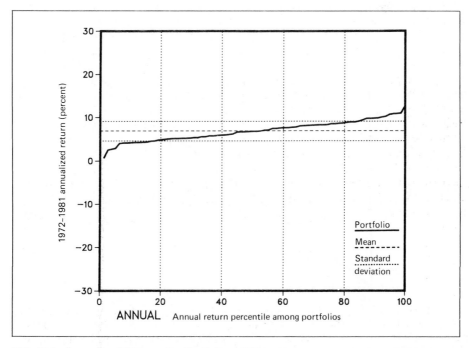

FIG. 17.4 Annualized Returns for Portfolios of 10

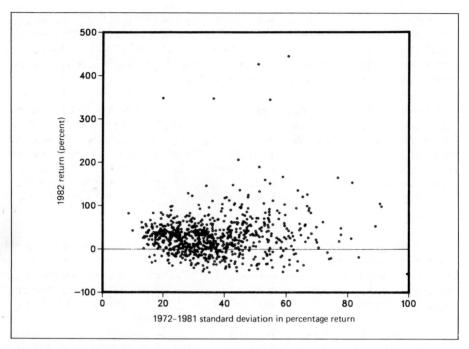

FIG. 17.5 Stock Volatility Predicts Return Dispersion

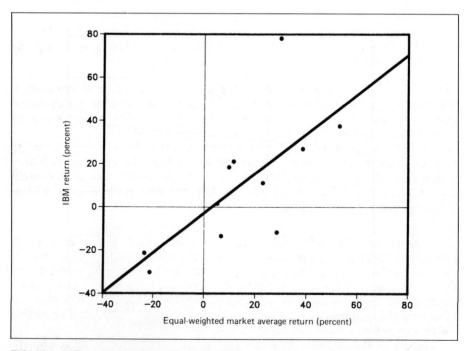

FIG. 17.6 IBM vs. Market Returns, 1972–1982

Figure 17.6 shows the strong positive relationship between annual returns for a single stock (IBM) and for the mean of the market as a whole. The slope of the diagonal best-fit line indicates the sensitivity of IBM to market risks. The scatter above and below the diagonal shows remaining risks. Both these characteristics have a modest degree of continuity over time.

Portfolio Return Standard Deviation. In 1952, Harry Markowitz wrote a paper on "portfolio selection" that sharply defined our notions of the role of each security in a portfolio. Stocks are held, he said, not in isolation, but within a portfolio of other holdings. The contribution of the stock's average return to that of the portfolio is direct. It depends only on the proportion of an investor's wealth placed in the stock at the start of a period. But the stock's contribution to portfolio risk, measured as standard deviation of return, is more subtle (for elaboration, see Chapter 14).

Systematic (Beta) Specific Risk. In the 1960s, it was discovered that over 30 percent of the variation in stock returns could be statistically explained by a single underlying factor, christened the market return. Sharpe, Lintner, and others developed a specialized model of portfolio returns in which the standard deviation of return each stock contributes to a portfolio has two main parts:

1 A systematic risk governed by the sensitivity of changes in the stock's return to changes in the market return. This sensitivity, known as beta, is the product of (1) the correlation coefficient between the market's and the stock's return, and (2) the ratio of the stock's standard deviation of return to the market's standard deviation of return.

2 The remaining specific risk peculiar to the company, or residual standard deviation after systematic risk is netted out, which can be diversified away through the insurance principle.

They also hypothesized that since specific risk could be diversified away, investors would not be paid for assuming it. Thus, differences in expected return ought to be primarily related to beta. This was the foundation of the Capital Asset Pricing Model (CAPM) (for elaboration, see Chapter 14).

In practice, in equal-weighted portfolios of 20 or more stocks, assuming diversification across industries, the portfolio's risk is largely determined by the average beta found within it. Although the beta estimated for individual stocks appear to be rather imprecise and unstable, the beta estimated for a large portfolio is extremely useful in predicting that portfolio's risk.

Capital Asset Pricing Model. Figure 17.7 illustrates a hypothetical set of alternative portfolios which could be selected for investment. The horizontal axis shows the standard deviation of portfolio return. The vertical axis represents the expected portfolio return. The curved line forming the upper-left boundary of the set indicates those alternatives which are efficient portfolios. These portfolios have the most return for a given degree of risk. The line itself is sometimes called the efficient frontier.

Figure 17.7 also shows what happens when a riskless investment, such as short-term Treasury bills, is added to the set of risky alternatives. By holding

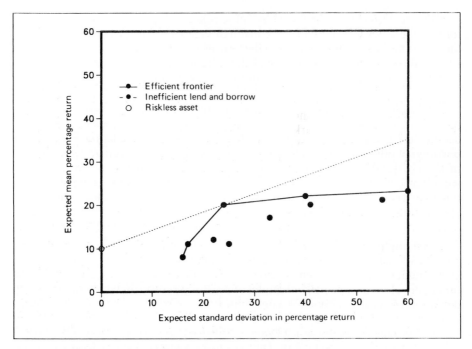

FIG. 17.7 Efficient Portfolios With and Without a Riskless Asset

varying degrees of bills, any point on the diagonal dotted line to the left of where it touches the prior efficient frontier (point of tangency) can be attained. Each point represents a unique combination of expected return and risk. If borrowing is allowed at the same interest rate (i.e., the investor can hold negative bills, or borrow at the same rate as the U.S. Government), then points on the diagonal to the right and above the prior efficient frontier are attainable. The addition of a riskless asset and borrowing consequently creates a potential improvement in the effective efficient frontier and straightens it out, or ''linearizes'' it.

The Argument for Index Funds. In a perfectly efficient market, given the existence of such a riskless investment and the ability to borrow at riskless rates of interest, each investor would have no incentive to hold any stocks but those represented in the portfolio at the point of tangency on his efficient frontier. He can adjust his risk simply by borrowing or lending the riskless asset. If the further assumption is made that investors have similar expectations of risk and return for each alternative portfolio and have similar tax brackets, that point of tangency will include the same investments for every investor. It will include the entire market of stocks in proportion to their market values. This is the market portfolio. Finally, if security risk is composed entirely of systematic risk and specific risk, individual securities will be priced according to their contribution of systematic risk to the market portfolio:

$$r_i = r_f + \beta_i (r_m - r_f)$$

where: r_i = expected return of stock i
r_f = expected risk-free return
r_m = expected return of the market portfolio
β_i = beta of stock i

This equation is a main conclusion of the CAPM. For example, suppose it is estimated that on average there is a 6 percent risk premium in the return expected (and demanded) from Standard & Poor's 500 (S&P 500) index of common stocks (a proxy for the market portfolio) and that for Treasury bills. Then the CAPM can be used as follows: If it is determined that portfolio A has a beta of 0.8 and portfolio B has a beta of 1.2, it will not be surprising if B has an average annual return 0.4 × 6 percent, or 2.4 percent higher than A.

Practical Value of CAPM. Obviously none of the assumptions behind the model are completely satisfied in practice, particularly the homogeneity of investor forecasts and tax brackets. However, the question is whether the conclusions of the model might be approximately satisfied.

While the evidence is quite strong that average long-term portfolio returns go up more or less linearly with increasing beta, the CAPM has turned out somewhat less useful in practice than its early promise. It is most useful for risk adjusting the returns of large portfolios in performance measurement. It seems least useful for decisions involving individual stocks, whose beta estimates are fairly unreliable.

The efficient market theory indicates that unmanaged portfolios will do about as well as the average professionally managed portfolio. The CAPM goes further and suggests that there is one best unmanaged portfolio, the market portfolio. In this sense, its widespread influence gives a strong impetus to the growth of so-called index funds. The latter are portfolios which attempt to replicate the performance of the market as a whole.

Intentionally Undiversified Portfolios. Suppose an investor decides to have only a few stocks, or a high concentration of stocks in the same industry, in his portfolio. This retains specific risk that other investors may diversify away. Theoretically, the portfolio will not be efficient. Yet, this is what almost all investors do to some extent. This practice is sensible because we assume:

1 That the transaction costs necessary to buy very small numbers of shares are disproportionately high; and
2 The investor has discovered "proprietary" information, that is, a market ineffi-ciency. In the extreme, perfect foreknowledge of earnings changes would justify holding just one stock.

INVESTMENT OBJECTIVES

Now investment objectives can be discussed, proceeding in top-down fashion to methods of achieving these purposes.

TABLE 17.1   Annual Percentage Return, 1926–1981

	Geometric Mean	Standard Deviation
Small stocks	12.1	37.3
Stocks	9.1	21.9
Corporate bonds	3.6	5.6
Treasury bills	3.0	3.1
Inflation	3.0	5.1

Source: Roger G. Ibbotson and Rex A. Sinquefield, *Stocks, Bonds, Bills and Inflation: The Past and the Future* (Charlottesville, Va.: Financial Analysts Research Bureau, 1982)

The major dimensions of investment performance are average return and risk, the latter usually measured as standard deviation of return, both being judged over a specified interval. These are the key issues for tax-exempt institutional investors, and those on which we focus here. Additional considerations treated here arise from investor tax circumstances, need for short-term liquidity, and a variety of legal and individual constraints appropriate for each investor or investing institution, most of which are beyond the scope of this work. A very important real-world complication is that most investment managers are not owners, but merely agents for owners, and overlay their own concerns on the investment process. Certain kinds of investments (e.g., bankrupt stocks or South African gold mines) might carry higher risks of embarrassment, yet otherwise might be attractive investments for the ultimate beneficiary or owners of the portfolio.

The first step in intelligently establishing risk and return objectives is to learn what performance is realistic (i.e., consistent with historical frequency distributions) and what the trade-offs between average return and standard deviation of return have been.

Portfolio Returns

Chapter 18 tabulates the long-term (1926–1982) results of holding large portfolios of common stocks, bonds, and Treasury bills. The average return before inflation is taken into account is shown in Table 17.1. The almost riskless Treasury bills had almost no return beyond inflation. Stocks had most risk and most return. This was especially true for stocks of smaller companies. Bonds were intermediate, but their risk and return were far lower than that of stocks.

The portfolio return of an equal-weighted portfolio is simply the arithmetic average return of the stocks that compose it. This concept does not carry over to the process of averaging returns over successive periods. Suppose an investor gets zero return for two years in a row. The average annual return is zero percent. Alternatively, suppose an investor gains 50 percent one year, then loses 50 percent of his wealth the next year. The resulting terminal wealth gain is not zero percent but a loss of 25 percent. The average return per year is a negative 13.4 percent.

The ratio of terminal wealth to starting wealth after a series of returns is determined by multiplying, not adding, the returns. The average return per time period is determined by taking the nth root of this ratio, where n is the number of time periods. This is the geometric mean of the individual returns, as shown in Table 17.1.

Given equal expected returns each period, the greatest expected multi-period return is given by the investment with the least expected year-to-year standard deviation in returns. An investment of higher risk must have a higher short-term expected return merely to stay even in expected return over a longer term.

This is only one example of the consequences of lengthening our time horizon from simple one-period risk-return analysis. Unfortunately, this theory is much less understood than single-period models. However, it is known from computer simulations that mixes of stocks, bonds, and Treasury bills are superior to pure ingredients for most levels of portfolio risk.

It is also known that the optimum mix shifts toward heavier use of stocks not only as risk tolerance is increased, but also as the time period is lengthened. That is, the higher average short-term return of equities appears to outweigh the negative impact of their higher short-term return dispersion.

Portfolio Objectives

Studies such as those in Chapter 18 give some notion of realistic portfolio objectives for risk and return, particularly when translated into real terms by netting out the inflation rate. These objectives can be modified for intermediate levels of risk, using commercially available studies of frequency distributions of returns by fairly large populations of mutual fund managers, investment advisors, and so forth. At a given level of risk, improving return objectives implies superior diversification, skill at locating market inefficiencies, or skill at selecting managers who have such skills. From the viewpoint of agent risk, it is wise not to set risk and return objectives unlikely to be met.

Selecting an appropriate point on the risk-return trade-off is an art, not a science. In general, long-term investors should take as much systematic risk as they can stand, because to do so has resulted in far higher average returns, as shown in Table 17.1. The key here is a realistic simulation and assessment of how the investor is likely to respond in times of negative returns. While large or wealthy investors are generally assumed better able to withstand temporary losses, this is not always the case. Each situation must be evaluated on its own merits.

The specification of investment objectives and time horizons is not easy. Investors often do not know how to articulate their risk preferences. In many cases the investor is, in fact, a client organization. Pension funds, for example, have been known to provide their investment managers with less than well-defined, or with contradictory, objectives. An investment manager for such a client may be forced to operate under an implicit definition of investment objectives, established by clearly communicating to the client the risk and return characteristics of the portfolio over time.

Given investment objectives, to derive an optimal portfolio based on the investor's after-tax efficient frontier of expected returns and risks sounds like a complicated, but essentially mechanical, process. This is incorrect. In practice the number of stocks is usually too large, their return distributions too little known, and the multiperiod problem too complex to optimize the portfolio fully.

Taxable Investors. What has been stated thus far implicitly assumes that returns realized through price gains are equal in desirability to those realized from dividends. This is only true for tax-exempt institutions such as pension funds. When capital gains are taxed at a lower rate, and taxes are not paid until the stock is sold, taxable investments should be biased against the purchase of stocks where a high proportion of returns is paid out as dividends. If this preference were reflected in the market, driving down dividend-paying stock prices, higher returns for high dividend stocks should be realized on a pretax basis, and to some extent this "yield tilt" seems to be found in practice, if allowances are made for differences in beta.

There seems to be an interplay between taxes and risk, including specific risk. The investor has the option of selling the stocks that have gone down to reduce taxes levied on regular income. On the other hand, the sale of stocks that go up can be deferred. The value of this option would make a portfolio of risky stocks more appealing to those in high income tax brackets than to tax-free investors, even if risk-return trade-off preferences on an after-tax basis were identical.

INVESTMENT POLICY

A policy is a guideline for a stream of similar decisions. After noting the importance of reducing trading costs, this section briefly indicates policy approaches to different levels of investment decision making. These are: stock selection; choice of covariant groups of stocks; asset class allocation; asset–liability matching; and managing the total income portfolio. At each level, the most fundamental decision is whether to make an active or passive selection. An active selection policy intentionally sacrifices some diversification benefit to achieve an expectation of a return greater than that normally available at a given risk level. It implies an expectation of market inefficiency. It need not imply frequent trading activity. So-called investment timing decisions are implicitly made whenever active selection is changed. However, investors with a policy of changing active selections in response to changes in stock prices or other ongoing stimuli are explicit "timers."

Trading Costs

Trading costs should influence every level of investment decision making. (See Chapter 10 for a discussion of trading markets.) They always seem to be higher than expected. In a very broad sense, equity trading costs include the total difference in portfolio return between what actually occurs during a period and what would have resulted from a pure equity portfolio composed of beginning-of-period investments. This total includes, first, brokerage commissions and, second, the lower return earned by interim cash needed as a buffer to effect transactions. The third trading cost is unfavorable price behavior. What is bought increases in price until the investor stops buying it, and may then sink back to its former price. And what is sold goes down until the seller stops selling it. In a portfolio with many stocks being traded during the period, the random specific risks will tend to cancel and allow this trading price impact to be revealed.

Evidence suggests that the round-trip cost to exchange one stock for another is typically between 2 and 4 percent of the price (Loeb, 1983). Without careful monitoring of total trading costs as defined here, the larger investor, whose price impacts may be great, can experience even higher costs. Active investment decisions are subject to an expensive discipline.

Security Selection

At the level of individual security selection, the investor can choose a passive or an active policy. If an active decision is to be made, the investor should review any stocks where above-average returns can be expected for a given level of risk. He seeks evidence of market inefficiency. The existing price of any security reflects a consensus view of the future. In actively selecting securities based on information, there are two key issues: Is the information right? and is it already embedded in the consensus? Experience suggests that investment research gives too little attention to the second issue.

There are many different specific approaches for actively selecting stocks. Only a few examples are noted here. None will work consistently for stocks that are well followed, and no detailed approach that works consistently is likely to remain useful over a long period.

Short-Term Earnings Forecasts. An investor who can accurately predict, not earnings per share, but the changes in earnings per share, over the next quarter to a year will capture a very large part of the intrastock variation in returns. It is not necessary to forecast total changes in earnings directly. A network of casual variables is antecedent to profit changes. For example, changes in sales volume will result in changes in profit because of fixed costs. Changes in industry product usage and market share jointly affect changes in sales volume. Market share is the result both of ability to get orders and ability to fill orders. Forecasts rooted near profits itself are information driven, and the information is extremely time sensitive. As one gets further upstream on the causal network driving profits, more stress is placed on insightful interpretation, and any inefficiencies found may endure until information on the next step downstream becomes public. Elaborate modeling of this type seems most useful when tied to realistic analysis of its past success in forecasting returns; otherwise, its labor intensity becomes busywork.

Competitive and Industry Analysis. Some investment research is aimed at a deeper understanding of the long-term factors that cause changes in profitability, perhaps best measured as changes in return on equity. It might be directed at changing competitve cost structures interacting with changing market shares, a change in industry segmentation, the emergence of a new technology, and so on. Usually only rough qualitative estimates of impact on stock price can be attempted, but this work focuses on nonconsensual interpretation more than on forecast accuracy. Such investors may have to be prepared to buy and hold stocks for 5 to 10 years to see their insights come to fruition.

Valuation Models. Models that purport to give a value for the stock against which prices can be compared may be useful. However, the value should not be taken very seriously in any individual case. When investment research is both economical and applied to large numbers of stocks, and trading costs are kept under control, it is not critical that the research be right on any one stock.

In its simplest form this might involve buying stocks with low P/E ratios. Despite the obvious contradiction with the efficient market hypothesis, academic studies have frequently indicated superior returns from such a strategy, even on a risk-adjusted basis.

Slightly more complex rules of thumb relate P/E to expected earnings growth rate. These are widely used (Bing (1971)). Another relates price-to-book (P/B) ratios to a normal P/B–ROE relationship (Wilcox (1983)).

A popular approach about which there should be more skepticism is the so-called total return method. This adds dividend yield to a sustainable growth rate in earnings to estimate total return. The fallacy here is the usual omission of easily forecastable changes in the P/E ratio (Wilcox (1983)).

A still more complex version brings to bear the CAPM. This method uses, as an indicator of normal return, the hypothetical overall market relationship between expected return and beta, the security market line. Stocks favored are those with the greatest excess of either total return or the internal rate of return from a dividend discount model over the return indicated by the security market line.

Finally, there is the dividend discount model, which seeks to capture total value as the time discounted present value of all future dividends. This also has a variety of subforms. (Further details of each of these models may be found from time to time in the *Financial Analysts Journal* and in Maginn and Tuttle (1983).

The chief danger of valuation models is that most of them, while purporting actively to value individual stocks, are biased toward or against specific large covariant groups of stocks that tend to move together. This effect is made obvious when long lists of similar stocks appear persistently to be either overvalued or undervalued. Use of such a model exposes the investor to covariant group risk which he might not be willing to accept if he were aware of it. For example, a low P/E stock group will usually suffer during a period when investment horizons lengthen; such a period favors the stable, high return on equity companies, which generally have high P/Es. On the other hand, the "total return" concept omitting expectable downward revisions in P/Es favors high return on equity companies. In practice some dividend discount models are heavily biased toward dividend-paying companies and away from growth.

Although such biased models can be used for implementation of covariant group strategies, misinterpreted, they make it appear as though the market is so inefficient as to misprice securities from their values for indefinite time periods. Good valuation models for individual stock selection should be unbiased with respect to covariant group risks. That is, they should point out good buys over a wide variety of industry groups and over a wide range of P/Es, dividend yields, betas, growth rates, and market capitalizations at all times.

Technical Analysis. Since the assessment of the internal dynamics of the market's own operation usually runs directly counter to the efficient market hypothesis in the weak or semistrong forms, the "chartist" is rather discredited. Nevertheless, use of unfamiliar internal market relationships that are not well worn, or use of unpublished data, may be justified. A good story is told by a broker who, having made a lifelong study of the "story" network, found that "hot" stocks tend to be bought early by accounts in Florida and late by medium-sized banks in the Midwest. He used the latter as a sell signal.

Seeking Out Thin Markets. Stocks that are not well followed by security analysts and that have small capitalizations and little trading volume should trade in less efficient markets. For such stocks (usually of smaller companies), ordinary financial analysis without extreme attention to avoiding the consensus might be argued to have some potential.

The apparent long-term excess returns produced by small stocks as a class, even without active selection, are of continuing interest to academics and practitioners alike. Even adjusting for higher beta, there seems to have been a long-term advantage to portfolios biased toward equal weighting of stocks rather than to portfolios where each stock's weight is in proportion to its market capitalization. Such a small-stock effect seems to reflect a reward for assuming specific risks, including liquidity risks, contrary to the tenets of the CAPM (Loeb (1983); Lustig and Leinbach (1983); and Arbel, Carvell, and Strebe (1983)).

In contrast to the five active approaches listed, passive stock selection implies that, once decisions are made at higher levels regarding asset classes and group rotation, the choice of individual securities from within a larger group is shaped only by the need for diversification of risk. Individual stocks within such a "buy" list are regarded as widely interchangeable and may even be chosen at random, depending on trading contingencies.

Covariant Groups of Stocks

Prices of stocks in the same industry tend to move up and down together. If we want to know what Dow Chemical will do next year, we want to know what will happen to the chemical industry overall. That is, individual stock returns seem to have not only systematic risks characteristic of the market as a whole and specific risks peculiar to the company, but group risks as well.

Groupings by industry are not the only clusters of return correlations that can be observed. James Farrell used a statistical technique called cluster analysis to categorize the returns of 100 large-capitalization stocks. He found four broad groupings of high intercorrelation of return after the specific effects of industry and the market as a whole were netted out. These he labeled:

- Stable
- Cyclical
- Growth
- Oil-related

It seems likely that additional clusters might emerge if this analysis is extended to greater numbers of stocks.

By concentrating his portfolio to hold disproportionate amounts of particular industries or of such superclusters, the investor can actively increase not only the portfolio's risk, but also its opportunities to take advantage of perceived market inefficiencies. Alternatively, passive, broad-based index funds can be used to avoid the covariant group level of investment decision. Most investment managers, however, give considerable attention to actively overweighting particular industries and other covariant groups. They practice investment strategy as opposed to the tactics of stock selection.

As in stock selection, there is a need both to be right and to avoid the consensus.

Industry Groups. At the industry level, the most appropriate analysis is probably focused on unforeseen changes in the long-term rate of growth or on changes in competitive pricing or cost structure. However, this is a very well-worked area indeed. A dozen good security analysts often specialize in a single industry and produce excellent consensus research. In fact, it is common for business strategy consultants to turn to investment research as a starting point in their industry-competitive analysis.

Groups by Established Descriptors. Figure 17.8 indicates correlations of the quarterly returns of Value Line stocks with prior year P/E ratios and dividend yields over a 12½-year period. It is obvious that doing nothing more than concentrating one's portfolio in the best half of a stock list ranked using a single descriptor such as these can produce extraordinary returns for three and four years in a row. P/E ratio and yield, along with some other simple descriptors, offer powerful leverage. Their use in stock screening can more dramatically affect portfolio returns than any practicable concentration of security analysis. The screens work when they focus the portfolio on a covariant group that will outperform the market. Valuation models can be a helpful adjunct to the exercise because they may give some indication of when the market price has moved relatively far from normal levels for a particular group. If the covariant group is well-known, investment policy may dictate getting in and out of it based on the state of the economy, market psychology, or technical indicators. In this case, the implied high rate of turnover makes us think of this more as timing than as selection. However, as defined here, timing is merely a change in selection.

Because of the efficient market principle, the expected return of a policy of frequent changes in selection usually is no higher than the expected return of a portfolio with fixed proportions of the various groups selected.

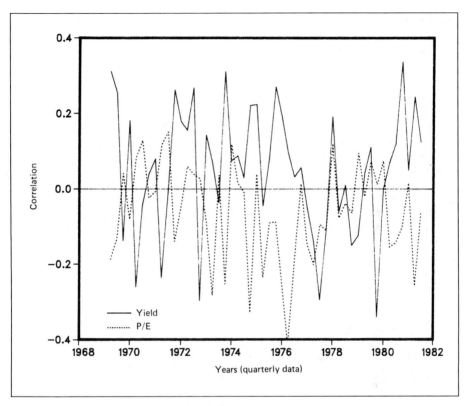

FIG. 17.8 Power of Yield and P/E to Predict Returns

Emerging Groups. A third type of covariant group has not yet been recognized because it is just emerging. A good example was furnished by inflation-sensitive stocks in the early 1970s. Only after the inflation rate had greatly accelerated did it become obvious to the market as a whole that some companies were better able to profit under the new environment. Concentration to favor a potential but not yet defined group attempts to exploit the market's inefficiency while it learns a new set of causal relationships for predicting profitability and growth.

Asset Class Allocation

Because the stock market's overall return varies quite substantially from year to year, the decision as to how much of an overall investment portfolio to put into stocks, bonds, or Treasury bills generally has more impact on the performance of a large portfolio than does stock selection or group strategy.

Switching in and out of stocks so as to sidestep years of declining stock prices would multiply 10-year portfolio returns several times if done perfectly. For example, Ibbotson and Sinquefield give terminal wealth for 10-year common stock returns ending in 1981 as 187.4 percent of an investment in common stock a decade earlier. If, in each year of common stock negative returns (1973, 1974, 1977, 1981), Treasury bills were held instead, terminal wealth would be increased to 470.5 percent of beginning investment. That is, there is a cumulative return of 87.4 percent versus a potential of 370.5 percent. This kind of potential offers strong motivation for investors and investment managers to try their hand at active market timing or rotation of asset classes. The passive alternative is the selection of an optimum mix for investment objectives (60 to 70 percent equities is typical for pension funds) and to hold it through thick and thin. This may require some occasional rebalancing to maintain portfolio risk at desired levels based on shifts of relative market values among stocks, bonds, and Treasury bills.

A decision between active and passive decision making at the asset allocation level should be influenced by a keen awareness of trading costs and, again, the need to avoid the consensus for forecasts to be useful. The following approaches are used, with varying degrees of success (for elaboration, see Chapter 16).

Economic Forecasting. The top-down economic forecast approach is time-honored. One forecasts change in Gross National Product (GNP) before deciding how much of the portfolio should be in equity, bonds, cash, and so forth. The efficient market doctrine suggests that such forecasts, if widely imitated, ought not to yield any advantage. Indeed, evidence suggests that economists are hard put to forecast changes in GNP, let alone the consequent implications for the stock market, which itself is normally regarded as a leading indicator of the economy. (Black, 1982.) Practical experience suggests that it is difficult to separate economists who have some ability to forecast the stock market from equally eloquent economists who do not.

Interest Rate Forecasting. To see that there is a strong correlation between changes in interest rates and returns from bonds, consider British consols, which have a fixed coupon but no date for repayment of principal. When interest rates double, consol prices are cut in half to yield the new rate. Similarly, existing long-term bonds go down in price to compete with new issues as interest rates increase. The net result is that bond portfolio returns go down as Treasury bill returns go up. Thus, a good forecast of interest rate changes ought to help us in asset allocation. Unfortunately, bond trading results in such an efficient market that almost all available information is already embedded in the current interest rate. Again, the record of interest rate forecasters as a class is poor.

The Fear-Greed Cycle. Seasoned equity investors claim to be able to recognize stock market peaks by the prevalence of optimism during certain periods. When the news is all optimistic, when there are many new firms being formed, these investors head for cover. Conversely, when the news is full of fear and anxiety, when there are numerous bankruptcies, this is the time to make a contrary bet and commit more resources to high-beta equities. The observation that even large institutions are governed by people with careers to protect and human emotions gives some credence to the fear–greed cycle as a source of market inefficiency. However, as indicated in the next section, skill in market timing is especially difficult to assess.

An alternative or a supplement to active asset allocation is to add more kinds of asset classes to the portfolio. This generally expands the possibilities for reducing risk and increasing return if the new asset's returns are little correlated with those of the prior portfolio. For example, real estate has been used in increasing proportions. Investments in real estate did very well during the accelerated inflationary decade beginning about 1972; at the same time, stocks and bonds both did less well than their long-term average.

International equity portfolios have substantially lower annual standard deviation of returns than do U.S. stock indexes alone, despite long-term higher returns. A market-capitalization weighted approach would put at least one-third of the U.S. investor's equity commitment outside the United States. More typical percentages applied by fund managers today are from zero to 5 percent. As a world capital market emerges through increased international trading, retaining such low percentages for foreign holdings represents an implied active asset allocation decision. This would only be optimal if the investor had superior information allowing him to predict superior risk-adjusted returns for U.S. equities.

Two new investment tools allowing risk-shifting will undoubtedly have greater roles in asset allocation decisions in the next few years. These are stock index futures and options on stock indexes. A stock index future is simply a contract to deliver or receive the equivalent of a very large portfolio of stocks at a specified date. One can take a position on either side of the contract. Puts (calls) are options to sell (buy) at a specified price within a specified time period.

Stock index futures allow low transaction cost changes in portfolio beta or in the degree of equity exposure without disturbing the underlying specific stock selections or covariant group exposure. This makes them potentially useful for active asset allocation purposes. Alternatively, taking a permanently renewed short position on stock index futures can be used to hedge away systematic risk. Thus, an investor with sufficient skills at group rotation or stock selection might do this to control total risk while focusing on the opportunities where he had the greatest edge.

Options on individual stocks are too specialized in their uses to discuss here. However, options on stock index futures or on the indexes themselves will probably be of general applicability. They allow even more flexibility than futures. Buying a put on a stock index will allow the construction of portfolios with high upside betas, but low downside betas. That is, those managers who so choose will be able to insure their portfolios against losses in bad years, while bearing some risk as to how great the gain will be in good years. Overall, the principal effect of market index options and futures on portfolio management will be to unbundle the security and covariant group selection from the asset allocation (or systematic risk) decision.

Asset–Liability Matching

The efficient portfolio concept applies to liabilities (negative assets) as well as to traditionally defined investment securities. However, most investors make implicit active decisions not to efficiently diversify their portfolio in this respect. Though our intentions are passive, we are active by default.

Long-term liabilities at fixed rates of interest are often not well matched to the long-term assets that are their security. For example, higher rates of inflation during the mid 1970s increased home values at the same time that accompanying higher interest rates reduced the market value of the mortgages. Homeowners enjoyed capital gains while banks suffered capital losses.

Not all long-term liabilities are at fixed rates of interest. Defined benefit pension funds nominally have a fixed obligation to employees. In fact, however, benefits go up with inflation.

Long-term bonds are not a hedge for benefit changes from accelerated rates of inflation because their prices move down when inflation moves up. Treasury bills are technically a good hedge for expected inflation, since the short-term interest rate reflects an expected inflation premium. However, their real return is too low for long-term use.

The pension fund may also invest in Guaranteed Investment Contracts (GICs) with an assured moderate rate of return from an insurance company, which can match its liability with an investment in bonds of similar maturity. If the weighted average maturity (the duration) is the same, this is called bond immunization. It reduces risk from interest rate changes. This is quite similar to the normal practice of a bank in matching its long- and short-term liabilities with long- and short-term assets. However, the pension fund may have only matched its assets and liabilities in dollar, or nominal, terms. Unlike purely financial intermediaries, its ultimate obligations may be in real terms. Changes in the rate of inflation will cause benefit schedules to be revised. Thus, in real terms, an investment like real estate, whose price increases with inflation, would better match the pension liability than does the GIC.

In the short term, stock returns fall because stock prices decline when inflation increases. However, in the long term, the income effect seems to predominate, as eventual higher return on equity is converted to a higher growth rate for nominal dividends. Stocks also might be considered useful long-term hedges against inflation.

Another liability risk of a pension fund arises from termination benefits if plants must be shut down. As indicated in the introduction, in this case a pension fund would benefit in terms of portfolio efficiency by not owning the parent company's stock. This example, interrelating noninvestment cash flows and investment returns, raises the issue of portfolio efficiency in a still broader sense.

Managing the Total Income Portfolio

In most cases securities are only a part of our total wealth. For example, the pension fund receives income from corporate contributions and has expenses in part determined by corporate actions. While recognizing there may be other reasons to hold parent company stock, from an investment view the securities usually should be diversified away from the operating business.

Analogously, private investors have human capital, which may earn a salary for them. Their most efficient portfolio would obviously tend to exclude shares in their employer, because here stock returns and changes in salary would tend to be highly postively correlated. The exceptions would be in cases of proprietary knowledge, or where not holding shares would subject the employee to sanctions.

Similar reasoning applies to systematic risk. An executive working entirely on predetermined salary and fringe benefits for a large, stable company may make very high-beta equity investments at a moderate total (including his human capital) portfolio risk. These securities would be too risky for the same executive if he were paid largely in stock options from a volatile start-up company rather than in stable salary.

PERFORMANCE MEASUREMENT

If it is impossible to identify reliable skill in obtaining extra risk-adjusted returns, efforts should focus only on risk control and efficient diversification to get the most return for the target portfolio risk. If skill can be identified, either in the investor himself or in other investment managers, it should be isolated so that efforts can focus on improving and utilizing it.

Identifying skill at exploiting market inefficiencies is critical. But this identification is very difficult because of the large intrinsic random component of stock returns. It is vital to separate skill from luck when most of what goes on is due to luck.

A more readily achievable task of performance measurement is to identify the inefficiencies introduced by trading costs and any management fees.

A third, fairly straightforward task is noting mismatches between investment activities and the investment objective in terms of risk tolerance.

Return Definition

Total return for a portfolio with no cash contributions or distributions during the period is simply end-of-period market value, including any cash, divided by beginning market value, including cash. Conventionally, subtract one and multiply by 100 to present a percentage return. It should be noted that dividends are included in ending market value if not distributed.

It is assumed that an investor adds $5 million in cash on the fifteenth day of the month to a portfolio valued at $100 million. At the beginning of the month the value was $95 million, and at the end, $100 million. What is the monthly return? It is not zero percent, but rather 2.6 percent.

$$\left[\left(\frac{100}{95}\right)^{15/30} \times \left(\frac{100}{100}\right)^{15/30} - 1\right] \times 100 = 2.6\%$$

Cash flow to or from the portfolio may be taken into account by dividing the period into one subperiod before the flow and one after it. A distribution is included in the ending market value of the first subperiod. A contribution is included in the beginning market value of the second subperiod. The returns of the two subperiods are calculated separately and then compounded by taking their product. This produces a time-weighted rate of return.

An Example of Performance Analysis. A concrete example of performance analysis is provided in Exhibit 17.1. It is quite detailed and is only slightly edited from "real life." It should be more helpful than an abstract discussion. Note, though, that the example deals with but a single three-month period. A sequence of several years of such analyses might be necessary to draw profound conclusions. Conventional statistical analysis of the results may be misleading. The apparently large number of observations from the several hundred stocks included in the portfolio do not eliminate what is called small sample error, since the observations of stocks are not statistically independent. This is the return intercorrelation problem again. For example, a high-beta portfolio will outperform the market for an extended period, as long as the market is rising, without demonstrating any skill at stock selection. Skill at asset allocation (i.e., market timing) will not be demonstrated during this period either, because the rise may represent a single event and thus, in some sense, only one statistical observation. However, by separating difference in returns across stocks into those correlated with beta and those uncorrelated with beta, a sample of residual returns can be constructed that better satisfies the statistical model of independent observations. Thus, beta-adjusted returns are of great interest. At a lower level, it is desirable to partition returns from covariant group rotation strategies from those based on security selection.

It should be noted that the term "variance" is used in the example as an "accounting variance from standard," as opposed to the concept of "statistical variance."

Using Performance Analysis Well

In using the foregoing analysis, it is important to keep in mind the influence of so-called small-sample error. Ideally, the investor should be able to present statistical confidence intervals around the accounting variances that would show the degree of uncertainty as to the performance likely to be realized in the future. Unfortunately, the tools to do this are not well developed. In their absence, the data should be treated with caution.

For a client interested in assessing an investment manager's performance, a good way to increase confidence in the measurement is to combine data from all portfolios managed in the same way for other clients. This reduces the influence of an essentially random selection of a subset of approved stocks actually held in a single-client portfolio.

EXHIBIT 17.1   A Performance Analysis

M E M O

RE: XXXXX Performance Analysis — Quarter Ending March 31, 1983

An analysis of our performance yields both some encouraging and perhaps some surprising results.

In an upward-moving market, our accounts continued to outperform the Value Line market-capitalization-weighted average. The difference may be analyzed as follows:

TABLE 1

ACTIVE ACCOUNT XXXXX PERFORMANCE

Quarter Ending March 31, 1983

	Percentage of Total	Return Variance
Value Line Cap-Wtd	10.0%	
Timing.		−0.1
Selection.		+2.8
XXXXX Holding-Wtd.	12.7	
Implementation		−0.1
XXXXX Average Actual	12.6	
Total		+2.6

"Timing Variances" are generated by the differences between Value Line capitalization-weighted beta and our holding-weighted beta multiplied by the slope of the best-fit equation for the period:

% return = 9.2 + 6.7 (Beta)

During this period we had a slight negative timing variance (−0.1 percent) based on a small low-beta bias during an up quarter.

The "Selection Variance" and "Timing Variance" together make up the difference between the returns of two idealized portfolios for the quarter, one weighted by initial market capitalization and the other by initial XXXXX holding values.

The "Timing Variance" is that return difference which can be accounted for by differences in portfolio sensitivity to the market (beta) for the period. The difference in beta multiplied by the slope of a best-fit line relating return and beta for the quarter. Betas are those provided by Value Line. Selection Variance is what remains of the gap between market-capitalization-weighted returns after Timing Variance is subtracted.

During the period, there was a healthy positive "Selection Variance" (2.8 percent) and only a small negative "Implementation Variance" (−0.1 percent). The latter was associated with a smooth trading implementation of a new strategy during the period.

The "Implementation Variance" is the difference between average account returns as reported to the client and the returns of 100 percent equity portfolios based on beginning-of-the-quarter performance of buys versus sales, and effects of tenders, bankruptcies, and so forth, which cause a stock to be dropped from the database during the quarter.

Surprisingly, however, the favorable selection variance of +2.8 percent was composed primarily of within-strategy stock selection variances (+2.0 percent) rather than across-strategy variances (+0.8 percent). Tables 2 and 3 detail these

(*continued*)

EXHIBIT 17.1   A Performance Analysis (*cont'd*)

variances by strategy. Note that the "999 Sale" strategy represents all Value Line stocks not included in our strategies.

TABLE 2

STRATEGY VARIANCES BY STRATEGY

Quarter Ending March 31, 1983

	Holding Share	Cap-Wtd Return	Cap-Wtd Beta	Beta Adjusted Cap-Wtd Return*	Difference from Market Cap-Wtd Return	Contribution to Strategy Variance
141 Yield	0.3089	9.87	0.859	10.77	0.75	0.23%
541 Cyclical	0.4936	11.07	1.063	10.55	0.53	0.26
641 Corp. Recov.	0.0561	15.41	1.054	14.95	4.93	0.28
741 Real	0.1100	10.01	0.971	10.13	0.11	0.01
999 Sale	0.0314	9.80	1.026	9.53	−0.49	−0.02
						0.75%

* The difference between capitalization-weighted return and this column were included in the overall timing variance.

TABLE 3

STOCK SELECTION VARIANCES BY STRATEGY

Quarter Ending March 31, 1983

	Holdings Share	Holdings Wtd Return	Holdings Wtd Beta	Beta Adjusted Holdings Wtd Return	Difference from Beta-Adjusted Cap-Wtd Return	Contribution to Stock Selection Variance
141 Yield	0.3089	9.86	0.840	10.85	0.08	0.02%
541 Cyclical	0.4936	14.35	1.056	13.89	3.34	1.65
641 Corp. Recov.	0.0561	17.43	1.064	16.92	1.97	0.11
741 Real	0.1100	10.99	0.966	11.14	1.01	0.11
999 Sale	0.0314	12.94	1.005	12.83	3.30	0.10
						1.99%

Not only were we fortunate in our strategies, we held the right amounts of each stock in these strategies. Interim monthly figures have indicated that an equal-weighted bias was a strong contributor to our favorable quarter.

The first two attached strategy selection charts are a useful graphical visualization of the material in Tables 1, 2, and 3.

The first figure [Figure 17.9] demonstrates quarterly market, holding-weighted, and actual returns plotted against beta, together with best-fits between returns and beta. (Note that individual Value Line stocks lying behind the best-fit line are not shown.) The full circle represents our holdings; the empty circle contrasts the Value Line market; and the ''X'' gives actual account average return.

After the summary chart, there is a more detailed figure [Figure 17.10] with a separate color for each strategy, including one for all Value Line stocks not in one of our strategies. The empty circles give market-capitalization-weighted portfolios incorporating the stocks in each strategy. The filled circles show our holding-weighted portfolios. In both cases, the weights are determined at the beginning of the quarter. The areas of each circle are proportional to the percentage of market-capitalization or our holding value contained within the strategy.

When favorable strategic selection has occurred, the filled circle is larger than the empty circle of the same color (strategy) of those strategies with the greatest vertical distance above the diagonal best-fit line. When favorable stock selection has occurred within the strategy, the filled circle has a greater vertical distance above the best-fit line than has the empty circle.

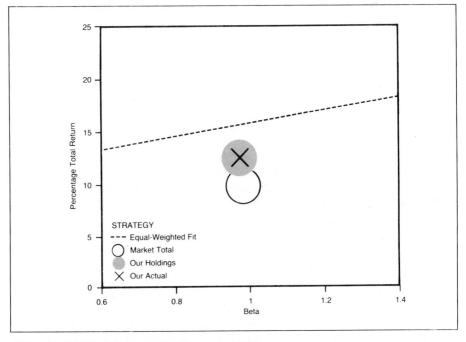

FIG. 17.9 Our Performance; First Quarter of 1983

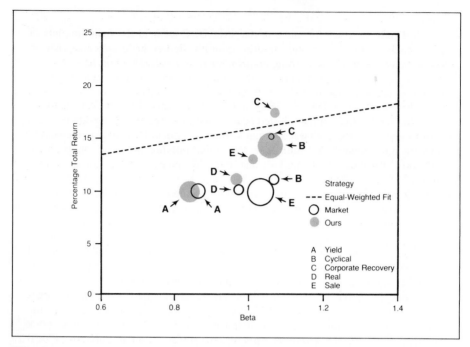

FIG. 17.10 Our Strategies vs. Market, First Quarter of 1983

Another way to increase confidence is to collect data at more frequent intervals. However, this increases the effective sample size only if many distinct investment decisions are being made for each period analyzed. And to the degree that results in adjacent periods are intercorrelated, this approach would not add effectively independent observations. In practice, for example, monthly analysis might be used for analyzing the power of a valuation model unbiased as to covariant group, quarterly analysis for assessing group strategy, and annual analysis for market timing. This implies, unless the skill level is very great indeed, that periods of 20 years may be necessary to detect skill at market timing, while individual stock selection power might be revealed in under two years.

Identifying trading costs on the other hand, may be done over a period of a few months. It is also possible to assess mismatches between investment holdings and risk tolerance for a large portfolio based simply on security return history, without any actual investment experience.

Detecting Mismatches With Investment Objectives

Investment returns are far harder to predict, and thus to control, than are investment risks. Management of the investment function should consequently begin with risk control. Reasonably-sized stock portfolios will have systematic risk quite close to their weighted average-measured security betas. Beta estimates are published for about 1,800 Value Line stocks. Betas for smaller firms can probably be estimated close enough for this purpose by regressing the stock returns measured quarterly over a five-year period against returns of the S&P 500. For long-term investments a correction of about one-third the deviation from one should be subtracted to allow for a tendency toward beta regression to the mean value over time. That is, a measured beta of 1.6 might be corrected to 1.4.

Specifying investment objectives to include a range for acceptable average portfolio beta calculated in this way will generally avoid the worst mismatches between investment objectives and actual holdings. If holding-weighted average beta lies outside such a bound, it is time to apply corrective measures. For example, a pension fund aiming at 6 percent real returns probably will have to accept betas on the order of one for a 100 percent equity portfolio. If unwilling to engage in market timing, this institutional investor might choose a practical range between 0.9 and 1.1.

The investor should also control the effective number of stocks in the portfolio, using a weighted average:

If x_ζ is stock ζ's percentage market value and ξ means the summation over all stocks, then:

$$\text{Effective Number } N = \frac{1}{\sum_\zeta (x_\zeta/100)^2}$$

Note that N will be smaller than the actual number, unless each stock has an equal percentage.

A potentially useful rule of thumb for large dollar portfolios might be to control the effective number to 20 or above. This is not a sufficient rule, however, to avoid group risk. If the investor has little skill in industry selection, the effective number of industry groups should also be pushed to 10 or more.

Detecting Changes in Areas of Focus

In operating businesses, greater experience in a particular activity usually implies higher effectiveness. While this thesis may not be valid in an efficient market, its influence is strong enough to cause client concern when an investment manager departs from his usual investment style. If indeed the manager has skill in finding one kind of market inefficiency, the argument runs, he is likely to have less of it when he tries something else. Overall, this view has probably done more harm than good in the investment arena. Over a period of years it is necessary to evolve, as competitors learn to do what you have already done.

Notwithstanding these protestations, over a short period, radical changes in style probably should be a signal for further inquiry, even if the manager is the investor himself. How should these changes in style be monitored?

At the broadest level, the most useful equity framework seems to be simply to plot the portfolios on a two-dimensional grid, as shown by Figure 17.11. The horizontal axis represents systematic risk, measured in beta with high beta on the right. The vertical axis represents specific risk, with high risk at the top. Specific risk is measured by the standard deviations of the residual returns unexplained by beta.

Portfolio measurements can be taken in two ways. They can be estimated at

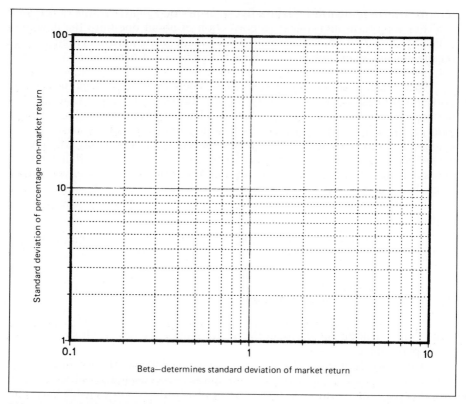

FIG. 17.11 Investment Style Grid

a point in time using weighted average historical data based on the stocks they contain. Alternatively, they can be estimated using portfolio returns over time related to those of the market portfolio, usually the S&P 500. The two approaches will not give identical results, but, if used consistently, both are sufficiently valid to pick up the kind of radical short-term changes sought.

The usefulness of detecting changes in focus is most apparent when investment decision making has been delegated to the professional investment manager. This raises a new set of practical issues.

WHO MAKES THE BIG DECISIONS?

Many large institutional pools of money (e.g., pension funds) are invested through a stable of professional investment managers. Over a long period, the typical result is the market return, perhaps minus transactions costs, and certainly minus fees. This judgment has a ring of truth, and it reflects a simple fact. If you want to have better returns than the market, you have to be different from the market. Of course, the danger is that being different might mean that you will be worse.

While large institutions face a fee structure that is minuscule in relation to the size of the assets managed, even this fee is probably too large if the result is a "closet index fund," an active fund that, because of its size, is in reality an index fund.

The investment management business is in danger of becoming a profession. While this is gratifying to its practitioners and perhaps even satisfying to its clients, it is not necessarily good investing. Efficiency is mechanical and deserves no mystique. The creativity and insight which sometimes leads to exploitation of market inefficiencies is worth more. But it is not likely to be produced in quantity through professional training, because the result will be self-canceling in the competition of the marketplace.

It should be remembered, in dealing with investment managers, that collectively they will not beat the market, because they make up too large a part of it. Much of the "track records" from which skill is asserted are the result of fortunate coincidences.

Nevertheless, professional investment managers can be extremely valuable, even if all they do is prevent the investor from making common, avoidable mistakes.

Types of Decisions That Should Be Delegated

The more the investor observes himself attempting to use in the investment area the lessons learned in a lifetime of business experience, the more he, or his institution, should delegate.

The large corporation, which has hired professional investment management to operate in-house, has the technical ability at least to cure the common mistakes. It could readily set up an in-house index fund and get market average returns. If transaction costs are held to a minimum, it is likely to rank in the top half of all money managers. One of the reasons why few do this may be the lack of distance from senior corporate management who impose their own egos and hard-won assumptions on the in-house investment manager who is facing a much more difficult task than the senior executive imagines.

The investor should himself make the decisions as to the most risk, both systematic and specific risk, that he can tolerate. He must determine the investment time horizon. He should in most cases proceed to set up a program of selecting and monitoring the performance of professional investment managers trying to give him the most return they are able within this risk level. Where demonstrations of skill are unconvincing, he should use low-cost passive tools, index funds. Because most professional managers are specialized by asset class, the investor will have to participate in, or take charge of, asset allocation. The portfolio should be widely diversified, including substantial amounts of other assets beyond U.S. stocks and bonds. Except for minor rebalancing to maintain overall proportions appropriate to risk constraints and time horizon, the major category asset allocation should probably be passive. Even if the potential is great, only demonstration of skill in this area makes it worthwhile to increase risks to the portfolio through market timing, and this skill takes too long to demonstrate practically.

The investor will need to restrict his managers to take account of his needs for asset–liability matching and total income portfolio needs. This is a neglected area but relatively straightforward. The client must convince the manager that he really does want to be treated individually in a way which is important to his overall investment objectives.

There are strong arguments for delegating any active group rotation and individual stock selection, but which managers have demonstrated ability?

Getting Behind Performance Records

The worst mistake in assessing demonstrated ability at stock selection or group rotation is to focus on overall performance. The investor should get behind the overall numbers, using tools such as the example performance analysis report, to see if the organization is really doing what it says and thinks it is doing.

The second-worst mistake is to stop at the performance records. After all, they contain a strong ingredient of random chance. Styles of investing, particularly those depending on biases toward one or two specific covariant groups, will often experience great success for three or four years and mediocrity or failure for the next few years.

Talk to the people involved. Find out how sympathetic they are to your assumptions. If you find yourself too comfortable, they probably would make the same mistakes you would. It is normal for a good professional investor who avoids consensus to have ideas the client sees as wrong. The manager should be keenly aware of common investment mistakes and be willing to stand up to the client in order to avoid them.

Another thing to look for is access to detailed records, which can be used to analyze performance at greater frequency or in detail. This not only helps to evaluate the manager; it is a sign that he is trying to help himself.

Finally, if possible, get data from other clients so you can estimate account performance dispersion. Even if the overall manager's specific risk is low, your account's risk may be high, unless there are proper internal controls. These can be assessed by observing the standard deviation in annual return across accounts. Based on practical experience, it is difficult to get below about 3 percent, so that would be good performance.

There are also professional consultants to help select an investment manager. They can be particularly helpful in selecting a list to interview, in collecting data from other clients, and in helping to serve as a bridge between two cultures, operating experience and investment experience.

Two Cultures

The emergence of large efficient securities markets represents a comparatively recent historical phenomenon to which our culture — our language, our patterns of thought, and our actions, have not yet adjusted.

The better able we are to rid ourselves of our preconceptions, the better we will perform in this environment. The following credo, derived in the course of the chapter, may serve as a reminder.

Good Portfolio Management

Foremost, a good investor respects the efficiency of the market and its high degree of randomness, and acts accordingly. At both the individual security and the portfolio level, the investor is on the lookout for performance reversals. Groups of stocks that have unusually good returns for several years will become mediocre, and vice versa. It is helpful to have standards of value that are not swept along with the crowd during periods of market rises or panics.

The good investor may abandon the search for market inefficiencies, keep trading to a minimum, and outperform over the long term most professional investment managers. Alternatively, if market inefficiencies are sought out, they will have a cost both in investment research effort and in the trading that results. The good investor will focus his attempts to discover inefficiencies on just those kinds of information in which he has a strong comparative advantage. He must have defensible reasons to believe he excels in collecting, interpreting, or implementing this information.

Investment consensus is not valuable. The good investor will strive to arrive at investment conclusions independently of other investors, perhaps going so far as to ignore published investment research and even whole avenues of approach well worn by competitors. His findings will reflect an assessment of difference from the consensus.

The good investor will try to avoid ascribing his best performance to skill. He will recognize that any definite use of information that has worked over a period of many years is likely to be eventually imitated away as the market continues inexorably toward greater efficiency. This means he must be sufficiently opportunistic to continue innovating if he is to retain his skills.

The good investment manager respects the value of diversification. His hallmark is to remove all risks that can be diversified at little cost or loss of opportunity. This usually requires a clear definition of where to make an active versus a passive decision. No implicit decision should be allowed to reduce diversification.

SUGGESTED READING

Arbel, Avner, Steven Carvell, and Paul Strebel. "Giraffes, Institutions and Neglected Firms." *Financial Analysts Journal* (May–June, 1983).

Ball, Ray, and Philip Brown. "An Empirical Evaluation of Accounting Income Numbers." *Journal of Accounting Research.* Vol. 6, No. 2 (Autumn, 1968).

Bing, Ralph A. "Stock Valuation: Theory vs. Practice." *Financial Analysts Journal* (May–June 1971).

Black, Fischer. "The Trouble with Econometric Models." *Financial Analysts Journal* (March–April 1982).

Brealey, Richard A., and Stewart Myers. *Principles of Corporate Finance* (New York: McGraw-Hill, 1981).

Cootner, Paul, ed. *The Random Character of Stock Market Prices*, rev. ed. (Cambridge, Mass.: M.I.T. Press, 1964).

Farrell, James L. "Homogeneous Stock Groupings, Implications For Portfolio Management." *Financial Analysts Journal* (May–June 1975).

Ibbotson, Roger G., and Rex A. Sinquefield. *Stocks, Bonds, Bills and Inflation: The Past and The Future*, The Financial Analysts Research Foundation (Charlottesville, Va.: 1982).

Lustig, Ivan L., and Philip A. Leinbach. "The Small Firm Effect." *Financial Analysts Journal* (May–June 1983).

Loeb, Thomas F. "Trading Costs: The Critical Link Between Investment Information and Results." *Financial Analysts Journal* (May–June 1983).

Maginn, John L., and Donald L. Tuttle, eds. *Managing Portfolios, A Dynamic Process* (New York: Warren, Gorham and Lamont, 1983).

Malkiel, Burton G. *A Random Walk Down Wall Street* (New York: W. W. Norton, 1981).

Markowitz, Harry M. *Portfolio Selection, Efficient Diversification of Investments* (New York: John Wiley and Sons, 1959).

Paynor, A. C., and I. M. D. Little. *Higgledy Piggledy Growth Again*. Oxford, U.K.: Basil Blackwell, 1966).

Sharpe, William F. *Investments* (Englewood Cliffs, N.J.: Prentice-Hall, 1978).

Wilcox, Jarrod W. "The PB-ROE Valuation Model." *Financial Analysts Journal* (Jan.–Feb. 1984).

18

Historical Returns on Investment Instruments

ROGER G. IBBOTSON
REX A. SINQUEFIELD
LAURENCE B. SIEGEL

INTRODUCTION

The twentieth century has seen a remarkable variety of world events, and they have affected capital markets as well as other institutions. The Great Depression, for example, was associated with an 84 percent decline in the value of common stocks, while the long growth era of 1948–1965 showed a 13-fold gain in the value of stocks with dividends reinvested. Dramatic events have occurred in other markets. In the 1970s, bond markets fell sharply in the face of rising interest and inflation rates, while holders of real estate equity found themselves suddenly wealthy. Collectibles and metals also were in vogue and enjoyed high returns in the 1970s; short-term money market instruments, after underperforming inflation for years, emerged as winners in the 1980s.

These short- and intermediate-term ups and downs of the various capital markets are interesting to the observer and exciting to the investor. They are, however, only part of the long-term picture. Given a long enough period of study, the capital market's enduring relationships, masked by the noise of short-period data, can be discerned.

Perhaps the easiest relationship to observe is that between return and risk. Investors are risk-averse, which means that given two assets that have the same expected return, all other things being equal, investors will buy the less risky one. A corollary of this observation is that investors expect higher returns for taking risk. Although there is no guarantee that these expectations will be realized, the set of common stocks called the Standard & Poor's (S&P) 500 outperformed riskless U.S. Treasury bills by an average margin of 6.0 percentage points per year in the period 1926–1982. This extra return (called a risk premium) may be interpreted as the price paid to investors for bearing the risk of stock ownership.

Scope of Study and Assumptions

This chapter presents the historical returns on a broad range of assets for long periods. S&P stocks, U.S. government bonds and bills, and inflation are studied for 1926–1982; corporate bonds in the United States are examined for 1926–1978, with some aggregate data for 1926–1981; non-S&P stocks, which include both listed and unlisted issues, are studied for 1947–1981; summary data are presented for real estate and other assets for 1947–1978; international stocks are studied for 1960–1981; and international bonds for 1975–1980.

For most asset categories, the relationship between return and risk is shown by displaying the standard deviation of returns as well as the mean return. Standard deviation is a statistical measure of the volatility of returns. The standard deviation is calculated such that, for a normal or bell-shaped distribution, two-thirds of the observations (returns) fall within (plus or minus) one standard deviation of the mean, and 95 percent fall within two standard deviations of the mean. For example, in Table 18.1, the standard deviation of 1947–1978 New York Stock Exchange (NYSE) returns is given as 17.73 percent, and the arithmetic mean return, 11.56 percent. These numbers indicate that two-thirds of the outcomes were within 17.73 percentage points (plus or minus) of 11.56 percent, and 95 percent were within two standard deviations (35.46 percentage points) of 11.56 percent. While the standard deviation of returns is not a flawless measure of risk, it is a useful estimate. During most historical periods, higher standard deviations have been associated with higher returns. (See Chapter 17 for a more detailed discussion of standard deviation.)

In this analysis, the historical risk–return relationship is not used to forecast the future. Such forecasts, however, have been made for stocks and bonds with considerable success. The underlying assumption of these forecasts is that the return paid to investors for taking risk is relatively constant over time and can be deduced from historical results, while the return paid to investors as compensation for inflation varies with the inflation rate. In addition, investors receive a real riskless rate of interest that has varied considerably over short periods but that has averaged zero over the long term. The sum of the inflation

TABLE 18.1   U.S. Capital Market Total Annual Returns, 1947–1978

	Arithmetic Mean	Geometric Mean*	Standard Deviation
Common stocks			
NYSE	11.56%	10.16%	17.73%
Over-the-counter	14.79	12.63	21.79
Total	11.79	10.34	18.02
Fixed income corporate securities			
Preferred stocks	3.31	2.92	9.20
Long-term corporate bonds	2.42	2.21	6.72
Intermediate corporate bonds	4.00	3.87	5.48
Commercial paper	4.29	4.27	2.37
Total	3.03	2.89	5.53
Real estate			
Farms	11.88	11.69	6.79
Residential housing	6.93	6.88	3.28
Total	8.19	8.14	3.53
U.S. government securities			
U.S. Treasury bills	3.53	3.51	2.11
U.S. Treasury notes	3.73	3.65	3.71
U.S. Treasury bonds	2.56	2.39	6.17
Agencies	4.08	4.01	3.92
Total	3.23	3.17	3.78
Municipal (state and local) bonds			
Short-term	2.45	2.44	1.37
Long-term	2.01	1.69	8.20
Total	2.02	1.75	7.62
Market total	6.97%	6.88%	4.65%

* Compound annual rate of return

Source: Roger G. Ibbotson and Carol L. Fall, "The United States Market Wealth Portfolio,"
The Journal of Portfolio Management (Fall 1979), p. 90

return, the real riskless rate of interest, and rate of return compensation for the risk of that asset is the expected return for the asset. An example of the use of this method of forecasting is found in *Stocks, Bonds, Bills, and Inflation*.[1]

There are other factors that influence the return on an investment in equilibrium. These include marketability, taxation, and management costs. Risk

---

[1] Roger G. Ibbotson and Rex A. Sinquefield, *Stocks, Bonds, Bills, and Inflation: The Past and the Future* (Charlottesville, Va.: Financial Analysts Research Foundation, 1982).

itself occurs across different dimensions: economy or beta risk; inflation or interest rate risk; residual risk; and other possible risks. The various assets discussed in this chapter are priced by the market according to the desirability of all their attributes. Thus, expected returns on a wide variety of assets are not determined solely by risk characteristics.

The aggregate market value of an asset category is another characteristic of interest to investors, who may want to study aggregate value out of general curiosity or because they want to hold assets in the approximate proportions in which they exist in the market. For example, U.S. government bonds have been falling as a percentage of total investment assets for 30 years. This is surprising in view of the growth of government in that period, but it reflects the great growth of the stock and real estate markets. Summary data on aggregate market values are presented here to highlight such trends.

RETURNS ON A BROAD SPECTRUM OF U.S. ASSETS

Ibbotson and Fall[2] studied the returns on stocks, bonds, and real estate for a 32-year period, 1947–1978. Figure 18.1 shows the growth (with reinvestment of income) of one dollar invested in each of these assets on December 31, 1946. Clearly, common stocks were the big winner over the period, with the dollar growing to $23.30 by the end of 1978. Real estate, which grew to $12.22, was second (although most investors bought levered real estate and had returns even higher than those of the stock market). Fixed income securities — government, municipal, and corporate bonds and preferred stocks — were disappointing performers, all net losers relative to inflation over the period.

A market wealth portfolio of the assets is shown in Figure 18.1, consisting of each of the assets represented in proportion to their aggregate market value for each year. The return on the market wealth portfolio is graphed along with the other assets in Figure 18.1 (market). The aggregate value of each asset category as a percentage of the total for all of the assets is graphed year-by-year in Figure 18.2. This graph shows that real estate is the largest component of the market. Common stock increased its proportion of the market over most of the period, while the fixed corporate security component (corporate bonds plus preferred stocks) declined. The municipal bond component rose during the early part of the period, before leveling off in more recent times. The U.S. government debt dropped in terms of relative wealth almost throughout the period.

Table 18.1 presents the geometric mean (compound) and arithmetic mean annual return of the components of the market wealth portfolio, along with the standard deviations of returns. This table breaks the broad categories into some of their component parts showing that over-the-counter stocks had the best performance of any asset subcategory, with an annual compound return of 12.63 percent. Farmland was a close second, 11.69 percent, with residential housing somewhat lower at 6.88 percent. (Coincidentally, 6.88 percent was also

---

[2] Roger G. Ibbotson and Carol L. Fall, "The United States Market Wealth Portfolio," *The Journal of Portfolio Management* (Fall 1979), pp. 82–92.

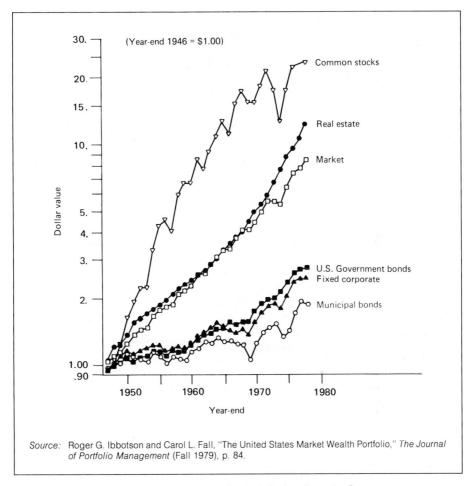

FIG. 18.1 Cumulative Wealth Indexes of Capital Market Security Groups

the compound annual return on the whole market wealth portfolio.) Both real estate components had relatively low standard deviations of returns, so it is reasonable to suppose that these assets had high returns and low risk. However, real estate price series are often produced using an appraisal method that artificially smooths price changes. Thus, while it is justified to conclude that real estate was a very good performer in 1947–1978, it cannot be concluded that these particular standard deviations are evidence of low risk in real estate investments.

Real estate has characteristics that distinguish it from stocks and bonds. Real estate, directly held, may not only be hard to sell; it requires management effort by the owner. Thus, buying it has some of the attributes of buying a business rather than just investing money. Real estate limited partnerships and investment trusts have arisen in response to investors' needs for a manage-

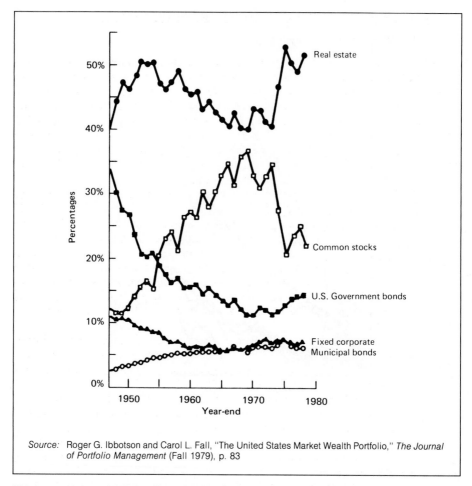

FIG. 18.2 Value of Capital Market Security Groups as a Percentage of the Total

ment-free investment vehicle in real estate. Some of these instruments preserve the favorable tax characteristics of real estate while others do not. The indices of real estate returns used represent directly held, nonleveraged real estate.

The fixed-income securities had uniformly poor returns, with short-term obligations outperforming long-term ones. It is not surprising that municipal bonds did the worst, since they have low yields because of their tax advantages.

The total for each major category is the market-value-weighted sum of the returns of its components. The market return is the market-value-weighted sum of all the component returns.

A 57-YEAR HISTORY OF STOCKS, BONDS, BILLS, AND INFLATION

As noted earlier, a long-period study can uncover relationships hidden in short-period data. The Ibbotson and Sinquefield book cited earlier, plus updates, covered the 57 years from 1926 to 1982, which included many types of events: a major depression; a world war; various periods of boom and bust; and low and high inflation and interest rates. Although there is no way of knowing what events will occur in the future, it is reasonable to assume that the historical events of a 57-year period are representative of the types of events that will occur. Thus, the relationships derived from this examination of capital market returns may be useful in predicting future returns.

This chapter presents capital appreciation and (where relevant) income returns for five asset categories: common stocks, represented by the S&P 500 common stock index; small company stocks, defined as the one-fifth of the stocks on the NYSE that rank as the smallest in terms of market value (price per share times number of shares outstanding); U.S. government bonds with approximately 20 years to maturity; long-term corporate bonds; and 30-day U.S. Treasury bills. In addition, similar data for the general price level (inflation) is presented. While the price level itself cannot be purchased, it represents a market basket of goods and services that can be purchased and serves as a benchmark for asset returns.

Figure 18.3 shows the growth of one dollar invested in four of the above-described assets on December 31, 1925. Stocks were the winner by a very large margin, with small company stocks growing to $763.83 by the end of 1982, with dividends reinvested and S&P 500 stocks growing to $162.22. This phenomenal growth was not without considerable risk. Returns on S&P 500 stocks for individual years varied from plus 54 percent (1933) to minus 43 percent (1931), and short holding periods for stocks variously showed large gains and losses. Total return indices of corporate and government bonds stood at $10.37 and $7.25, respectively, at the end of 1982. A substantial fraction of the return on bonds was achieved in one year, 1982, in which bond proceeds rallied sharply from their depressed levels and showed record one-year gains (see Table 18.2). Treasury bills and inflation both rose by approximately a factor of five over the period 1926–1982.

The graph in Figure 18.3 can be examined to reveal some specific market facts. The Great Crash of 1929–1932 cut the value of stocks drastically but, with dividends reinvested, the 1929 high was exceeded as soon as 1936 and was passed for the last time in 1943. Likewise, the so-called second great crash of 1973–1974, which was larger than any other decline since the Great Crash, was followed by a recovery that, in 1976, passed the previous peak. The year-by-year common stock returns appear to divide into three periods: the Depression and the first part of World War II, in which returns were poor and highly volatile; the wartime and postwar boom, in which returns were high and stable; and the current period of generally high inflation rates, 1966–1982, in which returns became more volatile, though not as much as in 1926–1941. The volatility of common stock returns is depicted in the bar chart in Figure 18.4.

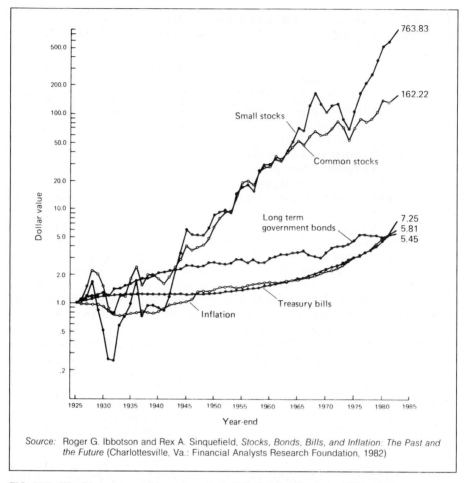

FIG. 18.3 Wealth Indexes of Investments in U.S. Capital Markets, 1926–1982

Standard & Poor's 500 stock returns were positive in two-thirds of the years (38 out of 57 years). The longest period over which a year-end investor in the S&P 500 total return index would have earned a negative return was the 14-year period 1929–1942. A month-end investor would have earned negative returns for an additional three months, from the beginning of December 1928 through February 1943.

The longest period for which an investor would have earned a negative return in real terms was more recent. It covers 18 years and 3 months, from the beginning of July 1964 through the end of September 1982. In nominal terms, the investor would have more than tripled his investment over that same period of time.

As shown by the inflation series in Figure 18.3, the first seven years of the study period were deflationary. This is one of the many deflationary times in American and world history; the persistence of high inflation rates in the 1970s

TABLE 18.2 Basic Series: Year-by-Year Total Returns, 1926–1982

(percentages)

Year	S&P 500 Common Stocks	Small Company Stocks	Long-Term Government Bonds	Long-Term Corporate Bonds	U.S. Treasury Bills	Consumer Price Index
1926	11.62	0.28	7.77	7.37	3.27	−1.49
1927	37.49	22.10	8.93	7.44	3.12	−2.08
1928	43.61	39.69	0.10	2.84	3.24	−0.97
1929	−8.42	−51.36	3.42	3.27	4.75	0.19
1930	−24.90	−38.15	4.66	7.98	2.41	−6.03
1931	−43.34	−49.75	−5.31	−1.85	1.07	−9.52
1932	−8.19	−5.39	16.84	10.82	0.96	−10.30
1933	53.99	142.87	−0.08	10.38	0.30	0.51
1934	−1.44	24.22	10.02	13.84	0.16	2.03
1935	47.67	40.19	4.98	9.61	0.17	2.99
1936	33.92	64.80	7.51	6.74	0.18	1.21
1937	−35.03	−58.01	0.23	2.75	0.31	3.10
1938	31.12	32.80	5.53	6.13	−0.02	−2.78
1939	−0.41	0.35	5.94	3.97	0 02	−0.48
1940	−9.78	−5.16	6.09	3.39	0.00	0.96
1941	−11.59	−9.00	0.93	2.73	0.06	9.72
1942	20.34	44.51	3.22	2.60	0.27	9.29
1943	25.90	88.37	2.08	2.83	0.35	3.16
1944	19.75	53.72	2.81	4.73	0.33	2.11
1945	36.44	73.61	10.73	4.08	0.33	2.25
1946	−8.07	−11.63	−0.10	1.72	0.35	18.17
1947	5.71	0.92	−2.63	−2.34	0.50	9.01
1948	5.50	−2.11	3.40	4.14	0.81	2.71
1949	18.79	19.75	6.45	3.31	1.10	−1.80
1950	31.71	38.75	0.06	2.12	1.20	5.79
1951	24.02	7.80	−3.94	−2.69	1.49	5.87
1952	18.37	3.03	1.16	3.52	1.66	0.88
1953	−0.99	−6.49	3.63	3.41	1.82	0.62
1954	52.62	60.58	7.19	5.39	0.86	−0.50
1955	31.56	20.44	−1.30	0.48	1.57	0.37
1956	6.56	4.28	−5.59	−6.81	2.46	2.86
1957	−10.78	−14.57	7.45	8.71	3.14	3.02
1958	43.36	64.89	−6.10	−2.22	1.54	1.76
1959	11.95	16.40	−2.26	−0.97	2.95	1.50
1960	0.47	−3.29	13.78	9.07	2.66	1.48
1961	26.89	32.09	0.97	4.82	2.13	0.67

(continued)

TABLE 18.2   Basic Series: Year-by-Year Total Returns, 1926–1982 (continued)

(percentages)

Year	S&P 500 Common Stocks	Small Company Stocks	Long-Term Government Bonds	Long-Term Corporate Bonds	U.S. Treasury Bills	Consumer Price Index
1962	−8.73	−11.90	6.89	7.95	2.73	1.22
1963	22.80	23.57	1.21	2.19	3.12	1.65
1964	16.48	23.52	3.51	4.77	3.54	1.19
1965	12.45	41.75	0.71	−0.46	3.93	1.92
1966	−10.06	−7.01	3.65	0.20	4.76	3.35
1967	23.98	85.57	−9.19	−4.95	4.21	3.04
1968	11.06	35.97	−0.26	2.57	5.21	4.72
1969	−8.50	−25.05	−5.08	−8.09	6.58	6.11
1970	4.01	−17.43	12.10	18.37	6.53	5.49
1971	14.31	16.50	13.23	11.01	4.39	3.36
1972	18.98	4.43	5.68	7.26	3.84	3.41
1973	−14.66	−30.90	−1.11	1.14	6.93	8.80
1974	−26.47	−19.95	4.35	−3.06	8.00	12.20
1975	37.20	52.82	9.19	14.64	5.80	7.01
1976	23.84	57.38	16.75	18.65	5.08	4.81
1977	−7.18	25.38	−0.67	1.71	5.12	6.77
1978	6.56	23.46	−1.16	−0.07	7.18	9.03
1979	18.44	43.46	−1.22	−4.18	10.38	13.31
1980	32.42	39.88	−3.95	−2.62	11.24	12.40
1981	−4.91	13.88	1.85	−0.96	14.71	8.94
1982	21.41	28.01	40.35	43.79	10.54	3.87

and early 1980s was unusual. It comes as a surprise to many that inflation rates (as measured by the Consumer Price Index, CPI), were negative in 50 different months since the end of World War II, and zero in 56 more months as of the end of 1981. There were three deflationary months in 1982. Before that, the last month with zero or negative inflation was January 1967.

The high inflation rates of 1966–1982 hurt the bond markets badly, and the spectacular recovery bull market of 1982 only recouped a small part of investors' losses. At the end of 1965, a 1925 one dollar investment in long-term government bonds had grown to $3.46 (including reinvestment of coupons), compared with $1.78 for the CPI. By the end of 1981, the gap had closed, with long-term government bonds at $5.16 and the CPI return index at $5.24. The 1982 market boosted the bond index to $7.25 and the CPI to only $5.45. Thus, over the long term, an investment in bonds has only slightly outrun inflation.

Figure 18.5 presents the geometric mean (compound annual) and arithmetic mean returns on the asset categories, along with standard deviations, showing that (in geometric mean terms) common stocks outperformed riskless U.S. Treasury bills by 6.0 percent per year. This may be thought of as the risk premium paid to investors for taking the investment risk of stocks rather than buying riskless securities. From the standard deviations and the distribution histograms, it is clear that stocks are riskier than Treasury bills. (The risk of Treasury bills is in fact overstated by the method used to produce Figure 18.5; while returns vary from period to period, the return for a given period is known in advance; that is, it is risk-free.) It is appropriate that common stocks return substantially more than Treasury bills; if they did not, no one would buy stocks.

Bonds, less risky than stocks because of their seniority in a firm's capital structure, do not command as high a risk premium. Long-term corporate bonds have outperformed Treasury bills by 0.5 percent per year over the study period.

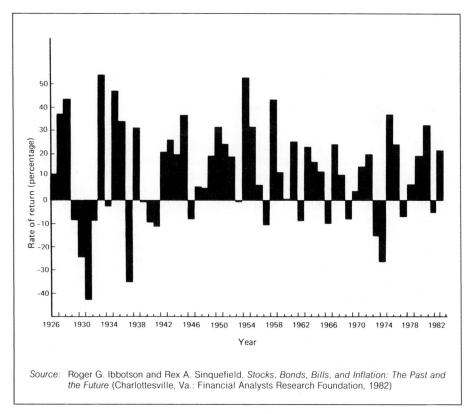

Source: Roger G. Ibbotson and Rex A. Sinquefield, *Stocks, Bonds, Bills, and Inflation: The Past and the Future* (Charlottesville, Va.: Financial Analysts Research Foundation, 1982)

FIG. 18.4 Year-by-Year Total Returns on Common Stocks

Series	Geometric Mean (%)	Arithmetic Mean (%)	Standard Deviation	Distribution
Common Stocks	9.3	11.6	21.5	
Small Stocks	12.4	18.3	36.7	
Long Term Corporate Bonds	4.2	4.4	7.6	
Long Term Government Bonds	3.5	3.8	7.4	
U.S. Treasury Bills	3.1	3.2	3.2	
Inflation	3.0	3.1	5.0	

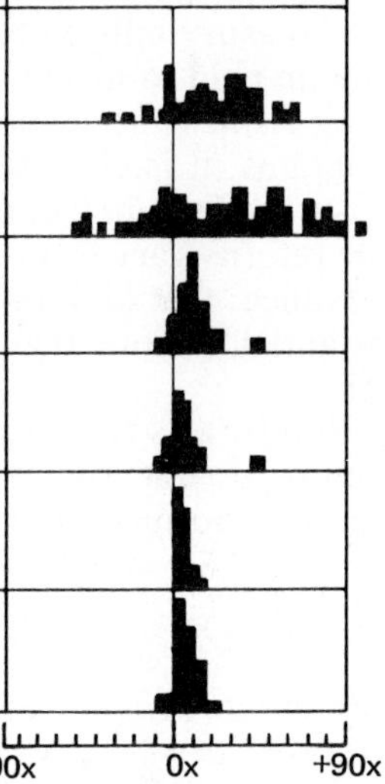

-90x   0x   +90x

Source: Roger G. Ibbotson and Rex A. Sinquefield, *Stocks, Bonds, Bills, and Inflation: The Past and the Future* (Charlottesville, Va.: Financial Analysts Research Foundation, 1982)

FIG. 18.5 Basic Series Investment Annual Returns, 1926–1982

This excess return may be regarded as a default premium for the default risk of corporate bonds. Long-term government bonds, which are virtually default-free, returned a 0.4 percent increment over short-term U.S. Treasury bills. This excess return may be thought of as the premium for the greater interest rate risk (i.e., the risk of price fluctuations) of long-term bonds, and is also called a maturity or liquidity premium.

Table 18.2 displays the year-by-year returns on stocks, government and corporate bonds, bills, and inflation presented in summary form earlier. These returns are converted to wealth indices (with year-end 1925 equal to $1.00) and displayed in Table 18.3. The numbers in this table, which show capital appreciation separately for stocks and government bonds, help illustrate the gains from the reinvestment of income (dividends and interest). While a $1.00 investment in common stocks at year-end 1925 would have grown to over $162 with dividend reinvestment, capital appreciation alone (without reinvestment) would have raised the value of the investment to only $11.02.

Inflation-adjusted total returns for the previously mentioned asset classes are presented year by year in Table 18.4. Wealth indices of these returns are displayed in Table 18.5. The by-now familiar dollar investment in common stocks in 1925 would have grown to $29.35 in 1925 dollars by the end of 1982. This means that the stock portfolio would have had more than 29 times as much

(text continues on page 18-20)

TABLE 18.3   Basic Series: Indexes of Year-End Cumulative Wealth, 1925–1982

(year-end 1925 = 1.000)

Year	S&P 500 Common Stocks		Small Company Stocks: Total Returns	Long-Term Government Bonds		Long-Term Corporate Bonds: Total Returns	U.S. Treasury Bills: Total Returns	Consumer Price Index: Total Returns
	Total Returns	Capital Gain		Total Returns	Capital Gain			
1925	1.000	1.000	1.000	1.000	1.000	1.000	1.000	1.000
1926	1.116	1.057	1.003	1.078	1.039	1.074	1.033	0.985
1927	1.535	1.384	1.224	1.174	1.095	1.154	1.065	0.965
1928	2.204	1.908	1.710	1.175	1.061	1.186	1.099	0.955
1929	2.018	1.681	0.832	1.215	1.059	1.225	1.152	0.957
1930	1.516	1.202	0.515	1.272	1.072	1.323	1.179	0.899
1931	0.859	0.636	0.259	1.204	0.981	1.299	1.192	0.814
1932	0.789	0.540	0.245	1.407	1.108	1.439	1.204	0.730
1933	1.214	0.792	0.594	1.406	1.073	1.588	1.207	0.734
1934	1.197	0.745	0.738	1.547	1.146	1.808	1.209	0.749
1935	1.767	1.053	1.035	1.624	1.170	1.982	1.211	0.771
1936	2.367	1.346	1.705	1.746	1.225	2.116	1.213	0.780
1937	1.538	0.827	0.716	1.750	1.194	2.174	1.217	0.804
1938	2.016	1.035	0.951	1.847	1.228	2.307	1.217	0.782
1939	2.008	0.979	0.954	1.957	1.271	2.399	1.217	0.778
1940	1.812	0.829	0.905	2.076	1.319	2.480	1.217	0.786
1941	1.602	0.681	0.823	2.095	1.305	2.548	1.218	0.862
1942	1.927	0.766	1.190	2.162	1.315	2.614	1.221	0.942

(continued)

TABLE 18.3 Basic Series: Indexes of Year-End Cumulative Wealth, 1925–1982 *(continued)*

(year-end 1925 = 1.000)

Year	S&P 500 Common Stocks Total Returns	S&P 500 Common Stocks Capital Gain	Small Company Stocks: Total Returns	Long-Term Government Bonds Total Returns	Long-Term Government Bonds Capital Gain	Long-Term Corporate Bonds: Total Returns	U.S. Treasury Bills: Total Returns	Consumer Price Index: Total Returns
1943	2.427	0.915	2.242	2.207	1.310	2.688	1.225	0.972
1944	2.906	1.041	3.446	2.270	1.314	2.815	1.229	0.993
1945	3.965	1.361	5.983	2.513	1.423	2.930	1.233	1.015
1946	3.645	1.199	5.287	2.511	1.392	2.980	1.238	1.199
1947	3.853	1.199	5.335	2.445	1.327	2.911	1.244	1.307
1948	4.065	1.191	5.223	2.528	1.340	3.031	1.254	1.343
1949	4.829	1.313	6.254	2.691	1.395	3.132	1.268	1.318
1950	6.360	1.600	8.677	2.692	1.366	3.198	1.283	1.395
1951	7.888	1.863	9.355	2.586	1.281	3.112	1.302	1.477
1952	9.336	2.082	9.638	2.616	1.262	3.221	1.324	1.490
1953	9.244	1.944	9.013	2.711	1.270	3.331	1.348	1.499
1954	14.108	2.820	14.473	2.906	1.325	3.511	1.360	1.492
1955	18.561	3.564	17.431	2.868	1.271	3.527	1.381	1.497
1956	19.778	3.658	18.177	2.708	1.164	3.287	1.415	1.540
1957	17.646	3.134	15.529	2.910	1.208	3.573	1.459	1.587
1958	25.298	4.327	25.605	2.733	1.097	3.494	1.482	1.615
1959	28.322	4.694	29.804	2.671	1.029	3.460	1.526	1.639
1960	28.455	4.554	28.823	3.039	1.124	3.774	1.566	1.663
1961	36.106	5.607	38.072	3.068	1.092	3.956	1.600	1.674
1962	32.955	4.945	33.540	3.280	1.122	4.270	1.643	1.695

Year							
1963	40.469	5.879	41.444	3.319	1.092	4.364	1.695	1.723
1964	47.139	6.642	51.193	3.436	1.084	4.572	1.754	1.743
1965	53.008	7.244	72.567	3.460	1.047	4.552	1.823	1.777
1966	47.674	6.295	67.479	3.586	1.036	4.560	1.910	1.836
1967	59.104	7.560	123.870	3.257	0.895	4.335	1.991	1.892
1968	65.642	8.140	168.428	3.248	0.846	4.446	2.094	1.981
1969	60.059	7.210	126.233	3.083	0.754	4.086	2.232	2.102
1970	62.465	7.222	104.226	3.457	0.791	4.837	2.378	2.218
1971	71.406	8.001	121.423	3.914	0.843	5.370	2.482	2.292
1972	84.956	9.252	126.807	4.136	0.840	5.760	2.577	2.371
1973	72.500	7.645	87.618	4.090	0.775	5.825	2.756	2.579
1974	53.311	5.373	70.142	4.268	0.748	5.647	2.976	2.894
1975	73.144	7.068	107.189	4.661	0.754	6.474	3.149	3.097
1976	90.584	8.422	168.691	5.441	0.815	7.681	3.309	3.246
1977	84.076	7.453	211.500	5.405	0.750	7.813	3.479	3.466
1978	89.592	7.532	261.120	5.342	0.682	7.807	3.728	3.778
1979	106.112| 8.459	374.614	5.277	0.615	7.481	4.115	4.281
1980	140.513| 10.639	523.992	5.069	0.530	7.285	4.578	4.812
1981	133.615| 9.605	596.717	5.162	0.475	7.215	5.251	5.242
1982	162.221| 11.023	763.829	7.245	0.589	10.374	5.805	5.445

TABLE 18.4   Inflation-Adjusted Year-by-Year Total Returns, 1926–1982

(percentages)

Year	Inflation-Adjusted S&P 500 Common Stocks	Inflation-Adjusted Small Company Stocks	Inflation-Adjusted Long-Term Government Bonds	Inflation-Adjusted Long-Term Corporate Bonds	Inflation-Adjusted U.S. Treasury Bills
1926	13.25	1.81	9.37	8.96	4.78
1927	40.08	24.41	11.12	9.63	5.23
1928	45.07	41.29	1.03	3.80	4.22
1929	−8.52	−51.46	3.18	3.04	4.52
1930	−20.09	−34.12	11.27	14.80	8.89
1931	−37.25	−44.38	4.58	8.37	11.59
1932	2.60	5.42	29.99	23.30	12.39
1933	53.25	141.98	−0.71	9.73	−0.37
1934	−3.42	21.81	7.77	11.54	−1.87
1935	43.28	36.14	1.93	6.44	−2.78
1936	32.34	62.79	6.21	5.45	−1.04
1937	−37.02	−59.33	−2.85	−0.39	−2.74
1938	34.82	36.61	8.50	9.12	2.80
1939	0.35	1.57	6.23	4.42	0.45
1940	−10.70	−6.16	5.07	2.40	−0.95
1941	−19.55	−17.23	−8.07	−6.44	−8.90
1942	10.14	32.45	−5.60	−6.18	−8.33
1943	22.22	83.55	−1.09	−0.36	−2.78
1944	17.30	50.57	0.69	2.57	−1.75
1945	33.43	69.96	8.31	1.77	−1.90
1946	−22.91	−26.17	−15.95	−14.39	−15.52
1947	−3.16	−7.47	−10.83	−10.56	−7.93
1948	2.67	−4.65	0.59	1.29	−1.92
1949	20.91	21.91	8.37	5.17	2.93
1950	24.62	31.35	−5.47	−3.51	−4.39
1951	17.23	1.88	−9.33	−8.16	−4.18

Year	Inflation-Adjusted S&P 500 Common Stocks	Inflation-Adjusted Small Company Stocks	Inflation-Adjusted Long-Term Government Bonds	Inflation-Adjusted Long-Term Corporate Bonds	Inflation-Adjusted U.S. Treasury Bills
1952	17.35	2.13	0.27	2.61	0.76
1953	−1.62	−7.13	2.99	2.77	1.18
1954	53.37	61.38	7.71	5.90	1.36
1955	31.11	20.00	−1.67	0.10	1.19
1956	3.63	1.38	−8.24	−9.44	−0.40
1957	−13.40	−17.08	4.29	5.50	0.11
1958	40.95	62.19	−7.72	−3.91	−0.22
1959	10.30	14.68	−3.71	−2.43	1.43
1960	−1.00	−4.73	12.11	7.47	1.16
1961	26.04	31.18	0.30	4.12	1.44
1962	−9.86	−13.00	5.60	6.65	1.49
1963	20.81	21.56	−0.43	0.54	1.44
1964	15.14	22.10	2.29	3.54	2.32
1965	10.31	39.06	−1.20	−2.35	1.97
1966	−13.03	−10.09	0.27	−3.08	1.36
1967	20.35	78.35	−11.90	−7.79	1.13
1968	6.07	29.92	−4.78	−2.06	0.46
1969	−13.84	−29.51	−10.58	−13.45	0.45
1970	−1.45	−21.88	6.28	12.25	0.98
1971	10.63	12.72	9.55	7.42	0.99
1972	15.09	0.96	2.21	3.73	0.41
1973	−21.77	−36.81	−9.13	−7.06	−1.75
1974	−34.78	−28.93	−7.08	−13.73	−3.78
1975	28.33	43.03	2.05	7.17	−1.14
1976	18.20	50.26	11.43	13.24	0.26
1977	−13.13	17.54	−7.01	−4.77	−1.56
1978	−2.29	13.25	−9.42	−8.41	−1.71
1979	4.55	26.86	−12.95	−15.58	−2.62
1980	17.87	24.40	−14.70	−13.49	−1.05
1981	−12.85	4.47	−6.66	−9.24	5.33
1982	16.81	23.17	35.14	38.48	6.42

TABLE 18.5   Inflation-Adjusted Indexes of Year-End Cumulative Wealth, 1925–1982

(year-end 1925 = 1.000)

Year	Inflation-Adjusted S&P 500 Common Stocks	Inflation-Adjusted Small Company Stocks	Inflation-Adjusted Long-Term Corporate Bonds	Inflation-Adjusted Long-Term Government Bonds	Inflation-Adjusted U.S. Treasury Bills
1925	1.000	1.000	1.000	1.000	1.000
1926	1.133	1.018	1.090	1.094	1.048
1927	1.586	1.267	1.195	1.215	1.103
1928	2.301	1.790	1.240	1.228	1.149
1929	2.105	0.869	1.278	1.267	1.201
1930	1.682	0.572	1.467	1.410	1.308
1931	1.056	0.318	1.590	1.474	1.459
1932	1.083	0.336	1.960	1.916	1.640
1933	1.660	0.812	2.151	1.903	1.634
1934	1.603	0.989	2.399	2.051	1.604
1935	2.297	1.347	2.553	2.090	1.559
1936	3.040	2.192	2.693	2.220	1.543
1937	1.915	0.892	2.682	2.157	1.500
1938	2.581	1.218	2.927	2.340	1.542
1939	2.590	1.237	3.056	2.486	1.549
1940	2.313	1.161	3.130	2.612	1.535
1941	1.861	0.961	2.928	2.401	1.398
1942	2.050	1.273	2.747	2.267	1.282
1943	2.505	2.336	2.737	2.242	1.246
1944	2.939	3.517	2.808	2.257	1.224
1945	3.921	5.978	2.857	2.445	1.201
1946	3.023	4.413	2.446	2.055	1.014
1947	2.927	4.084	2.188	1.832	0.934
1948	3.005	3.894	2.216	1.843	0.916
1949	3.634	4.747	2.330	1.997	0.943
1950	4.529	6.235	2.249	1.888	0.901
1951	5.309	6.352	2.065	1.712	0.864

Year	Inflation-Adjusted S&P 500 Common Stocks	Inflation-Adjusted Small Company Stocks	Inflation-Adjusted Long-Term Corporate Bonds	Inflation-Adjusted Long-Term Government Bonds	Inflation-Adjusted U.S. Treasury Bills
1952	6.230	6.487	2.119	1.717	0.870
1953	6.129	6.025	2.178	1.768	0.881
1954	9.400	9.723	2.306	1.904	0.893
1955	12.325	11.667	2.309	1.872	0.903
1956	12.772	11.828	2.091	1.718	0.900
1957	11.061	9.808	2.206	1.792	0.901
1958	15.591	15.906	2.120	1.653	0.899
1959	17.197	18.241	2.068	1.592	0.911
1960	17.025	17.379	2.223	1.785	0.922
1961	21.459	22.798	2.314	1.790	0.935
1962	19.343	19.834	2.468	1.890	0.949
1963	23.369	24.112	2.481	1.882	0.963
1964	26.906	29.440	2.569	1.925	0.985
1965	29.680	40.939	2.509	1.902	1.005
1966	25.813	36.808	2.432	1.907	1.018
1967	31.065	65.647	2.242	1.680	1.030
1968	32.949	85.289	2.196	1.600	1.035
1969	28.390	60.124	1.901	1.431	1.039
1970	27.977	46.967	2.133	1.521	1.049
1971	30.951	52.940	2.292	1.666	1.060
1972	35.621	53.447	2.377	1.703	1.064
1973	27.866	33.773	2.209	1.547	1.046
1974	18.174	24.003	1.906	1.438	1.006
1975	23.323	34.331	2.043	1.467	0.995
1976	27.569	51.586	2.313	1.635	0.997
1977	23.947	60.633	2.203	1.520	0.982
1978	23.399	68.666	2.018	1.377	0.965
1979	24.464	87.113	1.703	1.199	0.940
1980	28.835	108.371	1.473	1.023	0.930
1981	25.129	113.214	1.337	0.955	0.979
1982	29.352	139.449	1.852	1.290	1.042

purchasing power in 1982 as it had in 1925. In contrast, long-term corporate bonds would have had less than twice their original purchasing power after 57 years. Long-term government bonds and Treasury bills both posted small gains in inflation-adjusted terms over the period.

FOCUS ON STOCKS — NYSE, AMEX, OTC, AND INSTITUTIONAL PORTFOLIOS

Large and small stocks have had appreciably different histories. The large blue chip issues that make up the Dow Jones Industrial Average and the S&P 500 have been laggard performers since 1965, while smaller issues have raced ahead. In fact, as was pointed out in the last section, over long periods of time as well as most subperiods, small stocks outperformed large stocks. Further, according to research by Rolf Banz,[3] the higher betas of small stocks do not fully explain their higher returns. Thus, it frequently would have been preferable to hold small stocks.

Ibbotson and Fall examined the various markets for common stocks over the 1947–1978 period. Their work was updated to the end of 1981 by Ibbotson and Brinson.[4] Drawing on those results, the market was divided by exchange listing: NYSE-listed issues (including both S&P 500 and non-S&P 500 stocks); American Stock Exchange-(AMEX) listed issues; and issues traded over the counter (OTC). Annual returns were gathered for 1947–1981 for NYSE and OTC, and for 1963–1981 for AMEX. The year-by-year annual total returns for these series, with dividends reinvested, appear in Table 18.6. Wealth indices of these returns appear in Table 18.7.

The data in Table 18.7 shows that the wealth index of OTC stocks was more than twice that of NYSE stocks at the end of the 1947–1981 period. Translated into rates of return, OTC stocks returned 13.4 percent per year compared with NYSE's 10.6 percent. (See Table 18.1.) This relatively small difference in compound annual rates of return produces a large difference in wealth index values after 35 years.

The data for AMEX began in 1962, so the wealth index starts with one dollar invested on December 31, 1962. By December 31, 1981, it grew to $6.32, a compound annual return of 10.2 percent. Over the same 19-year period, a dollar invested in the NYSE wealth index grew to $4.37 (a compound annual return of 8.1 percent), and a dollar invested in the OTC grew to $12.11 (a compound annual return of 14.0 percent). Thus, OTC stocks were the best performers of the three groups over this 19-year period, a period in which substantial nominal returns were severely reduced by inflation.

Over both the 1947–1981 and the 1963–1981 periods, AMEX and OTC stocks had higher returns than NYSE stocks did. In general, non-NYSE stocks are smaller issues than NYSE stocks; this is consistent with other findings that small stocks outperform large ones.

---

[3] Rolf W. Banz, "The Relationship Between Return and Market Value of Common Stocks," *Journal of Financial Economics,* Vol. 9, No. 1 (Mar. 1981).

[4] Roger G. Ibbotson and Gary Brinson, *World Wealth: The History and Economics of Capital Markets* (University of Chicago Press, in progress).

TABLE 18.6   Year-by-Year Total Returns on U.S. Stocks

(percentages)

	Common Stocks			
Year	NYSE	AMEX	OTC	Total
1947	3.30	N/A	2.07	3.20
1948	2.32	N/A	−3.04	1.90
1949	20.21	N/A	16.26	19.90
1950	29.95	N/A	29.22	29.90
1951	20.95	N/A	15.72	20.57
1952	13.32	N/A	6.52	12.86
1953	0.37	N/A	3.29	0.55
1954	50.53	N/A	50.40	50.52
1955	25.26	N/A	18.88	24.87
1956	8.62	N/A	15.33	9.00
1957	−10.70	N/A	0.16	−10.79
1958	44.27	N/A	48.34	44.49
1959	12.87	N/A	9.53	12.69
1960	0.60	N/A	0.99	0.62
1961	27.17	N/A	36.28	27.63
1962	−9.38	N/A	−12.36	−9.54
1963	21.33	14.75	24.44	21.05
1964	16.29	15.07	25.87	16.69
1965	13.92	19.47	33.15	15.25
1966	−8.96	−5.86	0.90	−8.20
1967	26.96	56.27	56.38	30.46
1968	12.78	33.18	23.02	14.94
1969	−9.85	−22.51	1.67	−9.86
1970	1.40	−16.00	−12.54	−0.99
1971	15.89	21.60	40.65	18.17
1972	17.92	10.08	34.07	18.98
1973	−16.97	−28.25	−22.88	−18.19
1974	−26.85	−35.43	−38.50	−28.33
1975	37.73	39.56	37.48	37.78
1976	26.27	31.30	15.17	25.59
1977	−4.89	13.16	14.74	−2.82
1978	7.40	19.35	14.31	8.47
1979	21.82	62.32	31.91	24.21
1980	32.70	33.01	37.38	33.12
1981	−4.22	−5.28	−0.01	−3.90

Source: Roger G. Ibbotson and Carol L. Fall, "The United States Market
Wealth Portfolio," *The Journal of Portfolio Management* (Fall
1979) p. 88, for 1947–1978; Roger G. Ibbotson and Gary Brinson, *World Wealth: The History and Economics of Capital Markets* (University of Chicago Press, not yet published) for 1979–
1981

TABLE 18.7   Cumulative Wealth Indices of U.S. Stocks

(year-end 1946 = 1.000)

Year-End	Common Stocks			
	NYSE	AMEX*	OTC	Total
1947	1.033	N/A	1.021	1.032
1948	1.057	N/A	0.990	1.052
1949	1.271	N/A	1.151	1.261
1950	1.651	N/A	1.487	1.638
1951	1.997	N/A	1.721	1.975
1952	2.263	N/A	1.833	2.229
1953	2.271	N/A	1.893	2.241
1954	3.419	N/A	2.847	3.373
1955	4.283	N/A	3.385	4.212
1956	4.652	N/A	3.903	4.591
1957	4.154	N/A	3.429	4.096
1958	5.993	N/A	5.086	5.919
1959	6.765	N/A	5.571	6.670
1960	6.806	N/A	5.626	6.711
1961	8.655	N/A	7.667	8.565
1962	7.843	1.000	6.720	7.748
1963	9.517	1.148	8.362	9.379
1964	11.066	1.320	10.525	10.945
1965	12.607	1.578	14.014	12.614
1966	11.477	1.485	14.140	11.580
1967	14.572	2.321	22.113	15.108
1968	16.434	3.091	27.203	17.365
1969	14.815	2.395	27.657	15.653
1970	15.023	2.012	24.189	15.498
1971	17.410	2.446	34.022	18.315
1972	20.530	2.693	45.613	21.791
1973	17.047	1.932	35.177	17.826
1974	12.470	1.248	21.634	12.776
1975	17.175	1.741	29.742	17.603
1976	21.688	2.286	34.254	22.108
1977	20.628	2.587	39.303	21.484
1978	22.155	3.088	44.927	23.303
1979	26.989	5.012	59.263	28.945
1980	35.815	6.667	81.416	38.531
1981	34.303	6.315	81.408	37.028

*Year-end 1962 = 1.000

Source: Roger G. Ibbotson and Carol L. Fall, "The United States Market
Wealth Portfolio," *The Journal of Portfolio Management* (Fall
1979) p. 89, for 1947–1978; Roger G. Ibbotson and Gary Brinson, *World Wealth: The History and Economics of Capital Markets* (University of Chicago Press, not yet published) for 1979–
1981

While market averages such as the S&P 500, NYSE, and others accurately represent the activity of the stock market in general, they do not indicate how well specific investors fared. Investors generally hold portfolios that are more or less unrepresentative of the whole market, in an attempt to outperform the averages or achieve other investment goals.

Figure 18.6 shows how various classes of institutional investors' portfolios performed over one-, five-, and ten-year holding periods ending December 31, 1982. As expected, the dispersion of returns is much less for the ten-year holding period than it is for shorter periods. In 1982 alone, and in 1976–1982, special situations mutual funds had the highest returns, while income mutual funds had the lowest. There is, however, no evidence that one class of institutions performed better than another over the whole ten years. Furthermore, there is no evidence that institutions as a group outperform the market averages in the long run.

FOCUS ON BONDS — AN ANALYSIS OF THE CORPORATE BOND MARKET

A study by Roger G. Ibbotson examines the 1926–1978 period. Summary statistics from this study are shown in Table 18.8. The composite portfolio of all corporate bonds achieved a 3.43 percent compound annual return over the period. This was far lower than the return earned by stocks and just slightly higher than the inflation rate.

The set of corporate bonds is divided by industry, Moody's Investors Services's rating, and maturity category. Table 18.8 shows that, over the whole period, industrials had the highest return, and transportation issues had the lowest return. A dollar invested at year-end 1925 would have grown to $8.58 by 1978 if invested in industrial bonds, but to only half that much ($4.32) if invested in transportation bonds.

As expected, issues rated highest by Moody's had the lowest returns. The difference between Aaa-rated and below-Baa-rated issues is dramatic. A dollar invested in Aaa issues at year-end 1925 would have grown to only $1.45 by 1978, while the same dollar invested in the riskier below-Baa issues would have grown to $12.00. This is a vivid illustration of the principle that investors have been rewarded for taking risk. This estimate of standard deviation for corporate bonds is subject to substantial sampling error (due to small sample size) and should not be used as a measure of risk of these bond categories.

Results are displayed for two maturity categories: 5 to 14.99 years, and 15 years and more to maturity. (The sample for bonds with less than 5 years to maturity was too small to be used.) One can see that intermediate-term bonds (5 to 14.99 years) had a much higher return than long-term bonds. A dollar invested in intermediate-term bonds at year-end 1925 would have grown to $24.12 by 1978, compared with $6.86 for long-term bonds. This differential illustrates the extent to which long-term issues were hurt by rising inflation rates and, consequently, interest rates over the period.

The columns headed *Return in Excess of Yield* in Table 18.8 show the direction of the market. A negative return in excess of yield means that the

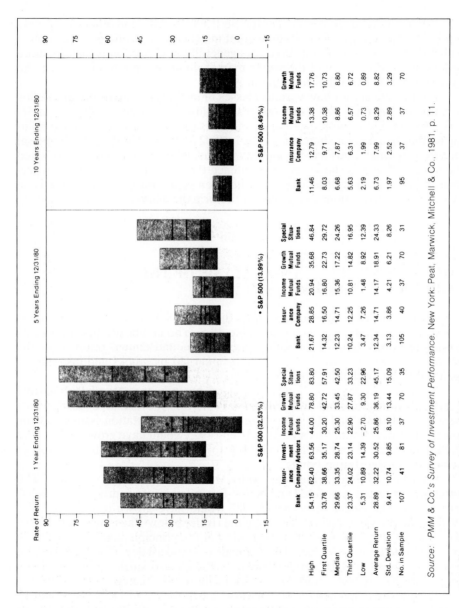

Source: *PMM & Co.'s Survey of Investment Performance.* New York: Peat, Marwick, Mitchell & Co., 1981, p. 11.

FIG. 18.6 Institutional Equity Fund Performance

TABLE 18.8   Corporate Bond Market, 1926–1978

Annual Percentage Returns

	Total Returns			Return in Excess of Yield	
Portfolio	Arithmetic Mean	Geometric Mean	Standard Deviation[a]	Arithmetic Mean	Geometric Mean
Composite	3.68%	3.43%	7.15%	−1.61%	−2.34%
Industry					
Utility	4.10	3.81	6.50	−1.16	−1.66
Industrial	4.36	4.14	6.83	−1.16	−1.35
Financial[b]	3.98	2.80	6.15	−1.82	−1.97
Transportation	3.32	2.80	9.93	−2.99	−3.46
Moody's rating					
Aaa	1.48	0.70	11.23	−2.93	−3.64
Aa	1.46	0.95	9.57	−3.10	−3.62
A	3.53	3.25	7.57	−1.57	−1.83
Baa	4.45	4.10	8.46	−1.21	−1.60
Below Baa	5.55	4.80	12.21	−2.94	−3.65
Maturity[c]					
5 to 14.99 years	6.47	6.19	8.11	0.57	0.28
15 years or more	3.93	3.70	7.73	−1.87	−1.93

(a) Standard deviations reflect a small sample size and thus do not exactly reflect the underlying dispersion of returns.
(b) Data for financial category is for 1950–1978.
(c) Results are omitted for 0 to 4.99 years to maturity due to small size.

Source: Corporate Bond Study 1926–1978 (Chicago: R. G. Ibbotson & Co., 1979), pp. 1–13

attained return was, on average, less than the market-anticipated return (i.e., the yield to maturity). In other words, the bond market went down. The return in excess of yield was negative for the composite portfolio over the period and for all of the components except intermediate-term maturity bonds. The bond market, then, was lower at the end of the period than it was at the beginning. That is, the bond yields rose. A look at the history of this market shows that the price trend was upward (bond yields went down) from 1926 to 1945; then prices fell sharply (and yields rose to unprecedented levels) in more recent years.

THE INTERNATIONAL VIEW — STOCK MARKET RETURNS IN 18 COUNTRIES

The U.S. stock market constitutes only about half of the world's common equities. Japan and the countries of Western Europe have important and active markets, and smaller markets are present in still other countries. In the period from 1960 through 1981, foreign stocks were very desirable for a U.S. investor to hold. Over the whole period, the stocks of 10 out of 15 foreign countries studied outperformed the U.S. stock market. This was partly because the foreign stock markets did well in their home currencies and partly because foreign currencies appreciated relative to the dollar.

Table 18.9 shows average annual returns for the 1960–1981 period for the United States and 17 foreign countries, as reported in a study by Ibbotson, Carr, and Robinson (with updates by Ibbotson and Siegel).[5] The countries are grouped by continental areas. The Asian and Pacific countries had the highest returns. Japan had the highest compound annual return over the entire period (15.6 percent); a dollar invested in Japanese stocks at year-end 1959 grew to $24.11 in 20 years. Hong Kong and Singapore, for which there are only 10 years of data, had compound annual returns of 20.6 percent and 22.7 percent, respectively, for 1970–1981. The Singapore return is higher than the highest return that a year-end investor in U.S. stocks could have earned in any 12-year period. (U.S. stocks returned a compound rate of 18.5 percent from the beginning of 1944 to the end of 1955.)

European countries varied widely in their stock market performance. Denmark led the group, with a compound annual return of 10.1 percent. Much of this gain was achieved in one year, 1972. The other countries of Europe had returns that fell between 4 and 10 percent per year, except for Italy. A dollar invested in Italian stocks grew to only $1.46 over the 22-year period, a compound return of 1.7 percent.

The North American region consists of the United States and Canada. Canadian stocks fared somewhat better than U.S. stocks, returning 9.7 percent per year. The United States, represented by a value-weighted portfolio of NYSE, AMEX, and OTC stocks returned 8.1 percent per year over the 22-year period.

It should be pointed out that the 1960–1981 period was a relatively poor one for common stocks in the United States. Had a different 20-year period been chosen, the United States might have been relatively a better place in which to invest in stocks. However, a span of 22 years is long enough to suggest that there are gains from international diversification in stocks, although such gains would not necessarily be expected to be as great in the future an they were in the decades of the 1960s and 1970s (see also Chapter 39).

THE INTERNATIONAL VIEW — RETURNS ON NON-U.S. BONDS

The idea that diversification across borders is a potentially good policy prompted a look at returns on international bonds as well as stocks. In the study by Ibbotson, Carr, and Robinson, the international bond market for 1975–

---

[5] Roger G. Ibbotson et al., "International Equity and Bond Returns," *Financial Analysts Journal* (July/Aug. 1982); and Roger G. Ibbotson and Laurence B. Siegel, "The World Market Wealth Portfolio," *The Journal of Portfolio Management* (Winter 1983).

TABLE 18.9   Annual Percentage Returns in U.S. Dollars, 1960–1981

Country	Arithmetic Mean	Geometric Mean	Standard Deviation
North America			
United States	9.59%	8.11%	17.52%
Canada	11.08	9.66	17.68
Europe			
Austria	8.95	7.59	17.70
Belgium	9.37	8.46	13.97
Denmark	11.98	10.14	23.84
France	6.59	4.51	22.11
Germany	9.31	7.52	19.73
Italy	4.85	1.72	26.81
Netherlands	9.63	8.20	18.04
Norway	15.94	8.99	48.34
Spain	10.47	8.64	19.39
Sweden	10.94	9.52	17.26
Switzerland	11.52	9.28	22.83
United Kingdom	13.57	9.02	33.19
Asia and Pacific			
Japan	18.88	15.57	30.71
Australia	10.58	8.06	23.42
Hong Kong*	35.69	20.64	60.65
Singapore*	35.31	22.68	63.54

* Data are for 1970–1981.

Source: Roger G. Ibbotson and Gary Brinson, *World Wealth: The History and Economics of Capital Markets* (University of Chicago, not yet published)

1980 was divided into three classes: foreign domestic (the domestic bonds of other countries); foreign cross-border (issued by the residents of one foreign country and denominated in currency of another); and U.S. dollar cross-border (issued by residents of a foreign country in U.S. dollars). A summary of the results of the study is presented in Table 18.10. In this table the first line, entitled "All Foreign Currencies — All Maturities," gives the return for the class of bonds as a whole. Each class outperformed U.S. domestic bonds. The two foreign currency classes also outperformed the U.S. inflation rate.

Each class of bonds is subdivided by currency and by maturity group. The foreign domestics are by far the largest of the three classes. Of the foreign domestics, Japanese bonds were the best performers, providing a compound annual return of 18.2 percent. British government (gilt-edged) bonds were a close second. In the foreign cross-border class, bonds issued in Japanese yen

TABLE 18.10   International Bond Returns, 1975–1980

Annual Percentage Returns in U.S. Dollars

	Arithmetic Mean	Geometric Mean	Standard Deviation
Foreign domestic			
All foreign currencies			
All maturities	17.17%	16.37%	11.82%
0 to 4.99 years to maturity	14.73	14.06	10.91
5 to 9.99 years to maturity	16.37	15.59	11.76
10 years or more to maturity	17.34	16.56	14.35
Pounds sterling			
All maturities	18.64	16.81	17.95
0 to 4.99 years to maturity	12.69	11.84	12.39
5 to 9.99 years to maturity	14.72	13.14	16.97
10 years or more to maturity	21.97	19.31	21.55
Deutschemarks			
All maturities	13.30	12.29	13.44
0 to 4.99 years to maturity	12.56	11.63	12.96
5 to 5.99 years to maturity	13.54	12.35	14.59
Japanese yen			
All maturities	19.29	18.21	13.70
0 to 4.99 years to maturity	17.91	16.90	13.33
5 to 9.99 years to maturity	19.57	18.48	13.77
Dutch guilders			
All maturities	12.08	11.06	13.63
0 to 4.99 years to maturity	11.88	11.14	11.60
5 to 9.99 years to maturity	11.40	10.48	12.94
10 years or more to maturity	12.16	11.04	14.23
Foreign cross-border			
All foreign currencies			
All maturities	12.50	11.66	12.28
0 to 4.99 years to maturity	12.81	11.93	12.56
5 to 9.99 years to maturity	14.60	13.57	13.46
10 years or more to maturity	15.16	13.85	15.19
Deutschemarks			
All maturities	13.59	12.50	13.92
0 to 4.99 years to maturity	11.93	10.96	13.32
5 to 9.99 years to maturity	13.65	12.52	14.26
10 years or more to maturity	14.05	12.62	16.02

	Arithmetic Mean	Geometric Mean	Standard Deviation
Swiss francs			
All maturities	17.07%	15.52%	16.43%
0 to 4.99 years to maturity	13.97	12.82	14.30
5 to 9.99 years to maturity	16.00	14.69	15.12
10 years or more to maturity	17.31	15.51	17.68
Japanese yen			
All maturities	19.11	18.05	13.55
0 to 4.99 years to maturity	18.21	17.21	13.19
5 to 9.99 years to maturity	19.25	18.20	13.53
10 years or more to maturity	18.74	17.65	13.74
Dutch guilders			
All maturities	12.63	11.62	13.53
Other currencies			
All maturities	4.53	4.17	8.34
U.S. dollar cross-border			
All U.S. dollar bonds			
All maturities	8.49	8.33	5.46
0 to 4.99 years to maturity	7.86	7.77	4.07
5 to 5.99 years to maturity	6.87	6.68	5.97
10 to 14.99 years to maturity	8.20	7.84	8.24
15 years or more to maturity	7.99	7.49	9.76
Yankee bonds			
All maturities	6.93	6.67	6.97
0 to 9.99 years to maturity	7.19	7.07	4.74
10 years or more to maturity	6.68	6.20	9.58
0 to 4.99 years to maturity	6.99	6.89	4.47
5 to 9.99 years to maturity	5.85	5.61	6.70
10 to 14.99 years to maturity	9.12	8.62	9.68
15 years or more to maturity	6.18	5.68	9.77
Dollar bonds			
All maturities	8.49	8.32	5.62
0 to 4.99 years to maturity	8.27	8.18	4.08
5 to 9.99 years to maturity	7.43	7.24	5.98
10 to 14.99 years to maturity	7.73	7.40	7.88
15 years or more to maturity	8.87	8.33	10.15
Floating-rate bonds			
All maturities	15.42	15.40	1.72

(continued)

TABLE 18.10   International Bond Returns, 1975–1980 (*continued*)

Annual Percentage Returns in U.S. Dollars

	Arithmetic Mean	Geometric Mean	Standard Deviation
U.S. domestic bonds (for comparison)			
Lehman Bros., Kuhn Loeb Index			
All maturities	6.35%	5.86%	9.74%
U.S. inflation rate (for comparison)	8.89	8.85	1.12

were the best performer, in this case by a substantial margin, due to declining Japanese inflation rates. In the U.S. dollar cross-border class, floating-rate notes (on which coupon rate is reset periodically according to current interest rates) greatly outperformed the other types of bonds. This was because the floating-rate characteristic of these bonds protected them from the accelerating U.S. dollar inflation of the 1975–1980 period.

The six-year period from the beginning of 1975 to the end of 1980 is not long enough to identify fundamental relationships. In this period, much of the high international bond return came from appreciation of foreign currencies against the U.S. dollar. It is not expected that the gain from international diversification in bonds will be consistently as great in the future as it was in 1975–1980 (see Chapter 37).

GOLD, SILVER, AND PORTFOLIO DIVERSIFICATION

A diversified portfolio of world assets would include not only stocks, bonds, and cash equivalents, but other assets such as real estate, gold, and silver. Ibbotson and Siegel constructed such a portfolio for the period from 1960 to 1980 and found that monetary metals, gold and silver, provided a tool for diversification that dampened extremes of year-by-year return. Table 18.11 shows the results. They constructed U.S., foreign, and world, market portfolios excluding monetary metals, then added metals in proportion to their market value to produce a world market portfolio including metals. The study shows that the portfolio excluding metals had returns which ranged from 17.5 percent in 1975 to −1.4 percent in 1974. This series had a compound annual return of 8.4 percent and a standard deviation of 5.4 percent. Adding gold and silver, the world market portfolio including metals had returns which ranged from 21.51 percent in 1980 to 0.99 percent in 1966. This second series had a compound annual return of 8.9 percent with a standard deviation of 5.7 percent. Thus, the inclusion of gold and silver had the effect of eliminating negative nominal one-year returns over the period studied, and produced a substantial incremental return with little rise in volatility.

TABLE 18.11 Year-by-Year Total Returns on World Assets, 1960–1980

(percentages)

Year	Equities United States	Equities Foreign Europe	Equities Foreign Asia	Equities Foreign Other	Equities Foreign Total	Equities Total	Bonds United States Corporate, Including Preferred Stock	Bonds United States Government	Bonds United States Total	Bonds Foreign Domestic Corp.	Bonds Foreign Domestic Gov't	Bonds Foreign Cross-Border	Bonds Foreign Total	Bonds Total
1960	0.83	13.65	38.50	-0.69	13.84	4.60	7.79	12.16	10.74	5.89	0.00	4.66	2.41	5.69
1961	27.52	15.11	-13.03	26.49	14.08	22.91	4.96	1.55	2.66	6.15	6.41	6.14	6.31	4.97
1962	-9.29	-2.35	4.68	-3.43	-1.86	-6.79	5.90	5.96	5.94	4.44	7.89	7.99	6.72	6.44
1963	21.04	7.08	8.78	19.19	9.18	17.04	3.59	1.69	2.32	11.24	4.03	6.03	6.49	4.94
1964	16.71	-2.13	10.93	16.12	2.25	12.11	4.75	3.83	4.15	5.55	1.71	5.90	3.28	3.61
1965	15.26	3.74	21.39	-1.27	4.46	12.15	-2.81	1.18	-0.26	4.04	1.90	1.88	2.65	1.54
1966	-8.21	-5.93	9.04	-3.92	-4.17	-7.18	-4.27	4.08	1.09	6.01	4.05	0.48	4.51	3.16
1967	30.45	18.98	-4.85	22.41	17.02	26.63	-3.91	-4.49	-4.29	4.20	0.58	3.71	2.03	-0.50
1968	14.95	35.05	26.43	27.46	32.76	19.63	2.69	1.93	2.21	5.77	3.71	6.28	4.57	3.62
1969	-9.86	1.51	34.15	8.26	6.43	-5.57	-7.50	-2.82	-4.64	2.80	-0.72	-0.08	0.50	-1.68
1970	-1.00	-9.04	-4.09	1.10	-6.40	-2.59	14.00	14.58	14.36	9.12	9.36	5.03	8.97	11.27
1971	18.16	27.33	48.41	7.59	26.68	20.77	11.71	9.75	10.52	24.29	21.47	15.70	21.93	16.77
1972	17.71	16.45	134.88	29.15	41.17	24.48	7.12	4.82	5.81	10.05	2.77	11.48	5.75	5.78
1973	-18.68	-7.78	-24.62	-5.72	-11.42	-16.38	1.22	2.03	1.68	7.69	5.30	7.18	6.24	4.30
1974	-27.77	-23.34	-19.75	-28.54	-22.99	-25.76	-5.70	8.23	2.38	3.62	2.49	5.33	3.08	2.79
1975	37.49	44.78	23.84	27.61	35.86	36.78	16.61	7.82	11.32	11.40	8.16	14.31	9.68	10.32
1976	26.68	-7.56	26.17	3.81	4.83	18.36	18.90	12.73	15.12	15.55	7.01	16.84	10.75	12.53
1977	-3.03	21.26	13.39	2.89	15.50	3.43	4.29	2.00	2.83	33.27	26.73	12.46	27.36	17.57
1978	8.53	25.51	51.13	21.06	34.62	18.25	0.44	2.05	1.49	21.38	22.40	9.24	20.82	13.70
1979	24.18	15.38	-5.57	49.75	11.29	18.77	-2.89	4.42	2.20	-6.65	0.75	2.03	-1.35	-0.20
1980	33.22	14.53	34.09	30.95	24.27	29.25	-1.14	3.38	2.14	12.19	3.83	4.26	6.18	4.88

(continued)

TABLE 18.11　Year-by-Year Total Returns on World Assets, 1960–1980 *(continued)*

(percentages)

| | Cash Equivalents | | | Real Estate | | | | Metals | | | Market Wealth Portfolios | | | |
| | | | | United States | | | Real | World | | | | | World, | World, |
Year	United States	Foreign	Cash Total	Business	Residential	Farm	Estate Total	Gold	Silver	Metals Total	United States	Foreign	Excluding Metals	Including Metals
1960	2.78	2.38	2.69	2.49	4.33	4.07	4.11	—	—	—	4.30	5.72	4.70	4.52
1961	2.36	2.92	2.49	2.69	4.69	9.10	5.41	—	13.19	0.21	10.69	8.60	10.04	9.69
1962	2.75	3.01	2.81	3.29	4.20	8.98	5.09	—	16.50	0.29	0.75	3.71	1.67	1.63
1963	3.13	3.37	3.18	4.29	6.03	9.79	6.62	—	7.50	0.15	9.62	7.25	8.89	8.60
1964	3.53	4.06	3.64	2.99	5.13	7.58	5.42	—	—	—	8.48	2.96	6.86	6.63
1965	3.92	4.93	4.12	4.09	5.61	12.64	6.91	—	—	—	8.35	3.32	6.96	6.74
1966	4.69	4.64	4.68	4.89	5.25	12.23	6.67	—	—	—	0.82	1.61	1.02	0.99
1967	4.48	0.41	3.73	6.39	6.29	10.30	7.12	—	59.67	1.26	12.30	7.15	10.98	10.68
1968	5.18	5.86	5.29	10.69	7.83	8.71	8.33	12.29	-4.85	11.72	9.66	15.19	11.01	11.04
1969	6.40	6.46	6.41	6.09	10.53	7.24	9.39	5.60	-7.65	5.24	0.72	3.09	1.27	1.40
1970	6.95	9.51	7.34	9.99	11.69	7.77	10.76	-12.29	-9.94	-12.24	7.32	2.35	6.16	5.56
1971	5.41	13.05	6.58	15.49	7.69	11.70	9.38	13.19	-14.72	-12.44	11.88	23.68	14.61	14.55
1972	4.20	4.50	4.25	9.49	6.34	18.94	8.93	42.23	42.45	42.22	10.96	19.73	13.06	13.88
1973	6.28	9.86	6.91	7.39	6.56	35.27	11.65	66.90	58.59	66.73	0.32	-1.58	-0.15	2.19
1974	8.06	9.75	8.38	8.09	13.21	19.80	13.79	63.29	39.81	62.85	1.64	-9.25	-1.35	2.17
1975	7.33	-0.15	5.68	8.86	13.02	18.52	13.44	1.13	-6.83	1.00	16.92	19.08	17.48	16.01
1976	5.44	4.86	5.33	8.02	7.31	19.54	9.70	-22.41	6.36	-22.00	13.58	8.30	12.26	9.51
1977	5.15	18.81	7.76	8.99	11.38	11.20	11.08	18.36	8.28	18.17	6.57	22.97	10.70	11.12
1978	6.60	19.92	9.57	12.17	14.22	18.18	14.76	30.55	25.90	30.47	11.28	24.92	14.96	15.89
1979	9.34	-2.48	6.48	14.52	18.92	19.70	18.60	58.83	367.45	63.91	16.94	2.40	12.70	16.14
1980	11.11	16.37	12.25	11.42	14.46	10.47	13.34	91.71	-24.78	87.43	15.39	12.67	14.59	21.51

Two factors contributed to this result. First, returns on gold and silver, shown in Table 18.11, were extraordinarily high during the period studied. There is no reason to believe that such a performance will be repeated in the next two decades; in fact, gold and silver began declining in 1981, the year after the end of the study. Second and more important, however, these metals have a correlation of almost exactly zero (specifically, 0.018) with the world market portfolio, excluding metals. Thus, while the performance boost realized over 1960–1980 from holding gold and silver should not be expected in the future, the reduction of risk due to diversification should continue, and it may make sense for certain investors to own gold and silver as a medium of diversification.

It is interesting to observe that the world gold supply had a market value of $1,655 billion at the end of 1980, or more than 14 percent of the investable world market wealth portfolio as measured in the Ibbotson and Siegel study. By way of comparison, U.S. stocks were valued at $1,381 billion and U.S. and foreign stocks combined at $2,430 billion. It is surprising that the market values gold so highly, since gold is principally a form of cash or "grease" for the world economy. Given the role of gold, its value by the market at two-thirds the aggregate market value of the world's equities is unexpected. While the authors are not asserting that gold in overpriced, they encourage the reader to form his own judgment on that issue.

CONCLUSIONS

In examining the behavior of most asset categories that investors hold, it is seen that over long periods of time capital at risk in business — common stocks — earns higher returns than less risky assets. Real estate, which is the most widely held tangible asset, also fares well. Bonds have low returns, and short-term money market instruments such as U.S. Treasury bills track inflation.

Over short periods of time, any specific asset class can outperform any other asset class. While it is interesting to compare realized returns on assets over any time period, it seems that the most reliable inferences are drawn from results over long periods of time.

Investors should buy and hold assets according to their needs and investment goals, and they should diversify their holdings to include more than one type of asset. An investor should not hold only those assets that went up the most in some past time period. It is very useful, however, for the investor to have access to historical return data in order to understand fundamental risk-return relationships and make intelligent investment decisions.

PART III

Short-Term Financial Management

19

Credit Analysis

ROY N. TAUB

INTRODUCTION

Credit analysis is performed for a very specific purpose. Credit ratings assigned to fixed income securities are intended to communicate to the investment community the analyst's opinions as to the relative likelihood that a borrower will make principal and interest payments in a complete and timely manner. The nature and provisions of the obligation and its relative position in bankruptcy are also taken into account.

Typically, the primary determinant of a credit rating is an analysis of the creditworthiness of the borrower. This chapter focuses on the key elements that go into the analysis of the credit quality of an industrial company. The basic form of the analysis is the same whether the security to be rated is a long-term debt issuer or a short-term obligation such as commercial paper. Some added factors concerning commercial paper are covered later in the chapter, as is the treatment of project financings.

RATING METHODOLOGY PROFILE

The key distinction between analyzing and rating the debt of a municipal entity and a corporation is the latter's vulnerability to competitive forces. This is especially true with regard to that broad category of rated corporate debt issues called industrials.

Analysis aimed at determining the capacity of an industrial borrower with regard to the timely payment of principal and interest can be organized (as it has by Standard & Poor's (S&P)) into a rating methodology profile addressing the following nine criteria:

1 Industry risk

2 Issuer's industry position/market position

3 Issuer's industry position/operating efficiency

4 Management evaluation

5 Accounting quality

6 Earnings protection

7 Leverage and asset protection

8 Cash flow adequacy

9 Financial flexibility

The first four categories are oriented to business analysis and the remainder to financial analysis. Thus, the rating process is not limited to the examination of various financial measures. Proper assessment of current and future debt protection levels requires that the financial statement analysis be performed within a broader framework. This involves a thorough review of the industries or business segments in which a company participates, a judgment as to the company's competitive position within the industry, and an evaluation of management. At times a rating decision may be heavily influenced by financial measures; at other times, analysis of the business risks and other subjective factors may dominate. The key point is that each rating analysis requires an independent qualitative weighting of the criteria categories.

ANALYZING INDUSTRY RISK

Industry risk is the strength of the industry within the economy and in relation to economic trends. It deals with the predictability or stability of industry revenues and earnings. To ascertain the level of industry risk, many issues must be addressed, including the extent to which the industry is in a growth, stable, or declining phase. Does the business display independent cycles as, for example, in the case of agriculture? If it moves with the economy in general, is it more or less volatile? Does it lead or lag economic trends, or does it have contracyclical tendencies?

Industry risk is perceived to be reduced to the extent it is demonstrated that the industry lags economic changes, thus giving management time to adjust inventories and spending. It is also reduced if the industry is recession-resistant or at least partially contracyclical.

Impact of Competition

The nature of competition plays an important role in the evaluation of industry risk. For example, is competition on a regional basis, as with cement; national, as with major appliances; or international, as with chemicals? Is competition based on price, quality of product, distribution capabilities, image, product differentiation, service, or some other factor? The basis for competition ultimately determines the long-term level of profitability attainable in an industry and helps the analyst to evaluate whether any firm's profit levels are based on long-term strengths or transitory conditions.

Furthermore, when the basis for competition changes, drastic effects can result for the participants. The auto industry is one example in which much of the competitive battle shifted in the mid-1970s from a national level influenced by marketing and styling to an international level based on quality, fuel economy, and price-sensitivity.

Finally, the ease or difficulty with which firms adjust to competitive shifts influence the risk level. For the auto industry, long lead times and costly product development heighten the risk-reward trade-off.

Regulation and the burdens or benefits it provides importantly influence risk levels. Broadcasters benefit from regulation in terms of franchise protection; oil companies are substantially constrained; and utilities are most seriously affected in an era of inflation and environmental consciousness. A change from regulation to deregulation may have profound effects on credit quality. The railroads are benefiting from partial deregulation, while both airlines and trucking are undergoing substantial stress. Another important assessment relates to the labor situation. Is the industry unionized? If so, are labor contracts negotiated on an industrywide basis, and what is the recent negotiating history? What are the vulnerabilities to strikes or other labor disruptions in related industries? A powerful, adversary labor presence in an increasingly cost-competitive industry tends to raise profit uncertainties and risk levels. Another factor in the study of industry risk is the analysis of raw material supplies. Does the industry have good control of key materials, or is there a dependence upon questionable foreign sources? Are there vulnerabilities that could develop from political pressures, environmental pressures, or energy-related problems?

Capital Needs

Another important component of industry risk analysis lies in determining the degree to which the industry is fixed-capital or working-capital intensive. Does the industry require heavy investment in fixed plant and equipment to generate sales, as in the chemical industry, or is the emphasis primarily in receivables and inventory, as in the textile industry? The beer industry, typically working-capital intensive, is also now fixed-capital intensive due to the expensive capacity-addition campaigns being waged by several large breweries. On the other hand, capital intensive industries such as automobile manfacturing need substantial working capital to finance slow-moving inventories.

Whatever the determinations, the answers to all these questions provide insights into the basic financing characteristics of an industry and offer a guide to financial expectations under varying economic conditions. Accordingly, the industry risk assessment often sets the stage for analyzing more specific company (debt issuer) risk factors. For example, if an industry is determined to be highly competitive, a careful evaluation of an issuer's market position is called for. If the industry has large capital requirements, examination of cash flow adequacy assumes major importance. This key role of the industry risk category makes it slightly more equal than other risk factors, even though any factor may be an overriding consideration for a given rating.

In general, favorably regarded industries have good, but not overly rapid, real growth prospects with a predictable revenue stream and a relatively stable competitive structure. An industry that can control its costs, particularly for key raw materials, and that enjoys a flexible pricing environment would be viewed as strong. Likewise, entrance barriers, not to be confused with large ongoing capital requirements, are judged to be positive attributes.

Ratings Evaluation

The industry risk evaluation of a company primarily serves to focus an analyst's attention on the relevant credit factors. Is there also a direct relationship between industry risk and debt ratings? Of course, a low industry evaluation does not preclude a company from obtaining a high debt rating, nor does a high industry evaluation automatically translate into a high rating. Nevertheless, industries that are viewed favorably have a disproportionate number of highly rated participants. On the other hand, poorly regarded industries typically contain few highly rated companies.

COMPETITION AS A RATING FACTOR — MARKET POSITION

Credit analysis proceeds from an evaluation of industry risk to a study of competition within a particular industry, and how the company being rated is positioned within that industry. This is measured in two ways: one is by market position; the other involves an analysis of relative operating efficiency, a topic that will be discussed in a later section.

The market position evaluation emphasizes the company's sales position in its major fields, its historical protection of that position, and its projected ability to maintain it. Devising an appropriate set of business unit and corporate comparisons is critical. Important use is made of the business segment disclosures contained in annual reports. Notwithstanding the limitations of this data for comparative purposes, it is regarded as helpful in discussions of market strategies with corporate managements.

Assessing Size

The purpose of market position analysis is the determination of what factors give one company competitive strength in its markets, based on the determinants of success in the markets themselves. Sheer mass is important only insofar as it can be shown to provide demonstrable advantages. If, for instance, an industry has a number of large but comparable-sized participants, there are no particular advantages or disadvantages related to size. Market strength generally results from one or more management skills such as technological strength, marketing expertise, cost control, or service orientation.

To the extent market shares are major rating considerations, strategies employed by corporations to keep or build their relative market positions are discussed in depth at meetings with management. Part of the ensuing analysis is to determine whether a company has a large enough portion of the market to influence the dynamics of the industry significantly. This is so whether the market is regional, such as crushed stone for road construction; national, such as household cleaners; or international, such as the major integrated oils. A company's ability and opportunity to utilize its market strength when dealing with its customers can then be assessed. While not everyone has world stature, there are many small companies that have impressively large market shares that lend considerable competitive benefits.

Market share analysis is much more than a numerical exercise, taking into account varying industry structures and the extent to which market share in a particular industry is a source of profitability. A smaller market share, built on high product differentiation, or market specialization, can be a source of great profitability, while a company with a "stuck-in-the-middle" market share will be highly dependent on cost structure and operating efficiency for profitability. Analysis of market position may also focus on research and development spending, when significant. The pharmaceutical industry is a classic example of an industry that requires an ongoing program of heavy spending to generate new products.

A single product often can be sufficient to create success and financial wealth in this industry. For industries dependent on continuing research and development (R&D), such as the drug industry, there is interest in the actual dollar trends of R&D spending, the percentage of sales this constitutes, the broad sectors in which the spending is concentrated, the record of productivity, and how all this matches up with competitors.

Companies that depend on profits from one product or service are inherently credit-dependent and limited unless they can effectively deploy their business resources to sustaining business success in products and markets that provide long-term protection for bondholders. Similarly, advertising and promotional expenditures are important considerations in evaluating market position for companies in the food processing, beverage, and tobacco industries. A change could signify a shift in competitive aggressiveness because of a loss in market share or in response to a change in advertising direction by a major competitor.

Leadership

Attitudes toward technological leadership are studied to determine if a particular company is an innovator or a follower. The latter may be the correct strategy for a small company whose product duplication is simple, but a leadership position usually translates into comparatively high market shares and higher margins.

During meetings with management, the company's relationships with its customers are examined by the credit analysts. Of benefit to credit quality is a diversity of major customers and an absence of customers representing significant credit risks. Where there is heavy dependence on one major customer, there is the risk that the loss of that customer could greatly alter the financial outlook, thus indicating credit vulnerability under stress. Therefore, the historical working relationship between supplier and customer is examined very carefully. (E.g., although a large percentage of Whirlpool's sales may be to Sears, it is also important to recognize that the two companies have a long-standing relationship, which has benefited both.)

Diversity is also analyzed in market position, but here it is product diversity rather than business diversity that is important. Usually, a company can better protect its position when it makes and markets a broad product line. Kellogg may only be a producer of ready-to-eat cereals, but its extensive line of offerings helps to secure it a major position with its industry. The benefits of diversity can, however, only be realized if sufficient financial and marketing support are given to the entire line.

OPERATING EFFICIENCY

The ramifications of market position vis-à-vis competition are also important. Essentially, an analysis of a company's historical operating margins is performed and a judgment is made as to its ability to maintain or improve them based upon cost or pricing advantages.

Operating efficiency analysis is used to determine what factors give one company a marketplace advantage or disadvantage in terms of sustaining profitability through periods of economic stress or serious competitive pressures. Statistically, a company's relative efficiencies can be measured in many ways: gross margins; operating margins; return on capital; labor costs in relation to sales; finished goods/sales; and ratio tools. But the reasons behind the numbers represent the essence of the analysis.

Production efficiency is a major consideration. An evaluation is made as to the extent to which a company is a high- or low-cost producer. The age of its plant and equipment often provides good insight into this evaluation, since modern, state-of-the-art facilities typically are far more productive than older, obsolete plants. While there are many examples, meat-packing stands out. This industry went through a revolutionary change that resulted in a complete transformation of the competitive structure. The impact was dramatic in the 1960s when Iowa Beef Processors introduced its boxed beef concept, based on new cutting techniques in modern single-story structures. The old-line packers such as Swift, Wilson, Armour, and Cudahy, operating in archaic, multistory, labor-intensive plants, were doomed to a competitive disadvantage. Older plants are not always a disadvantage, as indicated by DuPont, which has a long history of keeping its chemical facilities up-to-date through maintenance expenditure policies.

Another aspect of cost advantage can be traced to the relative degree of integration of manufacturing operations. At times this can result in significant advantages, such as backward integration into ethylene production of plastics. At other times it can be a costly and futile effort if either the supply of raw material can be obtained less expensively elsewhere, or if the market for the finishing product is depressed.

In evaluating these factors, discussions with management may focus on how much capital is being spent to bring facilities to the highest possible level of modernization. In addition, companies that have already met the strictest pollution control and Occupational Safety and Health Act of 1970 (OSHA) standards should have a better capacity to either expand or modernize facilities or to otherwise improve operating or production abilities.

When important, the analysis of operating efficiency may also include the labor situation, including availability, relative wage scales, and union relationships. The sources, total supply, and cost of raw materials are other major considerations. Generally, when supplies are abundant, such as for grain commodities, multiple sources selling at market provide the best margins. When sources are few, and supplies typically tight, long-term purchase contracts will usually result in a competitive edge.

How are companies viewed that operate in volatile markets? Here, the supply or market uncertainties are reflected in an assessment that industry risk is higher.

Over the past decade energy costs for many companies have become a far greater user of available dollars than other operating factors. For this reason, companies with a clear edge are those capable of using multiple energy sources or supplying their own energy requirements, possibly through a cogeneration facility that burns by-product or waste product, and those few who may still have low-cost, long-term supply contracts.

Price leadership is also taken into account in this category. While price leadership is generally a function of market share, price policy in itself is far more important to operating margins than it is to the total dollar sales position.

MANAGEMENT EVALUATION — A KEY TEST

According to many annual reports, corporate managements are often innocent victims of "depressed" market conditions, "unprecedented" interest rates, or "irresponsible" competition. Yet, in the final analysis management can, should, and will be held fully responsible for the corporation's results. This is because at some point management made all the basic decisions as to what business to be in, chose those strategies that should be followed to compete effectively, and determined how the business should be financed. Successful companies are constantly rethinking these issues; thus, an important focus of a credit evaluation is an assessment of management's sensitivity and responsiveness to change.

Meetings with management are needed to discuss industry outlook, business strategy, and financial forecasts and policies. This helps to accomplish a number of important analytical tasks. For example, competitors' forecasts of market demand can be compared with each other and with those drawn from independent econometric models. There is thus an opportunity to judge relative optimism regarding market growth and relative aggressiveness in seeking competitive advantage. Not least of all, it is possible to compare business strategies and financial plans over time for an understanding of why they changed and what they indicated regarding managment's approach to the future. From this ongoing process of meeting with different managements over the course of a year and the same managements year after year, distinctions between those with thoughtful solutions versus those with wishful approaches can be developed.

Establishing Credibility

One of the basic principles of management evaluation is that stated intentions can rarely substitute for demonstrated past performance. Since it obviously takes time for management to establish financial community credibility, how can the first-time issuer of bonds or commercial paper shortcut this process and obtain credit for the managerial effectiveness that he knows is fully deserved?

Essentially this calls for an ability to:

- Clearly articulate a corporate mission and illustrate how business objectives draw upon the organization's strengths.
- Detail essential workings of the budgeting and planning processes with emphasis on the system's responsiveness to cyclical and fundamental business shifts.
- Evidence an understanding of the direct relationship between risks inherent in the industries and businesses the company has chosen to participate in and the sorts of financial policies and practices that are appropriate to those circumstances. Since consistency, in terms of both philosophy and practice, is the foundation of credibility, the case is most effectively presented through use of examples that establish a pattern over time.

For many major industrial corporations, the issue of credit-standing policy, and thus debt ratings, is an appropriate subject for discussion at the executive committee or board of directors level. As a matter of financial policy, the question of which debt rating is optimal needs to be evaluated in terms of cost of capital, availability of capital, responsibilities to different classes of security holders and other constituencies, and management's objectives and values. How and why management resolves these issues is invariably an important rating consideration. It enables the analyst to evaluate where the long-term center of gravity is for credit quality and the basis on which a conservative financial policy may hold fast or be compromised.

There are obviously no universal answers to these issues, but it seems clear that in the minds of a number of industrial managements the AAA rating has become too costly for the perceived benefits. Thus, some companies chose to sacrifice their top credit ratings in the belief that growth and/or diversification opportunities were available at reasonable prices today, and could not prudently be foregone. Based on this pattern, managements in similar situations are questioned even more closely regarding their commitment to maintaining existing credit ratings. While no rating changes have occurred to date in the absence of a specific development, this is a future possibility.

The margin for error has narrowed considerably in recent years for the many firms that do not have the luxury of setting financial policy so as to qualify for their ideal debt rating. At current costs of capital, and considering the unstable economic outlook, a management decision to undertake or maintain a significant capital spending program using extensive short-term borrowings is akin to playing Russian roulette. Credit judgments assigned to the debt issues of companies following such risk-oriented practices must be revised accordingly.

MANAGEMENT AND CHANGE

In evaluating management, S&P's approach, for instance, is both cautious and deliberate. There is no attempt at either a management audit or to make overly simplistic judgments on managerial capabilities. Analysis focuses on the financial record as a reflection of management's success or failure, conservatism or aggressiveness, and areas of vulnerability. Of importance in this record is the extent to which it was the result of good management, was achieved despite management, or reflects a situation devoid of management influence. A financial record that indicates successful response to change is one of the better indications of favorable management performance.

Focus on Planning

Planning is another sector in which judgments are made. There is no attempt to analyze a company's entire planning process, but there is emphasis on the end result of financial plans, their integration into the business strategy and, of course, the reasonableness of the assumptions. Management plans are important as a concrete expression of corporate strategy and policy, and analytical judgments center not only on their realism but on the extent to which they support credit quality. Finally, the most sophisticated and well-thought-out plans will not overcome the weakness demonstrated when plans are not executed successfully, as viewed in yearly evaluations.

Business Scope

Management's view of its own business (Peter Drucker's perennial question, "What business are you in?") is the essential element against which a management's record of operations and plans can be evaluated. Countless companies have fallen into the trap of viewing their businesses as too limited by geography or industry. The countervailing trend today is for companies to view their business as too all-encompassing, leading them to attempt to do too much without the necessary financial resources or management skills.

Management's view of its business and objectives has to be backed by a demonstration that it can reasonably expect to meet its goals. Otherwise, achievement of objectives may be uncertain, indicating greater credit risk should unanticipated hurdles arise. Financial resources comprise only one element, and usually this is the test most easily met. The product plan and market strategy are evaluated to the extent that the analyst has adequate expertise to make a judgment as to realism, skepticism, or uncertainty. In many submarkets or for new products, many analysts do not have this expertise. Instead, they must look to whether existing and proven management skills, such as a demonstrated marketing expertise, a strong distribution or service organization, and operational or technological strengths, are in place or evident. If management requires new skills either to operate new businesses or to be successful in a major acquisition, additional uncertainty is perceived.

Management Credibility

Management credibility is a source of credit strength that is earned over time. Once earned, credibility allows for continuity of credit quality because it means management will do what it says to support creditworthiness when faced with stress or an important restructuring. However, credibility once lost is not easily restored. Credibility is gained when a company's actions are consistent with its plans and objectives as demonstrated by the record. Loss of credibility by a management cannot easily be remedied by a change in personnel, since the new management's policies and performance can only develop over time.

Changes in Policy

A most problematic issue in evaluating corporate credit quality is the increasing tendency of management policy to change because of (1) acquisitions or the threat thereof; (2) short-term performance pressures; (3) a changing of the guard; and (4) increasing economic pressures. There are no perfect analytical solutions, but such potential for management change can be dealt with as follows:

- Credit judgments should reflect some level of uncertainty regarding unforeseeable change.
- Nothing succeeds like success. A strong record of financial success and an analysis that the future will hold more of the same is important in understanding that management change is less likely to occur. Such change is more likely to occur for companies that are unsuccessful in meeting shareholder goals. Thus, for a company with consistently low earnings, very conservative debt usage may not be relied on as a credit strength over the long run.
- The evaluation should reflect an appreciation for management's own view of its business and the role it sees for credit quality. Certain managements have a long history of strong financial management and board of director support, while

others have opportunity-oriented financial management or see it as a limited staff function. Corporate cultures are usually slow to change. Most often they are backed up by extensive business reasons or a strong corporate philosophy, such as aversion to or preference for debt usage.

- Where business factors indicate that a change in management policy may become desirable, the issues should be discussed candidly and the evaluation reflected in the rating decision.

Organizational Considerations

Regarding the evaluation of top management, normally there is caution in second-guessing its structure and strategy. Analysts are confronted at times with situations where:

- There is substantial organizational reliance on an individual chief executive or financial officer who may be close to retirement.
- The finance function and finance considerations do not receive high organizational recognition.
- The transition to professional, organizational management from entrepreneurial or family-bound management remains to be accomplished.
- A relatively large number of changes occur in a short time.
- The relationship between organizational structure and management strategy is unclear.
- A substantial presence by one or a few shareholders exists, providing stability of ownership or constraints on management prerogatives. Depending on circumstances, this could have either positive or negative implications.

The organizational structure first and foremost needs to be understood in the context of the business environment, including past practices and future needs. Where appropriate, unresolved questions will be candidly discussed with management to develop this understanding. Where valid issues and questions still remain, these will be factored into the rating evaluation, albeit cautiously.

ACCOUNTING QUALITY

As part of a credit analysis, S&P, for instance, reviews accounting quality to determine whether ratios and statistics derived from financial statements can be accurately used to measure a company's performance and position relative to its competition. When feasible, adjustments are made to the income statement or balance sheet accounts to bring them into conformity with industry practice. Where quantification is impossible, conclusions are tempered with the assumption that apparent financial conditions may be understated or overstated. Thus, the study of accounting quality serves as a tool for ensuring that earnings protection, leverage, cash flow adequacy, and financial flexibility, as well as management performance, are being judged on a comparable scale for every company.

Ratings Are Not Audits

A rating is not an audit, and the rating process does not entail auditing a company's financial records. Ratings are based on audited data, generally for a five-year period. Analysis of the audited financials begins by reviewing the auditor's opinion and the summary of accounting policies. This opinion can be qualified or unqualified. A qualified auditor's opinion can indicate that the financial statements contain a departure from generally accepted accounting principles (GAAP), the effect of which is material; namely, that there has been a material change in accounting principles between periods or in the method of their application, or that there are significant uncertainties affecting the financial statements. Examples of major uncertainties contained in 1981 annual reports include:

- Litigation, such as health-related actions against Manville Corp. from its asbestos operations (the company subsequently entered Chapter 11 proceedings).
- Ongoing concern, such as Mego International, Inc.'s need to achieve certain sales and profitability goals and to maintain its new financial arrangements to sustain future operations (the company subsequently entered Chapter 11 proceedings).

In most cases major uncertainties are known well in advance of the auditor's opinion, reviewed in detail with management, and reflected in ratings. However, the qualified opinion does highlight, in the auditor's opinion, that the financial statements "present fairly" the consolidated results "subject to" the qualification.

Even when the auditor's opinion is unqualified, or clean, the reported values in the financial statements may be questioned or adjusted. These adjustments are made for the following reasons:

- To emphasize accurate credit analysis of current realities.
- To facilitate comparability among companies, particularly within the same industry.
- Because of the inherent limitations of accounting, such as the use of various estimates and approximations.

Two objectives of credits analysis are (1) to determine the quality of earnings; and (2) to determine the quality of assets and net capital position represented on the balance sheet. As a key to understanding financial statements, the footnotes and the summary of significant accounting policies are analyzed.

Accounting policies reviewed include:

- Consolidation basis
- Income recognition (e.g., successful efforts versus full cost in the oil industry, and percentage of completion versus completed contract in the construction industry)
- Depreciation methods
- Inventory pricing methods
- Amortization of intangibles
- Investment tax credit policy
- Employee benefits

Consolidation Principles

The principles of consolidation will indicate if any majority-owned subsidiaries are not consolidated, such as finance, insurance, or real estate subsidiaries. In the case of unconsolidated subsidiaries, the analytical approach might be (as decided on a case-by-case basis) to fully consolidate the entity, selectively consolidate the debt, or leave it unconsolidated. The factors determining the approach include:

- Whether standard industry accounting practice was followed;
- The operational and/or financial materiality of the subsidiary to the consolidated entity; and
- The amount of off-balance-sheet leverage being employed in the context of the unconsolidated operation.

Thus, for example, if a company had a finance subsidiary leverage at 10:1 debt/equity while the appropriate leverage was closer to 4:1, supranormal off-balance-sheet debt might well be added back to the parent company's financial statement.

Most industrial companies use straight-line depreciation for book purposes and accelerated methods for tax purposes. Therefore, companies that utilize acelerated depreciation methods for book purposes are generally considered more conservative. However, when analyzing different methods of depreciation or comparing companies in the same industry using the same method (i.e., straight line), a key factor in the determination of accounting quality is the estimated useful life for the major classes of assets. For example, if the industry norm is straight line over 10 years, and a company used 20 years, that company would be viewed as using a more liberal depreciation policy that overstates net income. Another important factor in the evaluation of depreciation methods is the assumed salvage value.

Inventory Pricing

Another area that involves substantial accounting alternatives is the inventory pricing method. In a period of rising prices, the LIFO method is viewed as the more conservative and appropriate method for income statement purposes. At the same time, there is recognition of the understated asset value, or LIFO reserve. For industries such as high technology, which have been experiencing declining prices, the FIFO method is deemed more conservative. Some large international companies have adopted LIFO on a worldwide basis, which is considered very conservative, while other companies have been quite selective in their choices of LIFO or FIFO methods.

The shortest amortization period used for intangible assets, such as goodwill, is viewed as the most conservative in terms of the income statement. Goodwill on the balance sheet is not viewed as adding asset protection unless the underlying business entity has a track record of generating favorable returns that support the value of the goodwill. Goodwill associated with broadcasting stations is a general example of goodwill that adds to asset protection.

Of the two methods of accounting for investment tax credits, the deferral method is preferred. However, since the majority of industrial companies are on the less conservative flow-through method, there is an adjustment to the equity base of companies on the deferral method by adding back the amount of deferred investment tax credits. This is not the case for utility-related operations.

Pension Policies

When analyzing pension funding policies, examine the firm's actuarial assumptions concerning rate of return and salary increments versus the industry norm. An unfunded liability is calculated by subtracting the market value of net assets available for benefits from the actuarial present value of accumulated plan benefits. This number, due to the exclusion of salary increments, is understated for all industrial companies. This consideration, plus the various allowable methodologies, information gaps, and plan assumptions involved, make it difficult at present to develop a representative pension liability estimate for use in the rating process.

Asset Valuation and Current Costs

Another area of importance in the review of accounting quality is the evaluation of undervalued assets due to accounting policies and/or principles. An example of this would include LIFO reserves and the assets of natural resource companies. With the high-average level of inflation over the last 10 years, most companies could claim to have assets on the books for an amount less than current replacement value of the assets. However, it is only the natural resource companies that have built-in undervalued assets by virtue of the accounting used by the industry. Using either the full-cost or the successful-efforts method of accounting, a petroleum company essentially puts its assets on the books at the finding cost, not at the current cost to acquire, as is the case with most other companies. This has serious implications regarding capital structure analysis. The approach to this industry's problem is to deemphasize the capital structure ratios and to focus on earnings and cash flow ratios as the key ratios. Thus, regardless of the value of the asset on the books, its true worth will be reflected in what it earns. Therefore, earnings and cash flow measures will better reflect debt-protection qualities.

A tool that may be useful in evaluating accounting quality is the supplemental information on inflation and changing prices. There is a preference for the current cost method, which attempts to adjust for specific price changes affecting the assets of a company. Inflation affects various specific prices in different ways. Consequently, information about changes in an index of general inflation does not provide sufficient information about the effect of inflation on an individual company. Therefore, constant dollar information is not as meaningful to the rating process for industrial companies. The experimental nature of current cost disclosures is recognized, as well as the significant number and scope of accounting alternatives available to management. Thus, rating decisions are not based solely on this largely unaudited data. However, in many cases, the depreciation number offers a rough estimate over time of the minimum capital a firm has to spend annually to maintain its current plant. Also, the difference between the current cost, the cost of goods sold, and the historical cost represents an approximation of the impact of switching to LIFO.

In summary, the results of the accounting quality review, whether qualitative or subjective, lay the foundation for a subsequent analysis of earnings protection, leverage and asset protection, cash flow adequacy, and financial flexibility.

Considerations for Non-U.S. Ratings

One of the primary challenges in analyzing international companies is an understanding of the various accounting systems under which non-U.S. companies report their financial results. Restatement of financial statements under U.S. GAAP is usually not required. However, analysis of the company's financial condition is facilitated by an explanation and quantification of significant differences from U.S. GAAP. In many instances, a meeting with external auditors is helpful. The basic point of reference in financial ratio analysis is, to a large extent, experience in domestic ratings. Thus, the additional information provided by management is used to adjust key financial ratios to facilitate comparison with U.S. and other foreign companies operating in similar industries.

The rating process, however, goes beyond financial ratio analysis. The starting point for analysis is an examination of the environment in which a company operates. As such, the financial system of the country is a major consideration. For example, in analyzing a Japanese company's capital structure, credit is given to the traditionally close relationship with its lead banks. In turn, this is tempered by the need to maintain this relationship with the banks, by the less developed capital markets in Japan as compared to those of the United States, and by the existing regulatory framework, which could limit the company's choice of financing alternatives.

EARNINGS PROTECTION

The importance of earnings protection in credit rating criteria centers on the consideration that in the long run, it is a company's earning power that attests to asset values, opens external financing sources, and provides credit protection. In analyzing earnings protection, several measurements are used to indicate a company's long-term earning power and the extent to which fixed charges are covered. The more significant measurements are:

- Returns on capital
- Profit margins
- Pretax coverage ratios
- Earnings on assets/business segments
- Sources of future earnings growth
- Inflation-adjusted earnings

Returns and Margins

Pretax return on average invested capital, and operating income as a percentage of sales, are ratios that indicate a company's financial health, regardless of the manner in which the company in capitalized. Obviously, all else being equal, a company that generates higher operating margins and returns on capital is considered to have a greater ability to generate equity capital internally, attract capital externally, and withstand business adversity. While the absolute levels of the ratios are important, it is equally important to focus on trends and how a ratio may compare to those of competitors. Various industries have different earnings protection characteristics and, therefore, what may be considered favorable for one business may be relatively poor for another. For example, the drug industry usually generates high operating margins and high returns on captial. The pipeline industry has high operating margins and low returns on capital.

However, companies in each of these industries can still have the same credit rating. These ratings naturally reflect not only analysis of earnings protection but also analysis of the other key risk categories.

Fixed Charges

Another key measurement of earnings protection is earnings in relation to fixed charges. There are several fixed-charge coverage ratios that are evaluated, but the two primary ratios are pretax interest coverage, and pretax coverage of interest and total rents. If preferred stock is outstanding and material, fixed charges are adjusted to include preferred dividends. Pretax earnings used in these ratios are adjusted to exclude the effect of unremitted equity income, gains and losses on repurchase of debt, unrealized gains and losses due to foreign currency translation, minority interests, nonrecurring or extraordinary gains and losses, and the effect of capitalizing interest. The objective is to more accurately reflect the ongoing earnings available to pay fixed charges. In the evaluation of earnings protection, it is necessary to go beyond the consolidated numbers, by examining the earnings and returns of various business segments in an attempt to highlight sources of profitability strength, weakness, or volatility. Problem areas will naturally lead to a series of questions that include: What is the nature of the business unit problem? What corrective actions are being taken, and how long will it take to get results up to expectations? What are the alternatives if management actions fail?

The analysis of earnings protection and the other financial categories evaluates both historical and projected performance. This allows a differentiation between the future and the past, and an assessment of changing business fundamentals and management strategies. All but a limited and declining number of companies whose debt is rated provide rating agencies with detailed financial projections. These are used for rating purposes only and are kept strictly confidential. Such projections provide insight as to management's view of its business, and are particularly useful in viewing differences in competitive strategy. In addition, industry analysts develop their own view of the future earnings outlook. Because ratings are an assessment of the likelihood of timely payment of interest and repayment of principal that will occur in the future, emphasis is placed on the evaluation of future performance. The rating analysis does not attempt to forecast performance in the most precise terms based on very specific economic assumptions. Rather, the forecast analysis emphasizes the range of expected future performances based on a probable range of economic scenarios.

Of particular importance are management expectations for sources of future earnings growth. There is an evaluation of whether existing businesses can provide satisfactory growth, particularly in a less inflationary environment, and to what extent acquisitions or divestitures may be necessary to achieve corporate goals. It is presumed that a corporation's central focus is to augment shareholder values over the long run. Thus, a lack of indicated earnings growth over the long run rather than on a year-to-year basis is considered a weakness. On its own, this may hinder a company's ability to attract financial and human resources. Equally important, limited earnings growth opportunities may lead management to seek earnings growth externally by taking on additional business and financial risks. Thus, demonstrated success in managing earnings growth through internal and external sources is viewed as a credit strength.

Inflation Adjusted Earnings

A quantitative tool that is beginning to be used in evaluating earnings protection is the supplemental information on inflation and changing prices. For industrial companies, the current cost method, which attempts to adjust costs for changes in specific prices, is more useful than the constant dollar method. The experimental nature of current cost disclosures is recognized, as well as the significant number and scope of accounting alternative available to management. Thus, no rating decision is based solely on this information.

However, it is especially interesting to compare current cost profits as a percentage of historical profits and price adjusted returns on assets for companies within the same industry. Interindustry comparisons produce expected results. Many captial-intensive industries have little or no earnings when cost of goods sold and depreciation are computed at current costs in the calculation of current cost earnings. Gains in purchasing power due to debt being greater than monetary assets are not included in the calculation. These gains, which some companies have added to current cost profits, will be realized only in the future, if at all, and the company still has to generate cash from its ongoing operations to pay off its debt.

In summary, the various measures of profitability are evaluated to determine whether, and to what extent, earnings protection is expected to be a credit strength or weakness in the future.

FINANCIAL LEVERAGE AND ASSET PROTECTION

The analysis of financial leverage and asset protection is one of the most direct and yet most difficult areas of financial analysis. It is direct because the distinction between liabilities and equity is well-defined and assets are easily related to outstanding debt. The difficult part is that certain unrecorded liabilities are "more real" liabilities than some recorded liabilities (i.e., pension liabilities versus deferred taxes) and the cumulative effect of inflation often has rendered reported asset and equity values of limited use. In such circumstances, what then is the value of analyzing financial leverage and asset protection, and specifically what measures should be emphasized in its analysis? The discussion will focus separately on leverage and asset protection.

Risk Indicator

Financial leverage, or, simply, the extent to which a firm borrows money to finance itself, has been used as an indicator of financial risk. The more (fixed) financial leverage (required payments) a company has the less able it may be to pay off its borrowed funds because it may be less able than a company with lower leverage to withstand diminution in asset values or cash flows and still meet its obligations. In the same vein, leverage has been used as a proxy to indicate the magnitude of fixed charges a company must service. Here again, it is an indicator of financial risk.

Another use of the leverage concept has been to measure the relative amount of equity supporting the asset base, or what generally is known as asset protection. A variation on this theme is asset protection relative to outstanding debt. In these instances the focus tends more toward viewing the company on a liquidating basis rather than as an ongoing concern.

Leverage can be viewed as an indication of the degree of risk a company is undertaking with its capital base. In effect, it is a statement by management of its risk-taking or risk-avoidance philosophy as actually practiced. Also, since ratings address primarily the risk of default and only secondarily whether or not a creditor will ultimately be paid off, leverage is viewed principally as a proxy for the level of fixed charges that must be serviced rather than as a measure of asset protection provided.

Creative Financing

Several ratios are used to capture the degree of leverage utilized by a company. They include:

- Long-term debt/capitalization
- Total debt/capitalization + short-term debt + off-balance-sheet liabilities (OBLs)

In this age of increasing reliance on short-term borrowing and various creative financing vehicles, the traditional long-term debt/capitalization ratio is losing its significance as a measure of permanent debt/capitalization. The ratio of total debt/capitalization + short-term debt is used to isolate those situations where permanent layers of short-term borrowing exist. Such layers finance not only seasonal working capital needs but also an ongoing portion of the asset base. Permanent layers of short-term debt occur for many reasons, including management philosophy (many financial officers believe that the days of the 1960s and early 1970s will recur, when short-term debt was consistently less expensive than long-term borrowings); reluctance to refinance long term when a substantial rate decline seems imminent (an argument made repeatedly in recent years and initiated when the cost-of-money spiral began); or, simply, an inability to obtain long-term financing.

The increasing use of creative financing is captured in the total debt + OBLs/capitalization + short-term debt + OBLs ratio. OBLs include:

- Capitalized operating rents
- Unfunded pension obligations
- Obligations under throughput and deficiency agreements and take-or-pay contracts
- Guarantees
- Debt of unconsolidated captive finance subsidiaries, joint ventures, and partnerships

The determination of total capitalized value of OBLs is not as simple as adding up all existing OBLs. The methodologies to determine the proper capitalized values are beyond the scope of this chapter. Simply put, each OBL is examined to determine the relevance of the activity financed to the mainstream business of the organization, and the likelihood of the necessity for financial support. Therefore, capitalized operating rents would be viewed as "real" liabilities, as would unfunded pension obligations. But debt of joint ventures, which by themselves are sound and stand-alone credits, may be viewed as much less onerous liabilities.

On the subject of creative financing, issues sold at original issue discounts (OIDs) should be mentioned. Analysis of financial leverage when OIDs have been issued requires a hybrid approach to ratio calculation. For purposes of capital structure analysis, OIDs are valued net of unamortized discount. However, when measuring the cash flow to debt relationship, the maturity value of the issue is considered.

The traditional ratio of total liabilities/tangible net worth is not included in the list of key ratios because of its great variability over various industries and among companies of similar strength. This variability reduces its value as an indicator of risk. The ratio also suffers because it includes many nondebt liabilities that do not generate fixed charges and that are serviced through normal asset liquidations rather than cash flow (i.e., accounts payable).

Mergers and Acquisitions

The surge of merger and acquisition activity in the past few years has produced large volumes of new preferred stock, much of which has features similar to debt obligations, specifically sinking funds. These "limited-life" preferreds are not automatically counted as equity for capital structure analysis, as are perpetual preferreds, but are classified as equity or debt, depending on their remaining average life. Limited-life preferreds with remaining average lives of 10 years or more are viewed as equity. Those under 10 years are classified as debt. Recognizing the high-cost nature of preferred stock, it is not considered reasonable to assume the preferred will be financed with additional preferred stock. Rather, the assumption is that it will be refinanced with some form of debt security.

Recent mergers and acquisitions have brought up another analytical challenge that is really part of the broader question: What are the "true" values of debt and equity in an environment of changing prices? The situation referred to here is where company *A* acquires company *B* and company *B* continues to be rated on its own statements. Current accounting standards allow company *B*'s assets and equity to be written up to reflect the acquisition price. Suddenly its equity has grown, its debt ratios have dropped, and management wants to add debt to bring the debt ratio back to preacquisition levels. Unfortunately, this company still has the same earning power as before. It really cannot support more debt and still support its credit rating. In this case the answer is clear; it is much less clear several years after the acquisition, as the ability to relate to preacquisition financial statements is lost. In these instances one must make year-to-year comparisons using statements that more accurately and consistently portray results on a current cost basis.

Effects of Inflation

Specifically related to financial leverage is the controversial issue of purchasing power gains on debt. While there is the reality that the cost of servicing debt is less of a burden in an inflationary climate, there is an equal, and perhaps more than offsetting, reality of the impact of inflation on a company's earning power. Experience to date suggests that inflation depletes more of a company's earning power (e.g., current cost earnings versus historical basis earnings) than is gained through purchasing power gains on debt. Moreover, a serious loss of earning power gives rise to questions as to the resilience of the corporation. This casts doubt on whether it can reach the day when it can pay off its debt with the cheaper dollars.

Management Philosophies

Beyond numerical analysis, the analyst ought to recognize the importance of examining management's philosophies and intentions toward leverage. Although it would appear that each corporation has set goals in this area, this is not the case. A surprising number of companies have not given this question serious thought, much less reached firm conclusions. Those who have set goals do not all have the wherewithal, discipline, or management commitment to achieve them. A company's leverage goals, then, need to be viewed in the context of past performance, the financial dynamics affecting its businesses, its current leverage position, and management's commitment to achieve those goals. For example, if a management states that its goal is to operate at 35 percent debt to capital, this fact should be brought into the analysis to the extent it appears plausible, attainable, and supported by the record. However, if a company is currently operating at 40 percent, has aggressive spending plans, mediocre profitability, and no hope of selling equity securities, that 35 percent goal should carry little weight. On the subject of equity securities, there is often a question about the treatment of convertible debt. At conversion they will be treated as debt; otherwise, they are debt, albeit at a reasonable capital cost. Many well-intentioned companies project short-time conversion but fail to accomplish it. Conversion is subject to enough variables beyond management's control that a prediction of when it might occur becomes a presumptuous exercise. Where convertible issues actually convert with regularity, the benefits to the equity base can be quite significant.

Another issue to address is, What is the maximum deviation from financial leverage objectives a company would tolerate in order to finance an acquisition?

Also related to this, Would management sacrifice or be indifferent to existing credit quality levels in order to meet growth and/or diversification goals? DuPont, General Foods, and Shell Oil are all examples of formerly AAA-rated companies that chose to view their ratings as a resource to be drawn on to achieve other goals. In some cases, analysis of a company's business outlook and position will suggest that management will be under much pressure to alter its capital structure goals, no matter how firm its stated policy or previous practice. This is particularly true of corporations with less internal cash flow flexibility, with limited sources of earnings growth, with overdependence on one or two industries, or with high vulnerability to economic cycles. By putting these considerations together and assessing a company's leverage record management policy and planning, a picture of where leverage is likely to be in the future can be derived.

Role of Asset Protection

The analysis of asset protection is not an exercise in appraising a company's assets in an attempt to gain a liquidating value for the company and, consequently, not a relationship between asset values and debt. A sensible approach to ratings presumes that a company is ongoing rather than in liquidation. Therefore, to calculate the liquidating value of assets in relation to debt is meaningless because the assets will not be liquidated to pay off debt. The one exception to this would be where a subsidiary or certain assets are to be sold. In such cases an attempt should be made to value the assets slated for disposal.

One approach to asset protection is an attempt to highlight materially undervalued or overvalued assets relative to book value so that leverage can be viewed in an alternate light reflecting the discrepancy. Examples included inventories, natural resource assets, intangible assets, and receivables. Where intangible assets are material in size, the first step is to determine whether the earnings support the value of this goodwill, then the decision to regard it at full or less than full value can be made. For most corporate assets, the liquidating or asset conversion values are of secondary relevance. Of primary importance are values of the assets on an ongoing basis, the best measure of which is long-term earning power.

The relationship between financial leverage and asset protection is straightforward; greater asset protection is a credit strength, which can offset nominally higher debt leverage. However, in evaluating this category, the leverage component of the analysis will predominate. While the asset protection analysis will tend to modify the leverage assessment, there is not a one-for-one trade-off between leverage and asset protection. Rather, the adequacy of leverage for a given rating category looks more importantly to cash flow adequacy, earnings protection, and financial flexibility.

CASH FLOW ADEQUACY

Cash flow is increasingly becoming the central focus of credit analysis. It is also the key variable in strategic planning decision making in corporate management. After all, cash flow is the sustaining element of corporate existence, without which a company's business life is threatened. This is particularly true today, for if a company's earnings and cash flow shrink, the shortfall needs to be financed with high-cost external capital from increasingly concerned lenders. Capital may not be available at any cost, or its high price may further reduce earnings and cash flow.

From a financial analysis standpoint, cash flow analysis in certain respects provides a better perspective on credit strength than earnings analysis. Because of alternative acceptable accounting treatments for such important segments as inventories, major contracts, depreciation, and investment tax credits, earnings as reported become somewhat of an artificial number. Cash flows may more accurately portray reality.

In fact, for industrial America net income would have represented only 93 percent of reported net in 1980 if such noncash earnings sources as unremitted equity in earnings of affiliates, gains on reacquisition of debt, capitalized interest, and foreign currency translation gains (or losses) were excluded. In 1982, if similar adjustments were made, the percentage would have been even lower, highlighting the need to emphasize cash flow analysis.

Cash flow adequacy can be viewed from two perspectives: in relation to debt and in relation to capital needs.

Cash Flow Ratios

Cash flow can be defined as the sum of adjusted net income, depreciation, depletion, amortization, and noncurrent deferred taxes. Thus, cash flow is more accurately a definition for funds from operations rather than the absolute amount of cash generated by a business (an amount which clearly differs from just net income plus noncash charges). If companies are viewed as ongoing entities, an analysis of funds from operations in relation to debt or capital needs is appropriate. At such time as the ongoing nature of a firm is in question, the focus of the analysis would change to an examination of the cash generated by the business from all sources rather than just from operations. The two ratios used to analyze cash flow in relation to debt are cash flow/long-term debt, and cash flow/total debt. In either ratio, the amounts used for the debt portion of the equation are the principal amounts of debt outstanding, not any one year's servicing requirements. An attempt is made to relate cash flow to permanent debt outstanding. Thus, the second ratio takes on primary significance in those instances where permanent layers of short-term borrowings are present. While the concept of debt service ratios has theoretical appeal, there are too many practical problems defining debt service in this age of evergreen bank commitments and high incidence of debt refinancing to make the ratio useful from a practical standpoint. The concept of debt service is addressed through a combination of the cash flow ratios and an examination of the debt maturity schedule in the analysis of financial flexibility.

What the cash flow/debt ratios describe in theory is how fast a firm could pay its debt if all cash flow were to be applied to debt repayment. Thus, a 25 percent cash flow/debt ratio would indicate that it would take four years for the company to pay its debt. It is simplistic, of course, to assume cash flow can be entirely devoted to debt repayment while excluding working capital, fixed capital, and dividend requirements. Nonetheless, when properly used, this ratio remains a highly important analytical tool.

For issues sold at original issue discounts, including zero coupon bonds, the analytical approach is to calculate cash flow/debt, including the full face value of the issue as debt. Cash flow will benefit from the effects of the amortization of the discount for a taxpaying issue in each year the bonds are outstanding. Since the amortization exists to provide for payment of the full face value of the issue, it is appropriate to compare the cash flow boosted by the amortization with the full liability that necessitates the amortization.

Cash Flow Variability

While the absolute level of cash flow in relation to debt is obviously significant, it is also important to examine the variability of cash flow. There is little creditor comfort in having a company exhibit 100 percent cash flow coverage of debt in one year only to see the coverage drop to 10 percent the next. Coverage at some stable intermediate level, perhaps 50 percent, in each of the years would be preferable. Cash flow/debt ratios of 50 percent for each of five years is preferable to cash flow ratios that range between 10 and 100 percent and yet average 50 percent over a five-year period. Almost certainly, the more consistent performer would be viewed more favorably. A corollary to this is the belief that a company that consistently exhibits a given level of cash flow coverage can probably utilize somewhat greater financial leverage than a company whose cash flow coverage averaged that same level, but was more variable.

The analysis of cash flow in relation to capital requirements begins with an examination of a company's capital needs defined to include working capital as well as fixed capital. While this analysis is performed for all debt issuers, it is critically important for fixed-capital- and rapidly growing working-capital-intensive firms. This is because these are significant customers of funds and strong candidates to fare poorly in a financing crunch. Since cash flow may be well short of needs for these companies, they face a key decision as to whether to cut back on spending and forego future income potentials and possibly a loss of competitiveness, or to press ahead and face the need to obtain external financing. Since either choice bears potential negative implications for credit quality, prior knowledge that capital requirements are outstripping cash flow is an important analytic input.

Companies, whose needs are predominantly for working capital, benefit by being able to finance a significant portion of their current assets through trade creditors. However, rapidly growing companies, such as many of the small- and medium-sized computer manufacturers, must rely on nontrade credit to a relatively greater extent. Despite strong profitability, the dynamic growth of these companies led to significant buildups in inventories and receivables that could not be financed internally or through trade credit. Had these companies used only debt to finance their growth, their financial leverage would have mushroomed. Wisely, many have chosen a combination of debt and equity and consequently preserved their credit ratings. A variation of this strategy has been to issue convertible debt supported by projections that earnings will continue to grow. This will enable a forced conversion of the convertible debt to equity at a future date. The convertibles, however, are treated as debt analytically while they are still outstanding.

Growth Rate Projections

The key to determining the working-capital requirements of a company is first to determine an expected growth rate that will translate into projected inventory and receivable levels from which trade financing sources can be computed. Inventory and receivable turnovers play an important role here. Turnovers are a function of economic conditions and management policies and procedures. The improvement of turnovers over the past several years would be no reason to project a continuation of the trend. Likewise, a declining trend does not necessarily mean that projected improvements will not be achieved. Individual circumstances must be examined in each case, including actual and projected management actions tempered by the credibility of management. The balance of growth will require external capital. Also, inventory levels necessary to support growth must be in place before the growth can occur. Thus, during rapid growth periods, inventory turnovers can be expected to decline.

Capital requirements for fixed-capital-intensive companies fall into two areas: the need to build new capacity, and the need to continually update and renew existing capacity. Given the high up-front costs to construct new facilities, it is unrealistic to expect that any but the strongest companies can finance such expenditures from internally generated funds. Nevertheless, it would be expected that once the capacity is on stream, the company would generate sufficient cash to allow some repayment of external financing funds. This does not always happen, however, either because of an extremely aggressive capital spending program for which external financing is required every year, or, more commonly, because the company finds itself in a cyclical trough at the very time its new capacity comes on stream.

Irrespective of current operating rates, a critical issue is whether or not a company is keeping its present capacity modern and efficient. In the face of a recessionary environment, a company may have to cut back capital spending to levels that can be internally financed to the detriment of keeping its plant in good operating order. While such a decision may have little near-term impact, it sows the seeds of long-term problems. Creditworthiness is evaluated for companies as ongoing enterprises. The expection is that they will provide funds on a year-in, year-out basis to maintain their capital investments at modern, efficient levels. Thus, cash flow adequacy is viewed from the standpoint of a company's ability to finance capital-maintenance requirements internally, as well as its ability to finance capital additions internally.

While capital additions are relatively easy to project, the concept of capital maintenance requirements is less easy to quantify, particularly in an inflationary environment. The amount of capital spending necessary to maintain current capacity can be related to the current cost depreciation expense reported in the financial statement footnotes describing the effects of changing prices. This number is viewed as a rough approximation for the actual number, which can only be derived from a detailed analysis of each company's individual circumstances.

The impact of inflation is not limited to its effect on fixed-capital requirements.

It also amplifies working-capital needs. A series of ratios can be used to analyze the impact of inflation on a company. Many of these ratios involve the concept of sustainable cash flow. The ratios are:

- Sustainable cash flow/total debt
- Sustainable cash flow/dividends
- Historical cost capital expenditures/replacement cost depreciation
- Capital requirements due to inflation/total capital dollars spent

Each of these ratios examines one particular aspect of cash flow adequacy.

Favorable cash flow adequacy requires high scores on both measures. For example, fixed-capital-intensive steel companies generate significant cash flows in relation to debt, even during periods of weak profitability. However, even in boom times, the capital generated internally is not sufficient to completely fund capital spending necessary to maintain modern, efficient facilities. These companies must limit spending, hoping to maintain their balance sheets while risking future problems, or they must finance needed spending, presumably with debt, and risk balance-sheet deterioration.

On the other hand, for those firms generating sufficient funds for capital needs, the cash flow/debt adequacy ratio can be very important. For example, there may be a very aggressive acquisition-minded company whose cash flow is very adequate in relation to its existing capital needs. However, the company may be highly leveraged, and cash flow may be very weak in relation to debt. In this instance, capital needs could include future acquisitions, and cash flow would be viewed as weak from that perspective.

Flexible Approach

Throughout this section, the focus has been on relating cash flow to needs in a static sense. In the real world, cash flow is variable, as are capital needs. Thus, while cash flow adequacy analysis is important, it does not have an overriding position in S&P methodology. Instead, it must be supplemented by an analysis of a company's flexibility to alter the timing of its capital requirements and to deal with debt repayments. These considerations are part of S&P's analysis of financial flexibility.

FINANCIAL FLEXIBILITY

Financial flexibility, an evaluation of a company's financing needs, plans, and alternatives under stress, is more than a summary of the previous three financial rating factors: earnings protection; financial leverage and asset production; and cash flow adequacy. This last category of the industrial rating methodology profile qualifies the bare financial ratios and links together business analysis, financial analysis, and external developments that confront all companies. It also encompasses a company's sources and uses of funds, such as divestitures and acquisitions beyond what is generated from, or employed in, ongoing operations. Also, this category recognizes a company's relative vulnerability to the vagaries of the capital markets. Benefits or detriments derived from a company's affiliation with other entities (e.g., a parent company) are considered at this point.

Unexpected Developments

Financial flexibility captures factors that might interfere with a company's normal financing plan. What are the company's options if internally generated funds are lower than expected, demand for the company's product does not slow, interest rates shoot up, or asset-based financing becomes unavailable? A firm that consistently generates enough cash flow to satisfy business needs, including growth in working-capital and capital expenditures, debt service, and dividends, has more flexibility than one that relies heavily on external funding.

Most industrial companies periodically tap the capital markets. Financial ratios are calculated for a period of three to five years to gauge financial flexibility. However, the specific timing of major expenditures and planned financing are compared. A company's ability to delay a capacity expansion or modernization program, without damaging its competitive position, is a plus. Likewise, prefinancing is generally viewed more favorably than gambling on the price and availability of funds during the quarter when they will be required. Volatile financial markets in recent years have prompted many previously infrequent borrowers to divide their financing needs into several pieces and accept the average cost. It is believed risky for a growing company to hold out for an interest rate that may not be seen for several years. Financial flexibility may be seriously jeopardized when a firm accumulates bank borrowings and commercial paper with the hope of funding out when market conditions improve.

Regardless of a company's degree of financial leverage, an imbalance within the debt or equity components can detract from financial flexibility. Reliance on short-term money or interest-sensitive funds of a longer maturity creates obvious risks. However, the use of short-term borrowing to finance a seasonal bulge in receivables and inventory, or to finance foreign operations in a local currency for which no long-term funds are available, would not be viewed unfavorably. An imbalanced capital structure might also result from an unusually short maturity schedule for long-term debt and limited-life preferred stock. Of course, there is no problem if maturing obligations, and all other cash requirements, will clearly be financed with internally generated funds. However, a growing business typically refunds maturing long-term debt with new long-term debt. It is generally assumed that limited-life preferred stock will also be refunded with long-term debt rather than new preferred, unless there is a reason to believe that the company's after-tax cost of preferred stock will always be no more expensive than debt. Moreover, the investor's appetite for preferred stock has been smaller and less dependable than his demand for debt securities.

A firm's access to various capital markets can augment financial flexibility. A company's experience with different financial instruments and different capital markets gives management alternatives if conditions in a particular financial market sour because of factors beyond the company's control. Ability to obtain a revolving credit commitment during the 1979–1980 credit crunch or to sell Eurobonds early in 1982 provided tangible benefits. Access to the common stock market is primarily a question of management's willingness to accept earnings per share dilution, rather than one of funds availability. When a new common stock offering is projected as part of a company's financing plan, there is an attempt to measure management's commitment to this financing vehicle, even at unattractive prices, based on past financing practices and the understanding of management's operating and financial strategies. A history of equity offerings and a favorable stock price trend lend credibility to a projected stock sale.

Asset Redeployment

A company's ability to generate cash through asset disposals may enhance its financial flexibility. Asset disposals will only provide added flexibility if it is believed that they can be accomplished under terms acceptable to the company's management. Stated intention to sell certain assets is not enough.

The credit analyst is usually not in a position to appraise asset values, but must be mindful of market conditions. For example, if there are many large coal properties on the market, the analyst may be skeptical of a firm's ability to raise cash by selling coal reserves. A well-known company's lack of success in selling businesses at acceptable prices causes a reluctance to attribute added flexibility automatically to that company because it is willing to divest some operations. All firms are viewed as going concerns and a company is not normally expected to repay debt by liquidating operations. It is not considered a strength if a company proposes to sell a business integral to its other operations. There is little benefit in selling natural resource properties or currently excess manufacturing facilities if these must be replaced in a few years.

A firm's financial flexibility may be impaired by an expectation that the company will make a sizable acquisition requiring external financing. Management's stated acquisition goals and past bids that were not consummated provide clues for estimating future actions. Additionally, management's growth objectives, the likelihood that existing operations will meet those objectives, and the company's debt leverage tolerance level are analyzed. Acquisitions may be essential to achieve real earnings growth in the future and to maintain an adequate return on capital. The modest (below 20 percent) debt leverage and large cash position (greater than outstanding debt) of many firms are not indicative of superlative financial flexibility when compared to their perceived need for new business opportunities.

Ownership

The affiliation of companies that on their own represent varying levels of credit quality provides a major analytical challenge. The best approach is pragmatic, primarily reflecting business realities rather than narrow legal commitments. The downstreaming of financial benefits to an apparently weaker subsidiary is generally at the discretion of a stronger parent company. Evaluation of each entity's financial flexibility, and ultimately its rating, is based on a case-by-case review of the owner's willingness and ability to provide support.

When Kennecott was acquired by Standard Oil of Ohio (Sohio), Kennecott's senior debt rating was raised to A – from BBB and Sohio's was lowered to AA – from AA. S&P concluded that the significance of Sohio's plans for investment in Kennecott justified giving substantial weight to ownership in Kennecott's rating, but that these plans did not constitute an unqualified commitment or willingness on the part of Sohio to risk its solvency for Kennecott. Furthermore, Sohio's large ongoing investment in Kennecott and the uncertain long-term returns would reduce Sohio's financial flexibility.

The Sohio/Kennecott situation was unusual because Sohio had explicit plans to help finance Kennecott's capital-spending program for several years after the acquisition. Customarily, acquired companies are expected to generate or borrow their own financing while paying a normal dividend to the parent company under these circumstances. Thus, no extra financial flexibility is attributed to a subsidiary simply because it is owned by a stronger company.

Hidden Risks

Standard ratios of financial leverage and asset protection incorporate certain off-balance-sheet liabilities, such as lease commitments and production payments, which can be readily measured. There are other potential liabilities, however, that cannot be easily quantified, but which may have a profound effect on many aspects of a company's operations and finances. Pension obligations and serious legal problems are two of the most prominent and slippery risk areas that the analyst confronts.

Unfunded pension obligations represent a claim on a company's future profits and cash flow. It may be necessary to finance them with added borrowing or by diverting internally generated funds from productive new investments. In either case, financial flexibility is reduced. Unfortunately, accountants continue to debate the proper financial statement and footnote treatment of future pension obligations. Financial Accounting Standard Board decisions to date give companies considerable leeway in selecting accounting methods, determining key assumptions, and reporting this data in published financial statements. The ability to satisfactorily quantify a company's liability or to make intercompany comparisons is limited because available information is so imprecise.

Nevertheless, pension liabilities are considered in the rating process. The pension question receives added emphasis when its impact is immediate. This burden must be considered when it hinders a company's ability to sell assets because a buyer is reluctant to assume this liability. Colt Industries experienced this problem when it sold Crucible Steel's Midland, Pa. facility, and the proceeds received from International Harvester's sale of its construction equipment business were significantly reduced by the estimated value of the previously unrecognized future pension liability. This off-balance-sheet item also has played a pivotal role in discouraging some managements from closing excess, inefficient, and costly manufacturing facilities. Such a closing may require the immediate recognition of future pension obligations, resulting in a substantial charge to equity. Whether or not management bites the bullet in this situation, the firm's financial flexibility is impaired.

A company's expected earnings protection and cash flow adequacy can be adjusted for the cash costs of resolving a major lawsuit against the firm. A complex web of suits, countersuits, and insurance protection, as well as the uncertainty inherent in all litigation, often requires the analyst to use a range of estimated costs. The intangible costs, however, must be reflected qualitatively in the assessment of a firm's financial flexibility. Disputes with suppliers or customers can have a long-term effect on a company's competitive position. Similarly, a well-publicized product failure may cost a company far more in lost sales than the payment to the injured individual. A potential liability that seems to threaten a firm's solvency because of its size, such as Westinghouse's uranium supply problems several years ago, will often limit the company's access to capital, at least temporarily. Manville's bankruptcy filing has undoubtedly heightened investor sensitivity to these issues. This event damaged the financial flexibility of other companies involved in major asbestos litigation, regardless of the anticipated outcome of their cases.

THE CREDIT RATING DECISION

The analytical framework described in the previous sections focuses the attention of the analyst on the important factors that determine credit quality. Even after the various factors have been evaluated for a particular debt issuer, there is no formula that leads to a credit rating.

Proper credit analysis must be forward looking. The various financial measures that are considered — return on capital, interest coverage, debt/capital, cash flow/debt, and so forth — show the analyst how a company has performed in the past and how much financial protection the company offers its creditors today. What a good analyst wants to know however, is how the company will fare in the future relative to its creditors. For that, financial analysis alone is typically not sufficient. That is why the analytical framework also stresses industry and business risk.

Table 19.1 shows the actual average financial performance over a period of years for industrial companies in the various S&P debt-rating categories. Ratings in the BBB category and higher are considered investment grade credits.

It should be noted that the range in performance for most rating categories is rather wide, and that there may be overlaps between categories. Clearly, ratings cannot and should not be determined by the financials alone.

For companies in industries that are viewed unfavorably or whose own business position is believed to be vulnerable, the financial standards for any given rating are often especially stringent. In fact, if the business risks are thought to be significant enough, typically they will be given far greater weight in the rating decision than the present financial performance, resulting in relatively low rating. Conversely, a company that is suffering through a couple of difficult financial years, but is believed to have maintained a sound business position, may have its rating maintained despite financials that are temporarily unsupportive. Each situation must be viewed on its own merits.

COMMERCIAL PAPER

The analytical approach involved in the determination of a commercial paper rating is comparable to the approach used in determining a long-term debt rating. The primary differences are the emphasis placed on liquidity and on

TABLE 19.1   Three-Year (1980–1982) Median Averages of Key Ratios by Rating Category

	AAA	AA	A	BBB	BB	B
Pretax interest coverage	14.44×	7.61×	5.47×	3.26×	2.43×	1.53×
Pretax interest and full rental coverage	7.46	4.42	3.33	2.31	2.06	1.34
Cash flow/long-term debt	250.94%	109.54%	68.18%	39.01%	27.73%	13.90%
Cash flow/total debt	138.56	75.13	55.68	33.60	24.55	11.18
Pretax return on average long-term capital employed	29.04	24.93	19.73	15.95	17.23	12.58
Operating income/sales	16.65	14.45	12.44	9.57	12.62	9.14
Long-term debt/capitalization	11.56	19.61	25.66	35.95	42.43	56.11
Total debt/capitalization including short-term debt	16.98	24.88	30.06	38.02	47.81	60.33
Total debt/capitalization including short-term debt (including 8× rents)	29.45	37.86	40.81	48.59	55.41	66.70
Total liabilities/tangible shareholders' equity and minority interest	76.43	97.31	104.11	127.86	182.02	276.66

Note: These are not meant to be minimum standards.

financial flexibility (and to some extent the shorter time horizon) in the commercial paper rating determination. While these can lead to meaningful distinctions in the two types of ratings for the same issuer, it would nevertheless be highly unusual for a company whose long-term debt is rated AA − or higher to have its commercial paper rated less than A − 1 + , and equally unusual for a company whose senior debt is not of investment grade quality to have its commercial paper rated even as high as A − 3. (The rating notations are those of S&P.)

While it is recognized that each commercial paper note is a short-lived instrument, the time horizon of the rating analysis is generally at least two years, with a substantial weight placed on fundamental credit factors. Thus, commercial paper ratings (like bond ratings) are expected to endure for a reasonable time rather than be changed frequently.

Purpose and Pattern of Use

Of primary importance in the analysis are the purposes of commercial paper issuance, its repayment sources, the relative size of the program, and the seasonal cycle of usage. The use of comparatively large amounts of commercial paper as a permanent financing source can have negative rating implications for the commercial paper rating, as well as for all rated debt obligations of a company. This reflects the concern that the shorter-term money is being used on an ongoing basis to fund a company's capital base, thereby constraining financing flexibility under adverse circumstances.

Conversely, if the use of commercial paper is clearly tied to a well-defined working-capital cycle, a company's commercial paper would warrant consideration of a relatively high rating. For instance, the certainty in predicting short-term cash flow and current asset liquidity for a commodity-oriented company may be much more precise than an evaluation of its ability to expand, compete, and maintain financial strength over a five-year period. In most such instances, the amount of commercial paper issued is directly related to the amount of inventory; therefore, if inventory is lower than projected, borrowings should be proportionately less. Grain and sugar companies are typical of this pattern. Other industries with strong seasonal borrowing patterns include enterprises in the leisure, retailing, consumer appliances, tobacco, and publishing fields.

Companies in the liquor industry have working-capital needs that are somewhat different from a typical seasonal borrower in that their operating cycle is two to three years. Borrowings are used to finance inventories that take that period to age, and this cycle has become accepted as normal. Cash flow is relatively more easy to predict as consumption trends rarely change radically from year to year.

A sizable number of industrial firms have formed finance or credit subsidiaries, generally to finance product sales. These subsidiaries raise funds in the commercial paper market under their own names. An ability to borrow at rates comparable to the parent company is one important premise of these subsidiaries. The achievement of this objective presumes that both parent and subsidiary will have equivalent ratings, despite the fact that the subsidiary may have more limited creditworthiness if evaluated independently. Thus, an understanding of the relationships between the two companies is key to a correct rating decision. In general, the more important the subsidiary is to the parent's economic fortunes, the less explicit and detailed formal support arrangements need be. Conversely, if the financing activities of the subsidiary are very much peripheral to the main business activities of the parent, a direct and strong support relationship would be important in evaluating the degree to which the parent company aids the creditworthiness of the subsidiary. The overriding rationale behind these approaches is that management's economic self-interest will assure support in the first case, whereas such inducement cannot be relied on in the second example.

Bank Line Coverage

An evaluation of bank line policy is an essential component of a commercial paper rating. For almost all companies, full bank line coverage of commercial paper borrowing is viewed as prudent financing practice, given the potential for disruption of the commercial paper market. The commercial paper market may become unavailable due to factors other than a company's own credit standing. In this event, a corporation could then quickly use its bank credit facilities to repay maturing commercial paper and continue to use these credit lines until the market was once again ready to accept the company's paper. It should be recognized, however, that the rating decision itself is not predicated on the strength or amount of bank lines, which, after all, are a supplementary source of funds and not a primary source of fundamental creditworthiness.

As a general policy, corporations are expected to maintain credit lines equal to all commercial paper, which will be outstanding during the period in question. However, there may be exceptions to this rule, each of which should be carefully considered and reviewed. Many corporations utilize commercial paper strictly to finance seasonal needs, with borrowings outstanding for only two or three months during the year. Borrowings will typically start at a low level and build to a peak, which may continue for only a few weeks, with all outstandings then repaid very rapidly. For these companies, there may not be a need to keep bank lines in place for a 12-month period to cover peak borrowings, which will only be outstanding for a very short time. In the case of financially strong issuers, a reduction of bank lines to some percentge of peak borrowings is considered reasonable.

PROJECT FINANCING

From a rating standpoint, project financings can be split into two basic types. The first is nonrecourse or "true" project financings. Here, cash flow from the project is the sole means of debt service, with no direct legal credit support by sponsors. The second type is credit-supported or recourse financings, which in the eyes of some observers are not true project financings. As with nonrecourse projects, the debt portion of the financing is expected to be serviced from project cash flow. If project cash flow is not sufficient, however, there is a direct legal obligation for project sponsors of other interested parties to step in and insure both completeness and timeliness of debt service.

Both types of project financings can, in turn, have rating implications from two different perspectives. In some instances project debt itself may be assigned a rating. In other cases the existence of project debt will have to be evaluated as to its impact on other debt ratings of a project sponsor or participant. Often, both will have to be considered.

Thus far, S&P has assigned relatively few ratings on nonrecourse project debt. The potential to rate any such project remains alive, however, with decisions being made on a case-by-case basis.

Economic Rationale

In analyzing a nonrecourse project financing, S&P would begin with the economic rationale for the project and, in particular, its importance to its sponsors. Normally, in making an economic analysis of a company, there exists the benefit of an historical operating record. In fact, S&P will not rate a company's debt if there is not at least a five-year track record.

For a new project, obviously there is no operating history. To circumvent this problem, a ratable project will often be one in which the project sponsors use the project output. S&P would have to be convinced that the project will supply its output to the project owners on a basis superior to alternatives in terms of both cost and availability. It would also be helpful if the financial obligations inherent in the project are small, relative to the economic damage that would be done to the sponsors if the project were allowed to go into default.

Another consideration would be the handling of completion risk. If the financing is to be done prior to the completion of the project, some sort of direct credit support would be necessary until the project has begun to operate.

S&P would generally not be favorably inclined toward projects using new technology nor ones in which there is a real chance of environmental, regulatory, or other political roadblocks. For a sizable project, the completion guarantee could be a substantial burden if there is a reasonable chance that it might have to be invoked due to technological or legal delays. It would also be undesirable to have such problems develop once the project has begun to operate and the guarantees are no longer in effect.

It is important also that the financing be structured to provide a high degree of confidence that payment of principal and interest will be made on a timely basis. This could be accomplished through a debt service reserve, an equity cushion, or some sort of insurance mechanism.

Creditworthiness of Sponsors

Finally, the analysis and rating of any project will still begin with, and be highly dependent upon, the creditworthiness of project sponsors and participants.

Most project finance debt that has been rated has been connected with credit-supported or recourse financings. Those ratings are generally heavily reliant on the credit standing of the sponsor(s). The ratings are largely dependent upon, and related to, the legal obligations of the sponsors, but they may also be affected by economic incentives, which might cause a sponsor to go beyond legal requirements in support of a project.

Common types of credit support are several guarantees, joint and several guarantees, take-or-pay contracts, throughput and deficiency agreements, and lease obligations.[1]

In general, the starting point of S&P's approach to rating credit-supported project debt is the credit standing of the sponsor or sponsors of the project. The next consideration is the nature of the liabilities and risks intrinsic to the project or to the financing structure, the economic incentives for participation in the project, and perhaps the relationships among the sponsors themselves. Evaluation is made as to any possible impact of project participation in the project, and perhaps the relationships among the sponsors themselves. Evaluation is made as to any possible impact of project participation or sponsorship on the credit rating of the sponsors. Out of that process will come a rating on project debt and/or a possible change in the bond ratings of the sponsors.

---

[1]*Several Guarantee:* A guarantee in which each of a group of guarantors is responsible only for its own specified portion of the obligation. For example, if company *A*'s debt of $100 million has a several guarantee of 50 percent from company *B*, 25 percent from company *C* and 25 percent from company *D*, the obligations of *B*, *C* and *D* are limited to $50 million, $25 million and $25 million, respectively.

Joint and Several Guarantee: A guarantee in which each of a group of guarantors is responsible initially for its own portion of the obligation, but also for as much as the entire obligation if other guarantors fail to perform. In the above example, *B*, *C* and *D* are each obligated for up to $100 million if two out of three of them fail to meet their obligation.

Take or Pay Contract: A contract that obligates an entity to pay a specified amount based on receipt of a product or material of some kind, whether or not that product is actually received. Such a contract is typically used to support a debt obligation.

Throughput and Deficiency Agreement: An agreement that obligates a group of entities to make payments based on a certain level of throughput through a pipeline, regardless of whether that throughput is actually achieved.

20

Cost Accounting Methods

ARTHUR J. SCHOMER

COST ACCOUNTING SYSTEMS

Cost accounting systems provide a powerful management tool for planning and controlling operations, product pricing, and similar decisions. If the cost system of a particular company is to meet these objectives effectively, the controller must carefully design and construct the system with these specific objectives in mind. He must also ensure that the collection and processing of appropriate production and inventory data is comprehensive, accurate, and timely (within practical limits), so that the system will be capable of producing meaningful information and meeting management needs. Too often a controller charges ahead with the mechanics of building a cost accounting system without carefully defining its goals or evaluating the complexities and alternative means of collecting and analyzing production data.

A cost accounting system is complex to design, install, and operate because it reflects the intricacies of the production operation. Because of the complexities and dynamics of the production activity, the system will never function perfectly, but it must function in a controlled, responsive, and reasonably accurate manner to justify the investment required for its development and operation. Not only an initial investment of time and effort, but also a commitment to keeping the system functioning properly and in tune with a dynamic production environment are necessary.

Types of Systems

Cost accounting systems can be characterized in several ways.

Job Cost vs. Process Cost. The distinction between job cost and process cost systems is based on the nature of the manufacturing operation to which the cost system will apply. Job costing is appropriate for companies producing custom products to order. Since each product is different and is produced in response to the customer's specifications, the actual cost of producing each order or job lot must be captured and reported. Identification of the cost of each job lot permits identification of the profitability of each order. It also permits evaluation of cost performance by comparison with the cost estimate on which the customer price quotation was based and provides a valuable tool in evaluating the quality of the cost estimating procedure itself.

Process costing, on the other hand, is appropriate to the manufacturing environment in which a standard line of products is offered for sale (i.e., mass production for stock in the expectation of customer orders). The primary emphasis is on the cost and efficiency of the process in each department, cost center, and operation over a period of time, rather than on each of the multitude of products and lots that may flow through the operation and cost center. That is not to say that the individual product is ignored. To the extent practical in the given situation, actual cost data should be captured by product in the detailed cost records, but the accumulation and reporting of costs should follow the process rather than the product.

Some companies have both job shop and mass production environments existing within the same plant. In such cases, a mixture of job and process costing techniques should be applied as appropriate to the individual phases of production.

Actual Cost vs. Standard Cost. Job or process cost systems can each be structured to accumulate actual costs only or, alternatively, to accumulate and record both actual costs incurred and standard cost allowances for the actual level and mix of production. In a standard cost system the emphasis is on the variances, which are the differences between the actual and the standard costs. A standard cost system is primarily a management control device, with variances highlighted and reported to management by cost element and by area of responsibility. Standard cost data is also useful in developing profitability reporting by business segment, in making pricing decisions, and in facilitating the development of a profit plan. If the standard cost system is properly structured, it can also provide valuable data for management decision analysis, which is discussed in more detail later in this chapter.

Absorption vs. Direct Costing. A given cost system can also be characterized as either an absorption costing or a direct costing system. The basic structural distinction between these two systems lies in the definition of factory costs capitalized through inventory. Absorption costing, which is required under generally accepted accounting principles (GAAP), includes all factory costs — direct material, direct labor, and factory overhead — in the costing of work in process and the finished goods inventory. Direct costing (also known as variable or marginal costing) capitalizes only variable manufacturing costs — direct material, direct labor, and variable factory overhead — through inventory. Under direct costing, fixed manufacturing overhead costs are expensed directly on the income statement in the period incurred. Variable costs are those costs that are expected to rise or fall proportionally with fluctuations in the level of production. Fixed costs are expected to remain more or less constant in the short run, since they represent the cost of operating capacity. A direct costing system is managerially oriented; the classification of costs according to cost behavior patterns (i.e., variable vs. fixed) provides a tool for profit planning and for use of the profit plan as a control device. Direct costing also provides the foundation for cost/volume/profit analysis and incremental cost analysis for decision-making purposes.

Systems Characteristics

This section describes the structure of each type of cost system discussed previously. Methods of accumulating and processing data required to operate a cost system are described later in this chapter.

Actual Job Cost System. An actual job cost system is structured to accumulate actual costs by job lot as incurred. The costs are recorded on a job cost sheet (Figure 20.1) by cost element and stage of production. Labor distribution records and material requisitions provide the source data for direct job charges. Overhead is applied on the basis of direct labor hours or dollars expended on the job or some other production measure appropriate to the particular manufacturing operation (e.g., machine hours). When the job is complete, the costs are totalled and divided by the actual quantity produced to determine the actual manufacturing cost per unit. This unit cost is used to cost finished goods inventory and to determine cost of goods sold. At the end of each month, total costs recorded on the cost sheets for uncompleted jobs represent work in process.

Typical journal entries for a job cost system include:

1 To record raw material used:
   Dr. Work in Process
   Cr. Raw Materials Inventory

STAR FURNITURE MANUFACTURING COMPANY

MANUFACTURED FOR: Harold's Department Store   ORDER NO. 110
PRODUCT: #105—Platform rockers
SPECIFICATIONS: Attached drawings and blueprints
QUANTITY ORDERED: 500
DATE ORDERED: 9/22/—   DATE WANTED: 12/10/—
DATE STARTED: 11/21/—   DATE COMPLETED: 12/5/—

DIRECT MATERIALS

Date	Department	Req. No.	Description or Stores No.	Quantity	Cost Per Unit	Total
11/12	Cutting	2947	support lumber oak and pine	500 pieces oak 10 ft	$1.80	$ 900.00
				250 pieces pine 8 ft	0.50	125.00
11/15	Assembly	3080	glue, pegs, and screws	500 standard	0.20	100.00
11/27	Upholstery	3407	upholstery cloth	3,000 yds	1.00	3,000.00
					Total materials cost	$4,125.00

DIRECT LABOR

Date	Department	Time Report Nos.	Description of Labor or Process	Hours	Rate	Cost
11/12–14	Cutting	867–901	power saw cutting	120	$2.75	$ 330.00
11/14	Planing	1125–1130	planing	50	2.50	125.00
11/15–21	Assembly	1360–1397	assembling frames	200	2.25	450.00
11/25–27	Upholstery	1480–1505	padding and upholstery	250	3.00	750.00
					Total labor cost	$1,655.00

APPLIED FACTORY OVERHEAD

Date	Department	Basis of Application	Hours	Rate	Cost
11/15	Cutting	$2 per direct labor hour	120	$2.00	$ 240.00
11/15	Planing	$3 per direct labor hour	50	3.00	150.00
11/22	Assembly	$1 per direct labor hour	200	1.00	200.00
11/29	Upholstery	100% of direct labor cost	—	—	750.00
			Total factory overhead applied		$1,340.00

SUMMARY ON JOB NO. 110

Materials	$4,125.00	Selling price		$10,850.00
Direct labor	1,655.00	Factory cost	$7,120.00	
Factory overhead	1,340.00	Marketing expenses	1,206.00	
Total factory cost	$7,120.00	Adm. expenses	905.00	
		Cost to make and sell		9,231.00
		Profit		$ 1,619.00

FIG. 20.1 Job Order Cost Sheet — Departmentalized Operation

2 To record the factory payroll:
Dr. Work in Process (for direct labor)
Dr. Manufacturing Overhead Control (for indirect labor)
Cr. Accrued Payroll

3 To record overhead expenses:
Dr. Manufacturing Overhead Control
Cr. Accounts Payable, Accumulated Depreciation, etc.

4 To record overhead applied to production:
Dr. Work in Process
Cr. Manufacturing Overhead Applied

5 To record finished production:
Dr. Finished Goods Inventory
Cr. Work in Process

6 To record cost of sales:
Dr. Cost of Goods Sold
Cr. Finished Goods Inventory

If job lots are shipped immediately upon completion of production, it is appropriate to bypass the finished goods inventory account and charge completed production directly to cost of goods sold. The manufacturing overhead control and/or the work-in-process accounts may be set up by department. These departmental control accounts are useful in isolating out-of-control conditions to a particular department. Departmental work-in-process data may help management evaluate levels of inventory investment and potential departmental bottlenecks. Departmental overhead data can be used to develop departmental overhead rates and to analyze and report on overhead costs by department.

The manufacturing overhead control account(s) should be supported by detailed expense accounts in a subsidiary ledger. It is also valuable from a managerial information and analysis standpoint to separate the overhead control and detailed records into fixed and variable expenses. Thus, a company's general ledger might have two overhead control accounts — fixed and variable — per department.

Actual Process Cost System. The classic actual process cost system relates to a continuous processing environment for the manufacture of one product. Under this system, costs are accumulated monthly by cost element for each department. Since costs are accumulated by process rather than by job, total departmental costs must be related to total departmental production for the month to develop a product unit cost for the department. This unit cost is needed to price the month-end departmental (work-in-process) inventory and to determine the cost of goods completed and transferred out of the department.

Unlike the job costing approach, in which unit cost is determined only when a job lot is completely manufactured, monthly product costing under process costing involves partial work effort on incomplete units. Therefore, an equivalent production count must be obtained. Equivalent production represents a restatement of partially completed units into equivalent work effort expressed in terms of completed units. For example:

Assume:	Units	Material	Labor and Overhead
Beginning work in process	2,000	$ 270	$ 625
Started this month	28,000	$16,650	$41,000
Completed and transferred	27,000		
Ending work in process	3,000	40% complete	25% complete

Equivalent Production:	Material	Labor and Overhead
Completed	27,000	27,000
Ending work in process — 3,000 @ 40% =	1,200	
— 3,000 @ 25% =		750
Total equivalent units	28,200	27,750

Cost/Equivalent Unit:

Material — $16,920($270 + $16,650) ÷ 28,200 = $0.60
Labor and overhead — $41,625($625 + $41,000) ÷ 27,750 = $1.50

Valuation of:

Ending work in process:

Material — 1,200 equivalent units @ $0.60	= $	720
Labor and overhead — 750 equivalent units @ $1.50 =		1,125
		$ 1,845

Completed and transferred:
27,000 equivalent units @ $2.10($0.60 + $1.50)   = $56,700

As goods are transferred from one production department to another, the transfer costs (calculated as in the illustration) are recorded as an additional cost element in the next department and are treated separately in the equivalent-production and cost-per-unit calculations.

In a multiproduct manufacturing situation, application of an actual cost system requires that costs be accumulated separately for each product produced in each department. This burdensome effort can be avoided by using a standard process cost system.

As with job costing, the variable and fixed overhead costs can be identified and accumulated separately in each department. The required journal entries for an actual process cost system are basically the same as those previously illustrated for job costing, except that costs and work-in-process accounts *must* be maintained by department. As goods move from one department to another, the preceding department's work-in-process inventory is credited and the subsequent department's work-in-process inventory is charged with the transfer cost (determined as in the illustration). This transfer cost is cumulative for *all* preceding departments, not just for the immediately preceding department. Also, if spoilage or other loss of units occurs *after* the first manufacturing step, the transfer cost "element" *per unit* must be adjusted by: (1) multiplying the quantity of lost units by the per-unit "transferred in" cost and (2) dividing the resulting dollar amount by the number of good units yielded in the process step in which the loss occurred.

Standard Cost System. Since the majority of factory environments involve mass production of multiple products with staging of partially completed materials or parts between departments, most firms have adopted a standard process cost system. A standard cost system records standard cost allowances throughout the flow of costs into work in process, finished goods, and cost of sales. As the standard cost allowances are recorded, actual costs incurred are closed out and the resulting variances are recorded on the books of account. As a result, the general ledger accounts serve as controls over the accuracy of the multitude of cost and inventory records and reports generated under a standard cost system. Variances are recorded by cost element and area of supervisory responsibility and thus provide a means of evaluating performance and identifying reasons for problem situations.

Standard Job Cost System. Under a standard job cost system, the standard costs for a particular job lot ideally will be the cost estimate data developed initially to cost the job and to quote a price to a customer. In some companies this system is not practical because the sales price quote is often based on preliminary, "rough" cost data. In such cases, the standard cost factors for the job lot will be developed in detail *after* the order is accepted. Often, a job shop factory can build up a given job cost standard based on a reference file of standard operations and raw material standards and yields.

Standard Process Cost System. Under a standard process cost system, industrial engineers develop a standard bill of materials (Figure 20.2) for each new product as the product is put into the line. Labor operations and time required per operation are also defined for the new product (Figure 20.3) based on appropriate engineering studies, with allowances for machine downtime, employee rest time, and so on. The objective is to establish realistic standards of performance under acceptable operating conditions and efficiency requirements. When industrial engineering support is not available, knowledgeable factory supervisory and staff personnel should develop the standards.

Overhead Budgets and Rates. Standard overhead rates are established on the basis of periodic overhead budgets. Separate overhead budgets should generally be established for each factory department or cost center, because types and levels of cost incurrence patterns differ from department to department. Futhermore, the appropriate basis for measuring production activity may vary from one department to another. That is, it may be appropriate to establish a standard overhead rate per labor hour in one department (e.g., assembly) and a standard rate per machine hour in another (e.g., metal stamping). Departmental budgeting also allows the controller to evaluate actual overhead spending levels by comparing actual costs with budget allowances based on each department's level and mix of production for a given month.

Product		Unit	Prepared by		Date		
Material/Part Number	**Description**	**Quantity**	**Unit**	**Price**	**Cost**		
	Total standard material cost						

FIG. 20.2 Standard Bill of Materials

OPERATIONS LIST

Stock Number		Description	Date Prepared	By	
Dep't No.	**Oper. No.**	**Operation Description**	**Machine Requirements**	**Standard Hours**	**Set-Up Hours**

FIG. 20.3 Operations List

TABLE 20.1   Variable Budget Manufacturing Overhead — Stamp and Press Department

Per Month	Per Direct Labor Hour	Total Budget
Budgeted production level — in direct labor hours		$10,000
Budgeted manufacturing overhead		
Variable costs		
Indirect labor — material handling	$0.15	$ 1,500
Overtime premium	0.05	500
Shift premium	0.10	1,000
Fringe benefits	0.67	6,700
Factory supplies	0.20	2,000
Power	0.30	3,000
Total variable costs	$1.47	$14,700
Fixed costs		
Supervision		$2,000
Indirect labor — mechanics		2,500
Fringe benefits		800
Heat and light		1,000
Depreciation		5,000
Rent		2,000
Total fixed costs	1.33	$13,300
Total monthly budgeted overhead	$2.80	$28,000

A breakdown of the overhead budget and standard overhead rates between fixed and variable cost components adds a valuable dimension to the standard cost system. Standard overhead factors categorized by cost behavior patterns form the basis for overhead control reporting based on actual production levels and provide expected cost behavior data for decision analysis. Table 20.1 is an example of a departmental overhead budget.

Updating Standards. Once developed, the standards must be periodically updated to reflect current operating conditions in a dynamic operating environment. However, continuous random updating of individual product standards can damage the effectiveness of the standard cost system by hampering meaningful analysis of variances from standard cost. Furthermore, every time product standard cost factors are changed, inventories must be revalued at the latest standards. To avoid an uncontrolled situation with "floating" standards, a regular schedule for updating should be established with at least annual review and revision. Many companies also review current standards quarterly or semiannually for possible updating.

Calculating Departmental Cost Allowances. Standard costs are allowed or earned for the number of good units of product manufactured in each depart-

Month of _____
Department _____

Product No.	Production Quantity Produced	Standard Unit Cost Material	Labor	Overhead	Standard Cost Allowed Material	Labor	Overhead
Total standard cost allowed							

FIG. 20.4 Standard Cost Allowed

ment. A common misconception about standard costing is that standard cost allowances are calculated *only* for units completely manufactured and placed in finished stock. On the contrary, standard cost allowances are determined at *each* stage of production by multiplying the quantity of each product processed at that stage by the predetermined unit standard cost factors for material, labor, and overhead for that stage of processing. Figure 20.4 illustrates the buildup of standard cost allowances for the production of one department.

Cost Flow and Recording. Figure 20.5 depicts the flow of cost data in the operation of a standard cost system. It shows the recording and flow of actual and standard costs and the resulting variances. The variances depicted by solid-line boxes on the chart are basic to most cost systems. The broken-line variances are optional, depending on the nature of the manufacturing process and the needs and desires of management. In some manufacturing situations, additional or modified types of variances are appropriate.

All of the accounts carried at standard cost as depicted in Figure 20.5 (i.e., all inventory accounts and cost of goods sold) function as control accounts and should be supported by detailed product quantity listings extended at the appropriate unit standard costs.

The following are representative journal entry requirements related to this flow of cost data (variances are indicated as debit or credit, depending on whether unfavorable or favorable):

1 To record the purchase of raw materials:
   Dr. Raw Materials Inventory (at standard)
   Dr./Cr. Material Purchase Price Variance
   Cr. Accounts Payable

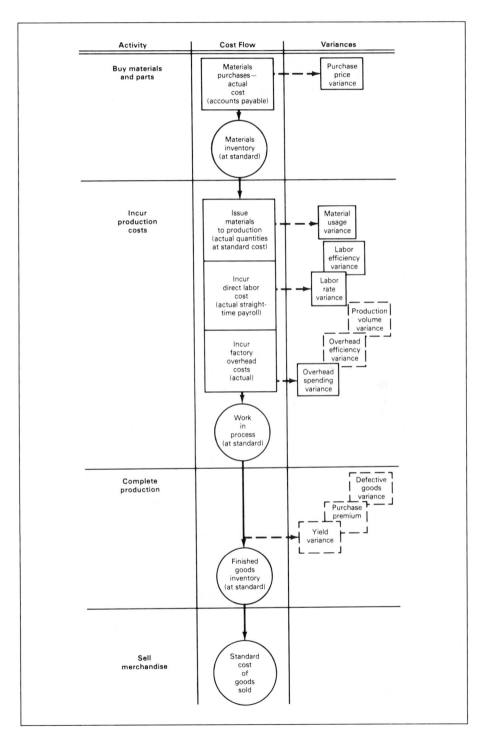

FIG. 20.5 Standard Cost System

2 To record raw materials used in production:
  Dr. Work in Process (at standard)
  Dr./Cr. Materials Usage Variance
  Cr. Raw Materials Inventory (actual usage at standard cost)

3 To charge direct labor cost to process:
  Dr. Work in Process (at standard)
  Dr./Cr. Labor Rate Variance
  Dr./Cr. Labor Efficiency Variance
  Cr. Direct Labor Cost Applied (actual cost)

4 To apply overhead cost to production:
  Dr. Work in Process (at standard)
  Dr./Cr. Overhead Spending Variance
  Dr./Cr. Overhead Efficiency Variance
  Dr./Cr. Overhead Production Volumn Variance
  Cr. Manufacturing Overhead Applied (actual cost)

5 To record finished production:
  Dr. Finished Goods Inventory (at standard)
  Cr. Work in Process (at standard)

6 To record cost of sales:
  Dr. Cost of Goods Sold (at standard)
  Cr. Finished Goods Inventory (at standard)

The work-in-process inventory should be segmented into separate accounts by department or, alternatively, by broad stages of production. This segmentation helps isolate possible accounting errors within particular production segments and enables management to determine the location and nature of any significant build-ups in inventory. In similar fashion, variance accounts should be detailed by department or cost center in order to identify the source and nature of significant nonstandard conditions and to assign responsibility for manufacturing performance.

Materials Purchase Price Variance. The materials purchase price variance represents the difference between the actual and standard unit purchase prices multiplied by the actual quantity of material purchased. It is calculated separately for each purchase of each type of raw material or part used in manufacturing. For example, assume the following transactions:

	Material A	Material B
Purchases — quantity	10,000 lbs	3,000 ft
— cost	$11,000	$1,200
Actual price/unit	$1.10/lb	$0.40/ft
Standard price/unit	$1.00/lb	$0.45/ft

The purchase price variance would be calculated as follows:

$$\text{Material } A: 10,000 \text{ lbs} \times (\$1.10 - \$1.00) = \$1,000.00$$
$$\text{Material } B: \ \ 3,000 \text{ ft} \times (\$0.40 - \$0.45) \ = \ \underline{(150.00)}$$
$$\text{Net unfavorable variance} \qquad\qquad\qquad \underline{\$ \ \ 850.00}$$

Month Ended _____					Product Line _____	
Material		Current Month			Year to Date	
Item	Code	Actual Cost	Standard Cost	Favorable (Unfavorable)	Actual Cost	Favorable (Unfavorable)
Totals						

FIG. 20.6   Purchase Price Variance Report

The journal entry to record the purchase is:

Dr. Materials Inventory	$11,350.00 [1]	
Dr. Material Purchase Price Variance	850.00	
Cr. Accounts Payable		$12,200.00

The purchase variance should be recorded as each invoice is entered into the accounts payable system. A monthly report should be issued by item, categorized by type of material and/or associated product line (Figure 20.6).

Because the purchase price variance is an outgrowth of the purchase function (as illustrated in Figure 20.5), it is an exception to the general rule that standard costs are allowed and variances determined at the time of production.

Materials Usage Variance. The materials usage variance identifies the efficiency of use of materials in each production step by comparing actual quantities of materials issued and used in production with the quantities that should have been used for actual production output (i.e., standard allowed). The difference between actual and standard materials quantities for each item is

---

[1] Material *A*: 10,000 lbs @ $1.00 = $10,000.00
  Material *B*: 3,000 ft @ $0.45 =   1,350.00
  $11,350.00

extended at the respective standard unit purchase price. To continue the illustration:

Material used — A	8,400 lbs
— B	1,600 ft
Units produced	500
Standard material quantities/unit:	
Material A	16 lbs/unit
Material B	3.5 ft/unit

The material usage variance would be calculated as follows:

Material A: (8,400 lbs − 8,000 lbs [2]) × $1.00 = $400.00
Material B: (1,600 ft − 1,750 ft [3]) × $0.45 = (67.50)
Net unfavorable variance: $332.50

The entry to charge the standard material cost to work-in-process inventory and to record the variance is as follows:

Dr. Work in Process $8,787.50 [4]
Dr. Materials Usage Variance   332.50
Cr. Materials Inventory $9,120.00 [5]

Material usage reports are issued weekly or monthly (or, in some cases, daily), showing usage and variances by responsibility area (e.g., department), as illustrated in Figure 20.7.

Direct Labor Variances. The labor rate variance represents the effect of deviation of actual hourly pay rates from standard (anticipated) rates for direct labor effort expended. Assume the following data for the same production department illustrated in the discussion of the materials usage variance:

---

[2] 500 units × 16 lbs/unit.
[3] 500 units × 3.5 ft/unit.
[4] Material A: 8,000 lbs @ $1.00 = $8,000.00
   Material B: 1,750 ft @ $0.45 = 787.50
                  $8,787.50
[5] Material A: 8,400 lbs @ $1.00 = $8,400.00
   Material B: 1,600 ft @ $0.45 = 720.00
                  $9,120.00

Material		Current Month			Year to Date	
Item	Code	Material Used (at Standard Price)	Standard Material Cost Allowed	Favorable (Unfavorable)	Material Used (at Standard Price)	Favorable (Unfavorable)
Totals						

Month Ended _____ Department _____

FIG. 20.7 Materials Usage Report

Actual direct labor hours	2,200
Actual direct labor payroll	$11,220
Actual hourly rate ($11,220 ÷ 2,200 hours)	$5.10
Units produced	500
Standard hours/unit	4
Standard rate/hour	$5.00

The labor rate variance is calculated by multiplying the actual payroll hours for direct labor by the difference between the actual and standard hourly pay rates. In the illustration:

$$2,200 \text{ hours} \times (\$5.10 - 5.00) = \$220$$
$$\text{unfavorable labor rate variance}$$

The labor usage (efficiency) variance is calculated by multiplying the standard hourly rate (to eliminate any rate variance effect) by the difference between the actual direct labor hours incurred and the number of hours that should have been expended to achieve the actual quantity produced (i.e., the standard labor hours allowance for the defective goods and the actual loss for the calculation of the defective goods variance. For purposes of the illustration, assume that the data presented previously for spoiled goods applies, except that the expected net sales value of the defective merchandise is $50 per unit. The standard allowance for defective goods would read:

$$[(\$77.575 - \$50.00) \times (100\% - 95\%)] \div 95\% = \$1.451$$

The defective goods variance would be calculated as follows:

Actual defective goods loss:	
50 units @ ($77.575 − $50.00)	$1,378.75
Standard defective goods loss allowance:	
450 good units @ $1.451	652.95
Unfavorable defective goods variance	$ 725.80

The journal entry to record the situation would be:

Dr. Finished Goods Inventory — 1st Quality	$35,561.70	[13]
Dr. Finished Goods Inventory — 2nd	2,500.00	[14]
Dr. Defective Goods Variance	725.80	
Cr. Work in Process	$38,787.50	[15]

If the expected sales value equals or exceeds the standard manufacturing cost, there is no loss, and no variances need be recorded.

Another operating condition often encountered involves companies that both manufacture and purchase merchandise for sale. If a company sometimes buys in finished form an item that it normally manufactures, it almost invariably results in a purchase price higher than the standard manufacturing cost for the item. This premium should be charged to a variance account as a nonstandard condition.

Some companies find the need to establish certain "variances" that represent differences between two or more sets of standards (rather than differences between actual and standard costs). As noted previously, it is not practical to update the cost accounting standards every time engineering standards are changed for a particular product or operation. Usually, such methods changes are reflected in the operating variances until the company's next periodic comprehensive update of the cost accounting standards. However, it is possible to measure actual costs against the updated operating standards in order to make performance reports more meaningful to the factory supervisors. If this is done, a "shadow" set of "standard-to-standard" variances must be recorded, accounting for the differences between the cost accounting standards and the current operating standards.

---

[13] 450 @ ($77.575 + $1.451).

[14] 50 @ $50.

[15] 500 @ $77.575.

Companies with multiplant operations often produce a given product in more than one plant location. Each plant will develop its own standard cost of manufacturing that product. Since the product will presumably be commingled in inventory regardless of where it is produced, one standard valuation for the product must be selected to value inventory and cost of sales. This standard can be the cost associated with the primary production location, or it can be a weighted average of the standard costs of all plants manufacturing the product. The weighting would be based on the projected production mix by location. As the product is manufactured and placed into finished stock, the individual plant work-in-process account must be relieved at that plant's standard cost. Finished goods inventory is charged at the selected inventory standard. The difference between the two standards represents a production location variance.

Disposition of Variance. For internal reporting purposes, the variances are usually closed directly to cost of sales each month. For external reporting purposes, good accounting practice requires that any significant variances be allocated among inventories and cost of sales as an adjustment to the previously recorded standard costs, unless a variance represents an abnormal condition that should not be capitalized through inventory.

Direct Cost System. As previously noted, a direct cost system values inventories at variable manufacturing costs only and expenses fixed manufacturing costs as costs of capacity. Emphasis is placed on cost behavior and its impact (actual or potential) on profitability. This is accomplished by focusing on the profit contribution generated by various products and operating segments of the business. The technique is particularly well suited for managerial decision analysis, as is illustrated later in this chapter.

Comparing Direct and Absorption Costs. By including only variable manufacturing costs in inventory, direct costing avoids the irrational swings in profitability that can result from significant changes in the level of inventory and the correspondent changes in the level of fixed (period) costs deferred through inventory. This is illustrated graphically and in financial statement form in Figure 20.11 and Table 20.2.

Figure 20.11 demonstrates that the amount of each quarter's period, or fixed, costs included in inventory fluctuates with the level of the inventory. Thus, in the first two quarters period cost deferred through inventory increased by $800,000 as a direct consequence of production exceeding sales during that period. In other words, $800,000 of the period costs incurred during the first six months was capitalized as a result of excess production, with a corresponding increase in net income. In the third quarter sales exceeded production, with the result that $1,500,000 of period costs previously deferred through inventory is now written off against income in addition to the period manufacturing overhead cost incurred in the third quarter. The fourth quarter again demonstrates the effect of an inventory build-up.

The impact of these inventory fluctuations on the income statement under absorption costing techniques is illustrated in Table 20.2. This table contrasts

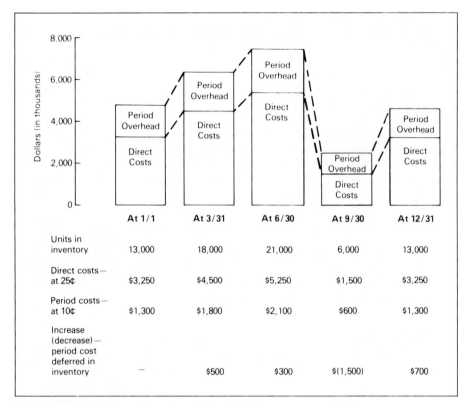

	At 1/1	At 3/31	At 6/30	At 9/30	At 12/31
Units in inventory	13,000	18,000	21,000	6,000	13,000
Direct costs— at 25¢	$3,250	$4,500	$5,250	$1,500	$3,250
Period costs— at 10¢	$1,300	$1,800	$2,100	$600	$1,300
Increase (decrease)— period cost deferred in inventory	—	$500	$300	$(1,500)	$700

FIG. 20.11   Illustration of Inventory Valuation Methods

absorption and direct costing income statements; it demonstrates that the quarterly pattern of net income follows the quarterly pattern of sales more logically under direct costing than under absorption costing. Under direct costing, each quarter is charged with its own period manufacturing overhead costs of $1,500,000 (no more, no less) because of the valuation of inventory at variable manufacturing costs and the flow-through of period costs to the income statement.

Table 20.2 also illustrates the difference in financial statement format under absorption versus direct costing. The gross margin under direct costing represents the profit contribution generated by sales after deducting all variable costs. This profit contribution is volume-related and is the amount available to cover period manufacturing costs and other fixed operating expenses and, it is hoped, to generate net income.

Direct Cost Income Statement. Table 20.3 further illustrates a direct costing income statement by operating segment of the company. The operating segments reported on (in this case, divisions) should be selected on the basis of the company's operating and marketing structure. Segments reported on might include manufacturing divisions, product lines, geographical regions,

TABLE 20.2   Absorption Costing vs. Direct Costing

COMPARATIVE INCOME STATEMENTS

	Quarter 1	Quarter 2	Quarter 3	Quarter 4	Total Year
Absorption Costing					
Sales	$ 6,000	$ 8,000	$12,500	$3,500	$30,000
Cost of goods sold:					
Beginning inventory	$ 4,550	$ 6,300	$ 7,350	$2,100	$ 4,500
Manufacturing costs	5,750	6,250	4,000	5,000	21,000
	$10,300	$12,550	$11,350	$7,100	$25,550
Ending inventory	6,300	7,350	2,100	4,550	4,550
	$ 4,000	$ 5,200	$ 9,250	$2,550	$21,000
Gross profit	$ 2,000	$ 2,800	$ 3,250	$ 950	$ 9,000
Other operating expenses	1,000	1,000	1,000	1,000	4,000
Net income (A)	$ 1,000	$ 1,800	$ 2,250	$ (50)	$ 5,000
Direct Costing					
Sales	$6,000	$8,000	$12,500	$3,500	$30,000
Cost of goods sold:					
Beginning inventory	$3,250	$4,500	$5,250	$1,500	$ 3,250
Direct costs	4,250	4,750	2,500	3,500	15,000
	$7,500	$9,250	$ 7,750	$5,000	$18,250
Ending inventory	4,500	5,250	1,500	3,250	3,250
	$3,000	$4,000	$ 6,250	$1,750	$15,000
Gross margin	$3,000	$4,000	$ 6,250	$1,750	$15,000
Period overhead	$1,500	$1,500	$ 1,500	$1,500	$ 6,000
Other operating expenses	1,000	1,000	1,000	1,000	4,000
Net income (B)	$ 500	$1,500	$ 3,750	$ (750)	$ 5,000
Difference (A − B)	$ 500	$ 300	$ (1,500)	$ 700	—
Units					
Beginning inventory	13,000	18,000	21,000	6,000	13,000
Produced	17,000	19,000	10,000	14,000	60,000
Available	30,000	37,000	31,000	20,000	73,000
Sold	12,000	16,000	25,000	7,000	60,000
Ending inventory	18,000	21,000	6,000	13,000	13,000

types of customers, and so on. The following features of Table 20.3 should be noted carefully:

- *All* variable costs (manufacturing, selling, etc.) should be deducted from sales to identify the profit contribution from each division's sales.
- Any period costs (manufacturing or otherwise) that are *specifically* and *wholly*

TABLE 20.3   Direct Cost Income Statement

THE PROFITABLE COMPANY
INCOME STATEMENT BY DIVISION

	Total Company	Division X	Division Y
Net sales	$900,000	$750,000	$150,000
Variable costs			
Variable cost of sales	$462,000	$417,000	$ 45,000
Variable selling expenses	90,000	67,500	22,500
Total variable costs	$552,000	$484,500	$ 67,500
Marginal contribution	$348,000	$265,500	$ 82,500
(Percentage of net sales)	(38.7%)	(35.4%)	(55.0%)
Period manufacturing costs	97,500	40,500	57,000
Divisional contribution	$250,500	$225,000	$ 25,500
(Percentage of net sales)	(27.8%)	(30.0%)	(17.0%)
Other period expenses			
Manufacturing overhead	$ 51,000		
Selling expense	76,500		
General and administrative expenses	57,000		
Total other period expenses	$184,500		
Net operating income	$ 66,000		
Other income and expense	4,500		
Net income before taxes	$ 70,500		
Provision for income taxes	35,500		
Net income	$ 35,000		

attributable to the support of an individual operating segment should be charged to that segment. Examples include (1) machinery and/or plant facilities devoted exclusively to a manufacturing division's product line and (2) advertising costs devoted exclusively to a product line or brand operating segment being reported on.

● All *general company* period (fixed) expenses are charged *only* to the total company and *are not* allocated to the segments, since to do so would necessarily involve arbitrary allocation decisions that would serve only to obscure the profitability analysis of an individual segment.

For Internal Use Only. Direct costing is not acceptable for external reporting purposes under GAAP or for income tax reporting, because it does not provide for "full" costing of inventory. This should not preclude its use as a valuable management tool, since it is a simple matter to adjust inventory valuation and income reporting to full costing. Table 20.4 shows one method of making such an adjustment, by allocating period manufacturing costs to inven-

TABLE 20.4 Inventory Adjustment

	(1) Standard Direct Labor Dollars	(2) Actual Period Costs
Opening inventory	$ 50,000	$ 5,000
Add: Current period	250,000	45,000
Total available	$300,000	$50,000 = 16.7%
Deduct: Cost of sales	200,000	33,000 @ 16.7%
Ending inventory	$100,000	$17,000

JOURNAL ENTRY

Dr. Period Cost Deferred in Inventory	$12,000	
Cr. Adjustment for Change in Level of Period Costs Deferred in Inventory		$12,000

tory on the basis of direct labor dollars. The table also shows the necessary journal entry to record the adjustment. This entry adjusts both inventory valuation and net income; the amount of the adjustment should be reported at the bottom of the direct costing income statement as a "reconciliation" with absorption costing net income.

Direct Standard Cost System. A direct standard cost system is a powerful management tool, since it integrates the features of both techniques into one system. The features of standard costing discussed previously in this chapter apply equally to absorption or direct costing except for overhead variance analysis and accounting. Since only variable costs are included in standard costs under direct costing, the overhead variances include only variable costs. The overhead variances illustrated previously under an absorption standard cost system would be modified as follows:

Two-variance approach:

Actual variable overhead	$14,900
Adjusted budget: 2,200 actual labor hours × $7.00	15,400
Favorable overhead spending variance	$ (500)

$7.00 × (2,200 actual hours − 2,000 standard hours) = $1,400
unfavorable overhead efficiency variance

Note that the efficiency variance is identical with that calculated under absorption costing, since under both systems only variable costs are used in the calculation.

One-variance approach:

Actual variable overhead	$14,900
Adjusted budget: 2,000 standard labor hours × $7.00	$14,900
Unfavorable overhead budget (spending) variance	$ 900

Note that the overhead production volume variance disappears under direct costing, since it represents merely an under- or over-absorption of fixed costs into inventory. With direct costing, fixed costs are not absorbed into inventory at all. The other distinction is the disappearance of the fixed cost portion of the spending variance. This variance regarding fixed costs can still be reported to management by cost element as an operating budget variance outside the structure of the formal cost system.

It should also be noted that the yield and defective goods variances would be calculated *excluding* fixed costs from the computations.

Implementing the Cost System

The development and implementation of an effective cost system requires considerable planning, structuring, and commitment over an extended period of time. The project tends to have definite stages that should be thoroughly understood and anticipated. With some variations in individual cases, these stages are:

1 Staffing the project;

2 Deciding on the fundamental characteristics and objectives of the system;

3 Determining appropriate data collection and data processing techniques;

4 Having management review and approve the system structure and objectives;

5 Developing the detailed system specifications;

6 Collecting and organizing the initial data;

7 Setting up the files; and

8 Performing the trial run.

Since most modern cost systems installed currently employ direct costing and standard cost techniques to some extent, implementation of a direct standard process cost system is assumed throughout this section. For the most part, however, this discussion applies with equal validity to cost system implementation in general.

Staffing the Project. The staffing structure can be either formal or informal, depending on the company environment. If the company style is structured, a working committee is appointed and a format of meetings and progress reporting is established. In either case, it is important to the success of the project that the implementation team include not only accounting and systems personnel but representatives of the various user functions as well. A typical team composition might include representatives from the manufacturing, purchasing, marketing, industrial engineering, accounting, and systems departments. Some functional representatives might participate only in those stages or aspects of the project that directly involve their function and responsibilities.

This working team or committee should report to a management committee that is responsible for overall guidance, direction, and control of all aspects of the implementation of the cost system. It is essential that management involvement and support be active and sustained throughout the project. Otherwise, lagging interest and resistance to change may become severe obstacles to a successful conclusion of the project.

Deciding on Systems Characteristics and Objectives. The systems objectives must be clearly defined at the outset. If not, the company runs the severe risk that the mechanics of the system will be developed without a clear perspective of what those mechanics may or may not achieve for the company. The work team must talk with the future users of the system (presumably represented *on* the team) to determine their needs. The objectives of the system regarding cost control, decision analysis, profit planning, profitability reporting, pricing analysis, and inventory costing should be clearly defined and documented.

The next step is to develop preliminary output report formats to be produced by the system in response to the user requirements. These formats should be reviewed with the user departments and modified as necessary on the basis of the reviews. Only then is the company ready to consider data collection and processing requirements to *meet* those objectives.

Determining Data Collection and Processing Techniques. Detailed information must be accumulated concerning materials used, labor effort expended, and production and flow of product through the plant. The data needed to meet the system objectives must be collected accurately and processed promptly. The choices regarding the methods of data collection and the degree of detail to be collected and processed will depend to a considerable extent upon the cost-benefit ratios involved. That is, the benefit to be gained from collecting each type of data must be weighed against the cost of that data collection effort. With recent advances in computer technology, it is more and more likely that most companies will be able to cost-justify computerization of some or all of the processing of cost system data. In addition, many companies may find it worthwhile to extend the use of computers to the data collection effort as well.

Identifying Materials Consumption. Materials consumed in production can be identified on the basis of requisitions of materials from stock. The requisition (Figure 20.12) should identify the type and quantity of material issued and the product and department for which the material was issued. If an actual cost system is involved, the requisition must also be priced, usually on a first in, first out or moving average cost basis. An inventory record maintained at the storeroom can be used to cost the requisition as the material is used. Alternatively, the factory office can cost the requisition.

An effective requisitioning system requires physical control over the materials storeroom in order to get a complete accounting for materials consumed. This often becomes difficult or impractical in a multishift operation. An alternative technique is reporting of materials as used in production, often on the same form used to record each stage of production. However, this is basically an uncontrolled method of reporting relying on factory rather than clerical employees.

STORES REQUISITION

Requested by
Department
Job No.

PAGE NO. _____ OF _____

Part No.	Description	Number Required	Stores Code No.	Delivered To	When Required	Price	When Issued	Per Unit	Total Amount	Comments	Completed By/When Issued/Authorization
										Total This Form	
										Total Brought Forward	
										Total Amount of Material	

FIG. 20.12 Group Stores Requisition

Another common alternative is the explosion of material consumption based on the actual quantity of production in the department using the particular item(s) of material. The explosion technique is simply a multiplication of the number of units of each product manufactured by the standard quantities of each type of raw material per unit of product. This technique depends upon frequent physical inventory counts, perhaps on a cycle basis, to identify material usage variances.Under these circumstances, it may not be possible to identify the particular departments or products responsible for the variances.

Some companies bypass the recordkeeping requirement for materials by taking complete monthly physical inventory counts. Combinations of these various methods of accounting for materials may be used for different material items, depending on cost significance and difficulty of obtaining the data.

Labor Distribution Reporting. Each direct labor employee prepares a labor distribution report (Figure 20.13) showing the time spent and operation performed on each production lot. This report is separate from time and attendance for payroll purposes. The hours noted on the distribution report are extended at the employee's actual straight-time hourly rate; the employees' hours and time charges are summarized by operation, cost center, and department. Each employee's total hours as reported on the labor distribution report should be reconciled to the payroll records to maintain control over the accuracy of the cost accounting records. Most companies summarize and record labor costs in this manner on a weekly basis. Any time spent by direct labor employees on indirect labor activities (e.g., maintenance) should be included on the distribution report and charged to the appropriate overhead accounts. In similar fashion, idle time (because of, for example, machine downtime) and overtime premium pay should be recorded as overhead costs.

A company with an incentive pay system accumulates incentive piece-work pay or incentive hours earned and records the cost in a manner similar to that just described for hourly workers. Any make-up or guaranteed pay supplements to such incentive pay are charged to overhead. In this type of situation there is no need for a labor efficiency variance. If incentive pay is earned on an hours basis rather than a piece-work pay basis, it will still be necessary to calculate a labor rate variance.

Some companies find it appropriate to have the factory foreman report on labor effort expended on a crew basis, with or without identification of individual employees involved. Although this usually simplifies the reporting effort, it also usually reduces reporting accuracy.

Production Data. Production data can be obtained from whatever type of production order records is used in the particular plant to control and report on the manufacturing process (Figure 20.14). The production data must be summarized by stage *and* product with whatever frequency is required by the reporting cycle, since this production data is needed to calculate standard cost allowances and determine variances. For example, if a company needs daily labor reporting, then it needs daily production data on which to base the daily standard hours and/or dollar allowances.

Overhead Data. Accumulation of overhead cost data usually presents the least difficulty. The prime requirement is an appropriate chart of accounts so that

EMPLOYEE NO.	ACCOUNT	EMPLOYEE NAME	SHIFT	YR/ MO/ DAY	WEEK	DIVISION	UNIT	T/K	DEPARTMENT

PART NUMBER	SPECIAL	EXPENSE FUNCTION	MJO	WORK ORDER	WORK CENTER	OPER.	QUANTITY	UNIT STANDARD	HOURS WORKED	CLOCK TIMES
										STOP START
										STOP START
										STOP START
										STOP START
										STOP START

AUTHORIZED SIGNATURE ______________________ DAILY JOB CARD

FIG. 20.13 Daily Job Card

Production Tag	Amount Scheduled	Amount Finished	Rate	
Machine No. _____ Operator No. _____				Out
Operation and No.				In
Labor Code No.				Out
Helpers' Code Nos.				In
Signature				Out
				In

FIG. 20.14 Production Ticket

manufacturing overhead costs will be accumulated by cost element, department, and cost behavior category (i.e., variable or fixed).

Use of Data Processing Facilities. The preceding discussion indicates that a voluminous amount of reporting and recordkeeping is required in order to operate a cost accounting system. Two problems generally arise because of this condition:

1 Difficulty in obtaining complete and accurate data about the production activity; and

2 The extensive effort of recording and analyzing the data and developing the detailed cost reports.

Many companies have utilized data processing facilities in order to cope with both of these problems. Several companies manufacture equipment specifically designed to collect data in the factory. The typical configuration consists of a central processing unit located either in the factory or in the office, terminals at appropriate work stations throughout the factory, a tape drive, and a printer. The factory employees use the terminals to enter into the system such data as time and attendance, labor distribution, units produced, and units transferred to the next operation or department. This data is printed out and recorded on magnetic tape or other electronic medium. At the end of the day, the data is transferred to the company's main computer facility for further processing and preparation of management reports.

Management Review and Approval. After the work team has established the objectives and defined the data collection and processing requirements and methods, the team should document this proposed system structure for presentation to the management committee. This presentation should include the expected one-time implementation costs (including cost of computer hardware and software required) and an estimate of the ongoing costs of operating the system.

Modifications to the system structure are common at this stage in response to management's appraisal of both the nature and the cost of the system. The work team is now in a position to develop the *detailed* system specifications.

Developing the Detailed Specifications. This step involves the detailed documentation of the nature and method of data collection, the method and steps required to process the data, and the procedures for generation and analysis of the appropriate management reports. If the system is computer-based, the specifications will include the layout of each of the computer files. All appropriate forms should also be designed at this time.

The Initial Data Requirements. The basic data files (manual or computerized) must be established before any processing of data can be accomplished. With a standard cost system, the primary effort involves development and documentation of the specifications for the manufacture of each product. The detailed product and operational standards must then be established on the basis of the specifications, so that standard cost allowances can be calculated as production data is gathered and processed through the system. The standard cost data must include:

- Material quantities and prices by operation and department (including an acceptable waste allowance);
- Labor time to perform each operation on each product;
- Departmental labor rates;
- Departmental variable and fixed overhead rates by cost element; and
- Spoilage or defective cost allowances by product (and, perhaps, by stage of operations).

Figure 20.15 illustrates a typical standard cost sheet format.

Style No. _____ Date _____

Description _____ Prepared by _____

Materials   Cost/ Dozen

Item	Description	Basic Yards	Waste Percentage	Total Yards	Price/Yd

Total material cost per dozen   _____

Direct labor and variable overhead

Operation	Direct Labor			Variable Overhead	
	Labor Time	Hourly Rate	Labor Cost	Percentage of Direct Labor	Overhead Cost

Total direct labor and variable
  overhead cost per dozen   _____   _____   _____

Total processing cost   _____

Allowance for loss on seconds: _____ % 2nds × $_____ loss/dz   _____

Total variable inventory cost   _____

Fixed plant overhead: $_____ direct labor cost × _____%   _____

Total inventory cost   _____

FIG. 20.15 Product Cost Sheet

Departmental Overhead Rates. Development of the departmental over-head rates requires establishment of overhead budgets upon which to base the rates. For a direct cost system, only the variable overhead costs will become part of the product standards. The rates should be based on production activity bases appropriate to each department's operation (e.g., direct labor hours, machine hours).

Inventory Records. Inventory files must be established and maintained for raw material, work in process, and finished goods. These inventories should be valued at standard cost as a starting point for operation of the cost system. This implies the need to establish the product standards by stage of operation so that work-in-process inventory may be properly valued. Once the inventory starting points are established, it is imperative that the company be prepared to continue the maintenance of these perpetual records, so the initial effort of establishing the inventories will have continuing value in the operation of the cost system. The journal entries described earlier in this chapter establish control accounts on the general ledger for all categories of inventory. During the operation of the cost system, the control accounts are used to verify the accuracy of the monthly valuation of all detailed inventories at standard cost. This procedure also serves to verify the accuracy of the data flowing through the cost system upon which the monthly journal entries (and thus the control accounts) are based.

The Trial Run. Once the data files are established, it is possible (and necessary) to begin processing actual data through the system, using the forms and procedures that comprise the detailed system specifications. This can be done in phases or on a comprehensive basis for a trial period. The phases might consist of separate implementation of collection and processing of:

- Production data
- Labor distribution data
- Material usage records
- Departmental overhead accounting

Another phasing-in approach is complete implementation of any or all of these data flows on a department-by-department basis.

The primary purpose of this trial run is not to collect accurate, useful cost information. Rather, it is to test the accuracy, reliability, and practicality of the cost system procedures. The results of this trial run should be carefully reviewed and evaluated to define possible bottlenecks and unexpected complications in the operation of the system and to uncover factory operating conditions not anticipated in the original system design.

Invariably, it will be necessary to modify the cost system on the basis of this trial run and evaluation. After modification, the system should again be tested thoroughly. This time the work team is interested in both the accuracy and practicality of the system and the reliability and meaningfulness of the data generated by operation of the system.

This process of testing, review, evaluation, and modification should be repeated as many times as necessary until the team is satisfied that the company has a working system.

This does not mean that the system development work is finished. In a sense, this effort is never finished. In the typical case it requires at least two years of operation of the system until management is completely satisfied with the established standards and the meaningfulness of the cost reports. In a broader context, a cost system is continually evolving, partly as a consequence of growing company sophistication in the use of such a system and partly because a factory operation is dynamic and the cost system must likewise be dynamic if it is to be a permanently useful management tool.

Pitfalls in Implementation. There are innumerable problems and pitfalls that may be encountered in as complex a project as implementation of a cost system. This section introduces the types of situations that may develop. If management is adequately prepared, problems of this type appear less formidable to cope with and to resolve.

Resistance to Change. Since installation of a cost system involves extensive change, it is likely to meet with extensive resistance from the factory workers and supervisors. The extensive demand upon them for discipline processing and collection of factory operating data will be met only if the factory personnel understand the reason for the system and the benefits that it entails for them and for the company. The success of the project depends on the work team demonstrating to the factory supervisors that the operation of the cost system will provide them with information to help them meet their responsibilities. During the trial run, management should pay careful attention to the extent and nature of the demands made upon the factory personnel by operation of the system, and it should make every effort to keep those demands within practical limits without degrading the quality of the system. At the same time, corporate management must demonstrate continuing involvement and support so that factory management will understand the importance that the company places on the objectives of the cost system.

Effect of Substitutions. Many companies find it necessary at times to substitute materials other than those originally specified for the manufacture of certain products. Unless the factory reporting system is structured to identify those substitutions (i.e., to identify the materials actually used), the cost reports and variance calculations and the perpetual inventory records will be inaccurate.

In similar fashion, it is essential to capture information regarding substitution of finished product in the fulfillment of customer orders. Otherwise the standard cost of sales will be calculated incorrectly and the finished goods perpetual inventory records will be inaccurate.

Material Losses. It is important to capture appropriate information regarding the production stage at which material losses occur. Otherwise, responsibility performance reporting will not be achievable and appropriate corrective action will not be possible.

Rework and Idle Time Costs. Failure to isolate rework labor cost from normal direct labor results in excessive build-up of unfavorable labor variances and an inability to identify the reasons for those variances. Failure to identify idle time of the direct labor force has similar consequences. The rework and idle time costs should be charged to variable overhead.

Coding Errors. A cost accounting system places a heavy demand for coding of direct and indirect costs incurred (both labor and expenses). This almost invariably results initially in a high incidence of coding errors. A continuing emphasis on clerical and factory staff training is necessary to overcome this system start-up problem.

Undue Emphasis on Product Costing. A common danger in both the design and implementation of a cost system is the placing of undue (or, at times, exclusive) emphasis on the product costing objective of cost accounting. Usually, the objectives of cost control and performance reporting deserve the primary emphasis in order to maximize the management usefulness of the system, as opposed to the "pure accounting" objectives.

DECISION ANALYSIS

The proper analysis of data relevant to a decision confronting management is one of the most important functions a financial executive can perform. The financial executive's ability to analyze data effectively is greatly enhanced by the operation of an effective cost system. A cost system utilizing both direct costing and standard costing techniques provides a valuable and comprehensive data base for this purpose.

As discussed earlier in this chapter, direct costing emphasizes cost behavior patterns (variable vs. fixed) in response to changing activity levels (e.g., production and sales volume). It also emphasizes profit contribution (sales minus variable costs), which is fundamental to many aspects of analysis for management decision making.

The availability of standard cost data facilitates the definition of expected cost patterns. Since decision analysis is a forward-looking technique, such a data base is invaluable. Standard costs represent, by definition, the costs that management expects to incur at desired levels of operating efficiency. Of course, if, in a given situation, management expects to incur variances from standard costs, those expected variances should be part of the projected cost data utilized in the analytical process.

Cost-Volume-Profit Analysis

The interrelationship of costs and volume, and the resulting impact on profitability, is at the heart of much of decision analysis. This interrelationship can best be understood by means of breakeven analysis. Breakeven analysis utilizes projected revenue and expense patterns to define the level of sales at which revenues and expenses are expected to equal each other; that is, the breakeven point. More importantly, though, this technique also defines the expected impact on profit, or loss, as the sales level moves above or below the breakeven point. There are two approaches to breakeven point determination: mathematical formula and charting. The breakeven formula approach emphasizes *only* the breakeven sales level, while a breakeven chart depicts the expected cost-volume-profit relationship over a range of activity levels.

The Breakeven Formula. The formula approach can be used to define the breakeven point either in sales dollars or in units. The sales dollar version of the formula is as follows:

$$\text{Breakeven sales amount} = \frac{\text{Total fixed costs}}{\text{Profit contribution as a}}$$
$$\text{percentage of sales}$$

To illustrate, assume:

Budgeted fixed costs	$200,000
Selling price per unit	10.00
Standard variable costs per unit	6.00

The profit contribution (also known as marginal contribution) is:

Selling price	$10.00	100%
Variable cost	6.00	60
Profit contribution	$ 4.00	40%

Therefore, breakeven sales are:

$$\frac{\$200,000}{40\%} = \$500,000$$

In words, $500,000 sales at a 40 percent contribution yields $200,000 of profit contribution, which is just sufficient to cover fixed costs of $200,000.

The breakeven sales units can be determined by use of the following formula:

$$\text{Breakeven units} = \frac{\text{Total fixed costs}}{\text{Profit contribution per unit}}$$

Continuing the illustration, breakeven units are:

$$\frac{\$200,000}{\$4.00} = 50,000 \text{ units}$$

Thus, 50,000 units at $4 profit contribuion per unit yields $200,000 total contribution, which is just sufficient to cover fixed costs of $200,000.

Either version of the formula can be modified to define the sales volume needed to achieve a target income level (pretax), by adding the target income dollars to the expected fixed costs. In the illustration, if it is assumed that management wants to know the sales level needed to achieve $40,000 of pretax income, then the calculations are:

$$\frac{\$200,000 + \$40,000}{40\%} = \$600,000$$

or

$$\frac{\$200,000 + \$40,000}{\$4.00} = 60,000 \text{ units}$$

In this case, the target sales dollars ($600,000) exceed breakeven sales dollars ($500,000) by $100,000. Since the breakeven sales level will, by definition, yield just enough profit contribution to cover fixed costs, the additional sales volume of $100,000, at 40 percent contribution rate, will generate $40,000 of pretax income. Similarly, 10,000 units above breakeven (60,000–50,000) at $4.000 contribution per unit equals $40,000.

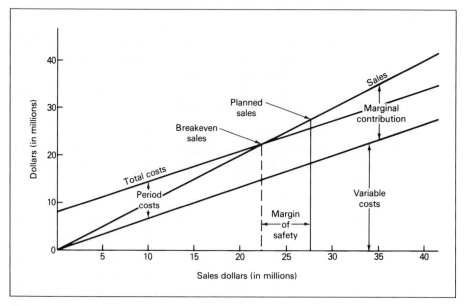

FIG. 20.16 Breakeven Chart of a Profit Plan

To summarize:

$600,000 sales* @ 40% profit contribution = $240,000

Fixed cost   200,000

Target income $ 40,000

* 60,000 units @ $10 selling price

The Breakeven Chart. The charting approach to breakeven analysis provides a more comprehensive picture of the inherent cost-volume-profit relationships. Figure 20.16 illustrates the breakeven chart of a company's profit plan. (The same technique can be utilized with historical data.) The vertical axis of the breakeven chart represents volume (usually expressed in sales dollars). The horizontal axis (in dollars) is used to plot and read the various relationships depicted in the chart. The first line drawn is the sales line; it is plotted by reading *both* axes as sales dollars. Next, the variable cost line is drawn, starting at zero (since by definition such costs rise or fall proportionately with volume) and plotting any additional variable cost points by multiplying the expected variable cost percentage by a given sales level. The difference between the sales and variable cost lines represents the marginal contribution (also known as profit contribution) at any given level of sales.

Period, or fixed, costs are plotted as a *constant* addition to variable costs at all levels of sale; this yields the total cost line. The breakeven sales point is simply that point at which the sales line crosses the total cost line. Stated another way, it is the sales volume level that provides just enough marginal contribution to equal the period costs.

The sales level inherent in the company's profit plan can then be identified as depicted on Figure 20.16. The difference between planned and breakeven sales is referred to as the margin of safety, since it represents the portion of planned sales that management can fail to achieve without operating at a loss. More importantly, perhaps, the chart depicts graphically the profit potential at each sales level above breakeven, and, conversely, the potential loss at any sales level below breakeven. In other words, it highlights the cost-volume-profit interrelationship.

Constraints of Breakeven Analysis. Breakeven calculations or charts are effective only as long as the underlying assumptions remain valid. Specifically, the following assumptions must remain static:

- Sales prices
- Product sales mix, and the resultant impact on a composite (weighted average) profit contribution rate
- Variable cost rate (i.e., spending and efficiency patterns)
- Level of period (fixed) cost

If any of these assumptions change, the analysis must be redone. Furthermore, the relationships depicted on a breakeven chart can be expected to be valid only within a "relevant" range of activity. That is, sales volume below or above a normal range of activity is likely to drastically alter the relationships underlying the chart. At very low volumes, operating efficiency might suffer (raising the variable cost percentage), any deferrable fixed costs will be put off in the interest of corporate survival, advertising costs may be increased, and management may offer significant price reductons to generate sales volume. At very high volumes, inefficiences might develop, and operating capacity may have to be increased to meet the production and sales demand.

Interpretation of Breakeven Charts. Figure 20.17 presents the breakeven charts depicting the cost-volume-profit relationships of two companies in the same industry. Note that the planned sales and expected operating profit are identical for both companies. However, one company has a low level of fixed cost (and a corresponding high ratio of variable costs to sales). This company's operations are labor-intensive, with relatively little factory automation. In contrast, the other company has high fixed costs because it is highly automated; it has a low rate of variable costs because of the degree of automation.

If the respective managements of each of these companies were unaware of their companies' underlying cost behavior patterns, they might be expected to react identically to marketplace conditions during the year. Examination of the implications of the two charts will reveal that very different responses may well be in order.

For example, the low-fixed-cost company has very little incentive to lower prices in order to attract additional sales volume, since operating profit increases at a very low rate on higher volume. The high-fixed-cost company has significant profit potential from increased volume and may benefit substantially from price reductions (and other forms of sales promotion).

Conversely, the low-fixed-cost company has a considerable margin of safety against falling sales. Since most of its costs are variable, it can lose a

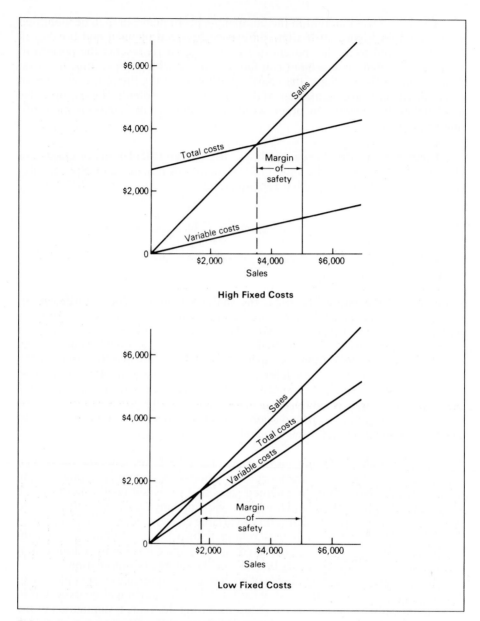

FIG. 20.17 Breakeven Charts of Two Companies

considerable amount of volume before reaching the breakeven point. The high-fixed-cost company has a strong incentive to maintain its planned sales level, since the fixed costs will remain substantially at the same level as volume drops, thus providing only a small margin of safety.

Other uses of the breakeven technique are illustrated in some of the examples presented in the following section.

It should be noted once again that the ability to project the impact on costs depends largely on the availability of reliable cost data, including an understanding of the cost behavior patterns of the company.

In a given situation, it may be that the company has sufficient idle capacity to fill the special order. If so, the incremental overhead costs will represent variable costs only. If capacity is not sufficient, management must project the increase in fixed costs that will be necessary to provide the required capacity. Also, the specific conditions of the order under consideration must be considered. Will a sales commission be paid on the order? Will the company or the customer pay shipping costs? Are there any other specific out-of-pocket costs (e.g., sales aids or advertising allowances) that the company must incur to obtain the order? If such costs are relevant, they must be included in the total of projected incremental costs.

Other critical factors that management must consider with respect to a marginal pricing decision are not always easily quantifiable. Nevertheless, they may be the determining factors in deciding whether or not to accept the order. Among these factors are the following:

- Will the customer expect the same low price on future orders, when the company may not have the idle capacity available? If so, the cost of providing that capacity may make the business undesirable.

- Will customers represented by the *base* volume (the 50,000 units, in this) expect to receive the favorable $6.00 selling price (as opposed to $8.00 at present)? If so, the company profits may disappear, since the *average* cost ($6.25) for all 80,000 units is more than the $6.00 selling price. The *total* sales of a company must, of course, cover *all* operating costs, both variable and fixed.

Make vs. Buy. A common problem facing many companies involves a decision to manufacture or purchase either a component used in the company's manufacturing process or a finished product itself. The relevant costs for the manufacturing alternative are those additional costs that will be incurred if the item is produced in-house. If the company has sufficient available capacity, only variable costs are relevant. Otherwise, the fixed costs related to the additional capacity required should be considered as well.

As with marginal pricing decisions, the *full* cost per unit for *all* production is not relevant, since much or all of the fixed cost incurred will not be affected by the decision to manufacture the part. To illustrate, if it is estimated that in-house production of a particular item will require $3.00 material cost and $2.50 direct labor cost per unit, and if the company's standard factory overhead rate is 200 percent of direct labor, then the full cost of manufacturing one unit will be:

Materials	$ 3.00
Direct labor	2.50
Overhead ($2.50 @ 200%)	5.00
Total cost	$10.50

If the same item can be purchased for $8.00, the company might logically decide to "save" $2.50 per unit ($10.50−$8.00) by purchasing the item.

However, if it is assumed that sufficient productive capacity exists to produce the item (e.g., without adding equipment, space, supervision, etc.) then only the variable overhead costs are relevant to the decision. Assume further that the company's 200 percent standard factory overhead rate comprises a 60 percent variable overhead rate and a 140 percent fixed overhead rate, then the proper cost analysis would be:

Materials	$3.00
Direct labor	2.50
Variable overhead ($2.50 @ 60%)	1.50
Total relevant cost	$7.00

On a *relevant* cost basis, the "manufacture" option now appears attractive ($7.00 cost to manufacture vs. $8.00 outside purchase price).

As with most incremental, or relevant, cost analysis, the direct financial analysis just presented may not tell the whole story. For instance, other considerations in a make versus buy decision might include:

- Is there another *more attractive* use for the available productive capacity?
- What is the expected *quality* of the product if manufactured, compared to acquisition from the outside vendor?
- How *reliable* is the outside source in terms of delivery commitments?

Nevertheless, without the availability of a reliable incremental cost analysis, management will be missing a vital component in its ability to make an informed, rational decision.

Other Incremental Decision Analysis. The analytical approach inherent in the preceding examples applies equally well to many other situations confronting management. For example:

- For a multiplant company, determining the plant at which to produce a particular product
- Whether to expand into a new product line (or to abandon an existing line)
- Whether to expand into a new territory
- Whether to market existing products to a new class of customers
- Whether to close a particular plant, or store, or warehouse

In all of these cases, the requirement is simply to determine the manner in which revenues and/or costs are expected to be affected by each decision alternative. The ability to make such a determination depends upon the availability of sound cost data and an understanding of the company's cost-volume-profit relationships.

SUGGESTED READING

Anderson, Henry R., and Mitchell H. Raiborn. *Basic Cost Accounting Concepts*. Boston: Houghton Mifflin, 1977.

Arnstein, William E., and Frank Gilabert. *Direct Costing*. New York: American Management Association, 1980.

Bierman, Harold, Jr., and Thomas R. Dyckman. *Managerial Cost Accounting*, 2nd. ed. New York: Macmillan, 1976.

Bulloch, James, et al. *Accountants' Cost Handbook*. New York: John Wiley & Sons, 1983.

Corcoran, A. Wayne. *Costs: Accounting, Analysis, and Control*. New York: John Wiley & Sons, 1978.

Davidson, Sidney, and Roman L. Weil. *Handbook of Cost Accounting*. New York: McGraw-Hill, 1978.

Horngren, Charles T. *Cost Accounting: A Managerial Emphasis*, 4th ed. Englewood Cliffs, N.J.: Prentice-Hall, 1977.

21

Cash Budgeting

JAMES D. WILLSON

RELATION OF CASH BUDGETING TO SHORT-TERM PLANNING

In the last decade there have been many changes in the business environment, some external and some internal, which are causing an upsurge in attention to the need for sound planning and control. Among these forces are increasingly volatile economic conditions; vastly changing rates of inflation; greater internationalism in business; more intense competition; a trend to decentralization in management; increased sophistication of management (both general and financial); and technological advances in computerization and communications. These developments require faster and better answers to alternative courses of action. Coupled with these dynamics are changes in capital markets, which make the raising of capital, in many circumstances, more difficult and costly. Hence, management must look to increased effectiveness in its operations, which means the employment of more sophisticated analysis in allocating capital to its highest and best uses, and more efficiency in managing the business assets and liabilities. Thus, sound budgeting, or planning and control, is a vital necessity.

A complete annual, or short-term business plan, usually is summarized in three or four basic financial statements:

1 The statement of estimated income and expense;

2 The statement of estimated financial position (i.e., the balance sheet);

3 The statement of changes in financial position, or estimated sources and uses of funds, or estimated cash receipts, disbursements, and cash balance; and (usually)

4 The statement of estimated capital appropriations and expenditures (i.e., the capital, or fixed asset, budget).

Hence, it can be seen that the planned cash statement is one of the three or four key financial statements, and reflects the need for cash planning or budgeting in the operation of the business.

IMPORTANCE OF CASH BUDGETING

While it may seem unnecessary to define the term "cash," it may help to clarify the perimeters of cash budgeting by describing cash as cash on hand and demand deposits in banks as of the close of business on the statement date. The essence of cash is its immediate availability as legal tender or purchasing power. Good cash budgeting provides that "excess" cash be placed in temporary investments, as briefly reviewed later in this chapter and more fully discussed in Chapter 24.

Why is cash budgeting important? To begin with, a business must operate within the limit of available funds. But the converse is true: The required funds must be made available to implement the planned activities. Hence, cash budgeting is intimately related to both short-term budgeting and strategic, or long-term, planning. Cash must be made available at the right time, in the right place, and at an acceptable cost. It follows, therefore, that cash availability must be planned. It cannot, or should not, simply be the residual of the short-term operational planning. Furthermore, it should not be the amount left over after planning receivable and inventory levels, related needs for capital assets, or accounts payable and accrued expenses. The proper cash balances as well as sources and uses must be planned.

A business needs a certain cash balance to meet the usual business requirements: to pay obligations promptly; to maintain required compensating balances, where applicable, with commercial banks; to retain flexibility in transferring funds among the various operating centers; and to meet other unexpected needs. To be sure, electronic fund transfer and other accelerated cash transfer techniques may reduce the amount of cash required for operations, but it should not be set at zero (or at a negative balance to reflect float) if only for psychological reasons.

In summary, as part of the financial planning operation, those responsible for cash budgeting should gain some awareness of what an acceptable ongoing cash balance should be, through discussions with the financial officers. In the planning process, of course, any excess would be reflected in the temporary investment category, producing some earnings. The required minimum cash balances should bear some relationship to activity levels such as sales or production. But knowledge of an acceptable balance is the starting point for cash budgeting.

PURPOSE OF CASH BUDGETING

In a general sense, as is evident from the preceding comments, the basic purpose of cash budgeting is to plan in such a way that the enterprise will have the necessary cash when required, and that appropriate plans may be set in force to invest effectively any excess, whether for the short term or long term. However, aside from this primary purpose, the following related or supplemental uses indicate some of the specific advantages of proper cash planning and control.

1 To indicate the timing and extent of funds needed to meet maturing obligations or uses such as payrolls, taxes, interest, accounts payable, and dividends;

2 To assist in planning for growth, including such requirements as working capital, new plant and equipment, or strategic acquisitions;

3 To identify the peaks and valleys, or seasonal fluctuations, in business activity that will require greater or lesser investments in receivables and inventory;

4 To facilitate the securing of funds on a more advantageous basis by knowing well in advance of actual requirements the extent and duration of cash needs;

5 To determine the extent and probable timing of funds available for temporary or other investments;

6 To assist in securing credit from banks or other lenders by identifying the sources and uses of funds, and the existence of an acceptable planning and control system;

7 To plan the reduction of indebtedness;

8 To coordinate the cash needs, and identify the excesses, of the divisions and subsidiaries or affiliates;

9 To permit the company to take advantage of cash discounts and forward or special purchases on a more advantageous basis;

10 To facilitate cash management and related investment of surplus funds; and

11 To assist in planning foreign exchange transactions and related hedges.

In summary, cash budgeting can be used to plan specific needs and take advantage of specific opportunities as they arise.

METHODS OF BUDGETING CASH

There are two principal methods of cash budgeting in general use, although various modifications or adaptations do exist. While the end product may be the estimated cash balance by period, such as week, month, quarter, or year, the two procedures differ basically as to starting point and extent of detail available. The two most widely used techniques are the following.

Direct Estimate of Cash Receipts and Cash Disbursements

By this method a detailed estimate is made as to each specific function, activity, cost, or income element. It is essentially a projection of the cash records, and is especially useful when the full magnitude of the swings or gyrations of both cash receipts and disbursements is necessary, as in cash short or lean situations. The procedure has the further advantage of more easily comparing actual receipts and disbursements with plan, and identifying each area of departure from planned performance. A cash budget prepared on a receipts and disbursements basis is illustrated in Table 21.1 on pages 21-6 and 21-7.

The Adjusted Net Income Method

This technique is also referred to as the source and use of funds method. As the name implies, the starting point is the statement of estimated income and expense, or the net income statement. The projected net income is adjusted for noncash transactions, such as depreciation and amortization, or deferred income taxes, to arrive at the cash flow, the internal cash generation before balance-sheet changes. Adjustments are made for expected changes in accounts receivable, inventories, and other balance-sheet items. Specific nonoperating uses and sources of cash are identified. In line with recent trends, this statement may be structured to identify funds provided or used by (1) operations; (2) financing transactions; and (3) investment transactions; to conform to some published formats in the nature of a statement accounting for changes in financial position.

A cash budget statement based on the adjusted net income method, and used for internal purposes, is shown in Table 21.2 on page 21-8. It is to be observed that the full magnitude of cash receipts or disbursements is not discernible. However, for most companies and executives (except possibly for certain financial executives concerned with cash management), such great detail may not be necessary for planning and control purposes.

As discussed later, there may be some merit in preparing cash statements based on both methods.

ESTIMATING CASH RECEIPTS

Whether done manually or by computer, and whether direct estimates of cash receipts and cash disbursements are made, or the adjusted net income method is used, certain specific transactions must be estimated either for impact on the financial statements, or to check the reasonableness of the financial statement balances.

Cash receipts in the typical commercial or industrial company will be represented primarily by (1) a limited number of transactions, each easily identifiable, and often of substantial relative size; and (2) voluminous transactions, each perhaps small in size, which are the principal sources of cash. Examples of limited transactions are: sales of fixed assets; commercial loans; sale of common or preferred stock dividends; and interest income. The more numerous transactions are typified by collections on accounts receivable, or cash sales. For most industrial or commercial firms, these latter two sources represent the greater recurring sources of cash.

Practically speaking, the larger, identifiable, and usually nonrecurring sources of cash must be predicted or estimated as to timing and amount, and appropriately reflected in the cash planning statement. Thus, proceeds from the sale of the fixed assets, bank loans, and sale of subsidiary are segregated in Table 21.1. Similarly, the cash received from the sale of long-term obligations are shown, separately identified, in Table 21.1. Usually, such receipts as dividends, interest income, and royalties are easily estimated, based on a review of the instruments and related documents, or the contracts, on an individual transaction basis.

Where the sources of cash are from numerous transactions, such as collections on accounts receivable, the procedure is somewhat different. Thus, an analysis of past experience and recent trends will indicate what share of sales probably will be for cash, and the month of collection of any receivable. This relationship may then be applied to the planned sales, by time period, to determine the probable proceeds of cash sales.

Collections on account must be analyzed to determine the typical pattern, which may be seasonal, and enable those responsible for cash collections to make reasonable estimates, based on experience and trends, and as applied to the credit sales reflected in the sales budget.

An example may be helpful. Assume that the analysis of cash collection experience in May for the past two or three years reflects this pattern:

Collections Period	Total May Credit Sales
May	3.4%
June	84.6
July	9.1
August	2.3
Cash discounts	0.5
Uncollectible	0.1
Total	100.0%

If the May sales for the planning year reasonably could be expected to follow the same pattern (or a somewhat modified one to reflect changing trends), then these or the adjusted percentages could be applied to estimated May sales to determine the month of probable cash collections. The same type of analysis (a

TABLE 21.1   Statement of Estimated Cash Receipts and Disbursements

THE JOHNSON COMPANY

STATEMENT OF ESTIMATED CASH RECEIPTS AND DISBURSEMENTS

Year Ending December 31, 19XX

(dollars in thousands)

	January	February	March	1st Quarter Total		December	4th Quarter Total	Year Total
Cash at beginning of period	$ 2,300	$ 4,000	$ 700	$ 2,300		$ 6,100	$ 5,000	$ 2,300
Cash receipts								
Regular								
Collections on account	$ 8,400	$ 7,200	$ 9,100	$24,700		$ 7,000	$21,300	$ 96,300
Cash sales	300	100	400	800		100	200	1,900
Dividends	1,400	700	1,400	3,500		800	2,700	12,100
Interest income	700	1,000	600	2,300		1,000	3,200	10,200
Subtotal	$10,800	$ 9,000	$11,500	$31,300		$ 8,900	$27,400	$120,500

Special							
Sale of fixed assets	$ 3,100	—	—	$ 3,100	—	$ 3,500	$ 6,600
Bank loans		$ 4,000	$ 4,000	4,000	—	2,000	6,000
Sale of subsidiary	2,200	—	—	2,200	—	—	2,200
Total cash receipts	$16,100	$ 9,000	$15,500	$40,600	$ 8,900	$32,900	$135,300
Total cash available	$18,400	$13,000	$16,200	$42,900	$15,000	$37,900	$137,600
Cash disbursements							
Accounts payable	$ 3,200	$ 4,000	$ 2,700	$ 9,900	$ 3,100	$ 8,700	$ 24,600
Payrolls — gross	8,600	7,100	8,800	24,500	7,400	22,900	82,400
Dividends on common stock	—	—	900	900	900	900	3,600
Interest expense	900	—	100	1,000	100	100	2,200
Capital expenditures	700	300	800	1,800	800	1,100	4,100
Payroll taxes and insurance	900	800	900	2,600	800	2,200	13,000
Other	100	100	200	400	600	700	1,700
Payments on indebtedness	—	—	—	—	—	—	4,700
Total cash disbursements	$14,400	$12,300	$14,400	$41,100	$13,700	$36,600	$136,300
Cash at end of period	$ 4,000	$ 700	$ 1,800	$ 1,800	$ 1,300	$ 1,300	$ 1,300

TABLE 21.2   Statement of Cash Sources and Uses

THE JONES COMPANY
STATEMENT OF ESTIMATED CHANGES IN FINANCIAL POSITION
Year Ending December 31, 19XX
(dollars in thousands)

Item	January	February	March	1st Quarter Total	December	4th Quarter Total	Year Total
Sources of cash							
Net income	$2,460	$2,070	$1,870	$ 6,400	$1,300	$5,200	$21,070
Depreciation	800	800	890	2,490	1,010	2,890	10,280
Deferred taxes	200	800	400	1,400	—	—	3,160
Internal cash generation	$3,460	$3,670	$3,160	$10,290	$2,310	$8,090	$34,510
Accounts receivable	700	800	100	1,600	(200)	(700)	2,900
Long-term obligations	4,000	—	—	4,000	—	—	4,000
Total sources	$8,160	$4,470	$3,260	$15,890	$2,110	$7,390	$41,410
Uses of cash							
Accounts payable and accruals	$3,800	$2,700	$2,100	$ 8,600	$ (790)	$ (210)	$18,700
Capital expenditures	900	1,020	870	2,790	270	840	6,000
Dividends	—	—	700	700	600	600	2,510
Purchase of treasury shares	—	500	—	500	1,000	1,400	2,900
Purchase of Aloha subsidiary	—	—	—	—	—	—	11,470
Total uses	$4,700	$4,220	$3,670	$12,590	$4,380	$2,630	$41,580
Increase (decrease) in cash and temporary investments	$3,460	$ 250	$ (410)	$ 3,300	($2,270)	$4,760	$ (170)
Cash position at end of period							
Cash	$1,100	$1,000	$1,010	$ 1,010	$ 970	$ 970	$ 970
Temporary investments	7,600	7,950	7,530	7,530	4,100	4,100	4,100
Total	$8,700	$8,950	$8,540	$ 8,540	$5,070	$5,070	$ 5,070

possible computer application) could be made for the planned sales for each month of the year to arrive at estimated collections on account for the planning year. The planned cash receipts for the month of May would be made up of these segments from May and prior month planned sales, as follows:

	Basic Sales Data		Estimated
Month of Sale	Applicable Collection Percentage	Monthly Sales (thousands)	May Collections (thousands)
January	0.6%	$21,460	$ 128.76
February	2.4	22,310	535.44
March	9.7	25,600	2,483.20
April	85.3	27,800	23,713.40
May	3.4	29,300	996.20
Total collections			$27,857.00
Cash discounts (April sales)	0.5		139.00
Uncollectible	0.1		29.30
Total			$28,025.30

By similar monthly calculations (a possible computer application) the amount of probable cash collections, provision for doubtful accounts, and estimated cash discounts may be planned, all as part of the short-term budgeting procedure, and as elements in the statement of changes in financial position (or statement of estimated cash receipts and disbursements), in the statement of estimated income and expense, and in the statement of estimated financial position. It should be noted that the planned cash collections or account must be known under either the direct estimating method or the adjusted net income method, to determine the estimated accounts receivable balances for the statement of estimated financial position.

It bears repeating that periodic analysis will be helpful in watching trends, including the impact of general economic conditions and patterns by type of customer or product line.

ESTIMATING CASH DISBURSEMENTS

In a sense, estimating cash disbursements is similar to estimating cash receipts in that there will be (1) the summarization of a series of regularly recurring transactions daily, weekly, or monthly; and (2) some less frequent, but usually individually significant, movements of cash. In the normal industrial or commercial firm, the voluminous regularity of recurring disbursements will relate to such items as:

1 *Accounts payable,* for inventories, fixed assets, supplies, and various operating expenses;

2 *Salaries and wages,* as related to direct labor, indirect labor, and various operating expenses;

3 *Accrued expenses,* such as taxes, insurance, professional expenses, royalties, interest expense, and retirement expense;

4 *Prepaid items,* including certain insurance and tax items. The less frequent disbursement transactions that must be planned and provided for include:

- Dividends
- Repayment of credit obligations (e.g., bank loans, bonds, etc.)
- Major capital expenditures
- Investments (e.g., stocks, bonds, etc.)
- Acquisitions
- Treasury stock purchases

The estimating of cash disbursements is an integral part of the financial planning process, closely associated with the preparation of the statement of estimated income and expense and the statement of financial position. It parallels the construction of functional and departmental budgets. Thus, when the purchase requirements for raw materials and purchased parts are known, the related accounts payable liability is determined, and, based on vendor terms, the cash requirements for this segment is calculated. The supporting tabulation, or computer run, for this segment of accounts payable is shown in Table 21.3. Comparable data are compiled for each major category of purchases and each expense account or department, based on the departmental budget, for all asset or expense accounts, which are generated through the accounts payable route.

Required disbursements for salaries and wages are determined on a comparable basis. That is, the payroll elements of the work-in-process inventory accounts, various operating expenses, or other accounts are determined, based on the functional budget. A review of the calendar, combined with company practice as to payment dates, will permit the estimating of the periodic accrual of payments. Thus, if the month ends on a Saturday, and company practice is to disburse salary payroll checks on the last day of the month, and hourly payroll on the succeeding Friday following the week salary payroll is disbursed, then an accrual would be required for only the one week and a day of the hourly payroll, and none for salaried personnel. A summarized work sheet (usually prepared by computer) for required salary and wage payments is shown in Table 21.4. Related calculations would be made for payroll deductions and so forth.

Similar summaries would be prepared for prepaid and accrual items.

Thus, it is evident that additions to asset accounts, or changes to the various expense accounts, by element, must be known by source (i.e., whether accounts payable, accrued salaries and wages, accrued expenses, requisitions, or prepaid items). Appropriate journal entries and payment schedules, where applicable, must be formulated and summarized following normal accounting practices. Average lag times, or payment terms, may be used in estimating payment dates (or computer applications may provide more accurate data). Major items may be tracked and accounted for on an individual basis (e.g., payments due large vendors).

TABLE 21.3   Estimate of Cash Requirements — Raw Materials and Purchased Parts

THE NMM MANUFACTURING COMPANY
ESTIMATE OF CASH REQUIREMENTS FOR RAW MATERIALS AND PURCHASED PARTS
Year Ending December 31, 19XX
(dollars in millions)

Month	Beginning Balance Accounts Payable	+ Purchases =	Total Estimated Liability	− Estimated Carry-Forward(a) =	Cash Required
January	$16,400	$ 37,300	$ 53,700	$12,400	$ 41,300
February	12,400	27,600	40,000	9,200	30,800
March	9,200	43,100	52,300	14,400	37,900
April	14,400	31,300	45,700	10,400	35,300
May	10,400	39,200	49,600	13,100	36,500
June	13,100	28,700	41,800	9,600	32,200
July	9,600	40,400	50,000	13,500	36,500
August	13,500	39,700	53,200	13,200	40,000
September	13,200	42,600	55,800	14,200	41,600
October	14,200	44,100	58,300	14,700	43,600
November	14,700	48,900	63,600	16,300	47,300
December	16,300	41,500	57,800	13,800	44,000
Total		$464,400	$621,800		$467,000

(a) Estimated at 33⅓ percent of monthly purchases

For those items not directly related to day-to-day operations, individual estimates and specific payment dates will permit proper scheduling. Thus, the known dividend disbursement dates would be used to identify the month, week, or day of payment. Dates for large maturing obligations are well-known in advance, and plans for required disbursements can be made. As an example, outstanding notes payable should be scheduled for payment when due or, if appropriate, when funds are available. A schedule for such payments is shown in Table 21.5. Similarly, purchase of stock or other investments can be individually planned. The summarization of planned disbursements or uses of cash for the two principal procedures are shown in Tables 21.1 and 21.2.

ILLUSTRATIVE ANNUAL CASH BUDGET

For the chief financial officer, responsible for the financial well-being of the enterprise, a summarized cash budget for the annual plan year, and/or for the long-term plan is essential. The specific format should be adapted to his needs or wishes, as well as for use by the board of directors and other members of top management.

TABLE 21.4   Accrued Compensation — Costs and Payments

THE WARE COMPANY
ACCRUED COMPENSATION — COSTS AND PAYMENTS
Year Ending December 31, 19XX
(dollars in thousands)

Item	January	February	March	1st Quarter Total	Year Total
Balance, beginning of period	$37,400	$32,890	$33,220	$ 37,400	$ 37,400
Add gross payrolls:					
Manufacturing	$49,400	$44,620	$50,260	$144,280	$579,130
Sales	14,310	12,010	14,970	41,290	167,800
Research and development	2,670	2,100	2,700	7,470	31,400
Engineering	4,820	4,730	4,910	14,460	59,430
Finance	3,700	3,120	3,740	10,560	44,570
Administration	7,890	7,400	7,930	23,220	94,900
Total additions	$82,790	$73,980	$84,510	$241,280	$977,230
Deduct payments:					
Salaries	$42,600	$42,600	$43,400	$128,600	$521,800
Hourly wages	44,700	31,050	34,690	110,440	452,710
Total payments	$87,300	$73,650	$78,090	$239,040	$974,510
Balance, end of period	$32,890	$33,220	$39,640	$ 39,640	$ 40,120

TABLE 21.5 Notes Payable — Planned Cash Receipts and Disbursements

THE WENDY MANUFACTURING COMPANY

NOTES PAYABLE ACTIVITY
Year Ending December 31, 19XX
(dollars in thousands)

Month	Beginning Balance	Borrowings	Repayments	Ending Balance
January	—	$1,300	—	$1,300
February	$1,300	2,100	—	3,400
March	3,400	3,800	—	7,200
April	7,200	—	—	7,200
May	7,200	—	$ 500	6,700
June	6,700	—	1,100	5,600
July	5,600	—	1,300	4,300
August	4,300	—	2,000	2,300
September	2,300	—	1,000	1,300
October	1,300	—	300	1,000
November	1,000	—	1,000	—
December	—	—	—	—
Total	—	$7,200	$7,200	—

A statement of estimated cash receipts and disbursements, the annual cash budget, is shown in Table 21.1 on pages 21-6 and 21-7. The following explanatory comments may be helpful:

1 The specific timing and magnitude of cash receipts is shown by month, segregated between the normal, recurring high volume, and the special or largely nonrecurring, receipts. It may be equally useful to present the same data by calendar quarter only, depending on circumstances.

2 The major application of cash disbursements, again reflecting the gross magnitude, is presented by months. The gross payable and accounts payable are identified, together with other important or monitored expenditures. These, too, could be presented by calendar quarter, if suitable.

3 For strategic planning, comparable data could be presented for a 5-, 10-, or 15-year planning period, by years, annually.

4 The cash balances at the beginning and end of each period is shown. This schedule can be adapted to reflect either "free" cash, or cash and temporary investments.

In summary, this format is devised to meet the specific needs of the management by identifying total cash movement and those items of importance the financial officer wishes to monitor.

A cash budget presented by months for an annual period, in the format of changes in financial position, also referred to as sources and uses of cash, is illustrated in Table 21.2. This form may be restricted to quarterly instead of monthly data and may relate, by years, to the strategic plan.

The benefits of this form are:

1 The statement reflects how much cash is generated from operations by identifying net income, and adjusting this figure for the noncash transactions, such as depreciation and deferred taxes.

2 The other sources and uses of cash are identified through the changes in the balance-sheet accounts.

3 The segregation of these other sources and uses identifies the important sources and uses, and those the management wishes to follow.

This format can be modified to more closely conform to the published data provided annually to the shareholders, as subsequently discussed in this chapter.

THE ANNUAL CASH BUDGET AS RELATED TO OTHER ANNUAL BUDGETS

At the outset of this chapter, it is stated that the annual cash budget is an integral part of the annual plan, or short-term plan; and that the statement of estimated cash receipts and disbursements, or its equivalent statement of changes in financial position, is one of the three or four key financial statements.

But it is also evident that the cash budget is in large part dependent on the operating budget, and on the planned level of assets and liabilities. For example, cash receipts cannot be usefully estimated until the planned sales, together with the planned terms of sale and probable collection period, are known. Cash disbursements cannot be determined until the magnitude of material purchases, inventory buildup, or expense levels and related payment terms are known. In actual practice, the cash budget is prepared after the operating plan or budget is known, and the asset requirements (e.g., receivables, inventories, and fixed assets) and liability limits have been calculated. The cash balances are, in a sense, a surge tank, with planned balances dependent upon business needs and borrowing capacity. In the planning process, borrowings are assumed if the cash level in any month is insufficient to meet the needs. Conversely, excess funds are assumed to be placed in temporary investments (or used to pay down a revolving credit bank obligation, etc). Hence, all segments of the annual plan are interdependent.

Failure to meet the operating plan will have an impact on available cash. If sales are below plan, the investment in accounts receivable will be less, and the amount of inventory probably will be higher. If the sales and earnings plan is not met, collections on accounts receivable will be less. Funds available for dividends and other uses will be less.

Because cash is so vital to many businesses, it usually is helpful to update continually the cash forecast, perhaps monthly or weekly. If a segment of the plan is not achieved, very often new cash plans are required which indicate, in many instances, a change in planned actions: more or less borrowings, restrictions on capital asset expenditures, rescheduling the payment of accounts payroll, and more intensive collection efforts.

A cash plan that reflects actual receipts and disbursements for the year to date, and the changed outlook for the balance of the year, all compared with the prior plan, is shown in Table 21.6.

CASH MANAGEMENT AS RELATED TO THE CASH BUDGET

The cash budgeting process described in this chapter relates principally to the planning of cash sources and uses for a year or perhaps several years. It also discusses cash planning for shorter periods such as months or weeks. However, it does not deal extensively with the day-to-day operational aspects of cash management. This latter function is discussed in Chapter 24.

Among other things, cash management has to do with the acceleration of converting accounts receivables into cash, management of the collection float, control of disbursements and the related disbursement float, control of actual cash balances (meaning available balances in the bank ledgers), and investment of surplus cash. Of course, consideration must be given to cash compensating balances, and commercial bank relationships. Obviously, cash management deals with the day-to-day operational needs of all the company management segments and is much more short-term oriented.

Cash budgeting, of course, must incorporate the results of good cash management. Hence, if the collection period is shortened, this should be reflected in the planned accounts receivable balances and the percentage of collections each month. Changes in the payment patterns also should be reflected in the planned accounts payable balances, as well as cash available for temporary investment, including investment income. In summary, then, cash budgeting reflects the results of good or poor cash management, but does not incorporate the operational aspects into the budget process.

TIME HORIZONS FOR CASH PLANNING

Cash budgeting or forecasting is an essential part of the financial management function. The time period covered by the cash plan obviously must be suited to the needs of the company. In general two factors govern the time horizon: (1) the purpose of the cash plan; and (2) the characteristics and financial position of the enterprise. If the purpose of the cash plan is to determine on a daily basis what funds are available for temporary investments, or what specific accounts

TABLE 21.6   Monthly Updating Cash Forecast

COOPER PETROLEUM COMPANY
CONSOLIDATED CASH PLAN
Year 19XX as of May 1, 19XX
(dollars in millions)

	Actual 1/1/XX 4/30/XX	Forecast May	Forecast June	Forecast July	Balance of Year	Present View 19XX	Prior Month's View 19XX
Cash receipts							
Sales revenue	$216.2	$51.4	$51.0	$52.0	$261.3	$631.9	$611.5
(Increase) or decrease in receivables	3.2	1.6	(0.8)	(0.6)	(1.4)	2.0	2.1
Estimated taxes collected for government	38.1	10.0	10.1	10.4	49.7	118.3	118.1
Sale of property and facilities	3.2	0.7	—	—	1.1	5.0	5.0
"R" inventory liquidation	—	—	—	—	6.0	6.0	6.0
All other receipts	31.8	6.6	9.6	7.0	39.8	94.8	85.1
Total	$292.5	$70.3	$69.9	$68.8	$356.5	$858.0	$827.8
Cash disbursements							
Raw material and purchased — product cost	$113.4	$19.0	$23.7	$22.5	$119.6	$298.2	281.0
Controllable operating expenses	68.8	19.4	19.5	17.2	92.3	217.2	209.6

Tax payments	8.1	1.3	0.9	0.8	9.8	20.9	20.8
Insurance	1.8	0.1	0.1	0.1	0.6	2.7	3.0
Interest	3.6	0.2	0.9	0.8	3.9	9.4	9.5
Payment of taxes collected for government	37.8	9.7	10.1	10.1	51.0	118.7	118.5
Purchase of treasury stock	—	0.6	1.1	0.1	1.2	3.0	3.0
Preferred dividend payments	1.7	—	—	0.8	0.9	3.4	3.4
Carved-out oil sale repayments (including interest)	9.2	2.3	2.4	2.3	11.9	28.1	28.1
Debt repayment	18.3	0.2	0.8	0.4	13.3	33.0	33.0
Capital expenditures	29.2	7.4	8.2	7.6	31.4	83.8	85.0
All other disbursements	25.3	4.1	8.6	5.3	26.7	70.0	68.2
Total	$317.2	$64.3	$76.3	$68.0	$362.6	$888.4	$863.1
Increase (decrease) in cash balance	$(24.7)	$6.0	$(6.4)	$0.8	$(8.1)	$(30.4)	$(35.3)
Ending cash balances							
Primary	$10.5	$11.8	$11.8	$11.8	$11.8	$11.8	$11.8
Field	6.1	6.0	6.0	6.0	6.0	6.0	6.0
Subsidiary	4.1	5.0	5.0	5.0	5.0	5.0	5.0
Temporary investments	29.9	33.8	27.4	28.2	22.1	22.1	17.2
Total	$50.6	$56.6	$50.2	$51.0	$44.9	$44.9	$40.0

payable are to be paid, then an extremely short-term plan may indeed be necessary, perhaps for the next week, by days. At the other extreme, if the objective is to get a general idea of the funds necessary for growth and expansion as contemplated in the strategic plan, then a long-range cash budget is necessary for perhaps a 5-, 10-, or 15-year period, by years. Incidentally, it is obvious that the extent of detail will vary with the time horizon and the purpose. In a cash lean company, or one with extreme fluctuations in receipts and disbursements, it may be necessary to identify the specific invoices and due dates for cash receipts estimating purposes. And the specific receipts, in some circumstances, may be matched by an identification of what specific accounts payable are to be paid. On the other hand, typically a long-term cash budget will involve the use of general and broad guidelines only. Thus, sales will be collected in, say, 45 days; or, accounts payable recorded in one month will be paid within 30 days. If the nature of the business is rather stable or is accurately predictable as to season, such as an electric utility, then a vast amount of detail and the very short-period cash plan may not be necessary. Moreover, in such circumstances, statistical techniques such as smoothing may be useful.

A typical pattern of cash-planning periods and related reports, for a company with sizeable daily cash receipts and disbursements, an active cash management program, and somewhat seasonal characteristics as to sales and inventory accumulation, might be summarized as follows:

A SHORT-TERM CASH FORECASTS

    1 *Daily cash forecast.* For close cash management and better planning of temporary investments, a daily forecast for a period of one or two weeks may be desirable.

    2 *Weekly cash plan.* For those circumstances where cash can be adequately planned on a weekly basis, a useful format is shown in Table 21.7.

    3 *Monthly cash forecast.* While the cash management officer may find daily or weekly cash forecasts desirable or necessary, other members of financial management may feel that a monthly cash forecast will satisfy their needs as to adequacy of the credit lines, review of cash activity, and planning of specific major transactions, such as long-term investments. A cash receipts and disbursements plan, indicating activity for the next three months and the balance of the year, is reflected in Table 21.6. This permits a continuous updating of the annual business plan cash segment.

    4 *Annual cash budget.* For most companies, an annual cash budget is a necessity. The cash budget, a key financial planning statement, may be in either the cash receipts and disbursements format, as shown in Table 21.1, or the change in financial position format (sources and uses of cash), as shown in Table 21.2. It may be presented for the year in total, compared with the prior year, or by fiscal quarters, if deemed necessary.

B LONG-RANGE CASH PLANS. For the companies that do formal strategic planning, a cash budget, by years, is prepared for the period of the strategic plan. This segment of the plan may cover a period of 5, 10, or 15 years, whatever time horizon is useful for planning purposes. The form is substantially similar to that the annual business plan, shown in Tables 21.1 and 21.2.

TABLE 21.7   Weekly Cash Forecast

THE JOHNSON COMPANY
CASH FORECAST
Weeks Ending July 30, 19XX
(dollars in thousands)

	Week Ending			
	7/9/XX	7/16/XX	7/23/XX	7/30/XX
Beginning balance	$3,700	$1,900	$2,000	$ 1,730
Cash receipts				
Collections on account	$ 800	$1,470	$1,250	$ 2,100
Receipts from divisions	1,900	2,310	1,430	2,870
Drawdown on credit agreement	1,400	2,380	2,230	(2,130)
Sale of fixed assets	300	—	—	—
Total cash receipts	$4,400	$6,160	$4,910	$ 2,840
Total cash available	$8,100	$8,060	$6,910	$ 4,570
Cash disbursements				
Payroll	$ 770	$ 850	$ 910	$ 1,260
Accounts payable	1,430	1,740	1,840	770
Capital expenditures	960	230	760	180
Interest expense	120	140	160	240
Dividends	—	—	470	—
Long-term debt	2,600	—	—	—
Advances to divisions	320	3,100	1,040	—
Total	$6,200	$6,060	$5,180	$ 2,450
Ending balance	$1,900	$2,000	$1,730	$ 2,120

For management purposes, it may be helpful to show the most probable cash budget, together with the optimistic and pessimistic scenarios. Cash planning for the long term is helpful in providing useful information to answer questions relating to:

- The extent, duration, and timing of long-term financing
- Advantageous timing for the liquidation of high-cost existing indebtedness
- Availability of cash for expansion
- Source of funds for major capital expenditures
- Funds available for cash dividends on common stock

FUNDS FLOW STATEMENTS

A comprehensive financial management system must include or consider not only cash, but also net income and financial positions. For this reason, some comments seem appropriate regarding funds flow statements.

It has been mentioned earlier that cash may be budgeted by the direct estimate of cash receipts and disbursements method or by the adjusted net income method. The latter essentially relates to the funds flow statement.

There has been considerable confusion in some areas as to the purpose and use of funds statements. Basically, it is a statement that identifies the sources and uses of funds affecting working capital, either in total or by element. Some of the confusion may have resulted from the multiplicity of titles given to the financial statement. While the Accounting Principles Board recommends the preferred title be Statement of Changes in Financial Position, [1] other past descriptions include:

- Statement of Source and Application of Funds
- Statement of Source and Disposition of Funds
- Statement of Changes in Working Capital
- Funds Statement

Additionally, there has been, and is, variance as to the concept of funds, whether, for example, "funds" should be interpreted as cash or its equivalent, or working capital.

Be that as it may, the Board concluded [2] that information concerning the financing and investing activities of a business enterprise, and the changes in its financial position for a period, is essential for financial statement users, particularly owners and creditors, in making economic decisions. It further opined that when financial statements purporting to present both financial position (balance sheet) and results of operations (statement of income and retained earnings) are issued, a statement summarizing changes in financial position should also be presented as a basic financial statement for each period an income statement is presented. Somewhat the same arguments can be made for presenting to the *management* and board of directors a statement of *planned* changes in financial position when presenting the statement of *planned* income and expenses, and statement of *planned* financial position. This funds statement serves to reconcile the income statement and the balance sheet. It also permits an analysis of changes in working capital that might not be evident from a review of the income statement or the balance sheet, each separately. But, as previously mentioned, the funds statement does not disclose the real magnitude of cash swings and the availability of funds to meet obligations. It is not necessarily a working statement for the use of financial management in the context of short-term cash management. Hence, there is much to be said for the use of both a funds statement and a cash statement in the financial planning and control of the enterprise.

---

[1] *AICPA Professional Standards,* Vol. 3, *Accounting* as of June 1, 1981 (New York: American Institute of Certified Public Accountants, 1981), p. 8053.

[2] Id.

These funds statements are gradually evolving into more understandable statements in the reports made to the shareholders of public companies. An example of the separation of cash provided by operations from financing and investment transactions, is contained in the 1982 Annual Report of CPC International, as shown in Table 21.8. A modified statement of changes in financial position, identifying the major sources and uses of cash, segregated between operating activities, investment activities, and financing activities is that used by the Northrop Corporation in presenting data to its shareholders in the first quarter 1983 interim report, as shown in Table 21.9. This type of statement effectively gets quite close in disclosure to a cash receipts and disbursement format. It well may be that the cash budget or planning statements used internally might include this same format, to give management a clearer perspective.

ENFORCING THE CASH BUDGET

In the control phase of budgeting, the usual procedure is to compare actual with plan (or flexible budget, or both) and take corrective action, where appropriate, to bring actual results in line with plan. Yet, the inability to meet the cash budget results usually from failure to meet other budgets: too much inventory; slow collections; or lower sales than expected. Hence the cash budget cannot be enforced independently of the other budgets of which it is the consequence. Therefore, appropriate action would be to:

1 Analyze the causes of not meeting the budget by area of responsibility.

2 Advise the responsible parties of the under-plan cash (or temporary investments) condition due to their individual activities, and suggest what each should do to get back on plan.

3 Update the current forecast (as in Table 21.6) to ascertain that sufficient cash will be made available to meet business needs; if not, advise the chief financial officer so that appropriate arrangements may be made.

It is often necessary to keep tabs on how cash requirements will be met. A sample weekly cash report is illustrated in Table 21.10. This provides a guide on where the company is not meeting the estimate and where it may require extra effort.

Another simple type of monthy control report, which identifies, within acceptable standard deviation limits, the planned month-end cash balances in the annual plan, before temporary borrowings and compares the actual balance, is illustrated in Figure 21.1.

To be sure, the enforcement of the cash budget generally requires adequate control of inventory, receivables, current liabilities, and income and expense, as well as of all items on the balance sheet — in other words, meeting the annual business plan.

But within the financial management area, the cash manager can be an important motivator in accelerating cash receipts and properly managing dis-

TABLE 21.8   Consolidated Statement of Changes in Financial Position

Years ended December 31

(dollars in millions)

	1982	1981	1980
Cash provided by operations			
Net income	$ 231.6	$218.4	$197.4
Non-cash charges (credits) to net income			
Depreciation	101.3	87.6	74.4
Gain on retirement of debt	(12.4)	—	—
Other	29.6	22.8	8.8
Decrease in noncurrent items due to changes in exchange rates	(45.8)	(39.1)	(2.9)
Changes in working capital			
Notes and accounts receivable	54.5	29.1	(56.5)
Inventories	25.7	76.8	(51.2)
Accounts payable and accrued items	(1.7)	(66.0)	42.3
Cash provided from operations	$ 382.8	$329.6	$212.3
Cash dividends	(101.4)	(91.7)	(81.1)
Cash provided by operations and retained in the business	$ 281.4	$237.9	$131.2
Financing transactions			
Long-term financing	$ 19.1	$141.5	$ 15.2
Short-term financing	(41.8)	(31.0)	92.9
Stock issued for debt	20.7	—	—
Payment of long-term debt	(72.5)	(30.6)	(16.8)
Net financing activities	$ (74.5)	$ 79.9	$ 91.3
Total cash available from operations and financing activities	$ 206.9	$317.8	$222.5
Investment transactions			
Capital expenditures	$ 216.6	$293.5	$235.9
Investment in affiliates	3.5	59.9	14.5
Sale of plants and properties	(17.7)	(47.6)	(8.7)
Deposit reclassified	20.0	—	—
Net cash used by investing activities	$ 222.4	$305.8	$241.7
Increase (decrease) in cash and temporary investments	$ (15.5)	$ 12.0	$ (19.2)
Cash and temporary investments at beginning of year	$ 80.7	$ 68.7	$ 87.9
Cash and temporary investments at end of year	$ 65.2	$ 80.7	$ 68.7

Source: CPC International Inc. and Subsidiaries

TABLE 21.9   Consolidated Condensed Statements of Changes in Financial Position

Quarters ended March 31

(dollars in millions)

	1983	1982
Operating activities		
Sources of cash		
Sales net of change in accounts receivable	$708.8	$498.2
Other income net	1.5	1.8
Decrease in progress payments	(25.4)	50.3
Decrease in advances on contracts	(51.7)	(19.9)
Cash provided by operating activities	$633.2	$530.4
Uses of cash		
Cost of sales, net of changes in inventories, payables and accruals	$770.7	$611.4
Less: Depreciation and amortization	(21.4)	(12.7)
Less: Amortization of unvested employee restricted award shares	(1.6)	(1.4)
Income taxes	3.9	(1.9)
Cash used by operating activities	$751.6	$595.4
Net cash used by operating activities	($118.4)	($ 65.0)
Cash dividends	(6.9)	(6.8)
	($125.3)	($ 71.8)
Investment activities		
Additions to property, plant and equipment	$ (74.2)	$ (40.7)
Carrying value of disposals of property, plant and equipment	0.1	0.2
Increase in other assets	(2.3)	(0.7)
Net cash used in investment activities	$ (76.4)	$ (41.2)
Financing activities		
Increase in short-term obligations	$ 82.9	$ (2.0)
Repayment of long-term debt	(2.1)	(2.2)
Net interest income	1.2	6.0
Issuance of common stock	2.0	2.0
Net proceeds from financing activities	$ 84.0	$ 3.8
Decrease in cash and cash items	($117.7)	($109.2)
Cash and cash items at beginning of period	124.6	194.3
Cash and cash items at end of period	$ 6.9	$ 85.1

Source: Northrop Corporation and Subsidiaries

TABLE 21.10   Comparison of Actual and Estimated Cash Activity

THE HICKS COMPANY
WEEKLY CASH REPORT
Week Ended November 16, 19XX
(dollars in thousands)

	Actual Week Ended 11/16/XX	Month to Date Actual	Month to Date Estimated
Beginning cash balance	$17,890	$ 32,511	$ 32,510
Cash receipts			
Government	$10,810	$ 18,310	$ 18,000
Wholesale	19,620	67,730	65,500
Retail	8,330	21,100	23,400
Total	$38,760	$107,140	$106,900
Cash disbursements			
Accounts payable — expenses	$12,330	$ 12,860	$ 12,300
Payrolls	12,660	37,010	36,900
Material purchases	1,890	19,340	14,300
Federal taxes	2,790	8,640	8,920
Capital expenditures	13,370	39,990	40,190
Other	1,060	2,030	2,000
Total	$44,100	$119,870	$114,610
Ending cash balance	$12,550	$ 19,781	$ 24,800
Estimated month-end balance			$ 30,000

bursements. The improved procedures, which ultimately should be recognized in the cash budget, usually result in lower required balances for operating purposes. Techniques accomplishing this, together with increased earnings resulting from more effective management of temporary investments, is discussed in Chapter 24.

COMPUTER MODELS FOR CASH BUDGETING

A basic question to be answered in cash planning is whether or not a computer model should be used. To begin with, it may be helpful to define a model or, more specifically, a financial model. An aircraft, ship, or bridge may be represented by a physical small-scale model, a representation in relief or in three dimensions, made of wood, plastic, metal, and so forth. Problems may be

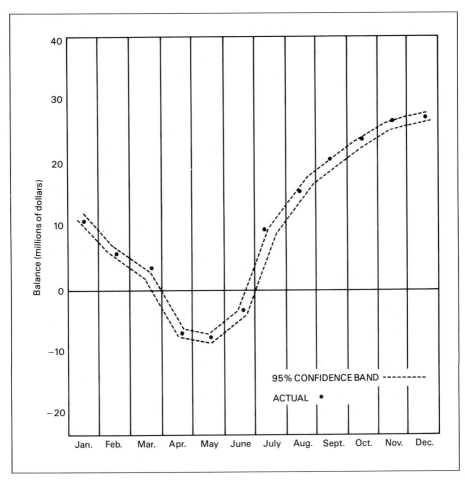

FIG. 21.1 Planned and Actual Cash Balances

resolved by studying such models and their workings. However, a business also may be represented by a financial model. This may be defined as the logic and data for the enterprise expressed in accounting terms. The output may be a projected financial statement: the income and expense statement; the balance sheet; or the cash flow statement; together with related supplemental data.

Financial models may be categorized as one of three basic types, depending largely on the intended usage: (1) deterministic, (2) probabilistic, or (3) optimizing. Most models for cash budgeting probably would be of the single dimension or one-case type, with the capacity to evaluate different assumptions given to it, and to provide the magnitude of impact on, in this case, the cash balance. It helps provide answers to "what if" questions. The other two types of models might be regarded as supplementing the deterministic one. Thus, a probabilistic model produces a range of answers, not merely one, and the probability associated with achieving it. Probabilistic models may play a part in determining the probability of achieving the planned cash balance. The optimizing model seeks the optimal or "best" answer by adjusting or substituting the variables in discrete amounts and testing the results to locate the best combination.

These models may be further classified as one of three types, depending on the time horizon and type of planning. Thus, a *strategic* model might deal with a five-year horizon, seeking the amount of required new funds, based on various long-range assumptions. A *tactical* model will be more detailed, and cover each month of the annual one-year business plan. It might deal with the impact of changing cash uses at different times in the year. An *operational* model might deal with the daily cash budget for a week or a month.

In the real world, a planning system might be regarded as a group of several models or programs, each of which may run alone or in conjunction with the other ones. One representation of a planning system is shown in Figure 21.2. In this instance the cash model is one of five; the others are the sales model, the manufacturing model, the cost model, and the profit model. In the illustration, the models or programs are represented by rectangles; the cylinders are storage areas for information; and the arrows identify the direction in which data flows. Each model refers to a specific area of budget responsibility, has its own sources of data, and its own output. Each model can transfer data to other models as needed, or operate on its own information.

The point to be made is that it is quite practical and useful to have a cash model for cash budgeting, related normally to the entire planning system.

Reasons for Using a Computer Model

A basic question is, Should we use a computer in cash budgeting? The answer probably is yes, and the reasons are simple. Proper cash planning, along with the other segments of business planning, must consider alternatives: possible changes in timing of major or cumulative cash receipts or disbursements; or changes in magnitude. Even in a small company the clerical burden is horrendous, when assumptions are varied and manual methods are used to determine the figures for the revised scenario. Thus, assume a cash budget is being prepared, by months, for a two-year period. A change in cash receipts in any one month affects the cash balance for each succeeding month of the planning period. And suppose there are many changes? Given the "ripple effect" of even a single change, the financial model can quickly calculate the new answer for all affected items, and produce the new amounts. The computerized burden is placed on the machine, and not on the financial staff.

The desirability of using computer models to assist in the budgeting and managing of cash is made cost effective by the extensive availability of the personnel computer and the many related and inexpensive software programs.

Some Applications of Financial Modeling

A financial model permits the user to simulate the future, using various assumptions or planned actions, and provides quantitative estimates of the impact of these planned events. In effect, various moves can be studied without putting money, material, or men at risk. Businessmen can consider very

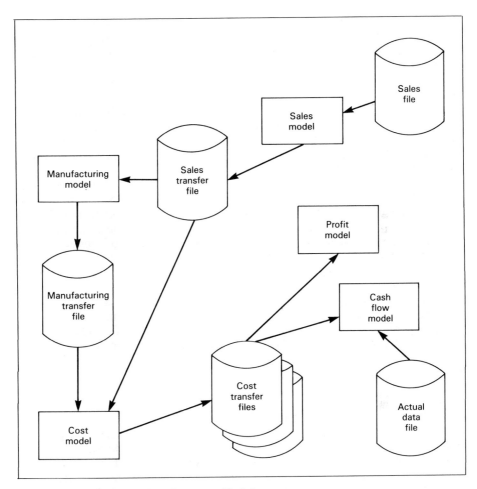

FIG. 21.2 Business Planning System — Models

quickly, and in great detail, the possible effect of selected potential actions. In addition, these financial models can be used to analyze past actions or performance to see where and why the problem occurred, and generally arrive at corrective steps.

Some of the financial models, which, directly or indirectly, bear on cash budgeting, include such segments as:

- Annual business plan, all functions
- Cash flow forecasting and analysis
- Sales planning and analysis
- Material and labor requirements
- Inventory planning and analysis
- Capital expenditure, evaluation, and analysis
- Merger and acquisition analysis

Computer models specifically involving cash budgeting and management can range from very simple to very detailed and complex, depending on the purpose served and the magnitude of the problems. Thus, a simple cash budgeting model may involve assumed cash receipts, using an average collection lag from the sales budget (as discussed earlier in this chapter) or an average lag in accounts payable, to arrive at estimated cash balances. Other models may track major sales to specific customers, or employ sophisticated statistical applications for smoothing cash flows to arrive at presumably more accurate budgets. Simple models can be effectively used in most companies. However, some circumstances may warrant extensive cash budget simulations to better reflect uncertainty and to simultaneously improve the accuracy of cash forecasting.[3]

In cash management, discussed in detail in Chapter 24, computer models often are used to predict disbursement float, determine optional geographic location of lockboxes, or determine changes in the collection system. In the cash budgeting function (in the planning and control phases), in a nonoperational sense, financial models have been developed to more easily provide planning and control data as follows:

Planning
□ Planning cash inflows:
  • In total for the time segments involved, by organization element — division, subsidiary, overall company
  • By major customers and specifically planned sales
  • By tracking accounts receivable
  • In tracing float

□ Planning short-term cash outflows:
  • By objective of expenditure, based on historical averages or pattern
  • By analysis of accounts payroll, accrual expenses, etc.
  • Forecasting disbursement float or check clearing time

□ Planning long-term cash requirements:
  • Acquisitions and mergers
  • Capital appropriations
  • Inflation impact

Control
□ Daily bank balances report
□ Actual versus planned cash receipts and disursements
□ Estimated daily working capital
□ Daily bank borrowings

The reader is referred to the currently extensive material on software programs, and capabilities of the smaller micro- and minicomputers.

---

[3] See, for example, David F. Scoot, Jr. et al., "Implementation of a Cash Budget Simulator at Air Canada," *Financial Management* (Summer, 1979), pp. 46–52.

SUGGESTED READING

"Financial Modeling Software: Tools for the Overworked Manager." *Personal Computing* (June 1981), pp. 22–28, 58–65.

Grand, Jeremy. "Using Computers to Manage Your Cash." *Journals of Systems Management* (Jan. 1983), pp. 32–33.

Nori, Rino. "Cash Management: Using Computers Gives More Bang to Your Bucks." *Data Management* (May 1982), pp. 28–30.

Stone, Bernell K., and Robert A. Wood. "Daily Cash Forecasting: A Simple Method for Implementing the Distribution Approach." *Financial Management* (Fall 1977), pp. 40–50.

Sweeney, H. W. Allen, and Robert Racklin, eds. *Handbook of Budgeting,* Chapter 16. New York: John Wiley & Sons, 1981.

Willson, James D. *Budget and Profit Planning Manual,* Chapter 19. New York: Warren, Gorham & Lamont, 1983.

———, and John B. Campbell. *Controllership, The Work of the Managerial Accountant,* Chapter 19. New York: John Wiley & Sons, 1981.

22

Financial Forecasting and Planning

DONALD E. REED

INTRODUCTION

All successful companies have clearly defined goals that identify where management wants to have the firm a certain number of time periods in the future. An integral and indispensable part of defining goals is the development of fairly detailed financial forecasts, beginning at the smallest business unit within a company and then consolidating the forecasts. As part of forecasting, both internal and external financing requirements and opportunities are identified. Anticipation of financing needs is beneficial both in the area of time planning and in the identification of appropriate types and sources of funds. It is often too late, for example, to recognize near the end of a quarter that during the next quarter substantial operating capital is required. Market opportunities could be missed or capital costs could be excessive and, as a result, the perceptions of the company in the financial marketplace as well as the value of the company to its shareholders could decline.

TABLE 22.1   Cash Flow Planning Sheet

	Year 1	Year 2	Year 3	Year 4	Year 5
Sales revenue					
Manufacturing cost	____	____	____	____	____
Gross margin					
Fixed costs					
Depreciation	____	____	____	____	____
Operating income					
Interest	____	____	____	____	____
Pretax income					
Tax	____	____	____	____	____
After-tax income					
Depreciation	____	____	____	____	____
Cash flow from operations					
Capital expenditures					
Dividends	____	____	____	____	____
Net cash flow	════	════	════	════	════

THE MODEL

Table 22.1 provides a way to look at the basic forecasting process. With minor alteration it can provide a profit and loss statement for financial accounting purposes and also can be used to derive a balance sheet on the same basis. The following sections describe the development of each line in the table and then show how the table is actually employed.

Sales Forecasting

The best and often the only good way of developing a sales forecast is to have the people who actually sell the product prepare the sales outlook. This, on the surface, seems to be fairly easy to accomplish. Most forecasts, however, tend to be straight lines with their slopes exactly equal to the direction sales took over the past two periods. That is, if 1983 sales were better than 1982 sales, most sales forecasts will show 1984 sales as better than 1983. The obverse is true as well. If a respected economic or econometric forecast from either internal or external sources can be used as an overlay or template, then the tendency to picture the immediate future may be modified.

The sales forecasting for a small, one product company is identical to that for a very large multiproduct firm. The forecaster is charged with answering the following questions: Given that the nation's economy will grow at x rate for y years and consumer spending (or basic steel or machine tools, etc.) will lead (be concurrent with or lag) gross national product (GNP) growth, who will buy the company's product and how much will they buy? In addition, given the forecast rate of inflation and the assessment of competitive and technological forces, what price, net of customer discount, is expected to be received for each product from each customer? Will all sales be made in domestic markets, or will there be any export sales?

The sales force should be required to provide its forecast with as much detail as can be developed for two reasons. First, management may wish to amend the forecast (although this should be done with trepidation, since the sales force knows the customers best). Second, the detailed forecast forms the basis of post-period audit. The audit can address such questions as: What happened to the sales to company X? Were volume expectations met? Did price increases hold up? What can be done to correct a wayward situation? The requirement to develop a detailed sales forecast forces the creation of a formal marketing plan, especially if management will be looking at performance based on the sales person's own forecast.

Manufacturing Cost

There are two basic types of direct manufacturing costs: variable and fixed. Variable costs are those that are volume sensitive. For example, for every extra ton of steel, so much electricity is needed, so many hours of labor, so much ore. By breaking out the factors that comprise variable costs, manufacturing costs can be forecast.

Again, the manufacturing people should be required to provide sufficient detail in variable cost to let management assess the forecast both on a prospective and retrospective basis. Fixed manufacturing costs are partially volume sensitive, but as the title implies, will not go away unless production ceases. Part of the labor expense (e.g., supervising efforts) will remain constant at most levels of production. Other fixed manufacturing expenses include a portion of utilities (e.g., lighting, heat, and water), manager's salaries, and attendant office expense. These costs are less sensitive to general economic conditions but cannot be blindly included in a forecast in disregard of the overall economic environment.

Gross margin or operating margin is simply sales minus manufacturing costs. For a multiproduct company, gross margin for a corporate forecast is the sum of each product line gross margin.

Fixed Costs

Two groups of costs generally do not vary with volume: direct fixed costs and indirect overhead costs. Typically, the direct fixed costs include a portion of labor expense, insurance, rentals, building expense (excluding depreciation), a portion of utilities, local property taxes, and office expenses at the manufacturing location. Indirect fixed costs would include wages and salaries of the corporate headquarters, which in a multiproduct company might be allocated to each operating location as a function of sales volume, employment levels, or assets employed. In addition, most corporate level overhead expenses fall into the category of country club memberships, donations, catering, and other nondiscretionary costs absolutely essential to maintain the espirit de corps of the senior corporate staff.

Excluded from fixed costs is depreciation, which, because of its effect on taxation and cash flow, needs to be calculated on a consolidated basis; that is, without regard to individual operating locations. Depreciation, on a tax basis, is included in analyses or forecasts of financial performance for operating locations where discounted cash flow or internal rate of return analyses are used to determine whether incremental investment at that location is justified.

Depreciation

Depreciation is a financial representation of the deterioration, in both a physical and economic sense, of the assets used in the production of a company's goods. In the context of financial planning, it can also be viewed as a cash generator because it is a deduction from income subject to tax; in other words, for every dollar of depreciation, the taxpayer can avoid 50 cents of income tax. Further, the generation of cash occurs at a level beyond the actual physical depreciation of the equipment. In the context of this forecasting procedure, all of these characteristics must be considered.

From the perspective of financial accounting, depreciation is a profit and loss item, or an operating expense; from the balance sheet perspective, the accumulation of depreciation reduces gross assets. Where depreciation is applied to producing assets, renewal capital expenditure can be estimated; that is, cash flow items that will require funding can be predicted.

At the same time, depreciation, for tax purposes, generates cash through the reduction of income taxes payable. The amount of depreciation appearing in a product line financial forecast must be adjusted for the corporation as a whole to develop the proper net income for tax purposes, and such adjustment can be substantial. In an emerging company with a fairly high level of new investment, the difference between tax basis and book basis depreciation can be substantial. In a more mature firm with a lower level of new net fixed investment, the reverse could be the case. Taxation as a percent of net book earnings would be much greater, thus causing cash requirements beyond that which would be inferred from a product line or profit center forecast of gross margin. The depreciation question should be given to the tax department or the firm's tax advisor for resolution, since the calculation of the amount of depreciation can be fairly detailed and subject to current tax regulations.

Operating Income

The line for operating income on Table 22.1 simply represents the profitability of operations, before the effect of interest, taxes, and external financing.

Interest and Finance Costs

The interest line on Table 22.1 has two elements: existing interest and interest and finance charges incurred as a result of new financing. The sum is derived both from this forecasting exercise and preparation of a balance sheet. In many corporations where the borrowing or finance function is centralized, the corporate treasury staff develops the interest expense number. In any event, computing this number is one of the last calculations performed, since business results plus investments made during the immediately preceding period will be the basis for the calculation of incremental finance charges. Unlike the sales and operating forecasts, which are relatively discrete from year to year, these calculations are done in series. In addition, a change in funds required or generated early in the planning period would require a recalculation of all succeeding years.

To this point, only the volume portion of interest expense has been addressed; equally important is the price portion. Unfortunately, consistently accurate forecasts of interest rates are nearly impossible to make. Anyone who ever achieved a dependable level of accuracy probably made so much money from his success that he took early retirement, and thereby ceased making accurate forecasts. Nevertheless, some attempt must be made to estimate both the direction and magnitude of change of interest rates, both short- and long-term. (See Chapter 13 for an analysis of interest rates.) Both categories of rates must be addressed, since it does not follow that all incremental borrowing will be either short- or long-term but rather some combination of the two, depending upon the desired complexion of the balance sheet.

The farther into the distance one gazes, the greater the need for corrective lenses; when it comes to interest rates, at a certain point even a radio telescope is inadequate to provide clarity. One suggested method of forecasting interest rates is to look forward on a quarterly basis for the first year of the plan and on an annual basis thereafter. However, some forecasters shy away from even the near term quarterly outlook and just pick an average rate for the year. Either method can be chosen because any misses in the interest rate forecast are bound to be offset by inaccuracies elsewhere in the assumptions, especially the more distant the horizon.

Taxation

For the most part, it is easiest to assume a 50 percent tax rate on net income. The actual rate can be made up of federal, state, and local income taxes as appropriate. For forecasting purposes, a rate of a flat 50 percent, although not exact, is reasonable. It should be kept in mind that for a single-product company, especially one with a relatively small net income, the assumed tax rate can be dramatically different from 50 percent. There are other, more complex considerations here, such as carry back or carry forward, investment tax credit, foreign tax credits, and dividend withholdings.

Maybe the best way to forecast taxes in a complex international company is to prepare the consolidated profit and loss statement, on a cash or tax basis, that can be reviewed by the company's internal tax department or outside accountant. That person can take into account all (or most) of the tricky tax considerations and some major swings in cash generation; as a result, the financing needs of the company can be predicted more accurately. The tax planning aspect is also important in determining the investment posture of the firm, its view toward tax-based leasing, venture capital, and other opportunities or requirements imposed on the firm. Therefore, even though the taxation part of the forecasting process is easily the most complicated, it cannot and should not be ignored.

Capital Expenditure and New Investment

There are five fairly straightforward elements in capital expenditure: maintenance capital, environmental requirements, expansion capital, new product investment, and external acquisitions. In each case an expenditure or event in the first year of the forecast will work its way through most of the cash flow categories in succeeding periods. Maintenance capital may reduce variable manufacturing costs, or just keep it even in some instances, while environmental expenditures may have no profit and loss effect other than an increase in tax depreciation and a consequent reduction in taxes. Expansion capital or new product investment will have an impact on every item in succeeding years' forecasts, and external acquisitions could change the complexion of the entire forecast as well as the balance sheet configuration.

Again, these items need to be built from the bottom, starting pretty much in the order previously shown. Usually, all but the last category, acquisitions, can and should be developed by the operating entities.

Dividends

Dividends on preferred and common stock are after-tax items. They are linked to the number of shares outstanding or, in the case of a privately or closely held company, are negotiated. Among the factors considered in computing dividends are: how much the company must retain for reinvestment, how much should be paid to maintain the market price of the stock, historical dividend policy, industry practice, and cash availability. (See Chapter 30 for an analysis of dividend policy.)

Dynamics

The calculation of corporate net cash flow is simple arithmetic, given a reasonably consistent generation of the basic numbers. The process, however, soon leads to iterations in series, as previously mentioned. The results of year 1 need to be developed before going on to year 2 and so forth. Furthermore, if extreme accuracy is desired, iterations within each study period will also be required; for example, if a significant investment is made in the first quarter, then cash required for the rest of the year, and the value of short-term investments, debt, or equity, will change, as will interest expense or dividends in quarters 2 through 4. A daily financial forecast would provide as much mathematical accuracy as possible, but obviously such effort would be fruitless. Monthly calculations for the three months following the forecast, then three quarters, then annual, should provide about as much information as can be used effectively and has some reasonable chance of being accurate.

Before proceeding from year 1 to year 2, however, financial statements on a basis compatible with those that would be published, would need to be prepared.

A CASE STUDY

What follows is a constructive example of the first part of the forecasting process: the attempt to predict operating events and consequent financing requirements.

Building the Estimates

The Zed Corporation has two divisions: Wonderful and Incredible. In November of each year the management of each division submits its five-year forecast of the business. Table 22.2 shows that the Wonderful Division enjoys steady growth both in volume and price. When the president of the Wonderful Division reviewed the economic forecasts he had received from both the corporate office and his own outside sources, he deduced that demand for his products would exceed the growth of the economy over the next five years. However, he also felt that his pricing policy would be determined more by the rate of inflation than by demand. Thus, with real GNP growth forecast at 5.5 percent and inflation at 4.5 percent, he forecast an annual average growth rate of 8.5 percent for sales volume, about 1.5 times that of the entire economy, but only a 4.5 percent average growth rate in price, equal to the increase in the Consumer Price Index.

He also felt that there was a need for maintenance capital over the next five years, but on a real basis, growing very slowly. Because he has adequate existing capacity to produce at his forecast sales levels, and because his plant produced absolutely no pollution, other capital expenditures were nil.

The president of the Incredible Division, on the other hand, felt that his product was in a much more competitive environment, with demand more a function of price. Even though he reviewed the same economic forecasts as his golfing buddy over at Wonderful, his outlook was very different, primarily because his products were much more sensitive to foreign competition. Because of these strong pressures, Incredible's president believed that within the next two to three years there would be a shakeout in the industry. Therefore, he wanted to be prepared to step in and take over that part of the market vacated by producers that he felt would eventually close their doors. He believed that his business prospects were not good for the first three years of the forecast period, but that in year three he would strongly recommend a significant expansion of capacity. That expansion would have to be financed from the corporate funds flow, either internal or external, and would just begin to throw off sizeable earnings after about a year of production. In addition, ongoing maintenance capital requirements would increase slightly. Again, he ran a pristine operation, so good in fact that it took in dirty air and water and returned them perfectly clean.

TABLE 22.2   Forecast for Wonderful Division

WONDERFUL DIVISION

FORECAST
(dollars in thousands)

	Year 1	Year 2	Year 3	Year 4	Year 5
Revenue					
Volume	1 mil	1.2 mil	1.2 mil	1.5 mil	1.5 mil
Price (dollars/unit)	1.0	1.05	1.20	1.30	1.42
Total revenue	$1,000	$1,260	$1,560	$1,950	$2,125
Manufacturing cost					
Variable (dollars/unit)	0.25	0.27	0.27	0.30	0.35
Fixed	125	125	125	160	200
Total manufacturing cost	$375	$449	$476	$610	$725
Gross margin	$625	$811	$1,084	$1,340	$1,400
Fixed capital	$100	$100	$100	$110	$110

Consolidating Forecasts

When the Vice-President — Finance of the Zed Corporation received the two division forecasts (Tables 22.2 and 22.3), he started the corporate financial forecast by preparing the skeleton format for the entire company, as shown in Table 22.1. It was fairly easy to fill in the revenue, manufacturing cost, and gross margin lines, those being nothing more than the combination of the two divisions' sales and manufacturing forecasts.

The first three lines of the corporate forecast equal the sum of the same lines from Table 22.2 and 22.3. He then gathered his own corporate expenses (Table 22.4) to develop the fixed cost line.

The next part of the cash flow forecast, depreciation, required some calculation. The V.P. knew, from the previous year's forecast, the amount of depreciation (tax basis) generated by existing assets. He then took the combined fixed-capital requirements of the divisions, shown in Table 22.5, and since all the fixed-capital requirements were machinery and equipment, he used the appropriate rates for five-year Accelerated Cost Recovery System (ACRS) equipment supplied by his tax manager, who also provided the amount of investment tax credit. In addition, the tax manager estimated the timing of the usage of the benefits (for this example ignoring the possibility of carry back or carry forward), which are a function of the date the equipment is placed in service. He assumed that all of the maintenance capital would be placed in service during the year of expenditure and would be immediately depreciable. However, the expansion capital needed by the Incredible Division, because of

TABLE 22.3   Forecast for Incredible Division

INCREDIBLE DIVISION
FORECAST
(dollars in thousands)

	Year 1	Year 2	Year 3	Year 4	Year 5
Revenue					
Volume	2.5 mil	2.5 mil	2.5 mil	3.1 mil	3.5 mil
Price (dollars/unit)	5.00	5.25	5.10	5.2	5.20
Total revenue	$12,500	$13,125	$12,750	$16,120	$18,200
Manufacturing cost					
Variable (dollars/unit)	1.50	1.55	1.55	1.60	1.55
Fixed	2,500	2,650	2,800	3,000	3,500
Total manufacturing cost	$6,250	$6,525	$6,675	$7,960	$8,925
Gross margin	$6,250	$6,600	$6,075	$8,160	$9,275
Fixed capital					
Maintenance	$300	$300	$ 350	$400	$500
Expansion			5,000		

TABLE 22.4   Projected Costs for Corporate Office

CORPORATE HEADQUARTERS
PROJECTED COSTS
(dollars in thousands)

	Year 1	Year 2	Year 3	Year 4	Year 5
Fixed costs					
Salaries	$2,500	$2,500	$2,650	$3,500	$3,750
Utilities, etc.	150	150	160	200	250
Selling, general, and administrative expense	1,425	1,049	999	1,300	1,000
Total	$4,075	$3,699	$3,809	$5,000	$5,000

the size and timing of the project, would not be spent until early the following year, and depreciation and investment tax credit would not be applicable until then.

Again, these calculations, also shown in Table 22.5, were performed simultaneously for all years of the forecast and added in to the corporate financial forecast.

TABLE 22.5   Combined Fixed Capital Requirements

	Year 1	Year 2	Year 3	Year 4	Year 5
Fixed-capital expenditures					
Maintenance	$ 400	$400	$ 450	$ 510	$ 610
Expansion	—	—	5,000	—	—
Environmental	—	—	—	—	—
Acquisition	—	—	—	—	—
Total	$ 400	$400	$5,450	$ 510	$ 610
Depreciation calculation (assuming five-year ACRS property)					
Year 1	$ 60	$ 88	$ 84	$ 84	$ 84
Year 2	—	60	88	84	84
Year 3	—	—	68	99	95
Year 4	—	—	—	827	1,212
Year 5	—	—	—	—	92
	$ 60	$148	$ 240	$1,094	$1,567
Depreciation (tax basis)					
Existing capital	$1,000	$750	$ 500	$ 250	$ 100
New capital	60	148	240	1,094	1,567
Total	$1,060	$898	$ 740	$1,344	$1,667
Investment tax credit	$ 40	$ 40	$ 45	$ 551	$ 61

Dynamics

At this point, the dynamic calculations began. The V.P.-Finance knew his cost of debt capital, debt outstanding at the beginning of the period, and dividend requirements (see Table 22.6, col. 1). From these figures he could calculate interest expense for year 1 of the forecast. He assumed, even though he knew that it was slightly inaccurate, that his divisions would not remit cash to corporate headquarters until the end of the year (earnings on cash are ignored). (See Chapter 24 for detailed analyses of the cash management process.) Therefore, he calculated the net cash flow for year 1 as follows. Since interest expense on outstanding debt was $170, pretax income in year 1 (Table 22.8, col. 1) was $1,570. He gave that number to his tax manager who calculated that year's tax, as shown in Table 22.7, col. 1. The V.P. took that amount, $745, plugged it back into his forecast, calculated after-tax income, and added back depreciation (a noncash item), thus deriving cash flow from operations. He then subtracted the amount required for capital expenditures and dividend payments (both after-tax items) and produced the first year's net cash flow, $485 (all shown in Table 22.8, col. 1).

TABLE 22.6 Interest and Finance Costs

CORPORATE HEADQUARTERS
INTEREST AND FINANCE COSTS
(dollars in thousands)

	Current Year	Year 1	Year 2	Year 3	Year 4	Year 5
NEW FINANCING						
Net cash flow	N/A	$ 485	$ 705	($4,169)	$1,599	$1,636
Source of funds						
Short-term debt	N/A	(285)	(215)	669	(669)	—
Long-term debt	N/A	(200)	(490)	1,000	(930)	(380)
Equity	N/A	—	—	2,500	—	—
Net cash position	—	—	—	—	—	$1,256
EXISTING FINANCING						
Short-term debt						
Amount	$ 500	$ 215	—	$ 669	—	—
Rate	0.10	0.10	0.10	0.10	0.10	0.10
Interest expense	$ 50	$ 22	—	$ 67	—	—
Long-term debt						
Amount	$1,000	$ 800	$ 310	$1,310	$ 380	—
Rate	0.12	0.12	0.12	0.12	0.12	0.12
Interest expense	$ 120	$ 96	$ 37	$ 157	$ 46	—
Total interest expense	$ 170	$ 118	$ 37	$ 224	$ 46	—
Equity						
Shares outstanding	1,000	1,000	1,000	1,250	1,250	1,250
Dividend ($1/share)	$1,000	$1,000	$1,000	$1,250	$1,250	$1,250
Market price (dollars/share)	$ 15	$ 12	$ 12	$ 10	$ 12	$ 15

TABLE 22.7   Income Tax Calculation

	Year 1	Year 2	Year 3	Year 4	Year 5
Pretax income	$1,570	$2,334	$3,173	$2,936	$3,537
Tax	$ 785	$1,167	$1,587	$1,468	$1,769
Investment tax credit	(40)	(40)	(45)	(551)	(61)
Net tax	$ 745	$1,127	$1,632	$ 917	$1,708

TABLE 22.8   Cash Flow Forecast

CORPORATE FORECAST OF CASH
(dollars in thousands)

	Year 1	Year 2	Year 3	Year 4	Year 5
Revenue	$13,500	$14,385	$14,310	$18,070	$ 20,325
Manufacturing cost	(6,625)	(7,336)	(6,551)	(8,570)	(10,075)
Gross margin	$ 6,875	$ 7,049	$ 7,759	$ 9,500	$ 10,250
Fixed costs	(4,075)	(3,699)	(3,809)	(5,000)	(5,000)
Depreciation	(1,060)	(898)	(740)	(1,340)	(1,667)
Operating income	$ 1,740	$ 2,452	$ 3,210	$3,160	$ 3,583
Interest	(170)	(118)	(37)	(224)	(46)
Pretax income	$ 1,570	$ 2,334	$ 3,173	$ 2,936	$ 3,537
Tax	(745)	(1,127)	(1,632)	(917)	(1,708)
After-tax income	$ 825	$ 1,207	$ 1,541	$ 2,019	$ 1,829
Depreciation	1,060	898	740	1,340	1,667
Cash flow from operations	$ 1,885	$ 2,105	$ 2,281	$ 3,359	$ 3,496
Capital expenditures	(400)	(400)	(5,450)	(510)	(610)
Dividends	(1,000)	(1,000)	(1,000)	(1,250)	(1,250)
Net cash flow	$ 485	$ 705	$ (4,169)	$ 1,599	$ 1,636

He then moved on to year 2 of the forecast. Again, the operating income line was complete so he had to derive the information from interest expense on down.

Table 22.6, col. 2 shows this process. The V.P.-Finance assumed that he would use the $485 to pay down $285 of short-term debt and $200 of long-term debt, in order to maintain a certain balance in these categories. The new interest expense was then $118. He followed the same process in year 2 to derive net cash flow as previously described. Moving along with great dispatch, the V.P.

continued the calculations for all but the last three lines of the forecast for year 3, at which time significant external funds would be required to finance the expansion at the Incredible Division.

The V.P. again assumed that all events occurred at year-end, and for the sake of illustration, he financed the net cash requirement from year 3 immediately at the beginning of year 4. The V.P. looked at his pro forma year-end balance sheet and determined that 40 percent of the incremental funds would be derived from debt and 60 percent from a new equity issue. (The split between these two sources is arbitrary at this point in the example, but will be addressed more fully later.)

From this point forward, the iterative process is the same as previously described, merely working down through interest, income, tax, and so on through to the end of the forecast period.

Having completed these tasks before lunch, the V.P. decided to take a break. Since he was an important fellow in the financial environment of the company, he had been invited to lunch by one of his friendly bankers. Even though the good V.P. knew that there was no such thing as a free lunch, he went anyway. He did recognize that he had a ton of work to do after lunch, so he limited himself to a meal of cold crabs and ice water. He would be ready to dive back into Financial Forecasting and Planning with clear head and sharp eye.

Financing Requirements

The V.P. returned to his office, rolled up his sleeves, and went to work on the second major part of his forecast, the implications of the upcoming year's activity on the Zed Corporation's balance sheet. (It should be noted that the numbers in the following tables are not consistent with those presented earlier. These numbers were created for illustrative purposes only.)

Being a public company with both debt and equity issues trading in New York, Zed needed to be aware of the impact that ratings for both debt and equity issues would have on the company's cost of funds. Without going into great detail, debt ratings are determined by a number of things, including quality of earnings, balance sheet strength, growth rates both historic and forecast, industry outlook, dividend policy, and strength of management. (See Chapter 19 for an analysis of credit ratings.) Only the balance sheet character could be influenced by the V.P. with any success, and that was his task for that afternoon.

The V.P. used all the divisional and corporate profit and cash flow data generated thus far to put together a corporate profit and loss statement, a source and application statement (Table 22.9), and finally, using both of these, a balance sheet for both the recent year-end and the next year-end (Table 22.10; Table 22.11 is a key or cross-reference between Tables 22.9 and 22.10). Since Zed was an industrial company subject to swings in overall economic activity and, thus, its earnings varied with economic cycles, it had to maintain liquidity and a strong equity base. A strong balance sheet was needed to provide adequate reserves to maintain the business when sales and earnings deteriorated, and thus maintain the current bond and stock ratings.

TABLE 22.9   Source and Application of Cash

ZED CORPORATION
SOURCE AND APPLICATION OF CASH
For the Period 19X4
(dollars in millions)

		Key
Sources of funds		
Pretax income	$ 255	1
Depreciation and amortization	50	2
Proceeds from stock issue	500	3
Proceeds from long-term debt	300	4
Total	$1,100	
Applications of funds		
Increase in working capital	$ 125	5
Purchase of fixed assets	825	6
Payment of taxes	150	7
Payment of dividends	100	8
Total	$1,200	
Increase (decrease) of cash	$ (100)	9

From the divisions' forecasts, the V.P. knew that 19X4 would not be a banner year, but he also knew that a major acquisition would take place nevertheless. His goal, then, was to try to maintain appropriate financial ratios during the year. The first thing he needed to know was the approximate size and character of the proposed acquisition. He was advised that the purchase would be of a private nature, could only be funded with cash, and that the total cost would be approximately $800 million. It was immediately obvious that even though he had enjoyed a splendid lunch that day with his friendly banker, even good old deep-pockets would not be willing to fund a cash requirement of that magnitude. He also knew that such an increase in debt (preferably long-term debt, since the bulk of the purchase was for producing assets) would severely increase the debt/equity ratio at a time when he could not really afford the risk or the debt service requirements.

His plan consisted of three parts: (1) raise equity to improve the ratios; (2) with the improved ratios, raise some long-term debt; and (3) use the proceeds of both to make the acquisition. He also knew that Zed's existing operations would be largely self-sustaining.

The question of the moment was how much equity and how much debt. From the balance sheet perspective, an equity issue of the full amount would be best. However, an $800 million issue was too big and would be very difficult to sell. The V.P. decided that if Zed could maintain its ratios during 19X4, future

TABLE 22.10   Balance Sheet

ZED CORPORATION
BALANCE SHEET
(dollars in millions)

	Dec. 31, 19X3	19X4 Activity	Dec. 31, 19X4
Assets			
Current assets			
Cash	$ 125	($100)	$ 25
Accounts receivable	2,625	250	2,875
Other	82	—	82
Subtotal	$2,832	$150	$2,982
Investment in unconsolidated subsidiaries	$ 422	$ 20	$ 442
Fixed assets	1,055	775	1,830
Intangibles	120	(5)	115
Other	238	(12)	226
Total assets	$4,667	$928	$5,595
Liabilities and stockholders' equity			
Current liabilities			
Short-term debt	$ 82	—	$ 82
Accounts payable	1,007	$125	1,132
Other	128	—	128
Subtotal	$1,217	$125	$1,342
Long-Term debt	$ 885	$300	$1,185
Other liabilities	222	(125)	97
Subtotal	$2,324	$300	$2,624
Stockholders' equity			
Capital stock (20 million shares at $1 par)	$ 700	$500	$1,200
Retained earnings	1,565	128	1,693
Foreign currency adjustment	78	—	78
Subtotal	$2,343	$628	$2,971
Total liabilities and stockholders' equity	$4,667	$928	$5,595

growth, both from existing operations and from the acquired company, would enhance the balance sheet satisfactorily. With an equity issue of about $500 million and then a debt issue of about $300 million plus forecast activity during the year, he felt that the major ratios of financial strength would be maintained as follows:

TABLE 22.11   Key to Activity

Balance Sheet 19X4 Activity (Table 22.10)	Source and Application Statement (Table 21.9)
Changes in assets	
■ Cash — decrease of $100	Item 9, net of all cash items
■ Accounts receivable — increase of $250	Resulting from increased sales (not shown) and reflected in Item 9 (increase in working capital)
■ Investment in unconsolidated subsidiaries — increase of $20	Earnings of subsidiaries during year included in Item 1
■ Fixed assets — increase of $775	Net of Item 6 (acquisition of Alpha Corp.) and Item 2 (depreciation)
■ Intangibles — Decrease of $5	Amortization of goodwill, included in Item 1
■ Other — decrease of $12	A plug item of no interest to anyone
Changes in liabilities and stockholders' equity	
■ Short-term debt — no change	A commercial paper program — have to keep name in market
■ Accounts payable — increase of $125	Resulting from increased production to support increased sales and reflected in Item 5
■ Long-term debt — increase of $300	Item 4, used to fund part of purchase of Alpha Corp.
■ Other liabilities — decrease of $125	Reduction of deferred taxes payable, appears as Item 7
■ Capital stock — increase of $500	Proceeds from new issue, Item 3, and used to fund part of purchase of Alpha Corp.
■ Retained earnings — increase of $128	Item 1 less annual taxes (not shown) and less dividends, Item 8, plus earnings from unconsolidated subsidiaries

	19X3	*19X4*
Current ratio	2.3	2.2
Long-term debt/Equity	0.4	0.4
Total liabilities/Equity	1.0	0.9

There are other considerations beyond financial ratios. A look at the ratio of market price of the stock to book value per share can by very helpful in assessing whether a large equity issue will be successful. The general industry environment should also be studied. For example, an automobile company could issue more shares at a higher price if the most recent period had been a good one for the auto industry. There is no single formula that allows the financial executive to identify precisely the best size or price of an external (public) financing. Nevertheless, all of these elements need to be taken into consideration.

Consistent with the company's policy of requiring five-year forecasts, the V.P.-Finance continued the process previously described. He produced a profit and loss statement, funds flow statement, and balance sheet for each of the remaining years in his forecast. Once it was completed, he packaged the whole thing, put it in his bookcase, and never looked at it again.

SUMMARY

Briefly, the steps to follow in preparing financial forecasts are:

- Ask the people who actually do the selling to prepare sales forecasts that take into account the state of the economy, not just what happened last year.
- Ask those responsible for manufacturing operations to provide complete data on the different product costs, based on volumes from the sales forecast.
- Compute depreciation on a consolidated basis, taking into consideration existing levels plus forecast new capital expenditures.
- Use operating income to measure the effectiveness of unit management.
- Base interest costs, which are both price and volume sensitive, on published forecasts. Such forecasts are usually free and sometimes fairly accurate. Using a consensus or average from several forecasts is the simplest way to obtain a figure. Interests costs must be projected in series; year 2 can only be calculated after year 1.
- Bring in a tax expert if the standard 50 percent assumption is inappropriate.
- Do not include capital expenditures in the forecast unless it is certain that the funds will, in fact, be spent.
- Look at industry dividend patterns as well as the company's history when projecting dividends.
- Be realistic in the breakdown or identification of future periods in the forecast. Monthly forecasting may be a good exercise for division management but can take more time to calculate, on a companywide basis, than its value to corporate management.
- Be realistic when looking at external funding alternatives. The markets may not have as much confidence in the company as management does.
- Use the forecast to plan both prospectively and retrospectively. Comparisons of actual performance to forecast performance can be used as guidelines in determining incentive compensation.
- Finally, look at the forecast and plan periodically after it has been completed. Revise it if the environment has changed significantly.

23

Financial Management in the Short Run

JAMES H. VANDER WEIDE

Managing the current assets and liabilities of a firm is the responsibility of the chief financial officer. This responsibility includes management of the firm's investment in cash, marketable securities, accounts receivable, and inventory, as well as its short-term borrowing alternatives. Because the task of managing the firm's current assets and liabilities is complex, responsibility for their management is frequently delegated to other individuals within the firm. For instance, a large firm might have a cash manager who is responsible for managing the firm's cash and marketable securities, a credit manager who is responsible for managing the firm's accounts receivable, and a purchasing manager who is responsible for managing the firm's trade credit. Responsibility for managing inventories is generally shared among employees in marketing, production, and finance.

This chapter describes the major economic factors that affect the financial manager's decisions regarding the firm's investment in current assets and liabilities. It provides an institutional framework necessary to make current asset and liability decisions; it also provides an introduction to some of the techniques and models that have proved useful in making these decisions.

CASH MANAGEMENT

The term "cash management" is frequently used quite broadly to refer to many of the decision-making problems covered in this chapter. For instance, the *Journal of Cash Management* includes all of the following as falling within the scope of cash management:

> [D]ay-to-day cash management (the collection system, disbursing system, concentration, disbursement funding and management of the overall cash balance), short-term financing and debt management, banking relations, services to support cash management (especially non-credit bank services), the evolving payment system (including payment system and depository institution regulation), short-term investments, money market instruments, money market trends and regulation, money market funds, financial futures, interest rate hedging, cash budgeting, cash planning, credit policy and management, payables management, inventory management, liquidity and overall working capital management, short-term planning, financial information systems and systems communications support for the short-term treasury area.

Clearly this definition covers more topics than can be covered in this chapter. Hence, cash management is defined here to include only the first category in the preceding definition; that is, the collection system, disbursing system, concentration, disbursement funding, and management of the overall cash balance.

Float

The term "float" refers to the delay in the transfer of value from the payor to the payee. (This concept is important to an understanding of cash management.) This delay is important to the financial manager because it represents funds that

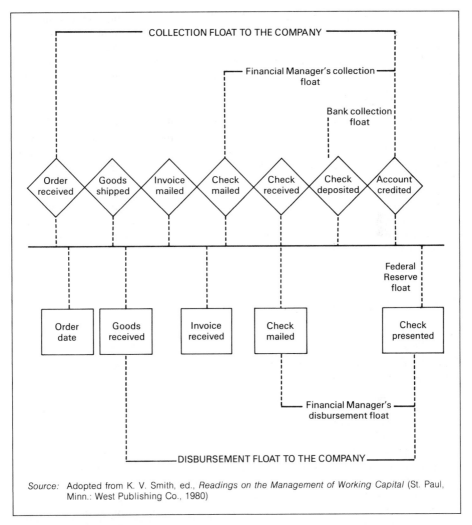

FIG. 23.1 Alternative Definitions of Float

the firm could otherwise be investing in interest-earning securities. In particular, by reducing the delay in the receipt of funds from its customers and increasing the delay in the payment of funds to vendors, the financial manager often can increase significantly the amount of funds available for investment.

Figure 23.1 illustrates the various delays that impede the transfer of funds from the payor to the payee. The horizontal line represents time and the diamonds and squares represent events that occur at various points in the collection and payment processes. The upper half of the figure displays a number of events in the process of collecting funds from the firm's customer; the lower half displays events in the process of disbursing funds to the firm's vendors. As shown in Figure 23.1, the financial manager should understand at least six definitions of float:

1 *Collection float to the company.* For many purposes, it is helpful to think of the collection process as beginning with the receipt of an order from the firm's customer. Thus, total collection float to the company is the delay in time between the receipt of an order and the credit of funds to the firm's bank account. This definition emphasizes that collection float can be reduced by prompt shipment and invoicing, as well as by prompt collection of the customer's check. This aspect of collection float is too often ignored because responsibility for shipping and invoicing falls outside the responsibility of the financial manager.

2 *Financial manager's collection float.* The delay between the time the customer mails the check and the time it is credited to the firm's account may be thought of as the financial manager's collection float. As demonstrated later, this delay can be significantly reduced by actions under the financial manager's control.

3 *Bank collection float.* Once the check has been deposited, the deposit bank must present it to the drawee bank for collection. This delay in bank collection of funds is called bank collection float. The financial manager is concerned with bank collection float because the firm's account is not actually credited until the funds are collected from the drawee bank.

4 *Disbursement float to the company.* On the payment side, the total delay between the time goods are received and the time the firm's account is debited is called disbursement float to the company. This definition emphasizes that the firm can often profit by using vendors who either invoice slowly or allow a long payment period. Delaying of accounts payable is a frequently used means of reducing the firm's financing needs; however, it must be used advisedly because it risks the ill will of crucial suppliers.

5 *Financial manager's disbursement float.* The term "financial manager's disbursement float" refers to the delay between the time the financial manager mails the check and the time the check is presented to the firm's bank for payment. Although extension of financial manager's disbursement float is a frequently used means of increasing the amount of funds available for investment, it has been criticized in recent years by Congress, the Board of Governors of the Federal Reserve System, and various consumer groups. It is essential that the financial manager understand both the risks and rewards of managing this aspect of float.

6 *Federal Reserve float.* For many years, the Federal Reserve System (Fed) has followed a policy of granting credit for check collection according to an "availability schedule" rather than according to the time it actually takes for the check to be presented. The difference between the time it actually takes the Fed to present the check and the time listed on its availability schedule is called Federal Reserve float. Positive Federal Reserve float is in essence an interest-free loan to the banking system. The benefits of this interest-free loan are frequently passed on to bank customers; however, since the Fed is currently taking steps to reduce or eliminate Federal Reserve float, these benefits are not likely to last for long.

Managing Cash Collections

In managing a cash collection system, the financial manager is concerned primarily with reducing the delay in the transfer of value from the customer to the

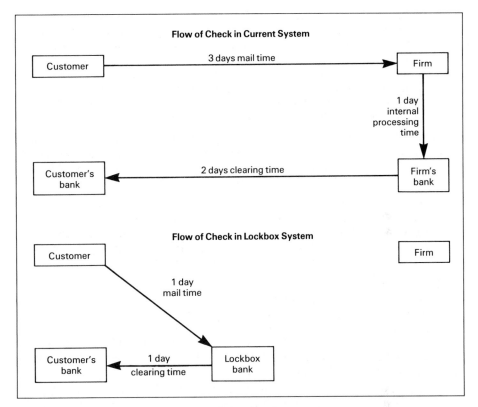

FIG. 23.2 Benefits of Using a Lockbox Collection System

firm. This is frequently accomplished by instructing the customer to remit payments to a postal address (lockbox) rather than to the firm's headquarters.

The goal of a lockbox collection system is to reduce the financial manager's collection float, which is composed of three elements: mail time, internal processing time, and availability time. Mail time is the time it takes for the check to arrive at the lockbox site, internal processing time is the time before the check is deposited to the firm's account, and availability time is the time before the account is credited with good funds.

The benefits of using a lockbox collection system are illustrated in Figure 23.2. The top of the figure shows what happens when customers are instructed to send their remittances to the firm's headquarters. The total financial manager's collection float in this case may be as much as six days, consisting of three days in mail time, one day in internal processing time, and two days in availability time. By locating a lockbox in the customer's immediate vicinity, the financial manager's collection float can be reduced to two or three days. As shown in the bottom half of Figure 23.2, this reduced float consists of one day of mail time, one day of availability time, and only a fraction of a day of internal processing time.

Lockbox Studies. It is common for financial managers to seek help from a bank cash management consulting department in designing a lockbox collection system. The consulting bank collects a sample of checks from the firm to determine the location of the firm's customers and the status of the firm's current collection system. These data are processed through sophisticated computer programs designed to find the optimal locations for the firm's lockboxes. Since the benefits of an efficient lockbox system can be substantial, the financial manager should try to understand the lockbox study process, so he can judge the quality of the lockbox study services he receives.

Managing Cash Disbursements

The potential savings to the firm from an efficient disbursement system are frequently as large as those found on the collection side. However, the problem of disbursement system design differs from that of collection system design in at least four ways:

1 The goal of the disbursement system is to *extend* the time between the date the check is mailed and the date on which it is presented to the firm's bank for payment. As a result, the optimal disbursement site is frequently remote from the payee, whereas the optimal collection site is close to the customer.

2 The disbursor also wants better control over its disbursement system. Once a check has been written, the check writer does not usually know when the check will be presented for payment; therefore he often keeps idle bank balances in order not to be caught short. There is great value in gaining control over this uncertainty, and some banks provide effective services to assist the financial manager in this regard.

3 Disbursement system design is further complicated by the fact that the firm has control over both the drawee bank and the location from which the check is mailed. Technically, the firm could both write the check on a remote bank and mail it from a remote location. In practice, however, financial managers are generally reluctant to extend mail times to their vendors. Thus, the optimal disbursement system is frequently based on presentation time alone.

4 The benefits of certain remote disbursement sites are likely to be eliminated in the near future as the Fed attempts to fulfill the mandate of Congress in the Depository Institutions Deregulation and Monetary Control Act of 1980 to greatly reduce Federal Reserve float. Thus, the firm may want to restrict its choice of disbursement sites to those whose benefits are unaffected by changes in Federal Reserve check clearing practices.

Benefits of Remote Disbursing

To illustrate the benefits of remote disbursing, consider a firm headquartered in New York that uses a New York disbursing bank for East Coast customers. The average presentation time for this firm is one day. By choosing a disbursement bank located in Raleigh, N.C., the firm extends its average presentation time to four days. This allows the firm to invest its funds for three additional days.

Federal Reserve Restrictions. In recent years, the Fed has sought in several ways to restrict the practice of disbursing from remote locations. First, it has exerted pressure on Fed member banks to cease offering the most obvious forms of remote disbursing services. Second, it has made a number of changes in its clearing procedures that partially reduce the benefits of remote disbursing. Third, it has announced its intention to make Federal Reserve float extension more costly to banks through direct charges and increased Federal Reserve availabilities. These changes in Federal Reserve policy must be recognized by a firm that is considering the redesign of its disbursement system.

Cash Concentration

Concentration banking is a process whereby funds deposited at regional field office or lockbox banks are transferred to a central cash pool where they can be managed more efficiently. The primary benefit of concentration banking is that it is far easier to manage one central account than many small regional accounts. With one central account, the financial manager can identify when the firm's total balances exceed the amount required to compensate the bank for services. The excess funds can then be invested in such money market instruments as Treasury bills (T-bills), commercial paper, and certificates of deposit (CDs). Concentrating the funds in one central pool facilitates the investment in instruments that trade only in units of $1 million or more. It is also easier for the financial manager to move funds to the firm's disbursement accounts from one central cash pool. Finally, by transferring funds to one central location under his control, the financial manager lessens the possibility of fraudulent use of field account funds.

Figure 23.3 shows the flow of funds in a representative concentration banking system. Funds collected from customers are either deposited at local depository banks in field office accounts or are sent to a regional lockbox bank. Data on the amount of funds deposited each day is collected by means of an information system maintained by either the corporation's headquarters or a third-party vendor. Knowing the amount of funds deposited, the financial manager can transfer funds to the concentration bank by using either a wire transfer, a depository transfer check (DTC), or the Automated Clearing House (ACH) system. The funds in the concentration bank may be used to maintain required compensating balances, for investment in short-term money market instruments, to pay down borrowings, or for disbursements to vendors.

The financial manager must make four kinds of decisions related to the concentration banking system. They include (1) the choice of transfer method, (2) the transfer schedule, (3) the design of a deposit information system, and (4) the choice of which concentration banks to use. An analysis of the economic issues involved in making these decisions is beyond the scope of this chapter; the article by Stone and Hill (1980) provides a lucid discussion of these issues.

MANAGING THE MARKETABLE SECURITIES PORTFOLIO

When the financial manager finds himself in a position of having a temporary funds surplus, he should invest in money market securities so he can earn interest until the funds are needed in the firm's main line of business. The amount

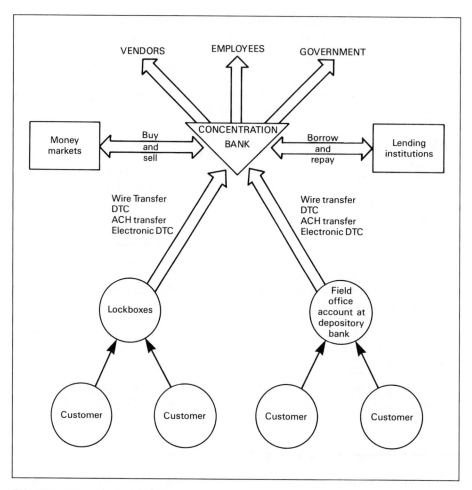

FIG. 23.3 Concentration Banking

of funds available for short-term investment, and the length of the investment period, depend on the time pattern of the firm's funds requirements and the method that is chosen to finance these requirements.

Figure 23.4 shows a typical time pattern of funds requirements. This pattern reflects a seasonal fluctuation about a long-term upward trend. The firm has three alternatives for meeting its funds requirements. Alternative *A*, represented by the top line in Figure 23.4, is a policy of relying entirely on long-term debt. Under this policy, there are extensive periods where the firm has surplus funds that must be invested in the money market. Alternative *C*, represented by the bottom line in Figure 23.4, is a policy of funding only the permanent component of funds requirements with long-term debt and funding all remaining require-ments with short-term debt. Under this policy, there are never any excess funds for money market investments. Alternative *B* is a middle-ground policy that is followed by many firms. Under this policy the firm finances all of its permanent

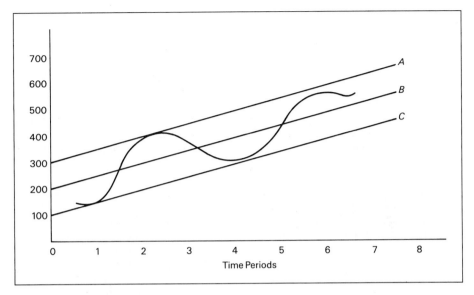

FIG. 23.4 Alternative Financing Strategies

funds requirements and some of its seasonal requirements with long-term debt. It can be seen from Figure 23.4 that under policy *B* there are some periods when the firm has surplus funds that need to be invested and there are other periods when the firm has to obtain additional short-term financing to meet its total funds requirements.

Reasons for Investing in Marketable Securities

The preceding discussion of background makes it apparent that there are at least three reasons why firms hold investments in marketable securities. These have frequently been labeled the "transaction motive," the "precautionary motive," and the "speculative motive."

Transaction Motive. The transaction motive arises from the high transaction costs associated with liquidating long-term securities and fixed assets such as property, plant, and equipment. Since the firm's surplus of funds is expected to be short-lived, the financial manager wants to be able to convert his investments into cash at short notice with little or no loss in value. Long-term securities, such as stocks and bonds, experience price changes of such a large magnitude that they are not suitable as a temporary store of value. The brokerage fee and other costs associated with selling real estate or disposing of other fixed assets make them ill-suited as a vehicle for investing temporary funds surpluses. On the other hand, the transaction costs and price fluctuations of money market securities are so small that these securities are an ideal investment for temporary funds surpluses.

Precautionary Motive. The funds requirements shown in Figure 23.4 generally are not known with certainty. Rather they represent the firm's best forecast of future funds requirements; the financial officer realizes that actual funds requirements may exceed the forecasted amounts by a substantial margin. Recognizing that arrangements for long-term borrowing take time and that short-term borrowing may not be available in times of emergency, some financial officers maintain a pool of investments in marketable securities as a precaution against unforeseen cash requirements. This precautionary need for a marketable securities portfolio has diminished in recent years, as more and more firms have ready access to the money markets as a source of short-term financing.

Speculative Motive. The third motive for holding a marketable securities portfolio is called the speculative motive. Some firms hold short-term marketable securities because they are speculating that long-term interest rates will soon rise. Thus, they borrow sufficient long-term funds at present low rates to cover their financial requirements well into the future, and they invest the surplus in marketable securities. The speculative motive is unlikely to be as strong a determining factor as the other two motives, since most financial managers believe that speculating on interest rate changes is not one of their responsibilities.

Criteria for Selecting Securities

The prior discussion suggests that money market securities must satisfy at least three criteria to be eligible for inclusion in the firm's marketable securities portfolio:

1 *Low default risk.* Since the firm intends to cash in its portfolio in the near future, the securities included in the portfolio clearly must have a low risk of default.

2 *Marketability.* For the same reason, the securities must have a high degree of marketability.

3 *Maturity.* Since long-term securities fluctuate in price to a much greater extent than short-term securities, it is generally considered appropriate to place the bulk of the short-term portfolio in securities that mature within a year. In fact, depending on the uncertainty of the firm's cash flows, a much shorter average maturity may be even more appropriate.

Alternative Strategies

In managing their marketable securities portfolios, financial managers employ a variety of strategies to increase portfolio yields while keeping risks and management costs to a minimum. For the purpose of discussion, it is convenient to group these strategies into four categories: passive, matching, riding the yield curve, and active.

Passive Strategies. In firms where the size of the marketable securities portfolio is rarely sufficient to justify large management costs, one of several passive portfolio management strategies may be used. These strategies require little action on the part of the financial manager. Their goal is to earn an acceptable yield on invested funds while minimizing the costs and risks of portfolio management.

One passive strategy that is used by many small firms is to invest any funds in excess of the required daily bank balance in an interest-earning account maintained by the bank. These accounts are frequently called sweep accounts because any amount in excess of the required daily balance is automatically swept into the interest-earning account. Although these accounts are extremely convenient for the financial manager, they generally earn an interest yield that is somewhat below the market rate. This is because the bank must invest the funds in money market instruments, and it requires an incentive to perform this service.

Another passive strategy, devised by Bernell Stone, is called the "K-day look-ahead strategy." This strategy recognizes that most banks allow firms to satisfy compensating balance requirements by averaging balances over a specified period, such as a month or a quarter. Since there is no need to meet the compensating balance requirement each day, the policy calls for the financial manager to let the balance amount drift up or down until a prescribed "control limit" is reached. At the time the control limit is reached, the financial manager looks at his cash forecast for the next K days, where K is a parameter whose value depends on the firm's ability to accurately forecast future requirements. If the balance is still expected to exceed the control limit in K days, securities are bought or sold in sufficient quantities that the target balance will be reached at the end of the K-day horizon. If, however, the balance in K days is expected to fall within the control limits, then no action is taken; that is, the amount in the account is allowed to drift for a while longer. Additional information about this policy, including some guidelines for choosing maturities, is found in Stone (1976).

Matching Strategy. The passive strategies just described allow a firm to earn some interest on its excess cash while incurring almost no risk of loss due to market fluctuations; however, the interest earned is generally quite low because the investment is essentially one day in length. Sometimes interest earnings can be improved at very little additional risk by investing in securities whose maturity is matched to the dates of expected cash outflows. Thus, if the financial manager expects a large cash outflow in two months, he might invest in a 60-day CD.

The matching strategy allows the financial manager to earn a higher yield on his investment by matching the maturity of his investment portfolio to periods of expected cash drains. This strategy is slightly more risky than the passive strategies, however, because the financial manager's cash forecast may be inaccurate. In this case, he would simply sell some of his investment before maturity, thereby incurring the risk of a possible loss. For securities with maturities of less than 90 days this risk is not large.

Riding the Yield Curve. The phrase "riding the yield curve" originally referred to a policy of buying securities with maturities beyond the investment horizon and selling them prior to maturity at the horizon. The strategy was based on the normal yield curve relationship, where yields on long-term maturities of a given security exceed those on short-term maturities. To understand this strategy, consider what would happen if the yield on a 30-day T-bill was 6 percent, the yield on a 60-day T-bill was 7 percent, and these rates were expected to stay the same over the next 30 days. Under these conditions, the financial manager could earn the higher yield on the 60-day instrument over the 30-day horizon, and sell the instrument at the horizon for a capital gain, because it would then be trading as a 30-day instrument.

Today, riding the yield curve refers more generally to a policy of speculating on shifts in the yield curve relationship. For example, if the yield curve were currently upward sloping and the financial manager expected the curve to flatten out as interest rates declined, he might extend the average maturity of his portfolio in anticipation of this change.

Two facts about riding the yield curve should be noted. First, studies (e.g., Osteryoung, Roberts, and McCarty, 1980) have shown that in practice, this strategy has not produced superior performance. The increase in yields from riding the yield curve has been minimal, while the increase in risks has been substantial. Second, if the financial manager follows this strategy in its speculative form, he should be aware that predicting interest rates is a specialized skill at which even experts frequently fail.

Active Strategy. The fourth type of strategy, followed only by firms whose marketable security portfolio is consistently large, is to buy and sell securities much like a money market dealer. This involves a willingness to (1) sell securities before maturity, (2) buy and sell securities for extremely short periods to take advantage of unusual conditions in the market, and (3) invest in a wide variety of sophisticated instruments, including futures and instruments denominated in foreign currencies. An active portfolio management strategy can be rewarding for the extraordinarily sophisticated financial manager, but it involves a high management cost because the skills required to play the game at this level are scarce and the necessary backup support is extensive.

Computer Aids to Short-Term Portfolio Management

Managing a short-term securities portfolio is a difficult task that involves the ability to process large volumes of data, to forecast future financial requirements, and to make complex interest rate calculations rapidly. Fortunately, computer models that significantly reduce the difficulty of this task have been developed. These models provide the following benefits to portfolio managers:

> 1 *Balance reporting.* In a world where firms may have cash in accounts at banks throughout the country, it is sometimes difficult for a financial manager to obtain timely information on the amount of funds he actually has available for investment. Computerized balance reporting systems, offered as a cash management service by many banks, provide information on deposit amounts in all the firm's

bank accounts via a computer terminal in the financial manager's office. In addition to simple deposit information, most balance reporting systems provide information on average cash balances vs. compensating balance requirements, lockbox collections, and cash disbursements.

2 *Portfolio information.* When a firm's portfolio is large, it is sometimes difficult to obtain adequate information on types and maturities of various securities, accrued interest, initial yields, and cash flows from maturing securities. Computer-based portfolio management systems provide ready access to this kind of information. They also allow this information to be fed into other files, such as a cash forecasting system or the firm's accounting records.

3 *Interest rate information.* Current market rate information on money market securities and foreign exchange is provided electronically by a number of firms for a fee. The information provided by these services is obviously essential to a financial manager who is following an active portfolio management strategy.

4 *Evaluating alternative strategies.* Computer models are now available that allow a financial manager to evaluate the financial impact of following alternative portfolio management strategies. Some of these models rely on sophisticated mathematical programming algorithms that help to find the portfolio strategy that maximizes return for a given level of risk.

ACCOUNTS RECEIVABLE MANAGEMENT

Accounts receivable management involves at least three kinds of activities on the part of the financial manager. On the policy level, the financial manager must decide how much the firm's investment in accounts receivable should be. In making this decision, the manager must identify the cash inflows and outflows associated with an investment in accounts receivable. The cash inflows result primarily from the increased sales that follow from credit financing. The cash outflows include the cost of the credit operation itself, the opportunity cost of the cash tied up in accounts receivable, the losses from bad debts, and the costs of collection efforts. Having identified the major cash flows, the manager must then evaluate them, just as he would any other capital budgeting project.

In practice, the financial manager must decide which customers are to get credit and which customers are not. If the manager decides to extend credit to an individual customer, he takes the risk that the customer will not pay off his debt. The cost to the firm of this occurrence depends on the variable costs per unit, the number of units sold to the customer, and the collection costs. If the manager decides not to extend credit to a particular customer, he loses the opportunity of making a profit on a sale. The lost profit depends on the average collection period, the profit per unit, the number of units sold, and the firm's cost of capital. The decision to extend credit to an individual customer, then, depends on the relative values of the costs of acceptance and the costs of rejection.

Finally the financial manager must constantly monitor the firm's accounts receivable to see whether the firm's investment in receivables is larger than expected. In performing this task, it is important that the manager use monitoring devices that distinguish between changes in payment patterns and changes in credit sales. If the financial manager believes that an increase in accounts receivable is due to a deterioration in customer payment patterns, he may implement a policy of more stringent credit standards at a time when this would be inappropriate. In a subsequent section, it is shown that this error is entirely possible.

Choosing How Much to Invest in Accounts Receivable

The amount of accounts receivable shown on the firm's books is the product of its average credit sales per day and its average collection period. If the firm has annual credit sales of $365,000 and the average collection period is 60 days, then the amount of its accounts receivable is $60,000.

The volume of average credit sales per day and the average collection period depend on both the level of economic activity and the firm's credit terms. A discussion of how the level of economic activity affects the volume of the firm's credit sales and its average collection period is beyond the scope of this chapter. The following subsection demonstrates how the firm's credit sales and its average collection period are affected by the firm's credit terms.

Credit Terms. Credit terms are the terms of the agreement whereby the firm extends credit to individual or business customers. It involves an agreement about the credit period, the form of the credit arrangement, the discount, and the discount period.

The credit period is the length of time between the invoice date and the due date, that is, the length of time for which credit is extended. The length of the credit period depends on competitive conditions in the industry, the costs of maintaining inventories, the cost of capital, and the economic conditions of the customer. In many industries, it is common practice for the credit period to be either 30 or 60 days; in some industries, such as clothing, the common practice is to use what is called seasonal dating. This allows the customer to accept goods from wholesale and pay for them only after they have been sold at retail.

The form of the credit agreement is usually a matter of industry practice, but it also depends on the credit standing of the customer. The most common practice is to grant credit "on open book," meaning that the seller invoices the buyer and records the amount on his accounts receivable ledger. In international business and some domestic industries, however, a more formal credit agreement known as a trade acceptance is common. The trade acceptance is actually a time draft on the buyer's bank account that is frequently originated by a letter of credit (from the buyer's bank) guaranteeing the amount. When the buyer's bank accepts this draft, it becomes known as a banker's acceptance, which then may be traded in the money market until it becomes due. Finally, for customers of unknown or poor credit risk, the seller may only extend credit against a promissory note.

To encourage customers to pay promptly, firms often offer a discount if payment is made within a certain prescribed period, known as the discount period. For instance, the seller might state that the buyer will get a 2 percent discount if payment is made within 10 days of receipt of the invoice, otherwise the full amount is due in 30 days. These terms are written in shorthand as: 2/10, net 30. Since forgoing the discount is, in this case, equivalent to borrowing for 20 days at 36 percent interest, terms of 2/10, net 30 are often sufficiently attractive to encourage payment within the discount period.

Evaluating Changes in Credit Terms. As noted previously, a firm's investment in accounts receivable may be evaluated using standard capital budgeting techniques. When using these techniques, the firm's financial manager must identify both the relevant cash flows and the cost of capital. The following examples explore how to evaluate the firm's investment in accounts receivable.

Example 1. It is assumed that a firm, Amco Inc., sells 110,000 widgets per year at $70 per unit. Amco's variable cost is $60 per unit and all its sales are on credit, with terms of net 30 days. However, the average collection period is 45 days because some customers are slow in paying. Under these assumptions, the average amount of accounts receivable on Amco's books is $7,700,000 × 45/365 = $949,315.

Now it is assumed that Amco is considering extending credit to customers with a slightly lower credit standing, a decision it believes will produce an increase in sales of 10,000 units and an average collection period of 60 days. (For convenience, it is assumed that there will be no bad debts.) Since Amco's plants are producing below capacity, there will be no increase in fixed costs associated with the increase in sales. Under the new policy, the average amount of accounts receivable carried on the firm's books is $8,400,000 × 60/365 = $1,380,822.

To analyze whether or not Amco should extend credit to these additional customers, a distinction must be made between the average amount of accounts receivable on the firm's books and its average investment in accounts receivable. As noted previously, the average amount of accounts receivable is the product of the firm's average credit sales per day and its average collection period. On the other hand, Amco's investment in accounts receivable is the product of its variable costs per day and its average collection period. This is because variable costs are the best measure of the dollars tied up in accounts receivable. Thus, Amco's investment in accounts receivable will increase under its new policy by ($1,380,822 × 6/7) − ($949,315 × 6/7) = $369,863.

An analysis of additional profits from Amco's proposed new policy is shown below.

Additional sales	$700,000
Profitability of additional sales	100,000
Additional investment in accounts receivable	369,863
Opportunity cost of additional investment at 25%	92,453
Net profits	7,547

Example 2. Suppose that Amco, Inc. is also considering offering a discount of 2 percent for payment within 10 days. Amco believes that 60 percent of its

customers will take advantage of the discount and that its average collection period will thus be reduced to 25 days.

Recall that Amco's investment in accounts receivable is less than the amount of accounts receivable shown on its books because of the difference between its selling price and its variable costs. Under its original policy, Amco's investment in accounts receivable is given by $7,700,000 \times (45/365) \times (6/7) = \$813,699$. If the firm adopts the discount policy, its investment in accounts receivable is $7,700,000 \times (25/365) \times (6/7) = \$452,055$. Thus, its investment is reduced by $361,644.

An analysis of the profits from the introduction of a discount is shown below.

Opportunity savings from reduced investment:
$0.25 \times \$361,644 = \$90,411$

Cost of discount:
$0.02 \times 0.6 \times \$7,700,000 = \$92,400$

Net savings:
$\$90,411 - \$92,400 = -\$1,989$

Amco should not adopt the discount policy because the cost of the discount exceeds the opportunity savings from the reduced investment in accounts receivable.

Selecting Individual Customers

Traditionally, decisions granting credit to individual customers have been based on the five Cs of credit: character, capacity, collateral, capital, and conditions. Information relating to the five Cs was generally obtained from personal interviews and a reasonably exhaustive analysis of the individual's financial condition. In the following sections, the five Cs of credit are defined and the weaknesses of this approach to credit granting decisions are discussed. Also, two different approaches that address these weaknesses are described.

The Five Cs of Credit. The first and most important of the five Cs, character, is related to personal characteristics such as honesty and integrity. It is meant to measure the individual's intent, or willingness, to pay. Information on this characteristic is obtained from personal interviews and credit references.

Capacity is a measure of the individual's ability to pay. An assessment of capacity is based on an analysis of the individual's income in relation to expenses. For corporate customers that can use the accrual method of accounting, it is advisable to investigate how income and expenses are translated into cash flows.

The third C of credit, collateral, has to do with assets that the individual might be able to pledge against the extension of credit. This is an extremely important characteristic in bank loans, but is relatively unimportant in the extension of trade credit. The assignment of assets is not a frequent practice in trade credit because the legal, accounting, and storage costs are simply prohibitive.

Capital is related to the resources that the customer can draw on in the event that income or cash flow proves inadequate. For a business customer, capital is generally measured by the amount of equity on its balance sheet, while for an individual customer capital is defined by the individual's net worth. Information on equity, or net worth, is also obtained from the customer's financial statements, but in this case the balance sheet is of more interest than the income statement.

The final C, conditions, is concerned with the economic climate in which the customer operates. If economic conditions are depressed, the individual's current income may be high but there is little likelihood that this level of income will continue. Thus, economic conditions are used to judge the sustainability of the customer's income.

Weaknesses of the Five Cs. The traditional five C framework ignores two important aspects of the credit granting decision. First, it ignores the significant costs of obtaining all the information required to evaluate character, capacity, collateral, capital, and conditions. As noted previously, assessments of character require either a personal interview or credit references, while assessments of capacity and capital require detailed analysis of the customer's financial statements. The cost of obtaining this additional information may well exceed its value.

Second, the five C framework does not specify how the information obtained can be translated into a credit granting decision. For instance, it does not say what should be done if the customer is strong in character and capacity but weak in capital. The credit scoring models discussed in the following sections are designed to alleviate this second weakness of the five C framework.

A Sequential Approach to the Credit Granting Decision. In situations where the cost of obtaining information is large compared to the amount of credit granted and the profit on the sale, a sequential approach to the credit granting decision may be used. In this approach, information is obtained in stages, beginning with a low cost source and, if necessary, moving to higher cost sources. For instance, the financial manager may begin by checking his company's credit history with this customer. If the credit history is either obviously good or obviously bad, the accept or reject decision can be made immediately without obtaining additional information. If the credit history is either mixed or nonexistent, however, it may be worthwhile to obtain additional information, such as credit references or financial statements.

The financial manager's sequential decision problem is depicted in Figure 23.5. The squares in this diagram represent decision alternatives and the circles represent chance events. The diagram should be read from left to right. The three alternatives at stage 1 are shown at the far left. If the manager chooses to investigate past experience, he encounters a chance event, namely whether the past experience is good, poor, or nonexistent. The manager then moves to a stage 2 decision, shown by the squares in the center of the diagram. If, at stage 2, he chooses to investigate further, he encounters another chance event, namely, whether the financial statements are sound or unsound. After considering the second chance event, the financial manager must make the final decision to accept or reject.

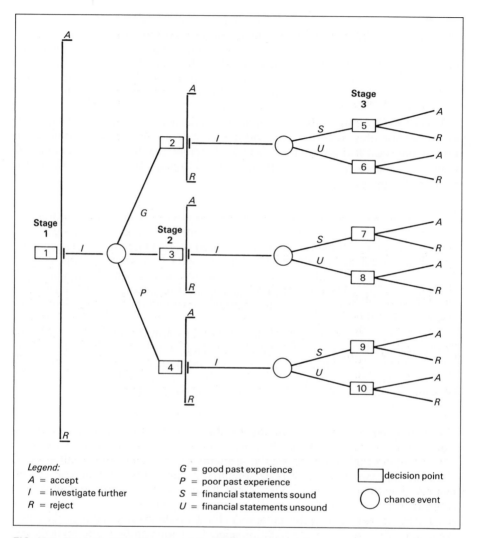

FIG. 23.5 Decision Tree Diagram of Credit Granting Decision

Although Figure 23.5 provides a useful overview of the financial manager's decision problem, some additional calculations are required before it can be determined what the best decision actually is. In particular, the costs associated with each decision at each stage of analysis must be calculated. Once these costs are known, the best decision at stage 1 is the one that minimizes the expected costs.

Credit Scoring Models

Suppose that a financial manager has obtained financial information on a particular credit applicant and found that the customer's financial leverage is above

TABLE 23.1   Profiles of Good and Bad Risks

Characteristics	Average Value for Each Group	
	Good Risks	Bad Risks
Average income (in thousands)	$34.73	$16.56
Average net worth (in thousands)	$116.45	$41.98
Years in present job	9.8	5.4
Number of dependents	1.6	3.3
Total debt/total net worth	21%	48%
Average age	43	37

the industry average, its operating leverage is below the industry average, and its liquidity is approximately the same as the industry average. Should the financial manager grant credit to this customer or not? It is difficult to answer that question without knowing how the customer's financial leverage, operating leverage, and liquidity relate to its ability to ultimately pay for the goods.

Because of this difficulty, many firms have begun to use credit scoring models to help them relate financial, demographic, and other information about the customer to the ability to repay. These models rely on a sophisticated statistical technique called discriminant analysis to determine a set of weights and a set of explanatory variables that best distinguish "good" customers from "bad" customers.

To develop a credit scoring model, the financial manager first must decide what distinguishes a good account from a bad account. Suppose he decides that a good account is one that is paid within three months and a bad account is one that is paid beyond three months or not at all. He must then develop a profile of characteristics that might be used in distinguishing good and bad accounts. For instance, he might find that good and bad accounts have the profiles shown in Table 23.1.

These figures demonstrate that the profile for good accounts is quite different from that for bad accounts, suggesting that this is an appropriate set of distinguishing characteristics. However, a set of weights that helps to determine a single credit score for each customer is still needed. This is where discriminant analysis is especially helpful.

Discriminant analysis works very much like a regression, where the dependent variable y takes on the value 1 or 0 depending on whether the account is good or bad. The goal is to determine a set of weights $a_1, \ldots, a_n$ that, when multiplied by the values of the independent variables $x_1, \ldots, x_n$ and summed best predicts the y values. Thus,

$$y = a_1x_1 + a_2x_2 + \ldots + a_nx_n$$

where the a's are chosen to minimize the cost of forecast errors.

Returning to the example, suppose that through the use of discriminant analysis, the set of weights given in Table 23.2 has been found.

TABLE 23.2   Characteristics of Credit Applicants

Characteristics	Weights
Income	7.31
Net worth	5.26
Years in present job	16.85
Number of dependents	−47.19
Total debt/total net worth	−20.76
Average age	4.9

To determine a particular credit score, the financial manager simply determines which questions were a "yes" for this customer and adds the points associated with those questions. When this is done for the set of customers in the study sample, the resulting credit scores will typically follow the distributions shown in Figure 23.6.

Since these distributions overlap, there will be some misclassifications unless the cutoff score F^* is set so high as to screen out many potential good customers. The final step then is to choose a cutoff score that minimizes the total cost of misclassifications. Because of the judgment involved, many firms choose two cutoff scores. If the customer's score exceeds the upper cutoff, the account is automatically classified as "good"; if it is below the lower cutoff, the account is automatically classified as "bad"; and if it falls between, further analysis is required.

There is no doubt that credit scoring models have proven useful in many applications. The principal advantage of credit scoring models is that they specify the relationship between customer characteristics in an objective, verifiable, and statistically sound manner. The principal disadvantage is that, like any statistical method, they are based on the assumption that future customers will behave in the same way as previous customers. Since this is not always true, credit scoring models must be used with a great deal of care.

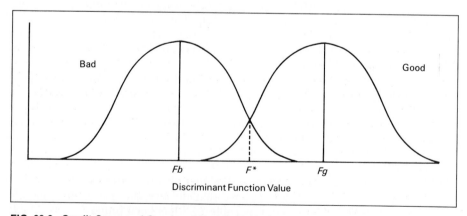

FIG. 23.6 Credit Scores of Good and Bad Customers

Monitoring Accounts Receivable Performance

The financial manager's third major activity with regard to accounts receivable management is to monitor the firm's accounts receivable performance. The two most widely used methods of performing this task are (1) calculating the accounts receivable turnover or its reciprocal, the days' sales outstanding, and (2) calculating the aging schedule of accounts receivable.

Days' Sales Outstanding

In the introduction to the accounts receivable section, it was noted that the amount of accounts receivable shown on the firm's books is equal to the product of the average daily credit sales and the average collection period; that is,

$$\text{Total accounts receivable} = \text{Average credit sales per day} \times \text{Average collection period}$$

Dividing both sides of this equation by the average credit sales per day, we see that the average collection period is given by

$$\text{Average collection period} = \frac{\text{Total accounts receivable}}{\text{Average credit sales per day}}$$

When looked at in this fashion, the average collection period is sometimes called the days' sales outstanding (DSO). It is used as a primary method of monitoring whether the firm's collection experience is improving or deteriorating.

To illustrate how the use of the DSO can provide misleading signals about the status of the firm's credit policy, consider the firm whose credit sales are shown here:

January	100	July	500
February	200	August	600
March	300	September	700
April	400	October	600
May	400	November	500
June	400	December	400

Assume that 20 percent of a given month's credit sales are collected in the current month, 40 percent are collected in the subsequent month, 30 percent in the following month, and 10 percent in the third month following the date of the sale. The set of numbers: 0.2, 0.4, 0.3, and 0.1 represent the payment pattern for the firm's customers, and under the previous assumption, this pattern is stable. Since, for any given month's credit sales, accounts receivable are just the proportion of the credit sales that have not been paid, a payment pattern of 0.2, 0.4, 0.3, and 0.1 implies a receivable pattern of 0.8, 0.4, and 0.1. Thus, the credit sales in January produce $80 of accounts receivable in January, $40 in February, and $10 in March; the credit sales of $200 in February produce accounts receivable of $160 in February, $80 in March, and $20 in April; and so on.

From the preceding discussion it is apparent that the accounts receivable shown on the books of this firm in any month are given by:

TABLE 23.3   Day's Sales Outstanding by Quarter for Different Averaging Periods

	Averaging Period		
Quarter	30 Days	60 Days	90 Days
1	$\dfrac{330}{10} = 33$	$\dfrac{330}{8.3} = 40$	$\dfrac{330}{6.7} = 49$
2	$\dfrac{520}{13.3} = 39$	$\dfrac{520}{13.3} = 39$	$\dfrac{520}{13.3} = 39$
3	$\dfrac{850}{23.3} = 36$	$\dfrac{850}{21.7} = 39$	$\dfrac{850}{20} = 43$
4	$\dfrac{580}{13.3} = 44$	$\dfrac{580}{15} = 39$	$\dfrac{580}{16.7} = 35$

$$REC_t = 0.8\ CS_t + 0.4\ CS_{t-1} + 0.1\ CS_{t-2}$$

where: REC_t = accounts receivable balance in month t
CS_t = credit sales in month$_t$
CS_{t-1} = credit sales in month$_{t-1}$
CS_{t-2} = credit sales in month$_{t-2}$

Applying this relationship to the credit sales in this example, the level of accounts receivable by month is as follows:

ACCOUNTS RECEIVABLE BY MONTH

January	290	July	600
February	240	August	720
March	330	September	850
April	460	October	820
May	510	November	710
June	520	December	580

Using these figures for receivables and credit sales, it is possible to calculate the DSO at the end of each quarter. The resulting figures are shown in Table 23.3 for averaging periods of 30, 60, and 90 days.

Although the firm's payment pattern was assumed to be constant, the use of the DSO indicates a volatile collection experience. If a 30-day averaging period is used for averaging credit sales per day, the credit experience is shown to deteriorate from quarter 1 to quarter 2, to improve from quarter 2 to quarter 3, and to deteriorate again from quarter 3 to quarter 4. The opposite results obtain if a 90-day averaging period is used. Only by using a 60-day averaging period is a conclusion consistent with the assumption of a constant payment pattern reached.

TABLE 23.4   Aging Schedule of Accounts Receivable by Quarter

Interval	Quarter 1	Quarter 2	Quarter 3	Quarter 4
0–30 days	73%	62%	66%	55%
31–60	24	31	28	35
61–90	3	8	6	10

The Aging Schedule. The aging schedule of accounts receivable displays the percentage of the firm's current accounts receivable that fall in different age categories. Under the assumptions made in the previous section, the aging schedule of accounts receivable at the end of each quarter is given in Table 23.4.

These figures indicate a deterioration in the payment patterns of the firm's credit customers. Once again, however, the original data were based on the assumption of a constant payment pattern. Thus, the aging schedule may also provide incorrect signals to the financial manager.

To explain why the two methods, DSO and aging schedule, produce misleading signals, consider the actual cash collections and accounts receivable balances that are generated from each month's credit sales under the assumption of a stable payment pattern of 0.2, 0.4, 0.3, and 0.1. These are shown in Tables 23.5 and 23.6. It is clear that the rows of these two tables contain the best payment pattern information, because they reflect the percentage of a given month's credit sales that are collected in subsequent months.

The two traditional methods of monitoring accounts receivable performance sometimes produce misleading signals primarily because they focus on the columns of Tables 23.6 and 23.7 instead of the rows. The aging schedule at the end of March is calculated by looking at the accounts receivable balance shown at the bottom of the March column of Table 23.7, and determining what percentage of this total is one month old, two months old, and three months old. The figures reveal that a relatively high percentage (240/330 = 73%) is one month old, but this is due primarily to the fact that credit sales in March are large compared to those of the previous two months.

The DSO takes the total accounts receivable at the bottom of the March column and relates this to the average credit sales over the last 30, 60, or 90 days. Since credit sales are rising, it is not surprising that the answer is sensitive to the length of the averaging period.

Payment Pattern Approaches. As the preceding discussion demonstrates, to get a correct signal of the payment patterns of the firm's customers, it is necessary to relate either cash collections or accounts receivable balances back to the credit sales that generated them; that is, data similar to those shown in the rows of Tables 23.6 and 23.7 must be gathered. Two approaches to accomplishing this have been recommended. The first, based on a payment pattern matrix, was developed by Llewellyn and Johnson (1972), while the second, based on a payment pattern regression, was developed by Stone (1976).

Suppose that the financial manager separates the accounts generating credit

TABLE 23.5   Monthly Cash Collections From Credit Sales

Month	Credit Sales	Jan.	Feb.	Mar.	Apr.	May	June	July	Aug.	Sept.	Oct.	Nov.	Dec.
October	600	60	—	—	—	—	—	—	—	—	—	—	—
November	500	150	50	—	—	—	—	—	—	—	—	—	—
December	400	160	120	40	—	—	—	—	—	—	—	—	—
January	100	20	40	30	10	—	—	—	—	—	—	—	—
February	200	—	40	80	60	20	—	—	—	—	—	—	—
March	300	—	—	60	120	90	30	—	—	—	—	—	—
April	400	—	—	—	80	160	120	40	—	—	—	—	—
May	400	—	—	—	—	80	160	120	40	—	—	—	—
June	400	—	—	—	—	—	80	160	120	40	—	—	—
July	500	—	—	—	—	—	—	100	200	150	50	—	—
August	600	—	—	—	—	—	—	—	120	240	180	60	—
September	700	—	—	—	—	—	—	—	—	140	280	210	70
October	600	—	—	—	—	—	—	—	—	—	120	240	180
November	500	—	—	—	—	—	—	—	—	—	—	100	200
December	400	—	—	—	—	—	—	—	—	—	—	—	80
Total		390	250	210	270	350	390	420	480	570	630	610	530

TABLE 23.6   End of Month Accounts Receivable Balances

Month	Credit Sales	Jan.	Feb.	Mar.	Apr.	May	June	July	Aug.	Sept.	Oct.	Nov.	Dec.
October	600	—	—	—	—	—	—	—	—	—	—	—	—
November	500	50	—	—	—	—	—	—	—	—	—	—	—
December	400	160	40	—	—	—	—	—	—	—	—	—	—
January	100	80	40	10	—	—	—	—	—	—	—	—	—
February	200	—	160	80	20	—	—	—	—	—	—	—	—
March	300	—	—	240	120	30	—	—	—	—	—	—	—
April	400	—	—	—	320	160	40	—	—	—	—	—	—
May	400	—	—	—	—	320	160	40	—	—	—	—	—
June	400	—	—	—	—	—	320	160	40	—	—	—	—
July	500	—	—	—	—	—	—	400	200	50	—	—	—
August	600	—	—	—	—	—	—	—	480	240	60	—	—
September	700	—	—	—	—	—	—	—	—	560	280	70	—
October	600	—	—	—	—	—	—	—	—	—	480	240	60
November	500	—	—	—	—	—	—	—	—	—	—	400	200
December	400	—	—	—	—	—	—	—	—	—	—	—	320
Total		290	240	330	460	510	520	600	720	850	820	710	580

TABLE 23.7   Payment Pattern Matrix

Month of Credit Sale	In Same Month	1 Month Later	2 Months Later	3 Months Later
		Percentage Collected		
January	0.20%	0.40%	0.30%	0.10%
February	0.19	0.39	0.31	0.11
March	0.18	0.38	0.32	0.12
April	0.17	0.37	0.33	0.13
May	0.16	0.36	0.34	0.14
June	0.15	0.35	0.35	0.15

sales by the month in which the credit sale occurred. He then determines what percentage of the accounts generating credit sales in January are paid in January and in each of the subsequent months. He also does this for February, March, and so on. The results are displayed in the form of the payment pattern matrix shown in Table 23.7.

Perusal of this matrix provides the financial manager with accurate information on trends in payment patterns. If, as shown here, the percentages collected in months 0 and 1 are declining, while those collected in months 2 and 3 are increasing, the financial manager is fairly safe in concluding that his customers' payment pattern is deteriorating. Of course, he must be careful that the change is of sufficient magnitude to represent a true trend, rather than a statistical aberration.

The payment pattern matrix requires that the manager be able to segregate accounts based on the month in which the credit sale occurs. In cases where this is not possible, Stone suggests the use of a payment pattern regression equation of the following form:

$$\mathrm{CC}_t = P_0\mathrm{CS}_t + P_1\mathrm{CS}_{t-1} + P_2\mathrm{CS}_{t-2} + P_3\mathrm{CS}_{t-3} \ldots + P_H\mathrm{CS}_H + C_t$$

where:

CC_t = aggregate cash collections in month t

CS_t = aggregate credit sales in month t

CS_{t-1}, CS_{t-2}, etc. = aggregate credit sales in previous months

$P_0, \ldots, P_1$, etc. = regression coefficients that indicate the payment pattern of the firm's customers

C_t = an error term

Stone suggests that the coefficients P_0 through P_H be estimated from a regression equation involving data from previous periods. The regression equation should then be used to forecast cash collections in future periods. As the actual cash collections are observed, the financial manager can calculate the forecast error in each future period. If these are persistently negative (or positive) for several months, the financial manager would be justified in concluding that his payment pattern had improved (or deteriorated).

INVENTORY MANAGEMENT

A firm's investment in inventories is frequently as large as, if not larger than, its investment in accounts receivable. It is the financial manager's responsibility to monitor the firm's inventory investment to ensure that the return on investment continues to exceed the cost of capital. The following sections describe several techniques that have been found useful for this purpose.

Rationale for Inventories

Firms hold inventories for three interrelated reasons. First, firms hold inventories of raw materials, goods in process, and finished goods in order to minimize natural delays in the ordering, production, and delivery of these items. If the firm held no inventories, it would have to delay the production process until it received an order from a customer. At that time, it would order the necessary raw materials, schedule production, and then make arrangements for delivery of the finished good. This delay is normally so long that the customer would surely seek to obtain the item elsewhere.

Second, firms frequently hold inventories to take advantage of quantity discounts. In many industries, suppliers offer discounts of as much as 10 percent to 20 percent to firms who are willing to take delivery of large quantities. If the discounts exceed the cost of holding the goods until they are sold, it is advantageous to accept this offer.

Third, firms in industries with seasonal demand frequently hold inventories to achieve the economies associated with a stable production schedule. If the firm can forecast the demand for its goods with reasonable accuracy, it can reduce the costs of changing work force levels, overtime pay, and frequent starting and stopping of the production process by producing at a constant level throughout the year. This means, however, that the firm's production exceeds its sales in periods of low demand, causing its inventories to increase.

Inventory Costs

The firm that decides to hold inventories incurs a variety of costs, which may be grouped into four categories: acquisition costs, holding costs, shortage costs, and management costs.

As the name suggests, acquisition costs include all the costs of acquiring the item to be held in inventory. These include the purchase price, the transportation or production cost, and the cost of maintaining the purchasing activity, including management time, telephone expenses, and so forth.

Holding costs include all costs of holding the item in inventory until it is sold. The costs of storage, shrinkage, security, and interest are all included in this category.

Shortage costs are the multitude of costs that the firm incurs when customers order an item that is out of stock. These costs include customers ill will, lost profits on sales, and higher than usual production or transportation costs. Because shortage costs are high, some firms hold inventories of sufficient

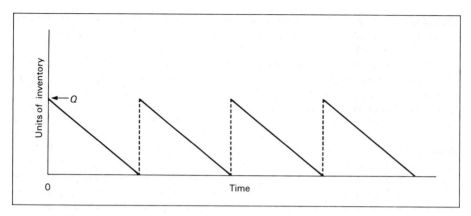

FIG. 23.7   Time Pattern of Triangle Beverage Company's Inventory

magnitude that shortage never occurs. Since this policy also involves substantial costs, the firm is better advised to treat the cost of shortage explicitly in its analysis.

The final cost of inventory management is the cost of management itself. For firms with thousands of different items in inventory, management costs may be significant. In an effort to reduce management costs, many firms have developed sophisticated computer-based inventory information and control systems. It is certainly worthwhile to consider such a system carefully.

Inventory Decision Models

The goal of inventory management is to minimize the total cost of the firm's inventory investment. Several models that help the manager accomplish this task are described in the following sections.

The Economic Order Quantity Model

The economic order quantity model is a simple, but widely used, approach to minimizing inventory costs. To illustrate its use, consider the inventory problem of the Triangle Beverage Co., a company that distributes approximately 156,000 cases of Butch Beer per year to over 12,000 retail outlets in the Southeast. Triangle purchases Butch Beer from the manufacturer at a cost of $4.50 per case, including transportation. The company believes that it incurs two kinds of inventory costs. Holding costs, which include interest, breakage, warehouse cost, pilferage, insurance, and taxes, amount to 25 percent of the firm's average inventory investment over the year. Acquisition costs, which include management time, paper, postage, telephone, and transportation, are about $25 per order.

The problem is to decide how many units to order at a time. If the firm chooses to order large quantities, it will incur a large investment in inventories, and thus its holding costs will be relatively high. However, if the firm seeks to minimize holding costs by making frequent orders for small quantities, it will incur excessive acquisition costs. The least cost order quantity clearly is one that balances the excessive holding costs associated with large orders with the excessive acquisition costs associated with small orders.

To analyze the inventory problem of the Triangle Beverage Company, it is helpful to be able to express the total inventory costs as a function of the order quantity. First consider holding costs. As shown in Figure 23.7, if the firm orders Q cases of Butch Beer at time 0, its inventory is Q at time 0 and gradually recedes to zero by the time the next shipment arrives. Thus, the firm's average inventory level is $Q/2$ and its annual holding cost, which is equal to the average inventory times the annual holding cost per unit, equals $C_H Q/2$, where C_H is the holding cost per unit. For the Triangle Beverage Company, the holding cost per unit equals 0.25 times $4.50, and so the annual holding cost is equal to $0.56 times Q.

The annual ordering costs are the product of the number of orders per year and the cost per order. Let D denote the annual level of demand (156,000 cases). Then the number of orders per year is equal to the annual demand divided by the quantity per order, that is, D/Q. Thus the annual acquisition cost equals

$$D/Q \times C_A$$

where C_A is the acquisition cost per order. Since C_A is $25 for Triangle Beverage, the annual acquisition cost is $(156,000/Q) \times \$25 = \$3,900,000/Q$. Furthermore, since the total inventory cost is simply the sum of the annual holding cost and the annual acquisition cost, the desired expression relating total costs to the quantity ordered is now at hand. It is

$$TC = \$0.56Q + \$3,900,000/Q$$

Using the above expression for total cost as a function of Q, the least cost order quantity can be obtained in one of two ways. First, the total cost equation can be used to calculate total costs associated with a number of different values of Q. For the case of Triangle Beverage Company, this has been done for nine values of Q ranging from 1,000 to 5,000. The results are shown in Table 23.8.

TABLE 23.8   Total Costs for Different Purchase Orders

Quantity (Q)	Holding Cost ($0.56Q)	Acquisition Cost ($3,900,000/Q)	Total Costs (TC)
1,000	$ 560	$3,900	$4,460
1,500	840	2,600	3,440
2,000	1,120	1,950	3,070
2,500	1,400	1,560	2,960
3,000	1,680	1,300	2,980
3,500	1,960	1,114	3,074
4,000	2,240	975	3,215
4,500	2,520	867	3,387
5,000	2,800	780	3,580

Total costs are lowest when 2,500 cases are ordered at one time. Under this policy, the firm will make approximately 62 orders a year or one order every 5.9 days.

The second method used in determining the least cost order quantity is to find the minimum value of the total cost function using calculus. When this is done, it is found that the least cost order quantity Q is given in general by the expression:

$$Q^* = \sqrt{\frac{2DC_A}{C_H}}$$

In this case, this equation yields:

$$Q^* = \sqrt{\frac{7,800,000}{1.13}} = 2,627$$

Although this appears to be somewhat more accurate than the first approach, the difference in cost between ordering 2,500 units at a time or ordering 2,627 units at a time is small, especially in light of the two simplifying assumptions that demand and cost values are known with certainty and that demand occurs at a steady rate throughout the year.

Lead Time in the Economic Order Quantity Model

The preceding analysis of the Triangle Beverage Company's inventory problem should be modified slightly to recognize the delay between the order and receipt of beer. It was determined that Triangle's best policy is to order roughly 2,600 cases every six days. Suppose now that it takes three days for the beer to be shipped from the manufacturer to Triangle's warehouse. It is evident that rather than waiting until its inventories are depleted, Triangle should place an order whenever its inventories reach a level of 1,300 cases. This is the number of cases that will be consumed during the shipment period. Since Triangle's inventory is depleted at the rate of roughly 2,600/6 cases per day, this is the same as saying that Triangle should place an order three days before receipt of a new shipment. The time between the placement of an order and the receipt of a new shipment is called the lead time in inventory analysis.

Quantity Discounts

It may be optimal for Triangle Beverage Company to order more than 2,600 units at a time if its supplier offers discounts for large orders. Suppose that Triangle's supplier offers a discount of $0.05 per case for orders between 3,000 and 4,000 cases, and a discount of $0.10 per case for orders greater than 4,000 cases. This discount must be reflected in the analysis of Triangle's least cost purchase quantity. The analysis shown in Table 23.9 reveals that an order quantity of 4,000 cases produces the optimal trade-off between the purchase cost savings of larger quantity orders and the increased inventory costs of these orders.

TABLE 23.9 Total Costs for Different Purchase Orders With Purchase Discounts

Quantity	Holding Cost	Acquisition Cost	Discount Cost Saving	Total Inventory Costs − Discount Savings
1,000	$ 560	$3,900	—	$ 4,460
1,500	840	2,600	—	3,440
2,000	1,120	1,950	—	3,070
2,500	1,400	1,560	—	2,960
3,000	1,590	1,300	$ 7,800	−4,910
3,500	1,855	1,114	7,800	−4,831
4,000	2,000	975	15,600	−12,625
4,500	2,250	867	15,600	−12,483
5,000	2,500	780	15,600	−12,320

Safety Stock

The assumption of known demand has been critical to this analysis so far. Demand uncertainty can be handled within the framework of the economic order quantity model through the inclusion of a safety stock. As shown in Figure 23.8, the firm never lets its inventory get down to zero. Instead it keeps a safety stock of S cases to protect against larger than expected demands. Of course, this also increases its average investment in inventory.

To see how the firm might determine the optimal safety stock to hold, suppose that Triangle Beverage believes the demand for beer over a six-day period is as shown below:

DEMAND FOR BEER OVER A SIX-DAY PERIOD

Demand	1,000	1,500	2,000	2,500	3,000	3,500	4,000
Probability	0.5	0.10	0.20	0.30	0.20	0.10	0.5

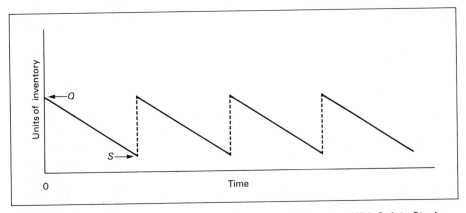

FIG. 23.8 Time Pattern of Triangle Beverage Company's Inventory With Safety Stock

TABLE 23.10   Expected Costs Associated With Various Safety Stocks

Safety Stock	Stockout	Stockout Cost (at $2)	Probability	Expected Stockout Cost	Additional Holding Cost	Total Cost
1,500	—	—	—	—	$840	$840
1,000	500	$1,000	0.05	$ 50	560	610
500	1,000	2,000	0.05	$100		
	500	1,100	0.10	100		
				$200	280	480
—	1,500	3,000	0.05	$150		
	1,000	2,000	0.10	200		
	500	1,000	0.20	200		
				$550	—	550

Suppose also that Triangle incurs a $2 cost per unit in lost sales or customer ill will every time demand exceeds the amount of inventory on hand.

Table 23.10 displays an analysis of the expected costs associated with safety stocks of 1,500, 1,000, 500, and 0 units. If the firm holds a safety stock of 1,500 units, there is no chance of a stockout and so the firm's stockout costs are zero. However, the holding costs of the extra 1,500 units in inventory are $840. If the firm holds a safety stock of 1,000 units, there is a five percent chance that it will incur stockout costs of $1,000. Adding the $50 expected stockout cost to the $560 additional holding cost yields a total of $610. By repeating a similar analysis for safety stock levels of 500 and zero, it is found that the optimal safety stock is 500 units.

MANAGING CURRENT LIABILITIES

Financial management in the short run also involves management of the firm's current liabilities, which may include trade credit in the form of accounts payable, various accruals such as wages and taxes payable, commercial paper, banker's acceptances, unsecured bank lines of credit, term loans, inventory loans, and funds advanced by pledging accounts receivable. These various short-term liabilities are not described in detail here, but the management of accounts payable and bank lines of credit, the two major manageable short-term liabilities for many firms, are discussed briefly.

Accounts Payable

Management of accounts payable can be improved through the recognition of three basic principles. First the financial manager should take full advantage of the credit period whenever no discount is offered for early payment. Second, the financial manager should take advantage of the discount, whenever the price savings exceeds the opportunity cost of the funds. Third, in making disbursements, the financial manager should choose disbursement banks that offer him both reasonable float and the ability to predict when disbursement checks will arrive.

Taking Advantage of the Full Credit Period. If no discount is offered, bills should never be paid before they are due. To see what is involved, suppose a financial manager has been presented with a bill of $100,000 that is due in 30 days. However, the financial manager intends to pay the bill within 10 days by selling some of the firm's marketable securities, which are currently yielding 10 percent. The cost of paying the bill in 10 days, rather than the 30 days allowed, is equal to the lost interest on the marketable securities. In this case, it is equal to:

$$\$100,000 \times 10\% \times 20/360 = \$555$$

If the manager handles accounts this way throughout the year, clearly the cost can be substantial.

Taking Advantage of the Discount. To see how the benefits of paying within the discount period can be compared to the opportunity cost of the funds, suppose that the financial manager in the previous example is offered a 2 percent discount for paying within 10 days. Thus, the financial manager will pay only $98,000 if he pays the bill within 10 days, but must pay an additional $2,000 if he pays by the thirtieth day. If he does not take the discount, the financial manager in essence is borrowing $98,000 for 20 days at an interest cost of $2,000. In terms of an annual percentage rate, this amounts to

$$2,000/98,000 \times 360/20 = 0.367 \text{ or } 36.7\%$$

If the firm's cost of capital is less than 36.7 percent, this is a bad deal, so the financial manager should take the discount.

Choice of Disbursement Banks. As noted in the discussion of cash management at the beginning of this chapter, the choice of disbursement banks can have a significant effect on the firm's earnings. In the previous example, suppose that the financial manager obtains the discount for early payment as long as the postmark date on the envelope is within 10 days of receipt of invoice. If he mails the envelope from a location that is distant from the payee and draws the check on a bank that is distant from the payee's bank, it may take an additional six days from the date of the postmark on the envelope for the check to be presented to the firm's bank for payment. If the financial manager can invest the full amount of the check for six days, the additional interest on this investment is:

$$10\% \times \$98,000 \times 6/360 = \$163$$

To allow the financial manager the opportunity to fund his account at the time the check is presented for payment, many banks offer a service known as a controlled disbursing account. To offer this service effectively, the bank must receive a high percentage of its presentments early in the day; it must be able to process these presentments rapidly, so it can notify the financial manager of the total presented that day; and it must be a member of the bank wire system so the financial manager can wire the funds to the bank by the end of the day. There are a great many banks that satisfy all three criteria.

Bank Credit Lines

A bank line of credit is an agreement with a bank that permits a firm to borrow up to a prespecified amount at any time before the end of the agreement. The total cost of the bank line of credit typically can be broken into two parts. First, the firm is charged an agreed upon rate of interest for the amount of funds actually borrowed; second, the firm is charged a fee for having the line available, whether it uses the line or not. The fee is often payable in either cash or compensating balances.

    Calculating the total cost of a bank line of credit is not always a simple task. First, the financial manager must decide whether he will pay for the fee in cash or balances. Second, if he decides to pay with balances, he must determine whether the balances required under the line exceed those he normally requires to do business. Finally, he must determine whether he wishes to purchase other services from the bank and, if so, whether the bank will allow the same balances to count in payment of the fee and the services.

CONCLUSION

In managing a firm's current assets and liabilities, there are many opportunities for making decisions that will affect the firm's bottom line performance and hence its market value. The financial manager can achieve the benefits of improved short-run financial management by thoroughly understanding the economic trade-offs involved in each short-run financial decision, and carefully evaluating the alternatives. The techniques discussed in this chapter should help him achieve this end.

SUGGESTED READING

Altman, Edward. "Financial Ratios, Discriminant Analysis, and the Prediction of Corporate Bankruptcy." *Journal of Finance* (Sept. 1968).

———. "The Z-Score Bankruptcy Model: Past, Present and Future." *Financial Crises: Institutions & Markets in a Fragile Environment*, eds. Edward Altman and Arnold Sametz, Chapter 5. New York: John Wiley & Sons, 1977.

Anderson, David R., et al. *An Introduction to Management Science: Quantitative Approaches to Decision Making*, 3rd ed. St. Paul, Minn.: West Publishing, 1982.

Austin, J., et al. "General Telephone's Experience With a Short-Run Financial Planning Model." *Cash Management Forum* (June 1980), pp. 3–6.

Boggess, William P. "Screen-Test Your Credit Risks." *Harvard Business Review* (Nov. -Dec. 1967), pp. 113−122.

Dyl, Edward A. "Another Look at the Evaluation of Investment in Accounts Receivable." *Financial Management* (Winter 1977), pp. 206−216.

Johnson, Robert W. "Management of Accounts Receivable and Payable." *Financial Handbook*, 5th ed., ed. Edward I. Altman, Chapter 28. New York: John Wiley & Sons, 1981.

Kramer, R.L. "Analysis of Lock-Box Locations." *Bankers Monthly Magazine*, Vol. 83 (May 1966), pp. 36−40.

Llewellyn, Wilbur G., and Robert W. Johnson. "Better Way to Monitor Accounts Receivable." *Harvard Business Review* (May-June 1972), pp. 101−109.

Magee, John F. "Guides to Inventory Policy." (I–III) *Harvard Business Review* (Jan.-Feb. 1956), pp. 49–60; (Mar.-Apr. 1956), pp. 103–116; and (May-June 1956), pp. 57−70.

Maier, S.F., and J.H. Vander Weide. "The Lock-Box Location Problem: A Practical Reformulation." *Journal of Bank Research*, Vol. 5 (Summer 1974), pp. 92−95.

———. "A Practical Approach to Short Run Financial Planning." *Financial Management* (Winter 1978), pp. 10−16.

Osteryoung, Jerome S., et al. "Riding the Yield Curve — A Useful Technique for Short-Term Investment of Idle Funds in Treasury Bills?" *Readings on the Management of Working Capital*, 2nd ed., ed. Keith V. Smith., Reading 15. St. Paul, Minn.: West Publishing, 1980.

Pogue, G.A., and R.N. Bussard. "A Linear Programming Model for Short-Term Financial Planning Under Uncertainty." *Sloan Management Review* (Spring 1972), pp. 69−98.

Smith, Keith V. *Guide to Working Capital Management*. New York: McGraw-Hill, 1979, pp. 141−172.

———. *Management of Working Capital*, Section 4. St. Paul, Minn.: West Publishing, 1979.

Stone, Bernell K. "Cash Management." *Financial Handbook*, ed. Edward I. Altman, Chapter 27. New York: John Wiley & Sons, 1981.

———. "The Payment Patterns Approach to the Forecasting and Control of Accounts Receivable." *Financial Management* (Autumn 1976), pp. 65−82.

———, Daniel M. Ferguson, and Ned C. Hill. "Cash Transfer Scheduling: An Overview." *The Cash Manager* (March 1980), pp. 3−8.

Stone, Bernell K., and Ned C. Hill. "Alternative Cash Transfer Mechanisms and Methods: Evaluation Frameworks." *Journal of Bank Research* (Spring 1982), pp. 7−16.

———. "Cash Transfer Scheduling for Efficient Cash Concentration." *Financial Management* (Autumn 1980), pp. 35−43.

24

Dynamics of Cash Management

PETER E. RASKIND

ROLE OF CASH MANAGEMENT

In a broad sense, cash management is the management of the *flow* of cash into and out of a firm. This function includes not only the management of the company's bank accounts, but also its portfolio of marketable securities, accounts receivable, accounts payable, and any other assets or liabilities that may produce or use cash in the near future. Since cash, marketable securities, and accounts receivable comprise a substantial portion of a manufacturing firm's assets, the cash management function is clearly central to a firm's everyday activities.

Despite the fact that cash management is a relative newcomer to financial management systems, recent high interest rates have focused increased attention on this subject. Together with improved capabilities on the part of providers of cash management services, formal cash management is now being practiced by firms with annual sales as small as $1 million. Larger firms typically have a staff of several people devoted to the cash management function, which can often contribute significantly to a firm's net income.

CASH BUDGETING

As described in Chapter 21, cash budgeting is essential to the short-term financial management function. In essence, the entire discipline of cash management assumes that the firm already has an idea of the cash balances and liquidity level that will be necessary in the short term. The goal of cash management, then, is to assure that the firm's liquid assets are sufficient for everyday operations, yet not so excessive as to produce opportunity losses for the firm in the form of forgone interest income.

MANAGEMENT SCIENCE / OPTIMIZATION TECHNIQUES

Most cash management optimization models begin with the assumption that the firm has already determined its liquidity needs. These models then address the division between cash and marketable securities. (Lockbox systems are discussed later in this chapter.) The best-known models for determining the optimal division between cash and marketable securities are the Baumol Inventory and Miller-Orr models.

Baumol Inventory Model

The Baumol model applies the concept of economic order quantity (typically used in inventory management) to the problem of optimizing the cash balance. In this model, the cost of carrying a cash "inventory" is traded off against the fixed costs of converting marketable securities into cash. The carrying cost of cash, of course, is the forgone interest that could have been earned had the cash been invested in marketable securities. The fixed costs of conversion to

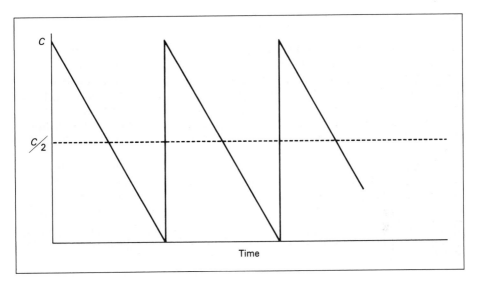

FIG. 24.1 Baumol Inventory Model

cash include not only explicit transactions costs charged by banks and brokers but also implied costs such as staff time.

Figure 24.1 depicts this model. It is assumed that over some period, the firm has a steady demand for cash. The firm "orders" cash by selling marketable securities and uses the cash until its cash balance is zero or some cushion level has been reached. At this point, the firm "reorders" and the process begins again.

The relevant question then becomes: What is the optimal "order" quantity C^* that minimizes total costs? That is, what order quantity balances the fixed order costs against the carrying costs of the cash inventory? To solve the problem, let:

i = interest rate per period

b = transaction cost of buying or selling any amount of securities

T = total amount of cash used over the time period

C = amount of securities sold in each sale transaction

There are T/C security sales during the period, producing transactions costs of bT/C. Since the average cash balance is $C/2$, the opportunity cost of holding this balance is $iC/2$. Therefore, total costs are:

$$\frac{bT}{C} + \frac{iC}{2}$$

If this equation is differentiated and the derivative is set equal to zero, the optimal value of C is found to be:

$$C^* = \sqrt{\frac{2bT}{i}}$$

The average cash balance is:

$$\frac{C^*}{2} = \frac{1}{2}\sqrt{\frac{2bT}{i}}$$

As expected, the equation for C^* implies that higher interest rates will lead to a lower cash balance. Similarly, higher transactions costs will result in higher cash balances.

To illustrate the use of the model, suppose that *ABC* Company disburses $1 million smoothly over a one-month period. The fixed cost for buying or selling securities is $50, and the interest rate on marketable securities is 12 percent, or 1 percent per month. Therefore:

$$C^* = \sqrt{\frac{2bT}{i}} = \sqrt{\frac{(2)(50)(1,000,000)}{0.01}} = \$100,000$$

ABC's average cash balance would equal $C^*/2$ or $50,0000. *ABC* would sell securities $1,000,000/$100,000 or 10 times during the month to obtain cash for disbursements.

The main drawback of the Baumol model is that cash does not flow into or out of a firm at a steady, known rate. For most firms, cash flow contains an element of variability, even randomness. The Miller-Orr model deals with the randomness of cash flow through the application of control-limit theory (again, a concept commonly used in inventory management).

Miller-Orr Model

Figure 24.2 illustrates the Miller-Orr control-limit model for cash balances. Over time, the cash balance (receipts less disbursements) wanders randomly between the control limits h and l. If the balance remains between these limits, no action is taken. If the balance reaches the upper control limit h, securities are purchased in the amount of $h - z$ in order to return the cash balance to z. If the cash balance reaches the lower limit l, securities are sold in the amount of $z - l$ in order again to return the cash balance to z.

If it is assumed that (1) the lower limit l is zero; (2) transactions costs for buying or selling securities are fixed and do not vary with volume, and (3) cash flows are completely random, then it can be shown that:

$$z = \sqrt[3]{\frac{3b\sigma^2}{4i}}$$

and $h = 3z$

where: b = transaction cost of buying or selling securities

  i = interest rate per day

  σ^2 = variance of daily closing cash balance

As expected, the cash balance increases as its variability increases.

To illustrate the use of the Miller-Orr model, suppose that the variance of *ABC* Company's closing cash balance is 25×10^8 (25 followed by eight zeros). If transaction costs for securities purchases/sales are $50 and interest rates are 12 percent annually or 0.033 percent daily, then:

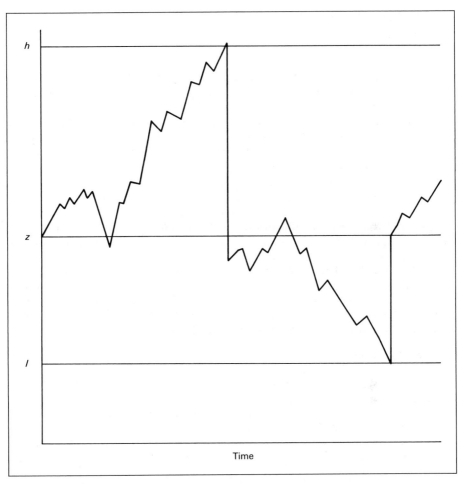

FIG. 24.2 Miller-Orr Control-Limit Model

$$z = \sqrt[3]{\frac{3b\sigma^2}{4i}} = \sqrt[3]{\frac{(3)(50)(25 \times 10^8)}{(4)(0.00033)}} = \$65,738$$

$$h = 3z = (3)(\$65,738) = \$197,214$$

Other Models

A variety of studies, including those performed by Fama-Eppen, Miller-Orr, Weitzman, and Frost, have extended the basic inventory and control-level models. In addition, it is possible to develop probability models that rely on management's subjective estimates of the probability of having to sell or buy securities given a current cash balance and a projected cash balance. Again, the aim is to minimize the total of opportunity costs (forgone interest) and fixed transactions costs.

Evaluation

The Baumol model clearly suffers from the assumption that the disbursement of cash will be smooth over time. For most firms, this assumption is quite unrealistic, since payrolls and other regular payments can make the disbursement level quite lumpy. Some of these difficulties can be mitigated by shortening the time period that is used, but the Baumol model is generally limited in its usefulness for practical cash management.

The Miller-Orr model improves upon the Baumol model in the sense that it assumes a randomness to the cash flow of the firm. The difficulty here is in estimating the value of σ^2, the variance of the daily closing balance. Historical surveys of closing balance positions may shed some light on the determination of σ^2, but the analysis and use of a "best guess" σ^2 will be error prone at best. The Fama-Eppen and other models come closer to modeling "real world" conditions but are also of limited use in everyday cash management.

Models for optimizing the firm's cash balance and marketable securities portfolio typically rest upon assumptions that are restrictive enough to limit their usefulness in practical cash management. Furthermore, the evidence available suggests that corporate cash management can be performed with similar results by following some "naive" rules rather than the output of the preceding models. However, these models do provide a conceptual framework for examining cash management problems and estimating acceptable solutions.

BANKING SERVICES AND HOW TO EVALUATE THEM

Since the early 1950s, commercial banks (and some nonbank corporations) have offered an increasingly sophisticated array of services designed to assist firms in their cash management. Over time, these services have become quite technical in nature, and they now permit firms to manage their cash position very closely on a day-to-day basis. The record high interest rates of recent years have created an ever widening awareness of cash management among corporations, and banks have responded to this growing market with continuous innovation and creativity.

For ease of presentation, cash management services are divided into the following categories: cash collection services, disbursement services, concentration services, control services, and investment services. The various services offered by banks can be categorized as in Table 24.1.

Collection Services

The major cash collection services that banks provide are lockbox, preauthorized checks, preauthorized electronic debits, electronic trade payments, and preencoded deposits.

TABLE 24.1   Categorization of Cash Management Services

Collection	Disbursement
■ Lockbox	■ Checking accounts
■ Preauthorized checks	■ Payable through drafts
■ Preauthorized electronic debits	■ Controlled disbursement
■ Electronic trade payments	■ Remote disbursement
■ Preencoded deposits	■ Zero balance accounts
	■ Electronic trade payments

Concentration	Control
■ Wire transfers	■ Information reporting
■ Depository transfer checks	■ Lockbox data transmission
■ Electronic depository transfers	■ Lockbox data pooling

Investment
- ■ Sweep accounts
- ■ Cash management accounts

Lockbox. The first lockbox arrangement began in the 1940s between Radio Corporation of America (RCA) and Chase Manhattan Bank. Since that time, lockbox has become the primary cash management service; it is used by virtually all corporations with over $100 million in sales (and many that are smaller) and is offered by virtually all banks with more than $1 billion in assets. Clearly, lockbox has proven to be a valuable service for corporations and banks alike.

The major purpose of a lockbox is the acceleration of the flow of useful cash from the various customers of a firm to the firm's bank accounts. Figure 24.3 illustrates how a lockbox can accelerate this flow. In the "Before Lockbox" case, customers of the firm mail their payments to the firm's headquarters, producing "mail float." If the firm is located in an area where mail service is poor, this mail float could be as high as four to five days. When the firm receives the payments, they are processed, posted to accounts receivable, collected into a bank deposit, and subsequently deposited at the firm's bank. This process can be termed "corporate processing float." Finally, the bank must send the deposited checks through the check collection system, producing "check collection float." In total, then, 4–8 days can elapse between the time that a payment is mailed and funds become available to the firm.

Using a lockbox, however, this collection float can be reduced to one to five days. Under a lockbox arrangement, a post office box is rented in the name of the firm at a post office near a bank. Customers of the firm are instructed to send their payments to this post office box (usually a location that enjoys good mail service). The bank picks up mail from the post office several times during the day and brings the mail back to the bank for processing. Many banks use a

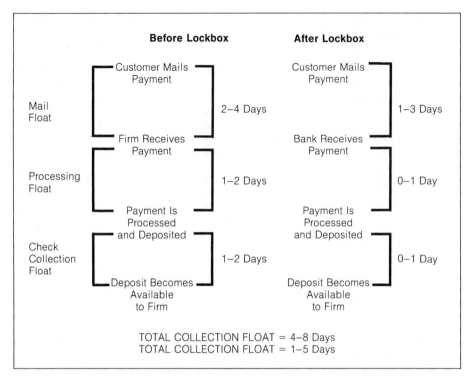

FIG. 24.3 Effect of Lockbox on Collection Float

unique zip code just for their lockbox customers in order to speed the Post Office's sorting of incoming mail.

Once the mail arrives at the bank, the following processing steps occur:

1 *Mail sorting.* The mail is sorted by customer, frequently with automated equipment.

2 *Deposit preparation.* Each envelope is opened and checks are removed. All the contents of the envelope are left inside to be sent on to the firm. The checks are batched together into a deposit.

3 *Deposit processing.* The dollar amount of each check is encoded as MICR characters on the bottom of each check. The checks are endorsed, microfilmed, imprinted with trace numbers, and photocopied. Then, the checks are sent on to the bank's check processing area to be cleared through the normal check collection channels. Typically, the bank's lockbox work schedules are arranged in order to channel checks to the bank's check processing area in time to meet key check clearing deadlines. In this way, the customer's deposit availability can be further improved.

4 *Deposit delivery.* The contents of each remittance envelope along with photocopies of the checks are sent to the firm by first class or express mail, courier, or

messenger services. The firm then uses this information to update its accounts receivable. In some cases, remittance data is transmitted electronically to the corporation by the bank (see the section on "Lockbox Data Transmission").

5 *Deposit reporting.* For the many firms that need to know their lockbox deposits on a same-day basis, the bank communicates the amount of the deposit through a telephone call, Telex message, or computer-based information reporting system.

By using a lockbox, then, a firm can reduce receivables float and increase the amount of cash available to invest or pay down borrowings. To illustrate the potential impact of a lockbox on the available cash balance, suppose that *ABC* Company generates $100 million in annual sales, all on credit terms. Further assume that, without a lockbox, six business days currently elapse between the time that a customer of *ABC* mails a payment to *ABC*'s headquarters and the payment becomes available for *ABC* to use. If a lockbox can reduce this time to three business days and the current investment/borrowing rate is 10 percent, then:

$$\text{Increase in available cash} = (\$100 \text{ million})(3/365)$$
$$= \$821,918$$
$$\text{Increased interest income/Decreased interest expense} = (\$821,918)(10\%)$$
$$= \$82,192$$

In addition, much of the processing burden for incoming payments can be shifted from the corporation to the bank.

It should be noted that banks are increasing automation of their lockbox processing. In particular, image processing technology appears to be quite promising not only for lockbox but for many other bank operations as well. Automated equipment photographs each incoming lockbox check and converts the photograph to a digitized image. The digitized image is a series of computer signals that allow the storage of the image on magnetic disk and the subsequent retrieval and reproduction of the image on computer terminals and paper. In this way, the physical checks can be released sooner into the clearing process while subsequent bank processing can be done using the check images. Although this technology is in its infancy, it should produce clearer photocopies of checks and, ultimately, better availability and lower costs for bank lockbox customers.

The evaluation of whether or not a lockbox is worthwhile rests on a comparison between the value of the increase in available cash versus the cost of operating the lockbox. Since most banks charge for lockbox services on a per item basis rather than on a dollars processed basis, firms who receive a relatively small volume of large dollar payments are most likely to find a lockbox worthwhile. However, if the firm can estimate the cost savings generated by its not having to process incoming payments, even a "retail" lockbox (large volume, small dollars per item) may be worthwhile.

For larger firms, multiple lockboxes in several areas of the country may be sensible. Again, the firm must examine the relative costs of operating the lockboxes versus the gains in available cash that the lockboxes will produce. Since there are many possible locations for lockboxes, different mail services for these locations, and different bank costs for operating the lockboxes at each location, an optimal lockbox system is complex to set up. Most major banks offer consulting services in which a lockbox optimization model is used to develop a lockbox system. These models are basically linear programming models that maximize availability gains subject to various constraints such as expenses and required locations. Expert consulting, together with management science techniques, can greatly ease the task of choosing locations for a multiple lockbox network.

Preauthorized Checks. Preauthorized Checks (PACs) are another service designed to speed the flow of incoming payments. Preauthorized checks are those written and deposited by the firm, drawn upon the firm's customers. This arrangement is authorized by the customer in advance, and places the responsibility for creating the payment check in the hands of the company to be paid rather than the payor. PACs are typically used for recurring payments such as insurance premiums and mortgage payments.

PAC services are usually available from the bank in two variations. (1) The bank maintains a master file of information regarding customers of the firm, their banks and bank account numbers, the amount for which the check should be created, and the date on which the check should be created. Then, the bank creates the checks in the proper amounts on the appropriate dates and deposits them to the firm's account. The check is then sent through normal check collection channels for payment. (2) The firm maintains its own file of customers and related data. It creates a computer tape which is sent to the bank for the subsequent creation of checks. This second method is used by firms that have fairly sophisticated computer facilities.

Like lockboxes, preauthorized checks must be evaluated in terms of their bank costs versus potential availability gains and cost savings for the corporation. By creating the check and immediately posting it to its accounts receivable, the firm should realize decreased collection time as well as reduced internal processing of incoming payments. In addition, bad debts may be reduced since the firm does not have to cajole its customers into issuing checks, but rather can create the checks of its own accord on the agreed dates in the agreed amounts.

Preauthorized Electronic Debits. A service very similar to PACs, preauthorized electronic debits (PADs) utilize the Automated Clearing House (ACH) for the settlement of electronic debits and credits rather than traditional paper check collection channels. The ACH is actually a collection of 32 regional ACHs spread throughout the United States. On a daily basis, each bank that is a member of the ACH submits to its local ACH a computer tape containing debits and credits that should be posted to accounts at other destination banks. The various ACHs route these debits and credits to the correct ACH for each destination bank, and each bank receives back from its local ACH a computer tape containing debits and credits to be posted to accounts at that bank. Figure 24.4 depicts the flow of electronic payments through the ACH.

The PAD service utilizes the ACH to speed up cash flow for the firm. If customers of the firm preauthorize the creation of a debit on their account and

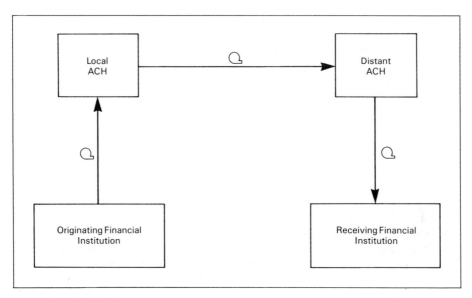

FIG. 24.4 Automated Clearing House Structure

if the customer's bank is an ACH participant, then the firm's bank can initiate debits through the ACH and credit the firm's account for these payments. Just like PACs, PADs place the responsibility for creation of the payment transaction in the hands of the payee rather than the payor, thus speeding up cash flow and reducing internal processing costs.

Why should a firm use preauthorized electronic debits rather than preauthorized checks? There are at least two reasons why PADs are often more desirable then PACs. First, PADs carry a certain one-day collection float. PACs are usually floated for at least one day and often two days. So PADs may produce more available cash to the firm then PACs. Second, most banks charge less for electronic debits than for paper items. Therefore, PADs may also be cheaper than PACs. It should be noted, however, that PADs can be used only when the customer's bank is an ACH participant and when the customer authorizes an electronic debit to his account. Many firms and individuals still desire paper evidence of a payment they have made; for example, a canceled check. In addition, the payer often does not want to give up the disbursement float that is currently being realized on paper checks that the payer is initiating. Over time, these attitudes should change as electronic payments become more common.

Electronic Trade Payments. In the past, preauthorized electronic debits were not terribly applicable for payments from one corporation to another since there was no way for the corporations to exchange electronically other information relating to the payment, such as invoices paid and discounts taken. Recently, however, the National Automated Clearing House Association

(NACHA) has introduced a system for exchanging corporate trade payments and related information on an electronic basis. While electronic trade payments are in their infancy, they are expected to gain acceptance as the costs of issuing, processing, and collecting checks continue to grow. Since access to the ACH is restricted to banks, electronic trade payments will be another cash management service offered by banks to corporations in the very near future.

Preencoded Deposits. In some cases, such as supermarkets and insurance companies, the volume of incoming checks is heavy enough that it is worthwhile for the firm to purchase the appropriate equipment and MICR-encode the dollar amount on the bottom of each check. Normally, this encoding is performed by the bank where the check is deposited, and the cost of encoding is included in the bank's price for an item deposited. Most banks charge a somewhat lower price for checks that are already preencoded when deposited. It should be noted that encoding equipment can be expensive; therefore, a careful investment analysis must be performed in order to determiine whether making preencoded deposits is sensible. Furthermore, encoding represents a significant operational burden for the firm that probably can be performed more efficiently by a bank. For some firms, however, preencoding deposited items may result in significant cost savings.

Cash Disbursement Services

There are several banking services available that assist firms in issuing, controlling, and slowing the disbursement of cash. These include checking accounts, payable through drafts, zero balance accounts, controlled/remote disbursement accounts, and electronic trade payments.

Checking Accounts and Account Analyses. Although checking or demand deposit accounts are not always thought of as a "disbursement" service, they represent not only the most common disbursement service but also the basis for other more specialized services. Furthermore, it is through balances left in the corporate checking account that the corporation compensates the bank for other banking services that are used.

While most of the features of the corporate checking account are well known and straightforward, it is worth paying special note to the concept of an account analysis. Since 1933, commercial banks have been prohibited from paying interest on checking account balances (also known as "demand deposits"). Since checking accounts were "free" for banks, checking account balances were quite valuable for a bank, a fact that did not go unrecognized by corporate treasurers. Over time, therefore, a quite formal system has arisen in most banks for assigning value to the checking account balances that a corporation leaves at the bank.

Table 24.2 illustrates a typical bank account analysis. During the month of December 198X, *ABC* Company carried an average balance of $50,000 in its corporate checking account. Average daily check collection float was $5,000, reducing available deposits to $45,000. The bank's reserve requirement for this

TABLE 24.2   Example of a Bank Account Analysis

ABC COMPANY
ACCOUNT ANALYSIS
December 198X

	Current Month	Year to Date
Average daily ledger balance	$50,000	$45,000
Average daily float	5,000	4,800
Reserve requirement (13.1%)	5,895	5,266
Average daily investable balance	$39,105	$34,934
Deposit credit (current earnings allowance is 10.0%)	$ 332	$ 3,843

Service	Volume	Unit Price	Total Cost	Balances Required
Maintenance	1	$15.00	$ 15.00	$ 1,766.13
Deposits	3	1.00	3.00	353.23
Items deposited	60	0.10	6.00	706.45
Wire transfers	6	6.00	36.00	4,238.71
Checks Written	400	0.10	40.00	4,709.68
			$100.00	$11,774.20

	Price Basis	Balance Basis
Deposit credit	$332	$39,105
Services rendered	100	11,774
Excess balances available to support other services or credit facilties	$232	$27,331

account for December was 13.1 percent or $5,895. This means that the bank had to leave $5,895 on a non-interest-bearing basis at the Federal Reserve Bank as reserves against this account. Therefore, the bank had $39,105 of "free" balances during the month that it could invest. Similar figures are also displayed for the year to date.

The next section of the account analysis assigns value to the balances. Each month, the bank chooses an earnings allowance rate (also called the analysis rate, the earnings credit, or the deposit credit). This rate is usually based on short-term money market rates, such as Treasury bill yields, and approximates the opportunity cost of leaving non-interest-bearing balances in the checking account. The earnings allowance rate is applied to investable balances in order to compute an earnings allowance or deposit credit. The earnings allowance represents the amount of services that a corporation could purchase from the bank without having to leave additional compensating balances. Essentially, the earnings allowance is implicit interest that the firm cannot remove from the bank in hard cash, but can use internally to buy services.

The last section of the account analysis details the various bank services that the firm used during the month, their prices, and the compensating balances that are required to support the use of each service (this can be verified using the price and volume of each service and the month's earnings allowance rate). Finally, the total balances required to support the services used are compared to the actual balances that were kept in the account. As Table 24.2 shows, *ABC* Company maintained "excess" balances of $27,331 for December 198X.

There are several important points to note about the account analysis. First, if excess balances are maintained over a given time period, banks do not compensate the firm for the excess in an explicit manner. Conversely, if the firm is in a deficit compensating balance position over some time period, many banks now bill the firm for the value of the deficit balances. So, it is extremely important that service use be estimated and balances maintained appropriately; hence the value of cash management!

Second, the precise format and computation of the account analysis varies widely from bank to bank. The earnings allowance rate, reserve requirement, number of days used and so on are all subject to the bank's discretion. It is entirely possible, then, that a service's price may be lower at one bank than another, although the service is actually more expensive in terms of required compensating balances. For example, suppose bank *A* and bank *B* use the following computation methods in their respective account analyses:

	Bank A	Bank B
Earnings allowance	10%	8%
Number of days in month	31	30
Number of days in year	365	365

Further suppose that bank *A* charges $1.00 for a particular service and bank *B* charges $0.80 for the same service. Bank *B* appears to be the cheaper service provider, but in fact:

	Bank A	Bank B
Service price	$ 1.00	$ 0.80
Monthly balance required to support service	117.74	121.67

If the firm is compensating the bank with balances for services that are used, bank *A* is actually the cheaper source, despite its apparently higher price. So, the analyst must be careful when comparing banks to take account of the different techniques that banks use in their account analyses. Of course, if the firm pays fees for services that are used, only the simple price of the service is relevant.

Finally, deregulation of the banking industry is quickly eliminating Regulation Q and the prohibition of interest on demand deposits. Once checking account balances become interest bearing, the need for a system of implicit interest as represented by the account analysis should disappear.

Payable Through Drafts. Payable through drafts are similar to checks but with one major difference. As long as a check has been signed by an authorized signer, it is payable on demand at the drawee bank. Payable through drafts, on the other hand, must be individually approved by the account holder and are drawn directly on the issuer. Mechanically, this means that the bank delivers to its customer payable through drafts that have been presented for payment that day. The firm must approve or disapprove each draft, and return them to the bank by some specified deadline, usually in the afternoon. The bank then pays the drafts that have been approved (debiting the firm's account) and returns the disapproved drafts.

Payable through drafts are usually used in situations where the firm needs to maintain control over outlying personnel who are making payments on the firm's behalf. For example, payable through drafts are often used by salespeople for paying travel expenses while on the road. Similarly, payable through drafts are often used by insurance companies for payment of insurance claims by adjustors. Finally, some firms use payable through drafts simply in an effort to elongate disbursement float, since most banks have an earlier deadline for same-day credit on payable through drafts than on regular checks.

Remote/Controlled Disbursement. Just as lockboxes reduce and control collection float, remote/controlled disbursement services are designed to elongate and control disbursement float. Since typical payment terms recognize the envelope postmark date as the relevant date for discounts taken and timely payment, it is worthwhile for the payor to attempt to extend the time between receipt of his payment and the ultimate collection of the check.

Remote disbursement services take advantage of the fact that certain locations are remote enough to make it difficult to present checks for payment in a timely way. This geographical advantage produces the effect of elongating disbursement float for the paying firm. During the 1970s, many firms were employing remote disbursement, sometimes to the point that East Coast payments would be drawn on West Coast remote points and West Coast payments drawn on East Coast remote points.

Of course, elongated disbursement float for the payor means elongated collection float for the payee. Typically, the burden of this increased collection float was shared between the payee and the Federal Reserve System (Fed). The Fed maintains a schedule by which it assigns float to checks that are presented for payment. Until recently, no check was ever floated by the Fed for more than three business days. Therefore, if a check actually took four days to collect, the payee would bear three days of float and the Fed would bear the additional day. The float that remote disbursement arrangements generated for the Fed became troublesome enough that the Fed began jawboning against remote disbursement. This, combined with other negative publicity, has caused most major banks to cease offering remote disbursement services, and today relatively few firms use these services.

Controlled disbursement services are now far more commonly offered by banks and used by corporations. The goal of a controlled disbursement service is not to elongate disbursement float but rather to improve the firm's control over daily disbursement and cash balances. Banks in Fed cities receive several presentations of checks for payment during each business day. In some parts of the United States, "city" items are presented by the Fed as late as noon. In addition, many banks collect together checks drawn on another bank and send those checks directly to the drawee bank instead of through the Fed. Most banks have established an "on us" deadline that determines whether checks sent directly to it will be credited immediately. Typically, this "on us" deadline is during the afternoon. Therefore, items drawn upon a corporate checking account may arrive at the bank from the Fed and other banks as late as 4 P.M.; even if they are promptly reported to the corporation by the bank, it may be too late in the day to invest excess cash or fund the account to avoid an overdraft. Since most firms (and banks) try to avoid overdrafts, the firm maintains excess balances in order to account for the uncertainty of daily debits against its account. This situation, of course, produces an associated opportunity cost for firms.

Controlled disbursement services rely on the fact that banks that are served by Regional Check Processing Centers (RCPCs) or that are located in Fed "country" points receive only one presentation of checks from the Fed, usually early in the morning. Furthermore, many RCPC banks will not accept direct shipments of "on us" checks for immediate credit. Therefore, once these presented checks are processed, the corporation can know in the morning all the disbursement debits that will be charged against its account that day. This timely notification of daily debits allows the corporation to fund its account in the exact amount necessary to cover the debits. The firm can manage its cash position with less uncertainty, and maximize cash available for investment or loan paydowns.

Most banks offer controlled disbursement services through branches of the bank that are served by RCPCs. In some cases (particularly in states that do not permit branching), controlled disbursement services are offered through an arrangement between a large "city" bank and a smaller RCPC bank. In this case, the corporation technically draws its disbursements against an account at the smaller RCPC bank, although the large bank actually performs all the processing and customer notification functions that are necessary.

Although controlled disbursement services enjoy a somewhat better reputation than did remote disbursement, they are also threatened by recently announced Federal Reserve plans to present items for payment as late as noon anywhere in the United States that is justified by dollar volume. This action represents a further effort on the Fed's part to reduce float in the nation's payments system. "Noon presentment" would certainly make controlled disbursement more difficult, but not necessarily obsolete. It remains to be seen whether the later deliveries of cash letters from the Fed to the banks will contain a material number of items, and whether firms will be willing to accept a service that contains some uncertainty as to daily debit totals. Furthermore, the Fed is considering whether or not to offer a service to "city" banks in which the Fed would capture on computer tape the MICR line from checks that will be delivered for presentment to the bank that day. The Fed would give the bank this information early in the morning in order that the bank could inform customers of the amount of debits that will be posted to accounts that day. However, the physical checks would be delivered by the Fed at the same times as deliveries are made now (up until noon or sometimes later). This MICR line capture service would allow banks to offer customers the same certainty that controlled disbursement currently permits, while allowing the Fed the processing time that it desires to sort and present checks to drawee banks for payment. Therefore, there is still some hope for controlled disbursement services.

Zero Balance Accounts. Many times a corporation wants to maintain several checking accounts for different purposes. For example, a firm may want to maintain separate disbursement accounts for different divisions in order to simplify accounting or spread check signing authority. However, the firm would rather not manage the balance in each of these accounts, thereby multiplying its cash management tasks. In this case, zero balance accounts can allow the firm to maintain separate accounts, but only manage one central concentration account. Essentially, zero balance accounts are accounts for which the bank will drive the balance to zero at the end of each day. For example, if *ABC* Company maintains a zero balance account for the disbursements of its *XYZ* Division, the bank will generate a credit each day to *XYZ*'s zero balance account in an amount sufficient to produce a net balance of zero. If debits for a particular day total $100,000, then a credit of $100,000 will automatically be generated in order to return *XYZ*'s balance to zero. This $100,000 would probably be transferred from *ABC*'s central concentration account. In this way, *XYZ* Division can perform its own disbursements from corporate funds without needing access to general corporate check stock. Separate accounts can be maintained with no danger of complicating the firm's cash management tasks and thereby producing excess bank balances.

Electronic Trade Payments. In the long run, the ACH should provide an efficient and inexpensive alternative to the current paper methods for settling corporate payments. In the short run, however, many corporations are resisting electronic trade payments because disbursement float will be lost. Over time, this situation will probably be resolved through different payment terms for paper and electronic payments. For example, firms may set terms of 2/10 net 30 for paper payments and 2/12 net 32 for electronic payments. Splitting payment terms would allow the payor and payee to share the float benefits and costs of electronic payments.

Concentration Services

Most large firms practice concentration banking; funds are collected at the most convenient and economical locations and then concentrated in a central concentration bank where they can be used for investment, loan paydown, or disbursement. Banks offer several services to assist in the daily concentration process: wire transfers, depository transfer checks, and electronic depository transfers.

Wire Transfers. The fastest method for moving funds between banks is wire transfer. By using wire transfers, a corporation can transfer funds on a same-day basis from outlying collection points to the concentration bank. The same-day feature of wire transfer services is particularly useful when the receipts at the local collection points (e.g., lockboxes) are largely immediately available funds. Then it is worthwhile to pay the relatively high cost of a wire transfer in order to immediately mobilize the funds. If, for example, the funds will become available in one day, there are cheaper alternatives for concentrating (see the following section, "Depository Transfer Checks"). Wire transfers can also be useful for payment to vendors when the day of receipt of the payment must be certain. Finally, wire transfers can be helpful for emergencies where funds must be transferred immediately.

Wire transfers are significantly more expensive than other mechanisms for concentrating funds. The distinguishing feature of wire transfer versus other concentration vehicles is a wire transfer's same-day availability. Therefore, some analysis is necessary in order to determine whether wire transfer is the most economical method for concentrating funds. This analysis is demonstrated in the next section on depository transfer checks (DTCs).

Depository Transfer Checks. DTCs represent an alternative for concentration that is cheaper than wire transfers. Essentially, DTCs are nothing more than checks that are drawn on a corporation's account at one bank and deposited at the same corporation's account at another bank. In this way, funds can be moved from one bank to another. In simplest form, DTCs operate as follows: A deposit is made in the firm's account at an outlying bank. The same day or later, personnel of the firm at the outlying location issue a check drawn on the outlying bank account and mail the check as a deposit to the concentration bank. The concentration bank then collects the check through normal check collection channels and the funds are moved from the outlying bank to the concentration bank. This arrangement is often called mail DTCs.

The drawback to mail DTCs is that while the check is in the mail to the concentration bank, valuable funds are laying idle at the outlying bank. In order to overcome this problem, most firms that use DTCs for concentration use an automated DTC service. For example, suppose *ABC* Company owns and operates apartment buildings all over the United States. Periodically, the superintendent of each building collects rent receipts and deposits them in a local bank. He then calls a designated telephone number and reports his location and the amount of the deposit. The number that the superintendent calls could be a bank, a nonbank provider such as National Data Corporation, or even the corporate headquarters. During the afternoon, this information is passed electronically to the concentration bank, which subsequently prepares checks drawn upon the local bank accounts. These checks are then deposited to the corporation's concentration account and clear through normal check collection channels. Usually, these checks clear in one day.

Clearly, the advantage of an automated DTC service over a mail arrangement is the saving of mail time. While a mailed DTC may spend two days in the Post Office system before it is received by the concentration bank, an automated DTC service creates the check and deposits it on the same day that the deposit was made at the local bank. This has the effect of reducing idle balances at the outlying banks and increasing investable balances for the firm.

If a corporation has receipts being collected and deposited at an outlying bank, how does it choose between wire transfer and DTC for concentrating funds? Consider the following example: *ABC* Company is a San Francisco distributor that has found it to be economical to operate a lockbox in Chicago. Although there is variation in both the amount and composition of receipts of the Chicago lockbox, a typical day's activity is as follows:

Funds immediately available	$ 20,000
Funds available in one day	80,000
Total lockbox receipts	$100,000

The Chicago lockbox is able to report this information each day to *ABC* Company early enough for *ABC* to wire out money if it so chooses. Suppose also that:

1 The total cost (both banks) for wire transfer of funds from Chicago to San Francisco is $14.

2 The total cost of a DTC is $2.

3 All investing/borrowing by *ABC* Company is done through its San Francisco bank.

4 *ABC* pays fees to its lockbox bank in Chicago and has no reason to leave compensating balances there.

5 *ABC*'s investment/borrowing rate is 10 percent.

The question then becomes, should *ABC* Company use wire transfer or DTCs to concentrate funds in San Francisco? If *ABC* wired out all the available funds on a given day, it would typically wire out $100,000 ($20,000 from today and $80,000 that has become available from yesterday's deposit). If *ABC* used DTCs that clear the Chicago bank in one day, an average available balance of $20,000 would arise in the Chicago bank. This idle balance carries an opportunity cost of 10 percent.

	Daily Bank Costs	Average Idle Balance	Daily Opportunity Cost
Wire transfer method	$14.00	$ 0.00	$0.00
Depository transfer check method	2.00	20,000.00	5.48

As can be seen in this example, the extra cost of a wire transfer is far greater than the opportunity cost of using a DTC that will clear in one day. Therefore, *ABC* Company should use the DTC method for concentrating its funds in San Francisco, despite the fact that an idle balance will be left in its Chicago account.

The choice of which concentration method to use depends, then, on the size of the transfer, the relative bank prices for the services, and current interest rate levels.

Electronic Depository Transfers. Depository transfers that are effected through the ACH are called electronic depository transfers (EDTs). (For a discussion of the ACH, see the section "PreAuthorized Electronic Debits.") EDTs are always floated one day according to ACH rules. In all other respects, except price, EDTs are exactly like DTCs. EDTs are usually cheaper than DTCs.

Control Services

All of the collection, disbursement, and concentration services described previously result in the movement of funds into or out of the firm. There is another class of services that does not produce funds movement, but rather helps the firm to control and monitor its cash position, and interacts with its accounting systems. These services include information reporting, lockbox data transmission, and lockbox data pooling.

Information Reporting Services. The concept of computerized information reporting services arose in the early 1970s. Since that time, their growth has been so explosive that virtually every firm with over $100 million in annual sales subscribes to at least one service. Most money center banks have developed and own proprietary systems that they offer to their customers. Chemical Bank in New York has also licensed its information reporting system to approximately 60 other banks that have banded together into an organization known as BankLink. Nonbank data processing firms, such as National Data Corporation and General Electric Information Services, also offer information reporting services.

Essentially, all the major information reporting services act as collection and distribution points for relevant cash management information. Typically, the major information reporting systems contain all of the following features:

1 *Multibank balance reporting.* Each day, all of the firm's banks input information regarding ledger balance, available balance, and float for each of the firm's accounts. The cash manager can then receive through a computer terminal a consolidated picture of his overall cash position as of the close of the previous day's business.

2 *Previous day debit and credit reporting.* Each of the firm's banks can provide data relating to debits and credits that were posted to the firm's accounts the previous day. Again the cash manager can receive this report through a computer terminal, and thereby track transactions that have occurred.

3 *Lockbox reporting.* Banks at which the firm maintains lockboxes can report in the amount of the daily lockbox deposits on a same-day basis. In this way, the

cash manager can make informed decisions regarding concentration transactions.

4 *Same day debit and credit reporting.* This service is very similar to previous day debit and credit reporting, but transactions are reported on the day that they occur. Most banks update the system on a periodic basis through each day with new debits and credits that will be posted to the firm's accounts that day. Banks vary quite widely in the sophistication of their same day reporting since it is quite dependent upon the sophistication of the bank's internal accounting systems. For example, some banks are able to report wire transfer activity but not check processing activity on a same-day basis. It should be mentioned that a firm would use same day reporting to receive controlled disbursement debit totals in the morning if controlled disbursement is being used.

5 *Depository transfer initiation and reporting.* Most information reporting systems also act as the mechanism through which depository transfers can be initiated and monitored. (See the preceding section, "Depository Transfer Checks.") In many systems, outlying offices of the firm can report deposits they have made at local banks through either a terminal, pushbutton telephone, or voice contact with an operator. The information reporting system then consolidates this information and transmits it to the concentration bank so that DTCs or EDTs can be initiated. Most systems also provide daily reporting to the corporate headquarters as to which locations reported deposits, the amount of the deposits, and so on.

6 *Wire transfer initiation.* This feature allows the corporate cash manager to initiate wire transfers through a terminal in the corporate office. The cash manager's wire instructions are transmitted through the computer to the bank's wire transfer area for execution. For high volume wire transfer users, this service can reduce errors and save time over instructions initiated by telephone.

7 *Target balance reporting.* Through historical experience, a firm usually knows approximately what level of compensating balances must be maintained each month to compensate the bank for services used. This feature of many information reporting systems helps the cash manager to monitor the firm's actual cash balance versus its target balance. In addition, this service often computes what level of balances would be necessary for the remainder of a month in order to meet the target balance.

8 *Money market reporting.* Many information reporting systems report current interest rates on money market instruments as well as foreign exchange rates. In a few cases, it is possible to purchase money market instruments by execution of instructions initiated through a computer terminal.

The decision to use a computerized information reporting service depends, of course, on the value of the information received. As with any cash management service, the analyst needs to compare the costs of using an information reporting system against the incremental interest income/saved interest expense that the firm will generate as a result of more timely information.

Lockbox Data Transmission. When a firm receives collections through one or more lockboxes, photocopies of the remittances received and other contents of the incoming envelopes are sent from the bank to the firm through the mail, a courier, or a messenger. (See the preceding section, "Lockbox.") The firm may receive the photocopies several days later and then update its accounts receivable to reflect payments that flowed in through the lockbox.

In some situations, this system can present operational problems for the firm. First, for a "retail" lockbox (large volume, small dollar value per remittance), there will be a large volume of payments that the firm must manually enter and post to its accounts receivable system. This can be an extremely time consuming, error prone, and expensive process. Second, even if the lockbox is "wholesale" (small volume, large dollars per remittance), there are many situations in which the firm needs to be aware of the payment from its customer as soon as possible. For example, if a firm's customer is experiencing financial difficulties, a firm may not be willing to ship goods until payment for the previous shipment has been received. In this situation, the time between the receipt of a payment at the lockbox bank and receipt of the photocopy by the firm may mean lost business for the firm.

Lockbox data transmission is designed to assist in both of the situations just described. In a lockbox data transmission service, the bank captures information that uniquely identifies the remitter and transmits this data to the firm along with the amount and date of the remittance. This computer transmission of lockbox data occurs on a same-day basis, thereby permitting the firm to update its accounts receivable system in a timely and automated fashion. Lockbox data transmission is not a service that directly speeds up a firm's cash flow, but rather it helps the firm to save processing time and costs and to improve accuracy.

In general, there are four typical service variations that banks often provide in terms of identifying the remitter for purposes of data transmission:

1 *MICR line information.* Here, the bank captures the MICR information from the bottom of each check passing through the lockbox. The MICR line is machine readable, and includes a transit/routing number identifying the bank upon which the check is drawn and the account number of the remitter at that bank. For wholesale lockboxes, the combination of transit/routing number and account number is usually sufficient to identify a specific remitter. By maintaining a computer file of MICR lines belonging to its customers, a firm can then use the information captured by the bank to update its accounts receivable on an automated basis.

2 *MICR line and invoice information.* In many cases, a firm asks the bank to capture not only MICR line information but also additional information such as the number of the invoice that was returned with the remittance. The addition of an invoice number should help the firm to attain a higher "hit ratio" of receivables successfully updated when the data transmission is used for receivables posting. This reduces the operational burden of posting manually payments that cannot be posted automatically because there is not enough information to assure accuracy.

3 *Optical character recognition.* As discussed previously "retail" lockboxes usually experience a relatively high volume of remittances. Good examples of retail lockboxes include insurance premium payments, mortgage loan payments, and charge card payments. For these types of payments, the MICR line is usually not a reliable method for identifying the remitter since consumers change banks and bank accounts far more often than corporations. Even if an invoice is returned with the payments, the cost of capturing this invoice information manually would be prohibitive. Therefore, banks utilize Optical character recognition (OCR) technology in which special equipment can "read" a line of information on a document that the consumer returns with his payment. This line of information contains the consumer's account number and the amount that he is expected to pay with the return document (for example, his account balance). The OCR equipment captures this line of information and an operator simply verifies that the actual payment matches the amount that was expected. In this way, the cost of capturing remitter identifying information can be reduced through the reduction of manual labor. In general, the OCR service is relatively inexpensive at most banks.

4 *Other detailed information.* In some cases, the firm requires information other than MICR or invoice data in order to post to its accounts receivable. Examples include the remitter's name, the remittance check number, or a remitter identification number. This information usually is not machine readable and, therefore, is quite costly for the bank to capture. As a result, specialized variations of the lockbox data transmission service tend to be relatively expensive for the firm.

Lockbox Data Pooling. For the firm that maintains multiple lockboxes and utilizes lockbox data transmission, it may be quite inconvenient to receive separate data transmissions from each lockbox bank. If errors occur, the firm may not be able to determine easily which bank should be involved. Furthermore, it may be expensive for the firm to maintain personnel in its data processing center to receive as many as 10 or 12 data transmissions, depending on the size of the firm's lockbox network.

Lockbox data pooling eliminates some of these difficulties by carrying the lockbox data transmission process one step further. Here, the bank that the firm designates as the "pooling" bank receives the lockbox data transmissions from each of the other banks in the lockbox network. The pooling bank combines all of this lockbox data, edits the data to verify that the transmissions have been completed, and generates one consolidated transmission to the firm. At this point, the firm can update its accounts receivable in the normal fashion. If errors or delays occur, the pooling bank is responsible for resolving the problems with the other lockbox bank. Typically the pooling bank is also a lockbox bank for the firm, although there is no reason why this must be true. The pooling bank usually charges extra for pooling lockbox data from other banks, in addition to the normal lockbox data transmission charges.

Lockbox data pooling is a quite sophisticated service that, as yet, is not offered by many banks or used by many firms. However, as the cost of data processing continues to fall, it seems reasonable to expect that more and more firms will find pooling to be an attractive alternative to multiple lockbox data transmissions.

Investment Services

Historically, banks have offered relatively few cash management services that were oriented toward investment transactions. Most cash management services were designed so that the firm could control and minimize its cash balance, but the responsibility for investing the excess rested squarely with the firm. Once the excess for a given day had been determined, it was the cash manager's responsibility to choose a suitable investment and initiate the investment transaction. It should be noted that this lack of automatic investment services offered by banks was not entirely due to an unavailability of suitable technology or simple oversight. Rather, banks have historically derived substantial income from excess balances maintained by corporate customers, and the banking industry was unlikely to promote new services that further reduced excess balances beyond their already low levels.

In recent years, however, deregulation of the banking industry and increasing competition for deposits from savings and loan associations and nonbanks have caused banks to offer increasingly attractive automated cash management accounts. The simplest form of these accounts is the sweep account; more complicated is the complete cash management account.

Sweep Account. A sweep account periodically transfers funds on an automated basis from a checking account to an interest-bearing account based upon the balance level in the checking account. In the typical case, the firm sets a minimum and maximum balance for its checking account. On any given day, if the closing balance exceeds the maximum that the firm has set, funds will be transferred to some interest-bearing investment in an amount that reduces the checking balance back to a maintenance level. Conversely, if the balance in the checking account falls below the minimum on any given day, funds are returned from the investment in order to restore the checking account to the maintenance level.

Sweep accounts often offer several investment options to which funds can be swept. For example, it may be possible to transfer funds to a money market account within the bank or to investments outside the bank such as money market mutual funds. Some sweep accounts offer investment alternatives such as preferred stock mutual funds or tax-exempt money market funds as investment options from a sweep account. In certain cases, it is possible to split funds that are being swept from the checking account into several different investments, and to return funds from those investments in the same proportions.

Obviously, a sweep account greatly eases the task of cash management for firms that usually have excess cash. It eliminates the need for the firm to monitor closely all flows of funds into and out of its checking account. Furthermore, the time that is spent choosing investments and monitoring a portfolio of marketable securities can be reallocated to other tasks within the firm. The firm needs only to channel funds into the sweep account and disburse from this account; any excess will be invested automatically.

There are several drawbacks to sweep accounts that should be noted. First, at this stage in their development as a cash management service, they are quite expensive for the firm to use. In some cases, this simply reflects defensiveness on the part of banks, but there is also some evidence that sweep accounts will be costly for banks to operate. So, there is a trade-off between the time savings and convenience of a sweep account and the bank's cost of having the account. Second, the yield that the firm can earn on the investment options associated with a sweep account will probably always be slightly less than the firm could earn if it searched actively for the best investment alternative each time an investment transaction was imminent. Clearly, this will represent an opportunity cost for the firm; however, the main goal of most firms is to earn profits based on their products rather than returns on marketable securities. Therefore, a small loss of return on short-term investments would probably be worthwhile for most firms because of time savings on the part of treasury personnel.

Cash Management Account. The cash management account is a natural extension of the sweep account in the sense that it offers not only investment options when checking balances exceed the maximum, but also credit options when checking balances drop below the minimum. For example, if the firm's closing balance on any given day is below the minimum that has been set, a drawdown under a line of credit may be created in order to return the checking balance to a maintenance level. In the case that the checking balance exceeds the maximum, funds would be transferred to an investment option that the firm has chosen.

Cash management accounts are also relatively new, and are currently being offered by some banks and brokerage firms. The convenience of these accounts for the firm should cause their growth to continue, particularly as banks acquire the internal systems necessary to process them efficiently on an automated basis.

CASE STUDY: ADLER BAKING COMPANY

Introduction

Adler Baking Co., a $270 million baker of breads and pastries, began to address the subject of its cash management system in late 1980. There was a general feeling among the firm's financial staff that Adler's cash management system contained inefficiencies that were leading to availability losses. The high interest rates prevailing at that time added to the firm's interest in reexamining its cash management system, since the opportunity costs of any availability losses were commensurately high. Consequently, Adler's treasurer requested that the cash management consultants from Midwest Bank, Adler's lead bank, study Adler's current cash management system and recommend improvements to it.

Business Background

Adler Baking Co. was founded in 1914 and is headquartered in Chicago. The firm bakes a full line of breads and pastries in its Chicago plant, and distributes them through nine regional distribution and marketing offices in Illinois, Indiana, Iowa, Wisconsin, and Missouri. For accounting and control purposes, each of these distribution offices is organized as a division, while headquarters in Chicago is referred to as "corporate."

Current Cash Management System

Figure 24.5 depicts Adler Baking Co.'s current cash management system. Table 24.3 presents a sample account analysis from a local bank used by an Adler division.

     Collection. Currently, the Chicago Division generates approximately $110 million in annual sales through distribution to major supermarket chains in the Chicago area. The other eight divisions each generate approximately $20 million in annual sales, largely through distribution to smaller chain stores and "corner" grocery stores. Each division is responsible for collecting and posting its own accounts receivable. Payments for Chicago Division sales are usually mailed by customers to the Chicago Division headquarters, where they are deposited in a Midwest Bank depository account on a daily basis by office

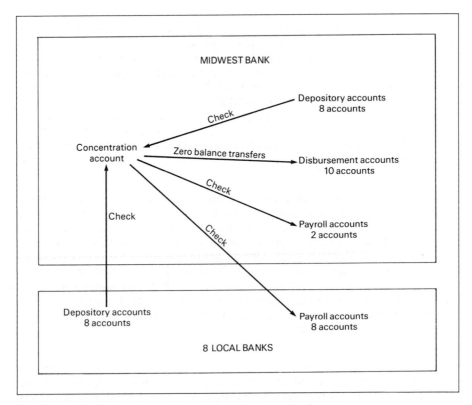

FIG. 24.5 Adler Baking Co. — Current Cash Management System

TABLE 24.3   Typical Local Bank Account Analysis

LOCAL BANK AND TRUST CO.

ACCOUNT ANALYSIS
Adler Baking Co. — Division 3

Average daily balances	$95,000
Balances required to support services used	14,000
Excess balances	$81,000

personnel. On a typical business day, 10 customer payments are received at Chicago Division headquarters; each payment averages $44,000. Payments to the other divisions are usually mailed to that division's office; sometimes they are given to truck drivers who deliver orders to customers. These payments are deposited in local banks on a periodic basis, usually once or twice a week.

Disbursement. Each division is responsible for its own disbursements, including payroll. The divisions maintain disbursement accounts at Midwest Bank upon which they issue checks for their various expenses. These disbursement accounts are tied to Adler's concentration account through a zero balance arrangement. Each day, funds are transferred to each division's disbursement account in the amount of the issued checks that have cleared that day. Payroll represents an exception to this process; payroll accounts are maintained at local banks and are funded by the division on the day before the payroll is issued. This funding is accomplished by depositing a check in the payroll account that is drawn on the division's disbursement account at Midwest Bank.

Concentration. Each time a division makes a deposit into a local bank, it is responsible for calling corporate and informing the cash management department of the amount of the deposit. Corporate then issues a check drawn upon the division's depository account and deposits the check into Adler's concentration account at Midwest Bank. One difficulty that Adler has been experiencing is a lack of consistency on the part of divisions in terms of reporting deposits to corporate. Occasionally, a division will report a deposit several days later or, occasionally, forget to report the deposit entirely. In these cases, corporate eventually discovers the deposit through an examination of the division's monthly local bank statements.

Control. On a daily basis, corporate telephones Midwest Bank to find out the balance in Adler's concentration account as of the day before. Adler uses this information to estimate the amount of cash that will be available for investment or loan paydown that day.

Proposed Cash Management System

After examining Adler's current cash management system, the Midwest Bank cash management consultants developed several recommendations that were designed to reduce bank charges and improve overall funds availability for the company.

Collection Recommendations. Since the Chicago Division was receiving a significant dollar volume of customer payments and manually depositing them to the depository account at Midwest Bank, the consultants suggested that Adler explore the option of a lockbox at Midwest Bank to receive these payments. The lockbox would not only lift some of the processing burden from Adler personnel, but also result in better funds availability for the firm, since Midwest Bank's lockbox processing is timed to meet key check clearing deadlines. Of course, a close study of the composition of the incoming payments would be necessary in order to determine whether a lockbox would be an economical proposition for Adler. However, based on a 15 percent investment/borrowing rate, a one day acceleration of the collection of the Chicago Division's $110 million in annual sales would produce $66,000 in additional interest income/reduced interest expense. So, the possible use of a lockbox appeared to merit some investigation.

Disbursement Recommendations. The Midwest Bank consultants recommended that the divisional payroll accounts be centralized at Midwest Bank and removed from the local banks. The practice of funding these accounts with a check drawn on the Midwest disbursement accounts was creating substantial idle balances at the local banks as Table 24.3 indicates. By moving these payroll accounts to Midwest Bank and placing them on a zero balance basis, these idle balances could be reduced or eliminated. It should be noted that if Adler wanted to leave excess balances at the local banks for nonfinancial reasons, this could be accomplished through the depository accounts at each local bank.

Concentration Recommendations. In order to improve the efficiency of Adler's concentration system, the Midwest Bank consultants recommended the use of automated depository transfers to move funds from the local banks to the Midwest concentration account. Through the use of Midwest Bank's computerized system, Adler employees at outlying divisions could report the daily deposits that were made into local bank accounts. Adler headquarters then could examine these reports, note any divisions that had not yet reported that day, and change any amounts that corporate staff wished to change. Finally, Midwest Bank would create depository transfers in order to move the funds from the local bank accounts to the concentration account. The consultants recommended that these transfers be accomplished through the ACH, since the float on electronic debits is certain and electronic entries are cheaper than similar paper transactions.

Control Recommendations. The consultants recommended that Adler utilize Midwest Bank's computerized information reporting system for several purposes. First, the system could be used for the concentration of funds as described previously. Second, Adler could eliminate its daily telephone calls to the bank by having its balance information reported through the automated system. Third, Adler could receive detailed debit/credit reporting that would allow it to spot errors sooner and accelerate its account reconciliation process. Finally, Adler could utilize the wire transfer feature of the system for any wire transfers that the firm might make.

WARNING SIGNS FOR A CASH MANAGEMENT TUNE-UP

Like an automobile, there are certain signs that should tip off the corporate treasurer or cash manager to the need for a cash management system tune-up. While the following checklist is certainly not exhaustive, it does contain many of the conditions that would indicate the potential for improvement in the firm's cash management system:

- Excess balances in bank accounts (as indicated by account analyses)
- Slower than desired receivables turnover
- Cash shortfalls that necessitate expensive borrowing (overdrafts)
- Poor investment yields (lower than market yields due to late-in-the-day "emergency" investing)
- Untimely receipt of information regarding balances, payments, etc.
- Poor forecasting of disbursements that will clear each day
- High labor costs for running the system
- High level of unavailable funds in bank accounts (excessive collection float)

Finally, banks and other providers of cash management services are regularly introducing new services that ease the task of cash management. The corporate treasurer can keep abreast of these developments through newsletters and other publications in order to keep the firm's cash management system running at peak efficiency.

SUGGESTED READING

Baumol, William J. "The Transactions Demand for Cash: An Inventory Theoretic Approach." *Quarterly Journal of Economics,* Vol. 65 (Nov. 1952), pp. 545–556.

Beehler, Paul J. *Contemporary Cash Management.* New York: John Wiley & Sons, 1983.

Eppen, Gary D., and Eugene F. Fama. "Solutions for Cash-Balance and Simple Dynamic-Portfolio Problems." *Journal of Business,* Vol. 41 (Jan. 1968), pp. 94–112.

Frost, Peter A. "Banking Services, Minimum Cash Balances and the Firm's Demand for Money." *Journal of Finance,* Vol. 25 (Dec. 1970), pp. 1029–1039.

Homonoff, Richard B., and David Wiley Mullins, Jr. "Applications of Inventory Cash Management Models." In Stewart C. Myers, ed., *Modern Developments in Financial Management.* New York: Praeger, 1976.

Miller, Merton H., and Daniel Orr. "A Model of the Demand for Money by Firms." *Quarterly Journal of Economics,* Vol. 80 (Aug. 1966), pp. 413–435.

PART IV
Long-Term Financial Management

25

How to Evaluate Long-Term Investments

DIANA R. HARRINGTON

Over the past few years, U.S. firms have been soundly criticized for failing to plan adequately for the long term. Managers of those firms, the critics accuse,[1] have been shortsighted, and much of the blame for their myopia has been placed on the techniques they use to analyze capital investments. Whether this criticism is justified or not is a matter of continuing debate.

Managers do not choose to make bad decisions, nor do they knowingly use techniques that will lead to them. While the debate continues, therefore, each manager will want to think again about the way in which capital investment

---

[1] See, for instance, Robert H. Hayes and William J. Abernathy, "Managing Our Way to Economic Decline," *Harvard Business Review* (July–Aug. 1980), pp. 67–77.

decisions are made. This chapter is intended to help the manager or investment analyst to make such decisions. It can also be used by the manager who is seeking an introduction to capital budgeting.

This chapter describes the most widely used techniques for analyzing corporate capital investments and the purposes of these techniques. Wherever these techniques can be misunderstood or misused, the potential problems are also described. Each section is accompanied by examples drawn from experience that demonstrate the techniques or point out the potential for problems.

INTRODUCTION TO CAPITAL BUDGETING

What Is a Capital Investment?

A capital investment is any outlay of money from which benefits are expected. To distinguish a capital investment from any corporate expenditure, it is usual to think of the benefits of a capital investment as continuing for some time, usually for more than a year.

Typically, the first thing to think of as capital investments are assets that will be recorded (capitalized) on the firm's balance sheet. Valued at its purchase price, such an asset (e.g., a building or equipment) is expensed (depreciated) over its useful life.[2] The investment is made with the expectation that it will generate some increase in benefits over the long term. The benefits can come from an increase in revenues or a decrease in costs.

While investments in physical plant, land, and equipment may come to mind first, firms also make investments in other firms (acquisitions), working capital (permanent increases in inventory, accounts receivable, or cash), advertising campaigns, marketing programs, and research and development, as well as in the added capacity to bear debt that each investment brings to the firm. Even though generally accepted accounting practices do not allow some of these investments to be capitalized and put on the firm's balance sheet as assets, they are, nonetheless, capital investments.

The Purpose of Capital Budgeting

Most firms have a formal capital budgeting process for two reasons. First, since the firm is just a reflection of its past investments, capital budgeting is an integral part of long-term strategic planning. Second, such investments are often large and can be difficult and costly to reverse once they are made. Thus, formal analysis is designed to help avoid costly errors.

In most firms the capital investment process consists of seven steps:

1 Identifying investment opportunities;

2 Estimating the benefits and costs associated with each opportunity;

3 Evaluating the benefits and costs;

---

[2] In fact, the useful life may be defined less by its economic value than by Internal Revenue Service rules.

4 Determining the relative attractiveness of each investment;

5 Choosing among investment alternatives;

6 Implementing the chosen investments; and

7 Evaluating the implemented investments.

These seven steps are repeated continuously in the ongoing firm. While each step is important in assuring that the best possible decisions are made, this chapter concentrates on those that are of most concern to the financial manager, steps 2 through 5.

COST/BENEFIT ANALYSIS

The manager's objective in making an investment is to create value for the firm's owners. To do so, the benefits from the investment must exceed its costs. The benefits and costs are those specific to the investment itself and are thus marginal (incremental) to those the firm would incur if the investment was not made.

Since cash is what a firm can use to invest, reduce debt, or pay expenses, it is cash, not promises of payment, that is of interest in capital budgeting. Most U.S. firms use an accrual method of accounting, in which revenues and liabilities are recorded when made, not when money is received or paid. There may be a lag of several months between the two. The benefits and costs from any investment are cash receipts and disbursements, not accrued revenues or expenses.

In addition, in evaluating a capital investment, concern is not with allocated expenses. For instance, over their life many investments will be charged with a portion of the firm's ongoing expenses, sometimes called overhead. If the investment neither increases nor decreases the overall corporate overhead, such an accounting allocation is not an incremental benefit or cost attributable to the investment and thus should be ignored. The investment analyst's job is not to forecast the revenues and expenses the firm's accountants will record but to estimate what the investment's cash cost and benefits will be over its life.

Forecasting Costs

Cash costs (outflows) are of two types: capital costs and operating costs. Capital costs include initial costs necessary to acquire the investment plus any subsequent expenditures that extend its life. Operating costs are the recurring cash outlays required once the investment is a part of the firm's operations.

An example of cash costs can be seen by examining the outflows from an investment being considered by the managers of the Trevi Corporation. Trevi prepares and packages horseradish for domestic consumption. Located in the northwestern United States, Trevi is one of the largest producers of ground horseradish in the world. Trevi's operations are seasonal and quite labor-intensive. To reduce this labor intensity, Trevi management is considering purchasing a labeling machine to replace the five full-time employees whose job it is to hand-place the labels on each jar of horseradish. The purchase price of the machine is $85,000, and the manufacturer says it will have a useful life of 5 years. The machine's life can be extended to 10 years if it has a major overhaul at a cost of $18,000 after 5 years. The cost of the machine and its overhaul are the capital costs.

For operating costs, the machine will use considerable electricity, forecasted at a cost of $1,000 per year, and require one full-time operator who will be trained by the manufacturer to operate the machine and perform basic repairs. The operator's training is included in the purchase price of the machine. Yearly salary and benefits for the machine operator are expected to be $11,000. The machine will be housed in a currently unused portion of the Trevi factory at no added cost to Trevi. Other operating costs (e.g., glue and labels) will remain the same whether the labels are placed by hand or by machine. The incremental capital and operating costs to Trevi are listed below:

LABELING MACHINE — CASH OUTFLOWS

Item	Cost	Timing
Purchase machine	$85,000	Before operation (year 0)
Overhaul machine	18,000	End year 5
Machine operator's salary	11,000	Yearly (years 1–10)
Electricity	1,000	Yearly (years 1–10)

Forecasting Benefits

Benefits can come from four different sources:

1 Revenues from increased sales;

2 Cost reductions from more efficient processes;

3 Cash received when replaced equipment is sold; and

4 Cash received when the investment is salvaged at the end of its useful life.

In the Trevi example, benefits from three of these sources will come from the investment in the new labeling machine; no added sales (Item 1) are expected as a result of the changed labeling process.

First, Trevi will no longer require four full-time workers to affix labels. The savings will be $8,500 per employee for a total of $34,000 per year. Second, the equipment currently used in the labeling operation, mainly tables, will be scrapped; management expects the equipment can be sold for $2,000. Since this equipment has been fully depreciated, taxes of $600 (capital gains tax on the salvage value) will be paid on this $2,000 cash receipt. Third, management expects any salvage value the new equipment may have at the end of its life to be offset by the costs of removing the equipment. Thus, the full value of the new equipment will be depreciated over its life: The machine will be depreciated using straight-line depreciation over the five-year economic life and the overhaul will be treated in the same way. The following summarizes the cash benefits (inflows) of the labeling machine to Trevi:

LABELING MACHINE — CASH INFLOWS

Item		Benefit	Timing
Reduced salaries and benefits		$34,000	Yearly (years 1–10)
Sale of old equipment			
Proceeds of sale	$2,000		
Taxes (at 30%)	(600)		
Net proceeds		1,400	Before operation (year 0)
Salvage value, new equipment		—	Year 10
Depreciation tax savings			
Labeling machine		17,000	Yearly (years 1–5)
[($85,000/5 years)(1 − 50% tax rate)]			
Overhaul		3,600	Yearly (years 6–10)
[($18,000/5 years)(1 − 50% tax rate)]			

The Economic Recovery Act of 1981 established a new system of depreciation, the accelerated cost recovery system (ACRS). While the system is based on accelerated depreciation, firms no longer have the option of selecting their method of depreciation. The Act prescribes depreciation rates for five asset classes. Firms not choosing to use ACRS must use straight-line depreciation.

To present a clear picture of the net after-tax cash flows from this investment to Trevi, the benefits and costs are combined in Table 25.1. The format used in this table is a useful and a frequently used way of presenting an investment's cash flows. Table 25.1 shows depreciation as a cost. Since depreciation shields income from taxes, it reduces the taxable income. It is, however, a noncash cost; thus, it is added back to the profit after taxes to determine the net cash flow. Alternatively, the depreciation tax shield could be added to the profit before depreciation and after taxes. For instance, in Table 25.1, the net profit in year 1 would change to $11,000 and the depreciation tax shield would be $8,500 ($17,000 × tax rate) for a net cash flow of $19,500.

In forecasting the cash flows, the manager seeks to make the best, most accurate forecast possible without overestimating or underestimating. The result is a forecast of the incremental costs and benefits that Trevi management expects from the investment in the labeling machine. Any expense allocations, such as overhead associated with the unused plant, would be incurred whether management chose to invest in this machine or leave that portion of the plant empty. Thus, such allocations are not incremental cash costs.

In addition, any cash already spent on the investment, such as research done to design or evaluate the labeling machine, is not a cost relevant to this project. This is a sunk cost, one that has no bearing on the marginal value of the investment, and thus is irrelevant to this decision. Trevi is not concerned with recovering sunk or irreversible costs but with creating value from any subsequent investment.

To demonstrate the estimation of costs and benefits, a simple example has been used. The costs of the machine are known (as they often are), and the wage and electricity costs and benefits can be forecasted with apparent ease. The latter, however, is rarely the case. While investment costs may be contrac-

TABLE 25.1   Cash Flows — Labeling Machine

(dollars in thousands)

	Year 0	Year 1	Year 2	Year 3	Year 4	Year 5	Year 6	Year 7	Year 8	Year 9	Year 10
Investment cash flows											
Machine	($85.0)										
Machine overhaul						($18.0)					
Salvage — old machine	2.0										
Taxes — old machine sale	(0.6)										
Salvage — new equipment											—
Annual cash flows											
Sales		—	—	—	—	—	—	—	—	—	—
Salary reductions		$34.0	$34.0	$34.0	$34.0	$34.0	$34.0	$34.0	$34.0	$34.0	$34.0
Wages and salaries		(11.0)	(11.0)	(11.0)	(11.0)	(11.0)	(11.0)	(11.0)	(11.0)	(11.0)	(11.0)
Electricity		(1.0)	(1.0)	(1.0)	(1.0)	(1.0)	(1.0)	(1.0)	(1.0)	(1.0)	(1.0)
Depreciation											
New machine		(17.0)	(17.0)	(17.0)	(17.0)	(17.0)	—	—	—	—	—
Overhaul		—	—	—	—	—	(3.6)	(3.6)	(3.6)	(3.6)	(3.6)
Taxable income		$ 5.0	$ 5.0	$ 5.0	$ 5.0	$ 5.0	$18.4	$18.4	$18.4	$18.4	$18.4
Taxes (at 50%)		(2.5)	(2.5)	(2.5)	(2.5)	(2.5)	(9.2)	(9.2)	(9.2)	(9.2)	(9.2)
Profit after tax		$ 2.5	$ 2.5	$ 2.5	$ 2.5	$ 2.5	$ 9.2	$ 9.2	$ 9.2	$ 9.2	$ 9.2
Noncash charges[a]		17.0	17.0	17.0	17.0	17.0	3.6	3.6	3.6	3.6	3.6
Net cash flow	($83.6)	$19.5	$19.5	$19.5	$19.5	$ 1.5	$12.8	$12.8	$12.8	$12.8	$12.8

(a) Depreciation tax shield

tual and thus known, two problems can make forecasting difficult: inflation and uncertainty. Indeed, difficulties with estimating the benefits and costs can at times render forecasts useless.

Incorporating Inflation

The term "inflation" means changes in the purchasing power of currency, in this case, the dollar. Over the life of the investment, costs and benefits may change considerably as inflation flares and wanes. For example, Trevi forecasted the salary for the new machine operator at $11,000 per year. In these forecasts, management assumed no increase in salary arising from inflation. What if management expected inflation to be 5 percent per year for the next 10 years? The salary forecast would not remain at $11,000 per year for 10 years. Then how would inflation be included in the forecasts?

Real cash flow forecasts (those made net of inflation) provide an estimate of the constant dollar costs and benefits anticipated from the investment. This is not a forecast of the investment's actual outflows and inflows as they will occur.

To estimate the actual cash flows, the nominal flows, the manager may choose to include the effects of the inflation forecast on each cost and benefit. To demonstrate the procedure, the Trevi investment can be used. Table 25.1 provided Trevi management's forecasts without inflation (real cash flow forecasts). To include an expected 5 percent inflation, each cash cost and benefit would be increased 5 percent per year. The resulting cash flows would be forecasted as shown in Table 25.2.

Table 25.2 shows cash costs and benefits that are all equally affected by inflation. The application of a single inflation rate to all cash flows may be too general if inflation affects the various costs and benefits in different ways. In that case, factor-specific indexes may be used. If the outlook for inflation is uncertain, the manager may use sensitivity or simulation analysis to evaluate the effect. These analytical tools are described in detail in Chapter 26.

Obviously, the cash flows in Table 25.2 are larger than those in Table 25.1. To the extent that depreciation provides a smaller tax advantage as inflation increases, the net cash flows are different, in real terms. However, that is the only factor that differentiates the two forecasts once it is recognized that they are based on different outlooks for inflation. Larger cash flows are not superior when based solely on a different forecast for inflation. Thus, it is critical that the inflation forecast be consistent for all costs and benefits and be explicit. In firms where a variety of functional specialists are making various cash flow forecasts, consistency can be a problem. Without an explicit forecast for inflation, each cash flow could be based on a different inflation rate. The result is cash flows that are inconsistent and generally useless for making decisions.

Incorporating Uncertainty

Whenever forecasts are made, there is a degree of uncertainty about what will actually occur. The more uncertain the forecast, the greater the manager's discomfort in making the estimate. However, the object is to make the best possible forecast given the information available. The larger the cash flow in

TABLE 25.2   Cash Flows — Labeling Machine
5 Percent Inflation

(dollars in thousands)

	Year 0	Year 1	Year 2	Year 3	Year 4	Year 5	Year 6	Year 7	Year 8	Year 9	Year 10
Investment cash flows											
Machine	($85.0)										
Machine overhaul						($21.9)					
Salvage — old machine	2.0										
Taxes on old machine sale	(0.6)										
Salvage — new equipment											—
Annual cash flows											
Sales	—	—	—	—	—	—	—	—	—	—	—
Salary reductions		$ 34.0	$ 35.7	$ 37.5	$ 39.4	$ 41.4	$ 43.4	$ 45.6	$ 47.8	$ 50.2	$ 52.8
Wages and salaries		(11.0)	(11.6)	(12.1)	(12.7)	(13.4)	(14.0)	(14.7)	(15.5)	(16.3)	(17.1)
Electricity		(1.0)	(1.0)	(1.1)	(1.2)	(1.2)	(1.3)	(1.3)	(1.4)	(1.5)	(1.6)
Depreciation											
New machine		(17.0)	(17.0)	(17.0)	(17.0)	(17.0)	—	—	—	—	—
Overhaul		—	—	—	—	—	(3.6)	(3.6)	(3.6)	(3.6)	(3.6)
Taxable income		$ 5.0	$ 6.1	$ 7.3	$ 8.5	$ 9.8	$ 24.5	$ 26.0	$ 27.3	$ 28.8	$ 30.5
Taxes (at 50%)		(2.5)	(3.1)	(3.7)	(4.3)	(4.9)	(12.3)	(13.0)	(13.7)	(14.4)	(15.3)
Profit after tax		$ 2.5	$ 3.0	$ 3.6	$ 4.2	$ 4.9	$ 12.2	$ 13.0	$ 13.6	$ 14.4	$ 15.2
Noncash charges(a)		17.0	17.0	17.0	17.0	17.0	3.6	3.6	3.6	3.6	3.6
Net cash flow	$ (83.6)	$ 19.5	$ 20.0	$ 20.6	$ 21.2	—	$ 15.8	$ 16.6	$ 17.2	$ 18.0	$ 18.8

(a) Depreciation tax shield

question and the more uncertain the forecast, the more the manager will seek expert help in making that forecast.

Trevi's labeling-machine forecast presented a relatively easy task, particularly because the labeling machine would not affect sales, only costs. Machine and wage costs and savings are often easier to forecast than sales increases. However, consider another investment that Trevi management had to evaluate.

For some time John Trevi's grandmother had been suggesting that the firm diversify. Their only product had been packaged ground horseradish, but Grandmother Trevi had suggested expansion into a line of food products, starting with her famous horseradish Yummies, a cookie laced with horseradish. The horseradish, in addition to providing considerable amounts of vitamins and minerals, gave the cookie a kind of zest. Grandmother Trevi believed that the cookie, a favorite among family and friends, would give Trevi entry into another market. Early success with the Yummies could be followed by other horseradish-based products, such as candy and soft drinks.

At Grandmother's prompting, management had forecast cash flows associated with the manufacture and sale of Yummies. The factory had space that was not being used. Since the building was an old dairy, it was designed to handle food processing and could easily be renovated to accommodate cookie production at a cost of $30,000. Added equipment would be needed, and used equipment was available for $90,000. Management believed that three full-time production workers ($8,500 per employee per year) and one supervisor ($15,500 per year) could produce the product.

Since the cookie would appeal to consumers who were concerned with their health and who might be more adventuresome than ordinary cookie-eaters, management had approached wholesalers who sold through camping and health food stores. The wholesalers were enthusiastic about the product and planned to concentrate on sales in the northwestern United States for the first year, after which, sales would be made across the United States. Selling costs were expected to be 10 percent of sales with a minimum of $20,000 per year. Together with the wholesalers, Trevi management had estimated the sales to be $150,000 the first year and $200,000 every year thereafter. The equipment was expected to be usable for 10 years. Management expected to sell the cookie for 50 percent more than it cost to produce. The benefits and costs, if there were no inflation, would be as shown in Table 25.3.

Obviously, Yummies' sales were the most uncertain forecast Trevi management had to make. While the acceptance by customers of a horseradish cookie makes the forecasting difficulty obvious, managers with less preposterous products often find themselves in an identical situation. The problem of making forecasts is exacerbated when going into a new business.

Having no experience of their own, managers who are striving to gain more confidence in their forecasts seek outside help. In addition to various experts inside the firm, one data source that is often used is the historical experience of others in similar businesses. Statistical data about other companies are available from marketing research firms. The data are aggregate (i.e., about firms or industries rather than products) and thus may be of limited use when a new venture is being undertaken.

A second source of data is the models and methods for determining product-market potential that have come into vogue over the last 10 years. Pio-

TABLE 25.3 Cash Flows — New Product
(dollars in thousands)

	Year 0	Year 1	Year 2	Year 3	Year 4	Year 5	Year 6	Year 7	Year 8	Year 9	Year 10
Investment cash flows											
Renovation	$ (30)										
Equipment	(90)										
Annual cash flows											
Sales		$150	$ 200	$ 200	$ 200	$ 200	$ 200	$ 200	$ 200	$ 200	$ 200
Cost of sales		(75)	(100)	(100)	(100)	(100)	(100)	(100)	(100)	(100)	(100)
Wages and salaries		(41)	(41)	(41)	(41)	(41)	(41)	(41)	(41)	(41)	(41)
Selling costs		(20)	(20)	(20)	(20)	(20)	(20)	(20)	(20)	(20)	(20)
Depreciation		(12)	(12)	(12)	(12)	(12)	(12)	(12)	(12)	(12)	(12)
Taxable income		$ 2	$ 27	$ 27	$ 27	$ 27	$ 27	$ 27	$ 27	$ 27	$ 27
Taxes (at 50%)		(1)	(13)	(13)	(13)	(13)	(13)	(13)	(13)	(13)	(13)
Profit after tax		$ 1	$ 14	$ 14	$ 14	$ 14	$ 14	$ 14	$ 14	$ 14	$ 14
Noncash charges(a)		12	12	12	12	12	12	12	12	12	12
Net Cash Flow	$(120)	$ 13	$ 26	$ 26	$ 26	$ 26	$ 26	$ 26	$ 26	$ 26	$ 26

(a) Depreciation tax shield

neered by consulting firms, such models as PIMS and the Boston Consulting Group's product-market matrix or experience curve can yield clues to what others have experienced or what the technology, market position, and relative competition may portend for expected revenues and costs.

The manager's job is to gather or create the best forecasts possible: not to be too conservative (overestimate costs and underestimate revenues) or too optimistic, but to be as accurate as possible in forecasting an unknown future. The forecasts will help the manager make decisions so long as they contain the best estimates of the marginal cash flows the firm will incur if the investment is made. Some methods used by managers to include differences in risk are discussed briefly later in this chapter. Chapter 26 discusses such formal methods as simulation analysis. For now, the best estimates made by Trevi management are used to demonstrate the process of capital budgeting.

CHOOSING AMONG INVESTMENTS: CREATING VALUE

Trevi managers have two possible investments. Should they make either or both of the investments? To decide, once the cash flows for the two investments have been made, management must have a way to measure and compare the value each investment will provide to the company's owners. There are a number of methods that could be used to compare the relative attractiveness of the investments. Each of the methods has advantages and disadvantages.

Accounting Rate of Return

One old measure of an investment's attractiveness, once widely used, is the accounting rate of return. The accounting rate of return is simply the average net book value over the life of the investment divided into the investment's average profits after tax. For Trevi's new product, the average investment over the project's life is $60,000 and the average profit is $24,700 ($13,000 + 9($26,000)/10). Thus, the accounting rate of return would be 41 percent. Managers using this method would compare the 41 percent to an average corporate accounting return (usually historical) or an industry average to judge the return's acceptability.

This method tells the manager very little about value. First, it ignores *when* the benefits and costs are received, and that is far too important to ignore. Second, it measures accounting returns, not cash flows; and it is cash, not accounting profits, the firm has to reinvest on behalf of its shareholders. The method is useful only in a firm where the managers are judged on the basis of accounting returns. Because a reward system is so important, the managers in such a firm will make investment decisions based on accounting returns regardless of the method used to analyze an investment's value. Since the accounting rate of return is not a measure of value, such a firm would be using conflicting methods for performance evaluation and capital budgeting. A better approach is to use performance review and reward systems that are consistent with the capital budgeting system and are based on value creation.

Benefit/Cost Ratio

The quickest way to compare investments is the benefit/cost ratio. To calculate this ratio, simply divide the benefits by the costs. If the ratio exceeds 1.0, the investment would be acceptable. The benefit/cost ratio for Trevi's labeling machine can be calculated by summing the net yearly benefits from Table 25.1 and dividing by the initial investment:

$$
\text{Benefit/Cost ratio} = \frac{\text{Benefit}}{\text{Costs}}
$$

$$
= \frac{\$143,500}{\$83,600}
$$

$$
= 1.7
$$

For Trevi's new product, the ratio would be 2 : 1. Both of these investments have forecast benefit/cost ratios exceeding 1.0 and thus would be acceptable using this measure.

Payback

A similar, but more widely used, measure is payback. Payback simply measures the time, in years, it takes to recover the initial investment. Using the inflation-free cash flows from Table 25.1, the payback for the labeling machine is 5.3 years and is calculated as shown in Table 25.4. Trevi's new-product payback period is shorter, 5.1 years.

It is up to Trevi management to decide whether a payback of either 5.3 or 5.1 years is adequate. The acceptable payback period is set by each firm's managements. In choosing among several projects with acceptable paybacks, managers generally favor investments with the shortest payback periods.

Payback is simple to use and can, in certain circumstances, be helpful. For instance, payback can indicate whether a firm is expected to recover its investment in time to make another investment or a payment on its debt. It is relatively useless, however, as a measure of value because it ignores all cash flows after the payback date and it ignores the timing of the benefits before the payback date. Two projects, A and B, with the cash flow patterns shown below, would both have paybacks of three years and, using this measure, would appear to be equally acceptable:

Year	Project A Net Cash Flow	Project B Net Cash Flow
0	($1,000,000)	($1,000,000)
1	999,999	—
2	—	—
3	1	1,000,000

Both the benefit/cost ratio and payback methods share this problem. The benefit/cost ratio treats cash received at all points in time as equivalent; yet,

TABLE 25.4   Payback — Labeling Machine

(dollars in thousands)

Year	Annual Cash Flow	Remaining Investment
0	($83.6)	($83.6)
1	19.5	(64.1)
2	19.5	(44.6)
3	19.5	(25.1)
4	19.5	(5.6)
5	1.5	(4.1)(a)
6	12.8	8.7
7	12.8	21.5
8	12.8	34.3
9	12.8	47.1
10	12.8	59.9

(a) Payback = 5.32 years (4.1/12.8 = 0.32)

investors prefer earlier to later receipts if the sums are the same size. Payback, on the other hand, attempts to include the investor's preference for earlier cash receipts by ignoring cash flows beyond the payback period. However, cash received at different times is not equally attractive, and later cash flows are not irrelevant. Neither payback nor the benefit/cost ratio adequately incorporate the time value of money.

Timing and Cash Flows: Discounting Techniques

Since investors have a preference for large versus small, and rapid rather than later returns, value depends on both the size and timing of the cash flows from an investment. Thus, investors need a method of analysis that takes into account the time value of money. Investors require a small return to compensate for a temporary lack of illiquidity, for deferring spending. To incorporate the investors' time value, a method called discounting can be used. For example, by applying a discount factor (R) of 5 percent to cash flows received in two years, it can be determined that a single dollar at that time would be worth 91 percent of the value of a dollar today (the present value). With n representing the number of years, the discount factor would be calculated as follows:

Discount factor $= (1 + R)^n$

$\qquad\qquad\quad = (1 + 0.05)^2$

$\qquad\qquad\quad = 1.10$

The present value (PV) of the cash flows (CF) would be calculated as:

$$\text{Present value} = \frac{CF_n}{(1 + R)^n}$$

$$= \frac{1.00}{(1 + 0.05)^2}$$

$$= \frac{1.00}{1.10}$$

$$= 0.91$$

This $0.91 can be compared with a dollar received today, worth $1.00, and with one to be received at the end of the year, worth $0.95. Discounting is simply the reverse of compounding. For instance, if an investor put $0.91 in the bank for two years at 5 percent compound interest, the future value, the sum at the end of two years, would be $1.00:

$$\text{Future value} = (1 + R)^n \times CF_n$$

$$= (1 + 0.05)^2 \times \$0.91$$

$$= \$1.00$$

Compounding and discounting, at one time a laborious process, are made quite simple by all but the most basic handheld calculators.

Present Value Payback. The most simplistic application of discounting is to include it in the payback measure, called present value payback. In this method, each year's net cash flow is discounted to its present value. The payback is then calculated, indicating the time it takes to recover the initial investment in present value cash benefits. The present value payback for Trevi's labeling machine, 6.4 years, is calculated in Table 25.5. The present value payback for Trevi's new product is 6.0 years.

While present value payback includes the time value of money, it also ignores cash flows beyond the payback date. Thus, it is only slightly better than payback itself. Only if management considers the investment as temporary, and a subsequent use of the funds is known, should payback or present value payback be used as a measure of relative attractiveness.

There is no need to discriminate arbitrarily against projects with large, but later, cash benefits. The net present value (NPV) internal rate of return (IRR), and return to net worth are discounting techniques that take both the time value of money and all the cash flows into account. Each of these methods gives a better measure of an investment's relative value to the investor than the methods discussed so far. Each, too, has its advantages and disadvantages.

Net Present Value. The NPV is, quite simply, the present value (the value in today's dollars) of the benefits minus the present value of the costs:

$$NPV = \frac{NCF_1}{(1 + R)^1} + \frac{NCF_2}{(1 + R)^2} + \cdots + \frac{NCF_n}{(1 + R)^n} - I$$

TABLE 25.5   Present Value Payback — Labeling Machine

(dollars in thousands)

Year	Cash Flow	Present Value Cash Flow[a]	Remaining Investment
0	($83.6)	($83.6)/$(1.05)^0$ = ($83.6)	($83.6)
1	19.5	19.5/$(1.05)^1$ = 18.6	(65.0)
2	19.5	19.5/$(1.05)^2$ = 17.7	(47.3)
3	19.5	19.5/$(1.05)^3$ = 16.8	(30.5)
4	19.5	19.5/$(1.05)^4$ = 16.0	(14.5)
5	1.5	1.5/$(1.05)^5$ = 1.2	(13.3)
6	12.8	12.8/$(1.05)^6$ = 9.5	(3.8)[b]
7	12.8	12.8/$(1.05)^7$ = 9.1	5.3
8	12.8	12.8/$(1.05)^8$ = 8.7	14.0
9	12.8	12.8/$(1.05)^9$ = 8.3	22.3
10	12.8	12.8/$(1.05)^{10}$ = 7.9	30.2

(a) Due to differences in the methods used for discounting by different calculators and computers, the numbers can vary slightly.

(b) Present value payback = 6.39 years (3.7/9.6 = 0.39)

where: NCF = yearly net cash flow (annual benefits minus costs),
        R = discount rate,
        I = initial investment, and
1, 2, . . . n = years from date of initial investment.

Using the Table 25.1 cash flows and a discount rate of 5 percent, the *NPV* for Trevi's labeling machine would be:

$$NPV = \frac{\$19.5}{(1+.05)^1} + \frac{\$19.5}{(1+.05)^2} + \frac{\$19.5}{(1.05)^3} + \frac{\$19.5}{(1.05)^4} + \frac{\$1.5}{(1.05)^5} + \frac{\$12.8}{(1.05)^6}$$

$$+ \frac{\$12.8}{(1.05)^7} + \frac{\$12.8}{(1.05)^8} + \frac{\$12.8}{(1.05)^9} + \frac{\$12.8}{(1.05)^{10}} - \$83.6$$

$$= \$30.14 \text{ or } \$30,140$$

This is the present value of the net worth that the labeling machine is expected to contribute to Trevi's owners by the end of the machine's 10-year life. The discount rate accounts for the investors' time value of money and thus takes the timing of the cash flows into account. The *NPV* of the new product is $68,380. Using a calculator with a net present value function makes calculating the *NPV* quite simple.

The *NPV* is a logical way of evaluating investments. It takes both the magnitude and the timing of the cash flows into account. Acceptable investments are those whose *NPV* is zero or greater. A net present value of zero

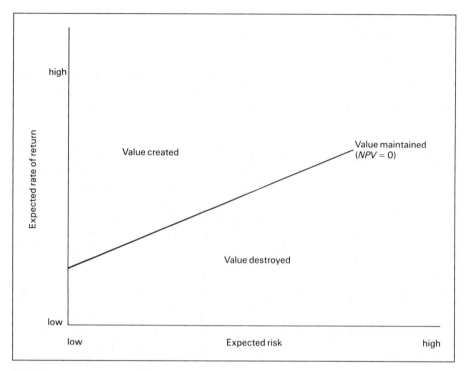

FIG. 25.1 Market Price of Risk

indicates that, at that discount rate, value is neither created nor destroyed; it is a sort of investment breakeven. *NPV*s greater than zero indicate value-creating investments. Figure 25.1 shows this graphically.

The labeling machine provides a return in excess of the 5 percent time value of money; it has a positive value. However, it is assumed that the investment is risk-free. This chapter later discusses how to incorporate risk into the analysis.

Present Value Index. Some managers find the dollar expression of the *NPV* hard to interpret and prefer to use a ratio. Taking the present value of all costs and benefits into account, the present value index (*PVI*) is essentially an adaptation of the benefit/cost ratio. For the labeling machine, the *PVI* would be:

$$PVI = \frac{\text{Present value net benefits}}{\text{Investment}}$$

$$PVI = \left(\frac{\$19.5}{(1.05)^1} + \frac{\$19.5}{(1.05)^2} + \frac{\$19.5}{(1.05)^3} + \frac{\$19.5}{(1.05)^4} + \frac{\$1.5}{(1.05)^5} + \frac{\$12.8}{(1.05)^6} + \frac{\$12.8}{(1.05)^7} \right.$$

$$\left. + \frac{\$12.8}{(1.05)^8} + \frac{\$12.8}{(1.05)^9} + \frac{\$12.8}{(1.05)^{10}} \right) \Big/ \$83.6$$

$$= \frac{\$113,740}{\$83,600}$$

$$= \$1.36$$

This means that, for each dollar invested, the labeling machine is expected to return $1.36 in benefits. The *PVI* for the new product is 1.57. Note that the *PVI* will change if the discount rate is changed.

Internal Rate of Return. The *IRR* measures the average rate of return the investment is expected to yield over its life. To calculate the *IRR*, the formula for the *NPV* is used, except that the *NPV* is set equal to zero and *R* is solved. *R* is the discount rate that equates the stream of net cash flows to the initial investment.

Solving for *R* by hand is somewhat more difficult than calculating the *NPV*. In fact, it is a trial-and-error process. First, the manager chooses an arbitrary rate (*R*) and calculates the *NPV*. If the *NPV* exceeds zero, a higher rate is chosen and used to discount the cash flows. If the *NPV* is below zero, a lower rate is used. The process continues until the rate that yields an *NPV* of zero is found. Obviously, calculators with an *IRR* function simplify the task.

The *IRR* for the labeling machine is 12.9 percent, and for the new product, 14.8 percent. An acceptable *IRR* (the hurdle rate) for a project with no risk would be a rate to compensate the investor for his illiquidity (i.e., the time value of money). As for risk, more about that later in the chapter.

While many believe the *IRR* is equivalent to the *NPV*, using it so can create problems. In comparing investments, if they are of different sizes, if the timing of the cash flows are different, or if there are negative and positive net cash flows alternating over the life of the project, using the *IRR* can give results that are misleading or difficult to interpret. For instance, if it cost $25,000 to overhaul the labeling machine in the fifth year, the investment would have negative net cash flows in both year 5 and year 0 and positive net cash flows in all other years. As a result of such alternating negative and positive net cash flows, more than one discount rate would allow the *NPV* to equal zero; there would be more than one *IRR*. While the results can be interpreted, most calculators and computers solve for only one *IRR* regardless of the fact that there may be several *IRR*s. Thus, the manager may believe he has adequate information on which to make an investment decision where he does not. For those and other reasons we will discuss, the *NPV* is superior to the *IRR* in measuring value.

However, many managers find the *IRR* attractive because it measures value as a rate of return, not as dollars of present value. Rates of return, so commonly used with capital market investments, are also a widely used method of describing an investment's attractiveness. For managers who like *IRR*, another measure, the return to net worth, holds promise.

Return to Net Worth. To calculate the return to net worth (*RNW*), the manager compares the total net worth the project would contribute to the firm by the end of its life to the initial investment. Since most investments have net benefits throughout their lives, the manager chooses a rate at which these cash flows could be realistically invested and compounds the interim cash flows to determine the ending net worth. Once the final net worth has been estimated, it is compared to the initial investment by using the *IRR* methodology.

Table 25.6 shows the *RNW* calculation for the labeling machine. Assuming the cash flows can be invested at 5 percent, the *RNW* for the labeling machine is 8.3 percent ($83.6 = $185.4/(1 + R)^{10}$), and for the new product, 9.9 percent. Obviously, the net worth, and thus the *RNW*, will be affected by the return the manager believes can be earned on the intervening net cash flows.

Table 25.7 summarizes the results of using each of the methods discussed in this section to evaluate Trevi's two investments.

Complications in Comparing Projects

Any investment that is expected to create value should be accepted. However, if the firm has limited funds to invest, or if the investments are alternative ways of doing the same thing and are thus mutually exclusive (i.e., only one will be chosen), the projects will have to be ranked by their relative values so that the managers can invest in those with the greatest value. The net present value method is best for ranking projects; it is consistent with the objective of maximizing value for the firm's owners. For the Trevi investments, each of the measures summarized in Table 25.7 suggests that the new product is the best investment.

The manager using any of the discounted cash flow methods must be aware that, for investments to be strictly comparable, they must have the same

---

TABLE 25.6   Terminal Net Worth — Labeling Machine

(dollars in thousands)

Year	Net Cash Flow	Value in Year 10[a]
1	$19.5	$ 30.2
2	19.5	28.8
3	19.5	27.4
4	19.5	26.1
5	1.5	1.9
6	12.8	15.6
7	12.8	14.8
8	12.8	14.1
9	12.8	13.4
10	12.8	12.8
Net worth in year 10		$185.1

(a) 5 percent investment rate

TABLE 25.7   Measures of Relative Investment Value

	Labeling Machine	New Product
Benefit/cost ratio	1.7	2.1
Payback	5.3 years	5.1 years
Present value payback	6.4 years	6.0 years
Net present value		
Discount rate 5%	$30,140	$68,380
Discount rate 10%	$ 9,240	$27,940
Present value index(a)	1.4	1.6
Internal rate of return	12.9%	14.8%
Return to net worth(b)	8.3%	9.9%

(a) 5 percent discount rate
(b) 5 percent reinvestment rate

lives and be of about the same size and risk. Whenever investment alternatives are of different lives, sizes, or risks, the analysis must be adapted.

Investment Life. Trevi's two investments were expected to have the same economic lives. However, assume that the new product is expected to contribute to Trevi shareholders' net worth for 15 years. How does the analysis change? The first step would be to forecast the cash flows as it is anticipated they would occur. Table 25.8 shows management's forecasts of new product B's cash flows. The NPV at a 5 percent discount rate is $107,300, and the IRR is 15.7 percent. Can this new product B be compared to the labeling machine? No, it cannot, for one reason; the forecasts are not descriptions of comparable strategies for investing the shareholders' funds. The labeling machine requires the investment of funds for 10 years; no description is provided for the use of those funds for the other 5 years. Thus, in comparing the machine project to the new product, which uses the funds for 15 years, the implicit assumption is that the funds remain idle for 5 years. Since this is unlikely, what will be done with the funds during those 5 years must be explicit. Failure to do so penalizes the project with the shorter life.

There are two approaches to equalizing the lives of the two projects. One is to assume the reinvestment of the net worth at the end of the labeling machine's economic life and to determine the net cash flow that would come from such reinvestment for the remaining five years. For instance, Trevi management might believe they will be able to earn a 7 percent real (net of inflation) return with little trouble. Higher returns may be available, but they can't be sure. At the end of the tenth year, the net worth from the labeling machine is $49,200, as shown in Table 25.9. If that money were invested at 7 percent, the

TABLE 25.8   Cash Flows — New Product *B*
15-Year Life

(dollars in thousands)

	Year 0	Year 1	Year 2	Year 3	Year 4	Year 5	Year 6
Investment cash flows							
Renovation	$ (30)						
Equipment	(90)						
Annual cash flows							
Sales		$150	$200	$200	$200	$200	$200
Cost of sales		(75)	(100)	(100)	(100)	(100)	(100)
Wages and salaries		(41)	(41)	(41)	(41)	(41)	(41)
Selling costs		(20)	(20)	(20)	(20)	(20)	(20)
Depreciation		(8)	(8)	(8)	(8)	(8)	(8)
Taxable income		$ 6	$ 31	$ 31	$ 31	$ 31	$ 31
Taxes (at 50%)		(3)	(16)	(16)	(16)	(13)	(16)
Profit after tax		$ 3	$ 15	$ 15	$ 15	$ 15	$ 15
Noncash charges[a]		8	8	8	8	8	8
Net cash flow	$(120)	$ 11	$ 23	$ 23	$ 23	$ 23	$ 23

(a) Depreciation tax shield

yearly net cash flow would be $3,400, and the net present value of the labeling machine with a 15-year life would be $39,180. This figure could be compared to the *NPV* of new product *B*.

Managers usually feel somewhat uncertain in forecasting the rate at which they can reinvest. Therefore, they use a second approach to equalize the lives. They assume that, at the end of the tenth year, the project with the longer life, the new product, is sold. The sale price is treated as the terminal value (a cash inflow) of the project. Whether the new product is actually sold is not relevant; the assumption of sale is made to determine the value at the end of the tenth year of the remaining five years of net cash flows.

While the terminal value approach is more widely used than the reinvestment approach, it is fraught with problems, such as how to measure the value of five years of prospective net cash flows. Managers often revert to the book value of the assets as an approximation of the remaining value of the investment. With new product *B*, the book value would be the undepreciated value of the renovated building and new equipment, $40,000. However, this value seems rather low for five years of net cash flows of $23,000 per year.

An alternative to using book value is to use the replacement value of the assets. However, in Trevi's case, and in many cases, this value is difficult to estimate.

Some managers use the liquidation value of the assets as an approximation of the value of the five years of net cash flows. It is difficult, however, to estimate the value at which the assets can be sold in 10 years, and it is difficult

Year 7	Year 8	Year 9	Year 10	Year 11	Year 12	Year 13	Year 14	Year 15
$200	$200	$200	$200	$200	$200	$200	$200	$200
(100)	(100)	(100)	(100)	(100)	(100)	(100)	(100)	(100)
(41)	(41)	(41)	(41)	(41)	(41)	(41)	(41)	(41)
(20)	(20)	(20)	(20)	(20)	(20)	(20)	(20)	(20)
(8)	(8)	(8)	(8)	(8)	(8)	(8)	(8)	(8)
$ 31	$ 31	$ 31	$ 31	$ 31	$ 31	$ 31	$ 31	$ 31
(16)	(16)	(16)	(16)	(16)	(16)	(16)	(16)	(16)
$ 15	$ 15	$ 15	$ 15	$ 15	$ 15	$ 15	$ 15	$ 15
8	8	8	8	8	8	8	8	8
$ 23	$ 23	$ 23	$ 23	$ 23	$ 23	$ 23	$ 23	$ 23

to believe that such a liquidation value would be close to the value of continuing to sell the new product.

The most frequently used way of approximating an investment's value at the end of the tenth year is to calculate the present value of the net cash flows for years 11–15 and to treat that value as a net inflow, just as if the business were sold at the end of the tenth year. With a 5 percent discount rate, this terminal value would be $99,580, and the cash flow forecasts would appear as in Table 25.9. If a 5 percent discount rate were used for these cash flows, the NPV would be $107,300. This value could then be compared to the NPV of the labeling machine.

Note that the NPV of $107,300 is the same as the NPV determined for the project with a 15-year life. So what has been done in two steps that could not have been done in one? Managers believe that later cash flows are more difficult to forecast than earlier ones; thus, they often discount the later flows at a higher rate. While there is some question whether this practice is the best way to deal with risk, if Trevi management had discounted the first five years of cash flows at 8 percent, the terminal value would be as shown below:

Method	*Terminal Value*	*Net Present Value (5%)*
Book value	$40,000	$ 70,730
Present value, years 11–15 (5%)	99,580	107,300
Present value, years 11–15 (8%)	91,830	102,530

TABLE 25.9   Terminal Net Worth — Labeling Machine

(dollars in thousands)

Year	Net Cash Flow	Value in Year 10 at 5% Rate
0	($83.6)	($136.2)
1	19.5	30.2
2	19.5	28.9
3	19.5	27.5
4	19.5	26.1
5	1.5	1.9
6	12.8	15.6
7	12.8	14.9
8	12.8	14.1
9	12.8	13.4
10	12.8	12.8
Terminal net worth		$ 49.2

Obviously, the method used to estimate the terminal value can change the net present value for the project considerably.

Investment Size. The problem of equivalent investment strategies extends also to investments of different sizes. To be comparable, investment sizes must be equivalent. For instance, if the *NPV* of an investment of $120 million is compared with that of an investment of $84 million, it is assumed that the firm leaves $36 million of its resources idle. Since this is unlikely, the problem is dealt with in a way similar to the first method used in equalizing project lives: by assuming a rate of investment for the unused funds from the smaller project. Trevi's two investments — the labeling machine and the new product — demonstrate the approach.

The first step is to make the two investments the same size. In Table 25.10, the cash flows from the labeling machine (the smaller investment) are subtracted from the larger cash flows. The last column, incremental cash flow, represents the costs and benefits from the larger investment. Trevi is spending an additional $42,900 in the first two years to secure a rate of return of 17.4 percent. This is an incremental present value of $38,240 (using a 5 percent discount rate). Trevi's management must now ask itself whether this is the best use of this additional investment, or whether these funds could be invested in another project to create shareholder value in excess of $38,240. This method is a somewhat laborious, and apparently arbitrary, approach. It is, however, the best method for dealing with investments of quite different sizes. None of the measures of value previously described can give the manager adequate information on which to base a decision without this kind of adaptation.

TABLE 25.10   Net Cash Flows

(dollars in thousands)

Year	New Product	Labeling Machine	Incremental Cash Flow
0	($120.0)	($83.6)	($36.4)
1	13.0	19.5	(6.5)
2	26.0	19.5	6.5
3	26.0	19.5	6.5
4	26.0	19.5	6.5
5	26.0	1.5	24.5
6	26.0	12.8	13.2
7	26.0	12.8	13.2
8	26.0	12.8	13.2
9	26.0	12.8	13.2
10	26.0	12.8	13.2

Differences in Risk. Except for the assumption that Trevi's investments were equally risky, risk has not yet been considered. Value depends on three things: the size of the expected returns; the timing of those returns; and the risk taken to gain those returns.

What is meant by risk is the possibility that the expected cash flows have either been over- or underestimated. Such misestimation results in returns that are lower or higher than expected. Investors prefer certain returns in addition to large and rapid returns. Moreover, they do not take risks unless paid to do so: the higher the risk, the larger the expected returns must be. In fact, there is a direct trade-off between risk and return. Figure 25.1 shows this trade-off graphically.

Of all the problems facing the manager when analyzing an investment, risk is the most troublesome. There is no ideal way of incorporating risk into the estimation of value, but there are several methods being used by managers.

In order to make the task as easy as possible, it is usually assumed that the risk of any investment is the same as the risk of the firm itself (i.e., that the cash flows are equally predictable). If that assumption is accepted, the firm's cost of capital can be used as a discount, or hurdle, rate. The cost of capital is simply the return required by the firm's capital providers (shareholders and creditors). These investors, like all investors, require a return for the use of their money (its time value) and for the risk that some or all of the money invested will not be returned. Thus, the investors' required return can be used as an indication of the firm's fair return for risk, rather than directly estimating each new investment's risk. Remember that to do this, it is assumed the investment's risk is equal to that of the firm.

ESTIMATING THE DISCOUNT RATE

Since new investment opportunities are being analyzed, the marginal cost of capital is being calculated (i.e., the cost if new money were raised in the capital markets). Since most firms use debt to finance a portion of the firm's assets, the costs of debt and equity and their relative proportions in financing the firm are needed to estimate the cost of capital.

Using Trevi as an example, estimate the cost of capital. Trevi is owned by members of the Trevi family. Thus, to determine their required return (the cost of equity for the Trevi Company), the family could be asked the following question: "What rate of return would be sufficient to prevent you from selling but not induce you to increase your current ownership position in Trevi?" The answer would be the shareholders' required rate of return and, thus, the Trevi Company's marginal cost of equity. Estimating the cost of equity for a publicly held firm can be difficult. The cost can change as market and firm circumstances change. Furthermore, the shareholders of a broadly held firm cannot be asked for their required return at each point in time. Thus, methods that rely on capital market data have been derived and are widely used. Chapters 14 and 18 discuss how such data can be used to estimate the cost of equity.

The Marginal Cost of Capital

An estimate of the marginal, after-tax cost of debt could be obtained from the firm's bankers or by inference from the yield-to-maturity on any publicly traded bonds Trevi might have. The cost of capital is the weighted average of the costs of debt and equity. For instance, if Trevi shareholders required a 15 percent return on equity, and Trevi's bankers said that new debt would cost 12 percent, and management expected to have 40 percent of its capital from debt sources, the after-tax cost of capital (with a tax rate of 50 percent) would be 11.4 percent, as shown in Table 25.11.

The 11.4 percent cost of capital rate is higher than the 5 percent discount rate used in analyzing Trevi's two investments. Two reasons might account for the difference: the 5 percent rate is both a risk- and inflation-free rate, and the 11.4 percent rate is neither. Five percent has been used as a risk- and inflation-free rate for the purposes of illustration. There is some disagreement among academics and managers about the size of the real risk-free rate. Estimates for the real rate begin at a low of 2.5 percent.

The inflation estimate included in the cash flow forecasts must be both explicit and consistent with the inflation forecast included in the cost of capital. If riskless debt (perhaps a Treasury bond) were yielding 10 percent and it were estimated that the real, inflation-free rate were 5 percent, then it might be inferred that investors were anticipating a 5 percent rate of inflation.[3] Thus, if an 11.4 percent discount rate were used, the cash flows must include the effects of a 5 percent rate of inflation. Alternatively, management could estimate an inflation-free cost of capital for use with real cash flows. Most managers,

---

[3] Chapter 26 will discuss methods for incorporating uncertainty into the forecasts. For now we will use the best estimates available to demonstrate the process of capital budgeting.

TABLE 25.11   Trevi Company — Marginal Cost of Capital

	Cost	Proportion	Weighted Cost
Debt (12% × 1 − tax rate)	6%	40%	2.4%
Equity	15	60	9.0
Marginal cost of capital			11.4%

however, prefer to include inflation both in the cost of capital and in the cash flows. Many, however, erroneously fail to make the inflation forecasts consistent, and the resulting data are useless for making decisions.

Using Trevi's marginal cost of capital of 11.4 percent as the discount rate for the inflated cash flows from Table 25.2, it is noted that the *NPV* for the labeling machine is $15,270. The *IRR* is 15.9 percent, but now it must be compared with the 11.4 percent cost of capital to determine its acceptability. With a 5 percent inflation rate, Trevi's new product would have an *NPV* of $44,700 and a 17.9 percent *IRR*.

Risk-Adjusted Cost of Capital

In using the corporate cost of capital as a discount rate, it is assumed that the projects are of the same risk and are as risky as Trevi's current business, but Trevi's two investments are neither risk-free nor equally risky: the returns from the new product, while potentially larger, are obviously less certain.

To compensate for these differences in risk, managers often arbitrarily change the corporate cost of capital to a rate they believe reflects the investment's risk. Many firms have a standard system for changing their cost of capital to a new, risk-adjusted, required return. An example is shown in Table 25.12. Managers of firms using similar methods for risk-adjusting hurdle rates believe that all new products are risky and that all cost reductions are less risky than average. If Trevi management used this scheme, they might choose to discount the labeling machine's cash flows at, for example, 11.4 percent and those from the new product at a higher rate, for example, 13.5. The resulting risk/return trade-off is shown in Figure 25.2. The return in excess of that required for the risk is each investment's contribution to the value of the firm. Stock market analysts call it excess, risk-adjusted return, or alpha. Shareholders call it value.

Conceptually this approach is very appealing. It does separate investments on the basis of their risk, and it is no longer assumed that all projects with the same returns are equally attractive. To use the method requires a measurement of the risk of the project or, at the very least, a measurement of the return required for the risk. Basing this required return on the kind of scheme shown in Table 25.12 creates problems. The method is arbitrary in two ways: It assumes that all investments in a given category are of equal risk and that a risk-adjusted rate can be estimated. Neither is true.

Determining the risk-adjusted discount rate is difficult. Unfortunately, some managers set such high rates for risky projects that they virtually exclude

TABLE 25.12   Risk-Adjusted Costs of Capital

Category	Level of Risk	Hurdle Rate
New products/lines of business	Higher than average	A rate higher than the firm's marginal cost of capital
Plant expansion	Average	Marginal cost of capital
Cost reductions	Low	A rate lower than the firm's marginal cost of capital

them from consideration. The result is inevitable: New products will not be accepted and cost reductions will. Since a firm's future depends on the investments it makes today, the implementation of such an implicit strategy may not be consistent with the firm's explicit strategy (e.g., growth in product-markets). Thus, some better method of incorporating risk is required.

Divisional Hurdle Rates. Two other risk-adjustment methods are in use: divisional and investment-specific hurdle rates. Managers of firms using divisional hurdle rates believe the divisional rate (i.e., a divisional cost of capital) better reflects the risks of that business than does the corporate-wide rate (i.e., the firm's cost of capital). A divisional rate may indeed be better in firms with diverse business interests, but a divisional or line-of-business cost of capital is more difficult to estimate than a corporate rate. In a division, there are no public investors to help determine the cost of capital. Thus, managers are often forced to turn to publicly traded firms in similar businesses as proxies for the division or line of business. If, for example, Trevi were considering diversifying and investing in farm machinery, say, the manufacture of horseradish harvesters, the firms shown in Table 25.13 might provide adequate proxies. The average costs of equity and debt and the average capital structure might be used to create an estimate of the divisional capital cost. Table 25.13 shows an example of such a calculation for the farm-equipment manufacturing businesses. Up to now, the marginal, not the book, value of the capital structure has been used in calculating cost of capital. Neither the book value (decisions past) nor current market value (the capital market's reflection of both the time at which debt was issued and the market value of equity) capital structure has been used. It is appropriate to use book value capital structure as a proxy for marginal capital structure only when the management is determined to maintain the book value capital structure. For the purpose of a divisional estimate, managers often use the average book value capital structure of the proxy firms as an *estimate* of the marginal capital structure since they find the market value capital structure difficult to estimate.

Divisional cost of *debt* can be estimated by using the proxies. The cost of

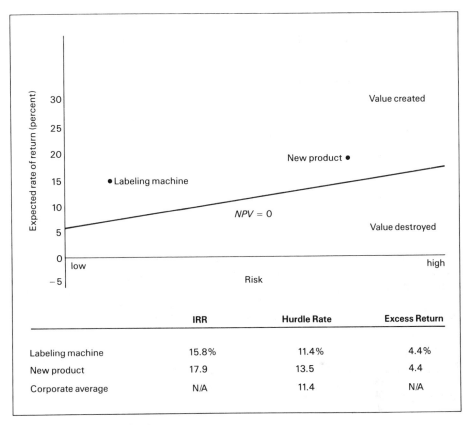

	IRR	Hurdle Rate	Excess Return
Labeling machine	15.8%	11.4%	4.4%
New product	17.9	13.5	4.4
Corporate average	N/A	11.4	N/A

FIG. 25.2   Risk-Return Analyses

debt for a firm is the cost of its newly borrowed funds. The 1982 historic cost of debt for a sample of firms in November averaged 10 percent. At the same time, bonds for the best risk firms (Aaa rated) averaged 11.7 percent, and debt for firms with lower ratings cost more (Baa firms had an average cost of 14.3 percent). Trevi's management might thus expect the cost of debt for its new venture to be 14.5 percent or more. After tax (at a 50 percent tax rate), the cost might be 7.25 percent.

Divisional cost of *equity* is more difficult to estimate. Three methods in common use for estimating the equity cost are described in Chapters 14 and 17, and estimates are shown at the bottom of Table 25.13.[4] All these estimates of

---

[4] Note that we are attempting to determine a marginal cost of capital for long-term investments. As short-term interest rates rose to unprecedented levels in the late 1970s and early 1980s, some firms were using discount rates as high as 25 percent. Obviously the inflation forecast contained in such a rate was very high. Only if management really believed that such an inflation rate would be maintained over the long term could so high a rate be justified. Even so, if such a rate were forecast, the cash flows from each investment would need to be increased at the same rate of inflation that was contained in the discount rate.

TABLE 25.13   Cost of Capital — Farm Equipment Manufacturers

(as of November 1982)

Company	Historic Cost of Debt	Debt Rating	Debt Proportion	Tax Rate	Dividend Yield	Estimated Growth(a)	Beta(b)	P/E
Allis-Chalmers	11.0%	Baa	29.0%	40%	7.0%	5.0%	1.20	11.9
Deere	8.0	Aaa	23.0	39	4.5	10.0	0.95	9.3
Hesston	11.0	N/A	37.0	48	2.0	10.0	1.10	NMF
International Harvester	10.0	N/A	41.0	NMF	nil	3.0	1.05	NMF
Average	10.0%		33.0%	42%	4.5%	7.0%	1.08	10.6

COST OF EQUITY

Method	Formula	Cost
Capitalization rate	$\dfrac{1}{\text{P/E ratio}}$	9.4%
Dividend discount	$\dfrac{\text{Dividend}}{\text{Stock price}} + \text{Growth}$	11.5(a)
Capital asset pricing	Risk-free + Beta(b) (market premium)	14.9

(a) Estimated growth in book value. This figure is used merely to illustrate the process.
(b) For a description of beta, see Chapter 14.

the cost of equity are made with industry averages merely to illustrate the process.

The proxy cost of capital is the weighted average of the various costs of capital. With bonds of the best firms (Aaa rated) yielding about 11.5 percent, Trevi management might expect its debt to cost 13 percent. Equity for this new venture would be more expensive than that for the average firm, about 16 percent. If Trevi expected to finance its new business as the industry does, and planned to borrow 30 percent of its capital, the weighted cost of capital might be 15.1 percent. This figure would be the divisional cost of capital and would then be used for evaluating investments in Trevi's farm equipment division.

Clearly, each business has investments whose risks are different. While a required return linked to the risk of each project is most appropriate, more managers find it easier to estimate and substitute a less project-specific required rate of return. The divisional rate is one such approach.

Problems With Risk-Adjusted Hurdle Rates. There are several problems in using risk-adjusted hurdle rates in general. For instance, a single, risk-adjusted rate assumes that risk increases over time; that is, that the investor requires increasing returns as time goes on, partly to compensate for illiquidity (time value of money). However, the risk of an investment may not increase geometrically over time. New products, for instance, may have significant uncertainty until after they are introduced and customer acceptance is known. At that point, risk may dramatically decline; the product either is accepted by consumers or not, but at least it is known. Later, as competition increases in importance, risk might increase again. The risk profile of such a new product might look like that in Figure 25.3. A single risk-adjusted discount rate is not consistent with this risk profile.

Changing levels of risk over time is only one of a number of problems encountered when risk-adjusted discount rates are used. Thus, new methods of incorporating risk analysis into capital budgeting are continually being developed. Some of those methods are discussed in Chapter 26. Until new methods are available for use by managers, a perplexing problem is encountered: Risk is an important part of determining relative value, but a part that has not yet been dealt with satisfactorily.

After all this analysis, how will Trevi management decide between the new product and the labeling machine? If sufficient capital, management time, plant space, and so on exist, they need not choose, since management forecasts that both projects will create value. If, however, they cannot invest in both, the decision is management's to make for its shareholders, based on how much risk the shareholders are willing to take. Obviously, the Trevi example was designed so both investments would have the same risk-adjusted return (4.4 percent in Figure 25.2). This risk-adjusted rate is a contribution to the value of the firm, and the choice between the labeling machine and the new product, Grandmother's Yummies, rests solely on the risks the owners are willing to take. If Trevi's owners are conservative, they are likely to prefer the labeling machine; it is less risky. If they are risk-takers, the new product may be preferred.

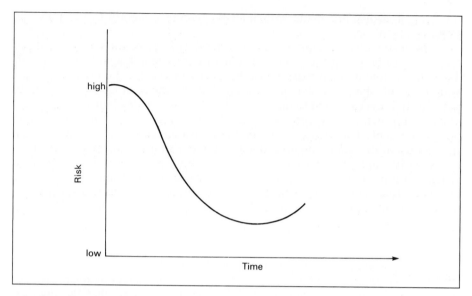

FIG. 25.3   Risk and Time

FINANCING INVESTMENTS

This whole method of analysis rests on one additional assumption, that the investment decision can be made without regard to how it is financed. Put another way, it assumes that, while the returns from a project change over time (as a result of changes in socioeconomic and political events), the costs of the firm's capital do not: The cost of capital, once that capital is obtained, will not change. Much of the time, and for many firms, this assumption is reasonable. During the late 1970s, however, as the returns from their businesses went down, some firms' capital costs went up. This was especially true for those that had debt written with a prime-plus-interest rate or if they had obtained short-term debt and subsequently rolled it over in an environment of increasingly volatile rates. This interrelationship of financing costs and investment returns is coming under increasing scrutiny, but until more research is done and experience gained, management generally uses a method of analysis that accepts the obviously erroneous assumption that investment decisions can be made without regard to financing decisions.

Two methods can be used to examine financing and investment decisions simultaneously: return to equity and adjusted present value.

Return to Equity

The return to equity method includes any cash outflows or inflows associated with the investment's financing in those cash flows from the project. The resulting net cash flows are those of the firm's owners and are discounted at the cost of equity (15 percent from Table 25.11).

To demonstrate the process, the analysis of Trevi's labeling machine can be reexamined. Without special financing, the project was expected to create value for Trevi's owners. If, however, the project had special debt financing available to it (e.g., because it was located in a disadvantaged area and could use Industrial Development Bond financing), the analysis would change. The principal of the debt would be a cash inflow at the beginning of the investment, and the interest and principal repayments would be cash outflows over the project's life. The added benefit would be the reduced cost of debt. For instance, if Trevi could obtain special financing of $50,000 for five years at a cost of 5 percent, the equity *NPV* would be $16,810. This amount is the return to equity, given the special financing. The full cash flow forecast is shown in Table 25.14.

Any form of financing has its costs and benefits. Depending upon the features of the debt or equity, the financing's costs and benefits would either reduce or increase the return to the equity holders.

Adjusted Present Value

To use the adjusted present value method for incorporating the financing into the investment decision, it should first be estimated what the value of the investment project would be if it were financed solely with equity. Thus, Trevi management would take the Table 25.2 cash flows and discount them at Trevi's cost of equity, 15 percent. The *NPV* of the all-equity-financed labeling machine is $2,670. Since the *NPV* is positive, the labeling machine would be acceptable even if it were financed with the more expensive equity. However, Trevi has the special loan available to finance the project. Interest cost is 5 percent and payments total $11,500 per year for five years. Ordinarily, Trevi would have to pay 12 percent to borrow funds; thus, the value (ignoring taxes for the moment) of the special debt financing is:

$$\text{Special rate loan } NPV = P - \sum_{t=1}^{n} \frac{I}{(1 + i)^t}$$

$$= \$50,000 - \sum_{t=1}^{5} \frac{11,500}{1.12}$$

$$= \$50,000 - \$41,450$$

$$= \$8,550$$

where: P = principal
I = annual payment
i = interest rate

The value of the project plus the special loan, the adjusted present value (*APV*) for the project, would be

$$APV = \text{All-equity } NPV + \text{Special rate loan } NPV$$

$$= \$2,670 + \$8,550$$

$$= \$11,220$$

TABLE 25.14   Net Present Value to Equity

Year	Earnings Before Interest and Taxes	Interest	Earnings After Taxes (tax rate = 50%)	Principal or Repayment	Investment	Noncash Charges	Net Cash Flow
0	—	—	—	$ 50.0	($83.6)	—	($33.6)
1	5.0	($2.5)	$ 1.2	(9.0)		$17.0	9.2
2	6.1	(2.0)	2.0	(9.5)		17.0	9.5
3	7.3	(1.5)	2.9	(10.0)		17.0	9.9
4	8.5	(1.0)	3.7	(10.5)		17.0	10.2
5	9.8	(0.6)	4.6	(10.9)	(21.9)	17.0	(11.2)
6	24.5		12.2			3.6	15.8
7	26.0		13.0			3.6	16.6
8	27.3		13.6			3.6	17.2
9	28.8		14.4			3.6	18.0
10	30.5		15.2			3.6	18.8

Since the adjusted present value is positive, the project would create value. Including the value of the interest tax deductibility, the adjusted present value would increase to $14,160.

Both methods, return to equity and adjusted present value, can account for the costs or benefits attributable to financing. Unfortunately, they do not deal with the problem of financing that has a changing (uncertain) cost.

CAVEATS

Forecasting the future of an investment is, to say the least, frustrating. Still, as investment is made in the shareholders' future, the probable effects of current actions must be examined. Since capital investments are large and often commit the firm to rather inflexible courses of action, methods have been developed to look at the future and consider the relative value of any investment. These techniques have gained widespread acceptance among managers for two reasons. First, in the process of forecasting what might occur, assumptions about the future are made explicit. Such explicit assumptions can expose poor judgment and losing strategies. Second, managers seek to create value for their shareholders and thus seek ways to measure it. Formal and systematic analyses help in ranking and choosing projects.

The methods can, however, be misused in several ways:

1 *Cash flows can be misestimated.* The manager, in an effort to be conservative, may underestimate returns, overestimate costs, or arbitrarily shorten the true economic life of a project in making the forecasts. Such conservatism creates bad forecasts. The manager's job is to forecast what he believes will be the investment's effect on the firm. Risk, the driving force behind conservatism in cash flow forecasting, must be dealt with in other ways.

2 *Risks can be overestimated.* Arbitrary adjustments to the required returns (hurdle rates) for investments can add unnecessarily high penalties for risk. Recent inflation has encouraged some firms to use hurdle rates as high as 25 percent. Unless a consistent inflation rate is used in the project's cash flow forecast, such a hurdle rate is illogical. Such rates reflect expected inflation that is inconsistent with the inflation reflected in the cash flow forecasts, and the resulting analysis is useless.

Cash flows must reflect the same macroeconomic outlook as that contained in the hurdle rate. Hurdle rates should be tailored to each investment and must reflect the return required for the risk of the given investment. While it is logical to find some scheme to categorize smaller investments (divisional or project-type required returns), the scheme must correctly reflect the risk of the investment opportunity and provide adequate information for making informed decisions.

3 *Some investments may be excluded.* Investments in hard assets, assets that will be capitalized, are frequently the only investments whose relative value is estimated. Investments in working capital, noncapitalized assets (e.g., research and development or advertising), and mergers or acquisitions often are analyzed using very different methods, and that should not be so. They are investments, and thus, their economic implications must not be ignored.

No short-term bias is inherent in the methods of investment analysis; bias creeps in only in their misuse. The techniques are flexible tools for exploring the potential of alternative courses of action.

SUGGESTED READING

Estimating the Cost of Equity and Debt

Brealey, Richard, and Stewart Myers. *Principles of Corporate Finance,* Chapters 4, 8, 9, and 21. New York: McGraw-Hill, 1981.

Harrington, Diana. *Modern Portfolio Theory and the Capital Asset Pricing Model: A User's Guide.* Englewood Cliffs, N.J.: Prentice-Hall, 1982.

———, and Brent D. Wilson. *Corporate Financial Analysis,* Chapter 5. Plano, Tex.: Business Publications, Inc., 1983.

Van Horne, James C. *Financial Management and Policy,* Chapters 2, 3, 20, and 21. Englewood Cliffs, N.J.: Prentice-Hall, 1980.

Weston, J. Fred, and Eugene F. Brigham. *Managerial Finance,* 7th ed., Chapter 16. Hinsdale, Ill.: The Dryden Press, 1981.

General Information About the Stock and Bond Markets

Fogler, H. Russell. *Analyzing the Stock Market.* Columbus, Ohio: Grid, 1978.

Sharpe, William F. *Investments,* 2nd ed. Englewood Cliffs, N.J.: Prentice-Hall, 1981.

Historic Data From the Stock and Bond Markets; Information About Comparable Firms

Arnold Bernhard & Co., Inc. *Value Line Investment Survey.*

Dun & Bradstreet. *Key Business Ratios.*

Ibbotson, Roger G., and Rex A. Sinquefield. *Stocks, Bonds, Bills and Inflation.* Charlottesville, Va.: Financial Analysts Research Foundation, 1982.

Robert Morris Associates. *Annual Statement Studies.*

Basic Capital Budgeting

Bierman, Harold, Jr., and Seymour Smidt. *The Capital Budgeting Decision,* 5th ed. New York: Macmillan, 1980.

Brealey, Richard, and Stewart Myers. *Principles of Corporate Finance,* Chapters 5–9. New York: McGraw-Hill, 1981.

Harrington, Diana R., and Brent D. Wilson. *Corporate Financial Analysis,* Chapters 4 and 6. Plano, Tex.: Business Publications, Inc., 1983.

Van Horne, James C. *Financial Management and Policy,* 5th ed., Chapters 5–8. Englewood Cliffs, N.J.: Prentice-Hall, 1980.

Weston, J. Fred, and Eugene F. Brigham. *Managerial Finance,* 7th ed., Chapters 13 and 14. Hinsdale, Ill.: The Dryden Press, 1981.

An Analysis of the Interrelationship of the Capital Budgeting and Planning Processes in a Single Firm

Bower, Joseph. *Managing the Resource Allocation Process: A Study of Corporate Planning and Investments.* Homewood, Ill.: Richard D. Irwin, 1970.

Descriptions of Various Approaches to Risk Analysis

Bower, Richard S. and J. M. Jenks. "Divisional Screening Rates." *Financial Management* (Autumn 1975), pp. 42–49.

Harrington, Diana R. "Stock Prices, Beta and Strategic Planning." *Harvard Business Review* (May–June 1983), pp. 157–164.

Hertz, David B. "Risk Analysis in Capital Investment." *Harvard Business Review* (Sept.–Oct. 1979), pp. 169–181.

Hull, J. C. *The Evaluation of Risk in Business Investment.* Elmsford, N.J.: Pergamon Press, 1980.

Weston, J. Fred. "Investment Decisions Using the Capital Asset Pricing Model." *Financial Management* (Spring 1973), pp. 25–33.

26

Project Selection Under Uncertainty

STEPHEN A. BERKOWITZ

INTRODUCTION

The Project Selection Process

Project selection is the process by which an organization assures that the resources it requires in order to engage in productive activity are available. The purpose of the project selection process is to coordinate the acquisition, divestiture, retirement, and transfer of assets to achieve the common adjectives of the organization.

In a small organization this can be accomplished by a single manager, either acting alone or with the advice of a relatively small staff. However, in larger organizations the project selection process can involve all responsibility center managers who participate in development of the operating and capital budget.

From an analytical standpoint, the project selection process is a process of ranking alternative investments according to criteria most closely aligned to the objectives of the organization. In private sector organizations, the criteria are likely to be profitability thresholds and compatibility with existing business. In the public sector, project selection criteria are likely to be client service thresholds, project costs, and compatibility with the organization's mission as reflected in authorizing statutes.

The product of the project selection process has both an analytical component and an administrative component. The analytical component produces a value that will be assigned to the expected cash flows associated with an opportunity to invest in a project. On the basis of this value, management will decide to accept or reject the project.

The administrative component of the project selection process produces assignments of responsibilities within an organization for undertaking projects. Typically, these assignments are formalized in the operating and capital budgets of the organization.

The financing requirements of both public and private sector organizations are directly related to the project selection process. The amount, timing, and cost of financing reflect the risk characteristics of the projects an organization has accepted.

The Nature of Uncertainty

Uncertainty can be described as a hierarchy of factors that influence project selection. There are three levels to the hierarchy:

1 Uncertainty regarding general economic conditions;
2 Uncertainty regarding specific industrial sectors of the economy; and
3 Uncertainty regarding the project-specific impacts on the firm.

Uncertainty regarding general economic conditions affects the analysis of all factors that contribute to project risk. As a result, factors located at lower levels in the hierarchy of uncertainty may have to be analyzed under several sets of assumptions about general economic conditions. This analytical strategy enables management to determine the sensitivity of project selection criteria to changes in economic conditions.

Assumptions about general economic conditions during the life of the project may be simple assumptions about the level of interest rates and the applicable federal, state, and local taxes. Where projects are large and involve substantial commitments of resources, the assumptions about general economic conditions may become much more complicated and require the use of large econometric models. These models use large systems of mathematical equations to specify the historical relationships among measures of economic activity and certain exogenous policy variables.

The models enable analysts to consider what might happen if current economic policies were changed. Among the factors most often extracted from a macroeconomic model are the following:

- Rate of inflation over the life of the project;
- Federal, state, and local marginal tax rates;

- Prevailing level of interest rates for corporate and public sector borrowers; and
- Level of national disposable income over the life of the project.

Uncertainty regarding the specific sector of the economy relevant to the investment project represents the second level of the hierarchy of uncertainty. The profitability of a specific industry and the risks associated with that industry are considered at this level. There are two common techniques for making assumptions about uncertain factors at the industry level:

1 A structural model of the industry to relate sales and service levels to general economic conditions; and
2 A time series model to identify the cyclical changes in factors affecting sales or service levels.

At the industry level in the hierarchy, it is also appropriate to address the institutional issues that affect the profitability of the industry. In many industries the most pressing institutional issue is that of government regulation. For example, public utilities are regulated as to the rate of return they can earn on capital investment.

In addition to rate-of-return regulation, there are regulations that affect an industry much in the same way as taxes; that is, they increase costs by requiring that permits or licenses be obtained and certain production standards be met. As firms are accorded procedural safeguards in the regulatory process, large amounts of data regarding the impact of regulations on specific firms are available from the public record.

Uncertainty regarding the impact of a project on the cash flows of a firm represents the third level in the hierarchy of uncertainties. Uncertain project cash flows, if significant with respect to the firm's cash flows, can affect the firm's cost of capital. When a firm accepts projects with risk characteristics that differ from the risks that the firm has accepted in the past, equity investors change their expected return requirements and providers of new debt capital will seek higher returns on new loans.

The Net Present Value (NPV) Framework

The three levels of uncertainties can be addressed within the NPV framework. To undertake an NPV analysis, it is necessary to reduce a project to a set of periodic cash flows expected over the life of the project. In most cases project life is defined as beginning when initial costs are incurred and lasting until the project is retired, or until the cash flows associated with the salvage or decommissioning of remaining assets have been realized.

Implicit in NPV analysis is the notion that cash flows occurring in the future are less valuable than cash flows occuring in the present. In a certain world there is an opportunity cost associated with deferred cash flows; that is, cash that is immediately available can be invested in some productive asset to earn a return. As cash inflows are deferred, the opportunity to invest cash receipts and realize returns are deferred. The cost of deferred cash outlays is also valued at less than the cost of immediate cash disbursements because the cash that will be used for the outlay can be invested until the actual disbursement is made.

Therefore, in a certain world, the appropriate rate would be a risk-free rate of return on investment. The return on U.S. Treasury securities provides a good proxy for the risk-free rate as payment of principal and interest is virtually certain. The maturity of the security selected for the proxy should be equal to the time period in which cash flows are measured (e.g., month, quarter, year). (See Chapter 25 for a discussion of the rudiments of capital budgeting.)

In an uncertain world, expected cash flows may not be realized. Thus, the difference between the value of an amount of cash available today and the same amount of cash available at some future date must reflect the possibility that future cash flows may not be forthcoming. Furthermore, expectations about the purchasing power of cash may change. As a result, investors seek a risk premium to compensate them for default risk (possible failure of cash flows to materialize) and for changes in the rate of inflation over the life of the investment.

Net present value provides a basis for evaluating whether the project costs occurring at the inception of a project are worth the project benefits that will be realized in the future. The NPV analysis also provides a basis for comparing the value of projects with cash flows expected according to different time schedules. Where judgments can be rendered regarding the value of nonpecuniary costs and benefits, they can be treated in the analysis in the same manner as expected cash flows. The following sections address techniques for using the NPV framework to accomplish project selection under conditions of uncertainty.

ESTIMATING THE VALUE OF PROJECTS UNDER CONDITIONS OF UNCERTAINTY

Future events cannot be predicted in the present with certainty. As a result, the economic value of projects that will generate future cash flows cannot be calculated with certainty.

However, the economic value of such projects can be estimated under conditions of uncertainty. This section presents a formal notion of uncertainty, hereafter referred to as project risk, and the following three methods for analyzing the economic value of project risk:

- Risk-adjusted discount rate method
- Certainty equivalent method
- Simulation and decision analysis

The Formal Notion of Risk

A project is risky if it can generate more than one possible set of cash flows. The amount of risk associated with a project is measured by the dispersion of possible cash flows around the expected value of the cash flows. The expected value of cash flow for a project in period t is calculated as follows:

TABLE 26.1   Expected Cash Flows From Two Sample Projects

CASE 1
Standard Deviation = 9273.62

Estimate	Probability	Expected Value
$10,000	0.10	$ 1,000
$30,000	0.25	7,500
$35,000	0.50	17,500
$45,000	0.10	4,500
$50,000	0.05	2,500

Mean = $33,000.00

CASE 2
Standard Deviation = 1224.74

Estimate	Probability	Expected Value
$31,000	0.15	$ 4,650
$32,000	0.15	4,800
$33,000	0.40	13,200
$34,000	0.15	5,100
$35,000	0.15	5,250

Mean = $33,000.00

$$E(R_t) = \sum_{x=1}^{n} P_{xt} \cdot A_{xt} \tag{26.1}$$

where: P_{xt} = probability that cash flow x will be realized in period t
$\quad\quad\quad A_{xt}$ = xth cash flow possibility in period t

Two projects with the same expected value may have very different levels of risk. This would occur when the possible cash flows of one project are more widely scattered around the expected value of the project than the possible cash flows of the other project. The standard deviation of possible cash flows measures the dispersion of cash flows around the expected value. It is calculated as follows for period t.

$$SD = \left(\sum_{x=1}^{n} (A_{xt} - \bar{A}_t)^2 \, P_{xt} \right)^{1/2} \tag{26.2}$$

The standard deviation can be interpreted in the same terms as the expected value of cash flows.

Assume two projects offer the possible cash flows listed in Table 26.1.

The expected value of both projects is \$33,000. To calculate the standard deviation for each project, the expected value $\bar{A}_t$ is inserted into the standard deviation formula yielding

$$SD = [(A_t - 33000_t)^2 P_{xt}]^{1/2}$$

Notice that since this example covers only one period, the time (t) subscript is understood to be i and could be dropped in the formula. The standard deviation for the first project is 9273.6. The standard deviation for the second project is 1224.7. The second project is therefore less risky. Since the expected values of the cash flows are equal, the second project is preferable as an investment if total risk is of concern to the decision maker.

If the expected values of the cash flows are not equal, the coefficient of variation may be used. The coefficient of variation is a summary measure of the relative dispersion of cash flows around the expected value. It is calculated as the standard deviation divided by the expected value. The coefficient of variation is 0.28 for the first project in the example and 0.04 for the second project. This measure of relative risk is particularly useful in comparing projects that are so different that their expected value and standard deviations are of different orders of magnitude.

The suppliers of capital to private and public sector organizations expect to earn returns on their capital investments commensurate with the risks they are assuming. The premium that suppliers of capital expect to earn over the returns they would expect from a perfectly safe investment is called a risk premium.

Should risk premiums not be forthcoming from their investment, suppliers of capital would have every incentive to withdraw their capital from the risky organization and invest it in a less risky asset. A withdrawal of capital occurs when investors no longer perceive that the company has the potential to offer adequate returns.

This suggests that the return an organization requires on invested capital be equal to the return required by its suppliers of capital. In effect, this is the rate of return expected by the capital markets on the debt and equity in the organization's capital structure. This rate of return is represented mathematically as the organization's weighted average marginal cost of capital. (See Chapter 34 for an approach that might be used when the constant capital structure assumption is untenable.) Under assumptions of stable capital structure, on any increment of capital investment, an organization expects to earn a percent return, K, calculated as follows:

$$K = E(W_e K_e) + E(W_d K_d) + E(W_h K_h) \tag{26.3}$$

where: W_e, W_d, W_h = weighting factors for equity, debt, and hybrid financing

K_e, K_d, K_h = costs of the marginal costs of equity, debt, and hybrid financings[1]

For the single-product organization that serves a single and homogenous

---

[1] Hybrid financings combine certain characteristics of debt securities with certain characteristics of equity securities. Examples include preferred stock and convertible debt securities.

market, K will be the appropriate discount rate for evaluating investments related to the organization's current business. However, such an organization represents an oversimplification of real-world organizations. Typically, organizations assume a wide range of risks associated with producing multiple product lines and servicing highly segmented markets.

As a result, some projects will be more risky than the cash flows generated by the organization as a whole and other projects will be less risky. The cost of capital to the organization expressed as a percent return to the investor is based on the cash flows from all projects. Therefore, if is was used to discount the riskier projects of an organization in a present value analysis, the resulting value of the project, that is, its ability to provide an *appropriate* risk premium, would be overstated. The converse would be true if it were used to discount the safer projects of an organization.

While it would be an administrative nightmare to calculate a unique risk premium appropriate for each project under consideration, it is entirely feasible to estimate a unique risk premium appropriate for investments in major product lines, or for investments affecting specific market segments.

Estimating a Risk-Adjusted Discount Rate—The CAPM Approach

The term "risk-adjusted discount rate" begs the issue of which risks are being discounted. If a firm invests in either a single asset or in assets whose returns are positively correlated to a high degree, then discounting project cash flows at a rate that reflects the total project risks is appropriate for obtaining the NPV of a project.

Firms with diversified holdings of assets or projects are exposed not to total risk, but only to systematic risk through an individual project. Systematic risk results from uncertainties regarding general economic trends, rather than from factors that have unique impact on individual projects.

The Capital Asset Pricing Model (CAPM) provides a theoretical basis for estimating the systematic risk associated with a project where the returns to the project are independent of returns to other investments. (See Chapter 14 for a complete analysis.) The CAPM specifies the rate of return on an asset expected by investors as:

$$R_j = i + \left[\frac{\bar{R}_m - i}{\text{Var}(m)} \right] [\text{Cor}(jm) \cdot \text{SD}(j) \cdot \text{SD}(m)] \tag{26.4}$$

where:

$\bar{R}_m$ = expected return on the value-weighted market portfolio of assets

i = expected returns on a risk-free asset

$\text{Var}(m)$ = variance for the market portfolio

$\text{Cor}(jm)$ = correlation between the expected returns on asset j and the expected returns on the market portfolio

$\text{SD}(j)$ = standard deviation of the probability distribution for asset j

$\text{SD}(m)$ = standard deviation of the probability distribution for the market portfolio

From the CAPM, William Sharpe has derived an estimating equation.[2] Recognizing that the term $[\text{Cor}(jm) \cdot \text{SD}(j) \cdot \text{SD}(m)][1/\text{Var}(m)]$ represents the covariance of two expected time series divided by the variance of one of the series, he suggested a regression procedure to estimate the expected return on an asset. The independent variable in the procedure is the historical risk premium realized on a value-weighted market portfolio. Mathematically, this relationship is expressed as follows:

$$(R_{jk}) = \bar{i}_k + B_j(\bar{R}_{mk} - \bar{i}_k) + \epsilon_{jk} \tag{26.5}$$

or, stated in the risk premium form,

$$R_{jk} - i_k = (B_j(\bar{R}_{mk}) - \bar{i}_k) + \epsilon_{jk}$$

where: B_j = slope of the line that describes the relationship of the risk premium expected for asset, to the market risk premium

R_{jk} = historical returns on asset j for period k

i_k = historical returns on the risk-free asset

R_{mk} = historical returns on a value-weighted market portfolio (e.g., the S&P 500)

ϵ_{jk} = error term $E\ (E_{jk}) = 0$

The least complicated way to use the estimating equation derived from the CAPM is to use data from a proxy company in lieu of the expected returns on asset j. It is often possible to identify companies that derive the predominant share of their revenues from investments similar to the project under consideration or from markets comparable to the markets that would be served by the project under consideration. This is sometimes referred to as the pure play technique. No company will possess risk characteristics identical to those of the project under consideration. Consequently, this procedure yields only an estimate of the appropriate required rate of return on equity on the project. (See Chapter 34 for a discussion of this.)

However, the ease with which this procedure can be implemented makes it a good first approximation. Where proxies are drawn from publicly traded companies, betas can be obtained from various investment advisory services, including Value Line Investment Survey and Merrill Lynch, Pierce, Fenner & Smith. Where no single company adequately serves as a proxy for risks associated with a project under consideration, the returns to a value-weighted industry portfolio can provide a usable proxy.

The current expected risk premium for the value-weighted market portfolio can be obtained from a study of returns on various investment vehicles over a 50-year period by Ibbotson and Sinquefield.[3] Recent updates have changed these figures only slightly. The current risk-free rate can be obtained from yields on recent Treasury bill offerings.

---

[2] A full description of the Capital Asset Pricing Model and its derivation is presented in Hames C. Van Horne, *Financial Management and Policy*, 6th ed. (Englewood Cliffs, N.J.: Prentice-Hall, 1983); Also see Michael C. Jensen, "Capital Markets: Theory and Practice," *Bell Journal of Economics and Management Science*, Vol. 2 (Autumn 1972), pp. 357–398.

[3] R. G. Ibbotson and R. A. Sinquefield, *Stocks, Bonds, Bills, and Inflation: The Past (1926–1976) and the Future (1977–2000)* (Charlottesville, Va.: Financial Analysts Research Foundation, 1982). See also Chapter 18.

The actual calculation of a risk-adjusted discount rate is relatively simple. Assume that a project was being considered in the consumer electronics industry. Also assume that a beta of 1.4 was estimated for a portfolio consisting of publicly traded firms in that industry. The expected risk premium on equity securities, drawn from the Ibbotson and Sinquefield study, is 8.3 percent, and the current risk-free rate is approximately 9.0 percent. The risk-adjusted discount rate R_j is calculated as follows:

$$R_j = 0.09 + 1.6 (8.3)$$
$$= 22.28$$

If the organization considering the investment has roughly the same proportion of debt in its capital structure as the proxy company, the expected return on equity for the proxy company can be used for calculation the weighted-average cost of capital. This in turn becomes the discount rate for calculating the present value of the asset.

If the capital structure for the proxy company differs from the capital structure of the organization considering the project, then the beta used in the CAPM to describe the relationship between the risk premium for the project and the risk premium on the market will have to be adjusted. When a project is financed with some proportion of borrowed funds, equity investors require higher expected returns than if the project was financed entirely with equity capital. Equity holders demand a higher rate of return because creditors will have first claim on cash flows generated by the project. As a result, higher expected returns are required to provide greater assurance that equity investors will realize their expected risk premium after creditors are paid.

To adjust the beta for leverage, the impact of debt on the beta of the proxy company must be removed. This "unleveraged" beta is then adjusted a second time to add the impact of debt in the capital structure of the company considering the project. The following procedure for adjusting an observed beta to allow for the risks associated with debt financing was developed by Robert S. Hamada.[4]

$$\beta_{adjusted} = \frac{\beta_{observed}}{1 + \frac{D}{E}(1 - t)} \qquad (26.6)$$

where: $\beta_{observed}$ = beta observed for the proxy company
D/E = ratio of the market value of debt to the market value of equity
t = effective tax rate for the proxy company

To adjust the beta to reflect the impact of debt on the probability of equity investors realizing appropriate returns from the project being considered, it is necessary first to calculate an unleveraged (debt-free) beta for the proxy company. Then it is necessary to adjust the beta again to reflect the proportion of debt in the capital structure of the organization considering the project.

Assume that the proxy company in the earlier example with a beta of 1.6 has a debt-to-equity ratio (at current market value) of 0.7 and pays taxes equal

---

4 For a full derivation of the adjustment for leveraged betas, see Robert S. Hamada, "Portfolio Analysis, Market Equilibrium and Corporation Finance," *Journal of Finance*, Vol. 24 (Mar. 1969), pp. 19–30.

to 28 percent of its cash flow. The unleveraged beta for the proxy company is calculated as follows:

unleveraged beta $= 1.6/[1 + 0.7 (1 - 0.28)] = 1.06$

The unleveraged beta is adjusted again to add the impact of the debt assumed by the organization considering the project. Using the unleveraged beta as the project discount rate would understate the expected returns if the organization considering the investment has significant debt. Assume the organization has a 0.33 debt-to-equity ratio. Insert the unleveraged beta into Equation 26.6 as the adjusted beta. Insert the debt-to-equity ratio of the organization considering the project into the equation as follows and perform the necessary algebraic manipulations:

$1.06 = $ Leveraged beta/1 $+ 0.33 (1 - 0.28)$
$1.31 = $ Leveraged beta

The adjusted beta is then inserted into the estimating equation derived from the CAPM. Assuming the value for the expected risk-free rate is 9 percent, and the value for the expected market risk premium, $E(r_m) - i$, is 8.3 percent, then the expected return on an equity investment in the project is estimated to be:

$E(R_j) = i + [E(R_m) - i]$
$E(R_j) = 9 + (1.31)(8.3)$
$E(R_j) = 19.87$

As the firm will invest both equity and debt capital in the asset, the weighted-average cost of additional capital is the appropriate discount rate for the project. A debt-to-equity ratio of 0.33 indicates a capital structure of one part debt to three parts equity. Thus, debt is 25 percent of total capital and equity is 75 percent of total capital. Assuming the firm must pay an interest rate of 15 percent on new borrowings, the weighted-average cost of debt is calculated as follows:

$K = W_d K_d (1 - t) + W_e [E(R_j)]$
$K = 0.24(15)(1 - 0.28) + 0.75(19.87) = 17.5\%$

The adjustment of the cost of debt, $(1 - t)$, reduces the interest rate to the after-tax effective borrowing cost. Thus, the risk-adjusted discount rate for the project is 17.5 percent.

The CAPM specifies the relationship of the expected returns on an asset to the returns expected from the value-weighted portfolio of market assets. However, the model was proposed under certain rigorous conditions that are not always met in the real world. The most signficant of these is the efficient, perfectly competitive capital market condition.

Where an organization is denied access to the traditional capital markets, it is subject to some unique pressures to generate cash flow. This gives rise to an element of risk that cannot be diversified away by investing in a portfolio of projects.

Where a firm faces some real possibility of insolvency, the projects it assumes must be considered on the basis of total risk, not just nonsystematic risk. The reason for this consideration is that investors assume not just project risks, but also the risk of transaction costs associated with the liquidation or reorganization of assets in the event of bankruptcy.

Implicit in the risk-adjusted discount method is the notion that project risks increase at a constant rate over the life of the project. As discussed later, this is not always the case, particulary for projects involving new technology.

Alternatives to the CAPM approach are available for specifying risk-adjusted discount rates. However, they rely heavily on the judgment of the investment analyst. The simplest of these alternatives is to employ, as the minimum estimate of the cost of equity capital, the nominal rate at which debt funds are made available to borrowers undertaking risks comparable to the project under consideration. Judgment is needed to define projects with similar risks.

As debt funds imply a fixed payment obligation not found in equity investments, this will understate the discount rate for projects with moderate risks. Lenders often price funds for high-risk investments to organizations that face a real possibility of bankruptcy, as if they will have to assume an equity position in the organization. Consequently, for very high-risk investments, the cost of debt capital may be an appropriate surrogate for the cost of equity capital.

Another alternative is to use the returns required by the organization on projects with a variety of risks as a guide for selecting a risk-adjusted discount rate. Assume that an organization has accepted three projects as follows:

- High-risk moon mining—expected return 30 percent;
- Medium-risk shoe manufacturing—expected return 15 percent;
- Low-risk government facility maintenance contracting—expected return 10 percent.

By judging the risks associated with the investment under consideration on a scale from 10 to 30 percent, it is possible to make a subjective judgment regarding the appropriate risk-adjusted discount rate. A survey of actual project histories within the industry in which a project is being considered may narrow the range within which subjective judgment is applied to estimate a risk-adjusted discount rate.

The Certainty Equivalent (CEQ) Method

A CEQ is the amount that an organization or an individual investor will accept with certainty in exchange for the rights to cash flows that bear some risk. Where future cash flows are converted to CEQs, an NPV is computed by discounting the CEQs at a risk-free rate.

An organization could invest in a project that had an expected net return of $800,000 one year in the future. It is willing to accept a certain payment of $600,000 one year in the future in exchange for the rights to the risky cash flow. The NPV of the CEQ would be calculated using the risk-free rate of 9 percent to discount the CEQ for the time value of money as follows:

$$NPV = \frac{\$600,000}{1 + 0.09} = \$550,459$$

To calculate the risk-adjusted discount rate that incorporates both the time value of money and the risk associated with the expected cash flows, use the following formula:

$$\frac{\text{Expected cash flow}}{CEQ} = 1 + r$$

$$\frac{800,000}{550,459} = 1.45$$

Thus, in this example the organization would discount risky cash flows at 45 percent.

The CEQ approach provides a structure for evaluating multiperiod cash flows where it is inappropriate to apply the same discount rate to the cash flows expected in each period. Investments in companies that face some possiblitity of bankruptcy, of expropriation of assets, or of failure in new technologies or new products often generate such cash flows. The traditional NPV approach assumes that cash flows in the future are more risky than cash flows in the present. This approach also assumes that risk increases at a constant rate throughout the project. This notion is evident in the mathematics of the NPV calculation:

$$NPV = \frac{\text{cash flow}_0}{(1 + r)^0} + \frac{\text{cash flow}_1}{(1 + r)^1} + \frac{\text{cash flow}_2}{(1 + r)^2} + \ldots + \frac{\text{cash flow}_n}{(1 + r)^n}$$

where: r = constant discount rate thereby reducing cash flows by a factor that increases proportionately each period

Investments in new technologies, as previously indicated, can incur large amounts of risk while the technology is being phased into operation and substantially less risk during operations. For example, a communications satellite may have a 20 percent probability of never attaining the orbit required to perform the functions for which it was designed. However, once it achieves that orbit and commences operations, it may face only a 2 percent probability of failure in each of the next eight years. Assuming a contractual obligation exists to purchase the available transponder capacity, the risks associated with cash inflows drop from 20 to 2 percent after operations begin.

The CEQ approach provides an alternative to NPV calculations involving multiple discount rates. The NPV of the CEQ of multiperiod cash flows is estimated as:

$$NPV = \sum_{t=1}^{n} \frac{CEQ}{(1 + r_f)} t \qquad (26.8)$$

where: CEQ = certainty equivalent

r_f = risk-free rate

Assume that an organization is investing in production facilities costing $9 million that are expected to generate positive cash flows of $3 million in each of five years. Improved scheduling is expected to reduce the amount of time that machines are taken off active production lines for maintenance. Thus, the standard deviation surrounding estimates of cash flows declines in the last two years from $2 million to $500,000. If the investment is evaluated according to the traditional NPV criteria, a discount rate of 20 percent might be assigned to the early cash flows and 9 percent to the later cash flows. The NPV of these cash flows would be calculated as follows:

$$NPV = -9,000,000 + \frac{\$3,000,000}{1.20} + \frac{\$3,000,000}{1.20^2}$$

$$+ \frac{\$3,000,000}{1.20^3} + \frac{\$3,000,000}{1.09^4} + \frac{\$3,000,000}{1.09^5} = \$1,394,513$$

The CEQ offered for the project cash flows, if immediately available, would reflect the value of the sum of the cash flows in the three early years discounted at a high rate, and the value of the cash flows in the two later years discounted at a lower rate. Thus, a firm might assign a CEQ of $10.4 million to these cash flows that result from this $9 million investment.

For some organizations the timing of risk taking can be critical for continued survival. While the CEQ approach offers no specific formula for estimating f_t (the amount an organization should be willing to forego to exchange a risky cash flow for a certain cash flow), it does provide a structure for incorporating estimates derived from technical data or from management preferences into the NPV framework.

Simulation and Decision Analysis Techniques

Simulation and decision analysis techniques are used to consider the impact of various forms of uncertainty on project returns. Unlike the risk-adjusted discount rate technique and the CEQ techniques that address relevant project risk, simulation techniques build an estimate of total project risks from the uncertainties associated with specific components of a project. For this reason, the simulation and decision analysis techniques can be used only for projects where the significant factors that give rise to costs and revenues are sufficiently well-specified to be incorporated in a model.

The model provides a formal definition of relationships among the significant factors that comprise a project. Where cash flows from the investment extend over more than one period, equations are included in the model to specify the relationship of factors affecting later period cash flows to factors affecting earlier period cash flows.

The Mechanics of Simulation. The simulation model typically takes the form of a set of simultaneous equations. The solution to these equations determines the cash returns to the investor. To enable the model to emulate conditions of uncertainty, equations are allowed to contain the following terms:

- *Constants* — representing known values;
- *Random variables with a known range* — representing chance occurences;
- *Unknown variables* — representing values that depend on relationships specified in the model and the values assigned to random variables.

A simulation begins by assigning a value within a specified range to each random variable.

Experience with analogous projects often provides the basis for setting the range within which random variables are allowed to vary. Where projects are unique, engineered values or the considered judgments of experts are used in lieu of experience to specify parameters for random variables.

For example, the interest rate on working capital loans may be allowed to vary between the lower bound of 200 basis points over the lowest prime lending rate for the last five years and an upper bound of 200 basis points above the highest prime rate for the last five years. Fixed direct production costs may be allowed to vary between the engineered standard for 60 percent capacity to the standard for 80 percent capacity.

This procedure generates sufficient data to provide unique solutions for the set of simultaneous equations in the simulation model. These solutions provide the values for critical unknown variables (e.g., cash available for return to investors and profits).

In its simplest form, a simulation can be performed by hand to test the sensitivity of critical unknowns to optimistic, pessimistic, and most likely assumptions regarding a small number of random variables. However, current computer technology enables analysts to perform simulations using large models with hundreds of equations and a large number of random variables.

In such simulations, thousands of "trials" are evaluated, each with a unique set of values assigned to the random variables. This provides a distribution of results for critical unknowns. This distribution of results can be transformed into a probability distribution to convey the likelihood that a critical unknown will fall within some range.

Level of Detail in a Simulation Model. Simulations can be performed on highly complex models with the computer technology available today. As a result, highly realistic representations of projects can be subjected to tests of investment returns under conditions of uncertainty. However, when models become increasingly complex, they become more costly to construct and require more computer resources for simulation trials. Therefore, there are practical limits to a model's complexity.

Furthermore, when simulation models become more complex, they become increasingly difficult to interpret. A larger number of variables in a simulation model increases confusion between the primary impact of a change in the values assigned to random variables and the impact of the interactions among factors allowed to vary.

There is no general rule for the optimum number of factors to include in a simulation model. The thing to remember is that there are costs associated with larger simulation models that are not present in smaller models.

Uses and Limitations. A simulation model provides a representation of an investment project. Over a larger number of trials, a simulation model generates a distribution of results.

Sufficient statistics (e.g., mean, mode, and variance) can be obtained from the results of performing numerous simulations, to enable management to evaluate the expected impact of alternative project structures on cash flows. For example, leased equipment may be substituted for purchased equipment to determine the least-cost method of obtaining production facilities, given uncertainties regarding interest rates.

While risk-adjusted discount rates and CEQ methods can be used to address the nondiversifiable component of risk, simulation techniques address only total risk. Thus, it provides little insight into the compatibility of one project with some portfolio of project commitments.

An NPV calculation can be performed on the expected cash flows that result from the simulation. The risk-free rate is the appropriate rate to use as a discount factor, since the uncertainty surrounding cash flows has been considered in the calculation of the expectation. However, if this calculation is used to accept or reject projects, then it is assumed, implicitly, that the expected value of the project is also the CEQ value of the project's cash flows. The expected value will not equal the CEQ value where the systematic risk (risk that cannot be diversified away) associated with a project is substantially different than the risk associated with the portfolio of projects that reflects the level of risk tolerated by the company's shareholders.

As a result, simulation techniques do not allow for the application of a general decision rule for the acceptance or rejection of projects. Rather, these techniques provide a structure within which sensitivity analysis can be performed to learn more about the components of risk associated with a project and to the factors most crucial to project success or failure.

Decision Analysis. Another structure for decomposing project risks into components amenable to analysis or judgment is the sequential decision tree. Many investment projects involve a series of investment opportunities available at different times during the life of a project. Each such opportunity has the potential for causing substantial changes in the size or timing of cash flows. A logical way to represent such a project graphically is the decision tree.

A decision tree consists of a series of nodes representing sequential decision points, and branches representing an action alternative under some environmental condition. A payoff or cost is associated with each branch of a decision tree. The probability that the payoff or cost will be realized is the probability of the environmental condition being achieved.

In the initial stage of the analysis, there is a simple probability of some condition being achieved. However, in all subsequent stages of the analysis, there is a joint probability of some condition being achieved. Later stage conditions are contingent upon the achievement of earlier stage conditions. Thus, the conditional probability of a later stage condition being achieved is the product of the probability of achieving the condition and the probabilities associated with the achievement of the earlier stage conditions necessary to reach the later stage.

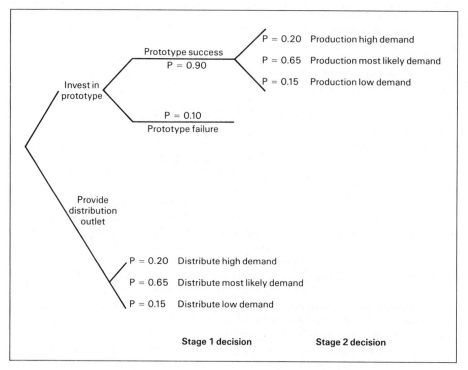

FIG. 26.1   Decision Tree

This calculation is best illustrated by an example. A company is faced with the requirement of adding a printing calculator to its product line in order to protect its market share of small business machines from erosion by competitors. The company estimates it will lose $100,000 in current year revenues if it does not announce its entry into the market. To meet this requirement, the company can either produce its own product (a 90 percent chance of success is assigned to the prototype model by the firm's design engineers), or distribute a competitor's product at a price that recovers distribution costs plus 2 percent gross margin. A $500,000 investment is required to construct the prototype. The company has three scenarios for product demand:

- High demand of 100,000 units given a 20 percent probability;
- Low demand of 60,000 units given a 15 percent probability;
- Most likely demand of 80,000 units given a 65 percent probability.

The standard margin for printing calculators (selling price less production cost) is estimated by the company to be $45 per unit. If the company elects to distribute a competitor's product, no initial investment is required.

From the decision tree presented in Figure 26.1, it is clear that there are two decision stages to be addressed by management. The first decision is to invest in building a prototype or distribute a competitor's product. The second decision is to select a level of production. Table 26.2 presents a table of the expected value of possible outcomes.

TABLE 26.2   Value of Possible Outcomes

Possible Outcomes	P(Outcome) × Cash Flow	
Invest in Prototype	Success — High demand	$(0.9)(-500,000) + (0.9)(0.20)(100,000)(45) = \$360,000$
	Success — Most likely demand	$(0.9)(-500,000) + (0.9)(0.65)(80,000)(45) = \$1,656,000$
	Success — Low demand	$(0.9)(-500,000) + (0.9)(0.15)(60,000)(45) = (\$85,500)$
	Failure	$(0.1)(-500,000 - 100,000) = (\$60,000)$
Distribute	High demand	$(0.20)(100,000)(45)(0.02) = \$18,000$
	Most likely demand	$(0.65)(80,000)(45)(0.02) = \$46,800$
	Low demand	$(0.15)(60,000)(45)(0.02) = \$8,100$

From this table it is clear that the development of a prototype and its subsequent product manufacture is riskier and potentially more rewarding than distributing a competitor's product.

An NPV framework can be incorporated into a decision tree by calculating the expected value of the NPV of a set of outcomes. If, for example, the payoff for a successful prototype followed by production to meet the most likely demand were to occur in period 1 and the risk-free rate were 10 percent, the expected value of the NPV of the payoff can be calculated as follows:

$$NPV = \frac{-\$500,000}{(1.1)^0} + \frac{-\$100,000(1 - 0.9)}{(1.1)^0} + \frac{(0.9)(0.65)(80,000)(\$45)}{(1.10)^1}$$

$$= \$1,404,545$$

where: $\$500,000$ = initial investment

90% = probability that the prototype will be marketable

65% = probability of the outcome being considered

$80,000$ = number of units to be produced

$\$100,000$ = penalty for not entering the market

$\$45$ = profit per unit

10% = risk-free rate

The decision tree technique, like the stimulation technique, is a method for structuring sensitivity analysis. As the number of decision nodes and alternatives increase, the analysis becomes geometrically more complex and costly to perform. Consequently, the analysis is useful when a project can be represented by a relatively small number of sequential (or dependent) decisions.

There are no unambiguous criteria for accepting or rejecting a project based on decision tree analysis. It can be argued that overlaying the decision tree with an NPV framework allows the analyst to select the branch that offers the highest discounted returns. However, discounting expected cash flows at the risk-free rate assumes that the CEQ cash flow equals the expected cash flow as with simulation analysis. This assumption can be true only for projects that have nondiversifiable risks equivalent to the risks acceptable to the firm as a whole.

PROJECT SELECTION: AN EXAMPLE

The NPV framework implies that cash flows expected in the future are more risky than cash flows expected closer to the present. The calculation of the NPV of a project also implies that the level of risk increases in each period at a constant rate measured by the discount rate at which cash flows are discounted.

Where projects are expected to face constant levels of uncertainty with regard to such factors as market share, costs of technology, and raw material costs, the risk-adjusted discount rate provides an appropriate summary measure of project risk.

If a major company wanted to invest in a project that uses known technology to produce a mature product such as disposable coffee cups, it would be appropriate to use a risk-adjusted discount rate in an NPV analysis. However, assume that this same company wanted to invest in a project to recycle disposable coffee cups. The expected cash flows associated with the project are presented in Table 26.3.

Assume that the company has a capital structure that consists of 50 percent debt and 50 percent equity. It can borrow funds at a 12 percent interest rate. Although the company faces a marginal tax rate of 46 percent, used to calculate the tax impact of project cash flows, it pays an effective tax rate of 28 percent. The effective tax rate is used to calculate the after-tax cost of debt capital. A portfolio of companies that recycle disposable paper and plastic products has a beta of 1.6 adjusted for the capital structure of the company considering the project. Using an expected risk-free rate of 9 percent and an expected equity risk premium ($R_m - i$) of 8.3 percent, the cost of equity capital, k_e, calculated from Equation 26.5 is:

$$K_e = i + B(R_m - i)$$

$$K_e = 9 + 1.6(8.3) - 22.28$$

Using the formula in Equation 26.3, the weighted-average cost of capital attributable to the project is calculated as:

$$K = W_e K_e + W_d K_d (1 - t)$$

$$K = 15(22.28) + 0.5(12)(1 - .28)$$

$$K = 15.46$$

The project offers an internal rate of return (IRR) of 22 percent. This is the discount rate that sets the NPV of project cash flows to zero. The NPV of the project using the risk-adjusted discount rate of 15.46 percent is $4,089,000.

It appears, using the risk-adjusted discount rate technique, that the company should accept the project. However, the technology for recycling disposable coffee cups has never been employed on a commercial scale.

The engineers responsible for developing the project have performed a simulation analysis and concluded that there is an 80 percent chance that the technology will work as expected and a 20 percent chance that an additional investment of $1 million will be required in year 2. The engineers also indicate that there is a 30 percent probability that total variable production costs will increase to 61 percent of sales revenue.

Under the least favorable cost assumptions, the project has an NPV of − $2,179.000 using 15.46 as the discount rate and yielding an IRR of 12.3 percent.

In considering the project, management came to the realization that the risk characteristics of the project change dramatically after the technology is proven. This is an example of a project that is very risky in the early years, with the potential of becoming substantially less risky after the technology is proven.

The risk-adjusted discount rate does not capture the change in project risks as uncertainty about the technology is resolved. Consequently, management decided to employ a decision tree analysis to ascertain the expected value of

TABLE 26.3   Disposable Cup Recycling Project — Cash Flows From Operations
(dollars in thousands)

	Year 1	Year 2	Year 3	Year 4	Year 5	Year 6	Year 7	Year 8	Year 9	Year 10
A. Sales	—	—	—	$36,198	$43,438	$52,125	$62,550	$68,805	$75,686	$83,254
B. Expenses (except depreciation)										
Direct labor	—	—	—	5,430	6,516	7,819	9,383	10,321	11,353	12,488
Materials	—	—	—	5,430	6,516	7,819	9,383	10,321	11,353	12,488
Indirect labor	—	—	—	1,810	2,172	2,606	3,128	3,440	3,784	4,163
Other manufacturing overhead	—	—	—	1,810	2,172	2,606	3,128	3,440	3,784	4,163
Sales and promotion	—	—	—	2,715	3,258	3,909	4,691	5,160	5,676	6,244
Administrative	—	—	—	1,810	2,172	2,606	3,128	3,440	3,784	4,163
Other	$1,000	$2,500	$5,000	—	—	—	—	—	—	—
C. Increases in current liabilities and nondepreciable assets										
Increase in accounts receivable	—	—	—	18,099	3,620	4,344	5,213	3,128	3,440	3,784
Increase in inventory	—	—	—	2,896	579	695	834	500	550	605
Increase in working cash balance	—	—	—	905	181	217	261	156	172	189
Decrease in current payables	—	—	—	3,628	724	869	1,043	626	688	757
D. Adjustments for other cash flows										
Decrease in cash proceeds	100	250	500	—	—	—	—	—	—	—
Cost of space	500	500	500	500	500	500	500	500	500	500
Executive time	250	100	100	300	100	100	100	100	100	100

E. Tax adjustments	—	—	—							
Taxes before depreciation				$ 7,909	$10,823	$11,656	$13,987	$15,418	$16,768	$18,444
Tax savings from depreciation		($143)	($500)	($1,214)	($1,214)	($1,214)	($1,214)	($1,214)	($1,071)	($714)
Cash outlays (B + C + D + E)	$1,850	$3,207	$5,600	$52,019	$38,118	$44,532	$53,561	$55,336	$60,882	$67,374
F. After tax cash flows (A − (B + C + D + E))	($1,850)	($3,207)	($5,600)	($15,821)	$ 5,320	$ 7,593	$ 8,989	$13,469	$14,804	$15,880
Net present value =	—									
Discount rate =	0.22000									
Sales				$36,198	$43,438	$52,125	$62,550	$68,805	$75,686	$83,254
Deductions										
Beginning inventory				2,896	3,475	4,170	5,004	5,504	6,055	6,660
Plus: Cost of production				14,479	17,375	20,850	25,020	27,522	30,274	33,302
Total manufacturing costs				$17,375	$20,850	$25,020	$30,024	$33,026	$36,329	$39,962
Less: Ending inventory				(2,896)	(6,371)	(4,749)	(5,699)	(6,338)	(6,555)	(7,211)
Cost of goods sold										
Selling and promotion				2,715	3,258	3,909	4,691	5,160	5,676	6,244
Administrative				1,810	2,172	2,606	3,128	3,440	3,784	4,163
Other	$1,000	$2,500	$5,000	—	—	—	—	—	—	—
Total deductions	$1,000	$2,500	$5,000	$19,004	$19,909	$26,787	$32,144	$35,289	$39,235	$43,158
Amount subject to tax				$17,194	$23,529	$25,339	$30,406	$33,516	$36,451	$40,096
Tax before depreciation				$ 7,909	$10,823	$11,656	$13,987	$15,418	$16,768	$18,444

TABLE 26.4   Summary of the Expected Value of Project Cash Flows [a]

(dollars in thousands)

Investment Cost		Production Cost		Conditional Probability	Sum of Cash Flow	NPV of Cash Flows	Value of NPV
		Low	0.7	0.56	$40,578	$13,258	$ 7,424
Low	0.8						
		High	0.3	0.24	22,345	3,593	862
		Low	0.7	0.14	39,578	12,937	1,811
High	0.2						
		High	0.3	0.06	21,345	3,273	196
					$34,908.1		$10,293

(a) Discounted at risk-free rate = 9.00% (IRR = 22%)

---

the project, assuming that only two environmental conditions could exist: the most likely condition, the technology works; and the worst case condition, that additional investments are required and production costs increase to 61 percent of sales. As indicated in Table 26.4 the decision tree analysis found that the expected value of cash flows is $34,908 and that the expected value of the NPV of cash flows is $10, 293.

Armed with this information, senior management assigned a CEQ value equal to the expected value of cash flows. This allowed senior management to place an economic value on the project equal to the expected value of cash flows discounted by the risk-free rate.

This analysis suggests that the project should be accepted by this company. Another company, with a more risk-averse management, would assign a lower CEQ value and might reject this project.

CONCLUDING COMMENT ON ESTIMATING CASH FLOWS

The various methods for evaluation of projects under conditions of uncertainty rely on reasonable estimates of project cash flows. Typically, this begins with an estimate of the revenues that can be derived from a project. Revenues are estimated by multiplying the price per unit and by the quantity of units expected to be sold at that price. This notion is complicated by the fact that most consumers (particularly of intermediate industrial product) are not passive "price takers." Rather, they seek the most advantageous "bundle" (i.e., actual products and related services, such as credit financing and transportation) at the least cost. As a result, for most products, greater quantities can be sold at lower rather than at higher prices. Sales can also increase by adding services or products to the bundle.

This suggests that revenue projections should consider the impact on cash flows of offering product bundles at a range of prices. The decision regarding the appropriate price will have to reflect assumptions about the competitive behavior of other firms offering similar products and substitutes. The appropriate price must also, in part, be determined by the cost of production at various levels of production.

Typically, the manufacturing division of a firm will seek to produce quantities that take maximum advantage of economies of scale to reduce unit production costs. Divisions that provide other components of the product bundles, such as financing, will also attempt to provide these components in cost-efficient quantities. For cash flow projections to be realistic, a level of production has to be assumed that reflects the demand for the end product of a project at a price that can be maintained as it is confronted with competitive behavior in the marketplace.

This implies that the product should be produced in quantities that allow for cost-efficient production of the entire product bundle. Otherwise, competitors will place products on the market at reduced prices that attract the consumers required to make the project venture feasible. The cash flow estimates that are subjected to the project selection techniques, discussed in this chapter, should reflect a price-quantity-production cost relationship that assumes sale of the product and assures that competitors have no opportunity to offer comparable products at a reduced cost.

No single analytical technique is appropriate to the analysis of all projects. However, the techniques discussed in this chapter allow management to structure an analysis of uncertainties surrounding a project. These techniques also force analysts to make explicit their judgments both about project risks and their perceptions of the level of risk desired by the firm's shareholders and creditors. Sophisticated analytical techniques are valuable where project cash flows have been estimated with rigor. However, where cash flow estimates are unrealistic, the application of rigorous project selection criteria will not assure that good projects are accepted and poor projects are rejected.

SUGGESTED READING

Blume, M. E. "On the Assessment of Risk." *Journal of Finance*, Vol. 26 (Mar. 1971).

Fama, Eugene F. "Risk-Adjusted Discount Rates and Capital Budgeting Under Uncertainty." *Journal of Financial Economics*, Vol. 5 (1977).

Hamada, Robert S. "Portfolio Analysis, Market Equilibrium and Corporation Finance." *Journal of Finance*, Vol. 24 (Mar. 1969).

Hertz, David B. "Investment Policies that Pay Off." *Harvard Business Review*, Vol. 46 (Jan.–Feb. 1968).

Jensen, M. C., ed. *Studies in the Theory of Capital Markets*. New York: Frederick A. Praeger, Inc., 1972.

Myers, S. C. "Postscript: Using Simulation for Risk Analysis." *Modern Developments in Financial Management*, ed. S. C. Myers. New York: Praeger Publishers, Inc., 1976.

Robichek, A. A., and S. C. Myers. "Conceptual Problems in the Use of Risk-Adjusted Discount Rates." *Journal of Finance*, Vol. 21 (Dec. 1966).

27

Managing the Capital Structure

MICHAEL M. JANSON
ANDREW J. KALOTAY
DENNIS E. LOGUE

INTRODUCTION

The way in which a business finances itself can have significant implications for the wealth of its shareowners. The more debt a company has, the greater the financial risk to its shareowners. The less debt the lower the financial risk. Also, the lower are the prospective returns to shareowners. Companies must perform a constant balancing act between debt and equity financing. While there are no rules regarding the proper proportion of debt and equity financing in a company, there are illuminating ways of looking at the choice between debt and equity so that managerial judgment can be brought to bear. This is the subject of this chapter.

    Once the financing mix is determined in its broadest terms (i.e., the percentage of total capital from debt and equity), there are many managerial issues that must also be considered. Companies just do not issue debt. The debt sold to the public or the money borrowed from the bank entails many decisions (e.g., collateral, coupon rate, maturity) and comes with much baggage, frequently in the form of covenants of various sorts. Introducing debt into a capital structure requires first an analysis of the desirability of debt and of the amount to be issued, and second, continuous management of the liability structure of the firm.

WHY DEBT?

Debt and Risk

Debt brings increased financial risk to the equity owners of a corporation. The existence of fixed interest expense means that returns to equity owners in a firm with debt (i.e., a firm with financial leverage) are more variable than they might otherwise be. Table 27.1 shows this.

The Advantage of Debt

While Table 27.1 shows debt in the capital structure makes equity ownership riskier, it also demonstrates one other very important feature. Principally, it shows company L pays less income taxes under all conditions. Since interest payments by businesses in the United States and in most other countries are deductible for income tax purposes, they produce a tax shield. Company U and company L are identical in all respects except for their capital structures. Because company L has debt in its capital structure, it pays less in taxes. This reduction in taxes redounds to the benefit of equity holders.

Ignoring the difference in taxes each pays, companies U and L should have identical values. If there were no corporate income taxes, the value of the equity in company U should equal the value of the debt plus the value of the equity for company L. The pie's size is independent of how it is sliced.

With taxation of corporate income, company L pays less to the government than company U does. Since less gets paid to a third party, a party that owns neither stock nor bonds, the market values of company L's stock and bonds must be greater than the market value of company U's stock.

In Table 27.1, consider the column showing normal conditions. Company U can give the people who own claims on its cash flows, in this case only shareholders, $120. Company L can give people who own claims on its cash flows, here bondholders and stockholders, $50 plus $90, or $140. This differs from what company U can distribute by $20, the difference in the tax payments the two companies make.

The increase in the total value of a company, the market value of its debt and equity is the capitalized value of the tax savings over the life of the debt when it issues debt. So, if a company sells debt and uses the proceeds to repurchase its own shares (this is the simplest case in which the company does not expand its asset base) the market value of the debt plus remaining equity will rise in value by the present value of the tax savings. Analytically, if the corporate tax rate is T_c and the company's ability to use the debt tax shield is no riskier than the debt itself, this is:

$$\text{Present value of interest tax shield} = \sum_{t=1}^{T} \frac{T_c \times \text{Interest rate} \times \text{Amount of debt}_t}{(1 + \text{Interest rate})^t} \quad (27.1)$$

TABLE 27.1 The Effect of Debt on Return on Equity

Company U

No debt
Equity: $1,000

	Normal Conditions	Depression	Boom
Sales	$1,000	$200	$2,000
Cost of goods sold	800	160	1,600
Gross profit	$ 200	$ 40	$ 400
Taxes at 40 percent	80	16	160
Net profit	$ 120	$ 24	$ 240
Return on equity (net profit equity)	12%	2.4%	24%

Company L

Debt: $500
Equity: $500
Interest rate: 10%

	Normal Conditions	Depression	Boom
Sales	$1,000	$200	$2,000
Cost of goods sold	800	160	1,600
Gross profit	$ 200	$ 40	$ 400
Interest	50	50	50
Profit before taxes	$ 150	($ 10)	$ 350
Taxes at 40 percent	60	0	140
Net profit	$ 90	($ 10)	$ 210
Return on equity	18%	−2%	42%

The equity in company L is riskier than the equity in company U. The range of returns to equity owners of company U over the business cycle is 2.4 percent to 24 percent. For company L, the range is −2 percent to 42 percent.

If the debt has an infinite life, or if the company intends to pay off existing debt by using the proceeds of new debt, the above simplifies to:

$$\text{Present value of interest tax shield} = \sum_{t=1}^{\infty} \frac{T_c \times \text{Interest rate} \times \text{Amount of debt}}{(1 + \text{Interest rate})^t}$$

$$= \frac{T_c \times \text{Interest rate} \times \text{Amount of debt}}{\text{Interest rate}}$$

$$= T_c \times \text{Amount of debt:} \qquad (27.2)$$

In this very simple case, the value of the firm, debt plus equity, should rise by the corporate tax rate (T_c) times the amount of debt.

Shareholder Value — An Example

Suppose a company has one million shares outstanding. Each share sells for $50, and earnings per share are $10. The market value of the company is $50 × one million, or $50 million. Now suppose the company decides to sell $20 million in debt and use the proceeds to repurchase stock. (For advantages of share repurchase over dividend payments, see Chapter 30.) The debt will be perpetual, and carries an interest rate of 12 percent. The corporate tax rate is 40 percent.

First, how much can a corporation offer for its own stock and leave the selling shareholders and remaining shareholders in identical wealth positions? The company will sell $20 million in debt. The value of the tax shield is T_c × interest rate × amount of debt/Interest Rate, or (0.4) (0.12) $20 million /0.12 = $8 million. There are one million shares outstanding, so if the firm offers $8 million/1 million shares or $8 per share more than the prevailing market price of $50, it will distribute the gain from financial leverage equally among all shareholders. The fair price is $58.

Second, how many shares can it repurchase? It has $20 million from the sale of debt, and will pay $58 per share, so it can repurchase 344,827 shares.

What will the firm be worth after the transaction? The firm had a value of $50 million when it started. The sale of debt created a tax shield worth $8 million, so the new total value of the firm must be $58 million.

How much is the remaining equity worth? The new market value for the firm's debt and equity is $58 million. The firm has $20 million in new debt outstanding, so the market value of the company's remaining equity must be $38 million ($58 million less $20 million).

Further, recall the firm repurchased 344,827 shares at $58 per share. Originally, it had one million shares outstanding, so it now has 655,173 shares outstanding. The per share price is $38 million (the market value of the equity)/655,173 shares, or $58 per share.

Effect on the Cost of Equity

In Chapter 9, one way shown to measure the cost of equity capital was to divide earnings by price. This is suitable for companies that are not growing, but only expanding. The difference between a growing company and an expanding one is the former is making most of its investments with positive net present values (see Chapters 25, 26, and 34), whereas the latter is making most investments with net present values equal to zero. Firms that are not growing may be expanding, but the return on investment just equals the capital cost.

In the example, the company had $10 per share in earnings and a price of $50. If the company is not growing, its cost of equity capital would be 20 percent. Its cost of equity after the capital structure change is higher because of increased risk.

The company's total earnings after taxes were $10 million ($10 per share × 1 million shares). Its pretax earnings would be $10 million/(1 − corporate tax rate), or $10 million/(1 – 0.4) or $16,666,667. After deducting interest of $2,400,000, after-tax income is $14,266,667 (1 – 0.4), or $8,560,000. There are 655,173 shares outstanding, so earnings per share are $8,560,000/655,173 shares, or $13.06. The earnings/price ratio has become $13.06/$58.00, or 22.5 percent, which reveals that the cost of equity has risen. (The ratio actually now understates the true cost of equity.) However, because debt is less expensive than equity, so the company should now be able to find positive net present value projects. Projects just barely acceptable using the cost of equity capital as a screening rate now become attractive because the new screening rate reflects the blend of low cost debt and high cost equity. The price/earnings ratio had been $50.00/$10.00, or 5X; it is now $58.00/$13.06, or 4.44X, again partially reflecting increased financial risk.

The cost of equity capital rises with debt. The price/earnings multiple falls. This is in large part because of the financial risk that debt brings to equity holders. The tax benefits of debt financing prevent the stock price from falling by the amount it should if only financial risk were considered. Although the cost of equity rises, the increase in cost is more than compensated by the increase in after-tax earnings because of the tax benefit associated with debt.

For all companies, and especially for companies that are truly growing, one of the best ways to estimate the cost of equity capital is using the capital asset pricing model (CAPM) (see Chapters 14, 16, and 17). Here, the cost of equity capital equals the risk-free rate plus the company's measure of systematic risk (beta) times the market risk premium, which is the expected return on a market portfolio less the risk-free rate. Analytically;

$$(27.3)$$

$$\text{Cost of equity} = \text{Risk-free rate of interest} + \text{Beta} \left(\begin{array}{cc} \text{Expected return on} & \text{Risk-free} \\ \text{market portfolio} & \text{rate} \end{array} \right)$$

Returning to the illustrative company, it is assumed that prior to debt financing its beta = 1.0, the risk-free rate is 10 percent, and the expected return on the market portfolio is 20 percent. Its pre-leverage cost of equity, using the CAPM is:

$$0.20 = 0.10 + 1.0 \ (0.20 - 0.10)$$

or, 20 percent.

If debt is introduced into the capital structure, it changes beta, the measure of systematic risk. (Recall how much more variable returns to shareholders were in Table 27.1 for company L.) The formula for the change in beta is:

Beta (levered) = $\hspace{6cm} (27.4)$
Beta (unlevered) $\times \ (1 + (1 - T_c))(\text{Market value of debt/market value of equity})$

Applying this formula to the illustrative company:

Beta (levered) = $1.0 \times [1 + (1 - 0.4)(20/38)]$

$\hspace{3cm} = 1.31$

Plugging the new estimate of beta into the CAPM produces:

Cost of equity = $1.0 + 1.31 \ (0.20 - 0.10)$

$\hspace{3cm} = 23.1\%$

This exceeds the cost of equity estimate given with the earnings/price approach, but not by a great deal.

The reason it is higher is as follows. Before the company issued debt, its cost of equity was 20 percent. Only projects that had a zero or positive net present value when cash flows were discounted at 20 pecent were acceptable. With debt in its capital structure, the company's new overall cost of capital is the weighted-average of its cost of equity and the after-tax cost of debt. This is lower than 20 percent.

$$\begin{array}{l} \text{Weighted-average} \\ \text{cost of capital} \end{array} = \text{Cost of equity} \left(\frac{\text{Market value of equity}}{\text{Market value of firm}} \right) +$$

$$\text{Cost of debt} \left[1 - T_c \left(\frac{\text{Market value of debt}}{\text{Market value of firm}} \right) \right]$$

(27.5)

For the illustrative company, this is:

$$\begin{array}{l} \text{Weighted-average} \\ \text{cost of capital} \end{array} = 0.231 \left(\frac{38}{58} \right) + 0.12(1 - 0.4) \left(\frac{20}{58} \right)$$

$$= 0.151 + 0.025$$

$$= 0.176, \text{ or } 17.6\%$$

The company's overall cost of capital, and thus its investment screening rate, has declined. Projects that were barely acceptable at a 20 percent screening rate now become very attractive; that is, they provide high positive net present values because the new investment screening rate is only 17.6 percent. The company can now grow. As a consequence, for companies that rearrange capital structure in this way, the cost of equity estimate provided by the earnings/price approach will understate the true new cost of equity.

This principle is one of the great motivating forces behind leveraged buy-outs: the purchase of a company by a small group of investors financed almost entirely with debt. In the preceding example, the trick would be to purchase the shares at less than the $58 per share price revealed by our analysis as the fair price.

Unfortunately, the analysis does not tell a company where to stop. It even suggests the more debt the better, because every dollar in debt adds value to the equity. Very few companies are financed with nearly 100 percent debt, however. What prevents companies from going to extremes in their decisions regarding debt financing?

Financial Distress

The poor-house is packed with those who had no regard for prudent debt limits. When a company runs out of cash, several things can happen, all bad. Debt increases the likelihood of running out of cash because interest payments are fixed obligations and cannot really be ignored by companies (for nations, this may be different matter). Moreover, the advantage to debt financing lies in the tax shield. If a company hits hard times and generates no taxable income, the advantage of debt disappears.

Too much debt can lead a company to bankruptcy. (See Warner (1977) and Chapter 35 for analyses.) If a company cannot meet its financial obligations, its lenders can force it into reorganization or liquidation. Reorganization is a very costly and time-consuming process, during which the operating effectiveness of the company may be impaired. Liquidation is a last resort, and in most instances shareholders end up with little or nothing at the conclusion of the process.

Reorganization and bankruptcy are often the results of having too much debt. However, few companies with too much debt, too great interest, and repayment obligations ever get to this stage. Nonetheless, they may face significant costs because of extreme debt burdens without ever going through the formal process.

First, when a company has much debt, lenders want not only their interest payments and debt repayments on time, but they also impose restrictions on the company (see Smith and Warner (1979) for a complete analysis), that can severely limit its operational effectiveness.

Debt convenants are customarily imposed to limit the risk of lenders. They are designed to keep cash and other liquid assets within the firm, and often to do so, the company is prevented from doing what might be in the best interests of shareholders. Common covenants include the following:

1 Restrictions on investment in physical assets

2 Restrictions on the sale of assets

3 Restrictions on mergers and acquisitions

4 Covenants requiring the maintenance of certain assets

5 Restrictions on the payment of dividends

6 Working capital minimums

Any of these could prevent a company from undertaking actions that benefit shareholders. The more debt the more covenants. If a company runs into a period of financial adversity, the covenants may bind it to such an extent that shareholders would be harmed. In addition, debt is a claim on corporate cash flows that is senior to equity claims, debt holders get priority in the distribution of cash.

Consider the following example. A company has $100 in debt and has two investment opportunities, both costing $105. Investment opportunity A has a present value of cash flows of $104 under any circumstance. Investment opportunity B has a present value of cash flows of $1,000 under most circumstances, but there is a 1 in 20 chance that the present value of cash flows will be only $60. If the company has previously not violated any convenants and is on good terms with all its lenders, it would choose B because of the likely benefit to shareholders. However, if its lenders have been contractually disappointed with the company, they may either prevent any new investment at all, or force investment A, because for them it is safe, despite the fact that it does not help shareholders; indeed, it may harm them because investment A has a negative present value.

Excessive debt can also influence potential buyers of a company's product. If a firm is short on cash and cannot borrow, and especially if its lenders have begun to exert pressure on it because it has violated a debt covenant or failed to make a timely interest or principal payment, prospective customers may fear that the company may not have sufficient resources to repair and maintain its product or to stock replacement parts. If a company's financial situation is sufficiently precarious, many consumers will simply choose not to deal with it, irrespective of the quality of the product. Alternatively, to sell its product, a company may have to discount the price, thus cutting its profit margin and thereby exacerbating the cash flow problem. Either consequence will further weaken the company's financial position.

Debt and the Corporate Life Cycle

A careful evaluation of capital structures shows a common pattern in the way highly successful companies have financed themselves. This pattern corresponds to the corporate life cycle.

When a company first begins, it typically is dealing in a new product market. In this introductory stage, the best companies will generally have very little debt. There is plenty of risk to shareholders in the product market, hence, no reason to add more risk by levering the capital structure. More important, at this stage of a company's life it has little taxable income, so the tax shield from any meaningful level of debt is irrelevant. In addition, in its introductory phase, a company must often move extremely quickly on new investment opportunities. If its actions are restricted by debt covenants, important projects may have to be delayed while the company negotiates with its creditors. On balance, many start-up companies view the expected opportunity losses on foregone projects as far more costly than avoided tax payments.

In the second stage of the life cycle, the growth stage, the company may add some debt as it expands output significantly. The company is still risky, however, so debt might be kept at very low levels. Again, the company may have little taxable income, so tax shields from the interest expense may have very little value.

The third stage is maturity. At this point, investment opportunities that promise spectacularly large net present values are relatively scarce. The value of the tax shields on debt financing rises, and the expected cost of having to pass up extraordinary opportunity falls. At maturity, the company should be distributing cash in reasonably predictable patterns. Therefore, an increasing portion of a company's capital structure is in the form of debt, and excess cash is distributed to shareholders in the form of dividends and share repurchases.

The fourth stage is decline. If a company can do it, now is the time to incur substantial debt, distribute the proceeds to shareholders, and allow the creditors to bear the very real risk of default. Lenders, of course, recognize this risk and will not lend the company all it wants. Nevertheless, at this stage debt financing is most ardently sought.

Tax Equilibrium

A company may reject an extreme leverage policy if it believes that the benefit of the corporate tax shield on interest payments is overstated. This could be true for several reasons.

First, the effective marginal corporate tax rate may be substantially below the statutory rate. This would be true to the extent the firm is able to manage its tax position cleverly, maintaining equality between its marginal and effective tax rates.

Second, the existence of personal taxes on interst income and on dividends and capital gains may, to some extent, offset the corporate tax advantage.

Suppose the statutory corporate tax rate is 46 percent, as it currently is in the United States. Further suppose a company could borrow at 10 percent from a nontaxable lender (the rate appropriate to the riskiness of its debt). Its after-tax cost of debt would then be interest rate X (1-corporate tax rate), or 0.10 (1-0.46), or 5.4 percent. Now suppose the lender faces a 50 percent statutory rate, currently the top personal rate in the United States. The lender evaluates the risk and decides a 10 percent after-tax return is appropriate. To provde the after-tax return of 10 percent, the company must pay an interest rate of 20 percent. The company's after-tax cost of interest is 0.20 (1 × 0.46), or 10.8 percent. The company's after-tax cost exceeds the investor's after-tax return. The tax authorities must be collecting more from the lender than the company itself is saving in tax payments. In this case, the advantage to debt financing is, in fact, negative because the interest rate that must be paid to compensate the lender for risk and tax payments is too high to allow shareholders to benefit from the tax shield associated with debt.

Merton Miller (1977) has worked out a full equilibrium integrating corporate taxes with personal taxes, allowing for differential personal taxes on interest income and on stock returns. Let T_c = the corporate tax rate, T_I = the tax rate on interest income, and T_g = the average of the tax rates on dividend income and capital gains, weighted by the proportion of total equity return from each source. For perpetual debt (analogous to equation 27.2):

$$\text{Value of tax shield on debt financing} = \left[1 - \frac{(1 - T_c)(1 - T_g)}{(1 - T_I)} \right] \times \text{Amount of debt} \qquad (27.6)$$

To illustrate, suppose $T_c = 0.46$, $T_I = 0.50$, and $T_g = 0.25$. The total market value of a company if it sold $100 worth of debt and used the proceeds to repurchase stock would rise by:

$$\text{Increase in value of corporation} = \left[1 - \frac{(1 - 0.46)(1 - 0.25)}{(1 - 0.5)} \right] \$100$$

In this full tax equilibrium, the value of the tax shield on corporate debt is lower for most realistic tax rates than it is when only the corporate tax rate is considered.

When this kind of analysis is brought to bear, it shows that the value of debt financing may be less than presumed by looking at only corporate tax savings. Trading off this smaller value against the expected losses from financial distress yields further insight as to why many firms are not as leveraged as they might otherwise be.

ASSESSING CORPORATE DEBT CAPACITY

Bond Ratings and Other Rules of Thumb

Some companies use standards set by rating agencies as a guide to how much debt they can have. (See Chapter 19 for a discussion of credit analysis and bond ratings.) The company must know what rating it wants to maintain and then adjust its debt/equity ratios accordingly. There is no simple formula for doing this; the ratio chosen depends on the judgment of company management. In addition, there is no assurance that the rating agency will use the same analysis management does when it establishes the company's rating.

Related to bond ratings are several other methods commonly used to determine debt capacity. These include (1) seeking advice from lenders and financial intermediaries (e.g., investment bankers), (2) examining the debt/equity ratios of comparable companies; and (3) assuming a debt capacity equal to historical norms.

For a full treatment of the deficiences of all these approaches, see Donaldson (1962, 1969). Generalizing these criticisms, all these approaches fail to consider what is actually in the best interest of the company's shareholders at the time the decision is being made.

For instance, its current bond rating might not be of concern to a company that has spectacular investment opportunities right now that will generate enough cash to undertake all future investment opportunities. Advice from outside financial experts may reflect their own concerns; that is, lenders worried about the security of their investments and investment bankers worried about the difficulty of selling low-rated debt may be too conservative. Furthermore debt/equity ratios of other companies in an industry may be inaccurate, or the companies sufficiently different in terms of product, production, investment, and research and development strategies, so as to provide no real guidance. Finally, historical practice may not be appropriate for the company, as its present operation or condition may be dissimilar to its historical situation.

Pro Forma/Adversity Analysis

A more useful approach to determining debt capacity is careful analysis of what happens to a company's liquid resources, cash flows, and ability to operate effectively when adversity strikes. The analysis is accomplished through the following general steps:

1 Estimate the level of revenues under adverse economic conditions, such as a broad-based cyclical downturn or intensifying competition, or both. This entails not only estimates of reduced unit sales, but also of any price reductions.

2 Estimate how quickly costs can be reduced. In many instances, costs cannot be cut as fast as revenues fall because of lags in the recognition of an economic downturn, lags in being able to lay off employees, work-in-process inventory, and investment and research and development spending which, if eliminated, would be very costly to reinstate.

3 Estimate the balance-sheet impact of a cyclical downturn. This includes estimating:

- Timing and extent of reductions in raw materials, work-in-process, and finished goods inventories.

- Timing and extent of liberalized credit terms, and slowing of other receivables.

- Timing and extent of reductions in capital spending plans.

4 Determine whether lenders will advance the company the implied amount of debt, and whether the covenants on such debt will so seriously bind that current organizational effectiveness and future prospects are debilitated.

During normal times a company wants enough unused borrowing capacity so that during cyclical downturns it can use this capacity to avoid foregoing good opportunities or selling stock at prices believe are temporarily depressed or with unusually large underwriter spreads.

Further general discussion of the concept of debt capacity can be found in Chapter 34 and in works by Donaldson (1969, 1971), Myers (1977), and Piper and Weinhold (1982).

ILLUSTRATION OF DEBT CAPACITY ASSESSMENT

One of the more difficult conceptual issues in assessing debt capacity is the fact that a company has to work backwards. It cannot directly estimate how much debt it can presently afford; rather, it must assess the amount of debt it can bear during a period of financial adversity, then work back to how much it can afford at the present time.

A complete assessment of corporate debt capacity is impossible here, but a stylized example, presuming a given debt/equity ratio as a starting point, is possible. (Material in Chapters 21 and 22 provide helpful insights into performing analyses of this type.)

The stylized scenario is presented in Table 27.2. It shows a company operating in a recessionary environment in which both its unit sales and selling prices decline. Costs cannot be reduced quickly enough to match its sales decline, and the company has investments that would be very costly to abandon from a competitive standpoint. Finally, the company feels that cutting the dividend would harm shareholders in the short run and make the company more vulnerable to a takeover bid.

As the company gets further into the recession, it will have to borrow more and more to sustain its investment plans and pay its dividends. If it abandons investment spending, it may fall behind its competitors. If it cuts its dividend, investors may interpret this more as signalling a permanent decline in profitability. In this case, the stock price could decline substantially. Of course, if the firm did not start with $2 million in debt, minor transitory borrowing or minor asset reductions might be able to get the company through the adverse economic period.

Table 27.3 illustrates the balance-sheet effects of the economic adversity and the attendant borrowing situation. The simplified assumptions are spelled out in the table itself.

The balance sheet at the end of the recession year shows very high debt relative to equity and little liquidity. The company can prevent these consequences by limiting investment spending or curtailing dividends. Alternatively, it could position itself better as it leaves the recession by reducing its debt.

A complete analysis requires estimating several different business cycle scenarios and several different initial debt positions. Further, management must

TABLE 27.2   Pro Forma Cash Flow Statements for a Period of Financial Adversity

(dollars in thousands)

	Actual	Recession Year 1	Recession Year 2	Recession Year 3[a]
Unit sales	100	90	85	95
Selling price	$ 50	$ 48	$ 45	$ 49
Revenues	$5,000	$4,320	$3,825	$4,655
Labor expense	(1,500)	(1,382)[b]	(1,250)	(1,396)
Raw materials	(1,500)	(1,500)[b]	(1,400)	(1,350)
Overhead	(500)	(500)	(450)	(425)
Depreciation	(600)	(600)	(600)	(600)
Earnings before taxes	$ 900	$ 338	$ 125	$ 884
Interest expense[c]	(300)	(300)	(350.6)	(384.3)
Profit before tax	$ 600	$ 38	($ 225.6)	$ 499.7
Tax (at 40 percent)	240	15.2	(90.2)[d]	199.9
Profit after tax	$ 360	$ 22.8	($ 135.4)	$ 299.8
Cash flow	$ 960	$ 622.8	$ 735.4	$ 899.8
Desired investment spending	600	600	600	600
Dividends	360	360	360	360
New borrowing or run down in liquid assets necessary to implement investment/ dividend decisions	—	$ 337.2	$ 224.6	$ 60.2
Total new debt or reduced assets (years 1–3)				$ 622

(a) Sales and prices stay down because of customer concerns over solvency (i.e., ability to get warrantee services, spare parts).
(b) Recession recognition lags; contracts with labor and raw materials suppliers keep costs up.
(c) Firm has $2,000 in debt outstanding; 15% floating interest rate. No change during recession.
(d) Rebate.

make some judgments regarding the tax shield advantage of the initial level of debt versus the potential costs of curtailing investment spending or dividends. In the scenario in Tables 27.2 and 27.3, the firm could maintain liquidity and low financial risk by not investing, by not paying dividends, or by selling new stock (though this may be undesirable given the impact that prospective future dividend cuts may have on the price of the stock). The company should evaluate the value of the tax benefits of debt relative to the lost value of cutting back what it can. If the latter exceeds the former, the company ought to consider reducing its original debt.

A full treatment of these issues can be found in Donaldson (1971).

TABLE 27.3   Pro Forma Balance Sheet for a Period of Financial Adversity

(dollars in thousands)

	Actual	Assumptions	End of Recession Year 2
Cash	$ 100	Minimum	$ 100
Marketable securities	100	Sold to meet requirements	—
Accounts receivable	417	60 days receivables (up from 30)	637.5
Inventory	834	90 days inventory (relative to sales, up from 60)	956.2
Plant and equipment (net)	3,758		3,758
Total assets	$5,209		$5,451.7
Accounts payable	$ 209	Suppliers want cash on delivery	—
Plug	—	New debt to support balance-sheet assets:	$ 762.3
Old long-term debt	2,000		2,000
New debt per table 27.2	—	Needed per Table 27.2, offset by marketable securities sales	522
Net worth	3,000	Per table 27.2	2,167.4
Total liabilities and net worth	$5,209		$5,451.7
Total debt to equity	$\dfrac{2,209}{3,000} = 0.74$		$\dfrac{3,284.3}{2,167.4} = 1.51$

LIABILITY MANAGEMENT

In its simplest terms, capital structure management addresses this question: Assuming the firm's investment strategy is fixed, how is the total market value of the firm related to the proportions of debt and equity? In its fullest sense, managing the right-hand side of the firm's balance sheet involves determining not only the aggregate amount of debt to incur but also the choice of maturities, the mix of fixed and floating rates, the use of options and, in general, the selection of structure from the rich variety of alternatives now available in the capital markets. Effective capital structure management focuses on the characteristics of the firm's debt in a portfolio context. This can mean, for example, that new debt issues are structured to offset the interest-rate risk of existing debt. It can also mean using techniques of active liability management on outstanding issues to alter the debt portfolio characteristics. This section deals with some specific topics in the area.

The conceptual problem of liability management bears a strong similarity to the problem of managing assets. In the case of assets, the usual objective is to maximize return (i.e., future value), while in the case of liabilities, the objective is to minimize the present value of costs. However, there are also several important practical differences. In the case of liabilities, the planning horizon is usually quite long, accounting standards and tax considerations can be extremely important, and the regulatory problems some firms (e.g., public utilities) face can create added difficulty. It should also be recognized at the outset that, in the absence of special provisions, the corporation usually cannot eliminate an outstanding liability at a reasonable price, that is, unlike an asset manager, the liability manager cannot completely restructure a portfolio without incurring overwhelming transaction costs.

Managerial Problems

In managing liabilities, two conceptually different problems can be distinguished, the structuring of a new issue and the retirement of an outstanding issue. The interest rate risk of the particular decision tends to be the dominant consideration.

The fundamental method for comparing alternative fixed-income securities is discounted cash flow (DCF) analysis (see Chapter 25). In the case of new issues, the present value (PV) of the alternatives are compared in the case of a refunding decision, the PV of the outstanding security is compared with the PV of the proposed refunding instrument. The major variables affecting the PVs are horizon of the study, the choice of of discount rate, and tax treatment of different flows. To avoid possible pitfalls, the analyst should assure that

1 The study horizon is identical for each alternative, and is at least as long as the maturity of the longest alternative (it can be longer).

2 The discount rate is approximately equal to the current after-tax cost of the security under consideration.

When the primary concern of the analysis is the interest rate sensitivity of the alternatives, the expected course of interst rates must be specified over the horizon. Once these are specified, maturing debt can be rolled over for the remainder of the horizon, and the PV of the rolled-over cash flows can be computed. Note that if interest rates are specified to remain at their current flat level, the future cost of debt is the same as the current cost. (In this special case, the choice of horizon can be shown to be irrelevant, provided the discount rate is exactly equal to the marginal cost of debt.)

Regarding the marginal cost of debt, the financial manager should be aware of two related considerations, namely the effect of the yield curve (see Chapter 13) and the effect of the various options associated with the issuer's traditional security on debt. Theoretically, the correct method of discounting is to apply the appropriate spot interest rate (see Chapters 12 and 13) to each cash payment, but computations involving the spot rates tend to be unjustifiably complicated. The long-term funding rate is most useful for discounting purposes. Admittedly, the use of the long-term rate will introduce a bias (e.g., if the yield curve is upward sloping, it will understate the present value of a cash flow). However, the bias tends to be consistent across all cash flows over the specified horizon, and the sign of the differential PV is seldom affected.

The second consideration is the influence of the various options, such as call and sinking fund acceleration provisions, upon the cost of the corporation's traditional long-term debt issue. These options tend to increase the nominal yield of the debt. The cost of these options cannot be measured directly by empirical means, since normally there are numerous confounding factors that prevent one from comparing a callable and a noncallable issue. However, for any specified model of interest rates, the cost can be determined by standard option-valuation methods (see Chapter 10). This raises a question concerning what is the appropriate model of interest rates, and there is reasonably strong empirical evidence that the logarithm of the long-term rate can be described as a random walk without a trend. Although the theoretical option values derived from this model are reasonable, there is no unanimity at this time concerning the behavior of interest rates. In fact, financial managers normally put a great deal of effort into developing forecasts to help choose the best time for their transactions. For most purposes, scenario analysis is thus the basic tool for valuation because it allows managers to gain an intuitive grasp of the nature of the uncertainty and its consequences without forcing them to be too specific with respect to future conditions.

Although it makes little practical difference whether the discount is at the pure cost of debt or at the cost of a new conventional issue, the latter is preferable. Using this, the PV of the resulting liabilities precisely equals the proceeds from the issue, and this results in substantial simplification of the resulting cash flow computations. Moreover, it circumvents possible pitfalls arising from deriving value from the mere issuance of a liability. (If the discount rate exceeds the cost of the issues, the difference between proceeds and PV of liabilities is positive.)

Refunding Considerations

As interest rates drift from the coupon rate of an issue, there may be an opportunity to reduce the cost of the issue by refunding it. There are two basic forms of refunding: the "high to low" case (when rates have declined) and the "low to high" case.

Accounting and Tax Considerations. Before considering these cases, the financial manager should be aware of their accounting and tax implications. In the high to low case the bonds are acquired at some premium above book (face) value. For accounting and tax purposes the premium is an expense, which under certain circumstances, such as a particular regulatory treatment in the case of utilities, can be amortized over time. To minimize the negative impact upon earnings, corporations normally will try to take advantage of such amortization provisions. At the same time, to maximize the cash flow benefit, they recognize the premium immediately for tax purposes. The high to low case is motivated by the opportunity to reduce interest expense; it is neither tax-driven nor accounting-driven, although it has important tax and accounting consequences.

In contrast, low to high refundings tend to be either accounting or tax driven. In this case the bonds are acquired below book value, and the resulting gain, or at least some fraction thereof, flows directly into earnings. If the bonds are purchased outright the gain is taxable, and the resulting tax obligations tend to reduce severely or completely the profitability of the transaction. However, it is possible to avoid any tax consequences upon the retirement of low coupon bonds. A well-known example of such a nontaxable event is provided by equity-for-debt exchanges. Since such an exchange qualifies as a reorganization, gains on the difference between purchase cost and book value are not taxable.

Since a low-to-high refunding tends to be tax driven, it is not surprising that such refundings can result in cash flow benefits only to a taxable issuer.

Tables 27.4 and 27.5 and Figures 27.1 through 27.3 illustrate the analysis that goes into a "high to low" refunding through a tender offer.

Interest Rate Risk of Refundings. Standard refunding studies assume that the maturity structures of the outstanding and refunding issues are similar. In theory, it is possible to construct a refunding issue with after-tax cash flows that precisely match those of the outstanding issue, thus eliminating any interest rate risk (some tax risk would remain, however). By constructing such matching liability streams, the need for discounting would be eliminated, since all future incremental flows sum to zero. The value of the transaction in this case is simply the proceeds of the refunding issue less the purchase cost of the outstanding issue.

In practice, the maturity structure of a new issue can be drastically different from that of the old one. Maturity extension is quite common, but in some cases the maturity is actually contracted. In either case, an element of interest rate risk is introduced. If maturity is extended and interest rates decline, the rate paid on the issue will be higher than prevailing market interest rates; if maturity is contracted and interest rates increase, the maturing new debt will have to be called at these higher rates.

A related consideration is the determination of the timing of a transaction. With the use of standard DCF methods, the profitability of a transaction under existing conditions can readily be determined. The usual risk of executing a profitable transaction at the present is a possibility of an opportunity loss, for rates could move in a direction that would result in an even more profitable transaction in the future.

A good illustration of this problem is provided in the calling (refunding) of high-coupon bonds. Since in this case the call price is independent of interest rates, the issuer's challenge is to call when rates reach a seasonal low. The situation is further complicated by the length of the planning horizon; by waiting for rates to decline the issuer must forego savings for the present.

Management of Sinking Funds

The rich structure of sinking fund (SF) issues provides a host of managerial opportunities. The SF feature is a double-edged sword. If rates rise, the sinking fund is a burden to the issuer, who must retire specified amounts over time. In the case of a public issue, the bonds can be purchased in the market, presumably at a discount. This opportunity is an obvious mitigating factor. However, since the issuer can make a market purchase whether or not there is a SF, the SF cannot be advantageous if rates rise.

A particular consideration concerning low-coupon SF issues is that they may be collected/hoarded by a single investor, who then could prevent the issuer from making market purchases. In that event, the SF payments are obtained by calling them at the specified SF call price, which is usually 100. (SF issues have two sets of call prices, one for optional redemption and the other for mandatory redemption.)

If rates decline, the SF is a valuable option to the issuer, for it enables him to call the specified amount at par, even if the bond is not refundable. When the bond is refundable, the issuer has the enviable option of calling some of the bonds at a premium and sinking the rest at par over time. The amount called at a premium depends, among other factors, upon the call price and the refunding rate.

Sinking fund issues often have an acceleration provision, allowing the issuer to retire at par a specified multiple of the mandatory amount, that is normally exercised as long as the refunding rate is below the coupon rate.

Defeasance

It is now possible for firms to remove from their balance sheets debt that has been "extinguished" through an arrangement termed "in-substance" defeasance. An in-substance, as distinguished from a legal, defeasance is an arrangement whereby the firm provides for the repayment of interest and principal on one or several of its long-term debt obligations. It achieves this by irrevocably placing essentially risk-free securities with a trustee to be used solely for satisfying debt service requirements. In 1982, shortly after several transactions by major companies were reported, the Securities and Exchange Commission (SEC) imposed a moratorium on in-substance defeasance until the Financial Accounting Standards Board (FASB) could consider the issues and adopt an accounting standard. In November 1983, the FASB issued *Statement of Financial Accounting Standards No. 76 — Extinguishment of Debt*. The statement set clear guidelines for determining when debt should be considered extinguished, and specified the criteria for accomplishing an in-substance defeasance. The SEC lifted its moratorium in December 1983 and issued *Financial Reporting Release No. 15 — Interpretive Release Relating to Accounting for Extinguishment of Debt*. SEC registrants contemplating in-substance defeasance should follow the guidelines established by this Release. (See Exhibit 27.1)

In-substance defeasance has been surrounded by controversy on several counts. Some have argued that the motivation for this transaction is not economic gain but rather improvement in reported earnings. They point out that the yield-to-maturity on the Treasury bonds placed in the trust is generally less than the company's marginal cost of borrowing and less than returns available elsewhere. Notwithstanding the apparently fatal implications of such objections, in-substance defeasance is more economic, on an after-tax basis, than repurchase of the corporate obligation. The advantage is chiefly due to the opportunity to defer and be taxed at the capital gains rate what would otherwise be ordinary gain upon reacquisition of debt.

Other controversies have arisen from the practical application of insubstance defeasance. In February 1984, a major U.S. corporation completed an

(text continues on page 27-22)

TABLE 27.4   After-Tax Present Value Savings or Loss

XYZ Company

TENDER OFFER ANALYSIS FOR 16⅛s OF 2021
AFTER-TAX PRESENT VALUE SAVINGS/LOSS

(No Refunding vs. Refunding)

(dollars in thousands)

Price	12.625		12.875		13.125	
	Amount	Percentage	Amount	Percentage	Amount	Percentage
108.500	$20,930	20.93%	$19,086	19.09%	$17,241	17.24%
110.500	19,869	19.87	18,006	18.01	16,142	16.14
112.500	18,808	18.81	16,926	16.93	15,043	15.04
114.500	17,748	17.75	15,846	15.85	13,943	13.94
116.500	16,687	16.69	14,766	14.77	12,844	12.84
118.500	15,626	15.63	13,686	13.69	11,745	11.74
120.500	14,566	14.57	12,606	12.61	10,645	10.65
122.500	13,505	13.51	11,526	11.53	9,546	9.55
124.500	12,444	12.44	10,446	10.45	8,447	8.45
126.500	11,384	11.38	9,366	9.37	7,347	7.35
128.500	10,323	10.32	8,286	8.29	6,248	6.25
Breakeven price $147.97			$143.84		$139.87	

Notes:

	Outstanding	Refunding Options		
		1	2	3
Coupon	16.125	12.625	12.875	13.125
Maturity	9/18/2021	4/1/2021	4/1/2021	4/1/2021
Remaining average life	37.464	37.000	37.000	37.000
Principal	$300,000	$109,301	$109,301	$109,301
Price	118.500%	100.000%	100.000%	100.000%

Discount rate	12.978% (7.008% after taxes)
Present value date	4/1/1984
Tax rates	46.00% marginal
Amount repurchased	$100,000
Issuance expense	0.875%

TABLE 27.5 Incremental Present Value Savings or Loss

XYZ COMPANY

GAIN/LOSS OF TENDERING NOW VS. WAITING UNTIL FIRST CALL
INCREMENTAL PRESENT VALUE SAVINGS/LOSS

(dollars in thousands)

	12.625		12.875		13.125	
Rate	Amount	Percentage	Amount	Percentage	Amount	Percentage
8.00	$-8,413	-8.41%	$-9,085	-9.08%	$-9,757	-9.76%
9.00	-7.767	-7.77	-8,445	-8.44	-9,123	-9.12
10.00	-7,120	-7.12	-7,805	-7.80	-8,489	-8.49
11.00	-6,474	-6.47	-7,164	-7.16	-7,855	-7.85
12.00	-4,455	-4.45	-6,317	-6.32	-7,221	-7.22
13.00	1,797	1.80	-143	-0.14	-2,084	-2.08
14.00	8.067	8.07	6,126	6.13	4,186	4.19
15.00	14,337	14.34	12,396	12.40	10,456	10.46
16.00	15,626	15.63	13,686	13.69	11,745	11.74
17.00	15,626	15.63	13,686	13.69	11,745	11.74
18.00	15,626	15.63	13,686	13.69	11,745	11.74
Breakeven internal rate of return	12.71		13.02		13.33	

Notes:

		Refunding Options		
	Outstanding	1	2	3
Coupon	16.125	12.625	12.875	13.125
Maturity	9/18/2021	4/1/2021	4/1/2021	4/1/2021
Remaining average life	37.464	37.000	37.000	37.000
Principal	$300,000	$109,301	$109,301	$109,301
Price	118.500%	100.000%	100.000%	100.000%

Discount rate	12.978% (7.008% after taxes)
Present value date	4/1/1984
Tax rates	46.00% marginal
Amount repurchased	$100,000
Issuance expense	0.875%

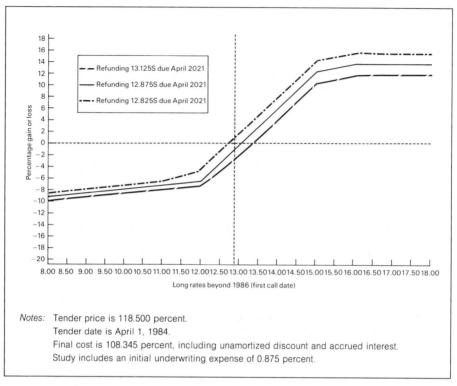

FIG. 27.1 XYZ Company's Gain/Loss of Tendering Now vs. Waiting Until First Call, 16⅛s of 2021

"instantaneous" in-substance defeasance. It defeased newly issued rather than old, low-coupon debt but still recorded a gain on the transaction for financial reporting purposes. It accomplished this by issuing 10-year bonds with a 7¼ percent coupon for 250 million deutsche marks (or about $91 million). With the standard underwriting spread for Eurobond issues of 3 percent, the all-in or effective cost of the issue was 7.7 percent. With the proceeds, the company bought German government securities at a yield of about 8.35 percent and used these to defease the bonds just issued. An immediate gain and a 65 basis-point arbitrage profit resulted from this transaction.[1]

Interest Rate Swaps

A relatively new technique of active liability management is the interest rate swap. The swap converts a floating-rate liability into an intermediate-term fixed-rate liability for one party and achieves the reverse for the other party. In effect, a borrower gains access to a particular market at a rate not achievable through traditional sources. (See Figure 27.4 and Exhibit 27.2)

---

[1] The FASB immediately moved to end instantaneous defeasances.

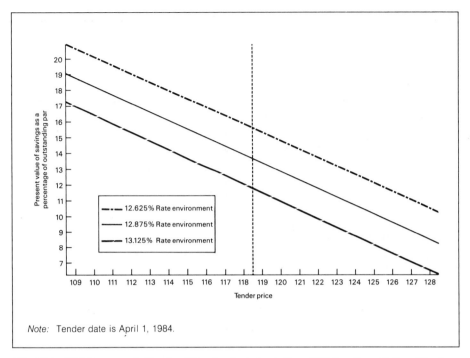

FIG. 27.2   XYZ Company's Tender Offer Analysis for 16⅛s of 2021 — Sensitivity of Savings to Tender Offer

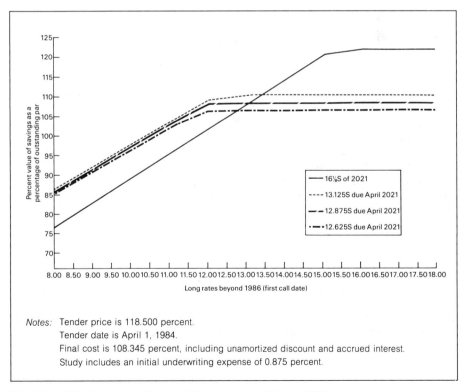

FIG. 27.3   XYZ Company's Tender Offer Analysis, 16⅛s of 2021

EXHIBIT 27.1   Illustrative Transaction

Suppose a company wants to achieve an in-substance defeasance of the following (hypothetical) issue:

Principal amount	$100 million
Coupon	6%
Remaining term	12 years
Conversion features*	None
Sinking fund	None (for simplicity)

Suppose also that 12-year U.S. Treasury bonds carrying a 6 percent coupon yield 11.5 percent and have semiannual interest payment dates that coincide with or slightly precede those of the corporate obligation. Such bonds would trade at 64.675 (rounded), or $64.675 per $100 of par amount. To defease the corporation obligation in substance, the company would:

• Purchase $100 million principal amount of the U.S. Treasury bonds for $64.675 million.

• Deposit the Treasury bonds in an irrevocable grantor trust with an independent trustee who is instructed to service the corporate obligation using the cash flows from the Treasury bonds.

As a result of this transaction:

• The $100 million face amount of the debt is removed from the balance sheet for financial reporting purposes. An extraordinary gain (pretax) equal to the difference between the carrying cost of the debt and the acquisition cost of the Treasury bonds is recognized. In the example, a pretax gain of $35.325 million is realized. A deferred tax provision related to the future capital gains tax liability on the Treasury bonds reduces the reported amount of the extraordinary gain.

• For income tax purposes, no gain or loss is recognized currently. The company remains legally obligated on the outstanding debt issue under its original terms. The interest expense on this debt will continue to be deductible from ordinary taxable income but will be offset (in the example, there is an exact offset) by the interest income on the Treasury bonds. There will also be a capital gains tax liability when the Treasury bonds mature.

---

  * The FASB concluded that convertible debt cannot be defeased in substance because of the inability to separate the debt obligation from the conversion option and because there will be no debt obligation if conversion is exercised.

An interest rate swap is a contract between two institutions in which each agrees to assume the interest expense associated with the other's preexisting or concurrently negotiated borrowings of equal principal amount. The swap agreement does not involve a transfer of the principal dollars, only the exchange of interest payments. The basis for the transaction requires that:

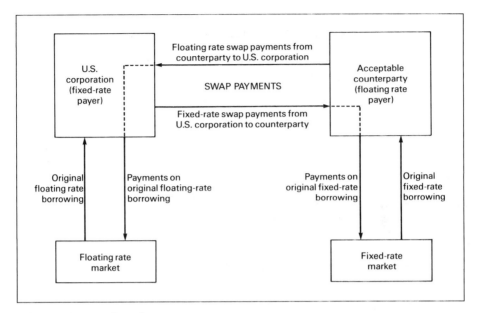

FIG. 27.4 Interest Rate Swaps

- Two parties want to borrow (or have borrowed) in two different markets.
- At least one of the borrowers can obtain better pricing than the other in one of the markets.

The second condition is relatively easy to establish. The public credit markets generally require greater yield differentials, or quality spreads, for borrowers of different credit strength than do commercial banks. That is, an A+ credit may have to pay 0.25 percent (25 basis points) more than a AA credit in the U.S. public intermediate-term market, while the credit differential might be 0.125 percent or less for a revolving bank line. If the two credits want to access different markets, the interest rate swap is a mechanism by which the differential quality spreads can be arbitraged and the savings shared.

For financial reporting purposes, the swap agreement itself is not reflected on the balance sheet of either party. Each party records only the original transaction through which it funds the swap. Net interest differential paid or received under the swap agreement is booked as an adjustment to interest expense. Potential withholding taxes can be a consideration in an interest rate swap with a foreign counterparty. Consultation with tax experts is advised.

The interest rate swap can be particularly useful to thrift institutions which have traditionally funded long-term interest-sensitive assets with short-term deposits. Savings and loan associations are attempting to reduce and better manage the risk inherent in this mismatch in a banking environment, which is becoming increasingly competitive and deregulated. A financial institution whose interest-sensitive assets are of longer duration than its interest-sensitive liabilities can reduce its rate risk by using interest rate swaps. It can enter into a "naked" swap agreement and simply convert a given amount of floating-rate

---

EXHIBIT 27.2   Illustrative Transaction

Suppose that a U.S. corporation wants to raise $50 million seven-year fixed-rate funds at the lowest possible cost. It determines that none of its traditional sources of fixed-rate funds can provide terms below 12.25 percent semiannual equivalent (SAE).

The U.S. corporation can draw on a syndicated bank facility at 0.375 percent over six-month London InterBank offered rate (LIBOR).

Suppose that an acceptable counterparty can borrow in the fixed-rate Eurobond market at an all-in cost (reflecting all transactions costs) of 11.012 percent. The counterparty wants to incur a floating-rate liability tied to six-month LIBOR. Its conventional sources of long-term floating-rate funds can do no better than 0.25 percent over six-month LIBOR.

An interest rate swap can be arranged that will result in reduced borrowing costs for both parties. Under the swap agreement, the U.S. corporation agrees to pay the counterparty's fixed-rate cost of 11.012 percent, while the counterparty pays the corporation six-month LIBOR less 0.125 percent. The resulting funds flows are shown in Figure 26.4.

As a result of the swap, the U.S. corporation converts its floating-rate liability to a fixed-rate obligation at a cost of 11.512 percent, or 74 basis points below what it could have achieved via traditional sources. The counterparty achieves a floating-rate liability at a cost of 0.125 percent under six-month LIBOR, a savings of 0.375 percent.

Additional savings are in fact available to the U.S. corporation in this transaction if it has access to floating-rate money such as commercial paper, which is less expensive than its syndicated bank line at six-month LIBOR plus 3/8 percent. For example, the spread between six-month LIBOR and a composite index for one-month commercial paper averaged −123.46 basis points from 1978 to 1983. To the extent that the commercial paper rate continued to be cheaper than its bank line, the corporation could issue paper to fund their floating-rate payments to the counterparty and thereby achieve greater net savings than nominally shown.

---

liabilities, such as Money Market Demand Accounts, into a fixed-rate obligation. It would increase interest expense and decrease its net margin and expected earnings by doing so, but would extend the duration of its liabilities and reduce the overall sensitivity of its earnings to an increase in rates. Another use of interest rate swaps for a savings and loan association involves the creation of a risk-controlled arbitrage. In this instance the swap is used to incur a fixed-rate liability, which is then used to support a fixed-rate asset with a positive spread. This transaction is intended to raise the expected profitability of the institution rather than reduce its riskiness.

Interest rate swaps have rapidly become a very effective liability management technique. While the agreement carries risk, it can be minimized through selection of strong counterparties. The risk is also reduced because it does not involve repayment of principal but only exchange of interest payments. Such transactions are, however, rather difficult to unwind and consequently can limit

---

EXHIBIT 27.3 Illustrative Transaction

Suppose that a U.S. corporation wants to incur a dollar-denominated liability. It first borrows Swiss francs through a public bond issue or a private placement in Switzerland.

Suppose an acceptable counterparty wants to borrow Swiss francs. It first borrows dollars through a public offering in the Yankee bond or Eurodollar bond market. The U.S. dollar offering will occur simultaneously with the Swiss franc offering by the U.S. corporation. Both issues will have identical maturity and redemption provisions.

In many cases, a prime international commercial bank will be interposed between the counterparties to isolate the credit of each.

On the pricing date of its Swiss franc issue, the U.S. corporation will arrange a standard forward contract with the bank intermediary to sell the net proceeds of the issue for U.S. dollars on the closing date of the offering. It will also enter into a series of forward contracts inputed by the swap to sell dollars and buy Swiss francs on each future interest payment date to meet its Swiss franc obligation.

The counterparty likewise sells the net proceeds of its U.S. dollar issue for Swiss francs and enters into a series of forward contracts to sell Swiss francs and buy dollars.

The net effect of the transaction is that the U.S. corporation obtains U.S. dollars at a fixed cost and incurs a dollar liability for financial reporting purposes. The counterparty receives a locked-in cost of Swiss francs.

---

management's flexibility with respect to the borrowing underlying the swap. The potential benefits of swaps seem to be well worth this limitation in many instances.

Currency Swaps

Currency-hedged bond offerings can give a borrower a lower cost of funds in a desired currency than would be available by directly entering the debt market in that currency. Hedged transactions combine debt financing with foreign exchange contracts. They can also be useful when a borrower is unable to enter a particular foreign currency market due to foreign exchange controls, unacceptable issuance delays, or simply when overly frequent use of a given debt market must be avoided (see Exhibit 27.3).

CLOSING REMARKS

The firm is obligated to repay the bondholder the principal amount of the loan at the promised time and to make timely payments of interest at the agreed rate while the debt is outstanding. The common shareholder has, of course, no assurance from the firm beyond the basic right of ownership, the right to decide matters of corporate policy. He or she can exercise this right either directly, by vote at regular shareholder meetings, or by delegating power of control to an elected board of directors. The firm has no specific financial commitments to its common shareholders regarding the future distribution of cash. It is this absence of specific commitment that makes common stock the fundamental basis of long-term financing. The ability to reduce or suspend common dividends without breaking a legal contract or interfering with the continuity of operations gives management a flexibility that it does not possess with fixed-charge debt obligations.[2]

Debt financing can be beneficial to shareholders because of the tax shields it carries. Because the likelihood of financial distress rises with the debt burden, however, there are limits to the amount of debt a company should have.

Even after the debt/equity choice is made, there are many management issues. These entail the maturities of the debt issues, refunding outstanding debt with new debt, tax reduction/earnings enhancement techniques, and other involving reducing interest expense and/or interest rate risk. These latter topics have just barely been touched. However, the last section of this chapter provides a good flavor of the opportunities and rewards that aggressive liability management can bring.

SUGGESTED READING

Donaldson, Gordon. *Corporate Debt Capacity: A Study of Corporate Debt Policy and the Determination of Corporate Debt Capacity.* Division of Research, Graduate School of Business Administration, Harvard University. Boston: 1962.

———. "Strategy for Financial Emergencies." *Harvard Business Review* (Nov.–Dec. 1969), pp. 67–79.

———. *Strategy for Financial Mobility.* Homewood, Ill.: Richard D. Irwin, 1971.

Hamada, Robert S. "Portfolio Analysis, Market Equilibrium, and Corporation Finance." *Journal of Finance* (Mar. 1969), pp. 13–31.

Miller, Merton H. "Debt and Taxes." *Journal of Finance* (May 1977), pp. 261–275.

Modigliani, Franco, and Merton H. Miller. "The Cost of Capital Corporation Finance, and the Theory of Investment." *American Economic Review* (June 1958), pp. 261–297.

———. "Corporate Income Taxes and the Cost of Capital: A Correction." *American Economic Review* (June 1963), pp. 433–443.

Myers, Stewart C. "Determinants of Corporate Borrowing." *Journal of Financial Economics* (Nov. 1977), pp. 147–175.

Piper, Thomas R., and Wolf A. Weinhold. "How Much Debt Is Right for Your Company?" *Harvard Business Review* (July–Aug. 1982), pp. 106–113.

---

[2] To put the capital structure in the context of stock options (see Chapter 11), note that common stock represents a residual claim on the firm's assets after all obligations to its bondholders have been satisfied. It can be viewed as a call option on the firm's assets where the exercise price is the bond redemption value. From this perspective, bondholders can be considered owners of the assets against which they have sold a call option.

Smith, Clifford W., Jr., and Jerold B. Warner. "On Financial Contracting: An Analysis of Bond Convenants." *Journal of Financial Economics* (June 1979), pp. 117–161.

Warner, Jerold B. "Bankruptcy, Absolute Priority, and the Pricing of Risky Debt Claims." *Journal of Financial Economics* (May 1977), pp. 239–276.

Further Readings on Capital Structure Management

Boyce, W.M., and A.J. Kalotay. "Optimum Bond Calling and Refunding." *Interfaces* (Nov. 1979), pp. 36–49.

Kalotay, A.J. "On the Advanced Refunding of Discounted Debt." *Financial Management* (Summer 1978), pp. 14–18.

———. "On the Management of Sinking Fund." *Financial Management* (Summer 1981), pp. 34–40.

28

How to Evaluate a Lease

Donald R. Kendall, Jr.

Companies need equipment and buildings. They can obtain the use of these assets either by buying or leasing them. Historically, leasing has been primarily associated with real estate (offices, warehouses, and stores), but since the 1960s it has been possible to lease almost any kind of capital asset. Estimates indicate that approximately 20 percent of all capital investment today is financed by leasing.

Leasing is similar to borrowing in many respects, including the creation of a fixed-payment obligation. When leasing is more advantageous than borrowing, it is generally due to tax or credit considerations. The lessee cannot effectively use the tax benefits of ownership; it cannot borrow 100 percent of the asset's cost based solely on its financial characteristics. As owner of the asset, the lessor has a stronger position than a general creditor in the event of disputes or bankruptcy and also benefits from the tax attributes of ownership and residual value of the asset. Certain lessees, the users of the asset, consider lease financing advantageous because they may be able to receive off-balance-sheet accounting treatment for the lease.

The author acknowledges the special assistance of Ross H. Goldstein and David J. McIhenny, Jr., in the preparation of the examples and in critically reviewing this chapter.

ADVANTAGES OF LEASING

Advantages to Lessees

The advantages of leasing to a lessee can be measured in terms of economic factors, accounting treatment, and qualitative factors. The economic advantage occurs through the ability to obtain the use of an asset at a lower after-tax cost than through ownership. This occurs through the indirect sale of the tax benefits that a lessee cannot effectively use to a lessor, who passes a portion of these benefits back to the lessee in the form of lower lease payments. Leasing can often be accounted for as an off-balance-sheet financing (i.e., neither an asset nor a liability appears on the lessee's balance sheet). The qualitative factors include financing through a new source of funds, the possibility of avoiding certain restrictive covenants in loan agreements, and the possibility of avoiding certain regulatory constraints.

Advantages to Lessors

Leasing is one of the few legal and acceptable means available to use efficiently a typically underused "asset," a company's tax capacity. A lease permits a company to use its tax base to invest in income-producing assets. Because tax capacity is a scarce resource, lessors are compensated for using their tax base as well as for investing their funds in a lease. Leasing is also attractive because it permits the lessor to particiate in an inflation-hedged investment, the future value of the leased asset.

TYPES OF LEASES

Leases take various forms but generally fall into two broad categories: (1) the sale and subsequent leaseback of an existing asset, and (2) the acquisition of an asset through a lease. Thus, the lease can be either an operating lease or a finance (full payout) lease.

Under a sale and leaseback arrangement, a firm sells an asset it owns (equipment, land, or buildings) to another company and simultaneously enters into an agreement with that company to lease the asset back. The sales price is frequently equivalent to the fair market value of the asset. The lessee (seller) receives the purchase price in cash and retains the use of the asset for the agreed-upon lease term. The lessor (buyer) receives predetermined lease payments, the tax benefits of ownership, and the residual value of the asset.

An operating lease generally includes maintenance and service as well as financing and is frequently arranged for a term significantly less than the asset's useful life. Computers, telephone systems, copiers, and automobiles are frequently financed through operating leases. As part of the lease, the lessor maintains and services the equipment. The payments in most operating leases do not fully amortize (or recover) the original cost of the equipment, and the leases frequently contain cancelation clauses. The lessor in an operating lease generally bears the risk of a decrease in residual value and technological obsolescence. Operating leases are frequently between the manufacturer and the user.

A finance lease is generally a net lease (the lessee provides all maintenance and services) and is fully amortized (i.e., the lease payments equal or exceed the cost of the equipment). The lessee selects the equipment it desires and negotiates the price and delivery terms directly with the manufacturer or distributor. The lessee then arranges for a financial institution to buy the equipment from the manufacturer and then leases the equipment from the financial institution for an agreed-upon lease payment and term. The financial institution or lessor will calculate its returns based on the lease payments, the tax benefits provided from depreciation and investment tax credit, and the anticipated residual value.

The finance lease, created as a new leasing vehicle by the Tax Equity and Fiscal Responsibility Act of 1982 (TEFRA), came into existence in 1984. In most respects, the finance lease is similar to a leveraged lease or guideline lease. However, it does permit the leasing of limited use property and permits a purchase option at a fixed price as long as the option is at least equal to 10 percent of the asset's original cost.

INTERNAL REVENUE SERVICE DEFINITIONS OF LEASING

A Brief History of Tax-Oriented Leasing

Leasing originally arose as a marketing device for manufacturers to aid in the sale and financing of costly equipment. It permitted purchasers to spread the payment of the purchase price over time and frequently permitted favorable off-balance-sheet accounting treatment. Tax-oriented leasing developed when Congress passed legislation providing tax benefits for the ownership of property. The Internal Revenue Code of 1954 first permitted various methods of accelerated depreciation; then, in 1962, a 7 percent investment credit was passed as an incentive for capital investment.

In issuing Revenue Ruling 55-540 in 1955, the Internal Revenue Service (IRS) established the first principles for determining who the tax owner (i.e., owner of the asset for tax purposes) is in a lease. The key concerns at that time were whether the lessee could deduct the full amount of the lease payments as rent, or only the interest portion as if the lease were really a conditional sale. Although the Revenue Ruling did not set criteria required to determine what a lease is, it did establish criteria to determine what it is not. Revenue Ruling 55-540 set forth the following conditions to classify a transaction as a purchase and not a lease:

- Portions of the payments are made specifically applicable to an equity interest to be acquired by the lessee;
- The lessee will acquire title to the leased property upon payment of a stated amount of rentals as required under the contract;
- The total amount that the lessee is required to pay for a relatively short period of use constitutes an inordinately large portion of the total sum required to be paid to secure the transfer of title;
- The agreed-upon rentals materially exceed the current fair market rental value.

- At the end of the lease term, the property may be acquired by the lessee under a nominal purchase option or under a purchase option requiring a small payment relative to the total rental payment; or

- Some portion of the rentals is specified as interest or is otherwise readily recognizable as the equivalent of interest.

These first leasing guidelines set forth the negative conditions of a lease and were used as a framework by the creators of a revolutionary new kind of lease, the leveraged lease.

The Leveraged Lease

Tax-oriented leasing took a quantum leap forward with the development of the leveraged lease in the 1960s. Through such a lease, the tax owner could borrow as much at 80 percent of the asset's cost and would still be entitled to 100 percent of the tax benefits of ownership. These transactions are structured so that a tax-intensive investor "buys" the tax benefits and the residual value for a small portion of the asset's cost; lenders lend the remaining portion of the asset's cost; and the lessee obtains the use of the equipment for a lower cost than ordinary debt financing. (See Figure 28.1.) Although these transactions could be extremely cost-effective to lessees who could not use the tax benefits of ownership, originally there was little formal guidance by the IRS as to how to properly structure leveraged leases. Private rulings were routinely given to provide comfort on the structure, but the IRS' position became more strict in the 1970s.

IRS Guidelines

Effective May 5, 1975, the IRS issued Revenue Procedure 75-21 to establish guidelines for issuing advance rulings on leveraged leases (guideline leases). Although compliance with the guidelines is not mandatory, they set forth specific criteria, which permit a transaction to be classified as a "true lease." These criteria include the following:

- The lessor must have made and maintained a minimum unconditional at-risk investment in the property equal to at least 20 percent of the cost of the property.

- The lessor must represent and demonstrate that an amount equal to at least 20 percent of the original cost of the property is a reasonable estimate of what the fair market value (residual value) of the property will be at the end of the lease term.

- The lease term plus any bargain renewal options cannot exceed 80 percent of the originally estimated useful life of the property.[1]

- The lessee may not have contractual right to purchase the property from the lessor at a price less than its fair market value at the time the right is exercised.

---

[1] In many leveraged leases, renewal options at a fair market rate are provided. These are not included in the 80 percent test, but renewals at a bargain rate are.

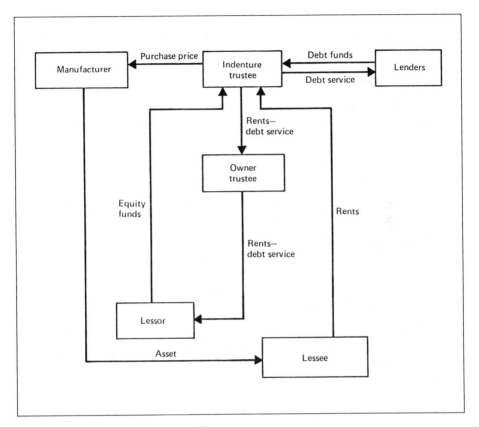

FIG. 28.1 Structure of a Leveraged Lease

- No portion of the cost of the property may be provided by the lessee.
- The lessee may not lend to the lessor any of the funds necessary to acquire the property or guarantee any indebtedness created in connection with the acquisition of the property by the lessor.
- The lessor must represent and demonstrate that it expects to receive a profit from the transaction, apart from the value of the tax attributes of the transaction.
- Uneven rents of more than 10 percent above or below the mean rents will be treated as prepaid or deferred rents.

Revenue Procedure 75-28 set forth the specific requirements for obtaining a ruling under Revenue Procedure 75-21 and set forth the limited use test. Under Revenue Procedure 75-28, leased property has to be demonstrated to be useful or usable by the lessor at the end of the lease term and capable of continued leasing or transfer to another party.

Revenue Procedure 79-48 was issued in 1979 to clarify the prohibitions against any investment by the lessee, which had been interpreted to take into account any improvements or additions. Normal repairs and maintenance had been permitted, but improvements were not. Revenue Procedure 79-48 set forth guidelines permitting lessees to make severable improvements (improvements not required to render the leased property complete for its intended purpose). Nonseverable improvements are permitted if required to comply with health, safety, or environmental standards, or if they do not substantially (defined as more than 25 percent) increase the productivity or capacity of the leased property or modify the leased property for a materially different use.

The IRS guidelines for obtaining an advance ruling for a leveraged lease have become increasingly complex and, for many lessees and lessors, less workable. The time response for obtaining a ruling has increased from as little as a few months shortly after the first Revenue Procedures were issued, to over a year in many instances. The guidelines' restrictions, in particular against favorable purchase options and lessee-provided funds, have clearly caused certain potential lessees to turn toward other less cost-effective sources of financing. Since the guidelines are not law, many lessees and lessors have been willing to violate them (e.g., including fixed-price purchase options in leases) or at least stretch them (e.g., leasing of facilities such as chemical plants and coke ovens, which could be potentially viewed as limited use assets), and rely solely on favorable opinions of tax counsel.

Recent Changes in Tax Law

One of the most dramatic changes in the leasing industry took place on August 13, 1981, when President Reagan signed into law the Economic Recovery Tax Act of 1981 (ERTA). In addition to greatly accelerating the depreciation benefits allowed for capital investment, ERTA created the safe harbor lease to permit companies to effectively transfer tax benefits if it cannot make use of them. ERTA eliminated the IRS guidelines for leasing and categorized a transaction as a lease if three safe harbor provisions were met. The three provisions are: (1) the lessor must maintain a minimum investment of 10 percent of the asset's adjusted basis throughout the lease term; (2) the lease term must not exceed the greater of 150 percent of the asset depreciation range (ADR) midpoint of the asset or 90 percent of its useful life; and (3) the lessor must be a corporation. It is estimated that approximately $50 billion of equipment was leased under the safe harbor leasing provisions for the 29 months between 1981 and 1983 they were operative.[2]

As a result of perceived abuses of the safe harbor leasing provision, Congress enacted certain provisions in TEFRA to gradually repeal safe harbor leasing as of December 31, 1983. In place of the safe harbor lease, TEFRA created the finance lease.

EVALUATION OF A LEASE

The objective of evaluation from the lessee's standpoint is to compare the attractiveness of leasing with alternative methods of financing, and from the

---

[2] Safe harbor leasing exists for mass transit equipment until 1987.

TABLE 28.1   General Assumptions

- Asset cost $100,000
- Lease terms 15 years
- Lease rate[a] 7.12%
- Lease factor[b] 11.06% payable annually in arrears
- Debt rate[c] 13%
- Debt term 15 years
- Debt portion 65% of asset cost
- Equity portion 35% of asset cost
- Investment tax credit 10% of asset cost
- Depreciation 5-year ACR for 95% of asset cost[d]
- Federal tax rate 46%

(a) Lease rate is the discount rate that equates the present value of the lease payments to the asset cost. Asset cost = $\sum_{t=1}^{y}$ lease payment/(1 + lease rate)^t where y = number of periods in the lease.

(b) Lease factor is the periodic lease payments expressed as a percentage of asset cost.

(c) The debt rate is the rate of interest currently being charged by lenders for a loan of 65 percent of asset cost for this type of asset and a lessee of the creditworthiness assumed herein.

(d) ACR = accelerated cost recovery. TEFRA provides that the depreciable basis of an asset be reduced by one-half of the investment tax credit (i.e., 100 − (10 ÷ 2) = 95) or that the investment tax credit for five-year property be reduced to 8 percent.

---

lessor's standpoint, to compare the attractiveness of an investment in a lease to other investment vehicles. In evaluating a lease from the perspectives of both the lessee and lessor, the same sample leveraged lease transaction is used. This example is representative of the types of leases that many companies evaluate annually. The general assumptions for this transaction are set forth in Table 28.1.

Lease vs. Own Analysis — Lessee's Perspective

In this section, using the sample leveraged lease as a basis of discussion, the cost of leasing is compared to the cost of owning. The present value of a full payout net lease (i.e., a finance lease that is fully amortizing and without maintenance provisions) versus that of ownership is analyzed. There are two key theoretical issues in the lease versus own analysis: (1) whether the investment (capital budgeting) and financing decision be commingled in analyzing the attractiveness of leasing, and (2) determining the appropriate discount rate for evaluating the leasing cash flows.

The investment and financing decisions should generally be treated separately. The desirability of an investment should be made on the basis of the net present value of its cash flow and without regard to the form of financing used to obtain the investment. The asset to be acquired will frequently produce the same revenue and have the same operating characteristics whether leased or owned (i.e., the same insurance cost is encountered whether the asset is leased or purchased). In the example, it is assumed that the acquisition of the asset meets the company's capital budgeting criteria.

It is often difficult to attach a specific financing to a specific asset; in effect, every asset is financed by the company's capital structure and its cost of capital. However, it is appropriate to compare leasing to 100 percent debt financing. Leasing does represent a contractual obligation to make payments. In most finance leases, it is the lessee's responsibility to pay the lessor a casualty value, which represents a return of, and on, the lessor's unrecovered investment if the asset is destroyed. Since leasing represents a contractual obligation to make payments, it also has an impact on a company's debt capacity and cost of capital in a manner similar to debt financing.

The appropriate discount rate is more difficult to determine, since a lease consists of various components: cash flows, financing flows, tax shields, and the loss of residual value in the asset. It can be argued that each flow should be evaluated using a different discount rate. For example, a case can be made for discounting the tax shields at a discount rate that reflects the company's ability to use those tax benefits. Since a company's ability to use tax benefits is constantly changing, it is often difficult to choose the correct discount rate. However, for theoretical and practical reasons, it is preferable to employ one discount rate, the after-tax cost of debt. It recognizes the fact that a lease is, in many respects, equivalent to debt financing; it is readily determinable and it permits the company to know the biases in advance. Much sensitivity analysis on the critical variables (in particular, the marginal tax rate and the asset's expected residual value) is recommended to detect any errors caused by the choice of assumptions and to verify the soundness of the lease versus own decision.

The net advantage (or disadvantage) of leasing is found by comparing the present value of ownership, assuming 100 percent debt financing, to the present value of leasing. Leasing tends to be advantageous for the following reasons.

1 The lessor, generally a high-bracket marginal taxpayer, can use the tax benefits of ownership more efficiently than can the lessee.

2 The lessor, possibly through past experience with similar equipment, perceives the residual value of the asset to be greater than that perceived by the lessee.

3 The lessor's required rate of return is less than the lessee's after-tax cost of debt.

In the lease versus own analysis, it is assumed that the asset cost is the same whether the asset is leased or owned. This is a fair assumption for large assets, but there may be certain situations where a leasing company can obtain a quantity discount and pass this savings along, at least in part, to the lessee through a reduced lease rate. The example also assumes that leasing is equivalent to 100 percent debt financing. A lease may actually use more or less debt capacity than the asset cost; that is, the present value of the lease payments may be other than the asset cost. The 100 percent debt financing assumption is a reasonable proxy in most examples and, as stated previously, sensitivity analysis is strongly recommended to test all the important assumptions and to verify any leasing versus owning decision.

TABLE 28.2   After-Tax Cash Flows of Leasing[a]

Year	Lease Payments	Tax Benefits (46%)	After-Tax Cash Flow
1983	—	—	—
1984	$ 11,602	($ 5,337)	$ 6,265
1985	11,602	(5,337)	6,265
1986	11,602	(5,337)	6,265
1987	11,602	(5,337)	6,265
1988	11,602	(5,337)	6,265
1989	11,602	(5,337)	6,265
1990	11,602	(5,337)	6,265
1991	11,602	(5,337)	6,265
1992	11,602	(5,337)	6,265
1993	11,602	(5,337)	6,265
1994	11,602	(5,337)	6,265
1995	11,602	(5,337)	6,265
1996	11,602	(5,337)	6,265
1997	11,602	(5,337)	6,265
1998	11,602	(5,337)	6,265
Total	$174,030	$80,055	$93,975

(a) Assumes no residual value.

The net present value of leasing is equal to the present value of the lease payments times one minus the tax rate, minus the residual value at the end of the lease term lost to the lessor reduced by any tax benefits provided from depreciating the purchase price of the residual value.[3] The net present value of ownership is equal to the present value of the debt service on 100 percent of the asset cost, less the tax shields provided by the interest and depreciation deductions and the investment tax credit.[4] The discount rate in both present value calculations is the after-tax cost of debt. Where the net present value cost of leasing is less than the net present value cost of owning, then leasing is advantageous.

Table 28.2 shows the lease payments and the after-tax cash flows of the leasing example from the lessee's perspective, assuming the lessee is fully taxable at a 46 percent marginal tax rate. Table 28.3 illustrates the after-tax cash flows of ownership, assuming the asset is financed 100 percent with debt.

---

[3] Net present value leasing $= \Sigma_{i=a}^{z}$ [Lease payment $\times$ (1 − tax rate) − (residual value − depreciation on residual value) $\times$ tax rate]/[1 + (debt rate $\times$ (1 − tax rate)^i].

[4] Net present value own $= \Sigma_{i=a}^{z}$ Debt service − [(interest + depreciation) $\times$ tax rate + investment tax credit]/[1 − debt rate $\times$ (1 − tax rate)^i].

TABLE 28.3   After-Tax Cash Flow of Ownership[a]

(1)	(2)	(3)	(4)	(5)	(6)
	Debt	Tax Deductions		Tax	After-Tax
Year	Service[b]	Interest	Depreciation[c]	Benefits[d]	Cash Flow[e]
1983	—	—	$14,250	($ 16,555)	($ 16,555)
1984	$ 15,474	$ 13,000	20,900	(15,594)	(120)
1985	15,474	12,678	19,950	(15,009)	465
1986	15,474	12,315	19,950	(14,842)	632
1987	15,474	11,903	19,950	(14,652)	822
1988	15,474	11,440	—	(5,262)	10,212
1989	15,474	10,916	—	(5,021)	10,453
1990	15,474	10,322	—	(4,748)	10,726
1991	15,474	9,653	—	(4,440)	11,034
1992	15,474	8,897	—	(4,093)	11,381
1993	15,474	8,042	—	(3,699)	11,775
1994	15,474	7,075	—	(3,255)	12,219
1995	15,474	5,984	—	(2,753)	12,721
1996	15,474	4,750	—	(2,185)	13,289
1997	15,474	3,355	—	(1,543)	13,931
1998	15,474	1,780	—	(819)	14,655
Total	$232,110	$132,110	$95,000	($114,470)	$117,640

(a) A positive (negative) cash flow represents an out flow (inflow).
(b) The asset is assumed to be financed with 100% debt amortized over 15 years on a level debt service basis at 13% interest.
(c) Depreciation equals 95% of the asset cost because TEFRA requires that the depreciable basis be reduced by ½ of the investment tax credit taken (10% in this case).
(d) 1983 tax benefits includes the 10% investment tax credit of $10,000.
(e) After-tax cash flow equals column (2) plus column (5).

Table 28.4 compares the after-tax cash flows of leasing to those of ownership, assuming the lessee is currently taxable (i.e., it can currently make use of the tax benefits of ownership). Table 28.4 shows that for all relevant after-tax discount rates and all residual value assumptions, ownership is more advantageous than leasing. This is the result that would be expected since in this example the lessee is able to use the tax incentives of ownership on a current basis. Since the lessor requires a return and cannot use the tax benefits more efficiently than can the lessee, in order for the lease to be beneficial to the lessee, the lessor would need to require a return below the lessee's debt cost or to perceive the asset's residual value to be significantly greater than that perceived by the lessee.

Table 28.5 shows the same lease example except that it assumes the lessee will be unable to use any tax benefits for 10 years, or in this example until

TABLE 28.4   Lease Vs. Own Analysis

Year	Lease After-Tax Cash Flow	Own After-Tax Cash Flow	Lease Advantage (Disadvantage) After-Tax Cash Flow
1983	—	($ 16,555)	($16,555)
1984	$ 6,265	(120)	(6,385)
1985	6,265	465	(5,800)
1986	6,265	632	(5,633)
1987	6,265	822	(5,443)
1988	6,265	10,212	3,947
1989	6,265	10,453	4,188
1990	6,265	10,726	4,461
1991	6,265	11,034	4,769
1992	6,265	11,381	5,116
1993	6,265	11,775	5,510
1994	6,265	12,219	5,954
1995	6,265	12,721	6,456
1996	6,265	13,289	7,024
1997	6,265	13,931	7,666
1998	6,265	14,655	8,390
Total	$93,975	$117,640	$ 23,665

NET PRESENT VALUE ANALYSIS OF LEASE ADVANTAGE (DISADVANTAGE)

Discount Rate	Residual Value (% of Asset Cost)				
	0%	10%	15%	20%	25%
0%	$ 23,665	$ 13,665	$ 8,665	$ 3,665	($ 1,335)
5	764	(4,046)	(6,451)	(8,856)	(11,261)
7.02	(5,023)	(8,637)	(10,446)	(12,252)	(14,059)
10	(11,274)	(13,668)	(14,865)	(16,062)	(17,259)

Note: 7.02% is the after-tax cost of debt (13% × (1 − tax rate)).

1994. The lessee is assumed to be able to use all tax benefits carried forward in 1994. This example shows that leasing is advantageous under most relevant discount rate and residual value assumptions. The residual value of the asset needs to exceed 50 percent of the asset's original cost in order for leasing to become more disadvantageous than ownership.

The present value method of analyzing the lease versus buy decision is practical and easy to use. It does, however, assume that one discount rate (i.e., the cost of debt) is appropriate to analyze all the cash flows (lease payments,

TABLE 28.5   Lease Vs. Own Analysis
(Lessee Not a Taxpayer Until 1994)

Year	Lease After-Tax Cash Flow	Own After-Tax Cash Flow	Lease Advantage (Disadvantage) After-Tax Cash Flow
1983	—	—	—
1984	$ 11,602	$ 15,474	$ 3,872
1985	11,602	15,474	3,872
1986	11,602	15,474	3,872
1987	11,602	15,474	3,872
1988	11,602	15,474	3,872
1989	11,602	15,474	3,872
1990	11,602	15,474	3,872
1991	11,602	15,474	3,872
1992	11,602	15,474	3,872
1993	11,602	15,474	3,872
1994	(47,105)	(91,696)	(44,591)
1995	6,265	12,721	6,456
1996	6,265	13,289	7,024
1997	6,265	13,931	7,666
1998	6,265	14,655	8,390
Total	$ 93,975	$117,640	$ 23,665

NET PRESENT VALUE ANALYSIS OF LEASE ADVANTAGE (DISADVANTAGE)

Discount Rate	Residual Value (% of Asset Cost)					
	0%	10%	15%	20%	25%	50%
0%	$23,665	$13,665	$ 8,665	$ 3,665	($ 1,335)	($26,335)
5	19,055	14,244	11,839	9,434	7,029	(4,996)
7.02	17,794	14,180	12,373	10,566	8,758	(277)
10	16,282	13,888	12,691	11,494	10,297	4,312

Note: 7.02% is the after-tax cost of debt (13% × (1 − tax rate)).

debt service, tax shields, and residual value). An attempt to overcome this deficiency is made by testing all the uncertain variables to ensure that the lease versus own decision is the same within relevant ranges for these variables.

Internal rate of return analysis (IRR) (see Chapter 25) is sometimes advocated as a lease versus own method, which does not require the choice of a discount rate. In the lease versus own analysis, this method employs an iterative process to find the discount rate that equates the present value of the outflows (i.e., after-tax lease payments, tax benefits of ownership [5] and residual value) with the cost of the asset. The IRR represents the after-tax cost of leasing. This method is also easy to use and can be used with different assumptions of residual value and other important variables.

Lessees who expect to remain in a low or zero taxpaying position indefinitely, sometimes use the lease rate or implicit interest rate of the lease as the lease versus own criteria. They compare the lease rate to their debt rate to determine whether leasing is attractive. This method is insufficient because it ignores the value of tax benefits and the lost residual value.

Evaluation of a Lease — Lessor's Perspective

A lease should be evaluated as an investment by the lessor. In traditional investments for capital or financial assets, the initial investment is followed by future positive inflows that exceed the initial outflow and provide a return on the investment. In a leveraged lease, however, the lessor has three components to its return: cash flow (rents in excess of debt service); tax shields (investment tax credit, depreciation, and interest deductions); and the expected residual value. In many leveraged leases, the tax payments in the later years exceed the cash flow resulting in cash outflows in those years. The resulting pattern of cash flows in a lease complicates the investment analysis considerably.

The cash flow pattern in a typical investment, such as a loan, will first be examined to illustrate more vividly the difference in cash flow of an investment in a lease. The loan in this example is for $100,000 and is payable at an annual interest rate of 13 percent on a level debt service basis and matures in 15 years (see Table 28.6 and Figure 28.2).

As the diagrams illustrate, the loan has a positive cash flow in each year, which is allocated in part to a recovery of the investment and in part to a return on the investment. The IRR of the after-tax cash flows is equal to 7.02 percent, which is the debt rate times one minus the tax rate. In the loan example, there is only one IRR. For any discount rate exceeding 7.02 percent, the net present value will be negative, and for any discount rate less than 7.02 percent, the net present value will be positive.

The cash flows to a lessor in a leveraged lease look quite different from the flows in a typical investment, such as a loan. Since the cash flows are comprised of "free cash" (rents in excess of debt service), tax shields, and residual value, the flows vary quite dramatically over the term of the lease. Table 28.7 and Figure 28.3 illustrate the cash flows in our sample leveraged lease.

Internal rate of return analysis of the after-tax cash flows often provides misleading and multiple solutions. This occurs because the cash flows change signs more than once, creating multiple roots (solutions) to the IRR. The IRR can also be misleading because it assumes that the positive cash flows in the early years can be reinvested at that rate. The example has two solutions to the IRR: 17.6 percent and 12.2 percent.

---

[5] The inflows from the ownership scenario are outflows in this method because they are considered unrealized or foregone positive after-tax cash flows.

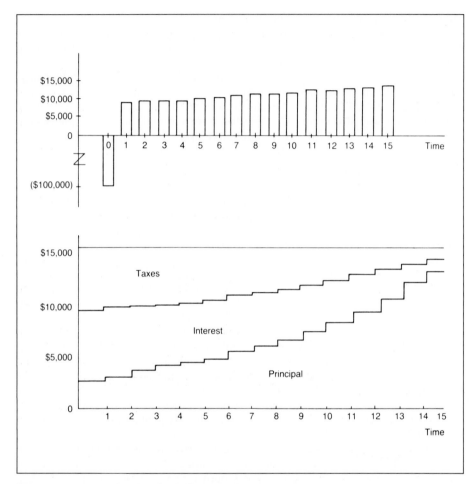

FIG. 28.2   Annual After-Tax Cash Flow of a Loan

Present value analysis can also be used to evaluate the leasing after-tax cash flows. However, since the investment is returned quickly, in this example the investment is recovered in 37 months; the discount rate assumed is automatically used for reinvesting the excess cash flows. The discount rate for present value purposes may not be the appropriate discount rate for reinvestment purposes for cash flows occurring in the future. Figure 28.4 illustrates the wide range of discount rates in which the present value of the after-tax cash flows is positive.

As a result of the imperfections in using IRR and present value analysis in evaluating a lease's after-tax cash flows, the sinking fund methodologies were developed. The sinking fund methods generally calculate a return on the investment from the initial positive cash flows. Once the investment plus a return is recovered, the remaining positive cash flows are placed in a hypothetical

TABLE 28.6   Annual After-Tax Cash Flow of a Loan

(1) Year	(2) Investment	(3) Debt Service(a)	(4) Principal	(5) Interest	(6) Taxes on Interest (46%)	(7) After-Tax Cash Flow(b)
0	($100,000)	—	—	—	—	($100,000)
1	—	$ 15,474	$ 2,474	$ 13,000	($ 5,980)	9,494
2	—	15,474	2,796	12,678	(5,832)	9,642
3	—	15,474	3,159	12,315	(5,665)	9,809
4	—	15,474	3,570	11,904	(5,476)	9,998
5	—	15,474	4,034	11,440	(5,262)	10,212
6	—	15,474	4,558	10,915	(5,021)	10,453
7	—	15,474	5,151	10,322	(4,749)	10,725
8	—	15,474	5,821	9,654	(4,441)	11,033
9	—	15,474	6,577	8,896	(4,092)	11,382
10	—	15,474	7,432	8,042	(3,699)	11,775
11	—	15,474	8,398	7,075	(3,254)	12,220
12	—	15,474	9,490	5,984	(2,753)	12,721
13	—	15,474	10,724	4,750	(2,185)	13,289
14	—	15,474	12,118	3,355	(1,543)	13,931
15	—	15,474	13,698	1,780	(819)	14,655
Total	($100,000)	$232,110	$100,000	$132,110	($60,771)	$ 71,339

(a) It is assumed that the loan is repaid on a level debt service basis; that is, principal and interest in each period are equal to the principal and interest in each other period.

$$\text{Loan} = \sum_{t=z}^{Z} \frac{\text{Debt service}}{(1 + \text{Interest rate})^t}$$

(b) After-tax cash flow is the sum of columns (2) + (3) + (6).

sinking fund, which is then reinvested at a specific rate and is used to pay the future negative cash flows (future taxes).

The example (see Table 28.8) uses the multiple investment sinking fund method, the sinking fund method most widely used by the leasing industry today. After recovering the investment (35 percent of asset cost) plus a 14.37 percent after-tax return on that investment, the remaining positive cash flows are placed in the sinking fund and are invested at a 3.24 percent after-tax rate. The multiple investment methodology looks ahead to the expected residual value and permits multiple investments in the future (see Table 28.8 — years 1995–1997) to be received plus the 14.37 percent return out of the residual value.

The sinking fund methodologies solve the reinvestment problems associated with both the IRR and present value methods. They provide more conservative

(text continues on page 28-19)

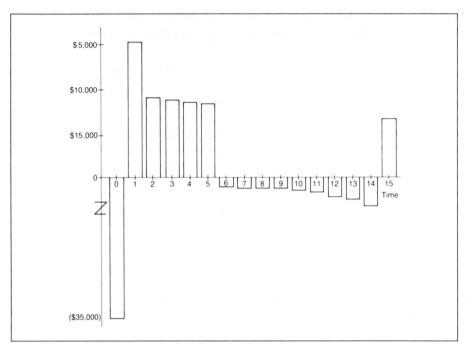

FIG. 28.3   Annual After-Tax Cash Flow of a Lease

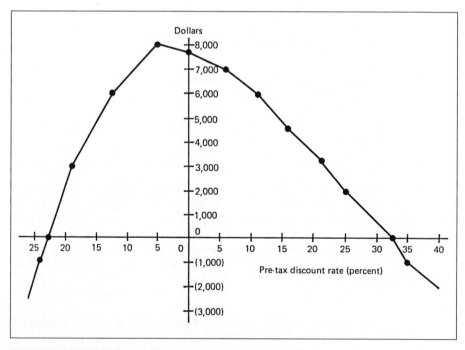

FIG. 28.4   Present Value of After-Tax Cash Flows of Leasing

TABLE 28.7 Lessor's After-Tax Cash Flow(a)

(1) Year	(2) Rental Income	Tax Analysis				Pre-Tax Cash Flow Analysis						
		(3) Depreciation	(4) Interest on Loan	(5) Taxable Income	(6) Taxes Paid(d)	(7) Rental Cash	(8) Debt Service	(9) Residual	(10) Before-Tax Cash(d)	(11) After-Tax Cash	(12) Investment	(13) Net Cash Balance
1983	—	$14,250	—	($14,250)	($16,555)(c)	—	—	—	—	$16,555	$35,000	($18,445)
1984	$ 11,062	20,900	$ 8,450	(18,288)	(8,413)	$ 11,062	$ 10,058	—	$ 1,004	9,416	—	(9,029)
1985	11,062	19,950	8,241	(17,129)	(7,879)	11,062	10,058	—	1,004	8,883	—	(146)
1986	11,062	19,950	8,005	(16,893)	(7,771)	11,062	10,058	—	1,004	8,774	—	8,628
1987	11,062	19,950	7,738	(16,626)	(7,648)	11,062	10,058	—	1,004	8,651	—	17,280
1988	11,062	—	7,436	3,626	1,668	11,062	10,058	—	1,004	(664)	—	16,616
1989	11,062	—	7,095	3,967	1,825	11,062	10,058	—	1,004	(821)	—	15,795
1990	11,062	—	6,710	4,352	2,002	11,062	10,058	—	1,004	(998)	—	14,796
1991	11,062	—	6,275	4,787	2,202	11,062	10,058	—	1,004	(1,198)	—	13,598
1992	11,062	—	5,783	5,279	2,428	11,062	10,058	—	1,004	(1,425)	—	12,173
1993	11,062	—	5,227	5,835	2,684	11,062	10,058	—	1,004	(1,680)	—	10,493
1994	11,062	—	4,599	6,463	2,973	11,062	10,058	—	1,004	(1,969)	—	8,523
1995	11,062	—	3,889	7,172	3,299	11,062	10,058	—	1,004	(2,296)	—	6,228
1996	11,062	—	3,087	7,974	3,668	11,062	10,058	—	1,004	(2,665)	—	3,563
1997	11,062	—	2,181	8,881	4,085	11,062	10,058	—	1,004	(3,082)	—	481
1998	31,062(b)	—	1,157	29,905(b)	13,756	11,062	10,058	$20,000	21,004	7,248	—	7,729
Total	$185,927	$95,000	$85,873	$ 5,054	($ 7,675)	$165,927	$150,873	$20,000	$35,054	$42,729	$35,000	

Additional Assumptions:

(a) The lessor's required rate of return is 14.37% after-tax assuming a 3.24% after-tax sinking fund reinvestment rate.

(b) Residual value is equal to 20% of the asset's original cost.

(c) Includes the $10,000 for the investment tax credit.

(d) After-tax cash flow is equal to column (10) – column (6).

TABLE 28.8 Multiple Investment Sinking Fund Method

Effective annual after-tax yield	14.367347%
After-tax sinking fund rate	3.240000%
Internal rate of return (after-tax)	17.55%
Residual value	$20,000

Year	Investment	After-Tax Cash	Investment Earnings	Repayment of Investment	Ending Investment	Sinking Fund	Sinking Fund Earnings
12/83	$35,000	$16,555	$3,767	$12,788	$22,212	—	—
12/84	—	9,416	2,645	6,771	15,441	—	—
12/85	—	8,883	1,699	7,184	8,257	—	—
12/86	—	8,774	672	8,102	154	—	—
12/87	—	8,651	2	154	—	$8,609	$ 114
12/88	—	(664)	—	—	—	8,239	294
12/89	—	(821)	—	—	—	7,698	280
12/90	—	(998)	—	—	—	6,960	260
12/91	—	(1,198)	—	—	—	5,995	234
12/92	—	(1,425)	—	—	—	4,770	199
12/93	—	(1,680)	—	—	—	3,245	156
12/94	—	(1,969)	—	—	—	1,379	103
12/95	—	(2,296)	2	(881)	881	—	38
12/96	—	(2,665)	180	(2,844)	3,725	—	1
12/97	—	(3,082)	605	(3,687)	7,412	—	—
12/98	—	7,248	83	7,412	—	—	248
Total	$35,000	$42,729	$9,655	$35,000			$1,926

solutions by permitting the lessor to choose a more realistic reinvestment rate. It must be pointed out that they are not free of fault, however. For example, if the residual value estimate is wrong, the analysis is incorrect.

At this point, it is reasonable to ask how the lessor determined the lease payments presented in Table 28.7. This is a fair question; yet, not an easy one to answer in simple terms. To derive the lease payments, the lessor must first determine its required rate of return, sinking fund reinvestment rate, the lessee's debt rate, and the amount of residual value it is willing to price in. Once it has determined these, it must then use trial and error to determine the amount of equity investment required to provide to the lessee the lowest lease rate consistent with the above assumptions. In the examples, it has been simplified and assumed that level rental payments and level debt service are acceptable. Many lessees today want the lowest present value of lease payments using uneven rentals and optimized (i.e., not level) debt service.

Lease evaluation computer programs are continually being updated and can easily handle the examples used herein.

ACCOUNTING FOR LEASES

On December 2, 1976, the Financial Accounting Standards Board (FASB) issued its Statement of Financial Accounting Standards No. 13, *Accounting for Leases*, establishing standards for the reporting of leases in financial statements. For purposes of this statement, a lease is defined as an agreement conveying the right to use property, plant, or equipment (land and/or depreciable assets) usually for a stated period of time. The implications of this statement are important because many previously off-balance-sheet leases are now recognized as obligations in the lessee's financial statements.

Lessees

In the case of the lessee, the statement generally requires that a lease be classified and accounted for as a capital lease (shown as an asset and an obligation on the balance sheet of the lessee) if it meets any one of four criteria:

- The lease tranfers ownership in the property to the lessee by the end of the lease term;
- The lease contains an option to purchase the property at a bargain price;
- The lease term is equal to 75 percent or more of the estimated economic life of the property; or
- The present value of the minimum lease payments is equal to 90 percent or more of the fair value of the leased property less any related investment tax credit retained by the lessor.

If the lease does not meet any one of these criteria, it is to be classified as an operating lease and not capitalized by the lessee. Rentals under an operating lease are expenses over the lease term. Future rentals must be disclosed in the footnotes to the lessee's financial statements.

Assets under capitalized leases are to be amortized in the same manner as owned assets. The capitalized value represents the present value of the minimum lease payments. Minimum lease payouts are to be allocated between principal and interest elements so as to produce a constant periodic rate of interest on the remaining balance of the obligation.

The lessee in the example would probably treat the sample lease as an operating lease, even though the lease is a full payout net leveraged lease. In examining the four FASB Statement No. 13 criteria, the lease clearly does not meet the first three: (1) it does not transfer ownership at the end of the lease term; (2) it does not contain a bargain purchase option; and (3) the lease term is less than 75 percent of the estimated economic life of the asset (in the example, it is assumed that the estimated economic life exceeds 20 years). Does the lease meet the 90 percent value test?

FASB Statement No. 13 requires that the lessee use the rate implicit in the lease as the discount rate unless the marginal cost of borrowing is lower. Since the lessee does not know the rate implicit in the lease (he must know the lessor's residual value assumption and the lessor will not tell him), the lessee's marginal cost of borrowing (13 percent in the example) may be used as the discount rate.

If the lease payments are discounted (11.06 percent of asset cost payable annually in arrears) at 13 percent, a present value of 71.5 percent of asset cost is derived. Since this is less than 81 percent (100 percent minus the 10 percent investment tax credit retained by the lessor times 90 percent), the lease fails the 90 percent test. As a result, the lease meets none of the criteria required to be a capitalized lease and will therefore be treated by the lessee as an operating lease and will be described only in the footnotes to the lessee's financial statements (not capitalized on the balance sheet as an asset and a corresponding liability).

Since the lessor's residual value assumption (20 percent of asset cost) is known, the lessor's implicit rate can be calculated. It is the IRR that equates the present value of the lease payments (11.06 percent) and the residual value (20 percent) to the asset's cost. In our example the lessor's implicit rate is 8.15 percent. Using this as the discount rate in the 90 percent test, the present value of the lease payments equals 93.8 percent. If the lessee knew the lessor's implicit rate, the lease in the example would be a capitalized lease and would appear on the lessee's balance sheet as an asset and a liability.

Lessors

In the case of the lessor, if a lease other than a leveraged lease meets any one of the preceding four criteria and also meets both of the following criteria, it should be classified and accounted for as a sales-type lease (if manufacturing or dealer profit is involved) or as a direct financing lease (if such profit is not involved):

- Collectibility of the minimum lease payments is reasonably predictable; and
- No important uncertainties surround the amount of costs yet to be incurred by the lessor under the lease.

Unearned income on sales-type and finance-type leases is to be amortized to income over the lease term so as to produce a constant periodic rate of return on the net investment in the lease. Leases that meet the criteria of direct financing-type leases, but which also include a long-term creditor that provides financing (normally nonrecourse as to the general credit of the lessor) on the leased property, are to be classified and accounted for as leveraged leases. All other leases are to be classified and accounted for as operating leases.

The lessor would treat the sample transaction as a capitalized leveraged lease since, from its perspective, the present value of the lease payments exceed the asset's cost less the investment tax credit times 90 percent. The lessor would treat its equity investment as an investment in leveraged lease on the balance sheet. Table 28.9 shows the income statement accounting treatment for the lease example from the lessor's standpoint. As this example indicates, the lessor allocates income to those periods in which it has an investment outstanding. FASB Statement No. 13 doesn't require the lessor to book a loss in any year if the lease is profitable over its term.

Figures 28.5 and 28.6 present flow charts illustrating the decision criteria for lessee and lessor classification of leases. These diagrams, prepared by the FASB, walk through each of the criteria discussed previously:

- Transfer of ownership at the end of the lease term
- Bargain purchase option at the end of the lease term
- The 75 percent test
- The 90 percent test

and for the lessor the additional tests of:

- Collectibility of rents
- Reimbursement of costs
- Is there a manufacturing profit?

SUMMARY

Leasing has played an important role in the United States in financing equipment and real estate. Evaluating a lease is difficult conceptually from both the standpoint of the lessee and the lessor. A lease permits a lessee to obtain the use of an asset by contractually committing to make lease payments to the lessor who owns the assets.

From the lessees perspective, the lease is similar in many respects to debt. Therefore, in evaluating leasing versus owning an asset, it is believed that leasing should be compared to ownership financed with 100 percent debt. Other variables that impact the results of the analysis, such as the lessee's projected tax position and the asset's expected residual value, should be tested using sensitivity analysis.

From the lessor's perspective, a lease is an investment that has an unusual after-tax cash flow pattern. Because of the multiple changes of sign in the

(text continues on page 28-25)

TABLE 28.9   Statement of Lessor's Lease Book Earnings

Date	Investment Cash	Lessor's Net Investment at Beginning Period	Annual Cash Flow			Components of Income		
			Cash Flow	Cash Flow Allocated to Investment	Allocated to After-Tax Income(a)	Pretax Income	Tax Effect of Pretax Income	Investment Tax Credit
12/1983	$35,000.00	—	$16,555.00	$13,378.39	$3,176.61	$22.03	($ 955.44)	$ 4,110.02
12/1984	—	$ 21,621.61	9,416.14	7,258.97	2,157.17	14.96	(648.81)	2,791.02
12/1985	—	14,362.64	8,882.97	7,582.94	1,300.03	9.01	(390.99)	1,682.01
12/1986	—	6,779.70	8,774.29	8,388.39	385.90	2.68	(116.07)	499.29
12/1987	—	(1,608.69)	8,651.49	8,651.49	—	—	—	—
12/1988	—	(10,260.18)	(664.27)	(644.27)	—	—	—	—
12/1989	—	(9,595.91)	(821.08)	(821.08)	—	—	—	—
12/1990	—	(8,774.83)	(998.27)	(998.27)	—	—	—	—
12/1991	—	(7,776.56)	(1,198.49)	(1,198.49)	—	—	—	—
12/1992	—	(6,578.07)	(1,424.74)	(1,424.74)	—	—	—	—
12/1993	—	(5,153.33)	(1,680.41)	(1,680.41)	—	—	—	—
12/1994	—	(3,472.92)	(1,969.31)	(1,969.31)	—	—	—	—
12/1995	—	(1,503.61)	(2,295.78)	(2,295.71)	—	—	—	—
12/1996	—	792.17	(2,664.68)	(2,809.31)	144.63	1.00	(43.50)	187.13
12/1997	—	3,601.48	(3,081.53)	(3,577.55)	496.02	3.44	(149.20)	641.78
12/1998	—	7,179.03	7,247.61	7,179.03	68.58	0.47	(20.64)	88.75
Total	$35,000.00		$42,728.94	$35,000.00	$7,728.94	$53.59	($2,324.65)	$10,000.00

(a) Lease income is recognized as 11.490010% per year of the unrecovered investment in each month in which the net investment is positive.

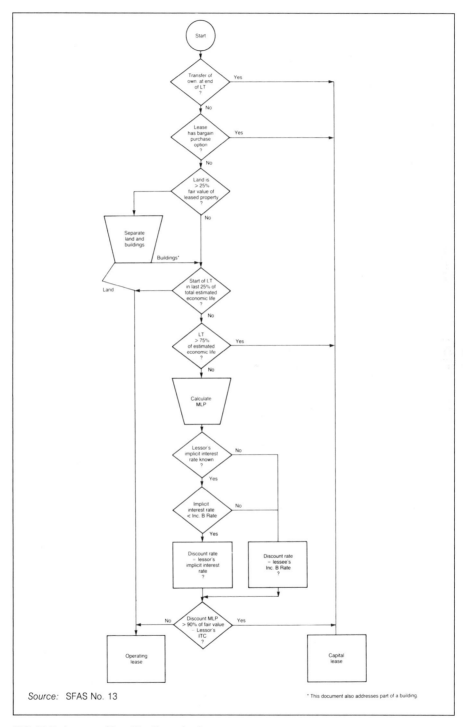

Start

Transfer of own. at end of LT ? — Yes

No

Lease has bargain purchase option ? — Yes

No

Land is > 25% fair value of leased property ?

No

Separate land and buildings

Buildings*

Land

Start of LT in last 25% of total estimated economic life ?

No

LT > 75% of estimated economic life ? — Yes

No

Calculate MLP

Lessor's implicit interest rate known ? — No

Yes

Implicit interest rate < Inc. B Rate — No

Yes

Discount rate = lessor's implicit interest rate ?

Discount rate = lessee's Inc. B Rate ?

Discount MLP > 90% of fair value – Lessor's ITC ? — Yes

No

Operating lease

Capital lease

Source: SFAS No. 13

* This document also addresses part of a building.

FIG. 28.5 Lessee Classification of a Lease

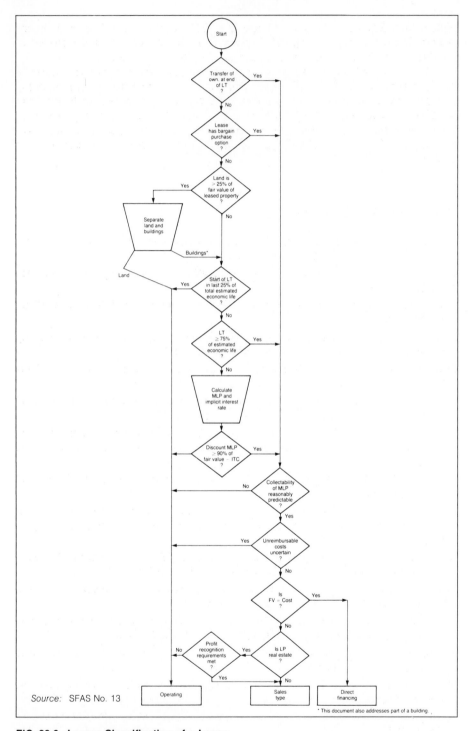

FIG. 28.6 Lessor Classification of a Lease

typical cash flows of a leveraged lease, the IRR and the present value analyses provide imperfect results. Sinking fund methodologies have been developed to satisfactorily analyze the unusual cash flow patterns of a lease.

As a result of the recent changes in tax law, and the reindustrialization of the United States, leasing will continue to play an important role in the financing of capital expenditures. Many companies that cannot effectively utilize the tax benefits of ownership will find leasing an economically attractive way to finance a new investment. Other profitable companies will perceive leasing as an attractive investment alternative providing tax shelter and deferral and residual value upside.

SUGGESTED READING

Athanasopoulos, Peter J., and Peter W. Bacon. "The Evaluation of Leveraged Leases." *Financial Management,* Vol. 9 (Spring 1980), pp. 76–80.

Bower, Richard S. "Issues in Lease Financing." *Financial Management*, Vol. 2 (Winter 1973), pp. 25–34.

Bower, Richard S., et al. "Lease Evaluation." *Accounting Review*, Vol. 41 (Apr. 1966), pp. 257–265.

Dyl, Edward A., and Stanley A. Martin, Jr. "Setting Terms for Leveraged Leases." *Financial Management*, Vol. 6 (Winter 1977), pp. 20–27.

Financial Accounting Standards Board. *Statement of Financial Accounting Standards Number 13 — Accounting for Leases*. Stamford, Conn.: 1976.

Gordon, Myron J. "A General Solution to the Buy or Lease Decision: A Pedagogical Note." *Journal of Finance*, Vol. 29 (Mar. 1974), pp. 245–250.

Honig, Lawrence E., and Stephen C. Coley. "An After–Tax Equivalent Payment Approach to Conventional Lease Analysis." *Financial Management*, Vol. 4 (Winter 1975), pp. 18–27.

Johnson, Robert W., and Wilbur G. Lewellen. "Analysis of the Lease-or-Buy Decision." *Journal of Finance,* Vol. 27 (Sept. 1972), pp. 815–823.

Keller, Thomas F., and Russell J. Peterson. "Optimal Financial Structure, Cost of Capital, and the Lease-or-Buy Decision." *Journal of Financial and Quantitative Analysis*, Vol. 13 (Dec. 1978), pp. 871–883.

Kim, E. Han, et al. "Sale-and-Leaseback Agreements and Enterprise Valuation." *Journal of Financial and Quantitative Analysis,* Vol. 13 (Dec. 1978), pp. 871–883.

Law, Warren A., and M. Colyer Crum. *Equipment Leasing and Commercial Banks*. Chicago: Association of Reserve City Bankers, 1963.

Miller, Merton H., and Charles W. Upton. "Leasing, Buying, and the Cost of Capital Services." *Journal of Finance*, Vol. 31 (June 1976), pp. 761–786.

Myers, John H. *Reporting of Leases in Financial Statements*. New York: American Institute of Certified Public Accountants, 1962.

Myers, Stewart C., et al. "Valuation of Financial Lease Contracts." *Journal of Finance*, Vol. 31 (June 1976), pp. 799–819.

Nevitt, Peter K. *On the Spot Leveraged Leasing*. San Francisco: Bank AmeriLease Group, 1977.

Schall, Lawrence D. "The Lease-or-Buy and Asset Acquisition Decisions." *Journal of Finance*, Vol. 29 (Sept. 1974), pp. 1203–1214.

Van Horne, James C. "Lease Financing." *Financial Management and Policy*, Chapter 23. Englewood Cliffs, N.J.: Prentice-Hall, 1971, pp. 576–601.

Vancil, Richard F. "Lease or Borrow: Steps in Negotiation." *Harvard Business Review*, Vol. 39 (Nov.–Dec. 1961), pp. 238–259.

——. "Lease or Borrow: New Method of Analysis." *Harvard Business Review*, Vol. 39 (Sept.–Oct. 1961), pp. 122–136.

Weston, J. Fred, and Eugene F. Brigham. "Lease Financing." *Managerial Finance*, Chapter 21. New York: Holt, Rinehart & Winston, 1981, pp. 850–874.

29

Mergers and Acquisitions

ROBERT CASE

WHY MERGE?

There are probably as many reasons why corporations merge and acquire as there are mergers and acquisitions. It is really only possible in an overview such as this to establish a framework for considering why a merger may or may not make sense, rather than to give a list of reasons for mergers.

The fundamental reason for an acquiror to make an acquisition is because the acquisition is expected to increase the *per share value* of the acquiror to its stockholders over the long term. Ultimately, this comes about in only one way: the discounted cash flows to be realized from operation of the acquired business exceed the cost of the acquisition.

The fundamental reason for a company to agree to be acquired, if the transaction is for cash, is that the selling shareholders have an immediate opportunity to be paid for some of the acquisition's expected benefits and to realize a premium which the stock price may not surpass for some time. In a transaction in which the seller receives the acquiror's stock, the seller, as one of the acquiror's shareholders, will also share in the benefits of the merger over time. It happens, therefore, that when the selling shareholders will end up owing a large portion of the combined company, the acquisition premium paid is usually much smaller.

In thinking about whether an acquisition will, on balance, create value to an acquiror's shareholders, several rules are becoming commonly accepted among analysts today:

Pure conglomerate acquisitions do not necessarily create new shareholder value. Shareholders of an acquiror already have the opportunity to invest in the acquisition target as an independent matter. By forcing those shareholders to make a both-or-none investment decision, management presents a less attractive investment profile to the market than if the two companies traded separately.

In order for a conglomerate acquisition to make sense, there must be some additional value created that is not present in either company on a stand-alone basis. If there is no such synergy, the combined companies will trade at a conglomerate discount, which is only eliminated when the unrelated businesses are divested or spun off. There were numerous examples of this in the late 1970s.

Countercyclical acquisitions do not necessarily create value. As discussed in Chapter 14, the capital market only assesses financial risk that is systematic (i.e., marketwide) in nature. Thus, mergers that tend to eliminate unsystematic (nonmarket related) risk do not improve the investment profile of a company. For example, a company that sells both umbrellas and suntan lotion may have less risk in its cash flows than a company that sells only one such product. Nevertheless, the risk involved (sunshine versus rain) is not one for which the market will demand a higher cost of capital. Therefore, a combined umbrella and suntan lotion company will not experience a lower cost of capital than the independent companies. Such a merger cannot be justified on purely financial grounds, although other bases (e.g., common management skills and economies of scale) may justify it.

The argument against countercylicality can be taken a step further. Even a combination of companies with countercyclical systematic risks (e.g., capital goods manufacturing and supermarkets) would appear not to create new value because each investor can also achieve a risk-balanced portfolio on his own.

The primary circumstance in which countercyclicality does create value is where there would otherwise be underutilized assets or skills in one or both companies. For example, an umbrella company may profitably combine with a snow-boot company to fill up unutilized capacity in manufacturing, sales, and distribution during the predictable off-season.

The market does not reward purely acquisition-induced growth. It is commonly recognized that companies with tremendous growth potential trade in the marketplace at earnings multiples far higher than companies with more mundane prospects. It is tempting, therefore, to conclude that a company that has exhausted its internal opportunities for fast growth can achieve equivalent results by a program of carefully timed acquisitions. The fallacy in this reasoning is that, unlike the situation of an established product with growing demand, each acquisition must stand on its own in terms of its contribution to a company's earnings and cash flow. Unless the circumstances are unique (e.g., a ready supply of acquisition targets that can be bought one by one, without competition), each acquisition is a nonrepeatable event. It is not like making and selling one more widget. Investors must continually rely on the ability of the company to pick good targets and negotiate favorable transaction terms. Because the likelihood of successfully carrying out a steady, predictable series of high-return acquisitions is quite low, the market discounts the earnings of companies that grow through acquisition at a much higher rate than those of companies that happen to be in product markets offering substantial growth within an area of demonstrated expertise.

Related diversification can be an important means of creating value in acquisitions. The most successful acquisitions typically involve situations in which the assets, skills, or knowledge of one company can be applied to the problems or opportunities of the other. For example, a target may have a strong sales force in place that can market many of the acquiror's products to new customers or in a new geographic region. This would be a revenue-increasing acquisition. Or the target may have a product or process uniquely suited to a need within the acquiror's business. This would be a cost-reducing acquisition. In many cases, the acquiror has the alternative of developing comparable skills, systems, or products on its own, but the speed and limited risk with which an acquisition can be consummated often more than offset the savings associated with internal development. Many acquisitions are both cost-reducing and revenue-increasing.

Acquisitions can be an important means of reaching a critical mass, where size is an important industry factor. In certain industries, long-run competitive success depends importantly on achieving a necessary critical mass in terms of sales, assets, customers, or some other factor. In the pharmaceutical industry, research and development (R&D) expenditures are critical to long-run survival and must be funded out of the earnings of a base of successfully established products. But a successful R&D program requires very substantial levels of spending, with minimum levels that cannot be met by smaller companies. Thus, there is a strong impetus to the achievement of size through acquisition. In commercial banking, overhead costs tend to decline and margins tend to increase as a percentage of lendable assets, up to very substantial bank sizes. The principal way that the large critical mass of customers, deposits, and loans necessary for efficient operation can be reached is through acquisitions of other banks.

Acquisitions are a tax-efficient means of investing excess corporate funds.
The U.S. Internal Revenue Code provides for double taxation of corporate
earnings: once at the corporate level in the form of the corporate income tax,
and again at the shareholder level in the form of capital gain and dividend taxes.
Shareholder taxes on corporate earnings can be deferred, however, if those
earnings are retained and reinvested within corporate solution. For example,
a company with $100 in excess cash could pay out $100 in dividends, but that
may leave shareholders with only $50 to invest (at a 50 percent marginal tax
rate). A more sophisticated company would buy some of its stock back in the
marketplace but, after capital gains taxes, may still only effectively distribute
$95. On the other hand, the full $100 may be reinvested productively by means
of an acquisition, and taxes at the shareholder level may ʰe deferred indefinitely.

This is not to say that a corporate management should always make acquisitions instead of paying dividends or repurchasing stock. It depends on
whether there are high-return alternatives available that can be effectively managed
by the corportion's executives. If there are no such alternatives, or if there is
a major risk that an acquisition program will overburden management and create
below-normal returns, it is better to pay out excess cash to shareholders and
let them reinvest it in other opportunities.

VALUATION OF A MERGER CANDIDATE

It is assumed that after lengthy searching, the ideal acquisition candidate is
found: Flexible Technologies Corporation. It is just the right size, fits a market
niche in which there is some knowledge and which should experience attractive
growth, and it has capable management who would work well in the organization.
There is a controlling stockholder who is willing to sell, but it must be decided
how much to offer him. How should the valuation process be undertaken?

Value to Whom?

There are many different concepts of value, which are largely distinguished by
determining who is the valuing party and how the value arises. Typically, there
are three different valuing parties in an acquisition situation: the buyer, the
seller, and a potential competing buyer.

Value to a buyer represents the discounted present value of the net cash
flows the buyer will ultimately realize and have freely available as a consequence
of making the acquisition. Those cash flows could be realized by operating the
business over a long period, liquidating all or part of the business, or restructuring
parts of both the buyer's business and the acquired business in a way that
creates synergy value in excess of that provided by the two businesses independently. It is important to note that the "buyer's value" represents the highest
amount the buyer should ever pay to acquire the company in question. Payment
of more than this would leave the buyer with a net economic loss for having
made the acquisition.

Value to the seller represents a similar discounted cash flow (DCF) calculation from the seller's viewpoint, including the many strategies for running the business and even making acquisitions of its own. In order for a transaction to be feasible, the seller's estimate of value must be below the buyer's by an amount larger than any taxes payable by the seller as a result of the sale. Clearly, a seller will not dispose of an asset for a price at which its net after-tax proceeds are below those realizable by retaining the asset.

Value to a competing buyer must always be kept in mind by both the buyer and seller in any merger negotiation. The key issue is whether the buyer with whom the seller is dealing is the buyer who is willing to pay the highest price. In order to be assured of success, the buyer should offer a price that is reasonably indicative of the full value of the business to that buyer. By the same token, a smart seller will not let a buyer know he is the only suitor in the negotiation.

Overview of Valuation Techniques

It is important to have an understanding of the nature and validity of the value that is estimated by each approach. The approaches to valuation to be considered are these:

1 Discounted cash flow
2 Acquisition multiples
3 Premium over market trading value
4 Liquidation value
5 Replacement value

The discounted cash flow approach is the most fundamental method of measuring value, since it measures the ultimate source of value: cash. It can be used validly in most situations, provided the underlying assumptions used to project the cash flows reflect the likely course of events.

Acquisition multiples are a means of establishing benchmark values for a company, based on multiples of earnings, book value, and so forth paid by other acquirors. The typical approach is "companies in the X industry trade at Y times earnings."

Premiums over market trading value typically measure the percentage premium paid to public stockholders. This measure is important in drawing support from shareholders to assure the success of a tender offer or merger. Liquidation values measure the amount of cash which could be realized if a company sold all of its assets and paid off its liabilities in the relatively near future. Finally, replacement values measure the cost of starting up a similar company from scratch.

In trying to make a valuation estimate, it is important to apply those methods most pertinent to the particular circumstances of the company under review. Thus, if the company has vast, underutilized natural resources, a liquidation approach will be material to the formation of a value judgment, even if the buyer does not plan to liquidate the company. On the other hand, if the company has little in the way of tangible assets, but has an important brand name and strong management skills, a DCF analysis will be much more relevant than a liquidation analysis. The purpose of having many techniques is to be able to choose those methods which best address the nature of the company in question. A second, and equally important, reason for the several approaches to value is to allow the analyst to confirm values generated by one technique with the results of a separate analysis. No matter how methodical the techniques may seem at times, there is little question that valuation is far more an art than a science.

Discounted Cash Flow Analysis

Discounted cash flow analysis is doubtless the most fundamental method of measuring value, since it is based on the source of value: cash. The values that DCF yields are often inappropriately referred to as "intrinsic" values. Such terminology has the unfortunate consequence of sidestepping the real issue, which is: Whose assumptions about the future should be used in estimating the cash flows? A value estimate is only as intrinsic to the business as a consensus is to the likely future cash flows. DCF has the useful characteristic that it can calculate numerous different values for a company, depending on whether the underlying assumptions are those of a seller, a buyer, or another potential owner. It is only because different perceptions of value exist that exchange takes place at all.

Definition of Scenarios. The first step in any DCF analysis is an evaluation of the historical operating characteristics of the company (e.g., growth, margins, and capital intensity,) and a projection of the behavior of these characteristics into the future. The projection clearly depends on a well-developed understanding of the industry and economic environment in which the company will be operating and a feeling for the operating strategy management has adopted and will use in the future.

The objective is to arrive at a set of basic operating ratios that will allow a projection of cash flows for the company. A typical set of such ratios include:

- Unit growth rate of sales
- Rate of price increases
- Cost of goods sold as a percent of sales
- Depreciation as a percent of net fixed assets
- Selling, general, and administrative expenses as a percent of sales
- Effective tax rate
- Working capital required as percent of sales
- Net fixed assets required as percent of sales

In order to integrate these operating ratios into a more general framework of the industry and economic climate, it is useful to make explicit assumptions about:

- Inflation
- Industry size and unit growth rate
- Market share changes within the industry

Unfortunately, it is not generally possible to project all of these industry- and company-specific factors with a high degree of certainty. While it is technically possible to perform many sensitivity analyses of value with respect to each assumption, financial analysts find it conceptually useful to group varying sets of assumptions into scenarios that logically belong together. For example, if unit sales do not grow as fast as expected, it may be because of increased competition, a factor that should be reflected in lower margins as well. Alternatively, it may be that part of the "value creation" of the acquisition consists of more stringent management of working capital and plant efficiency. A good DCF analysis would examine the impact on value if such efficiencies cannot be attained.

EXAMPLE. Flexible Technologies Corporation has the following historical operating record:

	Latest 5-Year Average
Unit rate of growth	7.0%
Rate of price growth	10.0
Operating income (% of sales)	22.5
Depreciation rate (% of net fixed assets)	12.0
Tax rate	46.0
Net working capital required (% of sales)	15.0
Net fixed assets required (% of sales)	40.0

It is also known that, over the five-year time horizon examined, the average inflation rate was 8.0 percent (and thus, real price increases were (1.10/1.08 − 1) × 100%, or 1.9%). Industry growth has averaged 7.0 percent, and Flexible's market share has remained steady at 11 percent.

For the future, two alternative scenarios are evolving in the industry. In the first "maturity" scenario, slackened demand and increasing competition will force Flexible to lower its prices and margins in order to maintain its market share. In the second "growth" scenario, continued high demand growth will continue for the next eight years, at which time the industry should mature.

These two scenarios can be quantified as follows:

Maturity Scenario. Assuming that, in the long run, unit demand growth is tied to population growth (assumed to be 1.5 percent), a maturity scenario can be described in which Flexible's unit sales growth declines to that 1.5 percent rate. Prices and margins must also reflect the maturity scenario. The implications of maturity can be seen by examining Flexible's return on invested capital, which has been above normal in recent years:

$$\text{Pretax return on assets (ROA), unleveraged} = \frac{\text{Operating income}}{\text{Sales}} \times \frac{\text{Sales}}{\text{Capitalization}}$$

$$= \frac{\text{Operating income}}{\text{Sales}}$$

$$\times \frac{\text{Sales}}{\text{Fixed assets} + \text{Net working capital}}$$

$$= \frac{\text{Operating income}}{\text{Sales}}$$

$$\times \frac{1}{\dfrac{\text{Fixed assets}}{\text{Sales}} + \dfrac{\text{Net working capital}}{\text{Sales}}}$$

$$= 0.255 \times \frac{1}{0.15 + 0.40} = 0.409$$

If industrial companies in mature industries generally are only able to earn unleveraged pretax returns of about 25 percent, margins can be expected to fall in Flexible's industry as well upon maturity:

$$\text{Future margins} = \frac{\text{Future ROA}}{\text{Present ROA}} \times \text{Present margins}$$

$$= \frac{25.0}{40.9} \times 22.5 = 13.8\%$$

Finally, it can be expected that this decline in margins would come about principally through price declines, assuming that Flexible's industry utilizes no unique factors of production whose costs will change at rates other than inflation.

The extent of real price decline can then be calculated from the amount of margin compression as follows:

$$\frac{\text{Future prices}}{\text{Current prices}} = \frac{1 - \text{Current operating margin}}{\text{Future operating margin}}$$

$$= \frac{1 - 0.225}{1 - 0.138} = 0.899$$

In other words, a real price decline of 10.1 percent will produce the expected fall in margins. Such a real price decline can be achieved cumulatively over a three-year period at a rate of 3.5 percent per year.

The maturity scenario assumptions are summarized in Table 29.1, where a three-year time is used for a smooth transition to the "long-run" assumptions. Other operating characteristics, such as asset turnover, depreciation, and tax rates, are assumed to remain constant.

Higher Growth Scenario. The higher growth scenario would assume continued high-unit growth of 7.0 percent for the next eight years, followed by an industry maturation period that would resemble the maturity scenario. The

TABLE 29.1 Summary of Maturity Scenario

	Year 1	Year 2	Year 3	Year 4 and Following
Unit sales growth	5.0%	3.0%	2.0%	1.5%
General inflation	7.0	7.0	7.0	7.0
Real price changes	(3.5)	(3.5)	(3.5)	0.0
Total price growth	3.3	3.3	3.3	7.0
Operating margin as percentage of sales	19.7	16.9	13.8	13.8

TABLE 29.2 Summary of Higher Growth Scenario

	Years 1–8	Year 9	Year 10	Year 11	Year 12 and Following
Unit sales growth	7.0%	5.0%	3.0%	2.0%	1.5%
General inflation	7.0	7.0	7.0	7.0	7.0
Real price changes	0.0	(3.5)	(3.5)	(3.5)	0.0
Total price growth	7.0	3.3	3.3	3.3	7.0
Operating income as percentage of sales	22.5	19.7	16.9	13.8	13.8

company's operating statistics would therefore be projected as shown in Table 29.2. Once again, other assumptions, such as asset turnover, depreciation, and tax rates, are assumed to remain constant.

Projecting Free Cash Flows. Once the scenarios are well defined, the next step is to project free cash flows (FCF) for each projection year. In any year FCF is the excess cash that can be removed from the business after meeting all investment, spending, and other operating requirements (exclusive of financing). Specifically, FCF is calculated as follows:

FCF = Net income after taxes

Plus: Noncash charges to income (deferred taxes, depreciation, amortization of intangibles, etc.)

Less: Capital expenditures

Less: Investment in net working capital (excluding cash and short-term debt)

EXAMPLE. Here is how FCF for Flexible Technologies Corporation (higher growth scenario) would be calculated for the first projection year. It is assumed that last year the balance sheet and income statement for Flexible was as shown in Table 29.3.

TABLE 29.3   Flexible Technologies Corporation Financial Summary

FINANCIAL POSITION, END OF YEAR 0

(dollars in thousands)

Current assets	$21,500	Short-Term Debt	$ 3,000
Net fixed assets	22,500	Other current liabilities	13,000
Total assets	$44,000	Long-term debt	5,000
		Deferred taxes	1,200
		Stockholders' equity	21,800
		Total liabilities and stockholders' equity	$44,000

INCOME STATEMENT, YEAR 0

(dollars in thousands)

Net sales	$55,000
Cost of sales	(33,900)
Selling, general, and administrative expense	(8,600)
Operating income	$12,500
Interest expense	(800)
Pretax income	$11,700
Income taxes	(5,400)
Net income	$ 6,300

For the projection of FCF, net income is first calculated:

Item	Assumption	Projected Value ($000)
Sales	7.0% unit growth and 7.0% price growth over year 0 value ($55,000)	$63,000
Operating income	22.5% of sales	$14,200
Interest expense	10.0% of total debt	(800)
Pretax income	Net of two items above	$13,400
Income taxes	46% of pretax income	6,200
Net income		$ 7,200

The next step is to identify noncash income and expense items and add them back.

Noncash Expense	Assumption	Amount ($000)
Depreciation	12.0% of net fixed assets	$2,700
Deferred income taxes	10% of income tax expense	600
Total noncash items		$3,300

TABLE 29.4 Summary Calculation of Free Cash Flow

(dollars in thousands)

Net income	$7,200
Plus noncash charges:	
Depreciation	2,700
Deferred taxes	600
Less: Investment in net working capital	(900)
Less: Capital expenditures	(5,400)
Free cash flow	$4,200

Adding noncash items to net income gives the *cash provided by operations* of $10,500.

Next, working-capital and fixed-asset investment requirements are projected:

Item	Assumption	Year-end Amount Required	Initial Amount Available	Investment Required
Net working capital	15.0% of sales	$ 9,400	$ 8,500 (a)	$ 900
Net fixed assets	40.0% of sales	25,200	19,800 (b)	5,400

(a) Based on current assets of $21,500 net of current liabilities of $13,000. Since operating requirements are calculated here, items such as short-term debt ($3,000) and excess investment cash (none available) are not included.

(b) Based on beginning amount ($22,500) less current year's depreciation ($2,700).

At this point, all of the components of Flexible's FCF have been calculated for year 1:

It is this $4,200 cash flow that the owners of Flexible are free to dispose of as they please. The ongoing stream of such FCFs makes up the economic value of Flexible in the acquisition marketplace. The following sections review how to discount these cash flows to arrive at a capitalized value for Flexible.

Weighted-Average Cost of Capital. This subsection will serve mainly to review concepts discussed more fully in Chapter 6.

The first point to keep in mind is that the owner of a company is free to vary the mix of financing used for the company. Because of its fixed repayment provisions, its seniority in liquidation, and the tax deductibility of interest, debt is a less expensive source of capital than equity. Most capital-using companies therefore employ some debt financing. However, as the proportion of debt to total capital increases, so do the risks of default, insolvency, and potential loss of control of the company by the stockholders. Therefore, financial theory posits that, for every company, there is an optimum level of debt, which appropriately balances the financial risk of debt with its cost advantages over equity. Experience suggests that, for a large group of industrial companies, optimum is somewhere in the range of 20 to 40 percent debt to total capital.

The *weighted-average cost of capital* (symbolized $\bar{k}$) is defined as the weighted-average cost of debt and equity:

$$\bar{k} = k_E \,(\% \text{ equity}) + k_D \,(1 - t) \,(\% \text{ debt})$$

where: k_E = cost of equity

k_D = cost of debt (pretax)

t = marginal tax rate

% debt = percent of debt to total capital

% equity = percentage of equity to total capital

The cost of debt, k_D, is typically the interest cost of medium- to long-term borrowing. The cost of equity, however, is more difficult to calculate. Recall that

$$k_e = r_f + B(r_m - r_f)$$

where: r_f = long-term risk free rate

r_m = long-term return on the market

B = systematic risk factor of the company and its industry

$r_m - r_f$, the long-term real return on the market, is usually estimated at around 5.5–6.0%. The best method of cutting through these abstract equations is to show how they are employed in the example.

EXAMPLE. Based on studies of the cyclical risks of Flexible Technologies Corporation and its industry, it is concluded that an appropriate debt/capital ratio is 30 percent. One of the several beta-estimating services is also examined, concluding that Flexible's industry is slightly more cyclical than the market as a whole, so that Flexible deserves a beta (at 30 percent leverage) of 1.15. Finally, it is noted that 10-year U.S. government bonds are currently trading to yield 8.5 percent (which defines the medium-term risk-free rate). Therefore, Flexible's cost of equity can be calculated:

$$k_e = r_f + B(r_m - r_f)$$
$$= 8.5 + 1.15(6.0)$$
$$= 15.4\%$$

Assuming that Flexible's medium- to long-term borrowing rate is 10.0 percent, the estimate for Flexible's weighted-average cost of capital is as follows:

$$\bar{k} = k_e(\% \text{ equity}) + k_D(1 - t)(\% \text{ debt})$$
$$= (15.4\%)(70\%) + (10.0\%)(1 - 0.46)(30\%)$$
$$= 12.4\%$$

Discounted Cash Flow Value Calculation. The value of the firm in total is equal to the sum of the values of its obligations to all contributors of capital, debt, and equity:

$$V_{\text{Firm}} = V_{\text{Debt}} + V_{\text{Equity}}$$

The DCF method, which employs a cost of capital representing the blended cost of debt and equity, is oriented toward valuing the *entire* firm, including both debt and equity. In other words, *DCF* calculates V_{Firm}. The method of determining the value of a firm's equity as it presently exists is a simple additional step:

$$V_{\text{Equity}} = DCF \text{ value} - V_{\text{Debt}}$$

where V_{Debt} is the market value of the outstanding debt of the firm at the time of valuation.

The *DCF* value of the firm is calculated as:

DCF value = Cash flow component + terminal component

= Present value of *unleveraged* FCFs for each projection year (discounted at $\bar{k}$)

+

The present value of the terminal value of the firm at the end of the projection period (discounted at $\bar{k}$)

The first component of the above equation, the cash flow component, follows almost immediately from the work done to project FCFs. The principal distinction is to note that *unleveraged* cash flows are discounted; that is, cash flows arrived at as if the company had no debt. For any projection year,

Unleveraged *FCF* = *FCF* + (interest expense)(1 − tax rate)

Thus, for the Flexible example in year 1:

Unleveraged *FCF* = \$4,200 + 800 (1 − .46)

= \$4,632

It is this series of cash flows that would be discounted.

EXAMPLE. The higher growth scenario assumptions lead to the unleveraged FCF calculations for Flexible as shown in Table 29.5. Discounting these unleveraged FCFs back to the present at a weighted-average cost of capital of 12.4 percent, produces a value of \$49.1 million which is the value that will be generated by Flexible's operation over the next 15 years.

The next step is to calculate the terminal value component of DCF value. This task is a bit more subjective. Typically, the book value, earnings value, and cash flow value of the company are estimated at the end of the projection period and an attempt is made to judge what the company might be worth then. The projection period is usually sufficiently long that reasonable variations in the estimation of terminal value have only a minor impact on the total DCF calculation.

A book value estimate is simply what the book value of all the debt and equity capital in the firm will be at the end of the projection period, assuming all the FCF has been paid out to the owners in the interim.

An earnings estimate is simply an attempt to estimate value by means of a price/earnings (P/E) multiple. The multiple chosen should be one typical of

TABLE 29.5   Detailed Free Cash Flow Projection for Flexible Technologies Corporation, Higher Growth Scenario

(dollars in thousands)

Year	Sales(a)	Operating Income(b)	Unleveraged Net Income(c)	Net Fixed Assets Required(d)	Net Working Capital Required(e)	Depreciation Expense(f)	Deferred Income Tax Expense(g)	Cash Provided by Operations(h)	Capital Expenditures(i)	Increase in Net Working Capital(j)	Free Cash Flow(k)
1	$ 62,970	$14,168	$ 7,651	$ 25,188	$ 9,445	$ 2,700	$ 652	$11,003	$ 5,388	$ 945	$ 4,670
2	72,094	16,221	8,759	28,838	10,814	3,023	746	12,528	6,673	1,369	4,486
3	82,540	18,571	10,029	33,016	12,381	3,461	854	14,344	7,639	1,567	5,138
4	94,500	21,263	11,482	37,800	14,175	3,962	978	16,422	8,746	1,794	5,882
5	108,193	24,343	13,145	43,277	16,229	4,536	1,120	18,801	10,013	2,054	6,734
6	123,871	27,871	15,050	49,548	18,581	5,193	1,282	21,525	11,464	2,352	7,709
7	141,819	31,909	17,231	56,728	21,273	5,946	1,468	24,645	13,126	2,692	8,827
8	162,369	36,533	19,728	64,948	24,355	6,807	1,681	28,216	15,027	3,082	10,017
9	176,037	34,679	18,727	70,415	26,406	7,794	1,595	28,116	13,261	2,051	12,804
10	187,220	31,640	17,086	74,888	28,083	8,450	1,455	26,991	12,923	1,677	12,391
11	197,180	27,211	14,694	78,872	29,577	8,987	1,252	24,933	12,971	1,494	10,468
12	214,147	29,552	15,958	85,659	32,122	9,465	1,359	26,782	16,252	2,545	7,985
13	232,574	32,095	17,331	93,030	34,886	10,279	1,476	29,086	17,650	2,764	8,672
14	252,587	34,857	18,823	101,035	37,888	11,164	1,603	31,590	19,169	3,002	9,419
15	274,323	37,857	20,443	109,729	41,148	12,124	1,741	34,308	20,818	3,260	10,230

Present value at 12.4% $49,093

(a) Sales projections based on prior year's sales, increased by previously described assumptions for unit sales growth, general inflation, and real price changes

(b) Calculated as a percentage of sales, with the percentage declining during years 9–11, as previously described for the higher growth scenario

(c) Calculated as 54 percent of operating income (assuming 46 percent effective tax rate). Interest expense has been ignored because the calculation here is of the amount of free cash flow available *without respect to how the company is financed.*

(d) Projected at 40.0 percent of sales

(e) Projected at 15.0 percent of sales

(f) Projected at 12.0 percent of previous year's net fixed assets

(g) Estimated at 10.0 percent of income tax expense (the latter being 46.0 percent of operating income)

(h) Net income plus depreciation expense plus deferred income tax expense

(i) Change in net fixed assets required plus depreciation

(j) Change in net working capital required

(k) Cash provided by operations, minus capital expenditures, minus increase in net working capital

a low-growth company in a mature industry, since the projection period is designed to include all of the high growth years in the company's life cycle.

A cash flow estimate is an attempt to find a multiplier of free cash flow that will appropriately determine value. The multiplier typically used is:

$$\frac{(1 + g)}{(k - g)}$$

where: g = rate of nominal growth of cash flows into perpetuity
          $\overline{k}$ = weighted-average cost of capital

This multiplier is the factor that capitalizes a cash flow stream growing at rate g (not too large) into perpetuity, at a discount rate of $\overline{k}$.

EXAMPLE. Returning to Flexible Technologies Corporation, the projections generate the following values for year 15.

   1 *Book value estimate*

Initial book value (debt and equity combined)	$ 29.8 million
Add: Cumulative unleveraged earnings, years 1–15	226.1
Less: Free cash flow extracted, years 1–15	(125.4)
Book value in year 15	$130.5 million

   2 *Earnings-based estimate*

Net income (unleveraged) in year 15	$ 20.4 million
Mature industry P/E ratio	6.0×
Implied value in year 15	$122.4 million

   3 *Free cash flow multiple*

Perpetual cash flow growth rate: 6.0% (slightly less than inflation)

Cash flow multiplier: $\dfrac{1 + 0.06}{0.124 - 0.06} = 16.6\times$

Times year 15 free cash flow	$ 10.2 million
Implied value in year 15	$169.3 million

Based on these alternative estimates, a single terminal value may be pegged as the median of the three, $130.5 million. Discounting this amount by 12.4 percent for 15 years, a terminal value component worth $22.6 million today is arrived at.

DCF value of firm = Cash flow component + Terminal value component
                     = $49.1 + $22.6 million
                     = $71.7 million

Therefore,

$$V_{\text{Equity}} = V_{\text{Firm}} - V_{\text{Debt}}$$
$$= \$71.7 - \$8.0^*$$
$$= \$63.7 \text{ million}$$

---

* At book value, which is assumed to approximate market value.

In summary, our DCF exercise has led us to the conclusion that, under the higher growth scenario, the economic value of 100 percent of the equity shares in Flexible Technologies Corporation is in the neighborhood of $63.7 million (or nearly three times the book value of $21.8 million). A similar exercise can be performed under the maturity scenario, which will obtain significantly lower values.

Acquisition Precedent

Buyers and sellers also look to other transactions in the same industry in order to establish valuation benchmarks in terms of the multiple paid of earnings, cash flow, book value, and so forth. Unlike DCF, this technique does not focus on the assumptions of the current or prospective owner about the future. Rather, such multiples represent an index of recent market prices paid by other acquirors and accepted by other sellers. From a potential seller's viewpoint, the multiples suggest a target price range at which other buyers have been willing to deal; conversely, for potential buyers, they suggest price ranges that are acceptable to other sellers.

Because each acquisition is unique, however, and buyers and sellers typically don't know all the factors and motives that went into the formulation of another acquisition price, acquisition multiples often suggest a wide range of values and must be used with care. Moreover, because the acquisition market is not continuous in time, the fact that a particular multiple was paid in the past does not necessarily mean that it still applies today. Unlike the stock market, there is no current P/E benchmark other than the most recent industry transaction, which may be several years old.

Several types of multiples are usually examined. Each multiple has its uses and limitations, and the appropriate choice often depends on the industry under analysis.

Earnings Multiples.   Prices paid as a multiple of earnings are typically the most useful for a broad range of industrial companies. An important requirement for such multiples to be meaningful is that the accounting principles underlying earnings be comparable across the sample of transactions. Table 29.6 gives a sample chart that records the multiple of earnings paid in a group of acquisitions in the soft-drink bottling industry. Column 8 ("P/E Offered") gives the information in terms of the multiple of earnings paid in each acquisition. The range varies from 7.4 to 26.0.

When a wide range of earnings multiples is presented by the transactions in an industry, it is important to understand, at least in a general sense, why the multiples paid are so different. In the soft-drink bottling industry, Table 29.6 clearly indicates that "large" acquisitions ($100 million or more) tend to occur at 15–18x multiples, while other small acquisitions occur at 9–11x multiples. An industry specialist would probably note that small soft-drink bottlers, which operate under territorial licenses, have a very limited acquisition market in which to sell, most commonly only to other bottlers in the area. On the other hand, once a bottler has reached a "strategic" size, it becomes an attractive acquisition candidate for a much broader range of acquirors, including consumer products companies and conglomerates.

Of course, other factors may be at work also. Companies with lower margins, which offer some room for efficiency improvements, may appear to sell for higher multiples of past earnings. What is unknown, of course, is what level of earnings was projected as reasonably achievable by the buyer after the acquisition.

A factor that may distort the comparability of earnings multiples is the amount of debt associated with an acquired company. For example, if a company with $10 million of net income and no debt were acquired for $100 million, we would say that the acquisition P/E ratio was 10x. If, however, that company had $50 million in debt on its balance sheet at an after-tax interest cost of $3 million, and the buyer therefore paid $50 million for the equity in the company, it would appear that the P/E multiple paid was 7x ($50 million paid for a company with $7 million in net income). Because a buyer and a seller usually have full control over the debt and equity financing of a company, debt on the books of an acquired company implicitly represents financing of the acquisition price. Therefore, it is preferable to restate acquisition multiples as gross acquisition price (including debt assumed) divided by unleveraged earnings (before interest expense and taxes).

Gross acquisition price = Price paid for equity + Market value of total debt owed by acquired company

Unleveraged earnings = Earnings before interest and taxes (EBIT)

  = Pretax earnings + Interest expense

Table 29.6 presents a calculation of unleveraged P/E ratios (gross acquisition price/unleveraged earnings) in column 9 (Price Paid Plus Debt/EBIT). Such ratios are particularly helpful when the acquisition candidate is a division of a larger parent company, and the division has no outstanding debt of its own.

Cyclicality may also distort the comparability of earnings and earnings multiples. If sales and margins tend to fluctuate widely but systematically through the business cycle, the timing of a transaction within the cycle may greatly distort the multiple paid. One common approach to this problem is to normalize earnings. The method typically involves the calculation of a five-year average operating margin (operating income/sales). The latest income statement is then recalculated as if the *average* operating margin had been in effect, rather than the actual one for that period.

Normalization must be used with care, however. For one thing, it is obviously based on counterfactual assumptions. For another, it depends critically on a variability in margins, which is cyclical and not secular. So if the industry under scrutiny is in fact in a permanent, long-term decline, it is misleading to assume that margins achieved in the past will, on average, be achieved again in the future. Finally, it is important to remember that a buyer will always pay less if the company is presently riding the cycle down than if the cycle is turning up, even if the seller insists that it "will all average out." This is because, in the "going down" case, the strong cash flows associated with the peak of the cycle are farthest away from the acquisition date, and the uncertainties of their timing and magnitude are greatest.

TABLE 29.6   Premiums Paid in Selected Acquisitions of Soft Drink Bottlers

Date of Announcement	Acquiree/Acquiror	Terms of Transaction	Revenues ($000) (CGR)[1]
11/2/76	Dr. Pepper Bottling Co. of Southern California[2]/Dr. Pepper Co.	Exchange 8/10 of one share of Dr. Pepper common stock for each share of Bottling Co. common	$ 38,569 (20.2%)
2/10/77	Pepsi-Cola Bottling Co. of Washington, D.C. Inc./ General Cinema Corp.	$20 cash for each common share	31,050 (13.0%)
6/26/77	Coca-Cola Midwest Inc./Twentieth Century-Fox Film Corp.	$26 cash for each common share	61,945 (18.8%)
9/27/77	Coca-Cola Bottling Co. of Mid-America[4]/Coca-Cola Bottling Co. of Los Angeles	$27 cash for each common and convertible preferred share	61,734 (27.0%)
10/17/77	Coca-Cola Bottling Co. of Los Angeles[5]/Northwest Industries	$40 cash for each common share and $78 cash for each convertible preferred share	184,106 (12.7%)
10/24/77	Coca-Cola Bottling Plants Inc. (South Portland, Maine)[6]/ Coca-Cola Bottling Co. of New York	Exchange of 12 shares of New York Coca-Cola common for each share of Coca-Cola Bottling (Maine)	19,069 (12.0%)
11/16/78	Atlantic Pepsi-Cola Bottling Co.[7]/Liggett Group	$35.04 cash and 1/10 share in Atlantic Telecasting Corp. for each common share	90,785 (25.6%)
6/27/80	PepCom Industries/ Suntory International	$38 cash for each common share	71,529 (10.1%)
11/24/80	Coca-Cola Bottling Co. of New York/ The Coca-Cola Co. and private investors	$10.375 cash for each common share	539,403 (16.8%)
11/6/81	Northwest Industries (Beverage Industries — Coca-Cola Bottling of L.A. & Buckingham Corp.)/ Beatrice Foods Co.	$580 million cash offer	529,649
5/10/82	Associated Coca-Cola Bottling/The Coca-Cola Co.	$35.93 cash for each common share	359,545 (16.8%)
10/15/82	Beverage Management Inc./ Fortsmann Little & Co.	$24.00 cash for each common share	198,207 (12.5%)

(1) Compound growth rate is based on last five years of operations prior to acquisition; it is computed using a log-linear least squares method.

(2) Data are from continuing operations only.

(3) Net loss in 1974 prevents use of log-linear least squares method; internal rate of return method yields 31.1 percent.

(4) Mid-America operated a canning division representing 35 percent of sales in 1973 and 16 percent in 1977.

(5) Data do not reflect purchase of Coca-Cola Bottling Co. of Mid-America by Coca-Cola Bottling Co. of Los Angeles.

(6) Data includes results of 49 percent interest in Mexican bottling operations accounted for on a one-line equity basis. These operations provided 37 percent of earnings in 1976.

(7) Data exclude results of television operations, representing 4 percent of sales and 11 percent of net income in 1978, which was spun off to Atlantic shareholders.

Source: Morgan Stanley & Co.

Latest Financial Information						
Net Income ($000) (CGR)[1]	Earnings Per Share	Aggregate Amount Offered ($ millions)	P/E Offered	Price Paid Plus Debt/Earnings Before Income Taxes	Price Paid/ Book Value	Premium Over Unaffected Market Price
$ 1,274 (N/A)[3]	$ 1.10	$ 12.1	9.5×	5.70×	1.47×	75%
2,093 (33.4%)	2.70	15.5	7.4	5.39	2.16	36
2,700 (21.3%)	2.55	27.7	10.2	5.44	1.72	96
2,560 (36.1%)	2.53	28.4	10.7	6.41	2.52	103
12,682 (12.8%)	2.58	204.0	15.5	8.34	2.43	84
1,367 (23.0%)	10.66	13.1	9.6	10.92	1.56	70
7,791 (47.6%)	2.07	123.4	15.8	10.40	4.15	94
6,434 (14.2%)	2.50	98.1	15.2	7.80	3.37	132
13,399 (22.0%)	0.70	235.8	17.6	9.41	1.64	66
22,300	—	580.0	26.0	13.99	2.28	—
28,967 (17.4%)	2.50	417.5	14.4	8.45	3.15	62
7,460 (3.4%)	1.75	98.4	13.2	7.72	2.04	—
		Range	7.4–26	5.4–14.0	2.0–4.2	36–132
		Median	13.8	8.1	2.2	80

Book Value Multiples. "Book value belongs in the library" is the common retort to a buyer or seller who insists on this measure of value. Because book values measure the net investment position of a company's stockholders rather than the prospective earnings and cash flow of a company, they are often dismissed by financial analysts as having less relevance to valuation than other ratios. Column 10 of Table 29.6 gives book value multiples paid in the acquisitions described there.

There are, however, a number of industries in which book value multiples are much more meaningful than earnings and cash flows. This is most commonly true for financial institutions such as banks, insurance companies, and securities firms. In such cases, the balance sheet values of most assets and liabilities are reasonably close to market values, so that book value represents a sort of liquidation value (see section on "Liquidation and Replacement Values"). Because such institutions typically have a franchise value in excess of what would be realizable in a liquidation, they are usually sold for a premium to book value that is much more systematic than any multiple of earnings.

A variation on this technique is often used, comparing prices paid for companies with their replacement cost book values. The concept involves revaluing all of a company's assets and liabilities to replacement cost or market values, and making the corresponding adjustment to book value. (The section on "Liquidation and Replacement values" demonstrates the method for calculating a company's replacement value.) The acquisition price is then calculated as a premium (or discount) to replacement value.

Multiples of Cash Flow. Outside of certain specialized industries, "cash flow" multiples are one of the least common forms of valuation. Why is this so, if one of the fundamental tenets of finance is that value is directly related to the discounted value of future cash flow? The reason for this apparent anomaly is the differing definitions of the term "cash flow." Accountants and stock market analysts typically refer to cash flow as meaning "cash flow from operations": net income plus noncash charges (depreciation, amortization of intangibles, and deferred tax expense). This value is the denominator of a cash flow multiple.

On the other hand, DCF values depend directly on FCF: cash flow from operations, less required investments in working capital, and in plant and equipment. It is only in industries where FCF approximates cash flow from operations (i.e., minimal required ongoing investment in working capital and plant and equipment) that cash flow multiples tend to be useful.

What industries are those? Typically, they are industries that undertake project-type investments (e.g., real estate and oil and gas). In these industries, massive amounts of capital tend to be invested initially (e.g., building an office complex and finding and developing a well), after which a steady stream of earnings and operating cash flows result, with relatively small investments required to maintain them. To the extent that companies in such industries spend massive amounts of capital year after year, they are investing in new projects that are not required to maintain the stream of cash flows from existing projects but, rather, are independently designed to augment earnings. Therefore, multiples of cash flow from operations can be a relatively accuratge guide to

TABLE 29.7   Average Acquisition Premium Offered Over Unaffected Market, 1978–1982

	Successful Bid	Unsuccessful Bid	Success Rate
Friendly bidder (agreed transaction)	61%	54%	76%
Hostile and unsolicited bidder	71	66	35

the value of such a company, excluding the value of assets and projects which are not yet past the start-up point.

Premium Over Market Trading Value

When an acquisition candidate is publicly traded, the market price of the stock is very important to the determination of a feasible acquisition price. Clearly, the buyer must pay a premium to market (why else would a shareholder tender his shares?), but how much of a premium is required? The answer depends on the attitude of the company's management (friendly or hostile to the acquiror), and the regulatory climate.

Before the Williams Act was passed in 1969, acquirors were usually able to buy companies successfully at premiums of 32 percent above the "unaffected" market price. (It is important to examine trading values that prevailed thirty to 60 days in advance of an acquisition announcement to be sure that the stock price was affected by acquisition rumors.) In that unregulated period, tender offers took place in very brief time spans, usually a matter of days, which allowed target company management little time to do other than capitulate.

Under the Williams Act, much longer periods were mandated for tender offers; for example, a bidder could not purchase shares until the fourth week of the offer. These longer time periods allowed management greater flexibility to seek a higher price through negotiation, litigation, or by finding a competing bidder willing to pay more (a "white knight"). In this era, acquisition premiums increased to an average of more than 50 percent above unaffected market. In regulated industries where there is a long approval process, the premiums are even higher (typically in excess of 70 percent).

Table 29.7 reflects the average premiums to market offered by successful and unsuccessful bidders in hostile and friendly acquisitions. Interestingly, hostile bidders tend to pay premiums even higher than friendly bidders, but their success rate is much lower. Thus, the prospect of resistance by a target appears to induce substantial premiums from bidders at the outset.

Market trading values are also useful as a benchmark in calculating the value of a privately held company or division. If a seller wishes to divest such a company, one of the alternatives will be to evaluate how much might be realized in a secondary public offering. Assuming that such an offering is feasible, the trading value of the shares in the company represents a minimum level of value that the seller be should willing to accept. Conversely, a buyer may not be willing to pay more than the fully distributed trading value of such a company, plus a reasonable acquisition premium, because that is the price at which other alternatives may be available in the market.

The significant question, of course, is just how much a private company would be worth in a public offering. The answer depends on current P/E ratios and market price/book value multiples prevailing for comparable companies whose stock trades in the secondary market.

Liquidation and Replacement Values

Two other valuation benchmarks buyers and sellers will look to are the liquidation and replacement values of a company. Liquidation value represents the amount of proceeds that could be realized by a stockholder if a company ceased operations, if all assets were sold at prevailing market prices, and if all liabilities and tax obligations were satisfied. Replacement value, on the other hand, represents the cost that would be incurred if one tried to replicate all of the assets and liabilities of a company by building them or purchasing them on the market. Broadly speaking, liquidation value represents a minimum value for a company, because the liquidation alternative is always available to its owner, whereas replacement value represents a maximum value for a company, the point at which an acquiror would build rather than buy.

In practice, the replacement value concept is awkward. What does it mean to build the equivalent of a 10-year-old plant with outmoded technology and capacities? What does it mean to replace a strong brand name and customer base? The best thing to do is to try to guess at the acquisition values of such items! Liquidation value is much more straightforward because it is a realistic alternative for most companies.

Table 29.8 represents a sample analysis of liquidation and replacement value. The methodology is straightforward; each asset and liability should be revalued to market value (which may differ between the liquidation and replacement alternatives), and add or subtract any additional "hidden" assets or liabilities not reflected in the balance sheet. For liquidation values, taxes must be paid on the difference between realized proceeds and the tax basis of each asset. The calculation of capital gain, recapture, and ordinary income tax liabilities, or the avoidance thereof, resulting from the liquidation is a technical subject not addressed here.

Excess Assets and Liabilities

The previous subsections have shifted back and forth between valuation techniques based on periodic flows (earnings and cash flows) and those based on momentary positions (balance sheets). It is important to remember that no single technique captures all of the aspects of the others, but that an integrated picture of a company's value must be built based on all of the techniques. An important requirement for integrating the values derived from the various techniques is to determine what elements of value any given technique leaves out, and to try to assess those items separately.

TABLE 29.8 Sample Calculation of Liquidation and Replacement Values

	Book Value	Liquidation Value		Replacement Value	
		Amount	Comment	Amount	Comment
Assets					
Cash	$ 50	$ 50	100% of book	$ 50	100% of book
Accounts Receivable	100	90	90% of book	100	100% of book
Inventory	80	56	70% of book	80	100% of book
Prepaid expenses	20	—	0% of book	20	100% of book
Total current assets	$250	$196		$ 250	
Net plant and equipment	$300	$150	Distress sale value	$ 500	Replacement cost
Investment in Hi-Tech Industries, Inc.	10	200	Hidden asset	200	Hidden asset
Goodwill	60	—	No value	90	Franchise value
Total assets	$620	$546		$1,040	
Liabilities					
Current liabilities	$150	$150	100% of book	$ 150	100% of book
Long-term debt	100	100	Redemption value	90	Market value
Deferred taxes	40	—	Separate tax calculation	—	No deferred taxes at start-up
Unfunded pension liability	—	20	Termination value	—	No pension liability on start-up
Total liabilities	$290	$270		$ 240	
Taxes on liquidation	—	50		—	
Net value to stockholders	$330	$226	Liquidation value	$ 800	Replacement value

To be specific, it is assumed that the company being valued has a $10 million operating profit each year ($5 million after tax), and the appropriate P/E multiple is 10x. The initial value estimate is $50 million. However, assuming there is also $5 million in excess cash on the balance sheet, not necessary to the business, as long as the interest earned on that cash is not already included in the $5 million profit figure, the company is actually worth $5 million more, or $55 million. If there is an unfunded vested pension liability of $3 million, that amount (after a 46 percent tax deduction) would reduce the value. In general, if there are excess assets or liabilities of a company, which play no part in determining the earnings or cash flows on which the basic valuation is made, such assets and liabilities must be separately added to (or subtracted from) the basic value estimate.

FINANCING AN ACQUISITION

During the decade of the 1970s, the subject of acquisition financing was, for the most part, a brief one: sellers wanted cash. Of course, a buyer had to arrange temporary bank financing to consummate the acquisition, and longer-term financing to replace it once the acquisition was complete, but it was a cash transaction.

In the 1960s, however, the reverse was true: with high stock prices, equity securities were the preferred medium of exchange. Recently, very large acquisitions (e.g., DuPont/Conoco) have tended to be financed with a mixture of cash and stock. Over time, all forms of consideration are used and new hybrids developed. The purpose of this section is briefly to outline the basic alternatives open to an acquiror in choosing the consideration to be paid.

There are four basic types of consideration that an acquiror can choose from: cash, debt, preferred stock, or common stock. Other instruments, such as convertible preferred, are hybrids of these basic types. The principal determinants of what type will be used are the identities and preferences of the buyer and the seller. If the buyer is a private or a foreign company without securities publicly traded in the United States, it will be constrained to utilize cash in the acquisition. If the buyer suffers from a low stock price, common equity will be ruled out, although notes or preferred stock may be workable. If the buyer's stock price is high, however, a common stock or convertible security acquisition may be opportune.

The seller's characteristics often have a more important effect on the appropriate choice of consideration. If the sale is a divestiture of a division or subsidiary by a large corporation, the seller will usually insist on cash for redeployment. On the other hand, if the sellers are dispersed public shareholders, it is often possible, if the acquisition is not exposed to competition, to have the shareholders accept more unusual forms of consideration (e.g., subordinated notes and preferred stock), commonly referred to as wallpaper. If the acquisition is at a very high price/earnings ratio, a buyer will typically want to achieve pooling accounting, which can only be done by using common stock (see the section on "Pooling Method Accounting"). Conversely, a low P/E acquisition is best accounted for as a purchase, which requires some consideration other than common stock. If many of the shares are held by taxable shareholders with low tax bases, then a tax-free acquisition is desirable, and can often be accomplished by using at least 40 to 50 percent equity securities (see the section on "Taxable and Tax-Free Transactions"). Conversely, if the seller's assets have a substantial write-up potential for tax purposes, without substantial recapture taxes (e.g., patents or natural resources), then economics will direct the acquisition into a taxable format, one which employs a minimal amount of equity securities (see the section on "The Step-up and Recapture Problem in Taxable Acquisitions").

Much of the choice of acquisition medium depends on its implications for such postmerger statistics as earnings pickup or dilution, and credit ratios. The calculation of such statistics is discussed in the section on "Accounting Treatment of Acquisitions and Pro Forma Analysis," but a brief summary of the rules of thumb is as follows: Cash and debt have the least dilutive effect on earnings, and the most negative effect on credit ratios (i.e., interest coverage, debt ratio, and the like). For a low or average P/E company, common stock can have the most dilutive effect on earnings, but the most favorable effect on credit ratios. Preferred stock is somewhere in between the two.

FEDERAL INCOME TAX ASPECTS OF ACQUISITIONS

Federal income taxes can have important effects on the parties to an acquisition transaction, and therefore must be carefully considered. This section highlights the principal forms of taxation faced by a seller and a buyer as a result of an acquisition, and the choices that must be made in structuring the transaction. There are two principal issues that must be resolved: (1) whether the selling shareholders are going to pay a tax on the gain they have realized upon sale (i.e., taxable versus tax-free transaction), and (2) whether the transaction should be designed to trigger depreciation recapture taxes.

Taxable and Tax-Free Transactions

The Internal Revenue Code provides that, in carefully defined circumstances, an acquisition can be accomplished without triggering income tax liability on the part of the selling shareholders. Such transactions are technically referred to as tax-free reorganizations and, broadly speaking, include the following types of acquisitions. (For clarity, the acquiror is X; the target is Y; and S is a dummy subsidiary of X, which exists for the purpose of consummating the transaction.)

> *"A" Reorganization (Merger).* Y merges into X, and the former shareholders of Y retain a continuity of interest in the new XY corporation (i.e., at least 40 to 50 percent of the aggregate consideration paid for Y consists of equity securities, preferred or common, of X).

> *"B" Reorganization (Stock Purchase).* X purchases 80 percent or more of the voting stock of Y, using only voting stock of X in payment.

"C" Reorganization (Asset Purchase). Y transfers substantially all of its assets, with or without Y's liabilities, to X in exchange for voting stock of X.

"(a)(2)(D)" Reorganization (Forward Triangular Merger). Y merges into S. X retains 100 percent of the ownership of S. Y's former shareholders receive equity securities in X in sufficient quantity (40 to 50 percent) to satisfy the continuity-of-interest test.

"(a)(2)(E)" Reorganization (Reverse Triangular Merger). S merges into Y. X receives all of the voting securities of Y as a consequence of the merger. Y's former shareholders receive solely voting stock in X.

Probably the most commonly used structures for tax-free acquisitions are the last two triangular mergers, because they are generally more flexible than the other forms, do not commingle the assets of the target with the assets of the acquiror, and do not require approval by the shareholders of the acquiror. The reverse triangular merger, however, is more restrictive in that it must be accomplished "solely for voting stock." (Technically, this applies only to the first 80 percent of shares acquired, but it is a rare occasion when this in practice does not mean all shares). Therefore, the most common type of triangular merger is the forward merger, in which equity securities of the acquiror (voting or nonvoting, preferred or common) may be used for as low as 40 to 50 percent of the aggregate acquisition price. The Internal Revenue Service (IRS) will give an advance ruling at the 50 percent level, but attorneys often will give opinions as to the tax-free nature of a transaction at levels as low as 40 percent based on experience with the case law.)

What happens to the selling shareholders in a tax-free reorganization? Generally speaking, if a shareholder receives an equity security in the acquiror, he maintains a carryover basis in the new security. If he receives cash or debt, he owes a capital gains tax on his gain. If he receives a mixture, however, he risks ordinary income (dividend) treatment on the cash portion. This is a complex area best left to tax experts and advisors.

The Step-Up and Recapture Problem in Taxable Acquisitions

It is assumed that X Corp. builds a new plant for $50 million. X may depreciate the full $50 million price in connection with the calculation of its taxable income. Alternatively, X buys the stock of Y Corp. for a price that reflects the $50 million value of Y's similar plant. However, Y has already depreciated its plant down to $20 million in net book value. How much remains for X to depreciate after the acquisition ($20 million or $50 million)?

The answer to the question just posed depends on whether X makes a 338 election to step up the tax basis of Y's assets to a level reflecting the purchase price X paid in the acquisition. The general principle operating here is that X should be in no different circumstances if it buys assets directly than if it buys a corporation containing those assets. X should have the opportunity to depreciate the assets based on the purchase price it paid for the assets or corporation. In practice, there are several important qualifications to this principle.

1 *Step-up is not available in tax-free reorganizations.* The theory behind a tax-free reorganization is that there is really no purchase and sale. Rather, there are two groups of shareholders who are combining their enterprises and are joint shareholders thereafter. Therefore, the old tax basis of each corportion's assets carry over after the combination.

2 *Step-up is mandatory in asset purchases.* If a buyer purchases the assets of another corporation in a taxable transaction, the purchase price is allocated among all of the acquiree's assets according to their fair market values, and such allocated price becomes the buyer's tax basis in the assets.

3 *Step-up is mandatory in mixed asset-stock purchases.* A Section 338 election is deemed by law to be made in any acquisition of a mixture of assets and stock.

4 *The election must be made rapidly.* An election must be made within 75 days after the closing of an acquisition.

5 *Step-up applies to all assets at all levels.* Once an election is made, it applies to all assets of all subsidiaries and tiers of subsidiaries of the acquired company. This rule, together with the no stock-asset mixtures rule, is designed to prevent selective step-up of only the most favorable subsidiaries.

Ordinarily, a step-up in the tax basis of the acquiree's assets is favorable from the standpoint of the acquiror. This is because additional tax depreciation is created, which reduces the acquiror's tax liabilities in the years after the acquisition. The principal cases in which a step-up would not be favorable are if the tax basis of the acquiree's assets are above the purchase price (thus creating a step-down in basis), or if the acquiree retains substantial unused tax loss carry forwards or tax credits, which are lost in a step-up.

Why is step-up a concern? Because the price exacted by the Internal Revenue Code for step-up transactions is a recapture tax. A recapture tax is the statutory obligation of the acquiree as of the moment of the acquisition. Recapture tax aims at preventing double depreciation of the same asset as a result of an acquisition; that is, it recaptures the depreciation tax benefit previously enjoyed by the corporation. The actual calculation of recapture tax liability is a highly technical process, which is best left to tax experts. The following is only an attempt to summarize what types of items are subject to recapture taxes.

1 *Depreciable personal property (including equipment).* Recapturable income includes the lesser of (1) the fair market value of such assets less their tax bases; and (2) the accumulated depreciation on those assets.

2 *Real property.* Recapturable income incudes the lesser of (a) the fair market value of the real property less its tax basis; and (b) the difference between the basis of the real property if it had been depreciated in a straight-line fashion, and its actual tax basis.

3 *LIFO Inventory.* Recapturable income includes the difference between last-in, first-out (LIFO) inventory value and fair market value.

4 *Domestic International Sales Corporation (DISCs).* Recapturable income includes the lesser of (a) the fair market value of the DISC less the tax basis of the DISC stock in the hands of the seller; and (b) the accumulated tax-deferred income of the DISC.

5 *Investment credits.* Investment tax credits taken in the past on property transferred in a step-up acquisition are recaptured as follows:

Period of Time Asset Held	Percentage of Tax Credit Recaptured
Less than 3 years	100
3–5 years	67
5–7 years	33
Over 7 years	—

6 *Other Items.* Specific rules exist for the recapture of unrepatriated foreign earnings, intangible drilling costs, expenses of mining exploration, gain on installment sales, and so forth. Such items are beyond the scope of this summary.

The actual operation of the recapture taxes is as follows. If the transaction is an asset sale, the recapturable income becomes taxable income to the selling corporation as of the moment of the sale. The result is that a certain portion of the seller's gain (the recapturable income) is taxed at ordinary income rates (presently 46 percent rather than at capital gains rates (presently 28 percent). In addition, recaptured investment tax credits directly increase the seller's tax liability.

If the transaction is a sale of stock, a 338 election by the acquiror within the 75 days following the closing causes the transaction to be treated for tax purposes as a sale of assets by the acquired corporation, so that the acquired corporation incurs the recapture tax liability. Because the acquired corporation is then owned by the acquiror, the acquiror in effect bears the cost of the recapture tax. In the case of a corporation selling a subsidiary, there has been some uncertainty recently as to who bears the liability, the selling corporation or the buyer, but this is usually resolved by an explicit agreement among the parties requiring the buyer, who makes the election, to bear the burden of the tax liability.

The step-up decision is usually reduced to a straightforward capital budgeting-type problem: Should a recapture tax be incurred today to achieve a certain depreciation-related tax savings in the future? A buyer must quantify the incremental tax depreciation it would expect to achieve as a result of the step-up election in each future year and compare the discounted present value of the associated tax savings with the immediate recapture liability. Only if the recapture liability is less than the present value of the tax savings should the 338 election be made.

The appropriate discount rate for a step-up analysis is one close to the company's borrowing cost for a similar length of time. This is because the riskiness of the cash flows associated with the tax benefits to be received is analogous in nature to the risk that the company will have some positive earnings available to be sheltered.

In general, there are only two situations where a step-up election makes sense today. First, a company may have undervalued assets which are not themselves subject to large amounts of depreciation recapture (e.g., timber, oil, and real estate). In such cases, the economics often favor paying the recapture tax because it is small in relation to the asset being substantially revalued. Second, the values of the acquired assets may be so far in excess of original cost that recapture represents only a fraction of the write-up potential. Since recapture is limited to original cost, the additional write-up potential may, on balance, make the election worthwhile.

Perhaps another way of making the last point is that if the acquired company principally holds depreciable personal property (including machinery and equipment), and the write-up potential of that equipment is not in excess of original cost, then a 338 election is almost certainly uneconomical. That is because the benefit of step-up (the depreciation tax shelter) is no larger in absolute dollars than the recapture tax paid today, and the benefit is further away in time.

ACCOUNTING TREATMENT OF ACQUISITIONS AND PRO FORMA ANALYSIS

One of the most important, and most misunderstood, reasons behind the decision to proceed or to reject an acquisition opportunity is the accounting impact the acquisition will have on the acquiror. More precisely, managers ask, "What effect will the acquisition have on my reported earnings per share?" and "Will my credit rating be affected?"

Efficient-market economists are inclined to argue that the market "sees through" accounting conventions to the underlying reality of an investment. This may be true, but it still does not mean that if a particular acquisition can be structured in two ways, one offering 30 percent initial earnings dilution and another offering only 8 percent, that a good manager will not choose the latter structure. The fact is that managers are very sensitive to an acquisition's impact on reported earnings, and they believe that the market *expects* them to behave in a manner that does not lead to drastic earnings declines. This is not saying that all acquisitions that improve earnings are good. Rather, the point is that few acquisitions that seriously impair earnings are feasible, even if desirable for other reasons.

There are two principal methods of accounting for acquisitions of control of a company. They are the *pooling* method and the *purchase* method. The pooling method applies almost exclusively to acquisitions using the acquiror's common stock. The purchase method, which is far more general, applies to all other forms of acquisitions. The pooling method is the simpler of the two, however, and so it is treated first.

Pooling Method Accounting

The theory of a pooling is that the two shareholder groups of the merged companies have fused their respective stakes, with a view to sharing jointly the benefits and risks of the combined venture thereafter. This may sound obvious, but it has very important consequences for the rules that determine when an acquisition must be treated as a pooling. The principal requirements of U.S. generally accepted accounting principles (GAAP) for when pooling treatment can, and must, be used are as follows:

1 *No subsidiaries.* Each of the combining companies must have been an autonomous corporation (not a subsidiary or a division of another corporation) for two years prior to announcement of the merger.

2 *Mutual independence.* No merging company may control more than 10 percent of the other prior to the merger.

3 *Timely completion.* The plan of merger must be consummated within one year, and all in one event.

4 *90 percent rule.* At consummation, the acquiror must issue its own voting common stock for at least 90 percent of the outstanding stock of the acquiree.

5 *No equity changes.* Neither merging company may have changed the interests of its voting common stock for two years prior to announcement of the merger in contemplation of the pooling (i.e., no recapitalizations, etc.).

6 *Repurchases.* Stock repurchases after the pooling are limited to "normal" amounts, but stock may not be repurchased for the purpose of effecting another business combination.

7 *No voting realignments or restrictions.* Each shareholder's vote must remain proportionate to that of other shareholders in a combining company after the pooling. Shareholders in the combining companies may not have their voting rights restricted in any way.

Assuming that a transaction satisfies these strict requirements, the important task for a financial manager in the position of evaluating the transaction is to determine its pro forma impact on the earnings and balance sheet of the acquiror.

Table 29.9 offers a relatively simple example of the pooling of balance sheets. The pooling method is a very straightforward consolidation method: Balance sheets are simply added together, line by line. The only adjustment commonly arising is the elimination of any intercompany investments, which are treated as treasury stock.

The income statement effect of a pooling is also simply calculated, as shown in Table 29.10. Comparable income statement items, down to net income, are simply added (assuming that each company prepares its statement according to the same accounting principles).

The key statistics for merger analysis can be derived from the combined income statement and balance sheet. The first is pro forma earnings per share (EPS). While earnings in the aggregate are additive in a pooling, the number of shares outstanding after the combination depends on the exchange ratio of the merger (i.e., the number of shares issued by the acquiror for each share of acquiree stock). Thus, in Table 29.10, if acquiror *A* has 40 million shares outstanding, acquiree *B* has 8 million shares outstanding, and *A* offers an exchange ratio of 2:1, then the combined *AB* will have 56 million shares outstanding after the acquisition. As the table shows, EPS of *A* are reduced from $1.00 per share with no transaction to $0.86 if the transaction takes place. This is dilution: EPS is diluted by 14 percent, pro forma, as a result of the acquisition. Ordinarily,

TABLE 29.9   Pooling of Interests Example — Balance Sheets

(dollars in millions)

	Prior to Merger A	Prior to Merger B	Merged A + B
Assets			
Current assets	$200	$100	$300
Net plant and equipment	200	100	300
Goodwill	100	50	150
Total assets	$500	$250	$750
Liabilities and shareholders' equity			
Current liabilities	$ 50	$ 30	$ 80
Long-term debt	100	100	200
Deferred taxes	100	40	140
Total liabilities	$250	$170	$420
Common equity	250	80	330
Total liabilities and shareholders' equity	$500	$250	$750

managers will examine combined EPS for several years into the future to determine when, if ever, EPS dilution disappears and pickup (the opposite of dilution) emerges. If a transaction promises no pickup for the forseeable future, there are probably serious questions as to either the price or the financial structure of the transaction.

Credit statistics (i.e., debt ratio, interest coverage, etc.) is the other set of statistics to be examined. It is important for a financial planner to know just how much financial flexibility is being gained or lost as a result of an acquisition. Table 29.10 calculates the "before and after" credit statistics. In a pooling, because the acquiror is issuing equity, the credit position of the combined entity is never worse than that of the weaker party to the transaction. Nevertheless, the acquisition of a much weaker company could impair the credit rating of a strong acquiror. As a general rule, however, poolings create more concern for earnings than for the credit position of the acquiror.

Purchase Method Accounting

If an acquisition does not fall into the pooling category, it must be treated as a purchase. The theory behind purchase accounting is that an investment has taken place on the part of an acquiror, and that the investment must be recorded at the acquiror's full cost. The cost of an investment must be allocated among the assets acquired as follows:

TABLE 29.10   Pooling of Interests Example — Income Statements

(dollars in millions except per share amounts)

| | Prior to Merger | | Merged |
	A	B	A + B
Sales	$300	$120	$420
Cost of sales	(100)	(50)	(150)
Selling, general, and administrative expense	(100)	(40)	(140)
Interest expense	(20)	(14)	(34)
Income before taxes	$ 80	$ 16	$ 96
Income taxes	(40)	(8)	(48)
Net income	$ 40	$ 8	$ 48
Earnings per share	$1.00	$1.00	$0.86
Dividends per share	$0.50	$0.30	$0.50
Number of shares outstanding (millions)	40	8	56
Market Assumptions			
Stock price per share	$10	$20	$10
P/E ratio	10×	20×	11.7×
Total market value	$400	$160	$560
Dividend yield	4.0%	3.0%	5.0%
Credit Statistics			
Debit ratio (see Table 29.9)	29%	56%	38%
Interest coverage	5.0×	2.1×	3.8×

Transaction Assumptions

A acquires B

Each share of B is converted into two shares
of A (i.e., exchange ratio is 2A:1B).

1 Adjust each acquiree balance sheet account to its fair value.

2 Any excess of purchase price over net fair value (fair value of acquiree's assets minus fair value of liabilities) is recorded as goodwill.

3 If the purchase price is below net fair value, noncurrent assets should be reduced proportionately. Negative goodwill is ordinarily not recorded.

4 Assuming the acquisition involved more than 50 percent of the target, the revalued target balance sheet is consolidated with that of the acquiror.

The acquisition and the revaluation process have implications for the earnings of the combined companies beyond the mere sum of the independent earnings streams.

1 Revaluations that alter the recorded value of depreciable assets of the acquiree must be amortized against future earnings according to the remaining life of the asset.

2 Goodwill must be amortized against future earnings over a period of time not to exceed 40 years.

3 Revaluations of liabilities (most commonly, bond discount or premium) must also be amortized into earnings over an appropriate period.

4 In each case, it is important to ascertain the tax effect of the particular adjustment to earnings. For example, goodwill incurred is not tax deductible and therefore reduces net income directly. Additional depreciation charges may also be non-deductible if no 338 election takes place in the acquistion.

Table 29.11 is a relatively self-explanatory example of the balance sheet adjustments associated with purchase accounting. The principal noteworthy facts of the example are that unfunded vested pension liability is recorded as a liability, and deferred taxes are eliminated. The logic behind the elimination of deferred taxes is that, if the acquiror makes a 338 election, the tax bases of the acquiree's assets will be revalued to fair value (i.e., the new book values). If no such election is made, then the recorded fair value of each asset should be reduced by the related tax liability incurred on a hypothetical disposition at fair value, so that deferred taxes are implicitly deducted from the asset side of the balance sheet.

Table 29.12 shows the corresponding combined income statements for a purchase. Each balance sheet revaluation creates a related income statement adjustment. The most important change, of course, is the interest on acquisition debt. Net income after the acquisition is less than that of the acquiror before the acquisition, and thus dilution takes place both in the aggregate and on a per-share basis. The credit impact of the transaction is also shown in the table.

Stock Price Impact

An interesting and useful analysis for both purchase and pooling transactions is to estimate the stock price impact the acquisition will have on the acquiror. If the acquiree is much smaller than the acquiror, the effect is usually minimal. On the other hand, a major acquisition can have a dramatic effect on the stock market's perception of a company.

An elementary fallacy is to assume that if a high-P/E company acquires a low-P/E company, the acquiror's P/E will be applied to the acquiree's earnings, thus boosting the value of the combined entity above the sum of the values of each company separately. At least in recent years, the market has not been fooled by such transparent devices. In reality, if there are no synergies or other improvements made as a result of an acquisition, the combination of two unrelated companies can often reduce the value of the combined enterprise below the sum of the values of the two taken independently, because the market has difficulty in assessing the true nature of the combined businesses. This is generally known in financial circles as the conglomerate discount.

One way to analyze the impact of an acquisition on a company's stock price is to calculate a weighted-average P/E for the combined company based
(text continues on page 29-38)

TABLE 29.11 Purchase Accounting Example — Balance Sheets

(dollars in millions)

	Prior to Merger		Adjust B to Fair Value	B as Adjusted	Purchase Price Allocation	Combined A + B
	A	B				
Assets						
Current assets	$200	$100	+10(a)	$110	−60(h)	$250
Net plant and equipment	200	100	+50(b)	150	—	350
Goodwill	100	50	−50(c)	—	+35(i)	135
Total assets	$500	$250	—	$260	+35	$735
Liabilities and shareholders' equity						
Current liabilities	$ 50	$ 30	—	$ 30	+10(j)	$ 90
Long-term debt	100	100	−10(d)	90	+100(h)	290
Pension liability	—	—	+5(e)	5	—	5
Deferred taxes	100	40	−40(f)	—	—	100
Total liabilities	$250	$170		$125		$485
Common equity	250	80	+60(g)	135	−135(i)	250
Total liabilities and shareholders' equity	$500	$250	—	$260		$735

Transaction Assumptions

A acquires *B*.

Each share of *B* is exchanged for $20 cash.

Total transaction size is $160, which *A* raises by issuance of $100 in long-term debt and $60 in excess cash.

A elects to step up the tax bases of *B*'s assets, incurring $10 of recapture taxes.

(a) Because *B* is on LIFO, *B*'s balance sheet understates the value of *B*'s inventory by $10.

(b) *B*'s fixed assets are worth 50 percent more as a result of long-term inflation effects.

(c) Goodwill incurred by *B* in its own past acquisitions has no identifiable value and therefore is eliminated.

(d) *B*'s outstanding fixed rate debt is worth less today because of general interest rate rises. It therefore must be revalued at a discount.

(e) *B*'s unfunded vested pension liability is added.

(f) *B*'s deferred tax liabilities are eliminated because *A* is making a Section 338 election to step up *B*'s tax basis. If *A* were not to make this election, deferred taxes would still be eliminated, but contra-assets essentially representing deferred taxes would be established for all assets where tax basis differs from fair value.

(g) This is a balancing adjustment reflecting the net effect on the fair value of *B*'s common equity.

(h) Transaction price of $160 is financed by $60 in excess cash and $100 in new long-term debt.

(i) Goodwill incurred = aggregate price paid ($160 + $10 recapture) less fair value of net assets acquired ($140).

(j) Recapture tax associated with *A*'s decision to step up *B*'s tax basis.

TABLE 29.12   Purchase Accounting Example — Income Statements

(dollars in millions except per share amounts)

	Projected Income Statements in Absence of Merger		Purchase Accounting Adjustments	Combined A + B
	A	B		
Sales	$300.0	$120.0	−6.0(a)	$414.0
Cost of sales	(100.0)	(50.0)	+8.4(b)	(158.4)
Selling, general, and administrative expense	(100.0)	(40.0)	−0.8(c)	(139.2)
Interest expense	(20.0)	(14.0)	+12.0(d)	(46.0)
Income before taxes	$ 80.0	$ 16.0		$ 70.4
Income taxes	(40.0)	(8.0)	−6.7(e)	(41.3)
Net income	$ 40.0	$ 8.0		$ 29.1
Earnings per share	$1.00	$1.00		$0.73
Dividends per share	$0.50	$0.30		$0.50
Number of shares outstanding (millions)	40.0	8.0		40.0

Market Assumptions

Stock price per share	$10	$20	$10
P/E ratio	10×	20×	13.7×
Total market value	$400.0	$160.0	$400.0
Dividend yield	5.0%	3.0%	5.0%

Credit Statistics

Debt ratio (see Table 29.11)	29%	56%	54%
Interest coverage	5.0×	2.1×	2.5×

Transaction Assumptions

A acquires B.

Each share of B is exchanged for $20 cash.

Total transaction size is $160, which A raises from $60 in excess cash and $100 in new long-term debt.

A elects to step up the tax bases of B's assets, incurring $10 of recapture taxes.

(a) Interest income forgone on $60 of excess cash (at 10 percent)

(b) Increased depreciation on B's fixed assets: $50 increase, amortized over remaining life of six years, tax adjusted at 50 percent

(c) Net change in B's goodwill amortization; assumes prior amortization of $1.7 per year and 40-year life for amortization of new goodwill ($35)

(d) Increased interest expense: $100 new debt and $10 tax liability, which must be financed, at 10 percent. In addition, amortization of debt discount will generate another $1.0 of interest expense.

(e) Income tax effect of all deductible items (all items other than goodwill and amortization of debt discount) at 50 percent

on the preacquisition P/Es of the two merging companies. The weights to use typically are the percentage contributions of each company to the preinterest operating earnings of the combined enterprise. The weighted-average P/E is applied to the pro forma EPS to generate a hypothetical stock price. While this method is simple to apply, it has a theoretical difficulty in that the P/E effect of changing leverage due to the acquisition is ignored.

Another method for analyzing the stock price impact of an acquisition focuses on the value created in an acquisition. It is assumed that company A wishes to acquire company B for cash, at a percentage premium P above market. A and B have current market values of V_A and V_B respectively. By making certain changes in the operation of B, A can ultimately realize synergies that increase B's value by the percentage S, but we assume that only a fraction of those synergies, Q, will be immediately recognized in the market. Then the market will perceive the gain from the acquisition as:

Perceived increase in value of A = Perceived value of B, including synergy gains − Price paid to acquire B

$$(1 + QS)V_B - (1 + P)V_B = (QS - P)V_B$$

As a percentage increase in A's stock price, this is:

% gain in A stock price = $(QS - P)V_B/V_A$

Management of A would not initiate the acquisition unless it believed the realizable gains from the acquisition (S) would outweigh the premium (P). But because acquiror stock prices commonly decline, at least temporarily, upon an acquisition announcment, this suggests that the market requires time to understand and digest the nature and amount of synergies the acquiror can achieve. In other words, the market begins with a Q value which is low or close to zero, and which only approaches one over time. Studies indicate that acquiror stocks do achieve abnormal positive returns as a result of acquisitions, but much more gradually as compared to acquirees.

LEGAL AND REGULATORY ASPECTS OF MERGERS

In the United States, corporations are private entities established at the behest of their founding shareholders, and governed in the context of a system which includes:

- A body of state statutory and judicial corporation law, which enables a corporation's formation, recognizes its rights as a legal entity, and offers "default" rules for internal governance. In choosing a state of incorporation, a founding group of shareholders chooses that body of law which best suits the needs of their corporation and its shareholders.

- Articles of incorporation, or the corporate charter, which define the basic rules of corporate governance and supplement or override the default provisions of state law.

- Bylaws, which provide rules of governance for the board of directors in some detail.

This section describes the legal mechanics of a business combination between two Delaware corporations, which is perhaps the single most common type of combination. Other state laws governing combinations generally parallel the Delaware rules.

Mergers and Consolidations

The most basic form of combination is achieved through a merger or consolidation. In a merger, two corporations, A and B, combine as follows:

1 The directors of corporations A and B approve an agreement of merger, which specifies, among other things:

- The terms and conditions of the merger;
- Designation of one corporation, for example, A, as the survivor;
- The number of shares of A or other consideration (e.g., cash) into which each share of B is to be converted as a result of the merger; and
- The timing and means by which the merger is to be carried out.

2 The shareholders of each corporation hold meetings at which the proposed merger is approved. The percentage of each corporation's outstanding shares that must approve the merger is 50 percent plus one vote, unless the charter specifies a higher percentage.

3 The surviving corporation files a certificate of merger with the Secretary of State of Delaware.

4 As a result of the filing, B ceases to exist and each share of B becomes a right to receive the consideration provided in the agreement of merger.

5 All of the assets and liabilities of B by operation of law become assets and liabilities of A, the survivor.

A consolidation is simply a merger in which there is no designated survivor but, rather, a newly created corporation that represents the combined A and B.

In the merger process just outlined, the most cumbersome aspect tends to be the requirement that each corporation obtain a vote of its shareholders to approve the merger. Delaware law has eased the shareholder vote requirement somewhat with a rule that if the merger does not cause the issuance of a number of survivor shares greater than 20 percent of the survivor's prior outstanding shares, then the shareholders of the survivor need not approve the merger.

A far more effective method of avoiding a shareholder vote by the acquiror, however, is the use of a holding company structure to effect a triangular merger. In this method of acquisition, the acquiror, A, establishes a dummy subsidiary, S, and causes S to merge with B. No new shares of S are issued. Rather, shares of the parent (A), or cash, are contributed to S and then used to redeem the B shares, which are canceled in the merger. Under this structure, even if the law requires the shareholders of S (a party to the merger) to vote, the sole shareholder of S is A, which is ruled by its board of directors. The requisite approval is therefore simple to obtain (a board meeting of A), and does not require the formalities of a public meeting of A's shareholders.

On the side of the target, B, the shareholder approval requirement is more difficult to circumvent in the context of a merger. If the target, B, is a subsidiary of another company, the formalities of a public shareholder meeting can be avoided because the directors of B's parent can approve a merger of B. If B is publicly held, however, the only real alternative open to the acquiror is a purchase of stock, typically by means of a tender offer. A tender offer, however, does not usually garner 100 percent of the target's stock, and therefore is usually followed by a merger to squeeze out the laggard or nontendering shareholders.

Some interesting factors come into play if A, the acquiror, owns a majority of B before the merger, as in a merger following a tender offer. A is then a controlling shareholder and controls the board of B. This type of transaction is generally referred to as a squeeze-out merger, because it represents a majority shareholder squeezing out the remaining shareholders from their position of ownership in B. While squeeze-out mergers serve many useful purposes, there is obviously a great potential for unfair treatment of the minority. That is because A, as a majority shareholder, is assured of success in the vote among B's shareholders to approve the merger. Moreover, if A owns more than 90 percent of B, B needn't even hold a shareholder meeting to permit A to merge out the minority under the short-form merger laws of many states (including Delaware). To assure that the consideration offered is fair, most states impose some substantive fairness requirements, and mandate appraisal rights for shareholders in such situations. Where A has been a controlling shareholder for a substantial period of time, the Securities and Exchange Commission (SEC) also requires extensive disclosure of the nature of such transactions under its Rule 13e-3.

Tender Offers

A tender offer is an offer made broadly to shareholders of a target for the purchase of their shares. The consideration offered is usually cash; if it is another security, such as stock of the acquiror, the offer is referred to as an exchange offer. Tender offers may be partial offers (seeking less than 100 percent control of the target) or any-and-all offers (seeking 100 percent control). Tender offers are extensively regulated by the SEC under the Williams Act. Some of the more important laws and regulations are:

- *Prorationing.* In a partial tender offer, the offeror must accept all shares tendered during an initial proration period on a prorata basis from each shareholder. For example, if the bidder is seeking 50 percent of the target's shares, and 80 percent are tendered during the proration period, each tendering shareholder will have ⅝ of his shares taken up under the offer. Under current rules, a bidder must offer prorationing throughout the entire period an offer is open, including any extensions.

- *Withdrawal.* An offeror must allow tendering shareholders to withdraw their shares for an initial period of the offer, currently 15 business days (approximately

20 calendar days). In addition, the initiation of a competing tender offer by a third party also causes the extension of withdrawal rights in existing offers for 10 business days following the initiation. Once withdrawal rights have expired, a bidder is permitted to purchase tendered shares (except in the case of offers involving prorationing, in which case the bidder may not purchase prior to expiration).

- *Minimum offer period.* Under current rules a bidder must keep its offer open for a minimum of 20 business days (approximately 27 calendar days).
- *Purchases outside the offer.* A bidder is prohibited from purchasing stock of the target during the tender offer except under the offer.

Unlike a merger, a tender offer does not require the approval of the board of directors of the target corporation. Instead, the offer is made directly to the shareholders, the ultimate owners of the corporation. The tender offer is therefore the means of accomplishing a hostile takeover, in which the board and management of the target company oppose the acquisition. Tender offers are quite flexible, however, and can be used in friendly acquisitions as well. Where an acquiror is afraid of a competing offer, the tender offer presents the fastest route to ownership of the target, because no proxy statement is prepared and no shareholder vote need be obtained. A tender offer is also less risky than a merger, because if an acquiror does not obtain a majority vote in a merger, it has nothing. It must completely reinitiate the proxy solicitation to raise the price. On the other hand, if an acquiror had made a tender offer, and receives about 40 percent of the shares, it has the option of simply increasing the price and extending the offer, and may buy those shares already tendered. A typical tender offer timetable is shown in Table 29.13.

Asset Sales

The third principal method for effecting a business combination is the asset sale. This is typically used when the business to be sold represents less than all of the businesses of a larger corporation (e.g., a single division). In some cases, the division's assets and liabilities are held in a separate subsidiary, in which case the only asset sold is the stock of the subsidiary. In the true asset sale, however, a buyer, A, agrees to buy specified assets and to assume specified liabilities of the seller, B. Because the only assets and liabilities transferred are those specifically agreed to in the purchase and sale agreement, that agreement becomes a critical document in the process. It often proves extremely difficult to negotiate the scope of the asset purchase agreement, especially when there are assets "shared" with other divisions of the seller, and where certain asset categories (e.g., inventory and receivables) can fluctuate in amount significantly prior to closing. In addition, many such sales require approval by third parties (e.g., secured lenders, other creditors, lessors, and holders of significant contracts), which will be transferred to the buyer as part of the sale. The combination of all of these factors causes asset sales to be the least preferred form of business combination. In pure outline, however, the concept is straightforward, and shareholder approval is often not necessary for either the buyer or the seller.

TABLE 29.13   Sample Timetable for Any-and-All Cash Tender Offer

Date	Event
D − 5 through D − 1	Bidder *A* announces its intention to make a tender offer for target *B*, at a specified price.
D-day	Commencement of offer: ■ Tombstone advertisement of offer is published in national newspapers. ■ Schedule 14D-1 is filed with SEC. ■ Offer to Purchase and transmittal documents are mailed to shareholders. ■ Filing is made for premerger antitrust review of the offer under the Hart-Scott-Rodino Act.
D + 15 calendar days	Hart-Scott-Rodino Act waiting period expires unless government requests supplemental information, in which case waiting period expires 10 days after compliance.
D + 15 business days (D + 19 to 21 calendar days)	Withdrawal rights expire at midnight.
D + 15 business days + 1 day (D + 20 to 22 calendar days)	Bidder commences purchase of tendered shares.
D + 20 business days (D + 26 to 28 calendar days)	Offer expires at midnight, unless extended.
Thereafter	Assuming success, bidder extends offer until 90 percent ownership reached. Upon reaching 90 percent ownership, short-form merger documents which bring ownership level to 100 percent are filed.

The steps involved in a typical asset sale are:

1 Buyer and seller reach agreement in principle with respect to the sale of a division. The agreement specifies broadly the price to be paid, principal terms and conditions of the transaction, and general principles for the determination of assets and liabilities to be transferred to buyer.

2 Buyer and seller file for antitrust clearance under the 1976 Hart-Scott-Rodino Antitrust Improvements Act (30-day waiting period).

3 Buyer and seller negotiate and execute purchase and sale agreement.

4 Boards of buyer and seller approve purchase and sale agreement.

5 Assets and liabilities of seller's division are transferred to buyer, and buyer makes payment, at closing.

Antitrust Review

While antitrust factors generally do not affect the design or valuation of a merger, they can have an important effect on the success or failure of an acquisition attempt. The typical attitude taken by businessmen is to determine in advance whether a proposed transaction is likely or unlikely to be challenged as a violation of the antitrust laws. If it is likely to be challenged, the proposal is usually dropped.

In order to assist businesses in planning mergers and acquisitions, the Department of Justice publishes detailed guidelines, which can be applied to a given fact situation, and which are intended to give indication as to how the Justice Department or Federal Trade Commission (FTC) will react to a given merger proposal. The guidelines were substantially revised in 1982, and are more lenient in many ways than their 1968 predecessors. The guidelines are summarized as follows:

1 *Horizontal mergers.* The principal factor involved in the analysis of a horizontal merger (one between competitors in the same industry) is the pre- and postmerger Herfindahl-Hirschman Index (HHI). The HHI is calculated as the sum of the squares of the market shares of all producers in an industry. Thus, if an industry had three producers with shares of 60, 30, and 10 percent, the HHI would be $60^2 + 30^2 + 10^2 = 4,600$.

If the merger is in an unconcentrated industry (postmerger HHI below 1,000, representing about 68 percent of U.S. industries), then it is unlikely to be challenged. If the merger is in a moderately concentrated industry (postmerger HHI between 1,000 and 1,800, representing 25 percent of U.S. industries), then it is likely to be challenged if the HHI increase is more than 100 points and other industry factors indicate an ease of collusion. Alternatively, if the industry is highly concentrated (HHI above 1,800, representing 15 percent of industries), then the merger is likely to be challenged if the HHI increase is 50 points or more. Finally, the Justice Department is likely to challenge any horizontal acquisition by a 35 percent share company of another firm with one percent share or more, if the acquiror is the leading firm in the industry and is more than twice the size of the second largest firm.

2 *Vertical mergers.* The Justice Department will ordinarily not challenge vertical mergers (transactions involving companies in a customer-supplier relationship) unless it creates barriers to entry, facilitates collusion, or is designed to evade rate regulation.

3 *Conglomerate mergers.* Conglomerate mergers will ordinarily be challenged only if they involve the elimination of a potential entrant, and (a) the industry HHI exceeds 1,800; (b) entry is difficult; (c) there are fewer than three other potential entrants; and (d) the market share of the acquired firm exceeds 5 percent.

The Department of Justice and the FTC evaluate proposed mergers through a prenotification procedure enacted in 1976 under the Hart-Scott-Rodino Antitrust Improvements Act. The procedure requires parties to a merger or acquisition to file economic data once they have reached an acquisition agreement. The government is required to permit the transaction to proceed within 30 days after filing, unless it makes a request for supplemental information or takes action to oppose the transaction. In the case of a cash tender offer, the 30-day review period is shortened to 15 days.

HOSTILE TAKEOVERS AND DEFENSE

Why Hostile Takeovers Occur

In the modern corporation, the separation of corporate ownership from corporate control is substantial, for good reason. The providers of equity capital consist of individuals, who utilize the stock market as a high-return use of savings; and institutions, such as insurance companies, mutual funds, and pension funds, which have substantial cash flows requiring investment. Institutions hire professional portfolio managers who aim to maximize their investment portfolios' values over relatively short periods. Portfolio managers and individual investors have a strong interest in the quality of management in each company in which they've invested because management's choice of policies and the implementation of them can greatly affect a company's value in the stock market. Portfolio managers and individual investors, however, have very little interest in actually heading up a major corporation or directing the use of its physical assets and purchased labor. Investors are relatively passive and shift their capital to those companies that appear to be adopting policies that generate the highest economic returns.

Corporate managers, on the other hand, have very substantial control over corporations and their policies, but often have very small ownership stakes in their companies. While the mandate of corporate management is to maximize the long-run value of their company, the separation of ownership and control permits managers to deviate somewhat from value maximization, resulting in opportunity costs identified by economists as "agency costs." Agency costs can be actual expenditures that are unnecessary or excessive, or they can represent the value of lost opportunities. For example, a manager might cause the expenditure of a large amount of funds on a monumental headquarters building, which he would not do if the funds employed were his own rather than those of a diverse and somewhat distant shareholder body. More seriously, a manager can make fundamental errors of corporate policy if he ignores the guidance of the capital markets, guidance which an owner-manager can hardly avoid. For example, he might embark on a "new plant-expansion" strategy involving the commitment of billions in capital when underutilized capacity already exists in the industry, which can be purchased and renovated at a fraction of the cost. Or he might fail to adopt any clear strategy at all and, as a result of changing business conditions, find his company outflanked by the competition in a few years.

The capital markets serve to protect against corporate mismanagement in several ways. Poorly managed companies obtain a low stock price (i.e, a low P/E or price/book value ratio) relative to the industry. Such companies are thereby effectively denied access to additional equity capital, except at exorbitant cost. Such companies become targets of opportunity for hostile takeovers. An acquiror that identifies a company with entrenched management and underutilized assets or skills can create substantial value by replacing that management with better operators. In order to do so, however, the acquiror must buy control of the company from its shareholders, by offering the shareholders a premium to sell their shares. In so doing, the acquiror splits the value it will be creating with the existing owners of the company. An entrenched management that expects to be ousted after an unsolicited acquisition usually opposes the acquiror's efforts, and thus, the situation develops into a struggle for control, referred to as a hostile takeover attempt. In spite of its bad publicity, the hostile takeover has many redeeming virtues. In particular, the hostile takeover can:

- Create new wealth in the hands of the shareholders of both the bidder and target companies.
- Cause assets to be transferred to better managers (or at least to managers who perceive themselves as better and are willing to stake a great deal of money on it).
- Cause assets to be shifted to higher and better uses on a large scale.
- Equitably share the benefits of such better management or better use of assets with the selling stockholders.
- Thereby cause all corporate managers to focus attentively on adopting policies that will maximize their companies' stock prices, in order to avert hostile takeovers.
- Induce greater accountability of management to shareholders.

The above analysis might be deemed the classical explanation for the hostile takeover. Its main defect is that it assumes target managements to be incompetent, or at least not very good at reading the signals of the capital and product markets. However, an acquiror may have many other good business reasons for advancing the acquisition proposal (e.g., business synergies, product line fit, and useful technology). The acquiror may wish to have the target management stay on, although if senior management departs, the acquisition would still be attractive. Cases like this still create important economic value, even if the value is unrelated to the capabilities of management. The mere fact that some hostile takeovers involve situations in which a target company was rather well managed does not disprove the thesis that hostile takeovers create new wealth in the hands of bidder and target shareholders that, in the aggregate, did not exist before.

Reasons for Defensive Measures

The above discussion of the merits of hostile takeovers is not intended to imply that defensive measures on the part of target managers are inappropriate. Managers of all companies are pleged to act in a manner that, in their business judgment, is in the best interest of their shareholders. Even the hypothetical manager, whose only goal is to maximize his stockholders' wealth, when faced with an unsolicited offer will employ some defensive tactics to obtain negotiating leverage on behalf of his numerous and unorganized shareholders. The appropriateness of a particular defensive action turns on the net gain that it is estimated to produce for target shareholders. That net gain is the probability-weighted increase in offer price resulting from the defensive action.

EXAMPLE. It is assumed that target company T has received an unsolicited acquisition proposal at $25 per share. Prior to the proposal, the stock of T was trading in the marketplace at $20. The board of T believes that if it takes action X, either the offeror or a third party will make an offer for T at $28 (70 percent probability) or all offers will be withdrawn (30 percent probability). The expected net gain resulting from taking action X therefore is:

(Gain) × (Probability of gain) − (Loss) × (Probability of loss)
     = ($28 − 25)(0.70) − ($25 − 20)(0.30) = $0.60

Because there is a positive net gain, the Board is therefore justfied in taking action X in spite of the risk it creates that the only offer in hand will be withdrawn.

In addition to this purely theoretical analysis of legitimate defensive measures, there are other reasons that may motivate a board of directors to reject or oppose an offer. Some are legitimate and some are not. (Legitimacy refers to commonly accepted reasons for a defensive action, especially reasons that are more likely than not to be accepted in a court of law reviewing a board's exercise of business judgment in taking a defensive action. This summary is not intended to represent the state of the law in any jurisdiction, however.)

Some legitimate motives for defensive actions include:

- Belief that target shareholders would realize greater value over time if they hold onto their stock instead of accepting a bidder's offer.
- Belief that a higher offer can be obtained in the near future.
- Belief that the bidder's offer is less than it appears, because it involves difficult-to-value securities, it is for less than all target shares, or it involves conditions that have a material risk of not being satisfied (e.g., regulatory approval).
- In situations where target shareholders would hold a continuing financial interest in the company, the belief that the new management would impair the value of the company.

Motives that probably do not support a business judgment to take defensive action, denying shareholders the power to decide to sell to a bidder, include:

- Desire of senior managers to retain their jobs, status, and perquisites.
- Fear that the bidder, in making restructuring changes, will "wreck the company" when all target shareholders under the offer would receive cash, which terminates their financial interest in the company.
- Fear that the bidder will close plants, lay off employees, terminate products, impose external management control, or alter salaries when shareholders would have no continuing financial interest in the company.
- Belief that the company should remain independent when shareholders will clearly be worse off over the long term than by accepting the offer.

Advance Preparation

The key to an effective takeover defense is advance preparation. There simply is not enough time, once a bid has been made, to prepare for all the actions that might be desirable in executing a good defense. The principal preparatory needs of a corporation involve the maintenance of appropriate charter provisions and active stock monitoring. Expert advice is usually required in each of these areas, so the following discussion is only intended as a general survey of the area.

Takeover-Resistant Charters. The fundamental determinant of a successful takeover effort is whether the bidder achieves control of the target's board. The means of doing so, once the bidder owns substantial stock in the target, are as follows:

- Bidder calls a special meeting of the target's shareholders at which bidder proposes to remove target's board and replace it with its own slate; or
- Bidder, which owns enough stock in the target to take shareholder action without a meeting, files a certificate of action without a meeting, which removes the target's board and replaces it with the bidder's slate.

Defensive charter provisions tend to be ones which make these processes more difficult for a bidder to initiate unless it owns a substantial amount of the company's stock. Typical defensive charter provisions include:

1 *Supermajority removal provisions.* These provisions require the vote of more than 50 percent of shareholders (e.g., 90 percent is an almost unattainably high voting requirement) to remove the board of directors unless the target has approved the bid in advance. Such provisions are primarily directed toward preventing an unsolicited bidder from making a tender offer for less than 100 percent of a company, and then only at a very generous price, which will attract nearly all the shares.

2 *Classified boards.* Such systems group the directors into three "classes," so that only one third of the board is up for election each year. Removal of directors not up for election is prohibited except for good cause. The implication of this system is that it will take a hostile bidder two annual meetings to elect a majority of the board, and thus deter those who would take control by exercising the influence of substantial minority (15 to 30 percent) blocks.

3 *No action without a meeting.* Requiring shareholders to call a special shareholder meeting causes a delay in the time a bidder can act to replace the board. This allows a target more time to play out its defensive strategy.

All of the above actions have a tendency to create delays in the speed at which a bidder can achieve board control. Ultimately, it would be unrealistic to expect board members not to resign in the face of a majority shareholder. However, a few extra days can make the difference in the success of certain defenses, such as a "pac-man" defense or finding a white knight.

Other defensive charter provisions are designed to deter would-be acquirors by interfering with important steps in their acquisition plans. For example, hostile takeovers are usually structured as a tender offer followed by a merger to obtain the remaining shares. Charter provisions aimed at interfering with this process include:

1 *Supermajority merger provisions.* Such provisions require high percentage votes (e.g., 80 percent) for shareholder approval of a merger following a hostile tender offer (typically defined in the charter as a tender offer made without the approval of the board prior to the acquisition of a 10 percent foothold). Thus, if the bidder received 60 percent of the shares in the hostile tender offer, it would still need approval of half the remaining nontendered shares (20 percent out of 40 percent) in order to complete the merger under an 80 percent supermajority provision.

2 *"Majority of the minority" provisions.* Such provisions require a merger following a hostile tender offer to be approved not only by a majority of shares, including the bidder's shares, but also by a majority of shares *not* owned by the bidder. In a sense, this provision disenfranchises a controlling shareholder from the voting power necessary to cause corporate action. For example, if the bidder owned 56 percent as a result of a hostile tender offer, a vote of more than 22 percent of the disinterested 44 percent of shareholders would be needed to approve the merger. The similarity in result to supermajority provisions is apparent. These are effectively "floating" supermajority provisions.

3 *"Fair value" provisions.* Such provisions are oriented toward assuring that the price paid in the second-step merger is at least equal to that paid in the initial tender offer. They are a reaction to recently developed bidders' tactics of encouraging quick tendering by offering more to those who sell early and don't wait to be merged out. Fair value provisions are designed to persuade shareholders not to tender into a hostile tender offer, because a better offer may come along shortly. Even if the initial bidder is successful, nontendering shareholders will be made whole in the second step. Shareholders can then be encouraged to hold out for a better offer, and, if enough shareholders fail to tender, a hostile offer can be defeated. Fair value provisions operate like supermajority merger provisions, in that they apply a supermajority vote requirement to the approval of any second-step merger in which the value paid is less than that paid in the preceding tender offer.

A more exotic form of defensive strategy requires more long-range planning. It involves the creation of two classes of stock: voting and nonvoting. The voting stock typically is held by a small group of founding family members or another trusted group (e.g., an employee stock ownership plan), which effectively retains control over the sale of the company. Nonvoting stockholders provide substantial additional equity capital and participate on an equivalent basis in any dividends or other distributions with the voting stockholders. At present, such unusual capital structures have the disadvantage of making a company ineligible for listing on the New York Stock Exchange.

A final defensive tactic that is often overlooked is reincorporation in states with more restrictive merger rules. The presence of such restrictive rules generally assists target managers who wish to delay or prevent a merger.

Nothing in the previous discussion of takeover defense is intended to recommend that companies generally rush to adopt "shark repellent" policies wholesale. Such policies, when used in quantity, can prove addictive and, in the long term, lead to lethargic company performance. There is a good deal of evidence to suggest that the presence of significant legal barriers to takeover leads to a lower stock valuation and a higher cost of capital. It is a truism that the best defense against a hostile bid is a high stock price.

Stock Monitoring. Companies fearing a hostile takeover are well-advised to undertake daily monitoring of their stock, especially by following transfers in and out of major depositories, such as Depository Trust Company. Such monitoring is aimed at the early identification of brokerage firms and institutions that are making extensive purchases of the stock and then usually withdrawing the shares from a depository to avoid the appearance of an accumulation. The means of tracking patterns of purchases and sales are technical, and companies are well-advised to employ professional advisers to assist in this area.

Responses to a Hostile Offer

Once a hostile approach has been made, there are a number of tactics at a board's disposal for taking defensive action. This section enumerates some of the more common responses and discusses their principal aspects.

Negotiate for a Higher Price or a Standstill Agreement. If a defense program is not successful in entirely maintaining the independence of the target, it may still be powerful enough to permit some negotiating leverage against the bidder. The target's board may determine that an acquisition by the bidder is acceptable if certain price objectives are met for the shareholders. Alternatively, the board may choose to be firm on maintaining the target's independence, and seek to prevent additional bidder stock purchases by means of a standstill agreement. In such an agreement, a bidder commits not to make further purchases of the target's stock for some period of time. In return, however, the target must usually make some concessions, such as a board seat for a representative of the bidder. Such arrangements typically only work successfully when the bidder has obtained a stake as large as 20 to 30 percent of the target, where the bidder is comfortable with its level of influence over the company, although still some distance from actual control.

Seek a White Knight. Often the only way to prevent shareholders from tendering into a hostile offer is to find them a better one. An offeror who comes in at the behest of target management to rescue a company from a hostile tender offer is commonly referred to as a white knight. Managements usually begin seeking white knights as soon as a hostile offer is made, because it often requires a great deal of effort, persuasion, and provision of information to find a company willing, on the basis of a quick analysis, to make a competing tender offer at a level higher than that of a hostile bidder. It is also important to have a white knight make its bid as soon as possible, in order to assure that it is not seriously disadvantaged in timing with respect to the initial offer. Of course, the Board's decision to agree to a white knight's offer is itself a difficult one, as it requires giving up any prospect of maintaining the company's independence.

Dispose of Key Assets. An important defensive technique, which is consistent with maximization of value to shareholders, is the sale of significant corporate assets to third parties. The basis of this defense is that if the asset disposed of is a principal factor in the bidder's pursuit of the target, the bidder may withdraw from the contest. On the other hand, if the asset was not essential to the bidder, the bidder may view such a sale more as a convenience than a discouragement, as it makes the target more liquid and easier to take over. An important aspect of an asset disposition involves the fairness of the value received by the seller for the asset. It is critical that the directors of the target believe that the price they are realizing for the asset enhances the value of their company for its shareholders. If the disposal is not at a fair price, then it is a waste of assets for which directors risk liability.

Self-Tender. A defensive self-tender is a tender offer made by the target for a portion of its own shares during the course of a hostile tender offer. The self-tender typically is made at the same price or at a higher price than the hostile bid. In theory, a self-tender should be an ineffective defense to a hostile offer. All a hostile bidder must do is wait to see how many shares are purchased in the self-tender and revise its own bid downward accordingly, to reflect the smaller company it is then acquiring.

In practice, however, a self-tender is a useful defense to a partial tender offer. That is because the current rules governing self-tenders often permit the self-tender to have a proration date earlier than that of the hostile partial offer. Consequently, the self-tender represents a more attractive offer to the market, and most shares are tendered to the self-tender. The hostile bidder must wait until the number of shares purchased under the self-tender is known before it can revise its offer, and this provides additional time for the target to bring in a white knight.

A self-tender also can make a partial acquisition very expensive, in an indirect way, when the bidder already has a significant foothold in the target:

EXAMPLE. Suppose hostile bidder A owns 20 percent of the target, T. A would like to increase its ownership of T to 40 percent through a partial offer. T has 10 million shares outstanding, trading at $20 before the offer, and A's partial offer is at $25 for 2 million shares.

- Prior to the offer, A owns 20 percent of T, and the stake is valued in the market at $40 million ($20 × 2 million shares).

- Were the offer to succeed, A would own 40 percent of T at an incremental cost of $50 million (2 million shares × $25). Presumably, the shares would again trade for $20 after the offer, so that the premium paid would be $10 million ($5/share times 2 million shares) on a total investment valued in the market at $80 million, or a 12.5 percent premium.

- If T makes a self-tender for 50 percent of itself at $25 a share, it will redeem 5 million shares. In making the tender, T is implicitly paying a premium of $5 per share out of its own capital to tendering shareholders. Consequently, the aggregate value of T after the offer will be $75 million ($200 million before offer — $125 million paid in self-tender), on a base of 5 million shares, for a posttender stock price of $15.

- In response to T's self-tender, A cancels its offer. A has now reached 40 percent ownership of T without buying a single share (2 million shares original stake out of 5 million outstanding). However, the market value of A's stake has fallen to $30 million. Thus, A has lost $10 million in market value to obtain a 40 percent stake, and has been forced to pay a 33.3 percent premium for its position.

"Pac-Man" Defense. A recent innovation in the tender-offer area is the utilization of a reciprocal hostile offer, more commonly known as the pac-man defense (named after the popular electronic game in which the pursued becomes the pursuer). In a pac-man defense, the target's basic threat is that unless the bidder withdraws (or raises its offer price), the target will proceed to acquire the bidder and oust the bidder's management. A necessary condition for the success of a pac-man defense is that the target have financial resources comparable to those of the bidder, or have a "deep-pocket" ally willing to lend its credit and credibility to the enterprise (as United Technologies did for Martin Marietta in 1982). In essence, a pac-man defense acknowledges the appropriateness of merging the two companies, but challenges the determination of which management will control the new enterprise.

Despite the game-like appellation, the decision to embark on a pac-man defense should only be undertaken with the most serious study and care. Such actions can obviously pose grave risks to the financial health of a target company if it succeeds in acquiring its pursuer.

Litigate. Both as an arena for implementing a tender offer defense and as a strategic weapon in itself, litigation pervades virtually all hostile takeover situations. The principal strategic aim of litigation is to obtain an injunction, temporary or permanent, or a temporary restraining order against the bidder's offer. The basis of the injunction is usually some alleged violation of law on the part of the bidder. Typical bases of litigation are:

- *Securities laws.* The bidder, in making its offer, has arguably violated one of the many laws governing the making of tender offers: disclosure of nonpublic information, or one of the many rules governing trading in the securities markets.

- *State tender offer laws.* Some states in the past have enacted laws specifically designed to impede hostile tender offers (e.g., requiring regulatory review and waiting periods). Most of these, however, have been struck down by the U.S. Supreme Court in recent years and, thus, are a rather unreliable form of defense.

- *Antitrust laws.* A target is permitted to argue that the proposed combination would probably violate the U.S. antitrust laws and, therefore, should be enjoined.

Other less common legal defenses arise in regulated industries (e.g., transportation, communications, defense, and nuclear energy), where there is public interest in the identity and reputation of the acquiror. In addition, federal antiracketeering laws have been stretched by targets in an effort to include within their scope acquirors who, either in the past or in the tender offer itself, have arguably committed multiple securities law violations.

SUGGESTED READING

Bebchuk. "The Case for Facilitating Competing Tender Offers." *Harvard Law Review*, Vol. 95 (1982), p. 1028.

Broderick. "Reorganizations from A to G." *Mergers and Acquisitions*, Vol. 16 (Winter 1982).

Easterbrook and Fischel. "The Proper Role of a Target's Management in Responding to a Tender Offer." *Harvard Law Review*, Vol. 94 (1981), p. 1161.

Jensen. *Corporate Control: Folklore vs. Science*. University of Rochester Economics Research Center. Rochester, N.Y.: 1983.

Jensen, ed. "Symposium on the Market for Corporate Control: The Scientific Evidence." *Journal of Financial Economics*, Vol. 11 (1983).

Manne. "Mergers and the Market for Corporate Control." *Journal of Political Economics*, Vol. 73 (1965), p. 110.

Mullins. "Does the Capital Asset Pricing Model Work?" *Harvard Business Review*, Vol. 60 (Jan.-Feb. 1982), p. 105.

Report of Recommendations. U.S. Securities and Exchange Commission, Advisory Committee on Tender Offers. 1983.

Salter and Weinhold. "Diversification via Acquisition: Creating Value." *Harvard Business Review*, Vol. 56 (July-Aug. 1978), p. 166.

Shay. "Setting the 'Right' Premium in an Efficient Market." *Mergers and Acquisitions*, Vol. 16 (1981), p. 23.

Weston and Chung. "Do Mergers Make Money?" *Mergers and Acquisitions*, Vol. 18 (Fall 1983).

30

Dividend Policy

PETER CAMPISI

Unless otherwise noted, the term "dividends" is used in this chapter to mean cash dividends paid to the holders of common stock. Except for the special case of liquidating dividends, state laws generally provide that dividends must be paid from past or present years' earnings, rather than from capital.

DEFINITIONS

Regular Dividends

Most dividend-paying companies remit regular dividends to their common shareholders. The amount of the regular dividend per common share is set by the board of directors, and its cash value is paid at regular (usually quarterly) intervals. Once a regular dividend rate per share is set by the board, it is very unlikely to be lowered. At a regular meeting, the board of directors will set (or confirm) the amount of the dividend declared, fix the date of payment, and specify the (earlier) record date. Dividends are distributed on the payment date to the owners of the shares as of the record date.

Special Dividends

Some companies elect to pay a special or extra dividend at (or after) year-end to bring total earnings payout for the year in line with the target payout ratio, once earnings for the year are known. Or, if earnings (or available cash) are higher than expected, management may recommend a special dividend for approval by the board of directors. The special nature of this type of dividend alerts shareholders that the payment should be treated as a onetime windfall. This tactic permits the company to convey some good news and fine tune its payout ratio, without increasing the regular dividend to a level that may not be sustainable. A company that routinely pays no regular dividend may occasionally choose to pay a special dividend.

Stock Dividends

Dividends of whole or fractional shares of stock do not represent cash payments, and create more shares without creating any additional value. A bookkeeping entry is made, merely transferring a portion of retained earnings to the capital stock account. The amount of the transfer is determined by the market value of the shares distributed, and the maximum size of the stock dividend is therefore limited by the level of the company's retained earnings. A hypothetical example is shown in Table 30.1.

TABLE 30.1   Balance Sheet Effects of 10 Percent Stock Dividend

	Before	After
Capital stock issued (par value $1)	$ 100,000	$ 110,000
Additional paid-in capital	2,000,000	2,990,000
	$2,100,000	$3,100,000
Retained earnings	5,900,000	4,900,000
Shareholders' equity	$8,000,000	$8,000,000
Shares outstanding	100,000	110,000
Market value per share	$100	$91

Note: Market value per share after the stock dividend is calculated by dividing aggregate value before dividend by the shares outstanding after the dividend. The results presented are consistent with reasonable expectations and empirical study.

TABLE 30.2   Balance Sheet Effects of One-for-One Stock Split

	Before and After	
Capital stock issued	$ 100,000	
Additional paid-in capital	2,000,000	
	$2,100,000	
Retained earnings	5,900,000	
Shareholders' equity	$8,000,000	

	Before	After
Shares outstanding	100,000	200,000
Par value	$1.00	$0.50
Book value	$80	$40

In a fully knowledgeable, perfect marketplace, since the value of the firm is unchanged by a stock dividend, the price of each of a greater number of shares should ultimately decline in proportion to the increase in shares outstanding; that is, the aggregate value of all the outstanding shares should be unchanged after a stock dividend, absent an expectation of higher earnings.

A stock dividend is very similar to a stock split. However, in a split, no adjustment is made to the capital accounts, but book value and par value per share are affected. Table 30.2 shows a hypothetical example of the effects of a stock split. When is a stock dividend really a split? The New York Stock Exchange regards stock distributions of 25 percent or more of the outstanding shares as stock splits.

Dividend Yield

Dividend yield is the annual dividend payment divided by the stock price. Usually, dividend yield is computed at a point in time by projecting the current quarterly dividend forward unchanged and dividing by the current stock price; that is, if the current quarterly dividend is $1 and the price is $40, the indicated annual dividend is $4 and the dividend yield is 10 percent per annum.

Payout Ratio

Payout ratio is the proportion of earnings the company pays to shareholders in the form of dividends and is usually calculated on a per share basis; for example, if earnings are $5 per share for the year and dividends for the year are $2, payout ratio is equal to 40 percent.

WHY DIVIDEND POLICY IS IMPORTANT

Consideration of why dividend policy is important must address the related issue of why (or even whether) actual dividend payments are important with respect to the valuation of the company in the marketplace, either inherently or as conveyors of information about the company.

Review of Theory

Until 1961, conventional wisdom in the financial world held that dividend policy was a causal factor of stock price movement. In October of that year, Miller and Modigliani[1] published a paper, which argued that dividend policy should have no impact on a company's market value, given a number of assumptions, most important of which includes the independence of the firm's investment policy from its dividend policy. Thus, dividend policy is irrelevant to share price, so long as the firm's investment decisions are unaffected by the decision to pay (or increase) dividends.

Prior to Modigliani and Miller, eminent thinkers and analysts, including Graham, Dodd,[2] and Gordon,[3] argued that more liberal dividend payouts were likely to be rewarded with investor willingness to pay higher prices for a company's common stock. The bird-in-the-hand premise, which argued for the certainty of current dividends versus the uncertainty of future dividends, seemed to be empirically supported, given strong statistical correlation between high dividend payouts and high price/earnings (P/E) ratios. However, the premise ignores the fact that companies whose future cash flows are in doubt, and whose stock represents a riskier investment, also tend to pay out less of their earnings in dividends. Conversely, companies whose investments yield more certain returns (i.e., are less risky) can safely afford a higher dividend payout rate.

More recent empirical work, including a study by Black and Scholes[4] published in 1974, supports the conclusion that expected returns on equally risky high- and low-payout stocks are not significantly different, and that valuation is unrelated to dividend yield.

Tax Effects

Should the differential between the tax on dividend payments and the lower tax on capital gains cause shareholders to prefer the latter to the former? For the individual investor, dividends are taxed as ordinary income in the year received, currently at a maximum tax rate of 50 percent. Long-term capital gains, on the other hand, are taxed in the year realized, at a maximum effective

[1] M. Miller and F. Modigliani, "Dividend Policy, Growth and the Valuation of Shares," *Journal of Business* (Oct. 1961), pp. 431–433.

[2] B. Graham and D. Dodd, *Security Analysis: Principles and Techniques,* 3rd ed. (New York: McGraw-Hill Book Company, 1951).

[3] M. Gordon, "Dividends, Earnings and Stock Prices," *Review of Economics and Statistics* (May 1959), pp. 99–105.

[4] F. Black and M. Scholes, "The Effects of Dividend Yields and Dividend Policy on Common Stock Prices and Returns," *Journal of Financial Economics* (May 1974), pp. 1–24.

tax rate of only 20 percent. (Under current law, to qualify for long-term capital gain treatment, the shares must be held for at least 12 months.) In a 1979 study, Litzenberger and Ramaswamy[5] argued that the higher tax on dividends versus capital gains actually makes investors dividend-averse, and that a dollar of dividends is therefore worth less than a dollar of capital gain, resulting in a relative market discounting of high dividend-yielding shares versus low dividend-yielding shares.

The long-standing argument as to whether investors prefer high, low, or no dividend yields is unlikely ever to be finally decided. In a recent work, using a sample of firms that had paid no dividends for at least 10 years, Asquith and Mullins[6] conclude that announcements of unanticipated dividends do result in increased shareholder wealth, at least in the short run. Much of the theory of finance, including the degree of preference of investors for dividends or capital gains, does not lend itself to final proof, in the sense that some theories of physical science may be proved (or disproved) in the laboratory by conducting the proper experiments under ideal conditions. Furthermore, as many of the empirical studies seek to evaluate investor preferences by measuring yields and total returns over many years, it may be that the preferences of investors in 1983 are different than those of investors in 1933; for example, preferences may be evolving as investors grow more sophisticated, or preferences may be, at least in part, cyclical in response to changing economic conditions and expectations.

It is likely that some investors prefer high dividends because of a bird-in-the-hand philosophy while, at the same level of investment risk, other investors prefer capital gains because of the reduced tax effect. Moreover, some of the very largest investors, which today account for a significant proportion of share ownership (e.g., pension funds and other trusts) are not taxed on either dividends or capital gains, and may well be indifferent between the two, concentrating instead on total return. With the universe of shareholding opportunities providing the investor community with a kind of equities supermarket in which high, low, or no dividend stocks may be purchased, investors may "shop" for the shares that provide them with the particular values they are seeking. In this scenario, if a company were to change its dividend policy, even in a major respect, rather than a drastic impact on share price (the literature fails to state with certainty the direction of the change), perhaps a change in the makeup of the aggregate community of investors holding the company's shares should be expected. This premise is consistent with what is referred to as clientele effect, a concept first suggested by Modigliani and Miller in 1961.

Information Effects

Because common dividends must be paid from earnings and not capital, it is not surprising that dividends of companies whose policy is to pay a portion of

[5] R. Litzenberger and K. Ramaswamy, "The Effects of Personal Taxes and Dividends on Capital Asset Prices, Theory and Empirical Evidence," *Journal of Financial Economics* (June 1979), pp. 163–195.

[6] P. Asquith and D. Mullins, Jr., "The Impact of Initiating Dividend Payments on Shareholders' Wealth," *Journal of Business* (Feb. 1983), pp. 77–96.

earnings to shareholders tend to rise irregularly over time as earnings are increased. Generally, there is a lag between an increase in earnings and a subsequent increase in dividends, indicating that companies are (properly) unwilling to increase the dividend until the board is convinced that the earnings increase is sustainable. This conclusion is supported by empirical evidence that extraordinary (unsustainable) spurts in earnings are usually not accompanied by extraordinary increases in the regular dividend (although a onetime or special dividend might be declared). Also, once a dividend level is established, companies are unlikely to reduce it, although further increases may be reduced or deferred if earnings growth is interrupted.

The earnings and dividends per share history of Black and Decker for 1972–1982 are shown in Figure 30.1, and are consistent with the previous comments. Although earnings increased by 40 percent in 1979, the dividend increase was only in line with prior years. Also, when earnings dipped in 1975, 1980, 1981, and 1982, the dividend was allowed to grow or remain unchanged.

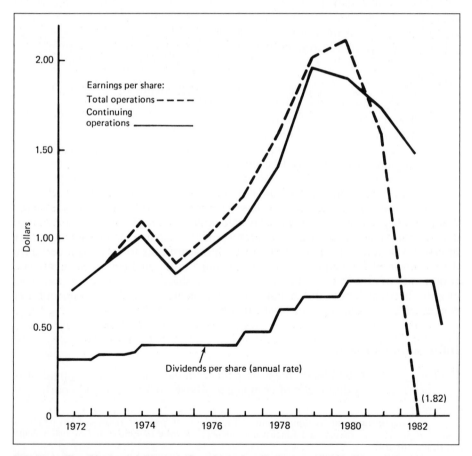

FIG. 30.1 The Black and Decker Manufacturing Company Dividends and Earnings per Share History

Not until a substantial decline in operating earnings was reported for fiscal 1982 (total earnings reflected a sizable loss for the year) did the company lower dividends by 30 percent, for the first quarter of fiscal 1983.

The practice of raising dividends in response to earnings increases is attributed to the so-called information effect of dividend announcements. By upping the dividend, management appears to be saying that the company's increase in earnings and cash flow is sustainable and can be expected to continue into the future. Therefore, the reasoning goes, the company can afford to raise its dividend payout now and into the future.

Dividend-Paying Behavior

Recent empirical work indicates that dividend-paying companies tend to establish a target range for the dividend payout ratio, while not trying to pay precisely the same percentage of earnings either each quarter or each year. Given a target payout ratio, the demonstrated occurrence of a lag in dividend increases versus earnings increases supports the theory that managements are reluctant to cut dividend payments in response to earnings decreases. Belief in the existence of the information effect of dividends is also supported by empirical evidence that cuts in dividends are uncommon even when earnings have actually declined. Concern over the information effect of dividends may even result in the subordination of the information effect of the underlying earnings themselves. A review of corporate annual reports reveals at least a few instances where dividends are actually increased in the face of declining earnings, apparently to convey management's confidence that the dip is only temporary.

The "No Dividend" Policy

While not proven in the scientific sense, recent work by academicians and other theorists argues compellingly that, beyond the very short run, managements cannot influence valuation (stock prices) through dividend policy. Some believe that the prevalence of dividend payments by U.S. corporations proves that the remittance of dividends is not irrational behavior. Others argue that dividends should not be paid except to communicate information that would otherwise not be available to investors.

Most current work, not surprisingly, supports a basic tenet of Miller's and Modigliani's work in 1961, namely that, since the profitability resulting from the company's investment decisions is the prime factor affecting its stock price, it is critical that dividend policy be considered only after investment policy has been established, and that forgoing a profitable investment in order to pay, or continue paying, a dividend is never justified.

In writings and corporate seminars, Joel Stern[7] argues that investors at large are dividend neutral and that those few investors who require income from their securities should either hold bonds (yielding higher returns with less risk) or periodically sell a portion of their stock portfolio and generate as much

---

[7] J. Stern, *Analytical Methods in Financial Planning,* 4th ed. (New York: Chase Manhattan Bank, N.A., 1980), pp. 8–10, 65–68, 79.

cash income as they need while incurring less taxation. Stern argues persuasively that, since corporations are reluctant to reduce them, dividends become the equivalent of a fixed charge similar to interest, and so inhibit management's financial flexibility; that is, dividend payments tend to be maintained, even in light of lower earnings, potentially causing rejection or deferral of a profitable investment.

Stern and his supporters contend that, when setting dividend policy, less is better than more and none is best, but they stop short of advocating that traditional payers of generous dividends abruptly eliminate them. Rather, they support a slowdown in the rate of increase or even maintenance at the current dollar level, allowing the payout ratio to decline over time as earnings rise. Clear and ample communication is most important, say the proponents and practitioners of the no (or low) dividend strategy, including corporate managements who have reduced or eliminated their dividends or have chosen not to begin paying any. The articulation of financial goals and strategies in corporate annual reports has become an increasingly popular way of explaining and communicating investment policy, management's return expectations, and dividend policy. Recent annual reports of the Dexter and Tandy Corporations, for example, clearly spell out investment and financial objectives, including financing and dividend policy. While Dexter's policy is to pay out 30–35 percent of earnings, Tandy reports that historically the company has not paid cash dividends. Both firms' common stock prices reflect P/E ratios well above the New York Stock Exchange (NYSE) average. This is no doubt the result of above-average investment returns, the achievement of rather aggressive operating and financial objectives, and importantly, lack of an inhibiting factor in their dividend-payment policies. While high-technology-oriented companies are often cited to illustrate the high P/E, low dividend anomaly with traditional financial theory, an investigation of NYSE issues will turn up a large number of nontech issues that also pay low or no dividends, yet carry above-average P/E ratios.

Dividend Policy and Investor Expectations

The value of a company's shares and the attractiveness of those shares to various investor groups depends on the expectations of market participants. Investors are adverse to unpleasant surprises, particularly with respect to their expectations for company earnings and investment returns. Importantly, investors need to believe that management is in control, conducting operations consistent with well-thought-out investment and business strategies and sound financial policy. In this context, dividend policy is important because the cash resources used for shareholder remittances could alternatively be allocated to capital investment. Also, the level and method of funding of dividends can impact the debt/equity ratio and cost of capital, underscoring the need for attention to dividend policy within the overall financial policy.

Management should never appear arbitrary or vague with respect to those elements of investor expectations within its control, including dividends. While investor clienteles probably can be identified who strongly prefer steadily growing dividends, or alternatively prefer all earnings to be reinvested, a clientele favoring random and arbitrary dividend distributions, if it exists, is likely to be very small.

SETTING A DIVIDEND POLICY

Over the years, empirical study and the development of financial theory have resulted in several plausible and often conflicting points of view on the desirability and effects of paying a portion of corporate earnings to shareholders in the form of dividends. Currently held positions range from the belief that dividends are harmful or do not matter (with respect to the price of the company's stock), to the belief that dividends are a worthwhile vehicle for communicating information not otherwise available to shareholders.

Factors Related to Corporate Dividend Policies

For those corporations that do choose to pay dividends, evidence exists that the payments result from some sort of dividend policy, whether articulated or not. Lintner[8] concluded from a series of interviews during the 1950s that corporations try to maintain a target payout ratio, although dividend increases typically are less than the proportional increase in earnings. By not strictly adhering dividend growth to earnings growth, dividends cuts are not as easily necessitated by unanticipated dips in earnings. In a 1972 study, Higgins[9] related dividend payout to funding requirements for capital investment. Assuming investment opportunities are such that capital growth and dividend payments exceed the company's capacity for internal financing, more generous dividend payouts will result in greater external funding and, assuming debt financing is used to replace dividend earnings, greater debt leverage.

Recent work by Rozeff[10] uses multiple regression analysis to test the relationship of several variables to the target dividend ratios of a large sample of U.S. companies. Rozeff assumed the target payout ratios equaled their actual average ratios over a seven-year period. He then demonstrated significant correlation between the targets and three independent variables: actual and forecasted growth, risk as measured by beta coefficients, and the proportion of shares held by insiders. Incidentally, industry grouping was shown not to be a significant determinant of dividend payout in Rozeff's study. Instead, it appears that companies in a given industry may independently arrive at common dividend payout policies due to similar characteristics of growth, risk, and ownership. Rozeff concludes that dividend payout ratios are not randomly distributed, more rapidly growing companies having greater investment expenditure levels will tend to have lower dividend payouts, companies exhibiting greater financial and operating leverage will also have lower payments, and higher dividend ratios will tend to be evidenced in companies whose equity is held by a greater number of shareholders.

The exhibited phenomenon of higher dividend payouts when there is less ownership by outsiders could result from a number of factors. Managements

---

[8] J. Lintner, "Distribution of Incomes of Corporations Among Dividends, Retained Earnings and Taxes," *American Economic Review* (May 1956), pp. 97–113.

[9] R. Higgins, "The Corporate Dividend-Saving Decision," *Journal of Financial and Quantitative Analysis* (Mar. 1972), pp. 1527–1541.

[10] M. Rozeff, "How Corporations Set Their Dividend Payout Ratios," *Chase Financial Quarterly* (Winter 1982), pp. 69–83.

may feel that a greater number of shareholders with proportionately less control over the business demand greater payout in return for surrendering control or, in restricting dividend payout, insiders may be acknowledging the heavier tax burden demanded from their own pocketbooks related to dividends versus capital gains. A third possibility is that ownership dispersion is a function of a company's life cycle. More mature companies may tend also to be less robustly growing and have their ownership distributed to a greater number of shareholders. It may be the lack of growth prospects, and concomitant lower requirement for investment capital, in more mature and less closely held firms that renders more cash available for dividends.

Integration With Investment and Financial Policy

To put dividend policy ahead of investment policy is to say that, at least under certain circumstances, a profitable investment in the business could be deferred in order to permit the dividend to be increased (or maintained). While not conclusive on the importance of dividends, most of the studies published in the past 20 years support the conclusion that investment returns, not dividends, are of primary importance in determining stock price and shareholder wealth. To accept this conclusion is to accept that dividend policy must follow investment policy. Since managements correctly want to reduce both volatility and financial risk, dividend policy's proper place is as one component of overall financial policy.

Management should first look at the menu of attractive investment projects available and at the projected internally generated funds flow available to finance the desired investments. A target capital structure or debt/equity ratio should be established which, together with the resulting measures of creditworthiness, such as interest coverage and the cash flow/debt ratio, provides management with sufficient financial flexibility in the face of business and economic uncertainty. The target capital structure will establish the cost of capital, and attractive investments therefore may be defined as all projects with investment returns exceeding the cost of capital. With the investment level and internal funds flow projected over a horizon of 5 to 10 years and the debt/equity ratio also pegged to an appropriate target[11] level (or range), the proportion of earnings available for dividends may be calculated as a residual. Because both (projected and actual) earnings and investment requirements can fluctuate from year to year over the planning horizon, it is wise to maintain flexibility by setting dividend payout at something less than the total residual funds available.

The residual method for determining the amount available for dividends assumes that all external financing is in the form of debt. Of course, it is possible to issue new stock to replace the equity lost through shareholder remittances. The net effect would be the replacement on the balance sheet of retained earnings with capital stock and surplus, minus transaction costs. Also, the residual method determines the amount available for dividends, not the amount

---

[11] The so-called "target" debt/equity ratio is also only one component of an overall financial policy, which supports the company's business strategy and investment policy. The debt-equity target should never be an objective in isolation; it is merely a convenient mathematical expression of a complex set of financial conditions and underlying assumptions.

TABLE 30.3   Company *A*'s Five-Year Plan

PROJECTIONS

	Year 1	Year 2	Year 3	Year 4	Year 5
Net income	$200	$230	$250	$300	$330
Capital investment	300	400	280	300	200

ACTUAL AT END OF YEAR 0

Shareholders' equity	$2,000
Total debt	$200
Debt/equity ratio	0.10 : 1.0
Target debt/equity ratio	0.25 : 1.0

that *should* be paid out. A discussion of the pros and cons of actually paying dividends appears later in the chapter.

Setting a Dividend Policy — Illustration

If management is able to project both profitability and funds requirements with sufficient certainty, the residual method may be used in a dividend-setting exercise as follows. For fictional company *A*, current debt and equity levels, earnings, and investment requirements are shown in Table 30.3 (amounts are assumed to be in thousands, millions, or whatever is relevant).

As shown in Table 30.3, management projects that company *A* will earn $1,310 during the next five years and capital investment requirements are expected to be $1,480. The pattern of annual earnings and investment flows illustrates the unlikelihood of management forecasting an earnings downturn, and the tendency to be more certain in predicting capital investment during the closer-in years when specific projects are identifiable, versus the out years for which some of the new ideas have yet to take shape. In this example, for simplicity, capital investment includes changes in working capital, as well as investment in new plant and equipment. Another simplifying assumption is that incremental debt is free of interest cost; that is, that the annual income projections are unaffected by the proportion of earnings paid out as dividends, which must be replaced by debt. To assume an explicit interest cost would have served only to complicate the example. In the real world, financing cost should never be ignored so cavalierly.

If company *A*'s forecasts come true, and no dividends are paid, shareholders' equity would be $3,310 after five years and total debt would be $370, assuming the shortfall of investment in excess of earnings is debt financed. The debt/equity ratio will have risen to 0.11:1, still well below the target level. While praiseworthy from the standpoint of rating agencies and creditors who view dividend outflows as an increased risk to lenders, this lower-than-desired leverage also keeps the company's cost of capital above target and presumably causes some otherwise profitable investments to be unattractive. Using very simple algebra, if dividends amounting to some $365 are paid to shareholders during the period, with added debt used to fund the extra outflow, the debt/equity ratio would be on target at the end of the five-year plan. The dividend amount is a residual of the calculation of the amounts of debt and equity in the total capitalization, given projected earnings, investment, and the target debt/equity ratio.

In the example, dividends totaling $365 for five years equal approximately 28 percent of earnings for the period. However, if dividends equal to 28 percent of earnings were paid out in each of the five years, the debt/equity ratio would have exceeded the target in the middle years, perhaps by enough to interfere with management's desired level of financing flexibility, the breathing room needed to adapt to unforeseen earnings downturns or unanticipated investment needs without a major dislocation of overall creditworthiness. Perceiving greater financial risk in the resulting higher debt level, the rating agencies might downgrade company A's bonds in response to some unplanned interim funding need, causing an increase in future financing costs. While a 28 percent payout may not be excessive for the five years as a whole, or beyond, assuming continued profitability, prudence seems to dictate a lower payout in the early years with an increase during the latter years, if warranted by more accurate (and farsighted) forecasts available at that time. Holding dividend payout to 20 percent of earnings for the first three years of the plan, before increasing to the full 28 percent if justified by the company's forecasts in year 4, would move the capital structure toward the target but not exceed it, providing company A with the full degree of financing flexibility intended by management, in setting 0.25:1.0 as its target for the debt/equity ratio. Such a strategy is also consistent with observed behavior, namely that corporate managements increase dividends at a slower rate than the rate of increase in earnings, after becoming more certain that the dividend amount, once established, will not have to be reduced. Table 30.4 shows company A's debt/equity ratios under the assumption of a 28 percent payout beginning immediately and alternatively assuming only a 20 percent payout for the first three years.

Communicating the Dividend Policy

Having set its dividend policy, what should company A do next? Whether the new policy results in dividends being paid for the first time, or in a change in amount, management should fully communicate its intention and expectations to shareholders and the investor community at large. Although, according to some studies, the actual dividend amount and its year-to-year change, or lack thereof, communicates information to investors, management should take important advantage of the dividend-setting event to assure that the right message is delivered and understood. Investors generally do not like surprises and will adjust stock prices abruptly in response to unexpected news. The daily stock market news broadcasts frequently report multipoint drops in price and high trading volume following an announcement of unexpectedly lower earnings. While recent studies maintain the irrelevance of dividends to stock prices, careful and explicit communication will serve to keep the company's dividend

TABLE 30.4 Company A Debt/Equity Ratios After Alternative Dividend Payouts

	Year 1	Year 2	Year 3	Year 4	Year 5
Net income	$200	$230	$250	$300	$330
Dividend payments:					
At 28 percent of net income	56	64	70	84	92
At 20 percent of net income	40	46	50	84*	92*
Debt/equity ratio:					
With 28 percent payout	0.17:1.0	0.26:1.0	0.28:1.0	0.29:1.0	0.25:1.0
With 20 percent payout	0.16:1.0	0.24:1.0	0.25:1.0	0.26:1.0*	0.23:1.0*

* As noted in the text, dividends are increased to 28 percent of earnings after three years, reflecting improved confidence in forecasts at that time.

action from being used arbitrarily or incorrectly as a surrogate for information regarding future earnings and returns, which do have important effects on stock valuation.

Assume, for example, that company A's dividend had historically been in the range of 25 to 30 percent of annual earnings. An unexplained drop to 20 percent would leave investors confused and likely to assume that management was trying to conserve cash in the face of anticipated lower earnings, since internal earnings and investment forecasts are seldom published. Instead, management could use a vehicle such as the annual report to explain that significant future earnings opportunities had been identified, which would require substantial capital investment outlays. If, in management's view, reducing earnings payout while simultaneously expanding leverage within prudent limits results in the expectation that shareholder wealth would improve, it is not unlikely that investors would have sufficient confidence based on their understanding of management's intentions to support or even bid up the price of the company's shares. Ultimately, management will have to earn credibility by consistently delivering the promised returns over time.

A 1981 article by Suzanne Wittebort[12] outlines the experiences of four companies of varying size, which combined a cut in the ratio of dividend payout with announcements of increases in investment levels and opportunities for higher returns and, in one case, a loss from discontinued operations. In each case, share prices were reported to improve. One of the companies, G. D. Searle, noted a change in its shareholder constituency, as growth-oriented investors replaced income-oriented investors, supporting the clientele effect originally suggested by Miller and Modigliani.

Much has been written about the importance and effectiveness of dividends as a device for communicating management's expectations with respect to investment returns. In recent years this view has been challenged by respected theorists including Merton Miller, who notes that investors may look for messages in dividends to confirm their own expectations of future earnings, rather than as a communication of the expectations held by management; and by the more controversial Joel Stern, who argues that anything management wants to convey to investors can be communicated clearly and unmistakeably (at far lower cost) by management's careful explanation of financial goals and expectations in vehicles such as the quarterly and annual reports.

Examples of such dissemination are no longer uncommon. The Dexter Corporation, founded in 1767, bills itself as the oldest company listed on the NYSE. Dexter's 1980 Annual Report discusses and quantifies the company's 1981 financial goals (including dividend payout expectations). The cover of the report shows a matrix of industry attractiveness and business strengths with Dexter's business units ranked from Invest/Grow to Harvest/Divest.

In its 1982 Annual Report, Tandy Corporation discusses its investment equation, which relates asset turnover and return on sales to return on assets and financial leverage, and notes that Tandy's average annual return on equity for the past 10 years was a very healthy 32.5 percent. So that shareholders will have no doubt as to management's views on dividends, the net income and

---

[12] S. Wittebort, "Do Investors Really Care About Dividends?" *Institutional Investor* (Mar. 1981), pp. 213–220.

earnings per share section of the discussion ends with the observation that historically the company has not paid cash dividends and that, while the board of directors periodically reviews the dividend policy, no change is contemplated at this time.

SHARE REPURCHASE VS. DIVIDEND PAYMENTS

If dividends are irrelevant (or even negative) to investors in determining stock prices, what about share repurchase? If dividends do not deliver any information which cannot be communicated effectively through an explicit message in the annual report or announced at the annual meeting, does share repurchase provide more useful information?

Since the company has the same aggregate income after completing a program to repurchase some outstanding shares, earnings per share will have increased, as the same income would be divided by fewer shares. The amount of share price increase for the remaining shares would be predictable, assuming the P/E ratio is unchanged. The relationships between share price, aggregate share value, earnings per share, and the P/E ratio may be used to derive the (equilibrium) price the company should offer for the number of shares to be repurchased. The market price after repurchase should, other things being equal, exactly match the repurchase price.

In the same way that regular dividends tend to become a onetime event from the standpoint of management decision making, and afterwards tend to be viewed as fixed costs, they are likely to be a nonevent for investors (i.e., notable only when they are changed). However, a stock repurchase program could serve to catch investors' attention and cause them to consider what message management is trying to communicate. One issue is whether the message could be communicated without the repurchase program, in the same sense that Stern argues for shareholder communication in lieu of dividends.

Company Point of View

From the company's viewpoint, assuming the decision has been made to distribute some earnings, share repurchase has the benefit of not becoming a fixed cost in the minds of management, as may be the case with regular dividends. Even if repurchase becomes a regular annual event, management has to consider current market price, available funds, and P/E ratio to determine the number of shares to be purchased and the likely impact on share price. It is hoped that this required mathematical exercise, and the need to justify the recommendation for each repurchase program, causes management to ask itself the question, "Is this something we really want to do? and, if so, why?"

Investor's Point of View

From the investor's standpoint, for those shareholders who would be subject to both capital gains and ordinary income taxes, the benefit of share repurchase is taxation at a lower rate. Perhaps as significant is that, for the individual shareholder, the tax and the realized gain are elective. Those shareholders who want a distribution can sell some shares, and get taxed at a lower rate to boot. Those shareholders who do not need the cash, or who would only have to reinvest it in the same or another company's shares, will simply let their investment ride and, if the mathematical relationship between earnings per share and the P/E ratio holds, they will see their shares increase in value.

A 1978 article by Miller and Scholes[13] demonstrates that, through a somewhat complex arrangement using personal leverage and tax shelters, it is possible for the individual investor to offset the income tax on dividends, thereby somewhat weakening the tax-related argument for share repurchase. It would seem, however, that most investors would prefer the simpler route of selling some stock when the need for cash arises. No doubt, fur*her empirical tests will help determine whether this is so.

Tax Effects

As previously noted, for individuals dividends are fully taxed at ordinary income tax rates, while only 40 percent of the gain on repurchased shares held for at least one year is taxed. Thus, under current law, the maximum tax rate on an incremental dividend is 50 percent, versus a maximum of 20 percent on the long-term gain portion only, in the case of share repurchase. Stated another way, if investors, having other income taxable at the maximum federal rate of 50 percent, share $1 million of a company's common dividends, IRS collects $500,000. If the same shareholders tender shares valued at $1 million in response to the company's offer to repurchase, assuming the shares were held for a year and had an original cost of $500,000, the IRS would collect only $100,000. The tax bite would be greater or less, if the stock had originally been purchased at a cost other than $500,000, but could not exceed $200,000 under any circumstances.

Earnings Effects

Ignoring transaction costs of both share repurchase and dividends, and assuming neither action affects company investment plans and prospects, the decision between distributing a like amount of cash (from equity) to shareholders as a dividend or through the repurchase of company stock has no impact on aggregate earnings. The accounting would differ within the equity section of the balance sheet, but total equity would be the same after either form of distribution. Interest income for the year would be equally lower or interest expense equally higher, depending only on whether the dividend or repurchase were funded from excess cash or new borrowings. However, as previously noted, in the case of repurchase, since the same aggregate earnings would relate to a reduced number of shares outstanding, earnings per share would increase. Shares held by the company as treasury stock do not figure in the earnings per share calculation.

---

[13] M. Miller and M. Scholes, "Dividends and Taxes," *Journal of Financial Economics* (Dec. 1978), pp. 333–364.

Share Repurchase — Illustration

As noted in the dividend-policy illustration, the level of dividend payment may be used to adjust the company's capital structure, contributing to the need for external financing and impacting the cost of capital. Share repurchase also impacts the debt/equity ratio, assuming repurchased shares are not replaced with newly issued ones. Depending on the size of the repurchase program, the effects on the capital structure and cost of capital can be significant. Combining share repurchase with debt financing has a double impact on the company's financial leverage. Thus, in terms of potential adjustments to the capital structure to reflect changing financial policy, share repurchase is similar to changing the channel on a television set, while adjusting the amount of the regular dividend is similar to moving the fine-tuning control.

Share Repurchase With Surplus Funds

Accounting for share repurchase is relatively simple and straightforward. Shares purchased and held in the Treasury (so-called treasury stock) are considered to be issued but not outstanding. The value of shares held in the treasury, computed at the actual purchase cost to the company, is shown as a subtraction in the calculation of shareholders' equity.

In the fictional company A dividend illustration, it was noted that, without dividends, the company's equity would have grown to $3,310 after five years while debt would have increased to only $370. The debt/equity ratio would have been 0.11:1.0. Assuming company A had not paid any dividends and, after successfully completing its five-year plan, had substantial surplus funds and a desire to reduce its cost of capital by increasing leverage up to the 0.25:1.0 target, the company could announce an offer to purchase shares with a market value of $1,830. After completion of the repurchase program, equity would equal $1,480, as shown in Table 30.5, and the debt/equity ratio would equal the 0.25:1.0 target.

Of course, a program to repurchase half or more of a company's outstanding equity would be very unusual, although not unprecedented. For example, during its fiscal years 1980–1982, Norton Simon, Inc. repurchased more that 20 million out of 48 million shares formerly issued and outstanding.

Share Repurchase With Debt Financing

The repurchase of shares using debt financing is a quick and simple means of adjusting the capital structure which, because of the leveraging effects of the debt, would require a much less dramatic purchase program than previously discussed using surplus funds.

As shown in Table 30.6, only $365 of treasury stock need be purchased with debt financing in order to move company A's debt/equity ratio to the target level, versus $1,830 worth of shares in the example using surplus funds and no debt. Although leverage is the same, total capitalization and financial capacity are very different, depending on the size of the share repurchase program.

TABLE 30.5   Balance Sheet Effects of Share Repurchase Using Surplus Funds

	Before	After
Cash and marketable securities	$2,000	$ 170
Total debt	$ 370	$ 370
Common stock issued	$ 250	$ 250
Additional paid-in capital	750	750
	$1,000	$1,000
Retained earnings	2,310	2,310
Treasury stock, at cost	—	(1,830)
Shareholders' equity	$3,310	$1,480
Total debt/equity ratio	0.11:1.0	0.25:1.0

Note: There is no change in the common stock issued account since repurchased shares remain authorized and issued. However, the number of shares issued and outstanding would decline by the number purchased and held in the Treasury.

TABLE 30.6   Balance Sheet Effects of Share Repurchase Using Debt

	Before	After
Total debt	$ 370	$ 735
Common stock issued	$ 250	$ 250
Additional paid-in capital	750	750
	$1,000	$1,000
Retained earnings	2,310	2,310
Treasury stock, at cost	—	(365)
Shareholders' equity	$3,310	$2,945
Total debt/equity ratio	0.11:1.0	0.25:1.0

Share Repurchase and Shareholder Communication

After the discussion of the desirability of communicating management's intended message associated with dividend activity, it should be obvious that anything as significant as a share repurchase program of the magnitudes previously discussed should be accompanied by a clear explanation of management's rationale and objectives. It could be pointed out, for example, that while management was pleased that internally generated funds had been sufficient to finance all identified profitable investment projects, the cost of capital had, with such modest financial leverage, increased to the point where otherwise attractive investments could not meet the company's evaluation criteria. In addition, other companies in the industry with lower costs of capital were increasing market share at the company's expense, as a result of their more aggressive investment programs. Alternatively, if truly surplus funds were on hand, management could explain that, since cash flow was anticipated to be sufficient to fund anticipated capital investment, the company felt it should distribute its surplus liquidity to those shareholders who perceived a need for a cash distribution, without establishing the expectation of a regular dividend, while at the same time discouraging possible predatory action by unwelcome suitors attracted by the company's cash stockpile.

If management's actions are reasonable, it should be able to anticipate a reasonable response from investors. There appears to be no better way to assure that investors accurately perceive and understand management's intentions than to spell out the rationale and objectives for a complex action such as share repurchase in a clear and honest communication document.

PROS AND CONS OF SHAREHOLDER DISTRIBUTIONS

So far it has been said that most companies pay regular dividends. (Many also undertake to repurchase some outstanding shares, at one time or another.) The relevance of dividend payments in market valuation of company shares has been debated for several decades, with recent work strongly supporting the theory that investment results, and not dividends, critically impact share prices. Dividend payments have been held to be appropriate and useful vehicles for communicating information to investors, although it is also argued that more direct communication is clearer and far less costly. How then is the practitioner of financial policy to advise his company? The following comments, which are principally directed at relatively large and widely held corporations, are observations of the pros and cons of distributing earnings to shareholders, either as dividends or in the form of share repurchase.

First of all, if a company has ample investment opportunities and to date has not established the practice of regular dividend payments, persuasive arguments for beginning to pay dividends do not come readily to mind. The importance of ample investment opportunities cannot be overstated. It implies that the number (and size) of investments yielding returns in excess of the cost of capital is sufficient to keep the company's leverage within its target range without building an increasingly large pool of surplus cash. If such a company were to pay dividends, it would only have to turn around and obtain replacement funds, with attendant transaction costs, in the capital markets. The company's investment-return record, supplemented by direct communication with investors, should obviate the usually offered reasons for paying out some earnings to shareholders.

For a company with an established policy of paying out a substantial portion of earnings in the form of dividends, it would not be a simple matter to abruptly end the payments. Assuming the existence of clientele effect, the company can be expected to have attracted a shareholder group that expects, and is not opposed to, the quarterly distributions. If, even after dividends, the company retains sufficient earnings such that, together with modest additional debt financing, the cost of capital can be maintained and all attractive investments undertaken, it is probably appropriate to continue the dividend practice. However, if new and larger investment opportunities were discovered, or if earnings declined, it would be completely reasonable to reduce or suspend dividend payments, a fact that should nonetheless be communicated to shareholders, together with management's explanation as to why such action is believed to be in their best interest.

What about the dividend-paying company with limited investment opportunities and an increasing pool of surplus cash? Certainly, investment opportunities can become limited in a company's traditional line of business, but there are no rules to prevent a company in one industry from making investments in another. Indeed, the company's shareholders are faced with this same challenge upon receipt of their dividends, but only after the distributed funds have been reduced by income taxes. Would it not be more in the shareholders' interest for the company to use those funds for new investments, which would generate future capital gains?

The previous observations apply in the specialized case of share repurchase also. A share repurchase program has three advantages over dividends, however. (1) The tax advantage relative to dividend payments together with the ability of shareholders to determine for themselves whether or not to participate. (2) Since share repurchases are more likely to be viewed by management as onetime events, they are less likey to be considered fixed costs that have to be maintained, even while attractive investments are deferred. (3) They provide a relatively quick and simple means of reshaping the capital structure and adjusting the cost of capital.

Early in this chapter the view was presented that dividend policy must be subordinated to investment policy and remain only one part of overall financial policy. The same is true of share repurchase. In the best of worlds, the availability of ample investment opportunities should, over time, be sufficient to enable a company to maintain its desired capital structure and achieve attractive investment returns. Ideally, the company that has temporarily found its investment opportunities to be limited, to the extent that surplus funds have accumulated or leverage has declined, and the cost of capital has increased, should be able to identify new fields for investment as a better and more satisfying remedial action than increased shareholder distributions. Much has been written regarding the value of dividends as communicators of management's expectations. It seems likely, when cash builds up or leverage declines in spite of a substantial dividend payout, and capital investment begins to level off, that the unstated message received by at least the most perceptive investors is that management is unable to identify any further acceptable capital projects and, not knowing what else to do, has tossed the reinvestment decision (along with the extra cash) back to the shareholders. If so, those same investors should be expected to look for other investment vehicles in which to increase their wealth.

A CHECKLIST

Old notions remain hard to dispel. Managers for whom dividend remittances still "feel right" would do well to consider the following checklist before initiating, increasing, or continuing the payment of dividends.

- [ ] What is the objective the company wishes to achieve in paying the dividend?
- [ ] Will paying the dividend cause us to pass up a profitable investment?
- [ ] Is the corporate debt/equity ratio on target? Will the dividend move the debt/equity ratio toward or away from the target?
- [ ] Do we have the cash, or will we have to borrow to make the payment?
- [ ] Will the dividend payment convey important information to investors? Are there other actions management can take that would convey the same information?
- [ ] Is the dividend payment consistent with management's objective of maximizing shareholder wealth?

SUGGESTED READING

Chase Financial Quarterly, Vol. 1, No. 2. New York: The Chase Manhattan Bank, N.A., Winter 1982.

Copeland, Thomas E., and J. Fred Weston. *Financial Theory and Corporate Policy*, Reading, Mass.: Addison-Wesley Publishing Company, 1979, pp. 327–371.

Soter, Dennis S. "The Dividend Controversy — What It Means For Corporate Policy." *Financial Executive* (May 1979).

Stern, Joel M. *Analytical Methods in Financial Planning*, 4th ed. New York: The Chase Manhattan Bank, N.A., 1980.

Weston, J. Fred, and Eugene F. Brigham. *Managerial Finance*, 4th ed. Hinsdale, Ill.: The Dryden Press, 1972, pp. 346–371.

31

Corporate Pension and Profit-Sharing Plans

Dallas L. Salisbury

Permission of the Employee Benefit Research Institute to incorporate its research findings in this chapter is gratefully acknowledged.

INTRODUCTION

As of September 1982, almost 750,000 pension plans were operating in the United States. Just under 200,000 were defined benefit plans, and 550,000 were defined contribution plans. Table 31.1 shows the growth of pension plans from 1956 to 1982.

By the end of 1981, pension assets totaled $850.1 billion. Nearly two thirds of all pension assets were held by private defined benefit and defined contribution plans in 1981, with most of the remainder concentrated in state and local government plans (Table 31.2).

Congress increasingly perceives this growth as threatening to federal tax revenues. Simultaneously, Congress is amending rules governing the Pension Benefit Guaranty Corporation (PBGC) to limit plan sponsor flexibility. Since 1921, the Congress has explicitly encouraged plan asset growth, but may now be acting in ways that will inhibit future growth.

The Financial Accounting Standards Board (FASB) continues to move in a direction that both tightens accounting for pensions and increases the degree to which these programs are viewed as part of the financial structure of the sponsor. This movement may have a significant effect on the future development of pensions.

A great deal is at stake. Over 68 percent of the full-time private sector work force between ages 25 and 64 is now covered by some form of employer pension. This retirement income protection constitutes one of the three major sources of retirement income; the two other major sources are individual savings and Social Security. Retirees' economic needs can also be supplemented by part-time employment, needs-related public transfer programs (such as Medicaid, Food Stamps, and Supplemental Security Income), and family support and assistance.

Public policy relative to Social Security, plan benefit guarantees, the tax treatment of private pensions, the regulation of pension assets, and allowance for voluntary versus mandatory plan provision will all affect the course of private plans in the future. The directions of policy may alter the balance between employer sponsorship and individual provision, between defined benefit and defined contribution plans, between public and private provision, between positive and negative real rates of return, and between aggressive and conservative asset allocation.

The end result will largely depend upon whether government considers only one retirement system component or all of them when reaching conclusions.

TABLE 31.1   Pension Plan Growth

Year	Net Total Plans Created	Defined Benefit	Defined Contribution	Total Plans	Percentage Growth in Total Plans
1956	4,944	2,983	1,961	35,503	16.2%
1957	6,074	3,347	2,727	41,577	17.1
1958	6,551	3,659	2,892	48,128	15.8
1959	6,792	3,554	3,238	54,920	14.1
1960	9,399	4,711	4,688	64,319	17.1
1961	8,652	4,545	4,107	72,971	13.5
1962	9,359	4,712	4,647	82,330	12.8
1963	10,250	5,399	4,851	92,580	12.4
1964	10,667	6,072	4,595	103,247	11.5
1965	12,496	6,983	5,513	115,743	12.1
1966	16,973	9,521	7,452	132,716	14.7
1967	19,214	10,690	8,524	151,930	14.5
1968	22,339	12,224	10,115	174,269	14.7
1969	26,245	13,723	12,522	200,174	14.9
1970	30,268	15,370	14,898	230,442	15.1
1971	37,329	20,888	16,441	267,771	16.2
1972	45,815	26,520	19,295	313,586	17.1
1973	55,475	31,608	23,868	369,061	17.7
1974	54,601	30,002	24,599	423,662	14.8
1975	21,931	10,769	11,162	445,593	5.2
1976	3,494	−4,180	7,674	449,087	0.8
1977	19,601	1,616	17,985	468,688	4.4
1978	50,398	5,103	45,295	519,086	10.8
1979	46,036	12,488	33,548	565,122	8.9
1980	56,063	14,552	41,511	621,185	9.9
1981	68,095	19,253	48,842	689,280	11.0
1982	56,693	18,451	38,242	745,973	8.2

Source: Employee Benefit Research Institute tabulations (Washington, D.C.: EBRI, 1983).

Social Security is now recognized as a necessary floor of retirement income protection for all those who have worked. Studies that set forth the policy issue as one of Social Security or private pensions detract from a constructive policy process. The appropriate question is how to make private programs, Social Security, and other system components work together. Analysis that fails to recognize the advantages that advance-funded systems provide in terms of cost allocation, and instead focuses only on the issue of aggregate savings, also detracts from a constructive policy process.

TABLE 31.2   Pension-Fund Assets: Selected Years

(dollars in billions)

Year(a)	Private Plans(b)	State and Local Government	Social Security OASDI(c)	Federal Civil Service	Total
1950	$ 12.0	$ 5.3	$13.7	$ 4.2	$ 35.2
1955	27.4	10.5	21.7	6.5	66.1
1960	52.0	19.3	20.3	10.5	102.1
1965	86.5	33.2	18.2	15.9	153.8
1970	138.2	58.1	32.5	23.1	251.9
1971	152.8	64.8	40.4	26.4	283.7
1972	169.8	73.3	42.8	29.2	315.1
1973	182.6	82.7	44.4	31.5	341.2
1974	194.5	94.0	45.9	34.6	369.0
1975	210.7	108.2	44.6	38.3	401.8
1976	248.8	120.8	41.1	45.8	456.5
1977	290.2	130.5	35.9	52.6	509.7
1978	321.3	148.5	31.7	60.6	562.1
1979	424.0	169.7	27.7	64.0	685.4
1980	500.3	198.1	24.6	73.0	796.0
1981	520.2	222.1	23.8	84.4	850.1

(a) End-of-year totals

(b) Total includes insured and noninsured plans.

(c) Old Age, Survivors' and Disability Insurance. Federal disability insurance is only included in totals from 1960 on.

Sources: Asset totals from Board of Governors of the Federal Reserve System, *Banking and Monetary Statistics, 1941–1970*, and *Annual Statistical Digest*, various years

RETIREMENT BENEFITS AS A MANAGEMENT TOOL

Retirement income programs help meet the economic security needs of the elderly. Employer-sponsored programs have developed because both employers and employees value them. Employers have found that retirement programs meet moral and social needs as well as corporate business needs.

- Management of work force size and composition is made easier by retirement programs. Older workers leaving employment may do so with future income assured, so that they can live in dignity. Younger workers can move up the ladder into jobs left vacant by the retirees. Productivity and morale may be enhanced.
- Management of taxes for both the employer and employee is enhanced by pension programs. Contributions to plans, like wages, are tax deductible. Unlike wages,

they are not treated as current income to the employee, and income tax on fund earnings is also deferred until the employee actually receives a cash benefit.

- The quality of labor-management relations can be enhanced by the provision of retirement income programs. Pension programs are so widespread that employees now expect them to be provided. As a result, they are valuable in attracting and retaining employees.

- Economic efficiency can be achieved by means of the group nature of pensions that lower administrative costs, the ability to integrate plans into the total compensation package, and the assurance that employees have funds to augment Social Security.

LEGAL FRAMEWORK

In 1921, Congress began to encourage the creation of private pensions with the Revenue Act, which made pension trust investment earnings nontaxable for stock bonus or profit-sharing trusts, a provision supported by statute in the Revenue Act of 1926. The 1926 Act allowed reasonable contributions intended to fund benefits for past service to be deducted from corporate taxable income. The Revenue Acts of 1938 and 1942 made additional changes, and all were incorporated into the Internal Revenue Code of 1954. The most recent major legislation was the Employee Retirement Income Security Act of 1974 (ERISA).[1]

Before ERISA was passed, regulation of private plans was limited in scope. Reporting and disclosure of plan information was required, and plans were to be maintained for the exclusive benefit of employees, but regulatory administrative expense was minimal. ERISA introduced four major changes: (1) the scope of reporting and disclosure was increased dramatically with accompanying administrative cost increases of as much as 1,000 percent. (2) Fiduciary responsibility provisions of the law caused major changes in the operation of plans and the costs of gaining permission for many transactions. (3) Costs were increased dramatically through the minimum standards specified in ERISA which required early participation, shortened vesting of benefits, and mandatory advance funding of all liabilities. (4) ERISA's creation of the PBGC at once changed the nature of a plan sponsor's pension liability.

ERISA also, for the first time, extended the advantages of tax deferral to individuals by creating Individual Retirement Accounts (IRAs) for those not participating in an employer pension plan. The Economic Recovery Tax Act (ERTA) of 1981 expanded the availability of IRAs to those participating in an employer pension plan and increased the amounts that could be contributed. The law also allows employers to provide Simplified Employer Pensions, which make use of IRA accounts, as a means of encouraging joint employer and employee involvement. During 1981, the government also took actions that allowed establishment of salary reduction plans for the individual with tax deferral. These may compete with IRAs and employer-sponsored plans.

---

[1] Employee Retirement Income Security Act of 1974, Pub. L. No. 93-406, 88 Stat. 829 (1974) [hereinafter referred to as ERISA].

The passage of ERISA had readily identifiable effects: (1) Many small employers termined pension plans in order to avoid their costs. (2) The formation of new defined benefit pension plans practically stopped from 1975 to 1979 and formation still remains far below pre-1974 levels. (3) The formation of defined contribution pension plans accelerated with more net plans created between 1975 and 1981 than between 1956 and 1974. (4) Plans are much better funded, benefits are more secure, and the incentives are great for an employer to terminate a fully funded plan.

Most recently the Tax Equity and Fiscal Responsibility Act of 1982 (TEFRA)[2] imposed new per employee limits on the total amount of employer tax deductions permitted for contributions to both defined benefit and defined contribution plans. These limits have been incorporated into the Internal Revenue Code at 1983–1985 levels of $30,000 for defined contribution plans, $90,000 for defined benefit plans, and $112,500 if an employer has both plan types. Beginning in 1986, these limits will be indexed on the same basis as Social Security retirement benefits (under current law the limits will be indexed to the Consumer Price Index (CPI)).

The employee is not taxed for the amount of employer contribution made on his behalf. Thus, while the employee's cash earnings are subject to both federal income and payroll taxes, the employer contributions are tax-free at the time of the contribution to the tax-qualified pension plan. It is important to note that the taxes are deferred for the individual, not forgiven. The deferral serves to make retirement saving more attractive than regular saving. When benefits from the plan are paid to the employee at separation from the company, or retirement, benefits are taxed as income unless rolled over into some other tax-deferred retirement program. For the newly retired, this income is usually less than 100 percent of preretirement earnings and therefore is taxed at a lower rate than preretirement earnings.

TYPES OF PLANS

The Pension Universe

Three major types of pension plans exist today in the United States:

1 Defined benefit employer pensions — those that promise a given benefit upon retirement with the contribution fluctuating and the employer bearing the risk of poor investment returns. These include multi-employer plans where several employers provide benefits through a single pension plan. A multi-employer pension plan is one that:

   ● More than one employer is required to support;
   ● Is maintained under one or more collective bargaining agreements;
   ● Must cover a substantial number of employees in an industry in a particular geographic area; and

---

[2] See Tax Equity and Fiscal Responsibility Act of 1982 (TEFRA), Pub. L. No. 97-248, 96 Stat. 419 (1982).

- Employer's contributions to a single fund are set forth in a labor agreement.

2 Defined contribution employer pensions — those that promise a given contribution with the ultimate benefit fluctuating and the employee bearing the risk of poor investment returns. Profit-sharing plans are one form of defined contribution plan.

3 Individual pensions — generally defined contribution in approach — with the employee making contributions *and* bearing the risk of poor investment returns. This includes IRAs and Keogh plans for the self-employed.

An IRA is an individual pension plan that can be set up by any worker regardless of employer pension provision. IRAs are offered by many types of financial institutions, including commercial and thrift banking institutions, mutual funds, life insurance companies, and credit unions. The IRA permits an individual to contribute up to $2,000 per year to an account, and to take a personal federal income tax deduction equal to the amount of the contribution. In addition, earnings on the total assets in an IRA are tax-deferred until retirement, when distributions from the account are taxed at regular rates. A person with an unemployed spouse may contribute an extra $250 per year to an IRA.

A Keogh plan is a pension plan that can be set up by a self-employed individual, or an owner-employee of a Subchapter S corporation. Annual contributions to these plans may be a maximum of $30,000 or 25 percent of total compensation, whichever is less, for defined contribution Keoghs; and for defined benefit Keoghs, $90,000 or 100 percent of total compensation, whichever is less. TEFRA has put Keogh plans on a basis of parity, in most respects, to corporate plans.

Employer pension programs provide several kinds of benefits: early and normal retirement, survivors, disability, and other ancillary benefits. In addition, many plans coordinate their benefit or contribution structure with Social Security. These plans are said to be integrated with Social Security.[3]

The Major Differences Between Defined Benefit and Defined Contribution Plans

The most important differences between defined benefit and defined contribution plans are these:[4]

- Achievement of retirement income objectives;
- Cost;
- Ownership of assets and investment risk;
- Provision for ancillary benefits;
- Facility for postretirement benefit increases;
- Employee acceptance; and
- Benefits and length of service.

---

[3] For a complete discussion of integration, see James H. Schulz and Thomas D. Leavitt, *Pension Integration: Concepts, Issues and Proposals* (Washington, D.C.: Employee Benefit Research Institute, 1983).

[4] For a detailed treatment see Dallas L. Salisbury, ed., *Economic Survival in Retirement: Which Pension Is for You?* (Washington, D.C.: Employee Benefit Research Institute, 1982).

TABLE 31.3   How Pension Plans Work — Career Pay

	Employee *A*	Employee *B*
Before taxes		
1. Final earnings rate	$25,000	$15,000
2. Pension benefit: $150/year × 30 years	4,500	4,500
3. Social Security (primary only; age 65)	8,148	7,212
4. Retirement income (line 2 + line 3)	12,648	11,712
As percentage of final earnings (line 1)	50.6%	78.1%
After taxes		
5. "Net pay" — line 1 less Social Security		
and federal income taxes (1981 rates)	$19,324	$12,382
6. Pension benefit, net of income tax		
(1981 rates)	4,500	4,500
7. After-tax retirement income (line 3 + line 6)	12,648	11,712
As percentage of net pay (line 5)	65.5%	94.6%
8. After-tax income including Social Security		
for spouse age 62	$15,703	$14,416
As percentage of net pay (line 5)	81.3%	116.4%

Source: Towers, Perrin, Forster & Crosbv

Achievement of Retirement Income Objectives. Many employers feel that the primary objective in adopting a retirement plan is to provide future retirement income to employees. In addition, they have an interest in using such programs to help maintain the organization's efficiency and vitality. Such goals require that plans be available for long periods of benefit accumulation. For career employees who do not change jobs frequently, the defined benefit plan provides a known result with minimum employee risk. Defined benefit plans calculate the ultimate benefit based upon formulas. Examples of such formulas are as follows:

- Flat benefit pension: $12 per month per year of service.
- Career pay pension: For an integrated plan, the formula might be one percent of the employee's earnings up to the Social Security wage base plus 2 percent of such earnings in excess of the Social Security base for each year of plan participation; and for a nonintegrated plan, 1.5 percent per year.
- Final pay pension: For an integrated plan, the formula might be 1.5 percent of the employee's final five-year average earnings times the years of service (or plan participation) minus one-half of the primary Social Security benefit. For a nonintegrated plan, the percentage might simply be 1.25 percent.

Table 31.3 provides examples of what can be achieved with an integrated career plan; Table 31.4 indicates what can be achieved with an integrated final pay plan.

The flat benefit formula is most frequently found in union-negotiated plans. The career pay and final pay formulas are more often found in plans for salaried employees. The latter is most common today.

The adoption of a pension plan does not guarantee that benefits will be sufficient to support an individual fully during retirement. The defined benefit approach does, however, allow the employer the ability to design a plan that attempts to meet stated retirement income objectives.

Defined contribution plans base contributions on predetermined fixed formulas. There are several types of defined contribution plans. A common type is profit sharing. In these plans, annual contributions are based on the sponsor's profitability. Generally, the size of the employer's payment to the plan is derived from a predetermined formula, although it may be decided at the employer's discretion. Allocation of the employer's total contribution is based upon a formula that is usually related to the employee's compensation.

The money purchase pension plan is a second major type of defined contribution plan. Annual contributions to money purchase pension plans are usually based on annual compensation. For example, sponsors may contribute 10 percent of total annual compensation to the plan. A lump-sum distribution may be made of the final account balance. If an annuity is purchased, the monthly benefit will vary depending on factors such as age and retirement date, but not, as a result of a recent Supreme Court decision, because of sex.

A third major type of defined contribution plan is the thrift or savings plan,

TABLE 31.4   How Pension Plans Work — Final Pay

	Employee A	Employee B
Before taxes		
1. Final earnings rate	$40,000	$15,000
2. Social Security (primary only; age 65)	8,148	7,212
3. Pension benefit: 50 percent of final five-year average earnings, less 50 percent of Social Security	12,885	2,862
4. Retirement income (line 2 + line 3)	21,033	10,074
As percentage of final earnings (line 1)	52.6%	67.2%
After taxes		
5. "Net pay" — line 1 less Social Security and federal income taxes (1981 rates)	$28,765	$12,382
6. Pension benefit, net of income tax	11,858	2,862
7. After-tax retirement income (line 2 + line 6)	20,006	10,074
As percentage of net pay (line 5)	69.5%	81.4%
8. After tax income including Social Security for spouse age 62	$23,061	$12,778
As percentage of net pay (line 5)	80.2%	103.2%

Source: Towers, Perrin, Forster & Crosby

which typically permits employees to contribute from 2 to 6 percent of their pay voluntarily. Employer contributions are usually a fixed percentage of employee contributions — most commonly 50 percent, but sometimes higher. Thrift and savings plans are frequently offered as supplemental protection when employers also offer other defined benefit or defined contribution plans.

Stock bonus plans are a fourth type of defined contribution plan. These bonus plans permit employers to contribute shares of company stock to a plan. The shares are then allocated to individual participant accounts, usually based on a percentage of annual compensation. Employee Stock Ownership Plans, Tax Reduction Act Stock Ownership Plans, and Payroll-Based Employee Stock Ownership Plans are the most common stock bonus plans.

Under most defined contribution plans, there is no way of knowing in advance how much will be in the employee's account at retirement. The size of the account can be affected by the amounts contributed, the impact of investment gains or losses, or the value of distributed plan forfeitures.

Employers adopt defined contribution plans for a number of reasons:

- The employer may use the plan to supplement an existing defined benefit plan;
- The employer may view it as a first step toward retirement income security for his employees;
- The employer wishes to avoid long-term funding and liability commitments and requirements;
- The employer needs a program that provides for short-term workers.

Cost. The employer who adopts a defined benefit plan accepts an unknown cost commitment. The costs of promised benefits are influenced by investment rates of return, the number of employees working to retirement, the nature of future government regulatory changes, and the future employee pay levels.

Variable costs and concomitant risk are deterrents to the adoption of a defined benefit plan. Employers do attempt to minimize unknowns by projecting future interest earnings, mortality rates, personnel turnover, and salary increases, and by so doing establish a reasonably level funding pattern. Moreover, the fund assets and liabilities of the plan are evaluated periodically — usually annually — and contributions can be adjusted on a regular basis. The employer is permitted, within the limits of the law, to vary contributions from year to year and thus achieve a certain contribution flexibility — although not, of course, to the same degree as under a defined contribution plan.

The employer who adopts a defined contribution plan knows exactly what the cost is each year. The employer pays an established amount on a regular basis and does not need to concern itself with the future. This cost-control feature appeals to many employers, particularly to those that are relatively new and small.

Ownership of Assets and Investment Risk. The ownership of plan assets differs between defined benefit and defined contribution plans. In the defined contribution plan, the contributions can be viewed as a deferred wage once vested as a nonforfeitable benefit. The full asset value of the individual account can be viewed as being "owned" by the employee.

In the defined benefit plan, the promised benefit, when vested, can be viewed as the deferred wage. It is here, however, that the difference in risk becomes important. The employer with a defined benefit plan is obligated to pay a stipulated future benefit and must accept any investment risk involved in meeting that obligation. If the fund established to provide the promised benefits earns a lower-than-expected yield, or suffers capital losses, the employer will have to make additional contributions.

The employer with a defined contribution plan, on the other hand, has committed to the payment of a stipulated contribution. In terms of benefit adequacy, it is the employee who bears the risk thereafter. Favorable investment results will increase benefits; unfavorable results will decrease them.

Because the employer-sponsor of a defined benefit plan is at risk for the payment of the promised benefit, the employer can be viewed as "owning" the assets. The employee can be viewed as "owning" the ultimate benefit. Participants in a defined benefit plan own the right to collect the stream of income, not the right to own or control the assets.

Provision for Ancillary Benefits. Plans must, by law, make some provision for the payment of benefits in the event of death or preretirement termination. Most plans provide for the payment of early retirement and disability benefits as well. To receive ancillary benefits, employees usually must meet eligibility requirements, limits for which are prescribed by law. Most plans require that employees work a specified length of time before they qualify for benefits. Defined benefit programs normally require longer waiting periods for employees before they are entitled to benefits, or are vested, than defined contribution plans. Defined contribution plans usually pay the vested employee's individual account balance in full upon death, termination, retirement, or disability. Defined benefit plans generally distribute the vested benefit as a stream of level monthly payments, deferred until the employee reaches normal retirement age. The more liberal eligibility and vesting requirements under defined contribution plans serve to make these plans more generous providers of ancillary benefits than do defined benefit plans. Many employees whose age and service would not qualify them for early retirement, death, termination, or disability benefits under a defined benefit plan do qualify for such benefits under a defined contribution plan. Many employees prefer full and immediate payment under the defined contribution plan to the continuing income provided by the defined benefit plan.

The defined benefit plan offers certain advantages to the employer. First, by making ancillary benefits a function of the normal benefit formula, the employer can tailor the plan to meet employee needs and employer objectives. Second, since the defined benefit plan incorporates ancillary benefits, it is a more cost-effective vehicle for providing retirement income benefits. Fund monies are not dissipated, to the extent they may be under a defined contribution plan, by the payment of benefits that might be considered by the employer to be of secondary importance. The defined benefit plan can coordinate ancillary benefits with similar benefits payable from other benefit plans. If, for example, the employer has a three-times-pay group life insurance plan, or a long-term disability plan providing 60 percent pay continuance, the defined benefit pension plan can be designed to reflect the liberal benefits already provided. The employer with a defined contribution plan cannot react in the same fashion.

The defined contribution plan can be designed to coordinate with separate plans, but coordination of plans is more difficult because there is no certain benefit. As a result, the total benefit provided by the combined plans in any given circumstance may be more or less than was intended or needed.

Facility for Postretirement Benefit Increases. Over the past few years, inflation has brought the financial plight of the pensioner into sharp focus. Retired employees living on fixed pensions, or on incomes derived from the investment of a lump-sum distribution at retirement, have been seriously hurt by the declining value of the dollar. The automatic increases in Social Security benefits provided for by law have helped, but often not enough for above-average earners.

Most employers are both aware of and concerned about the financial problems of their pensioners. Few, however, are able to provide automatic cost-of-living adjustments under their plans because of the prohibitive cost that would be involved. If they are provided, the initial benefit is generally reduced to balance costs. What many are willing to do, on a voluntary basis, is grant periodic ad hoc benefit increases after retirement that take inflation into account. Due to the monthly benefit payment approach of defined benefit plans, adjustments can be made easily, if resources are available.

The employer with a defined contribution plan is likely to have provided lump-sum settlements to retired employees. The employee may purchase a partially indexed annuity, but this would require a reduction of the amount of the initial benefit.

Employee Acceptance. Defined benefit plans are complex by nature. Numerous government regulations intended to protect employee rights have added to that complexity. To many employees, the promised benefit often seems remote and the current dollar value of that benefit is not apparent.

As employees approach retirement, they usually grow to understand and appreciate the defined benefit plan. In some cases, however, an employer may conclude that the expensive benefit being provided does not reap a fair return in terms of employee motivation and retention.

Defined contribution plans, too, are often complex and subject to most of the same government regulations. However, the complexity of such plans is less apparent to the employees. They have individual accounts with known values expressed in dollar, not benefit, terms. These accounts are usually payable to them in a lump sum on death, disability, termination, or retirement. Employees may instinctively prefer a $50,000 cash payment to a monthly benefit of $400, even though the value of the latter may be the same or greater.

Benefits and Length of Service. The defined contribution plan offers distinct benefit advantages to those employees who change jobs frequently. Under this type of plan, vesting provisions are generally more liberal. It is the rare plan that does not provide at least partial vesting after two or three years of company service. Also, vested benefits are normally paid in a lump sum at termination. Thus, prudent employees can hedge against future inflation by investing that money when they receive it.

By contrast, employees covered under defined benefit plans usually do not become fully vested until they have completed a minimum of 5 to 10 years of service. Instead of being paid immediately, the vested benefit takes the form of deferred monthly income. Since the amount of that income is usually frozen at the time of termination, the employee is fully exposed to the effects of future inflation.

Defined benefit plan benefit formulas frequently anticipate the possibility of late-age hirings, and some are designed to provide fully adequate benefits for as few as 20 or 25 years of service.

For the employee who makes a permanent job commitment fairly late in working life (e.g., at age 40 or 45), this offers an advantage. Under defined contribution plans, the employee hired at age 40 or 45 is less likely to accrue adequate benefits under that single plan. The compounding effect of monies held under defined contribution plans is such that the employee with 20 years of participation may retire with a benefit that is only one half, or less, of that received by an employee with 30 years of participation, even assuming similar earnings.

Combined Plans. An increasing number of employers believe that the most effective retirement program is one that combines the two types of plans, making maximum use of the particular cost or benefit advantages of each.

An employer could, for example, adopt a defined benefit plan providing a very modest level of benefits, and supplement such benefits under a defined contribution plan. In this manner, the cost risk under the defined benefit plan would be minimized and the combined retirement benefits could meet the necessary standards of adequacy.

Alternatively, an employer with a defined contribution profit-sharing plan could adopt a defined benefit plan solely to guarantee a certain minimum level of retirement benefits (e.g., 40 percent of final pay) from both plans combined. In this case the defined benefit plan is called a floor plan. Its purpose is to make up any retirement benefit deficiencies in the primary defined contribution plan. Minimum benefit objectives can be met with certainty under this particular combined plan approach, but cost control is lacking. Even slight deficiences in expected benefit levels under the profit-sharing plan can result in sharp cost increases under the defined benefit makeup plan.

Pension Integration With Social Security

Employee pension plans are usually integrated with Social Security. In other words, they are designed to take into account the substantial benefits provided by the Social Security system. This is done by adjusting either the level of benefits under the plan formula or the amount of contributions allocated to each employee's account. (This depends on the form of the plan itself.)

Integration is a complicated process. It reflects the complexities of pension plans, Social Security, and tax law. However, considering the size of Social

Security's benefits and costs, it may be a practical necessity. Integration may be accomplished in one of three ways.

Excess Plans. A plan's benefits may be based only on that part of pay that exceeds the Social Security wage base. This is called an excess plan. An example of such a plan is one that provides a pension equal to 25 percent of the employee's pay in excess of the Social Security wage base.

Step-Rate Plans. A plan that gives credit for all levels of pay may use a stepped-up rate for the part of pay in excess of the Social Security wage base. This is called a step-rate plan. An example of such a plan is one that provides a pension equal to 25 percent of pay up to the Social Security wage base and 50 percent of pay in excess of the wage base.

Offset Plans. As an alternative, the plan may calculate total benefits without considering Social Security, but then subtract a part of Social Security from the result. This is called an offset plan. An example of such a plan is one that provides a pension equal to 50 percent of pay minus 50 percent of the Social Security benefit received.

Excess and step-rate plans often must be amended as Social Security benefits change. The offset methods has the advantage of automatically adjusting integration in a way that reflects changes in Social Security. As a result, many defined benefit retirement plans, which had earlier been integrated by the step-rate method, have been changed over to the offset method. This is now the most widely used approach.

Integration Limits for Tax-Qualified Plans

The Internal Revenue Code provides that the formula used by a tax-qualified pension plan may reflect differences in pay levels and length of service, and may also be integrated with Social Security. However, the result must provide as high a proportional benefit for the typical employee as for employees who are highly paid or are officers or stockholders. The IRS interprets the Code and sets the integration limits to prevent discrimination in favor of officers, shareholders, and the highly compensated.

IRS regulations allow a plan sponsor to adjust benefits for that part of Social Security that is provided by the sponsor's own tax payments. This translates into the following maximum limits.

Flat Percent and Unit Credit Integration

Flat Percent Plans. Where the plan benefit is a flat percent of the employee's highest five-year-average pay, credit may be taken for 37-1/2 percent of the part of wages covered by Social Security. The basic limits for flat-percent plans are reduced proportionally if the employee has less than 15 years of service.

Unit Credit Plans. For a plan where the benefit is based on a unit credit per year of service, the IRS assumes that the average employee has between

35 and 40 years of service. The previous flat-percent plan limit of 37-1/2 percent is therefore divided by 37-1/2 years to reach the unit credit plan limit, which is one percent of the highest five-year-average pay per year of service.

Where the benefit per year of service is based on the employees' career-average pay, credit may be taken for 1.4 percent of Social Security wages, multipled by years of service.

A step-rate plan could provide a pension equal to one percent of the part of career-average pay covered by Social Security and 2.4 percent of the excess for each year of service.

The 1.4 percent limit based on career-average pay exceeds the one percent limit based on highest five-year-average pay because it is estimated that the highest five-year average would exceed the career average in that proportion.

Offset Benefit Limits. The basic rule for integrating a plan by the offset method is that the benefit formula may be offset by as much as 83-1/3 percent of the employee's primary Social Security benefit. For this purpose, the IRS assumed that an employee's total benefits from Social Security, including old-age, survivors', dependents', and disability benefits would be worth approximately 166-2/3 percent of his old-age benefits alone, and that employer taxes provide half of the cost.

Defined Contribution Limits. Integrated plans in which the contributions are allocated to individual employee accounts may use either the excess, or the step-rate, approach. The allocation of contributions is adjusted to achieve integration, and credit is allowed for the actual employer rate of Social Security Old Age, Survivors' and Disability Insurance tax (5.4 percent in 1983).

Adjustments in Basic Limits. The IRS rules include actuarial adjustments in the previous limits where the plan benefits:

- Start before age 65;
- Include disability benefits;
- Include survivor benefits during active service (other than those required by law);
- Include survivor benefits after retirement;
- Are supported in part by contributions from the employee;
- Are based on highest average pay measured over fewer than five years; or
- Use an integration level higher than the Social Security wage base.

Integration Level. The amount of the Social Security wage base recognized in integrating excess and step-rate plans is called the integration level. In view of the fact that the Social Security wage base has increased some tenfold since the system was established, and may continue to rise with average pay levels, there are several ways of estimating an employee's full career-covered wages for integration purposes.

- All plans may use the average of Social Security wages during each employee's work history, or a reasonable approximation of it.

- Plans based on pay in all years of coverage may use the employee's actual Social Security wage base in each such year.
- Any plan may establish a single integration level for all participants, providing that it does not exceed anyone's individual average.

PARTICIPATION AND VESTING

An understanding of private pensions must be built upon distinctions between coverage, participation, and vesting. Coverage refers to workers whose employers sponsor a pension plan and whose job classification permits plan participation after minimum age and service criteria are satisfied. Participation refers to workers who have satisfied age and service requirements in at least one retirement plan. Vested participation refers to active participants with nonforfeitable rights to employer-financed pension benefits.

Minimum Standards

Under ERISA, both the Department of Labor and the IRS are responsible for enforcing standards for participation, vesting, and earnings benefits in retirement plans. The law also created a method of payment of benefits that plans must include in some situations, and imposed funding obligations on employers that sponsor certain types of plans. These minimum standards represent a further effort to protect plan participants.

The minimum standards are the outside limits. An employer can still adopt a plan with more liberal provisions.

Participation Requirements. ERISA does not require that all employees be covered by retirement plans. It is permissible, for example, to design a retirement plan covering only hourly employees. ERISA does require that if an employer sponsors a plan for some or all of its employees, employees must be brought into the plan after they meet certain minimum age and service requirements.

The age at which employees become eligible for retirement plan membership cannot be higher than 25 in most situations, nor can employees be required to have completed more than one year of service for eligibility. (An exception is available for plans that give participants full rights to their benefits immediately; such plans may require three years of service.)

Introduction of these minimum standards has made it possible for more employees to become eligible for retirement plan coverage.

Minimum Vesting Standards. When participants have met certain conditions set forth in the plan, and thus are entitled to all or part of their benefits, they are said to be vested in those benefits. Participants who terminate employment after they are vested in plan benefits may, in some cases, receive the benefits immediately. In other cases, they may get benefits at a later date.

A plan must now satisfy one of three alternative vesting requirements (although exceptions apply):

- Full vesting after 10 years of service, with no vesting before the 10-year requirement is met;
- Graduated vesting from the time the participant completes 5 years of service, so that full vesting occurs after 15 years; or
- Graduated vesting under the rule of 45, which requires that vesting start when the participant has at least 5 years of service, and his age plus his years of service equal at least 45, so that full vesting occurs when the participant has at least 10 years of service, and his age plus his years of service equal at least 55. (Under the rule of 45, a participant must be at least 50 percent vested after 10 years of service and 100 percent vested after 15 years of service, regardless of age.)

Full vesting also occurs at normal or early retirement and, in some plans, at death or disability. Loss or suspension of benefits is permitted in some situations, however. If a participant dies before benefits begin, there is no general requirement that a death benefit be payable. Benefits to retired participants may be suspended during reemployment in some circumstances. Participants who take their own contributions out of the plan may, if they are not sufficiently vested, lose the part of the benefit plan provided by the employer.

Following the passage of ERISA, most private defined benefit pension plans adopted the 10-year vesting standard, while defined contribution plans frequently provide vesting after four to six years.

The Tax Equity and Fiscal Responsibility Act of 1982 introduced the concept of top-heavy plans and the imposition of complex rules for such plans. A top-heavy plan, where a few employees receive a large share of plan benefits, must meet one of two new vesting schedules for all accrued benefits: Either 100 percent vesting after three years of service, or graded vesting of at least 20 percent after two years, 40 percent after three, 60 percent after four, 80 percent after five, and 100 percent after six years.

FUNDING

Pension plan funding is the systematic accumulation of assets or resources against which benefit claims can be made. Some public employer programs and Social Security are funded on a pay-as-you-go basis; they use current revenues to pay benefits. Private pensions are advance-funded: they set aside assets in trusts for future payment of benefits. Funding plays a major role in assuring retirement income security and represents a crucial difference between most private pensions and Social Security. For example, a plan that is fully funded is unaffected by changes in worker/beneficiary ratios.

Funding differs in complexity and importance between defined benefit and defined contribution plans. When benefits are fixed in advance, based upon pay and service, or fixed-dollar amounts, the contribution becomes a function of calculations dependent upon numerous actuarial assumptions and the selection of a specific actuarial funding method.

TABLE 31.5   Amortization Periods for Liabilities in Defined Benefit Plans Under ERISA

Type of Liability	Number of Years
Initial unfunded liability	
Plan started before January 1, 1974	40
Plan started after January 1, 1974	30
Liability from plan amendments	30
Gains and losses from:	
Anticipated vs. actual experience	15
Changes in actuarial assumptions	30

Source: Employee Retirement Income Security Act of 1974, Section 302.

The funding of the defined contribution pension plan is very straightforward and requires simply that an agreed-upon contribution be made and credited to the account of the individual employee. The funding of the defined benefit pension program requires the accumulation of assets to satisfy future promised benefit disbursements. The level and rate at which the defined benefit plan must accumulate assets depends on the actuary's valuation procedures, assumptions about future events, valuation of assets, cost methods, and gains and losses over time.

Advance Funding Objectives

Private pensions are advance-funded for a number of reasons:

- To improve benefit security;
- To allocate costs across a worker's years of employment and to allow for management of costs;
- To provide a disciplinary restraint on promises;
- To provide budgetary flexibility; and
- To utilize tax incentives.

Funding Standards

Private pension plans are subject to the funding standards established in ERISA (see Table 31.5). These standards require contributions for benefits as they accrue, as well as payment for the amortization of unfunded actuarial liabilities. These latter liabilities can arise from plan amendments liberalizing benefits, changes in actuarial assumptions, and actuarial losses from poor investment performance. For liabilities created after 1974 through plan amendments or changes in actuarial assumptions, the amortization period is 30 years, and for investment losses, 15 years. The standards also impose limits on the maximum contribution amount that can be deducted from taxable income. These maximum limits through 1986 are $30,000 for defined contribution plans and $90,000 for defined benefit plans. Beginning in 1986, these limits will be indexed to the CPI.

Risk to Shareholders

Because the contribution to a defined benefit plan can vary over time and because the employer must make the plan whole in the event of poor investment performance, there is shareholder risk. Additionally, in the event of termination of a plan that is not fully funded, the Pension Benefit Guaranty Corporation may lay claim to as much as 30 percent of the net worth of the company.

Because the defined contribution plan requires a fixed contribution each year and because there is no further obligation in the event of either poor investment performance or plan termination, there is more limited shareholder risk.

As in most cases, risk is balanced by potential value in that the defined benefit plan sponsor can reduce contributions if investment returns are better than expected. Also, the sponsor can adjust actuarial assumptions on a year-to-year basis in order to adjust contribution levels.

Accounting Standards

The funding requirements under ERISA and the federal tax provisions deal with the plan sponsor's cash contributions to the plan. Generally Accepted Accounting Principles (GAAP), on the other hand, deal with appropriate charges for pension cost. Accounting Principles Board (APB) Opinion No. 8, paragraph 43, states that pension cost charged for accounting purposes "may vary from the amount funded."[5]

The accounting profession's formal role in prescribing pension cost accounting standards dates back to 1956, when Accounting Research Bulletin No. 47 was issued. In this bulletin, titled "Accounting for Costs of Pension Plans," the Committee on Accounting Procedures stated that pension "costs based on current and future services should be systematically accrued during the expected period of active service of the covered employees" and that "costs based on past services should be charged off over some reasonable period, provided the allocation is made on a systematic and rational basis and does not cause distortion of the operating results in any one year."

Accounting for pension costs is currently governed by APB Opinion No. 8, which provides that:

- The minimum annual provision for pension cost is, essentially, the sum of:
  (i) normal cost plus

---

[5] Financial Accounting Standards Board, Statement of Financial Accounting Standards Nos. 35, 36.

(ii) an amount equivalent to amortizing actuarial accrued liabilities arising from adoption of the plan or any subsequent amendments over respective periods of 40 years (until fully amortized), and

(iii) interest equivalents on the difference between prior provisions and amounts funded;

- The maximum annual provision for pension cost is the sum of:

(i) normal cost

(ii) 10 percent of any increases or decreases in actuarial accrued liabilities arising from adoption of the plan or any subsequent amendments (until fully amortized), and

(iii) interest equivalents on the difference between prior provisions and amounts funded.

Both the Internal Revenue Code and GAAP recognize that cash contributions into the separately established pension fund may differ from pension expense charges. In private plans, balance sheet reserves allocated for future payment toward the pension obligation may be accumulated when this happens. For federal tax purposes, pension costs reported as expenses in one tax year can be taken as a deduction in that year, even though not actually paid into the separately established trust until the following tax year. In order to be deductible in the tax year of expense, the actual cash contributions must be made prior to the date of tax return filing, including extensions.

In addition to normal year-by-year pension expense accruals, GAAP may require additional balance-sheet reserves under certain circumstances:

1 Pension contributions required to meet minimum funding requirements of, or required to support, a federal income tax deduction, may, by management decision, differ from pension expense charges required to meet GAAP.

2 Special pension expense charges are required in extraordinary situations under GAAP. Accounting Principles Board Opinion No. 8, paragraph 331, reads: "Actuarial gains and losses should be recognized immediately if they arise from a single occurrence and not directly related to the operation of the pension plan and not in the ordinary course of the employer's business."

3 Additional special pension balance-sheet reserves are required in certain acquisition situations under GAAP. Acounting Principles Board Opinion No. 16, paragraph 88, states that "accruals for pension cost" should be reflected as "liabilities assumed"; and footnote 13 of that opinion defines that "an accrual for pension cost should be the greater of (1) accrued pension cost computed in conformity with the accounting policies of the required corporation for one or more of its pension plans or (2) the excess, if any, of the actuarially computed value of vested benefits over the amount of the pension fund."

Disclosure Rules

Funding standards and accounting rules differ considerably from disclosure requirements. Pension disclosure rules help financial analysts, stockholders, and other interested individuals evaluate the sponsoring firm's financial health in the light of its fixed contractual obligations. Requirements governing pension disclosure have evolved considerably since the passage of ERISA and may evolve further when the Financial Accounting Standards Board (FASB) completes its current reevaluation of pension accounting and disclosure rules. While the IRS requires detailed disclosure of a plan's financial status (in Forms 5500 and 5500C), IRS data are not linked in any way with information on the financial status of the plan's sponsor or sponsors.

What firms must disclose on their balance sheets about their pension obligations generally differs from how these obligations must be computed by the accountants. Prior to the enactment of ERISA, the only required public disclosures of pension funding are found in APB Opinion No. 8, which required footnote disclosure of: "the excess, if any, of the actuarially computed value of vested benefits over the total of the pension fund and any balance-sheet pension accruals, less any pension prepayments or deferred charges," and in the Securities and Exchange Commission (SEC) requirement that the amount of the unfunded actuarial accrued liability be disclosed in the financial statements of publicly held corporations on Form 10-K.

Neither of these disclosures was particularly useful. The APB No. 8 requirement did not require the firm to disclose any actuarial assumptions used in arriving at the disclosed amount, and did not indicate how the pension fund assets were to be valued for disclosure purposes. Furthermore, disclosure of only the excess of vested benefits over assets did not indicate how vested benefits and assets had changed over time. The SEC requirement was criticized by the FASB because the amounts "can vary considerably or be non-existent depending on the actuarial cost method selected, without any differences in other facts or circumstances"; this requirement has since been repealed.

To elicit more useful information, FASB Statement No. 36 was issued for fiscal years beginning after December 15, 1979. This statement requires the following footnote disclosure as of the most recent date for which the data are available:

- The actuarial present value of vested accumulated plan benefits;
- The actuarial present value of nonvested accumulated plan benefits;
- The plans' net assets available for benefits;
- The assumed rates of return used in determining the actuarial present values of vested and nonvested accumulated plan benefits; and
- The date that the benefit information was determined.

The definitions of net assets and accumulated plan benefits are contained in FASB Statement No. 35. "Net assets" are defined essentially as "fair value" on an accrual basis. "Accumulated plan benefits" are defined as "those future benefit payments that are attributable under the plan's provisions to employees' service rendered up to the benefit information date."

Pension Plans and Inflation

Inflation affects pension plan funding in two ways:

1 It erodes the real value of benefits paid to pensioners, reducing their purchasing power; and

2 It can influence the cost of pension provision by the employer.

In addition, inflation may also reduce the amount of a pension benefit for a future retiree, depending on the method used to calculate the pension.

Retiree Income

Retirees receiving benefits from private pension plans are on fixed incomes; as prices rise during periods of inflation, their need to purchase goods and services remains constant; thus, their purchasing power shrinks. While most private pension plans do not provide full indexation of benefits paid to retirees, ad hoc adjustments are common, reducing retirees' exposure to inflation. In addition, a retiree who receives Social Security benefits does receive full indexation of these payments with respect to inflation. For those lower income retirees who receive the substantial portion of their retirement income from Social Security, protection of purchasing power from inflation is quite good.

Benefit Formulas and Costs

Different retirement income programs respond differently to inflation because of the various methods used to determine benefit levels and to fund benefit costs. Many defined benefit plans use formulas that adjust benefits to wage changes as they occur, whether they result from inflation or real wage gains. Retirees who receive benefits that were defined in nominal terms years ago or that are based in part on earnings early in their careers may find that inflation has eroded the purchasing power of their pensions.

The method used by career-average plans, which relate the initial retirement benefit to the wages earned by an employee over his career, is a major factor in determining the impact of inflation in such plan benefits. For these plans, the real purchasing power of benefits calculated on the basis of average wages over the career is diminished by rising prices.

The effectiveness of final earnings plans in providing inflation-adjusted benefits is limited for some employees who change employers. Given inflation, workers who change jobs will tend to have lower retirement benefits under plans that base benefits on years of service and final earnings than workers who remain with one firm. This is because the final earnings of the earlier jobs will be lower than the final earnings of the preretirement job. For employees with long tenure, however, final earnings plans significantly aid in providing inflation-adjusted benefits.

It should be noted that final earnings plans, when viewed as a price adjustment mechanism, introduce a distortion in the sense that they provide a relatively greater return to employees whose earnings increase relatively rapidly during the later years of their careers. An alternative method for maintaining the real value of pension benefits prior to retirement, which would not involve this particular distortion, is to use a price or wage adjustment mechanism to adjust wages received over the career, and then to average the adjusted wages.

Unexpectedly high inflation in the years just before retirement can cause contributions to increase very rapidly, as expectations of final earnings are adjusted upward. If early contributions are based on low inflation expectations, the contributions of later years must increase not only to reflect adjusted future expectations, but must also compensate for the lower earnings plans and, to a lesser extent, to career-average earnings plans because contributions to both are set in anticipation of the level of wages in the years prior to retirement.

In order to fund adjustments, realistic assumptions about future inflation rates and the rate of return on investments must underlie the determination of contributions to prefunded defined benefit plans.

Benefits under defined contribution plans equal the sum of the contributions and accrued investment earnings on the worker's retirement account, minus administrative costs. The rate of return on investments largely controls the response of defined contribution plans, Keoghs, and IRAs to inflation. If contributions are invested over a period of high inflation and low rates of return, pension benefits may be worth less in real terms than the contributions were worth in real terms when they were made.

The cost impact of introducing full, automatic cost-of-living adjustments into retirement income programs is not insignificant, even at rates of inflation that are moderate by the standard of recent experience in the United States. This fact is illustrated by Table 31.6. Inflation adjustments in private pension plans must be financed through additional contributions and/or higher (nominal) rates of return on the invested assets of pension funds.

It may also be necessary to adjust additional contributions to employer-sponsored plans for inflation. To the extent that rates of return on pension fund investments are not high enough to allow fully funded benefit increases, any inflation adjustment would have to be accompanied by the creation of a past service liability, which would have to be amortized.

VALUATION OF PLAN ASSETS AND LIABILITIES

Actuarial Valuation Procedures

An actuarial valuation measures the adequacy of a plan's assets and expected future contributions relative to its current and projected benefit obligations. To accomplish this, the actuary must convert a number of future flows into present value terms and incorporate projections of various possible future events.

Actuarial valuation procedures are essentially the same for any set of actuarial assumptions and any actuarial cost method. The actuary first projects salaries (where applicable), Social Security benefits, and service duration. The formulas determining plan benefits are then applied to these projections to predict the benefit payable for each employee should the employment terminate at any future year of potential employment. Next, the actuary applies the probabilities of retirement, death, or employment termination at each age. The actuary then applies life-expectancy factors to predict how long benefits will be paid after retirement. All expected benefit payments are then converted to

TABLE 31.6   Cost Impact on Hypothetical Private Pension Plans of Instituting Cost-of-Living Adjustments

Rate of Inflation	Percentage Increase in Plan Costs
2%	18.9%
3	29.4
4	41.3
5	53.6
6	68.2

Note: The calculations are based on the following assumptions:

(1) Interest rate of 6 percent;

(2) Retirement age of 65;

(3) Proportion of participants who are male equals 75 percent;

(4) Proportion of annual contributions allocated to normal cost equals 60 percent; and

(5) Proportion of past-service liability already funded equals 50 percent.

Source: Edward H. Friend and Company, *Quarterly Newsletter,* Vol. 1, No. 4 (3rd quarter 1976), Tables 2 and 3

values as of the valuation date, yielding present values of future benefits. Finally, the actuary compares the actuarial present values to the available assets, as valued for actuarial purposes, and develops future company contribution requirements with an allowance for future employee contributions if applicable.

Actuarial Assumptions and Gains and Losses.   Actuarial assumptions represent the actuary's forecast of economic and other events affecting plan costs. As a means of regulating actuaries, ERISA created a Board for the Enrollment of Actuaries, an examination, and the requirement that an actuary must be enrolled in order to be able to sign actuarial reports submitted to the government.

ERISA placed responsibility for selecting actuarial assumptions squarely on the actuary for purposes of minimum funding. Section 302(c)(3) states:

> For the purpose of this part, all costs, liabilities, rates of interest and other factors under the plan shall be determined on the basis of actuarial assumptions and methods which, in the aggregate are reasonable (taking into account the experience of the plan and reasonable expectations), and which, in combination, offer the actuary's best estimate of anticipated experience under the plan.

Key actuarial assumptions include:

- Investment return assumption;
- Salary projections (if applicable);
- Social Security projections (if applicable);
- Retirement rates by age;
- Disability rates;
- Mortality rates; and
- Employee turnover rates.

Until recent years, assumptions concerning investment returns, salary projections, life expectancies, or mortality rates were considered the major actuarial liabilities. Because of the recent experience with high inflation and corresponding high interest rates, rate-of-return assumptions have become particularly controversial in the actuarial community. The higher the interest-rate assumption is, both absolutely and relative to the salary projection, the lower the contribution that must be made. Recent trends toward more liberal early retirement benefits and age-discrimination legislation have also added retirement-age assumptions to the list of the most significant actuarial assumptions in terms of their effect on necessary contribution levels.

Since the actuarial process represents a forecasting or projection process, it is virtually certain that the emerging experience under the plan will vary from the actuarial expectation, notwithstanding the actuary's attempts to minimize these deviations by careful forecasting. The funding process, therefore, incorporates a procedure for recognizing and amortizing these emerging deviations, which are called actuarial gains and losses. Each specific actuarial cost method defines how the actuarial gains and losses will be amortized.

Actuarial Value of Assets. The funding status of a defined benefit plan measures the adequacy of assets relative to accumulated benefits. Actuaries generally use asset values based upon some form of historical average rather than either historical cost or current market value, since the latter may not be representative of long-term experience. Although the FASB has allowed current market value of snapshot asset disclosure under GAAP, the longer-range funding process requires an entirely different concept. The actuary must account for unrealized asset appreciation or depreciation in the value of plan assets to reflect the expected long-term value of assets. To eliminate the effect of short-term volatility, the actuary may elect to recognize asset appreciation or depreciation gradually over several years.

Actuarial Cost Methods. Actuarial cost methods channel the present value of future company contributions between the portion identified as "normal cost," or the portion accrued in the current year and funded over the future work life of employees; and the portion accrued in past years, or "unfunded past service cost," and funded over a specified period. These cost concepts are defined differently in each method.

There are basically four actuarial cost methods used in defined benefit plans, although there are variations within each. The methods differ in how they allocate costs over the worker's service life (level payments or varying amounts) and in the length of time over which costs are allocated.

Unit Credit Method. Under the unit credit method, the benefits (projected or unprojected) of each individual included in an actuarial valuation are allocated by a consistent formula to each valuation year. The actuarial present value of benefits accumulated or acquired in a valuation year is called the normal cost. The actuarial present value of benefits accumulated in all periods prior to a valuation year is called the actuarial accrued liability. Under this method, the actuarial gains (losses), as they occur, generally reduce (increase) the unfunded actuarial accrued liability.

Entry Age (Entry Age Normal) Method. The present value of projected benefits, using the entry age method, is allocated on a level basis over the earnings or service of the individual between entry age and assumed exit or retirement age. The portion of this actuarial present value accrued in a valuation year is called normal cost; the remainder is called the actuarial accrued liability. Under this method, the actuarial gains or losses, as they occur, reduce or increase (respectively) future normal costs.

Attained Age Method. Under the attained age method, the excess of the actuarial present value of projected benefits over the actuarial accrued liability for each individual included in an actuarial valuation is allocated on a level basis over the earnings or service of the individual between the valuation date and the assumed retirement date. The portion of this actuarial present value, which is allocated to the current year, is called the normal cost. The actuarial accrued liability is determined using the unit credit actuarial cost method. Under this method, the actuarial gains (losses), as they occur, reduce (increase) the unfunded actuarial accrued liability. The differences that regularly arise between the normal cost under this method and the normal cost under the unit credit actuarial cost method will affect the determination of future actuarial gains (losses). Under a variation of this method, the frozen attained age actuarial cost method, the actuarial gains (losses) as they occur, reduce (increase) future normal costs.

Aggregate Method. The excess of the actuarial present value of projected benefits of the group included in an actuarial valuation over the attained value of assets, using the aggregate method, is allocated on a level basis over the earnings or service of the group between the valuation date and assumed exit. This allocation is performed for the group as a whole, not as a sum of individual allocations, as is done in other methods. That portion of the actuarial present value allocated to a valuation year is called the normal cost. The actuarial accrued liability is equal to the actuarial value of assets. Hence, by definition, no unfunded liability ever exists. Under this method, the actuarial gains (losses), as they occur, reduce (increase) future normal costs.

Inflation may alter the value of pension-fund assets already invested in different financial instruments, as well as the rate of return on those investments.

An increased rate of inflation increases the effective corporate income tax rate because, in periods of rising prices, the rules for calculating business expenses generally understate depreciation allowances and the material costs of the products sold. The offsetting effect from the decline in the real value of corporate liabilities is not expected to be great enough to offset the increase in the effective tax rate. This higher effective tax rate reduces the real return on corporate equity, and stock prices fail to maintain the former real rate of return. Consequently, a pension fund holding corporate equities suffers a capital loss.

For the same reason, historically, investment in bonds has not provided pension funds with yields that compensate for inflation. Holders of outstanding corporate liabilities may suffer a capital loss from increased inflation, but some ambiguity exists about the yields on new issues.

Potential Solutions

One proposed method for maintaining real rates of return in the face of inflation is to give pension plans access to index bonds whose nominal return is fully indexed to the inflation rate so that a constant real rate of return is guaranteed. Financial investments in indexed domestic corporate bonds are not currently available.

Although it is possible for the federal government to issue such bonds, this could disrupt capital markets. It is possible that the real yield for such securities would be driven to zero or actually become negative; in this case, pension funds' financial position may not change at all. New capital market innovations, such as index bonds, stand little chance of being authorized.

Other potential solutions to the inflation problem for private pensioners have been discussed, including:

- Provision of a maximum annual adjustment;
- Recognition of a CPI change in excess of same base rate;
- Adjustment of benefits based on a fraction of CPI change; and
- Application of a fully indexed increase to the first X dollars of pension benefits.

These adjustments would lead to higher costs for the plan sponsor that might result in lower initial benefits in the future.

The present practice of ad hoc increases may actually be the best approach, allowing the sponsor to respond when financially able. Over three-fourths of plan sponsors do provide ad hoc increases.

Actuarial Simulations

The purpose of the actuarial process for defined benefit pension plans is to allow management to allocate costs in a systematic and manageable way over time. Each of the actuarial methods previously described creates a different picture of liabilities over time and a different flow of contributions.

Simulations can be done with ease, given the present state of computers. The actuarial assumptions previously noted can be varied for each model. This allows a company to assess how much contributions would change if the interest assumption were raised, for example, from 7 to 9 percent. The same testing can be done of all assumptions.

Pension decisions are increasingly being pushed into the financial realm, with an eye toward effects on the balance sheet and the bottom line. As a result, simulations are also being used to assess the ability of certain investment strategies to stabilize and lower the level of plan contributions over time; for example, the technique of bond immunization (see the next section).

PLAN ASSET MANAGEMENT

Investment Objectives

The particular objectives of trusteed private pension plans may vary, depending on the individual plan, but all have these primary objectives:

- Preservation of capital — short-run fluctuations in the value of the portfolio are not critical, but the long-run goal of assuring participants' benefits is paramount.

- Assurance of long-term growth of portfolio value — accumulated reserves are expected to grow through compounding of income and new contributions, to assure that participants' benefit payments can be met.

It is also important to note that plan investment objectives and policy are related to the requirements of the prudent man rule under ERISA; the primary goal is to protect the interests of beneficiaries and participants in the plan.

Supplementary objectives include diversification to minimize the risk of loss, and protection against inflation to preserve the value of the portfolio over the long term. Liquidity, immediate recovery of principal, is not important for most funds, since generally only a small portion of plan participants are retired beneficiaries drawing benefits from the fund. The amount of annual distributions from the plan can be projected with some certainty; thus, cash flow needs from the portfolio are easily managed.

Developing an investment policy can help to meet plan objectives. The investment policy is generally a formal statement outlining factors pertinent to the plan's objectives.

Beyond the basics, such as the plan's purpose (providing pension income), the type of plan, and the plan's age, factors such as industry characteristics (whether static, declining, or growing) and company characteristics/financial status, all have an influence on the plan's investment posture.

Work force characteristics play an important part in setting investment policy, since they relate to short- and long-term liquidity needs. Key factors include: work force growth or decline (and at what rate), employee attitudes towards early retirement, distribution of work force ages, and average retirement age.

The actuarial interest assumption is another crucial factor in investment policy decisions, since it refers to the actuary's best estimate of factors needed to determine the amount and timing of expected benefits, thus significantly affecting the company's level and timing of contributions to the plan. Vesting provisions of the plan also affect liquidity needs and should be considered in the context of investment policy.

Investment restrictions, beyond those of ERISA, may also be factored into investment policy decisions. These restrictions might include international investments, investments with social criteria, limits on mortgages, small firm stocks, or holdings in certain industries. A clearly defined list of restrictions helps to direct the investment manager.

Investment return objectives constitute another aspect of overall investment policy. Rate-of-return goals should include overall fund performance over predetermined time frames, and should also be segmented by each portfolio component (e.g., stocks and bonds). These returns are most useful when compared to the actuarial assumption, the CPI, and several relevant national indexes. These combined measures will help realistically to evaluate the performance of the fund and its manager(s).

The Prudent Man Rule

Part of ERISA's mandate includes standards of fiduciary conduct, known as the prudent man rule.[6] Under this rule, fiduciaries include anyone exercising discretionary authority or control with respect to the management of a plan or its assets. Thus, those encompassed within this rule may be officers and directors of a plan, members of a plan's investment committee, designated plan trustees, and investment managers who have been delegated responsibility for managing plan assets.

The prudent man rule may be summarized as follows:

1. The fiduciary shall discharge his duties solely in the interest of the participants and beneficiaries and —

   a. for the exclusive purpose of:

      i. providing benefits to participants and their beneficiaries; and

      ii. defraying reasonable expenses of administering the plan;

   b. with the care, skill, prudence, and diligence under circumstances then prevailing that a prudent man acting in a like capacity and familiar with such matters would use in the conduct of an enterprise of a like character and with like aims;

   c. by diversifying the investments of the plans as to minimize the risk of large losses, unless under the circumstances it is clearly prudent not to do so; and

   d. in accordance with the documents and instruments governing the plan insofar as such documents and instruments are consistent with the provisions of ERISA.

---

6 ERISA § 404(a)(1)(B), 88 Stat. 829 (1974), 29 U.S.C. § 1104(a)(1)(B).

Upon the enactment of ERISA, trustees feared that taking factors into consideration other than immediate net return on the individual investment might not qualify under the "exclusive benefit to plan participants and their beneficiaries" covenant.

Final regulations issued by the Department of Labor, however, alleviated these concerns. These regulations implied that the relative riskiness of a *specific* investment or investment course of action does not render such investment either prudent or imprudent.[7]

In addition, the regulations noted that the prudence of an investment decision should not be judged without regard to the role that the investment plays within the overall plan portfolio.

The fiduciary requirements of the prudent man rule under these regulations will be satisfied if the fiduciary has given appropriate consideration to the facts and circumstances regarding a particular investment.

"Appropriate consideration" includes:

1. A determination by the fiduciary that the proposed investment is reasonably designed as part of the portfolio; that the fiduciary has considered the risk of loss and the opportunity for gain associated with the investment; and

2. Consideration of the following factors as they relate to the investment:

   a. the composition of the portfolio with regard to diversification;

   b. the liquidity and current return of the portfolio relative to the anticipated cash flow requirements of the plan; and

   c. the projected return of the portfolio relative to the funding objectives of the plan.

Prohibited Transactions

Sections 406 and 407 of ERISA are designed to prevent conflicts of interest between persons having relationships with pension plans. These persons, known as parties-in-interest, include fiduciaries, counsel, or employees of the plan, persons providing services to the plan, the employer of any employees covered by the plan, an employee organization with members covered by the plan, and several other special categories of persons.

Plan fiduciaries are prohibited from causing the plan to engage in any of five types of direct or indirect transactions between the plan and a party-in-interest, if the fiduciary knows the nature of the transaction. These five types of transactions are:

- Sale, exchange, or lease of any property;
- Lending of money or extension of credit;
- Furnishing of goods, services, or facilities;
- Transfer to, or use by, or for the benefit of a party-in-interest, plan assets;
- Acquisition or retention of any employer security or employer real property in violation of Section 407(a) of ERISA.

---

[7] Department of Labor Regulations, ERISA §§ 2250, 404a-1, 42 Fed. Reg. 54,122.

There are several statutory exemptions to the prohibited transactions provisions that cover a wide range of investments and activities. These include a maximum 10 percent limitation on the amount of pension-plan assets invested in qualifying employer securities, and qualifying employer property, as defined in Section 407(d) of ERISA.

Other exemptions extend to use of certain pooled funds run by potential parties-in-interest (such as banks), advisory services provided by securities broker-dealers, and other related service operations.

Plans may also apply to the Department of Labor for individual exceptions on particular transactions.

ERISA affected pension-plan operations in other ways, such as funding requirements and contribution limits, which are explained earlier in the chapter.

Social Investing and the Prudent Man Rule

The fidicuary responsibilities of trustees under the prudent man rule have raised many concerns over the role of socially responsible investments in a pension portfolio.[8]

The phrase social investing can be interpreted in many different ways. It has been classified within three categories:

1 Totally neutral investment policies, focusing purely on financial factors;

2 Socially sensitive investment policies, which include factors other than traditional investment criteria as secondary considerations;

3 Socially dictated investment policies, which sacrifice safety, return, marketability, or diversification to serve some particular objective.

Social investments can take three major forms:

1 Inclusionary investments, where a particular investment is made for its social impact;

2 Exclusionary investments, where a particular investment is either removed from a portfolio or not made because of its implications (e.g., an investor that bars all investments in companies with interests in South Africa because of apartheid is following an exclusionary approach);

3 Investments made for proxy purposes, where the investor wishes to exert influence through voting control of outstanding common stock, to achieve a desired outcome on a particular issue or transaction.

Interpretations of the prudent man rule as applied to social investing have permitted such investments when social considerations are secondary to financial returns. Investments made have, for the most part, been inclusionary in nature. Socially dictated investment policies, which sacrifice returns, generally conflict with the intent of the prudent man rule under ERISA.

---

8 See Dallas L. Salisbury, ed., *Should Pension Assets Be Managed for Social/Political Purposes?* (Washington, D.C.: Employee Benefit Research Institute, 1980); and Salisbury, *Setting Pension Investment Policies: Joint Control and Management Issues*, Industrial Relations Research Association, Proceedings of the Thirty-Fourth Annual Meeting (Dec. 28–30, 1981).

The Investment Portfolio

The types of investments most frequently used to meet investment objectives take the form of corporate equitites and bonds, which together accounted for 77.5 percent of the total assets of private trusteed pension plans in 1981 (Table 31.7).

Small and Large Plans. Nearly every plan portfolio component varies in importance with the plan's size. Small plans (with fewer than 100 participants) hold 15.6 percent of assets in cash and other deposits, while plans with 5,000 or more participants hold only 1.6 percent of their assests in cash (Table 31.8). Holdings of U.S. government securities increase with plan size, accounting for 4.9 percent of small-plan assets and 8.4 percent of the assets of plans with 10,000 or more participants. Corporate equities are twice as important in the largest- as in the smallest-plan category for which data are available; 17 percent of the assets of plans with 100 to 499 participants are held in equities, while plans with 10,000 or more participants hold 39 percent of their assets in equities. This particular difference might be due to the larger plans' greater ability to diversify risks and, perhaps, to their greater sophistication.

Interest in pooled funds (e.g., insurance company accounts and master trusts) also varies fairly consistently with plan size, with smaller plans holding nearly twice as much of their assets in this form as larger plans. Party-in-interest investments, in turn, increase in importance with plan size, rising from 4.9 percent of smaller-plan assets to 10.2 percent of assets in the largest plans.

Defined Benefit and Defined Contribution Plans. Defined benefit and defined contribution plans exhibit different investment patterns. Although all types of large plans in a Greenwich Research Associates (GRA) survey held over 40 percent of their assets in the form of common stocks, defined contribution plans invested more heavily in the sponsor's stock (Table 31.9). Defined benefit pension plans use guaranteed investment contracts significantly less than do defined contribution plans. Profit-sharing plans invest over 20 percent of their assets in guaranteed investment contracts (GICs), and thrift plans invest over 30 percent. Defined benefit pension plans, in contrast, are more likely to invest in bonds than in GICs.

IRS data show similar differences between the investment patterns of defined benefit and defined contribution plans, though here again, IRS asset distributions differ from those available from other sources. IRS data do show, for example, that defined benefit plans, at least those with 100 or more participants, are more concentrated in corporate securities than are defined contribution plans, and that defined contribution plans invest less in bonds than do defined benefit plans (Table 31.10). IRS and GRA asset distributions are difficult to compare directly, however, because IRS data are considerably more detailed. Party-in-interest investments, for example, account for nearly 29 percent of defined contribution plan assets (Table 31.10), and these investments are distributed quite broadly across the asset spectrum. Inclusion of these assets in individual asset categories could reduce the differences between the GRA and IRS data.

(text continues on page 31-37)

TABLE 31.7 Distribution of Private Trusteed Pension Plan Assets, 1950–1981

(dollars in billions)

Year	U.S. Government Securities		Corporate Foreign Bonds		Corporate Equities		Mortgages		Currency, Deposits, and Other Assets		Total
	Total	Percent	Total	Percent	Total	Percent	Total	Percent	Total	Percent	Total
1950	$ 2.0	33.2%	$ 2.8	40.1%	$ 1.1	15.7%	$0.1	1.4%	$ 0.7	9.5%	$ 7.1
1955	3.0	16.3	7.9	42.1	6.1	33.2	0.3	1.8	1.1	5.9	18.2
1960	2.7	7.0	15.7	41.1	16.5	43.4	1.3	3.4	1.9	5.0	38.1
1965	3.0	4.1	22.7	30.8	40.8	55.4	3.4	4.6	3.8	5.2	73.6
1970	3.0	2.7	29.4	26.6	67.1	60.8	4.2	3.8	6.6	6.0	110.4
1975	10.8	7.4	35.8	24.4	88.6	60.4	2.4	1.6	9.4	6.4	146.8
1977	20.1	11.3	42.1	23.6	101.0	57.1	2.5	1.4	11.7	6.6	178.3
1980	30.9	10.8	58.1	20.3	175.8	61.3	3.7	1.3	18.4	6.4	186.8
1981	40.5	13.7	61.7	20.9	167.0	56.6	3.9	1.3	21.6	7.3	294.8

Source: Board of Governors of the Federal Reserve System, *Flow of Funds Accounts, Assets and Liabilities Outstanding*

TABLE 31.8   Percentage Distribution of Private Trusteed Pension Plan Assets, 1977(a)

Type of Investment	Number of Participants					
	Less than 100	100 to 499	500 to 999	1,000 to 4,999	5,000 to 9,999	10,000 and over
Cash and other deposits	16.8%	7.0%	4.5%	2.7%	1.8%	1.9%
Net receivables	7.8	6.7	5.8	4.9	4.3	3.2
U.S. Government securities	5.3	8.8	8.9	8.8	9.0	9.5
Municipal and state securities	N/A	0.1	0.1	0.1	0.2	0.1
Corporate debt	27.8	14.5	15.3	16.4	16.1	14.9
Stock (common and preferred)	27.8	21.1	24.9	30.4	33.1	39.2
Real estate and mortgages	3.4	1.6	1.3	1.3	1.8	3.4
Interest in pooled funds	17.3	22.8	20.8	16.5	14.1	10.6
Other loans and investments(b)	21.6	11.4	11.6	10.0	9.5	5.5
Party-in-interest investments(c)	N/A	6.0	6.7	8.8	10.2	11.6
Total Assets (dollars in billions)	$37.0	$18.0	$12.7	$44.5	$23.7	$129.9

(a) Totals include trusteed assets of partially insured plans. Numbers may not add due to rounding.

(b) Includes shares of registered investment company, loans other than mortgages, buildings and depreciable property, and unclassified investments

(c) Includes employee stock ownership arrangements as well as holdings of employer stock in other types of plans and holdings of employer property

Source: Internal Revenue Service disclosure data; Employee Benefit Research Institute tabulations

TABLE 31.9 Percentage Distribution of Plan Assets Among Types of Investments by Plan Type, 1980

Type of Investments	Defined Benefit Plans	Profit-Sharing Plans	Savings and Thrift Plans
Common stock			
Sponsor's stock	1.1%	19.6%	35.3%
Other common	46.3	21.3	11.7
Bonds	21.4	12.1	6.3
Guaranteed investment contracts	8.1	27.1	35.1
Insured benefits	5.2	1.0	2.5
Real estate	2.2	1.0	—
Cash and equivalents	14.4	15.0	7.2
Other assets	1.4	1.0	0.7

Source: Greenwich Research Associates, *Large Corporation Pension Plans — 1982 Report to Participants* (Greenwich, Conn.: GRA, 1983).

TABLE 31.10 Percentage Distribution of Private Pension Plan Assets in Defined Benefit and Defined Contribution Plans, 1977[a]

Asset Type	Defined Benefit Plans		Defined Contribution Plans	
	Small[b]	Large[b]	Small	Large
Cash and other deposits	14.7%	1.8%	15.6%	3.7%
Net receivables	5.8	3.2	7.8	4.9
U.S. government securities	5.9	7.8	4.6	8.3
Municipal and state securities	N/A	0.1	N/A	.2
Corporate debt	20.1	15.1	28.3	7.2
Stocks (common and preferred)	20.1	31.8	28.3	21.3
Real estate and mortgages	2.3	2.5	3.5	1.5
Interest in pooled funds	18.2	12.8	15.3	7.3
Other loans and investments[c]	17.4	5.9	21.2	9.2
Party-in-interest investments[d]	N/A	2.9	N/A	28.9
Unallocated insurance contracts	15.6	16.1	3.3	7.4
Total assets (dollars in billions)	$11.8	$210.0	$27.2	$62.2

(a) Excludes insured plans funded through allocated insurance contracts

(b) Small plans have fewer than 100 participants; large plans have 100 or more.

(c) Includes shares of registered investment companies, loans other than mortgages, buildings, and depreciable property, and unclassified investments.

(d) Includes employee stock ownership arrangements as well as holdings of employer securities in other types of plans and holdings of employer property.

Sources: Internal Revenue Service disclosure data; Employee Benefit Research Institute tabulations

TABLE 31.11 Dollar and Percentage Distribution of Life Insurance Company Assets and Assets Held in Pension Reserves, 1950–1980(a)

Year	Government Securities		Corporate Bonds		Corporate Equities		Mortgages and Real Estate		Other Assets		Total	Insurance Company Assets Held in Pension Reserves	
	Total	Percentage	Total	Percentage	Total	Percentage	Total	Percentage	Total	Percentage	Total	Total	Percentage
1950	$16.1	25.2%	$ 23.2	36.3%	$ 2.1	3.3%	$ 17.5	27.3%	$ 5.0	7.9%	$ 64.0	$ 5.6	8.8%
1955	11.8	13.1	35.9	39.7	3.6	4.0	61.5	35.5	7.0	7.7	90.4	11.3	12.5
1960	11.8	9.9	46.7	39.1	5.0	4.2	45.5	38.0	10.5	8.8	119.6	18.9	15.8
1965	11.9	7.5	58.2	36.7	9.1	5.7	64.7	40.8	14.9	9.3	158.4	27.4	17.2
1970	11.1	5.3	73.1	35.3	15.4	7.4	80.7	38.9	27.0	13.1	207.3	41.2	19.9
1975	15.2	5.2	105.8	36.6	28.1	9.7	98.8	34.1	41.4	14.4	289.3	72.2	25.0
1977	23.6	6.7	137.9	39.2	33.8	9.6	107.9	30.7	—	—	—	101.5	28.9
1980	33.0	6.9	179.6	37.5	47.4	9.9	146.1	30.5	73.1	15.2	479.2	165.8	34.6

(a) Includes general and separate accounts. Totals do not add to 100 percent due to exclusion of miscellaneous assets.

Sources: American Council of Life Insurance, 1981 Life Insurance Fact Book and 1981 Pension Facts (Washington, D.C.: ACLI, 1982).

TABLE 31.12   Investment of Life Insurance Company Separate Accounts Used Solely for Group Pension Contracts, 1980

(dollars in billions)

Accounts Invested Primarily In	Total	Percentage
Common stocks	$14.4	46.6%
Publicly traded bonds and private replacement debt	2.9	9.4
Real property and real estate mortgages	5.0	16.2
Short-term investments	1.4	4.5
Mixed portfolio (common stocks and publicly traded bonds)	1.4	4.5
Other	5.8	18.8
Total	$30.9	100.0%

Source: American Council of Life Insurance, *1981 Pension Facts* (Washington, D.C.: ACLI, 1982).

Insured Plans. Pension plans (defined benefit and defined contribution) managed by life insurance companies are managed either as part of their general investment accounts or in separate accounts. Insurance company general accounts are invested to meet anticipated life insurance, annuity, and pension obligations. Pension assets managed as part of a general investment account must therefore meet insurance company investment and reserve requirements specified in state laws. Those managed in separate accounts, however, are not commingled with the general assets of the insurer; and thus are not subject to the limitations imposed by insurance regulation.

In 1980, pension assets accounted for almost 30 percent of insurance company general accounts and over 80 percent of separate accounts. Almost 20 percent of pension assets managed by insurance companies are held in separate accounts.

Over two-thirds of general accounts assets are invested in fixed-income securites, such as corporate bonds and mortgages (Table 31.11). Corporate equities represent only about 10 percent of insurance company assets.

Several accounts permit insurance companies to make a broader range of investments than do general accounts. Perhaps for this reason, the investment patterns of pension funds invested in separate accounts resemble those of private trusteed plans. Like trusteed plans, pension plans held in separate accounts are heavily invested in common stocks and corporate debt, with nearly two-thirds of total assets held in this form (Table 31.12). Unlike trusteed plans, however, pension plans invested in separate accounts held over 16 percent of total assets in mortgages and real property in 1980, while trusteed plans held only over 3 percent.

New significance has been accorded old investment vehicles, and new vehicles and techniques have been developed to meet pension funds' special needs in the rapidly evolving capital markets. Some of these are described as follows:

- *Short-term investments.* Many investors have invested in short-term securities such as Treasury bills, commercial paper, certificates of deposit, bankers' acceptances, and repurchase agreements. These securities are purchased directly from issuers or through funds that sell shares in a portfolio of short-term securities.

- *Options and futures contracts.* When common stock and long-term bonds display relatively poor performance, some investors purchase and sell options and futures contracts as a way to augment the inflation-adjusted performance of the underlying security. The use of options and futures contracts is becoming more prevalent among pension funds.

- *Participant-directed accounts* permit participants in profit-sharing and thrift plans to select alternative investment vehicles for their pension accounts. Typically allowing a choice of stock, bond, and money market funds, this approach shifts some of the pension fiduciary burden to the participants, while permitting individuals to chose pension investments that complement other forms of individual savings.

- *Bond immunization* is a technique that permits a pension-plan sponsor to purchase a portfolio of corporate or government bonds that is carefully matched in maturity and return to its maturing pension obligations. This technique requires the isolation of pension liabilities by year of maturity. It also requires detailed information on a large number of long- and short-term bonds so that sponsors can select the appropriate bonds for purchase.

- *Original issue discount bonds (OIDs)* are long-term bonds with relatively low or zero coupons that are sold at substantial discounts, generally 40 to 60 percent of par. They have been issued by firms seeking lower interest costs, including the tax advantages of amortizing the difference between discount and par over the life of the bond. Pension funds benefit because these bonds are only redeemable at par, thus reducing the risk of redemption prior to maturity and reducing investment risk. Because OIDs permit investors to lock in reinvestment rates, some pension plans use them as a form of guaranteed investment contract.

- *Guaranteed investment contracts* promise a fixed rate of return annually. Some contracts offer a rate of return that is adjusted in relation to movements in the CPI. Pension plans have purchased these contracts to reduce the volatility of their portfolios and to reduce the reinvestment risk of fixed income securities.

- *Mortgage pass-through securities* provide to investors a share in a pool of residential mortgages. Although many institutions purchase these securities, pension funds have not been major purchasers. The Government National Mortgage Association mortgage securities, backed by federally insured loans, have grown rapidly in recent years. The Federal National Mortgage Association is also packaging and selling pools of conventional mortgages using pass-through securities. Private firms have also begun to pool residential mortgages for resale to institutional investors such as pension plans and insurance companies.

- *Real Property.* During recent periods of high inflation, many investors have directly purchased real property. Pension fund managers are increasingly interested in real-property investments, particularly real estate, though this interest may have peaked. Because these investments provide claims on tangible assets, they may retain their value during a period of inflation, but they may also be fairly volatile.

half the amount of the participant's benefit. In return for the death benefit protection, the amount of the participant's benefit usually is reduced when benefits begin. A participant who does not want the benefit at retirement must take action under the terms of the plan to elect an alternative method of receiving benefits.

Plans are also required, in some situations, to make available death benefit protection for participants who die after meeting the plan's early retirement conditions but before actual retirement. Again, employers are permitted to reduce participants' benefits to cover the cost of this protection.

Plan participants must be given a notice explaining both of these provisions in detail. The provisions are included in plans in an effort to avoid situations in which a participant unknowingly leaves a surviving spouse with no income.

Minimum Benefit Standards. ERISA imposes a standard that plans must meet for the rate at which benefits are earned by participants. In general, benefits must be earned evenly over the course of the participant's period of plan participation. ERISA deals only with the rate at which the benefits are earned; it does not deal specifically with the levels of benefits employers may provide through their retirement plans.

TEFRA also created a requirement that "top-heavy" plans provide participants with a minimum benefit. Regulations are yet to be issued specifying the benefit levels.

Protection of Participants. Plans are required to have an appeals procedure that participants can follow if a claim to all or any part of their benefit is denied. Participants must be given a written explanation of the reason for the denial, and then have the right to request a reconsideration of the decision. If the claim is still denied, the participant has the right to file suit in federal or state court to enforce it.

ERISA prohibits anyone, including the employer, from discriminating against a participant who has exercised his rights under the law, this section or any other. If a participant is fired or otherwise discriminated against for exercising his rights, he may seek assistance from the Department of Labor or file suit in a federal court.

GUARANTEES AND PLAN TERMINATIONS

Pension Guarantees

While the funding process is the most important way to assure benefit security in private sector retirement programs, defined benefit plan pension benefits are also guaranteed by the PBGC. The PBGC guarantees most of the benefits of defined benefit private pension plans but does not cover defined contribution plans or public-employer plans.

Most defined benefit pension plans pay premiums to the PBGC based upon the number of plan participants. These premiums are intended to be sufficiently adequate to assure the PBGC's continued operation on an independent basis. While it receives no federal appropriations, the PBGC does have the authority to borrow up to $100 million from the Treasury.

Vested retirement benefits in terminated single-employer plans were guaranteed up to $1,381 per month in 1982. The guarantee limit is adjusted upward annually to reflect increases in the Social Security wage base. The guaranteed benefits are subject to certain limits, including amendment phase-in rules, and cover temporary supplemental benefits payable until Social Security commences.

Plan termination triggering PBGC payments can arise under different circumstances:

- *Voluntary plan termination* occurs whenever the employer has permanently discontinued or announced its intent to discontinue all contributions to the plan. A termination notice must be filed with the PBGC.

- *Involuntary plan termination* can be ordered by a federal court whenever the PBGC finds that a plan is not meeting minimum funding standards; continued operation of the plan increases the potential loss to the PBGC; the plan is unable to pay benefits; or $10,000 or more in benefits is distributed to an owner of the sponsoring firm. Plan termination is not mandatory; however, the PBGC has considerable latitude in determining whether an unstable plan should continue operation.

In the event that plan assets are insufficient to meet the benefit obligations of a terminated plan, the sponsoring employer must pay the plan up to 30 percent of its net worth. This obligation is equivalent in priority to a tax lien, and thus potentially affects the credit standing of the plan sponsor.

SUGGESTED READING

Accounting and Reporting by Defined Benefit Pension Plans. Financial Accounting Standards Board, Statement of Financial Accounting Standards Number 35. Stamford, Conn.: 1980.

Allen, Everett T., et al. *Pension Planning. Pensions, Profit Sharing, and Other Defined Compensation Plans*. Homewood, Ill.: Richard D. Irwin, 1976.

American Council of Life Insurance. *Pension Facts 1982*. Washington, D.C.: American Council of Life Insurance, 1983.

Bankers Trust Company. *Corporate Pension Plan Study. A Guide for the 1980's*. New York: Bankers Trust, 1981.

———. *A Review and Comparison of Employee Savings Plans*. New York: Bankers Trust, 1979.

Bassett, Preston C., and Mario Leo. *Financial Aspects of Private Pension Plans*. New York: Financial Executives Research Foundation, 1975.

A Bibliography of Research: Retirement Income and Capital Accumulation Programs. Employee Benefit Research Institute, Educational Pamphlet. Washington, D.C.: 1981.

The Conference Board. *Profile of Employee Benefits*. New York: The Conference Board, 1982.

Cooper, Robert, and Melody Carlsen. *Pension Fund Operations and Expenses — A Summary Report*. Brookfield, Wis.: International Foundation of Employee Benefit Plans, 1980.

Coopers & Lybrand. *Employer Accounting for Pension Costs and Other Post-Retirement Benefits*. New York: Financial Executives Research Foundation, 1981.

Cottle, Sidney, et al. *Pension Asset Management: The Corporate Decision*. New York: Financial Executives Research Foundation, 1980.

Defined Benefit and Defined Contribution Plans: Understanding the Differences. Employee Benefit Research Institute, Educational Pamphlet. Washington, D.C.: 1981.

The Employee Retirement Income Security Act. Employee Benefit Research Institute, Educational Pamphlet. Washington, D.C.: 1981.

The Flexible Compensation Plan. Employee Benefit Research Institute, Educational Pamphlet. Washington, D.C.: 1981.

Greenwich Research Associates. *Large Corporate Pension Funds — 1981 Report to Participants*. Greenwich, Conn.: Greenwich Research Associates, 1982.

Hewitt Associates. *1982 Profit Sharing Survey — 1981 Experience*. Chicago: Profit Sharing Council of America, 1982.

Howard, Bion B. *A Study of the Financial Significance of Profit Sharing, 1958–1977*. Chicago: Profit Sharing Council of America, 1979.

Integrating Pension Plans with Social Security. Employee Benefit Research Institute, Educational Pamphlet. Washington, D.C.: 1981.

Johnson and Higgins. *Funding Costs and Liabilities of Large Corporate Pension Plans*. 1981 Executive Report. New York: 1982.

Korczyk, Sophie M. *Retirement Income Opportunities in an Aging America: Pensions and the Economy*. Washington, D.C.: Employee Benefit Research Institute, 1982.

Latimer, M. W. *Industrial Pension Systems in the United States and Canada*. New York: Industrial Relations Counselors, Inc., 1933.

Logue, Dennis E. *Legislative Influences on Corporate Pension Plans*. Washington, D.C.: American Enterprise Institute, 1971.

Mamorsky, Jeffrey D. *Pension and Profit Sharing Plans — A Basic Guide*. New York: Executive Enterprise Publications, 1977.

McGill, Dan. *Fundamentals of Private Pensions*. Homewood, Ill.: Richard D. Irwin, 1971.

———. *Social Security and Private Plans: Competitive or Complementary?* Homewood, Ill.: Richard D. Irwin, 1977.

Metzger, Bert. *Profit Sharing in 38 Large Companies*. Evanston, Ill.: Profit Sharing Research Foundation, 1978.

The Multiemployer Plan. Employee Benefit Research Institute, Educational Pamphlet. Washington, D.C.: 1981.

Myers, Robert J. *Indexation of Pension and Other Benefits*. Homewood, Ill.: Richard D. Irwin, 1978.

The Pension Plan. Employee Benefit Research Institute, Educational Pamphlet. Washington, D.C.: 1981.

The Profit Sharing Plan. Employee Benefit Research Institute, Educational Pamphlet. Washington, D.C.: 1980.

Salisbury, Dallas L. "The Private Pension System in the United States." *Benefits International* (Sept. 1982), p. 5.

Salisbury, Dallas L., ed. *America in Transition: Implications for Employee Benefits.* Washington, D.C.: Employee Benefit Research Institute, 1982.

———. *Economic Survival in Retirement: Which Pension Is For You?* Washington, D.C.: Employee Benefit Research Institute, 1982.

———. *Should Pension Assets Be Managed for Social/Political Purposes?* Washington, D.C.: Employee Benefit Research Institute, 1980.

Schieber, Sylvester. *Social Security: Perspectives on Preserving the System.* Washington, D.C.: Employee Benefit Research Institute, 1982.

———, and Patricia George. *Retirement Income Opportunities in an Aging America: Coverage and Benefit Entitlement.* Washington, D.C.: Employee Benefit Research Institute, 1981.

Schulz, James. *Pension Integration: Concepts, Issues, Proposals.* Washington, D.C.: Employee Benefit Research Institute, 1983.

The Social Security Program. Employee Benefit Research Institute, Educational Pamphlet. Washington, D.C.: 1981.

Treynor, Jack, et al. *The Financial Reality of Pension Funding under ERISA.* Homewood, Ill.: Richard D. Irwin, 1976.

U.S. Chamber of Commerce. *Employee Benefits 1981.* Washington, D.C.: U.S. Chamber of Commerce, 1982.

32

Asset/Liability Management in Financial Institutions

E. Michael Caulfield

A significant challenge confronting financial institutions is the management of assets and funds in an environment of deregulation, competitive pressures, interest rate volatility, and periodic stress in worldwide credit markets. In this environment, asset/liability managers must deal with both interest rate and liquidity exposure in situations where one mistake could irreparably damage the institution. At the same time, overly conservative management practices can be a major drawback because effective and aggressive management can be a powerful competitive weapon and is often an important prerequisite to financial success.

The concept and practice of asset/liability management means different things to different people in the financial industry. As used here, asset/liability management deals with the management of the entire balance sheet in an integrated fashion. As such, it encompasses such topics as liquidity management, interest rate risk management, and capital management.

A HISTORICAL PERSPECTIVE

The practice of asset/liability management can largely be viewed as a response to the focal concerns of the period. A recurring requirement is the management of liquidity: providing the ability to meet commitments, whether these arise from creditors or depositors, for funds at a reasonable cost.

Asset Management

Through the late 1960s, the management of liquidity at large institutions occurred on the asset side of the balance sheet. Liquidity requirements were largely satisfied by investing a specified portion of funds in money market instruments and marketable securities, including obligations of the U.S. Treasury and state and local municipalities. Portfolio securities were bought and held until they either matured or were sold to meet liquidity needs. Much of the discussion and research focused on managing the investment portfolio and developing optimal strategies to increase portfolio returns relative to maturity constraints dictated by liquidity requirements. Portfolio management approaches that were practiced and debated included "ladders" (whereby portfolio maturities are evenly spaced) and "dumbbells" (whereby maturities are split between very short maturities, such as those under 3 years, and very long maturities, such as those over 20 years). These liquidity management approaches are still used by many smaller institutions.

Beginning in the early 1970s, both investment portfolio research and practice shifted to emphasizing the virtues of active portfolio management. Under active portfolio management approaches, securities are continually bought and sold (swapped) in order to maximize portfolio returns over time, again given specified risk constraints. This approach focuses on the relative value of individual securities in the portfolio, as well as the projected total holding period return of individual securities, in order to maximize return per unit of risk assumed. Various kinds of swaps are executed in order to accomplish portfolio objectives: substitution swaps involving similar securities, intermarket swaps involving instruments in different markets, rate anticipation swaps involving altering the maturity of the securities portfolio, and pure yield pickup swaps involving essentially similar securities.

Liability Management

The introduction of the negotiable certificate of deposit (CD) in 1961 by Citibank heralded a new era for financial institutions. As a money market instrument, negotiable CDs allow money center and other large regional institutions to acquire funds in the money market to meet commitments. An institution that maintains its good name in the credit markets can raise funds to finance asset growth as well as to repay maturing obligations. In this scheme, the acquisition of liabilities provides the raw material for asset expansion. At larger institutions, liability liquidity has essentially supplanted asset liquidity. Although smaller financial institutions do not have as many options for acquiring funds as do their larger counterparts, they can often issue CDs to access regional pockets of funds.

With the advent of liability management at large institutions, the management of the investment portfolio acquires an added dimension: the size of the portfolio becomes a significant variable in the investment decision. Portfolios are viewed as self-sustaining leveraged investment vehicles, and portfolio returns are evaluated against the marginal cost of financing.

Spread Management

As deposit instruments were deregulated in the late 1970s, the cost of an increasing portion of financial institution deposits became subject to open market interest rates. As a result, a large number of financial institutions, notably savings and loans (S&Ls), were caught funding fixed-rate assets (primarily long-term mortgages) with variable-rate funds when interest rates soared in the 1979–1982 time period. For many, the earnings implications of this rate mismatch were so great that they had to be bailed out by federal regulators. The lesson of the S&Ls was not lost on commercial bankers, who escaped the S&Ls' harrowing experience only by fortuitously possessing a significant amount of variable-rate assets.

As the risks associated with ignoring interest rate exposure became all too apparent in an environment of volatile interest rates, the focus of asset/liability management in the late 1970s shifted to managing and controlling the spread between asset yields and funds costs. Interest sensitivity or gap management became the dominant concept used in managing exposure to interest rates. By focusing on the interest rate pricing sensitivity of assets and liabilities and the resultant net mismatch position, the risk embedded in the balance sheet of an institution could be managed in an integrated fashion. At many institutions, significant efforts were made to capture the interest rate sensitivity profile of assets, funds, and off-balance-sheet commitments in an effort to gauge the effect of changes in short-term interest rates on the income stream of the institution.

Interest Rate Exposure Management Under Deregulation

The essence of interest rate exposure management in a deregulated environment lies in managing the net interest rate risk of a portfolio of assets and funds under liquidity constraints while simultaneously attempting to satisfy the requirements of a fickle and demanding market. The role of financial institutions as an intermediary causes a recurring interest rate risk management problem.

As Figure 32.1 illustrates, in order to fulfill most efficiently their role as an intermediary, financial institutions need to be able to warehouse funds during periods of excess liquidity to satisfy loan demand during liquidity crisis periods. Furthermore, they need to be able to transform the interest rate characteristic of funds in order to simultaneously satisfy depositors' and borrowers' rate preferences.

Customers who are users of funds often desire to borrow money at fixed interest rates for periods longer than customers who are providers of funds desire to invest (often at the perceived trough in the rate cycle). There are also occasions when the opposite problem occurs: the supply of fixed-rate long-maturity funds from investors exceeds the demand for such funds from borrowers

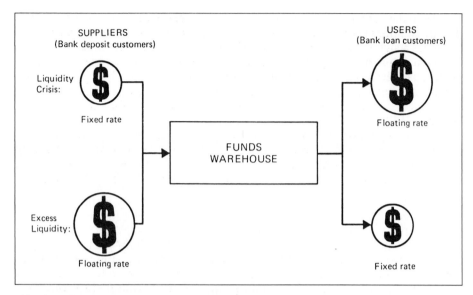

FIG. 32.1   The Financial Institution as Intermediary

(often near the perceived peak in rates). Institutions that desire to create only variable-rate assets, such as variable-rate mortgages and installment loans to match variable-rate liabilities, run the risk of alienating both customers who request fixed-rate financing and depositors who require fixed-rate investments.

Until very recently, the response to the problem of an abundance of fixed-rate funds has centered around the creative use of portfolio securities to hedge risk positions. This approach has limitations, however, due to the accounting treatment of portfolio gains and losses. The most recent and most promising response has resulted from the emergence of two off-balance-sheet tools: financial futures and interest rate swaps. These tools permit differentiation of interest rate characteristics and final maturity, thus allowing the effective interest rates of the embedded assets and funds to be transformed. This transformation enables an institution to bridge the gap between the demands of the marketplace and the objectives of management.

Recently, an integrated portfolio approach to asset/liability management has engendered some significant creative efforts in the area of applying portfolio risk management concepts, such as immunization and duration, to the problem of managing risk exposure.[1] This approach compares the duration of assets to that of liabilities in order to estimate the effect of a change in interest rates on the net market value of the asset/liability portfolio. Using this approach, some

---

[1] *Duration* is defined as the average maturity of the present values of a stream of cash payments and can be viewed as a measure of the price elasticity of an asset or liability for a given change in the rate used to discount the cash flows. Two assets or liabilities with identical durations will experience the same price change for a given change in interest rates. Duration concepts are widely used in attempts to "immunize" fixed-income portfolios; that is, achieve a predetermined rate of return over a specific time horizon.

theorists have argued that the duration of assets should always be shorter than that of liabilities; for example, financial institutions must be asset sensitive in order to stabilize the market value of the firm's shareholders equity over a complete interest rate cycle. The underlying theory holds that higher levels of income in periods of high interest rates are required to offset the market's higher required rate of return and that lower levels of income during periods of low interest rates will be neutralized by a reduction in the required rate of return.

In a deregulated environment, asset/liability management emphasizes the formulation of creative strategies and tactics that respond to a demanding marketplace, as well as the deliberate structuring and management of investment and funding activity to maximize profit within acceptable risk parameters.

ASSET/LIABILITY MANAGEMENT CONCEPTS

The objective of asset/liability management is the formulation of policies and the implementation of strategies that maximize returns while maintaining reasonable levels of liquidity and assuming reasonable levels of interest rate risk. From a practical standpoint, the task boils down to managing sources and uses of funds within specified risk parameters.

Liquidity Management

Financial intermediaries are in the business of investing long term and funding short term. To a greater or lesser degree, funds mature before assets and institutions assume liquidity risk arising from the requirement to roll over maturing liabilities. Consequently, the acquisition and deployment of funds must first and foremost be performed in a fashion that ensures the liquidity of the institution.

In the classic textbook definition, liquidity is the condition of having sufficient cash or liquid assets to pay debts or to assume obligations. In the real world, liquidity has been defined as something you always have until you really need it: once liquidity is perceived to be absent, it becomes a significant challenge to keep creditors at bay and keep the institution a going concern. Specific liquidity problems arise as a result of the market's lack of confidence in an institution's ability to repay debt obligations. This perception normally stems from operating losses experienced by the institution either from loan-related activity or unsuccessful interest rate or foreign exchange gambles.

The analysis of liquidity problems experienced by individual institutions is instructive because it illustrates several basic principles of managing sources and uses of funds. These principles include the following:

1 The reputation of the institution is critical in determining its access to money market sources. Management must neither engage in activity nor assume risks that could potentially blemish the institution's name in the money markets.

2 Diversification of funding sources is essential. Some investors are more sensitive than others with respect to which financial institutions they will lend money. The most sensitive will cease lending at the first sign of a problem, while others tend

to be more forgiving. The same attribute applies to markets; the domestic money market tends to be more sensitive than the Euromarket. By diversifying its funding sources, an institution can take advantage of differences in sensitivity to credit quality across markets and investors.

3 Liquidity premiums exist for a reason. Longer maturity funds will usually cost more than shorter maturity funds. However, in periods of crisis, it is reassuring to management to know that the longer maturity funds will remain within the institution. Liquidity premiums may be viewed as representing the cost of insurance for providing funds on a rainy day.

4 A certain amount of funds must be deployed in easily liquidated assets. For smaller institutions, this means that funds must be invested in short-term money market instruments such as Treasury bills, bankers acc :ptances (BAs), CDs, and Euro placements that, combined with funds sold in the federal funds market, can easily be converted into cash. For larger institutions, funds deployed as a liquidity cushion can also be invested in short-term, transaction-oriented commercial loans (money market loans) that provide for higher returns with commensurate risk, as long as these commitments can be terminated without complete damage to the lending relationship. It is important to note that these liquid investments often degrade an institution's return on assets, a situation consistent with reduced levels of risk.

Although the principles previously noted are useful in the management of required balance-sheet liquidity, liquidity management really boils down to assessing two factors: potential sources of funds and potential demand for funds that will be present in a liquidity crisis. These two factors will vary with the nature of the liquidity crisis (i.e., whether it is institution-specific or system-wide in nature).

In an institution-specific liquidity crisis, the problem confronting management lies in raising cash to meet deposit outflows as investors flee to safer havens. In preparing for this kind of crisis, a liquidity analysis is performed comparing sources of cash (primarily asset conversions) to demand for cash (cash needed to satisfy deposit outflows). All assets that can be converted into cash via maturity or sales are grouped together according to time-period availability. Simultaneously, all deposits that mature and are not likely to be rolled over are similarly grouped. The net cash difference represents the liquidity surplus (if positive) or liquidity deficit (if negative) to the institution. In the event a liquidity deficit is reported, a liquidity crisis scenario would require that the financial institution borrow either under previously arranged lines of credit or at the Federal Reserve's discount window.

In Table 32.1, the funds excess/(deficit) line shows that the cumulative demand for funds exceeds the cumulative supply of funds available from maturing assets and asset sales through the sixth month. This situation will generally occur in any institution-specific crisis. Therefore, managers should continually ensure that their institutions will have adequate outside liquidity sources in the event a crisis occurs. The approximate amount of external funding that must be located in any time period can be determined from this type of analysis.

A systemwide liquidity crisis provides for a different scenario. In this situation, many institutions are competing against one another in a mad scramble

TABLE 32.1 Institution-Specific Confidence Crisis — XYZ Bank's Maturity Schedule

(dollars in millions)

	Current Levels	Cumulative Maturing and Not "Rolled"		
		1 Month	3 Months	6 Months
Funds				
Purchased funds	$2,000	$350	$600	$ 900
"Core" funds	3,000	350	375	375
Total	$5,000	$700	$975	$1,275
Assets				
Liquid assets	$1,000	$400	$500	$ 850
All others	4,000	20	100	175
Total	$5,000	$420	$600	$1,025
Funds excess (deficit)		($280)	($375)	($ 250)

to acquire funds to fulfill surging demand for credit. The problem confronting bank management is to raise sufficient cash to finance loan growth despite a scarcity of supply.

In assessing this type of crisis, the liquidity analysis compares sources of funds (primarily liquid and marketable assets) to funds requirements (primarily incremental loan demand). One method of determining the potential increase in loans outstanding is to assess the likely usage of lines of credit and commitments based upon alternatives available to customers. This method assigns low expected utilization rates to the highest credit-quality customers and progressively higher expected utilization rates to lower credit-quality customers. This information is then combined with the institution's committed facility profile to calculate expected usage.

Table 32.2 shows a typical report used to track projected increases in loan demand in a system-wide liquidity crisis. It should be noted that medium credit-quality loans account for the majority of the increase. In general, these customers have fewer alternate sources of credit than do high credit-quality customers. From this phase of the analysis, management knows that it must acquire at least sufficient funds to allow for a $700 million increase in loan demand.

The analysis then compares the incremental funds requirement from both loans and deposit outflows (perhaps owing to a contraction in the funds market) to potential sources of cash, thereby providing a glimpse of the potential liquidity pressure on the institution by time period. The liquidity deficit largely represents the borrowing requirement at the Federal Reserve's discount window.

Table 32.3 shows that system-wide liquidity crises place pressure on institutions to locate sufficient funds to satisfy increased loan demand. It is noted that the bank's cumulative six-month net position is a deficit of $300 million. Thus, in order to satisfy loan demand, management must have ensured that

**TABLE 32.2   Systemwide Liquidity Crisis — PQR Bank's Projected
Increase in Loan Demand**

(dollars in millions)

		Commitment Usage			Loan Demand Increase	
Credit Quality	Firm Commitments	Current	"Crisis"	Increase	Amount	Percentage of Total
High	$2,000	5%	10%	5%	$100	14%
Medium	2,000	40	60	20	400	57
Low	1,000	60	80	20	200	29
Total	$5,000				$700	100%

the institution will possess sufficient strength to acquire the $300 million from outside sources without undue strain.

There is, of course, an easy answer to the problem of the amount of liquidity an institution should maintain. Many institutions have developed liquidity measures of one kind or another and use those measures to keep track of their position. These measures usually compare liquid assets to volatile sources of funds or relate volatile sources of funding to loans and investments. The following ratios are representative of the ones commonly utilized by commercial banks to evaluate liquidity exposure:

- Liquid assets/deposits + Short-term borrowings
- Purchased funds − Liquid assets/loans + Investments

TABLE 32.3   Systemwide Liquidity Crisis — Potential Liquidity Pressure

(dollars in millions)

	Cumulative Requirements/Sources		
	1 Month	3 Months	6 Months
Fund Requirements			
Loan growth	$117	$234	$ 700
Deposit outflows	50	150	300
Total	$167	$500	$1,000
Fund sources			
Liquid assets	$300	$350	$ 600
All others	20	40	100
Total	$320	$390	$ 700
Net excess (deficit)	$153	($110)	($ 300)

It is important to keep in mind that liquidity management is an art rather than a science. Liquidity management is necessarily subjective; to pretend that it is anything else would be foolish. All too often, misplaced emphasis on return on assets and shortsighted least-cost funding have left institutions with no options in liquidity crises. Clearly, liquidity is an element that must be managed with a view toward external market conditions. Sometimes one needs more; other times less will suffice. One major tool that has been utilized to help conceptualize these conditions is the interest rate cycle.

Interest Rate Cycle Management

Investment and funding decisions take place in a marketplace in which the forces of supply and demand for securities combine to produce a given set of interest rates. The maturity pattern of interest rates for a given type of security (such as U.S. Treasury obligations) can be depicted by plotting the yields for these securities for varying maturities. This picture, known as a yield curve, reflects two factors: the market's expectation of the future level of short-term interest rates and the liquidity premium demanded by investors. The liquidity premium exists because long maturity securities are riskier than short maturity securities (i.e., their market value is more sensitive to changes in the level of interest rates than is that of short maturity securities). Because investors demand to be compensated for assuming additional risk, a premium is added to the purely expectations-based level of interest rates, with the result that the yield curve tends to be positively sloped, with long-term rates higher than short-term rates. The magnitude of the liquidity premium is difficult to estimate and tends to vary across types of securities. Nevertheless, prior to the recent volatile rate environment, the interest rate on U.S. Treasury obligations with a maturity of six months contained a liquidity premium of approximately 25 to 50 basis points versus the same obligation with a maturity of three months.

The shape of the yield curve tends to fluctuate with the business cycle. At troughs in the cycle, the yield curve tends to be positively sloped due to both the liquidity and the future rate expectation factors. At peaks in the interest rate cycle, although liquidity considerations continue to exert a positive influence, expectations of lower future interest rates are often sufficiently strong to produce a flat, or even a negatively sloped, yield curve.

Asset/liability managers are often tempted to take advantage of positively sloped yield curves by investing long (at fixed rates) and funding short. Although this strategy can be profitable in the short run, it is important to note that, to the extent that the market's implicit forecast of increasing short-term interest rates is realized, diminishing funding spreads will be experienced. Over time, consistently employing this type of strategy will allow the institution to earn nothing more than the embedded liquidity premium. When the yield curve is inverted (negatively sloped), asset/liability managers are similarly tempted to take advantage of the shape of the curve by funding long and investing short. This strategy contains the additional attraction of adding liquidity to the balance sheet by locking up long maturity funds. Of course, the risk in this approach derives from the fact that market expectations call for declining short-term interest rates. A decision to fund with long maturities could result in an institution holding extremely costly funds as asset yields decline.

The market's expectation of the future level of short-term interest rates embedded in the yield curve is referred to as the implied forward rate. By computing the implied forward rate, management can compare its own forecast of interest rates to the market's projection (see Chapters 6 and 13).[2] This comparison facilitates the evaluation of the effects of investment and funding strategies. Because risk management decisions are performed at the margin, strategies designed to incur interest rate risk are normally implemented only if there are significant differences between market and internal interest rate expectations.

Asset/liability management decisions are influenced by anticipated changes in the level of interest rates. Over a long time frame, interest rates tend to move in a cyclical fashion, with the level largely determined by the demand for credit by business borrowers. A typical interest rate cycle has four phases: a low rate phase, a rising rate phase, a high rate phase, and a falling rate phase. As shown in Figure 32.2, there are different investment and funding strategies that should be implemented in order to maximize economic returns to the institution over the entire rate cycle.

There are probably quite a few asset/liability managers who could recite verbatim the strategies contained in Figure 32.2. Unfortunately, one finds few institutions that have been able to practice those strategies consistently. In fact, strategies practiced by the banking industry as a whole have typically been far from optimal, with wrong decisions the rule rather than the exception. To appreciate why such a state of affairs exists, one must first recognize that the predominate force that drives commercial bank income and balance-sheet activity is loan demand. Bank management's concern with providing adequate funds to fund loan growth and with providing adequate income when loans are scarce has largely dictated investment and funding strategy and has confounded asset/ liability management strategists everywhere.

When interest rates are at peak levels and securities prices are correspondingly at low levels, banks have historically tended to be net sellers of securities because funds have been needed to finance loans. Conversely, when interest rates are low and securities prices are correspondingly high, banks have tended to be net buyers of securities because they have required an investment outlet for funds in the absence of loan demand. This mistake is compounded by the temptation to extend investment portfolio maturities in search of higher yields. Although not as apparent, similar errors of judgment tend to be made in funding. At peaks in the interest rate cycle, long maturity rather than short maturity funds tend to be sought because funds are perceived to be hard to obtain and

---

[2] Given a particular yield curve, it is possible to compute the implied forward interest rate by using the following general formula:

Money Market Instruments (*Simple Interest Basis*)

$$1 + F (DF/360) = [1 + RL (DS + DF)/360]/[1 + RS (DS/360)]$$

where F = forward interest rate; RL = rate on long maturity instrument; RS = rate on short maturity instrument; DS = time period of short maturity instrument (days); and DF = time period of forward period (days).

Coupon Securities

$$(1 + F/2) \exp YF*2 = [(1 + RL/2) \exp (YS + YF)*2]/[(1 + RS/2) \exp YS*2]$$

where F = forward interest rate; RL = rate on long maturity instrument; RS = rate on short maturity instrument; YS = time period of short maturity instrument (years); YF = time period of forward period (years).

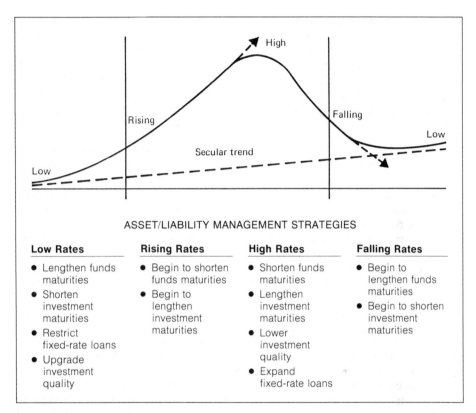

ASSET/LIABILITY MANAGEMENT STRATEGIES

Low Rates	**Rising Rates**	**High Rates**	**Falling Rates**
• Lengthen funds maturities	• Begin to shorten funds maturities	• Shorten funds maturities	• Begin to lengthen funds maturities
• Shorten investment maturities	• Begin to lengthen investment maturities	• Lengthen investment maturities	• Begin to shorten investment maturities
• Restrict fixed-rate loans		• Lower investment quality	
• Upgrade investment quality		• Expand fixed-rate loans	

FIG. 32.2 The Interest Rate Cycle

hold. At troughs in the interest rate cycle, with most institutions awash in liquidity, long maturity funds are rarely sought because few desire to pay a liquidity premium when it is deemed to be unnecessary and when bank earnings tend to be under pressure.

Asset/liability management theory suggests that bank managers structure the balance sheet to be as illiquid as possible (long maturity assets/short maturity liabilities) at the peak of the interest rate cycle and as liquid as possible (short maturity assets/long maturity liabilities) at the trough of the cycle. Unfortunately, to implement successfully the correct types of strategies in the real world requires not only that bank management possess firm convictions on the future course of interest rates but also that it possess the courage to act in the face of pressures pulling it in exactly the opposite direction.

INTEREST RATE RISK MANAGEMENT — THE MISMATCH

All financial institutions are confronted with exposure to changing interest rates to some degree. Much of this risk arises naturally out of the general course of business. First, customers are usually free to deposit funds in a multitude of deposit instruments. Moreover, borrowers often have the option of selecting from a variety of loan maturities. As we noted earlier, often the demands of customers and the requirements of depositor are diametrically opposed. Finally, financial institutions generate a significant amount of both non-interest-bearing funds and fixed rate interest bearing funds without specified final maturities. In this general process of intermediation, it is impossible for the maturity structure of assets and liabilities to coincide. As a result, changes in the level of interest rates will affect the amount of net interest income a particular institution will achieve in any given time period.

Although the sources of involuntary risk exposure are primarily located in the domestic market, the conceptual framework that has evolved to identify and manage interest rate risk — the mismatch — has its origins in the Euromarket. Offshore funding managers who are responsible for managing a pool of assets and funds (called a book) have traditionally had a relatively straight-forward task. In the Euromarket, practically all assets (in the form of either interbank placements or commercial loans) and funds (in the form of time deposits) are acquired at fixed interest rates for specified periods of time. Unlike in the domestic market, in the Euromarket it is possible for a manager to run a so-called matched book (i.e., a book in which the interest rate maturities of assets are precisely matched with those of similar liabilities).

Interest rate risk is assumed when the terms of the assets and funds do not match exactly; hence, the origin of the term "mismatch." For example, a decision to lend money for a six-month period and simultaneously to acquire funds for a three-month period would create a forward three-month gap or mismatch. In this example, interest rate risk is present because the asset yield is fixed for a six-month period, while the supporting deposit must be rolled over at an uncertain interest rate three months hence. The opposite type of mismatch would be created, for example, by taking in a three-month deposit and lending the proceeds out overnight.

By carefully monitoring the interest rate maturity structure of assets and funds, the funding manager can assess the degree of mismatch risk assumed and adjust this position by either acquiring or lending funds. A negatively gapped or mismatched book (one in which fixed-term assets exceed fixed-term liabilities) is structured to capitalize on stable (the return being the liquidity premium) or declining interest rates. Conversely, a positively gapped or mis-matched book is structured to capitalize on rising interest rates. One area of caution is important to consider: In a high rate environment, the compound interest effect on financing a six-month asset with overnight funds can fully offset the perceived spread income.[3] Although it can take a variety of forms, the monitoring and control process is usually accomplished via a gap-reporting mechanism similar to the one shown in Table 32.4.

Table 32.4 shows a negatively gapped funding book (i.e., projected term assets exceed projected term funds in most time periods). The excess term assets are to be funded with funds at unknown interest rates. As a result, the position is structured to take advantage of stable or falling interest rates.

---

[3] In order to calculate the realized spread precisely, both assets and funds must be converted to effective annual yields and costs. For example, a six-month asset earning 18 percent has an annualized yield of 18.81 percent and overnight funds costing 17 percent have an annualized cost of 18.53 percent.

TABLE 32.4 ABC Eurodollar Bank Gap Report

(dollars in millions)

		Projected Outstanding		
		Term Assets	Term Funds	Gap
Week	1	$896	$714	$182−
	2	830	665	165−
	3	809	585	224−
	4	730	513	217−
	5	676	478	198−
	6	626	409	217−
	7	593	384	209−
	8	562	336	226−
	9	519	300	219−
	10	460	282	178−
	11	428	248	180−
	12	421	243	178−
	13	395	217	178−
Month	1	804	607	197−
	2	592	376	216−
	3	429	249	180−
	4	279	174	105−
	5	250	168	82−
	6	175	106	69−
	7	100	85	15−
	8	84	83	1−
	9	79	78	1−
	10	73	74	1
	11	51	54	3
	12	47	47	—

Although each of the offshore units is viewed as a separate book, the risk positions of aggregate units are usually consolidated into one centrally managed Eurodollar book. The degree of risk in this book, and in each of its component books, is controlled through the establishment of gap limits. The magnitude of these gap limits varies with management's assessment of its ability to predict the direction of future interest rate movements. Therefore, the gap limits in nearby months are higher than those in more distant months. For example, the limits associated with the funding book in Table 32.4 might be $300 million at one month and decline to $100 million in six months.

Recently, there has been a growing tendency to apply the funding book concept to domestic risk management activities. The movement toward this approach has been driven by an increase in the proportion of money market priced assets and funds on the domestic balance sheet. This increase is primarily the result of the emergence of "cost plus" lending arrangements in the domestic market (arrangements in which commercial loans are priced at rates based on the C.D., London interbank offered rate (LIBOR), and federal funds rates instead of the prime rate) coupled with the market pricing of small denomination consumer deposits.[4] Thus, conceptually, domestic risk management has increasingly lent itself to the Eurodollar-type mismatch position management framework.

Many large institutions now run a domestic funding book that is managed in a fashion similar to a Eurodollar book. Indeed, some institutions maintain multiple domestic funding books to provide for decentralized decision making. Of course, where multiple books exist, the risk positions are ultimately consolidated into one domestic book to derive the mismatch position of the domestic funding book.

The major obstacle to managing a domestic funding book in a manner analogous to a Eurobook lies in determining the interest rate maturity of assets priced off the prime lending rate. The pricing tenor of the prime rate is impossible to determine because the prime rate is an administered rate. The prime rate changes in response to changes in money market rates, with a lag reflecting the delayed response of bank liability costs to changes in open market rates. One institution's response to the problem has been to derive a theoretical funds matching scheme based upon an examination of funding combinations that over time would have minimized the variance associated with the spread between the prime rate and the cost of matching funds. In this scheme, prime priced loans are presumed to be "match funded" with a pool consisting of 57 percent 30-day CDs and 43 percent 90-day CDs that are constantly rolled over. Once the prime rate obstacle has been overcome, a domestic funding book can be created, with a format similar to the one shown in Table 32.4.

Table 32.5 shows a domestic funding book whose risk position has been described in a manner similar to that used to describe the risk position of the Eurobook in Table 32.4, that is, the gap between assets and funds. However, it can be seen from Table 32.5 that, in calculating the gap in a domestic funding book, the funding manager must also account for prime priced assets and funds without specific maturities. As in the case of Eurobooks, the mismatched position in the domestic funding book is manipulated to take advantage of expected interest rate movements.

Mismatched positions can be broadly grouped into two categories: strategic and tactical, according to intent and duration. Strategic mismatches are implemented to take advantage of longer-term cyclical movements in interest rates. This type of mismatch position is normally created by buying investment portfolio securities and financing them with short maturity funds when interest rates are perceived to be at a cyclical peak. Long maturity funds are then used to displace these short maturity liabilities when interest rates are perceived to be at a cyclical trough. In the case of portfolio securities, the strategic mismatch created is designed to allow fixed-rate assets to be funded at progressively lower costs as interest rates decline, thereby generating wider net interest margins. In the case of long maturity funds, the mismatch is designed to allow fixed-rate funds

---

[4] LIBOR represents the rate at which banks operating in London are willing to lend funds to other top-quality banks in the interbank market.

TABLE 32.5   ABC Domestic Bank Risk Position

Projected Average Outstanding
(dollars in millions)

		Prime Priced	Term Interest-Bearing Assets	Term Interest-Bearing Funds	Funds Without Specified Maturity	Gap/ Mismatch
Week	1	$645	$2,250	$2,000	$700	$195−
	2	527	2,250	1,925	700	152−
	3	408	2,100	1,875	700	67−
	4	299	2,100	1,820	700	121
	5	201	2,095	1,780	700	184
	6	176	2,070	1,720	700	174
	7	151	2,030	1,600	700	119
	8	128	2,025	1,550	700	97
	9	104	2,025	1,500	700	71
	10	81	1,995	1,465	700	89
	11	52	1,993	1,415	700	68
	12	34	1,993	1,370	700	43
	13	10	1,993	1,315	700	12
Month	1	470	2,175	1,905	700	40−
	2	152	2,049	1,630	700	129
	3	44	1,994	1,391	700	53
	4	—	1,875	1,230	700	55
	5	—	1,874	1,125	700	49−
	6	—	1,873	1,050	700	123−
	7	—	1,872	975	700	197−
	8	—	1,846	950	700	196−
	9	—	1,845	950	700	195−
	10	—	1,814	949	700	165−
	11	—	1,813	945	700	168−
	12	—	1,793	940	700	153−
Quarter	5	—	1,775	910	700	165−
	6	—	1,720	875	700	145−
	7	—	1,690	835	700	155−
	8	—	1,575	800	700	75−

to fund assets that are progressively rolled over at higher yields as interest rates rise. Although strategic mismatches on the asset side can be implemented using a variety of instruments, such as fixed-rate term loans or tax-exempt and corporate securities, U.S. government securities are normally preferred because of their absence of credit risk, their high degree of marketability, their protection against early call or repayment, and their self-financing characteristic (i.e., they can be funded with repurchase agreements). Of course, positioning fixed-rate loans and corporate securities would require the concurrence of the lending areas because of the credit risk involved.

Tactical mismatches are implemented to capitalize on short-term (six months or less) opportunities in the money markets. These opportunities may arise as the result of differing expectations on interest rates, perceived anomolies in the shape of the yield curve, or disparities in the supply and demand for selected money market instruments.

Large institutions have a great deal of flexibility in creating tactical mismatches because of their ability to create what are essentially leveraged investment vehicles and to manage the structure of their funding. Within constraints, these institutions can acquire loans and investments as they please, knowing that these assets can be easily financed by acquiring funds in the money markets. Consequently, large institutions can create mismatches by simply electing not to acquire matching maturity funds. In the Eurodollar market, tactical mismatches are created by placing term deposits, which are funded overnight, or by acquiring longer maturity funds to fund short-dated assets. In the domestic market, tactical mismatches are frequently implemented by positioning whichever asset is perceived to be "cheapest" in a given maturity (e.g., Treasury bills, CDs, BAs, Eurodollar CDs, or Eurodollar Time Deposits) and proceeding to fund it with shorter maturity funds. The following table shows the effect of a decision to adjust the domestic risk position shown in Table 32.5 by adding $100 million in six-month Eurodollar time deposits, which are initially funded with a 30-day deposit. The $100 million additional mismatch that has been created in the two- to six-month time period is observed.

The funding book is now more negatively gapped. It should be noted that weeks 8–13 and months 3–4 are now negatively rather than positively gapped. This type of tactical mismatch might be implemented if the interest rate on the six-month Eurodollar time deposit was unusually high versus the interest rate on the one-month deposit and interest rates were expected to decline or remain stable over the next six months.

At large institutions, interest rate risk is managed from a global perspective. Domestic and Eurodollar positions are managed separately but are aggregated and reported on a consolidated basis. This type of management framework provides each funding manager with a considerable degree of autonomy while providing for a necessary measure of centralized coordination and control. Global risk reporting allows management to closely monitor corporate-wide risk, thereby ensuring that the aggregate size of the rate risk bet does not exceed acceptable parameters.

Smaller institutions do not have as many options as large money center institutions. They cannot add assets and associated funding at will. Furthermore, unlike the larger institutions, smaller institutions are deposit driven (i.e., much of their asset activity is a function of what they take in as deposits). Therefore, their interest rate risk management process focuses largely on structuring loan and investment activity to avoid undesired mismatches that arise from inflows of consumer and commercial deposits.

In recent years, as the profile of consumer deposits shifted toward shorter maturities, much of the risk management activity at smaller institutions has been oriented toward ensuring an appropriate level of variable rate assets. This process has, in many instances, resulted in new consumer products, such as

TABLE 32.6 ABC Domestic Bank Risk Position, $100 Million Additional Mismatch

Projected Average Outstanding

(dollars in millions)

		Prime Priced	Term Interest-Bearing Assets	Term Interest-Bearing Funds	Funds Without Specified Maturity	Gap/Mismatch
Week	1	$645	$2,350	$2,100	$700	$195−
	2	527	2,350	2,025	700	152−
	3	408	2,200	1,975	700	67−
	4	299	2,200	1,820	700	21
	5	201	2,195	1,809	700	113
	6	176	2,170	1,720	700	74
	7	151	2,130	1,600	700	19
	8	128	2,125	1,550	700	3−
	9	104	2,125	1,500	700	29−
	10	81	2,005	1,465	700	11−
	11	52	2,003	1,415	700	32−
	12	34	2,003	1,370	700	57−
	13	10	2,003	1,315	700	88−
Month	1	470	2,275	2,005	700	40−
	2	152	2,149	1,630	700	29
	3	44	2,094	1,391	700	47−
	4	—	1,975	1,230	700	45−
	5	—	1,974	1,125	700	149−
	6	—	1,973	1,050	700	223−
	7	—	1,872	975	700	197−
	8	—	1,846	950	700	196−
	9	—	1,845	950	700	195−
	10	—	1,814	949	700	165−
	11	—	1,813	945	700	168−
	12	—	1,793	940	700	153−
Quarter	5	—	1,775	910	700	165−
	6	—	1,720	875	700	145−
	7	—	1,690	835	700	155−
	8	—	1,575	800	700	75−

variable rate mortgages and variable rate installment loans, in addition to the standard prime priced commercial loan. However, because of insufficient demand, substantial amounts of funds are invested in both money market instruments and longer-term floating rate instruments, such as floating rate corporate notes and bank CDs, in order to mitigate mismatch risk.

In the past, smaller institutions have typically avoided running aggressively managed mismatch positions because they have been comfortable with the margin levels they have experienced by running a "neutral" risk position book. However, the continuing process of deposit deregulation has changed that situation. Because of escalating deposit costs, even small institutions now find themselves battling for incremental yield. Hence, the task confronting management is all the more formidable. Management not only must invest funds to contain mismatch risk, but must also be prepared to create and assume mismatch risk, when appropriate, to maximize income over time. Since risk management largely takes place on the asset side of the balance sheet, the maturity profile and composition of assets must be constantly evaluated against that of liabilities and must be restructured as appropriate. This task requires that cash instruments be bought and sold in an efficient fashion. Unfortunately, small institutions operating in the cash market operate at a disadvantage because of high transaction costs. However, this disadvantage largely disappears when two of the most powerful off-balance-sheet risk management tools in existence today are used: financial futures and interest rate swaps.

OFF-BALANCE-SHEET RISK MANAGEMENT TOOLS

Two risk management tools came of age in the early 1980s that provided asset/liability managers with previously unknown flexibility. Although they are very different instruments, from an asset/liability management perspective, financial futures and interest rate swaps share one common feature: they allow for the differentiation of interest rate risk and maturity risk. Using these tools enables financial institution management to manipulate the effective interest rate maturity of embedded assets and liabilities without altering the balance sheet. Most importantly, liquidity need not be sacrificed for the sake of managing interest rate exposure. The emergence of these off-balance-sheet tools now permits liquidity and interest rate risk to be managed separately.

Financial Futures

Much has been written about the development and subsequent dramatic growth of the financial futures markets (see Chapter 12). It is not the intention to review the history and evolution of these markets. However, by providing an overview of the variety of potential futures applications, some of the sense of excitement possessed by many in the business can be conveyed.

Futures markets in financial instruments have been attractive to many money market and capital market participants because they represent a relatively uncomplicated method of assuming an interest rate position. The attractions of the futures market include the absence of credit risk, a variety of contracts and delivery dates, good liquidity due to easily transferable positions, and relatively low transaction costs.

Participants can utilize futures positions either to speculate (to assume risk) or to hedge (to transfer risk to another party). A hedge is initiated by assuming an economic position in the futures market that is equal in scope but opposite in effect from the position to be hedged in the cash market. The offsetting position in futures is designed to neutralize the risk associated with holding a particular cash market position. Although hedged positions will reduce interest rate exposure, there remains some amount of residual risk known as basis risk. Basis risk stems from the fact that although cash prices and futures prices tend to move in a parallel fashion over time, they rarely move precisely in tandem.

Most financial institutions obtained their initial exposure to the futures market through their dealer activities. Short position in futures are commonly used to hedge cash market inventory positions and in conjunction with arbitrage and hedged trading activities. Some examples of these activities include selling short Treasury bill contracts to hedge a long position in cash Treasury bills and holding a long position in the 10-year Treasury note contract against a short position in intermediate-term Treasury securities. Currently, many institutions actively employ futures as a temporary substitute for anticipated asset or liability transactions. For example, futures are commonly employed when a funding manager desires to issue a large amount of CDs in anticipation of rising interest rates and is temporarily unable to do so because of market conditions. He can sell short an appropriate number of CD futures contracts to hedge his position and wait to issue CDs when market conditions improve. As interest rates rise, he can unwind his position by buying back the futures contracts. He will thereby realize a profit on the futures transaction to offset the higher cost that resulted from issuing the CDs at a later date.

From an asset/liability management perspective, there are two kinds of hedges that can be implemented using futures: asset hedges and liability hedges. An asset hedge is designed to transform the effective interest rate maturity of an asset; a liability hedge is designed to transform the effective interest rate maturity of a liability. Conceptually, the process is relatively straightforward. To extend the effective maturity of an asset, futures contracts are bought; to reduce the maturity of an asset, futures contracts are sold. Conversely, to extend the effective maturity of a liability, futures contracts are sold; to reduce the effective maturity of a liability, futures contracts are bought. Within this framework, the objectives and goals of management will dictate the type of hedge that is implemented. Asset or liability hedges can be conceptualized as falling into one of two categories: those designed to maintain the market value of the asset or liability and those designed to reduce net interest income risk.

Futures contracts in both short- and long-term instruments are being used by financial institutions in a variety of ways. The applications essentially fit into one of the following four categories:

Hedge Objective	Examples	Futures Position	Effect
Rate on anticipated funding	CDs, money market deposit accounts, six-month certificates, long-term debt	Short	Maturity extension
Value of existing funding	Six-month certificates, long-term CDs	Long	Maturity reduction
Rate on anticipated investment	Investment securities, money market instruments	Long	Maturity extension
Value of existing investment	GNMAs, investment securities	Short	Maturity reduction

In funds management, futures contracts are commonly used to hedge undesired maturity risk. One common application has been to change the effective maturity of consumer deposits, such as six-month money market certificates (MMCs), that must be consistently marketed for competitive reasons. When the desired maturity risk of the MMC is less than six months, Treasury bill, CD, or Eurodollar contracts can be bought to adjust that risk. For example, suppose an institution issues $10 million of six-month MMCs and desires to convert the maturity risk from 182 days to 60 days. The excess maturity risk of 122 days can be hedged by buying 13 Treasury bill contracts.[5] After 60 days have elapsed, the institution would unwind the position by selling the contracts. The gain or loss on the transaction would be amortized over the subsequent 122 days. Other common applications in the funds management area include using futures to create inexpensive synthetic variable rate CDs by issuing CDs and simultaneously buying the CD contract, and to hedge the risk associated with future requirements for fixed-rate funding either associated with forward term loan products or anticipated debt issuance.

The availability of futures contracts to manage risk eases the task of operating the funds warehouse shown in Figure 32.1. Fixed-rate term deposits can prudently be garnered at perceived peaks in the interest rate cycle to fund short-term commercial loans because effective funds maturities can be shortened. Similarly, rate sensitive deposits such as MMCs or money market deposit accounts (MMDAs) can be utilized at perceived troughs in the interest rate cycle to fund fixed-rate consumer loans because effective funds maturities can be extended.

From an asset management standpoint, futures contracts can be utilized to protect the market value of assets such as mortgages or investment securities pending sale. In addition to hedging assets acquired in the normal course of business, futures can be utilized intentionally to create short-term assets by buying deliverable securities and simultaneously selling contracts with the intention of delivering the securities. One example of this type of transaction is purchasing a Treasury bill maturing in September that is deliverable under the June contract and holding it until delivery. Such transactions are undertaken to create yields higher than those available on a comparable maturity cash market asset.

In their most powerful application, futures contracts can be utilized to adjust the effective interest rate maturity of an entire portfolio of assets and liabilities to any desired level of risk. The use of futures in this fashion is referred to as macro or strategic balance-sheet hedging (in contrast to microhedging which addresses specific components of the balance sheet). Although macrohedging is theoretically possible, there are a number of obstacles that hinder its implementation.

Because of the absence of uniform accounting rules on futures transactions, many different accounting conventions are used. For example, the Comptroller of the Currency requires national banks to utilize mark-to-market accounting whereby gains and losses on futures positions are recognized each day. On the other hand, the accounting profession believes that the accounting treatment

---

[5] In this example, excess maturity risk of 122 days is neutralized by assuming a "long" position in Treasury bill futures. Thirteen contracts are bought because the value of a Treasury bill contract reflects a $1 million 91-day instrument (122 days/91 days × 10 = 13.4 contracts).

for futures should conform to the characteristics of the assets and/or liabilities being hedged, and that deferral accounting (whereby gains and losses are not recognized until the position is closed out) should be permitted for bona fide hedges of assets/liabilities carried at cost.

As a result, many commercial banks use two sets of books, one set for regulatory reporting and one for financial reporting. The two sets are required because mark-to-market reporting will often result in substantial degrees of income volatility as interest rates fluctuate. A problem arises because macrohedges, which are implemented to adjust risk positions, contain an element of ambiguity and tend to be difficult to define concretely. Moreover, they are likely to be altered with some degree of frequency as interest rate expectations change. As a result, some accountants have suggested that macrohedge positions be accounted for on a mark-to-market basis.

Perhaps more significantly, there is no clear consensus on how to measure, let alone hedge, overall balance-sheet risk. A fundamental question related to measurement of risk is whether one should focus on the time interval mismatches and therefore attempt to hedge net interest income risk, or instead focus upon portfolio cash flow (and maturity) and attempt to hedge market valuation/economic risk. Hedge theory indicates that futures can be used to create an offsetting economic position, but there is no precise methodology for hedging risk. Unanswered questions include these: Which contracts should be utilized? Nearbys or deferreds? A strip of contracts or multiples of a single contract? Short-term contracts or weighted long-term contracts? Finally, what about basis and yield curve risk? Although using futures to immunize the balance sheet against interest rate risk is promising, much work remains to be done in this area.

As a result of these two concerns, the approach to hedging adopted by many institutions is to implement specific hedges within the context of an overall risk management framework. Many smaller institutions utilize futures to accomplish objectives that cannot be implemented in the cash market. Futures provide these institutions with a source of fixed-rate financing by allowing them to hedge the risk of rolling over shorter maturity funds. For large institutions, futures hedges are implemented as an alternative to hedges using cash market instruments. The use of futures in this fashion frequently boils down to a question of efficiency and price (relative value), and more often than not, futures win.

Interest Rate Swaps

The interest rate swap market is in a much more embryonic state than the financial futures markets. Although the first swap was probably implemented in 1979, the swap market did not become a significant market until 1982, when the volume of swap transactions reached an estimated $5 billion.

An interest rate swap is a transaction in which two parties exchange interest payments on an agreed-upon amount of underlying (notional) principal. One party agrees to pay a fixed interest rate to the other party who, in turn, agrees to pay a floating interest rate. A swap is generally contracted for a term of 3 to 10 years, with most transactions running 5 or 7 years. Interest payment

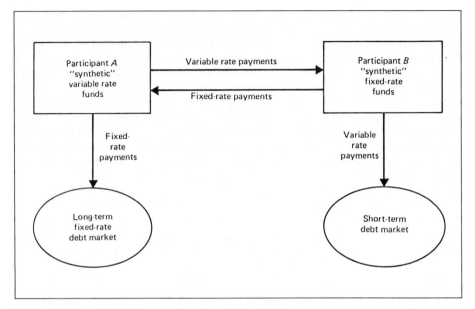

FIG. 32.3 Interest Rate Swaps: Cash Flow Schematic

obligations are settled periodically (usually every six months) by the remittance of the net obligation by one party.

The economic rationale underlying a swap transaction is straightforward. A swap attempts to match two parties that possess different *relative* financing advantages in long-term fixed-rate markets and short-term floating rate markets. One participant will normally have a significant cost advantage over the other when it comes to acquiring long-term fixed-rate funds, but will have a smaller comparative advantage in the shorter-term credit markets. By leveraging upon the ability of the more creditworthy participant to access longer-term markets, a swap allows the less creditworthy party indirectly to obtain fixed financing rates, which would otherwise be unavailable to the institution.

Figure 32.3 shows the structure of the cash flows associated with a swap. Participant *A* initially borrows in the fixed-rate market and is, therefore, able to provide fixed-rate funding for participant *B* via the swap. Similarly, participant *B* initially borrows in the variable rate market and provides variable rate funding to participant *A*. Thus, through the swap mechanism, participant *A* acquires funding at a "synthetic" variable rate while participant *B* acquires funding at a "synthetic" fixed rate. By implicitly agreeing to service one another's debt, both parties benefit from the transaction. As shown in Figure 32.4, participant *A* obtains commercial paper rate funding at a 50-basis-points saving, and participant *B* receives fixed-rate funding at a 35-basis-point cost reduction compared to alternative sources of fixed-rate funding.

The economics of a swap transaction work because no principal is involved. As a result, companies that are more creditworthy are comfortable with the concept of providing indirect fixed-rate financing for weaker companies. In addition to the favorable economics, swaps are attractive to many companies because they can offer the companies fixed-rate funds for maturities that otherwise are not available. Furthermore, swaps provide companies with an important degree of flexibility because they do not disturb traditional financing arrangements.

From a financial institution's perspective, interest rate swaps represent an intriguing risk management tool. Smaller institutions can utilize swaps to create potentially significant amounts of long-term fixed rate financing that would otherwise be available only at prohibitive cost. The implications of this are enormous. Institutions can potentially offer fixed-rate term financing to both commercial and retail customers in virtually all market environments. More importantly, as an asset/liability management tool, swaps allow institutions to adjust gaps or mismatch positions without altering the underlying asset or liability positions.

Larger financial institutions with access to intermediate or long maturity funding can often utilize swaps to create variable rate funding at advantageous interest rates. More importantly, the acquisition of long maturity variable rate funding reduces the liquidity risk that stems from continually rolling over short maturity funds. A hypothetical swap between a large commercial bank and a smaller S&L is shown in Figure 32.5.

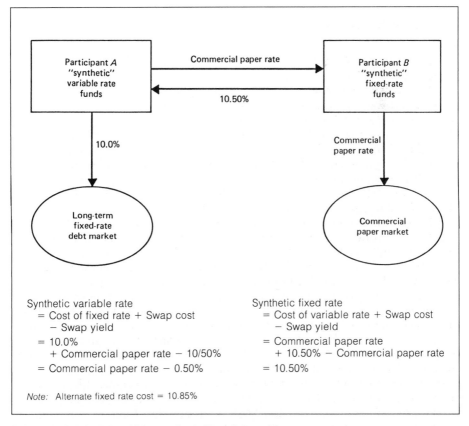

FIG. 32.4 Interest Rate Swaps: Cash Flow Schematic

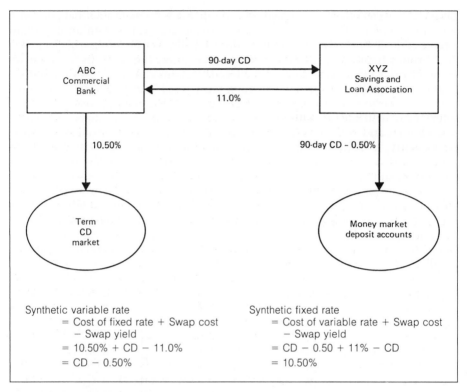

FIG. 32.5 Hypothetical Swap

In the previous example, the S&L is able to acquire term fixed-rate funds at a cost of 10.5 percent. The 10.5 percent rate is not guaranteed, however, because it is predicated upon the S&L pricing its MMDA at 50 basis points below the national market 90-day CD rate. Thus, this particular transaction contains an element of basis risk because the party's actual borrowing cost is not identical to the floating rate index.

Despite their many advantages, interest rate swaps do not represent the ultimate asset/liability management tool for financial institutions. One disadvantage of a swap results from the fact that unlike a futures position, the swap transaction is irreversible. Moreover, swaps tend to be transacted in large amounts, typically $25 million and over, primarily to spread legal expenses over a larger principal amount. Finally, the swap is not an entirely riskless transaction from a credit standpoint. The more creditworthy party assumes the risk that the weaker party will not default on the transaction. This risk is sometimes mitigated by requiring the less creditworthy party to pledge collateral amounting to approximately 15 percent of the principal amount. It is important to note, however, that an economic loss will be experienced only in the event of a default coupled with an adverse movement in interest rates. For the party providing fixed-rate financing, an adverse movement would result if interest rates declined, because that situation would require previously acquired fixed rate funds to be redeployed at lower interest rate levels.

INFORMATION SYSTEMS AND ANALYTICAL TOOLS

One of the cornerstones of effective asset/liability management is management information. Management information should at a minimum define both the liquidity and interest rate risk position of the institution and enhance management's ability to implement decisions to manage those risks.

Asset/liability management information must be both comprehensive and timely. For smaller institutions, the information requirements are less severe than is the case with larger institutions. In many cases, monthly reporting of risk positions will suffice. For larger institutions, risk position reports must be available at least on a weekly basis, if not on a daily basis.

Interest rate risk reporting assumes a variety of formats. One common format is the one shown previously in Tables 32.4 and 32.5. The major advantages of this type of reporting structure are twofold: the gap intervals are well-defined, and the effect of changing interest rates and matching/mismatching strategies are easily simulated.

Table 32.7 shows the types of information that might appear in a Eurodollar book risk position report. This report contains yield and cost information of embedded assets and funds. In this reporting framework, asset yield information is reported after subtracting the credit spread associated with the asset in order to obtain a benchmark rate to measure funding performance. For example, a loan priced at LIBOR + 0.5 would appear on the report with a yield/benchmark funds cost of LIBOR because the credit spread of 0.5 percent would be netted out. One of the more useful pieces of information contained in this report is the break-even rate associated with the gap or risk position. In the case of a negative gap, the break-even rate represents the maximum rate at which funds can be acquired for the position to generate funding profits. In the case of a positive gap, the break-even rate represents the minimum rate at which excess funds can be invested for the position to be profitable. By providing a projection of the interest rates at which the deficit/excess will be funded/invested, the risk manager can obtain an estimate of the anticipated profitability of the position. In this example, the combination of the embedded risk position and the 8.50 percent projected overnight funding (O/N) rate will provide for $303,000 of funding income in the first month, assuming no additional activity.

One of the more powerful tools available to a risk manager is the ability to simulate the effect of changing interest rates, as well as the effect of alternative investment and funding strategies, on the profitability of his position. The effect of a different set of interest rate assumptions can quickly be gauged from the column titled, "Income Sensitivity to One Percent Change in Funds Cost." The information presented in this column can be utilized in conjunction with the projected income information as an indicator of potential risk and return. In addition, reports such as the one shown in Table 32.8, providing for the effects of an alternative interest rate scenario, are helpful.

In this case, it is observed that because the risk position has been structured to take advantage of stable or declining interest rates, the effect of a declining interest rate scenario on the profitability of the position is clearly evident. Assuming a 7.50 percent overnight funding rate in month 6, the funding spread increases to 116 basis points from the 47 basis points shown in Table 32.7. In

(text continues on page 32-29)

TABLE 32.7 ABC Eurodollar Bank Gap Report I
(amount: dollars in millions; income: dollars in thousands)

Month	Term Assets		Term Funds		Gap		O/N Funding			Income Sensitivity to 1% Change in Funds Cost
	Amount	Benchmark Funding Rate	Amount	Effective Rate	Amount	Break-Even Rate	Rate	Funding Spread	Income	
1	$804	9.33%	$607	9.00%	$197—	10.35%	8.50%	0.45%	$303	$164
2	592	9.39	376	9.09	216—	9.91	8.50	0.52	254	180
3	429	9.51	249	9.24	180—	9.88	8.70	0.50	178	150
4	279	9.61	174	9.41	105—	9.94	8.80	0.43	100	88
5	250	9.70	168	9.55	82—	10.01	9.00	0.33	69	68
6	175	10.02	106	9.75	69—	9.92	9.25	0.47	38	57

TABLE 32.8 ABC Eurodollar Bank Gap Report II

(amount: dollars in millions; income: dollars in thousands)

Month	Term Assets		Term Funds		Gap			O/N Funding			Income Sensitivity to 1% Change in Funds Cost
	Amount	Benchmark Funding Rate	Amount	Effective Rate	Amount	Break-Even Rate	Rate	Funding Spread	Income		
1	$804	9.33%	$607	9.00%	$197—	10.35%	8.50%	0.45%	$303		$206
2	592	9.39	376	9.09	216—	9.91	8.00	0.70	344		222
3	429	9.51	249	9.24	180—	9.88	7.75	0.90	320		192
4	279	9.61	174	9.41	105—	9.94	7.50	0.92	214		88
5	250	9.70	168	9.55	82—	10.01	7.50	0.82	171		68
6	175	10.02	106	9.75	69—	9.92	7.50	1.16	169		57

TABLE 32.9   ABC Eurodollar Bank Gap Report III

(amount: dollars in millions; income: dollars in thousands)

Month	Term Assets		Term Funds		Gap		O/N Funding			Income Sensitivity to 1% Change in Funds Cost
	Amount	Benchmark Funding Rate	Amount	Effective Rate	Amount	Break-Even Rate	Rate	Funding Spread	Income	
1	$854	9.34%	$607	9.00%	$247—	10.18%	8.50%	0.48%	$345	$164
2	642	9.40	376	9.09	266—	9.83	8.50	0.55	296	180
3	479	9.51	249	9.24	230—	9.80	8.70	0.53	211	150
4	279	9.61	174	9.41	105—	9.94	8.80	0.43	100	88
5	250	9.70	168	9.55	82—	10.01	9.00	0.33	69	68
6	175	10.02	106	9.75	69—	9.92	9.25	0.47	38	57

addition to simulating the effect of interest rate changes, simulating the effect of different investment/funding strategies is also valuable. The reporting system should be designed to capture the effect of hypothetical strategies provided by the user. Table 32.9 shows the effect of a decision to lend $50 million at 9.50 percent for a three-month period to be funded overnight. It should be observed that the larger gaps in the first three months increase the sensitivity of net interest income to a change in funds cost.

In the context of day-to-day decision making, another piece of useful information is the effect on profitability of a hypothetical decision to reduce mismatch risk to zero for a selected time period. Generating this information requires that the current funding/investment rates be provided. The report format should then highlight the level and maturity of funds/investments that must be made to neutralize the risk as well as the associated income effects. One example of this type of reporting is shown in Table 32.10.

In addition to risk reporting mechanisms, one analytical tool that many asset/liability managers utilize is the linear program. Linear programs are designed to allow for optimal investment and funding decisions, given a forecast of interest rates and internal constraints. The constraints usually specify the maximum and minimum levels of various types of investments/funds. One or more of the constraints may be relaxed to determine the effect on the optimal decision. In addition, the interest rate scenario may likewise be altered to gauge the impact on optimal strategy.

The major benefit of linear programming models is that they generate "shadow prices" (i.e., the amount of income that would accrue if the particular constraint were relaxed by one unit). As such, linear programs can be a valuable tool in disciplining managers to be cognizant of the cost associated with the constraints they are imposing in the risk management process. As with all analytical tools, the information generated must be tempered with management's judgment in order to produce worthwhile decisions.

REQUIREMENTS FOR EFFECTIVE ASSET/LIABILITY MANAGEMENT

An attempt has been made to present a glimpse of the nature of asset management. Although it is hoped that some of the thoughts have served to illuminate the arena and stimulate discussion, there is acute awareness that management styles, practices, and problems differ across institutions.

There are some strongly held beliefs concerning the requirements for effective asset/liability management. These include:

- An understanding of the relevant issues and problems at the highest levels of the organization.
- A long-term commitment of resources to assist in the management of risk and return, including the development of management reporting and analytical tools.
- The delegation of responsibility for decision making and implementation to the appropriate financial market personnel.

TABLE 32.10   ABC Eurodollar Bank Gap Report: Risk Reporting

(amount: dollars in millions; income: dollars in thousands)

| | Term Asset | | Term Funds | | | Funds Purchased This Maturity | | Term Funding | | | |
| | Amount | Benchmark Funding Rate | Amount | Effective Rate | Gap Amount | Amount | Effective Rate | Scheduled Balance New Term Funds Amount | Effective Rate | Funding Spread | Period Income |
Month											
1	$804	9.33%	$607	9.00%	$197–	19–	9.00%	197	9.37%	0.24%	$161
2	592	9.39	376	9.09	216–	36	9.10	216	9.34	0.21	103
3	429	9.51	249	9.24	180–	75	9.25	180	9.38	0.21	76
4	279	9.61	174	9.41	105–	23	9.40	105	9.48	0.17	40
5	250	9.70	168	9.55	82–	13	9.50	82	9.50	0.17	35
6	175	10.02	106	9.75	69–	69	9.50	69	9.50	0.37	54

- A commitment to focus upon longer-term time horizons in decision making.
- A willingness to actively explore new techniques, tools, and concepts.
- A firm belief that there is no free lunch.

SUGGESTED READING

Hayes, Douglas A. *Bank Funds Management*. Ann Arbor, Mich.: University of Michigan Press, 1980.

Hempel, George H., ed. *Funds Management Under Deregulation*. Washington, D.C.: American Bankers Association, 1981.

Light, J.O., and William L. White. *The Financial System*. Homewood, Ill.: Richard D. Irwin, 1979.

Stigum, Marcia L. *The Money Market: Myth, Reality and Practice*. Homewood, Ill.: Dow Jones-Irwin, 1983.

————, and Rene O. Branch, Jr. *Managing Bank Assets and Liabilities*. Homewood, Ill.: Dow Jones-Irwin, 1983.

33

Real Estate Finance

KERRY D. VANDELL

INTRODUCTION

The nature of real estate as a good has dictated that financing, the use of debt capital, be a major component of the market. Real estate is a long-lived durable; thus, its purchase price represents the capitalized value of its future flow of benefits. This implies that the purchase price is generally large relative to the resources or liquid assets of the investment entity, making financing necessary for purchase. Real estate is also often an investment good. Thus, even if investors had the resources to purchase outright, the opportunities for financial leveraging to increase returns to equity often make it desirable to enter into credit markets.

Because real estate is involved in all physical activities, the amount of capital invested in it is quite large. It has been estimated that in 1981, the value of all real estate holdings in the United States was $5,847 billion, which represents 69 percent and the largest single component of the total net stock of fixed reproducible tangible wealth. The debt component of real estate investment is similarly large. In 1982, mortgages accounted for $1,652.1 billion, which represents 29.2 percent and the largest single component of total credit (Table 33.1). The growth since 1960 in the use of credit for real estate purchases, especially for commercial real estate, illustrates even more clearly how dominant the real estate credit sector of the economy has become. In 1960, real estate credit accounted for only 26.8 percent of total credit outstanding. Mortgage credit increased by 690.9 percent by 1982 as compared to only 625.2 percent for total credit.

This secular relative growth in mortgage credit outstanding has in part been due to trends in inflationary expectations, which have forced investors and households to shift their demand toward durables such as real estate, considered a hedge against inflation. In part, also, it has been due to the fact that real estate in general, and housing in particular, has (until recently, some would say) been viewed as a favored credit sector. A structure of regulations, laws, and institutions has grown up around a policy of insuring that an ample supply of cheap credit would be available to the residential sector.

THE PROVIDERS OF CREDIT

Table 33.2 is a summary of the activities of the institutions traditionally involved in real estate financing.

Savings and Loan Associations

Savings associations (S&Ls) were *the* dominant holders of one- to four-family loans in 1982, holding $398.5 billion, or 35.8 percent of all such loans and with 82.6 percent of their mortgage portfolio in such loans (Table 33.3). They also dominated the multifamily loan market, with over one quarter of all such loans, even though less than 8 percent of their mortgage portfolio was in such loans.

This heavy concentration in residential lending is not due simply to historical preferences and expertise. It was reinforced by tax laws and regulatory restrictions, which have been changed considerably in recent years. Today, how-

(*text continues on page 33-6*)

TABLE 33.1   Growth in Selected Types of Credit

(dollars in billions)

Type of Credit	1960		1982		Percentage Increase
	Total	Percentage of Total	Total	Percentage of Total	
Corporate and foreign bonds	$ 90.2	11.6%	$ 570.6	10.1%	532.6%
State and local government obligations	70.8	9.1	449.4	7.9	534.7
Consumer credit	65.1	8.3	428.0	7.6	557.5
Federal debt	243.1	31.2	1,372.7	24.3	464.7
Real estate credit	208.9	26.8	1,652.1	29.2	690.9
Residential mortgage loans	162.7	20.9	1,248.9	22.1	667.6
One- to four-family homes	141.9	18.2	1,112.4	19.7	683.9
Apartments	20.8	2.7	136.5	2.4	556.3
Mortgages on commercial properties	33.4	4.3	296.4	5.2	787.4
Farm properties	12.8	1.6	106.9	1.9	735.2
Other debt	101.8	13.1	1,183.3	20.9	1,062.4
Total credit outstanding	$779.9	100.0%	$5,656.1	100.0%	625.2%

Source: Federal Reserve Board; U.S. League of Savings Associations

TABLE 33.2   The Institutions of Real Estate Finance

The Providers of Credit	Types of Lending / Investment	Size of Mortgage Portfolio (Year-End 1982) (billions of dollars)
Savings and loan associations (S&Ls)	One- to four-family and multifamily loans; residential construction loans; moving into consumer and commercial lending; income property loans; equity ownership	$482.4
Commercial banks	Commercial lending; consumer lending; income property construction financing; some one- to four-family and income property mortgages; interim financing; loan warehousing	301.7
Mutual savings banks	Commercial lending; consumer lending; one- to four-family and multifamily mortgages; construction lending; greater concentration in FHA/VA loans than S&Ls or commercial banks	94.5
Life insurance companies	Securities market investments; commercial and multifamily mortgages; farm lending; interim financing and equity shares in joint venture arrangements; some residential lending through GNMAs or other mortgage pools or through larger conventional loans	141.9
Real estate investment trusts	Commercial and multifamily construction and permanent loans; income property equity ownership; interim, gap, and wraparound financing	2.4
Mortgage companies	Originators of residential and commercial construction, interim, and permanent financing; servicing of loans	16.5
Pension funds	Securities market investments; small proportion of portfolio in income property loans and equity ownership; some FHA/VA loan purchases and GNMAs	18.1

The Providers of Credit	Types of Lending / Investment	Size of Mortgage Portfolio (Year-End 1982) (billions of dollars)
Federal National Mortgage Association (FNMA)	Secondary market for FHA/VA one- to four-family loans, conventional residential loans, FHA multifamily loans, condominium and planned unit development loans, inner-city conventional residential loans (in gentrifying neighborhoods), conventional and GNMA mortgage-backed securities, subsidized loans through tandem program	$ 71.8
Government National Mortgage Association (GNMA)	Secondary market for subsidized one- to four-family and multifamily FHA loans; management and liquidation of old Home Owners' Loan Corporation loans; packaging and selling GNMA mortgage-backed securities	4.2
Federal Home Loan Mortgage Corporation (FHLMC)	Secondary market for conventional one- to four-family loans, FHA/VA one- to four-family whole loans and participations, multifamily FHA/VA or conventional whole loans and participations	4.8
Farmers' Home Administration (FmHA)	One- to four-family, multifamily, and commercial loans in rural or small town areas; farm loans	1.8
Federal Housing Administration/Veterans Administration (FHA/VA)	A few direct one- to four-family or multifamily loans; primarily defaulted loans from insured programs	5.2
Federal Land Banks	Farm loans and direct one- to four-family loans in rural or small town areas	50.4
State and local housing agencies	One- to four-family and multifamily loans; some commercial property and farm loans	45.9
Credit unions	Consumer lending; some one- to four-family residential loans	5.5
Individuals	Recent growth in one- to four-family and farm loans, both first and second liens	122.1

(continued)

TABLE 33.2   The Institutions of Real Estate Finance (continued)

The Mortgage Insurers	Purpose
Federal Housing Administration (FHA)	Insures residential loans, both one- to four-family and multifamily; loans on mobile homes, elderly, condominium, subsidized rental, and owner-occupied housing, nursing homes, hospitals, land development, and group medical practices
Veterans Administration (VA)	Guarantees losses incurred by private lenders through default on one- to four-family home and mobile home loans
Farmers' Home Administration (FmHA)	Insures or guarantees rural farm and home loans, loans for assisted rental and cooperative housing, and business and industrial development loans
Private mortgage insurance (PMI) companies	One- to four-family loan insurance
Commercial PMI companies	Mortgage insurance and lease guarantees on commercial property
Federal Savings and Loan Insurance Corporation (FSLIC)	Deposit insurance at federally chartered S&Ls and other member institutions
Federal Deposit Insurance Corporation (FDIC)	Deposit insurance at federally chartered commercial banks and other member institutions

ever, the S&L industry is undergoing a transition toward a more competitive financial system in a number of ways:

- In 1981, savings associations found themselves with a negative profit margin for the first time (although profit margins had been dropping gradually over the previous 20 years). This loss is primarily attributable to a rapid increase in the cost of savings deposits. While the spread between net operating income and the cost of savings stood at 1.8 percent in 1979, by 1981 it had dropped to 0.1 percent.
- Because of recent economic and regulatory conditions, S&Ls are being forced to change their historical lending patterns. Secondary market activities, both buying and selling, have increased, reflecting a desire for liquidity and higher yields. In 1978, S&Ls for the first time became net sellers of mortgages, indicating a changing portfolio composition.
- Finally, the basic "borrow-short, lend-long" problem of the S&L industry, which has periodically resulted in severe disintermediation during tight money periods,

is also gradually being dealt with. On the asset side, S&Ls are beginning to offer variable rate notes of various types and to diversify into short-term consumer lending. On the liability side, an increasing proportion of deposits are being indexed to various competitive rates such as those of Treasury bills. Mortgage money will likely become more expensive as deposit costs become competitive in the postderegulation world, but the swings in mortgage lending which occurred in the past will increasingly arise more from the demand side of the market than from the supply side.

As restrictions are eased and management gradually ventures forth, the nation's S&Ls will acquire a new image. New asset sources, including consumer and commercial lending, income property lending, and even equity ownership in property, will be tapped. Many S&Ls will specialize in various roles beyond those of the traditional single-family home lender, such as family financing center, real estate venture capitalist, commercial banker, mortgage banker, and even developer.

Commercial Banks

Commercial banks in 1982 still specialized in commercial lending rather than mortgages; only 18.8 percent of their assets were in mortgage credit (Table 33.3), but because of their dominance in the credit markets, they still made up a substantial share of the mortgage market. Their mortgage assets totaled $301.7 billion, or 18.3 percent of total mortgage credit outstanding. One- to four-family home loans still made up the bulk of their mortgage loans (58.7 percent), but they were less concentrated in this regard than the S&Ls. Their primary area of emphasis was commercial property (chiefly construction) loans, with a third of their mortgage portfolio in such loans. Commercial banks also held a third of the total commercial property loan market.

Until the Depository Institutions Deregulation and Monetary Control Act of 1980 was passed, national banks were effectively restricted to a relatively small portfolio of long-term mortgage lending (except for loans to manufacturing or industrial businesses or Federal Housing Administration (FHA) or Veterans Administration (VA) loans). The restrictions were less severe for second liens and construction loans. Because demand deposits make up a substantial share of commercial bank liabilities, this effectively limited their ability to extend longer-term credit.

Therefore, permanent financing has been limited by commercial banks to only a small proportion of their mortgage portfolio, except during slack periods in commercial loan demand. They frequently provide loans for residential purchase as a favor to large customers. Several have also developed inner-city lending programs, often in conjunction with the Federal National Mortgage Association (FNMA) repurchase agreements, as part of a commitment to the local community or for public relations purchases. Some, especially smaller banks, do have a regular program of residential lending, but only on terms more restrictive than S&Ls. Commercial lending also is usually only limited to those cases in which the bank is the primary creditor of a firm and mortgage financing is provided as part of a general credit package.

Construction financing is a different matter. Classified as ordinary commercial loans by regulation, these loans are short term (under three years) and floating

TABLE 33.3   Mortgage Credit Outstanding and Other Assets by Type of Property and Lender, 1982

(dollars in billions)

(Percentage of portfolio in each property type and percentage provided by each lender in parentheses)

Lender	Non-mortgage Assets	(Percent-age of Total)	Mortgage Assets by Type of Property					
			Residential Properties			Commercial Properties	Farm Properties	Total
			One- to Four-Family	Multifamily	Total			
Savings associations	223.6	(31.7)	398.5(a) (82.6)(b) (35.8)(c)	36.0 (7.5) (26.4)	434.6 (90.1) (34.8)	47.9 (9.9) (16.2)	* (0.0) (0.0)	482.4 (100.0) (29.2)
Commercial banks	1,306.1	(81.2)	177.1 (58.7) (15.9)	15.8 (5.2) (11.6)	193.0 (64.8) (15.5)	100.3 (33.2) (33.8)	8.5 (2.8) (8.0)	301.7 (100.0) (18.3)
Mutual savings banks	79.7	(45.8)	64.1 (67.8) (5.8)	15.0 (15.9) (11.0)	79.1 (83.7) (6.3)	15.3 (16.2) (5.2)	* (0.0) (0.0)	94.5 (100.0) (5.7)
Life insurance companies	421.7	(74.8)	16.7 (11.8) (1.5)	18.8 (13.2) (13.8)	35.6 (25.1) (2.9)	93.5 (65.9) (31.5)	12.8 (9.0) (12.0)	141.9 (100.0) (8.6)
Real Estate Investment Trusts	5.3(d)	(68.8)	0.1 (4.2) (0.0)	0.8 (33.3) (0.6)	0.9 (37.5) (0.1)	1.5 (62.5) (0.5)	0 (0.0) (0.0)	2.4 (100.0) (0.1)
Mortgage companies	—	—	9.4 (57.0) (0.8)	2.7 (16.4) (2.0)	12.1 (73.3) (1.0)	4.4 (26.7) (1.5)	0 (0.0) (0.0)	16.5 (100.0) (1.0)
Pension funds(e)	586.9	(97.0)	5.7 (31.5) (0.5)	5.8 (32.0) (4.2)	11.6 (64.1) (1.0)	6.5 (35.9) (2.2)	0.1 (0.6) (0.1)	18.1 (100.0) (1.1)
Federal National Mortgage Association	—	—	66.5 (92.6) (6.0)	5.3 (7.4) (3.9)	71.8 (100.0) (5.7)	0 (0.0) (0.0)	0 (0.0) (0.0)	71.8 (100.0) (4.3)
Government National Mortgage Association	—	—	0.7 (16.7) (0.1)	3.6 (85.7) (2.5)	4.2 (100.0) (0.3)	0 (0.0) (0.0)	0 (0.0) (0.0)	4.2 (100.0) (0.3)
Federal Home Loan Mortgage Corportation	—	—	4.7 (97.9) (0.4)	* (0.0) (0.0)	4.8 (100.0) (0.4)	0 (0.0) (0.0)	0 (0.0) (0.0)	4.8 (100.0) (0.3)

Pools for mortgage-backed securities	—	192.8 (89.0) (17.3)	7.9 (3.6) (5.8)	200.7 (92.6) (16.1)	7.0 (3.2) (2.4)	8.9 (4.1) (8.3)	216.7 (100.0) (13.1)
Farmers' Home Administration	—	0.8 (44.4) (0.1)	0.2 (11.1) (0.1)	1.0 (55.6) (0.1)	0.4 (22.2) (0.1)	0.4 (22.2) (0.4)	1.8 (100.0) (0.1)
Federal Housing Administration/ Veterans Administration	—	1.9 (36.5) (0.2)	3.2 (61.5) (2.3)	5.2 (100.0) (0.4)	0 (0.0) (0.0)	0 (0.0) (0.0)	5.2 (100.0) (0.3)
Federal Land Banks	—	3.1 (6.2) (0.3)	0 (0.0) (0.0)	3.1 (6.2) (0.2)	0 (0.0) (0.0)	47.3 (93.8) (44.2)	50.4 (100.0) (3.1)
State and local credit agencies	—	28.4 (61.9) (2.6)	13.1 (28.5) (9.6)	41.5 (90.4) (3.3)	3.0 (6.5) (1.0)	1.4 (3.1) (1.3)	45.9 (100.0) (2.8)
Credit unions	83.1 (93.8)	5.5 (33.9) (0.5)	0 (0.0) (0.0)	5.5 (73.3) (0.4)	0 (0.0) (0.0)	0 (0.0) (0.0)	5.5 (100.0) (0.3)
Finance companies	213.1 (92.8)	9.4 (0.8)	2.7 (16.4) (2.0)	12.1 (100.0) (1.0)	4.4 (26.7) (1.5)	0 (0.0) (0.0)	16.5 (100.0) (1.0)
Individuals(f)	—	122.1 (11.0)	0 (0.0) (0.0)	122.1 (100.0) (9.8)	0 (0.0) (0.0)	0 (0.0) (0.0)	122.1 (100.0) (7.4)
Other(f)	—	4.6 (9.2) (0.4)	5.4 (10.8) (4.0)	10.0 (20.1) (0.8)	12.3 (24.7) (4.1)	27.5 (55.2) (25.7)	49.8 (100.0) (3.0)
Total(g)	—	1,112.4 (68.0) (100.0)	136.5 (8.3) (100.0)	1,248.9 (75.6) (100.0)	296.4 (17.9) (100.0)	106.9 (6.5) (100.0)	1,652.1 (100.0) (100.0)

(a) Total credit outstanding
(b) Proportion of total mortgage portfolio of institution
(c) Proportion of total mortgage credit outstanding for property type
(d) Financial assets only
(e) Includes state and local retirement funds and private pension funds
(f) Certain debt listed in the "other" holders category may in fact be held by individuals. Breakdown unavailable.
(g) Entries may not add due to rounding
* Less than $50 million

Source: Federal Reserve Board

rate, set two to five points above prime. Commercial banks are the largest construction lenders, and this makes up a substantial portion of their real estate activities.

Another major share of real estate-related activity is in the area of interim financing and loan "warehousing." Commercial banks work very closely with mortgage bankers in providing interim development and construction loans for projects until the permanent lender takes over at project completion. The bank usually requires a firm commitment from the permanent lender for extension of long-term financing before the construction loan is made. This commitment is either in the form of an advance or forward commitment or a standby commitment. An advance or forward commitment is a firm statement of obligation by the permanent lender. The standby commitment is an agreement by the bank to purchase the construction loan at a discount from the mortgage banker if an institutional lender cannot be found by a specific time. Interim loans secured by advance or standby commitments are often specially designated as mortage inventory loans (as compared to other construction loans originated directly with the developer), and the practice of making such loans is known as warehousing.

Mutual Savings Banks

In 1982, Mutual Savings Banks (MSBs) maintained a portfolio profile between that of S&Ls and commercial banks, with mortgages totaling $94.5 billion making up 54.2 percent of their assets; one- to four-family residential loans making up 67.8 percent; and commercial loans 16.2 percent of their mortgage portfolio respectively (Table 33.3). The MSBs, largely concentrated in the Northeast, were heavily committed to multifamily mortgages in comparison to S&Ls and commercial banks. However, because of their small share of the credit market and limited growth over the last few years, they only provided 5.7 percent of total mortgage credit balances.

MSBs are virtually all state-chartered mutual institutions although, in 1978, they were permitted the option of conversion to federal chartership. Thus, their lending patterns largely reflect state rather than federal regulating restrictions, as well as historic preferences and areas of expertise. MSBs have historically preferred single-family rather than multifamily loans; only the largest have ventured into multifamily and income property financing. Of all the major lenders, they have been the most receptive to FHA/VA loans; about one quarter of their loan portfolio is made up of such loans.

Life Insurance Companies

Life insurance companies (LICs) made up 8.6 percent of the mortgage market as of year-end 1982, with mortgages outstanding totaling $141.9 billion (Table 33.3). Although only 25.2 percent of their asset portfolio was in mortgages, there are indications that such lending will increase, primarily through additional investments in commercial mortgages. Only 11.8 percent of their mortgage portfolio was in one- to four-family home loans. This had declined from the 1950s when they were heavy investors in FHA/VA mortgages. However, new investments are taking place in this area in the form of Government National Mortgage Association (GNMA) certificates and blocks of conventional loans. Life insurance companies were most heavily committed to commercial and multifamily lending, with these categories making up 65.9 and 13.2 percent respectively of their mortgage portfolio. Of all of the major institutional lenders, the LICs have been historically most involved with farm lending, providing 12 percent of such credit and holding 9 percent of their mortgage portfolio in such loans.

The long-term nature of LICs' policy liabilities render them natural investors in long-term instruments such as mortgages. Furthermore, greater certainty of cash flows enable them to plan their investment activities better, although even LICs become less active during tight money periods in making commitments for purchase. They traditionally have participated as front money partners in joint venture arrangements to develop income properties. This is a form of limited or general partnership, usually with a developer, in which the LIC provides the interim and permanent financing in exchange for a share of the development profit and possibly an equity share in the project.

The residential loans LICs are making today tend either to be in GNMA mortgage-backed securities, in other mortgage pools, or in larger conventional residential loans with loan/value ratios under 75 percent.

Nontraditional Mortgage Lenders

Nontraditional sources of mortgage lending recently have become a much more important part of the mortgage market. These include real estate investment trusts (REITs), mortgage companies, pension funds, secondary market institutions, federally supported agencies, mortgage pools, credit unions, and individuals. Altogether, by year-end 1982, these sources held over one third of total mortgage indebtedness, including over four fifths of all farm lending and over two fifths of all residential credit. A description of the mortgage-lending activities of each of these sources follows:

Real Estate Investment Trusts. REITs held only $2.4 billion or 0.1 percent of total mortgage credit outstanding in 1982, most of which was concentrated in multifamily and commercial lending (Table 33.3). This figure dropped from $16.2 billion or 2.2 percent in 1974, due to the gradual falling out among the REITs, which occurred beginning in the tight money period of 1974–1975.

The basic REIT concept has been around since the late nineteenth century, but it was not until 1961 that REITs meeting certain requirements were permitted to act as conduits for income for the trust and not be taxed twice as a corporation. In order to qualify for this privilege, a REIT had to distribute at least 90 percent of its annual net income to shareholders, hold at least 75 percent of its assets in mortgages or equity ownership of real estate, receive at least 75 percent of its earnings from real estate assets, and meet certain other requirements. This allowed REITs to become the "mutual funds" of real estate and to grow significantly into the 1970s. Most REITs tended to specialize as either equity REITs, investing primarily in real estate equities; or mortgage REITs, investing in short-term construction or development loans, permanent financing and, to some extent, interim (or gap) and wraparound mortgages.

Problems arose in 1974 from several sources, including a general contraction in the economy, high interest rates, an inversion in the yield curve, overbuilding, and inappropriate structuring of management fees. The result was considerable reduction in share values, some bankruptcies, some conversion to corporate status to permit the carrying forward of losses, and the required forbearance by a number of sponsoring companies. Much "fall out" is still occurring as loan losses are taken and some liquidations take place. However, many REITs today, through sound conservative management policies, are providing decent returns to their shareholders and permitting restoration of public trust.

Mortgage Companies. As of year-end 1982, mortgage companies held $16.5 billion or one percent of all mortgage debt, primarily in residential credit (Table 33.3). However, this figure is misleading, since mortgage companies, sometimes called mortgage bankers, are in the business of originating loans to sell, not in holding inventory. They originate residential loans at the same rate as commercial banks, including about three quarters of all FHA/VA loans. They are second to commercial banks in the origination of income-property loans. Mortgage bankers are not to be confused with mortgage brokers (although they may sometimes perform as mortgage brokers also), in that mortgage brokers do not actually originate notes but merely bring the buyer and seller together, thus facilitating the sale of a note.

Mortgage companies undertake a variety of functions beyond mortgage loan origination and resale. They service loans, including any paperwork required upon prepayment or default. They may also write hazard insurance, broker loans or property, manage property, act as leasing agents, or act as appraisers. These functions are all attendant to property transfers, and, because of relatively little government regulation, mortgage companies that find these subordinate functions desirable also find them allowable.

In originating a loan, the mortgage company generally has received a takeout commitment or standby commitment from the mortgage investor to repurchase the loan. In some cases the investor actually advances the money to the mortgage company; in other cases the mortgage company must use its own limited funds or, more frequently, borrow through the sale of commercial paper or through advances from commercial bank lines of credit. In the case of lines of credit, often the mortgage company must secure the advance through already originated mortgages (usually a pool of FHA/VA mortgages), in a practice called warehousing. Borrowing must also take place in those relatively rare instances in which the mortgage company does not yet have a purchaser and must inventory the loan temporarily until a purchaser is found.

There are several major sources of revenue for mortgage companies. The loan origination fees and loan servicing fees are usually primary. The former are usually a percentage of the loan amount plus explicit costs for various transaction services. These are generally standard at one percent for FHA/VA loans but vary considerably for other loans. They are charged to the borrower. Loan servicing fees are usually based upon a percentage of outstanding loan balance. This is usually negotiable between the mortgage company and the secondary market purchaser. It should be noted that this fee declines as the mortgage amortizes. Beyond a point, it does not cover the marginal cost of

FHLMC has several programs of purchase for either whole loans or participations. These are over-the-counter programs in which delivery is mandatory.

- The *single-family whole loan program* involves whole interests in single-family conventional or FHA/VA mortgages that must be delivered within 60 days. Servicing fee to the seller is 0.375 percent. Prices are adjusted to provide FHLMC's required yield.

- The *multifamily whole loan program* involves whole interests in eligible multifamily conventional or FHA/VA loans. The servicing fee is lower in recognition of the economies of scale inherent in servicing larger loans, 25 basis points for the first $250,000 of unpaid principal and 12.5 basis points for the balance.

- The *Class A participation program* involves purchases of 50 to 85 percent interest in eligible multifamily conventional mortgages that must be delivered within 30 days. Service fees are the spread between the nominal rate and FHLMC's required net yield. Maximum volume per contract is $5 million.

- The *Class B participation program* involves purchases of 50 to 85 percent interest in single-family conventional mortgages along with multifamily purchases not to exceed 50 percent of the total.

- The *Class C participation program* is like the Class A program except it is designed for smaller loan packages, between $100,000 and $750,000.

In addition to immediate purchases, FHLMC, like FNMA, issues commitments for 6 to 24-month periods for delivery at the seller's option. These are for all types of eligible conventional and FHA/VA loans. Net yields are determined by an auction process similar to that established by FNMA.

FHLMC relies upon several sources of capital for its mortgage purchase activities. These include $100 million of capital shares issued to the 12 district Federal Home Loan Banks, borrowings from the Federal Home Loan Banks, issuance of GNMA guaranteed mortgage-backed bonds, sale of mortgages from its loan portfolio, issuance of debt securities, issuance of participation sale certificates, and issuance of Guaranteed Mortgage Certificates (GMCs). FHLMC participation sale certificates extend the mortgage-backed securities concept to conventional loans. The certificates are backed by FHLMC-owned mortgage participations and are fully guaranteed by FHLMC. Guaranteed Mortgage Certificates are also fully backed by FHLMC and are being offered for sale to nontraditional mortgage investors in an effort to increase conventional mortgage marketability.

Other Lenders.   In addition to the major institutional primary and secondary mortgage market participants previously discussed, there are numerous other, relatively minor, participants, some of which have become more important in recent years in originating certain types of loans:

Federal agencies together held about 3.5 percent of the total outstanding mortgage debt as of year-end 1982. They include:

- The Farmers Home Administration, which held $1.8 billion in one- to four-family, multifamily, commercial, and farm credit loans as of year-end 1982.

- The Federal Housing and Veterans Administrations, which, as of year-end 1982, held $5.2 billion of direct one- to four-family or multifamily loans, primarily defaulted loans from various programs that FHA/VA had assumed.
- The Federal Land Banks which held $50.4 billion in one- to four-family and farm credit loans as of year-end 1982.

Most states and many localities now have *housing agencies*, sometimes called housing finance agencies, which have been established to provide housing for low- to moderate-income households. As of year-end 1982, state and local credit agencies held $45.9 billion, or 2.8 percent of all mortgage debt.

Credit unions have traditionally served the installment credit needs of their members, but, since 1977, federally chartered credit unions have also been permitted to make home mortgages. As of year-end 1982, credit unions held only $5.5 billion in residential mortgage loans, roughly 6 percent of their assets; but this could change considerably in the future.

Individuals were originally the primary source of mortgage lending, but they had shrunk in importance by the 1960s. However, in recent years, they have again become important in certain markets, especially the residential and farm markets, as stringent credit terms or lack of credit availability have forced sellers to take back notes, oftentimes at below-market terms, to assure sale.

THE MORTGAGE INSURORS

The use of a government agency to insure or guarantee loans rather than for direct lending is attractive, both because it reduces actual government budgetary outlays and leverages private dollars. Such insurance lowers risk to the lender, allowing more lending at a lower cost and more lenient terms.

The Federal Housing Administration

The Federal Housing Administration (FHA), established in 1934, was the first government mortgage insurance agency. Its creation was an effort to reestablish confidence in the devastated mortgage market. The Title I program insured home improvements and repairs and small nonresidential construction projects. The Title II program was for permanent financing for purchase. Title II set up the Mutual Mortgage Insurance Fund, which was funded as a loss reserve paid out of premiums of 0.5 percent of the outstanding loan balance. The 203(b) program, the basic unsubsidized program for one- to four-family homes, has been eminently successful. Today, it insures the lender for up to 97 percent of the first $25,000 of acquisition cost (including closing costs) and 95 percent of the remainder, up to a maximum of $67,500 ($90,000 in high-cost areas). In the event of default, the lender receives from the FHA debentures in the amount of the net loss after the foreclosure sale.

Over the years, numerous additional mortgage insurance programs have been added to the FHA offerings to accomplish specific objectives. These have ranged from multifamily and mobile home insurance (Section 207), elderly housing insurance (Section 231), condominium insurance (Section 234), and hospital insurance (Section 242) to various subsidized housing programs for low- and moderate-income rentals and ownership (Sections 221, 235, 236, 237), even to mortgage insurance for nursing homes (Section 232), land development (Section 1000), and group medical practice facilities (Section 1100).

The Veterans Administration

The Servicemen's Readjustment Act of 1944 authorized the Veterans Administration (VA) to guarantee home loans to veterans. Since this is a guarantee, not an insurance program, there is no insurance premium paid, nor is there an insurance fund pool.[2] All losses are paid by the federal government. The current guarantee is for $27,500 or 60 percent of the loan, whichever is less.

The Farmers Home Administration

The Farmers Home Administration (FmHA) was established in 1946 to provide financing through insurance, guarantees, or direct loans to the farm population. Originally, the programs were for farm or home purchase, but they have evolved today into a number of areas, some of them unrelated to farming operations. The loans may be made in rural areas, including towns and villages under 20,000 in population.

The main credit programs of the FmHA are insured loans for farm purchase and house purchase, assisted rental and cooperative housing loans, and guarantees for business and industrial development. In each case, the borrowers must not be able to obtain credit at a reasonable price elsewhere. Furthermore, if credit subsequently becomes available, they must refinance. Because the terms on FmHA credit are often below market, FmHA credit often dominates the rural market, especially for smaller home loans.

Private Mortgage Insurance

Private mortgage insurance (PMI) was in force prior to the Depression, but disappeared at that time due to bankruptcies or simply cessation of activity. In 1957, the Mortgage Guaranty Insurance Corporation (MGIC) was organized as the first of a new breed of private mortgage insurors. MGIC typically insures fully amortizable first mortgages on one- to four-family properties made up to 95 percent of property value. The top 20 percent of the loan is insured. When the loan is paid off below 80 percent of value, the insurance policy may be dropped.[3] Generally, the insurance is not used for loans below an 80 percent

---

[2] Although a VA insurance program does exist, it is negligible in volume. There also is a small direct-loan program, which has become more important in capital-short areas. Most loans are for single-family homes, but there is also a mobile home program, and veterans can theoretically jointly purchase larger multifamily projects.

[3] Value may have appreciated since origination. It may therefore be desirable for the borrower to seek an appraisal and apply for policy cancellation prior to payment of the loan down to 80 percent of original value.

TABLE 33.4   Growth in Mortgage Insurance

(dollars in billions)

Year-End	One- to Four-Family FHA/VA	Percent-age of Total	Private Mortgage Insurance	Percent-age of Total	Total	Insurance as a Percentage of Home Mortgage Debt
1960	$ 56.4	99.5%	$ 0.3	0.5%	$ 56.7	40.0%
1965	73.1	95.7	3.3	4.3	76.4	34.6
1970	97.3	93.0	7.3	7.0	104.6	35.1
1971	105.2	91.6	9.6	8.4	114.8	35.0
1972	113.0	86.6	17.5	13.4	130.5	35.1
1973	116.2	80.9	27.4	19.1	143.6	34.5
1974	121.3	78.3	33.6	21.7	154.9	34.5
1975	127.7	76.1	40.0	23.9	167.7	34.2
1976	133.5	73.0	49.3	27.0	182.8	32.8
1977	141.6	69.3	62.8	30.7	204.4	31.2
1978	153.4	65.6	80.5	34.4	233.9	30.6
1979	172.9	64.5	95.2	35.5	268.1	30.5
1980	195.2	65.0	105.3	35.0	300.5	31.3
1981(a)	205.9(b)	64.3	114.3	35.7	320.2	31.5(b)

(a) Preliminary
(b) September 30

Source: United States League of Savings Associations

loan/value ratio, in accordance with FNMA and FHLMC regulations. Premium fees range from 25 to 100 basis points up front and an annual premium of 0.25 percent.[4] In the event of default, the insurer holds the option of taking title to the property, paying the lender the full amount of the loss (including administrative costs), or leaving title with the lender and paying 20 percent of the outstanding loan balance.

Thirteen other private mortgage insurance companies have developed since 1957, and residential PMI has enjoyed a substantial resurgence. As of year-end 1981, PMI made up 35.7 percent of total mortgage insurance outstanding (Table 33.4).

Commercial Private Mortgage Insurance

PMI on income properties failed badly in the Depression and did not reappear until 1967, when MGIC created the Commercial Loan Insurance Corporation to offer both mortgage insurance and lease guarantees. The original insurance

---

[4] An alternative plan, which is less common, pays 2.5 percent "up front" for a 10-year term.

program was similar to MGIC's residential program, insuring the top 20 percent of an income-property loan for a noncancelable, five-year term premium of 1.75 to 2.90 percent or for an up front premium of 1.2 percent and 0.5 percent annually at the beginning of each year.

The Depository Insurors

The federal depository insurors, the Federal Savings and Loan Insurance Corporation for S&Ls and the Federal Deposit Insurance Corporation for commercial banks, were established in 1934 and 1933, respectively, to reestablish depositor confidence. The limit on insurance for any one account is periodically reset to reflect inflation. It currently stands at $100,000.

MORTGAGE INSTRUMENTS

Not only have conditions and needs shaped institutions dealing in mortgage credit, they have also shaped the instruments which convey that credit. Mortgage instrument types can be differentiated in several ways: (1) by stage in the development process, from acquisition of raw land, through development and construction, to permanent financing; (2) by property type; and (3) by term structure, with terms including the interest rate, maturity, payment schedule, method of amortization, loan/value ratio, presence or absence of insurance, precedence of claim, nature of the security, property included, and presence or absence of equity claim. Table 33.5 shows an overview of mortgage instruments.

Financing Various Stages of Development

Loans for Purchase of Agricultural Land. Mortgages for land expected to be held primarily for agricultural uses are generally from four sources. The first is through federal government agencies, such as the Federal Land Banks and the FmHA, which insure or guarantee loans made by private lenders or lend directly in some instances. These constitute the largest source of credit. The loans are generally fixed-interest rate, fully amortizable, long-term loans for a high proportion of value. Payment levels are commonly adjusted, however, to coincide with fluctuations in farm income and are made less frequently than monthly. In some cases, sinking fund reserves are paid in to offset the lean years.

Life insurance companies, commercial banks, and individuals are also active in farm lending. Individuals constitute the second largest source of farm lending and have become more important in recent years during restrictive credit conditions.

Predevelopment Loans or "Front Money." Once land becomes ripe for development, the potential developer must obtain and expend certain funds prior to acquiring a development and construction loan. These are required for land acquisition, planning the development, and preparing the necessary doc-

(text continues on page 33-26)

TABLE 33.5　Instruments of Real Estate Finance

Instrument	Purpose	Characteristics	Lender
BY STAGE OF DEVELOPMENT			
Agricultural land	Purchase land to be held for agricultural uses	Fixed-rate, fully amortizable, long-term, high loan/value ratio	LICs, commercial banks, individuals
Front money	Land acquisition, planning, preparing documentation for development	Installment sale, interest only and short-term with balloon payment, blanket mortgage, joint venture, equity "kicker," option to purchase, sometimes from own capital or credit lines	Seller, own capital, credit lines, some institutional money in conjunction with construction loan
Construction loan	Cash flow needs for materials and labor during development	Interest tied to prime plus fixed fee, periodic draws as work is completed, short-term, interest only, balloon payment	S&Ls, commercial banks, mortgage companies, some REITs
Gap financing	Finance development between construction and permanent financing	Short-term, interest only plus fee, balloon payment, interest tied to prime	Traditional construction or permanent lenders
Permanent financing	Finance purchase over life of property	Fixed-rate, fully amortizable, long-term, high loan/value ratio or one of a variety of alternative mortgage instruments	S&Ls, MSBs, LICs, secondary market institutions, nontraditional lenders, some commercial banks, etc.
BY TYPE OF PERMANENT FINANCING INSTRUMENT			
Fully amortizable fixed-rate mortgage	Permanent financing on most residential properties, many commercial properties	Fixed-rate, fixed payment, fully amortizable, long-term, high loan/value ratio	Most permanent financing institutions

Type	Purpose	Characteristics	Typical lenders
Junior mortgage	Finance difference between down payment and purchase price not covered by first lien	Usually short-term, only partially amortizable, or interest only; balloon payment, sometimes direct reduction loan, higher rates	Permanent lenders, finance companies, individuals
Open-end mortgage	Permit additional later borrowing for additions, modifications, repairs	Principal added to original note, same maturity, usually no interest adjustment	Permanent lenders (used infrequently because of lack of control)
Wraparound mortgage	Finance difference between down payment and purchase price not covered by first lien, permit purchase at lower rate than market	Short- or long-term, interest charged on both principal amount *and* spread between new interest rate and rate on outstanding first mortgage	First mortgage lender, other permanent lenders, finance companies, individuals
Blanket mortgage	Raise debt capital in excess of security available from a single property, economies of scale in acquisition of multiple properties	Multiple properties act as security, partially paid off as property developed and sold (usually in excess of proportion of value)	Permanent mortgage lenders
Package mortgage	Finance both land and improvements *plus* specific fixtures and appliances	Standard permanent financing features, enumeration of fixtures covered	Permanent mortgage lenders
Participation mortgage	Provide lender with opportunity for additional yield in exchange for lower contract rate, share in upside potential return	Actual or potential sharing of cash flow or reversion with the lender/investor	Permanent mortgage lenders, especially LICs, pension funds; individual investors or investor groups
Land installment contract	Permit sale in less desirable markets	Not true mortgage, title not transferred until payment completed	Individuals, finance companies, and others active in inner-city lending
Leasehold mortgage	Raise capital using leasehold as security	Higher interest than freehold mortgage, especially without subordination agreement; ground lease is subordinated to fee mortgage, making possible acquisition of loan to cover value of land and improvements	Landowners, individuals, permanent lenders

(continued)

TABLE 33.5   Instruments of Real Estate Finance (continued)

Instrument	Purpose	Characteristics	Lender
Land or rental trust certificate	Means of sharing ownership of land or leases among individuals	Owner leases parcel to tenant who agrees to build, issues land trust certificate to investors on basis of lease security representing fractional interest in development; rental trust certificates similar for ownership of leasehold	Owners of parcels of land or leaseholds
Personal loans	Raise capital for improvements, repairs, sometimes purchase	Personal property or assets used as security; usually short-term, high rate	Finance companies, commercial banks, credit unions, individuals
Housing and industrial development bonds	Finance housing or industrial development seen in public interest at below-market rate	Tax-exempt issues sold in marketplace; proceeds recast as long-term low-interest mortgages	Housing finance agencies, industrial development corporations
Securities issues (real estate bonds)	Issued to individual investors, means of raising additional capital, backed by first mortgages	Bonds structured as typical bonds; payment to individual investors depends upon mortgage cash flows	Developers/owners; more recently GNMA, FNMA, FHLMC, mortgage companies
Sale-leaseback financing	To split interests in property in most tax-effective manner	Sale and immediate leasing to seller or third party	Investors, companies without interest in equity ownership, landowners
Alternative Mortgage Instruments (AMIs)			
Graduated payment mortgage (GPM)	Tilt payment stream to better correspond with borrower's income during the first few years	Long-term, low down payment, fixed interest rate, graduated payment first few years known a priori	Traditional permanent lenders, FNMA, FHLMC
Variable rate mortgage (VRM)	Increase yield flexibility for lenders	Long-term, low down payment, interest rate fluctuates according to an index rate, either payments or maturity variable	Traditional permanent lenders, FNMA, FHLMC
Reverse annuity mortgage (RAM)	Allow elderly borrowers to withdraw equity as an annuity	Typically an annuity which draws down equity through monthly payments to owner; all principal and interest due upon sale of home or death of owner	Few made; traditional permanent lenders, LICs

Price level adjusted mortgage (PLAM)	Reduce early payments to permit purchase and higher loan amounts	Long-term, low down payment, offered at real interest rate, balance outstanding indexed to consumer price index; payments increase at rate of inflation	Traditional permanent lenders; few made because of tax problems
Graduated payment adjustable mortgage loan (GPAML)	Graduate payments according to borrower needs, yet adjust yields to make attractive to lenders	Long-term, low down payment; combines GPM and VRM; payments graduated but yields adjusted; maturity adjusted accordingly	Traditional mortgage lenders; few made
Accelerated equity buildup mortgage	Reduce time of repayment and ultimate interest costs in exchange for lower rate	Intermediate term, low down payment, graduated payment increases beyond level necessary to amortize loan at term	Traditional permanent lenders
Shared appreciation mortgage (SAM)	Allows below-market rate in exchange for share of equity ownership; "copurchaser" mortgage allows two singles to share in purchase	Like "bullet" loans; written for long amortization periods but often due in 5–10 years; lower down payment traded in exchange for payment to lender of return on capital and share of capital gains; "copurchaser" mortgages written like traditional loans	Traditional permanent lenders, investors and investor groups
Balloon mortgage	Low-payment for borrower, quick recovery of capital by lender	Payments interest only or partially amortized; outstanding balance due prior to loan maturity	Traditional permanent lenders, sellers, individuals
Wraparound mortgage	Roll over lender's money, make purchase possible	Rate "blended"; assumption of existing first lien, plus additional amount to cover remainder of purchase price less down payment; rate on total amount below market but above existing note	Traditional permanent lenders
Buydown	Permit sale	Seller or builder "buys down" interest payments for a period by paying lump sum to lender	Seller/builder
Seller financing	Permit sale	Take back or purchase money mortgage, either first or second lien	Seller

umentation for development and subsequent financing. Considered together as "front money," this is probably the most ad hoc and riskiest stage in capital acquisition. It includes both loans and other arrangements.

Speculative or development land acquisition is especially difficult. Financing for outright land purchase must almost exclusively be through seller financing, an installment sale, or some other means of participation by the landowner. Seller financing would frequently be interest only and short term with a balloon payment due upon project completion. Sometimes the developer takes out a blanket mortgage covering all the land. As he develops individual portions of the site and obtains permanent financing, he repays the seller that portion of the note plus a margin, which lowers the mortgage balance. Traditional institutional lenders sometimes participate in such lending. As an alternative, the landowner may enter into a joint venture with the developer as the land contributing partner. He could even put up part of the capital for the project and often receives an equity share of the development. Actual title transfer to the joint venture may not take place until after development.

A variety of other schemes have also been devised to minimize the cash needs of the developer, yet provide adequate return to the landowner. One includes a variety of options arrangements whereby the developer secures control of the land by paying the seller for an option to purchase for a specific amount within a specific time frame, usually with no recourse in the event financing or other arrangements fall through. Often, possession of an option for land purchase is sufficient for provision of interim financing.

Beyond the costs of land acquisition, a variety of other up front services need to be paid for. For these, the developer must rely on a variety of other ad hoc sources of capital including his own capital and regular bank credit lines, though these are often inadequate or costly.

Development and Construction Financing. If a construction lender obtains assurances that (1) the project has a commitment for permanent financing; (2) the developer has an acceptable track record and credit rating; and (3) sufficient front money is available, he will provide a 6- to 12-month development or construction loan (usually with provisions for extensions, in some cases up to three years). Development and construction loans are similarly handled. They are sometimes considered together (e.g., for tract builders), but in the case in which the subdivider is different from the builder, they are handled separately. The purpose of the construction/development loan is to handle cash flow needs for materials and labor during development.

Construction loan rates are frequently tied to prime, usually two to five points over prime depending on the property type, conditions in the market, and riskiness of the project. In addition, there is a fixed fee, generally one to two points, to cover origination costs. This creates an incentive for the lender to roll over the loan as quickly as possible. Advances are made in the form of "draws," which can be structured in a variety of ways but usually bear some relationship to the amount of work completed on the project. Repayments of interest are made regularly, usually monthly, but in some cases are deferred until project completion. Upon project completion, the full amount of loan principal becomes due.

The providers of construction credit are typically major institutions: S&Ls and commercial banks for single-family loans (S&Ls if they are to retain permanent financing); commercial banks, S&Ls, and mortgage companies for multifamily loans; and commercial banks for nonresidential income properties.

Standby or Gap Financing. When the developer may not be able to or want to obtain permanent financing, he must seek temporary standby or gap financing, usually available through traditional construction or permanent lenders. Standby or gap financing would not be necessary if construction lenders always required a permanent commitment prior to lending. For various reasons, however, they do not. Instead, to compensate for the added risk, they may request additional fees on the construction loan, or a standby commitment by a permanent lender that need not be honored. In the case in which the permanent takeout commitment is "split level" (i.e., in stages until rents reach a certain level), the construction lender may agree to finance the "gap" for a fee.

Permanent Financing. Permanent financing makes up the bulk of the mortgage market, over 90 percent of outstanding credit and two thirds of originations. While interim financing is almost always less than three years in duration, permanent loans today are frequently contracted for periods of 25 to 30 years and sometimes longer. Although permanent financing is last chronologically, frequently it must be obtained first as a prerequisite to obtaining construction funds. Before making a permanent loan commitment, a lender must be assured that (1) the track record and financial capability of the developer are acceptable; (2) the proposed development plans and cost estimates are sound; and (3) market conditions are such that the project will be economically viable. Lenders require developers to prepare a submission package, which offers evidence on these questions. Although such packages are supposedly objective, they are virtually always favorable to the developer (otherwise he would not take the time to prepare it or consider the project in the first place). Fee incentives to market analysts also sometimes affect the objectivity. Thus, the lender must evaluate the submission package based on his own best judgments about current and future market conditions before deciding whether to make the loan and on what terms.

Types and Characteristics of Permanent Financing Instruments

The Fully Amortizable Fixed-Rate Mortgage. By far, the most common type of permanent financing for both residential and commercial properties is the fully amortizable, long-term fixed-rate note. Its characteristics are: (1) a level payment stream throughout the mortgage term, with no balloon payment at any time; (2) a constant interest rate applied to the outstanding balance; (3) payment of both the interest on the outstanding balance and a portion of the principal in each payment, with the principal payment increasing over time as the outstanding balance (hence, interest payment) declines; and (4) full amortization at the end of the fixed term.

This mortgage type proved advantageous during noninflationary periods in that it never required refinancing nor required the borrower to come up with a large cash payment, hence reducing default risk. It also provided certainty to the borrower and lender as to the nominal payment levels expected over time. With an extended maturity, it could provide low payment levels approaching those of the interest-only note.

Typically, the interest rate on such notes is quoted on an annual basis, but payments and amortization are paid monthly. Hence, the actual interest paid is one twelfth of the annual rate. The payment can be calculated from tables of mortgage constants (the payment necessary to amortize a loan of $1) or from the formula

$$Q = \frac{Lr}{1 - (1 + r)^{-T}}$$

where: Q = monthly payment

L = loan amount

r = annual contract rate/12

T = term to maturity in months

For example, a $100,000 loan for 30 years at 12 percent would have a monthly payment Q of $(100,000) \{(0.12/12)/[1 - (1 + 0.12/12)^{-360}]\}$ = $1028.61. The term after the principal amount represents the mortgage constant, which is available in any set of financial tables, sometimes as the "installment to amortize." This is for a monthly pay note. An annual pay note would make use of the annual contract rate and maturity in years to calculate the annual payment.

The outstanding balance at the end of time t is simply the present value of the remaining stream of mortgage payments over the remaining term of the note. This can be calculated as the monthly payment Q times the present value of a monthly annuity discounted at the contract rate r for the remaining term of the loan $T - t$, or

$$B_t = Q \times MPVA_{T-t}^r$$

To determine the outstanding balance on the previous loan after the fifth year (month 60), one would calculate

$$B_{60} = Q \times MPVA_{300\ mo.}^{12\%} = (1028.61)(94.9466) = \$97,662.97$$

In order to obtain the amount of loan paid off between periods t and $t+k$, $P_{t,t+k}$, the analyst needs merely to subtract the present values of the payment annuities for these periods, or equivalently the outstanding balances after these periods:

$$P_{t,t+k} = B_t - B_{t+k}$$

For the previous loan, to determine the principal paid off during the fifth year (between months 48 and 60), this would become

$$P_{48,60} = B_{48} - B_{60} = 98,248.01 - 97,662.97 = \$585.04$$

Of course, during the fifth year, the amount of interest paid would be the difference between the total annual mortgage payment $12Q$ = $12,343.32 and $P_{48,60}$ = $585.04 or $11,758.28.

Alternative Mortgage Instruments. Alternative Mortgage Instruments (AMIs) may differ from the fixed-rate note in a number of ways. The interest rate and/or payment level may be variable, the term to maturity may be adjustable, the loan may not be fully amortizable (e.g., with a required balloon payment), or a combination of these.

The term *AMI* has come to be applied to single-family residential mortgages, and most of the recent innovations in mortgage design have been in that area; but many of these designs have been adopted from mortgage types that have long been in use in commercial or limited types of residential markets. AMIs are discussed in more detail later in this chapter.

Junior Mortgages. Junior mortgages are those written upon a property which take secondary status relative to the first mortgage with respect to claims for debt owed. These may be second mortgages, third mortgages, and so forth, depending on their order of precedence. One form of junior mortgage is the take-back or purchase-money mortgage, which involves seller financing. Although "seconds taken back by the seller" and "purchase-money mortgages" are terms often used interchangeably, they may be very different. A true purchase-money mortgage involves a lien of especially high priority in most states; in order to achieve the status of a second mortgage, a specific waiver must be written in.

Terms on junior liens are usually strict (except in the case of seller financing when the seller needs to consummate the sale). They are often short term and not fully amortizable. In fact, they are often interest-only, balloon-payment notes, especially in cases where the second is a temporary arrangement. Sometimes, too, they are direct-reduction loans, with interest being paid on the original loan amount and not on the outstanding balance. Rates and yields are typically high, reflecting the additional risk created by the junior position on claims and, in some cases, the market power of the lender. In the event of default on the first note, the second mortgage holder must either hope the foreclosure sale will provide sufficient proceeds to satisfy his debt claim also, or must exercise his right of reinstatement by taking over payments on the first loan and foreclosing himself or by attempting to work out a foreclosure arrangement with the mortgagor.

There is a growing market developing in the resale of second notes, especially those taken back by home sellers in the recent tight money period. Second mortgage companies have become active in the purchase of these notes from sellers eager to get out free and clear, sometimes at discounts of up to 50 percent. These notes are beginning to be packaged and sold to investors as a high-risk, high-yield security.

The Open-End Mortgage. The open-end mortgage permits additional later borrowing for additions, modifications, or repairs. This is added to the original note, usually with no adjustment in interest. Such notes are broadly permitted, but used infrequently, in part because of the lack of control by the lender over subsequent borrowings, in part because of rising interest rates, which make the lender hesitant to advance additional sums at the old rate. This type of loan has proved useful, however, for financing rehabilitation of residential structures in gentrifying neighborhoods.

The Wraparound Mortgage. The wraparound note (WRAP) is so named because the new second mortgage is "wrapped around" the first mortgage, which is typically at a low interest rate relative to market rates. The existing first mortgage remains in force. In some cases the first mortgage does not have a due-on-sale clause, and the seller or lender continues to make payments on it, while advancing an additional amount equal to the difference between the purchase price and the amount available through down payment plus the first mortgage. A higher interest rate is charged in recognition of its junior debt position or changed economic conditions. However, the interest rate is charged on the *full amount* of the debt, resulting in a return on the additional amount advanced of the interest on that amount plus the spread in interest on the amount of the first mortgage.

In other cases the existing first mortgage is subject to a due-on-sale clause but is assumable with lender approval. The lender of the WRAP is often the first mortgage lender who advances an additional amount, charging a below-current-market rate on the entire amount loaned. This is attractive to the borrower, obviously. It is attractive to the lender because (1) it provides a high yield on the additional amount advanced; and (2) it rolls over an existing low-interest note for a new note at a higher rate. The new rate is not market, but the alternative may be no sale.

The Blanket Mortgage. The blanket mortgage involves a single mortgage covering several parcels of real estate. It is used most frequently by developers who have one loan on a development, part of which is paid off after each individual lot is subdivided, developed, and sold. Usually, the lender requires that the amount paid off be in excess of the proportion of the sales price of the parcel to the total development value. This is to reduce the risk exposure.

There are at least two other occasions in which blanket mortgages are sometimes used. Debt capital in excess of the security available from a single property is sometimes raised through the issuance of a blanket mortgage. In addition, corporations sometimes handle their property development and ac-quisitions on the basis of a single blanket note.

The Package Mortgage. The package mortgage has features in common with both the open-ended and the blanket mortgage. It involves financing covering the whole real estate package, including both land and improvements as well as specific fixtures and appliances. These items must qualify as fixtures under law and be specifically enumerated in the mortgage.

The Participation Mortgage. Participation or equity participation loans, sometimes called equity kickers, have become quite common in recent years, first for commercial markets and, more recently, even for home purchase.

Participations all have in common the feature that cash flows to the lender not only through interest and principal flows but also through flows tied to property performance, either rents or appreciation. There are a variety of arrangements that can be made: (1) the most common is one in which the lender receives a percentage of the net or gross income from the project, usually over a threshold break-even level; (2) he may participate through a given percentage of capital gains from resale; (3) he may obtain a given percentage of equity ownership; (4) he may arrange a sale buy-back agreement in which the lender/investor buys a property from the developer, then resells it under a long-term installment sale while retaining title, making money off the favorable terms of the installment sale; or (5) he may enter into a joint venture with the developer, agreeing to provide certain front monies for an equity share of the project. The equity ownership position may be actually taken or (more frequently) remain only potential in the event of lack of performance on the part of the developer. While the intent of the equity participation loan is for the lender to gain some of the upside potential of a project, it must be remembered that, unless properly structured, it could force the lender also to share in the downside risk.

Nonmortgage Alternatives for Permanent Financing. In addition to the common mortgage financing arrangements, there are a variety of less traditional forms of debt financing for property acquisition, which do not (in a legal sense) include mortgage financing.

- *The Land installment contract*[5] transfers legal title from the seller to the buyer only after all contractual payments are made. The buyer retains equitable title and all rights of occupancy.
- *The Leasehold mortgage* uses the leasehold interest as a security. The leasehold can be valued by anticipating cash flows from the leasehold and risks associated with the potential interruption of that cash flow. Leasehold mortages are riskier than fee mortgages if the lease is subject to being canceled because of nonperformance by the tenant or default on the fee mortgage by the owner. A *nondisturbance agreement* or *subordination agreement* is necessary to insure the lease will continue in such cases. Sometimes for large projects, *subordinated ground leases* are established, in which the landowner subordinates his interest in the land to the fee mortgage, making possible acquisition of a loan to cover both the value of the improvements and the land.
- *Land trust certificate* and *rental trust certificate* are means of sharing ownership of a parcel of land (land trust certificate) or sharing ownership of leases (rental trust certificate) among a number of individuals. Land trust certificates work in the following way: An owner of a parcel leases it on a long-term basis to a high-quality tenant who agrees to build. The lease is sufficient security to back the issuance of land trust certificates to investors representing fractional interests in the development. Equitable title passes with the certificates, but legal title is given to a managing trustee. Rental trust certificates are similar except that ownership of leases or subleases is divided rather than fee interests. Each rental trust certificate represents a fractional share of equitable ownership of a lease. Legal ownership rests again with the managing trustee.
- *Personal loans* or consumer installment loans, which make use of assets beyond the property itself as security for the debt, are frequently used in the real estate market to finance improvements, repairs, or even purchase.

---

[5] Also called real estate contract, contract for deed, agreement to convey, land contract, or installment sales contract.

- *Housing and industrial development bonds* are available through a number of programs that provide revenue for the development and/or purchase of real estate through the issuance of tax-exempt bonds by governmental or quasi-government agencies. The tax exemption allows the cost of capital so raised to be lowered by several percentage points.

- *Securities issues*, in the form of real estate bonds, have been in existence for many years. In most cases they were issued by developer/owners to individual investors and backed by first mortgages as a means of raising additional capital. This traditional financing vehicle, however, suffered during the Depression and the REIT problems of 1974–1975.

  Today the real estate bond and debenture concept is being used more conservatively. GNMA mortgage-backed securities are being guaranteed by the federal government to increase the marketability of residential loans. In addition, FHLMC, FNMA, and some private mortgage companies are also developing residential mortgage bond programs.

- *Sale-leasebacks* involve the purchase of a property and immediate leasing back to the seller or a third party. The tax advantages of sale-leaseback are a major motivating factor in its frequent presence. In many cases it is a practical means to split interests in such a way that high-bracket investors can receive the benefits of depreciation and interest deductions through fee ownership, while low-bracket or tax-exempt individuals and institutions can benefit from the sale of those rights. Sometimes, in the case of a land sale and leaseback, only the land may be sold to a low-bracket owner, while the building is sold to a high-bracket investor. Those who wish to participate primarily in the capital gains expectations of long-term ownership in land would be interested in such an arrangement.

  One variation of the sale-leaseback technique is the subordinated ground lease arrangement, used often in shopping center developments. The owner of the land leases it back to the developer, keeps the land, but agrees that the land is to be mortgaged, with the developer obtaining the proceeds for additional capital.

Alternative Mortgage Instruments

From the Depression until quite recently, the standard means of financing residences in this country was the fully amortizable fixed-rate mortgage (FRM). However, beginning in the mid-1960s, volatility in interest rates and the economy, and increasing inflationary expectations, created problems for the FRM. Its inflexible yield and cash flow structure were partly responsible for periodically severe disintermediation at savings institutions. In addition, the "tilt effect," increasing current real payment levels that reflect rising inflationary expectations in the interest rate charged, began pricing numerous households out of the home-ownership market. A number of proposals began to be made to permit a variety of AMIs that would respond to these problems.

The Graduated Payment Mortgage. The Federal Home Loan Bank Board (FHLBB) in 1978 issued regulations permitting federally chartered S&Ls to issue Graduated Payment Mortgages (GPMs), which would resemble FRMs in that their rate would be a fixed, long-term rate, but payments would be graduated

TABLE 33.6   Comparison of Monthly Payments and Amortization: GPM vs. FRM

Loan terms: $100,000, 30-year maturity, 12 percent, GPM 7.5 percent graduation over five years

Year	GPM Payments	FRM Payments	GPM Outstanding Balance	FRM Outstanding Balance
1	$ 791.38	$1,028.61	$102,646.57	$99,637.12
2	850.73	1,028.61	104,875.34	99,228.22
3	914.54	1,028.61	106,577.49	98,767.46
4	983.13	1,028.61	107,625.63	98,248.16
5	1,056.86	1,028.61	107,871.63	97,663.22
6–30	1,136.13	1,028.61	—	—

over the first few years of the note to better match income trends. Several alternative plans were offered, the most popular being the five-year graduation period plan with rates of graduation at 5 and 7.5 percent. A comparison of the payment stream for the 7.5 percent graduation GPM to that for the standard FRM is provided in Table 33.6 for a $100,000 loan at 12 percent. It should be noted that the 7.5 percent graduation plan produces an initial payment of 23 percent ($237.23) below the FRM payment. The payment level then rises until it is 10 percent ($107.52) *above* the FRM level in years 6 through 30. The calculation of the initial payment for the GPM is determined by the formula:

$$Q_1 = L \div \left[(MPVA\ _{12\,mo.}^{i\%})(MSFF\ _{T\,yr.}^{u\%}) + \frac{(1 + g)^T (MPVA\ _{N-T\,yr.}^{i\%})}{\left(1 + \dfrac{i}{12}\right)^{12T}} \right]$$

where: Q_1 = first year's monthly payment

L = loan amount

$MPVA\ _{12\,mo.}^{i\%}$ = monthly present value of an annuity factor at $i\%$ (annual) for 12 months (i is the contract loan rate)

$MSFF\ _{T\,yr.}^{u\%}$ = monthly sinking fund factor at $u\%$ (the sinking fund rate) for T years (T is the period of graduation)

$$u = \frac{1 + g}{(1 + i/12)^{12}} - 1$$

g = rate of graduation

N = total term of the loan in years

The Variable Rate Mortgage and its Derivatives. In April 1981, the FHLBB authorized variable rate mortgages (VRMs), which permitted adjustment in interest rates over time in accord with an index rate, and imposed few restrictions. The only restrictions placed upon adjustable rate mortgages (ARMs) for commercial banks and adjustable mortgage loans (AMLs) for S&Ls were a one percent cap on the upward interest rate adjustment every six months and a requirement that lenders lower rates immediately if the interest rate index declines.[6]

The ARMs and AMLs were quite readily adopted during the most recent tight-money period of 1981 to 1982; however, lowered rates in late 1982 again forced many lenders to return to issuance of FRMs.

Other Instruments. A variety of other AMIs have been authorized by the FHLBB, or proposed since 1979, which have been intended to meet specific needs of borrowers and/or lenders under different economic scenarios:

The Reverse Annuity Mortgage (RAM). The RAM is designed for elderly borrowers with high amounts of liquid equity tied up in their residences. The most common RAM is designed as an annuity which draws down the equity in the form of monthly installments payable over a 10-year period. Interest accrues on the withdrawal, and all principal and interest become due upon the sale of the home, or the death of the owner and the transfer of the estate.

The Price Level Adjusted Mortgage (PLAM). The PLAM is offered at a low interest rate (the real interest rate, excluding inflationary expectations and a premium for bearing inflationary risk) and the balance each month indexed according to the Consumer Price Index (CPI). Payments then increase at the rate of inflation, remaining constant in real terms. This eliminates the tilt effect, substantially lowering initial monthly payments.

The Graduated Payment Adjustable Mortgage Loan (GPAML). The GPAML combines characteristics of the GPM, in that payments are indexed according to a payment rate, which is set ex ante, and the VRM, in that interest accrues at a separate debit rate that may be adjusted over time according to an index.

The Accelerated Equity Buildup Mortgage. This mortgage type is another form of the GPAML that has received some attention. The payment stream on this loan increases over time beyond the level necessary to amortize the loan over the term, paying off the loan more quickly. Because the loan is effectively short term, the lender will likely provide an interest rate reduction to encourage acceptance.

The Shared Appreciation Mortgage (SAM). The SAM allows the lender to offer a below-market rate in exchange for a share in the appreciation of the unit. Often, such loans have a contingent interest feature in which the borrower must pay the lender a share of the appreciation of the property upon sale or

---

[6] As an alternative to increasing monthly payments, the lender could lengthen the term or increase the outstanding balance. He could also separate the period of interest adjustment from that of payment adjustment (e.g., the interest rate could change every three to six months but the payments change only every one, two, or three years). This, of course, could result in negative amortization.

EXAMPLE: **Calculation of Payments and Outstanding Balance for the Price Level Adjusted Mortgage (PLAM)**

Loan terms: $100,000, 30-year maturity, rate of inflation 9 percent, real rate 3 percent

Year 1: Q_1 = Monthly payment $= \dfrac{Lr}{1 - (1 + r)^{-T}} = \dfrac{100,000\,\dfrac{(0.03)}{(12)}}{1 - \left(1 + \dfrac{0.03}{12}\right)^{-360}}$

$$= \$421.60$$

Outstanding balance prior to CPI adjustment $= Q_1 \times MPVA_{N - 12}^{r\%} = 421.60 \times 232.23734$

$$= \$97,912.20$$

Nominal outstanding balance after CPI adjustment $= \$97,912.20\,(1.09)$

$$= \$106,724.30$$

Year 2: Q_2 = Monthly payment $= \dfrac{106,724.30\,\dfrac{(0.03)}{(12)}}{1 - \left(1 + \dfrac{0.03}{12}\right)^{-348}}$

$$= \$459.55$$

Outstanding balance prior to CPI adjustment $= Q_2 \times MPVA_{N - 24}^{r\%} = 459.55 \times 227.13468$

$$= \$104,379.38$$

Nominal outstanding balance after CPI adjustment $= \$104,379.38\,(1.09)$

$$= \$113,773.52$$

etc.

Note: Figures may not add exactly due to rounding.

---

refinancing. The loans are generally written for long amortization periods but, like bullet loans in commercial lending, are due in 5 to 10 years.

There are two variants of the SAM in existence. The first is the Rich Uncle program, which exists in a variety of forms, all of which provide that, in exchange for a lower down payment, the homeowner shares appreciation with a coinvestor, which may be either an individual or a partnership, and also pays him a small return on his invested capital. The second variant of the SAM is the copurchaser mortgage in which two singles share in the purchase of a specially designed home.

The Balloon Mortgage. The balloon mortgage involves some lump-sum principal repayment at the end of a shortened term. Two types are prevalent:

(1) the interest-only balloon, in which payments cover interest only with a typical maturity of three to five years; and (2) a partially amortized balloon, based upon fixed or variable rates, in which the loan amortizes partially according to a normal, that is, 30-year, term but is due in full in 15 or fewer years.

Wraparound Mortgages (WRAPs). Under the WRAP or "blended" mortgage arrangement, the home buyer assumes the holder's low-interest rate mortgage from the lender plus an additional principal amount, bringing the loan up to the required amount. The rate on the assumption may be increased a percentage point or so, and the remainder of the principal will be loaned at a higher market rate.

Other Alternative Financing Mechanisms. Although technically not really included among the set of previous AMIs, a set of alternative financing mechanisms for home purchase has arisen out of necessity during the recent period of credit stringency. These have included such techniques as buydowns, seller financing, and installment land contracts.

With a buydown, the builder or seller "buys down" for a certain number of years (usually one to five) a certain proportion of the interest payments by paying a lump sum up front to the lender. Seller financing includes take back or purchase-money mortgages, either firsts or seconds. With an installment land contract, title passes only after the last payment is received. In the event of default, possession is much more easily taken than if foreclosure had to be formally undertaken.

ANALYSIS OF REAL ESTATE INVESTMENTS

The market for investment real estate has evolved very rapidly over the last decade. Decisions for investment and financing were once made solely on the basis of simple rules of thumb or instinct. Because the economic and financial environment was relatively stable, the rules of the marketplace relatively simple, and because inflation bailed everyone out, such decision criteria generally proved acceptable. However, economic instability, deregulation, and increasing competition have changed this situation, requiring the development and use of more exacting and generalized decision criteria.

As with all investments, the judgment of whether or not to invest, borrow, or lend in real estate is not just based upon a simple measure of expected profitability. It involves a trade-off between returns and risk associated with the investment, and a variety of other, usually subordinate, objectives such as cash flow, wealth constraints, and nonpecuniary returns. In addition, each investor type has its own particular set of weights and measures for these objectives, depending upon its risk aversion, set of portfolio opportunities, expertise, tradition, wealth, and cash flow situation. Accordingly, each also has its own particular set of analyses that is relevant to its decision-making needs. There are three basic types of studies that are generally undertaken by either the investor/borrower or lender, or both, in the course of decision making about a real estate investment. These include:

1 The Market Analysis

2 The Valuation Analysis (the Appraisal)

3 The Feasibility Analysis

The Market Analysis

The market analysis is probably the most basic of all the studies and is included in virtually all real estate decision making. It is essential because it provides the basis for the numbers which go into all the other studies. Its product is an estimate of current and future market and economic conditions. Both macrolevel (national, regional, and city) and microlevel (neighborhood and site) influences are recognized as important. The first task in any market analysis is to delineate the market area within which each of these influences operates and to insure that the parcel of interest lies within the market area.

At the national and regional level, the factors which seem most important for most types of real estate investments are economic and financial market conditions and economic development activities in various sections of the country. Examples here include inflationary expectations, current and future rates on mortgages and other borrowing, unemployment, changing economic structure, migration patterns, tax laws and other regulations, and technological evolution.

At the neighborhood level, the prevalent influences include conditions external to the subject property, which influence its desirability and marketability by affecting the physical environment within which it is situated and with which its usefulness is intimately related. These are often considered separately as demand and supply side influences.

Demand factors are those that influence the behavior of the demanders or consumers of space. These would include population growth or decline, income levels and trends, wealth, changing tastes and attitudes toward particular patterns of consumption, accessibility, the existence of nearby support facilities, the provision of necessary raw materials or services, the nearby location of a market for goods produced, condition and type of surrounding land uses, and the quality of life available in the immediate area.

On the supply side of the market, the market analysis is concerned both with the factor costs of production and the current and future available stock and price of competing real estate in the market area. Factor costs would include the cost and availability of land; the existence, availability, and cost of a suitable labor force for production (or service provision); operating and maintenance costs; taxes; and the cost of capital for real estate development or firm operations.

Once the demand and supply conditions are fully assessed and projected, their interaction within the market can be examined to develop estimates of current and future market conditions. Such conditions would include vacancy rates, construction rates, unsold inventory, absorption rates, rent/price trends, and conversion or redevelopment trends.

Valuation Analysis

The product of the appraisal is generally a recommended "highest and best" use, or type and intensity of use that provides the highest return to the investor, along with an estimate of market value. The market value is that price which a property would be expected to bring if exposed to sale under conditions currently typical for the market. The market value is always estimated under the highest and best use.

The appraisal makes use of the market analysis for input; it is used in turn as input into the feasibility analysis. An appraisal is useful because what a particular investor should pay for a property could be greater or less than the market value estimate, and their relationship can tell the investor a lot about his investment strategy. Furthermore, the investor is concerned about subsequent resale, which relates to a general investor, hence involving a market value estimate. Finally, the lender must be concerned about the adequacy of the property as security for the debt; therefore, he must have some estimate of what the property could be expected to bring if exposed to the market at a foreclosure sale.

There are three general methodologies for appraisal which have been developed and are of use for particular types of properties:

1 The Market Comparison Technique

2 The Cost Analysis Approach

3 The Income Approach

The Market Comparison Technique. This technique is based upon the principle of substitution: Properties with similar characteristics in the same market tend to sell for similar prices. It involves acquiring information on a number of recent sales in the same market to be used as comparables, adjusting these for various differences (e.g., time of sale, characteristics of property or neighborhood, and financing characteristics) to make them as similar to the subject property as possible, and weighting the adjusted value estimates in some way to achieve an estimated market value for the subject property. The market comparison technique is useful in all markets in which there is a relatively active market (i.e., many recent sales) and in which sales and other information is readily available. It is the technique which usually dominates in the single-family residential market. An example of a single-family residential appraisal using the market comparison technique is shown in Figure 33.1.

The Cost Analysis Approach. This technique is based upon the principle of contribution: The value added to a property by an attribute equals the marginal cost of production of the attribute less accrued depreciation. It involves estimating the replacement cost or reproduction cost new [7] of the structure, less accrued depreciation from various sources, plus the estimated land cost. Theoretically, the technique is applicable to all markets but provides less certain

---

[7] The replacement cost may differ from the reproduction cost new in that technologies and styles of building may change over time. The cost to replicate an older building (reproduction cost new) may be greater than the cost of producing a similar building with today's technology and style providing exactly the same utility as the older building (replacement cost). With such structures, replacement cost is the more appropriate cost estimate.

The undersigned has recited three recent sales of properties most similar and proximate to subject and has considered these in the market analysis. The description includes a dollar adjustment, reflecting market reaction to those items of significant variation between the subject and comparable properties. If a significant item in the comparable property is superior to, or more favorable than, the subject property, a minus (-) adjustment is made, thus reducing the indicated value of subject; if a significant item in the comparable is inferior to, or less favorable than, the subject property, a plus (+) adjustment is made, thus increasing the indicated value of the subject.

ITEM	Subject Property	COMPARABLE NO. 1		COMPARABLE NO. 2		COMPARABLE NO. 3	
Address	815 Pleasant Valley	3213 Tam O'Shanter		2819 Forest Grove		2800 Valley Ridge	
Proximity to Subj.		4 Blocks North		4 Blocks East		5 Blocks East	
Sales Price	$--		$160,000		$124,000		$110,000
Price/Living area	$-- Ø		$ 58.78 Ø		$ 53.24 Ø		$ 51.74
Data Source	Inspection	MLS/Realtor		MLS/Realtor		MLS/Realtor	
Date of Sale and Time Adjustment	DESCRIPTION	DESCRIPTION	+ (-) $ Adjustment	DESCRIPTION	+ (-) $ Adjustment	DESCRIPTION	+ (-) $ Adjustment
Date of Sale and Time Adjustment	3-83	9-82		11-82		10-82	
Location	good	similar		similar		similar	
Site/View	good	view of club -9,000		similar		similar	
Design and Appeal	good	similar		similar		similar	
Quality of Const.	good	similar		similar		similar	
Age	14	11		9		10	
Condition	good	superior	-4,000	inferior	+3,000	inferior	+3,000
Living Area Room Count and Total	Total 9 / B-rms 3 / Baths 2	Total 9 / B-rms 5 / Baths 3½	-1,750	Total 8 / B-rms 4 / Baths 2½	- 750	Total 8 / B-rms 4 / Baths 2½	- 750
Gross Living Area	2,514 Sq. Ft.	2,722 Sq. Ft.	-5,200	2,329 Sq. Ft.	+4,625	2,126 Sq. Ft.	+9,700
Basement & Bsmt. Finished Rooms	none	none		none		none	
Functional Utility	good	good		good		good	
Air Conditioning	central	central		central		central	
Garage/Car Port	none	2 car garage	-4,000	2 car garage	-4,000	2 car garage	-4,000
Porches, Patio, Pools, etc.	typical	pool	-15,000	pool	-15,000	similar	
Special Energy Efficient Items	typical	similar		similar		similar	
Other (e.g. fireplaces, kitchen equip., remodeling)	1 WBFP typical kitchen	similar		similar		similar	
Sales or Financing Concessions	n/a	assumption	-1,000	VA		conventional	
Net Adj. (Total)		☐ Plus; ☒ Minus	$ -39,950	☐ Plus; ☒ Minus	$ -12,125	☒ Plus; ☐ Minus	$ 7,950
Indicated Value of Subject			$ 120,050		$ 111,875		$ 117,950

Comments on Market Data ___ These adjusted sales range from $111,875 to $120,050

This appraiser estimates market value at $117,500

INDICATED VALUE BY MARKET DATA APPROACH .... $ 117,500

Source: Federal Home Loan Mortgage Corporation (Form 7), Federal National Mortgage Association (Form 1004)

FIG. 33.1 Using the Market Comparison Technique to Estimate the Market Value of a Single Family Residence

estimates of value for older properties, in which depreciation is considerable and construction technology has changed. It is the primary means of appraising unique nonincome producing properties for which neither an active market nor a rental stream exist that may provide the basis for value. Such properties include mansions, churches, schools, special use properties, and institutions.

The appraiser generally has less confidence in the depreciation estimate than in any other component of the cost analysis value estimate. This is both because of data limitations and limitations in appropriate techniques of analysis. There are three types of depreciation that may be attributed to a structure (land is considered indestructible; hence, it has no depreciation):

- *Physical deterioration* relates to physical wear and tear and the wearing out of a structure or a component.
- *Functional obsolescence* relates to the adequacy of the structure to perform the purpose for which it was originally intended because of a change in construction and component technology.
- *Locational obsolescence*, sometimes called economic obsolescence, relates to the loss in value due to the property's inability to perform the use for which it was originally intended because of locational factors in the environment.

The cost analysis technique is shown in Table 33.7 through the appraisal of a church building.

The Income Approach. This technique is based upon the principle of anticipation: Value is theoretically equal to the present value of all future net benefits derived from use of the property. In other words, value (V) is a function of income (I) or some other measure of benefits: $V = f(I)$. It involves development of an estimate of income to be derived from the property and an estimate of the capitalization rate (R) or discount rate to be applied to the income to yield the estimate of value. In the case of the capitalization or "cap" rate, the transformation is direct:

$$V = \frac{I}{R}$$

The income approach, of course, is only applicable to income-producing properties or properties for which a number of comparable properties are income producing.

There are a variety of techniques of income capitalization that have evolved in response to specific needs. Generally, these relate to (1) the particular income measure used; (2) the particular capitalization rate used; (3) the method of obtaining the capitalization rate; (4) whether the property is considered as a whole or by components, as defined by the land and the structure, or the mortgage and equity interests; (5) the pattern of income over time; and (6) the economic life.

The simplest capitalization technique—*direct capitalization*—makes no explicit assumption about the time pattern of income over time or about the economic life of the property. It instead allows the market to define an overall rate (OAR) by observing the ratio of net operating income to sales prices of comparable properties and applies this OAR to the first year expected net operating income (*NOI*) of the subject property:[8]

$$V = \frac{NOI}{OAR}$$

The *NOI* is defined as the gross potential income (*GPI*) from all sources (contract rent plus miscellaneous property revenues), less a vacancy and collection loss (*Vac*) based upon current market conditions (to obtain an estimate of

---

[8] Oftentimes, explicit comparisons are not carried out in the development of an estimate of the *OAR*. Rather, "word of mouth" or some other technique is used.

TABLE 33.7   Using the Cost Analysis Technique to Estimate the Market Value of a Church Building

The church building is 10 years old and in good condition, but located in an area undergoing transition to commercial uses.

Reproduction cost new (from comparable new construction, including hard and soft costs and site development: $67/sq ft × 10,000 sq ft)			$670,000
Less: Depreciation			
1. Physical deterioration			
Curable[a]			
Repainting	$5,000		
Repairs	3,000		
		$ 8,000	
Incurable[a]			
Structural decay = 1.5% per year or 15% on the incurable base ($670,000 − $8,000 = $662,000) 0.15 × $662,000		99,300	
Total physical deterioration		$107,300	
2. Functional obsolescence			
Curable			
Modernize trim (cost to cure)	$7,500		
New sound system (retro-fit cost)	2,000		
		$ 9,500	
Incurable			
Inefficient heating/air-conditioning system ($3,200 cost per year at 12% for 15-year life of system) 6.811 × 3,200		21,800	
Total functional obsolescence		$ 31,300	
3. Locational obsolescence			
Physical life of new church at ideal site (67 years)			
Present value of benefits at 12% (8.329)			
Physical life of new church at present site (30 years)			
Present value of benefits at 12% (8.055)			
Percent loss in benefits $\left(\dfrac{8.329 - 8.055}{8.329} = 3.3\%\right)$			
on depreciable base (reproduction cost new less physical and functional already taken or $670,000 − $107,300 − $31,300 = $531,400)			
Total locational obsolescence (0.033 × $531,400) =		$ 17,540	
Total depreciation			$156,140
Depreciated structure value			$513,860
Value of site by market comparison			150,000
Value of church property			$663,860

(a) "Curable" means curing the defect is economically desirable. The amount of depreciation is the cost to cure. "Incurable" means the cost to cure is in excess of the value contributed if cured. The amount of depreciation in this case is the present value of the loss of benefits by keeping the defect.

**TABLE 33.8   Calculation of Net Operating Income
Midrise Office-Building Development**

Revenues		
Rent (64,000 sq ft. × $17.00/sq. ft.)		$1,088,000
Parking fees ($250/space × 300 spaces)		75,000
Total gross potential income (GPI)		$1,163,000
Less: Vacancy and collection losses (4.5% of GPI)		52,335
Effective gross income (EGI)		$1,110,665
Expenses		
Fixed		
Property taxes	$ 72,500	
Insurance	13,900	
Total fixed costs	$ 86,400	
Variable		
Maintenance and repairs	$ 92,800	
Utilities	96,000	
Management (4% of EGI)	44,427	
Security (by contract)	25,000	
Total variable costs	$258,227	
Total fixed and variable costs		344,627
NOI prior to reserves for replacement		$ 766,038
Reserves for replacement		
Blacktop replacement (every 15 years, sinking fund in 8% account, at cost of $120,000; SFF = 0.036830)	$ 4,420	
Carpet replacement (every 10 years at cost of $100,000; SFF = 0.069029)	6,903	
Total reserves for replacement		11,323
NOI after reserves for replacement		$ 754,715

effective gross income), less fixed and variable operating expenses (*OE*), less reserves for replacement (*Res Repl*).

$$NOI = GPI - Vac - OE - Res\ Repl$$

Fixed operating expenses include those expenses, such as property insurance, property taxes, and exterior maintenance, that would be incurred regardless of whether the property is occupied or not. Variable operating expenses include those expenses that vary according to occupancy, such as property management and utilities. Reserves for replacement include a reserve for components that will need replacement over relatively long periods as they reach the end of their physical lives. An example of an NOI calculation is shown for an office-building development in Table 33.8.

Straight capitalization takes explicit account of the economic life of the subject property, the time pattern of income, and usually separates consideration of the building and land. *Straight capitalization, straight-line recapture* assumes a linearly declining income stream to a residual (constant) level attributable to return on the land at the end of the economic life of the building. *Straight capitalization, sinking fund recapture* assumes a constant income stream, dropping to the constant return on the land at the end of the economic life of the building. In either case, the NOI stream is divided into that proportion attributable to return *on* the land (NOI) and return *on* and *of* the building (NOI_B).

$$NOI = NOI_L + NOI_B$$

The return *of* is an amount in excess of the return *on* capital invested in the building. It represents the gradual return of a wasting asset. Each of these NOI components is then capitalized at an appropriate, *land capitalization rate* (IR_L) or *building capitalization rate* (BCR) to determine the value of the land and building respectively.

The land capitalization rate is determined through market observation. The building capitalization rate is composed of the return *on* the building (IR_B), estimated through market observation (usually somewhat higher than IR_L because of greater risk of capital invested in improvements), and the return *of* the building or rate of recapture (RR).

$$BCR = IR_B + RR$$

In straight-line recapture, RR is simply the inverse of the remaining economic life of the building. In sinking fund recapture, it is the sinking fund factor (SFF) for the economic life of the building and IR_B.

Straight capitalization is usually either land residual or building residual in that it makes use of an externally developed estimate of building value (usually through the cost analysis technique) or land value (usually through market comparisons for raw land sales) to back out the residual value of the land or building, respectively.

One widely used application of the land residual technique is the *highest and best use analysis,* in which a variety of possible land uses or development densities are assumed. In each case, the improvements value is estimated using the cost analysis technique, and a residual value to land is backed out. That use or density which results in the highest residual value to land is the highest and best use of the site. It also results in the greatest profitability to the investor and determines the market value of the site. Table 33.9 shows the use of the straight capitalization, sinking fund recapture, land residual technique in determination of the highest and best use of a 1.8 acre site.

The *annuity capitalization technique* involves discounting the property income stream back to a present value estimate at an appropriate discount rate (*not* in general the OAR) determined from market observation of the internal rate of return (IRR) required to attract investment to that particular type of investment. Like straight capitalization, it may separately value land and improvements using a land or building residual technique, or it may treat them together. One variation is the property residual technique, which assumes the property is resold at the end of the economic life of the building (or, alternatively, at the end of the holding period of the typical investor).

The final income property valuation technique, *mortgage-equity analysis,*

TABLE 33.9   Highest and Best Use Analysis Making Use of Straight Capitalization, Sinking Fund Recapture, Land Residual Technique 1.8 Acre Raw Land Site

	Alternative Use Category		
	5-Story Office Building	10-Story Office Building	15-Story Office Building
Construction cost (V_B)	$2,225,000	$4,250,000	$6,300,000
Estimated revenues (GPI)	$ 414,413	$ 732,000	$1,064,217
Estimated expenses (E)[a]	$ 62,000	$ 122,000	$ 210,000
Estimated NOI $(NOI = GPI - E)$	$ 352,413	$ 610,000	$ 854,217
Return on building (IR_B)[b]	0.10	0.10	0.10
Economic life of building	40 years	40 years	40 years
Return of building (RR)[c]	0.02259	0.02259	0.02259
Building capitalization rate $(BCR = IR_B + RR)$	0.12259	0.12259	0.12259
NOI attributable to return on and of the building $(NOI_B = V_B \times BCR)$	$ 272,763	$ 521,008	$ 772,317
NOI attributable to return on the land $(NOI_L = NOI - NOI_B)$	$ 79,650	$ 88,992	$ 81,900
Return on the land (IR_L)[b]	0.09	0.09	0.09
Estimated land value $\left(V_L = \dfrac{NOI_L}{IR_L}\right)$	$ 889,000	$ 988,800	$ 910,000
Highest and best use (highest estimated land value)		*	

(a) Includes vacancies, operating expenses, and reserves for replacement
(b) From market observation
(c) Sinking fund factor at economic life and IR_B

---

separates consideration of the property into its financial components, the mortgage and equity components. This technique provides an estimate of the OAR under specific assumptions about holding periods and cash flows over time. The *Ellwood* mortgage equity technique makes use of the following formula for representation of the OAR:

$$OAR = Y - MC \overset{+}{\underset{-}{}} (\tfrac{dep}{app} \times SFF_{@Y,HP})$$

where:

Y = required before-tax equity yield rate, or the before-tax IRR to equity required to attract capital to the market, obtained through market observation

M = loan/value ratio (L/V)

EXAMPLE: Use of the Ellwood Mortgage-Equity Technique to Estimate Value of an Office Property

It is assumed the required equity yield rate (Y) to attract capital to the office market is currently 18 percent. The property can be financed through an assumable 12 percent, 25-year note for 70 percent of value. The expected holding period is 10 years. During this time the property is expected to appreciate 40 percent.

The mortgage constant f for a 12 percent, 25-year rate is 0.126384. The proportion of the loan paid off P over the 10-year holding period is 0.12246. The sinking fund factor at 18 percent over 10 years is 0.042515. Therefore:

$$C = Y - f + P \times SFF_{@Y,HP} = 0.18 - 0.126384 + (0.12246)(0.042515)$$

$$= 0.05882$$

$$\text{and } OAR = Y - MC \pm \left(\frac{dep}{app} \times SFF_{@Y,HP}\right)$$

$$= 0.18 - 0.70(0.05882) - (0.40 \times 0.042515)$$

$$= 0.12182 \text{ or } 12.18 \text{ percent}$$

---

dep, app = proportional depreciation or appreciation of the property over the holding period

$SFF_{@Y,HP}$ = sinking fund factor at the equity yield rate (Y) over the holding period (HP)

C = $Y - f + P \times SFF_{@Y,HP}$, or the mortgage coefficient, where P is the proportion of the original mortgage balance paid off by the end of the holding period, and f is the mortgage constant[9]

Ellwood tables have been developed which provide estimates of the basic rate ($Y - MC$), C, $SFF_{@Y,HP}$, and P for various loan/value ratios, mortgage terms, holding periods, and required equity yield rates. The *Ellwood* technique is used quite frequently by the appraisal profession, partly due to the greater availability of data for mortgage and equity rates than for required return rates on the physical components of the property.

The Feasibility Analysis

Feasibility analysis uses as input the market analysis and the appraisal. In most general terms, its intent is to determine whether the specific use is feasible (i.e., meets the investor's criteria for acceptability).

There are several products of a feasibility analysis that are useful for investment decision making. The first, and probably most widely used, is the estimate of *investment value,* sometimes referred to as *justified investment*

---

[9] A second mortgage-equity technique, the Akerson formulation, is written in the form $OAR = Mf + EY - MP \times SFF_{@Y,HP} \pm \frac{dep}{app} \times SFF_{@Y,HP}$, which can be easily shown to be equivalent to the *Ellwood* formulation. E represents the equity/value ratio and the other terms are defined in the text.

price. This may differ from the estimate of market value for a number of reasons, including the investor's tax situation, his set of expectations about future market conditions, his risk aversion, and such constraints as cash flow requirements, down payment limitations, and a limited set of investment alternatives. To the extent that the feasibility analysis is below the market value estimate and the investor is confident about the parameters going into his analysis, the feasibility analysis is telling him that perhaps he is not the investor to invest in this market or that he is unlikely to be the successful bidder. To the extent that the investment value is above the market value estimate, he must ask himself whether his situation is unique and would not be recognized by the general market. If so, then he may incur a windfall return from investment. If not, however (the more general case), it means that somewhere in his analysis, there are parameters and expected market conditions that deviate from those recognized by the general market.

Other products of the feasibility analysis include various measures of the investor's return on equity and on the total investment, measures of risk associated with the investment, and various other measures that relate to the diverse set of objectives of the investor.

Projecting Cash Flows. The previous discussion on appraisal shows how net operating income (*NOI*) flowing from an investment is calculated. Because feasibility analysis is specific both to the individual site and the individual investor, it is necessary to proceed beyond *NOI* and take into account the impact of both debt service and taxes. Calculation of the *before-tax cash flow* (*BTCF*) or *cash throw-off* (*CTO*) is the first step beyond calculation of the *NOI*. *BTCF* is simply *NOI* less the debt service payment.

$BTCF = NOI -$ Debt service

This is what the investor actually puts into his pocket prior to paying his income taxes. Debt service, of course, varies with the mortgage type and terms. It may be fixed or graduated in nominal terms with the payment stream certain a priori, as with the fixed rate mortgage or the graduated payment mortgage, or it may be highly uncertain, as with the variable rate mortgage or price level adjusted mortgage.

The *after-tax cash flow* (*ATCF*) is the net income received by the investor after payment of income taxes. It is simply the *BTCF* less income tax payments (or plus tax savings) attributable to the specific investment.

$ATCF = BTCF -$ Tax

The tax due is simply the investor's marginal tax rate (*MTR*) times taxable income (*TI*) from the investment.

$Tax = MTR \times TI$

Taxable income is the income the IRS considers is being made from the investment and equals the *NOI* less deductions, which include interest (*Int*) and depreciation (*Depr*).

$TI = NOI - Int - Depr$

TABLE 33.10   Comparison of Pre-1981 and Current Tax Law Affecting Residential and Commercial Income Property

	Pre-1981 Tax Law	Current Tax Law
Residential property		
Depreciable life	30–40 years(a)	15, 35, or 45 years
Maximum depreciation method		
New property	200% declining balance	175% declining balance(b)
Existing property	125% declining balance	175% declining balance(b)
Recapture	Excess depreciation	Excess depreciation(c)
Component depreciation	Permitted	Not permitted
Commercial property		
Depreciable life	30–40 years(a)	15, 35, or 45 years
Maximum depreciation method		
New property	150% declining balance	175% declining balance
Existing property	Straight line	175% declining balance
Recapture	Excess depreciation	All depreciation, if investor has used accelerated depreciation
Component depreciation	Permitted	Not permitted

(a) Could be shorter on existing properties with shorter economic lives

(b) Up to 200 percent declining balance for low-income housing

(c) For low-income housing, recapture reduced by one percent for every month held past 100 months

Source: William B. Brueggeman, Jeffrey Fischer, and Gerald Stern, "Choosing the Optimal Depreciation Method Under 1981 Tax Legislation." *Real Estate Review* (Winter 1982), pp. 32–37

---

which can alternatively be written

$$TI = BTCF + Amort - Depr$$

in which *Amort* is the annual amortization of the note through debt service payments.

It should be noted that taxable income could be greater or less than *BTCF*, depending upon whether amortization is greater or less than depreciation. A tax shelter is said to exist any time that

$$TI < BTCF \text{ or, equivalently, } Amort < Depr$$

It should be noted also that if depreciation is large enough and amortization small enough, taxable income could become negative, and outside income could be tax sheltered.[10] This suggests that a desirable strategy for the investor would be

---

[10] This differs somewhat from some definitions of tax shelter. It does not say that outside income is necessarily sheltered ($TI < 0$), only that the income the IRS considers to have been made is less than that actually received.

to minimize amortization and maximize depreciation to the extent permitted by law. Appropriate depreciation methods were considerably changed in the 1981 Tax Reform Act. These are summarized in Table 33.10.[11]

There are a number of additional tax considerations that affect the *ATCF*, including investment tax credits, minimum tax requirements, tax credit provisions for rehabilitation expenditures, and investment interest limitations. The reader is referred to the appropriate Internal Revenue Code sections for greater detail on these. The development of the after-tax cash flow stream for an office-building development over a five-year holding period is shown in Table 33.11.

Estimating Proceeds from Sale. The reversion or proceeds from sale, like the cash flow, may be on either a before-tax, before-financing basis (gross reversion, corresponding to *NOI*), a before-tax, after-financing basis (net before-tax reversion, corresponding to BTCF), or an after-tax, after-financing reversion (net after-tax reversion, corresponding to *ATCF*). The formula for each is:

Gross reversion	= Sales price − Sales commission − Other nondebt and nontax transaction costs
Net before-tax reversion	= Gross reversion − Outstanding mortgage balance − Prepayment penalty − Other debt-related transaction costs
Net after-tax reversion	= Net before-tax reversion − Tax on sale − Any tax-related transaction costs

The tax due on sale has been revised considerably by the 1981 Tax Reform Act. If straight-line depreciation has been used,

$$\text{Tax on sale} = (\text{Adjusted sales price} - \text{Remaining book value}) \times 0.40 \times MTR$$

The adjusted sales price is the sales price less transactions costs, such as sales commission, and any loan prepayment penalties that are permitted as deductions by the IRS. The remaining book value, of course, is the depreciated value of the property as of the date of sale. It should be noted that this tax is at a lower capital gains tax rate. Thus, the advantages of taking depreciation deductions include both the time value of the deduction and the lower tax rate on income generated at resale.

In the event that 175 percent declining balance depreciation has been taken, however, the recapture provision applies, reducing these capital gains tax advantages. In such a case:

For residential properties—

Tax on sale = (Adjusted sales price − Remaining book value under straight-line depreciation) × 0.40 × *MTR* + (Remaining book value under straight-line depreciation − Remaining book value under accelerated depreciation) × *MTR*

---

[11] Note: As this volume was going to press, the Tax Reform Act of 1984 was being signed into law, which will modify several of these provisions, including an extension to 18 years (from 15) of the minimum allowable depreciable life. The interested reader is urged to consult the current tax code to keep abreast of these changes.

For commercial properties—
Tax on sale = (Adjusted sales price − Purchase price) × 0.40 × *MTR* + (Purchase price − Remaining book value) × *MTR*

The last term in each equation is the recapture term. The intent of this provision is to recapture income taxes lost by the taking of excess depreciation. The provision is more severe in the case of commercial properties. In fact, it is so severe, it has effectively rendered the taking of accelerated depreciation for these properties undesirable.

Measures of Return, Value, and Other Investment Criteria. Now that all cash flows proceeding from the investment have been developed, it is possible to develop estimates of various measures of return, investment value, and other investment criteria. Two sets of criteria are relevant here: traditional cash flow criteria and contemporary investment criteria.

Traditional Cash Flow Criteria. These include multipliers and financial and profitability ratios used either by lenders (to evaluate the risk they face in lending and their acceptable loan size) or by equity investors (to determine a property's market or investment value and profitability). Those most frequently applied are defined and categorized in Table 33.12. These criteria become less useful during inflationary, tight money periods because a greater share of total returns comes from (unmeasured) capital gains, because market standards tend not to fully adjust to reflect market conditions, and because the time value of money is not taken into account. During such periods, heavier reliance on contemporary investment criteria is suggested.

Contemporary Investment Criteria. These criteria all make use of the time value of money. They include:

- *Present Value Criteria,* which result in a present value (*PV*) estimate of future benefits;
- *Internal Rate of Return Criteria,* which provide an estimate of the IRR on the cash flows from an investment; and
- *Modified Return Criteria,* which estimate returns modified to correct for certain shortcomings in the IRR measures.

The *PV* of an investment is defined by the relationship

$$PV = \sum_{i=1}^{T} \frac{CF_i}{(1 + R)^i} + \frac{\text{Reversion}}{(1 + R)^T}$$

where:
CF_i = cash flow during period i
T = holding period
Reversion = reversion upon resale
R = discount rate, a rate observed in the market as the return necessary to attract capital to this type of investment

(*text continues on page 33-53*)

TABLE 33.11   Calculation of Revenues and Expenses Over Holding Period
Midrise Office Building Development

	Year 1	Year 2	Year 3	Year 4	Year 5
Revenues					
Base rent	$1,088,000	$1,088,000	$1,280,000	$1,280,000	$1,280,000
Escalations	—	32,000	34,560	37,325	40,311
Parking fees	75,000	81,000	87,480	94,478	102,037
Total gross potential income	$1,163,000	$1,201,000	$1,402,040	$1,411,803	$1,422,348
Less: Vacancy and collection losses	(52,335)	(74,462)	(84,122)	(77,649)	(71,117)
Effective gross income	$1,110,655	$1,126,538	$1,317,918	$1,334,154	$1,351,231
Expenses					
Property taxes	$ 72,500	$ 79,025	$ 86,137	$ 92,167	$ 98,619
Insurance	13,900	15,151	16,515	18,001	19,621
Maintenance and repairs	92,800	101,152	110,256	116,871	123,883
Utilities	96,000	105,600	116,160	130,099	145,711

Management	44,427	45,062	79,075	80,049	81,074
Security	25,000	25,000	25,000	32,500	32,500
Total expenses	$ 344,627	$ 370,990	$ 433,143	$ 469,687	$ 501,408
NOI prior to reserves for replacement	$ 766,038	$ 755,548	$ 884,775	$ 864,467	$ 849,823
Less: Debt service(a)	(505,960)	(505,960)	(505,960)	(505,960)	(505,960)
Before-tax cash flow	$ 260,078	$ 249,588	$ 378,815	$ 358,507	$ 343,863
Plus amortization	16,620	19,102	21,954	25,233	29,002
Less: Depreciation(b)	(525,000)	(463,750)	(409,646)	(361,854)	(319,638)
Taxable income	$ (248,302)	$ (195,060)	$ (8,877)	$ 21,886	$ 53,227
Tax (savings)(c)	(124,151)	(97,530)	(4,439)	10,943	26,614
Plus before-tax cash flow	260,078	249,588	378,815	358,507	343,863
After-tax cash flow	$ 384,229	$ 347,118	$ 383,254	$ 347,564	$ 317,249

(a) Mortgage terms: $3,500,000 note at 14 percent, 25-year maturity
(b) 175 percent, 15-year depreciation permitted under the Accelerated Cost Recovery System
(c) Investor assumed to be in 50 percent tax bracket

TABLE 33.12   Traditional Investment Criteria: Multiplier and Ratio Analysis

	Used Primarily by Equity Investor	Used Primarily by Mortgage Lender
Before Tax and Financing	Gross rent multiplier $= \dfrac{\text{Investment}}{\text{GPI}}$ Effective gross rent multiplier $= \dfrac{\text{Investment}}{\text{EGI}}$ Overall rate of return (rate of return on total capital) $= \dfrac{\text{NOI}}{\text{Investment}}$	Operating expense ratio $= \dfrac{\text{Operating expenses}}{\text{EGI}}$
Before Tax After Financing	Payback period $= \dfrac{\text{Equity capital}}{\text{BTCF}}$ Equity dividend rate (rate of return on equity) $= \dfrac{\text{BTCF}}{\text{Equity capital}}$	Debt coverage ratio $= \dfrac{\text{NOI}}{\text{Debt service}}$ Break-even ratio $= \dfrac{\text{Operating expenses + Debt service}}{\text{EGI}}$ Loan/value ratio $= \dfrac{L}{\text{Investment}}$
After Tax and Financing	After-tax dividend rate $= \dfrac{\text{ATCF}}{\text{Equity capital}}$ Gross yield on equity $= \dfrac{\text{ATCF + Principal repayment}}{\text{Equity}}$ Average after-tax return on equity $= \dfrac{\left(\dfrac{\Sigma\text{ATCF + AT Rev.} - \text{Equity}}{\text{Holding period}}\right)}{\text{Equity investment}}$	

Definitions: GPI = gross potential income   BTCF = before-tax cash flow   AT Rev. = after-tax reversion
               EGI = effective gross income   ATCF = after-tax cash flow   Investment = purchase price
               NOI = net operating income   L = loan amount

Essentially, this relationship discounts the future cash flows at the opportunity cost of capital and brings them to the present. The criteria may be applied on a before-tax, before-financing basis, in which case the present value becomes an estimate of the market value of the property.[12] The appropriate cash flow in such a case is the *NOI*. The reversion is the gross reversion. This is the annuity capitalization, property residual, technique.

If the criteria are applied on a before-tax, after-financing basis, the present value becomes an estimate of the market value of the equity component of the property.[13] The appropriate discount rate is the required before-tax equity yield rate (*Y*). The appropriate cash flow measure is the before-tax cash flow (*BTCF*). The appropriate reversion is the net, before-tax reversion. This is recognized as a generalized mortgage-equity capitalization method. The mortgage amount is then added to the equity value to determine the total property value.

Finally, if the criteria are applied on an after-tax, after-financing basis, the present value becomes an estimate of the investment value of the equity, which is added to the mortgage amount to result in an estimate of the *investment value* of the property, the subjective value of the property by the invididual investor.[14] The appropriate cash flow is the *ATCF*. The reversion is the net after-tax reversion. The discount rate is the after-tax equity yield rate currently appropriate for markets of this type.

The *internal rate of return* (*IRR*) of an investment is defined by the relationship

$$\text{Investment cost} = \sum_{i=1}^{T} \frac{CF_i}{(1 + IRR)^i} + \frac{\text{Reversion}}{(1 + IRR)^T}$$

where: CF_i = cash flow during period i
  T = holding period
 Reversion = reversion upon resale

Essentially, this relationship determines the required discount rate in order to equate the present value of the cash flows (including the reversion) to the initial outlay. Again, the criteria may be applied both on a before-and after-tax and financing basis.

The before-tax, before-financing *IRR* is known as the *internal rate of return on total investment*. The appropriate cash flow, reversion, and investment cost are the *NOI*, gross reversion, and purchase price, respectively. This measure is the internal rate of return counterpart to the *OAR*, but generally is higher than the *OAR*.

The before-tax, after-financing *IRR* is known as the *before-tax equity yield rate* (*Y*) for the subject property. The *BTCF*, net before-tax reversion, and down payment are the appropriate measures of cash flow, reversion, and in-

---

[12] This is true only so long as the cash flow estimates are those made by a typical investor in the market, the discount rates are those of a typical investor, and the proposed use is the highest and best use. Otherwise, the present value is an estimate of the investment value.

[13] *Ibid.*

[14] If, however, cash flow estimates, discount rates, financing terms, and tax rates are those for a "typical" investor in the market, and the use is the highest and best use, then the present value is an estimate of the market value.

vestment cost. This measure corresponds to the equity dividend rate among the traditional cash flow investment criteria, respectively, but is generally higher.

Finally, the after-tax, after-financing *IRR* is known as the *after-tax equity yield rate* for the subject property. The *ATCF*, net after-tax reversion, and down payment are the relevant parameters in determination of this IRR. The after-tax equity yield rate most closely resembles the after-tax equity dividend rate among the traditional cash flow investment criteria but again is usually higher.

The decision rule using the *IRR* measures is: If the after-tax equity yield rate indicated for the property is the same or greater than the required hurdle rate, then purchase at the required asking price. Comparison of the indicated IRR on total investment and the before-tax equity yield rate with their respective hurdle rates also provides information about the relationship between the asking price and the market value.

The *IRR* criteria clearly are superior to traditional cash flow investment criteria in that they take into account future cash flows and reversion, as well as current cash flows, and they consider the time value of money. However, the *IRR* is often considered inferior to the present value criteria in that it implicitly assumes all dollars received are reinvested at the *IRR*, which may not be true, especially for projects with relatively high or low returns. Also, under certain cash flow patterns, multiple rates of return may result.

In an attempt to overcome these shortcomings of the *IRR*, several modified return procedures have been developed, which make different assumptions about the reinvestment rate. One of the most frequently used, the financial management rate of return (*FMRR*), assumes cash flows are at first reinvested at a "safe" (liquid) rate for a period until they can accumulate to an amount sufficient to reinvest in a typical real estate project. The *FMRR* is defined only for the after-tax, after-financing cash flow streams and reversion. To obtain the *FMRR*, cash flows are future valued at the appropriate rate to the terminal year of the investment and summed to a terminal value. The *FMRR* is then defined as

$$FMRR = \sqrt[T]{\frac{V_T^*}{D_0^*}} - 1$$

where: T = holding period
           V_T^* = terminal value
           D_0^* = initial investment

The advantage of these modified return measures is that they can better replicate what the firm actually does with its cash receipts. However, they are sometimes criticized for not adequately replicating reality, or for providing mathematical overkill on data that may be in itself very tentative.

Using Feasibility Analysis to Structure the Investment

The alternative measures of return are only the first set of useful results from the feasibility analysis. It is useful also for structuring the investment with respect to taxes, financing, management and redevelopment decisions, and risk.

Tax Planning. The intent here is to minimize and/or defer income tax payments in such a way that the after-tax equity yield rate (or other suitable measure of return or investment value) is maximized. Numerous tax treatment alternatives exist, which may be tested against the base case to evaluate optimal tax structuring. These include choice of tax year, choice of accounting method, capitalizing versus expensing cash expenditures, property exchanges, installment sales, sale-leasebacks, and division of interests in syndications.

Financial Planning. A second major exercise necessary in structuring an investment is financial planning, an attempt to use debt creatively to maximize the investment value or equity yield of the project within constraints imposed by risk or other considerations. This can be accomplished by (1) reducing the amount of equity in the project (assuming it can be used to generate other higher returns elsewhere); or (2) reducing the rate paid for borrowed funds. Some of the most common techniques for doing this are refinancing the existing note at a lower rate, going to an interest-only note, extending the maturity, or adding a second mortgage. In each case, the assumption is that the cost of borrowed funds is lower than what the property is returning on a free-and-clear basis. If it is not, then negative financial leveraging is being employed.

Maximum financial leveraging would be unambiguously desirable if it were not for several factors, which render its use undesirable beyond a certain point. First, trade-offs are often implicit between the amount of debt forthcoming as a proportion of property value and its cost, because of the increased risk of default. Whether leveraging is increased depends upon how costly the debt is, relative to the return provided by the reduction in equity investment. Second, increased use of debt can substantially increase the volatility of expected returns; hence, the riskiness of the investment. Therefore, beyond a point, even though expected returns may be increased, increased risk associated with the investment may make a higher discount rate appropriate, thus lowering the measure of project desirability.

Risk Analysis. The investor may also use the feasibility analysis to assess project risk. A thorough risk analysis can help the investor to assess the magnitude of the uncertainty in various return or profitability measures and to determine their source. It can also aid in determining how well the project hedges the existing portfolio of investments.

Traditional Risk Criteria. A number of traditional risk criteria in the form of financial ratios have been used for years, especially by lenders, as rules-of-thumb for lending and setting loan terms. These include the debt-coverage ratio, the operating expense ratio, the break even ratio, and the loan/value ratio. While inadequate in and of themselves to assess risk of default, they each proximate in various dimensions the ability of a property to withstand unforseen adverse fluctuations in income, expenses, or market value.

Sensitivity Analysis. Sensitivity analysis attempts to test the degree of impact of uncertainty in various parameters on various measures of return or other criteria. It is usually carried out by varying the values of the input variables in the basic discounted cash flow model and observing how this affects such output as market value, investment value, after-tax equity yield, and debt/coverage ratio. Usually, the analyst's judgment is used to select optimistic, most probable, and pessimistic values for each parameter. Runs are made, first varying each parameter individually to assess marginal impacts, and then varying all together to determine combined effects. One problem with the latter exercise is that it exaggerates the likely variability in returns by assuming all parameters are perfectly correlated, which they are not.

Monte Carlo Simulation. Monte Carlo simulation explicitly assigns a probability distribution of future values to each of the parameters in the analysis. The probability distributions are obtained through surveys, estimation techniques, or the analyst's best judgment. A number of computer runs are made under the assumed set of probability distributions. In each, a set of parameter values are randomly selected according to the probability distribution. The return and other outputs are then observed. Over a number of runs, the outputs begin to approximate a probability distribution over their range. Like sensitivity analysis, Monte Carlo simulation assumes the parameters are independently distributed.

SUGGESTED READING

The Appraisal of Real Estate, 8th ed. Chicago: American Institute of Real Estate Appraisers, 1983.

Arnold, Alvin L., et al. *Modern Real Estate*. Boston: Warren, Gorham & Lamont, 1980.

Brueggeman, William B., et al. "Choosing the Optimal Depreciation Method Under 1981 Tax Legislation." *Real Estate Review* (Winter 1982), pp. 32–37.

Brueggeman, William B., and Leo D. Stone. *Real Estate Finance*, 7th ed. Homewood, Ill.: Richard D. Irwin, 1981.

Colton, Kent. "Financial Reform: A Review of the Past and Prospects for the Future." *AREUEA Journal*, Vol. 8 (1980), pp. 91–117.

Dennis, Marshall W. *Mortgage Lending Fundamentals and Practices*. Reston, Va.: Reston Publishing Co., 1981.

Dougall, Herbert E., and Jack E. Gaumnitz. *Capital Markets and Institutions*, 4th ed. Englewood Cliffs, N.J.: Prentice-Hall, 1980.

'82 Savings and Loan Sourcebook. Chicago: United States League of Savings Associations, 1982.

A Guide to Fannie Mae. Washington, D.C.: Federal National Mortgage Association, 1979.

Jaffe, Austin J., and C. F. Sirmans. "Improving Real Estate Investment Analysis." *Appraisal Journal* (Jan. 1981), pp. 85–94.

———. *Real Estate Investment Decision Making*. Englewood Cliffs, N.J.: Prentice-Hall, 1982.

Maisel, Sherman J., and Stephen E. Roulac. *Real Estate Investment and Finance*. New York: McGraw-Hill, 1976.

McKenzie, Joseph A. "A Borrower's Guide to Alternative Mortgage Instruments." *Federal Home Loan Bank Board Journal*, Vol. 5, No. 1 (Jan. 1982), pp. 16–22.

Messner, Stephen D., and M. Chapman Findlay, III. "Real Estate Investment Analysis: IRR versus FMRR." *The Real Estate Appraiser* (July–Aug. 1975), pp. 5–20.

Phyrr, Stephen A. "Real Estate Risk Goes Scientific." *Real Estate Review*, Vol. 3, No. 3 (Fall 1973), pp. 62–67.

———, and James A. Cooper. *Real Estate Investment*. Boston: Warren, Gorham & Lamont, 1982.

Seldin, Maury, ed. *The Real Estate Handbook*. Homewood, Ill.: Dow Jones-Irwin, 1980.

Smith, Halbert C., et al. *Real Estate and Urban Development*, 3rd ed. Homewood, Ill.: Richard D. Irwin, 1981.

Vandell, Kerry D. "Toward Analytically Precise Definitions of Market Value and Highest and Best Use." *Appraisal Journal* (Apr. 1982), pp. 253–268.

34

Financial Strategy

DENNIS E. LOGUE

The financial objective of the business organization is maximization of owners' wealth. This chapter discusses strategies that are helpful in doing so.

FREE CASH FLOW

For a publicly held corporation where ownership and management are separate, the financial objective implies that managers must strive to maximize the amount of free cash flow "available" to investors over time. (See Treynor (1981).) Free cash flow is the amount of cash generated by the business in excess of that necessary to be reinvested to sustain the base business. This free cash flow can either be distributed to investors through cash dividends or share repurchases, or it can be retained in the business to generate growth in sales and earnings, hence raising share values. If cash is retained, the benefits of the retention should be weighed against the price of retention (the cost of not distributing cash to investors); in other words, the estimated return on invested funds must be compared to investors' required returns.

In publicly held corporations, managers are agents of shareholders; they work for, and should work on behalf of, shareholders. There is probably no other corporate objective, aside from shareholder wealth maximization, that the owners, if polled, could unanimously agree upon. As a consequence, any financial objective other than shareholder wealth maximization (achieved, of course, in accordance with legal and moral norms) is simply unlikely to meet owners' desires.

While the financial objective of the corporation is unambiguous, it does not automatically produce a guide for action. The objective must be recast in terms that relate to specific types of business decisions. More importantly, it must be couched in probabilistic terms, that is, in terms of choices that are more or less likely to increase owners' wealth rather than in terms of choices that unambiguously affect owners' wealth by a given magnitude.

Financial decision making is not like physical estimation. In physics, certain actions have perfectly predictable consequences: A rock dropped from the top of a building will hit the ground. In business decisions, one can never be perfectly confident of the consequences of any nontrivial decision; a new marketing program is likely to increase sales, but it may not.

Shareholder wealth maximization, therefore, is a tricky business. First, factors over which one has some degree of control and that seem to associate with the financial objective must be identified. Second, the likely impact of decisions on those factors must be estimated. Pursuit of the objective is, thus, not a purely physical process.

The financial manager plays a vital role in the process of value creation for shareholders. Most importantly, the financial manager should substantively participate in the capital allocation process, the financing process, and the general behavior of the business organization. Before considering these areas of influence on value creation, a brief discussion of the things that affect stock prices and, as a result, shareholder wealth, is relevant.

STOCK PRICES

Enhanced stock value (and/or increasingly large distributions of cash) is the financial objective of the corporation. In many instances, stock prices also govern: (1) executive compensation and job security; (2) shareholder relations; (3) access to capital; (4) acquisition strategy; and (5) ability to resist takeovers. (See Branch and Gale (1983).) Accordingly, corporate strategy and, particularly, financial decision making must be designed to influence stock prices beneficially.

Market to Book Ratios

High or low stock prices, per se, have no significant meaning. A company whose shares are selling for $100 each can split its stock five for one and have its shares selling for $20 each. It remains the same company, however. Thus, the concept of a high or low stock price must be discussed in the context of a benchmark.

For the benchmark, the ratio of the market price of the stock to per share book value is used, commonly referred to as the market to book ratio. (Sometimes, this is referred to as the q ratio.) A market to book ratio of greater than 1.0 implies that the company is adding value. Ignoring for the moment accounting complications, inflation, and the like, a market to book of greater than 1.0 means that investors put up $1.00 and management transforms it into a market value of more than $1.00. On the other hand, a market to book ratio of less than 1.0 is a signal that management may be engaging in a value-destruction process because $1.00 is transformed into a market value of less than $1.00.

Care must be taken in interpreting market to book ratios. First, identification of value-creating and value-destroying processes must be done "at the margin." That is, companies may have low market to book ratios as a consequence of poor prior decisions, but if recent and new capital allocation decisions could be explicitly priced separately from prior allocations, the market to book ratios of the new could be substantially above 1.0. Unfortunately, when evaluating a company, it is sometimes impossible to disentangle the effect of the new and the old decisions upon worth. All that it may be possible to assert is if a company's market to book is rising (all other things remaining the same), relative to other companies in the same industry its new decisions are likely better than its old decisions.

A second caution in evaluating market to book ratio is accounting problems. Two identical firms could have different market to book ratios simply as a result of different accounting methods for depreciation and inventory, hence, different ways of determining book value. Similarly, inflation could lead to serious distortions in book value of what an investor puts into a company either directly or indirectly through corporate earnings retentions. (See Chapter 15 for a treatment of these problems.)

Despite these cautions, market to book ratios provide at least some clues as to what companies might be doing to enhance shareholder wealth.

Factors Affecting Stock Prices—Market to Book Ratios

Examination of historical data to identify what factors lead to high and low market to book ratios is a useful exercise. It can reveal past and present hallmarks of successful and unsuccessful companies. It also may provide insights into what companies ought to do in developing and implementing their overall strategies.

Branch and Gale provide very useful data in an excellent recent study on factors affecting stock prices. Figure 34.1 is adopted from that study.

The value creation process is affected by management's ability to identify and follow through on sound capital projects and to finance those projects in a least-cost way.

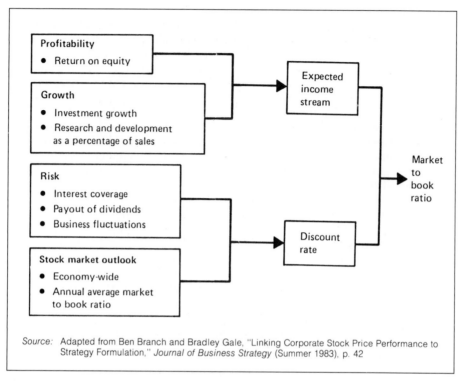

Source: Adapted from Ben Branch and Bradley Gale, "Linking Corporate Stock Price Performance to Strategy Formulation," *Journal of Business Strategy* (Summer 1983), p. 42

FIG. 34.1 Key Determinants of Stock Prices

To see how strongly each factor associates with shareholder value creation, Table 34.1 has been constructed. It shows for the period 1974–1981 just how strongly some of the variables noted in Figure 34.1 affected average market to book ratios for the companies in the Branch and Gale study. Clearly, profitability combined with investment growth and expenditures on research and development created value for shareholders. For instance, for companies that had high returns on equity and high annual growth in investment, the average market to book ratio was 1.83. If new investment and old investment was equally beneficial to owners, this implies a $1.00 newly put into the firm would be transformed into a value of $1.83. This is clearly value creation. On the other hand, a firm that spends virtually nothing on research and development and has a low return on equity (again, if new and old decisions are homogenous) is value destroying: a $1.00 put into the firm is transformed into a value of 59 cents.

Branch and Gale also show that management of capital structure has a meaningful role in market to book determination. As shown in Table 34.2, high profitability firms with high payout ratios create value, as do firms with high interest coverage. In contrast, low payout firms with low profitability seem to be destroying value, as they retain $1.00 that could otherwise be given to shareholders and transform its market value into 60 cents.

The Branch and Gale study demonstrates that market to book ratios, useful measures of whether management is creating or destroying wealth, are strongly

TABLE 34.1   Factors Influencing Stock Price: Average Market to Book Ratios for Companies in These Categories, 1968–1981

Average Return on Equity	Annual Growth in Investment		
	12 Percent and Over	8 to 12 Percent	0 to 8 Percent
15 percent and over	1.83	1.41	1.14
10 to 15 percent	1.17	0.96	0.83
9 to 10 percent	0.81	0.67	0.57

Average Return on Equity	Annual Average Ratio of Research and Development to Sales		
	2.0 Percent and Over	0.5 to 2.0 Percent	0 to 0.5 Percent
15 percent and over	2.02	1.49	1.35
10 to 15 percent	1.25	0.92	0.90
0 to 10 percent	0.73	0.63	0.59

Source: Adapted from Ben Branch and Bradley Gale, "Linking Corporate Stock Price Performance to Strategy Formulation," *Journal of Business Strategy* (Summer 1983), p. 42

TABLE 34.2   Financing Decisions Relation to Average Market to Book Ratios

Return on Equity	Dividend Payout Ratios (Dividends/Earnings)		
	40 Percent and Over	25 to 40 Percent	0 to 25 Percent
15 percent and over	1.92	1.47	1.49
10 to 15 percent	0.99	0.94	1.03
0 to 10 percent	0.66	0.60	0.60

Average Market to Book Ratio	Interest Coverage (Profits Before Interest and Taxes/Interest Obligations)
1.5 to 2.0	12 × up
1.0 to 1.5	6 × to 12X
0.5 to 1.0	6 × down

Source: Adapted from Ben Branch and Bradley Gale, "Linking Corporate Stock Price Performance to Strategy Formulation," *Journal of Business Strategy* (Summer 1983), p. 42

influenced by return on equity, investment growth, research and development spending, dividend payout, and leverage. Other studies also suggest that value creation is affected by the degree of proprietariness of a product (e.g., whether it has extensive patent protection, whether the marketing team has successfully differentiated the product in the marketplace, and whether there are significant barriers to other firms' competing).

Factors associated with high market to book ratios are the consequences of other decisions. They are not generally decision variables themselves. A company cannot decide to have a high return on equity. Moreover, simply spending lots of money on research and development, although it is a hallmark of a value-creating enterprise, will not automatically lead to higher market to book ratios. In the best firms, high research and development spending is a response to creative identification of new opportunities, not rote behavior. There are, however, ways to make decisions that will tend to produce desired results. As noted before, there is not in business a perfect one-for-one correspondence between action and outcome. However, much can be done to narrow the range of possible outcomes resulting from particular decisions. (See Rappaport (1981).)

One other factor that seems to be a hallmark of value-creating firms deserves special emphasis. In an excellent book, William Fruhan (1979) offers a list of "Hall of Fame" firms. There are firms that have produced high returns on equity over a long period, and that have given investors extraordinary rewards. His study uncovered 72 New York Stock Exchange firms that produced return on equity of 15 percent or more in every year over the period 1966–1975. One feature common to all these firms was the generally narrow focus of their businesses. To be sure, there were some very large companies on the list, IBM for example. However, there were no conglomerates; no companies with a collection of extremely divergent businesses, wildly different technological production, and marketing bases. Indeed, 82 percent of the "Hall of Fame" firms derived 50 percent or more of their sales from a single line of business.

The empirical inference from this study is supported by the observations in the Peters and Waterman book (1982), and by Logue's and Tapley's analysis (1983): Large multidivisional, multi-industry companies are hard to manage, and all too often fail to create substantial value for their shareholders.

The necessary managerial control mechanisms in such companies often get in the way of creativity and inventiveness. This insight into value creation is something that ought to be kept in mind in decisions regarding acquisitions and new business development.

Management Action

Finance theory provides many useful insights into the decisions managers might make in order to maximize shareholder wealth. Indeed, many of the chapters in this book, particularly Chapters 25, 26, 27, and 29, give the theoretical foundations for these techniques and offer guidance on how to use them. They are highlighted together here, however, in summary form, because these are the key elements in implementing a value-creating strategy.

First, managers should assure that new projects undertaken as well as continuing businesses generate sufficient cash flows to compensate investors for waiting and for risk, and that they cover their capital costs. This entails making

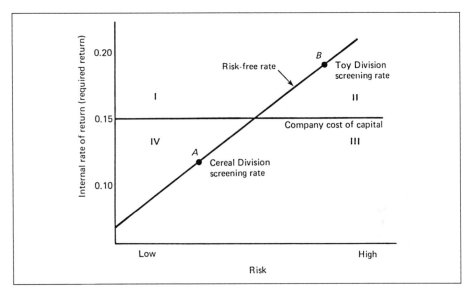

FIG. 34.2 Relation Between Required Return and Risk

forecasts of future free cash flows and making estimates of the appropriate capital costs. The former can be done using techniques discussed in Chapters 21 and 22; the latter can be done using either the dividend growth model, treated in Chapter 16, or the capital asset pricing model, discussed in Chapters 14, 26, and 27. Of course, these estimates must be adjusted for the effect of capital structure, the debt/equity ratio, on the cost of equity.

It is important to emphasize that, for most firms, capital costs will not be the same for every project. Each project has different risk characteristics, so the capital cost, often referred to as the screening rate, hurdle rate, or discount rate, should be different for each project. As a practical matter, it is cumbersome to estimate different screening rates for each different project. So business firms that sensibly distinguish risks among projects typically set up different screening rates for different divisions of a business. It is easiest to see why this is important by examining the consequences of not doing so.

Suppose *X* has two divisions: a cereal division and a toy division. The former has low risk and consequently deserves a low screening rate; the latter has high risk and deserves a high screening rate, 10 and 20 percent, respectively. The company's overall cost of capital is 15 percent.

Figure 34.2 shows the relationship between required return and risk. In this context, and only for illustration, the internal rate of return is used as a capital budgeting decision criterion.

If the company uses its cost of capital as a screening rate for the toy division, it will accept projects in Sector II. These will be undertaken despite the fact that they would not be if the company were only a toy company. Similarly, the company will turn down projects that fall into Sector IV, despite the fact that they would be economically worthwhile even if the company were only a cereal company, with a cost of equity of 10 percent.

The immediate consequence of using the single rate of 15 percent for both divisions is overinvestment in toys and underinvestment in cereal. If the true rate for toys should be 20 percent, but the company is willing to accept 15 percent, many poor projects will be undertaken. Similarly, good projects will be passed up in the cereal business. Over time, the company will become a toy company, and its overall cost of equity will rise to 20 percent. However, investors will realize substandard returns over the transition period.

The financial experts who have addressed this problem (see Bower and Jenks (1975) and Harrington (1983)) recommend that companies identify firms within the same industry plays as their divisions. Then they should estimate the screening rates for these proxy companies. Finally, the company should apply these screening rates, adjusted for capital structure differences, to project evaluations for company divisions.

Another action financial managers should take to create value deals with financing the company. Use of prudent amounts of debt is beneficial because interest costs are tax deductible. For elaboration, see Chapter 27.

Managers can also create value by monitoring corporate performance. The financial manager should do whatever possible to assure that the potential positive net present values produced by outstanding projects are not dissipated by other corporate actions; that is, that the enterprise not be allowed to drift toward satisficing, a condition in which free cash flows are maintained just at the level that compensates investors for risk, with any excess being used unproductively.

Finally, corporate financial officers should frequently check the prices of their company's stock. This provides a valuable and objective evaluation of corporate performance. If the market to book ratio is less than 1.0, corporate strategy and its implementation should be carefully reevaluated. If the low ratio cannot be explained by a generally depressed market or attributed to the fact that good news about the company has been withheld (for competitive reasons) from the market and is known only by senior management, some changes are in order. If the market to book ratio exceeds 1.0, the company should thoroughly examine what factors have contributed to its success and what must be done to continue that success.

The following sections detail the actions managers can take to create value through capital project evaluation, financing, and monitoring.

CAPITAL PROJECTS

There are five stages in the development of capital projects, new ways to employ corporate financial and other resources.

Stages in Capital Deployment

The Idea. The first stage is conceptualization and identification. Here the idea is born. The potential market the new product or process will serve is identified. The key initial questions are whether (1) the idea is technologically feasible; (2) there is a market for the output; (3) it can be financed and, in general, (4) it may pay to give the project further consideration.

Strategic opportunities can be identified by the marketing, production, or research and development group. Although financial managers typically have not played a substantial role in this stage of capital projects, they also have much to offer. For instance, financial managers could identify potentially attractive business opportunities by examining market to book ratios of companies already in the business. The high market to book ratio in 1981 and 1982 of Apple Computer probably played some role in tempting other computer companies into the personal computer business. Similarly, the financial manager may be able to warn the company away from potential businesses that are not economically sensible, as a consequence of stock analysis. Generally, the analysis found in Michael Porter's excellent book (1980) ought to be applied most rigorously at this stage of the capital process. Broadly, the best chances of identifying value-creating projects arise when, in addition to healthy and growing demand for a product or service,

1 There is little threat of additional entrants to a business.

2 There is little threat of substitute products and/or services.

3 There is the strong possibility that the product or services will give the company bargaining power over buyers.

4 There is the strong possibility that the product or service will give the company bargaining power over its suppliers.

Estimation. The second stage in capital deployment entails in-depth investigation of the project idea. This might also be termed the design and planning stage. In this stage, the details of the project are estimated (e.g., how big a factory, how much it will cost, and how many more employees). Also, estimates of prospective cash flows are necessary. This entails forecasting market demand for the output, responses by competitors, the life cycle of the product or service, and so forth. (See Chapters 21, 22, and 23 for elaboration.)

Evaluation. The third stage of the process is evaluation. This is where the financial manager has the most to offer, and it is the area that has received the greatest attention by financial economists.

Various aspects of this stage have been treated in Chapters 25 and 26, and further aspects will be covered in a later section of this chapter.

Implementation. This is the fourth stage of the capital allocation process. It entails actually bringing the project on stream, within budget.

Control. This is the last stage of capital allocation. It is important, although few firms do it systematically. It entails not only budgeting for production but also continuous reevaluation of the economic sense of the project. (See Chapter 20 for a detailed analysis.)

While firms may carefully estimate cash flows before undertaking the project, it is also important to do ex post audits of how well a project is doing relative to the assumptions that motivated the project in the first place. Questions regarding the quality of cash flow estimates and biases in the evaluation procedures should be addressed. Without such an ex post audit, systematic errors in capital evaluation procedures can persist, thus prompting a firm to continue investing in a business where the inherent economics no longer justify it. Moreover, with no audits, projects may be continued that would be better abandoned or sold to some company that can make better economic use of the assets devoted to the project.

Project audits are not difficult, and they may be quite revealing to any company intent upon creating value for shareholders.

Because project evaluation is the stage in the capital allocation process that can be influenced most directly by the financial manager, this stage will be scrutinized further here.

Three Benefits From Investment

A capital project brings three benefits to investors. (See Myers (1977)) for a technical elaboration.) The first is the stream of pure economic benefits. This is the after-tax operating cash flows discounted at a rate appropriate to the riskiness of the project. In this case, the discount rate is the rate that would obtain if the project was financed entirely by equity capital.

The second benefit is the interest payment tax shield associated with the incremental debt capacity a project brings. If two projects are identically attractive in terms of the first benefit, they may still differ with respect to the second. Indeed, the debt capacity differences among projects may be sufficient to produce different internal rankings of project desirability. The value of the tax shield is determined as the value of tax savings attributable to interest deductions discounted at a rate consistent with the riskiness of the tax savings. Riskiness is a consequence of the company's ability to use its tax shields, and to do so, it must have taxable income. The correct discount rate in most instances will fall between the investor's yield on the debt of the company and the pure equity discount rate.

The third advantage of a capital project is the explicit timing of the cash flows. In a world of perfect capital markets and no transaction costs, the costs associated with raising or placing capital, any pattern is acceptable, and specific patterns have no value. If capital markets are imperfect, however, either because of serious structural deficiences or because of transaction costs, there may be a pecuniary advantage to a particular pattern.

Suppose, for example, a company has two good investment opportunities this year. Both have the same pure economic benefits and tax shield benefits. Suppose further that the company looks ahead to the next year and discovers another good investment opportunity that from all viewpoints is desirable, this could change the company's otherwise indifference to the two projects this year. If one of these projects produces enough cash after one year to allow the company to avoid costly capital raising activities, (ie., bank negotiations, public security issue preparation costs, and underwriter's fees), that project should be given credit for this. Similarly, if acceptance of any project is expected explicitly to lead to future capital market transaction costs or financial penalties (that may arise as a consequence of a bond indenture violation, for example), that project's evaluation probably ought to reflect this.

As a practical matter, this last component of project attractiveness is likely very small, perhaps negligible for most American companies. However, it may be very large for smaller companies domiciled in countries where capital markets are primitive. It may be estimated or applied with judgment. One reasonable way for a manager to apply judgment is by asking herself how much she would be willing to pay for insurance to avoid running the risk of costly capital issue transactions.

The Case of Pencil Stub, Inc.

To help put the material in the last two sections into perspective, a stylized illustration is offered.

The Idea. Ollie Palmer, Chief Financial and Planning Officer at Pencil Stub, Inc. (PSI), had just returned from a long meeting with Don Watson, Director of Manufacturing at PSI, and Bea Trevino, Vice-President — Marketing at PSI. Both presented some preliminary notions regarding their possible programs for the coming year.

Watson mentioned that while driving to work that day, he noticed an advertising billboard extolling the virtues of Stump Grinders. He thought that perhaps with PSI's manufacturing expertise, distribution system, and tie-in marketing possibilities, the Stump Grinder business was a natural product addition for the firm.

Trevino had indicated that her sales people were returning from calls to retailers asking about Stub-Crunchers, a new product marketed by PSI's arch rival, Vader Lead, and several smaller specialty manufacturers. It seems the retailers would just as soon buy Stub-Crunchers from PSI, since they preferred to buy most of their other products in this category from PSI as well.

Palmer called Sally Mac, Planning Director at PSI, to his office and asked for a very preliminary evaluation of the two prospective opportunities.

Sally Mac began by identifying other companies that produced the two products, and then tried to determine whether there was any money to be made in either. She produced the evaluation shown in Table 34.3.

She reported orally: "While the market for Stump Grinders will grow fast and become quite large, rivalry will be intense. Moreoever, because of low capital requirements and high technology input, there's nothing to prevent some entrepreneurial engineering school professor from producing a better product in a year or two and doing severe damage to all competitors. Better to do some further investigation on Stub-Crunchers where we've got a chance to shine."

Estimation. Ollie Palmer reported these results to Trevino and Watson. Despite some grousing by Watson (he was "turned on" by the engineering challenges of the Stump Grinder), they agreed it might be worthwhile to give some further thought to the Stub-Cruncher. Watson was to do the engineering, and Trevino, the market analysis.

After several weeks of sporadic work, Watson had succeeded in pulling together the engineering estimates. There was plenty of extra space in existing buildings, so no new plant was necessary, although immediately expensable

TABLE 34.3   Preliminary Report

	Stub-Crunchers	Stump Grinders
Companies in industry	5	3
Profitability		
Average market to book ratio of firms	1.3	0.9
Return on equity	21 percent	14 percent
Capital requirements	High	Low
Technological requirements	Medium	High
"Proprietariness" (ability to differentiate product)	Medium	Low
Size of market	100 units	50 units
Growth	15 percent per year for 5 years	30 percent per year for 5 years
Dominant firm	No firm with more than 23 percent of market	Yes: Giant Co. with 50 percent of market
Attractiveness	Good; opportunity to become dominant firm; power over retailers through tie-in marketing	Poor; too much like a commodity; tough battle for market share with Giant Co., high technology component could result in quick capital obsolescence

building modifications costing $10,000 were necessary. One new machine would be required immediately; it would cost $5,000 and have a useful life of five years. It would enable production of up to 25 units per year, with extra shifts. Additional machines would be purchased when needed to meet rising demand or to replace worn-out equipment. Watson estimated direct labor and material costs at $300 per unit. Further, he estimated that no other overhead costs would change.

Trevino talked with her sales and market research people. They projected a 10-year product life cycle, with maturity setting in by year 6. Their selling projections were:

	Year 1	Year 2	Year 3	Year 4	Year 5	Years 6–10
Total market	115	132	152	175	190	200
PSI market share	10%	15%	20%	25%	25%	25%
PSI units	11	20	30	44	48	50
Selling price	$600	$625	$630	$630	$630	$575
Sales revenues	$6,600	$12,500	$18,900	$27,720	$30,240	$28,750
Marketing expense	$1,000	$1,500	$2,000	$2,000	$2,200	$2,500

Armed with these projections, Palmer went to the Treasurer and asked her to have one of her people work out the free cash flows after taxes and allowing for any working capital changes. These are shown in Table 34.4

Evaluation. Upon Palmer's receipt of the free cash flow estimates, he turned to one of his subordinates, Ken Hogan, for a financial evaluation.

Hogan's first task was estimation of the correct screening rate. He did not want to give effect to the project's financing, so he wanted to use a pure equity rate. He gathered the following data:

Competitor Companies (Only in Stub-Cruncher Business)	Stock Beta	Debt/Equity (D/E) at Market Values
1	1.5	1.0
2	1.3	0.9
3	1.6	1.2
4	1.4	1.1
Average	1.45	1.05

To determine the beta that would prevail if the project was not financed with any debt, Ken applied the following formula:

$$\beta \text{ unlevered} = \frac{\beta \text{ levered}}{[\,1 + (1 - t)DE\,]}$$

where: t = marginal tax rate

   D = market value of debt

   E = market value of equity

Since these companies had a marginal tax rate of 40 percent, he did the following computation to approximate the unlevered equity cost.

$$\beta \text{ unlevered} = \frac{1.45}{[\,1 + (1 - 0.4)D/E\,]} = \frac{1.45}{1 + 0.37}$$

$$= 1.06$$

To determine the pure equity discount rate, the rate reflecting only business risk, he applied estimates of the risk-free return and the return on the market portfolio based upon data in Chapter 18.

He estimated it to be:

Pure equity rate = 0.09 + 1.06 (0.16–0.09)

= 0.164, or 16.4%

He then applied this rate to the free cash flow estimates in Table 34.4 and found a present value of $9,803.49. Since the pure economic benefits are highly positive, the investment seemed wise.

The second step in the evaluation is giving credit for any additional tax shields attributable to its financing. PSI, Ken knew, had a policy of financing

TABLE 34.4   After-Tax Free Cash Flow Assuming Remaining in Business 10 Years

	Year 0	Year 1	Year 2	Year 3	Year 4	Year 5	Year 6	Year 7	Year 8	Year 9	Year 10
Investment	$(5,000)	—	$(5,000)	—	—	$(5,000)	—	$(5,000)	—	—	—
Building expense	(10,000)	—	—	—	—	—	—	—	—	—	—
Disposition of saleable equipment	—	—	—	—	—	—	—	—	—	—	$ 2,000(a)
Working capital changes	—	($1,000)	(500)	—	—	—	—	—	—	—	1,500
Sales revenue	—	6,600	12,500	$18,900	$27,720	30,240	$28,750	28,750	$28,750	$28,750	28,750
Incremental costs											
Labor and materials	—	(3,300)	(6,000)	(9,000)	(13,200)	(14,400)	(15,000)	(15,000)	(15,000)	(15,000)	(15,000)
Marketing expense	—	(1,000)	(1,500)	(2,000)	(2,000)	(2,200)	(2,500)	(2,500)	(2,500)	(2,500)	(2,500)
Pretax cash flow	($15,000)	$1,300	$ (500)	$ 7,900	$12,520	$ 8,640	$11,250	$ 6,250	$11,250	$11,250	$14,750
Tax payments of cash flows(b)	4,500	(120)	(900)	(2,360)	(4,208)	(4,956)	(3,700)	(3,200)	(3,700)	(3,700)	(5,100)
After-tax free operating cash flows	($10,500)	$1,180	$(1,400)	$ 5,540	$ 8,312	$ 3,684	$ 7,550	$ 3,050	$ 7,550	$ 7,550	$ 9,650

Note: These cash flows reflect continuing investment in the project.

(a) Book value of machine purchased in year 7

(b) These include adjustments for tax credits, depreciation, etc.: 10 percent tax credit; 40 percent income tax rate; 20 percent capital gains rate; five-year straight-line depreciation. Assumes losses in this line offset taxes in other parts of business.

new investment with 50 percent debt at book value: in this case $7,500 could be borrowed. Ken further knew that the company's board would not want to have debt with a maturity of more than three years. Finally, he knew that interest expense would be 10 percent and the loan would be a bullet type, interest only for three years, then principal repayment.

To compute the value of financing, the reduction in income taxes attributable to interest payments, Ken developed the following chart:

	Year 0	Year 1	Year 2	Year 3
Loan	$7,500	—	—	—
Repay	—	—	—	($7,500)
Interest	—	$750	$750	750
Tax shield at 40 percent	—	300	300	300

Finally, Ken figured the ability to take advantage of the tax shields was about as risky as the overall business of PSI. PSI's overall unlevered cost of equity was 14.5 percent, so he applied this discount rate to the tax benefits. The value of the interest tax shield associated with the debt financing was $690.69.

Ken Hogan reported back to Ollie Palmer that the investment looked good, and gave details. Ollie, however, was worried about year 2 when the cash flows were negative. Further planning suggested he would have a problem meeting the indenture requirements on extisting loans and would have to renegotiate the loans as a consequence. He estimated it would cost an extra $100 in year 2 as a result of temporarily higher interest rates connected to the renegotiation. Since this was fairly certain, he chose to discount this by 9.5 percent, the rate on two-year government bonds. The pattern of cash flows would cost in present value terms $100/(1.095)^2$, or $83.40.

Overall, the financial evaluation was:

Value created = Pure economic benefits + Value of financing − Value of cash flow timing

10,410.78 = 9,803.49 + 690.69 − $83.40

The Stub-Cruncher project seemed to be a good one. If valued as an independent firm, its market to book ratio would be 25,410.78/15,000, or 1.69.

Implementation. The implementation went smoothly. Trevino and Watson worked well together.

Control. After three years in the business, Palmer, now President of PSI, observed things were not going well with Stub-Crunchers. Prices had come down much faster than anticipated, and raw material costs were rising spectacularly. Tevino had left the company to start her own firm, and her replacement was not the marketing genius she had been.

Palmer ordered Ken Hogan, the new Chief Financial Officer, to reevaluate the project. After extensive investigation, Hogan produced results showing the value of remaining in the business to be +$1,221. Alternatively, if PSI got out of the business it could sell the machines and patents for $1,800 after-tax. The decision was made to sell.

Summary. This highly stylized description, while substantially simplified, does point out the steps managers should take in allocating capital in a manner that creates shareholder value.

While the foregoing has focused upon specific projects, financial strategy also must be concerned with the totality of projects and with planning for capital allocations over time. The question that should be uppermost in financial executives' minds is whether what the company anticipates doing over the long run makes sense for shareholders. The following analysis might prove helpful. (This material is largely derived from Rappaport (1981) though it is available in many places.)

Value of Firm Equity

For simplicity, it is assumed the firm will operate forever, maintaining roughly constant business risk, financial leverage, and no growth. Growth here is defined not as expansion, which is feasible, but as an ability to invest funds at rates in excess of the weighted-average cost of capital. The weighted-average cost of capital is the cost of equity times the proportion of equity in the capital structure plus the after-tax cost of debt times the proportion of debt in the capital structure. (See Chapters 25, 26, and 27 for elaboration.)

$$\text{Stock value} = \frac{\text{Cash flow after taxes}}{\text{Weighted-average cost of capital}} - \text{Debt}$$

This can be elaborated by allowing M to represent cash flow before taxes divided by sales (gross margin), S to represent sales, and k to represent weighted-average cost of capital. Then,

$$\text{Stock value} = \frac{M(1 - T)S}{k} - \text{Debt}$$

Rappaport shows that the change in shareholder wealth, or stock value, equals:

$$\text{Change in stock value} = \frac{\Delta M(1 - t)\Delta S}{k} - \frac{(f_t + W_t)S_t}{1 + k}$$

where: f = capital expenditures minus depreciation per dollar of sales increase, assumed to take place at the end of period

W = cash required for net working capital for each dollar of sales, assumed to take place at the end of the period

When:

$$\frac{M(1 - T)}{k} = \frac{(f_t + W_t)}{1 + k}$$

a breakeven margin is obtained. This is the minimum gross margin necessary to make investment worthwhile. The minimum gross margin (M_{min}) can be obtained by solving this equation:

$$M_{min} = \frac{(f + W)k}{(1 - T)(1 + k)}$$

returns will tend to be acquired, fail, or go into liquidation if they allow themselves to slip into any of the last three models.

The Market for Corporate Control. If the financial managers of firms in the second, third, or fourth categories cannot impose strict cost/benefit criteria to price cuts, marketing expenses, and operating expenses, the offending company may be a target for takeover by another company.

In a careful review article, Jensen and Ruback (1983) report that in acquisitions of all sorts, shareholders of acquired firms experience substantially positive returns. This is attributable to the premium paid by acquiring firms. At the same time, shareholders in acquiring firms tend not to lose, despite the premium. What allows acquirers to avoid loss while acquirees gain is not known. However, it is reasonable to conjecture that, in part, investors expect the acquiring company to eliminate the wealth-dissipating practices of the displaced management. Other factors, such as exploitable economies of scale or scope, may contribute to this finding, but benefits from the displacement of inefficient management through the competitive process cannot be dismissed.

The moral is that financial managers should be very keen to prevent their firms from falling into a nonshareholder wealth-maximizing mode. It is far less costly to the economy and less threatening to managers' careers for firms to operate efficiently on their own rather than to accomplish efficient allocation of corporate resources through expensive takeover processes.

Incentives

In very large corporations, successful implementation of a corporate strategy requires that senior management motivate divisional and other profit-center managers to share their goals and aspirations for the company. If the men and women running profit centers pursue objectives that conflict with corporate goals, even the most wisely developed corporate strategy may be doomed. Information gathering and processing as well as investment and program decisions by these people may not reflect what is really important to the success of the firm from the shareholders' view.

It is not only that what lower echelon managers do may be harmful; the problem is substantially more subtle than that. Rather, it is what they fail to do—potentially great projects that never get presented, good ideas that never get thought—that can do the gravest damage to achievement of corporate objectives.

Most major U.S. corporations have formal incentive compensation and bonus plans. A substantial portion of income for managers can derive from their performance relative to the standards defined in the plan. Many managers like the system because they have figured out how to manage it. This is one horn of the dilemma: Many compensation schemes are, for the most part, tied to measures of profit-center performance that may be very poor indicators of the true contribution these managers make to the achievement of the most fundamental corporate goal: enrichment of its owners. The incentives built into these plans may actually be counterproductive; they may create a conflict between senior management's objectives and those of their subordinates. The other horn of the dilemma revolves around the need for boards of directors to evaluate top managers over short intervals and for top managers to monitor and assess the quality of the contribution made by subordinate managers.

Corporate Goals. In a market economy, maximization of owners' wealth is (or should be) the primary objective of any corporation's management. There may be other objectives, but if managers grossly fail to satisfy shareholder expectations, they often find themselves under siege by a potential acquirer, and possibly unemployed. One is hard pressed to produce examples of companies that are highly successful by other criteria but that experience sustained share price depreciation over a long period while the rest of the market is rising.

There are many formulations of potentially winning strategies. Whether any of these causally correlate with owners' wealth, no one knows for sure. All represent attempts to focus managerial attention on tangible, explicit factors about which they may be able to do something in an effort to enhance shareholder wealth. Under the guidance of these strategies managers can focus on increasing market share, investing heavily in rapidly growing markets, or identifying a market niche, whereas the objective of maximizing shareholder wealth alone does not really provide direct insight for action.

More often than not, broad corporate strategic thrusts are accompanied by a set of specific, measurable financial goals. A target return on investment, for instance, is a frequently cited goal. A specific return on equity capital is another. (Whether these financial goals are perceived as primary or are viewed as constraints on behavior cannot be known, except in careful case-by-case examination.) These goals may not govern share price behavior. Accomplishment of such goals may conflict with the shareholders' goal by diverting energy from doing those things owners might really prefer.

Just as important (and perhaps substantially more important) as the translation of the overall corporate goal into an outline of strategy for senior managers is the translation of the corporate goal into guides for action for lower echelon managers, the people who run divisions of large corporations, most particularly. Not only must the goals be set for them, but senior management must provide tangible rewards for meeting those goals.

If senior managers have difficultly in relating to the concept of shareholder wealth maximization and find problematic the identification of activities that ultimately will enhance shareholder wealth, then the problem of the division manager, or any profit-center manager for that matter, is even more complex. The manager must not only manage an ongoing activity but must also spend significant time and resources identifying the new business directions in which the profit center should be moved. New products need to be developed, new investment projects must be identified, analyzed, and presented to senior management, and other activities must be dedicated to the future prosperity of the profit center. Senior managers must provide direction here. They must provide guidelines for the sort of developmental work they want lower echelon managers to undertake. They must at least broadly define the kinds of products and projects junior managers should review. They must specify whether these managers should "blue-sky" or remain within very tight boundaries regarding proposals forwarded to a corporation's senior decision maker.

Incentive Plans. Pay for measurable performance has become quite common in American industry. Use of stock options for very senior managers is widespread. Indeed, many subordinate managers also have options or stock positions. With stock options, the total value of executive compensation is linked quite directly to increases in share price. if investors bid up a stock's price, those executives who hold stock options benefit.

With such stock-related compensation plans, executives who have them are at least partially compensated by owners who file daily reports, by buying or selling shares, on how they seem to be doing. In part, however, compensation of even top management depends upon the balance sheet/income statement criteria set up by the board. Below the top rungs of management, however, there is virtually no market assessment of performance, no meaningful assessment of an individual's contribution to shareholder wealth maximization. The market rewards or penalizes an entire corporation; it cannot differentiate among divisions. There are only the measurable financial goals that may not correlate precisely and in the short run with share price increases.

Over the last decade, incentive compensation plans for those below the top echelons of a corporation have proliferated. Indeed, for many mid-level executives, the incentive component of compensation comprises a significant fraction to total compensation.

Ideally, incentive compensation should be geared toward contributing to the overall corporate goal of shareholder wealth maximization. However, shareholders are far removed from the performance of a manager who runs a profit center employing about one hundredth or less of the corporation's resources. Thus, in setting incentive plans, those in charge try, at least implicitly, to find substitutes for the securities markets, measurable items they believe correlate with that which security market investors prize. In brief, senior managers attempt to establish shadow markets so that subordinates can be evaluated and rewarded. If established incorrectly, shadow markets can create very serious problems and may thwart the strategic thrusts of the company.

Where senior managers establish corporate strategy, where they set the approach and measurable goals they believe will cause increases in share values, they may be wrong. They may choose to concentrate on things neutral or even detrimental to shareholder wealth; that is, the true model of security price formation may differ from what they think matters. Nonetheless, what they think matters and what actually does matter may not be mutually exclusive. In fact, by pursuing what they think matters, they may in the process also be acting upon what does matter. Pursuit of the wrong things or of the right things in the wrong way may not prevent the stock market value of the firm from increasing, because all along the way the right things may be getting done.

Wrong beliefs by senior managers about the things that affect investor expectations and share prices can, however, prompt the development and design of incentive plans for subordinate managers that do, in fact, induce behavior that can destroy corporate value, or that does not contribute as much to the incentive plans as optimal behavior might.

Customarily, the shadow market developed by senior managers to reward subordinates relies upon measurable, objective criteria and accounting and financial data accumulated over periods far shorter than those with which investors are most seriously concerned. (See, e.g., Rappaport (1983).) Typically, such plans entail bonus awards for meeting return on investment targets or working capital reduction targets or any of a variety of other shortsighted financial objectives. These are set on the sometimes mistaken belief that the data govern stock prices. To the extent that subordinate managers themselves aim for maximum compensation (constrained perhaps by some other motivations) determined on the basis of their achievement of set financial targets, they may do things that deleteriously affect stock prices, but which positively affect their compensation. When wrong beliefs about what governs stock values work their way into incentive compensation formulae, senior managers will not be getting the most they can from subordinates, and the overall corporate objectives may be thwarted.

Illustration of the Problem. Suppose senior managers believe share price to be influenced heavily by return on investment (ROI). Further suppose this criterion is built into subordinate managers' incentive awards, leading division managers to skimp on plant maintenance or quality control expenditures. The short-run consequences are high bonuses; the long-run consequences could be devastating. Sensible senior managers, however, would question the subordinate regarding what was done to achieve higher return on investment, and disqualify the bonus award if it was destructively achieved.

A more subtle illustration is now considered, and a more damaging situation because senior managers may never have the information to override subordinates' recommendations.

Suppose there are two strategically logical but mutually exclusive investment alternatives that a subordinate might present to senior management. Both are equally risky; thus, the appropriate discount rate for each in a discounted cash flow evaluation is 20 percent. The first is a simple investment, that is, a plant expansion using known technology. It costs $1 million and will generate $225,000 in after-tax cash flows for 15 years starting at the end of the year. The present value of the after-tax cash flows is $1,051,981.34, discounting at 20 percent. The net present value is the present value of cash flows less the cost, or $51,981.34. It is economically satisfactory; it should enhance shareholder wealth. The alternative is the development of a small pilot plant to produce the same product, but which uses a new technology that may reduce unit production costs by a great deal. It requires an investment of $750,000 a year for three years, but is expected to generate after-tax cash flows of $1 million per year beginning in year 4 and continuing for 12 years. In addition, the existing plant must be used more intensively during the new plant construction period, and $500,000 in additional working capital to finance larger inventories is needed. (It is assumed this $500,000 is recoverable at the end of the third year.) Present value of after-tax cash flows starting in year 4 is $2,568,981, including recovery of extra inventory investment. The present value of outlays, including the working capital investment, is $1,896,213. The net present value is $699,778.

By discounted cash flow criteria, the second project is the better one. However, this project may never even be shown to senior management for approval. Indeed, the executive in charge may not even develop the data necessary to evaluate the second investment, because a potential negative effect on incentive compensation during the next several years is expected.

If subordinates are evaluated on return on investment criteria, the first investment gets the nod. It produces a return on investment of 22.5 percent early on, and more in later years as the expenditure is depreciated. For the first three years, the second investment only adds to the investment base of the manager and produces no return. In the fourth year, it could really pay off, but if the manager has been transferred or promoted, he may not care because his compensation may not reflect this courageous decision. Moreover, the current incentive portion of total compensation may be harmed because more investment must be carried without a corresponding short-term rise in after-tax cash flow. Chances for promotion may be injured, so the manager may recommend the first investment rather than the second.

Some companies will provide a grace period for a project such as the second. They will not assess the amount spent on the project against the manager's performance measure until the project is complete. However, even then, the manager may still be penalized because of the increase in working capital required during the construction period, again an increment to investment perhaps without a concomitant rise in returns.

Incentive plans based on short-run performance and/or incentive plans based on misbeliefs about what investors are seeking may prompt lower echelon managers to recommend projects that, while satisfactory, may be less productive than alternatives. The better projects may not even be shown to top management if undertaking them may adversely influence compensation. Even worse, some managers may not even expend the resources to uncover and evaluate better, more foresighted projects, in the belief that they may not enhance, or may even detract from, personal records.

Some Possible Remedies. Some, perhaps many, companies' incentive schemes actually provide incentives that prompt low echelon managers to make decisions and recommendations that, while not positively damaging to shareholders, may not be as beneficial as they might otherwise be. One reason these incentives exist is that control measures constructed for subordinates must be easily measurable even though they might only loosely correlate with share values. Therefore, senior managers may trade off great prospects for simple measures useful in monitoring and evaluating subordinates' behavior. The question that emerges is, What might senior managers and corporate strategists do to bring lower echelon control, evaluation, and monetary incentive mechanisms more closely in line with those applied by the capital market to the overall corporation itself?

In the first instance, it is tempting to assert that, rather than cash awards, subordinates might be rewarded with stock or stock options. This, at least, would provide them with the incentive to bring to the attention of top managers projects with potentially large but distant payoffs. However, a substantial "free-rider" problem could result. The contribution of any one profit-center manager to corporate performance is typically small. The hard work and effort of one manager may be offset by the lack of effort of others. Accordingly, incentive payments based on aggregate corporate performance, in view of the fact that most managers affect only tiny portions of the aggregate, may not be effective. Thus, ownership claims (e.g., stock-based compensation), may not have as much impact on individual behavior and performance as might be desired in large corporations.

However, at least three possibilities remain for resolving the incentive dilemma fostered by the need for monitoring devices, on the one hand, and for stimulus to creativity, on the other. First, there is an acceptance strategy. It recognizes imperfections in the internal, shadow market of corporate divisional contribution to shareholder wealth, but it values control and short-run monitoring more highly than the potentially missed opportunities caused by poorly constructed incentives. In this instance, senior managers would make an environmental assessment directed at identifying possibilities for investments that may have large expected net present values. If they conclude that there are few, if any, legitimate "bonanzas" on the horizon in view of their current business portfolio, top management probably should also conclude that the value of short-run monitoring, accomplished through the most commonly used, easily measurable indicators, exceeds the value of missed opportunities. The businesses most likely to reach such conclusions are commodity type, that is, nondifferentiable product and transaction-oriented businesses, such as those engaged in deal making, where there are no true proprietary product claims.

A second approach suitable for non-commodity-type businesses is an information-intensive approach. Incentive schemes can be set on a net present value basis. This would provide a close link between subordinate decisions and security market values. The investment in information could be very substantial, however. This would require a market-like evaluation of each division (see Piper and Fruhan (1981)). To run such a scheme, the far off, high payoff investment, for instance, would have to be monitored very carefully as it slowly develops. The assumptions that initially justified the decision would have to be retested, at least annually, to determine whether they still apply. The costs of such a system might be very high in terms of top management time and, because of the difficulties involved in such evaluations, may result in unfair or biased decisions regarding the quality of performance. Nonetheless, this general approach could move the shadow market of performance assessment more nearly in line with the real market. Indeed, at least at the division level, the aggregate shadow market values of the divisions could not exceed the market value of the corporation. Incentive payments could equal some fraction of the net present value of each decision or project as each comes on stream.

A third possibility, quite radical, is a "divide and conquer" or "partial spin-off" approach. Markets economize on information. Any fair incentive system, any incentive system that pushes managers to align their personal interests with those of owners, can either intensively generate and use information or can rely upon markets. Yet, very few companies have voluntarily moved to market-based systems, and this is what gives this possibility its radical flavor.

Rather than owning 100 percent of the stock of its divisions, parent corporations could break down their divisions into minimum efficient operating units. The parent corporation would retain about 51 or more percent of the stock, allowing the remainder to be publicly traded. Division managers, at least, could then be evaluated by the same market-type standards as are senior managers. The parent firms would, of course, retain nearly as much control as is now maintained, except that shuffling resources among divisions must entail fair treatment of the outside owners. Since each division would be a comparatively small entity, the division manager could evaluate subordinates either by using objective, measurable information or by subjective judgments based on familiarity with the business. But the incentive to make myopic decisions, at least at the division level, should be reduced, and because of the increased proximity of each profit-center manager to ultimate ownership, profit-center managers may more easily internalize the interest of owners. Division managers could then be rewarded with stock ownership, without fear about free-riders in other divisions.

The perceived drawback to this approach is the limitation it places on senior managers in moving resources from business unit to business unit. If, for instance, top managers wanted to transfer ownership of a plant from one division to another, a price would have to be set so that the outside owners of the losing division could be compensated. As a practical matter, the loss of cash resources would only be proportional to the share of outside ownership. For instance, division *A*, with 20 percent outside ownership, transfers to division *B* a plant worth $100; division *A* gets the $100 and declares a dividend of $100. The holding company receives $80 and outside owners get $20. Thus, the drain on corporate cash resources is only $20. (There is nothing special about cash relative to any other equal value resource; if corporations need cash, they can always sell stock or bonds. Moreover, virtually every discussion of interdivisional or transfer pricing of resources urges the use of fair market values. This should not pose a real problem to senior corporate managers sincerely trying to use corporate resources efficiently.

SUMMARY OF STEPS IN IMPLEMENTING FINANCIAL STRATEGY

These are the steps managers must take to make decisions aimed at creating value for shareholders:

1 Develop an understanding of the factors that beneficially influence market prices.

2 Develop sensible estimates of screening rates for evaluating capital investments.

3 Use present value methods to make investment decisions.

4 Use prudent amounts of debt in the capital structure.

5 Assure that corporate behaviors are justified on cost/benefit criteria.

6 Explore different methods for monitoring and compensating subordinate managers.

SUGGESTED READING

Asquith, Paul, and David W. Mullins, Jr. "The Impact of Initiating Dividend Payments on Shareholders' Wealth." *Journal of Business* (Feb. 1983), pp. 77–96.

Black, Fischer, and Mary P. Dewhurst. "A New Investment Strategy for Pension Funds." *Journal of Portfolio Management* (Summer 1981), pp. 26–34.

Bower, Richard S., and Jeffrey Jenks. "Divisional Screening Rates." *Financial Management* (Autumn 1975), pp. 42–49.

Branch, Ben, and Bradley Gale. "Linking Corporate Stock Price Performance to Strategy Formulation." *Journal of Business Strategy* (Summer 1983), pp. 40–50.

Constantanides, George M. "Capital Market Equilibrium with Personal Tax." *Econometrica* (forthcoming).

Donaldson, Gordon. "Strategies for Financial Emergencies." *Harvard Business Review* (Nov.–Dec. 1969), pp. 67–79.

Fruhan, William E., Jr. *Financial Strategy*. Homewood, Ill.: Irwin, 1979.

Harrington, Diana R. "Stock Prices, Beta and Strategic Planning." *Harvard Business Review* (May–June 1983), pp. 157–164.

Jensen, Michael C., and William H. Meckling. "Theory of the Firm: Managerial Behavior, Agency Costs, and Ownership Structure." *Journal of Financial Economics* (Oct. 1976), pp. 305–360.

Jensen, Michael C., and Richard S. Ruback. "The Market for Corporate Control." *Journal of Financial Economics* (July 1983), pp. 5–50.

Logue, Dennis E. "Shareholder Wealth and Management Compensation." *Journal of Corporate Accounting* (Winter 1984), pp. 38–45.

———, and T. Craig Tapley. "Performance Monitoring Costs, the Agent's Agency Problem, and the Timing of Cash Flows." Working paper (1983).

Masulis, Ronald W. "The Effects of Capital Structure Change on Security Prices." *Journal of Financial Economics* (1980), pp. 139–178.

———. "Stock Repurchase by Tender Offer: An Analysis of Causes of Common Stock Price Changes." *Journal of Finance* (May 1980), pp. 305–319.

———. "The Impact of Capital Structure Change on Firm Value: Some Estimates." *Journal of Finance* (March 1983), pp. 107–126.

Myers, Stewart C. "Determinants of Corporate Borrowing." *Journal of Financial Economics* (1977), pp. 147–175.

———. "Interaction of Corporate Financing and Investment Decisions — Implications for Capital Budgeting." *Journal of Finance* (Mar. 1974), pp. 1–25.

Peters, Thomas J., and Robert H. Waterman. *In Search of Excellence*. New York: Harper and Row, 1982.

Piper, Thomas R., and Wolf A. Weinhold. "How Much Debt Is Right for Your Company?" *Harvard Business Reveiw* (July–Aug. 1982), pp. 106–113.

———, and William E. Fruhan, Jr. "Is Your Stock Worth Its Market Price?" *Harvard Business Review* (May–June 1981), pp. 124–132.

Porter, Michael. *Competitive Strategy*. New York: The Free Press, 1980.

Rappaport, Alfred. "Corporate Performance Standards and Shareholder Value." *Journal of Corporate Strategy* (Spring 1983), pp. 28–38.

———. "Selecting Strategies that Create Shareholder Value." *Harvard Business Review* (May–June 1981), pp. 139–149.

Strebel, Paul. "Using the Stock Market to Assess Strategic Position." *Journal of Corporate Strategy* (Winter 1983), pp. 77–83.

Treynor, Jack L. "The Financial Objective in the Widely Held Corporation." *Financial Analysts Journal* (Mar.–Apr. 1981), pp. 68–71.

35

Bankruptcy Liquidation and Reorganization

MICHELLE J. WHITE

INTRODUCTION

A central tenet in economics is that competition drives markets toward a state of long-run equilibrium in which those firms remaining in existence produce at minimum average costs. In the process of transition to long-run equilibrium, inefficient firms, firms using obsolete technologies, and those producing products that are in excess supply, are eliminated. Consumers benefit because, in the

I am grateful for research support from the National Science Foundation Law and Social Sciences Program under grant number SES-8208930.

long run, goods and services are produced and sold at the lowest possible price. The mechanism through which this "productive destruction" of unprofitable firms most often occurs is bankruptcy, the legal process applied to firms unable to pay their debts. This chapter discusses and analyzes U.S. bankruptcy procedures, taking both positive and normative viewpoints.

The concern in particular is with economic efficiency as a goal, and with bankruptcy as a means to that goal. Does bankruptcy act as a screening device that identifies and eliminates inefficient firms? If so, then bankruptcy procedures promote long-run economic efficiency. However, if bankruptcy procedures tend to prolong the existence of failing firms, or to prolong the operations of high-cost producers, then their effect would be to delay and obstruct the transition to long-run equilibrium and to tie up capital unnecessarily in unproductive uses.

While most shutdowns of firms involve a bankruptcy, in fact there is no necessary connection between the two. Firms normally file for bankruptcy because they cannot meet financial obligations currently due. This usually means that the value of their liabilities is equal to or greater than that of their assets, since otherwise they could borrow to pay current obligations. In contrast, economists normally pose two tests for whether and when a firm should shut down. The first is that assets should move from lower value to higher value uses. Thus, even a profitable firm should shut down if the assets it uses (its workers, its equipment, or its site) are more valuable in some other use. Examples are a bank occupying a desirable retail location that could be used more profitably as a restaurant, or a Hula-Hoop manufacturer whose capital can be retooled more profitably to produce garden hoses. In these cases, shutdown need not involve a bankruptcy if the firm either has assets equal to its liabilities, or does not but is owned by a conglomerate that is profitable overall. The prospect of achieving a higher return for owners of the firm's capital in some other endeavor provides the motivation for the shutdown.

The second test for whether a firm should shut down applies specifically to firms that are losing money, and concerns the optimal timing of the shutdown. Economists argue that firms should eventually shut down if revenues do not cover both fixed and variable costs, but should not immediately shut down unless revenues fail to cover variable costs alone. If revenues cover variable costs but not total costs, and if the firm has specialized capital equipment having no alternative use, then it should continue operating, but the specialized capital should not be replaced when it wears out. An example is a firm owning machinery for producing double knit polyester textiles.

In these latter cases, a bankruptcy is usually involved. If a firm that has been losing money ceases to operate, and liquidates, then the value of its assets is normally less than that of its liabilities, and a bankruptcy filing is necessary to release its owners from the obligation to pay its liabilities in full. If the firm attempts to continue to operate despite a loss, then a bankruptcy filing will prevent creditors from disrupting its operations, by suing for repayment of the amounts owed them and attempting to collect by foreclosing on the firm's equipment. Some firms with a loss might be efficient potentially, but risky. For example, a firm developing a new product might experience delays or cost overruns. If investors feel that the project eventually will be profitable, they will lend more money to it. Whether it survives depends both on its prospects and on investors' valuation of its prospects.

However, the U.S. bankruptcy system is not necessarily structured to encourage failing firms to shut down at the best time from an economically efficient standpoint. For example, a failing firm has outstanding subordinated bonds that are publicly traded. In the past the proceeds of the bond issue were used to finance equipment purchases (i.e., to pay fixed costs). The failing firm later uses the equipment to secure new loans to finance variable costs, such as wages. The bondholders cannot prevent this because they cannot foreclose on the equipment. If the firm continues to lose money and finally shuts down, it will have no free assets left with which to pay the claims of its bondholders. This shifting of claims across creditors' classes allows the firm to continue to operate while, in effect, it consumes its free assets. However, this is inefficient if its assets are not specialized and would be more valuable in some other use. Thus, the bankruptcy system encourages some failing firms to continue to operate too long.

Conversely, it is also possible that the bankruptcy system might encourge some firms to shut down too early. Here, a particular creditor whose loans to the firm are decisive in providing working capital must decide that its claims are more valuable if the firm shuts down immediately. This outcome could be inefficient if the firm's capital is specialized and has no alternative use. This possibility is less likely than that of too early a shutdown because if the firm's capital is specialized, it will be worth little in liquidation.

Once a firm files for bankruptcy, there are two alternative procedures. The first is bankruptcy liquidation, under which the firm shuts down, its assets are sold, and the proceeds are distributed to creditors according to a predetermined formula. The second is bankruptcy reorganization, under which the firm continues to operate after the bankruptcy filing, and an agreement is made to compensate creditors partially for their claims. Reorganization in bankruptcy is a curious procedure from an economic standpoint, since it has the effect of prolonging the operation of firms that, being financially shaky, are quite likely to be economically inefficient as well.

The previous discussion suggests an economic justification for bankruptcy reorganization; that is, financially insolvent firms having specialized capital can continue to operate until their capital is worn out. In other words, bankruptcy reorganization might be used as a temporary transition to liquidation. These firms' revenues from continued operation can cover variable but not fixed costs, but only if a bankruptcy filing protects the firm from lawsuits by fixed-cost creditors. However, it will be seen that reorganization in bankruptcy is used much more widely than just as a transition to liquidation for insolvent firms having specialized capital.

THE LAW AND ECONOMICS OF CORPORATE BANKRUPTCY: LIQUIDATION

In a formal sense, bankruptcy is a procedure that allows firms to be discharged from some or all of their debts if they turn over their assets to the bankruptcy court for distribution to creditors. In order to qualify for bankruptcy treatment, the court must be convinced that the debtor's liabilities exceed its assets and that no means exist for creditors to be paid in full. As soon as the bankruptcy filing occurs, creditors are prevented (stayed) from initiating or continuing with individual lawsuits against the debtor. The bankruptcy filing has the effect of substituting the body of bankruptcy law for that of normal commercial and tax law, which govern nonbankruptcy situations. Thus, the normal obligations of a firm to fulfill its contracts with other parties and to pay taxes are suspended and replaced by a different set of obligations.

In its simplest form, a bankruptcy liquidation procedure for a failing firm would consist of the firm's filing for bankruptcy, shutting down its operations, and turning over its remaining assets to the bankruptcy court's appointed trustee. The assets would then be sold and the proceeds distributed to creditors who would each be paid an equal percentage of the face value of their claims. Creditors in a bankruptcy liquidation do not receive ownership of the firm itself or of its assets; rather, they receive the *value* of the firm's assets after sale by the trustee. Only if some amount remained after creditors were paid in full would equity holders receive anything. In general, equity holders are expected to receive nothing in bankruptcy liquidation. If they are expected to receive something, then the firm should not be in bankruptcy in the first place. (This is the case at the time of the bankruptcy filing. *Ex post*, the value of equity could be positive if, for example, the firm reorganizes rather than liquidates.)

The bankruptcy-mandated equal sharing of assets among creditors differs from the distribution of assets that results under normal commercial law. If there were no bankruptcy filing, then unpaid creditors would have the right to sue the debtor for the amounts owed them. This means that the first creditors to sue (actually the first to succeed) would probably be paid, perhaps in full, while creditors suing later would certainly receive less, or perhaps nothing at all if the debtor's assets were already exhausted.

For example, a firm has two creditors, A and B, each of which is owed $500. The liquidated value of the firm's assets is $250. Under bankruptcy law, each creditor would receive $125, or a 25 percent payoff rate, and equity holders would receive nothing. Under commercial law, if creditor A received a judgment against the firm first, then it would get $250, or a payoff rate of 50 percent. Creditor B and equity holders would receive nothing. The distribution pattern of assets to creditors in the example is thus more equal across creditors in bankruptcy as opposed to out of bankruptcy. Clearly, bankruptcy law and most bankruptcy situations are more complicated than this bare bones example, but it can now be asked how and whether bankruptcy law furthers the goal of encouraging long-run economic efficiency in markets.

The remainder of this section sets out several approaches to this question and explores them in the context of bankruptcy liquidation.

The Collective Negotiations Approach

One approach to thinking about the economic efficiency of bankruptcy procedures follows the tradition of legal economic analysis (see Posner (1972); Jackson (1982) has used this approach to analyze bankruptcy law). Here is asked what agreement the firm's creditors and equity holders would have negotiated concerning procedures to be followed in the event of bankruptcy had they all gotten

cussed, cause the value of the firm to fall.[3] However, Scott (1977) has pointed out that the value of the firm may rise if secured debt is substituted for unsecured debt ranked according to the me-first rule. The reason is if all or most debt is secured, then administrative costs in bankruptcy will be low or zero, since there are few free assets for the bankruptcy trustee to sell. However, the firm's value is defined as the present value of future revenues minus expenditures, including expected administrative costs in bankruptcy but excluding debt service costs. Therefore, reducing bankruptcy administrative costs increases the value of the firm to debt and equity holders.

Despite the fact that administrative claims in bankruptcy are paid to outsiders, creditors and shareholders would probably agree in an ex ante bargaining situation to provide for these costs to be paid before other claims in bankruptcy. Clearly, the processing of the bankruptcy and the liquidation of the firm's assets will proceed most smoothly and generate the highest payoff for creditors if the persons responsible for it expect to be paid for their services. This can be accomplished by giving them priority over all other creditors.

Coalition Behavior

There is the view that in a bankruptcy, some interests go unrepresented, at least at certain stages of the process. This can result in inefficient decisions being made, which do not maximize the value of the firm. In this view, it is assumed that a subset of interested parties, a coalition, controls the behavior of the firm. The coalition is most often composed of equity holders and some particular group of creditors but, in the simplest case, may be composed of equity holders alone. It is also assumed that the firm's investment policy can vary, whereas the previous section assumes that the firm's investment policy is fixed.

An example emerges from the fact that managers are often thought to act in shareholders' interests (i.e., to maximize the value of equity). However, the value of the firm equals the combined value of debt plus equity. Therefore, managers may have incentives to make decisions that increase the value of equity at the expense of a decrease in the value of debt and perhaps in the total value of the firm. Economically efficient bankruptcy rules should discourage managers from using bankruptcy (or the potential of bankruptcy) to benefit equity at the expense of debt in a way which lowers the overall value of the firm.

Under certain assumptions, the me-first rule and the equal-sharing rule in bankruptcy both have this efficient property. For example, it is assumed that managers wish to maximize the value of equity, the amount of debt is fixed, the firm's investment policy is fixed, and debt claims are paid in full before equity receives anything in bankruptcy. Then maximizing the value of equity

[3] See E. H. Kim et al., "Capital Structure Rearrangements and Me-First Rules in an Efficient Capital Market," *The Journal of Finance* (June 1977), pp. 789–810; A. H. Chen and E. H. Kim, "Theories of Corporate Debt Policy: A Synthesis," *The Journal of Finance* (May 1979), pp. 371–384; J. B. Warner, "Bankruptcy Costs: Some Evidence," *Journal of Finance* (May 1977), pp. 337–348.

is equivalent to maximizing the value of the firm, since the value of equity equals the value of the firm minus the value of debt, and the latter is fixed.

However, if the firm's investment level can vary, then these simple bankruptcy rules are no longer economically efficient. As an example, a firm that has assets of $100 and liabilities of $90 is considering investing in a risky project. If the project is undertaken, it has a 50 percent chance of increasing the value of the firm's assets to $150 and a 50 percent chance of decreasing the value to $50. In the latter case, the firm will file for bankruptcy. The project costs $10 and will be equity-financed. For simplicity, it is assumed that the interest rate is zero.

The project, if undertaken, lowers the value of the firm's debt from $90 with certainty to a 50 percent chance of $90 and a 50 percent chance of $50 or $70. However, the project raises the value of equity from $10 with certainty to a 50 percent chance of $60 ($150 − $90) and a 50 percent chance of zero, or $30, minus costs of $10, or $20 net. The project is therefore worthwhile from the viewpoint of equity, but it reduces the value of debt from $90 with certainty to an expected value of $70. Also, the project is economically inefficient, since it lowers the combined value of debt plus equity from $100 ($90 + $10) to $90 ($70 + $30 − $10).

In the example, the project is attractive from the viewpoint of equity, since it redistributes value from debt to equity; that is, the value of debt falls and that of equity rises. However, from a value-maximization standpoint, the project wastes resources.

It is further assumed that the project is to be debt-financed. All other assumptions remain unchanged. (1) If the new loan follows the me-first rule and takes lowest priority, the value of the loan is $10 if the outcome is successful and zero if bankruptcy occurs, for an expected value of $5. In this case the loan would be unattractive to lenders and would not be made. (2) If the loan takes equal priority with prior loans (the equal-sharing rule), its value is $10 if the firm survives and $5 if bankruptcy occurs, for an expected value of $7.50. Again, the loan would not be attractive to a lender. (3) If the loan is secured by a lien on an asset worth $10, the loan is always repaid $10 whether or not bankruptcy occurs, and would be attractive to a lender. However, the loan violates the me-first rule.

It has already been established that the project is economically inefficient regardless of how it is financed, since it causes the firm's overall value to fall. However, from the viewpoint of equity, the project varies in attractiveness depending on how it is financed. The project is worth $20 to equity if it is financed either by a new equity issue or by a fully secured loan. The project is worth more to equity if it is financed by an unsecured loan, which takes last priority under the me-first rule, or equal priority with other debt under the equal-sharing rule. In either of these cases the expected value of equity with the project is $25 (0.50 ($150 − $90 − $10) + 0.50 (0)). It has been shown that a lender would not find the loan attractive if it took equal priority or last priority in bankruptcy, but the world is an uncertain place and creditors sometimes make mistakes.

Two conclusions emerge from this example. First, managers and equity owners may find it desirable to undertake economically inefficient projects, that lower the overall value of the firm. This occurs because the project makes the firm's earnings stream more risky and increases the probability of bankruptcy. Equity benefits, since if a good outcome occurs, equity holders get the firm's high earnings. If a bad outcome occurs, limited liability allows equity holders to avoid bearing the firm's losses, which are shifted to debt. Second, projects such as the one previously analyzed are even more attractive to equity when they are financed by unsecured loans that follow the me-first rule. However, the me-first rule does not work perfectly in screening out inefficient projects. Some inefficient projects may be attractive even when they are fully financed by equity, which does not violate the me-first rule.

These results can be generalized somewhat. It is assumed that the firm's own earnings stream without the new investment and the earnings stream of the new investment are both subject to uncertainty, the cost of the investment is known, and the firm has debt outstanding. Whether the investment is worthwhile from an economically efficient standpoint depends upon a comparison of its expected earnings relative to its costs. All parties are risk-neutral, and bankruptcy administrative costs are positive.

If the earnings stream of the project is positively correlated with that of the firm, then the effect of undertaking the project is to make the firm's combined earnings stream *more* risky. This hurts debt holders by increasing the probability of bankruptcy. It benefits equity holders by increasing the expected value of equity, so part of the return to equity holders from the project is a transfer from debt holders. This transfer gives managers an incentive to undertake the project even in some cases where it is economically inefficient, if the transfer from debt holders to equity holders is large enough to offset the difference between the project's cost and its expected benefit.

If the project is financed by equity or by a fully secured loan, the project is least likely to be attractive from the standpoint of equity. It still may be attractive, however, despite the fact that it is economically inefficient. If the project is financed by unsecured debt under the me-first rule or the equal-priority rule, the project is even more attractive to equity holders. In these cases the debt holder is less likely to find the investment attractive. Thus, the me-first rule discourages the undertaking of economically inefficient projects. However, some such projects are attractive to equity holders even if their financing does not violate the me-first rule.[4]

It has been shown when managers act in the interests of equity, economically inefficient investment projects may be attractive to the firm because they cause transfers from debt holders to equity holders. This analysis of investment incentives by firms is formally identical to the analysis of the effect of bankruptcy on incentives for conglomerate mergers. In the merger case, the new investment project is the purchase of an existing firm. It can be shown in this case that some mergers are attractive to equity holders because they increase the value of equity at the expense of a decrease in the value of debt. This occurs when the combined firm has a higher probability of bankruptcy. In this case the

---

[4] See M. J. White, "Public Policy Toward Bankruptcy: Me-First and Other Priority Rules," *Bell Journal of Economics* (Autumn 1980), pp. 550–564. In the opposite case where the firm's and the investment's earnings streams are negatively correlated, equity is likely to pass over economically efficient investments because they cause transfers from equity to debt by reducing the probability of bankruptcy. From a public policy standpoint this distortion is less serious, however, since other firms will find these projects attractive, especially new firms.

overall value of the firm can rise or fall. Scott (1977) shows that, in general, conglomerate mergers only increase overall firm value if the merger causes the probability of bankruptcy to fall or if the merger causes expected bankruptcy costs to fall, due to economies of scale in bankruptcy administrative costs.[5]

Managers generally have an incentive to continue the firm's operations as long as possible, even if it is losing money and will eventually file for bankruptcy. Such continued operation could be attractive to equity at the expense of debt if dividends continue to be paid after the firm's liabilities exceed its assets. Continuation may be attractive to managers at the expense of both creditors and equity holders if managers keep their jobs longer, even though the continued operation wastes assets. Usually, continued operation of a financially weak firm involves a coalition of equity and some particular set of debt interests.

Bulow and Shoven (1978), and White (1980), have analyzed coalition models of failing firms' decisions to liquidate in bankruptcy versus continuing operations for one more period. They show that it is possible for a coalition of managers representing equity and some particular group of debt holders to make economically inefficient decisions either to continue to operate the firm when its assets are more valuable in some other use or to shut the firm down when its assets have no more valuable use. The latter case may result, for instance, if a particular secured creditor providing working capital has a claim on an asset whose value is greater if the creditor can foreclose on it immediately, even though the firm's assets are generally more valuable in their current use.

The more common case, however, is coalition behavior delaying the firm's shutdown too long. A particular lender whose unsecured loan has come due may know that the firm is failing and that the lender will be paid little in a bankruptcy liquidation. Thus, the lender agrees to roll over its loan in return for conversion of the principal from unsecured to secured status. This benefits the lender by making its loan less risky and benefits managers and equity by allowing the firm to continue for at least one more period, during which its financial condition could improve. This conversion of the crucial lender's status from unsecured to secured is unlikely to reduce overall transactions costs. It would probably not be agreed to in ex ante bargaining by creditors and equity holders, since its main effect is to increase the value of the late creditor's claim at the expense of unsecured creditors generally. This is because the free assets used to secure the late creditor's claim were purchased with the proceeds of earlier, unsecured creditors' loans. However, continued operation of the firm hurts creditors generally if the firm is losing money.

Recent changes in commercial law have made it easier for coalition rescues of failing firms to occur. While a failing firm is likely to have most of its long-lived equipment already subject to secured creditors' liens, the Uniform Commercial Code (UCC), Article 9, adopted by most states during the 1960s, allows liens to be written in general terms to apply to short-lived assets, such as raw materials, inventory, or accounts receivable, that change form frequently.[6] (Previously, secured creditors' liens had to describe the asset in detail, so only

---

[5] Scott also considers the effects of tax consideration and redistribution across types of creditors on incentives for merger.

[6] See A. Schwartz, "Security Interests and Bankruptcy Priorities: A Review of Current Theories," *Journal of Legal Studies* (Jan. 1981), pp. 35, 45–49.

long-lived assets could be used as security.) As a result, creditors of failing firms can convert late loans to secured status by taking liens on inventory and accounts receivable. These liens can be written to include after-acquired assets of the firm so that if inventory is sold, the lien also covers the new accounts receivable. However, if the firm is losing money, such rescues can quickly absorb all its free assets. Thus, when such firms finally do file for bankruptcy liquidation, their total liabilities will be well in excess of their assets, and secured liabilities alone may equal the value of assets. Few free assets will be available to pay the claims of unsecured creditors, whose payoff in bankruptcy liquidation will be very low. These hypotheses are tested in the following discussion.

Bankruptcy rules can encourage firms to shut down when it is economically efficient for them to do so and to avoid inefficient investment projects. This can be accomplished by abolishing the limited liability of equity holders in bankruptcy. This would make decisions that cause transfers from debt to equity unattractive, since equity holders would have to cover creditors' losses. However, such a drastic change has other drawbacks and appears unlikely.

Alternatively, the examples previously discussed suggest that the firm's incentives are generally more efficient when either (1) the me-first rule is followed for all loans; or (2) all loans, past and present, are secured.

In the all-secured case, in order to obtain a new loan, the firm must either have free assets available equal to the amount of the loan, or the loan itself must create new assets sufficient to provide the needed security. The former occurs if a previously secured loan is rolled over with the same security. The latter occurs if a new asset, such as equipment or inventory, is purchased with the loan proceeds. In either circumstance, if the value of the asset equals the principal of the loan, the firm repays the loan fully regardless of whether or not bankruptcy occurs. The incentive to undertake any project is the same as if it were financed by equity. In particular, the firm cannot operate past the point where the value of liabilities exceeds that of its assets. It cannot prolong its operations at the cost of using up free assets that would otherwise be paid to unsecured creditors. The firm's incentives are economically efficient in this situation. However, the transactions costs of securing all claims are likely to be very high. Such a rule would particularly harm small trade creditors, since there are high fixed costs to secure any claim.

In the all-unsecured case, all loans are unsecured and the latest loan ranks last. Here, the failing firm will find it difficult to raise a new loan, since the last lender is only repaid in bankruptcy if all prior loans are repaid in full first. Since the last creditor is unsecured, it cannot be repaid by the firm transferring to it free assets purchased with the proceeds of earlier unsecured loans. Thus, the firm can only continue if it has assets equal in value to the total of its liabilities, including the last creditor's claim. Managers' incentives are not always economically efficient in this case. Some risky investments (continuation included) may still be attractive because they make the firm's earnings stream more risky and increase the probability of bankruptcy. However, the firm cannot prolong its operations by transferring free assets across creditors' groups in violation of the me-first rule.

Thus, with either all loans secured or all loans unsecured but taking priority according to the me-first rule, managers' scope to make inefficient decisions by transferring value across creditors' groups or between creditors and equity holders is considerably reduced. In practice it has been seen that a mixture of secured and unsecured debt is used, with many ways of violating the me-first priority ordering. Assuming that the mixture of debt types is here to stay, the efficiency of managers' incentives could be improved by going back to the pre-UCC rule that only long-lived assets could be used to secure loans. This would make it more difficult for firms to finance late projects at the expense of early creditors. Since late loans are generally used to provide working capital, they could not be secured. Before the UCC was adopted, there was a tracing requirement, which stipulated that the asset used to secure a loan had to be traceable to that creditor's loan. This prevented new creditors from securing their loans with claims on old capital.

THE LAW AND ECONOMICS OF CORPORATE BANKRUPTCY: REORGANIZATION

Bankruptcy reorganization is a process by which all or part of the failing firm continues to operate after the bankruptcy filing. A settlement with unsecured creditors is arranged, giving them partial payment on their claims and, sometimes, equity in the reorganized firm. New loans can be more easily obtained to finance the firm's operation after the bankruptcy petition, since postpetition creditors take priority over all prepetition creditors if the reorganized firm fails and files for bankruptcy in the future. Old equity is usually retained but may be diluted by new issues. Old secured creditors are prevented by the bankruptcy "stay" from foreclosing and removing their lien assets except with the bankruptcy court's approval. Usually, the old management remains in control of the firm.

The negotiations framework is again considered. If all creditors and equity holders could meet ex ante to agree on a procedure for bankruptcy reorganization, they would have to agree on (1) the circumstances under which the firm could reorganize rather than liquidate if bankruptcy occurs; and (2) how much, if anything, creditors and equity holders would receive in a reorganization.

One obvious point of agreement for all parties might be that reorganization rather than liquidation of the firm should occur if and only if the value of the firm's assets is greater in reorganization than in liquidation. In this case if any party is harmed by reorganization, it should be possible for other parties to compensate the harmed party and still remain better off. The previous discussion suggests that firms that are more valuable in reorganization than in liquidation are those that have specialized capital with no alternate use, but not yet worn out. These firms would be more valuable if liquidation were delayed and the firms continued to operate until the capital is worn out. For these firms, reorganization would be a temporary transition to liquidation.

However, reorganization is often thought to benefit a much wider class of firms. Managers of failing firms usually agree that the assets of failing firms are worth more if they reorganize rather than liquidate, because reorganization avoids the disruption that accompanies shutting the firm down, dismissing its workers, and disturbing its relationships with suppliers and creditors. Thus, transactions costs, broadly defined, are lower in reorganization. However, in theory it should be possible to liquidate a failing firm by selling it on the open market as a going concern rather than by shutting it down and selling its assets piecemeal. This could give creditors the benefit of the higher value without a formal reorganization. It is also often thought that the reorganizing firm should retain the same management to minimize disruption. However, to the extent that failing firms are likely to have had bad management, replacing the firm's managers would seem likely to increase the value of its assets.

Creditors meeting ex ante to discuss a procedure for reorganization would probably realize that coalition problems loom large. Equity holders and managers have an incentive to avoid liquidation at all costs, because equity is inevitably wiped out and managers' jobs and shares are lost in liquidation. A coalition of managers and equity holders can delay or avoid liquidation by converting unsecured to secured debt, by making risky investments that have a small chance of a very high return, or by engaging in unnecessary litigation. Alternatively, if they expect that liquidation is inevitable, they may waste the firm's resources generally.

Managers can also form coalitions with groups of creditors, usually those supplying working capital. Reorganization is often attractive to such a coalition because, after the bankruptcy petition, new postpetition loans incurred with the court's permission take priority over older loans and sometimes over administrative expenses if a liquidation occurs later. Thus, bankruptcy reorganization enables the last unsecured creditor to rank highest rather than lowest among unsecured creditors, thereby jumping the me-first queue. An example of this would be retailing chains, which often file for bankruptcy reorganization under a threat from unsecured inventory suppliers that they will otherwise cut off the firm's credit.

Equity holders and unsecured creditors generally can also benefit from reorganization at the expense of secured creditors. The latter prefer liquidation, since they can then reclaim their lien assets immediately. These assets remain with the firm if it reorganizes, and often depreciate in value over time. Thus, secured creditors are usually made worse off if the firm reorganizes, since they are forced to lend to a risky enterprise.

Further, reorganization is often attractive to managers and equity holders at the expense of particular suppliers, customers, and debt holders of the firm. This is because firms reorganizing in bankruptcy have the right to reject any contracts they have made with other parties, as long as the contracts are not substantially completed. These "executory contracts" can be rejected by firms reorganizing in bankruptcy purely because they are unprofitable. In contrast, firms not in bankruptcy can reject contracts only if they are impossible to perform, and then they are liable for damages to the other party.

The right of bankrupt firms to reject contracts means, for example, that loans incurred in the past at above current market interest rates can be paid off even if they have not yet matured, while loans incurred in the past at below current market interest rates can be retained. Those who loaned above market rates would not be better off if the firm liquidated, since their claims would still be for face value. Those who loaned below market rates might prefer liquidation, since they would have a claim for full face value in liquidation, even though the current market value of their claims would be less than face value.

This "decontracting" aspect of bankruptcy reorganization has been used more widely in recent years. There have been several recent instances of firms filing for bankruptcy reorganization primarily as a means of rejecting collective bargaining agreements, thereby reducing workers' wages to nonunion levels. (This has occurred notably in the airline and meat-packing industries, both of which have a mixture of unionized and nonunionized firms.) Failing firms also frequently close down unprofitable lines of business and reject as executory contracts their obligations to suppliers and customers.

Similarly, in several instances firms have used bankruptcy reorganization to reduce liability to tort claimants. The most famous instance is the Manville Corporation, which justified its bankruptcy filing with a study showing that potential liability to its own and to customers' workers who contracted asbestos disease exceeded the value of its assets. Tort claims and the claims of holders of rejected contracts who seek money damages are treated similarly in bankruptcy reorganization; both rank as general unsecured claims.

Finally, tax considerations provide an additional incentive for firms to reorganize rather than liquidate. Firms that reorganize are allowed to retain their tax loss carry-forwards, while firms that liquidate do not. Having a tax loss carry-forward makes a firm valuable either because its own future profits (if any) will be free of the corporate profits tax or because the firm becomes an attractive merger target for an already profitable suitor. The tax consideration potentially benefits all parties having a stake in the firm at the expense of the U.S. Government if the reorganization is chosen.

In general, coalition-type issues imply that managers, equity holders, and some groups of creditors are likely to prefer reorganization to liquidation because it makes them better off at the expense of those not in the coalition (possibly including the U.S. Treasury). Other groups of creditors, workers, or suppliers are made worse off. However, reorganization may not make creditors and equity holders as a whole better off, so it may be economically inefficient.

Given the considerations set out here, what provisions are creditors and equity holders likely to agree on ex ante? Unsecured creditors are likely to agree that allowing reorganization is desirable in many cases; otherwise, managers can delay a bankruptcy liquidation long enough that unsecured creditors will receive little when it occurs. (This is a second-best consideration.) As previously noted, managers are able to postpone liquidation of failing firms by obtaining loans for working capital from previously unsecured creditors who convert their loans to secured status. As a result, unsecured creditors in general receive a low or zero return in liquidation. This means that their expected opportunity cost if the firm reorganizes is very low. If unsecured creditors' payoff in liquidation were higher, they would be more likely to oppose reorganization.

For the same reason, unsecured creditors are likely to allow equity interests to remain intact even when debt claims are cut back. This implies giving up the protection of the absolute priority rule, under which equity is eliminated unless all creditors are paid in full. In this case creditors would require that no dividends be paid to equity while the reorganization plan remained in effect. Unsecured creditors are also likely to allow the old management to remain if reorganization occurs. This is because if managers anticipate that they will be replaced in a reorganization, they will avoid reorganization by all means available, that is, by depleting the firm's free assets for as long as possible and then filing for liquidation. Thus, reorganization with management intact is a means of overcoming the agency costs that arise as a failing firm moves toward bankruptcy.

Creditors would probably want an independent appraisal of the firm's assets to be made, both to verify that the firm is worth more if it reorganizes and to determine how much the firm can pay to old creditors. In a liquidation, the firm's assets would be sold on the open market, so their value would be known. In a reorganization, the assets are not sold, so it is more difficult to determine their value. Creditors might decide to require limits on how much or what types of new investment a reorganized firm is permitted. Extensive new investment in new lines of business would suggest the existence of assets that could be used instead to pay old creditors a higher return. Unsecured creditors are likely to agree on some sort of less than unanimous voting procedure to approve a firm's reorganization plan. Such a provision prevents small groups of creditors from holding out for greater compensation than others having the same priority receive. In contrast, secured creditors are likely to demand payments or claims equal to the market value of their lien assets in return for allowing the reorganized firm to retain the assets. Since each secured creditor has an individual lien on some capital asset, they are not likely to agree on a majority voting rule. Rather, each one will favor negotiating individually with the firm.

The previous discussion suggests several conclusions concerning the economic efficiency of reorganization. First, it is likely that too many firms will reorganize; that is, more will reorganize than just those whose assets are more valuable if they continue to operate than if they liquidate. This happens for a variety of reasons: Equity holders and managers always prefer reorganization; tax considerations always favor reorganization; and unsecured creditors are generally unlikely to oppose reorganization, since their expected return in liquidation is low. This means that some firms are likely to reorganize even though their assets are more valuable in some other use. Also, assuming that most reorganized firms are required to remain in the same line of business, it means that reorganization in bankruptcy has the effect of slowing the movement of resources from less efficient to more efficient uses.

Second, secured creditors are the only group of creditors likely to oppose strongly reorganization of failing firms. Thus, their role is critical in determining whether failing firms reorganize or liquidate. It is interesting to note that the statutory rights given to secured creditors to oppose reorganization plans have varied quite a bit over the last few decades and were strengthened under the new Bankruptcy Code, discussed in the following section.

One situation in which secured creditors are unlikely to oppose reorganization is where the firm's capital is specialized and has no alternative use. Then, secured creditors do not benefit from foreclosing on the capital. However, secured creditors will probably have to agree to a reduction in their previous rental or interest payments from the firm in order for the firm's revenue to be sufficient to pay postpetition (variable cost) creditors in full.

Finally, creditors and equity holders might also agree ex ante that the transactions costs of reorganizing could be reduced by avoiding a formal bankruptcy filing altogether. If the firm appears to be failing, the parties could get together outside of bankruptcy and renegotiate their claims. The type of plan they would agree on would probably be similar to that which would be arrived at in a formal bankruptcy reorganization proceeding. This is because all creditors would realize that if the informal negotiations failed, the firm would file for a formal reorganization. To reduce transactions costs, creditors would probably be willing to bind themselves to vote in favor of any formal reorganization plan that was substantively the same as an informal reorganization plan negotiated before the bankruptcy filing. Obviously, many firms have succeeded in reorganizing without ever filing in a bankruptcy court (e.g., International Harvester and Chrysler), but their reorganization plans were probably very close to the terms that would have emerged in a formal reorganization.

The features of a reorganization procedure that creditors, equity holders, and management might agree to ex ante have been previously discussed. However, bankruptcy reorganization, unlike liquidation, is mainly statutory law rather than judge-made law. This means that the procedure can change as congressional concerns change over time. For example, Congress has been concerned to encourage the reorganization of failing firms as a means of saving jobs. This concern may not be economically rational, since reorganized firms often lay off many of their workers, while liquidation of failing firms releases resources to move and generate jobs in new uses.

This bias in favor of reorganization creates a trade-off between compensating the firm's old creditors versus increasing the chance of the reorganization plan being successful by conserving the firm's capital. The more that secured and unsecured creditors give up, the less new capital needs to be raised to finance the reorganization plan, and the more likely it is to be successful. In particular, managers can often prevent secured creditors from foreclosing on their lien assets by arguing that the reorganization effort is infeasible without these assets. Given this trade-off, it is not surprising that creditors are sometimes compensated less than they would have agreed to in voluntary negotiation.

The discussion implies that regardless of the exact decision rule applied to secured creditors in reorganizations, firms having relatively more secured debt in their capital structures are more likely to liquidate, and those having relatively more unsecured debt are likely to reorganize. This is both because secured creditors are more likely to oppose reorganization and because they are in the best position to block a proposed reorganization plan. This hypothesis is tested in the following section.

THE NEW BANKRUPTCY CODE

This section considers major changes in bankruptcy law and procedures made by the new Bankruptcy Code. The Bankrutpcy Reform Act of 1978 replaced the previous bankruptcy legislation, the Chandler Law of 1938, and constituted the first major revision of U.S. bankruptcy procedures in 40 years. The Chandler Law is referred to as the old Bankruptcy Act (old Act), and the post-1978 reform as the new Bankruptcy Code (new Code). The new Code took effect in late 1979.

Liquidation

The bankruptcy liquidation procedure under the new Code is known as Chapter 7. It replaces a procedure known as straight bankruptcy under the old Act.

The Liquidation Priority Rule. The order of distribution of a liquidated firm's assets to creditors is governed by the liquidation priority rule. Under the rule, the firm's assets are sold and the proceeds are used to pay creditors' claims in full in the following order: (1) administrative costs of bankruptcy, including lawyers', trustees', accountants', and court fees and "expenses of preserving the estate" (i.e., postpetition loans to the firm); (2) loans to the firm arising in the ordinary course of business after the bankruptcy filing if the filing is involuntary; (3) claims for wages and salaries up to specified limits; (4) claims for contributions to employee benefit plans up to specified limits; (5) claims by customers for deposits; (6) claims by governmental units for taxes of any type; (7) claims of unsecured creditors; and (8) equity claims. Claims falling in categories 2 through 6 are known as priority claims.

Claims are for the face value of the amount owed plus accrued interest, except that accrual of interest stops at the time of the bankruptcy filing. Claims of each class are paid in full before the next class receives any payment. Creditors in the last class to receive payment have their claims prorated.

The new Code added the priorities for employee benefits and for customer deposits and raised the limit on the wage priority to $2,000 per employee. The limit on the new benefit priority is also $2,000 per employee. The new Code recognizes subordination agreements among unsecured creditors where they exist. These give rise to subclasses of unsecured creditors, each having priority over lower subclasses. Where there is no explicit agreement, that creditor's claim ranks last in the class. Both the old Act and the new Code also recognize the claims of secured creditors to highest priority over the proceeds from sale of their particular lien assets. If the proceeds do not cover the amount of the secured creditor's claim, then the remainder becomes an unsecured claim. Secured creditors are allowed to claim their lien assets directly if the value of the claim exceeds the value of the asset. If the value of the asset exceeds the claim, the trustee sells the asset but the creditor is entitled to interest after the bankruptcy filing.

Administration of Bankruptcy Liquidation Cases. When a firm files for bankruptcy liquidation, a trustee is appointed. The trustee acts as an independent contractor who locates and evaluates the firm's assets and decides whether to take possession of and liquidate, or to abandon, each asset not subject to a lien. The trustee is also empowered to examine all transactions of the firm for six months prior to the bankruptcy filing and to cancel any that were fraudulent or that benefited insiders at creditors' expense. This is known as the avoiding power of the trustee. Trustee's fees and expenses must be covered by the proceeds of assets liquidated; no funds are provided by the court. Trustees receive a fee equal to a declining proportion of the value of the assets they liquidate.

Under this system, trustees have an incentive to spend time and incur expenses in searching for assets only to the point where the value of an extra expenditure of time brings in enough extra assets such that the fee as a proportion of the value of the extra assets compensates trustees for their time. If the fee is a low proportion of assets, trustees have little incentive to spend time on search. But more effort by trustees in general could generate a higher payoff to unsecured creditors in liquidation cases, which in turn would increase the expected return to future creditors of similarly situated firms. Thus, a system that encourages too little search by trustees raises the borrowing cost by firms in general.

The new Code experiments with changing the administration of bankruptcy cases. For 5 years in 10 geographic districts, administration is to be overseen by an official called the U.S. Trustee, who is independent of the bankruptcy court. In these districts, the U.S. Trustee appoints trustees for individual liquidation cases. The intent of this change is to meet the criticism that bankruptcy judges (who previously appointed trustees) both administer and adjudicate bankruptcy cases and thus may be subject to conflicts of interest. In the experimental districts, the U.S. Trustee rather than the bankruptcy judge appoints trustees and evaluates their performance. However, the problem — that trustees in individual cases have an inadequate incentive to search for assets — remains under the experimental system. The new Code adopted a maximum compensation schedule for case trustees of 15 percent of the first $1,000 of liquidated assets, 6 percent of the next $2,000, 3 percent of the next $17,000, 2 percent of the next $30,000, and one percent of any additional amount. These amounts are clearly very low except in large cases.[7] Trustees sometimes hire themselves as attorney on the case as a means of increasing their compensation by charging for their time spent on legal work. However, this leads to many fruitless lawsuits being filed, which delays completion of the bankruptcy process and payment of creditors.

What compensation scheme would improve trustees' incentives? A simple economic analysis of the trustee's role as an independent contractor suggests that for the marginal unit of effort, the trustee should receive the full value of the proceeds. Then the trustee will stop searching for assets when the value of the proceeds equals the opportunity cost of his time. This suggests that trustees should receive a rising proportion of the value of the extra assets the locates and liquidates. The actual payment system does exactly the opposite, thus discouraging effort at the margin by trustees.

Reorganization

Consolidation of Chapters. Under the old Act, there were two separate business reorganization procedures, Chapters X and XI. Chapter X was intended to be used by large firms having publicly held debt or equity, and Chapter XI to be used by smaller, closely held firms. Chapter X was a more formal procedure, including mandatory appointment of an independent trustee to supervise the firm's operation and involvement by the SEC to advise on the fairness of the reorganization plan. As a result, managers invariably preferred Chapter XI, under which they remained in control of the firm. The SEC sometimes initiated litigation over which Chapter would be used, with managers preferring Chapter XI and the SEC maintaining that the public interest could only be protected in a Chapter X proceeding. The new Code combines the old Chapters X, XI, and

---

[7] See N. Ames et al., *An Evaluation of the U.S. Trustee Pilot Program for Bankruptcy Administration: Findings and Recommendations*, U.S. Department of Justice, Consultants' study (Cambridge, Mass.: Abt Associates, 1983).

XII (used by firms holding mainly real property) into a single procedure for business rehabilitation, known as Chapter 11. Chapter 11 combines many features of the old Chapters X and XI, which greatly reduces the role of the SEC.

Management's Role. The new Code allows current management to remain in charge of the firm (as debtor-in-possession) or a trustee to be appointed to oversee management. The former prevails in most cases, but the latter is possible if an interested party shows cause (such as showing that the management has made preferential transfers to certain creditors or is stealing the assets of the firm). In all Chapter 11 arrangements, a committee of unsecured creditors is appointed by the judge or the U.S. Trustee to oversee the firm. Other interests, such as equity holders or secured creditors, can also request that additional committees representing them be appointed. (Although tort claimants could petition for representation, workers whose wages are cut or whose jobs are terminated are not represented.)

The Reorganization Plan. Under the old Chapter XI, only the firm's management could propose the reorganization plan. This put creditors in the undesirable position of choosing between accepting management's plan and rejecting the plan and forcing the firm into a liquidation. (Litigation could have been instituted to move a firm to a Chapter X arrangement, but this was done very rarely.) The new Code attempts to put creditors in a better bargaining position by allowing them to propose their own reorganization plans after a 180-day period of exclusivity by management. This change is probably only important to large firms, since only then are individual creditors' claims large enough to make it worthwhile for them to spend time and effort formulating an alternative plan. Furthermore, if creditors as a group attempt to join forces to formulate a plan, free rider problems crop up, since some creditors may refuse to share the costs.

Valuation of the Firm in Reorganization. Under any reorganization plan, proponents must argue that the firm is worth more if it continues to operate than if it is shut down and its assets liquidated. In reorganization, the firm is valued by estimating the flow of future after-tax earnings and discounting them by using an appropriate interest rate to determine the net present value of future earnings. If old equity interests are to be maintained, the net present value of future earnings must also exceed the total value of creditors' claims.

In many reorganization cases, these valuations are a formality. The alternative value of the firm's assets if it liquidates is determined by estimating the amount they would bring if sold piecemeal at auction. Since this amount is invaribly very low, it justifies the firm reorganizing even if its estimated future earnings will provide only a low payoff to old unsecured creditors. The actual payoff rate to old creditors, however, is determined by bargaining.

Use of the Firm's Assets. Under the old Chapter XI, reorganization plans had to keep the firm operating without selling or closing down any major portion of its assets. Under the new Code, any disposition of the firm's assets is allowable.[8] This is an important change from an economic standpoint, since for the first time it allows bankrupt firms an alternative between liquidating and selling their assets piecemeal versus reorganizing and retaining essentially the same asset structure. Under the new Chapter 11, parts of the firm can be shut down and other parts retained, and any or all parts of the firm can be sold as a going concern. This change allows reorganizing firms to use their assets in whatever way maximizes profits. The change improves economic efficiency by removing requirements that tied the firm to using its capital in an obsolete industry or technology.

Unsecured creditors are likely to favor reorganization plans that pay them at least their (low) expected return in liquidation and to favor some type of majority or strong majority voting procedure for approving reorganization plans as a means of avoiding holdout problems. Secured creditors are likely to oppose most reorganizations except when the capital on which they hold liens is specialized and has no alternate use.

The old Chapter XI procedure made it relatively easy for a reorganizing firm to retain assets subject to secured creditors' liens. The reason was that Chapter XI, intended only for smaller companies, did not allow the claims of secured creditors to be cut back at all. Since their claims could not be cut back, they were not given the right to vote on the reorganization plan. The old Chapter X procedure allowed secured creditors' claims to be cut back, but required that they consent to the reorganization plan if their claims were cut back. It contained a "cramdown" procedure, however, which was similar to the new Chapter 11 cramdown, discussed in the following section.

This often led to abuses, such as in the well-known *Yale Express* case.[9] Here, a trucking firm in bankruptcy reorganization argued that its trucks were necessary for the success of the reorganization plan. The secured creditor who had a lien on the trucks was therefore stayed by the court from foreclosing. However, the reorganization plan provided for payments to the creditor that were less than what the trucks could be leased for elsewhere and also below what Yale had agreed to pay before its bankruptcy filing. Thus, the secured creditor was forced to agree to a reorganization plan, which it would not have agreed to voluntarily, but which it did not have the right to vote on. In other similar cases, secured creditors' liens were moved from more liquid to less liquid assets, or were made subordinate to a new postpetition creditor's lien on the same asset.

Thus, Chapter XI bankruptcy reorganizations were popular, at least in part, because they allowed the firm to cut back secured creditors' claims without full compensation. This benefited managers and equity holders, but it was economically inefficient in that it kept assets tied up in what was not necessarily their most valuable use. In the *Yale Express* case, for example, the firm's capital, trucks, was not at all specialized and probably was more valuable to some other firm with better management. One of the main aims of the new

---

[8] This was known as the "Pure Penn doctrine." The justification for it was that Chapter XI provided less procedural protection for creditors; therefore firms were not allowed to make drastic changes such as selling off major parts of their business. (In re Pure Penn Petroleum Co., 188 F.2d 851 (2d Cir. 1951.))

[9] In re Yale Express 370 F.2d 433 (2d Cir. 1966).

Code was to provide better protection to secured creditors. The new Code changes the requirements for firms reorganizing to keep assets that are subject to secured crditors' liens.

Requirements for Adoption of a Reorganization Plan Under the "Unanimous Consent Procedure."

Under the new Code, there are now two procedures for adopting a reorganization plan. The first is referred to as the unanimous consent procedure (UCP) and requires consent by all classes of creditors. The second is aptly named cramdown and provides for a plan to be adopted despite the objection of some creditors' classes.

Under the UCP, secured creditors' claims may be cut back, but if so, they have a right to approve or disapprove the reorganization plan. If their claims are not impaired, then they are deemed to approve the plan. Secured creditors are treated individually rather than as a class.

Unsecured creditors also have the right to vote on the plan if their claims are impaired. To approve the plan, they must vote in favor by a two-thirds margin and with a majority in number of claims voting in each subclass.

The treatment of priority (tax and wage) claims is also changed. Under the old Chapter XI, these had to be paid in full at the time of adoption of the plan. Under the new Chapter 11, priority claims can be cut back, but if so, they must vote in favor of the plan. In particular, the new Code provides for tax claims to be paid in installments over a period of up to six years. (However, this is less of a change in substance than in form, since previously, tax creditors often voluntarily reduced their claims.)

Chapter 11 also incorporates a standard for treatment of dissenting minorities within a class or subclass of unsecured creditors that accepts the plan. Dissenting unsecured creditors must receive value equal to what they would get if the firm liquidated under Chapter 7. (This is referred to as the best interests of creditors test.)

Equity claims also have the right to vote on the plan if their claims are impaired. They must vote in favor of the plan by two thirds of those shares voting. Equity interests are deemed to reject the plan if their shares are eliminated. However, equity must be eliminated if the firm's outside appraisal shows that its liabilities exceed its assets. (It should be noted that the market value of equity may be positive even if the value of the firm's assets is less than its liabilities. This is because the market anticipates that equity claims will be maintained in reorganization and that equity in the future may have value.)

It is interesting to note the role of equity in a Chapter 11 UCP reorganization plan. Equity is deemed to vote for the plan if the old shares remain intact, even if they are diluted by the issuance of new shares to creditors. If equity is eliminated, then it is deemed to reject the plan and the plan cannot be adopted by unanimous consent of all classes. Cramdown must then be used, and it is a more expensive procedure. Thus, the new Chapter 11, like the old Chapter XI, contains a built-in bias in favor of retaining old equity interests. Given that firms filing for bankruptcy usually have liabilities exceeding their assets, this statutory bias in favor of maintaining old equity interests seems difficult to explain.

If all classes (and subclasses) of creditors accept the plan, it is submitted to the bankruptcy court for approval under the UCP, which in this case is a formality. How does approval of a plan under the UCP of Chapter 11 compare to approval under the old Chapter XI procedure? The old Chapter XI procedure required only a simple majority vote by unsecured creditors (instead of a two-thirds majority), so unsecured creditors were in a somewhat stronger bargaining position vis-à-vis managers. (Management could pay off creditors to obtain the requisite majority, but this became expensive as the majority requirement was strengthened.) Also, secured creditors now have the right to disapprove the plan if their claims are impaired, putting them in a stronger bargaining position. The result would seem to be that fewer firms in bankruptcy will adopt reorganization plans under the new UCP than they did under Chapter XI of the old Act. This hypothesis is tested in the following section.

Cramdown. Under the new Chapter 11, cramdown comes into play if an impaired class of creditors does not vote for the reorganization plan by the required margin or if management anticipates this outcome. The new Code provides that a reorganization plan can be confirmed by the bankruptcy court as long as each dissenting class is treated according to the "fair and equitable" standard.

This standard differs by class. For secured creditors, it requires that they retain their prebankruptcy liens and that they receive periodic cash payments equal to the amount of depreciation on the property. For each class of unsecured creditors, it requires either that they receive compensation equal to the amount of their claims or that they receive some lesser amount, but that all lower-ranking classes receive nothing. For equity, the requirement is that their interest be eliminated if any higher-ranking class receives partial payment.

Thus, the use of cramdown introduces a form of the liquidation priority rule into the bankruptcy reorganization context. Normally, reorganization is associated with a "relative priority rule"; that is, higher-ranking creditors receive less than full payoff, while lower-ranking creditors receive something, and equity interests are maintained. Under cramdown, however, an "absolute priority rule" is introduced if any creditors' groups vote to reject the plan. This means that unless all higher-ranking classes either receive approximately full payment of their claims or else consent to partial payment, then no lower-ranking classes can receive anything.

In practice, the use of cramdown raises the transactions costs of the bankruptcy process substantially. While the bankruptcy court is likely to confirm a UCP plan with only cursory information concerning the firm's finances, the same court is likely to probe further before confirming a plan that uses cramdown. Valuations of the firm's assets by outside appraisers, testimony by experts, and so forth are likely to be necessary if cramdown is used. Cramdown is therefore a realistic alternative only for very large firms that can afford these high fixed costs.

However, cramdown appears to be a possibility in one other context. If a firm's management and its creditors are unable to agree on a reorganization plan, the firm can either shift to a Chapter 7 liquidation or it can continue operating while a buyer is sought for it as a going concern. Sale of the firm in itself provides a valuation of its assets. The proceeds can then be distributed to creditors in order of the liquidation priority rule. Legally, the resulting distribution is a reorganization. In practice it constitutes a liquidation that avoids the high disruption costs and the long delays associated with a formal bankruptcy liquidation. The data discussed in the following section suggest that this type of informal reorganization has become fairly common under the new Code.

A problem with the cramdown procedure is if equity is to be eliminated, then it is not clear who owns the firm and whose interest management represents. Managers have an incentive to find a buyer for the firm that promises the best deal for managers, rather than the highest price for the firm's assets. Thus, agency problems reappear in bankruptcy situations where cramdown is used.

BANKRUPTCY TRENDS FOR THE U.S. ECONOMY

There are two main data sources concerning aggregate bankruptcy levels. The first is provided by the Dun & Bradstreet Corporation (D&B) in its annual *Business Failure Record*. D&B data include the number of firms that failed, their liabilities, and other characteristics. The data include as failures all firms that ceased operations with loss to creditors, were involved in a bankruptcy proceeding, or reduced creditors' claims in a voluntary agreement; that is, without filing for bankruptcy. However, the data exclude many small firms, many service firms, and all firms in banking, insurance, real estate, farming, and several other sectors. Also, by definition, the term "liabilities" excludes long-term, publicly held debt.

Table 35.1 lists historical failure trends for the United States since the 1930s. Since the 1930s, the failure rate has always been below one percent (or 100 per 10,000 firms) per year and usually below 0.5 percent per year. Thus, business bankruptcies are relatively rare events. During the period 1950 to 1980, the number of failures was essentially trendless, fluctuating between about 9,000 and 11,000 per year. The failure rate rose from 1945 to 1960, but then declined steadily from 57 per 10,000 firms in 1960 to 28 in 1979. The average level of liabilities per failure was increasing in nominal terms over the 1950 to 1980 period and also increased in real terms, although at a slower rate. Thus, on average, larger firms were failing. The proportion of firms failing that were in business for five years or less was stable at about 53 to 57 percent.

Since 1980, the number of firms failing and the failure rate have jumped. The failure rate in 1982 was 89 per 10,000, compared to 61 in 1981, 42 in 1980, and 28 in 1979. The number of failures rose from under 12,000 in 1980 to over 25,000 in 1982. Thus, the recent recession has had a much more serious effect on business failures than any of the previous post-World War II recessions. The failure rate in 1982 was not far below that in 1933 (89 per 10,000 firms versus 100, respectively).

The second important data source concerning bankruptcy emerges from the U.S. bankruptcy courts. A statistical report on its operations is published each year. Table 35.2 gives the number of bankruptcy filings by type each year since 1970.

During the period 1970 to 1982, the total number of bankruptcy filings

TABLE 35.1   Failure Trends for the U.S. Economy, 1933–1982

(dollars in thousands)

Year	Number of Failures	Failure Rate per 10,000 Listed Concerns	Average Liability per Failure	Average Real Liability per Failure	Percentage of Failures in Business 5 Years or Less
1933	19,859	100	$ 23	$ 92	N/A
1940	13,619	63	12	41	N/A
1945	809	4	37	98	N/A
1950	9,162	34	27	77	68%
1955	10,969	42	41	67	57
1960	15,445	57	61	89	59
1965	13,514	53	98	132	57
1966	13,061	52	106	138	57
1967	12,364	49	102	129	55
1968	9,636	39	98	119	54
1969	9,154	37	125	144	53
1970	10,748	44	176	192	55
1971	10,326	42	186	194	54
1972	9,566	38	209	209	56
1973	9,345	36	246	233	57
1974	9,915	38	308	268	60
1975	11,432	43	383	304	57
1976	9,628	35	313	237	55
1977	7,919	28	391	279	53
1978	6,619	24	402	267	53
1979	7,564	28	353	216	55
1980	11,742	42	395	221	54
1981	16,794	61	414	212	49
1982	25,346[a]	89[a]	N/A	N/A	N/A

(a) Preliminary

Sources: The Business Failure Record (New York: Dun & Bradstreet Corporation, 1983); *Economic Report of the President* (Washington, D.C.: U.S. Government Printing Office, 1983), p. 166. For GNP price deflator used to construct average real liability per failure data, 1972 = 100.

increased from 194,000 to 380,000, or 96 percent. This includes both business and personal bankruptcies. Starting in 1980, the data break out business versus nonbusiness bankruptcy filings. There were about 44,000 business bankruptcies in 1980, about 13 percent of the total; and 69,000 in 1982, about 18 percent of the total. Despite the widespread publicity given to the rise in the number of personal bankruptcies since the adoption of the new Code, the number of

TABLE 35.2 Bankruptcy Filings by Chapter of the Old Bankruptcy Act and the New Bankruptcy Code

Year and Type	Total Filings	Straight Bankruptcy or Chapter 7		Chapter X	Chapter XI or 11		Chapter XIII or 13	Chapter XII
		Involuntary	Voluntary		Involuntary	Voluntary		
1970	194,399	1,085	161,366	115		1,262	30,510	58
1971	201,352	1,215	167,149	179		1,782	30,904	120
1972	182,869	1,094	152,840	105		1,361	27,373	92
1973	173,197	985	144,929	101		1,458	25,632	92
1974	189,513	1,009	156,958	163		2,171	29,023	172
1975	254,484	1,286	208,064	189		3,506	41,178	280
1976	246,549	1,141	207,926	141		3,235	33,579	525
1977	214,399	1,132	180,062	96		3,046	29,422	640
1978	202,951	995	167,776	75		3,266	30,185	650
1979	226,476	915	182,344	63		3,042	39,442	669
1980	331,098	1,157	248,000		203	6,150	75,584	—
Business	43,629		33,698		5,878		4,052	
Nonbusiness	287,463		215,460		471		71,532	
1981	363,847	1,177	259,487		160	9,881	93,139	—
Business	48,014		34,062		8,928		5,022	
Nonbusiness	315,832		226,602		1,113		88,117	
1982	380,212	1,471	256,173		278	18,543	103,738	—
Business	69,207		44,941		16,622		7,636	
Nonbusiness	311,004		212,703		2,199		96,102	

Source: Administrative Office of the U.S. Courts, "Bankruptcy Statistical Tables" (1980)

business bankruptcies has risen faster. The data also highlight the difference in coverage between the D&B data and the comprehensive U.S. courts data; in 1981, for example, the D&B data indicate that there were 16,800 business failures, but Table 35.2 indicates that there were 48,000 business bankruptcy filings.

Table 35.2 breaks down bankruptcy filings by Chapter and indicates whether the bankruptcy filing was voluntary or involuntary. Voluntary bankruptcies are filed by debtors themselves, and involuntary bankruptcies are filed by creditors. The latter have the effect of forcing the debtor into bankruptcy. Both business and personal bankruptcies can be involuntary, but the overwhelming majority are filed voluntarily.

Bankruptcy liquidations are given in columns 3 and 4. They are referred to as straight bankruptcies under the old Act and as Chapter 7 filings under the new Bankruptcy Code. Since 1980, the proportion of all business bankruptcies filed as liquidations has fallen from 0.77 in 1980 to 0.65 in 1982. However, many firms that file for bankruptcy reorganizations later shift their filing to liquidations.

Chapters X, XI, and XII were all business reorganization procedures under the old Act; they were combined into the single Chapter 11 under the new Code. There were always very few Chapter X cases, an average of 122 per year from 1970 to 1979, compared to 31,700 per year under Chapter XI during the same period. Use of Chapter X declined in the late 1970s from 189 cases in 1975 to 63 in 1979. However, since Chapter X cases always involved large firms, their relative importance was greater than the numbers alone suggest. Use of Chapter XII, which applied to firms holding mainly real estate, increased rapidly during the 1970s, from 58 in 1970 to 669 in 1979.

Chapter XIII, replaced by Chapter 13, is used mainly by individuals having regular income. It provides a bankruptcy reorganization procedure for individuals, allowing them to pay off a portion of their debts over time. Use of Chapters XIII and 13 increased rapidly during the period 1978 to 1982.

Unfortunately, the bankruptcy court statistics do not provide any kind of breakdown on characteristics of firms going through bankruptcy proceedings. To pose and answer questions concerning characteristics of firms filing for bankruptcy, or treatment of creditors in bankruptcy, survey data must be used.

TREATMENT OF CREDITORS IN BANKRUPTCY

Here, data concerning how creditors fared in bankruptcy reorganization and liquidation cases are discussed and hypotheses previously developed are tested. The data consist of samples of bankruptcy cases collected separately by White and by Abt Associates as part of a report to the Department of Justice (DOJ) evaluating the experimental U.S. Trustee system.[10]

White's data consist of four separate groups of firms: (1) those that liquidated in bankruptcy under the old Act (straight bankruptcies); (2) those that reorganized

---

[10] See M. J. White, "Bankruptcy Costs and the New Bankruptcy Code," *Journal of Finance* (May 1983); N. Ames et al., note 7 *op. cit.*

under Chapter XI of the old Act; (3) those that filed for liquidation under the new Code (Chapter 7); and (4) those that filed for reorganization under the new Code (Chapter 11). In all cases the firms filed in the Bankruptcy Court of the Southern district of New York (Manhattan). Each of the four groups was restricted to incorporated firms but included all firms in that category for which complete data were available. For the two Code samples, the data include all incorporated firms that filed for bankruptcy from January 1980 to July 1982. For the Act samples, the data include only cases that completed the bankruptcy process; that is, they had confirmed reorganization plans under Chapter XI, or the trustee had completed liquidating the firm's assets and the bankruptcy court had paid the proceeds to creditors. The Act reorganization cases all had plans confirmed during 1977–1980 and the Act liquidation cases all were closed during 1978–1980. The data were obtained from bankruptcy court records and, for the Code samples, from the records of the U.S. Trustee as well.

The DOJ data consist only of Code cases filed during the period July 1980–June 1981. There are two separate samples: (1) cases filed under Chapter 11; and (2) business or involuntary cases filed under Chapter 7. In each, the sample consists of 30 cases selected randomly from each of 18 bankruptcy court districts across the country. The DOJ samples differ from the White samples in that noncorporate as well as incorporated firms are included in the Chapter 11 DOJ sample and some involuntary personal cases were included in the DOJ Chapter 7 sample.

The first issue to be examined is the overall financial condition of firms at the time they file for bankruptcy. Table 35.3 gives these data. The data come from schedules of assets and liabilities submitted by managers to the bankruptcy court at the time of, or shortly after, the firm's bankruptcy filing. These data have several problems. First, in most cases no one checks them, so they are subject to managers' attempts to make the firm's situation look better or worse than it is. Also, the asset data is generally by book value, which may bear little relationship to market value for bankrupt firms. However, these are the only data available concerning firms' financial status at the time they enter bankruptcy. The values for secured liabilities, priority liabilities, and unsecured liabilities do not add up to the value for total liabilities both because of rounding and because postpetition liabilities are not broken out. The latter more commonly occur in reorganization cases but also occur occasionally in liquidations, especially if a reorganization was attempted but failed.

Columns 1 and 2 are examined first. Here, firms that filed for bankruptcy under the old Act are classified according to whether they eventually liquidated or reorganized under old Chapter XI. The category of firms liquidating includes some that originally filed under Chapter XI but later converted to a liquidation because no reorganization could be agreed on with creditors. The data indicate that firms that liquidated had liabilities far in excess of their assets, while firms that reorganized had liabilities about equal to their assets. (The ratios are 2.1 versus 1.15) Firms liquidating also had a much higher proportion of their assets subject to secured creditors' liens (0.75 versus 0.30). On average, firms liquidating were smaller than those reorganizing.

Next, the two middle columns concerning firms filing for bankruptcy under the new Code are examined. Here, the composition of the samples differs somewhat, since the data consist of all firms that filed for bankruptcy rather

TABLE 35.3   Financial Characteristics of Firms Filing for Bankruptcy Under the Old Bankruptcy Act and the New Bankruptcy Code

(dollars in thousands)

	(1) Firms Liquidating Under the Act (White)	(2) Firms Reorganizing Under the Act, Chapter XI (White)	(3) Firms Liquidating Under the Code (White)	(4) Firms Filing to Reorganize Under the Code (White)	(5) Firms Liquidating Under the Code (DOJ)	(6) Firms Filing to Reorganize Under the Code (DOJ)
Number of firms	90	95	73	45	500	500
Total liabilities	$1,551	$1,835	$710	$2,226	$72	$357
Secured liabilities	$548	$480	$182	$1,072	$10	$154
Priority liabilities	$65	$40	$46	$68	$1	$17
Unsecured liabilities	$1,047	$1,309	$481	$1,100	$35	$118
Assets	$736	$1,592	$437	$1,643	$10	$257
Total liabilities/assets	2.1	1.15	1.6	1.35	7.3	1.4
Secured liabilities/assets	0.75	0.30	0.42	0.65	1.0	0.60
Percentage of firms with priority liabilities/assets greater than 33 percent	28%	9%	37%	11%	—	—

than firms that have completed the bankruptcy process. Thus, some small firms filing to liquidate may never have their cases closed, since no one has an incentive to push no-asset cases through the bankruptcy process. This probably accounts for the smaller size of firms liquidating in the Code sample as compared to the Act sample. Also, some firms are included in column 4 even though their reorganization plans are not yet confirmed and may never be.

Again, the ratio of total liabilities to assets is greater for firms liquidating than for those filing to reorganize. Comparing column 3 to 4, the ratios are 1.6 and 1.35, respectively. However, on average the liquidation sample has a lower rather than higher ratio of secured liabilities to assets (0.42 to 0.65).

The last two columns indicate characteristics of the DOJ samples. Here, the average size of firms filing both to liquidate and reorganize is much smaller than in the White samples. The reason for this is not entirely clear; presumably the inclusion of nonincorporated firms and of involuntary filings of individuals reduces the average size figures in the DOJ samples. Also, firms for which the data were incomplete are included in the DOJ samples but not in the White samples. These firms are likely to be small. The DOJ data classify firms on the basis of their original Chapter of filing, rather than on which procedure was actually used.

The relative magnitudes here show a similar picture to that already discussed, however. Firms filing to reorganize in the DOJ sample are larger than firms filing to liquidate. The ratio of total liabilities to assets is higher for firms filing to liquidate than to reorganize (7.3 to 1.4) and the ratio of secured liabilities to total assets is higher for firms filing to liquidate than to reorganize (1.0 to 0.60).

Thus, the data appear to show that firms liquidating have liabilities well in excess of their assets at the time of the bankruptcy filing and have relatively more secured liabilities than firms reorganizing. The data support the general picture that firms that finally liquidate avoid bankruptcy as long as possible, while firms that reorganize initiate the bankruptcy process earlier. The results concerning the importance of secured liabilities are mixed, however.

The data in Table 35.3 also suggest that, for many firms that liquidate, priority obligations (mostly taxes due) play an important role. Overall, priority liabilities are always below 10 percent of the value of assets listed for all samples in Table 35.3. However, in the White liquidation sample of column 1, 28 percent of all liquidation cases have priority liabilities amounting to more than 33 percent of the value of assets. For the White reorganization sample in column 2, the corresponding figure is only 9 percent. Under the old Act, priority liabilities had to be paid in full at the time the reorganization plan went into effect. This meant that having a high level of priority liabilities generally barred a firm from reorganizing. Furthermore, the data suggest that, for failing firms attempting to delay filing for bankruptcy, the end of the process may have occurred because a tax creditor succeeded in foreclosing on the firm's assets for nonpayment of tax claims. The samples in columns 3 and 4 of firms filing under the new Code tell a similar story. Here, the proportion of firms liquidating that have priority liabilities greater than one third of their assets is 37 percent, while for firms reorganizing the corresponding figure is 11 percent. Under the new Code, priority liabilities are somewhat less a bar to reorganizing, since they can be deferred, but the data suggest that they are still important.

Data concerning the characteristics of firms as they complete the bankruptcy

**TABLE 35.4   Characteristics of Firms Completing the Bankruptcy
Process Under the Old Act
(White Data)**

(dollars in thousands)

	Firms Liquidating	Firms Reorganizing
Number of firms	90	95
Average time spent in bankruptcy	6 years	2 years
Priority liabilities filed by creditors ("approved claims")	$145	$38
Unsecured liabilities filed by creditors ("approved claims")	$1,001	$839
Total value of liquidated assets[a]	$106	N/A
Total administrative costs	$22	$10
Payoff rate to secured creditors[b]	31%	N/A
Payoff rate to priority creditors		
Percentage of cases having payoff greater than zero	50%	100%
Average payoff rate on approved claims for those cases having positive payoff	11% ⎫	
Expected payoff rate overall	6% ⎬	96%
Payoff rate to unsecured creditors		
Percentage of cases having payoff greater than zero	29%	100%
Average payoff rate on approved claims for those cases having positive payoff	14% ⎫	cash: 9%
Expected payoff rate overall	4% ⎬	installments: 24%
Administrative costs/liquidated value of the firm's assets net of administrative costs	0.21	
Administrative costs/amount paid to creditors under the reorganization plan		0.03
Administrative costs/total liabilities at filing	0.01	0.005

(a) Net of postpetition claims. This information is not available for firms that reorganized, since their assets are not sold.
(b) Includes only cases where secured assets were sold by the bankruptcy trustee

process under the old Act are now examined. Table 35.4 gives data concerning the same sample of firms that constituted columns 1 and 2 in Table 35.3. Here, however, the data report financial characteristics as these firms completed the bankruptcy process. This sample is of particular interest because it is the only data set for which the characteristics of firms both at the time of their bankruptcy filing and at the time their cases were closed (or the reorganization plan went into effect) are known.

The data given in Table 35.4 are generated in a different way from those reported in Table 35.3. In both liquidation and reorganization cases under the old Act, creditors had to file their claims with the bankruptcy court. Managers of the firm had the right to contest these claims and the bankruptcy judge decided disputed cases. Liabilities that went through this process were referred to as approved claims. However, claims not filed by creditors never appeared in the approved claims record. Creditors sometimes neglected to file claims (especially in liquidation cases) if the anticipated return did not justify their effort. The approval process was contested more vigorously in reorganization cases than in liquidation cases, since in the latter, the firm had been shut down and no manager had a continuing interest in the firm.

In liquidation cases under the Act, the funds generated by the trustee from sales of assets were turned over to the court for distribution to creditors. In reorganization cases, the amount to be paid to creditors at the time the reorganization plan was approved was turned over to the court for distribution to creditors. Thus, the data in Table 35.4 are verified and refer to actual dollar amounts, but exclude some unfiled liabilities. The administrative cost and payoff rate data are generated by the court in the process of paying out these funds.

The liquidation cases are considered first. Here, the mean level of approved unsecured liabilities in Table 35.3 (1,047,000 per firm) as listed by managers is very close to the mean level of unsecured claims in Table 35.4 (1,001,000 per firm). However, for priority liabilities, the mean level listed at the time of the bankruptcy filing is much lower than the average level of approved priority claims as filed by creditors ($65,000 to $145,000). Thus, past due priority claims appear to be an even more important reason for failing firms actually closing down than the data in Table 35.3 indicate.

The administrative costs of operating the bankruptcy system appear very high. On average, six years elapse for liquidating firms between the bankruptcy filing and the date when the case is closed. The administrative costs of operating the bankruptcy system average about $22,000 per liquidation case. This figure includes the trustee's fee, the trustee's expenses, attorneys' fees, accountants' fees, court fees, appraisers' and auctioneers' fees, and so forth. The total value of liquidated assets given in Table 35.4 is the dollar amount of all assets located and sold by the trustee, net of administrative costs and any postpetition claims. (Postpetition claims could have been incurred if the firm attempted to reorganize and continued to operate for a period before converting to liquidation.) This amount includes the value of assets subject to secured creditors' liens if the assets were sold by the trustee. On average, administrative costs of liquidation amount to about 21 percent of the value of assets liquidated. Administrative costs are about 1.0 percent of total liabilities at the time of the bankruptcy filing.

Comparing Tables 35.3 and 35.4 data on assets, it is also found that for firms liquidating, the value of assets as listed at filing averages $736,000 per firm, while the liquidated value of assets net of administrative costs is $106,000. Taking the former as a measure of book value and the latter as a measure of market value, the average ratio of book value to market value of assets for firms liquidating is about 6.9.

Finally, the payoff pattern for creditors in liquidation cases is examined. For secured creditors, the payoff rate is given only for situations where the trustee sells the asset, rather than the creditor claiming the asset directly. (Only when the trustee sells the asset is a secured claim filed with the bankruptcy court at all. This occurs in two extreme cases: if the asset is worth more than the secured creditor's claim, or if the cost to the creditor of repossessing the asset is greater than its value. Usually, the creditor claims the asset directly.) The average payoff rate is 31 percent. For priority creditors, 50 percent of the sample of cases report a positive payoff rate. For these cases, the average payoff rate as a percent of approved claims is 11 percent. Thus, the overall expected payoff rate on approved priority claims is 6 percent. For unsecured creditors, only 29 percent of liquidation cases have positive payoff rates. For these cases, the average is 14 percent. Thus, the overall expected payoff rate on approved unsecured claims is 4 percent. The low payoff rate to unsecured creditors (see Table 35.4) generally supports the hypothesis that failing firms convert unsecured to secured claims as a means of delaying or avoiding bankruptcy. At the time they file for bankruptcy liquidation, few free assets are left to pay the claims of unsecured creditors. The long time period required to complete the bankruptcy process probably exacerbates this, since there is ample time for assets to "disappear" before sale by the trustee.

Now the Act reorganization sample is examined. Table 35.4 also gives data on the levels of approved priority and unsecured claims. Here, the approval process is often actively pursued, with managers contesting filed unsecured claims and negotiating with priority creditors to voluntarily reduce the level of claims filed. Since approved priority claims must be paid in full in reorganization, bargaining over approved claims presents the main opportunity for managers to reduce these claims. The more that claims are cut back at the approval stage, the higher the payoff rate that the firm can offer to unsecured creditors for the same total expenditure.

For firms reorganizing, the bankruptcy process is faster, two years on average from filing to approval of the reorganization plan, and administrative costs are lower. Since no trustee is appointed in Chapter XI reorganization cases, the only administrative costs were court fees and, in some cases, fees of lawyers representing committees of unsecured creditors. The costs of managers' time spent on the reorganization and cost of disruption do not appear. Administrative costs on average amount to 3 percent of the amount paid to creditors under the reorganization plan and to 0.5 percent of total liabilities of the firm at filing.

Finally, payoff rates in reorganization average 95 percent for priority creditors as a percent of approved claims. This figure is below 100 percent because some priority claims are voluntarily reduced after the approval process is completed. For unsecured creditors, the average payoff rate is 9 percent in cash (i.e., paid when the reorganization plan is approved) and 24 percent in installments. Installments are paid usually over a 3 to 10-year period, without interest. They are risky, since the reorganized firm may later attempt to renegotiate or may liquidate. Nonetheless, the payoff rate to unsecured creditors here is well in excess of that which unsecured creditors receive in liquidation cases.

Next is the characteristics of incorporated firms completing the bankruptcy process under the new Code, shown in Table 35.5. This sample consists of the same firms whose characteristics at the time of the bankruptcy filing are reported in Table 35.3, columns 3 and 4. However, the firms here are classified in greater

TABLE 35.5 Characteristics of Firms During the Bankruptcy Process Under the New Code (White Data)

(dollars in thousands)

	(1) Firms Liquidating	(2) Firms That Converted From Chapter 11 to Chapter 7	(3) Firms With Confirmed UCP Reorganization Plans	(4) Firms With Unconfirmed UCP Reorganization Plans	(5) Firms With Liquidating Reorganization Plans
Number of firms	54	19	26	4	15
Total liabilities at filing	$493	$1,328	$1,917	$1,509	$2,954
Secured liabilities	$82	$466	$629	$470	$2,003
Priority liabilities	$24	$107	$61	$52	$83
Unsecured liabilities	$383	$761	$1,221	$989	$920
Total assets	$300	$825	$1,651	$938	$1,819
Total liabilities/assets	1.6	1.6	1.16	1.6	1.6
Secured liabilities/assets	0.27	0.56	0.33	0.48	1.1
Percentage of firms with priority liabilities/assets greater than 33 percent	37%	37%	11%	0	13%
Payoff rate to unsecured creditors					
Cash	—	—	0.16	0.10	0.13
Installments	—	—	0.18	0.09	
Administrative costs/amount paid to creditors under the reorganization plan	—	—	3.4%(a)	3%	10%(b)
Average time spent in bankruptcy up to confirmation of the reorganization plan	—	—	17 months	—	—

(a) Data available for 15 cases only
(b) Data available for five cases only

detail according to the outcome or latest status of the bankruptcy procedure. None of the firms that originally filed to liquidate under Chapter 7 have completed the bankruptcy process. The firms that originally filed to reorganize under Chapter 11 are classified according to the following outcomes: (1) They have converted to a Chapter 7 filing, presumably because no reorganization plan could be agreed upon. (2) They have confirmed reorganization plans adopted under the UCP. (3) They have failed to adopt a reorganization plan under the UCP and are in the process of selling the firm and paying creditors according to the absolute priority rule (firms with liquidating reorganization plans). (4) They have reorganization plans that have not yet been confirmed (and might never be).

Cases classified under (3) are the most interesting, since they represent a new category of liquidating reorganizations that did not exist under the old Act. These firms operate under the control of their prebankruptcy managers (no trustee or examiner is appointed), and generally they are sold or are attempting to sell the firm as a going concern with the court's approval. From a legal standpoint, these cases appear to fit somewhere between reorganization cases under the cramdown procedure and failed reorganization attempts, which under the Code should convert to Chapter 7 liquidations. However, allowing these liquidating reorganizations to remain in Chapter 11 represents an economic efficiency gain in that the bankruptcy procedure can proceed more quickly and cheaply and because the firm may be worth more as a going concern. However, there is a potential for agency problems/conflicts of interest to develop if former shareholders are the purchasers of the firm, as occurred in several cases in the sample. Also, managers have an incentive to find a buyer that will retain the old managers, rather than a buyer that will pay the highest price.

Table 35.5, columns 1 and 2, break the group of firms liquidating into two subgroups — those that filed originally under Chapter 7 and those that filed originally under Chapter 11 but converted to Chapter 7. Both subgroups of firms have high ratios of total liabilities/assets, 1.6 for both, and high percentages of firms having priority liabilities in excess of one third of the value of assets, 37 percent for both. However, the group of firms that filed originally to liquidate under Chapter 7 have low ratios of secured liabilities/assets; the average is 0.27, while the group that converted have a higher average ratio of 0.56. It is possible that for many of the former group, secured creditors have already foreclosed on their lien assets. Since both subgroups consist of firms that have not yet officially completed the bankruptcy process, no payoff rate or administrative cost data are available. (These data are generated at the conclusion of the bankruptcy process.)

The firms reorganizing under the new Code, shown in columns 3 through 5 of Table 35.5 are now examined. The subgroup of firms having confirmed UCP plans, column 3, is similar in financial characteristics to the comparative groups of firms reorganizing under old Chapter XI; they have relatively low levels of total liabilities/assets (1.16) and secured liabilities/assets (0.33), and only a small proportion of them have priority liabilities greater than one third of assets (11 percent). For these firms, payoff rates to unsecured creditors averaged 16 percent in cash and 18 percent in installments. This is slightly better than the return received by these creditors in cases under the old Act, where the figures were 9 percent in cash and 24 percent in installments. Thus, unsecured creditors appear to be in a somewhat better bargaining situation under the new Code, perhaps because of the existence of the liquidating reorganization possibility.

Priority creditors in all these cases received full payment of their claims either in cash or in installments paid up to six years later. Since the new Code abolished the approval procedure for claims, that is, creditors no longer need to file their claims with the bankruptcy court unless the claims are disputed, there is no clear indication in the records whether priority creditors are voluntarily agreeing to reduce the amount of their claims, as often occurred under the old Act.

Another aim of the new Code is to speed up and reduce the costs of the bankruptcy process. The data (admittedly fragmentary) shown in Tables 35.4 and 35.5 do not suggest that the process is any cheaper for reorganization cases, however. Administrative costs for the firms with UCP reorganization plans were about 3.5 percent of the amount paid to priority and unsecured creditors under the plan, similar to the figure for the Code sample. However, the amount of time between bankruptcy filing and adoption of the plan is less for the Code sample of firms reorganizing than for the Act sample, 17 months versus 2 years on average. This may be the effect of the U.S. Trustee intervening to speed the process. (The DOJ study (1983) also came to this conclusion.)

Column 4 of Table 35.5 gives data on a small number of firms that had filed reorganization plans with the court, but whose plans had not yet been adopted.

Finally, column 5 of Table 35.5 lists the characteristics of firms that had failed to adopt reorganization plans and instead were sold, usually as going concerns. These firms generally have high levels of both total liabilities/assets (1.6) and secured liabilities/assets (1.1). The payoff rate to unsecured creditors averaged 13 percent (usually all in cash); a return between what they could expect to receive under a UCP reorganization plan and a straight Chapter 7 liquidation, but closer to the former than the latter. Since the firms in column 4 were generally in worse financial shape than those in column 5 at the time of filing, the payoff rate to creditors seems relatively high. This suggests that the liquidating reorganization alternative to liquidation under Chapter 7 has made unsecured creditors better off by giving them an alternative to the low return they can expect to receive in a Chapter 7 liquidation proceeding. This gives them a greater incentive to vote against the reorganization plan. It should be noted that administrative costs in this case appear to be midway between the levels in UCP reorganizations and Chapter 7 liquidations.

In comparing the data concerning the Act versus Code samples of firms in bankruptcy, the main results are the following:

First, for firms reorganizing, the bankruptcy procedure appears to have been speeded up under the new Code. However, it is impossible to distinguish whether this is due to the provisions of the new Code itself or the effect of the U.S. Trustee system, instituted experimentally in the Southern District of New York. For firms liquidating, no cases filed under the new Code had closed, so no evidence concerning timing is available. Administrative costs appear to be about the same as previously.

Second, the data support the hypothesis discussed earlier that firms filing for bankruptcy liquidation have total liabilities well in excess of their assets rather than equal to their assets, as finance theorists usually assume. Firms reorganizing, in contrast, have much lower levels of total liabilities/assets, although the average is slightly above one. This comparative pattern reappears in the White Act and new Code samples and in the DOJ samples of firms liquidating versus reorganizing.

Third, firms liquidating generally have higher levels of secured liabilities/ assets than firms reorganizing. The former are also more likely to have priority liabilities in excess of one third of their assets. This pattern appears in the White Act samples and DOJ samples. The White Code samples indicate a low level of secured liabilities/assets for firms liquidating. However, the finer break- down in Table 35.5 shows that, for firms originally filing under Chapter 11, the higher the level of secured liabilities/assets, the more likely that the firm would either convert to a Chapter 7 liquidation or use the liquidating reorganization procedure, rather than adopt a UCP reorganization plan.

Fourth, the evidence suggests that firms filing for bankruptcy are less likely to reorganize under the new Code than under the old Act. In the White Act sample, over half of all firms completing the bankruptcy process had adopted reorganization plans and thus continued operating. In the White Code sample, only 25 of 118 firms filing for bankruptcy, less than one-quarter, adopted re- organization plans under the UCP. All the rest followed some type of liquidation, either shutdown and piecemeal sale of assets by a trustee or sale of the firm as a going concern. The evidence suggests that fewer failing firms, than previously are continuing to operate in essentially their prebankruptcy form under the new Code. Since it was previously argued that too many failing firms continued to operate under the old Act and thus delayed the movement of resources to more productive uses, this change should improve the economic efficiency of the bankruptcy system generally.

FEDERAL TAXES AND BANKRUPTCY

Debt, Taxes, and Bankruptcy Costs: Theoretical Issues

Most firms in bankruptcy have been losing money for at least several periods and are not currently paying U.S. corporate income taxes. However, in models of the optimal capital structure of firms generally, both bankruptcy and corporate income taxes play important roles.

The basic idea is that firms have a tax incentive to issue debt over equity. Interest payments on debt are deductible expenses to the firm, while dividend payments on equity must be paid from after-tax profits. This makes equity more expensive to the firm than debt. Firms therefore prefer to issue debt over equity, and in the absence of bankruptcy, they would be expected to finance themselves with a nearly all-debt capital structure. However, the higher the proportion of debt in the firm's capital structure, the more risky it becomes from the viewpoint of holders of its debt. Therefore, debt holders demand a higher interest rate as the firm's debt/equity ratio rises. For each firm, a point therefore exists where the marginal dollar of equity converted to debt yields a tax savings just equal to the higher interest cost associated with the firm's higher risk. At the point where this equality holds, the firm's debt/equity ratio is optimal in that the value of the firm (debt plus equity) is maximized. (This point is not without controversy. See Chapter 27.)

The trade-off between tax savings from extra debt versus greater financial risk stemming from higher expected bankruptcy costs, while conceptually clear, has proved difficult to quantify. On the tax side, personal as well as corporate tax rates and the tax treatment of income versus capital gains are all relevant in estimating the tax advantage to corporations of using debt over equity. While debt payments are tax deductible to the firm, they are taxable at income tax rates to the bondholder. The return on equity, however, receives more favorable personal tax treatment than the return on debt. This suggests that the tax advantage of using debt over equity is smaller than would appear from corporate tax considerations alone.

On the bankruptcy cost side, there has been debate over whether the costs of liquidation or reorganization are relevant and over whether these costs are large enough to offset the tax advantage of debt over equity. Haugen and Senbet (1978) propose that bankruptcy costs should be defined as the minimum cost of the firm going through bankruptcy liquidation or reorganization. They argue that the bankruptcy costs of reorganization are smaller than those of liquidation, since no transfer of ownership or dismantling of the firm occurs in reorganization. They conclude, therefore, that bankruptcy costs are too small to offset the tax subsidy to debt over equity and, consequently, too small to support an optimal debt/equity ratio for the firm. However, they present no data to support their argument.

Empirical Studies of Bankruptcy Costs

There have been several empirical studies attempting to establish the level of bankruptcy costs.

Warner (1977) examined data on court-approved bankruptcy administrative costs for a group of railroad reorganization cases occurring from the 1930s through the 1950s. Warner compared these costs to the total market value of the railroads' debt and equity. He found that administrative costs amounted to 5.5 or 2.5 percent of the market value of the firm, depending on whether market value data at, or three years before, the date of the bankruptcy filing was used, respectively. Warner thus concluded that bankruptcy costs were low. Other studies of bankruptcy administrative costs reported higher cost levels, but for samples of small firms. (See Stanley and Girth (1971) and Van Horne (1976).)

The data discussed in Table 35.4 can be used to provide further evidence on bankruptcy administrative costs. Firms undergoing bankruptcy are much smaller on average than Warner's railroads, and few of them have publicly traded debt or equity. However, the amount paid to creditors under the terms of the reorganization plan (if a reorganization) or after sale of the firm's assets by the trustee (if a liquidation) provides a proxy for what the market value of these firms would have been at the date of the bankruptcy filing if their debt and equity were publicly traded. The results suggest that bankruptcy administrative costs are lower for firms reorganizing under Chapter XI than for Warner's railroads, one percent. For firms liquidating, however, administrative costs are much higher, 20 percent.

Why are Warner's figures higher than the results given here for firms reorganizing under Chapter XI? Before the adoption of the new Code, railroad reorganizations occurred under special legislation which provided for a very formal procedure, more like the old Chapter X than the old Chapter XI. (This was known as Section 77.) This meant extensive court scrutiny of the reorganization, close involvement by lawyers and trustees representing many creditors' groups, and an average time lapse from bankruptcy filing to approval of the plan of over seven years. Thus, Warner's data combined with White's data suggest the existence of diseconomies of scale in bankruptcy administrative costs, due both to more active contesting of large than small claims and to use of a more formal reorganization procedure in large cases. While the new Code combined all of these procedures into the new Chapter 11, it is probably nonetheless true that administrative costs rise at a faster rate than do increases in the size of the bankrupt firm's liabilities. As claims get larger, it is more worthwhile to represent them actively in the bankruptcy proceedings.

Other authors have argued that bankruptcy costs in total are substantially greater than the data on court-approved administrative costs in bankruptcy would suggest. Gordon and Malkiel (1981), for example, make direct use of the trade-off between the firm's tax incentive to replace equity with debt and the increase in expected bankruptcy costs resulting from the extra debt. They assume that the first dollar of debt contracted by the firm causes zero bankruptcy costs and the last dollar of debt contracted by the firm causes bankruptcy costs equal to the tax advantage per dollar of debt over equity. In between, extra dollars of debt cause linearly increasing bankruptcy costs to be incurred, starting with zero and ending at the cutoff point implied by the equality. (The firm's total capitalization is assumed to remain fixed; only its debt/equity ratio changes.)

Then total bankruptcy costs can be estimated by the area under the bankruptcy cost function, which in this case is a triangle. This triangle of "deadweight" costs represents the total loss to the economy in wasted resources caused by the bankruptcy system, including all administrative costs, lost managerial time, disruption costs, costs of continuation of inefficient operations, and diversion of assets into inefficient uses. Gordon and Malkiel calculate the size of the triangle for the entire U.S. economy. The height of the triangle is the tax incentive per year of replacing a dollar of equity with a dollar of debt, assumed to be $0.014 in 1975 dollars. The base is the total amount of corporate debt, which was $440 billion in 1975. The resulting estimate of total bankruptcy costs is 3.1 billion per year in 1975 dollars.

Another approach to estimating bankruptcy costs is used by White (1983). She uses a coalition model of firm behavior to argue that firms choose reorganization over liquidation too often from a social standpoint, because reorganization benefits managers and equity holders. To the extent that failing firms' assets may be more valuable if they liquidate rather than reorganize (and thereby release their assets to move to more valuable uses), bankruptcy costs are created over and above administrative costs. White refers to these costs of inefficient decision making ex ante bankruptcy costs and argues that they may affect firms generally, including some firms that never actually file for bankruptcy. White calculates upper-bound estimates of ex ante bankruptcy costs and exact (not upper bound) estimates of bankruptcy administrative costs (or ex post bankruptcy costs). She estimates that aggregate ex ante bankruptcy costs for the entire United States as of 1980 under the terms of the old Act were bounded from above at $35 billion per year, compared to about $1 billion for aggregate ex post bankruptcy costs per year. Thus, bankruptcy administrative costs alone underestimate total bankruptcy costs by up to a factor of 40. White also repeats the calculations for 1980 using values prevailing under the new Code. The results suggest that the upper bound on ex ante bankruptcy costs fell to about $22 billion per year upon adoption of the new Code, while ex post bankruptcy costs remained about the same. Thus ex post bankruptcy costs under the new Code still underestimate total bankruptcy costs by a large factor, up to about 27.

These estimates of total U.S. bankruptcy costs are upper-bound levels and are likely to exaggerate the extent of deadweight costs due to bankruptcy. However, it should be noted that total U.S. corporate income tax receipts were about $80 billion in 1980. Viewing bankruptcy costs as the deadweight cost of collecting the corporate income tax, the analysis suggests that the corporate income tax may be an extremely inefficient way for the government to collect taxes: for each dollar of tax receipts, up to $0.35 of resources is wasted in bankruptcy costs.

Tax Changes Under the 1980 Bankruptcy Tax Act

Once a firm is failing, corporate income taxes give it an incentive to reorganize rather than liquidate in bankruptcy. The reason for this is that its net operating loss carry-over is lost in liquidation but remains usable if the firm reorganizes under certain conditions. The carry-over can either offset future taxable earnings of the firm or it can make the firm an attractive merger target, since the carry-over will shelter the merger partner's otherwise taxable profits. This tax incentive for failing firms to reorganize results from the asymmetrical treatment of profits and losses under the U.S. corporate income tax. Profits are taxed, but losses do not result in tax refunds unless the firm either paid taxes in the past that can be refunded or makes profits in the future.

The tax incentive of failing firms' managers and equity holders to reorganize can lead to economically inefficient outcomes, since the gains from reorganization result in part from transfers rather than from more efficient use of resources. The transfer in this case is to the firm from the U.S. Government.

A further problem with the tax subsidy to reorganization is that firms must satisfy tests requiring continuity of ownership and business in order to retain their tax loss carry-forwards in reorganization. If a reorganized firm merges with a profitable firm, the merger can be challenged by the Internal Revenue Service (IRS) on the basis that its sole purpose is tax avoidance. If successful, the challenge can lead to disallowance of the carry-over. The continuity-of-business test is the most significant from an economic standpoint. It gives reorganizing firms an incentive to continue their existing lines of business to avoid possible challenge. This, however, is inefficient because it delays or prevents reorganizing firms from moving their assets to new and more valuable uses, so they may make economically inefficient decisions concerning asset utilization to insure that they retain the net operating loss carry-forward and its associated tax subsidy.

The tax incentive provided to failing firms to reorganize again reflects Congress's preference for saving existing firms in financial distress. This preference appears to go to ridiculous lengths at times. Penn Central, for example, after selling off its railroads to the government, was able to avoid the continuity tests and became mainly a tax carry-over shell in search of profits to shelter from taxes. It subsequently purchased several profitable companies that could use the carry-over. In contrast, the Reagan Administration has discussed selling off Conrail, the nationalized rail network composed mainly of former Penn Central track. Any successful bidder would probably want Conrail mainly because of its accumulated losses, which can shelter the acquirer's profits. The bidder will probably try to sell off parts of the railroad (probably to state or local governments).

The job-saving effectiveness of such transactions is rather doubtful. For example, the Chrysler Corporation, which benefited both from its tax loss carry-forward and from explicit government aid in the form of loan guarantees, cut its employment level by 45 percent from 1978 to 1980, compared to decreases of 15 to 18 percent during the same period by General Motors and Ford. The rescue of Chrysler at substantial government expense seems to have rescued rather few jobs. Had Chrysler filed for bankruptcy under Chapter X or XI, it seems unlikely that job losses would have been any higher.

The Bankruptcy Tax Act of 1980 made several important changes in the tax treatment of firms in bankruptcy. These changes, described briefly in the following discussion, had a mixed impact on the tax incentive of failing firms to reorganize rather than liquidate.

The Act changed the tax treatment of debts discharged in reorganization. Forgiven debts received a subtle tax subsidy before 1980. Creditors whose claims were cut back by the reorganization plan could deduct these losses from taxable income. However, the reorganized firm itself did not have to recognize the discharged debts as taxable income. The latter provision differs from the usual treatment of discharged debts, which are normally taxable as income if no bankruptcy is involved.

The 1980 law requires that discharged debts be recognized as income, although in a way which affects the firm's future rather than its present tax liability. Debt discharge amounts must be used to reduce either the firm's depreciable asset basis or its net operating loss carry-over. Thus, there is deferred recognition of tax liability due to debt discharge. This change reduces, but does not eliminate, failing firms' preference for reorganization over liquidation, as well as the reorganized firm's tax advantage over competitors that have never filed for bankruptcy.

The new law makes it easier for firms undergoing bankruptcy reorganization to exchange equity for debt. Such an exchange, which gives creditors at least partial ownership of the reorganized firm's assests, is the classic assumption made by finance theorists concerning bankruptcy. As previously pointed out, such an exchange does not occur in bankruptcy liquidation, where creditors receive the value of the firm's assets after liquidation by the trustee rather than ownership of the assets themselves. In reorganization, such an exchange was possible, but was discouraged by tax considerations. Issuing stock to prior creditors such that they received voting control of the firm violated continuity-of-ownership requirements. Also, if stock were issued in exchange for debt, then creditors were not allowed to deduct their losses from taxable income even if the stock issued to them had a far lower value than the prior debt claims.

The new law makes it easier for firms undergoing bankruptcy reorganization to issue stock for debt, since there is no longer a requirement that voting control of the reorganized firm remain with its prior shareholders. Also, an explicit procedure is provided by which either the bankruptcy court or the parties themselves can place an explicit value on the new shares issued. (Either the IRS must have an opportunity to intervene in the proceeding or the parties making the agreement must have opposing interests.) Old creditors can therefore receive shares in the reorganized firm in partial exchange for debt claims, but still recognize as a loss for tax purposes the difference between the face value of old debt and the value of the new shares issued to them. These rules differ somewhat for trade creditors versus security holders.

The new law eases requirements for continuity of ownership and generally facilitates the merger process for firms undergoing bankruptcy reorganization. It does this by introducing a new type of tax-free reorganization (the G reorganization), which allows a bankrupt firm to merge with another firm and retain its prior depreciable asset basis and its operating loss carry-over (except for reductions due to debt discharge), while easing the previous continuity-of-ownership requirements. The acquiring firm can issue its own stock or its own debt, or the stock of a subsidiary or a parent firm in return for the assets of the bankrupt firm. Continuity of ownership is satisfied if the bankrupt firm's creditors, rather than its shareholders, receive the acquiring firm's stock or debt. However, the continuity-of-business rules still apply, since the bankrupt firm must transfer to its merger partner either an active business or substantially all of its assets in order to qualify for favorable tax treatment. Thus, the new law still inhibits firms in bankruptcy reorganization from closing down an inefficient business or selling obsolete assets. The firm cannot liquidate all its assets and still qualify for a G reorganization, although the Act provides for partial sale of assets, if such a sale leaves the firm with "a more manageable business."

Thus, the new Act loosens its previous tight grip, but still probably hampers the transfer of assets in reorganization from less valuable to more valuable uses. From an economist's viewpoint, there seems to be no reason at all for limiting favorable tax treatment to bankrupt firms that retain their prior asset structure. Either all bankrupt firms should be treated favorably or none should, thus eliminating the artificial tax incentive for bankrupt firms to continue operating economically obsolete lines of business.

BANKRUPTCY PREDICTION MODELS

Predicting bankruptcies for individual firms has been a topic of interest both to researchers in finance and to market practitioners. The ability to predict future bankruptcies would clearly be useful both to potential investors buying the publicly traded stocks and bonds of risky firms and to potential lenders to such firms.

A problem in predicting bankruptcy, however, is that while many firms do go bankrupt each year, the data previously discussed suggest that bankruptcies are still quite rare. The rate of failure in the D&B data shown in Table 35.1 as a percent of the total number of firms is always below one percent per year. Also, since large firms are less likely to go bankrupt than small firms, the percent of liabilities of firms that go bankrupt is probably even lower. If the goal of the bankruptcy prediction study is to provide guidance for investors, then only a few dozen of the 40,000 to 60,000 business bankruptcies that occur each year are of interest, since only these few have publicly traded debt or equity.

Model Specification

Bankruptcy prediction models typically start with a sample of firms that went bankrupt and a second matched sample of firms that did not go bankrupt during the same period. Data from financial statements are collected for both samples of firms. The financial data pertain to the firm's condition one or more periods prior to the period when the firm either went bankrupt or avoided bankruptcy. Discriminant analysis is then used to estimate a function, usually assumed to be linear, which maximizes the likelihood that all firms are classified in the correct bankruptcy status group given their financial characteristics.

Suppose $x_{1i} \ldots x_{ni}$ refers to the set of n financial variables for each of i firms. The results of discriminant analysis are in the form of a set of constant discriminant coefficients, $b_1 \ldots b_n$, determined such that the likelihood of correct classification is maximized. These results can be aggregated to yield the equation:

$$z = b_0 + b_1 x_{1i} + b_2 x_{2i} + \ldots + b_n x_{ni}$$

where the b's are constants and the x_i's are variables.

Using the estimated coefficients and the data concerning the x_i's for individual firms, a z_i value can be calculated for each firm in the sample. Observing whether each firm actually filed for bankruptcy or not, a cutoff point or range, say z_1 to z_2, can be determined. Then for individual firms, values z_i above some z_1 imply that the firm is predicted to go bankrupt, while values z_i below some z_2 imply that the firm is predicted to avoid bankruptcy. For values z_i in the z_1 to z_2 range, the result is indeterminate.

These predictions can be used to test the accuracy of the model in predicting bankrupt versus nonbankrupt status either for firms in the original sample or for firms not in the original sample. The accuracy of the model can be measured by determining what percent of firms are correctly classified; that is, were predicted by the model to go bankrupt and did or were predicted to avoid bankruptcy and did. Errors include those firms predicted to avoid bankruptcy that went bankrupt (type I) and those firms predicted to go bankrupt that avoided bankruptcy (type II).

For example, Altman (1977) estimated the following model for a sample of 33 bankrupt and 33 nonbankrupt firms:

$$z = 1.2x_1 + 1.4x_2 + 3.3x_3 + 0.6x_4 + 1.0x_5$$

where the x_i's are, in order, working capital/total assets; retained earnings/total

U.S. dollar or the British pound, is expressed or measured in terms of a given weight of gold or silver or some other commodity. For example, the United States was on the gold standard in the latter part of the nineteenth century because the domestic legislation provided that the $10 coin contain 232.2 grains of gold. Thus, the term "arrangement" is the most comprehensive or inclusive term for the variety of payments practices extant at any moment; the term "system" involves the legal-based set of payments arrangements, and the term "standard" applies with those systems that involve commodity monies, such as gold or silver.

Payments arrangements and systems have evolved over the centuries as traders and investors have sought to reduce the costs and risks of international payments. Changes in technology have facilitated the reduction in these costs. At times changes in national policies have reduced these costs; at other times, however, these costs have increased.

This chapter presents a historical approach toward the changes in the foreign exchange value of the U.S. dollar. For nearly 200 years the U.S. dollar was pegged to gold; hence, the foreign exchange value of the U.S. dollar was set by its relation to the price of gold compared with the foreign currency's relation to the price of gold. At the time of the Civil War, the link between the U.S. dollar and gold was broken, with the result that the U.S. dollar then floated in the foreign exchange market. During World War I, many countries broke the link between their currencies and gold; once again national currencies floated. In the 1970s, the currencies of the major industrial countries again began to float.

INTERNATIONAL PAYMENTS BEFORE WORLD WAR I

The U.S. Gold Standard

From 1792 to 1973, the foreign exchange value of the U.S. dollar in terms of the currencies of most other major countries was based on the relationship between the U.S. dollar and commodity gold. The U.S. Coinage Act of 1792, one of the first laws passed by the U.S. Congress, provided for the establishment of a mint and stipulated that the principal U.S. coin would be the $10 eagle, which weighed 270 grains standard for coin containing 11/12 gold or 247 1/2 grains of fine or pure gold. (There are 480 grains of gold in a troy ounce.) Gold was legal tender for all payments. At that time the weight of the British sovereign was 123.274 grains of gold 916 2/3 thousands fine. Since both the U.S. dollar and the British sovereign had values expressed in terms of gold, the price of the British sovereign in terms of the U.S. dollar could be inferred from the ratio of the price of each currency in terms of gold, so the U.S. dollar price of one pound was $4.86 once an adjustment was made for the difference in the fineness or gold content of the two coins.

In 1834, the U.S. Congress reduced the gold content of the eagle to 258 grains standard or 232 grains of pure gold. Legislation in 1837 fixed the gold content of U.S. coins at the ratio of 9/10, which meant the U.S. gold parity, the dollar price of gold, was $20.67, which remained the U.S. gold parity until 1933. Legislation in 1849 provided for a double eagle ($20), a quarter eagle ($5), and a gold dollar ($1).

As long as the U.S. dollar price of gold was fixed at $20.67, the United States was on the gold standard. Gold was an important component of the U.S. money supply but not the dominant component because the use of gold in payments was less convenient and more costly than the use of bank notes or U.S. Treasury notes.

The Use of Bills of Exchange

Similarly, the use of gold in international payments, such as between the United States and Great Britain, was modest during this period. Most international payments involved transactions in bills of exchange, which were comparable to a postdated check. U.S. firms with payments to make in London in 30 or 60 days for the purchase of goods would buy sterling-denominated bills of exchange that U.S. exporters were selling in New York and Philadelphia and other U.S. port cities. The exporters had received these sterling bills from British importers, and had shipped them back to the United States to exchange for U.S. dollars. U.S. importers with payments to make in London compared the U.S. dollar price of the sterling-denominated bill of exchange with the dollar price of making the payment by shipping gold. The use of bills of exchange for international payments was more efficient than the use of gold, since the shipping costs were lower and the bills of exchange could be replaced if lost (and hence, they were less expensive to insure). Moreover, the bills earned interest while en route, while gold did not.

Effects of the Civil War

Payments in gold were suspended December 1861, eight months after the beginning of the Civil War. The cessation of gold specie payments reflected that wartime finance would lead to a significant increase in the U.S. money supply and the U.S. price level; the dollar price of gold began to increase. The U.S. authorities could not maintain the fixed price of gold in terms of dollars at a time when virtually all other U.S. prices were increasing; from 1861 to 1864 the U.S. price level more than doubled. Since Great Britain continued on the gold standard and the sterling price of gold remained unchanged, changes in the dollar price of sterling were reflected in changes in the dollar price of gold, which doubled from 1860 to 1864.

The similarity in the increase in the U.S. dollar price of the British pound and the increase in the U.S. domestic price level focuses on the concept of the "real exchange rate," which is the nominal or market exchange rate adjusted to reflect the differences in the domestic and foreign price levels. From the point of view of the competitive position of producers in different countries, stability of the real exchange rate is likely to be more important than stability of the nominal exchange rate. Both the nominal measure and real exchange rates for the period 1860–1878 are shown in Figure 36.1. The depreciation of the U.S. dollar after the Civil War appeared smaller than might be inferred from the increase in the U.S. price level relative to increase in the British price level.

In January 1879, the U.S. Congress passed legislation that the U.S. dollar be convertible into gold at the pre-Civil War parity of $20.67. The return to gold convertibility at the traditional parity was possible because the U.S. price level

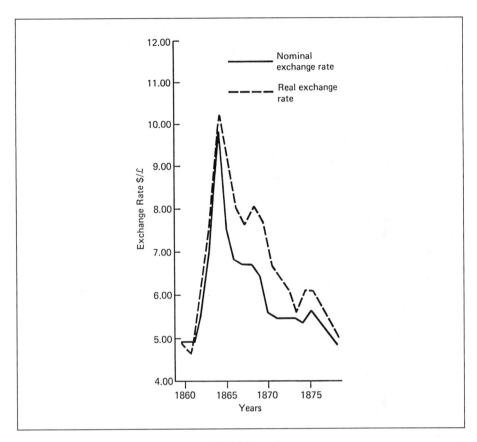

FIG. 36.1   The U.S. Dollar Price of the British Pound

had fallen relative to the British price level following the end of the war; at the same time, the dollar had appreciated and the dollar price of gold declined. The gold parities of the major countries and the foreign exchange value of the U.S. dollar in terms of other countries is shown in Table 36.1.

Cable Transfers

In the 1870s, two changes in technology reduced the costs of international payments. One was the move to steam from sail as the power for ocean transport, with the result that the time and costs of shipping both gold and bills of exchange across the Atlantic declined. The second was the development of the Trans Atlantic Cable, which introduced a new way to make more immediate payments. The telegraph or cable transfers could be used to signify changes in the ownership of bank deposits abroad. Thus, an American importer with a payment to make in London could buy a sterling deposit from a bank in New York; the New York bank could cable the London bank to transfer ownership of its deposit to the party designated by the American importer. The availability of

TABLE 36.1   Parities of Major Currencies Under the Gold Standard

Country	Unit	Weight[a]	Fineness[b]	Value of One Pure Ounce	Dollar Parity
United States (1879)	1 dollar	1.672	0.900	$20.67	—
Great Britain (1816)	1 pound	7.988	0.917	3/17/10½	$4.86
France (1878)	1 franc	0.3226	0.900	FF107.1	$0.193
Germany (1871)	1 mark	0.398	0.900	DM86.8	$0.238
Italy (1878)	1 lira	0.3226	0.900	IL107.1	$0.193
Netherlands (1875)	1 florin	0.672	0.900	DF51.4	$0.402

(a) Weight of standard coin in grams
(b) Fineness of standard coin = proportion pure gold

Source: M. L. Mühleman, *Monetary Systems of the World* (New York: Charles H. Nicoll, 1894), as adapted by Mayer, Dusenberry, and Aliber, *Money, Banking, and Economic Activity*

the cable meant that international payments could be made within a day or two, whereas payments made by shipping bills of exchange usually required a two-week lead time.

INTERNATIONAL PAYMENTS FROM WORLD WAR I TO WORLD WAR II

World War I Gold Embargo

Soon after World War I began, the belligerent countries in Europe wanted to hoard gold for military and security reasons, so they lifted the requirement that their currencies be convertible into gold, much as the United States had at the beginning of the Civil War. Moreover, they embargoed gold exports. Once national currencies were no longer convertible into gold, they were no longer effectively pegged to each other. During most of the war, these currencies traded at prices that were from 2 to 10 percent below their prewar values in terms of the U.S. dollar. Intervention by various national monetary authorities in Europe combined with exchange controls that restricted payments abroad by their residents (which were intended to conserve holdings of gold and foreign exchange for the war effort) limited the depreciation of these currencies.

Because of the war, the imports of European countries increased sharply relative to their exports, with the excess of imports over exports financed by selling securities and by borrowing. The British Government, for example, requisitioned the foreign securities owned by British residents. Before the war, trade between the United States and Great Britain was denominated in sterling, which meant that U.S. exporters and importers acquired the exchange risk, since they received and made payments in sterling. Once the war began, trade and payments were regulated on a centralized basis; British importers needed government approval before they could buy foreign goods. British holdings of dollars became concentrated in the hands of the British monetary authorities. U.S. exporters sold their goods to British importers for dollars and U.S. importers paid in dollars; the British importers and exporters acquired the exchange risk.

The Postwar Period: A Shaky Return to Parity

At the end of World War I, there was widespread sentiment for a return to the gold standard, and at the national parities for gold that had prevailed before the war. One problem that forestalled the ability of countries to peg their currencies at their prewar parities was that, since inflation rates had differed greatly among countries during the war, either the price levels in Western Europe would have to decline or the U.S. price level would have to increase so that the prewar gold parities would once again be appropriate. In real or price-level adjusted terms, the currencies of the European countries had appreciated extensively. Without this required change in the relationship among national price levels, the currencies of the countries in Western Europe would have been overvalued and these countries would continue to incur payments deficits.

Moreover, there was concern that the return to the gold standard would be jeopardized by a prospective gold shortage. Since the price level after the war was significantly higher than before the war, the fear was that a shortage would follow because the increase in gold mining costs would cause the volume of new gold production to diminish, while the demand for gold would increase relative to silver and other metals because the prices of these other materials had increased with the general price level.

Several League of Nations conferences in the early 1920s developed recommendations designed to facilitate the return to the gold standard. Measures to economize on the use of gold both by private and by national central banks were intended to cope with the possible shortage of gold. One recommendation was that the use of gold in domestic payments within countries be reduced. A second recommendation was that some central banks, especially the newer ones in the countries established in Central Europe from the breakup of the Austro-Hungarian Empire, should hold their international reserve assets in the form of foreign exchange (i.e., liquid assets such as bank deposits, Treasury bills, or bankers acceptances denominated in sterling or in the U.S. dollar) rather than gold. The arrangement whereby some central banks held in liquid assets denominated in sterling or in the U.S. dollar rather than gold as part of their international reserve assets became known as the gold exchange standard.

The period between World War I and World War II was one of great disorder in international monetary arrangements. Soon after World War I, the British authorities ceased supporting sterling, and the currency depreciated by more than 20 percent. Soon after the end of the war, a number of defeated belligerents, including Austria and Germany, were subject to hyperinflations and were forced to adopt new currencies. Both Great Britain and France sought to return to the gold standard at their prewar parities. Large fluctuations occurred in the foreign exchange value of the British pound and the French franc in terms of the U.S. dollar. (See Figure 36.2.)

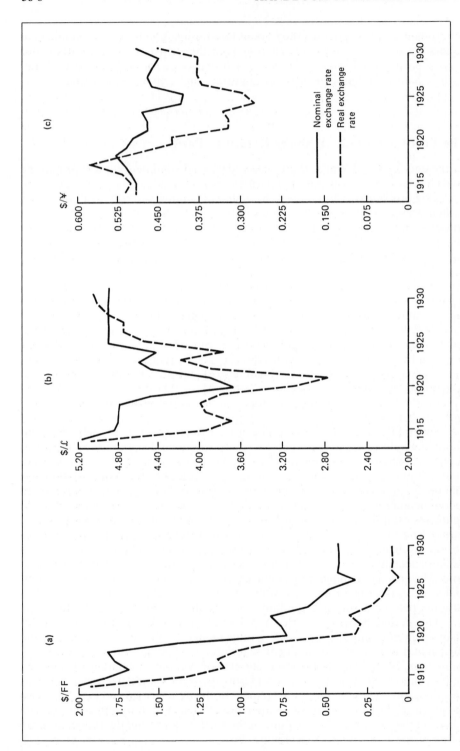

FIG. 36.2 Price Levels and Exchange Rates, 1913–1930: (a) France; (b) United Kingdom; (c) Japan

Great Britain succeeded in going back on gold at its prewar parity in May 1925; but there was general belief that sterling was overvalued, so the maintenance of the prewar parity required high interest rates in London, with the consequence that unemployment in Great Britain exceeded 10 percent.

France, in contrast, had stabilized the value of its currency in terms of gold in late 1926 after the French franc had depreciated very sharply as a result of speculative attack. At its new parity, the price of the U.S. dollar in terms of the French franc was nearly five to six times higher than at the beginning of the war; the French franc was widely regarded as undervalued.

Once the French franc was again pegged to gold, a system of pegged exchange rates had been established. However, there was considerable tension associated with the structure of exchange rates because of the belief that the British pound was overvalued and the French franc undervalued. To avoid attracting funds from London, the French, like the Americans, pursued a low interest rate policy. As a result, the U.S. authorities provided modest loans to the Bank of England, and the French authorities agreed that the Bank of France would hold deposits in the Bank of England.

The system of pegged exchange rates arranged at great cost finally began to unravel in the early 1930s. In spring 1931, the Austrian schilling was subject to a speculative attack by investors concerned by the closing of the Credit Anstalt, the leading bank in Austria. Banks in Germany had made substantial loans to the Austrians. As the likelihood that these banks would be able to collect on these loans declined, some investors withdrew funds from banks in Germany. Germany responded by tightening exchange controls. Speculative pressure was deflected to Great Britain and to the foreign exchange value of sterling. In September 1931, the British ceased supporting sterling at its parity because the economic costs of the levels of unemployment associated with the contractive monetary policies were deemed too high. When sterling depreciated, the competitive position of British firms in world markets inevitably improved and that of its trading partners worsened. The consequence was that speculative pressure then was diverted to the United States and to other countries whose currencies remained pegged to gold. U.S. exports declined and U.S. imports increased in response to the improved competitive position of British producers in world markets. The United States was subject to an outflow of gold by investors who anticipated that the U.S. authorities would be forced to follow the British example and stop selling gold at the established U.S. parity.

Nationalization of U.S. Gold Holdings

Immediately on taking office in March 1933, President Roosevelt closed the banks (to forestall further runs on the banks) and nationalized U.S. gold holdings; all U.S. citizens were required to sell gold to the U.S. Treasury at the established parity. The U.S. dollar was then floating in the foreign exchange market, much as it had in the time of the Civil War, and the dollar depreciated modestly. In late summer 1933, the U.S. authorities sought to increase the dollar price of gold to raise the U.S. price level. The hope was that a higher U.S. price level would promote the U.S. economic recovery, and thus lead to an increase in employment and a decline in the rate of business failure. To raise the dollar price of gold, a subsidiary of the U.S. Government's Reconstruction Finance Corporation began to buy gold. As the dollar price of gold increased, the foreign exchange value of the U.S. dollar declined in terms of currencies that were still pegged to gold (e.g., the French franc).

In January 1934, the U.S. authorities decided to peg the price of the dollar at $35 per ounce of gold. The speculative pressure became diverted to the French franc and to other currencies that also were pegged to gold; these countries, France, the Netherlands, and Belgium, comprised the Gold Bloc. Eventually, in September 1936, they abandoned their gold parities.

"Beggar-Thy-Neighbor" Policies

The sequence of changes in exchange parities in the 1930s became known as beggar-thy-neighbor policies, which implied that individual countries devalued their currencies as a way to increase their exports and employment at the expense of their trading partners. Most countries, however, devalued only after their currencies were subject to speculative attack.

One response to the decline of competitive power when trading partners depreciated currencies was increased reliance on tariffs and exchange controls to limit payments deficits. Controls of international payments were increasing; the international economy was fragmenting or disintegrating behind tariff preferences, exchange controls, and uncertainty about future exchange rates.

At the outbreak of World War II at the end of the 1930s, the price of the U.S. dollar in terms of the currencies of most other countries was not very different from the pattern that had prevailed a decade earlier, before the Great Depression began. The dollar price of sterling was $4.8662 in 1928 and $4.8894 in 1938. The parity of the French franc had been 25.50 francs to the U.S. dollar in the late 1920s; by the late 1930s, the parity was 35.90.

By the beginning of World War II, the United States had become the dominant international financial power. The U.S. dollar was strong. The United States had a large payments surplus. United States official holdings of monetary gold were nearly 60 percent of total worldwide official holdings, and much higher than those of the next largest 10 holders combined. The price of gold in terms of the U.S. dollar and most other currencies was 75 percent higher than it had been in the previous decade. If there had been a gold shortage in the 1920s, there was a gold glut in the late 1930s evidenced by the very sharp increase in the U.S. gold holdings from $3.9 billion at the end of 1929 to $16 billion at the end of 1930. In some ways the increase in gold effected in the 1930s through the sequence of exchange rates changes could be viewed as an unplanned response to the concern with the gold shortage in the period immediately after World War I.

POSTWAR ECONOMIC PLANNING AND THE BRETTON WOODS SYSTEM

One of the motives for the extensive planning during the early 1940s for the international economic arrangements for the postwar period was the belief that one of the causes of World War II was the economic dislocations of the interwar period, and the combination of high employment, substantial variability in exchange rates, and the growth in trade barriers and exchange controls. The planners in the United States, Great Britain, and their wartime allies recommended the establishment of three multinational institutions: the International Monetary Fund (IMF) to deal with exchange rates and international payments; the International Bank for Reconstruction and Development (the World Bank) to finance postwar reconstruction; and the General Agreements on Tariffs and Trade to provide a framework for negotiating changes in tariffs and other commercial policy arrangements.

The Bretton Woods system, established by the Articles of Agreement of the IMF in 1944, followed the U.S. proposal that a multinational institution manage a pool of national currencies from which a member country might borrow to help finance its payments deficits. The rationale was that the more readily a country might borrow, the less likely this country would follow the "beggar-thy-neighbor" exchange rate policies associated with the 1930s. The Articles of Agreement provided that each member country would state a value or a parity for its currency in terms of gold or the U.S. dollar and would undertake to prevent the foreign exchange value of its currency from deviating from this parity by more than one percent in spot exchange transactions within its territory. Each member would change the foreign exchange value of its currency only in accord with stipulated procedures, and usually with the approval of the IMF. (Eventually, the view developed that the member country had to be in fundamental disequilibrium before it might change its parity.) Each member country would agree not to apply exchange controls on international payments by its residents after an initial postwar transitional period.

On becoming a member of the IMF, each country was obliged to subscribe to the capital of the IMF. The amount of its capital subscription was determined on the basis of a formula which included a country's share of world trade and its share of world monetary gold holdings. Each member paid for one fourth of its capital subscription in gold and the remaining three fourths in its own currency in the form of a non-interest-bearing demand note. Each member could borrow currencies owned by the IMF in proportion to its own quota. In deciding whether to approve the request for loans, the IMF was not supposed to be concerned with the member's domestic economic or social policies. Each member was obliged to sell its currency to the IMF in exchange for gold, and the IMF might borrow currencies from its members over and above their amounts made available through the capital subscription.

Under the Bretton Woods system, international payments between traders and investors in different countries involved transfer of ownership of demand deposits in banks located in different countries and denominated in different currencies. A British importer with a payment to make in the United States would buy dollar demand deposit with a British pound demand deposit; this exchange of deposits would involve a transaction with the commercial banks. The commercial banks might have acquired the dollar deposits from an exporter in London with a receipts from sales in the United States, from another bank, or from the Bank of England. The Bank of England would have sold dollars to limit the decrease in the foreign exchange value of sterling significantly below its parity. Similarly, a Japanese importer with a dollar payment to make would buy a dollar deposit from a commercial bank in Tokyo or New York, which might have obtained these dollars from another bank in Tokyo, from a Japanese exporter, or from the Bank of Japan, which would have sold dollars to prevent the yen from depreciating significantly below its parity.

Under the Bretton Woods system, each member country could hold its international reserve assets in the form of gold or of liquid assets such as demand and time deposits and banker's acceptances, denominated in U.S. dollars, British pounds, or some other currency. There were no limits on the volume in reserve assets a country might acquire. In addition, there was no mechanism to supply countries as a group with international reserve assets comparable to the central bank mechanisms within each country that supply its residents with money.

The 1950s and the 1960s were decades of rapid growth in world trade and income. Trade barriers and payments controls were reduced. Germany and Japan, which had been occupied after World War II, became integrated into the international economy. The world price level was reasonably stable. After 1949, changes in exchange parities were quite infrequent (most countries had devaluated their currencies in September 1949 to compensate for the more rapid increase in price levels in Western Europe than in the United States). Thus, the British pound was devalued once in 1967; the French franc twice, once in 1959 and again in 1969. The German mark was revalued twice, once in 1961 by 5 percent and again in 1969 by about 10 percent. The foreign exchange values of the Swiss franc, the Japanese yen, and the Italian lira were not unchanged. Only a few countries permitted their currencies to float, and then usually for a brief period, pending the return to a new parity. (The exception was Canada, which permitted its currency to float from 1950 to 1962.) Because most changes in exchange rates involved devaluations, the foreign exchange value of the U.S. dollar was modestly higher in 1970 than in 1950.

The prosperity of the world economy during these several decades was sometimes attributed to the stabilizing features of the Bretton Woods system. It was seen as a modern day counterpart to the gold standard, which, many believed, was the cause of the growth of the world economy in the 30 years prior to World War I. The opposing interpretation was that the rapid economic growth facilitated adherence to a system of pegged exchange rates by the various national authorities.

Yet, this system of apparently stable economic arrangements was subject to two different types of pressures in the late 1960s, each of which centered on the United States. One was a growing shortage of international reserve assets, especially gold (much like the gold shortage anticipated after World War I). Because of the absence of any mechanism that might produce increases in the supply of reserves in response to increases in the demand, other countries could add to their holdings of gold and foreign exchange only if the United States incurred payments deficits. U.S. gold holdings declined from $23 billion in 1950 to $11 billion at the end of 1970. Over this same period, foreign holdings of liquid dollar assets increased from $9 billion to $68 billion.

The combination of the decline in the U.S. gold holdings and the increase in the dollar holdings of foreign central banks and foreign private parties was a consequence of the devaluations of the currencies of the countries in 1949, which, of course, greatly improved the competitiveness of foreign goods in the U.S. market.

U.S. PAYMENTS DEFICITS IN THE 1960s

In 1959, the United States began to adopt various measures to limit U.S. payments abroad and to reduce U.S. gold sales. Through the 1960s, increasingly more restrictive measures were adopted to achieve the same objectives. Initially, procurement under various U.S. foreign aid programs was tied to U.S. sources. U.S. military forces abroad bought more goods in the United States than in the countries in which they were stationed. Germany and other U.S. allies were encouraged to buy more military equipment in the United States to offset U.S. military expenditures in their countries. In 1963, the U.S. authorities applied a tax of 1 to 2 percent to U.S. imports of foreign securities. In 1965, voluntary controls were applied to capital outflow of U.S. firms. In 1968, mandatory controls were applied to the foreign investments of U.S. banks, firms, and residents.

One response to the combination of taxes on U.S. purchases of foreign securities and to the exchange controls on outflow of funds from the United States was that the market in dollar deposits and other financial instruments began to develop rapidly in London and other foreign financial centers. The primary reason for the growth in the dollar-denominated deposits in London, Frankfurt, Singapore, and other offshore centers was that the banks that produced these deposits did not encounter some of the costs incurred when dollar-denominated deposits were produced in the United States. Foreign firms and governments found they could borrow dollars in London and other offshore centers at a lower interest cost than in the United States. Foreign owners of dollar assets found they could obtain higher interest rates on dollar deposits in London and Luxumbourg than in the United States. Thus, one consequence of the types of measures to limit U.S. payments abroad was that the offshore market in dollar deposits and other types of dollar securities increased.

The U.S. payments deficits persisted despite the wide variety of measures taken to reduce U.S. payments abroad and to increase foreign payments to the United States. Eventually, the view developed that the U.S. payments deficits would decline only if a mechanism were established that enabled other countries to satisfy their demand for reserve assets without forcing the United States to incur payments deficits.

The establishment of Special Drawing Rights (SDR) within the framework of the International Monetary Fund as a new reserve asset was intended to meet this problem. SDR would be a store of value for national central banks; $10 billion of SDR was produced over a three-year period beginning in 1969 and was then distributed to IMF members in proportion to their quotas in the Fund. SDR was a unit-of-account, with the value of SDR determined on the basis of the foreign exchange values of the currencies of the major industrial country. SDR would be transferred among countries in the settlement of payments imbalances; thus, the Bank of England might sell SDR to the U.S. Treasury to obtain dollars for exchange market support.

One of the ironies was that just as the SDR arrangement was being implemented to reduce the likelihood that the U.S. payments deficits could be attributed to the demands for reserve assets, the U.S. inflation rate began to increase. The U.S. demand for imports surged.

BREAKDOWN OF THE BRETTON WOODS SYSTEM

Shortly after the devaluation of sterling in November 1967, the private demand for gold increased sharply, apparently in the belief that the monetary price of gold was too low and that its price would increase. In the 30 years since the U.S. gold parity was set at $35 in 1934, the U.S. price level had increased by 150 percent. For the first time in the postwar period, the private demand for gold exceeded new gold production, which meant that official institutions would be obliged to sell gold from their reserves to maintain a market price close to the U.S. parity; otherwise, the price would rise. Throughout the 1950s and indeed until 1965, the private demand for gold was smaller than new production, so official gold holdings were increasing, although at a declining rate. When the private demand at $35 exceeded new production, the U.S. authorities were reluctant to sell gold from U.S. stocks to maintain the $35 parity, so they took the lead in developing a two-tier gold price system. The U.S. gold parity of $35 would be retained for transactions between official institutions, while private parties were obliged to buy and sell gold at a free market price. Central banks would no longer arbitrage gold from their official reserves to the private market to prevent the free market price from rising above $35. The free market price varied between $35 and $43. With a free market price higher than the official parity, monetary authorities were reluctant to sell gold to finance their payments deficits.

The second pressure leading to a breakdown in the Bretton Woods system was that, in the late 1960s, the U.S. price level began to increase more rapidly than the price levels in other major industrial countries, which meant that a change in the price of the U.S. dollar in terms of most other currencies would be necessary. Either the dollar price of gold would have to be increased while the price of gold was more or less constant in terms of the currencies of other industrial countries, or the currencies of the other industrial countries would be devalued. There was substantial reluctance in the United States to raise the dollar price of gold. The U.S. authorities believed that just as other countries had devalued their currencies relative to the dollar when their currencies had become overvalued, so they should revalue their currencies relative to the dollar when their currencies had become undervalued. The monetary authorities in other industrial countries took the contrasting view that the dollar price of gold should be increased. Their rationale was that they had been obliged to devalue their currencies when their price levels increased more rapidly than those of their trading partners, and they felt the United States should follow the same course. This impasse over whether the United States or its major trading partners should take the initiative in changing the alignment of the exchange rates lasted from 1968 through mid-1971. In the interim the cumulative U.S. payments deficits totalled $40 billion, with the consequence that the foreign dollar holdings increased rapidly.

Under the Bretton Woods system, countries subject to persistent payments deficits were eventually obliged to devalue their currencies when they could no longer finance their payments deficits. Countries with persistent payments surpluses were under far less pressure to revalue their currencies, although some were concerned with the domestic economic consequences of these surpluses. The United States was in an exceptional position, for it might incur payments deficits without limit as long as the countries with the payments surplus were willing to acquire dollar assets. In April 1970, Canada permitted its dollar to float. More than a year later, Germany and the Netherlands also permitted their currencies to float.

In August 1971, the U.S. Government adopted a package of measures designed to break the impasse over the frozen exchange rate structure. The U.S. Treasury's gold window was closed, and the U.S. Treasury indicated that it would no longer sell gold to foreign official institutions at the $35 parity. More-over, the U.S. Government applied a 10 percent tariff surcharge to dutiable imports, with the implication that this tariff would be withdrawn after the other industrial countries permitted their currencies to be revalued. At the time, the European countries and Japan ceased pegging their currencies in the foreign exchange market, and their currencies appreciated. Controls were applied to limit increases in prices and wages in the United State so that the improvement in the U.S. international competitive position that resulted from the changes in exchange rates would not be offset by a resurgence in the U.S. inflation rate.

By the end of 1971, these other currencies had appreciated, and the U.S. authorities and their counterparts in other industrial countries agreed to a new set of currency parities. Effectively, the other currencies were revalued by 12 percent, or the U.S. dollar was devalued by 12 percent. The U.S. authorities raised the dollar price of gold by 8.6 percent to $38.00, although the U.S. Treasury's gold window remained closed. The U.S. Treasury was not willing to deal in gold at that price. Finally, there was agreement on the need for a new international monetary system, one that could cope with crises much more readily than the Bretton Woods system had. A committee was established within the framework of the IMF to develop proposals for such a system.

The new set of pegged exchange rates negotiated in late 1971 lasted about one year and broke down when investors shifted funds to German marks in response to a sharp increase in interest rates on mark-denominated assets. Early in 1973, the authorities ceased pegging their currencies because the domestic costs of attempting to maintain a system of pegged exchange rates were too high. The plan for a new monetary system, commissioned under the Smithsonian Agreement in 1973, was almost obsolete at its release because it was based on a system of pegged exchange rates. Such a system was not likely to be feasible at a time when the inflation rates in the major countries were approaching 8 to 10 percent and more.

THE POST-BRETTON WOODS SYSTEM

Floating Exchange Rates

The dominant feature of the period since the move toward floating exchange rates in the first quarter of 1973 has been the volatility of the movements in the foreign exchange value of the U.S. dollar (see Figure 36.3), similar to exchange rate movements during the 1920s. The antecedents to the decisions to permit currencies to float during these two eras differ significantly. The movement to floating exchange rates after World War I reflected the very sharp differences

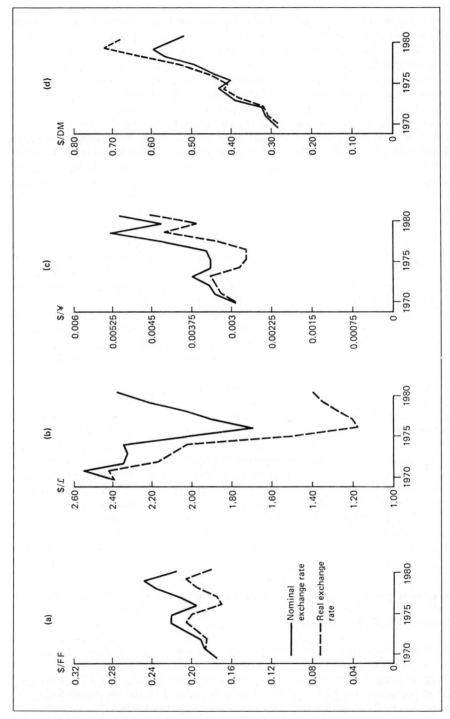

FIG. 36.3   Changes in Exchange Rates, 1970–1980: (a) France; (b) United Kingdom; (c) Japan; (d) West Germany

among countries in their inflation rates during the war. The differences among countries in their inflation rates in the 1960s were much more modest. For example, the largest difference in any one year between the inflation rates in the United States and Germany in the late 1960s and the early 1970s was 8 percent, and the annual difference averaged about 3 percent. However, the average annual variation in the mark price of the dollar was 10 percent. Moreoover, the U.S. inflation rates in the 1970s and 1980s ranged from 5 to 15 percent, whereas (except for the period immediately after World War I) the U.S. price level was reasonably stable in the 1920s. In the 1970s, two oil price shocks had a modest impact on the world price level, perhaps increasing the inflation rate by two to three percentage points; however, the United States and most of its major trading partners were experiencing double-digit inflation rates before the first oil price shock.

Although the major industrial countries permit their currencies to float, more than 100 countries (usually the smaller ones), continue to peg their currencies to reduce the uncertainty that their traders and investors incur in the foreign exchange market. Currencies are pegged to the U.S. dollar, the French franc, the SDR, or to an alternative market basket of currencies. The choice of the currency to peg to is largely determined by trading patterns; countries tend to peg their currencies to that of a nearby trading partner.

One other significant feature of the period with floating exchange rates was the sharp variability of the market price of gold. Private investors bid up the price of gold from $43 at the end of the 1971 to $200 when the inflation rate was increasing in 1973 and 1974. When the anticipated inflation rate declined, the market price of gold declined almost $100. In 1976, the market price of gold again began to increase when the worldwide inflation rate began to increase. The gold price peaked at $970 an ounce in January 1980. Then, with the decline in the inflation rate, the price of gold began to fall. The price of gold in 1983 ranged from $350 to $400, or as a minimum, more than 10 times higher than the 1960s parity of $35. One consequence of the surge in the level of the gold price was that the value of gold reserves of national central banks increased. Although few central banks traded gold, many began to calculate the value of their gold holdings on the basis of the market price of gold, with the consequence that the gold component of international reserves was more than 10 times larger than in the 1960s.

One consequence of the oil price increase was that the oil exporting countries generated large payments surpluses, which led to a surge in their holdings of international reserve assets. Initially, there was concern that the oil exporting countries would acquire a large share of the system's reserve assets; however, their oil export earnings could be used to finance either the increase in their commodity imports or the increase in their imports of securities, including bank deposits. Cumulatively, the oil exporting countries had payments surpluses that approached $200 billion in the 1974–1983 period. The surge in their reserves led to a sharp increase in their deposit holdings in the major international banks, and with these deposits the banks in turn were able to increase their loans to many of the developing countries.

The consequence was that commercial bank loan finance, or "liability management," was replacing the use of owned reserves in the financing of payments deficits, which reduced the importance of the IMF.

TABLE 36.2   Value of International Reserves

(U.S. dollars in billions, end of year)

	1960	1965	1970	1975	1980	1982
Gold	$37.9	$41.8	$37.0	$ 41.8	$ 42.5	$ 36.5
Foreign exchange	18.5	24.0	45.5	162.4	378.4	325.1
Reserve position in the International Monetary Fund	3.6	5.4	7.7	14.8	21.4	28.1
Special drawing rights	—	—	3.1	10.2	15.0	19.5

Source: International Financial Statistics

Non-Gold International Reserve Assets

A third significant aspect of the 1970s was the surge in the non-gold component of international reserves. In the 1960s, one means proposed to correct the shortage of international reserves was that the major countries permit their currencies to float. Then they would no longer need to intervene in the foreign exchange market to maintain the foreign exchange value of their currencies. The irony is that the period of floating exchange rates would be associated with a sharp increase in the value of international reserve assets. In part, the increase in this component of reserves resulted from the large OPEC surpluses; in part, from purchases of dollar assets in the late 1970s by those central banks that wanted to limit the appreciation of their currencies. Most of the increase was denominated in the U.S. dollar, although there was continued growth in the volume of reserves denominated in a few other currencies.

Within a decade, the urgency of the reserve shortage that had led to the establishment of SDR had disappeared. Individual countries still had problems financing their payments deficits, but the concern that there would be a reserve shortage diminished. Indeed, the probability was high that the unplanned growth in reserves had led to a reserve glut, although few countries appeared to have reserves they found excessive. Over the postwar period, IMF quotas had increased about as rapidly as world trade. Because of the surge in the price of gold and increases in dollar and other reserve currency holdings of various central banks, however, the share of IMF reserves in the total worldwide reserves declined. (See Table 36.2.)

Alternative Exchange Rate Arrangements

In the 1960s, the major countries in Western Europe joined in an economic community and made great strides in reducing the barriers that segmented their economies; tariffs on intra-European trade were reduced or eliminated, as were many other non-tariff barriers. There was a community-wide tariff on imports from other countries; there was a Common Agricultural Policy; and there were steps toward fiscal harmonization (e.g., each country adopted the value-added tax as a form of indirect taxation). Also an initiative toward a common monetary policy took the form of a joint float. Some members of the community pegged their currencies to each other so as to reduce the uncertainty associated with intra-European trade and financial transactions. (See Table 36.3.)

Once it became evident that the industrial countries would permit their currencies to float for the indefinite future, member countries of the IMF were no longer adhering to their IMF commitments. To legitimatize the current practices in the foreign exchange market, a new amendment (the so-called Second Amendment, the First Amendment having been the establishment of the Special Drawing Right) to the Bretton Woods system was adopted; member countries were allowed to pursue any type of exchange rate system. Many countries continued to peg their currencies; however, the major countries permitted their currencies to float. There was concern that countries might attempt to manipulate the foreign exchange value of their currencies to facilitate the achievement of their objectives in a style reminiscent of the "beggar-thy-neighbor" policies of the 1930s. Therefore, the IMF was charged with multilateral surveillance of the exchange market practices of its members; the IMF needed a role in the world of floating exchange rates.

With the move to floating exchange rates, however, the IMF no longer has the obligation to police and to maintain a system of pegged exchange rates. The role of the IMF is increasingly oriented to the problems and the policies of the developing countries. In the last several years, the IMF has been preoccupied with their external debt problems.

One counterpart to the volatility of the movement in exchange rates was the growth in the volume of protectionist import measures. The increase in the demand for protection reflected that when a country's currency appreciated sharply, in real terms as well as in nominal terms, the competitive position of firms producing in that country declined. Foreign producers could increase their share of the domestic market because changes in the exchange rate gave them a price advantage of as much as 25 or 30 prcent. To forestall the decline in market share (or even the downward pressure on domestic prices, wages, and profits), the producers sought tariff protection.

In recent years exchange rates have been extremely volatile. National authorities and analysts have been puzzled by changes in exchange rates that are considerably larger than would have been predicted or inferred from the differences in the changes in national price levels. There is very little evidence that the large swings in exchange rates are a consequence of official intervention by central banks and the various national monetary authorities; rather, the intervention of the national monetary authorities was undertaken to limit the sharp movements in the exchange rates.

THE FUTURE OF THE INTERNATIONAL
MONETARY SYSTEM

One of the lessons from the last decade is that a system of pegged exchange rates is difficult to maintain during a period of inflation, especially when the inflation rates are significantly different among countries. As inflation rates become more

TABLE 36.3   Exchange Rate Arrangements
(end of period)

Classification status(a)	1980	1981 Qtr 3	1981 Qtr 4	1982 Qtr 1	1982 Qtr 2	1982 Qtr 3	1982 Qtr 4	1983 Qtr 1	1983 Qtr 2	1983 April	1983 May	1983 June	1983 July	1983 August
Currency pegged to														
U.S. dollar	39	39	38	39	37	37	38	37	36	37	36	36	36	36
French franc	14	14	14	14	13	13	13	13	13	13	13	13	13	13
Other currency	4	5	5	5	5	5	5	5	5	5	5	5	5	5
Pound sterling	(1)	(1)	(1)	(1)	(1)	(1)	(1)	(1)	(1)	(1)	(1)	(1)	(1)	(1)
Special drawing rights	15	15	15	15	16	16	15	14	14	14	14	14	12	12
Other currency composite	22	21	21	21	23	23	23	24	25	24	25	25	27	27
Exchange rate adjusted according to a set of indicators	4	4	4	4	4	4	5	5	5	5	5	5	6	6
Cooperative exchange arrangements	8	8	8	8	8	8	8	8	8	8	8	8	8	8
Other	34	36	37	38	39	39	38	39	39	39	39	39	38	38
Total (b)	141	143	143	145	146	146	146	146	146	146	146	146	146	146

(a) Excluding the currency of Democratic Kampuchea, for which no current information is available. For members with dual or multiple exchange markets, the arrangement shown is that in the major market.

(b) Including the currency of Democratic Kampuchea

nearly similar, the range of movement in the exchange rates will diminish. The costs of pegging exchange rates is also likely to diminish; thus, the monetary authorities may again seek to peg their currencies. Within the European community, the exchange rate pegging operating is likely to be more extensive, with the result that the European currencies and the Japanese yen may be pegged to the U.S. dollar.

SUGGESTED READING

Aliber, Robert Z. *The International Money Game*. New York: Basic Books, 1983.

International Monetary Fund. *Annual Reports* (various years). Basle, Switzerland.

———. *International Financial Statistics* (various issues). Washington, D.C.: Bank for International Settlements.

Jack, D. T. *The Restoration of European Currencies*. London: P. S. King & Son Ltd., 1927.

Mayer, Thomas, et al. *Money, Banking and the Economy*. New York: W. W. Norton, 1984.

Solomon, Robert. The International Monetary System 1945–1976. New York: Harper and Row, 1977.

37

Foreign Exchange Markets and Foreign Currency Exposure

RITA M. RODRIGUEZ

E. EUGENE CARTER

Money denominated in one currency is bought and sold with money denominated in another currency in the foreign exchange market. When a Dutch company pays for goods bought from a British company, guilders are exchanged into sterling for payment. This conversion from one currency into another is typical of the transactions that take place in the foreign exchange market. Few of the foreign exchange market activities involve a transfer of actual currencies in circulation; when they do, most of these cases are accounted for by travelers who find it difficult to have their personal checks accepted in foreign countries. Most transactions occur through changes in the ownership of bank deposits. In our example, the settlement of the transaction typically results in a change in ownership of guilder deposits at a Dutch bank and sterling deposits at a British bank. The exchange market interconnects the markets for deposits in different currencies, the money markets of those currencies.

This chapter discusses some of the institutional aspects of the foreign exchange market, including the mechanics of foreign exchange quotations. It also discusses the nature of the relationship between the exchange market and the money markets for different currencies and theories of how rates are determined. A brief review of techniques is presented for forecasting exchange rates. Finally, various measures of corporate foreign exchange exposure and alternatives for coping with that exposure are discussed.[1]

INSTITUTIONS IN THE FOREIGN EXCHANGE MARKET

Currency is bought and sold in the spot exchange market for immediate delivery (in practice, two days later); and in the forward exchange market for delivery at some specified date in the future. The rates at which these currencies are bought and sold are the spot exchange rate and the forward exchange rate. Currencies also can be bought and sold in the currency futures market.

As an example of how the spot and forward exchange markets work, it is assumed that an exchange trader quotes the following exchange rates:

Spot rate	FF5.00/$
30-day forward rate	FF5.02/$

The following transactions are assumed: (1) buy francs against dollars (sell dollars) for spot delivery; and (2) sell francs against dollars (buy dollars) for delivery 30 days later. Both transactions are for FF100,000. The cash flows today, day 1, and 30 days later, day 31, for the two currencies are as follows:

		Currencies	
Date	*Transaction*	*Dollars*	*French Francs*
Day 1	Buy francs against dollars spot	−$500,000	+FF100,000
	Sell francs against dollars for delivery in 30 days	NCF	NCF
Day 31	Sell francs against dollars as per contract on day 1	+$502,000	−FF100,000

Note: + = cash inflow; − = cash outflow; NCF = no cash flow

The exchange rates and the amounts of each currency were determined when the transactions were closed on day 1.[2] The cash flows take place on the delivery or value date. The spot date is assumed to be on day 1 immediately after the transaction is closed. The forward value date specified in the forward transaction is day 31 in this example. Once a forward transaction has been closed at a given rate, the cash flows at delivery will take place at that rate.

Normally, the exchange rate on a forward transaction will not be the same as the actual spot rate which appears on the day of delivery, although there are some unverified theories noted later that consider the forward rate to be an unbiased predictor of the expected future spot rate.

The foreign exchange market resembles the over-the-counter market in securities. There is no centralized meeting place (except for a few places in Europe and the futures market of the International Monetary Market of the Chicago Mercantile Exchange) and no fixed time of operation. Trading occurs over the telephone or by telex. The currencies and the extent of participation of each currency in this market depend on local regulations, which differ from country to country. Only a few countries have established full convertibility of their currencies for all transactions. The currencies with restricted convertibility play a very small role in the foreign exchange market.

Commercial Bank Participants

The primary participants in the foreign exchange market are the few major commercial banks that actually "make the market." In the United States, about a dozen banks in New York (plus Exxon) and another dozen banks located in other U.S. cities have traders who maintain positions in 12 or 15 major currencies and, to a lesser extent, in other currencies. These banks operate in the foreign exchange market at the retail level in dealing with their customers: corporations, exporters, and so forth. At the wholesale level, they maintain an interbank market as well. Contact in this market in the United States is usually made through one of the handful of foreign exchange brokers. (The broker receives a small commission.) By maintaining the anonymity of seller and buyer until the deal is completed, the broker provides a fuller market than if the banks were to contact other banks directly. When dealing with institutions in other countries, banks usually deal directly with each other without the intermediation of brokers.

Currency Futures Market

The futures market in the Chicago Mercantile Exchange is an alternative to the forward exchange market. The International Monetary Market (IMM) of

---

[1] For a detailed explanation of the foreign exchange market, see Heinz Riehl and Rita M. Rodriguez, *Foreign Exchange Markets and Money Markets* (New York: McGraw-Hill, 1983). This section is based on Rita M. Rodriguez and E. Eugene Carter, *International Financial Management*, 3rd ed. Chapter 5. (Englewood Cliffs, N.J.: Prentice-Hall, 1984).

[2] It is assumed that delivery on a spot transaction takes place immediately after the contract is closed. This departure from the usual two days taken for delivery on a spot transaction will help simplify the presentation.

this Exchange deals in eight currencies: Swiss francs, German marks, French francs, British pounds, Dutch guilders, Canadian dollars, Mexican pesos, and Japanese yen. For the average individual who just walks into a bank and asks to purchase SF110,000 for delivery in three months, having access to a bank's exchange trader is unrealistic, and so the IMM is an option.

Trading in futures is similar to trading in the forward exchange market. The major characteristic that distinguishes the futures market from the forward exchange market is that a margin or security deposit must be maintained with a broker as a guarantee of one's ability to fulfill a contract. This margin is a security designed to cover any initial loss created by adverse price movements. The Exchange establishes an initial margin and a maintenance margin per contract in each currency. Each currency has a contract size which is set by the Exchange. The original margin is approximately 2 1/2 percent of the value of the contract. If the initial margin for a sterling contract is $1,500 and the maintenance margin is $1,000, someone buying or selling sterling contracts with these margin requirements initially deposits $1,500 per contract with a broker as margin. If the equity in the contract declines to under $1,000, there is a "margin call" from the broker requesting an additional amount to restore the $1,500 margin. If the contract is liquidated at that point, the additional margin becomes a realized loss. Conversely, gains in the price of the contract can become realized gains. These adjustments are computed daily, and margin calls are settled on a daily basis. This situation is in contrast to the transactions with the commercial banks' exchange traders, where there are no margin requirements and where the gain or loss in a forward exchange contract is not settled until maturity.

The gains or losses that a speculator in the IMM may suffer in a given day are also limited by the Exchange, which establishes limits on the amount that the price of specific contracts can move per day. For large changes in prices, the Exchange provides for larger limits for two days, and then a day of trading without limits if required, after which the normal limits are reinstated. For example, the contract size for the British pound is £25,000. The normal limit of price fluctuation in a given day is $0.05/£ or $1,250 per contract. After two successive days of the contract losing or gaining $1,250 per day, the maximum price change allowed on the third day increases to 150 percent of the normal limit, $1,875. If, at the end of the third day, the closing price has changed to the allowed limit, the maximum price change permitted on the fourth day is increased to 200 percent of the normal limit, $2,500. Finally, on the fifth day of sustained maximum price changes, the price of a contract is allowed to float without limit before normal limits are established again on the sixth day.

The amounts traded in the futures market are multiples of the contract size of each currency, and no fractional contracts are traded. The futures market also establishes specific dates of delivery, which are the third Wednesday of March, June, September, or December. Custom-made contracts in a given amount for specific dates of delivery are not possible in the IMM. As a matter of fact, currencies are treated by the Exchange in the same way as any other commodity (e.g., cocoa beans), where actual delivery of the contracted merchandise only takes place in a very small percentage of the transactions. Most transactions are settled before maturity.

Transactions in the futures market involve a commission paid to the broker, which is negotiated between the customer and the broker. As in the stock market, brokers discourage small transactions by imposing relatively high commissions.

Some individuals are forced to operate through the IMM because of lack of an alternative in commercial banks. Some large businesses have found it advantageous to transact through the IMM on some occasions. Sometimes, the IMM is very active relative to the banks, and its spreads between bid and offer price become narrower than the banks' market. As one might guess, there is arbitrage between the IMM and the banks' market. However, major multinationals still consider the size of their transactions too large for the IMM to handle without destabilizing the market. The IMM is a very active market with more than half of the outstanding contracts often changing hands on a daily basis, but its size is still relatively small.

Foreign currency options (as opposed to futures) are traded in a variety of currencies in both the United States and Europe. On the Philadelphia Stock Exchange, for example, contracts for half the size of the corresponding futures contracts on the Chicago Board — Options Exchange are traded with up to nine months maturity in marks, sterling, yen, Swiss francs, and Canadian dollars. Options can be exercised at any time during the contract life, and require a deposit subject to normal margin requirements. The futures contract must be exercised, and the purchaser must continually make up the margin balance; hence, a wrong price move could result in the speculator losing far more than the original investment, as he cannot simply walk away from the futures contract as he can an option contract.[3]

Other Participants

The other important participants in the foreign exchange market are the various countries' central banks. These institutions frequently intervene in the market to maintain the exchange rates of their currencies within a desired range and to smooth fluctuations within that range. The extent of this intervention depends largely on the exchange rate regime followed by the given country's central bank (e.g., fixed rates and freely floating rates) (see Chapter 36 for a detailed analysis).

The other participants in the foreign exchange market are nonfinancial business and individuals who deal in the market through commercial banks.

FOREIGN EXCHANGE QUOTATIONS

Meaning of Foreign Exchange Quotes

A foreign exchange quotation is the price of one currency expressed in terms of another currency. Quotations are generally made in terms of local currency per unit of foreign currency. Thus, in the United States, exchange rates are quoted in terms of American dollars per foreign monetary unit (e.g., $0.20/FF);

---

[3] See "Currency Options: W.C. Fields Had a Phrase for It," *The Economist* (Oct. 30 1982) p. 76f.

and in France the quotations are made in terms of French francs per unit of foreign exchange (e.g., FF5.00/$). But in the United Kingdom, foreign exchange prices are quoted in terms of foreign monetary units per pound sterling (e.g., $2.20/£, FF11.00/£).

To avoid confusion, it is useful to make clear which currency in the quotation plays the role of the unit of account and which currency is the unit for which the price is being quoted. Following U.S. practice, a quote can be made clearer by placing the currency used as a unit of account in front of the quoted price, and the unit of the currency being priced after the quote.[4] Thus, in the United States, prices for various articles are quoted as follows: $15,000/car, $0.70/tomato, and so forth. In the same manner, a quote for the deutsche mark can be expressed in American dollar terms, as follows: $0.30/DM. The unit of account (the local currency) is the U.S. dollar and the unit of currency being priced (the foreign currency) is the deutsche mark.

A foreign exchange quote involves a joint statement about two currencies. A change in the price of one currency implies a change in the price of the other currency that appears in the quote. For example, if the price of the mark against the dollar moves from $0.30/DM to $0.32/DM, it can be said that the mark has appreciated relative to the dollar by $0.02. This is the same as saying that the dollar has depreciated relative to the mark. When the quoted number increases, this implies an appreciation in the value of the currency used as the item purchased or sold (mark), but a depreciation for the currency used as the unit of account (dollar).

To translate the previous quote of $0.30/DM from American terms to German terms, the reciprocal of 0.50 is taken. This gives the reciprocal rate. If

$$\frac{\$}{DM} = 0.30$$

then

$$\frac{DM}{\$} = \frac{1}{0.30} = DM3.33/\$$$

Thus, the quote $0.30/DM in American terms, and the reciprocal quote DM3.33/$, in German terms.

The exchange rate between two currencies can be obtained from the rates of these two currencies in terms of a third currency. The resulting rate is called the cross rate. Suppose an American trader in New York quoted exchange rates of $0.50/DM and $2.20/£. From these quotes, DM/£ and £/DM can be obtained as follows:

$$\frac{DM}{£} = \frac{DM}{\$} \times \frac{\$}{£} \quad \text{and} \quad \frac{£}{DM} = \frac{£}{\$} \times \frac{\$}{DM}$$

---

[4] This practice is not observed in many countries where the position of the two currencies in a quotation is reversed. That is, the unit of account or local currency appears after the quoted number.

Thus,

$$\frac{DM}{£} = \frac{1}{0.30} \times 2.20 = DM7.3333/£$$

and

$$\frac{£}{DM} = \frac{1}{2.20} \times 0.30 = 0.1364/DM$$

DM7.3333/\$ and £0.1364/DM are the cross rates computed from the direct quotes of \$/DM and \$/£ given previously. As expected, 7.3333 is the reciprocal of 0.1364, and vice versa.

Comparing Quotes From Different Traders

The computation of reciprocal rates and cross rates facilitates the comparison of quotes given by different sources when each quote is expressed in different terms. As an example, the following quotes given by two traders in their respective local terms are considered:

New York	*Frankfurt*
\$0.31/DM	DM3.35/\$

To compare the two quotes directly, they are first expressed in the same terms, that is, DM/\$. This requires the computation of the reciprocal rate of \$/DM in New York. The DM/\$ rate for the two traders are:

New York	*Frankfurt*
DM3.2258/\$ (= 1 ÷ 0.031)	DM3.35/\$ (as originally given)

When buying dollars against marks, it is preferable to deal with the trader in New York; when selling dollars against marks, it is preferable to deal in Frankfurt.

A discrepancy in quotes between two traders offers an opportunity to profit by buying one currency against another from one trader at one price and reversing the transaction with the other trader at a higher price. Such a transaction is called arbitrage. For individuals with access to those rates, there is no risk whatsoever in this arbitrage transaction because all the relevant rates are known in advance. There is no investment required, since the purchase of each currency is financed with the sale of the other currency. The individual who performs those transactions is the arbitrageur. In the DM/\$ example, the arbitrageur will want to do the following:

New York	*Frankfurt*
Buy dollars	Sell dollars
Sell deutsche marks	Buy deutsche marks

To make the comparisons in terms of \$/DM, the following is done:

New York	*Frankfurt*
\$0.31/DM (as originally given)	\$0.2985/DM (= 1 ÷ 3.35)

The same conclusion holds as when the quotes were expressed in terms of DM/$. For individuals interested in one specific transaction (such as buying dollars against deutsche marks) and for arbitrageurs willing to buy and sell each currency simultaneously, the quotes offer the following incentives: Buy deutsche marks against dollars from the trader in Frankfurt and sell deutsche marks against dollars to the trader in New York.

The transactions induced by the difference in the traders' quotes will tend to force a change in the market rates. In Frankfurt, the transactions will tend to increase the price of deutsche marks against dollars (decrease the price of dollars against deutsche marks). In New York, the tendency will be for a decrease in the price of deutsche marks against dollars (increase in the price of dollars against deutsche marks). These trends will continue until the exchange rate between the deutsche mark and the dollar is approximately the same for the two traders in the two cities. The pervasiveness of these pressures is such that, given modern communication, large discrepancies among the quotes offered by different traders for the same currencies rarely occur in the market. When they appear, they disappear rapidly.

Pressures to equalize rates develop when there are more than two currencies and cross rates. For example:

New York	Zurich
$0.60/SF	SF1.67/$
$0.31/DM	SF0.52200/DM

There are three quotes to be compared: dollars to Swiss francs, dollars to deutsche marks, and Swiss francs to deutsche marks. The comparison of dollars to Swiss francs just requires the computation of the reciprocal of the Swiss francs to dollars quoted by the trader in Zurich. However, the comparison of dollars to deutsche marks requires the computation of a cross rate from the Zurich quotes for Swiss francs to dollars and Swiss francs to deutsche marks offered by the trader; and the comparison of Swiss francs to deutsche marks for the New York trader requires the computation of a cross rate between the quotes for dollars to Swiss francs and dollars to deutsche marks. The three relationships for the two traders produce the following quotes:

	New York	Zurich
Dollars/Swiss franc	$0.60/SF	$0.60/SF[a]
Dollars/deutsche mark	$0.3100/DM	$0.3120/DM[b]
Swiss francs/deutsche mark	SF0.51770/DM[c]	SF0.52200/DM

Notes: (a) In Zurich the exchange rate is SF1.67/$, so $/SF = 1/1.67 = $0.60/SF.
  (b) In Zurich, $/SF = $0.60/SF (from note (a)) and SF/DM = SF0.52200/DM. Then, DM/SF = 1/0.5200 = DM1.9231/SF and $/DM = ($/SF)/(DM/SF) = 0.60/1.9231 = 0.3120/DM
  (c) In New York, $0.31/DM = DM3.2258/$ and $0.60/SF = SF1.67/$, so SF/DM = (SF/$)/(DM/$) = 1.67/3.2258 = SF0.51770/DM

Reading down the list of quotes, it is noticed that:

1 There is no arbitrage incentive between the Swiss franc and the dollar;

2 The deutsche mark against the dollar is higher for the Zurich trader than for the New York trader; and

3 The deutsche mark commands a higher price in terms of the Swiss franc with the Zurich trader than with the New York trader.

There are two arbitrage opportunities:

1 Buy deutsche marks against dollars in New York; sell deutsche marks against dollars in Zurich; and

2 Buy deutsche marks against Swiss francs in New York; sell deutsche marks against Swiss francs in Zurich.

There are incentives in the same direction for individuals interested only in a specific transaction. For example, a manager interested in buying deutsche marks against francs would rather deal with the trader in New York than with the trader in Zurich.

The pressures generated in the market by these transactions will tend to reduce the discrepancies between quotes given by the two traders. Large purchases of deutsche marks for francs from the trader in New York will tend to increase the quote of the deutsche mark against the franc from the trader. The opposite transaction with the trader in Zurich will make the trader decrease the initial quote of the deutsche mark against the franc. The trends will continue until the quotes are similar for both traders.

Relationship Between Spot and Forward Rates

The foreign exchange market provides exchange rate quotes for spot delivery and for delivery at various forward value dates. The relationship between the forward rate and the spot rate is usually expressed in the form of a percentage per annum premium or discount of the forward rate over the spot rate. A foreign currency is at a forward discount against a given currency when the forward price of the foreign currency is lower than its spot price. The opposite is true in the case of a forward premium.

For example, if the spot rate of the French franc is $0.20 per French franc, then the quote of U.S. $0.19 for three-month French francs shows a discount in the forward rate of the French franc against the U.S. dollar. That is, a unit of French francs buys fewer dollars for delivery in three months than for immediate delivery. This quote also shows that the U.S. dollar is at a forward premium against the French franc. One U.S. dollar buys more French francs for delivery in three months than for immediate delivery.

The percentage per annum discount ($-$) or premium ($+$) in a forward quote in relation to the spot rate is computed as follows:

$$\text{Forward premium} = \frac{(\text{Forward rate} - \text{Spot rate})}{\text{Spot rate}} \times \frac{12}{\text{Number of months forward}}$$

The following rates are assumed to prevail in the market for sterling:

Spot rate	$2.20/£
Three-month forward rate	$2.19/£

Then, the forward discount of sterling against the dollars is:

$$\frac{2.19 - 2.20}{2.20} \times \frac{12}{3} = -0.018 = -1.8\% \text{ per annum}$$

The first term in the equation converts the difference between the forward rate and the spot rate into a percentage of the spot rate. The second term annualizes this percentage. This annualization process permits comparison of the premium or discount on the forward rate with interest rates, which traditionally are expressed on a per annum basis.

Bid and Offer in Foreign Exchange Quotes

A foreign exchange trader will usually quote two numbers: the price at which he is buying and the price at which he is selling a given currency. The first price is the bid price; the second price is the offer or ask price. In either case, the currency for which the bid or offer price is given is the unit of the item priced. In the bid quote $0.30/DM, the trader is willing to buy deutsche marks at the price of $0.30 per mark. However, this is tantamount to being willing to sell dollars at the price of $0.30 per mark. Implicitly, the quote also establishes the offer price for the currency used as unit of account. Similarly, the trader's offer price per mark implicitly quotes the rate at which dollars would be bought per mark.

In transactions among traders, usually only the last digits of the bid and offer rates are quoted; the rest is understood. These last digits are called points. For example, the quotation of the spot dollar/lira rate might be 936/946. Given that lira quotes are usually given with six decimal places, this means the trader is willing to buy liras at $0.000936 per lira and sell liras at $0.000946 per lira. Equivalently, he is willing to sell U.S. dollars at $0.000936 per lira and buy U.S. dollars at $0.000946 per lira.

A foreign exchange dealer receiving a call asking for a quote is under a general moral obligation to quote and to deal at the rate quoted. He need not deal for unlimited amounts, but if the dealer is asked the price at which he will buy a given currency and then offers to transact only a small amount, it is clear that the dealer prefers to be at the other end of the transaction, in this case, to sell that currency. A good dealer provides a prompt response (to avoid giving the caller the opportunity to shop around) and narrow spreads. Otherwise, it is obvious on which side of the transaction he wishes to be. Quotations are stated both to buy and to sell. Given the narrow spreads, a dealer will very often sell when a buy is preferred, and vice versa.

The quotations for forward rates can be made in terms of the amount of local currency at which the quoter will buy and sell a unit of foreign currency, as described previously. This is called the outright rate and is used by traders in quoting to customers. The forward rates also can be quoted in terms of points of discount and/or premium from spot, called the swap rate, and used in interbank quotations. The outright rate is the spot rate adjusted by the swap rate.

To find the outright forward rates when the premiums or discounts on quotes of forward rates are given in terms of points (swap rate), the points are added to the spot price if the foreign currency is trading at a forward premium;

if trading at a forward discount, the points are subtracted from the spot price. The resulting number is the outright forward rate.

It is usually well-known to traders whether the quotes in points represent a premium or a discount from the spot rate, and it is not customary to refer specifically to the quote as a premium or a discount. However, this can be readily determined in a mechanical fashion. If the first forward quote (the bid or buying figure) is smaller than the second foward quote (the offer or selling figure), there is a premium; that is, the swap rates are added to the spot rate. Conversely, if the first quote is larger than the second, it is a discount. A 5/5 quote would require further specification as to whether it is a premium or a discount. This procedure assures that the buy price is lower than the sell price and the trader profits from the spread between the two prices. When asked for spot, one-, three-, and six-month quotes on the French franc, a U.S.-based trader might quote the following:

0.2016/9   2/3   6/5   11/10

In outright terms these quotes would be expressed as follows:

Maturity	Bid	Offer
Spot	0.2016	0.2019
One-month	0.2018	0.2022
Three-month	0.2010	0.2014
Six-month	0.2005	0.2009

It should be noted that the one-month forward franc is at a premium against the dollar, whereas the three- and six-month forwards are at discounts.

DETERMINANTS OF EXCHANGE RATES

Relationship Between Foreign Exchange Markets and Money Markets

In a competitive market, financial return is directly linked to the amount of financial risk in the investment. Trades with no financial risk are not expected to produce a financial return. If funds with a given financial instrument are borrowed and the proceeds invested immediately thereafter in another financial instrument with the same risk and maturity, there is no risk, but neither should there be any net return. The interest rate on the borrowings and the investment should be the same except for the usual spread between bid and offer rates. For example, if a bank borrows 90-day dollars in the interbank market and invests in a 90-day dollar placement with another bank of comparable credit standing, a net return would not be expected. If a net return were possible from this transaction, profits would be possible without risk and without any investment of risk capital. Thus, there would be profits for arbitrageurs, who would soon move the market toward an increase in the borrowing rates and a decrease in the investment rate. This trend would continue until the two rates were approximately the same and profit from arbitrage between the two rates was eliminated.

The exchange market gives us access to money (bank deposits) in any currency traded in the exchange markets. Therefore, this market should also be subject to the principle that financial return is related to the amount of financial risk in the investment. If funds are borrowed in one currency and the proceeds invested in another currency, there should not be any net return if there is no financial risk. However, in such a transaction there is a financial risk: the currency in which the investment is made may depreciate against the currency of the borrowings before maturity of the transaction. For example, if a bank borrows 90-day deutsche marks in the interbank market at 11 percent and invests the proceeds in a 90-day dollar placement with another bank of comparable credit standing at 13 percent, the bank's risk is that the dollar could depreciate against the deutsche mark before day 90. Such a depreciation of the dollar could convert the initial 2 percent interest gain into a net loss. In contrast to the earlier transaction in which both borrowings and investment were made in dollars, when there are two currencies, there is a risk. There may be a gain or loss depending on the fluctuations in the spot exchange rate.

To make the operation of borrowing in one currency and investing in another riskless, an exchange rate must be initially locked in at which the currency of the investment can be exchanged into the currency of the borrowing upon maturity. This can be done in the forward exchange market. Today, a rate can be locked in at which dollars can be converted into deutsche marks 90 days hence. The rate at which that exchange transaction is made on day 91 is today's 90-day forward rate. This forward transaction will eliminate the risk created from borrowing in marks and investing in dollars. The forward transaction converts the whole operation into a riskless one, and there should not be any financial return associated with it.

Interest Rate Parity

In the previous example there was a net interest gain from borrowing marks at 11 percent and investing in dollars at 13 percent. If the return on the total transaction, including the forward transaction, is near zero, it is known what the forward rate must be relative to the spot rate at which the marks are converted into dollars initially. The forward rate of the dollar against the mark must be at a 2 percent per annum discount relative to the spot rate. Thus, the forward discount on the dollar (premium on the mark) must equal the interest differential between the two currencies in favor of the dollar, and interest rate parity (IRP) exists. In this condition, it is not possible to realize any profits from borrowing in one currency and investing in another one without undertaking some risk.

If a net return were possible from borrowing in one currency and investing in another with a cover in the forward market, there would be an incentive for covered interest arbitrage to take place. To see what happens when the relationship between the forward premium/discount and the interest rate differential is not maintained, and interest rate parity does not hold, consider the following situation:

Spot rate	$0.30000/DM
90-day forward rate	$0.30225/DM
90-day interest rates	
Deutsche marks	11% per annum
U.S. dollars	13% per annum

To compute the per annum percentage premium (discount) of the 90-day mark against the dollar, the formula presented before can be used:

$$\text{Forward premium (discount)} = \frac{\text{Forward rate} - \text{Spot rate}}{\text{Spot rate}}$$

$$\times \frac{12}{\text{No. months forward}}$$

$$= \frac{0.30225 - 0.30000}{0.30000} \times \frac{12}{3}$$

$$= 0.03 = 3\% \text{ per annum}$$

Thus, the premium of the forward deutsche mark against the dollar, 3 percent, is larger than the interest differential of 2 percent in favor of the dollar, and there is an incentive to profit from covered interest arbitrage.

For example, the arbitrageur could realize one percent profit by doing the following:

Borrow dollars	−13%
Convert dollars into deutsche marks spot	
Invest deutsche marks	+11
Sell deutsche marks forward against dollars at a premium for deutsche marks	+ 3
Net profit	+ 1%

The cash flows associated with this interest arbitrage are presented in Table 37.1. Working with $100,000 initially, the net profit of $271 for 90 days, represents a net profit of about one percent per annum (271/100,000 × 12/3 months = 0.01). The principal amount on which the arbitrageur can earn this one percent is limited only by the amount he or she can borrow at the current rate.

As the amounts involved in this interest arbitrage increase, the following patterns will develop. In exchange markets:

1 The spot rate of the deutsche mark against the dollar will tend to appreciate as deutsche marks are bought against dollars.

2 The forward rate of the deutsche mark against the dollar will tend to depreciate as deutsche marks are sold against dollars.

Both movements tend to decrease the initial forward premium of the deutsche mark against the dollar.

TABLE 37.1   Cash Flows in a Covered-Interest Arbitrage Operation

		Currencies	
Date	Transaction	Dollars	Deutsche Marks
Day 1	■ Borrow dollars at 13 percent per annum for 90 days	+100,000	—
	■ Sell dollars against deutsche marks spot	−100,000	+333,333
	■ Invest deutsche marks at 11 percent per annum for 90 days	—	−333,333
	■ Sell deutsche marks against dollars for delivery in 90 days	NCF	NCF
	Net cash flows	—	—
Day 91	■ Investment of DM333,333 matures		
	Interest = 0.11 × 333,333 × 3/12 = 9,167	—	+342,500
	■ Borrowing of $100,000 matures		
	Interest = 0.13 × 100,000 × 3/12 = 3,250	−103,250	—
	■ Deliver on forward contract from Day 1	+103,521	−342,500
	Net cash flows	+ 271	—

Note: + = cash inflow; − = cash outflow; NCF = no cash flow

In money markets:

1 The interest rate for the dollar will tend to increase as dollars are borrowed.

2 The interest rate for the deutsche mark will tend to decrease as more funds are available to invest in deutsche marks.

Both of these movements will tend to increase the initial interest differential between the deutsche mark and the dollar.

Over time, the returns on a covered basis on the two currencies will move toward each other. At that point, the discount on the forward rate of the currency with the high interest rate will equal the interest differential in its favor. The swap rate expressed as a percentage of the spot rate will equal the interest differential. For example, if all the necessary adjustments produced by interest arbitrage are assumed to occur through changes in the forward rate (i.e., the interest rate and the spot rate remain constant), the new forward rate in the example can be calculated. It must be a 2 percent premium on the mark against the dollar; the swap rate must be 2 percent of the spot rate.

Swap rate for 12 months $= +2\%$ (spot rate)

$\qquad\qquad\qquad\qquad\quad = +2\%$ (0.30000)

$\qquad\qquad\qquad\qquad\quad = +0.00600$

Swap rate for 90 days $\quad = 0.00600 \div 12/3 = 0.00150$

Then, new forward rate $= $ Spot rate $+$ Swap rate

$\qquad\qquad\qquad\qquad\quad = 0.30000 + 0.00150$

$\qquad\qquad\qquad\qquad\quad = 0.30150$ or \$0.30150/DM

An alternative:

$$\begin{array}{l}\text{Forward premium} \\ \qquad\text{on mark}\end{array} = +2\% = \dfrac{\text{New forward rate} - \text{Spot rate}}{\text{Spot rate}}$$

$$\times \dfrac{12}{\text{No. of months forward}}$$

$$= \dfrac{X}{0.30000} \times \dfrac{12}{3}$$

$$\text{New forward rate} = +2\% \text{ (Spot rate)} \left(\dfrac{\text{No. months forward}}{12}\right) + \text{Spot rate}$$

$$= +2\% \text{ (0.30000)} \left(\dfrac{3}{12}\right) + 0.30000$$

$$= 0.30150 \text{ or } \$0.30150/DM$$

This shows the roots of the term "swap transaction." When a covered interest rate transaction takes place, what is done in the forward market is the opposite of what is done in the spot market. For example, if in the spot market marks are sold against dollars to generate dollar proceedings, the cover in the forward market involves a purchase of marks against dollars. Buys equal sells for each currency. There is just a temporary swap of one currency into another, deutsche marks into dollars in this case. The rate for this swap is the swap rate, the difference between the forward and the spot rates.

When there is an opportunity for covered interest arbitrage, there is an incentive to invest in the higher-interest currency to the point where the discount of that currency in the forward market is less than the interest differential. If the discount in the forward market of the currency with the higher interest rate becomes larger than the interest differential, then it pays to invest in the lower-interest currency and take advantage of the excessive forward on this currency.

Covered interest arbitrage involves no risk: From day 1 all the relevant interest rates and exchange rates are known, even though some of the cash flows do not take place until later in the future. This arbitrage requires no investment; the funds to begin the arbitrage are borrowed. Anybody with access to borrowed funds and investment outlets at those rates can profit from covered interest arbitrage. Given the large number of major banks that have access to these markets and modern information systems, opportunities to profit from covered interest arbitrage are seen rarely in the market. When they do appear, they disappear rapidly.

Interest rate parity holds among currencies only when dealing in net interest rates accessible to banks. These rates are the net of costs associated with taxes, exchange controls, reserve requirements, and so forth. Hence, interest rate parity can be observed best when comparing Eurorates among banks of comparable credit standing. Except for the Eurocurrency interbank market, national financial markets are usually not completely free, and strict interest rate parity does not hold. In these cases the forward discounts and premiums reflect other factors, such as political risk, in addition to interest differentials. This is particularly so in periods of heavy speculation about a future change in the spot rate.

Purchasing Power Parity

When markets are open and competitive, interest rate parity as discussed earlier should hold. Some people might argue that there is a relationship among interest rates that matches the parity relationships previously discussed in terms of the interbank market for funds, and that relationship holds rather well even with various impediments to the transfer of funds, transactions costs of various types, and informational requirements. The state of general interest rate parity becomes a function of how competitive one thinks the world as a whole is.

The issue of the general competitiveness of the world goods market becomes even more critical in the related concepts of purchasing power parity (PPP). Essentially, PPP relies on a comparison of relative inflation rates among different countries. In the simplest example of only one product, the price of the good should be the same regardless of where it is purchased and what currency is used to purchase it, ignoring items such as transportation costs and taxes. If a good were more expensive in country A than country B, buyers would tend to purchase the product in country B, driving up the price in B. The resulting reduction in demand for country A's product would tend to lower the price there. Over time, as export revenues in A declined and rose in B, there would be a tendency for the currencies of the two countries to adjust until the price of the good in both countries would be the same.

A sufficiently large number of traded goods in relation to the total goods of a country, and sufficiently small transportation costs, might move the currencies in the direction indicated. It might also be presumed that the trading account is the major determinant of the country's balance of payments, ignoring the other accounts, which are discussed later. However, even if the international trading sector is not that large and the transportation effects are somewhat large, relative national changes in costs (in terms of such a general index as the relative consumer price index) should be reflected in the foreign exchange rates, and changes in relative national costs should be reflected in changes in foreign exchange rates, whatever the initial exchange rate. As inflation rises more rapidly in one nation, the cost of that nation's goods rise, and the value of its currency in local purchasing power declines. One would expect this decline to be reflected in an adjustment of its foreign exchange rate vis-à-vis other currencies over time as well, in order for some sort of PPP to exist. This does not mean that all costs are comparable. Indeed Americans concerned about the rising cost of the average single-family home in relation to median national income (about three years income per home) can note that the typical single-family home in Switzerland costs more than 10 times the average annual income. However, it means that the average consumption bundle in one country will have changes in its costs that parallel changes in its exchange rate versus other currencies in line with changes in those other countries' price indices.

Related to this concept is the Fisher effect, named for the economist Irving Fisher, who suggested that interest rates were a combination of a real interest rate and the expected inflation rate. Hence, there is a link between PPP and IRP, and the common link is the nation pairs' differential inflation rate.[5]

Balance of Payments Analysis

A nation's balance of payments statement provides information about the possible course of its exchange rate movements under the classic argument that a debtor nation needs a convertible foreign exchange in order to continue to trade internationally. As it continues with deficits in its balance of payments accounts, there will be pressure to depreciate, or devalue, if the exchange parity is pegged to some major freely convertible currency; the terms are often used interchangeably. Opposite pressures apply to the net creditor nation, which will receive pressure from its trading partners to appreciate (upvalue) its currency.[6]

A balance of payments statement is similar to a corporate sources and uses of funds. Any transaction involving two nations involves offsetting debit and credit entries for each single nation's balance of payments account. Since the balance of payments must balance, what is meant by the terms "deficit" or "surplus" is the net balance of the autonomous accounts, what are assumed to be the motivated transactions. The other accounts are presumed to have compensating activities, accommodating autonomous transactions. Thus, an exporter sells merchandise, but in turn receives (buys) an account receivable, or a foreign currency, from the customer.

Current Account. For most nations, the major account within the current account is merchandise trade. Trade is a function of relative prices, relative incomes, and the response of production and consumption in the economies to changes in prices and incomes. Barriers to trade exist, of course, and changes in those barriers would be presumed to have an effect on trade, with an influence on the exchange rates. Intangible trade items are called trade in services and include travel, whether business or vacation (one is presumed to be importing scenery when one travels abroad), transportation of goods and people, and interest and dividends. Finally, gifts of immigrants to their families, the repatriation of funds of migrant workers to their clans, and untied government aid are part of the unilateral transfer account, for which there is no offsetting product or service returned.

Capital Account. Direct investment is defined for balance of payments purposes as a purchase of 10 percent or more of the ownership of a foreign business. Whether motivated by a determination to protect market share, or directly in search of profit opportunities, this longer-term commitment of funds is also influenced by issues such as trends in relative national income, costs of funds, availability of raw materials, general expansion of markets, and so forth. Portfolio investment, by contrast, involves purchase of bonds or stocks

---

[5] Algebraically these relationships can be presented in simple form. See Rodriguez and Carter, *op. cit.*, pp. 139–143.

[6] This section summarizes the concepts. For additional detail, see Rodriguez and Carter, *op. cit.*, pp. 10–55. See also Riehl and Rodriguez, *op. cit.*, pp. 122–139.

with an original maturity of at least one year (and where the stock would not otherwise be considered part of direct investment). Relative interest rates, security and liquidity of the capital markets, as well as the trends in these areas are all major factors in determining changes in portfolio investment. Finally, short-term capital flows involve purchase of accounts of less than one year's maturity when issued. Sometimes this flow involves acceptance of a receivable from a customer, as noted earlier. At other times, there will be a need for funds in the future, and the firm buys a foreign government note whose maturity matches the firm's need for foreign funds. In other cases, there may be a purchase of the foreign note as a speculation on the value of the foreign currency. As might be gathered, determining which transactions are autonomous and which are compensating becomes especially difficult in this area of short-term capital flows.

Official Reserves. Whether the nation's central bank intervenes because of mandated intervention in a fixed exchange rate environment or moves to counter an inappropriate appreciation or depreciation of the currency in a floating environment (and such intervention is done in coordination with other central banks), the official reserve accounts are really the short-term capital flows of the nation. These accounts will rise when foreigners wish to have more of the nation's currency: The central bank receives other currencies that are convertible in exchange for its own, hence increasing its official reserve balance. An American buying a French bond increases the official reserves of the French Government by the dollars he has used to buy the French debt. When foreigners turn in those debts (or French currency, in our example), France loses official reserves of other currencies. Ultimately, if the process continues, the French Government would be forced to let the franc depreciate, improving the competitiveness of French goods and attracting foreign capital to France. Thus, governments are presumed to be studying the balance of autonomous accounts, recognizing longer-term pressures on their official reserve accounts that may provoke a currency alignment under duress, and may take actions to adjust the parities of their currencies long before the lack of reserves forces them to do so. In the 1980s, nations are increasingly concerned with unemployment, inflation, and a range of variables, and the foreign exchange rate is one variable that may be used to affect these other economic accounts. There are many complaints that the U.S. dollar is overvalued, hurting U.S. exports. Yet a strong dollar may be seen as part of the Federal Reserve's commitment to keeping inflation under control, and it helps to attract long-term capital to the United States, which in turn, of course, helps make the dollar even stronger. In the meantime, union leaders and exporters complain about diminished sales and resulting unemployment.[7]

---

[7] The various policy issues involved here are beyond the scope of this chapter. For many years after World War II, the United States was in a special position, for the huge reservoir of U.S. dollars in other nations' official reserve accounts (which theoretically could have been turned into the Treasury at any time in exchange for gold and hence implied a weak U.S. dollar) were desired by foreign nations. The dollar was the only freely convertible currency which other nations trusted. The United States, thus, bought up huge amounts of foreign equity, ending up with the securities while the foreigners had dollars. Eventually, a crisis developed when everyone recognized

Balances in the Balance of Payments. As suggested before, the problem in transactions lies in deciding what is autonomous and what, if anything, is compensating. Typically, there are three balances of interest: the balance on trade, the balance on the current account, and the balance on current account plus direct investment. These figures are taken arbitrarily as representing the collection of autonomous transactions for a nation during one period. Whether one or more of these balances is in deficit and what the level of the deficit is compared to a previous period are of interest. Stages in the business cycle are important, for the United States tends to emerge from recessions sooner than other nations, and while it is emerging, rising U.S. relative incomes mean larger imports by Americans, hurting the U.S. trade accounts. Other nations are attractive for long-term capital purposes. Hordes of bankers race to lend to growing areas, as they did to Mexico and Brazil in the 1970s. In these nations, weak trade and current account balances are less important than the perception that other nations have government authorities committed to lend and invest in Mexico and Brazil. Even more than Israel, Egypt is dependent upon U.S. aid to support its balance of payments. To the extent the world believes U.S. aid will continue to these nations, their currencies are not put under the pressure they would otherwise face. Other comments in the following paragraph outline some of the variables one considers when analyzing a nation's balance of payments as a guide to the probable course of its currency's exchange rate.

Other Factors

Major participants in the market can reinforce trends by their own actions. When central banks make agreements, when the central bank of a nation known to have large franc reserves is known to plan to liquidate them, or when the trading desk of a major corporation or a commercial bank is known to be bearish on a currency, then there will be adjustments in the parities of the currencies independent of any basic IRP, PPP, or balance of payments element. Indeed, if the franc is expected to fall because of the sale of franc reserves by another central bank, there may be adjustments in the parities between the U.S. dollar and, say, the Mexican peso, because of anticipated changes in the franc/dollar rate. While these factors may be logically acknowledged ex post, ex ante, it is difficult to filter them. The situation is analogous to the 30-second nightly news bulletin about the stock market and the money supply. After the fact, if the money supply rose sharply and the stock market fell apart, it is because of investor worries about a new round of inflation. If the stock market rose, it is explained by increased availability of credit and increasing confidence in the economy. The problem is to anticipate ex ante (1) what the important factors are, and (2) what the reaction will be in the foreign exchange markets.

---

that U.S. gold reserves were grossly insufficient to redeem the paper dollars, that the dollars paid nothing, and that if other nations suddenly turned in their dollars those continuing to hold dollars would be stuck with depreciated paper. A solution to upvalue gold (i.e., devalue all the currencies relative to gold) had the problem of (1) rewarding those nations, such as France, which had most badgered the United States by turning in dollars and holding gold; and (2) rewarding such major gold producers as South Africa and the Soviet Union. The lurching adjustments in the parity of the dollar versus its trading partners in the 1960s and 1970s stemmed from this basic dilemma. How to adjust was a continuing problem, as even the Watergate tapes made clear.

FORECASTING EXCHANGE RATES

In this section, how corporate officers determine the exposure of their firms are outlined and approaches for forecasting exchange rates are provided. The bibliography suggests further reading, and within those readings a number of approaches are presented in detail. Also included are surveys of how managers do forecast exchange rates.

This section provides ideas on how to forecast exchange rates, indicating the issues to be considered and how they interact. It is necessary to consider such macroeconomic issues as monetary and fiscal policy, and the adjustment of prices to changes in the policies. This section also indicates how different views of "how the world works" determine views of exchange rate changes. Ultimately, it also deals with some major macroeconomic variables, and includes a discussion of how those items might affect exchange rates, as well as the rapidity with which prices adjust over time.

The Forward Rate as Predictor of the Future Spot Rate

The forward rate might be viewed as the predictor of the future spot rate, either because of a belief that no one can really predict the rate, or from the view that interest rate and PPP hold. In either case, the firm manager might not wish to worry about exchange rates, especially if each item in the balance sheet or income statement that is denominated in a currency other than the parent company's home currency is relatively small in relation to the total assets of the firm. Even if one can forecast rates that differ from the forward rate on occasion, and if there are substantial accounts involved such that the change in the foreign exchange rate is a concern, management may feel that the transaction costs are too great. Thus, the bid-ask spread and the cost of monitoring exchange rates for the important currencies together are too great in relation to the few forward exchange positions that the firm ultimately takes with successful outcomes.

If IRP and PPP hold, and there is a relatively open economic environment, then it follows that the forward rate is the best unbiased predictor of the future spot rate. Again, the point is not that the forward rate is always "right" in terms of the subsequent spot rate, but simply that it is right on average, and unbiased (i.e., the errors between the prediction and the actual average to zero). This outcome implies what is commonly called market efficiency, and is a position often held by many economists and finance scholars for reasons discussed earlier.

There are several recent studies involving periods and currencies that suggest that the forward rate has not been an unbiased predictor of the future spot rate. There are suggestions that certain filtering rules involving changes in forward and spot rates, and changes in interest rates provide information that, if followed, make it possible to outguess the forward rate in predicting the future spot rate. These studies then imply some form of inefficiency in the markets, or else that there is a risk premium in the forward rates. What is not settled, if the risk premium excuse for deviations from PPP and IRP is accepted, is what form of premium should exist. One receives a return to stock that is greater than debt because of risks of being an owner rather than a creditor.

One receives a risk premium for lending long term over short term (the traditional upward sloping yield curve) because of the greater risks regarding changes in the intervening short-term and long-term rates that affect both the ultimate and the intermediate value of a long-term debt. But the foreign exchange forward or spot position involves two parties on opposite sides of the issue, where the only differential is neither time nor risk, but the currency. It is not clear why there should be a risk premium for holding one form of money versus an interchangeable form.

Short-Run Deviations from IRP/PPP

Another position maintains that IRP/PPP hold in the long run, but in the short run there may be deviations from the equilibrium. Here, the analyst would forecast the correct future spot rate, and take action if the forward rate deviates substantially from that forecast.

The key in forecasting the future spot rate would be different relative inflations in the two countries, with the assumption that interest rates and foreign exchange rates would eventually follow those inflation differentials. The prime concern would typically be monetary policy, and here there are divergent judgments. For example, an expansion in the money supply in one economy might signal an increase in inflation even with relatively high unemployment, if one assumes that there will be increased demand for other goods in any case, and limited substitutability of workers and resources in the short run into production of the other goods. Others would focus on that increase in the money supply as accommodating demand for goods and transactions that is anticipated, and hence believe it is not inflationary. Moreover, over the last 20 years a school of economics focusing upon rational expectations has argued that policy makers' expected actions are already captured in market prices because the market anticipates the increase in the money supply. Hence, there is no impact on the interest or exchange rates. Indeed, if the increase in the money supply is less than anticipated, the result for inflation may be benign.

Aside from the difficulty of forecasting monetary policy and the impact of monetary policy on inflation in one nation, there must be another forecast for the other economy. In addition, other factors, such as industial capacity, unemployment, fiscal deficits, consumer spending, and capital spending must be forecast because such items affect expectations about future money supply, interest rates, and inflation. There are feedbacks and interactions among these variables and among the changes in these variables over time. There are arguments about the speed of adjustments to these changes, even if everyone agrees upon the nature of the changes portended for the future state of economic affairs. There are frequently sticky prices, with lagged adjustments to new outcomes and anticipated movements of various external factors. There is an adjustment in the short run of existing quantities and prices of goods as these external factors appear. There may well be substantial short-run volatility in such factors as producers and consumers work off existing stocks of a variable in relation to some perceived new equilibrium level of prices and output. (Such an explanation is consistent with the reasons why national price levels and changes in price levels are more stable than foreign exchange rates, which tend to overshoot in adjusting to new anticipated inflation rates.)

Even if one could agree on the model and the adjustment process, as well as the link to exchange rates, there are two problems. First, as Keynes pointed out, in the long run we are all dead. There is a series of short runs, and there is no guarantee that the equilibrium point will be realized at the maturity date of the forward contract. Second, for reasons outlined later, managers are often concerned about the values of forward contracts prior to maturity, since balance sheet reporting dates require a valuation of those contracts. Again, there is no guarantee that the desired equilibrium will be reached by that intervening date, which may make the manager uncomfortable as stockholders perceive commitments to currency positions where the commitments seem unrelated to any sensible economic outcome currently visible.

Forecast Rates

Another approach is to forecast rates explicitly and act when forward rates are substantially different from those forecast. Although relative interest and inflation rates are important, a large number of other variables are explicitly forecast. The other variables, in turn, may relate to or be influenced by interest and inflation rates, but larger long-run factors are seen as driving them. In any case, analysts who explicitly forecast foreign exchange rates use a wide range of factors to look at monetary policy as previously discussed, but will also study the factors listed in the following sections.

Foreign Exchange Intervention. Because of capital flows and domestic output levels of products and services, central bankers increasingly have the foreign exchange rate as a target variable. Both export and import industries have concerns about the rate, and the bankers respond by focusing upon the "proper" rate. Hence, forecasting future rates depends upon forecasting central bank intervention that can affect the foreign exchange rate. Although there is widespread disagreement over both the desirability and the efficacy of intervention, there certainly can be an impact for some period of time from increased demand for one currency and supply of another currency, which is what intervention involves.

Anticipated Balance of Payments Trends. In addition to the importance of trade flows, there are changes in capital flows. Major investment capital or aid capital flows can sustain economies well beyond what their current account would warrant: Israel and Brazil in recent years are two obvious examples. However, judgments about safe economies or probable appreciating currencies, such as were widely held views in the late 1970s regarding both the yen and the deutsche mark, and the Swiss franc, will result in sustained movement of funds into those currencies on a speculative basis as well, and these patterns must be anticipated. Forecasting current account, trade account, and other balance of payments figures for the future will have an effect upon one's view of the future spot exchange rate, for the traditional balance of payments analysis leads to judgments about whether a government can maintain an exchange rate for the foreseeable future or must let the currency appreciate or depreciate.

Where the currencies are pegged to some other reference currency, there is a deliberate judgment about whether the nation's monetary authorities will explicitly adjust the parity by devaluation or revaluation.

Others' Reactions. A major factor in exchange rates is what others think capital flows will be, and what they think others will think they will be. Again paraphrasing Lord Keynes, the desirable stock is based on what one expects others to anticipate still others will want, and so forth. The analyst following this view of the world will spend a great deal of time talking with bankers and other corporate officers for an indication of how the world should be viewed, as well as for learning what the other person believes others in his field believe.

Advisory Services. Many banks operate foreign exchange advisory services, which provide consulting advice to corporations on long-run trends in foreign exchange rates and on possible actions to take to control "damage." Traders, in contrast, are concerned with short-run movements, hence they may not pay much attention to advisory services. Most of the services are highly computerized, involving complex models that incorporate substantial tax and other issues to help the corporation manager anticipate what positions should be handled in which ways. Surveys of the services, and corporate managers' reactions to them, are discussed in several references in the bibliography. Again, a large number of corporate managers surveyed in one study indicated that the advisory services were useful not so much in forecasting rates (which the managers felt they could do as well given their own international banking sources), but for indicating what other informed people believed about the future course of rates.

MEASUREMENT OF CURRENCY EXPOSURE FOR A CORPORATION

Definition of Exposure

Exposure to exchange risk occurs as a result of several different factors. Highly liquid assets (cash, accounts receivable, or foreign exchange contracts that give the right to receive foreign currency at some future date) are all tangible accounts that represent a risk until the date of transfer. Thus, if the parent is a U.S. firm and it (or its subsidiary) owns deutsche mark-denominated assets, there is a risk in the dollar value of those assets arising from changes in the deutsche mark/dollar rate. Similarly, if the firm's liquid liabilities or near-term cash outflows are denominated in deutsche marks, there is a change in the debt status of the parent with changes in the exchange rate. In these situations, there is a cash or near-cash account, or a foreseeable cash flow. The cash flows (arising from either the balance sheet account changes or from an anticipated action on the part of the firm such as payment of a dividend to the parent) represent a type of exchange exposure often called transaction exposure.

In contrast, translation exposure arises from the need to consolidate state-ments, and from the historical cost basis of accounting. Regardless of the near-term, business-related cash flows of the business, there are assets and liabilities denominated in another currency, and there is the question of how those accounts can be valued at each balance sheet date. The assets and liabilities will, it is hoped, give rise to cash flows in the future, but it is not the accountant's accepted role to estimate such future cash flows. Rather, the goal is the orderly and consistent preparation of balance sheets from period to period based on historic costs and certain rules. There was little problem prior to 1971, but with the managed floating exchange rate system since that date, the manner in which statements were consolidated has become very critical to multinational managers.

Examples of Exposure

Table 37.2 presents hypothetical data for a subsidiary where the initial exchange rate between the local currency (LC) and the dollar is LC1/$. Hence, accounts have the same numeric basis in both currencies as shown in the first two columns. A sharp deterioration of the local currency then results in a new exchange rate of LC2 per dollar.

Column A shows the effect on the parent's accounts when all the asset and liability accounts are translated at the new, current (C) exchange rate as opposed to the historic (H) rate at which the assets were acquired. This method of translation, often called the equity method, results in a change in the equity in proportion to any change in the exchange rate, since the accounting identity of assets equal liabilities plus equity must hold. The assets are worth half, the liabilities are only half as great, so the difference is also reduced by half, resulting in the $250 exchange loss shown.

Fundamentally, the only accounts that affect the exposure of the firm are those accounts translated at the current exchange rate, since the dollar value of the other accounts does not change with variations in the LC/$ exchange rates. When assets translated at the current rate exceed liabilities translated at the current rate, there is a net asset position; the opposite gives rise to a net liability position.

One view is that long-term fixed assets, such as plant, should not be translated at a current rate. The rationale is that, whatever the ultimate effect on cash flows of changes in exchange rates, short-term variations in that rate hardly denominate an accurate value of a major fixed asset such as a plant, whose historic accounting cost may bear little relationship to any market value. Accordingly, if plant value is excluded from the translation, the firm's exposure becomes a net liability position, as shown in column B. Notice that the net effect on the firm is again the difference between exposed assets and exposed liabilities (i.e., those assets and liabilities translated at a current exchange rate) times the change in the exchange rate.

A definition of exposure called the monetary-non-monetary method would exclude both plant and inventory in our simple example, as shown in column C. The rationale is that nonmonetary assets and liabilities are inherently difficult to value in a market sense, so applying a market (current) exchange rate to their balance sheet account is inappropriate. In this example, notice that this action would further increase the net liability position of the firm, resulting in an exchange gain of $150, because the dollar value of the net debtor position

TABLE 37.2 Balance Sheet Translation Under Alternative Accounting Rules

	Initial Valuation Spot: LC1.00/$		Subsequent Alternative Dollar Valuations Spot: LC2.00/$*				
	Local Currency	Dollars	A	B	C	D	E
Assets							
Cash	LC 60	$ 60	$ 30(C)	$ 30(C)	$ 30(C)	$ 30(C)	$ 30(C)
Accounts	140	140	70(C)	70(C)	70(C)	70(C)	70(C)
Inventories	160	160	80(C)	80(C)	160(H)	160(H)	80(C)
Total current assets	LC 360	$ 360	$180	$180	$260	$260	$180
Net plant and equipment	640	640	320(C)	640(H)	640(H)	640(H)	640(H)
Total assets	LC1,000	$1,000	$500	$820	$900	$900	$820
Liabilities plus equity							
Short-term debt	LC 180	$ 180	$ 90(C)	$ 90(C)	$ 90(C)	$ 90(C)	$ 90(C)
Long-term debt	320	320	160(C)	160(C)	160(C)	320(H)	320(H)
Total liabilities	LC 500	$ 500	$250	$250	$250	$410	$410
Equity	LC 500	$ 500	$500	$500	$500	$500	$500
Exchange gains (losses)	—	—	(250)	70	150	(10)	(90)
Total equity	LC 500	$ 500	$250	$570	$650	$490	$410
Total liabilities plus equity	LC1,000	$1,000	$500	$820	$900	$900	$820

* Valuation basis: H = historical rate of LC1.00/$; C = current rate of LC2.00/$

of the firm is reduced with the decline in value of the currency in which the debt is denominated.

Column D presents the results from excluding long-term debt, often rationalized on the grounds that even long-term monetary accounts will be valued only later than one year; the exchange rate next year (let alone 20 years in the future) is not known, so it is inappropriate to use an historic exchange rate. In the example, the net exposure position is 20, resulting in a loss of 10.

Finally, column E shows the current-non-current method of translation, in which near-term accounts (i.e., all current accounts) are translated at current exchange rates while all long-term accounts, both monetary and nonmonetary, are translated at the historic (cost) rate. Again, the firm has returned to a net asset position, and there is an exchange loss for the period.

United States Financial Reporting Standards

Prior to 1971, the issue was not significant to most corporate managers because there was relatively limited volatility in exchange rates. There were sometimes sharp exchange adjustments but there was not the consistent volatility of rates witnessed in recent years with the managed floating arrangements. For reporting purposes prior to 1974, even the volatility of exchange rates was not a central concern of the managers since virtually any method of consolidation could be used, and any resulting gain or loss typically could be charged directly to the equity account rather than flowed through the income statement. Firms could (and did) use different methods of consolidation for subsidiaries in different countries, and could change their methods of consolidation from one year to the next. From 1974 to 1981, under Financial Accounting Standard 8, the translation convention was closest to column C, in the previous example. Of greater significance for most firms, however, was a requirement for exclusion in exposure calculation of plant, but inclusion of long-term debt often assumed to finance that plant. This practice left the typical firm in a net liability position. In contrast to the example in Table 37.2, the dollar was generally weak during this period, meaning that firms often showed substantial exchange losses as a result of the relatively larger dollar value of their debt as the dollar sank. Most importantly, this foreign exchange loss had to be reported as such on each period's income statement. For many firms, such exchange losses represented a significant portion of net income.

In part responding to criticism, the Financial Accounting Standards Board (FASB) issued Statement 52, which became binding upon all firms after 1981. This method essentially paralleled column A, with all accounts translated at the exchange rate prevalent at the period's end. Income statement accounts were translated at the average exchange rate of the period. Moreover, any resulting gain or loss was charged to an equity reserve account rather than entered in the period's income statement. (See Chapter 41 for details on this topic.)

Whatever the convention, notice that there is *no cash flow* associated with the reported gain or loss. Moreover, the effect on the gain or loss is a function not just of the accounts translated at the current rate, but of the size of the balances in those accounts and the ultimate net figure.

The discussion of exchange rates earlier involved concepts such as IRP and PPP. Strong adherents to those theories usually argue that a concern for exchange risk management is misplaced, at least where the exposure is a relatively small part of the firm's total asset base. Management costs and the transaction costs using the bank market or the IMM are significant. Furthermore, to the extent that the forward markets are good predictors of the future spot rate, there is no benefit; the price received for selling an asset such as deutsche marks to move the firm from a net asset position to a zero exposure position is fully consistent with the value. Selling a stock everyone agrees is worth very little usually results in a price consistent with that consensus valuation!

Nevertheless, many managers feel they have market forecasting ability superior to that given by a simple market model, or that the market is heavily influenced by other short-term factors, or that the assets are a significant portion of their firm's total asset such that the exposure is extreme. As a result many managers from time to time will hedge both cash flow exposures and balance sheet exposures. We now turn to some of the techniques used to affect those exposures.

TECHNIQUES FOR MANAGING EXCHANGE RISK

Hedging Cash Flows

Table 37.3 presents sample money and forward market rates using both Euromarket and domestic quotations. Notice that the three-month swap rate for dollars versus pounds is $0.0275/£. This figure is a 5.50 percent discount of the pound versus the dollar from the spot rate of $2.0000/£, and 5.50 percent is also the difference in the Eurodollar and Europound three-month money market rates.

Forward Exchange Markets. Suppose the firm wishes to hedge an anticipated £1 million receipt in pounds due in three months from a U.K. customer. The firm would enter a contract to sell pounds for dollars at the three-month forward rate of $1.9725/£. At maturity, the firm would receive $1,972,500 from the bank in return for the £1 million receipt from the customer that is turned over to the bank. This receipt represents a 5.50 percent per annum discount from the spot rate of $2.0000/£. As discussed earlier in this chapter, the firm could also use the IMM, selling pound contracts forward to offset the receipt of pounds from the customer.

Money Markets. The simplest way of using the money markets to hedge the pound exposure is to borrow pounds, convert the pounds to dollars, and invest the dollars. When the pound receivable is collected, it is used to repay the pound loan. Using the Euromarkets in the example, the firm would borrow pounds at 12.50 percent, convert them to dollars, and invest them at 7 percent, the same cost as computed for the forward market hedge.

The Eurorates are available in the interbank market, and the firm in our example may have to pay an extra 1.50 percent to borrow pounds, bringing

---

TABLE 37.3   Hedging a Future Pound Cash Inflow

Problem: Cover a three-month receivable in pounds

RATE SCENARIO

Money market, three-month maturity

Eurodollars, interbank	7.00%
Domestic dollars, base rate	7.50
Europound, interbank	12.50
Domestic pound, interbank	10.50

Foreign exchange market

Spot rate	$2.00/£
Three-month swap rate (5.5 percent per annum discount on the pound)	$0.0275/£
Three-month forward rate	$1.9725/£

OPTIONS

(1) Cover in the forward market; sell pounds against dollars forward at $1.9725/£.

(2) Cover in the spot exchange and Eurocurrency money market:
   (a) Using interbank rates, borrow pounds at 12.50 percent, exchange into dollars, invest dollars at 7 percent.
   (b) Using nonbank borrowers' rates, borrow pounds at 14 percent, exchange into dollars, invest dollars at 7 percent.

(3) Cover in the domestic money market. Using nonbank borrowers' rates, borrow pounds at 12 percent, exchange into dollars, and invest dollars at 7 percent.

---

the total cost to 7.50 percent for the money market hedge. The freely traded Euromarket interbank rates should have this relationship between the money market and forward market hedges. However, the nonbank firms who have to pay the premium typically would find that a forward market hedge costs less. The problem is that the bank that has loaned the money to the customer has a full credit risk in the money market hedge; in the forward contract, the risk is only a difference in timing when the bank closes the contract and when the customer fulfills his obligation. There is only a question of rates and rate changes over the period, rather than the risk of losing the full amount hedged. To the extent that the firm manager borrows pounds, converts them to dollars, and deposits them with the same bank, there is obviously much less risk to the banker. In this situation, the 1.50 percent normally will be smaller.

Suppose the U.S. firm actually had a need for dollars, and would be borrowing domestic dollars at the same time. One solution would be to sell forward pounds at the 5.50 percent annual rate computed earlier. Domestic dollars could be borrowed at 7.50 percent, plus, say, 2 percent to cover compensating balances (which in part offset the bank's reserve requirements) and direct fees. The total cost is then 15 percent. If the Eurodollars were borrowed instead, then the absence of reserve requirements and possibly reduced fees could result in a dollar loan cost of 7 percent plus (say) 1.50 percent in fees, for a total hedge-plus-borrow cost of 14.00 percent.

Another option involves borrowing Europounds instead of Eurodollars, at a rate of 12.50 percent plus the 1.50 percent fee, or 14.00 percent. The pounds are sold for dollars on the spot market. Thus, whether Europounds are borrowed and converted to dollars, or Eurodollars are borrowed with a three-month forward pound sale, the cost is the same.

The pattern shown here usually holds; that is, the firm finds it cheaper to borrow in the Euromarkets with a hedge involved rather than hedge and borrow domestic dollars.

Where a country has export controls on its funds, such as suggested in these data for the pound, the domestic rate is expected to be substantially lower than the Euromarket, as shown. Suppose the firm has a wholly owned U.K. subsidiary. If the pound receivable is owed to the subsidiary, which in turn has a payable to the parent in the same currency and same amount, then access to the domestic market is possible. The subsidiary might borrow pounds at 10.50 percent plus the 1.50 percent fee, prepay the liability to the parent, and then collect the receivable when due to repay its own debt. The parent converts the pounds to dollars and invests them at the 7 pecent dollar rate. With this access to the domestic market, the total cost is 5 percent, less than the forward market hedge and the money market hedge using the Euromarkets. This is an example of a leading payment, discussed more fully in the following section. It should be noted, however, that the affiliate must be willing and able to use the domestic market to prepay its obligations to its nonresident owners. Transactions with a subsidiary involving a currency expected to appreciate gives rise to reverse actions, delaying payment (and hence conversion) of the currency involved while the parent is borrowing in its domestic currency. This process is called lagging.

Hedging Balance-Sheet Exposure

Background. There are no cash flows directly involved in the balance-sheet exposure. Rather, the accounting conventions, which dictate how the firm's assets and liabilities denominated in other currencies will be valued for the sake of consolidation with the parent, create balance-sheet exposure. Moreover, the tools available for coping with these net asset or net liability positions are the same as those discussed earlier for coping with real cash flows. However, the cash flows to the firm from dealing with these reported exchange gains and losses are different.

Money Market and Foreign Exchange Market Hedges. Table 37.4 shows how a firm manager might use the foreign exchange market to hedge a net asset (long) position of local currency (LC) 400. He will use the forward market, but the results would be similar in the money market. Thus, he will sell the LC against dollars in the forward market. At the value date, there will be an adjustment made between the spot rate at which the LC is bought and the value contracted in the forward contract. During the interim, however, the manager has neutralized his exposure in LC (the net asset position) by having an offsetting

TABLE 37.4   Hedging Balance-Sheet Exposure: Cash Flow and Reporting Effects

Date	Transaction	Currency	
		Local Currency	Dollars
	INITIAL SITUATION		
	Spot rate: LC4.00/$		
	One-year forward rate: LC4.40/$		
Day 1	■ Balance-sheet position: LC400 = $100		
	■ Hedge: Sell local currency against dollar, value date day 360		
	SITUATION A		
	Spot rate: LC4.40/$		
Day 360	■ Balance-sheet position: LC400 = $90	NCF	NCF
	■ Sell local currency against dollars from day 1 contract	−440	+100
	■ Buy local currency against dollars spot	+440	−100
	Net cash flows	—	—
	Reported exchange gain (loss)		
	Translation gain (loss) ($90 − $100)	−$10	
		—	
	Cash gain (loss)	−$10	

SITUATION B
Spot rate: LC4.00/$

Day 360

	NCF	NCF	Reported exchange gain (loss)
■ Balance-sheet position: LC400 = $100	−440	+100	
■ Sell local currency against dollars from day 1 contract	+400	−100	
■ Buy local currency against dollars spot			
Net cash flows	−40	—	
Translation gain (loss)			—
Cash gain (loss) (−LC40)			−$10
			−$10

SITUATION C
Spot rate: LC3.60/$

Day 360

	NCF	NCF	Reported exchange gain (loss)
■ Balance-sheet position: LC400 = $111	−440	+100	
■ Sell local currency against dollars from day 1 contract	+360	−100	
■ Buy local currency against dollars spot			
Net cash flows	−80	—	
Translation gain (loss) ($111 − $100)			+$11
Cash gain (loss) (−LC80)			− 22
			−$11

Note: + = cash inflow; − = cash outflow; NCF = no cash flow

debt, the obligation to deliver (pay) LC under the forward contract. Had he used the money market, he would have borrowed the LC, transferred the funds to the parent firm's currency of account, and had the LC debt, which offsets the firm's net asset position. Again at maturity, he would have repaid the debt by exchanging the parent currency (i.e., dollars) for LC on the spot market. The cash flows and costs again may be slightly different in the money and forward markets depending upon the competitiveness of the banks, the accessibility to various capital markets, and so forth. The point is that either approach can offset the balance-sheet exposure.

The cash flows, however, are very different for these balance-sheet hedges and the real cash flow hedges discussed earlier. The manager has entered a forward contract to sell LC on the day of his financial report, day 360 in Table 37.4. The contract rate represents a discount on the LC compared with the dollar, for the contract rate is LC 4.40/$ compared with the spot rate of LC 4.00/$. There is no cash flow on day 1, when the hedge is entered.

Three possible outcomes are now examined, which differ only in the spot LC/$ rate on day 360. It is on day 360 that the actual cash flows appear. The differences in the reported exchange gains and losses on day 360 are also noted, depending on what has happened to the spot rate.

In the first scenario, it is assumed that the spot rate has indeed depreciated to the LC 4.40/$ forward contract rate. He buys LC at the 4.40/$ rate, which offsets the sale of LC in the forward contract at the same rate. Thus, there is no cash loss on this transaction. However, the net assets of the balance sheet must be translated at the lower exchange rate, giving rise to a $10 translation loss. The total reported exchange loss is the sum of these two items, cash and balance-sheet translation, $10.

In the second scenario, the manager faces an exchange rate that is unchanged at the end of the year. Thus, he faces no translation loss on the net asset position of his firm, since all the accounts are valued at the same exchange rate as began the fiscal year. However, he is committed to deliver local currency at a rate of LC 4.40/$, yet his purchase at the spot rate will be at the rate of LC 4.00/$. Hence, he has a cash loss on the forward contract of $10. The combination of the loss on the forward contract and no loss on the translation of the balance sheet again produces a reported exchange loss of $10.

In the third scenario, the LC has appreciated to LC 3.60/$, producing a translation gain when the $100 net asset position is valued at the appreciated rate. This gain is $11. On the other hand, there is a substantial loss on the forward contract, since the local currency sold at LC 4.40/$ under the forward contract must now be purchased in the spot market at LC 3.60/$. This purchase will produce a cash loss of approximately $22, for a combined reported exchange loss of $11.

It should be noted that, regardless of the change in the spot rate, the manager has locked in a reported exchange loss of about $10, ignoring some of the rounding and simplifying assumptions. This outcome demonstrates that the forward contracts do not prevent a loss. Rather, they simply lock in a known loss (or gain) regardless of what occurs subsequent to the spot exchange rate. The only time any accounting translation loss would be avoided is when the forward contracts are contracted at a rate identical to the spot rate today. Furthermore, the contract does not have to be closed or to mature at the end of the fiscal year, as shown in this example. The accounting firm will value the contract at its then value, based on the forward rate price which occurs on day 360 in any case. Ultimately, the cash flows associated with the contract will take place in one form or another. Finally, the cash loss or gain is a real factor, as opposed to the pure translation of the balance-sheet accounts. As a result of these factors, many managers have sought alternatives to the financial market hedges described.

Altering the Balance Sheet. Exposure is a function of the net of the asset and liability accounts translated at the current exchange rate. Accordingly, any action to change the size of the asset and liability accounts translated at the current exchange rates will alter the balance-sheet exposure of the firm. All accounts are eligible for adjustment, but the most common adjustments will take place in the cash, accounts receivable, or inventory accounts. The simplest adjustment would be to transfer some cash to the parent's currency, even though the currency might actually be left in the local country where the subsidiary is operating. If there is a block on converting the currency and holding it, then the subsidiary may declare a dividend if that is permitted. In either case, unless management of cash has been casual, there will typically not be a sufficient amount of cash available to substantially alter the firm's exposure. Reducing receivables would reduce the amount of exposed assets, assuming the cash so released was converted to the parent's currency. Receivables could be reduced by granting fewer credit sales, shorter credit terms, or attempting more rapid collection of accounts. All of these approaches have a cost in terms of customer ill-will, and presumably lost sales. Over time, inventories could also be at a lower level in the balance sheet. Again, customer ill will from stock-out conditions would have a cost as well.

Increasing liabilities by stretching suppliers, adding debt, or the like all serve to reduce the net asset position by adding liabilities in the other currency. In all these cases the cash raised in the local currency must be converted to the parent's currency for exposure to be reduced. Otherwise, the same amount of local currency liability and assets is simply added, leaving the net exposed asset position unchanged. Moreover, the leading and lagging payments described earlier from a subsidiary to a parent can also be used to external sources. Thus, additional debt in the local currency can be used to furnish cash to reduce accounts payable in other than the local currency. Prepayment of these accounts is part of the leading process. In contrast, one would lag payments in the associated local currency, which would have the effect of increasing the accounts payable from their normal level, increasing total liabilities and reducing the net asset exposure.

Over the longer term, sales might be denominated in another currency, or the local currency price may be adjusted by a currency adjustment factor reflecting depreciation of the currency. Similarly, payables in a relatively hard currency can be adjusted over time by seeking better credit terms from the supplier, or an invoice in the same local currency, or the like.

Clearly, none of these adjustments are free, for customer and supplier ill will, as well as explicit debt costs, are present. Nevertheless, these techniques are all part of the tools available to the international financial office in coping with balance-sheet exposure. The new accounting standards, which no longer require each income statement to bear the gains or losses from foreign exchange movements, may reduce the use of these techniques considerably. Thus, over time, managers will consider the long-run exposure of their operation from existing in that nation in that currency, and react accordingly in terms of investments, invoicing, credit terms, and the like.

SUGGESTED READING

Aliber, Robert Z., ed. *The International Market for Foreign Exchange.* New York: Praeger, 1969.

Antl, Boris, and Richard Ensor, eds. *The Management of Foreign Exchange Risks*, 2nd ed. London: Euromoney Publications, 1982.

Babbel, David F. "The Rise and Decline of Foreign Currency Options." *Euromoney* (Sept. 1980), pp. 141–149.

Calderon-Rossell, Jorge R., and Moshe Ben-Horim. "The Behavior of Foreign Exchange Rates." *Journal of International Business Studies* (Fall 1982), pp. 99–111.

Chicago Mercantile Exchange, International Monetary Market of the. *The Futures Market in Foreign Currencies.* Chicago: The Chicago Mercantile Exchange (undated).

———. *Trading in International Currency Futures.* Chicago: The Chicago Mercantile Exchange (undated).

———. *Understanding Futures in Foreign Exchange.* Chicago: The Chicago Mercantile Exchange (undated).

Coninx, Raymond G. F. *Foreign Exchange Today.* New York: John Wiley & Sons, 1979.

Coombs, Charles A. *The Arena of International Finance.* New York: Wiley Interscience, 1976.

Cornell, Bradford, and Marc R. Reinganum. "Forward and Future Prices: Evidence from the Foreign Exchange Markets." *Journal of Finance* (Dec. 1981), pp. 1035–1045.

Craig, Gary A. "A Monetary Approach to the Balance of Trade." *American Economic Review* (June 1981), pp. 460–466.

Cumby, Robert E., and Maurice Obstfeld. "A Note on Exchange Rate Expectations and Nominal Interest Differentials: A Test of the Fisher Hypothesis." *Journal of Finance* (June 1981), pp. 697–703.

"Currency Options: W.C. Fields Had a Phrase for It." *Economist* (Oct. 30 1982), p. 76f.

Dalal, Ardeshir J. "Decision Rules for an Investor in Forward Exchange Markets." *Journal of International Economics* (Sept. 1979), pp. 539–558.

Dam, Kenneth W. *The Rules of the Game.* Chicago: University of Chicago Press, 1982.

Dillon, Laura White. "The Do's and Don'ts of Foreign Exchange Trading." *Institutional Investor* (Jan. 1980), pp. 161–164.

Dufey, Gunter, and Ian H. Giddy. *The International Money Market.* Englewood Cliffs, N.J.: Prentice-Hall, 1978.

Einzig, Paul. *The Dynamic Theory of Forward Exchange*, 2nd ed. London: Macmillan, 1967.

———. *A Textbook on Foreign Exchange.* London: Macmillan, 1966.

Feiger, George, and Bertand Jacquillat. "Currency Option Bonds, Puts and Calls on Spot Exchange and the Hedging of Contingent Foreign Earnings." *Journal of Finance* (Dec. 1979), pp. 1129–1139.

Giddy, Ian H. "Research on the Foreign Exchange Market." *Columbia Journal of World Business* (Winter 1979), pp. 4–6.

Grubel, Herbert G. *International Economics*, rev. ed. Homewood, Ill.: Richard D. Irwin, 1981.

Gupta, Sanjeev. "A Note on the Efficiency of Black Markets in Foreign Currencies." *Journal of Finance* (June 1981), pp. 705–710.

Gurwin, Larry. "Death of a Banker." *Institutional Investor* (Oct. 1982), pp. 258–275.

Hodrick, Robert J., and Sanjay Srivastava. "An Investigation of Risk and Return in Forward Foreign Exchange." Working paper, Graduate School of Industrial Administration, Carnegie-Mellon University. Pittsburgh, Pa.: 1983.

Kolb, Robert W., et al. "Managing Foreign Interest Rate Risk." *Journal of Futures Markets* (Summer 1982), pp. 151–158.

Krueger, Anne O. *Exchange-Rate Determination.* Cambridge, Eng.: Cambridge University Press, 1982.

Levich, Richard M. "Are Forward Exchange Rates Unbiased Predictors of Future Spot Rates?" *Columbia Journal of World Business* (Winter 1979), pp. 49–61.

———, and Wihlborg, Claus, eds. *Exchange Risk and Exposure.* Lexington, Mass.: D. C. Heath, 1980.

McFarland, James W., et al. "The Distribution of Foreign Exchange Price Changes: Trading Day Effects and Risk Measurement." *Journal of Finance* (June 1982), pp. 693–714.

Officer, Lawrence H. "The Purchasing Power Parity Theory of Exchange Rates: A Review Article." *International Monetary Fund Staff Papers* (Mar. 1976), pp. 1–60.

Riehl, Heinz, and Rita Rodriguez. *Foreign Exchange and Money Markets.* New York: McGraw-Hill, 1983.

Rodriguez, Rita M. *Foreign Exchange Management in U.S. Multinationals.* Lexington, Mass.: D. C. Heath, 1980.

———, and E. Eugene Carter. *International Financial Management*, 3rd ed. Englewood Cliffs, N.J.: Prentice-Hall, 1984.

Sampson, Anthony. *The Money Lenders.* London: Hodder & Stoughton, 1982.

Solomon, Robert. *The International Monetary System.* New York: Harper and Row, 1982.

Walker, Townsend. *A Guide for Using the Foreign Exchange Market.* New York: Ronald Press, 1981.

38

International Financial Markets

RICHARD ZECHER

LEE THOMAS

INTRODUCTION

Basic Concepts

This chapter examines the structure of international financial markets and the way in which a balance is obtained internationally between the supply of and the demand for funds. It discusses the institutions that have evolved internationally, as well as who uses them and for what purposes, and describes data on financial flows worldwide.

Financial markets are simply those markets in which financial assets are traded. Financial assets are claims on other economic units that are held as a store of value and a source of income. Any financial market that admits foreign transactors is part of the international financial system and, broadly defined, might be called an international financial market. The distinction between national and international financial markets is somewhat arbitrary. Still there are some distinctive features of what are generally considered "international" rather than "linked national" financial markets. An international financial market is one in which a substantial portion of the instruments traded are foreign to the country in which the market is located. International financial markets are distinguished from their national counterparts not only by the types of claims that are traded — claims denominated in currencies other than that of the country in which they trade — but also by their participants, which may include (1) foreign as well as domestic individual investors, financial institutions, governments, and government agencies; (2) multinational as well as national corporations; and (3) international organizations.

International financial markets include exchange, money, and capital markets. The exchange markets (discussed in Chapter 37), as their name suggests, exist to exchange national monies. The international money and capital markets exist to trade, respectively, short-term and long-term assets and liabilities denominated in foreign currencies. They operate in parallel with national money and capital markets, which trade similar assets denominated in their respective home currencies only. The Euromarket, the most important international financial market, is an offshore money market that exists to facilitate trades of short-term bank deposits and loans.[1] The international capital market includes markets for foreign bonds and Eurobonds. This chapter focuses on the Euromarket and international capital markets.

Internationally traded financial assets exist in part because savings must be channeled among countries. Some of the economic agents that participate in international financial markets are surplus-savings entities with income in excess of spending. Others are deficit-savings agents that wish to spend more than their current income. In a world without international financial markets, capital transfers from surplus-savings units in one country to deficit-savings units in another country might be difficult or costly to achieve. This implies that the marginal product of capital might differ among countries. Such a situation is inefficient because global gains could be realized by shifting capital from low-yielding to high-yielding allocations. That is, capital should move to areas where its productivity is highest until its risk-adjusted after-tax yield is equal everywhere.

Internationally traded assets may also be used to channel savings within a single country, in which case the transactors' motive is generally to avoid regulations or taxes that are imposed on domestic investors or financial institutions. Avoiding regulations and taxes is one of the chief reasons the offshore markets — the most important category of international financial markets — have grown so quickly.

A third reason why investors demand internationally traded assets is the increasing importance of international diversification as the financial environment becomes riskier. International financial markets simplify the job of spreading risks across currencies and across countries.

---

[1] "Offshore" means that Euromarket institutions trade only credit instruments denominated in foreign currencies; a Eurobank in, for example, the United Kingdom would trade instruments denominated in all currencies other than pounds sterling. Currently the Euromarkets are the center of international activity for short-term (one year or less) deposits and loans, and they are becoming increasingly important for longer-term loans as well.

THE EUROMARKETS

At the heart of the international financial markets is a group of offshore money markets called the Eurocurrency markets. Eurocurrencies are deposits denominated in currencies other than those of the country in which the deposit is made. Banks that take foreign-denominated deposits use them to make foreign-denominated loans, called Euroloans. It has never been unusual for the two kinds of financial-market participants — borrowers and lenders — to look to foreign markets to obtain better yields, lower risks, or cheaper finance. Even so, until fairly recently there were no markets *devoted* to the purchase and sale of assets denominated in foreign currencies *only*, as the Eurocurrency markets are.

As Table 38.3 and Figure 38.2 show, the Eurodollar is by far the most important Eurocurrency, distantly followed by the deutsche mark and Swiss franc. Although the dollar's share of the Euromarket has been slowly falling, Eurodollars currently account for about two-thirds of the externally denominated liabilities of the 10 major European banks included in the Bank for International Settlements (BIS) statistics on the European Euromarkets. Thus, the following discussion tends to focus on the Eurodollar markets, even though the analysis is generally applicable to other Eurocurrencies as well.

Size

How big is the Euromarket? This may be a straightforward question, but it is difficult to give a simple answer. There are three sources of data on the size of the Euromarket. The first is the Bank of England's *Quarterly Bulletin*, which reports highly detailed statistics pertaining to the London-based U.K. Euromarket, the most important in the world. A second and broader estimate of the size of the Euromarket appears in the annual report of the BIS, published every June. The BIS statistics cover a number of European countries including Belgium-Luxembourg, France, Germany, Italy, the Netherlands, Sweden, Switzerland, and the United Kingdom. Both of these sources of information exclude the newer and rapidly growing markets in North America and Asia.[2] The third and most comprehensive data currently available are published monthly by the Morgan Guaranty Trust Co. of New York.

Morgan Guaranty constructs two major measures of Euromarket size. The first is the gross measure, which represents the total foreign-currency liabilities of banks in the BIS countries plus Canada, Japan, Singapore, the Bahamas, the Cayman Islands, and Panama. The second measure (net measure) excludes redeposits of interbank holdings, which are deposits at one Eurobank that have been lent by another Eurobank. Unfortunately, these data are not reported in the extensive detail that the Bank of England and the BIS provide. In addition, because the Euromarket is defined differently in each of these three sources, each one reports different values for the size of the market.

(*text continues on page 38-11*)

---

[2] Recent BIS statistics partially include newer markets, but non-U.S. banks outside Europe are still excluded.

TABLE 38.1 Geographic Distribution of the Euromarket Foreign Currency Assets and Liabilities of Banks

(U.S. dollars in millions)

	1975	1976	1977	1978	1979	1980	1981
Assets							
Belgium-Luxembourg	$ 39,070	$ 49,420	$ 66,950	$ 90,120	$119,090	$139,670	$ 145,890
France	39,020	47,990	62,210	80,780	100,440	118,770	120,440
Germany	10,640	14,330	17,280	20,770	21,710	21,510	23,810
Italy	14,980	12,290	14,780	22,160	28,320	29,690	35,570
Netherlands	17,350	22,000	27,180	36,560	44,480	50,810	53,330
Sweden	2,570	2,920	3,180	3,390	4,780	6,450	6,460
Switzerland	16,260	18,370	23,010	31,410	31,900	30,070	31,370
United Kingdom	118,240	138,000	159,210	202,850	270,000	333,640	401,230
Canada	13,390	17,070	17,720	21,890	25,020	34,840	36,800
Japan	18,830	19,560	18,150	25,720	34,080	48,690	63,610
United States	1,440	1,790	2,360	3,930	2,420	4,210	5,170
Caribbean and Far East	51,090	74,930	91,090	106,520	127,640	141,000	171,830
Total	$342,880	$418,670	$503,120	$646,100	$809,880	$959,350	$1,095,510

Liabilities

Belgium-Luxembourg	$ 37,860	$ 47,530	$ 65,470	$ 88,020	$119,180	$ 141,430	$ 147,810
France	38,110	48,660	62,970	78,790	99,600	121,700	132,250
Germany	9,310	13,730	15,230	18,880	23,430	23,500	24,820
Italy	15,040	14,950	21,520	27,800	35,250	43,620	46,760
Netherlands	16,370	19,580	25,470	35,550	44,580	52,400	53,640
Sweden	1,750	2,290	3,410	4,520	7,810	10,760	12,220
Switzerland	12,020	15,290	18,010	26,870	30,780	31,790	30,990
United Kingdom	128,210	148,620	171,360	213,420	281,970	346,720	413,570
Canada	12,070	14,620	16,700	22,350	29,730	40,610	56,870
Japan	25,210	27,160	24,470	30,320	46,670	67,880	87,220
United States	560	750	810	2,230	1,920	3,750	3,740
Caribbean and Far East	50,960	74,080	91,660	107,480	128,840	142,990	175,790
Total	$347,470	$427,260	$517,080	$656,230	$849,760	$1,027,150	$1,185,680

Source: Bank for International Settlements, *Annual Reports*

TABLE 38.2   The Asian Currency Market

(U.S. dollars in millions)

	1975	1976	1977	1978	1979	1980	1981	August 1982
Assets								
Loans to nonbank customers	$ 3,472.5	$ 4,386.6	$ 5,281.2	$ 6,376.8	$ 8,484.0	$12,402.3	$19,452.2	$ 23,667.3
Loans to banks in Singapore	270.1	414.4	573.4	866.6	1,100.4	1,084.7	1,495.2	1,316.9
Loans to non-Singapore banks	8,659.3	12,198.7	14,679.1	18,963.1	26,993.3	38,467.6	60,677.9	69,921.0
Other	195.5	354.4	484.6	833.6	1,585.0	2,438.6	4,149.9	5,403.2
Total	$12,597.4	$17,354.1	$21,018.3	$27,040.1	$38,162.7	$54,392.6	$85,775.2	$100,308.4
Liabilities								
Deposits of nonbank customers	$ 2,067.7	$ 1,960.3	$ 2,254.6	$ 3,600.0	$ 5,771.3	$ 9,322.1	$13,659.0	$ 16,444.1
Deposits of banks in Singapore	584.0	799.2	1,382.8	1,442.6	1,881.8	1,304.3	1,817.5	1,552.0
Deposits of non-Singapore banks	9,710.3	14,268.0	16,967.5	20,544.6	27,543.1	39,575.3	64,548.8	76,172.9
Other	235.4	326.6	413.4	1,452.9	2,966.5	4,190.9	5,749.9	6,139.4
Total	$12,597.4	$17,354.1	$21,018.3	$27,040.1	$38,162.7	$54,392.6	$85,775.2	$100,308.4

Source: Monetary Authority of Singapore

TABLE 38.3   Denomination of Euromarket Assets and Liabilities

(U.S. dollars in millions)

Year End	Dollars	Deutsche Marks	Swiss Francs	Pounds Sterling	Total Nondollars	All Currencies
			ASSETS			
1968	30,430	3,920	1,820	610	7,270	37,700
1969	47,630	5,990	2,980	580	10,540	58,170
1970	60,370	10,110	5,080	610	17,880	78,250
1971	71,500	16,220	8,180	1,620	28,630	100,130
1972	98,000	20,390	7,780	2,180	33,840	131,840
1973	132,110	31,410	15,000	3,080	55,510	187,620
1974	156,230	34,950	14,420	2,050	58,940	215,170
1975	190,180	41,620	15,430	1,980	67,950	258,130
1976	224,020	48,680	17,930	2,150	81,300	305,320
1977	268,430	70,350	23,640	5,310	116,410	384,840
1978	339,520	97,430	27,890	7,300	162,450	501,970
1979	427,960	124,430	38,660	11,140	211,770	639,730
1980	518,730	122,930	49,620	12,970	232,510	751,240
1981	593,530	120,280	60,020	13,120	246,520	840,050
			LIABILITIES			
1968	26,870	3,010	2,290	800	6,840	33,710
1969	46,200	4,640	4,030	810	10,520	56,720
1970	58,700	8,080	5,720	940	16,590	75,290
1971	70,750	14,630	7,760	2,110	26,970	97,720
1972	96,730	19,540	8,810	2,210	35,200	131,930
1973	131,380	32,020	17,160	4,560	60,720	192,100
1974	156,430	34,380	18,290	3,590	64,340	220,770
1975	189,470	39,940	15,290	3,140	69,200	258,670
1976	230,040	47,230	15,880	3,980	80,610	310,650
1977	278,840	68,680	22,720	6,870	117,360	396,200
1978	348,590	93,000	27,890	10,320	162,220	510,810
1979	436,630	127,940	40,710	15,180	229,200	665,830
1980	548,360	125,260	51,620	23,820	252,140	800,500
1981	631,520	117,130	68,110	18,330	259,970	891,490

Source: Bank for International Settlements, *Annual Reports*

Table 38.4 and Figure 38.3 present evidence of the rapid growth of the Euromarkets, as reported by Morgan Guaranty. Both the absolute size of the market (gross and net) and the rate of growth are impressive. The gross quantity of Eurocurrency bank liabilities outstanding at the end of 1981 was almost $900 billion. This is nine times the stock outstanding only a decade previously.

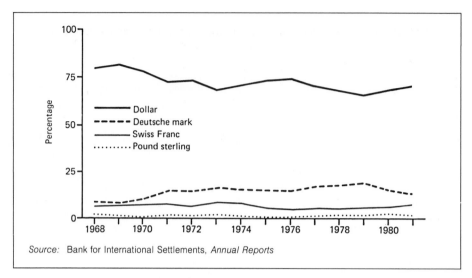

FIG. 38.2 Currencies' Shares of the Euromarket

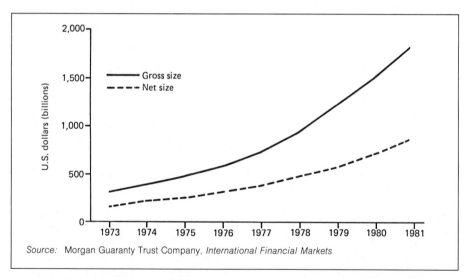

FIG. 38.3 Estimated Size of the Euromarket Measured by Banks' Foreign Liabilities

Definitions and Institutions

The term "Eurodollars" conjures up images of suitcases of currency smuggled across the Atlantic and there circulating hand to hand, as dollars do in the United States. This vision is wrong in many respects. Both "Euro" and "dollar" are misleading.

First, the term "Euromarkets" refers to *all* offshore money markets, not just those in Europe. Eurodollars include dollar-denominated assets trading in

**TABLE 38.4   Estimated Size of the Euromarket Measured by Banks'
Foreign Liabilities**

(U.S. dollars in millions)

Year End	Net Size	Gross Size
1973	$160,000	$ 315,000
1974	220,000	395,000
1975	255,000	485,000
1976	320,000	595,000
1977	390,000	740,000
1978	495,000	950,000
1979	590,000	1,235,000
1980	730,000	1,525,000
1981	890,000	1,860,000

Source: Morgan Guaranty Trust Company,
International Financial Markets

many financial centers in Europe and Asia. The London market, however, is still the most important.

Second, Eurodollars are not dollars strictly defined, but are dollar deposits, although they do include some very short-term (overnight) deposits. Eurodollars do not include any of the assets (currency and checkable deposits) incorporated in the narrow definition of U.S. money, M1. Eurodollars can represent dollars in the sense of money only if a more inclusive definition of money is used; overnight Eurodollar deposits are included specifically in the broader measure of U.S. money, M2.

The Euromarket is most analogous to the federal funds market in the United States, since it is primarily an interbank market. That is, most of the deposits in the Euromarkets are held by other banks. However, the analogy between the Euromarkets and the domestic federal funds market is not adequate, since the Euromarkets perform many other functions including (and very importantly) lending to and taking deposits from nonbank entities.

The first international money market developed for dollars in London. Trading in other currencies (e.g., deutsche marks and Swiss francs) followed. Since then Eurocurrency markets have evolved in other cities in Europe, Asia, Canada, and the Caribbean, and recently in the United States.

Ironically a major early boost was given to the Eurodollar market by the Soviet Union. After World War II the Russians and Eastern Europeans were, like most of the world's transactors, forced to negotiate their trades in dollars. Therefore, they needed to maintain dollar-denominated bank deposits. The danger from their perspective was that these dollar deposits, if maintained at U.S. banks, could be seized in the event of a political crisis, just as the Carter Administration froze Iranian assets in 1979. To prevent this from occurring, the Russians deposited their dollars in European banks, especially in London.

Fear of governmental interference with onshore deposits for political reasons may have been an important stimulus for the foundation of the Euromarkets, but is not the reason these markets flourished. In fact it could be argued that there is *no* reason why these markets *must* exist. It would certainly be possible for U.S. banks to hold all dollar deposits, British banks all pound deposits, and so on, with banks providing the necessary international facilities (exchanging currencies, providing forward exchange markets for hedgers, and clearing international checks) for their own nationals. A major reason the Euromarkets have come into existence and flourished is simply that they permit transactors to avoid costly government taxes and regulations. Eurodollars are traded outside the United States and so can be traded without the restrictions imposed on dollar instruments traded by U.S. residents. The most costly and restrictive regulations on U.S. banks, deposit rate ceilings and non-interest-bearing reserve requirements, are circumvented by creating a market outside the legal jurisdiction of U.S. authorities.

Importance of the Euromarkets

It has been argued that, strictly speaking, there is no need for Euromarkets. All the functions of these markets could be performed even if such markets did not exist, with each bank accepting deposits and making loans only in its domestic currency. It does not follow, however, that these markets have no economic importance.

The Euromarkets facilitate financial intermediation, the most important function of any financial market. Because the Euromarkets exist, it is easy for the excess savings of the residents of one country to be channeled into investments in other countries. Without the Euromarkets international interest differentials would still trigger this flow of savings and investors would still diversify internationally, but the process might not be as efficient.

The Euromarkets also aid purely domestic intermediation, since they provide a channel (and one remarkably free of regulation) between domestic borrowers and domestic lenders. It is odd to think that one effect of the substantial regulation of U.S. financial markets is to virtually guarantee that some capital channeled from savers in St. Paul to borrowers in Minneapolis will travel via London or even Singapore!

International financial markets have also performed one function that has received little attention. When only domestic financial markets exist, the currency in which an asset is denominated also corresponds to the jurisdiction in which that asset is trading. This makes international diversification more difficult. To purchase assets denominated in deutsche marks in domestic financial markets, an investor must necessarily purchase German assets. As a result, currency risk is inextricably connected to political risk. Through the use of offshore international markets, currency and political risks are much more separable.[3] An investor can purchase assets denominated in deutsche marks that are not

---

[3] Political and currency risks are not perfectly separable in practice, even in the offshore markets. As an example, all dollar denominated transactions, even in the Euromarkets, use the clearing mechanism in New York and therefore could in principle be controlled to some extent by the U.S. authorities.

TABLE 38.5 Maturity Distribution of the Euromarket, United Kingdom Only, November 1982

Maturity	U.K. Banks' Foreign	
	Assets	Liabilities
Less than 8 days	14.98%	20.67%
8 days to less than 1 month	16.12	20.52
1 month to less than 3 months	25.61	29.49
3 months to less than 6 months	16.33	18.87
6 months to less than 1 year	6.71	5.98
1 year to less than 3 years	6.62	2.60
3 years and over	13.63	1.87
All maturities	100.00	100.00

Source: Bank of England, Quarterly Bulletin

subject to the jurisdiction of German authorities, or he can purchase German financial assets (i.e., assets trading in German markets) that are not denominated in deutsche marks. The flexibility this separation affords permits investors to diversify their portfolio more easily with respect to national currencies and political risks.

Participants

Two classes of transactors participate in the Euromarkets. Creditors, or funds suppliers, hold Eurocurrency deposits, which are simply claims against banks denominated in currencies other than those of the host country. Debtors, or funds users, hold foreign-currency-denominated loans. These groups are not distinct: The large Eurobanks that are the major Euromarket participants both borrow and lend.

Funds are normally placed in the Eurocurrency market as time deposits. Table 38.5 shows that most of these deposits are relatively short term (about 90 percent are for less than six months) and it is common for depositors to "roll over" or reinvest time deposits as they mature. Transactors generally effect transfers by wire.

Funds suppliers to the Euromarket also hold negotiable Euro certificates of deposit (Euro CDs), but these constitute a much smaller fraction of the market. These investments are more liquid than time deposits, since they can be sold by the original purchaser before maturing. This feature is especially appealing to nonbank lenders. Because Euro CDs are more desirable for depositors, they sell at slightly lower yields than comparable time deposits; the differential is usually quite small.

In earlier years only the largest multinational corporations had access to the Euroloan market. As credit evaluation information systems have improved and the volume of funds available in the Euromarket has expanded, the markets have become more open to smaller and less well-known borrowers. It has become common for many otherwise completely domestic firms to use the Euromarkets to supplement other funding sources, expecially when domestic credit conditions are tight. Even so, most of the private nonbank borrowers are still multinational corporations or firms engaged in international trade. Typically Eurodollar loans are unsecured and are not amortized. Therefore only good credit risks have access to these markets.

Because borrowers in the Euroloan market are of top quality, they can easily transfer their business to the onshore debt markets. There are many advantages to borrowing in the Euromarkets. These markets provide flexible terms regarding maturity, repayment, and currency of denomination. The banks that make Euroloans are also able to provide many other services needed by international customers, such as exchanging currencies and providing forward coverage. Finally the market is very large and the terms offered are usually competitive.

A second group of borrowers — governments and government agencies — is especially attracted by another feature of the Euromarkets: Borrowers seldom are burdened with restrictions on the use of funds obtained. International organizations are often willing to provide loans at bargain interest rates to government borrowers, but there are usually restrictions attached that governments may find offensive or burdensome.

Euromarket Interest Rates

There are actually two sets of interest rates determined in the Euromarkets: deposit and loan rates. The spread, or difference between the two, represents the cost of providing intermediation and the profits of the intermediaries.

Profit margins are small for intermediaries in the Eurodollar market. The existence of close domestic substitutes for Eurodeposits — Treasury bills and federally insured domestic certificates of deposit — means that deposit rates have an unbreachable floor. Since borrowers who acquire Eurodollars have good enough credit ratings to have access to the U.S. markets, Eurodollar lending rates must be less than or, at most, equal to the loan rates charged in the United States. Thus banks participating in the Euromarket must pay as much or more to borrow funds and must charge less or, at most, as much interest on their loans, when compared with their operations in the onshore market. Intermediation in these markets is profitable only because of the cost advantage provided by the absence of regulations and taxes and by the high volume of trading that permits substantial economies of scale to be realized.

Since borrowing and deposit rates are close, it is reasonable to talk about what determines *the* Euro interest rate for a particular currency and a given maturity, even though the spread is not fixed. Euromarket deposit rates for dollar, deustche mark and Swiss Franc denominated deposits are illustrated in Figure 38.4. Euromarket interest rates depend on the demand for and the supply of funds in these markets. Funds are supplied through Eurodeposits and demanded in the form of Euroloans.

The supply of Euromarket funds depends largely on the home interest rate, as markets are sufficiently integrated to eliminate unreasonable spreads between domestic and offshore markets. This high interest elasticity simply means that

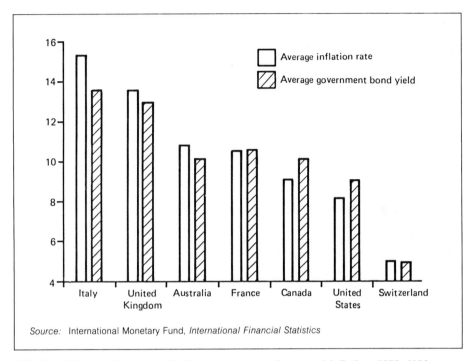

FIG. 38.4 Historical Relationship Between Interest Rates and Inflation, 1972–1982

if the Eurodollar rate were to rise by even a small amount relative to domestic U.S. interest rates, large quantities of funds would flow from the domestic to the offshore markets. This would reduce the spread between the two. Symmetrically, a decline in Eurodollar rates relative to U.S. rates moves funds into the domestic markets.

According to the efficient markets hypothesis, there are no recurring opportunities in well-organized financial markets to obtain higher expected returns without also bearing greater risk. Extensive evidence confirms that this provides a good description of the real world. The implication is that Eurodeposit rates cannot be higher than corresponding onshore deposit rates unless there are other equilibrating differences. If funds are deposited in both the United States and Euromarkets and the rates on Eurodeposits are higher, it must be that Eurodollar deposits are riskier or less convenient than deposits in the United States. Banks are willing and able to pay higher rates to Euromarket depositors primarily because these deposits do not carry legal reserve requirements.

One risk that attaches more to offshore than to onshore deposits is political risk. A U.S. depositor in the United States must always contend with the unlikely chance that the U.S. Government will interfere with the cash flows he expects his deposit to produce. The same depositor in the London Euromarket assumes the risk that *either* the U.S. Government, *or* the U.K. Government will act to confound his expectations. Further, countries may unexpectedly impose regulations on nonresidents that do not apply to domestic investors.

Euroloans are typically short- to medium-term (see Table 38.5) and are often quoted in floating rate form, usually as a fixed percentage over the London Interbank Offer Rate (LIBOR). Many banks fund, or acquire deposits to back their loans, in the London interbank market. LIBOR is the rate a top quality bank must pay to acquire (buy) deposits from other banks. Variable rate loans, quoted relative to LIBOR, protect banks, which are typically short-funded, from unexpected increases in interest rates. Deposits in the Euromarket are transformed by Eurobanks either into loans to other banks, through the interbank market, or into loans to nonfinancial borrowers.

In practice LIBOR is not a single interest rate. Instead there are different rates for each bank that transacts in the interbank market. Each bank's cost of buying deposits in this market depends on the market's appreciation of its unique risk characteristics. Ordinarily the rates for major banks are all close. At times, however, substantial differences may open in offer rates; this situation, known as tiering, generally indicates turbulent financial conditions.

The cost of funds a bank charges a nonfinancial borrower depends on the bank's perception of the riskiness of the loan. However, the spread above LIBOR that a borrower must pay is only loosely related to the borrower's riskiness, because the spread is an inexact measure of the borrowing cost. There are two reasons for this: First, banks usually charge fees in addition to interest, so the stated interest rate on a loan may be higher depending on the size of the other fees charged. Second, since LIBOR is not a single rate, the effective cost of a loan depends on *which* LIBOR the contracted spread is based upon.

Conclusions

The development and growth of the Euromarkets are monuments to the adaptability of financial institutions to their economic and regulatory environment. When regulations are costly or burdensome, they may well be circumvented. In addition, as the world financial environment becomes riskier, the development of institutions that will facilitate risk reduction or transfer can be expected. Both the level of regulation of domestic financial markets and the increasing riskiness have been instrumental to the success of the Euromarket system.

Looking ahead, these markets can be expected to remain important, although their explosive growth phase has probably ended. It is likely that the forces that have encouraged funds to flow through international instead of domestic financial markets will remain important. International markets offer substantial benefits that their domestic rivals to not provide. They have far more access to foreign capital and they remain relatively independent of the monetary, fiscal, and regulatory actions of governments. Domestic transactors can diversify using foreign financial markets, but the international markets simplify and expedite the process.

INTERNATIONAL BONDS

A potential debt issuer has three options: He can issue his debt in his own currency in the domestic market, issue it in a foreign currency in a foreign

TABLE 38.6   New International Bond Issues

(U.S. dollars in millions)

	1977	1978	1979	1980	1981	1982
			AMOUNT			
Eurobonds	$17,771	$14,125	$18,726	$23,970	$31,616	$49,839
Foreign bonds	16,205	20,154	22,264	17,950	21,369	25,975
Total	33,976	34,279	40,990	41,920	52,985	75,814
			PERCENTAGE			
Eurobonds	52.3%	41.2%	45.7%	57.2%	59.7%	65.7%
Foreign bonds	47.7	58.8	54.3	42.8	40.3	34.3
Total	100.0	100.0	100.0	100.0	100.0	100.0

Source: Morgan Guaranty Trust Company, *International Financial Markets*

market, or issue it in the Eurobond market in any currency he wishes. Most bonds are still issued in domestic markets. Until about 1960, issuing bonds in foreign markets was the primary method for obtaining foreign debt capital. Since then truly international instruments (Eurobonds) have surpassed (in new issues) foreign bond issues. The relative growth of the Eurobond market is documented in Table 38.6.

International bonds are defined by the currency in which they are denominated. An international bond is one that is denominated in a currency other than the borrower's; thus the international bond market comprises both Eurobonds and foreign bonds. Foreign bonds are those traded within their own currency domain, for example, pound bonds issued by non-British residents trading within the United Kingdom or dollar bonds issued abroad but trading in the United States. Eurobonds are denominated in a currency other than either the issuer's or the holder's. For example, a dollar denominated bond sold by a German issuer in the New York market is a foreign bond; if the bond was sold in the London market, it would be called a Eurobond. Some Eurobonds are payable in a basket of currencies, which is an artificial standard of value representing many currencies; others have clauses permitting payment to be made in one of a list of currencies. These instruments may help the borrower, the lender, or both to diversify some of their exchange risk. They are international assets in every respect: They have no natural home and no single associated currency of denomination.

Eurobonds are distinct from domestic and foreign bonds in a number of ways. First, they are generally sold to multinational investors from many countries. Second, they are usually sold by multinational syndicates. Because they are denominated in many currencies and sometimes in baskets of currencies, Eurobonds afford international investors the flexibility to choose the currency of denomination for their holdings. This feature is a unique and major advantage of the Eurobond market, since otherwise investors would need to deal simultaneously in many domestic bond markets to enjoy the same gain from diversification. This last attribute has been a major element in the rapid growth of the Eurobond market, as has the ability of borrowers to reduce the costs of issuing their debt by avoiding some registration expenses.

Table 38.6 shows that international bond issues increased from $34 billion in 1977 to nearly $76 billion in 1982. Eurobond issues have increased much more rapidly; as a result, their share doubled between 1972 and 1982, from about one-third to two-thirds of all new international bond issues.

Eurobonds

Eurobonds should not be confused with Euroloans issued by banks in the Eurocurrency market. Eurobonds are held directly by lenders, while Euroloans are intermediated by the banking system. A Eurobond holder has a direct claim on the borrower. A Eurodeposit holder has a claim on a bank, which itself has a claim on the borrower to whom the bank has loaned funds. The Eurobond market is much smaller than the Eurocurrency market.

Eurobond markets have existed since the late 1950s, but they received a major boost from the U.S. interest equalization tax, which was passed to counteract U.S. balance-of-payments problems in 1963 and remained in effect until after fixed exchange rates were discarded in 1973. The tax applied to American holders of foreign securities; this encouraged borrowers, especially multinational corporations, to sell their debt, including dollar debt, to non-U.S. residents. By the time the tax was eliminated in 1974, the Eurobond market was already well established.

Eurobonds are usually sold (placed) by multinational syndicates of banks and other financial institutions. The bonds are generally sold simultaneously to investors worldwide, most going to countries other than those of either the borrower or the lender. The bond purchasers (lenders) often hold the bonds in nonresident investment accounts. Table 38.7 shows that borrowers include corporations, governments, government agencies, and international organizations. U.S. corporations have represented a small fraction of this total; in 1982, U.S. company debt represented only about one-fourth of the total new Eurobond issues. However, the dollar is still the dominant currency of denomination for Eurobonds. Table 38.8 shows that more than three-fourths of all Eurobond issues in 1982 were dollar denominated.

The terms on Eurobonds can be deceptive. The interest is often quoted as a margin (spread) over LIBOR, and the rate is adjusted every few months as interest rates change. The quoted spreads are often small, but it is important to observe that the borrowers bear the interest-rate risk for these variable rate loans. In addition, the low spreads do not include the various fees that the participating banks charge. These include commitment fees and management fees that can add 100 to 150 basis points to the cost of the loan. The spread and fees depend on the borrower's credit standing and the term of the loan. It is uncommon for spreads to exceed 125 basis points and most are under 100 basis points. Governments can often borrow at 30 to 80 basis points above LIBOR.

The Eurobond markets are independent of the Eurocurrency markets, but they have evolved for similar reasons and perform similar functions, permitting international borrowers and lenders to transact with very little governmental

TABLE 38.7   New Eurobond Issues, by Category of Borrower

(U.S. dollars in millions)

Category of Borrower	1973	1974	1975	1976	1977	1978	1979	1980	1981	1982
					AMOUNT					
U.S. companies	$ 874	$ 110	$ 268	$ 435	$ 1,130	$ 1,122	$ 2,872	$ 4,107	$ 6,178	$12,596
Foreign companies	1,309	640	2,903	5,277	7,347	4,540	7,183	9,032	12,882	13,231
State enterprises	947	542	3,123	3,930	4,667	3,291	4,524	5,839	7,496	13,529
Governments	659	482	1,658	2,228	2,936	3,643	2,433	3,045	2,629	7,107
International organizations	404	360	615	2,186	1,691	1,529	1,714	1,947	2,431	3,376
Total	$4,193	$2,134	$8,567	$14,056	$17,771	$14,125	$18,726	$23,970	$31,616	$49,839
					PERCENTAGE					
U.S. companies	20.8%	5.2%	3.1%	3.1%	6.4%	7.9%	15.3%	17.1%	19.5%	25.3%
Foreign companies	31.2	30.0	33.9	37.5	41.3	32.1	38.4	37.7	40.7	26.5
State enterprises	22.6	25.4	36.5	28.0	26.3	23.3	24.2	24.4	23.7	27.1
Governments	15.7	22.6	19.4	15.9	16.5	25.8	13.0	12.7	8.3	14.3
International organizations	9.6	16.9	7.2	15.6	9.5	10.8	9.2	8.1	7.7	6.8
Total	100.0%	100.0%	100.0%	100.0%	100.0%	100.0%	100.0%	100.0%	100.0%	100.0%

Source: Morgan Guaranty Trust Company, *International Financial Markets*

TABLE 38.8   Denomination of New Eurobond Issues

(U.S. dollars in millions)

Currency	1973	1974	1975	1976	1977	1978	1979	1980	1981	1982
				AMOUNT						
U.S. dollar	$2,447	$ 996	$3,738	$ 8,932	$11,627	$ 7,290	$12,565	$16,427	$26,830	$42,930
Deutsche mark	1,025	344	2,278	2,661	4,131	5,251	3,626	3,607	1,277	2,487
Dutch guilder	194	381	719	502	452	394	531	1,043	529	645
Canadian dollar	0	60	558	1,407	655	0	425	279	634	1,181
European composite unit	99	174	371	99	28	165	253	65	309	1,301
Other	428	179	903	455	878	1,025	1,326	2,549	2,037	1,295
Total	$4,193	$2,134	$8,567	$14,056	$17,771	$14,125	$18,726	$23,970	$31,616	$49,839
				PERCENTAGE						
U.S. dollar	58.4%	46.7%	43.6%	63.5%	65.4%	51.6%	67.1%	68.5%	84.9%	86.1%
Deutsche mark	24.4	16.1	26.6	18.9	23.2	37.2	19.4	15.0	4.0	5.0
Dutch guilder	4.6	17.9	8.4	3.6	2.5	2.8	2.8	4.4	1.7	1.3
Canadian dollar	0.0	2.8	6.5	10.0	3.7	0.0	2.3	1.2	2.0	2.4
European composite unit	2.4	8.2	4.3	0.7	0.2	1.2	1.4	0.3	1.0	2.6
Other	10.2	8.4	10.5	3.2	4.9	7.3	7.1	10.6	6.4	2.6
Total	100.0%	100.0%	100.0%	100.0%	100.0%	100.0%	100.0%	100.0%	100.0%	100.0%

Source: Morgan Guaranty Trust Company, *International Financial Markets*

interference. The very stringent reporting requirements of the Securities Act of 1933, and the costs that attend meeting these requirements, are largely avoided in the Euromarkets. In addition, most Eurobonds are in bearer form, and there is no withholding of taxes due on Eurobond interest.

Normally, 30 percent of U.S. interest payments on bonds is withheld for income taxes. In order to enjoy relief from tax withholding, U.S. firms that wish to issue Eurobonds currently must establish financing subsidiaries. If a U.S. corporation intends to use Eurobond-derived funds outside of the United States, to avoid withholding tax it is sufficient to establish a U.S.-registered foreign income corporation. If the funds are destined to be used within the United States, however, U.S. corporations virtually always establish a financing subsidiary located in the Netherlands Antilles (N.A.), a group of islands off the coast of northern South America.

The arrangement works as follows: The N.A. subsidiary of a U.S. corporation issues Eurobonds under the parent's guarantee and then lends the proceeds back to the parent. Interest payments from the parent to the subsidiary are exempt from U.S. withholding under the terms of the tax treaty between the United States and the Netherlands Antilles. These interest payments are then passed on by the subsidiary to the bondholders. Interest payments from the subsidiary to the bondholders are also exempt, since they are made by a non-U.S. corporation.

Under current rules, an N.A. subsidiary must meet certain requirements to qualify for this favorable treatment:

1 It must be independent of the parent. It must have a separate Board of Directors, and the parent and subsidiary cannot commingle funds in the same bank account.

2 It must be more than a corporate shell; thus there must be reasonable equity in the subsidiary.

3 It must pay N.A. corporate income taxes, but these taxes can then be treated as a credit toward U.S. corporate taxes by the parent.

The U.S. Treasury has been increasingly anxious to end the operations of N.A. subsidiaries in recent years, since they result in a drain on U.S. tax revenues. The Treasury is constrained, however, because many foreigners would simply refuse to purchase Eurobonds issued by U.S. corporations if taxes were withheld. Representatives of the United States and the Netherlands Antilles have been meeting to revise the existing tax treaty, but the ultimate result of these meetings is still in doubt.

Growth in the international financial markets, and particularly in the Eurobond markets, has brought forth new and sophisticated instruments, such as Euro-commercial paper, floating rate issues, and warrant-attached issues. Other in-novative ideas unique to the international markets are multiple-currency bonds and bonds issued in a basket of currencies.

Although most Eurobonds are still single-currency issues, multiple-currency and basket-currency bonds are growing in importance as Table 38.9 documents. A multiple-currency bond is payable in one of a number of currencies, at the lender's discretion. Obviously the lender will request payment in whichever currency has appreciated the most when the bond becomes payable. In doing

TABLE 38.9   International Bond Issues Denominated in Currency Cocktails

(U.S. dollars in millions)

International Bond Issues Denominated In:	1973	1974	1975	1976	1977	1978	1979	1980	1981	1982
Arab currency-related unit (ARCRU)	—	$ 12.0	—	—	—	—	—	—	—	—
European composite unit (EURCO)	$ 64.7	67.9	—	—	—	—	—	—	—	—
European currency unit (ECU)	—	—	$ 36.8	—	—	—	—	—	$236.1	$823.4
European unit of account (EUA)	99.9	168.4	390.9	$83.8	$33.5	$202.8	$305.8	$79.8	125.5	12.3
Special drawing rights (SDR)	—	—	173.0	—	—	32.1	106.6	19.6	386.1	—
Total	$164.6	$248.3	$600.7	$83.8	$33.5	$234.9	$412.4	$99.4	$747.7	$835.7

Source: Organization for Economic Cooperation and Development, *Financial Market Trends*

so, the lender not only avoids exchange rate risk, but even profits from changes in the exchange rate at the expense of the borrower.

For basket-currency bonds, on the other hand, the denomination of the repayment is set before the loan is made. Currency baskets, such as the European currency unit and special drawing right, are artificial measures of value comprising many currencies. Table 38.9 shows the composition of these two "currency cocktails." Denominating a bond in a basket of currencies permits both borrower and lender to diversify away some of the exchange risk that attends issuing liabilities denominated in foreign currencies or holding assets denominated in foreign currencies. Exchange risk could be diversified by holding and issuing portfolios of differently denominated bonds, but currency-basket issues simplify the process. Since the foreign-exchange markets have proved highly turbulent in the flexible rate period, the advantages of such diversification are obvious.

THE STRUCTURE OF INTERNATIONAL EXCHANGE AND INTEREST RATES

The most important determinants of interest rates in international financial markets are rates in the domestic markets. Only capital controls, tax treatment, and regulatory differences permit interest differences to exist between otherwise identical assets trading onshore and offshore. Such influences are not important for most currencies. It follows that different prices or returns between assets traded on the international markets and similar assets trading in domestic markets must come from the different tax, regulatory, or risk characteristics among these assets. Arbitrage between domestic and foreign markets would quickly eliminate unreasonable rate differentials should they appear. Differences do exist, however. In the Euromarkets, for example, deposit rates can simultaneously be higher and loan rates lower than comparable domestic rates because of tax and regulatory differences among markets.

If all the world's investors were risk-neutral, all assets would be perfect substitutes. Then there would be only one (after-tax) interest rate for all assets. But in actuality investors are not risk-neutral. The return to any asset can be divided into the "pure" interest rate and a risk premium proportional to the asset's systematic risk — that portion of the asset's risk that does not vanish when it is held in a well-diversified portfolio of assets. The risk premiums in international markets derive from the following (overlapping) sources:

1 Is the asset onshore or offshore? This may be important (a) because governments may guarantee onshore assets (as the Federal Deposit Insurance Corporation guarantees bank deposits in the United States) and (b) because the offshore market may be perceived as being riskier, since it often is distinguished by the absence of government controls, regulations, and reserve requirements.

2 In what currency is the asset denominated? The interest rates for an asset denominated in a currency that is expected to depreciate will be higher than the rate for a comparable asset denominated in an appreciating currency. The holder of a foreign asset receives a total return — measured in units of his home currency — composed of interest plus any changes in the exchange rate. Strong currencies

often are associated with countries with low expected future inflation. Figure 38.4 shows that low inflation countries also tend to have low interest rates. If there is a risk of inflation or exchange rate depreciation for other reasons, interest rates will be high.

3 What is the maturity of the asset? The term structure of interest rates describes the relationship between yield and maturity (or, more strictly, the related concept of duration). Longer-term assets are more sensitive to changes in interest rates, and may therefore be seen as riskier than short-term assets. In addition, longer-term interest rates incorporate expectations of future short-term rates. These influences operate equally in domestic and international markets.

Foreign and domestic assets are clearly substitutable to some degree for most investors. As a result, interest rates in different countries are interdependent. Interest rates in different countries are also linked to exchange rates. The interest rate and exchange rate relationship between similar assets denominated in different currencies is captured by the concepts of "closed" (covered) and "open" (uncovered) interest-rate parity.

Closed Interest Rate Parity

Closed parity, also called covered parity, is a relationship between interest rates in two countries and the forward and spot exchange rates for their currencies. It is an arbitrage condition, and so must hold as long as assets can be freely traded. According to closed interest parity, the forward premium or discount equals the interest differential. The forward premium or discount is the annualized percentage difference between the spot and forward exchange rates.

Assume that the interest rate received for depositing deutsche marks (DM) for one year is 9 percent, while a dollar denominated deposit earns 7 percent. A lender in the United States could deposit his funds in the dollar account, or he could first convert them to deutsche marks and thus earn a 2 percent bonus. Should he do so, he might lose not only the 2 percent but a great deal more, should the deutsche mark decline against the dollar over the next year. To protect himself against any future changes in the exchange rate, the investor might choose to sell his deutsche marks forward for dollars. This guarantees the number of dollars his deposit will produce one year hence.

These two investments — one a dollar deposit, the other a deutsche mark deposit combined with a forward contract to sell deutsche marks one year in the future for dollars — have equal risks. They must therefore have equal expected returns. It follows that the dollar will sell at a 2 percent premium in the forward market, so that a transactor must pay or give up 2 percent of the current exchange rate in order to sell deutsche marks forward for dollars. If the spot exchange rate is DM2.40/dollar, the one-year forward rate will be 2.448 (2.40 × 1.02).

The forward discount or premium on Eurodeposits of various maturities, compared with the associated interest rate differential on a dollar deposit, is shown for a typical day in Table 38.10. Exact correspondence between the discount or premiums on the forward exchange is not to be expected, since the quotes are not exactly simultaneous and differences insufficient to warrant

TABLE 38.10   Interest Rate Differentials and Forward Exchange Premiums Compared, May 13, 1983

	United States	Canada	Germany	Japan	United Kingdom	Switzerland	France
One month							
Eurodeposit rate	8.750	9.000	4.750	6.063	10.313	4.125	13.000
Difference from U.S. rate	—	-0.250	4.000	2.688	-1.563	4.625	-4.250
Forward dollar discount*	—	-0.39	4.56	2.89	-1.69	5.03	-4.07
Three months							
Eurodeposit rate	8.813	9.000	4.938	6.125	10.188	4.375	14.000
Difference from U.S. rate	—	-0.188	3.875	2.688	1.375	-4.438	-5.188
Forward dollar discount*	—	-0.26	3.89	2.72	1.33	-4.62	-4.83
Six months							
Eurodeposit rate	8.875	9.125	4.063	6.125	10.188	4.375	16.250
Difference from U.S. rate	—	-0.025	4.813	2.750	-1.313	4.500	-7.375
Forward dollar discount*	—	-0.28	3.78	2.65	-1.14	4.44	-6.92
Twelve months							
Eurodeposit rate	9.698	9.313	5.375	6.250	10.188	4.313	17.625
Difference from U.S. rate	—	-0.375	4.313	3.438	0.500	-5.375	-7.938
Forward dollar discount*	—	-0.27	3.43	2.58	0.91	-4.49	-7.60

* Percentage per annum. If covered interest arbitrage holds exactly, the forward dollar discount should equal the corresponding interest rate difference.

arbitrage will generally exist. But the relationship is very good despite these problems; the largest discrepancy is less than one half of 1 percent per year.

Open Interest Rate Parity

Closed interest parity is an arbitrage condition, but open or uncovered interest rate parity, first described by Irving Fisher early in the 20th century, is not. Therefore, open interest parity need not hold with nearly the same precision. Open interest parity is a condition that relates the observed interest differential to the expected future change in the exchange rate.

Returning to the previous example, a depositor has the choice of earning 9 percent from a deutsche mark deposit or 7 percent from a dollar deposit. If he anticipates the deutsche mark will decline by exactly 2 percent relative to the dollar over the relevant period, his anticipated return from either deposit is the same. According to open interest parity, interest rates in various countries will be bid up or down until total anticipated returns, including expected exchange rate changes, are equal in all currencies. Thus, the interest differential must be a measure of the market's expected change in the exchange rate. In the example, according to open interest parity the dollar is expected to appreciate by 2 percent against the deutsche mark over the next year.

Open interest parity is only valid if investors are indifferent to risk. Investing in deutsche marks at 9 percent is not the same as investing in dollars at 7 percent, even if the exchange rate is *expected* to change by 2 percent. The former course is riskier for a U.S. investor who intends to repatriate his funds into dollars. Empirical studies present mixed evidence but many have found that the interest differential or forward exchange rate premium or discount is not an unbiased predictor of the change in the exchange rate, indicating that open-interest parity is not always satisfied.[4]

Term Structure

The theories of the term structure of interest rates that apply to domestic markets (described in Chapter 13) are also applicable to international financial markets. In addition, there are some interesting relationships between term structures in different markets that are important in international markets but not in domestic ones.

Recall that according to open interest parity, the interest differential between otherwise identical deposits in dollars and deutsche marks reflects the expected change in the exchange rate. Although in actuality this is not the only element that explains interest rate differences, it is the most important. A comparison of term structures in the two currencies should reveal an approximation of the market's aggregate prediction of the future course of the exchange rate for those currencies.

For example, assume the deutsche mark-to-dollar exchange rate is expected to fall over the coming year by 3 percent, reflecting an appreciation of the

---

[4] For example, see the studies by Bilson, Cornell, Jacobs, and Cumby and Obstfeld cited in the bibliography.

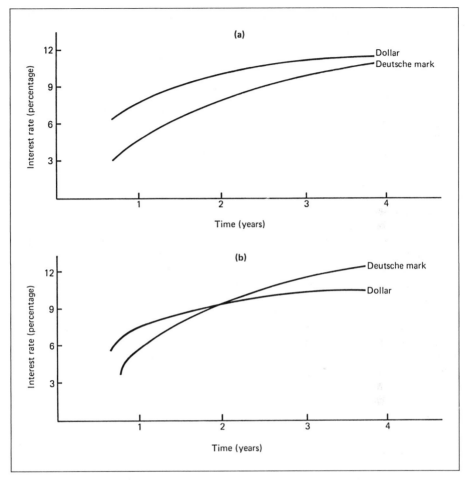

FIG. 38.5 Sample Yield Curves for Two Exchange Rate Changes: (a) One-Time Exchange Rate Change; (b) Exchange Rate Reversal

German currency. Assume further that investors do not expect the exchange rate to change thereafter.

If the one-year dollar deposit rate is 9 percent, the one-year deutsche mark deposit rate will be approximately 6 percent (open interest parity), reflecting the anticipated future strength of the deutsche mark. If a two-year dollar deposit yields 10 percent per year, or approximately 21 percent over two years, a two-year deutsche mark deposit must yield 18 percent (21 percent − 3 percent), or about 8.6 percent per year. The implied yield curves in this case are shown in Figure 38.5(a). It is observed that this case — an expected one-time-only change in the exchange rate — corresponds to gradually diminishing distances between the yield curves for dollar and deutsche mark deposits.

Many other relationships are possible. Perhaps the most interesting case corresponds to yield curves that cross, as they do in Figure 38.5(b). This illustrates a reversal of the expected exchange rate change. In the case shown, the deutsche mark is expected to be higher than its current value against the dollar over the next two years. Thereafter, the market expects the dollar to be higher than the current exchange rate against the deutsche mark.

RISKS IN INTERNATIONAL FINANCIAL MARKETS

An investor bears risk whenever the actual cash flows produced by an investment project may not equal the cash flows anticipated. Risk is generally measured by the variance of an uncertain future cash flow stream.

In general an investor can expect to increase his portfolio's return only if he is also willing to bear more risk. The implications of this fact are more complicated than is generally understood, however. One of the important techniques an investor can use to mitigate risk is to hold a diversified portfolio rather than to concentrate on one asset. The total risk attached to any asset can be partitioned into a systematic (or nondiversifiable) portion and its unsystematic (or diversifiable) risk. Since the latter can in principle be eliminated by sufficient diversification, only systematic risk enters into the market's pricing of an asset. Higher expected returns attach to assets with higher systematic, not total, risk.

It is common to classify risks by their source of origin. Some, such as interest rate risk, exist in all markets. Others, such as political risk, exist in all markets but are more important in international financial markets. Finally, there are risks such as exchange risk that are unique to the international environment.

Interest Rate Risk

Interest risk derives from mismatched maturities. Generally, a lender's liabilities (deposits held by its depositors) are of shorter term than its assets (loans to borrowers). As a result, if interest rates rise, lenders must pay higher interest to acquire funds while their interest income remains relatively fixed.

Interest risk is not unique to international financial intermediaries, and neither are the interest risk reduction tactics. A firm can avoid or reduce interest rate risk in any of the following ways: First, it can match the maturities of its obligations and assets. This is ordinarily not possible, since one of the chief functions of an intermediary is to perform maturity transformation by lending long-term and borrowing short-term. Second, banks can make variable rate rather than fixed-rate loans. Most Euroloans are quoted this way, as a fixed percentage above LIBOR, the banker's cost of funds. Third, intermediaries can hedge using the futures markets. This strategy is increasingly used by major banks.

Political Risk

All investments involve political risks, but international investments bear them in a highly magnified measure. Restrictions on the repatriation of interest or principal apply only to foreign investing, and seizure of assets — either directly or through unreasonable taxation — are often directed specifically toward foreign investors.

The vast majority of international financial transactions occur in stable environments, such as London or Singapore, where political risks are small. This is no coincidence, and the existence of such stable locations for international investing mitigates political risk. Further, much of the thrust of the research on the functioning of the financial markets in the last 20 years suggests that participants will be adequately compensated for any risks they bear. There is no reason to think that political risk differs in this regard.

Political risk is closely related to country risk, which is the risk that a sovereign borrower will be unable (or unwilling) to meet its obligations. There is very little legal action creditors can take in this instance, since there is no global civil court system that can rectify breaches of contracts made by countries. However, lenders do have some means of enforcing payment: They can threaten to deny future loans, even refusing to grant the short-term loans usually made to finance trade. This not only would deny defaulting countries access to the world's financial markets, but would also effectively deny them access to the goods markets. In addition, country loans are usually syndicated and bear cross-default clauses, according to which a default on any of the country's loans ordinarily makes all other loans immediately due. As a result, a country cannot ordinarily default against one creditor without involving all its other creditors.

Exchange Risk

Exchange risk arises when a firm or investor has a future cash flow (payable or receivable) that is denominated in a foreign currency. For financial markets, the relevant cash flows are those associated with financial assets and liabilities.

Assume that an American firm has deposited DM1 million in the Euromarket as a 60-day deposit in a London bank. If the spot exchange rate is DM2.40/dollar, the deposit is currently worth $416,667. If the exchange rate were to change to DM2.42/dollar when the 60 days have passed (quite a modest movement in the current exchange-market environment), the deposit would yield only $413,223, plus interest. On the other hand, had the deutsche mark appreciated to DM2.38/dollar over the 60 days, the deposit would have produced $420,168, plus interest. Risk — the chance of incurring a loss — also implies the opportunity to realize an unexpected gain. Exchange market movements can easily dwarf the interest paid or received on assets and liabilities in the computation of total return.

Since 1973, exchange rate movements have become increasingly important to international investors as the dollar has been permitted to float against the world's major currencies. Since then, and even more so in recent years, exchange rate variations have been so large and unpredictable that they have often dominated other sources of returns on international investments. Figure 38.1(a) shows the increased volatility of the dollar against three of the major foreign currencies in recent years.

One obvious way for an individual or firm to avoid exchange rate risk is to select the dollar as the currency in which it deposits or borrows its funds. Another is to use forward cover to eliminate currency exposure. These techniques are well known. It is less well known that by diversifying internationally and therefore accepting exchange risk, an investor may actually reduce the overall riskiness of his portfolio. Chapter 39 deals with international diversification.

CONCLUSION

This chapter has examined the operation of the international financial markets, which operate parallel to, complement, and compete with domestic financial markets.

International financial markets provide several services. Some of those services, such as intermediating between borrowers and lenders, are almost identical to those provided by domestic markets. Others, such as facilitating international diversification, duplicate services that domestic markets can provide but that can be more conveniently supplied by the international markets. Finally, the international financial markets offer some services that are unavailable in domestic markets, such as severing the political risks of assets from their exchange risks.

International financial markets have grown dramatically since World War II and now provide a global village marketplace, bringing together suppliers and users of funds on a worldwide basis. The integration and rapid growth of global financial markets continue a long historical trend that was interrupted by the World Wars and the Great Depression in the first half of the 20th century. The growth in the size and sophistication of these markets in the postwar years has more than made up for the fragmentation that occurred during the earlier period of war, economic protectionism, and isolationism.

A major boost to international trade and finance in the postwar period was the reduction in trade restrictions accomplished under the General Agreement on Tariffs and Trade. The lowered trade barriers, reinforced by rapid progress in cutting the costs of international information flows and transportation, led to the complete globalization of many markets (e.g., commodities and, significantly, financial services). During this period international trade grew faster than the global economy, generating a rapid rate of growth in the demand for international financial services.

Since the early 1970s, the growth in international trade and finance has been enhanced by the breakdown of the Bretton Woods fixed exchange rate system (the gold-based dollar). The 1970s and early 1980s was a period of high inflation and of increased risks associated with high and variable interest rates and unstable exchange rates. This much riskier international monetary regime induced producers and consumers to diversify internationally. The United States, for example, saw a doubling of the proportion of its GNP exported and imported over this period.

At the same time, the more inflationary and riskier environment released enormous creative energies in global financial markets to meet the demands of doing business in such an atmosphere. New international financial markets developed, new trade-finance products were introduced, and whole new financial industries specializing in "risk products" (e.g., financial options and futures) grew from infancy to maturity. In turn, these changes placed great stress on the regulation of financial markets, particularly in highly regulated markets such as those in the United States. The greatest stress has been placed on regulations that are anticompetitive in nature; that is, those that fix prices (e.g., Regulation Q interest ceilings) and those that bar entry either by geography (restrictions on interstate banking) or product line (restrictions on investment banking activities by commercial banks).

The inflationary and risky environment of the monetary regime ushered in over a decade ago has played a major role in shaping the global financial markets of the current period. A key question for the future, perhaps the single most important question, is whether the inflationary and financially risky environment of the recent period will continue, or whether it will be replaced by a more stable regime.

SUGGESTED READING

Adler, Michael C., and Bernard Dumas. "Portfolio Choice and the Demand for Forward Exchange." *American Economic Review* (May 1976), pp. 332–339.

Aliber, Robert Z. "Exchange Risk, Political Risk, and Investor Demand for External Currency Deposits." *Journal of Money, Credit, and Banking* (May 1975), pp. 161–179.

————. "The Interest Parity Theorem: A Reinterpretation." *Journal of Political Economy* (Dec. 1973), 1451–1459.

————. "International Banking: Growth and Regulation." *Columbia Journal of World Business* (Winter 1975).

Argy, Victor, and Zoran Hodjera. "Financial Integration and Interest Rate Linkages in Industrial Countries, 1958–71." *IMF Staff Papers* (Mar. 1973), pp. 1–73.

Awanohara, Susumu. "Does the Asia Market Serve Asia and Asean?" *Far Eastern Economic Review* (Apr. 6, 1976), pp. 65–69.

Bank for International Settlements. *Annual Reports.*

Bank of England. *Quarterly Bulletin* (various issues).

Bhattacharja, Anindya. *The Asian Dollar Market.* New York: Praeger, 1977.

Bilson, John F. "The 'Speculative Efficiency' Hypothesis." *Journal of Business,* Vol. 54, No. 3 (1981), pp. 435–451.

Campbell, Mary. "Luxembourg — City State of Finance." *The Banker* (Feb. 1975), pp. 189–195.

Cooper, Richard N. "Implications of the Euro-dollar for Monetary Policy and the U.S. Balance of Payments Deficit." *National Monetary Policies and the International Financial System,* ed. R. Z. Aliber. Chicago: University of Chicago Press, 1974.

Cornell, Bradford. "Spot Rates, Forward Rates, and Exchange Market Efficiency." *Journal of Financial Economics* (Aug. 1977), pp. 55–66.

Cumby, Robert E., and Maurice Obstfeld. "A Note on Exchange-Rate Expectations and Nominal Interest Differentials: A Test of the Fisher Hypothesis." *Journal of Finance,* Vol. 36, No. 3 (June 1981), pp. 697–703.

Dooley, Michael P. "Note on Interest Parity, Eurocurrencies, and Capital Controls." *International Finance Discussion Paper, No. 80.* Washington, D.C.: Federal Reserve Board, Feb. 1976, p. 7.

Dufey, Gunter, and Ian H. Giddy. *The International Money Market*. Englewood Cliffs, N.J.: Prentice-Hall, 1978.

Edwards, Franklin R. "The New International Banking Facility." *Columbia Journal of World Business* (Winter 1981), pp. 6–18.

Einzig, Paul. *The Euro-bond Market*. New York: St. Martin's Press, 1969.

———. *The Eurodollar System*. New York: St. Martin's Press, 1973.

"Eurodollars: Enter Commercial Paper." *Economist* (June 17, 1970), pp. 83–84.

Fisher, Irving. *The Theory of Interest*. New York: Macmillan, 1930.

Frankel, Jeffry. "The Diversifiability of Exchange Risk." *Journal of International Economics*, Vol. 9 (1979), pp. 379–393.

Franklin, Allen. "The Lender of Last Resort Facility in the Context of Multinational Banking." *Columbia Journal of World Business* (Winter 1975), pp. 120–127.

Frenkel, Jacobs. "The Forward Rate, Expectations, and the Demand for Money: The German Hyperinflation." *American Economic Review* (Sept. 1977), pp. 653–70.

Frenkel, Jacob A., and Richard M. Levich. "Covered Interest Arbitrage: Any Unexploited Profits?" *Journal of Political Economy* (Apr. 1975), p. 325.

———. "Transactions Costs and Interest Arbitrage: Tranquil Versus Turbulent Periods." *Journal of Political Economy* (Dec. 1977), pp. 1209–1226.

Friedman, Milton. "The Euro Dollar Market: Some First Principles." *Morgan Guaranty Survey* (Oct. 1969).

Friedrich, Klaus. "A Quantitative Framework for the Eurodollar System." *Princeton Studies in International Finance, No. 26*. Princeton: Princeton University Press, 1970.

Giddy, Ian H. "An Integrated Theory of Exchange Rate Equilibrium." *Journal of Financial and Quantitative Analysis* (Dec. 1976), pp. 883–892.

Goodstadt, Leo. "How Hong Kong Came of Age as a Euromarket Center." *Euromoney* (Feb. 1982), pp. 54–63.

Grauer, F. L. A., et al. "Sharing Rules and Equilibrium in an International Capital Market Under Uncertainty." *Journal of Financial Economics* (June 1976), pp. 233–257.

Hendershott, Patric H. "The Structure of International Interest Rates: The U.S. Treasury Bill Rate and the Euro-dollar Deposit Rate." *Journal of Finance* (Sept. 1967), pp. 455–465.

Hewson, John, and Eisuke Sakakibara. *The Eurocurrency Markets and Their Implications*. Lexington, Mass: D. C. Heath, 1975.

Hoffmeyer, Eric. "Monetary Cooperation and the Euromarkets." *Euromoney* (Sept. 1975), pp. 70–74.

Jacobs, Rodney. "The Effect of Errors in Variables on Tests for a Risk Premium in Forward Exchange Rates." *Journal of Finance*, Vol. 37, No. 3 (June 1982), pp. 667–677.

Kaserman, David L. "The Forward Exchange Rate: Its Determination and Behavior as a Predictor of the Future Spot Rate." *Proceedings of the American Statistical Association* (1973), pp. 417–422.

Kindleberger, Charles P. "The Formation of Financial Centers: A Study in Comparative Economic History." *Princeton Studies in International Finance, No. 36*. Princeton, N.J.: Princeton University Press, 1974.

Kwack, Sung. "The Structure of International Interest Rates: An Extension of Hendershott's Tests." *Journal of Finance* (Sept. 1971), pp. 897–900.

Lee, Boyden E. "The Eurodollar Multiplier." *Journal of Finance* (Sept. 1973), pp. 867–874.

Levy, H., and M. Sarnat. "International Diversification of Investment Portfolios." *American Economic Review* (Sept. 1970).

Lichtenstein, Cynthia C. "U.S. Banks and the Eurocurrency Markets: The Regulatory Structure." *The Banking Law Journal* (June 1982), pp. 484–511.

Little, Jane S. "The Impact of the Eurodollar Market on the Effectiveness of Monetary Policy in the United States and Abroad." *New England Economic Review* (Mar.–Apr. 1975), pp. 3–19.

Lutz, Friedrich A. "The Euro-Currency System." *Banca Nazionale del Lavoro, Quarterly Review* (Sept. 1974), pp. 183–200.

Machlup, Fritz. "The Eurodollar System and Its Control." *International Monetary Problems*, eds. Fritz Machlup, et al. Washington, D.C.: American Enterprise Institute, 1972.

Marston, Richard C. "Interest Arbitrage in the Eurocurrency Market." *European Economic Review* (Jan. 1976), pp. 1–13.

Mathis, F. John, ed. *Offshore Lending by U.S. Commercial Banks*. Washington, D.C.: Robert Morris Associates, 1975.

———. *Offshore Lending by U.S. Commercial Banks*, 2nd ed. Washington, D.C.: Bankers' Association for Foreign Trade, 1981.

Mayer, Helmut W. "The BIS Concept of the Eurocurrency Market." *Euromoney* (May 1976), pp. 60–66.

———. "Some Theoretical Problems Relating to the Euro-Dollar Market." *Princeton Essays in International Finance, No. 79*. Princeton, N.J.: Princeton University Press, 1970.

McKinnon, Ronald. *Money in International Exchange*. New York: Oxford University Press, 1979.

Monetary Authority of Singapore. *Monthly Digest of Statistics*.

Morgan Guaranty Trust Co. *World Financial Markets* (monthly publication).

Niehans, Jurg, and John Hewson. "The Eurodollar Market and Monetary Theory." *Journal of Money, Credit and Banking* (Feb. 1976), pp. 1–27.

Officer, Lawrence H., and Thomas D. Willett. "The Covered-Arbitrage Schedule: A Critical Survey of Recent Developments." *Journal of Money, Credit and Banking* (Mar. 1970), pp. 247–257.

Park, Yoon S. *The Euro-bond Market: Function and Structure*. New York: Praeger, 1974.

Ruckdeschel, Fred B. "Risk in Foreign and Domestic Lending Activities of U.S. Banks." *Columbia Journal of World Business* (Winter 1975), pp. 40–54.

Santomero, Anthony M. "The Error-Learning Hypothesis and the Term Structure of Interest Rates in Eurodollars." *Journal of Finance* (June 1975), pp. 773–784.

Solnick, Bruno H. "An Equilibrium Model of the International Capital Market." *Journal of Economic Theory* (Aug. 1974), pp. 500–524.

———. *European Capital Markets*. Lexington, Mass.: D.C. Heath, 1973.

"South East Asia: The Dragon Awakes." *Euromoney* (May 1976 supplement).

Stem, Carl H., et al., eds. *Eurocurrencies and the International Monetary System.* Washington, D.C.: American Enterprise Institute, 1976, p. 308.

Stulz, Rene. "The Forward Exchange Rate and Macroeconomics." *Journal of International Economics*, Vol. 12 (1982), pp. 285–299.

Van Horne, James C. *The Function and Analysis of Capital Market Rates.* Engelwood Cliffs, N.J.: Prentice-Hall, 1970.

Westerfield, Janice M. "An Examination of Foreign Exchange Risk Under Fixed and Floating Regimes." *Journal of International Economics* (May 1977), pp. 181–200.

Willms, Manfred. "Money Creation in the Euro-Currency Market." *Weltwirtschaftliches Archiv,* Vol. 112 (1976), pp. 201–230.

Yassukovich, Stanislas. "Could the Euromarkets Leave London?" *Euromoney* (Oct. 1981), pp. 240–253.

Yeager, Leland. *International Monetary Relations: Theory, History and Policy.* New York: Harper and Row, 1976.

39

International Portfolio Diversification

V. R. ERRUNZA

International diversification has general appeal to the investment community. First, the limited risk reduction potential at home, due to generally high correlations among security return distributions within an economy, suggests international diversification as a natural next step. Second, performance across various national markets has varied significantly during most time periods, thereby providing an opportunity for improving investment results. Finally, since international capital markets are not fully integrated, it is possible to improve the reward-risk ratio by selective global management of the investment portfolio. Potential improvement in reward-risk ratio can result from low return correlations among securities from different markets, investment in foreign markets that outperform home markets, or selective investment in markets that command a higher reward-risk ratio. Examples of the latter markets include those which are not fully integrated within the world capital market, that is, smaller developed markets and many of the newly emerging markets.

Even though investment portfolios in recent years have become more international, an average portfolio consists primarily of domestic assets with some diversification into developed country (DC) markets and negligible investments in securities of less developed countries (LDCs).[1] This reluctance to hold a truly global portfolio can be traced to currency and political risk; capital controls; the less developed nature of foreign markets, implying among other things inadequate liquidity, depth, regulation, information, and efficiency; and perceived inordinate transaction costs.

ADVANTAGES OF INTERNATIONAL DIVERSIFICATION

The National Factor

Pioneering works of Markowitz (1959) and Tobin (1958) demonstrated that holding a diversified portfolio of risky assets leads to substantial risk reduction without sacrifice of expected return. However, the potential is limited by the generally high correlations among return distributions of assets within an economy. The proportion of the risk (measured by return variance) that is nondiversifiable (i.e., marketwide risk) for a typical U.S. security is about 30 percent. As reported in Table 39.1, estimates of systematic risk for other countries are generally higher. The relatively higher systematic risk for DCs and LDCs vis-à-vis the United States reflect lower diversification opportunities on non-U.S. markets. This can be attributed to a smaller number of regularly traded securities that constitute each market index, and the less diverse nature of firms that reflect a narrower economic base.[2]

The World Factor

To the extent that world economies are not completely tied together, the potential exists for further risk reduction through international diversification. A large part of the total risk that is systematic in the domestic sense can be eliminated in the global context. Table 39.2 reports the systematic risk for various markets based on two different world indexes. Even though from a theoretical viewpoint as well as for practical management reasons the world index should be capitalization-weighted, in general investors do not and would not hold a market-capitalization-weighted world portfolio, in view of the situation that world markets are not fully integrated. They would tend toward a portfolio heavy with domestic assets. Since the U.S. market dominates a market-capitalization-based world portfolio, the other extreme case, that is, the equally weighted portfolio, illustrates gains from international diversification under widely differing

---

[1] The terms *less developed countries' markets* and *emerging markets* are used interchangeably.

[2] Data on LDCs is based on one major stock exchange of the country. For full details on LDC data, see V. Errunza, "Emerging Markets — A New Opportunity for Improving Global Performance," *Financial Analysts Journal* (Sept.–Oct. 1983), pp. 51–58.

TABLE 39.1   National Systematic Risk Estimates

Argentina[a]	0.56	Japan[b]	0.27
Australia[b]	0.34	Korea[a]	0.40
Austria[b]	0.37	Mexico[a]	0.50
Belgium[b]	0.49	Netherlands[b]	0.40
Brazil[a]	0.43	Norway[b]	0.46
Chile[a]	0.50	Spain[b]	0.40
Denmark[b]	0.31	Sweden[b]	0.42
France[b]	0.46	Switzerland[b]	0.51
Germany[b]	0.44	Thailand[a]	0.60
Greece[a]	0.41	United Kingdom[b]	0.37
India[a]	0.42	Zimbabwe[a]	0.32
Italy[b]	0.43		

Note: The figures represent the average proportion of variance of individual
security returns explained by the national index of the country whose
securities are being assessed.
(a) 1976–1980
(b) 1969–1973

Sources: Vihang Errunza and Etienne Losq, "International Asset Pricing Under
Mild Segmentation: Theory and Test," Working Paper, McGill University, Montreal (Dec. 1982); Donald Lessard, "World, Country and Industry Relationships in Equity Returns," *Financial Analysts Journal*
(Jan.–Feb. 1976)

weighting schemes. A small portion of the domestic nondiversifiable risk is
systematic for all countries in the world context. For most emerging markets,
the national risk almost evaporates in terms of a global portfolio, thereby
suggesting that investors hold a very broad portfolio.

Correlation Coefficients

The potential diversification gains by assessing return correlations among various
markets can be probed as follows. Traditionally, low correlations among markets
have provided the rationale for diversifying internationally. Table 39.3 reports
pairwise correlations among DCs and LDCs. Although correlations among DCs
are not very high, over time they have increased due to greater economic
synchronization. On the other hand, the emerging markets are generally much
less correlated with those of the United States and other DCs. The results thus
confirm previous findings that investors should hold a global portfolio that
includes the emerging markets.

Realized Returns

So far in this chapter only the risk reduction potential of international diversification has been looked at, but what about returns? Given low correlations,

TABLE 39.2   Proportion of Variance of National Indices Explained by Alternate World Factors

	Equally Weighted	Market Capitalization Weighted
Emerging markets		
Argentina	0.07	—
Brazil	0.07	—
Chile	0.01	0.03
Greece	0.10	0.02
Hong Kong	0.32	0.27
Jordan	0.14	0.19
Korea	0.05	0.07
Mexico	0.20	0.13
Singapore	0.46	0.38
Spain	0.13	0.06
Thailand	0.01	0.06
Zimbabwe	0.01	—
Developed markets		
Australia	0.40	0.03
Austria	0.34	0.11
Belgium	0.45	0.29
Canada	0.39	0.52
Denmark	0.34	0.24
France	0.39	0.39
Germany	0.33	0.21
Italy	0.21	0.15
Japan	0.28	0.25
Netherlands	0.44	0.48
Norway	0.25	0.21
Sweden	0.18	0.16
Switzerland	0.47	0.29
United Kingdom	0.38	0.42
United States	0.22	0.78

Source: Vihang Errunza, "Emerging Markets — A New Opportunity for Improving Global Portfolio Performance," *Financial Analysts Journal* (Sept.–Oct. 1983)

investors would generally be willing to accept a somewhat lower return from a foreign market vis-à-vis a domestic market, unless the volatility of foreign markets more than offset the risk reduction benefits. As Table 39.4 reports, more than two-thirds of the markets had higher realized returns than the United States during 1976–1980. This result is not new or surprising; similar findings have appeared frequently in the literature. Thus, in addition to risk reduction benefits, international diversification also leads to higher returns — a no-miss situation.

Global Portfolio Performance

How would volatility of foreign markets affect the reward-risk ratio? Table 39.5 reports performance of various internationally diversified portfolios constructed from respective national indexes on an equally weighted and market-capitalization-weighted basis. There is evidence of increasing benefits in terms of risk reduction and higher returns as more markets are included in the portfolio. The benefits decline as one moves from equal weighting to market capitalization weighting due to the lower capitalizations of most non-U.S. markets, especially the emerging markets (see the section on Foreign Securities Markets). A portfolio of developed countries, with Mexico, Korea, Hong Kong, Singapore, and Spain is included in Table 39.5, since investments in these emerging markets are feasible and are included in some of the available funds.

INTERNATIONAL ASSET PRICING MODELS

Two approaches to international asset pricing models (IAPM) have been used primarily: Markets are fully integrated; and markets are segmented due to barriers to portfolio investment flows. We discuss major contributions briefly under each of these approaches. (Original references should be consulted for a complete discussion.)

Integrated Markets Approach

In his pioneering work, Solnik (1974b) developed an IAPM under a set of simplifying assumptions of perfect capital markets, homogeneous investor expectations, unlimited short selling, no transaction costs, no capital controls, unlimited borrowing and lending at the risk-free rate in each country, and investor consumption limited to home country.

Solnik ignores home currency inflation and shows that

> All investors will be indifferent between choosing portfolios from the original assets or from three funds, namely:
> — A portfolio of stocks hedged against exchange risk (the market portfolio)
> — A portfolio of bonds, speculative in the exchange risk dimension
> — The risk-free asset of their own country (Solnik, 1974b, p. 520)

TABLE 39.3   Correlation Coefficients — Monthly U.S. Dollar Total Returns, 1976–1980

	United States	Japan	Canada	United Kingdom	Germany	Spain	France	Hong Kong	Singapore
United States	1.0								
Japan	0.151	1.0							
Canada	0.641	0.144	1.0						
United Kingdom	0.380	0.326	0.459	1.0					
Germany	0.230	0.415	0.258	0.358	1.0				
Spain	0.110	0.232	0.188	0.258	0.111	1.0			
France	0.369	0.533	0.493	0.507	0.428	0.152	1.0		
Hong Kong	0.274	0.434	0.218	0.390	0.344	0.217	0.330	1.0	
Singapore	0.419	0.446	0.423	0.404	0.343	0.265	0.371	0.732	1.0
Argentina	−0.019	−0.109	0.244	−0.129	−0.229	0.025	−0.070	−0.006	−0.026
Brazil	−0.033	0.022	0.052	0.221	0.012	−0.108	0.112	0.064	0.166
Chile	−0.176	−0.067	−0.041	−0.170	−0.048	−0.078	−0.137	−0.148	−0.086
Greece	−0.009	0.224	0.016	0.294	0.370	0.041	0.040	0.146	0.216
Jordan	0.342	0.245	0.369	0.255	0.213	0.116	0.420	0.051	0.266
Korea	0.229	0.169	0.133	0.205	0.319	−0.173	0.245	−0.079	0.114
Mexico	0.223	0.224	0.210	0.406	0.199	0.199	0.187	0.254	0.278
Thailand	−0.358	0.083	−0.307	0.038	0.277	−0.046	−0.021	−0.097	−0.024
Zimbabwe	0.002	−0.034	0.040	−0.043	0.037	0.266	−0.099	−0.005	0.081

Source: Vihang Errunza, "Emerging Markets — A New Opportunity for Improving Global Portfolio Performance," *Financial Analysts Journal* (Sept.–Oct. 1983)

In a manner analogous to the capital asset pricing model (CAPM) (see Chapter 14), Solnik shows that a security's risk premium is proportional to its international systematic risk. Grauer, Litzenberger, and Stehle (1976) derive closed-form valuation equations assuming individuals have multiplicative utility functions with consumption preferences defined over many commodities. An international Sharpe-Lintner capital asset pricing model is derived which states that "without loss of generality, the real rate of return on the *j*th asset may be decomposed into a component perfectly correlated with the real rate of return on the international market portfolio and a component uncorrelated with the real rate of return on that portfolio." (Grauer, Litzenberger, and Stehle, 1976, p. 241) The preceding statement also holds for returns in nominal terms.

Stulz (1981b) develops an intertemporal model of international asset pricing that allows consumption opportunity set to differ across countries. The "consumption opportunity set" is defined as the set of goods available for consumption, current prices, and the distribution of their future prices. In the spirit of preceding IAPMs, Stulz (1981b, p. 397) derives the equilibrium pricing relationship: "The expected excess real return of a risky asset is proportional to the covariance of the home currency return of that asset with changes in world real consumption rate."

Argentina	Brazil	Chile	Greece	Jordan	Korea	Mexico	Thailand	Zimbabwe
1.0								
0.214	1.0							
0.186	0.071	1.0						
0.006	0.100	0.060	1.0					
−0.168	0.114	0.040	0.183	1.0				
−0.228	0.097	−0.037	−0.027	0.079	1.0			
0.081	0.071	−0.051	0.038	0.113	0.040	1.0		
−0.216	−0.090	−0.152	0.219	−0.158	0.102	−0.066	1.0	
−0.024	−0.021	0.105	0.079	−0.242	−0.168	−0.040	−0.132	1.0

In a recent study, Adler and Dumas (1983) assume investors' consumption preferences to be nationally heterogeneous with maximization of time-additive von Neumann-Morgenstern expected utility of lifetime consumption. They show that "every investor in the world holds a combination of the universal logarithmic portfolio with weight α and his personalized hedge portfolio which constitutes the best protection against inflation as he perceives it, with weight $1 - \alpha$." (Adler and Dumas, 1983, p. 27)

The logarithmic portfolio is independent of the behavior of commodity prices and hence is identical for every investor. It implies that the (M-V) efficiency frontiers of all investors have one common point. The personalized hedge portfolio of an investor is the one with a nominal rate of return having the highest correlation with his perceived inflation rate. This second portfolio is therefore investor specific.

Empirical verifications of IAPMs under full integration have been inconclusive. Solnik's (1974a) test results for European securities are weakly consistent with predictions of his model. Stehle (1977) developed sophisticated procedures to test the competing hypotheses of integrated versus segmented world capital markets. He finds weak support in favor of international pricing of New York Stock Exchange (NYSE) stocks.

TABLE 39.4 Realized Returns — U.S. Dollar Terms, 1976–1980*

Emerging Markets	Annualized Market Return	Developed Markets	Annualized Market Return
Argentina	97.3%	Australia	20.0%
Brazil	4.8	Austria	5.5
Chile	122.6	Belgium	0.9
Greece	3.2	Canada	17.0
Hong Kong	41.4	Denmark	1.7
Jordan	40.4	France	10.3
Korea	30.3	Germany	5.2
Mexico	47.0	Italy	13.8
Singapore	29.8	Japan	19.7
Spain	−18.6	Netherlands	11.3
Thailand	21.5	Norway	16.6
Zimbabwe	30.4	Sweden	1.7
		Switzerland	11.0
		United Kingdom	18.8
		United States	8.0

* Returns are annualized by compounding mean monthly returns; they are not adjusted for withholding or any other taxes. Official exchange rates as reported by the International Monetary Fund are used for conversion.

Source: Vihang Errunza, "Emerging Markets — A New Opportunity for Improving Global Portfolio Performance," *Financial Analysts Journal* (Sept.–Oct. 1983), p. 53

TABLE 39.5 Gains From Diversification, 1976–1980

(U.S. dollars)

Portfolio	Number of Countries in Portfolio	Equally Weighted Portfolios		Market Capitalization Weighted Portfolios	
		Annual Return	Monthly Standard Deviation	Annual Return	Monthly Standard Deviation
United States	1	8.0%	4.15%	8.0%	4.15%
Developed countries	15	10.6	3.68	11.5	3.51
Developed countries Mexico, Korea, Hong Kong, Singapore, Spain	20	13.6	3.72	12.1	3.51
Developed countries and 12 emerging markets (world portfolio)	27	19.6	3.05	12.5	3.46

Notes: (1) Results on a U.S. portfolio are based on U.S. index as published by Capital International S.A., Geneva, Switzerland.

(2) For a list of 12 emerging markets and 15 developed countries, see Table 39.4.

Source: Vihang Errunza, "Emerging Markets — A New Opportunity for Improving Global Portfolio Performance," *Financial Analysts Journal* (Sept.–Oct. 1983), p. 54

Segmented Markets Approach

Even though market segmentation at the domestic level might safely be ignored, it is much harder to avoid at the international level due to severe restrictions on foreign portfolio investments in many countries; lack of substantial international portfolio investments due to official controls, investor apathy, or high transaction costs; and partial segmentation of the real (goods and factor) markets. Further, the predictions of IAPMs based on full integration do not hold; that is, investors do not seem to hold a well-diversified world market portfolio; rather, their holdings tend toward a disproportionate share of the home country assets. Finally, as reported earlier, empirical tests of the integration hypothesis have been inconclusive and do not allow rejection of the segmentation hypothesis. The issue of segmentation has been treated primarily in three ways:

Welfare Gains From Bridging Investment Barriers. Adler and Dumas (1975) calculate value maximizing foreign acquisition and show that it would not be welfare maximizing for home investors. Lee and Sachdeva (1977) show that when home firms behave as pure competitors at home, home welfare is maximized and host country investor welfare is generally minimized. Neither study characterizes an equilibrium relationship between risk and return. Stapleton and Subrahmanyam (1977) calculate numerical, as opposed to analytical, solutions for capital market equilibrium for different market structures, and find that segmentation caused by investment restrictions produces incentives for firms to merge.

Equilibrium Risk-Return Trade-offs. Black (1974) and Stulz (1981a) employ a continuous parameter of segmentation in the form of a proportional tax to develop IAPMs. Black's model is somewhat artificial in that the tax is on net foreign position, whereas Stulz does not specify risk-return trade-offs for assets not traded by all investors. Errunza and Losq (1982b) assume the cost of investing abroad to be prohibitively high; that is, a class of investors is unable to trade in a subset of securities. In this limiting case (mild segmentation) of the more general framework of Stulz, the problem is completely solved and allows Errunza and Losq to study the impact of mild segmentation on portfolio optimality and asset pricing. No investor will hold the world market portfolio in any of the preceding models.

Errunza and Losq (1982b) also derive testable hypotheses based on their IAPM under mild segmentation. They state that "the results are not statistically inconsistent with theoretical expectations, and thus lend tentative support to the mild segmentation hypothesis." (Errunza and Losq 1982b, p. 23)

Pricing of Multinational Corporate Equities. Investment in multinational corporate (MNC) shares as an indirect vehicle to achieve international diversification in the presence of capital flow controls has been put forward as a hypothesis for quite some time. In an attempt to verify this hypothesis, Hughes, Logue, and Sweeney (1975) relied on traditional risk-adjusted performance measures, whereas Agmon and Lessard (1977) and Jacquillat and Solnik (1978) used international analogs of return-generating processes. The results have been inconclusive and difficult to deal with at the empirical level, as suggested by Errunza and Yalovsky (1978) and Adler (1981).

Since the idea of indirect diversification via the MNC is intuitively very appealing, Errunza and Senbet (1981) investigated the existence of monopoly rents (arising from imperfections in the product, factor, and financial markets, as well as differential international taxation) from foreign operations in a market-value theoretic framework. They argue that "if the U.S. market is well functioning, investors must accept a smaller *equilibrium* expected return on multinational stocks than on otherwise equivalent but purely domestic stocks. In other words, they pay a price *premium*." (Errunza and Senbet, 1981)

Since the diversification services provided by MNCs are priced out in an equilibrium, it is not possible to detect these pricing effects empirically using either the traditional performance measures or the international analogs of return-generating processes. Their empirical test, based on a market-value theoretic framework, establishes the existence of monopoly rents from international operations and provides initial evidence of the relative contribution of barriers to capital flows (vis-à-vis other factors) toward monopoly rents of multinational involvement.

Summary

The theoretical and empirical contributions on international asset pricing can be summarized as follows:

- World capital markets are neither fully integrated nor completely segmented.
- Both national and world factors play a part in pricing of domestic securities.
- Investors do not (and should not) hold a world market portfolio of risky assets but tend toward a portfolio heavy in home assets.
- MNCs derive monopoly rents from international operations and serve as a vehicle for international diversification.

FOREIGN SECURITIES MARKETS

This section provides some data on market size, liquidity, and transaction costs for a number of developed and developing markets. Details on individual firms can be obtained from Capital International Perspective (CIC) (developed markets) or International Finance Corporation (IFC) data bank (emerging markets).[3]

Market Size

How large are these foreign markets? Table 39.6 reports market capitalization figures in U.S. dollars. All these markets appear small in comparison to the

---

[3] *The Capital International Perspective* (Geneva, Switz.: Capital International S.A.). The details on the IFC data bank can be obtained from the Capital Markets Department of IFC, The World Bank Group, Washington D.C., or the author of this chapter.

TABLE 39.6   Market Capitalization, 1980

(billions of U.S. dollars)

Large capitalization		Small capitalization	
Japan	$357	Mexico	$18
United Kingdom	190	Spain	16
Canada	113	Brazil	13
Medium capitalization		Sweden	12
Germany	71	Belgium	10
Australia	60	Chile	9
France	53	India	6
Switzerland	46	Argentina	4
Hong Kong	42	Korea	4
Singapore	27	Greece	3
Netherlands	25	Philippines	2
Italy	25	*Very small capitalization*	
		Jordan	1.6
		Zimbabwe	1.5
		Thailand	1.2
		Portugal	0.2
		Indonesia	0.1

Source: International Finance Corporation data bank, The World Bank Group, Washington, D.C.

trillion-plus capitalization of the United States. Among foreign markets, Japan, the United Kingdom, and Canada are quite large, while many of the European markets are not big. In fact, some of the smaller European markets and many of the emerging markets are of comparable size. The very small LDC markets are included to watch for future potential. Of course, in many of the medium and small markets, there are a few very large firms that might be of interest to investors.[4]

Liquidity

The critical question here has to do with how much and in which securities one can invest without adversely affecting prices or experiencing undue delays in order of execution at the time of investment and on liquidation. Tables 39.7 and 39.8 provide data on equity trading volume and turnover. In terms of trading volume, Japan, the United Kingdom, and Canada make up the top three. However,

---

[4] Among LDC markets included in the IFC data bank, over 200 firms have market capitalization of at least $25 million. For many non-U.S. markets, capitalization figures are upward-biased due to nontrading, and downward-biased due to incomplete reporting.

TABLE 39.7 Equity Trading Volume, 1980

(billions of U.S. dollars)

High volume		Low volume	
Japan	$157	Netherlands	$5
Medium volume		Australia	5
United Kingdom	36	Singapore	4
Canada	28	Mexico	3
Hong Kong	19	Brazil	3
Germany	15	India	3
France	14	Belgium	2
Italy	10	Korea	2
		Sweden	2
		Chile	1.5
		Spain	1.5
		Argentina	1.1
		Very low volume	
		Philippines	0.6
		Thailand	0.3
		Zimbabwe	0.2
		Jordan	0.1
		Greece	0.1
		Indonesia	0.01
		Portugal	0.002

Source: International Finance Corporation data bank, The World Bank Group, Washington, D.C.

the emerging markets move up the ladder a bit. In terms of turnover, the picture is quite different. Three of the top five and six of the top ten markets are of the emerging type, suggesting a highly active nature and consequent liquidity. Again, as in the case of market size, most medium-to-small markets are characterized by a reasonable number of very heavily traded firms.[5]

Transaction Costs

Transaction cost components vary from market to market and also change over time. Table 39.9 reports available information on world markets. Unless otherwise noted, the reported cost figures are for buyers and sellers; that is, the cost

---

[5] Among LDC markets included in the IFC data bank, over 130 firms have average daily trading volume in excess of $100,000. This does not include off-the-floor trading or trading on other exchanges within the country.

TABLE 39.8   Annual Trading Volume as Percentage of Market Capitalization (Turnover), 1980

High turnover		Low turnover	
Hong Kong	50%	Sweden	15%
Korea	49	Indonesia	14
Japan	44	Singapore	14
India	44	Zimbabwe	11
Medium turnover		Spain	9
Italy	38	Jordan	9
Philippines	31	Australia	8
United States	31	Greece	3
Argentina	29	Portugal	1
Thailand	26		
France	26		
Canada	25		
Brazil	21		
Germany	21		
Belgium	21		
Netherlands	20		
United Kingdom	19		
Mexico	18		
Chile	16		

Source: International Finance Corporation data bank, The World Bank Group, Washington, D.C.

---

estimates are only for one side of the round-trip trade. In some of the markets, cost components such as stamp duties, surcharges, taxes, and custody fees are not reported due to lack of data. Finally, the average bid-ask spread data are also not reported. Since we would generally expect a wider spread for thinner markets (securities), its impact would be somewhat unequal across markets (securities).

Based on these figures, the transaction costs, excluding bid-ask spread, do not seem to be very different across world markets.

BARRIERS TO FOREIGN PORTFOLIO INVESTMENTS

Despite well-documented evidence of the higher expected returns and lower risk of an internationally diversified portfolio, an average investor holds primarily domestic assets. A common explanation for this behavior is that there are too many barriers to going abroad, and the expected returns and risk do not ap-

(*text continues on page 39-18*)

TABLE 39.9   Transaction Costs on World Markets

Country	Types of Charges on Securities Transactions	Costs
Austria[a]	Brokerage, credit institutions commission, turnover tax	1.25% and 0.70% on stocks for domestic private clients and foreign banks, respectively; custody fees of 1% for private customers and 0.5% for banks
Australia[a]	Brokerage	$5 plus fixed percentage of transaction amount (e.g., 2.5% on first $5,000, 2% on next $10,000)
Belgium[a]	Brokerage, safekeeping, and custodial charges	Brokerage depends on whether transaction is spot or forward, and stock price; fee schedule depends on transaction amount; fixed duty of BF 100 per transaction, listing stamp duty of 0.025%, and tax of 0.35% (0.17%) for spot (forward); base rate of 2.5% for custodial charges
Denmark[a]	Commission and stamp duty	Shares on main list, 0.5%; other Danish shares, 1% of market price; stamp duty of 0.25% of market price in multiples of Kr. 200
France[a]	Commission, stamp duty, and value added tax	Stocks on Paris exchange, 0.215% for transaction amount over FF2.2 million; stamp duty of 0.15% for transaction amount over FF1 million; value added tax of 17.6% on the commission
Hong Kong[a]	Stamp duty, commission, custody, and handling charges	Stamp duty of HK$3 per HK$1,000 of transaction amount; brokerage commission of 0.5%; safe custody fees of HK$10 minimum and HK$2,500 maximum; handling commission for registration and return of HK$20 per request

Japan[a]	Commission and handling charges	Commission depends on transaction value with ¥125,000 plus 0.55% for transaction of ¥100 million or more; handling charge also varies with transaction value with 0.1% plus ¥39 for ¥5,000 or more transaction value
Norway[a]	Commission, stamp duty	0.75% of principal net amount and 1% stamp duty (foreign brokers exempted from duty)
Singapore and Kuala Lumpur[a]	Commission, stamp, transfer, and custody charges	Commission of 0.75 cent, 1.25 cents, and 1.25% of value for share prices of under 50 cents, 50–99 cents, and $1 and upwards on big board contracts; contract stamp of $1 per $1,000; transfer stamp of 20 cents or 30 cents per $100 of transaction value in Singapore and Malaysia, respectively
Sweden[a]	Commission	0.5% of transaction value
Switzerland[a]	Commission, stamp, and tax, custody and administrative fees	Commission of 1% or 0.625% of transaction value for shares with price of SFR 150 and over SFR 150, respectively; stamp and tax of SFR 0.90 and SFR 1.65 per SFR 1,000 value for Swiss and foreign securities, respectively; custody and administrative fees of SFR 1.25 and SFR 1.50 a year per SFR 1,000 for regular and numbered accounts, respectively
United Kingdom[a]	Commission, stamp, and value added tax	Commission depends on transaction value with 1.5% on first £7,000, 0.5% on next £93,000, 0.4% on next £150,000, etc.; stamp duty of 2% on purchasers with 1% for overseas residents; value added tax of 8% on commission for U.K. resident clients and individuals within European Economic Community (but not institutions); other overseas residents exempt from value added tax

(continued)

TABLE 39.9   Transaction Costs on World Markets *(continued)*

Country	Types of Charges on Securities Transactions	Costs
West Germany[a]	Commission, brokerage, custody, and delivery charges	Commission of 0.5% and brokerage of 0.1% of countervalue
Korea[b]	Commission	Ranges between 0.7% and 1%
Mexico[b]	Commission	Commission depends on transaction size; minimum is M$60 plus 0.5%
Portugal[c]	Commission	Approximately 1% of value
Thailand[c]	Commission	0.5% of transaction value
Brazil[c]	Commission	Ranges between 0.5 and 2.5% of transaction value
Chile[c]	Commission	1.6% of value — negotiable on large amounts
Jordan[c]	Commission, surcharge, and stamp tax	Commission of 0.65% and 0.5% for value of 20,000 dinars and over 20,000 dinars, respectively; 0.35% surcharge on all transactions; 0.15% stamp tax on par value of contract

Philippines[b]	Commission	Brokerage commission of 1.5% — another 1% frequently charged on transactions by foreign parties
Indonesia[b]	Commission	1% of transaction value
Nigeria[b]	Commission	1.5% of transaction value — paid, in many cases, several months after the transaction on receipt of share certificates by the buyer
Kenya[b]	Brokerage, contract, stamps, stamp duty	Brokerage fee ranging from 5 cents per share for shares under Ksh.1.50 to 1.50% for shares over Ksh.20; contract stamps of 50 cents for contracts under Ksh.2000 and Ksh.1 for each Ksh.10,000; 0.5% stamp duty
Zimbabwe[b]	Commission	1% of transaction value

Sources: (a) *Investing in Foreign Markets*, 2nd ed. (New York: ABD Securities Corporation, 1981).
(b) Antoine van Agtmael, "Investment Banking in Emerging Securities Markets," *Euromoney* (Fall 1983).
(c) Author's discussions with various stock exchange authorities

propriately take into account the additional costs and risks of holding foreign securities.[6] The obstacles most frequently cited are

1 Currency fluctuations

2 Political risk

3 Capital controls

4 Market efficiency

5 Information

Currency Fluctuations

If one assumes that markets are perfect and fully integrated, the securities would be priced globally, and the expected return and risk would appropriately account for the additional costs and systematic components of risks for the foreign investor. Under this scenario, investors need not actively manage risk from currency fluctuations. There are four theorems that interlink exchange rates, prices (absolute and relative), and interest rates.

1 Relative version of the purchasing power parity (PPP) theorem states that expected relative inflation (between two countries) would be offset by a corresponding change in exchange rates between the two currencies; that is, a higher rate of inflation would lead to an appropriately declining exchange rate.

2 The Fisher effect states that differential interest rates between two countries reflect differential expected inflation rates.

3 The interest rate parity theorem (IRPT) states that the forward margin (forward rate minus spot rate over the spot rate) should equal the interest rate differential between the two currencies. Interest arbitrage generally ensures this relationship.

4 Forward rate as an unbiased predictor of future spot rate states that the forward rate should equal the expected future spot rate. If it does not, actions of speculators will move the forward toward the expected future spot rate.

If all the preceding relationships hold, anticipated exchange fluctuations would not be relevant. This is because in a perfect capital market they would be appropriately reflected in asset prices.

Since an efficient market sets prices on the basis of anticipations about the future, the market performance would be affected to the extent that realizations deviate from expectations. Thus, an investor may wish to manage exposure to unanticipated (by market) changes or events.

The current wisdom, however, suggests that world equity markets are

---

[6] A general discussion of the barriers is found in V. Errunza, "Gains from Portfolio Diversification into Less Developed Countries' Securities," *Journal of International Business Studies* (Fall–Winter 1977), pp. 83–99; D. Lessard, "International Diversification," *The Investment Manager's Handbook*, ed. S. Levine (Homewood, Ill.: Dow Jones-Irwin, 1980), pp. 359–383; and A. van Agtmael and V. Errunza, "Foreign Portfolio Investment in Emerging Securities Markets," *Columbia Journal of World Business* (Summer 1982), pp. 58–63. Discussion of political risk is found in V. Errunza and B. Rosenberg, "Investment Risk in Developed and Less Developed Countries," *Journal of Financial and Quantitative Analysis*, Vol. 17 (1982), pp. 741–762.

neither fully integrated nor completely segmented. Under this setting, it is likely that asset prices in each market may not be set so as to take into account all of the costs and systematic risk aspects of currency risk.[7] Since it is generally believed that exchange risk does not affect the home investor, its systematic component may not carry an appropriate risk premium. However, if purchasing power parity holds in the long run and stocks are a good hedge against inflation, exchange risk is neutralized in the long run. Investors may wish to hedge against short-term disequilibrium either by going into a forward contract or borrowing in the foreign money market. For forward hedge one enters into a forward contract either for the amount of investment or for the expected future proceeds; each alternative unfortunately entails some residual exchange risk. The cost of forward hedge is the difference between forward margin and the expected change in exchange rate. Similarly, for a money market hedge one borrows in the currency of investment an amount equal to the investment or the expected future proceeds. The cost of this hedge is equal to the difference between interest rates (home minus foreign interest rate) and the expected change in exchange rate.

Irrespective of the structure of world capital markets, currency risk may not be important if

1 There is no systematic component to exchange risk; that is, movements in security prices are totally independent of movements in exchange rates. In this case the exchange risk need not be priced.

2 The international investor holds a well-diversified portfolio. He may then be able to diversify away most of the exchange risk, thereby reducing the importance of currency fluctuations on the performance of his portfolio.

Finally, an active manager might wish to exploit the currency dimension either by holding open currency positions (via forwards or money markets) or holding assets denominated in such currencies. The motivation may come from the belief that he can successfully outguess the markets or that markets are inefficient.

Political Risk

Traditionally, the issue of political risk has played a critical role in direct or portfolio investment. Many prospective investors shy away from politically unstable regions of the world and may in the process forgo significant opportunities to diversify their portfolios. The key question is that of how well the politically unstable market is functioning.

If markets are perfect, the systematic component of political risk would be priced appropriately. For example, heightened expectations of expropriations would bring falling stock prices and the consequent increase in expected returns, as investors (both domestic and foreign) shift out of stocks into other domestic

---

[7] On the other hand, as demonstrated in V. Errunza and E. Losq, "International Asset Pricing Under Mild Segmentation — Theory and Test," Working Paper, McGill University (Montreal, Can.: 1982), the equities of markets that do not allow foreign portfolio investments offer super risk premium in addition to the usual marketwide systematic risk premium.

or international assets. To the degree that political risk may also affect other domestic assets and that investors hold a disproportionately larger share of home assets (see section on International Asset Pricing Models), the political risk would weigh more heavily on domestic investors. Thus, in a well-functioning market, internationally diversified investors would be at an advantage vis-à-vis domestic investors.

On the other hand, if domestic investors have no other alternatives (i.e., they cannot invest in foreign securities or there are no other viable options at home), prices might not fully reflect the probability of expropriation and thus understate the risk (and expected return) for a foreign investor. Again, the internationally diversified investor is better equipped to diversify away the political risks of individual domestic markets.

Capital Controls

There are many types of institutional barriers aimed at restricting and at times prohibiting portfolio capital flows across countries. The U.S. interest equalization tax, investment pounds sterling in the United Kingdom, Japanese controls on portfolio capital flows, as well as negative interest rates on Swiss accounts are well-known examples of developed markets.[8] The restricted list of Mexico; the minimum investment time period requirement in Argentina and Chile; major restrictions in Korea (except for investment trusts), Brazil (except for investment depository receipts), Greece and India (except for nonresident Indians) are some examples of controls in emerging markets. Table 39.10 reports existing controls on LDC markets. It should be noted that rules on foreign investments are currently under review to attract foreign investors in many emerging markets.

The tax treatment of dividends and capital gains are summarized in Tables 39.10 and 39.11. Based on the figures reported, dividend withholding taxes or capital gains taxation does not seem to constitute a major cost obstacle to investment in foreign markets.

Market Efficiency

From the viewpoint of the foreign investor, the critical question is that of whether prices are fair and reflect all available information appropriately and quickly. This is because domestic investors are relatively better informed about securities on their own market, and hence would be expected to post superior performance (vis-à-vis the market and foreign investor) if possible.

Rigorous tests (weak, semistrong, and strong form) using differential information sets are primarily available for the U.S. market. For non-U.S. markets, the tests are largely limited to the random walk (weak form) variety. Tests of the European (Solnik, 1973) and the smaller developing markets (Errunza and Losq, 1982a) have consistently reported the difficulty of using past price changes to forecast the future. Although the smaller European markets and the emerging markets reveal somewhat greater serial dependence, they cannot be exploited by formal trading rules.

---

[8] For further details, see *Investing in Foreign Markets* (New York: ABD Securities Corporation, 1981).

With respect to the relationship between risk and return, the available evidence has generally provided weak support to the various IAPMs. Further, tests based on individual foreign markets show greater realized returns for riskier securities. Thus, foreign markets appear to be reasonably well functioning, and in the global context, securities are priced in a world market structure that is neither fully integrated nor completely segmented.

Finally, with respect to portfolio performance, it can be evaluated either in the global context or in the context of individual markets. Given current knowledge about the structure of world capital markets, it is impossible to define the benchmark portfolio at the global level. Which markets should be included and in what proportions? At the individual market level, most European funds are diversified into foreign securities, whereas extremely few funds exist in the developing markets.

To summarize, foreign security prices behave so as to be consistent with the random walk hypothesis. The relationship between risk and return is in line with the modern asset pricing theory (CAPM) within many markets that have been studied to date. Whether portfolio managers can consistently outperform relevant benchmarks in the global or in the individual market context is unclear, since reliable portfolio performance results for foreign markets are unavailable.

Information

Availability, timeliness, and quality of information is on the rise worldwide. There are many reasons, the most important being investor (domestic and foreign) demand. Computer systems are commonplace even among the developing markets. Daily, monthly, and quarterly data on exchange activity is easily available on many markets. Capital market laws and internationalization of the big accounting firms have improved disclosure and quality of information. Investment advisors and technical staffs at brokerage houses are common in most markets. Despite these changes, the local norm prevails in terms of operation of the exchange (e.g., no specialists and limited moves), financial reporting (e.g., inflation accounting, consolidation practices), and information dissemination (e.g., family-groups-friends network). Thus, even though information barriers are less severe today, special knowledge, interpretation skills, and local contacts are necessary for the management of the global portfolio.

ACHIEVING INTERNATIONAL DIVERSIFICATION

There are primarily three ways to achieve international diversification. They are:

1 Direct approach
2 International mutual funds
3 MNC shares

To assess the effectiveness of each alternative, two benchmark portfolios are needed. First, the truly global portfolio representing the ideal, and second, the

TABLE 39.10   Foreign Investment Restrictions and Tax Barriers

Country	Foreign Portfolio Investment	Repatriation Restrictions	Withholding Tax on Dividend	Tax Treaty With United States	Capital Gains Tax
Asia					
Hong Kong	Free	None	None	N/A	None
Singapore	Free	None	0%	No treaty	None
Malaysia	Free up to 10% of capital	None	0%	No treaty	None
Philippines	Relatively free, certain share limitations	Registration (automatic) required	15–35%	Treaty signed but not ratified	None
Thailand	Relatively free, limitations on certain shares	Registration required	20%	N/A	25%
Korea	Restrictive but changing	Registration required	25%	N/A	20–25%
Indonesia	Not allowed	N/A	N/A	Under discussion	N/A
India	Not allowed	N/A	25%	Not applicable	N/A

Latin America					
Argentina	Maximum 2% of capital of any company; foreign ownership, 20% maximum	Minimum period	17.5%	No treaty	None (?)
Brazil	Restricted to special mutual funds (Decree 1401)	Three-year minimum investment, 40% per year	15%	No treaty	15% (−60%)
Chile	Relatively free	Registration required; three-year minimum investment before repatriation	None	No applicable treaty	None
Mexico	Allowed in certain B-shares	None	21%	N/A	None
Venezuela	49% maximum	14% per year	20%	N/A	No withholding
Middle East					
Egypt	N/A	N/A	40.55%	N/A	None
Jordan	Approval easily granted	Easy	None (?)	N/A	None

(continued)

TABLE 39.10   Foreign Investment Restrictions and Tax Barriers *(continued)*

Country	Foreign Portfolio Investment	Repatriation Restrictions	Withholding Tax on Dividend	Tax Treaty With United States	Capital Gains Tax
Turkey	N/A	N/A	38%	N/A	None
Africa					
Kenya	N/A		15%	N/A	10%
Nigeria	N/A		12.5%	N/A	20%
Zimbabwe	Approval easily granted	Registration required	20%	N/A	30%
Europe					
Greece	All foreign investment requires approval	Special approval required	38–41%	38–41%	30%
Portugal	N/A	N/A	N/A	18%	None
Spain	Allowed, 50% per company	None	16.5%	No treaty	None (?)

Source: Antoine van Agtmael, "Investment Banking in Emerging Securities Markets," *Euromoney,* (Fall 1983). p. 23.

truly domestic portfolio representing the minimum acceptable performance. The ideal is, of course, not achievable at present due to capital controls, and the pure domestic portfolio is not readily available due to inclusion of foreign securities and multinationals (trading on local markets) in broad domestic indexes.[9]

Direct Approach

It is possible to achieve limited international diversification by investing in markets devoid of capital flow controls. Time and again, past studies have shown the benefits of going abroad. For example, a U.S. investor's gains from diversification into major world markets are significantly increased by further diversification into some of the smaller (available) exchanges. For results based on a passive strategy see Table 39.5. Of course, one would have to adjust these results to reflect costs of managing a personalized portfolio.

International Mutual Funds

Just as it is more expensive to have a customized domestic portfolio vis-à-vis buying into a mutual fund, it is also very costly to hold a personalized international portfolio. The cost reduction and professional management arguments that favor investments in national mutual funds are even more convincing in the global context. The availability and recent performance of international mutual funds is reviewed next.

Many U.S. and European funds have some investment in foreign securities. There are also international funds as well as specialized funds from developed countries (e.g., Japan fund) and LDCs (e.g., Mexico fund). Table 39.12 provides recent performance data on some international funds. Of the eight funds in operation for five years or more, two invest primarily in the Pacific region, one invests in Canadian firms, and the remaining five have European and some Far Eastern securities in their portfolios. A far cry from a truly global portfolio! In terms of performance, these funds on an average did not perform as well as the average equity fund, the Dow-Jones industrials (DJI), or the S&P 500. However, the average equity fund had some foreign stocks and multinationals in the portfolio and the DJI and S&P 500 include many multinational stocks. Hence, the performance comparison is not very appropriate and should be interpreted with caution.

Investment in emerging markets is just beginning. Table 39.13 provides portfolio compositions of U.S. funds in LDCs and funds that specialize in LDC markets.

MNC Shares

MNCs derive part of their revenues from foreign operations. Hence, investments in MNC shares should provide the benefits of diversification. Since capital flow controls are generally more severe for portfolio investments, compared to foreign

---

[9] See discussion in V. Errunza and M. Yalovsky, "International Diversification and the Multinational Corporation," Working Paper, McGill University (Montreal, Can.: 1978).

TABLE 39.11 Dividend Taxation

Company's Domicile

Shareholder's Domicile		Australia	Austria	Belgium	Canada	Denmark	France	Germany	Hong Kong	Italy	Japan	Luxembourg	Netherlands	Norway	Singapore	Spain	Sweden	Switzerland	United Kingdom	United States
Australia	−		20	15	15	30	15	15	0	30	15	15	15	25	0	15	30	35	15	15
	=		C	C	C	C	C	C		C	C	C	C	C		C	C	C	C	C
Austria	−	30		15	25	10	15	25	0	30	20	15	15	15	0	15	10	5	15	15
	=	D		C	C	C	C	C		C	C	C	C	C		C	C	C	C	C
Belgium	−	15	15		15	15	15	15	0	15	15	15	15	15	0	15	15	15	0	15
	=	DC	DC		DC	DC	DC	DC		DC	DC	DC	DC	DC		DC	DC	DC		DC
Canada	−	15	20	15		15	15	25	0	30	15	15	15	15	0	15	15	15	0	15
	=	C	C	C		C	C	C		C	C	C	C	C		C	C	C		C
Denmark	−	30	10	15	15		0	15	0	15	15	15	15	15	0	15	15	0	15	15
	=	C	C	C	C			C		C	C	C	C	C		C	C		C	C
France	−	15	15	15	15	0		15	0	15	15	15	15	10	0	15	0	5	15	15
	=	C	C	C	C			C		C	C	C	C	C		C		C	C	C
Germany	−	15	20	15	25	15	0		0	30	15	15	15	15	0	15	15	15	0	15
	=	C	C	C	C	C				C	C	C	C	C		C	C	C		C
Hong Kong	−	30	20	20	25	30	25	25		30	20	15	25	25	0	15	30	35	0	30
	=																			
Italy	−	30	20	15	25	15	15	25	0		15	15	0	25	0	15	15	15	0	15
	=	C	C	C	C	C	C	C			C	C		C		C	C	C		C

Country		(1)	(2)	(3)	(4)	(5)	(6)	(7)	(8)	(9)	(10)	(11)	(12)	(13)	(14)	(15)	(16)	(17)	(18)
Japan	I	15	20	15	15	15	15	0	15	15	15	15	15	0	15	15	15	0	15
	=	C	C	C	C	C	C	—	C	C	C	C	C	—	C	C	C	—	C
Luxembourg	I	30	15	15	25	30	15	0	30	20	15	15	25	0	15	30	35	15	15
	=	C	C	C	C	C	C	—	C	C	D	C	C	—	C	C	C	C	C
Netherlands	I	15	15	15	15	15	15	0	30	15			15	0	15	15	15	15	15
	=	C	C	C	C	C	D	—	D	C	C		C	—	C	C	C	C	C
Norway	I	30	15	15	15	10	15	0	30	15	15	15		0	15	15	5	15	15
	=	D	C	C	C	C	C	—	C	C	D	C		—	C	C	D	C	C
Singapore	I	15	20	15	15	15	15	0	10	15	15	15	0	0	15	15	15	15	30
	=	C	D	C	C	C	C	—	C	C	D	C	—	—	D	C	C	C	D
Spain	I	30	15	15	25	15	15	0	30	15	15	15	15	0		15	15	15	30
	=	C	C	C	C	C	C	—	C	C	D	C	C	—		C	C	C	C
Sweden	I	30	10	15	15	15	15	0	15	15	15	15	15	0	15		5	15	15
	=	C	C	C	C	C	C	—	C	C	C	C	C	—	C		C	C	C
Switzerland	I	30	5	15	15	0	15	0	15	15	15	5	5	0	15	5		15	15
	=	D	C	C	C	—	C	—	C	C	D	D	D	—	C	C		C	D
United Kingdom	I	15	15	15	15	15	15	0	15	15	15	15	15	0	15	15	15		15
	=	C	C	C	C	C	C	—	C	C	C	C	C	—	C	C	C		C
United States	I	15	10	15	15	15	15	0	15	15	7.5	15	15	0	15	15	15	15	
	=	C	C	C	C	C	C	—	C	C	C	C	C	—	C	C	C	C	

Notes: I Indicates the effective rate of dividend withholding tax

       II Describes the treatment of the foreign withholding tax in the share's country of residence

       D indicates deduction for foreign tax paid; i.e., the shareholder's country of residence imposes its tax on net foreign dividends.

       C indicates credit for foreign tax paid; i.e., the shareholder's country of residence imposes its tax on gross foreign dividends but the amount of this tax is reduced by the amount of the foreign dividend withholding tax

Source: Capital International Perspective, (Geneva, Switzerland, Capital International S.A., 1981), p. 444

TABLE 39.12   Total Reinvested Cumulative Performance

(dollars in millions)

Mutual Fund	Total Assets			Percentage Changes				
	March 31, 1983	Dec. 31, 1982	March 31, 1982	10 Years (June 1973–June 1983)	5 Years (June 1978–June 1983)	12 Months (June 1982–June 1983)	1st and 2nd Quarter 1983	2nd Quarter 1983
First Investors International	$ 3.8	$ 1.1	$ 0.4	*	*	55.02	31.90	14.06
Transatlantic Fund	31.1	27.8	30.3	100.62	68.97	31.98	23.01	7.58
Templeton Foreign	10.1	1.7	*	*	*	*	22.30	10.27
Canadian Fund	25.4	24.0	20.8	116.59	121.19	73.31	21.47	11.12
United International Growth	72.3	66.8	56.8	194.99	169.68	55.47	20.35	10.05
Scudder International	99.0	79.1	56.5	84.42	92.37	42.66	19.91	6.35
Putnam International Equities	40.2	38.1	32.6	231.44	108.80	50.19	19.14	9.35
Kemper International Fund	31.3	26.5	20.4	*	*	41.65	18.54	10.12
Principal World	0.1	0.1	*	*	*	*	16.79	9.17
Keystone International	31.3	31.1	28.0	107.19	90.39	46.47	16.06	10.61
G.T. Pacific Fund	14.4	13.9	11.2	*	39.68	20.10	14.72	10.50
T. Rowe Price International Fund	99.6	101.0	69.4	*	*	37.61	13.34	8.06
Merrill Lynch Pacific	41.5	40.0	33.9	*	79.26	36.70	13.15	12.25
Mass Financial International TR-Bond	42.4	37.4	33.8	*	*	27.35	0.66	1.33
Trustees Commingled International	10.0	**	**	**	**	**	-0.92	**
International — total	$552.5	$488.6	$394.1	139.21	96.29	43.21	17.95	9.34
Equity funds average				319.91	176.82	69.04	25.95	13.02
Dow Jones Industrials, unmanaged				134.98	100.84	58.56	19.57	9.36
S&P 500, unmanaged				161.36	129.45	61.22	22.23	11.10

 * Fund was not in existence for period covered.
 ** Trustees Commingled International was offered on May 16, 1983.

Source: "Special Second Quarter 1983 Report, Lipper-Mutual Fund Performance Analysis." (Westfield, N.J.: Lipper Analytical Services Inc., June 30, 1983)

TABLE 39.13   Institutional Investment in LDC Markets, December 1980

(Percentages of total non-U.S. portfolio)

	Hong Kong/ Singapore	Southeast Asia	Mexico	Spain	Other
Aetna Warburg	3%	—	—	—	—
Brown Brothers	12	—	—	—	—
Battery-March	4	—	—	2	—
BEA Associates	1	—	4	1	—
Fiduciary	9	—	—	—	—
IDS-Gartmore	21	—	—	—	—
Mellon Pictet	6	—	—	—	—
Kleinwort Benson	13	3%	4	1	—
Rowe-Price Fleming	—	14	—	—	—
Scudder	4	—	3	—	—
State Street	—	—	—	—	—
Specialized funds					
Mexico Fund	—	—	100	—	—
Jardine S.E. Asia	86	2	—	—	—
Jardine International Pacific Securities	34	—	—	—	—
G.T. Asia	16	10	—	—	—
Save & Prosper Jardine Far Eastern	28	—	—	—	—
Singapore Growth	86	—	—	—	—
Jardine Philippine	—	100	—	—	—
G.T. Philippine	—	100	—	—	—
Philippine Investment Co.	—	100	—	—	—
Brazil Funds	—	—	—	—	100

Source: Capital Markets Department, International Finance Corporation, The World Bank Group, Washington, D.C.

direct investments, MNCs should provide more complete diversification opportunity in comparison to currently available international mutual funds and customized portfolios. Available evidence suggests that MNCs derive monopoly rents from international operations and serve as a vehicle for international diversification.

With respect to the extent of benefits, as Jacquillat and Solnik (1978) report: "Variability of returns measured by the standard deviation of the U.S. multinational portfolios is usually 90% of the risk of a purely domestic U.S. portfolio of the same size."

Even though MNCs are not a perfect substitute for the idealized international portfolio that typically exhibits 30 to 50 percent of the risk of the U.S. domestic portfolio, MNCs do provide international diversification services. Costs of investment in MNC portfolios would also be significantly lower than in the idealized international portfolio, which in reality cannot be bought at present. Thus, in view of the existing restrictions on capital flows, the high costs of personalized portfolios, as well as the nonavailability of a global portfolio, investment in MNCs deserves careful consideration.

FUTURE PROSPECTS

Crystal-ball gazing can be dangerous. However, some safe speculations are:

- Economic interdependence will continue its rise among nations of the world.
- Capital markets in general and smaller emerging markets in particular will continue to evolve and become more efficient.
- World capital markets will become more integrated.
- Rapid economic growth will lead to increasing opportunities in emerging markets.

What do these developments mean in terms of diversification benefits and strategy? First, there is some evidence of increasing correlations among securities of developed markets; however, in view of the influence of a strong national factor in each market, it is unlikely that the international diversification benefits would disappear over time. With respect to the emerging markets, correlations have remained at rather low levels over the last two decades and can be expected to provide substantial risk reduction potential over the foreseeable future.

Second, as markets develop and become more efficient, the information costs and perceived risks from inefficiencies in asset pricing would tend to diminish, thereby increasing the attractiveness of diversification.

Third, with increasing world market integration and the consequent pricing of, primarily, the global systematic risk, a domestic portfolio would be expected to provide inferior performance. Of course, with perfect markets, the diversifiable component of domestic systematic risk will not command any risk premium.

Finally, despite poor performance of some emerging markets over the last two years due to global and domestic economic and political problems, emerging markets are coming of age and should be seriously considered for inclusion in a global portfolio. Their rapid economic growth can be expected (as in the past) to translate into superior performance reminiscent of the "Japanese" experience. In addition, the mildly segmented nature of emerging markets would provide super risk premiums to international investors. Of course, one would expect these risk premiums to dissipate slowly as markets move toward total integration.

SUGGESTED READING

Adler, M. "Investor Recognition of Corporate International Diversification: Comment." *Journal of Finance*, Vol. 36 (Mar. 1981), pp. 187–191.

———, and B. Dumas. "International Portfolio Choice and Corporation Finance: A Synthesis." *Journal of Finance*, Vol. 38 (June 1983), pp. 925–984.

———. "Optimal International Acquisitions." *Journal of Finance*, Vol. 30 (Mar. 1975), pp. 1–20.

Agmon, T., and D. Lessard. "Investor Recognition of Corporate International Diversification." *Journal of Finance*, Vol. 32 (Sept. 1977), p. 1049–1056.

Black, F. "International Capital Market Equilibrium with Investment Barriers." *Journal of Financial Economics*, Vol. 1 (1974), pp. 337–352.

Errunza, V. "Emerging Markets — A New Opportunity for Improving Global Portfolio Performance." *Financial Analysts Journal* (Sept.–Oct. 1983), pp. 51–58.

———. "Gains from Portfolio Diversification into Less Developed Countries' Securities." *Journal of International Business Studies* (Fall–Winter 1977), pp. 83–99.

———, and E. Losq. "The Behavior of Stock Prices on LDC Markets." Working Paper, McGill University. Montreal, Can.: 1982.

———, and E. Losq. "International Asset Pricing Under Mild Segmentation — Theory and Test." Working Paper, McGill University. Montreal, Can.: 1982.

———, and B. Rosenberg. "Investment Risk in Developed and Less Developed Countries." *Journal of Financial and Quantitative Analysis*, Vol. 17 (1982), pp. 741–762.

———, and L. Senbet. "The Effects of International Operations on the Market Value of the Firm: Theory and Evidence." *Journal of Finance*, Vol. 36 (May 1981), pp. 401–418.

———, and M. Yalovsky. "International Diversification and the Multinational Corporation." Working Paper, McGill University. Montreal, Can.: 1978.

Grauer, F., et al. "Sharing Rules and Equilibrium in an International Capital Market under Uncertainty." *Journal of Financial Economics*, Vol. 3 (June 1976), pp. 233–256.

Hughes, J., et al. "Corporate International Diversification and Market Assigned Measures of Risk and Diversification." *Journal of Financial and Quantitative Analysis* (Nov. 1975), pp. 625–649.

Jacquillat, B., and B. Solnik. "Multinationals are Poor Tools for Diversification." *Journal of Portfolio Management* (Winter 1978), pp. 8–12.

Lee, W., and K. Sachdeva. "The Role of the Multinational Firm in the Integration of Segmented Capital Markets." *Journal of Finance*, Vol. 32 (May 1977), pp. 479–492.

Lessard, D. "International Diversification." *The Investment Manager's Handbook*, ed. S. Levine. Homewood, Ill.: Dow Jones-Irwin, 1980, pp. 359–383.

———. "World, Country and Industry Relationships in Equity Returns: Implications for Risk Reduction Through International Diversification." *Financial Analysts Journal* (Jan.–Feb. 1976), pp. 2–8.

Markowitz, H. *Portfolio Selection: Efficient Diversification of Investments*. New York: John Wiley & Sons, 1959.

Solnik, B. "An Equilibrium Model of the International Capital Market." *Journal of Economic Theory*, Vol. 8 (Aug. 1974), pp. 500–524.

———. "The International Pricing of Risk: An Empirical Investigation of the World Capital Market Structure." *Journal of Finance*, Vol. 29 (May 1974), pp. 48–54.

———. "Note on the Validity of the Random Walk for European Stock Prices." *Journal of Finance* (Dec. 1973), pp. 1151–1159.

Stapleton, R., and M. Subrahmanyam. "Market Imperfections, Capital Asset Equilibrium and Corporation Finance." *Journal of Finance*, Vol. 32 (May 1977), pp. 307–321.

Stehle, R. "An Empirical Test of the Alternate Hypotheses of National and International Pricing of Risky Assets." *Journal of Finance*, Vol. 32 (May 1977), pp. 493–502.

Stulz, R. "A Model of International Asset Pricing." *Journal of Financial Economics*, Vol. 9 (Dec. 1981), pp. 393–406.

———. "On the Effects of Barriers to International Investment." *Journal of Finance*, Vol. 36 (Sept. 1981), pp. 923–934.

Tobin, J. "Liquidity Preference as Behavior Towards Risk." *Review of Economic Studies* (Feb. 1958), pp. 65–86.

van Agtmael, A., and V. Errunza. "Foreign Portfolio Investment in Emerging Securities Markets." *Columbia Journal of World Business* (Summer 1982), pp. 58–63.

40

International Banking

PHILLIP A. WELLONS

INTERNATIONAL BANKING ACTIVITIES

Introduction: What Is International Banking?

Banking is international when it involves more than one country. This simple definition is accurate on the whole, but fuzzy on the margins. A loan by a U.S. bank to a Japanese borrower appears to be quintessentially international. Even if the U.S. bank is lending yen from its branch in Tokyo to a local resident, most bankers accept this as international. But when a U.S. bank in California lends to a local subsidiary of a Japanese semiconductor producer, many bankers treat the loan as domestic even if the Japanese parent guarantees the loan. The world of banking is not organized into neat compartments.

International bankers share a common culture and a common language, English, regardless of their home country, and Anglo-American law provides the legal infrastructure even for transactions between European banks and Asian borrowers. The dollar is the dominant currency. Many international bankers spend as much time traveling as they do in their own homes and offices. They have their own trade journals, replete with gossip. They even dress alike. Functional and sometimes dysfunctional, the common culture knits together the disparate players in a global industry.

The story of international banking since the 1960s is dramatic. Massive change emerged from the clash of two forces: the integration of the world economy and nationalism. The dynamism of the first often obscures the intensity of the second. Both shaped the industry: the range of activities and customers, the distribution of assets and liabilities, the risk and return on credit, the nature of competition, even the peculiar administrative issues.

Range of Activities

Types of Activities. As financial intermediaries, the banks act abroad in the same general ways as at home: as principals, brokers, or advisers. The precise range of activity varies with the laws of the home and host countries, but in general banks have been less restricted in international activities than they have on the domestic front. International operations, however, tend to have a different mix. Wholesale banking dominates over retail banking. Since much of the money is purchased, transactions among banks are more important than their domestic activities.

Groups of Clients. The demand for international, as opposed to domestic, banking services comes much more from the business sector than from households. The high transaction costs associated with international operations may also price some smaller firms, as well as individuals, out of the market. So it is not surprising that the major customers of international banks have been big companies, governments, and other financial institutions. Big firms seek finance for trade, investment, acquisitions, and to some extent, working capital. National governments seek credit for current and capital expenditures. Individuals and purchasers of real estate are less significant.

The relative importance of each group varies with the type of activity. For example, in the syndicated Eurocurrency market, public sector borrowers have historically overshadowed private borrowers. In 1976, private borrowers raised only 29.3 percent of $20.5 billion in Eurocredits. In 1982, private borrowers raised 42 percent of a total of $148 billion,[1] much of it to finance corporate takeovers.

Players: Which Banks Do It?

Describing the banks that provide international services is a bit like describing the elephant and its nearest living relative, the hyrax, a small, furry animal about the size of a rabbit. True, they are related, but one sees the differences first.

Among the thousands of banks in the world, the number engaging in some sort of regular international activity is in the hundreds; for most that activity represents a small part of their total operations and they are small players in the world arena. By 1982, 196 U.S. banks had foreign branches. Few have branches in more than one or two foreign countries, and these tend to be financial centers. A study of banks in 1975, for example, revealed that only 84 had offices in five or more countries.[2] While the number has risen, the concentration is still clear.

The largest banks have offices in over 50 countries, leading some analysts to distinguish between international banking, which any bank can do from its headquarters, and multinational or transnational banking, which is possible only with a large network of offices in a variety of countries.[3] With few exceptions, banks with the largest networks also have the most assets. Some 20 to 40 of the world's largest banks dominate international banking. In 1982, the three largest U.S. banks — Citicorp, BankAmerica Corporation, and Chase Manhattan Corporation — were the three top lead managers of syndicated loans. Together, the three led 408 loans amounting in value to 13 percent of all loans syndicated that year.[4]

Individual banks cannot measure their market share accurately. Because data about international markets are inadequate, asset size is sometimes used as a proxy for international position, but is inadequate, as Table 40.1 shows. For 1982, the G-5 countries (France, Germany, Japan, United Kingdom, and United States) were the homes of the largest banks and of the main lead managers of syndicated credits. But size alone did not confer leadership on the banks. Some smaller banks were leaders and some of the largest were not.

---

[1] *Borrowing in International Capital Markets*, Table 12 (Washington, D.C.: International Bank for Reconstruction and Development, July 1979); and "Annual Financing Report 1983," *Euromoney* (Apr. 1983), p. 30.

[2] United Nations Center on Transnational Corporations, *Transnational Banks: Operations, Strategies and Their Effects in Developing Countries*, Table I-1 (New York: United Nations, 1981).

[3] See, for example, Organization for Economic Cooperation and Development, "The Internationalisation of Banking," *Financial Market Trends*, Vol. 25 (June 1983), p. 1.

[4] "Annual Financing Report 1983," *Euromoney* (Apr. 1983), p. 28.

TABLE 40.1   Home Countries of the Largest Banks, Ranked by Assets and by Lead Managements, 1982

Home Country	Assets — Number in:				Lead Management — Number in Top 50
	Top 20	Next 30	Next 50	Total	
Japan	7	8	9	24	9
France	4	—	3	7	5
United Kingdom	3	2	—	5	8
United States	3	4	9	16	15
West Germany	1	5	5	11	3
Canada	1	3	1	5	4
Brazil	1	—	—	1	—
Netherlands	—	3	1	4	—
Switzerland	—	2	1	3	—
Italy	—	2	4	6	—
Hong Kong	—	1	—	1	1
Australia	—	—	4	4	1
Spain	—	—	3	3	—
Sweden	—	—	3	3	—
Belgium	—	—	2	2	1
Israel	—	—	2	2	—
India	—	—	1	1	—
Austria	—	—	1	1	1
Greece	—	—	1	1	—

Sources: Asset ranks: "The 1983 Global Banking Rankings," *Institutional Investor* (*International*) (July 1983), p. 138; lead manager ranks: "Citicorp displaces Chase," *Euromoney* (Apr. 1983), p. 28

The History of International Banking

International banking today evolved from a structure that dates at least to the middle of the last century and, in some senses, much further back. The predecessors of most of today's large banks started during the Industrial Revolution. In the 1800s, the major banks were based in Europe, growing with the colonial empires of the time or in the financial centers of industrial Europe. As part of a program to catch up with the economic and political power of the United Kingdom and France, the governments of Germany and Japan promoted their banks at the turn of the century, with consequences for international banking today.

Two great world wars and the Great Depression changed the face of the world economy and reshaped international banking. Most of the major banks survived the shocks. By the mid-1940s, however, German banks had twice lost their international assets and networks and the Japanese banks had lost theirs once. The loss of empire forced the French and British banks to rethink their strategy. The period from the end of the war to the late 1960s was a time of consolidation for banks from Europe and Japan. The same period saw the U.S. banks blossom overseas, drawn by the expansion of foreign trade and investment by U.S. companies, pushed by restrictions at home on banking and foreign capital flows, sustained by the role of the dollar in the Bretton Woods monetary system, and protected by a Pax Americana.

The largest U.S. banks saw their dominance challenged in the early 1970s. Smaller U.S. banks and the largest European and Japanese banks responded to the American presence, to recessions at home, and to new opportunities abroad by building international networks. The first oil shock, which occurred in 1973–1974, slowed the challengers' expansion, but by the late 1970s international banking was highly competitive, with many players and narrowing returns. The economic carnage that followed the second oil shock reintroduced a note of caution, however. Many newcomers dramatically reduced their international operations, while the larger, older banks became more selective in their lending.

The Aggregate Dimensions Today

At the aggregate level, international banking grew fast during the last 15 years, to the point where its size alone attracts attention. In 1982–1983 its growth stopped, at least temporarily.

The Growth of the Euromarkets. One of the biggest markets is the Eurocurrency market. It is mainly an international short-term capital market of currency deposited in banks outside the country that issued the currency. A U.S. dollar deposit in a bank in Nassau or Hong Kong is a Eurodollar (despite the prefix, the term applies wherever banks are permitted to hold deposits in currencies other than that of their residence). Indeed, the dollar dominates, its share averaging 77 percent since 1971.

Appearing initially in the 1950s, the market grew quickly in the 1960s, as holders of dollars chose to deposit them outside the United States. From 1965 to 1971, the market grew each year by 37 percent (compounded annually); from 1971 to 1979, the annual growth slowed a bit to 30 percent; then from 1979 to 1982, growth slowed dramatically, to only 18 percent each year.

As this is a short-term market, its main source of funds has always been other banks: 70 percent in 1972, 72 percent in 1982. Most funds are deposited overnight or for periods as short as one week. In 1972, central banks and nonbanks shared the remainder (12 and 18 percent, respectively), but by 1982 central banks provided only 4 percent of the funds and nonbanks provided 24 percent. Largely by agreement, central banks have pulled out of the market.

The main users of funds in the Eurocurrency markets, after one nets out interbanks funds, are nonbanks which represented 41 percent of all uses in 1972, growing to 62 percent in 1982. Central banks and other banks had been significant early users (41 percent of all uses in 1972), but their share dropped to 28 percent in 1982. Borrowers in Europe who converted the Eurofunds into local currency went from 18 percent in 1972 to 10 percent in 1982. The decade ending in 1982 saw the rapid growth in borrowers outside Europe and outside the financial sector.[5]

Banks' International Assets and Liabilities. The best aggregate measure of international banking is in the combined reports by major industrial countries of their banks' "international claims and liabilities." Available since the mid-1970s, these data show the growth of lending and funding, the regional distribution, the major borrowers by country and income group, and the cost and maturity structure of the loans. The data extend beyond Eurocurrency operations to include other forms of cross-border lending, such as loans in the currency of the country where the bank resides.

Trends. In less than 10 years, international loans, as a share of total bank loans, rose from 8.7 percent in 1973 to 17.4 percent in 1981. As Figure 40.1 shows, international lending grew at an annual rate that fluctuated between 20 and 30 percent, roughly paralleling world economic growth and the dramatic shifts in payments imbalances after the two oil shocks of the 1970s. Only in 1982 did this growth stop. In the net flow of all credit across borders, international bank lending has dominated throughout the period. Bonds have always been a small portion of the flow, geographically focused on issuers in industrial countries. The net flows fall far short of gross lending. In 1981, for example, net flows of $165 billion contrast with gross flows of $1,542 billion (or $940 billion if one excludes redeposits among banks).[6]

Distribution by Income Group. The more industrialized the borrowing country's economy, the more the economy is likely to have borrowed. In Table 40.2, one sees the dominant position of industrial countries as borrowers, followed by developing countries. In general, industrial countries are net suppliers of funds to the banks, while developing countries and eastern European countries are net borrowers. Oil exporting countries vary, depending on the size of their surplus and on whether the country has a large population.

Developing countries began to attract special attention in the early 1980s when it became apparent that many could not service their debt on schedule. All countries do not borrow to the same extent, even those with similar economies. Lending is concentrated in a few countries, those that are more industrialized and those that export oil. Table 40.3 illustrates this concentration. Indeed, at the end of 1981, four countries — Mexico, Brazil, Argentina, and South Korea — accounted for 52 percent of the $278 billion in claims of banks on nonoil developing countries.

Geographic Distribution. Since banks lend more to countries that are more industrialized, the banks' assets are concentrated in industrialized regions. In

---

[5] The source for statistics in this section is Morgan Guaranty Trust Company, *World Financial Markets* (various issues).

[6] The source for data in this section is R. C. Williams and G. G. Johnson, *International Capital Markets: Developments and Prospects, 1982*, International Monetary Fund, Occasional Paper 14. (Washington, D.C.: July 1982).

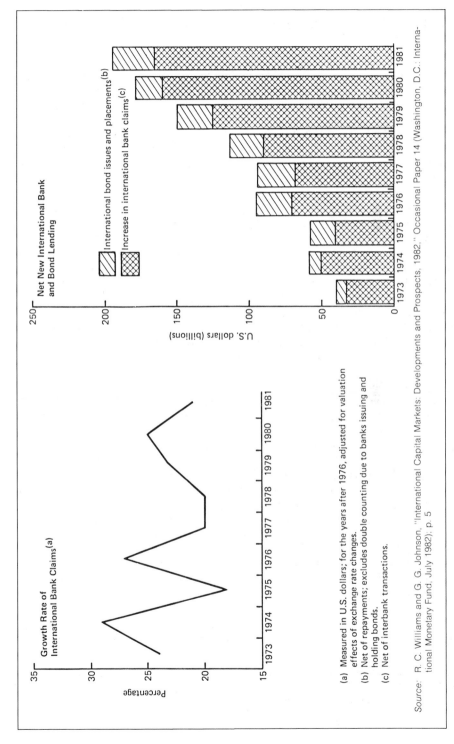

FIG. 40.1 Net Lending Through International Capital Markets, 1973—1981

Source: R. C. Williams and G. G. Johnson, "International Capital Markets: Developments and Prospects, 1982," Occasional Paper 14 (Washington, D.C.: International Monetary Fund, July 1982): p. 5

(a) Measured in U.S. dollars; for the years after 1976, adjusted for valuation effects of exchange rate changes.

(b) Net of repayments; excludes double counting due to banks issuing and holding bonds.

(c) Net of interbank transactions.

TABLE 40.2   Distribution of Banks' International Loans and Deposits by Type of Country

(U.S. dollars in billions)

Borrowing Country	Borrowers 1978	Borrowers 1981	Depositors 1978	Depositors 1981	Net Position 1978	Net Position 1981
All	$90	$165	$90	$165	—	—
Industrial	38	100	67	141	−$30	−$42
Nonoil developing	25	50	14	10	10	41
Oil exporting	15	4	3	4	12	—
Centrally planned	7	5	2	—	5	4

Source: R. C. Williams and G. G. Johnson, "International Capital Markets: Developments and Prospects, 1982," Occasional Paper 14 (Washington, D.C.: International Monetary Fund, July 1982), Table 9

TABLE 40.3   Bank Lending to Nonoil Developing Countries

(U.S. dollars in billions)

Country Group	1978	1981
All	$25	$50
Major exporters of manufactures	13	24
Net oil exporters	5	19
Low income	2	1
Other	5	7

Source: R. C. Williams and G. G. Johnson, "International Capital Markets: Developments and Prospects, 1982," Occasional Paper 14 (Washington, D.C.: International Monetary Fund, July 1982), Table 11

1981, of the $278 billion banks loaned to developing countries, those in the Western Hemisphere took over half (58 percent), while Africa only took 10 percent. All international banks are not equally exposed in the various regions.

Banks from different home countries are more closely tied with some regions than with others. Compared to all banks, those from France have a larger share of their loans in francophone Africa, while those from Germany have more in eastern Europe, Japan in eastern Asia, and the U.S. in Latin America. These differences in relative exposure attest to the impact of the home country's trade and foreign investment on its banks' international lending.

The share of U.S. banks in loans to developing countries and to eastern

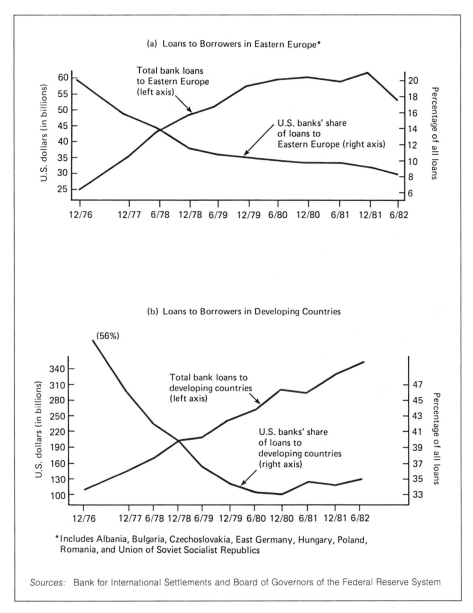

FIG. 40.2 U.S. Banks' Shares of Selected Cross-Border Loan Markets: (a) Loans to Borrowers in Eastern Europe; (b) Loans to Borrowers in Developing Countries

Europe declined a lot during the late 1970s. In part this was intended by the U.S. banks, which had been very active in the mid-1970s and benefited from the entry of other banks. In part, it reflected the changing pattern of competition among international banks, as more banks from Europe and Japan, in particular, entered the market. Figure 40.2 shows these trends in both regions.

TABLE 40.4   Short-Term Claims as a Share of All Claims on Selected Groups of Countries

Country Group	Short-Term Share (end of period)	
	1978	1981 (June)
All	44.1%	46.6%
Nonoil developing	44.3	46.1
Nonoil developing — 6 largest	34.5	44.6
Oil exporters	47.6	54.7
Centrally planned	43.6	39.5

Source: R. C. Williams and G. G. Johnson, "International Capital Markets: Developments and Prospects, 1982," Occasional Paper 14 (Washington, D.C.: International Monetary Fund, July 1982), Table 41

Distribution by Maturity. Just under half of international banks' loans are short term. During the few years for which data are available, the trend for some groups of countries has been toward shorter maturities, as Table 40.4 shows. In part, this shortening was a response of borrowers to high interest rates, in part the increased concern of banks about the risks of longer-term lending. In the case of the biggest developing country borrowers, however, the shift to shorter tenures merely increased their vulnerability, as is demonstrated by the experience of Brazil after September 1982.

Maturities fluctuate with general credit conditions. In tight markets, they shorten; in easy markets, they lengthen. Figure 40.3 illustrates this.

Prospects. For almost a decade, banks' international loans — particularly to developing countries — grew by an average of 25 percent each year. Lending dropped dramatically at the end of 1982. In 1983, most observers expected that lending would simply grow much more slowly in the future. Prudential concerns are seen as paramount. Too much of the banks' capital is seen as being at risk, particularly in lending to developing countries. The International Monetary Fund (IMF) calculated that during the three years to the end of 1981, the banks' claims on the 20 largest nonoil developing countries increased from 50 percent of bank capital to 70 percent. The two largest countries alone accounted for 40 percent of capital by 1981. Although there was a large variation among banks, lending by banks as a group had grown by 25 percent each year, while capital grew by only 10 percent a year. As a result, the IMF estimated that banks' international lending would grow only by 15 percent in the near future.[7] Such a view was consistent with opinion surveys that asked bankers in the United States which geographic markets they expected to target for growth in

---

[7] *Ibid.*, pp. 15, 44.

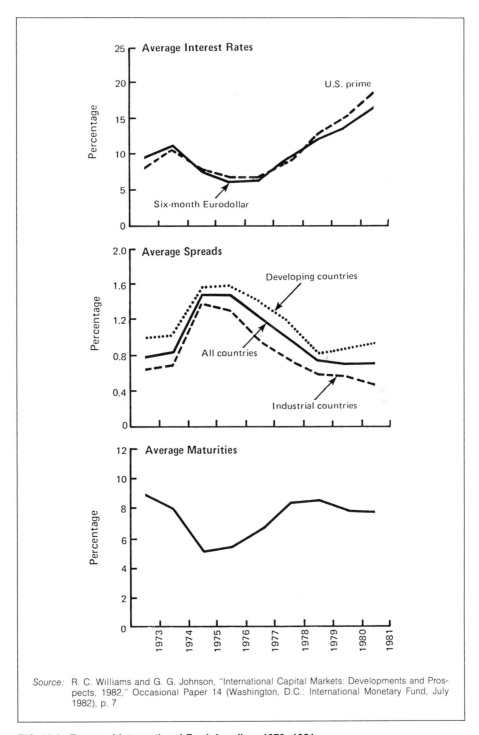

Source: R. C. Williams and G. G. Johnson, "International Capital Markets: Developments and Prospects, 1982," Occasional Paper 14 (Washington, D.C.: International Monetary Fund, July 1982), p. 7

FIG. 40.3 Terms of International Bank Lending, 1973–1981

the future. All respondents, foreign bankers as well as local, ranked developing countries at the bottom of the list. Most focused on local or regional customers.[8]

Major Issues in International Banking

International banking is no longer left to bankers. Justifiably or not, the banks' activities of the last 15 years have alarmed many people. It is asserted that the banks shape economic and political life today as they did before the Great Depression. Heads of state now keep informed on aspects of international banking that they once saw as arcane. People concerned with economic development and the stability of the world economy see the handiwork of international banks and sometimes tremble. Their concerns only deepen as banks struggle with new technologies, arguably creating a city of tomorrow in which many people would prefer not to live. The tendency toward greater concentration in the industry is viewed with alarm, yet there is concern about the consequences of strong competition.

Highly technical, the games that specialists once played in private are now under a public spotlight. This is the context of international banking in the 1980s. The major issues are sketched below.

Internationalization and National Interests. Students of finance see international banking markets as among the most integrated and open markets that exist. Evidence of this internationalization of banking appears above. Where once there had been little competition across national boundaries and few substitutes or potential new entrants, now they are legion.[9] Banks are now called Eurobanks and their Eurolending "sever[s] the nationality of the bank from the nationality of the currency in which it deals. . . . "[10] In this view, banks are another form of multinational corporation, active in markets outside their home and host countries, and content to act against the interests of any country, home or host, if such an act serves the bank's own purposes. Set against this view of international banks is one that relates the activities of almost all such banks to their home countries. The banks respond mainly to home government policy or to ties with other economic factors at home (notably the multinational corporations). Whether the banks are independent, or an integral part of their home country's political economy, is relevant to competition among banks and to the nature of credit allocation worldwide.

Economic Imbalances and the Banks' Role as Intermediary. Since no country is ever in balance of payments equilibrium, the world needs some device to manage the imbalances. International banks have always helped with this function and in the 1970s they played the role with a vengeance.

---

[8] Seung H. Kim and Stephen W. Miller, *Competitive Structure of the International Banking Industry* (Lexington, Mass.: Lexington Books, 1983), p. 158.

[9] P. Crane and S. Hayes, "The New Competition in World Banking," *Harvard Business Review* (July-Aug. 1982), p. 88.

[10] Gunter Dufey and Ian H. Giddy, *The International Money Market* (Englewood Cliffs, N.J.: Prentice-Hall, 1978), p. 10.

TABLE 40.5   Current Account Financing of Nonoil Developing Countries, 1973–1983

(U.S. dollars in billions)

	1973	1978	1983
Current deficit	−$11.3	−$41.3	−$67.8
Increase in reserves	−10.4	−17.4	−7.2
Errors and omissions	−3.8	−2.8	−16.5
Total to finance (= 100%)	−$25.5	−$61.5	−$91.5
Selected sources			
All external debt	$11.4	$40.8	$50.8
Long-term credit from private financial sources	6.5	19.5	39.1
Short-term credit	8.3	4.9	N/A

Source: "World Economic Outlook," Occasional Paper 21 (Washington, D.C.: International Monetary Fund, May 1983), Table 25

The first oil shock increased the oil producers' current account surplus from $18.6 billion in 1973 to $82.1 billion in 1974. That year, the U.S. Treasury Department estimates that the Organization of Petroleum Exporting Countries (OPEC) had an investable surplus of $60.25 billion, of which they are known to have invested $26.70 billion in commercial banks in the United States and in the Euromarkets.[11] After the second oil shock, a somewhat smaller portion of larger surpluses in nominal terms was also "recycled" through international banks. The banks played an important role in the international economy; no other financial institutions were so well placed to identify good lending opportunities and to mobilize the large volume of funds needed by deficit countries. Developing countries in particular lacked access to other financial markets.

As a result, after 1973 banks became an ever more important source of funds for developing countries. From 1973 to 1977, for example, private credit (mainly from banks) rose from 19 percent of the flow of funds to developing countries to 39 percent. During the same period, the more traditional sources declined: official aid dropped from 40 to 30 percent of all flows, while direct investment fell from 29 to 18 percent.[12] Banks were the new development financing agencies.

By 1983, the banks had moderated their role in financing development and recycling petrodollars — more accurately described as current account financing — but they were still important. Table 40.5 gives a sense of the banks' position in the previous decade. It suggests that private financial sources,

---

[11] *Estimates of the Disposition of OPEC Investable Surpluses, 1974–1979*, U.S. Treasury Department, Office of International Banking and Portfolio Investment (June 13, 1980). OPEC current account data are from the International Monetary Fund, *International Financial Statistics*.

[12] Organization for Economic Cooperation and Development, *Development Cooperation Review* (various issues).

mainly banks, helped to fund not only the current deficit but also the increase in reserves held by the countries, normally considered a healthy trend because it serves as a cushion in bad times. Because the banks lend relatively more to the newly industrializing countries (NICs), their contribution to the NICs' current account financing was even greater. At its apex in 1978, bank lending was 130 percent of the NICs' current deficit.[13] By virtue of their role, the banks had become the object of political attention worldwide.

The Impact of Technological Change. Despite many rhetorical flourishes heralding the new age of electronic banking, it has far to go before it is a commonplace in world markets. Compared to domestic markets, where retail and corporate banking are replete with evidence of the new technologies, international banking has only just begun to draw on them.

On the verge of thoroughgoing change, international banking is shaped today by a technological infrastructure. The interbank and exchange markets are world markets, integrated institutionally by a communications network unavailable even 15 years ago. Banks can now instruct correspondent banks abroad to settle payments using a network called Society for Worldwide Interbank Financial Telecommunications (SWIFT). But SWIFT illustrates the limits of the technology in international banking: it does not tie into either bank's computers and cannot actually transfer payments. It merely shortens the time in which instructions are transmitted. The prospect of technological change in banking has attracted attention and created debate.

Among bankers, the issues are managerial and strategic. At the operational level, the question is how electronic banking can speed transactions, reduce costs, integrate existing services, and create new opportunities in the international sphere. Cash management and trade-related services seem to offer the most potential. At the strategic level, the question is how technology propels banks into a whole range of information services that are not traditionally a part of banking. The shift may be one of several forces moving at least the large international banks away from direct intermediation and into competition with a range of other information-providing institutions and nonbank financial intermediaries.

Among governments, the issues concern the structure of the banking system, management of the money supply, and prudential regulation. Examples include concern about the impact of new technologies on competition among banks, on existing specializations among financial and other institutions, and on more general issues of concentration and antitrust. Central banks are concerned about managing liquidity in a world which is even more integrated.

Competition and Cooperation Among Banks. International banking requires of the players a mix of competitive and cooperative relations that some see as oligarchic, or unstable, or both. One example is loan syndication, which draws on teamwork as well as competition. The concentration of lending and particularly of managerial roles in a relatively small number of very large banks, the fact that many of these are part of an oligarchic structure at home, the tendency of bankers to move as a group, is sometimes presented as evidence that even

---

[13] R. C. Williams and G. G. Johnson, *op. cit.*, Table 11, p. 32.

in international banking a few of the largest institutions manage many of the markets. By implication, this invites at the least monopoly rents and at the most an inefficient allocation of credit. It may also insulate the large banks from appropriate control by the affected governments.

The same phenomena lead others to argue that the structure of international banking contributes to the instability of the world economy and so undermines nations. Through the process of syndication, the large lead banks draw many smaller banks into loans they otherwise could not make, since they lack the capacity to analyze the risks and to identify the opportunities. This herd mentality, sometimes called oligopolistic reaction, leads to excess. Loans are in excess, and efforts to escape countries with loan problems are also in excess. The result is radical swings in access to credit; in times of trouble the borrowing country lacks the essential for recovery, liquidity.

The upshot is simple: International banking has itself created several major issues that are important to the industry but are also important to many groups outside the industry. National governments, opposition parties, major multinational corporations, even the press, are sensitive to the activities of international banks to a degree unprecedented since World War II. International bankers face an environment that is not merely risky, but sometimes hostile.

INTERNATIONAL CREDIT: MAJOR MARKETS AND SERVICES

Introduction

Today credit is still at the heart of international banking. In the future, the large commercial banks' role as a direct intermediary may diminish. The change some foresee is systemic, as commercial banks shift to operations outside the flow of funds, such as leasing and guaranteeing. The change others foresee is that most banks will specialize more, while the largest will move closer toward universal banking that will include even direct equity investment.

International Credit Services and Markets One may cut international credit services and markets several ways:

1 Current credit, which is largely self-liquidating (letters of credit, advances, acceptances);

2 Longer-term financing, either for general purposes (notably payments imbalances), for noncurrent assets (most notably projects), or for acquisitions (notably by big U.S. companies);

3 Interbank transactions (either placing funds with a bank or replacing a bank as a holder of a note); and

4 Specialty loans (such as shipping, real estate, trade, or even agribusiness).

Each has different risks, returns, and processes.[14]

---

[14] Robert Morris Associates and Bankers' Association for Foreign Trade, *Preparing a Bank's Written International Lending Policy* (Philadelphia: Robert Morris Associates, 1977).

Risk Associated With International Credit. Banks that lend abroad expose their investment and earnings to risks absent from, or greater than, domestic credit, since they encounter variables not present in domestic markets. Funding is in many currencies, raised in uncontrolled world money markets. Foreign banks and borrowers are subject to the vagaries of national economic performance and to government policy. The governments themselves are subject to political reversals.

Until 1982, however, bankers pointed out that problem loans were regularly lower for international assets than for domestic assets. For example, on average from 1978 to 1982 among the 10 leading U.S. banks, international earnings were 48 percent of total earnings, foreign branch loans were 46 percent of all loans, overseas deposits were 51 percent of total deposits, but international net loan losses were only 22 percent of total net loan losses.[15] After 1982, foreign problem loans made this argument less compelling. On balance, it appears that the stream of international earnings is somewhat more variable than are domestic earnings.[16]

To manage the risk associated with international lending, banks have devised several techniques:

1 Better information should improve judgments about risk.

2 Pricing and maturity reflect risk, although in general the price ranges are narrow.

3 Allocation, the bank's decision to lend or not, reflects risk judgments. The very weak borrowers simply lack access to credit in any volume under any terms.

4 The law seems to offer some sense of safety, if increasingly complex contracts are anything to go by.

5 Shifting risk may also mitigate it.

6 Official help, explicit or implicit, is often sought.

7 Finally, to deal with risk that is not otherwise moderated, banks look to the self-interest of all parties in keeping the system intact and their access to it assured.

The following sections explore the international aspects of credit risk and the techniques to manage the risk. There are three aspects: the credit itself, the country, and liquidity or funding.

Credit Risk: Soverign Lending and Interbank Lending. Foreign borrowers present banks with special problems, many of which are informational. Compared to borrowers in the bank's home country, foreign borrowers use different accounting procedures, adhere to different conventions of behavior and performance, and operate in markets with a different structure. Without an office or experience in Bangkok, a U.S. bank based in Flagstaff, Arizona finds it difficult to judge a prospective borrower in Thailand.

Banks try to solve the information problem by following the lead of banks that have experience with the borrower or offices in the borrower's country: the large banks with international networks. Formally, smaller, regional banks

---

[15] Salomon Brothers Bank Securities Department, *A Review of Bank Performance: 1983 Edition* (New York: Salomon Brothers, May 1983).

[16] Gunter Dufey and Ian H. Giddy, *op. cit.*, p. 61.

make international loans by participating in syndicates led by international banks. Informally, the smaller banks simply lend to a foreign borrower that has already borrowed from a large bank. The follower, however, does not shift the risk to the leader; indeed, leaders specifically renounce such a shift. Yet to maintain their status as leader and win the fees that accompany such a role, the lead banks must maintain credibility so that followers continue to rely on leaders.

Pricing of course reflects risk, but allocation seems to be preferred by banks as the way to deal with the unknown. The range in price differences is relatively small. In Eurocredits, the differences are reflected in the spread over the bank's cost of funds and in fees for attendant services. An early example is found in loans made during 1972–1973 to four state-owned energy companies in different countries. The National Iran Oil Company paid a spread of 0.87 percent, Petroleos Mexicanos paid 0.63 percent, Algeria's Sonatrach paid 1.00 percent, and Indonesia's Pertamina paid 1.50 percent.[17] The range is less than one percent. Rarely do spreads exceed 2.5 percent and fees add another 1.5 percent. By this point, many lenders have already dropped out.

Syndication became a much less popular process in international banking after the second oil shock raised the stakes for many banks. Replacing syndicates are "club deals," in which large banks take larger pieces of a syndicate for their own portfolio. According to one journal, "In the main, deals are turned into club deals because syndication has gone badly."[18] In 1982, 15 percent of all Eurocredits were club, most in the private sector and in Latin America.

To keep borrowers and lenders in the game when circumstances change for the worse, banks designed a nuclear option, the cross-default clause. That is, the loan will be in default if the borrower defaults on any other loan. An imminent default on a single loan will focus the attention of all lenders. There is also a fail-safe device: in each syndicate, a majority must determine that default has occurred. Thus the banks can act as a group but neither the borrower nor a rogue bank — despite recent lawsuits — can push the button alone.

Credit risk is subject to regulation by home governments, which tend to be more lenient toward international loans than domestic ones. Bank examiners look for problem loans, but in many countries they are less meticulous when the loans are abroad. Also less enforced abroad are rules designed to reduce the risk of asset concentration. Countries often limit their banks' lending to individual borrowers. The common method is to limit lending to a fixed share of capital, such as 10 percent. Some countries, however, do not extend these rules to international loans. Germany exempts loans made through a bank's foreign subsidiaries. At best, governments are half-hearted policemen of world credit risk.

Borrowers generate risk peculiar to their group. In international lending, sovereign risk and risks associated with interbank operations draw special attention.

For centuries, soverign lending — credit to governments — created special opportunities and risks, as banks lending to Philip II of Spain discovered when

---

[17] P. A. Wellons, *Borrowing by Developing Countries on the Euro-currency Market* (Paris: Organization for Economic Cooperation and Development, 1977).

[18] "Annual Financing Report," *Euromoney* (Apr. 1983), p. 323.

public borrowers became illiquid.[19] The sovereign differs from private borrowers in important ways:

1 Legal standing: In some countries, the sovereign is immune from suit, so lenders may find collection less tractable.

2 Decision making: Governments act more on the basis of noneconomic criteria, forcing lenders to anticipate a wider range of factors that will influence the government's behavior in the future.

3 Performance measures: Profitability is not the criterion of success for the sovereign, so banks must employ qualitative as well as quantitative measures to judge a government.

4 Life expectancy: Even when bankruptcy destroys a government, the state endures and may repay a debt.

5 Relationship with lender: The sovereign may regulate important local operations of the bank or its corporate customers, so it can offer nonprice rewards or sanctions.

6 Access to funds: When threatened with a financial crisis, governments may be able to play on their importance to a major power, possibly helping the lenders.

One would expect the risks of lending to sovereigns to differ from private sector risk.

Banks argue that the risk of sovereign lending is less: firms disappear after bankruptcy, leaving the lender with 10 cents on the dollar. Countries continue to exist, and if they want access to international trade in the future they must play by the rules today. With the exception of a single loan to Ghana in 1966, no sovereign borrower has repudiated its debt since World War II. In a rescheduling, the lender hopes to eventually get its dollar back, in full. Prices reflect this judgment by the banks: rarely does the government pay more than private borrowers.

Even if the borrower is a public sector company whose debts are not legally those of the central government, bankers argue that those debts are safer than private sector loans. The case of Pertamina in 1975 illustrates this: Despite bitter political rivalry between the state oil company's leader and government ministers, and even though some loans were not registered, Indonesia stood behind Pertamina's massive external debt. Few governments will permit a major state industry to default, because the government's own credit standing would then suffer.

Despite the no-default rule for sovereigns, the home governments of some banks have tried to reduce concentration of assets by treating loans to the sovereign and certain parastatals as loans to a single borrower. Banks would then be bound by a single loan limit. The U.S. Government tried this in the late 1970s, with little success. As U.S. lenders to Mexico, for example, reached their limits for its government, the government orchestrated borrowing by public firms which met the definition of independence under U.S. law. These firms

---

[19] See Fernand Braudel, *The Mediterranean and the Mediterranean World in the Age of Philip II*, trans. Sian Reynolds (New York: Harper and Row, 1972).

in turn made their credit available to the Mexican government. Fulfilling the forms, all parties nevertheless violated the spirit of the U.S. law.

Banks extended their no-default rule beyond national borders to encompass lending to governments within a major power's sphere of influence. Mother Russia's umbrella was invoked for loans to eastern Europe where, bankers argued, the U.S.S.R. would not abandon an allied government on a rainy day. Events in Poland demonstrated that Russian support was far less encompassing than lenders had hoped.

In sum, banks perceived sovereign loans as less risky. These perceptions were shaped by actual loan loss experience, coupled with beliefs about national and world politics. Bankers believed that some credit risks shifted from the lender to future governments or to major world powers. The debt crisis of mid-1982 did not destroy these beliefs, but it may have forced lenders to discriminate more carefully among governments.

Interbank lending, much more significant in international than domestic banking, creates risks not found in the domestic banking system. There are two reasons for this: no central regulatory authority exists and common conventions are weak. One study identified risks at two levels: (1) the individual bank, and (2) the market. The study suggested that depositing banks fail to analyze user banks carefully, a serious problem given the proliferation of medium-sized banks from many countries. The study found that this reduced "transparency," which it defined as the ability to ascertain "the ultimate sources and uses of funds. . . ."[20] This in turn created greater instability in the market as a whole.

Banks try to manage the problems of interbank risk in four ways: diversification, pricing, reliance on official help, and reliance on mutual self-interest. Banks began to discriminate among deposit-taking banks in 1975, after several bank crises. Since then, this tiering of rates waxed and waned. Depositors also relied on understandings among central banks about official responsibility in the event an individual bank encountered problems. Events in 1983 involving the central bank of Italy cast doubt on the integrity of these understandings. Finally, the largest banks police the market, tracking the exposure of participants and warning their own authorities if one seems to be overexposed.[21]

The second nation involved in international banking introduces a set of variables treated as peculiar to this part of the industry: country risk.

Country Risk. The literature and practice of country risk analysis is like the meat counter of a delicatessen: There is so much bologna that many people do not even buy the good cuts.

The term, country risk is defined as "a spectrum of risks arising from the economic, social and political environments of a given foreign country . . . having potential favorable or adverse consequences for foreigners' debt and/ or equity investments in that country. . . ." These are "distinct from considerations

---

[20] Group of Thirty, *Risks in International Bank Lending* (New York: Group of Thirty, 1982), p. 21.

[21] See, for example, Joan Spero, *The Failure of the Franklin National Bank* (New York: Columbia University Press, 1979).

relating to a given borrower's credit-worthiness."[22] Many organizations other than banks analyze country risk, some using the synonym political risk.[23]

For each country, banks must determine which assets are at risk, not an easy matter given the variety of assets. According to a study in 1977, banks generally treat "most unguaranteed balance sheet and off-balance sheet items as exposure to the country wherein the borrower or potential borrower resides." Most banks include risk assets such as "loans, advances, casual and arranged overdrafts." Banks are less consistent about such balance sheet items as "minimum risk transactions, placements with foreign branches and/or subsidiaries of [other] banks," about such risk assets as "shipping loans supported by various charter party assignments," and about some special off-balance-sheet items such as "contingent liabilities arising from forward exchange contracts, management of fiduciary accounts and intra-bank placements."[24]

Analysts of country risk measure it in many different ways. A study in 1982 identified five approaches by banks.

1 Unstructured: Analysis is case by case.

2 Checklist: Countries are scored by standard measures.

3 Qualitative: The country's unique attributes and problems are evaluated.

4 Structured/qualitative: A common format combines economic and political data, opinion, and statistics.

5 Covariance: World events are weighed for their impact on the bank's portfolio in the country.

Other approaches include treating the country like a company or assessing its vulnerability to an abrupt halt in the flow of finance. The 1982 study concluded that the choice of approach is a function of the bank's size and skills and its involvement in international banking.[25]

In the literature, one sees a progression away from simple quantitative measures to more complex and qualitative measures. One approach is to group countries that are alike in terms of risk. Another is to identify countries that are likely to reschedule. Both raise difficult problems of comparing countries that differ along many dimensions. The dominant approach is to use indicators of economic performance to determine whether a country is like other countries that already rescheduled their debt. In this sense, it is based on precedent.

Early studies looked to debt-related indicators: the debt-service ratio (debt service payments divided by exports);[26] groups of related debt indicators (e.g.,

---

[22] Association of Reserve City Bankers, *Country Exposure Measurement and Reporting Practices of Member Banks* (New York: Association of Reserve City Bankers, Mar. 1977), pp. 11–12.

[23] See, for example, Stephen J. Kobrin, *Managing Political Risk Assessment* (Berkeley, Cal.: University of California Press, 1982).

[24] Association of Reserve City Bankers, *op. cit.*, p. 9.

[25] Group of Thirty, *op. cit.*, p. 44. This drew on earlier classifications of country risk analysis.

[26] C. Frank and W. Cline, "Measurement of Debt Servicing Capacity: An Application of Discriminant Analysis," *Journal of International Economics* (Feb. 1971).

debt service/imports divided by disbursements/imports;[27] and best/worst cases (the best case against rescheduling compared to the strongest case for it).[28] Some argued that one must look for the characteristics of the economy at the onset of a payments crisis: big fiscal deficit, fast growth of bank credit, unadjusted exchange rates, or wage growth exceeding productivity.[29] In any event, the question was whether the country under analysis resembled countries that had rescheduled debt.

Other analysts looked for factors that would suggest a tendency to reschedule. Some used weighted checklists,[30] others drew on individual indicators such as export growth.[31]

The analysis of strategic options available to a country presented a very different technique in concept and execution. The analyst would examine scenarios under which a country might choose to default or reschedule. The approach could be either deductive [32] or inductive. Although a few large multinational companies use this approach, even the large banks are reluctant to allocate the resources needed to do a careful job.

Data are a major problem for country analysis systems. Comparable data below the most macroeconomic level are hard to find. Many variables are hard to quantify. Efforts to do so lead to charges that quantifications are emotional or value laden. Most analysts are new and those with established reputations, such as the IMF, will not share their studies. The largest banks rely on their own analysis.

Once the country analysis is completed, there is some question as to whether bankers will apply it to lending decisions in a regular way. One study found that even the most careful country analysis yields to growth imperatives in the banks.[33] How then does one explain the costly analysis? In one view, a country analysis exists to justify marketing decisions after the fact, if a loan goes bad. When the technique is used, country analysis helps banks decide country limits, but not evaluate portfolio quality or set prices.[34] One reason might be a residual skepticism about the science. According to one study,

---

[27] P. Dhonte, "Describing External Debt Situations: A Roll-Over Approach," *I.M.F. Staff Papers* (Washington, D.C.: International Monetary Fund, 1975).

[28] C. Fisk and F. Rimlinger, "Nonparametric Estimates of LDC Repayment Prospects," *Journal of Finance* (Mar. 1979), p. 429.

[29] Y. Maroni, "Approaches for Assessing the Risk Involved in Lending to Developing Countries in Historical Perspective," *Proceedings of a Symposium on Developing Countries' Debt* (Washington, D.C.: U.S. Export-Import Bank, Aug. 1977).

[30] *A Survey of Country Evaluation Systems in Use*, U.S. Export-Import Bank, Policy Staff Analysis (Dec. 22, 1976).

[31] G. Feder and R. Just, "A Study of Debt Service Capacity Applying Logistic Analysis," *Journal of Development Economics* (Mar. 1977).

[32] R. Freeman, *Optimal International Borrowings with Default*, Board of Governors of the Federal Reserve System, International Finance Discussion Paper No. 126 (Washington, D.C.: Jan. 1979).

[33] Multinational Strategies, Unpublished Report (New York: 1983).

[34] *A Survey of Country Evaluation Systems in Use*, U.S. Export-Import Bank, Policy Staff Analysis (Dec. 22, 1976), p. 21.

spread rankings taken from the market predict debt repayment problems better than models using economic statistics.[35]

Liquidity or Funding Risk. Having advanced credit, banks bear the risk that they will not be able to fund it at an acceptable interest rate, in the appropriate currency, or at all. Of course, judicious mismatching of assets and liabilities presents earning opportunities as well as risks. Banks approach these risks and opportunities in different ways.

Banks pass on much of the risk that the cost of funds will change. Much of the medium-term lending is at floating rates; if the bank chooses it can fund for periods that match the three- or six-month rollover periods of these loans. This ingenious shifting of risk to the borrower effectively translates a funding risk into a credit risk: whatever the prevailing rate may be, the borrower must be able to service the debt.

Floating rates do not always protect the bank. In the mid-1970s, for example, Japanese banks as a group paid more for deposits than did others. Yet the Eurosyndicates in which they participated fixed the base rate as that paid by certain prime banks. When the spread paid by the borrower was less than the extra deposit costs to Japanese banks, they lost money on the loan.

Access to funds in the appropriate currency is a major concern to non-U.S. banks, because most Eurocurrency loans are in dollars. Eurocredit agreements solve this problem by exculpating the lenders: if they cannot raise funds in the appropriate currency, they may offer alternatives. Non-U.S. banks tend to be cautious in lending dollars; U.S. banks have the Federal Reserve Board as a lender of last resort, so they do not have a currency risk when they lend dollars.

Access to funds at all is a serious concern for each individual bank, but it is less a problem for the banking system as a whole. Depositors may avoid any bank they decide is too risky, although they rarely do so. Such an event would be the coup de grace for a bank already in trouble. At the systemic level, some voices said in the early days of the Eurocurrency markets that those markets might dry up; for example, by act of state. Lawyers solved the problem by passing this risk on to the borrower: the loan would cease to be valid if the lush Eurocurrency markets turned to desert. It was probably a Pyhrric victory — the borrower could hardly be expected to repay suddenly. But the war did not have to be fought. Funds diverted from the Eurocurrency markets would reenter from their new destination.

Returns Associated With International Banking. Cross-border loans appear to generate lower margins than domestic loans, at least in the case of U.S. markets. Domestic markets in many developing countries and in some industrial ones offer much higher returns because the markets are protected and local banks inefficient.

Evidence that foreign margins are lower is found in individual reports of

---

[35] Monroe Haegle, cited in Chris C. Carvounis, "The LDC Debt Problem: Trends in Country Risk Analysis and Rescheduling Exercises," *Columbia Journal of World Business* (Spring 1982), pp. 15, 18.

banks. As mentioned above, for the 10 largest U.S. banks from 1978 to 1982, overseas deposits were 52 percent of all deposits, but international earnings were only 48 percent of all earnings, which suggests a slightly higher return on domestic deposits. The annual report of Citicorp, one of the nation's largest banks, suggests the same: during 1978–1982, the net spread on domestic assets averaged 4.26 percent, while net international spread averaged only 2.50 percent. (The net spread is the difference between the cost of funds and earnings on the assets. The distinction between domestic and international assets is somewhat arbitrary.)

Narrower margins do not necessarily indicate less profitable loans. Wider margins would be essential at home, where retail lending incurs higher administrative costs than international wholesale lending. Despite lower margins, international operations could still contribute more to after-tax earnings. At Citicorp during 1976–1978, as a share of the total, U.S. after-tax operating earnings were 25 percent, against U.S. assets of 38 percent. (By 1980–1982, Citicorp's strategy had changed and so had the role of the United States. The domestic share of after-tax operating earnings was up to 42 percent against 38.6 percent of assets.)

While the most important element in pricing credit is the cost of funds, the runner-up seems to be the competitive environment. According to one study, in pricing, the most sensitive to the competition and to their own long-run profit objectives are the large banks based in money centers like New York and Chicago. On the other hand, foreign banks in the United States are less sensitive to competition when they price, presumably because they are funding home firms or sister branches. All banks surveyed — money center, regional, foreign — ranked capital requirements as the item of least concern in pricing. This was at a time when public concern about inadequate capital was reaching a crescendo.[36]

Major Types of International Credit Markets

During the 1960s and 1970s, banks ventured into many new loan markets, developing some and abandoning others. The period saw rapid change. The banks, able to copy one another's innovations and in need of cooperation, prevented the leaders from staying very far out in front. Their major credit markets are described below.

Trade Finance. The elder statesman of international finance, trade credit led many banks abroad. A dynamic postwar world economy and the gradual opening of borders offered banks new opportunities. Table 40.6 gives a sense of the growth of trade, twice as fast as gross national product (GNP), and also of the abrupt slowdown that occurred after 1973. One reason for the shift in assets toward developing and oil exporting countries should be clear: after 1973, their imports grew faster than those of industrial countries.

---

[36] Seung H. Kim and Stephen W. Miller, *op. cit.*, p. 150.

TABLE 40.6   The Growth of World Trade

| | Annual Average Change in Volume | | | |
| | Imports | | Exports | |
Countries	1963–1973	1974–1983	1963–1973	1974–1983
World	8.8%	3.0%	8.8%	3.0%
Industrial	9.4	3.7	9.2	2.2
Oil exporters	9.6	−5.2	9.4	14.4
Nonoil developing	6.9	5.5	6.7	3.6

Source: "World Economic Outlook," Occasional Paper 21 (Washington, D.C.: International Monetary Fund, 1983), p. 176

TABLE 40.7   Share of Total World Trade

| | Exports | | | Imports | | |
Countries	1963	1973	1981	1963	1973	1981
Industrial	64.1%	68.0%	61.7%	64.2%	69.6%	64.8%
Oil exporters	—	7.3	13.7	—	3.6	7.6
Nonoil developing[a]	20.4[b]	11.9	13.5	20.9[b]	14.5	16.3
East Europe	12.2	10.0	9.1	11.7	9.9	8.8

(a) Nonoil developing countries includes oil exporters in 1963.
(b) Data for oil exporters and nonoil developing are combined.

Source: S. J. Anjaria, et al., "Developments in International Trade Policy," Occasional Paper 16 (Washington, D.C.: International Monetary Fund, Nov. 1982), p. 71

Directions and Kinds of Trade Finance. As most trade is within the industrial world (see Table 40.7) one would expect the banks' trade financing to reflect this balance. In fact, it is necessary to distinguish between short- and long-term finance. The sparse data about trade financing suggest that within the industrial bloc most trade is paid in cash and the little financing is short term. A study in 1975 showed that 80 percent of U.S. exports to developed countries were in cash. Of the financed portion, the supplier loaned 47.9 percent, U.S. banks provided the buyer only 7.5 percent, while foreign banks loaned 36.0 percent. Most of this financing was short term (see Table 40.8).

Banks serve trade either as agents or as principals. As depository institutions, banks facilitate payment. The importer may issue a bill of exchange drawn on its bank and due on shipment. Alternatively, the importer's bank may issue a letter of credit promising to pay the exporter if the proper shipping documents

TABLE 40.8   U.S. Export Financing, Third Quarter, 1975

Portion of payment financed

All exports	36.5%
To developed countries	20.7
To developing countries	56.0

Sources of financed portion

Institution	Developed Countries	Developing Countries
Exporters	47.9%	18.4%
Foreign banks	27.3	36.0
Exim Bank	13.9	22.1
U.S. banks	4.9	7.5
Other	6.0	16.0

Source: U.S. Department of Commerce, Bureau of the Census, "Characteristics of Financing U.S. Exports, Third Quarter, 1975" (Washington, D.C.: U.S. Government Printing Office, May 1978). Exports were $23.3 billion.

are presented to the bank. The exporter's own bank, called the advising bank, may be asked to confirm the letter of credit, thus taking any risk on itself. As principal, the bank may provide credit to the exporter, taking accounts receivable as security. It may act as a factor, buying the exporter's credit claims on the buyer at a discount.[37] The bank's ability and willingness to lend to the supplier or the buyer will depend on its capacity to evaluate the risk. A world network is thus valuable.

Compared to trade among industrial nations, a much higher portion of trade with developing countries and with eastern Europe is financed. A U.S. study described 56 percent as being financed. Of this, much less was suppliers' credit and more was bank loans (see Table 40.8).

For developing countries, financing plays a greater role not just because the countries need money but because of what they import. Developing countries (including OPEC) and the eastern European countries import relatively more capital goods and fewer consumer goods. Capital goods are more expensive, take longer to produce, and longer to pay off. Some of these imports are goods and equipment for enormous projects of plant and equipment or for mineral exploitation. They cost hundreds of millions of dollars and take five or more years to complete. Financing becomes more significant and must be on a longer-term basis, matching the life of the goods.

For trade in capital goods, banks provide medium- and long-term finance and use mechanisms that differ from short-term credit. One useful study identified three types of facilities according to the locus of risk:

---

[37] Charles J. Gmur, ed., *Trade Financing* (London: Euromoney, 1981).

1 The exporter bears the risk:

   a Foreign currency credits

   b Secured bank overdrafts

   c Discount of trade receivables

2 The exporter participates in the risk:

   a Governmental export guarantee schemes

   b Credit insurance

3 The financial institution bears the risk:

   a Confirming house facilities

   b Buyer credits

   c Export leasing

   d Forfeiting [38]

International banks from most countries are involved in all of these operations. They may act as agent or depository (in the cases where the exporter bears the risk), as principal (when they confirm, lease, or forfeit), or both. Each operation has its own forms, laws, and practices. Some are arcane, few deserve special attention.

Forfeiting occurs when the bank takes a nonrecourse note; generally, the buyer promises to pay the exporter at some point in the future and the exporter sells that promissory note to the bank at a discount, but the bank forfeits any claims against the exporter if the buyer fails to pay. Forfeiting is "often chosen for small or medium sized project finance."[39] Some London consortium banks have developed forfeiting as a specialty.

Leasing usually involves a bank through a leasing subsidiary. It is most common in the United States, because of tax laws there, but is also found in Europe and east Asia. According to one study, 20 percent of all investments in the United States are leases, against 9 percent in France, and 5 percent in Germany. The bank may lend up to 75 percent of the value of the equipment, which is security for the loan. The bank may also act as trustee for either the owner or the lender. Large leases are syndicated.[40] Leasing is small but not insignificant for major U.S. banks. In 1982 Manufacturers Hanover Corporation reported lease financing of $3.1 billion on total lending of $45.7 billion, while Citicorp reported lease financing of $1.8 billion on a total of $79.2 billion.[41] Banks do not disclose the portion attributable to international activities.

Project Finance. Financing large projects brings many of these trade facilities together. True project finance makes payment contingent on the cash

[38] Robert H. Miller, "Financing Trade in Capital Goods," *Trade Financing*, ed. Charles J. Gmur (London: Euromoney, 1981), pp. 83–84.

[39] Charles J. Gmur, "Forfeiting," *Trade Financing*, ed. Charles J. Gmur (London: Euromoney, 1981), p. 117.

[40] Charles M. Gmur, "Leasing," *Trade Financing*, ed. Charles J. Gmur (London: Euromoney, 1981), p. 106.

[41] Manufacturers Hanover Corporation, *Annual Report 1982*, p. 71; and Citicorp, *Annual Report 1982*, p. 55.

flow of the project, putting a premium on careful evaluation of the risks associated with that project. More common is financing for a specific purpose, such as a big hydroelectric plant or an aluminum refinery, but if the project fails repayment is from other resources, such as the local government's budget or the parent companies' assets.

Project finance places the banks in the middle of a complicated technical package, both in terms of the way the project works and the types of financing that are needed. Whether the project is to construct plant and equipment, such as a steel mill, or to exploit raw materials, such as a coal lode, the bank must understand the production process, the available technology, the industry structure, and the project's position in it. Financing options would include the range sketched above. Some of the largest banks in the United States and the United Kingdom have large project finance units, staffed with engineers who specialize in particular industries, such as energy. Elsewhere, even the largest banks rely on bankers to appraise the projects. Most people agree that the leaders are a few large U.S. banks, but whether the technical skills give banks a competitive edge is a matter of debate.

Large projects also place the bank in a complex set of financial institutions, public and private. The bidding process is important, because the bank's role and revenues hinge on whether its exporting customer wins the project. If it does, the bank leads the bank syndicate and works with the official export credit and insurance agencies, earning fees for its role. If the customer loses, the bank may be out in the cold; certainly, the prospect of fees for leading evaporates.

To finance large projects, banks often compete along national lines. Since in many countries the largest banks are the house banks for major firms, banks and firms are already linked in national groups. Particularly when the country has only one national champion, the firm and its banks compete with groups from other countries. The bigger the project, the more important it becomes to the home government (exports mean jobs). Often the success of the erstwhile supplier hinges on the home governments' willingness and ability to offer attractive subsidized credit as a complement to the private credit. Thus the bank's competitive position is a function of its home firm's competitiveness and its home government's subsidies.

Official Export Credit. Since 1981, the financial press has resounded with articles trumpeting the export credit war. Official export credit agencies have operated since the 1920s and 1930s; the U.S. Export-Import Bank opened its doors in 1934. These official agencies differ from country to country. Some provide export insurance or bilateral aid as well, but most provide credit, at longer terms than banks are usually willing to give. Some lend directly to the seller or buyer, others rediscount through domestic banks. They are funded in different ways, most by a combination of user fees, interest payments, and money from the central government. Some official export agencies operate within annual budgetary limits, while others have no limit on the exports they can support.

Almost 50 years after founding their export credit agencies, the governments of the major industrial countries decided "to avoid destructive competition that was leading to an export credit terms race," in the words of their forum, the

TABLE 40.9   Guidelines for Selected Official Export Credits Compared to Market Rates on Domestic Corporate Bonds

End of Year	Minimum Interest Rate on Loans Repayable Over 5 to 8.5 Years by Country Group			Domestic Corporate Bond Yields		
	I	II	III	United States	Japan	France
1978	8.00%	7.75%	7.50%	9.25%	6.94%	10.27%
1979	8.00	7.75	7.50	10.75	8.34	12.92
1980	8.75	8.50	7.75	13.00	8.60	15.23
1981	11.25	11.00	10.00	15.50	7.70	17.33
1982	12.40	11.35	10.00	11.75	7.55	15.91

Notes: Group I countries have relatively high per capita incomes. Group II countries have intermediate incomes per capita. Group III countries have low per capita incomes.

Sources: Organization for Economic Cooperation and Development, press release concerning the meeting of participants held May 5–7, 1982; Morgan Guaranty Trust Company, *World Financial Markets*, various issues

Organization for Economic Cooperation and Development (OECD). In 1976, they agreed informally to minimum interest rates, maximum maturities, minimum down payments, and maximum local-cost financing terms for most "officially supported export credits."[42]

The 1976 consensus became an "arrangement" in 1978. Signatories agreed that, if they intended to offer a credit with more concessions than the guidelines permitted, they would notify the others beforehand and explain the action. The guidelines varied with the maturity of the loan and with the borrowing country's income, so more concessions were available to poorer countries. For loans maturing within 5 to 8.5 years, Table 40.9 illustrates how the guidelines, which were the same for all countries, evolved as market rates changed.

For several reasons, some suggested by Table 40.9, the signatories did not embrace the consensus with gusto. The U.S. and German Governments pushed for market rates to end what were seen as market-distorting subsidies. Countries like Japan were forced to raise their domestic rates to comply with the consensus threshold. Others, like France, felt limited. The French Government used its domestic credit controls to promote exports: excluded from the ceilings were export credits, so banks took advantage of this route to grow. Occasionally, a country concluded that it would have to offer greater concessions to win exports and exceeded the guidelines but notified other signatories at the last minute to preserve the competitive edge. Many turned to mixed credits.

Mixed credits, the use of commercial credit and foreign aid as well as official export credit, allowed an exporting country to wheel out all its guns in

---

[42] Organization for Economic Cooperation and Development, *The Export Credit and Financing Systems in OECD Member Countries* (Paris: Organization for Economic Cooperation and Development, 1982).

TABLE 40.10 World Trade by Commodity

Commodity	Share in World Exports			Developing Countries' Percentage in 1980
	1963	1973	1980	
Agriculture	29%	21%	15%	52%
Minerals	*	6	5	N/A
Fuels	18*	11	24	N/A
Manufactures	53	61	55	9

* Data for minerals and fuels are combined.

Source: S. J. Anjaria, et al., "Developments in International Trade Policy," Occasional Paper 16 (Washington, D.C.: International Monetary Fund, Nov. 1982), Tables 1, 2, 26

the credit war. Banks in countries willing to deploy such weapons had yet another competitive advantage, if they could mobilize it. No one knew how much trade was affected, but the practice grew for years. This new assault on free competition diverted aid to countries that otherwise would not have received it. Free marketeers and third worlders joined forces. In mid-1983, the OECD announced guiding principles for associated credits:

1 Aid would be for projects that were part of the country's development program.

2 Aid must provide a grant element equal to at least 20 percent of the financing.[43]

The OECD relied on shame to encourage compliance; no sanctions existed to ensure it.

Trade Finance by Commodity. The discussion so far concerns manufactures, which account for only half of all trade. As Table 40.10 shows, trade in fuels is substantial and trade in agricultural commodities and nonfuel minerals is also important.

Banks that finance commodity trade encounter a very different world from the capital goods trade. The customers differ. The exporter is more often a developing country (see Table 40.10). A trading company is much more likely to be involved in the transaction and trade in a commodity is often managed by a few producing countries and a few firms.

The industry structure, often oligopolistic and highly organized in the producer states, dictates different competitive relationships among the banks. In the case of the grain trade, for example, a few U.S. banks dominate the financing; they operate in close contact with their customers, a secretive group for whom

---

[43] *DAC Adopts Guiding Principles for the Use of Aid in Association with Export Credits and Other Market Funds*, Organization for Economic Cooperation and Development, Press Release (Paris: June 14, 1983).

financial costs are very important because a fraction of a point can win or lose a sale. The central role of agricultural cooperatives in many countries introduces a new competitor for the commercial banks: the cooperatives' bank. In France, Crédit Agricole — one of the five largest banks in the world — has become quite active internationally.

Credit for commodity trade tends to be short term and tends to be self-liquidating in that it is outstanding while the goods are in transit and is paid when the goods arrive. As developing countries became net importers of food, however, developed producers began to offer longer-term credit or even aid. In the early 1980s, the U.S. Commodity Credit Corporation guaranteed private loans for commodity exports to certain developing countries. Banks responded by arranging syndicates and a few U.S. banks took positions of leadership. Only in 1982 did the U.S. Government use credit subsidies as a weapon in agricultural trade analogous to export credits in manufactured trade.

Barter. As countries run increasingly short of funds, they turn to barter. Estimates as to the amount of world trade that is bartered range from 5 to 20 percent.[44] Some international banks have small barter units; Citicorp, for example, opened one in 1981. From a bank's perspective, barter is a poor alternative to financial intermediation. Maintaining such a unit, however, allows the bank not only to participate in an expanding activity, but to offer a service tied directly to other trade-related services they offer. To the extent banks define their competition broadly to include trading companies and information-based firms, the banks will need to offer barter services.

Interbank Markets. Historically related to trade finance, interbank credit dominates the Eurocurrency market in sheet volume. According to Morgan Guaranty Trust Company, at the end of 1982, banks' claims on other banks amounted to $1.4 trillion of a Eurocurrency market of $2.1 trillion (see Figure 40.1).

Banks lend to other banks in several ways. First, they may place funds with the banks, either as time deposits (TDs) or as certificates of deposit (CDs). Almost all short term, the TDs make up most of the $1.4 trillion. A survey in 1982 revealed that half the banks in the sample normally redeposit with other banks 40 percent or more of the interbank deposits they take. This trading seemed excessive to 40 percent of the people interviewed.[45] According to one view, however, even if this trading results merely from the banks' desire to be in the market, it "serves a pure information function" by providing "traders with information about . . . market demand and supply" and other banks "and their techniques."[46]

The trade-related interbank operations described above — confirming or opening letters of credit, for example — are the second form of bank-to-bank

[44] Peter Truell, "Barter Accounts for a Growing Portion of World Trade Despite its Inefficiency," *Wall Street Journal* (Aug. 15, 1983), p. 21.

[45] Group of Thirty, *How Bankers See the World Financial Market* (New York: Group of Thirty, 1982), p. 56.

[46] Gunter Dufey and Ian H. Giddy, *op. cit.*, p. 226.

lending. Correspondent banking flourished long before the Eurocurrency markets. Many banks continue to rely on it as their principal form of international activity.

Banks also offer a wide range of other facilities. One writer identified eight:

A *Loans for the bank's own needs, liquidity or otherwise.*

    1 Standby credit lines, available to the bank under set circumstances and terms. Non-U.S. banks look to U.S. banks for this kind of help should dollars become tight.

    2 Term loans secured by collateral such as securities.

    3 Loans for the bank's own needs (e.g., construction).

B *Loans for a particular customer of the bank.*

    4 Loans for preexport financing.

    5 Loans for projects may be funneled through a bank.

    6 Loans for the government or its agencies sometimes are channeled through a bank.

C *Loans for unspecified customers of the bank.*

    7 Revolving loans to finance customer's trade needs.

    8 Loans to be loaned on to the customer, either in the foreign or the domestic currency. The best-known example is the Resolution 63 loans in Brazil, but other countries with exchange controls have similar facilities. [47]

Thus, banks use interbank lending as a surge pot when they cannot place funds to better advantage elsewhere, as a way to learn about other banks, and even as a long-term investment. As banks in developing countries drew increasingly on interbank funds, the balance may have shifted somewhat away from the traditional form of bank-to-bank loans. In the survey cited above, 56 percent of all bankers interviewed said interbank activity "is becoming more risky because . . . [of more borrowing] by banks that are relatively higher risks." To protect themselves, most banks set overall and daily limits on placements by bank and by country.[48]

The working of the interbank market came under scrutiny during the debt crises of 1982–1983. In the crises, the interbank market proved the least manageable as banks and their governments tried to reschedule credits and keep the borrowing countries liquid. The debate split the creditors: one group argued that all credit, including the interbank loans, should be rescheduled over the medium term; another insisted that for the interbank market to remain viable, its short-term quality had to be preserved and its debts honored as they came due. The positions reflected the relative importance of interbank lending to each bank; for example, the Swiss banks opposed rescheduling.

---

[47] Charles S. Ganoe, "Loans and Placements of Foreign Banks, *Offshore Lending by U.S. Commercial Banks*, F. John Mathis, ed. (Washington, D.C.: Bankers' Association for Foreign Trade and Robert Morris Associates, 1975).

[48] Group of Thirty, *op. cit.*, p. 57.

Personal Wholesale Markets. In the late 1970s, when many entrants cut spreads in the Eurocredit market, the established banks searched for wide-margin alternatives. Bankers to the rich had a long tradition; in the ninteenth century, for example, British banks had followed wealthy customers to their Mediterranean watering holes and opened branches. By the late twentieth century, large personal fortunes were to be found in oil exporting nations and, because of the disparity of income distribution, even in other, poorer developing countries.

The competitive advantage lay with banks that could offer safety and stability. At the turn of the decade, the largest U.S. banks offered both. If the government of one's home country seemed to look hungrily at one's assets (which happened in industrial countries such as France as well as in developing countries such as Mexico), one sought safety in the large financial markets of the United States. The size of those markets and the size of the large U.S. banks also offered diversity and therefore stability. Assembling people in special units to interpret their diverse services to the rich, the largest U.S. banks set out to capture a share in the personal wholesale market at the end of the 1970s.

Balance of Payments Finance. It is a truism that every hard currency loan affects the balance of payments, albeit one ignored by many who finance projects. Balance of payments finance came to mean, however, lending to countries for general purposes rather than a specific use. Balance of payments loans took root in the late 1960s, flowering in the aftermath of the first oil shock. During 1974–1977, loans for general purposes, including those to financial institutions, were 51 percent of all published Eurocredits.[49]

Balance of payments loans are low-cost, high-volume, and, the lender hopes, low-maintenance loans. The basic analysis is of the country in question; once done, it can be updated at intervals. The industry and technical expertise essential to project lending are unnecessary. The detail of retail banking is absent. Through a syndicate, a bank simply buys a participation. Scale economies are easily realized: the same input permits small and large investments. For banks intent on gaining market share, balance of payments finance was the vehicle; the loans were often jumbos, $100 million was common, and multiples surprised no one.

As early as the mid-1970s, however, lenders started to say they preferred loans for projects over balance of payments loans. As most project loans were not contingent upon the performance of the project, the distinction makes little economic sense, although it may be politically important.

For the economy that must service a loan, whether it is project related or general purpose, the important question is the marginal impact of the financing. If a loan for a sound project that would have been carried out in any event only frees government funds for consumption or a bad investment, the loan is at greater risk than project analysis alone would suggest.

The political value of project lending, however, may be high compared to balance of payments lending. The bank's regulators and shareholders will see something tangible, so will the borrowing country, and so will the bank's important

---

[49] *Borrowing in International Capital Markets*, Table 8 (June 1977), and Table 12 (July 1979) (Washington, D.C.: International Bank for Reconstruction and Development).

customers, the suppliers to the project. Indeed, every creditor — banks, export credit agencies, even aid agencies — wants projects. Not only are there too few to go around; the countries also need untied funds.

Bonds and Notes. Compared to international lending, the market for bonds and notes differs in structure, demand, and, since many major banks are not active, competitive dynamic. International bonds are of two types: foreign bonds, which are issued in a national capital market by nonresidents, and Eurobonds, which are issued outside the country in whose currency the bonds are denominated. Table 40.11 shows the composition of each type.

The Eurobond market is relatively open, unregulated, and competitive, but the foreign bond market, subject to the rules of the country of issue, is much more managed. Despite its position offshore, the Eurobond market reflects the laws of the banks' home countries. U.S. commercial banks are rare among the lead managers: In 1982, 13 of the top 40 leaders were from the United States, but only five were commercial banks. The preeminent position of U.S. investment banks reflects the Glass-Steagall Act, which separates investment and commercial banking in the United States. The same is true of Japanese banks.[50] In the foreign bond market, the banks from the country of issue often hold dominant positions, at least in Europe and Japan. In the U.S. foreign bond market, the U.S. banks play a relatively smaller role. The capital markets of Europe and Japan are more managed than is the U.S. market.[51] Table 40.12 suggests the differences in the two markets.

Other Services Associated With Credit. The goal of banks in the 1980s has been to offer services on which they can earn fees. Banks have been imaginative in pursuing this goal. In addition to lending, some have taken very small equity positions in firms as investments. This international venture banking created administrative problems for the banks without the commensurate rewards. However, given the debt problems of many borrowers, banks may once again find their loans transformed into equity.

OFFICIAL POLICIES TOWARD INTERNATIONAL BANKING

The Importance of International Banking

In the space of 10 years, from 1970 to 1980, international banking assumed a prominence in the world unprecedented during the past half-century. National governments responded, as usual, more slowly.

---

50 "Annual Financing Report 1983," *Euromoney* (Apr. 1983 supplement), p. 2.

51 Philip Wellons, "International Bankers: Size Up Your Competitors," *Harvard Business Review* (Nov.–Dec. 1982), pp. 95–103.

TABLE 40.11   International Bonds, by Type

(U.S. dollars in billions)

	1977	1978	1979	1980	1981[a]
Eurobonds	$19.5	$15.9	$19.5	$22.2	$11.4
Straight	80.6%	69.6%	65.8%	64.2%	60.6%
Floating rate notes	9.4	16.0	21.6	19.1	24.3
Convertibles[b]	6.0	8.2	8.3	11.7	11.6
Special placements	3.7	5.3	4.3	4.5	3.5
Other	0.2	0.9	—	5.2	—
Foreign bonds	$16.6	$21.5	$21.1	$16.2	$ 9.1
Straight	94.4%	87.9%	84.5%	86.9%	82.5%
Floating rate notes	0.4	0.6	0.6	0.6	1.0
Convertibles[b]	1.4	3.9	10.1	6.9	7.9
Special placements	12.0	3.7	3.6	3.5	6.5
Other	1.7	3.9	1.2	2.0	2.1

(a) Data for 1981 are through June only.
(b) Includes warrants

Source: R. C. Williams and G. G. Johnson, "International Capital Markets: Developments and Prospects, 1982," Occasional Paper 14 (Washington, D.C.: International Monetary Fund, July 1982), p. 51

The Role of International Operations for Banks.   For the large U.S. banks, international banking was very important by the mid-1970s. At the start of the decade, only in one bank, Citicorp, did overseas earnings exceed 25 percent of total earnings. By 1976, at seven of the largest banks the share was over 40 percent, reaching almost 80 percent for the two New York giants, Citicorp and Chase Manhattan Corporation. By 1982, for the 10 largest banks the share was 55 percent.[52] For smaller U.S. banks and for most non-U.S. banks international banking contributed less to earnings and accounted for a smaller share of assets. But the number remained significant for many. German banks, for example, said they wanted to keep international operations at about 30 percent of the bank's balance sheet.

The Importance of International Banking to the World Economy.   In the growth, employment, prices, and stability of the world economy, international banking also played a key role after 1973.

The most renowned case of the banks' contribution to growth and employment during the 1970s is their so-called petrodollar recycling after the two

---

[52] Thomas Hanley, *United States Multinational Banking: Current and Prospective Strategies* (New York: Salomon Brothers, June 1976); and Salomon Brothers Bank Securities Department, *A Review of Bank Performance: 1983 Edition* (New York: Salomon Brothers, May 1983).

TABLE 40.12   International Bond Issues by Major Currency

Currency	Total 1977	Total 1981	Eurobonds 1977	Eurobonds 1981	Foreign Bonds 1977	Foreign Bonds 1981
U.S. dollar	55.5%	58.8%	63.3%	81.6%	44.1%	25.6%
Deutschemark	18.6	5.6	26.8	3.7	8.7	8.3
Swiss franc	13.7	17.1	—	—	28.5	41.8
Yen	3.9	6.5	0.6	2.4	7.4	13.2
Pound sterling	0.6	3.4	1.1	2.9	—	4.1
French franc	0.2	1.3	—	—	0.0	0.0

Source: R. C. Williams and G. G. Johnson, "International Capital Markets: Developments and Prospects, 1982," Occasional Paper 14 (Washington, D.C.: International Monetary Fund, July 1982), pp. 50, 74

oil shocks. Most commentators tend to focus on the way banks financed the payments deficits of the nonoil exporting developing countries. Banks also financed industrial countries; indeed, at the behest of their home governments, the largest banks of France and the United Kingdom arranged jumbo loans for public sector borrowers in order to finance their country's deficits. The immediate impact seemed laudable. By intermediating, the banks permitted many economies to adjust to the oil shocks with less disruption and unemployment. In retrospect, the delay was a mixed blessing. Some observers believe policy adjustments were delayed by unconditional bank financing, and that as a result a number of countries that are heavy borrowers will find the less buoyant financial markets making difficult adjustments necessary in the next few years.[53]

As the banks eased the pain of adjustment, they may also have fanned world inflation. Specifically, the large fiscal deficits and growth in international reserves are said to have created "an uncontrolled expansion of world money and credit" which is inflationary.[54] The world's money supply certainly grew fast during the 1970s, but the cognoscenti argue about the role of the banks. Much of the debate centers around the extent to which nonbank borrowers of, for example, Eurodollars use those funds within or outside the United States. It appears that when nonbanks use Eurocurrency loans to finance transactions outside the country of origin, they create liquidity. Even for the dollar, however, this multiplier may not be very high.[55] An OECD study concluded that "the market's potential as an autonomous source of monetary disturbances is modest."[56]

---

[53] Organization for Economic Cooperation and Development, *Financial Market Trends*, Vol. 25 (June 1983), p. 16.

[54] *Ibid.*, p. 15.

[55] Gunter Dufey and Ian H. Giddy, *op. cit.*

[56] Organization for Economic Cooperation and Development, *Financial Market Trends*, Vol. 25 (June 1983), p. 15.

TABLE 40.13   Asset Distribution of U.S. Banks, End of 1982

(dollars in billions)

	Assets			
			Latin America	
	Total	**Outside United States**	**Total**	**Top Four Countries**
All U.S. banks	$1,820.1	$351.6	$81.8	$66.1
Nine largest U.S. banks	634.1	204.5	50.0	40.5

	Maturity Distribution in Top Four Latin American Countries		
	1 Year	**1 to 5 Years**	**5 Years or More**
All U.S. banks	$36.6	$17.5	$10.6
Nine largest U.S. banks	21.4	11.7	6.5

Sources: Federal Financial Institutions Examination Council, "Country Exposure Lending Survey: December 1982," Statistical Release E.16 (Washington, D.C.: June 1, 1983); Board of Governors of the Federal Reserve System, *Federal Reserve Bulletin*, Vol. 69, No. 7 (July 1983), Table 1.25

As an integral part of world trade, and as the means by which savings are mobilized and value preserved, the international banking system is vital to the real economy of the world. Threats to the system's sound functioning are seen on both sides of the banks' balance sheets. On the liability side, fears arise every so often that a concentration of deposits — from OPEC nations, for example — may endanger not merely a single bank but a nation's banks. In reply, bankers ask how the deposits would leave the banking system without destroying the wealth of the holders.

On the assets side of the balance sheet, the fear is that many of the big borrowers will not service their debt. Defaults by several, it is said, would damage the lenders beyond repair. The exposure varies by bank, but many of the world's largest banks are very exposed in a few countries that are already unable to make their payments on schedule.

Should there be a wave of defaults, the danger to banks' assets is serious. In four Latin American countries (Mexico, Brazil, Argentina, and Venezuela), the nine largest U.S. banks had assets at risk equal to 6.5 percent of their total assets. Their equity capital, however, equaled only 4.5 percent of total assets.[57] These nine banks loom large in the U.S. banking system: they account for one-third of the assets of all U.S. commercial banks (see Table 40.13). Of their $40.5 billion in unguaranteed loans to the four countries, half is due in the first year. The U.S. banks may be among the most exposed banks in Latin America,

---

[57] Salomon Brothers Bank Securities Department, *Industry Analysis* (Mar. 4, 1983 and May 31, 1983).

but major banks from other countries are exposed in other regions (German banks in eastern Europe, for example). International banking has become important to the governments of the major industrial states, as well as to the borrowing countries and to the countries that are hosts to the banks.

Host Country Policies: The Problems and the Response

For the country that hosts the branch, subsidiary, or representative office of a foreign bank, the alien presence in the domestic banking system raises a wide range of issues. Should entry be permitted at all? Should the foreign banks be allowed to carry on the same business as domestic banks? Should they be subject to the same restrictions as the domestic banks? What is the effect of foreign banks on competition among banks within the country, on the stability of the banking system, or on macroeconomic management? If the host is a developing country, the issue is whether the foreign bank promotes the development program or undermines the nation's control over its economic destiny.

The Range of Controls. Host governments regulate foreign banks along many dimensions of activity:

Ownership and Control of Domestic Banks. Many countries require a majority of a bank's shares to be owned by the citizens. This forces foreign banks into joint ventures with local residents. As many of the largest banks were established in host countries decades before the host government passed these rules about local ownership, it is newcomers who find their control restricted. While the rule is common in developing countries, one finds it in developed countries as well. Canada is an example.

Entry and Expansion. Governments sometimes prohibit new banks from entering unless a public purpose is served. Grandfathering again protects the established banks. In the OECD, "by and large, regulatory policies . . . have moved in the direction of a more liberal treatment over the past two decades, though perhaps . . . not as extensive as the . . . liberalization of international capital movements and integration of capital . . . markets might have warranted."[58] In developing countries, there is no pretense toward liberalization. Restrictions have increased over the past 15 years.

Geographic Markets. Host governments sometimes confine foreign banks to specific regions of the country, such as a city or a state. Indonesia, for example, restricted foreign banks based in Jakarta, the capital, from soliciting deposits beyond a radius of 50 miles from the city. India confines foreign banks in Bombay to the city. The rules protect the deposit base of local banks. The benefits, however, are sometimes reversed. In the United States, for many years the laws against interstate branching effectively restricted U.S. banks but not the operations of foreign banks in various states. Finally, some gov-

---

[58] Organization for Economic Cooperation and Development, *Financial Market Trends*, Vol. 25 (June 1983), p. 10.

ernments require foreign banks to serve unprofitable regions, for example, poor or rural areas, as a quid pro quo for access to lucrative, protected urban or industrial markets.

Service Segment. Foreign banks may be restricted to particular services, such as wholesale lending. While the dominant position of local banks in industrial countries often makes such laws unnecessary, in developing countries the foreign bank may be preferred by local depositors as safer and more efficient. While local laws usually protect the local banks, sometimes governments use foreign banks to promote change in the domestic banking system. Nigeria created a type of merchant bank, of which foreign banks could own part, to force more imaginative and efficient operations from the local commercial banks (some foreign-owned). By practice rather than by law, host governments may channel their parastatal companies' business to local rather than foreign banks. Foreign banks must, of course, abide by local rules that limit banks to particular lines, such as commercial banking or investment banking. In Japan, the German universal banks must have two legally separate units, one for commercial banking and the other for underwriting.

Cost and Pricing. The monetary authorities of many countries regulate what banks can pay for deposits and charge for loans. Regulators use ceilings, rediscount rates, and reserve requirements. They distinguish among banks. Foreign banks, sometimes ineligible for facilities, are affected because they rely particularly on "bought money as a funding vehicle. . . ."[59]

Exchange Transactions. By regulating capital flows in and out of the country, central banks sometimes limit foreign banks' access to liquidity in local currency and to demand for loans. Since many host governments see foreign banks as conduits to tap foreign savings, they often encourage the foreign banks to bring funds into the country. Since the governments fear that foreign banks may act as conduits by which multinational firms and residents avoid exchange controls, the governments give the banks' expatriation of funds a special scrutiny, but often have a sense of impotence. Suppose that Zambia, for example, places a ceiling on interest payments for foreign loans, but South Africa does not. Suppose a firm has subsidiaries in both countries and both borrow dollars from a foreign bank, but the legal limit on interest payable in Zambia is below the market rate for the borrower. The Zambian subsidiary pays interest at the legal limit and uses transfer pricing to pay the difference to the South African subsidiary, which in turn pays a higher interest rate to the foreign bank. The mere possibility of this sort of transaction makes host governments in developing countries very sensitive about foreign banks operating on their soil.

Safety and Soundness. Regulators require domestic banks to operate in a prudent manner and expect foreign banks doing local business to operate the same way. The host bank regulator, however, may devote less attention to the

---

[59] *Ibid.*, p. 11.

safety and soundness of foreign branches or even subsidiaries on the understanding that ultimately the home governments are responsible for them.

Concentration. In a few countries, antitrust policies prevent a small number of banks from dominating the industry. The United States is the prominent example. Foreign acquisitions, either of going concerns or banks in distress, raise antitrust issues for regulators. In practice, however, the regulators have often allowed acquisitions by large foreign banks instead of large U.S. banks. In most countries, concentration in the banking industry is much less of an issue.

Investors. In some countries, of which again the United States is the prime example, banks are obliged to reveal information about their performance to public shareholders and bondholders. Quite the opposite is true in the home countries of many banks, where bank secrecy is valued. The prospect of coming into the public spotlight is a barrier to entry, but the big U.S. market is a lure to which more and more foreign banks have succumbed.

The world looks like a crazy quilt of laws to a bank in more than a few countries. What is the overall impact? How protected are the markets for international banking? In an effort to determine the relative openness of host countries to foreign banks in the late 1970s, one scholar concluded that 63 countries, with 45 percent of the world's GNP, were open or relatively open; 51 countries with 21 percent of the world's GNP were restrictive; and 24 countries with 34 percent of the world's GNP were closed.[60] The latter consist mainly of Communist countries or Socialist nations in which the government owned major commercial banks. Openness to banks was also related to the importance of trade: countries with a high import-GNP ratio tended to be more open. Most important was the government's perception of the cost to the economy, as opposed to the benefits, of opening to foreign banks. Where the prospective costs looked high, the banks were held at bay despite possible benefits.

Compliance. As the example of Zambia and South Africa suggests, host governments are skeptical about their ability to enforce compliance with their rules. Since the ingenuity of bankers, faced with restrictions at home, led to the growth of the Eurocurrency market, a similar inventiveness is not surprising in their host countries.

The extent of noncompliance is unknown, however. Most host countries are reluctant to admit that their laws are flouted. Occasionally the press reports, for example, that after a police raid in Teheran uncovered 20 bankers at work in the representative office of a foreign bank, the bank was forced to reduce its staff to six bankers, a more normal size for such an office. Interviews suggest that institutional forms designed to limit activity, representative offices only, for example, have limited effect. In a recent celebrated lawsuit, an employee

---

[60] Adrian T. Tschoegl, *The Regulation of Foreign Banks in Countries Other Than the United States*, Working Paper No. 233, University of Michigan, Graduate School of Business Administration (Ann Arbor, Mich.: Aug. 1980).

of Citibank in Europe accused the bank of evading local tax laws through a complex series of transfers into and out of tax havens. One hears of "missionary money" used to repatriate profits blocked by exchange controls: if a missionary society based in London, for example, wishes to transfer funds to a country with exchange controls, the foreign bank will keep the sterling in London and use local deposits to fund the society's local currency needs. The sterling balance in London becomes the foreign subsidiary's repatriated earnings. There is no way to know how much of this takes place.

Reciprocity. As in the trade in goods, host governments sometimes allow foreign banks to engage only in activities open to the host's banks in the home country of the foreigner. As a study by the U.S. Comptroller of the Currency showed, it is an immense, cumbersome task to determine whether reciprocity exists.[61]

Home Country Policies

While the host countries' rules constrain international banking, the policies of a few home countries have a much more profound effect on the industry as a whole. The hosts, acting in their own interests, affect operations only within their borders. The governments of five or six countries, the major industrial states, shape the markets and activities of their banks at a global level.

The Range of Policies Despite a tendency to think of home countries' policies toward banks in terms of prudential regulation, in practice many other home policies also affect international banking.

Prudential Regulations. The safety and soundness of its banking system is of great importance to each home country, but the systems for encouraging prudent behavior vary widely. Some home governments rely on informal, consensual methods (the United Kingdom is an example), others on formal rules that apply across the board to all banks (Germany and the United States), others use a combination (Japan), and still other governments rely on bureaucratic or administered processes (France). The systems used at home carry over to international banking, although in diluted form.

Prudential controls over international banking have increased during the past 10 years, but much more slowly than might have been expected, given the growth of the market, and mainly in response to crises. U.S. regulators were the first to react to the 1974 crisis; they coordinated their activities, started a data base to consolidate the international banking operations of U.S. banks, developed a staff of examiners familiar with foreign countries, and started to classify countries: strong, moderately strong, and weak. If they find the bank's exposure in weak or only moderately strong countries exceeded a certain share of capital, they inform the board of directors. In the United Kingdom, the Bank

---

[61] Steven J. Weiss, "A Critical Evaluation of Reciprocity in Foreign Bank Acquisitions," *Foreign Acquisitions of U.S. Banks* (Richmond, Va.: Robert F. Dame, 1981).

of England shifted its staff, built competency in the analysis of country as well as credit risk, and began to raise the proverbial eyebrow at loans concentrated in certain countries. In Japan, the Finance Ministry and Bank of Japan kept careful track of every international loan made by their commercial banks, discouraging some loans according to criteria that were at least in part prudential.

The regulators of banks from the other major home countries, however, exercise very limited power over their banks' international operations. Despite the crises, French and German regulators held back. The French regulator of banks examines the international lending of the smaller French banks but leaves the large banks to their own devices on the theory that they know more than he does about country risk. The German authorities have fought for years to get the banks to consolidate their accounts (they need not report foreign subsidiaries' operations). Done for the past few years by gentlemen's agreement rather than the force of law, consolidation of accounts is only the first step in Germany toward prudential regulation of international banking.

Structural Policies. Home governments regulate the structure of the banking industry along several dimensions: service line, geographic market, and concentration, as described above. These rules affect, indeed sometimes prompt, the international operations of banks: limited at home, the banks turn abroad. To the extent that banks are allowed to have close ties to particular groups of customers — equity as well as debt, management as well as outside lender — barriers exist to entry by banks from other countries.

Macroeconomic Policies. Many macroeconomic policies employed by the home governments affect the international activities of their banks. There are two sorts of policies: those that influence the domestic economy, such as demand management through fiscal or monetary tools; and those that affect the balance of payments of the home country, such as export promotion or import substitution policies on the trade side or rules restricting loans to foreigners or deposits by foreigners on the side of the capital account. Monetary policies affect demand for banks' services at home and the relative cost of funds at home and abroad. Trade-related programs tie the lender to home firms. Capital account policies determine whether the banks' home currency is available as a reserve currency.

National Security. In times of crisis or overt, continuing hostility, home governments look to their international banks as tools or weapons. The simple idea is that one's banks should not lend to one's enemy or be vulnerable to enemy action. At the time of the war in the Falkland Islands, the United Kingdom Government restricted U.K. bank lending to Argentina. Over a protracted period, the U.S. Government prohibited, as "trading with the enemy," loans by banks to such countries as Cuba. During the year that Iran held U.S. diplomats hostage, the U.S. Government embargoed Iranian deposits at U.S. banks so the funds could not be suddenly withdrawn to the detriment of the banks, as it was argued at the time.

Security interests prompt home governments to bend their banks' lending capacity to national purpose. Again the idea is simple: money is power and we should reward our friends. No state department or foreign ministry, however, has the authority of the imperial powers of a century ago. Then, in the words of a German bank director in 1906, "the first move made is to ask the consent of the Foreign Office for carrying on the [loan] negotiations."[62] Now bureaucratic power over international banking has shifted within home governments from the foreign ministries to the treasuries and central banks. Only in the U.S. Government does a staff of specialists exist in the State Department; in the British Foreign Office, one man followed international banks in the early 1980s. In Japan, the Finance Ministry has a monopoly over this function. As a result, today the foreign ministries lack the formal power as well as the technical expertise to manipulate the international lending of their banks. Nevertheless, they try. One method is to build coalitions with the trade ministry and export credit bank. In Germany, lending to countries in eastern Europe was an integral part of the Ostpolitik.

The Impact of National Policies. As one would expect, the impact of home policies on international banking varies a lot depending on whether all work in the same direction. If not, as in the United States, bankers experience the frustration of contradictory policies but also independence. In the words of one U.S. banker, "We get inconsistent signals from Washington. . . . Take the classification of various countries. . . . Ivory Coast is loaned up to its eyeballs according to the Comptroller and Fed, but the Eximbank just made a new loan there. It would be a lot easier if the signals were consistent, but thank goodness they are not."[63]

At the other extreme is the country in which these diverse policies are coordinated toward a common objective. Coordination is a relative thing, given policies with multiple goals. One could imagine, however, a country in which:

- Domestic regulations such as capital-asset ratios do not apply outside the borders.
- Monetary policies encourage lending to finance exports, and export credit agencies subsidize interest rates.
- Banks own shares of the major companies, allowing them to rely less on short-term profits and more on market share.
- Strong economic performance encourages depositors to place funds with the banks.

Banks from such a country — Japan and sometimes France would be examples — could offer very fine spreads. Banks from a country with the opposite characteristics would be at a competitive disadvantage.[64] One looks to the national strategy to weigh this.

Home country policies could be protective, defensive, or aggressive. When the laws have an extraterritorial reach, however, they may conflict with the

---

[62] Herbert Feis, *Europe: The World's Banker* (New York: W. W. Norton, 1965), p. 174.

[63] Quoted in P. A. Wellons, *World Money and Credit: The Crisis and Its Causes* (Boston: Harvard Business School, 1982), p. 172.

[64] For an elaboration of this argument, see P. A. Wellons, "International Bankers: Size Up Your Competitors," *Harvard Business Review* (Nov.–Dec. 1982), p. 95.

laws of other jurisdictions where the banks do business. In the words of the OECD, "problems of conflict of jurisdiction remain considerable. . . . Existing legal uncertainties provide a further incentive for . . . strengthening . . . supervision . . . of both local business of foreign [banks] and the worldwide business of domestic banks."[65]

Multilateral Policies

For more than a decade, bank regulators from major industrial countries have met to share data and coordinate policy toward international banking. Although far from a resounding success, these efforts have improved mutual understanding of different policies and have improved information available to regulators about the activities of the banks.

The Bank for International Settlements (BIS) gathers data about the aggregate foreign exposure of banks. The data allow a very rough sense of trends in lending, after a delay of six months. They are good enough for one to see the shift over a period of three years from long-term to short-term credit to Mexico, which ultimately suffered a debt crisis. They did not allow anyone to pick up a surge in short-term lending in the six months leading up to the crisis.

The main forum regulators use to coordinate policy is the BIS' Committee on Banking Regulation and Supervisory Practices. Members from 12 industrial countries attend. In its own words, the committee

> Does not attempt far-reaching harmonization of member countries' supervisory techniques. Rather, it aims to establish broad principles [while members work out details]; it attempts to identify gaps in the supervisory coverage of international banking and to recommend corrective action; and it provides an opportunity for the supervisors who attend . . . to learn of each other's techniques and profit from each other's experiences.[66]

From this Committee emerged an understanding called the Basle Concordat (Basle is the headquarters of the BIS). In essence, the Concordat said: all foreign banks should be supervised; the host must supervise joint ventures with foreign banks; where authority overlaps, the host takes first responsibility for liquidity problems and for the solvency of foreign joint ventures or subsidiaries, but the home is responsible when the parent has a moral commitment or where the unit is a foreign branch; and, finally, supervisors will cooperate.[67]

After time and events revealed weaknesses in the Concordat, new guidelines were published in 1983 by the Cooke Committee, named for its chairman, Peter Cooke, of the Bank of England. In effect, the new concordat placed more

---

[65] Organization for Economic Cooperation and Development, *Financial Market Trends*, Vol. 25 (June 1983), p. 13.

[66] From *Record of Proceedings*, International Conference of Banking Supervisors (London: July 5, 1979), quoted by Robert R. Bench, "A Framework and New Techniques for International Bank Supervision," *Central Banking Seminar*, Vol. 2, (Washington, D.C.: International Monetary Fund Central Banking Department, June 28–July 13, 1982), p. 64.

[67] Robert R. Bench, *ibid.*, p. 65.

responsibility on the host, without removing from the home responsibility for a branch's solvency or the liquidity of its own banks worldwide.[68]

"Calculatedly vague" describes the position of the Concordat on the question of who will be lender of last resort in a crisis. One study concluded that the system now is the "worst of all possible worlds" in that "institutions that pretend to be LLRs [lenders of last resort] for international banking activities . . . cannot control the risk exposure of international banks, and . . . will not be able to perform LLR functions . . . when a crisis hits." The authors argued for effective LLR facilities or, as a fallback, "an explicit acknowledgement of where LLR responsibilities stop, combined with a general policy of reliance on private market mechanisms and maximum disclosure."[69] This very American solution is one that they recognized many regulators would oppose.

Joint action extends no further. Despite occasional efforts by governors of the Federal Reserve Board, the Cooke Committee has never consented to work toward uniform rules about capital adequacy, leveraging, and reserves. One reason is that offshore banking centers exist. Regulators fear that if they should tighten up controls on banks operating in their jurisdiction, the banks would simply move their business elsewhere. London is not prepared to relinquish its preeminent position as a financial center and the Bank of England chairs the Cooke Committee.

Regulation by Offshore Financial Centers

Some countries have chosen to become financial centers. To attract banks, they hold to a minimum the rules that govern operations of the banks outside the financial center, or "offshore," as it is called. Normally there are no reserve requirements or prohibitions on capital movements. Often there are limited taxes. Despite the Concordat, regulators in financial centers have little interest in the quality of the banks' offshore portfolios; it is not clear whether the smaller centers, such as Panama or Singapore, accept responsibility for the liquidity of joint ventures. Although this is changing, the countries themselves lack access to unlimited hard currency funding. Recent legislation in the United States permitted the establishment of international banking facilities (IBFs). These IBFs appear to have become the location of most new international dollar lending.

Strategic Implications for International Banking

The complex weave of regulation constrains international banks, but it also frees them. Should a country choose, it can improve the competitive stance of its banks; such a choice is usually made to accomplish a broader purpose than

---

[68] See Peter Montagnon, "Central Banks Try to Close the Loopholes," *Financial Times* (Aug. 17, 1983), p. 8.

[69] Jack Guttentag and Richard Herring, *The Lender of Last Resort Function in an International Context*, Working Paper No. 9-81, University of Pennsylvania, The Wharton School (Philadelphia: 1981).

helping the banks, such as to increase employment by promoting exports. Many policies affect the banks' access to markets (service or geographic) and affect the growth of those markets. The impact on profitability follows. The complexity may increase uncertainty and risk, but it also increases opportunity for the banks.

STRATEGY, STRUCTURE, AND OPERATIONS

Major Strategic Differences Among Banks

Competition can be fierce in international banking. One expects this in an industry with many and varied firms. Intense rivalry is normal when "competitors diverse in strategies, origins, personalities, and relationships to their parent companies have differing goals and differing strategies. . . . They may have a hard time reading each other's intentions accurately and agreeing on a set of 'rules of the game' for the industry."[70]

Among banks with international activities, there seem to be three groups. They are less strategic groups, in the traditional sense, than banks of roughly similar size and capability. In many cases, their strategies seem more closely parallel to those of peers from their home country than to the strategies of banks based elsewhere.

Straddling the market are about 20 to 40 banks of world class. They have global networks in common (but not necessarily a developed branch network). They diverge on whether to provide universal financial services or to specialize in such services as wholesale lending. As multinational companies, these banks face the most trying structural problems: how to integrate diverse activities. Some tried a matrix organization, only to discard it as cumbersome. Just before Citicorp moved away from the matrix, Japan's Sumitomo Bank opted for it on the advice of an American consulting firm. Others diversify the entire bank along regional lines, placing the home market in one such region. Still others fully integrate along market lines, such as markets for individuals and markets for institutions. No bank appears convinced it has resolved the administrative problems to its satisfaction.

A second set is more aptly called international banks. They have units abroad but lack a global network. They have developed geographic and service niches. Examples include the Swiss banks, specializing in financial markets and Europe; the regional banks from Texas, specializing in energy finance and lending in Latin America; those like Bank of Boston that specialize in domestic markets and trade finance in Latin America. Like other firms whose foreign business is not fully integrated into the company, they tend to have an international division.

Finally, there are many domestic banks with small international operations. For them, the structure reflects the low status of international banking. The international staff is small, ancillary to the main purpose of the bank.

---

[70] Michael Porter, *Competitive Strategy* (New York: The Free Press, 1980), p. 19.

Administrative Problems Associated With International Banking

International banking raises many administrative problems. The following paragraphs review the most visible of these problems.

Growth: Marketing vs. Prudence. Fashionable as it is to upbraid banks for lending to countries that later rescheduled, one blessed with hindsight should recall the organizational dynamic. The following describes the process in one of the largest New York banks:

> [O]ne staff office, under the vice chairman and outside IBG [the international banking group], sets cross-border limits for countries at an annual budget review. It assesses risk but ignores earnings. Each regional division head in IBG has ultimate responsibility for pricing decisions by his officers in the various countries. These were the guys who tried to hold back the eroding spreads and they are the ones who argue for higher exposure limits if conditions change after the budget. For [my] segment, no one person or office really calculates risk and return.[71]

The organizational setup is critical: the analyst of risk is a staff person known to all his colleagues to be trained in the dismal science. Not only has he warned against countries that hindsight shows were too risky, but this economist has also warned against countries that hindsight shows are still sound. Set against this Cassandra is a line person who wants to improve the earnings of the bank. An imbalance in power is built into the administrative structure of the bank.

Dealing with uncertainty is what international banking is supposed to be about. Solutions reflect the basic strategy of the bank: is it after fast growth of market share, of assets, or of earnings? At what part of the market does it aim? Most international banks are still in search of a successful solution. Unless one concludes that banks will win a low-cost bailout on bad country loans, it appears that many banks have not devised a structure to relate country risk and return effectively.

Customer Groups: Multinational Corporations vs. Local Client. Inherent in an international bank network is a conflict between those who serve customers with global activities and those whose markets are confined to a particular region, like a country.

The typical conflict arises when the multinational corporation (MNC) needs funds in a country where local currency is a scarce commodity for foreign banks. The MNC expects a price that reflects its global standing and the benefits of its worldwide business to the bank. The country manager wants to earn wider margins by lending to local customers. Because the domestic market is often protected, the rate difference between the MNC and the local borrower is not due entirely to risk.

---

[71] Quoted in P. A. Wellons, *World Money and Credit: The Crisis and Its Causes* (Boston, Mass.: Harvard Business School, 1983), p. 99.

For the bank as a whole, the issues are several. Who decides which customer and banker gets priority, what criteria are used? When bankers are rewarded for contribution to earnings, how does one reward an opportunity foregone for the greater good of the bank? In big banks, authority is often lodged in a regional chief with a line of appeal for the other interests.

Exposure: Headquarters vs. Field. The more a bank sprawls across the world, the more issues of centralization and decentralization come to the fore. All multinational firms confront this problem and banks are no exception. One question is how much authority to grant local officers who expose the bank through credit and foreign exchange operations. Banks resolve this by setting limits: the officer based in Singapore can lend up to $5 million without seeking approval from a senior officer. Banks provide guidelines for loan limits and for processes. A second question is where to locate the senior officer. Some banks have gone so far as to place executive vice presidents in the field, near their soldiers.

Funding: Common Pool vs. Autonomous Sources. An integral part of the bank's view about centralization is its procedure for funding loans. Does the bank have one cost of funds for all units, to maintain a standard hurdle rate on loans, or is each unit on its own, able to tap any funding source in the world and working at arm's length with other units in the same bank? Depositors distinguish between a bank's foreign branches and its subsidiaries as to which must pay more. If in practice a bank is morally liable even for its subsidiaries' liabilities, does it make sense to fund through the subsidiaries? Despite the new technology linking money markets around the world, liability management remains complex.

Revenue: Interest vs. Fees. Gone is the international banker of yore, who would arrive on a distant shore, test the wind, and decide whether to lend. Replacing this legend is a team of specialists scattered around the bank, one the credit officer who will analyze the borrower, another the merchant banker who will syndicate the loan. The loan generates regular interest payments, while the syndication generates a single fee.

The organizational problem lies in integrating the services and rewarding each banker according to performance. Banks solve the problem in different ways. Some allocate earnings among those involved according to a formula. Others double count, allocating all earnings to each unit or person involved. A third group simply lumps together all earnings, allots them to the credit officer, and judges the merchant banker by different criteria. The solution is a function of the strategy of each bank, which includes goals about the quality of life in the bank.

Marketing: Service vs. Geographic. One problem of marketing is much like the problem of rewarding fee- and interest-generating operations. The largest banks, world class, by the previous definition, have concluded that their wide networks and range of services create scale economies and barriers to entry. One caveat remains: the banks must be able to reap the benefits.

A common example of the marketing problem involves the link between trade financing and the customer base, domestic and foreign. Suppose a customer of Banque Nationale de Paris's branch in Strasbourg, France needs foreign currency financing for exports to Latin America. Dollar credits might make the export more competitive. How does BNP's manager begin to know the range of dollar-based services that might be available from the offices of the sprawling bank.

The administrative problem is to enhance the bank's marketing of its services by managing massive amounts of data. The goal is to take advantage of potential scale economies. Most banks are still coming to grips with the problem at an organizational level. The revolution in technology heightens the problem without providing an obvious solution.

Networks: Full Ownership vs. Minority Interest. Banks that emerged from national systems that prize control, or banks that rely on control to coordinate idiosyncratic strategies, face a special administrative problem when confronted by host governments with local ownership rules.

The administrative issue is whether to build a network of wholly owned units or, alternatively, to seek or accept partners. In practice, the banks use joint ventures or consortia to enter new markets.[72] Partners are expected to provide knowledge of an unfamiliar market and access to unknown customers. Once established, however, the banks opt for their own units.

The dilemma for foreign banks arose with local laws mandating citizens as shareholders. In the mid-1970s, some banks insisted on control and withdrew from countries that denied them full or at least majority ownership. Many, however, proved willing to share ownership.

The banks that shared ownership appear to have felt compelled to do so: they acted to keep market share or to enter. A study indicated that of all entities owned by 84 transnational banks in 1975, in 31 percent the banks shared ownership. The proportion was equal for entities in developed and developing countries. At the time, banks with the greatest propensity to share ownership were either already established in the host by virtue of colonial networks and therefore captives of a sort (U.K. and French banks) or trying to break in rapidly to new markets (Japanese banks). Banks with the least propensity to share specialized in money and capital market operations in Europe (Swiss banks).[73]

Conclusion

Much of the story of international banking involves the coordination and packaging of services in an extremely complex environment. Although some banks are streamlining and, in U.S. financial markets, intermediaries are unbundling ser-

---

[72] See Marianne Odjagov, Foreign Ownership of U.S. Transnational Banks," Unpublished Dissertation, Harvard Business School, 1978.

[73] United Nations Center on Transnational Corporations, *op. cit.*, pp. 60–61.

vices, the trend in international banking still seems to be in the opposite direction. Those that dominate the industry of international banking are giants by any measure.

In another age, the elephant and its nearest relative today, the little hyrax, had a cousin who failed to adapt to changing times. It was called the mammoth. In the future, size alone may not be the prerequisite or the measure of success in international banking.

SUGGESTED READING

The following books are a useful introduction to a cross-section of issues about international banking.

Banking and the Euromarkets

Aliber, Robert Z. *The International Money Game*, 3rd ed. New York: Basic Books, 1980.

Hogan, W. P., and T. F. Pearce. *The Incredible Eurodollar*. London: George Allen & Unwin, 1982.

Johnston, R. B. *The Economics of the Euro-Market*. New York: St. Martin's Press, 1982.

Kim, Seung H., and Stephen W. Miller. *Competitive Structure of the International Banking Industry*. Lexington, Mass.: Lexington Books, 1983.

Mendelsohn, M. *Money on the Move: The Modern International Capital Market*. New York: McGraw-Hill, 1980.

Administrative Issues and International Banking

Davis, Stephen I. *The Management Function in International Banking*. London: Macmillan, 1979.

Policy Issues

Key Issues in International Banking. Federal Reserve Bank of Boston, Proceedings of a Conference Held October 1977. Boston: 1977. (Several interesting papers concerning U.S. banking abroad, foreign banking in the U.S., risk in international lending, and regulation.)

The History of International Banking

Feis, Herbert. *Europe the World's Banker 1870–1914: An Account of European Foreign Investment and the Connection of World Finance with Diplomacy Before World War I*. New York: W. W. Norton, 1965. (First published in New Haven, Conn.: Yale University Press, 1930.)

Kindleberger, Charles P., and Jean-Pierre Laffargue. *Financial Crises: Theory, History, and Policy*. Cambridge, Eng.: Cambridge University Press, 1982.

Country Risk

Nagy, P. J. *Country Risk—How to Assess, Quantify and Monitor It*. London: Euromoney, 1979.

Lending to Developing Countries

Cohen, Benjamin. *Banks and the Balance of Payments: Private Lending in the International Adjustment Process*. Montclair, N.J.: Allanheld Osman, 1981.

Organization for Economic Cooperation and Development. *Debt Problems of Developing Countries*. Paris: Organization for Economic Cooperation and Development, 1974. (This provides a useful typology of the kinds of debt problems a developing country can encounter.)

United Nations Center on Transnational Corporations. *Transnational Banks: Operations, Strategies, and Their Effects in Developing Countries*. New York: United Nations, 1981.

Banks from Different Industrial Countries

Bronte, Stephen. *Japanese Finance: Markets and Institutions*. London: Euromoney, 1982.

Channon, Derek F. *British Banking Strategy and the International Challenge*. London: Macmillan, 1977.

Textbooks

Dufey, Gunter, and Ian H. Giddy. *The International Money Market*. Englewood Cliffs, N.J.: Prentice-Hall, 1978.

Useful Sources of Industry Information

Bank for International Settlements (various series on international bank flows).

Bank of England. *Quarterly Bulletin* (for data about banks based in the United Kingdom).

Euromoney (London monthly).

Federal Reserve Board (various series on U.S. bank flows).

Institutional Investor, International (New York monthly).

Morgan Guaranty Trust Company. *World Financial Markets* (New York monthly).

Organization for Economic Cooperation and Development. *Financial Market Trends* (Paris, three times a year).

41

International Accounting

LEE H. RADEBAUGH

INTRODUCTION TO THE INTERNATIONAL DIMENSIONS OF ACCOUNTING

The quality of financial managers' decisions is obviously enhanced if the managers have access to quality information. It is the job of the corporate controller to provide this information for internal as well as external users. All the functions with which the controller is concerned have international as well as domestic relevance. It is easy to assume that what is done domestically must be done exactly the same way internationally. However, that assumption ignores the cultural, educational, legal/political, and economic variables that affect U.S. business abroad. There are a number of factors that influence the quality of information generated for a multinational firm, such as different accounting standards and disclosure practices worldwide, foreign currencies, and other environmental factors that determine the way that subsidiaries and subsidiary managers are evaluated. In addition, the tax function has some interesting international ramifications. These issues are incorporated in the discussion of four key topics: financial accounting issues (such as accounting for foreign currency transactions and the translation of foreign currency financial statements), reporting inflation results, and reporting geographic segments and export revenues; differences in accounting standards and disclosure practices worldwide; taxation issues; and management performance measurement.

FINANCIAL ACCOUNTING ISSUES FOR INTERNATIONAL OPERATIONS

Statement of Financial Accounting Standards No. 52

The concepts of foreign exchange markets and foreign exchange exposure are discussed in Chapter 37. This chapter looks more closely at the specific accounting concepts that are connected to foreign exchange.

In December 1981, the Financial Accounting Standards Board (FASB) issued *Statement of Financial Accounting Standards No. 52 — Foreign Currency Translation*, which supersedes FASB Statement No. 8, the controversial standard on translation issued in 1975. The new standard deals with two major issues: accounting for foreign currency transactions and the translation of foreign currency financial statements. The latter area involves the most changes from FASB Statement No. 8, so the former is dealt with first. Foreign currency transactions involve two major problems: accounting for normal sales and acquisitions with settlement due in a foreign currency, and accounting for forward contracts.

Accounting for Foreign Currency Transactions. U.S. companies may become involved in international transactions without having foreign operations. These companies do so through import/export activities and the financing of operations by borrowing foreign currency. The most important international transactions are the sale or purchase of merchandise, capital assets, or services; the payment or receipt of dividends, royalties, and management fees; and borrowing or lending money. The assumption is that these transactions are to be settled in foreign rather than domestic currency, giving rise to some interesting accounting and reporting problems.

Four issues need to be resolved in accounting for transactions denominated in a foreign currency: (1) the initial recording of the transaction, (2) the recording of the foreign currency balances at subsequent balance sheet dates, (3) the treatment of any foreign exchange gains and losses, and (4) the recording of the settlement of foreign currency receivables and payables when they come due. Although there are various ways to deal with each of the problems identified above, FASB Statement No. 52 is clear on what to do. According to FASB Statement No. 52, it is important that each firm decide on its functional currency. The functional currency is defined as "the currency of the primary economic

---

TABLE 41.1   Foreign Currency Transaction

Assume the following exchange rates:

$2.25/pound sterling	spot rate on January 1
$2.20/pound sterling	spot rate on January 31
$2.22/pound sterling	spot rate on February 15, the settlement date

On January 1, the XYZ Company purchased capital equipment from a British exporter for 500,000 pounds sterling with payment to be made on February 15.

January 1	Equipment	$1,125,000	
	Accounts payable		$1,125,000
January 31	Accounts payable	25,000	
	Gains		25,000
February 15	Loss	10,000	
	Accounts payable	1,100,000	
	Cash		1,110,000

---

environment in which the entity operates; normally, that is the currency of the environment in which an entity primarily generates and expends cash."[1] For firms involved in import/export operations, the functional currency is normally the currency of the country in which it is based. Thus, a U.S. company buying a piece of capital equipment from Germany would normally consider the U.S. dollar as its functional currency, since most of its transactions take place in the United States.

Once the functional currency has been defined, it is relatively easy to account for foreign currency transactions. FASB Statement No. 52 requires that assets, liabilities, revenues, and expenses be recorded in the functional currency at the exchange rate in effect on the transaction date. At each subsequent balance sheet date, balances denominated in a currency other than the functional currency should be adjusted to reflect the current exchange rate. In practice, an acquisition of merchandise or capital assets is recorded at the exchange rate in effect on the transaction date, as is the liability. At subsequent balance sheet dates, the merchandise or capital asset remains at the initial recorded value, but the liability — which is still denominated in the foreign currency — is adjusted to reflect its value at the new exchange rate. Any gains or losses on that adjustment are recorded as a gain or loss to be taken to the income statement. Table 41.1 illustrates how these journal entries might look.

Four things should be noted from this example. First, the equipment is recorded at the original spot rate and its value does not change even though the exchange rate does change. Second, the account payable is changed at the balance sheet date to reflect the new exchange rate. Third, each time this balance

---

[1] *Foreign Currency Translation,* Financial Accounting Standards Board, Statement of Financial Accounting Standards No. 52 (Stamford, Conn.: 1981).

is computed, a gain or loss is determined and the amount is recorded as a gain or loss in the income statement. Fourth, the amount of cash actually expended is determined by the spot rate in effect on the day of payment.

It is worth noting two other standards relating to this issue that were introduced in 1983. International Accounting Standard (IAS) 21, which was issued by the International Accounting Standards Committee (IASC, described in the later section, "Harmonization of Standards") in July 1983, is very similar to FASB Statement No. 52. However, IAS 21 allows firms to adjust the carrying amount of assets acquired in a foreign currency for exchange losses arising from severe devaluations or depreciations. This would hold as long as the carrying amount does not exceed the lower of replacement cost and the amount recoverable from the use or sale of the asset. In addition, a firm that acquires an asset for a price in a foreign currency and hedges the price with a forward contract may carry that asset at the forward rate rather than the original spot rate. The liability then is carried at that same rate.[2] These practices are generally followed in Statement of Standard Accounting Practice No. 20, *Foreign Currency Translation*, which was issued by the British in April 1983.

Accounting for Forward Exchange Contracts. To this point, the discussion has dealt primarily with the spot market in recording transactions. The forward market is a market that exists to facilitate future transactions in currencies. The forward rate is an exchange rate quoted by the foreign exchange trader and his customer for transactions that take place beyond the two business days covered by normal spot market transactions. The forward rate is a contractual rate that may or may not equal the spot rate in effect when the contract comes due. The contract allows a firm to "lock in" an exchange rate so it can plan its purchases and sales more precisely when future spot rates are difficult to determine.

There are four major reasons to enter into a forward contract: to hedge a foreign currency commitment; to hedge the receivable or payable attached to a foreign currency transaction, such as the one described in the preceding section; to hedge a net investment in a foreign operation; or to speculate.

An example can explain how the forward contract affects the firm. Assume that the spot exchange rate is $2.25/pound sterling and that the 45-day forward rate is $2.20. In this situation, the pound sterling is selling at a discount in the forward market because the forward rate is less than the spot rate. (If the forward rate were $2.30/pound sterling, the pound sterling would be selling at a premium in the forward market.) If a firm enters into a contract with the foreign exchange trader to deliver dollars (the contract payable) in order to receive pounds sterling (the contract receivable), then it records this executory contract as a memorandum entry. No formal entry is made in the books until the contract is actually fulfilled. The amount denominated in foreign currency (the contract receivable in this case) is recorded at the spot rate on the date of the contract, and the amount denominated in dollars (the contract payable) is recorded at the forward rate. The difference between the two is the discount or premium, depending on what the two rates actually are.

---

[2] *Accounting for the Effects of Changes in Foreign Exchange Rates,* International Accounting Standards Committee, International Accounting Standard No. 21, Paragraph 31 (London, Eng.: 1983).

In the case of a foreign currency commitment, assume that a U.S. importer agrees to purchase capital equipment from a British manufacturer as soon as it is completed, with payment to be made in pounds sterling. To protect against a possible adverse movement in exchange rates, the importer enters into a contract to deliver dollars in exchange for pounds sterling, with settlement to take place around the same time that the machinery is to be delivered. The forward contract locks the importer into a fixed dollar equivalent for the machinery regardless of what the exchange rate is when the transaction is finally recorded. Because the forward contract is designed to hedge a foreign currency commitment (neither of which is recorded in the books at this point), the forward rate actually sets the value of the equipment as well as the amount of payment. Thus if the spot rate is $2.25 at the commitment date and $2.22 at the date of the transaction, and the forward rate is $2.20, then the acquisition of capital equipment costing 500,000 pounds sterling is recorded at $1 million, an amount fixed by the forward contract.

Sometimes a forward contract can be used to hedge the payment of a transaction already recorded, such as the one in Table 41.1. In that case, the equipment has been purchased, but settlement of the liability will not take place for 45 days. That leaves the firm open to a foreign exchange risk, as shown in the example. In this case, the forward contract can eliminate the risk. The only cost of the contract is the premium or discount plus transaction costs on the contract. The premium or discount will be written off over the life of the contract and taken directly to income. The gain or loss on adjusting the account payable will be offset by a loss or gain on the forward contract. In essence, the capital asset is recorded at the spot rate when the transaction is recorded, and the amount of cash needed to settle the liability is set by the forward contract. The difference between the spot rate and the forward rate (the premium or discount) is the amount taken to the income statement.

If a U.S. parent decides to enter into a forward contract or other foreign currency transaction to hedge an investment in a foreign entity, the parent may include any gain or loss on the contract as a separate component of stockholder's equity. (This new account is explained in the next section.) If a firm enters into a forward contract to speculate on currency changes rather than to hedge an exposure, any gains or losses on that contract are recognized immediately in income. This gain or loss is determined by comparing the book value of the contract with its new market value, and then updating that market value each time a balance sheet is prepared.

Translation of Foreign Currency Financial Statements. The previous section deals with amounts receivable or payable in foreign currency where conversion will take place eventually. Conversion implies that one currency is actually exchanged for another, usually through the foreign section of the commercial bank with which the firm deals. Translation implies that one currency is expressed or restated in terms of another currency. The only thing that happens in translation is that the unit of measure changes, not the properties of the item being measured.

There are many reasons why a financial statement should be expressed in a currency other than the one in which it is issued. Restatement may assist the reader of the financial statements. Some companies issue financial statements in the parent currency but include appropriate exchange rates so readers in other countries can translate the statements into their own currency. The management of a multinational company (MNC) may wish to see the results of a foreign operation stated in the parent currency in order to facilitate cross-national comparisons. If a multinational enterprise is to prepare consolidated financial statements, it needs to express the statements of its operations in a common currency before combination or consolidation can occur.

In the process of translation, all local currency balance sheet and income statement accounts are restated in terms of the parent currency by multiplying the local currency amount times the appropriate exchange rate. The process of translation is governed in the United States by FASB Statement No. 52, which applies two different translation methods, the temporal method and the current rate method (sometimes referred to in Europe as the "closing rate" method).

The process of translation has gone through some interesting changes in the United States since the early 1930s. Initially, firms were required to use the current/noncurrent method of translating foreign currency financial statements. Under that method, current assets and current liabilities are translated at the current rate (the rate in effect at the balance sheet date), and noncurrent assets and liabilities are translated at the historical exchange rate (the rate in effect when the transaction actually took place). During the 1960s, the theory behind this method was criticized as not being appropriate, given the purpose of translation and the characteristics of assets and liabilities. Thus the monetary/nonmonetary method began to have some influence. Briefly, this method recommends that monetary assets and liabilities be translated at the current exchange rate, and nonmonetary assets and liabilities be translated at the historical exchange rate. The accounts primarily affected by the change in methods are inventory (translated at the current rate under the current/noncurrent method and the historical rate under the monetary/nonmonetary method) and long-term debt (translated at the historical rate under the current/noncurrent method and the current rate under the monetary/nonmonetary method). Although the current/noncurrent method was not significantly changed during this time, the Accounting Principles Board in the United States did allow long-term debt to be translated at the current rate when a significant change in exchange rate took place after the liability was booked.

During this same period, the current rate method was very popular in Europe and the United Kingdom. Under this method, all assets and liabilities are translated at the current exchange rate. Net worth, as is true in all other translation methods, is the only section of the balance sheet translated at historical exchange rates.

In the early 1970s, the monetary/nonmonetary method gained substantial credibility through the issuance of Accounting Research Study (ARS) No. 12 by the American Institute of Certified Public Accountants (AICPA). ARS No. 12 recommended the adoption of the temporal method, which is very similar to the monetary/nonmonetary method. Basically, this method translates monetary assets and liabilities at the current exchange rate. All assets and liabilities carried at past exchange prices (their historical cost) are translated at the historical exchange rate, and assets and liabilities carried at current exchange prices (such as current values) are translated at the current exchange rate. Table 41.2 summa-

TABLE 41.2   Translation Methodologies

	Current/ Noncurrent Method	Temporal Method	Current Rate Method
Current assets			
Monetary	C	C	C
Nonmonetary	C	H	C
Noncurrent assets			
Monetary	H	C	C
Nonmonetary	H	H	C
Current liabilities			
Monetary	C	C	C
Nonmonetary	C	H	C
Noncurrent liabilities			
Monetary	H	C	C
Nonmonetary	H	H	C

C = Current exchange rate, the rate in effect on the balance sheet date
H = Historical exchange rate, the rate in effect when the asset is acquired or the liability incurred

rizes these major translation methodologies. The temporal method, as shown in the table, is similar to the monetary/nonmonetary method and assumes that nonmonetary assets and liabilities are carried at past exchange prices. If they were carried at current exchange prices, a different exchange rate would be used.

In October 1975, the FASB issued *Statement of Financial Accounting Standards No. 8 — Accounting for the Translation of Foreign Currency Transactions and Foreign Currency Financial Statements*, a standard that was to become one of the most controversial ever issued by the Board. According to FASB Statement No. 8, the objective of translation was the following:

> For the purpose of preparing an enterprise's financial statements, the objective of translation is to measure and express (a) in dollars and (b) in conformity with U.S. generally accepted accounting principles the assets, liabilities, revenues, or expenses that are measured or denominated in foreign currency.[3]

The translation methodology employed was the temporal method, and any gains or losses arising from translating the financial statements were to be taken directly to the income statement in the quarterly as well as the annual statements.

FASB Statement No. 8 resulted in a uproar from the business community. In 1978 when the FASB asked for public comments on its first 12 standards, most

[3] *Accounting for the Translation of Foreign Currency Transactions and Foreign Currency Financial Statements*, Financial Accounting Standards Board, Statement of Financial Accounting Standards No. 8 (Stamford, Conn.: 1975), p. 3.

of the comments it received were related to FASB Statement No. 8. Several issues were raised in the comments. The major concern was that immediate recognition of all gains and losses resulted in a distortion of operating results and misleading information, which in turn led to poor economic decisions. Most critics felt that gains and losses on foreign currency transactions should be taken directly to the income statement but that gains and losses on translating foreign currency financial statements should somehow be taken out of income.

Another concern was that certain accounts were not being translated properly. Inventory, for example, was translated primarily at historical rates. Thus a rate change in one period might not affect operating profits until the period in which the inventory was sold. This distortion of operating results was perplexing to managers. Many controllers were also concerned about the complexity involved in keeping track of historical costs and historical exchange rates for inventory, an asset which turns over fairly quickly. The preference was to translate inventory at current rates.

Another account that gave rise to concern was long-term debt, which was translated at current rates and thus exposed to foreign exchange losses. Many respondents felt that it was unfair to translate a fixed asset at historical rates and thus have that asset sheltered from any foreign exchange gains or losses, whereas the debt used to acquire the asset was exposed to an exchange gain or loss. The consensus was that the asset should be translated at the current rate in order to match the exposure of the debt, or that the gain or loss on the debt should somehow be taken out of income.

As a result of the comments received concerning FASB Statement No. 8, the FASB decided to reconsider the statement, and FASB Statement No. 52 was issued in December 1981. To justify the new standard, a new set of objectives was developed. They are to:

> Provide information that is generally compatible with the expected economic effects of a rate change on an enterprise's cash flows and equity, and . . . reflect in consolidated statements the financial results and relationships of the individual consolidated entities as measured in their functional currencies in conformity with U.S. generally accepted accounting principles.[4]

The change in objectives essentially allowed firms more flexibility in determining how to translate their foreign currency financial statements; it also allowed the firms two translation methods to choose from.

The choice of translation method depends on an understanding of the functional currency and how it relates to the currency in which the parent's financial statements are issued. There are several "currencies" that need to be defined in order to avoid confusion in the remainder of the discussion. The "reporting currency" is the currency in which the consolidated company prepares its financial statements. In the case of a U.S.-based MNC, this would be the U.S. dollar. The "local currency" is the currency of a particular country being referred to. For example, the local currency of Brazil would be the Brazilian cruzeiro. The "functional currency," is the currency of the primary

---

[4] *Foreign Currency Translation,* Financial Accounting Standards Board, Statement of Financial Accounting Standards No. 52 (Stamford Conn.: 1981), p. 3.

economic environment in which the entity operates. In most cases, the functional currency of a foreign subsidiary is the local currency, but it can also be the reporting currency. This is elaborated on later. The final currency to define is the "foreign currency." This is a currency other than the functional currency of a firm. For example, a foreign currency of a subsidiary operating in France which uses the French franc as its functional currency might be the German deutsche mark.

The functional currency is the key to the process of translation in FASB Statement No. 52. The FASB has given some general guidelines on how to decide what is the functional currency, but it is up to management to make the choice and defend it. Exhibit 41.1 identifies several criteria that firms can use to decide whether the parent or local currency is to be selected as the functional currency.

As mentioned earlier, the functional currency is that of the primary economic environment in which the entity operates. Thus a French corporation that produces and sells for the German market might consider the German deutsche mark as its functional currency, in this case the currency in which it keeps its books and records. The functional currency will be translated into the reporting currency of the U.S. parent company (the dollar) using the current rate method.

If, because of the nature of the subsidiary, management decides that the functional currency is something other than the local currency of the subsidiary, then the books and records have to be translated into the functional currency using the temporal method, which is the same as the method required under FASB Statement No. 8. In most cases, the functional currency probably is considered to be the parent's reporting currency, the U.S. dollar in the case of a U.S.-based MNC. It is possible for the functional currency to be something else, however. For example, the German subsidiary of a U.S. firm could set up a sales office in Switzerland to handle export sales of goods produced in Germany. In this case, the Swiss franc is the local currency, but management might decide that the functional currency is the deutsche mark. The statements of the Swiss company will be translated into deutsche marks using the temporal method. However, these cases are not typical in terms of the overall translation problem.

A final criterion for translation involves operations in highly inflationary countries. The Board decided that operations in these countries, defined as having a cumulative rate of inflation of 100 percent over a three-year period, should be translated into the reporting currency under the temporal method. The reason is that currencies in highly inflationary countries tend to devalue against the U.S. dollar at a rate that is similar to the rate of inflation. Under the current rate method, assets would quickly lose dollar value since they would be translated at the new exchange rate every time a balance sheet was released to the public.

The determination of the functional currency in most developing countries is contingent on the ability to accurately measure inflation over the three-year period. The Board chose to allow firms to make the decision on classification, taking into consideration the level of inflation as well as trends. No guidance was given on the index to use, although one would probably assume the use of the consumer price index, an index whose accuracy is open to dispute in some countries. It is interesting to note that the British prefer firms to use the closing rate method in highly inflationary countries after making adjustments for price

EXHIBIT 41.1   Criteria for Selection of the Functional Currency

a. Cash flow indicators

    (1) *Foreign Currency* — Cash flows related to the foreign entity's individual assets and liabilities are primarily in the foreign currency and do not directly impact the parent company's cash flows.

    (2) *Parent's Currency* — Cash flows related to the foreign entity's individual assets and liabilities directly impact the parent's cash flows on a current basis and are readily available for remittance to the parent company.

b. Sales price indicators

    (1) *Foreign Currency* — Sales prices for the foreign entity's products are not primarily responsive on a short-term basis to changes in exchange rates but are determined more by local competition or local government regulation.

    (2) *Parent's Currency* — Sales prices for the foreign entity's products are primarily responsive on a short-term basis to changes in exchange rates; for example, sales prices are determined more by worldwide competition or by international prices.

c. Sales market indicators

    (1) *Foreign Currency* — There is an active local sales market for the foreign entity's products, although there also might be significant amounts of exports.

    (2) *Parent's Currency* — The sales market is mostly in the parent's country or sales contracts are denominated in the parent's currency.

d. Expense indicators

    (1) *Foreign Currency* — Labor, materials, and other costs for the foreign entity's products or services are primarily local costs, even though there also might be imports from other countries.

    (2) *Parent's Currency* — Labor, materials, and other costs for the foreign entity's products or services, on a continuing basis, are primarily costs for components obtained from the country in which the parent company is located.

e. Financing indicators

    (1) *Foreign Currency* — Financing is primarily denominated in foreign currency, and funds generated by the foreign entity's operations are sufficient to service existing and normally expected debt obligations.

    (2) *Parent's Currency* — Financing is primarily from the parent or other dollar-denominated obligations, or funds generated by the foreign entity's operations are not sufficient to service existing and normally expected debt obligations without the infusion of additional funds from the parent company. Infusion of additional funds from the parent company for expansion is not a factor, provided funds generated by the foreign entity's expanded operations are expected to be sufficient to service that additional financing.

f. Intercompany transactions and arrangements indicators

(1) *Foreign Currency* — There is a low volume of intercompany transactions and there is not an extensive interrelationship between the operations of the foreign entity and the parent company. However, the foreign entity's operations may rely on the parent's or affiliates' competitive advantages, such as patents and trademarks.

(2) *Parent's Currency* — There is a high volume of intercompany transactions and there is an extensive interrelationship between the operations of the foreign entity and the parent company. Additionally, the parent's currency generally would be the functional currency if the foreign entity is a device or shell corporation for holding investments, obligations, intangible assets, etc., that could readily be carried on the parent's or an affiliate's books.

Source: Financial Accounting Standards Board, *Statement of Financial Accounting Standards No. 52 — Foreign Currency Translation* (Dec. 1981), pp. 26, 27. Copyright by Financial Accounting Standards Board, High Ridge Park, Stamford, Conn. 06905, U.S.A. Reprinted with permission. Copies of the complete document are available from the FASB.

level changes. IAS 21 also prefers that approach but permits the U.S. approach as well.

In summary, the current rate method of translation is used for operations where the functional currency is defined as the local currency, and the temporal method is used for operations in countries where the functional currency is defined as the reporting currency or some other foreign currency and where the operations are located in highly inflationary countries. Once the functional currency has been defined for a particular operation, it can change only when the circumstances on which the decision was based also change. This prevents firms from changing their translation methodologies in order to smooth earnings; it also is in harmony with the concepts of consistency and comparability between periods.

Before a numerical example of the translation process is presented, some important details should be discussed. So far, the balance sheet process has been discussed without delving too much into the income statement. Under the current rate method, the income statement is translated at the average exchange rate for the period. The average rate used depends on whether the translation process occurs on a monthly, quarterly, or annual basis. The longer the time period, the more important the concept of weighting the exchange rate in order to account for the cyclical nature of business. The average rate applies to all income statement accounts, including cost of sales and depreciation expense. Another point is that translation gains and losses are not included in income as is the case with the temporal method. However, gains and losses from foreign currency transactions are included in income. Translation gains and losses are included as a separate component of stockholders' equity.

The temporal method of translation involves several differences from the current rate method. Although revenues and most expenses are translated at the same average rate that would be used under the current rate method, cost of sales and depreciation expense are handled differently. Cost of sales is translated at the exchange rate in effect when the inventory was purchased. This is normally an average rate that is older than the one used for revenues and other expenses. Depreciation expense is translated at the rate in effect when the fixed assets were acquired, which is the original historical exchange rate. In addition, translation gains and losses and transaction gains and losses are recognized in the income statement in the period in which the exchange rate changes, rather than included as a separate component of stockholders' equity, as is the case with the current rate method.

The illustration in Tables 41.3 and 41.4 shows the difference between the current rate and temporal methods for translating foreign currency financial statements. It should be pointed out that the process of translation and consolidation is a complex situation that cannot be adequately covered in a short chapter. Most of the international public accounting firms have developed detailed implementation guides that add considerably more detail than is presented in this simple illustration. However, the illustration is designed to point out some key aspects of the translation process.

In a simplified way, the foreign exchange gain in the illustration is derived as a plug figure. In the case of the temporal method, the ending retained earnings balance must be $174,000 in order for assets to equal liabilities plus owners' equity. The determination of the foreign exchange gain is as follows:

Retained earnings, December 31, 1982	$174,000
Net income	(99,750)
Retained earnings, January 1, 1982	(57,875)
Foreign exchange gain	$ 16,375

That amount is carried directly to the income statement.

The determination of the translation adjustment under the current rate method is more complex in the year of transition to FASB Statement No. 52, but then it is relatively easy to maintain. The illustrations in Tables 41.3 and 41.4 provide information on calendar year 1982 only, so some assumptions must be made in order to determine the accumulated translation adjustment. It should be noted that the Board decided not to restate prior retained earnings balances in the year of transition but to keep the retained earnings figure as reported in the prior year's balance sheet and then determine the accumulated translation adjustment as follows.

Assume that net assets for December 31, 1981 were 252,500 in local currency (LC) or $486,875. Table 41.5 shows how the beginning accumulated translation adjustment on January 1, 1982 would be determined before recognition of 1982 translation adjustments.

Next, the accumulated translation adjustment for December 31, 1982 must be determined. The difference between the beginning and ending balances reflects the translation adjustment arising during the year. Table 41.6 shows how the closing balance is determined and then provides an analysis of the balance.

As can be seen in Tables 41.3 and 41.4, the temporal and current rate methods treat the translation adjustment very differently. Under the temporal method, the translation adjustment appears in owners' equity via the income statement and retained earnings, whereas under the current rate method, the translation adjustment appears as a separate component of owners' equity.

TABLE 41.3   Balance Sheet, December 31, 1982

	Local Currency	Temporal Method Exchange Rate	Temporal Method U.S. Dollars	Current Rate Method Exchange Rate	Current Rate Method U.S. Dollars
Assets					
Cash and receivables	LC100,000	2.05(a)	$ 205,000	2.05	$ 205,000
Inventory	125,000	2.03(b)	253,750	2.05	256,250
Net fixed assets	300,000	1.95(c)	585,000	2.05	615,000
Total	LC525,000		$1,043,750		$1,076,250
Liabilities and owners' equity					
Current liabilities	LC115,000	2.05	$ 235,750	2.05	$ 235,750
Long-term debt	100,000	2.05	205,000	2.05	205,000
Capital stock	220,000	1.95	429,000	1.95	429,000
Retained earnings	90,000	—	174,000		172,875
Equity adjustment from translation	—		—	—	33,625
Total	LC525,000		$1,043,750		$1,076,250

Assume that the beginning retained earnings balance is $57,875

(a) Current or year-end balance sheet rate
(b) The average rate during the period that the ending inventory was purchased
(c) The rate when fixed assets were purchased and capital stock was issued

TABLE 41.4   Income Statement, 1982

	Local Currency	Temporal Method Exchange Rate	Temporal Method U.S. Dollars	Current Rate Method Exchange Rate	Current Rate Method U.S. Dollars
Sales revenue	LC700,000	2.00(a)	$1,400,000	2.00	$1,400,000
Cost of sales	(437,500)	2.04(b)	(892,500)	2.00	(875,000)
Depreciation	(45,000)	1.95	(87,750)	2.00	(90,000)
Other expenses	(160,000)	2.00	(320,000)	2.00	(320,000)
Net income before foreign exchange gain (loss)	LC 57,500		$ 99,750		$ 115,000
Foreign exchange gain (loss)	—		16,375		—
Net income	LC 57,500		$ 116,125		$ 115,000
Retained earnings, December 31, 1981	32,500		57,875		57,875
Retained earnings, December 31, 1982	LC 90,000		$ 174,000		$ 172,875

(a) Weighted average rate during the year
(b) Average rate during the period when the merchandise that was sold was initially purchased

TABLE 41.5   Accumulated Translation Adjustment, January 1, 1982

Net assets, December 31, 1981	LC252,500	
Exchange rate, December 31, 1981	2.00	
Net assets at current rate		$505,000
Less: Reported net worth, December 31, 1981		
Capital stock	$429,000	
Retained earnings	57,875	
		486,875
Accumulated translation adjustment, January 1, 1982		$ 18,125

TABLE 41.6   Accumulated Translation Adjustment, December 31, 1982

Net assets, December 31, 1982	LC310,000	
Exchange rate, December 31, 1982	2.05	
Net assets at current rate		$635,500
Less:		
Capital stock, December 31, 1982	$429,000	
Retained earnings, December 31, 1982	172,875	
		601,875
Accumulated translation adjustment, December 31, 1982		$ 33,625

ANALYSIS OF ACCUMULATED TRANSLATION ADJUSTMENT

Balance, January 1, 1982	$18,125
Add: Adjustment for 1982	15,500(a)
Balance, December 31, 1982	$33,625

(a) This is the difference between the opening and closing balances.

The Board requires an analysis of changes in the separate component of equity for the period, including the beginning and ending amount of the cumulative translation adjustments and the aggregate adjustment for the period resulting from translation adjustments. In a separate financial statement, in notes to the statements, or as part of a statement of changes in equity, the following information must be disclosed:

a. Beginning and ending amount of cumulative translation adjustments
b. The aggregate adjustment for the period resulting from translation adjustments and gains and losses from certain hedges and intercompany balances
c. The amount of income taxes for the period allocated to translation adjustments

d. The amounts transferred from cumulative translation adjustments and included in determining net income for the period as a result of the sale or complete or substantially complete liquidation of an investment in a foreign entity.[5]

Statement No. 52 must be implemented for fiscal years beginning on or after December 15, 1982, although firms were encouraged to implement the standard before then. The date of implementation determined what kinds of prior period adjustments needed to be made and how that information had to be disclosed in the annual report to shareholders. Even though FASB Statement No. 52 was adopted by the Board, the vote was four in favor and three against adoption of the standard. The three dissenting Board members would have preferred some modifications to FASB Statement No. 8 rather than a standard that allows two different translation methods.

It is important to realize that FASB Statement No. 8 has not disappeared entirely. Many people mistakenly believe that FASB Statement No. 52 has adopted the current rate method and eliminated the temporal method of translation. That is true only if the functional currency is defined as the local rather than the reporting currency of the parent company. Thus FASB Statement No. 52 is actually more complex than FASB Statement No. 8, since it still uses the temporal method of translation for some subsidiaries while allowing the current rate method for others. The new component in stockholders' equity may also cause some confusion to financial statement readers, since that section of the balance sheet is normally preserved for capital stock and retained earnings.

The impact on the financial statements of using the current rate method rather than the temporal method depends on a number of factors, such as the size of net worth and the degree of fluctuation in exchange rates. Table 41.7 summarizes the dollar amounts for the balance sheet and income statement under the temporal and current rate methods and provides some ratios for purposes of comparison. The differences appear slight due to the relatively small difference between the current and historical exchange rates.

In 1982, for example, IBM adopted FASB Statement No. 52 and disclosed in its annual report that 85 percent of its operations abroad were translated by the current rate method. The translation adjustment included in 1981 stockholders' equity was a negative $622 million (3.5 percent of total stockholders' equity), and in 1982 it was $1,307 million (6.5 percent of total stockholders' equity). The amount, while small compared with total stockholders' equity, will continue to increase as long as the dollar strengthens against major currencies. In addition, IBM disclosed that the accounting change increased net income $449 million and earnings per share $0.75 in 1982. The exact impact on stockholders' equity and earnings is going to vary from company to company, but the IBM example is not atypical of U.S. MNCs during a period of a strengthening dollar.

In addition to this new complexity, the current rate method, if selected for translation, does not totally eliminate the impact of exchange rate changes on the income statement, even though translation gains and losses are taken directly to equity. This is so because the income statement still must be translated into dollars. If the local currency is weakening relative to the dollar, the dollar equivalent of net income will fall. Many firms experienced this phenomenon in Europe during the recession of 1981. In that case, income in local currency was

[5] *Ibid.*, pp. 12, 13.

TABLE 41.7   Balance Sheet and Income Statement Comparisons

BALANCE SHEET COMPARISON

	Temporal Method		Current Rate Method	
	Amount	Percentage of Total Assets	Amount	Percentage of Total Assets
Assets				
Cash and receivables	$ 205,000	19.6%	$ 205,000	19.0%
Inventory	253,750	24.3	256,250	23.8
Net fixed assets	585,000	56.1	615,000	57.2
Total	$1,043,750	100.0%	$1,076,250	100.0%
Liabilities and owners' equity				
Current liabilities	$ 235,750	22.6%	$ 235,750	21.9%
Long-term debt	205,000	19.6	205,000	19.0
Capital stock	429,000	41.1	429,000	39.9
Retained earnings	174,000	16.7	172,875	16.1
Translation adjustment	—	—	33,625	3.1
Total	$1,043,750	100.0%	$1,076,250	100.0%

INCOME STATEMENT COMPARISON

	Temporal Method		Current Rate Method	
	Amount	Percentage of Total Sales	Amount	Percentage of Total Sales
Sales revenue	$1,400,000	100.0%	$1,400,000	100.0%
Cost of sales	(892,500)	(63.7)	(875,000)	(62.5)
Depreciation	(87,750)	(6.3)	(90,000)	(6.4)
Other expenses	(320,000)	(22.9)	(320,000)	(22.9)
Foreign exchange gain (loss)	16,375	1.2	—	—
Net Income	$ 116,125	8.3%	$ 115,000	8.2%

not rising very much because of the recession, so the strong dollar exacerbated the weak profit picture resulting in small dollar increases in some cases and dollar declines in others.

From the standpoint of the controller and treasurer, the method of translating operations does not affect the basic cash flows of foreign operations. Dividends are declared on local currency profits, and they are converted into dollars at the spot rate in effect when the dividend is sent to the parent. However, the method of translation does affect the financial statements, possibly affecting investment and credit decisions by management as well as external users. Thus, an understanding of FASB Statement No. 52 is important.

Inflation Adjusted Financial Statements

In September 1979, the FASB issued *Statement of Financial Accounting Standards No. 33 — Financial Reporting and Changing Prices*. This standard requires firms to disclose as supplementary information the effects of general price level and current cost changes on certain accounts and account balances. Under FASB Statement No. 33, firms are required to disclose the following: (1) information on income from continuing operations adjusted for general price level changes; (2) the purchasing power gain or loss on net monetary items; (3) information on income from continuing operations on a current cost basis (cost of goods sold at current cost and depreciation expense of property, plant, and equipment); (4) the current cost amounts of inventory and property, plant, and equipment; (5) increases and decreases in the current cost amounts of inventory and property, plant, and equipment net of inflation; and (6) certain summary information for the five most recent years. When applying this standard to foreign operations, management first needs to decide on the functional currency of the foreign operation. If the functional currency is the local currency, then the current rate method of translation is used. Current cost information is determined in the local currency and translated into dollars at the current rate. General price level adjustments need not be made, so the financial statements are simply translated into dollars at the current rate, using the historical cost and local currency financial statements unadjusted for inflation. If the functional currency is the reporting currency, the current cost financial statements are still made, and the adjusted statements are translated into dollars using the current rate method of translation. However, the general price level adjustments are handled differently. The local currency financial statements are first translated into dollars using the temporal method of translation, and the statements are then adjusted to reflect general price level changes in the U.S. dollar. This method is known as the translate/restate method, as opposed to the restate/translate method used for current cost adjustments.

Geographic Segment and Export Revenues Disclosures

A final piece of important disclosure that appears in the annual and Form 10K reports relates to the firm's international operations and export revenues. The guidelines for such disclosures are found in *Statement of Financial Accounting Standards No. 14 — Financial Reporting for Segments of a Business Enterprise*. This statement includes disclosure requirements for industrial segments and major customers as well as geographic segments and export revenues. The latter two are most germane to this chapter.

In order to disclose information about foreign segments, foreign revenues must be at least 10 percent of consolidated revenues, or identifiable assets must be at least 10 percent of consolidated assets. If these conditions hold, then revenue from sales to unaffiliated customers, revenue from intercompany sales, operating profit or loss, and identifiable assets must be disclosed for each geographic segment. A firm may choose to lump all its foreign operations into one segment, or it may disaggregate the data into several segments by individual country or groups of countries. The decision to aggregate or disaggregate is left to management. The tendency in the absence of more stringent requirements is to divide foreign operations into a few segments. The level of aggregation is usually so high that investors cannot really use the information to project revenues or profits or to determine the level of risk in foreign operations. However, the capital markets apparently do not consider this to be a big problem. Most firms prefer to disclose as few segments as possible in order to keep from disclosing much profit information by country. One way to give more information about firm revenues without disclosing profit information, as is rquired in FASB Statement No. 14, would be to disclose more highly disaggregated sales revenue data in the business narrative.

Information must also be disclosed about export revenues from the United States to other countries. U.S. export revenues must be disclosed if they are 10 percent or more of consolidated revenues. This disclosure can be made in the aggregate, or the export revenues can be broken out in more detail, such as by continent or country. This type of disclosure is rare for U.S. firms, since their export revenues are such a small part of total revenues. It would be more common to find this type of disclosure for the large exporters, such as the aircraft companies.

DIFFERENCES IN ACCOUNTING STANDARDS AND DISCLOSURE PRACTICES

Differences in Accounting Standards

It is evident from reading annual reports from countries around the world that accounting standards and practices vary, sometimes significantly, from country to country. Variations exist not only in the amount and type of information disclosed but also in the underlying standards on which the financial statements and accompanying footnotes are based. It is important to keep these two types of variations in mind, since there is a big difference between form and substance. Accounting standards and practices determine how economic events are recorded in the books and records of the company, whereas disclosure requirements determine how the information is presented to the various user groups, including investors, creditors, employees, and government.

The MNC face the dilemma of balancing its need for uniform information for reporting purposes in the United States with the requirements for reporting that exist in the country where the foreign subsidiary is located. Standardized U.S. requirements come from two basic sources: management and investors. Management obviously wants uniform information in order to evaluate and control foreign operations. For this reason most companies go to great lengths to develop detailed accounting manuals that are used worldwide.

In spite of the need for uniform standards and practices for home office use, the MNC must also allow its local affiliates to keep financial records according to local standards in order to satisfy the demands of local capital markets, government regulators, taxing authorities, and so forth. These standards could vary significantly in different countries depending on the local accounting standards. This results in multiple sets of books to satisfy home office and local country requirements.

Reasons for Differences in Accounting Standards

Accounting objectives, standards, and practices depend ultimately on the users of the financial statements and the extent of user group influence over the setting of standards. It is impossible to identify all the factors that influence accounting or to rank the factors since each country is unique, but a number of factors are very important. The major factor leading to greater harmonization in accounting is the development of international capital markets. Investors seem to have an insatiable appetite for information, and firms that want to raise capital on international markets are obliged to disclose information that is consistent with those markets. In general, this means that firms must develop statements based on accounting and disclosure practices that are in harmony with the United States and the United Kingdom. Although there are differences in practices between these two countries, they are similar and are based on providing information for investors.

Accounting standards and practices are influenced by many factors. Some of the most important are the nature of firms, major enterprise users, the government, and local environmental and business influences. In countries where there is no organized capital market and family owned or closely held firms predominate, accounting tends to be creditor and management oriented. In some of the European countries, employees are major enterprise users of information, and they have been able to get some interesting employee-related disclosures guaranteed by law. Governments play an important role in the development of accounting standards, especially in countries where the accounting profession is not highly developed. In other countries, such as France, the government essentially sets accounting standards via tax legislation. Local environmental influences, such as high rates of inflation in some Latin American countries, have also been influential in the setting of standards. Colonial influences, such as the British in the Commonwealth countries and the French in their former colonies, can also be important in setting standards and practices.

Major Types of Differences in Accounting Standards

Accounting varies not only in the format and amount of information disclosed but even more importantly in the underlying standards on which the information is based. Differences in standards do not imply superiority or inferiority but simply differences. Some standards that are perfectly reasonable in the U.S. environment would be inappropriate elsewhere due to differences in the business system and other elements of the environment. In a recent study of annual reports for countries around the world, major differences related to consolidation practices, accounting for goodwill, deferred taxes, long-term leases, discretionary reserves, inflation, and foreign currency translation were enumerated.[6]

Consolidation practices include not only whether or not majority owned subsidiaries are consolidated with parent company results but how less than majority owned investments are recorded on the books of the parent. In some cases, such as Peru, consolidated financial statements are actually not allowed. There are three options on presenting the accounts of the group to outsiders: (1) present parent company financial statements only, (2) present parent company financial statements but include consolidated financial statements, or (3) present consolidated financial statements only. The consolidated statements normally

---

[6] Frederick D.S. Choi and Vinod B. Bavishi, "International Accounting Standards: Issues Needing Attention," *Journal of Accountancy* (Mar. 1983), p. 65.

include domestic and foreign operations, but separate domestic and foreign consolidated statements also could be presented.

It is relatively common to see financial statements in Europe presented according to the second option. U.S. companies never provide parent company results but disclose consolidated statements only. The IASC in its standard on consolidation in 1976 recommended that consolidated statements be presented; this standard caused many countries, such as Japan, to move away from parent company statements only and include consolidated statements as well in their external reporting. The problem with parent company statements only is that firms can hide the results of intercompany transactions. As pointed out with reference to Japanese companies before the passage of their consolidation standard in 1977,

> During periods of slack turnover, some parent companies have been known to ship merchandise to their subsidiaries and list the goods as sold, even though the subsidiaries didn't have any customers on hand. Workers also could be transferred from a parent to a subsidiary to lower unit costs. And managers skipped over for promotions in the head office could be transferred to subsidiaries, where their performances couldn't be as easily seen.[7]

As an example of the difference between consolidated and unconsolidated earnings, Toshiba, a large Japanese MNC, showed an unconsolidated net income of $30 million in 1976, but on a consolidated basis the company had a $13 million loss.[8]

Even though many countries where only parent company financial statements were issued now require consolidated statements, there is still a difference in the way the results of less than majority owned subsidaries are presented. In the United States, a parent company that owns more than 20 percent of the voting stock of another corporation but has less than a controlling interest in that corporation must include its equity interest in the income or loss of that corporation in the parent's income for the year. If it owns less than 20 percent of the voting stock of the corporation, it reports income only when received in the form of a dividend. The former is known as the equity method of accounting and the latter as the cost method. It is very common outside of the United States and the United Kingdom for companies to use the cost method exclusively. This is a far more conservative method of recognizing income from foreign operations and has its roots in the conservative business environment of these countries. In some countries, such as Japan and Germany, companies are required each year to remit a minimum dividend to shareholders based on the reported income of the company. It makes sense not to recognize foreign source income until it has been remitted in the form of a dividend; otherwise the parent would have to use parent company cash flows to pay dividends on foreign income reported to the shareholders. Thus the cost method is a more popular way of reporting the earnings of nonconsolidated foreign operations.

Accounting for goodwill involves the timing of recognition of expenses. In the United States, it is common to write off goodwill over 40 years, whereas in

---

[7] Masayoshi Kanabayashi, "Japanese Firms 'Disown' Subsidiaries to Protect Results," *Wall Street Journal* (Feb. 6, 1977), p. 6.

[8] "Japan's Accounting Shakeup," *Business Week* (Apr. 25, 1977), p. 114.

other countries it is common to write off goodwill as an expense in the year of acquisition or to write it off over five years rather than 40 years.

As pointed out by Choi and Bavishi, deferred taxes are used extensively in Canada, the United States, and the United Kingdom, but are used sparingly if at all in most other countries. There appears to be a greater acceptance of deferred taxes in industrial countries. However, there are still different interpretations on which type of expenses should be considered for deferred tax treatment. Currently, capitalizing long-term leases is rarely found outside of the United States, Canada, and Mexico,[9] but an international standard recently passed by the IASC may alter that practice worldwide.

The extensive use of reserves internationally is interesting. The United States largely abandoned the use of reserves with the adoption of the all-inclusive income statement under the assumption that investors should rely on earnings to make sound investment decisions and reserves tend to smooth and distort earnings too much. In many countries, reserves fall into three categories: hidden, legal, and free. Hidden reserves arise as a result of understating assets and overstating liabilities. The purpose of such a conservative balance sheet is to bring more expenses into the income statement, thereby reducing taxable and distributable earnings, leading to a more liquid balance sheet. This is especially beneficial to creditors who tend to be the major source of capital for most firms outside of the United States. These hidden reserves arise by depreciating assets very quickly, undervaluing inventories (as is the case in Sweden), and recognizing contingencies as actual expenses and liabilities.

Legal reserves arise from the articles of incorporation of the firm. Many countries require that a certain percentage of earnings be appropriated in a legal reserve before dividends are declared, thus reducing the dividend base of the firm. This results in higher liquidity. It is common for the firm to include even higher reserve requirements in the original articles of incorporation to ensure even better liquidity.

Free reserves as a variation of legal reserves and result from a variety of factors, including the fact that shareholders may vote for a higher reserve level at the annual meeting. These reserves result in a more conservative balance sheet with relatively high liquidity and in an income statement that is often smoothed in order to show what management wants to show. In some countries, such as Switzerland, there is wide management discretion in determining the size of the hidden reserves; in others, such as France and Germany, the hidden reserves are actually a product of tax accounting, which tends to show a faster write-off of fixed assets.

It is virtually impossible to recast accurately financial statements from one country's generally accepted accounting principles (GAAP) to another's using only published financial statements. Some non-U.S. companies have issued special financial statements for U.S. readers in order to raise money in the U.S. capital markets. N. V. Philips, a Dutch MNC, uses replacement value accounting in its primary statements, so it provides approximate historical cost balance sheet and income statement data for American shareholders. In addition, it provides other adjustments to bring the financial statements even more in line with U.S. GAAP. The information is provided in Dutch guilders and then

---

9 Frederick D.S. Choi and Vinod B. Bavishi, *op. cit.*, p. 68.

TABLE 41.8   Selected Data From the 1979 Annual Report of N. V. Philips Gloeilampenfabrieken Comparing Dutch With U.S. Generally Accepted Accounting Principles

(guilders in millions)

	Dutch GAAP	U.S. GAAP
Fixed assets	11,853	11,299
Inventory	10,468	10,400
Trading profit	1,851	2,044
As percentage of sales	5.6%	6.1%
Profit after tax	666	781
As percentage of sales	2.0%	2.3%
Net profit	619	711
As percentage of stockholders' equity	5.5%	6.8%
Net profit after other adjustments for U.S. GAAP	619	627

translated into dollars at the year-end exchange rate. Table 41.8 illustrates some key data from Philips' 1979 annual report.

Disclosure of Information

Of immediate concern to the financial executive is the disclosure of information in different capital markets. The Securities and Exchange Commission has set a high standard of disclosure that probably will be sufficient for most capital markets. Disclosure requirements may necessitate information being prepared in accounting terms different from those in the United States and may also require information different from that disclosed in the United States. In any event, the following issues need to be addressed for each capital market:

1 Can the company's financial statements be in English or do they have to be translated into the local language? IBM's annual report is translated into French, German, and Japanese. Its stock is listed in the United States, Austria, Belgium, Canada, the United Kingdom, France, Japan, Switzerland, the Netherlands, and Germany. Philips provides its annual report in Dutch, English, German, and French.

2 Can the company's financial statements be in dollars or do they have to be translated into local currency units? It is most common to have the annual report given in the currency of the parent company rather than have the figures translated into another currency. The Swedish Match Company, a Swedish MNC, publishes an English-language annual report in Swedish krona rather than dollars, but it includes the year-end exchange rate for a number of different currencies. As noted previously, Philips publishes its English-language annual report in Dutch guilders, but it has a section devoted to U.S. readers which publishes some income statement data in dollars as well as guilders. The year-end exchange rate is used for these purposes.

3 Can the company's financial statements be presented according to U.S. GAAP, or do they have to be recast in terms of local GAAP?

Most firms rely on their footnote disclosures to explain how the financial statements have been generated. However, some firms have thought it necessary to provide more information than that when issuing capital stock in the United States. Once again, Philips has an extensive section on replacement value accounting, since its financial statements are based on replacement values rather than historical costs. Royal Dutch Petroleum Company, the parent of Shell Oil, has a section on replacement value accounting in which it describes its method of accounting for inflation and then explains how that method differs from that required in the United Kingdom and United States and commonly practiced in the Netherlands.

Harmonization of Standards

The different accounting standards and practices discussed in the preceding sections illustrate how difficult it is for the MNC to keep books worldwide that are consistent with home country and local country requirements. In fact, the Royal Dutch/Shell Group of Companies reflects a synthesis of the accounting principles of the Netherlands, the United Kingdom, and the United States. Its extensive operations in all three countries have forced it to take a multinational approach to accounting rather than adopt the standards of any one country. Obviously, Royal Dutch/Shell would benefit from an international harmonization of standards, so it would not have to develop its own standards.

The harmonization process is currently occurring on an international and regional basis. However, wide differences in the nature of accounting standards make harmonization a difficult process to pursue. As pointed out by Nobes and Parker (1981), there are systems that are microbased and those that are macrobased. The microbased systems rely on business economics, as in the Netherlands, or on business practice, as in the United Kingdom and the United States. The U.K. influence has spread to Austria, New Zealand, and other Commonwealth countries, whereas the U.S. influence is noticeable in Canada, Mexico, the Philippines, and Japan. The macrobased systems are heavily influenced by government and oriented to uniformity rather than choice. They are subdivided into those that are economics based and those that are tax and legal based. Sweden, which relies on heavy fiscal incentives, is an example of a system that is economics based. West Germany is based on the law. Since the law is considered by the Germans to be true and fair, the legal principles are very detailed and all encompassing. Tax-based systems are typified by the systems in Spain, Italy, and France.[10]

The International Accounting Standards Committee. Founded in 1973, the IASC's main objective has been to formulate standards to be observed in the presentation of audited financial statements, and to promote their acceptance

---

[10] Christopher Nobes and Robert Parker, *Comparative International Accounting* (Homewood, Ill.: Richard D. Irwin, 1981), p. 213.

and adherence. The founding members of the IASC were professional organizations from Australia, Canada, France, Japan, Mexico, the Netherlands, the United Kingdom, Ireland, the United States, and West Germany. Since then, a number of professional organizations from more than 50 countries have joined the IASC. Thus, the IASC is a group of private accounting bodies rather than a group of governments setting accounting standards. To date, the IASC has set 20 standards covering a variety of topics. There have not been any major differences between IASC standards and those issued by the United States, so there is good reason to assume that adherence to FASB standards implies adherence to IASC standards as well. However, the AICPA rather than the FASB is the U.S. representative to the IASC. Thus far, the IASC has attempted to narrow alternative practices rather than standardize principles. Given the political nature of standard setting and the strong national pride in accounting standards, this process of harmonization is probably the wisest one to take.

The United Nations. The United Nations has become involved in the process of setting accounting standards through the Commission on Transnational Corporations of UNESCO. The Commission is concerned with "securing international arrangements for the operations of transnational corporations and furthering understanding of the nature and effects of their activities."[11] A portion of the Commission's activities relates to accounting disclosure, most specifically to nonfinancial disclosure, such as the structure of the MNC, the main activities of its entities, employment information, accounting policies, and transfer pricing policies. The major financial statement disclosures are not that different from what is already accepted good practice internationally. The Commission has been working on these disclosures for several years, but no final standards have been passed. The major difference between these standards and those of the IASC is the heavy input of the developing countries and their concerns over the influence of the MNC. Once standards have been issued, individual countries could write these standards into national law. So far, that has not been the case with IASC. As a result, the operations of this Commission bear watching.

The Organization for Economic Cooperation and Development. The Organization for Economic Cooperation and Development (OECD), which comprises most of the industrial countries of Western Europe, plus Canada, the United States, and Japan, has a code of conduct for multinational enterprises that deals in part with accounting issues. The OECD guidelines are very similar to those already in use in most of the industrial countries, and U.S. companies should have no trouble adhering to those guidelines simply by complying with already existing accounting standards and disclosure practices in the United States. The OECD, like the IASC, has no enforcement mechanism, so its standards depend on the desires of the individual states.

The European Economic Community. The European Economic Community (EEC) is one of the most interesting of the political attempts at harmoni-

---

[11] *World Accounting Report* (Sept. 1982), p. 9.

zation. One of the original goals of the 10-member EEC was the free flow of capital. Obviously, this objective would be difficult in the face of widely different accounting standards. The EEC is empowered to set directives, which are orders to the member states to bring their laws into line with EEC requirements within a certain period, usually two years. A series of directives has been issued; the Fourth Directive deals specifically with accounting issues. Adopted in 1978, the basic aim of the Fourth Directive was to provide the framework for a common standard of accounting disclosure. The major areas covered by the Fourth Directive are the format of accounts and valuation rules. The directive requires firms to present a balance sheet and income statement (but not a statement of changes in financial position) and accompanying footnotes. It allows a country to choose from among two balance sheet and four income statement formats, with additional options for large firms, as opposed to medium and small firms. The directive is a compromise between the heavily legalistic German and French views of accounting and the relatively flexible true-and-fair view of the financial statements prevalent in the United Kingdom. Not all the member countries have adopted the Fourth Directive, and the British and Dutch have adopted such a liberal version that firms can essentially do whatever they are doing currently.

U.S.-based MNCs need to be concerned about the Fourth Directive because their subsidiaries in various countries will be required to adhere to the version of the directive legislated in each country. This means that different subsidiaries will be generating financial statements according to different national laws, creating the problem of different sets of books.

Two other directives now being developed could have an impact on U.S. firms. They are the Seventh Directive, which will prescribe the method of consolidation required in the EEC, and the Directive on Informing and Consulting With Employees. The latter directive has not been issued in draft form at this time. The Seventh Directive should provide a much narrower scope of alternatives than the Fourth Directive allows in the format and content of financial statements. For U.S. MNCs, the only major problem that could arise in the Seventh Directive is how firms will be required to consolidate their European operations, since a parent company located in the United States may have several operations throughout the EEC. The solution to that problem is still being debated.

INTERNATIONAL TAX ISSUES

Taxation has a strong impact on the choice of (1) location in the initial investment decision; (2) legal form of the new enterprise, such as branch or subsidiary; (3) method of finance, such as internal as opposed to external sourcing and debt as opposed to equity; and (4) method of arranging prices between related entities.[12] Tax planning is crucial since it can have a profound effect on profitability and cash flow. In the international situation, the tax accountant must not only be familiar with the laws of his own country but must be able to provide manage-

---

[12] Albert J. Radler, "Taxation Policy in Multinational Companies," *The Multinational Enterprise in Transition,* eds. A. Kapoor and Philip D. Grub (Princeton, The Darwin Press, 1972), p. 30.

ment with information about similar laws in the countries where the firm is currently operating or is considering expanding. In addition to laws governing domestic source income, the tax accountant must be familiar with laws governing foreign source income.

Reducing Taxes on Export Earnings

The law is currently in a state of flux in the United States concerning tax breaks for export revenues. The major incentive in force is the domestic international sales corporation (DISC), a piece of tax legislation passed in 1971 with the express intent of assisting U.S. exports. A DISC can be incorporated in any state with a nominal capital of $2,500; at least 95 percent of the DISC's gross receipts and assets must be export-related. Prior to the Tax Reform Act of 1976, the DISC was able to defer 50 percent of its income until it was declared as a dividend to shareholders. Currently, the deferral applies only to incremental income. Basically, this means that DISC receipts must continue to grow in order for a company to continue to receive DISC benefits.

In 1973, the mood began to swing against the DISC domestically as well as internationally, and the U.S. Government contemplated a replacement for it. The most likely replacement is the foreign trade company (FTC), an entity being considered in legislation. The FTC would have to be incorporated outside the United States and maintain an office outside the United States as well. If the residency requirement is met, the FTC would not be subject to U.S. tax on a portion of its foreign trading company income, defined as income from the sale, exchange, or other disposition of export property, as well as other specified forms of income. Relatively liberal transfer pricing rules would apply to the income of the FTC, and other interesting tax breaks would also apply.

Taxation of Foreign Operations

Two important tenets relating to the taxation of foreign source income are the deferral principle and the tax credit principle. The deferral principle implies that income is not taxed until received by the U.S. shareholder. According to the tax credit, a firm gets credit for income taxes that have already been paid to a foreign government on income earned in that foreign country.

In addition to exporting goods and services directly to the foreign buyer from production in the United States, an MNC may choose to produce and sell in the foreign country through a branch of the parent or through a foreign corporation in which the parent has an equity interest. The income or loss of a foreign branch must be combined with the parent's income for tax as well as book purposes. In most cases, however, a U.S. corporation does not declare income for tax purposes from a foreign corporation until it actually receives a dividend. This is the principle of deferral.

The Tax Credit. There are two kind of taxes that a firm needs to keep track of internationally: taxes on income and all other taxes. Only taxes on income can be used for the tax credit, which results in a dollar for dollar reduction of the U.S. tax liability. All other taxes must be deducted from income to arrive at taxable income. It is also possible for a firm to consider foreign income taxes as deductions from income, but it is often to the firm's advantage to use those taxes as credits.

The tax credit applies to all income that must be recognized by the parent. The credit is available for income of foreign branches as well as for income of foreign corporations. The amount of tax that can be considered as creditable is a combination of the corporate income tax paid to the foreign government as well as any withholding tax paid on the dividends remitted to the U.S. investing firm by the foreign corporation. However, the upper limit on the credit is what the U.S. investor would have paid in U.S. taxes on that foreign source income. Any excess credits can be carried back two years and carried forward five years. This is why some firms may prefer to treat their foreign income taxes as deductions rather than credits.

Subpart F Income. The second key tenet of international taxation is the concept of deferral of foreign source income until it has been remitted as a dividend. One important exception to this principle involves passive or Subpart F income. In the 1950s and 1960s, many U.S. MNCs set up operations in tax haven countries in order to take advantage of low tax rates. Countries such as Switzerland, Panama, and Hong Kong offered a variety of incentives, such as low or no corporate income taxes or taxes on domestic rather than foreign source income. Thus firms set up operations in these countries to shield their income from U.S. taxation. As a result, the U.S. government passed a law requiring certain types of income to be included in U.S taxable income when earned by the foreign corporation rather than when remitted as a dividend. This income, known as Subpart F income because of its relevant section in the Internal Revenue Code, must be earned by a controlled foreign corporation (CFC) in order to be considered for special treatment. A CFC is a foreign corporation with more than 50 percent of its voting stock owned by U.S. shareholders, defined as persons or companies that hold at least 10 percent of the voting stock of the foreign corporation. If the foreign corporation does not qualify as a CFC, the U.S. investor has full access to the deferral principle, irrespective of the nature of the income earned. If the foreign corporation is a CFC, however, the income must be divided into Subpart F and other income. Subpart F income includes the following: (1) insurance of U.S. risks, (2) foreign base company personal holding company income, (3) foreign base company sales income, (4) foreign base company services income, (5) foreign base company shipping income, (6) boycott-related income (from the Arab boycott of Israel), and (7) foreign bribes (related to the Foreign Corrupt Practices Act).

Foreign base company personal holding company income is dividends, interest, royalties, and similar income that arises from holding rights rather than actually producing or selling goods and services. Foreign base company sales income arises from the sale or purchase of goods produced and consumed outside the country where the CFC is incorporated. Foreign base company services income arises from contracts utilizing technical, managerial, engineering, or other skills. The other forms of foreign base company income are rather specialized and not of as broad an interest as the forms just defined.

The Impact of Tax Treaties

A thorough study of international tax issues uncovers a variety of different tax practices worldwide. These differences exist in terms of how to define taxable income and tax deductible expenses, statutory tax rates, different types of taxes, and whether or not income is taxed more than once, as is the case in the United States where corporations are taxed on income earned and shareholders are taxed again when dividends are declared. In addition, countries have different policies on how to tax income earned from abroad and how to tax income earned locally by foreigners. Differences in philosophy on how income should be taxed have given rise to treaties between countries to minimize the effect of double taxation on the taxpayer, protect each country's right to collect taxes, and provide ways to resolve jurisdictional issues.

The United States has at least 26 tax treaties with 38 countries. Among other things, tax treaties have an impact on dividend, interest, and royalty payments. In West Germany, for example, the withholding rate not only on dividends and royalties but on the interest on certain loans is 25 percent, whereas the interest on loans secured by real property and interest from a permanent establishment such as an operating subsidiary in Germany are subject to a 50 percent rate. In the tax treaty with the United States, however, the withholding rate on dividends is reduced to 15 percent, and interest and royalty payments are totally exempt from withholding tax. The dividend rate rises to 25 percent under certain circumstances, but the benefits to a U.S. corporation are obvious in the case of royalties and interest.

PERFORMANCE EVALUATION AND CONTROL

Financial executives are not only concerned with the use of accounting information for external reporting purposes; they also need to use that information for a variety of internal purposes, such as capital budgeting (discussed in Chapter 22) and performance evaluation and control. Five key problems that affect the quality of the information used are: (1) accounting requirements in different countries, (2) the size and importance of operations all over the world, (3) the organizational structure of the firm, (4) the purpose of each subsidiary (especially as it concerns profit centers, (5) and different currencies.

As mentioned earlier in this chapter, accounting standards are very different in different countries. Most of the people hired by a firm to perform accounting functions have been trained in the system of the local country and may have great difficulty relating to a U.S.-based system. Also, a firm is usually required to keep its books and records in the currency and language, and possibly in the GAAP, of the country in which it operates.

The size and importance of the foreign operations can be critical, especially in deciding how complex the reporting of the operations should be. It is common for an MNC to transfer its internal reporting system worldwide because it is easier and cheaper, and management is already familiar with it at the home office. However, that system might be extremely burdensome to a relatively small operation in a country where management is not very sophisticated in the generation and use of accounting data. It might be too much to ask the local operation to use a sophisticated system. Thus management must be sensitive to adjustments that need to be made in the amount, complexity, and timing of information requested from abroad.

The information system has to be suited to the structure and philosophy of the firm. For example, if a firm operates through a highly decentralized structure, its information and control requirements are different from those of a highly centralized firm. Largely autonomous subsidiaries do not require as much control from the parent and therefore need not transmit information as frequently or in as much detail to the parent. Similarly, firms organized along product lines have different lines of data transmission than firms organized along geographic lines. Firms with a matrix structure need to develop reports that take into account product as well as geographic flows of data.

Concerning transfer pricing, the price that one related enterprise charges another, there appears to be a movement toward vertical integration of MNC operations as firms attempt to shore up sources of supply of key materials and components. In addition, the search for cost advantages has led to greater disaggregation of the production process to capitalize on the unique comparative advantages that firms have to offer. Thus with increasing frequency, semifinished components and finished goods are transferred across national borders from one entity to another controlled by a common parent. A key consideration for each government involved as well as the firm itself is how the transfer price is set.

Because such transfers do not occur at arm's length, there is obviously room for price manipulation. Governments are concerned because the price attached to a transfer could affect excise taxes (such as border taxes and value added taxes) as well as corporate income taxes. Companies are concerned because transfer prices affect direct cash flows for payments of goods, taxes, cost structures affecting its competitive position, and evaluation of management performance.

Different conditions in the home country of each subsidiary could lead to different transfer pricing decisions, assuming that the firm has the discretion to set arbitrary prices. Tax authorities tend to have the greatest influence in prohibiting companies from setting prices arbitrarily; the preference is to have an arm's length price instead. Management itself may prefer an arm's length price for two basic reasons. First, it is often difficult to set priorities for transfer prices. For example, goods being shipped to a politically unstable country where there are low corporate income tax rates are subjected to conflicting possibilities: The unstable environment would imply a high transfer price to get goods out, whereas the low tax rate would imply a low transfer price in order to concentrate profits.

The second reason for wanting an arm's length price is performance evaluation. Arbitrary transfer prices affect net income as well as the asset base in calculations of return on investment. Thus management performance is evaluted in areas where management has no control when arbitrary transfer prices are used. As a result, many firms prefer to use cost plus or some other way of setting arm's length prices on its intracorporate transfers.

The last area of concern is that of currency. Management is obviously concerned about the ultimate dollar results of its operations worldwide, since

TABLE 41.9   Possible Combinations of Exchange Rates in the Control Process

Rate Used for Determining Budget	Rate Used to Track Performance Relative to Budget		
	Actual at Time of Budget	Projected at Time of Budget	Actual at End of Period
Actual at time of budget	A-1	A-2	A-3
Projected at time of budget	P-1	P-2	P-3
Actual at end of period (through updating)	E-1	E-2	E-3

Source: Donald R. Lessard and Peter Lorange, "Currency Changes and Management Control: Resolving the Centralization and Decentralization Dilemma," *Accounting Review* (July 1977), p. 630

reports to shareholders and home country creditors are made in the reporting currency, the U.S. dollar. However, there is a big gap between the initial transactions that occur in the local or foreign currency and the final results in dollars. In addition, there is the problem of setting budgets, monitoring performance, and evaluating performance of local subsidiaries and their management.

The issue of currency is a critical one. The choice of currency used in evaluations depends a great deal on the evaluation technique being used. As opposed to using just the local currency or just the parent currency, many firms use both currencies. The choice of currency to set budgets and track performance is more complex and includes top management's attitude toward dollar accountability. Table 41.9 illustrates the possible combinations of exchange rates that can be used in the control process.

The options that make the most sense are A-1, A-3, P-2, P-3, and E-3. Under options A-1, P-2, and E-3, the same exchange rate is used to set the budget and track performance. In the case of option A-1, the exchange rate in effect when the budget was set is used to translate actual results into dollars. Thus management sees the information in dollars, but local managers are not responsible for exchange rate changes. Option E-3 is very similar in philosophy except that the budget in dollars is updated to reflect the current rate in order to match actual performance translated at the current rate. Option P-2 is slightly different in that while management is not held responsible for exchange rate changes, it is required to project exchange rates. Top management must decide who is responsible for projecting the rate, but there appears to be no attempt to hold anyone responsible for an inaccurate projection.

Options A-3 and P-3 introduce the element of accountability for exchange rate changes. In both cases, a different rate is used to track performance than is used to set the budget. For option A-3, management is accountable for the total fluctuation between the rates in effect when the budget is established and when actual performance is recorded. Top management must decide where to assign responsibility for exchange fluctuations, since A-3 includes operating as well as currency variances. The assumption is that the operating manager is responsible for any currency changes. If that is the case, then the corporate or regional finance staff needs to provide assistance to local management on exposure management techniques. Care must also be taken to ensure that local management does not do something to minimize exchange exposure that might adversely affect operating performance.

For option P-3, the same kinds of issues exist as for option A-3. The difference is that with option P-3 management is required to forecast or project the exchange rate. The currency variance that shows up when budget costs are compared with actual costs is the difference between what management forecasts the rate to be and what it actually is. Thus the corporate finance staff needs to provide assistance to local management in protecting the exchange rate.

As pointed out previously, some companies prefer to use local currency rather than information translated into dollars when setting budgets and monitoring results. This is partly because they believe the translation process distorts the relationships among accounts that exist in local currency. The introduction of the current rate method in FASB Statement No. 52 results in dollar statements that maintain the same relationships that exist in local currency. That may add more credibility to dollar financial statements in performance evaluation.

CONCLUSION

As financial executives make decisions concerning asset management and funds positioning in the highly volatile and complex international environment, they must rely on the accuracy, reliability, and timeliness of the accounting data supplied by the accounting group. Differences in accounting standards worldwide complicate the recordkeeping process, since firms must keep one set of books in accordance with local standards and another set to assist in preparing consolidated financial statements according to the parent company's external reporting requirements. In addition, comparability of international results for internal purposes is enhanced when common standards are used for preparing internal reports.

Multinational firms are also faced with a variety of specific accounting problems that are a direct result of their international operations. Foreign currency is a big issue as firms must account for foreign currency transactions and the translation of foreign currency financial statements. As pointed out earlier in this chapter, FASB Statement No. 52 adds a new dimension to the issue as firms have the option of translating foreign currency financial statements using the current rate method or the temporal method made popular by FASB Statement No. 8, depending on the characteristics of the foreign company whose statements are being translated. Under the current rate method, many of the disadvantages of the temporal method are eliminated, especially since foreign exchange translation gains and losses are put in a separate component of shareholders' equity rather than recognized in income.

Foreign tax principles are important, because the tax practices and incentives that a country has to offer may have an impact on the location of a foreign operation and the timing of various dividend and interest flows to the parent company. Tax treaties should be studied closely to find out how best to protect parent cash flows.

Finally, the performance evaluation of subsidiaries and subsidiary management is complicated by transfer pricing decisions and foreign currencies. A number of international variables encourage the setting of arbitrary rather than arm's length prices for intracorporate transfers in order to position funds more effectively. However, these arbitrary prices can injure performance evaluation. Thus management needs to be aware of the effect of intracorporate transfer prices on subsidiary and management performance. Exchange rate changes also should be considered in performance evaluation, since they can distort the picture that corporate management sees. Thus a decision must be made as to who is accountable for dollar results, and whether or not local currency results are relevant for making decisions.

As can be seen, the same issues that accountants face in a domestic context must be dealt with in an international context. However, in the international context, variables such as different accounting standards and foreign exchange can create numerous complexities that affect the accuracy, reliability, and timeliness of the accounting data on which the financial group needs to rely.

SUGGESTED READING

American Accounting Association. *Notable Contributions to the Periodical International Accounting Literature — 1975–78.* Sarasota, Fla.: American Accounting Association, 1979.

Arpan, Jeffrey S., and Lee H. Radebaugh. *International Accounting and Multinational Enterprises.* New York: John Wiley & Sons, 1981.

Burton, John C., ed. *The International World of Accounting: Challenges and Opportunities.* Reston, Va.: The Council of Arthur Young Professors, 1981.

Choi, Frederick D.S., ed. *Multinational Accounting: A Research Framework for the Eighties.* Ann Arbor, Mich.: UMI Research Press, 1981.

Choi, Frederick D.S., and Gerhard Mueller. *Essentials of Multinational Accounting: An Anthology.* Ann Arbor, Mich.: University Microfilms International, 1979.

———, and Gerhard Mueller, *Essentials of Multinational Accounting: An Anthology.* Ann Arbor, Mich.: University Microfilms International, 1979.

Daley, Lane A., and Gerhard G. Mueller. "Accounting in the Arena of Global Politics." *Journal of Accountancy* (Feb. 1982), pp. 40–53.

Morsicato, Helen Gernon. *Currency Translation and Performance Evaluation in Multinationals.* Ann Arbor, Mich.: UMI Research Press, 1980.

Nobes, Christopher, and Robert Parker, eds. *Comparative International Accounting.* Homewood, Ill.: Richard D. Irwin, 1981.

Persen, William, and Van Lessig. *Evaluating the Financial Performance of Overseas Operations.* New York: Financial Executives Research Foundation, 1979.

Watt, George C., et al. *Accounting for the Multinational Corporation.* New York: Financial Executives Research Foundation, 1977.

42

Investment/Financing Decisions for Multinational Corporations

MARK R. EAKER

INTRODUCTION

The international dimension of capital budgeting introduces a number of elements that complicate the decision process. Those elements do not invalidate the use of standard capital budgeting techniques, but they do make necessary the explicit recognition of some of the assumptions that are usually invoked in their domestic applications. The procedures and guidelines recommended in this chapter do not come out of a well-developed theoretical model of foreign investment. Instead the recommendations take into account the problems facing managers who must make investment decisions and the amount of information that is most likely to be available to them at the time those decisions are made.

Capital budgeting involves two broad categories of estimates: First, the analyst must determine the relevant cash flows; second, he must estimate the appropriate discount rate or required rate of return. Both these estimates are affected by the international elements of a project in a variety of ways. Should the cash flow and cost of capital estimates be for the project or for just those aspects that directly affect the parent? How should inflation and exchange rate fluctuations be taken into account? What is the best way to reflect the added risk of doing business overseas? How do special tax and financing arrangements enter into the capital budgeting calculus? Answers to each of these questions are provided in subsequent sections of this chapter.

MOTIVES FOR INTERNATIONAL INVESTMENT

Operations in distant and culturally different places are inherently more difficult than domestic operations. Consequently domestic companies have a competitive advantage. Why, then, do firms invest overseas?

Possible Competitive Advantages of Foreign Firms

There are several possible compensations for incurring the risk and problems of foreign investment. Some industries are characterized by economies of scale; that is, firms with larger market shares globally are able to operate more efficiently, with lower cost structures. A large multinational corporation (MNC) therefore has an advantage over smaller, local firms because of its lower unit costs of production. Moreover, local production might be the only way to capture or maintain market share. Many firms shift from an export orientation to overseas production because trade barriers restrict or threaten their access to current or potential markets. If competitors establish production facilities inside the trade barriers, then they might be able to expand their market share, reduce costs, and compete more effectively in all other markets. This is one example of defensive foreign investment, overseas expansion motivated by a desire to protect market position.

Another advantage that firms can exploit is superior knowledge or technical expertise. This might be the result of research and development activities or skills related to the marketing of products. Knowledge intensive industries, such as chemical, pharmaceutical, and electronics, have been major sources of foreign investment activity. So have consumer products industries where brand identification and promotion skills are important. Both types of knowledge — production and marketing — can be exploited in order to compensate for the additional difficulties of overseas investment. They might provide reduced operating costs or product differentiation of overseas investment. They might provide reduced operating costs or product differentiation which allow the firm to compete even with a higher cost structure.

Although the advantages of superior knowledge explain how firms can successfully compete overseas, they do not necessarily explain why. Those same advantages can be utilized to expand export sales, but it is when export sales are threatened by restrictions or competition that overseas production is desirable.

Another primary motive for overseas expansion is directly related to cost reductions. Foreign investment is often necessary in order to secure low-cost raw materials such as petroleum, bauxite, or rubber. Without access to those materials firms find themselves at a competitive disadvantage in comparison to vertically integrated competitors. Labor can be viewed in this context as a raw material, so establishing foreign operations to take advantage of lower overseas labor costs fits into this category.

Related to cost reductions is the need to establish overseas offices and facilities to serve customers located abroad. Even companies that primarily market through export channels have found that after-purchase relationships with customers require in-country operations. This is true even for nonmanufacturing companies such as banks, which have followed the flag as their domestic customers have expanded overseas.

Another motive for overseas investment is to take advantage of subsidies offered by foreign governments. In order to attract technology, jobs, and foreign exchange, many countries offer foreign firms special tax treatment, tariff protection, or below market financing. These subsidies frequently represent crucial considerations when a firm is evaluating an overseas location. Without the added inducement, the project would not be justified, but with it, the project is acceptable.

A final motive for direct foreign investment is the desire to diversify one's wealth position. Modern financial theory has shown the advantages of holding a diversified portfolio of assets. Just as there are potential gains from diversification across industries, there are gains from diversification across national borders. Unfortunately, there are a number of factors that make it difficult for individual investors to own securities in other countries.

Many nations have restrictions on capital flows that disallow portfolio investment. In addition, capital markets in most less developed countries and even many developed nations lack depth and breadth. There are relatively few traded securities and large concentrations of ownership among them that make it almost impossible for investors to acquire assets in those countries even where formal restrictions are absent.

Investment even in developed countries is hard to accomplish. Tax rules are different from nation to nation, and information about securities is not as available in other countries as in the United States. Consequently, although investors believe that there are benefits to international diversification, they are unable to diversify their own portfolios.

An alternative to individual diversification is to invest in MNCs. With their legal staffs and industry knowledge, these companies are able to engage in direct investment despite the information barriers that thwart individuals. The logical extension of this argument is that shareholders desire management to diversity in order to substitute for individual diversification which is blocked by formal and informal barriers.

There is no direct evidence that firms are in fact motivated by the diversification issue. It is, however, an interesting and theoretically satisfying argument. The academic research on the topic has focused on the empirical question as to whether MNCs are a good vehicle for diversification. The results are mixed.

Disadvantages Related to Foreign Operations

In the introduction to this section it was stated that firms face added difficulties related to overseas operations. It is worthwhile to list some of them so that they will be kept in mind when cash flow forecasts and risk adjustment are discussed in subsequent sections.

1 The firm is perceived as being foreign, which causes resentment among consumer groups, domestic competition, and government officials. Often those interest groups or stakeholders mistrust the foreign parent.

2 Foreign operations are physically very far from headquarters. Information is harder to gather and disseminate so managerial control is more difficult.

3 Cultural differences exist which need to be considered in determining organizational design and personnel policies.

4 A new set of *tax and legal* rules must be learned and incorporated into financial planning and firm policy.

5 Transactions occur in a foreign currency, which adds to the uncertainty of cash flows.

6 The firm must operate in a different political environment. A failure to understand that environment and its laws could lead to severe penalties.

In addition, if the political atmosphere is less stable than in the home country, the firm must deal with a rapidly changing environment. To keep up with events requires resources expended on information gathering.

ASSESSMENT OF FOREIGN CASH FLOWS

A frequent shortcoming of cash flow forecasts is that they fail to identify all the potential benefits and problems related to an overseas investment. It is likely that fewer errors will be made if the motivation for the project is kept in mind at the time the cash flows are estimated.

The major difficulty faced by analysts evaluating foreign investment cash flows is the divergence between the cash flows generated by the investment project as a freestanding local project and the cash flows accruing to the parent. Several factors contribute to the differences; some are controlled by the investor and others are determined by the firm's operating environment. Regardless of the source of the discrepancy, it is important for the investor to recognize that those cash flows which affect his position are the relevant ones to include. Estimation of those cash flows involves a three-stage process which begins with a forecast of the total or freestanding project flows and ends with the investor cash flows. That process requires an identification of the factors that cause the two cash flows to diverge and a procedure for converting estimated foreign currency flows into the home currency of the investor.

Sources of Divergence

Interdependencies. As indicated in the preceding section, overseas investment is often prompted by defensive motives: reaction to trade restrictions or

TABLE 42.1   Incremental Cash Flow Analysis

	Current Export Sales	Sales With Expansion		Sales Without Expansion
Units	4,000	1,000	6,000	1,500
Price	$60	$50	$50	$50
Revenue	$240,000	$50,000	$300,000	$75,000

competitive pressures. In those cases some of the sales generated by the project are cannibalized from export sales formerly made by existing divisions of the firm. Sales that are taken away from other units but that would have been maintained without the overseas expansion should not be included among the project's revenues. At the same time, if those sales would have been lost due to trade restrictions or competition, they are correctly attributed to the project.

An example can help clarify this point. A firm is contemplating an overseas investment that will have sales of 6,000 units per month at a price of $50 per unit. The firm currently services that market with export sales of 4,000 units at a price of $60 per unit. A major competitor is establishing a facility in the same region in order to avoid import quotas which will be in place in the next year. If the firm does not follow suit and make the investment, its estimated export sales will be 1,500 units at $50 per unit. If it does make the investment, export sales will fall to 1,000 units. What is the amount of sales revenue that should be credited to the foreign investment?

The correct answer is the amount that is incremental to the project compared to what would be generated if the project were not undertaken. That amount is $275,000 per month, the difference between the $350,000 total sales with the expansion and the $75,000 that would be realized without it. The $275,000 represents the $300,000 in sales that the investment generates, less the $25,000 that is cannibalized from existing sales. The remaining decline in export sales ($165,000) is not deducted from the project because those sales would be lost even if the investment were not made. This example is summarized in Table 42.1.

Changes in sales revenues are utilized in the example to illustrate interdependencies, but they are only one side of the cash flow equation. In a more complete analysis, costs are also considered. If costs were higher at the foreign operation, then the increase would have to be taken into account when cash outflows were estimated. It is the net impact on total cash flows that is relevant.

Interdependencies also show up through transfer pricing. Once foreign operations are established, it is likely that intracompany transactions will cross international borders. Firms establish transfer prices at which those transactions clear between the operating entities. Because of tax effects and currency restrictions, those transfer prices are not always set at market levels. Transfer pricing might be used to shift earnings from a high tax jurisdiction to a low tax jurisdiction. An internal effect of that pricing policy is to reduce stated cash flows in the high tax country and lower them in the lower tax country. From a corporate viewpoint the tax reduction increases total cash flows, but without careful analysis the source of the cash flows might be identified incorrectly. Again, an example is helpful.

A firm is considering an overseas assembly plant that will buy components from the parent. The market price of the component is set at $30, at which price the contribution margin for the parent is $8. After assembly, which adds $10 to the cost, the subsidiary will sell the finished product for $50. The effective tax rates in the parent's and subsidiary's countries are 30 percent and 40 percent, respectively. At the existing transfer price the after-tax cash flows for the corporation are $11,60: $5.60 at the parent level and $6.00 at the subsidiary level. Because of the differences in tax rates, a higher transfer price would lead to higher after-tax cash flows for the corporation as a whole. At a transfer price of $40, the subsidiary's profits are eliminated entirely, whereas the parent's after-tax earnings rise to $12.60. If the $40 transfer price is used in evaluating the overseas project and the subsidiary is not credited with its share of the final cash flows, the investment will be turned down. As an extreme case, suppose all the sales are dependent on building the assembly plant (because of trade restrictions). The correct cash flows to the project then would be the full $12.60, even though none of these show up on the subsidiary's books. Because of the presence of interdependencies, it is important to identify accurately the amount and source of all relevant cash flows.

Remittance Restrictions. Countries frequently impose limits on the amount of funds that subsidiaries can pay to their overseas parent in the form of dividends. These policies are generally part of a more comprehensive program to reduce a balance of payments deficit. Descriptions of restrictions in force and changes in policies can be found in *Exchange Arrangements & Exchange Restrictions*, published annually by the International Monetary Fund. Exhibit 42.1 is an excerpt from the section on Argentina in the 1982 report. At the time that an investment decision is being made, it is important that current restrictions are understood and that some estimate is made of the probability of continuing restrictions or future restrictions being imposed. The latter necessarily involves an evaluation of the host country's balance of payments position.

Restrictions come in a variety of forms, usually allowing only a maximum percentage of annual earnings, retained earnings, or sales to be paid. Whatever their form, they have the effect of deferring the receipt of cash flows and thereby reducing the value of those flows. The amount of the loss is determined by the severity of the restriction, the length of time that receipt of the flows is delayed, and the opportunity available for investing the blocked funds before repatriation. For example, assume that an investment with a 10-year life generates annual net cash flows of $1 million. Restrictions on dividends limit payments to $400,000 each year for the first nine years, but allow payment equal to accumulated retained earnings at the end of the tenth year. The appropriate cash flows to consider in this case are then $400,000 per year for the first nine years and $6,400,000 in the last year. If the funds can be reinvested during the interim, the additional interest income should be included. If the $400,000 can be invested at 10 percent and those earnings are also available for dividends at the end of the tenth year, the final cash flow will be $6,400,000 plus $2,303,600 in interest.

In the example, cash flows and earnings are considered to be the same. That is usually not the case because of the presence of noncash expenses such as

EXHIBIT 42.1   Exchange Restrictions

CHANGES DURING 1981

January 19. Regulations on inward foreign investment were relaxed as follows: (a) examination and approval of foreign investments were centralized in the Under Secretariat for Foreign Investment in the Ministry of Economy; (b) preference would be given to new investment in priority sectors and to ventures involving at least 51 percent of local participation; and (c) repatriation of capital would be allowed after an initial three-year period, provided that the continuity of the local firm was assured (Decree No. 103 of the Ministry of Finance).

February 3. The Argentine peso was devalued by 10 percent against the U.S. dollar and at the same time a schedule of daily buying and selling regulation rates was announced for the period February 3–August 31, 1981. The Central Bank was to intervene in the foreign exchange market if the buying or selling rates exceeded the band created by the announced regulation rates (Circular No. R. C. 929 of the Central Bank of Argentina).

March 20. Foreign exchange purchases exceeding US$20,000 in each case were made subject to a written declaration of purpose (Telephone Communication No. 4486 of the Central Bank of Argentina).

April 1. The tariff reform program initiated in January 1979 was suspended.

April 2. The following changes were made in the exchange arrangement: (a) the practice of preannouncing the exchange rate was discontinued, and it was decided that the Central Bank would determine daily the spot selling and buying regulation rates of the Argentine peso for the U.S. dollar; (b) the rates would be adjusted by small amounts at frequent intervals in the future; and (c) the spot selling rate of the peso against the U.S. dollar was adjusted by 30.1 percent and the spot buying rate by 32.4 percent. (Foreign exchange earnings on exports declared to the Junta Nacional de Granos by April 1, 1981 that either paid export taxes or received rebates would be converted at the exchange rate prevailing on April 1, 1981 — Communication A, No. 16 of the Central Bank.)

April 2. The following measures were introduced in conjunction with the depreciation of the peso: (a) a 12 percent tax was imposed on exports of cereals, meat, and other products, to be gradually reduced for cereals beginning May 1, 1981, eliminated for grain cereals by November 1, 1981, and for coarse grain cereals by March 1, 1982; (b) a 10 percent tax was levied on exports of various food products including wheat flour, vegetable oils, and cereal products; (c) export rebates for specified products, including fruits, tomatoes, cotton, tea, milk, and wool, were reduced by 3 percentage points; and (d) with the exception of those for motor vehicles, import duties at the maximum levels were reduced by 12 percentage points but to levels which may not be below 43 percent (Communication A, No. 16 of the Central Bank).

(continued)

EXHIBIT 42.1   Exchange Restrictions *(continued)*

April 2. The declaration requirement for foreign exchange purchases exceeding US$20,000 was eliminated (Communication B, No. 35 of the Central Bank).

May 29. Authorization was granted for risk-contract exploration and development of uranium by foreign private companies in joint ventures with the Argentina Nuclear Agency on a 50-50 basis; a maximum of 25 percent of the production must be exported and the balance would be required to be sold to the Nuclear Agency.

Source: Exchange Arrangements & Exchange Restrictions (Washington, D.C.: International Monetary Fund, 1982)

---

depreciation. The disparity between earnings and cash flows creates some ambiguity about which cash flows are available for repatriation. If the dividend restriction establishes a limit on payments which is based on earnings, the positive cash flow related to depreciation will not be available to the firm for repatriation. Unless these funds can be used beneficially elsewhere in the country, it will usually be in the parent corporation's interest to keep depreciation expenses low in order to maximize after-tax income available for foreign dividends. There is no general rule to follow which fits all cases, but it is necessary to understand fully whatever restrictions exist and their implications.

Taxation. Differences in tax rates have already been shown to enter the cash flow calculations. Effective tax rates in different countries vary a great deal. From the standpoint of a U.S. investor, the tax rate that applies is usually the higher of the two effective rates. The United States gives credit for foreign taxes but only up to the maximum U.S. rate. Therefore any taxes beyond that rate reduce the return to the investor.

Subsidies. Decisions to invest in particular projects are often influenced by inducements offered by the host country. As indicated in the preceding section on motives for foreign investment, these can take a variety of forms. Given sufficient subsidies, projects that otherwise would not be acceptable become viable investments. For potential investors a key question is whether or not the subsidies can be taken away if the host country has a change of policy. The current government may offer a tax benefit that is of substantial value if it stays in effect for the life of the project. It serves as the necessary incentive to attract capital or technological knowledge. Once the investment has been made, the government may alter the tax laws or impose a new restriction that offsets the original subsidy.

Potential investors need to evaluate the subsidy and the probability that it will be eliminated. A very conservative approach is to accept only those projects that would be viable without the subsidy. A more reasonable method is to adjust the cash flows in order to take account of the risk or probability of losing the subsidy at some future time. Being aware of the importance of the subsidy also allows the investor to take steps to reduce the impact of its loss.

Exchange Risk and Cash Flows

In the various examples presented previously the cash flows are given in dollars even though it is clear that they are generated in some other currency. Conversion from local currency into dollars is consistent with the view that parent or investor cash flows are the relevant cash flows to analyze. A U.S. investor ultimately wants to have dollars to distribute to its shareholders. That much is straightforward. What is not so simple is the process by which estimated foreign currency flows are valued in dollars. That requires forecasts of inflation and exchange rates, as well as the impact of changes in both on the operating cash flows. In addition, the appropriate choice of currency for cash flow measurement is related to the choice of a discount rate. Therefore the analysis that follows discusses both the numerator and the denominator of the capital budgeting formula. Because the task is so formidable, it is important to start with a very structured approach. Once the basic framework is established, it is possible to build more complicated relationships into the analysis.

To evaluate the investment using the net present value (NPV) criterion, an analyst has several options. Those options are:

1 To use real foreign currency cash flows and a real foreign currency discount rate;
2 To use nominal foreign currency cash flows and a nominal foreign currency discount rate;
3 To use real dollar cash flows and a real dollar discount rate;
4 To use nominal dollar cash flows and a nominal dollar discount rate.

Real cash flows are nominal flows adjusted for inflation using the inflation rate expected or experienced in that country. The four options are not as different as they might appear at first. Economic theory explicitly links inflation rates, exchange rates, and interest rates to one another. If those theoretical relationships are valid empirically, then the choice of one of the four options is immaterial: Each would lead to the same outcome. Because the empirical evidence is in support of the theoretical relationships, some authors have suggested using option 1, since it requires the least information. That option makes both inflation and exchange rate forecasts unnecessary. Unfortunately, the use of real foreign currency cash flows can obscure some important and relevant factors that might influence the desirability of a particular project. As a result the approach suggested here is to use option 4, and most difficult of the options. It requires that both inflation rates and exchange rates be forecast, but the extra effort greatly enhances investment evaluation. In the following sections, the theoretical relationships among exchange rates, inflation, and interest rates are introduced and used to show under that conditions the four NPV calculations are equivalent.

Fisher Effect

The Fisher effect relates interest rates to inflation expectations. Specifically, it hypothesizes that the nominal rate of interest consists of a real or noninflation-related component and an inflation premium related to price expectations. An algebraic representation and numerical example are:

$$(1 + i) = (1 + r)(1 + \pi) \qquad (1.236) = (1.03)(1.20) \tag{42.1}$$

where: i = nominal rate of interest, here 23.6 percent

r = real rate of interest, here 3 percent

π = expected inflation, here 20 percent

Equation 42.1 is true for both the home and foreign country. When foreign country variables are used, they are denoted by an asterisk(*). In the theoretical literature it is usually assumed that r and r^*, the real rates of return, are equal. Accordingly, the Fisher effect for the foreign country is:

$$(1 + i^*) = (1 + r)(1 + \pi^*) \qquad (1.1124) = (1.03)(1.08) \tag{42.2}$$

Purchasing Power Parity

Purchasing power parity (PPP) relates the exchange rate between two countries to their differential inflation rates. A change in the exchange rate between two time periods is determined by the relative inflation rates in the two countries. The nation experiencing the higher rate of inflation has a depreciating currency. The nation with the lower inflation rate sees its currency strengthen. PPP can be expressed as:

$$X_t = \frac{X_0(1 + \pi)^t}{(1 + \pi^*)^t} \qquad 2 = \frac{1.80(1.20)}{1.08} \tag{42.3}$$

where: x_0 = exchange rate expressed in home currency (dollars) per foreign currency unit at time 0, here 1.8:1.0

x_t = exchange rate at time t years from 0, here 2.0:1.0

Alternative Cash Flow Measures

Once these relationships have been developed, it is straightforward to show that if they are valid the four alternative cash flow calculations are equivalent. First this is done analytically, then it is demonstrated through an extended example.

Beginning with option 1, the NPV of the real cash flow in the base year, C_0, denominated in the foreign currency is

$$\frac{C_0}{(1 + r^*)^t} \tag{42.4}$$

To account for inflation, it is necessary to adjust both the cash flow and the discount rate. Therefore, the nominal flows are:

$$\frac{C_0(1 + \pi^*)^t}{(1 + r^*)^t(1 + \pi^*)^t} \tag{42.5}$$

Since the numerator and denominator both have been multiplied by the same number, the discounted value of the cash flow has not changed. But the denominator is the right-hand side of the Fisher equation, so in fact Equation 42.5 is equal to:

$$\frac{C_0(1 + \pi^*)^t}{(1 + i^*)^t} \tag{42.6}$$

which is the mathematical representation of option 2. Therefore, options 1 and 2 are equivalent.

Option 3 is calculated by converting the foreign currency cash flows into dollars and discounting at the real U.S. rate.

$$\frac{C_0 X_0}{(1 + r)^t} \tag{42.7}$$

Making use of PPP, Equation 42.7 becomes

$$\frac{C_0(1 + \pi^*)^t X_t}{(1 + r)^t(1 + \pi)^t} \tag{42.8}$$

which is the nominal foreign currency cash flows converted to dollars and discounted at the nominal dollar rate, that is, option 4.

To arrive at an NPV figure using option 4, it is necessary to forecast the base year cash flows, C_0; inflation in the foreign country, π^*; and future exchange rates, X_t. Because of the Fisher effect, there is no need to forecast home currency inflation, since the denominator in Equation 42.8 is equal to $1 + i$, and i, the home nominal rate, is available. For all intents and purposes, however, forecasting X_t requires some measure of π to compare with π^*, so a home inflation forecast is in fact necessary.

These relationships and the advantages of using nominal dollar flows can be clarified with an example. Assume that an investment in a French project requires a cash outlay of $1 million or 5 million francs at the current spot rate. Sales revenues from the project, which as a five-year life, are estimated to be 3 million francs per year at today's prices, while costs are 1.2 million francs. Both revenues and costs are expected to change by 12 percent per year in line with French inflation. Inflation in the United States is 5 percent. For a project of this type the required real rate of return is determined to be 3 percent.

With the preceding information, it is possible to evaluate the project according to each of the options. The only additional values necessary to do the various calculations can be arrived at by assuming that the Fisher effect and PPP hold. The cash flows, discount rates, and NPVs are summarized in Table 42.2.

Examination of the numbers reveals that all four options give the same result. That being the case, it is easy to understand why some people advocate using real cash flows and real returns. That method requires the least amount of information and the least amount of forecasting. It is important to understand, however, that the equivalent results were derived because the economic relations, PPP and the Fisher effect, were assumed to hold perfectly and because the cash flows were of a simple form.

Validity of the Economic Assumptions

There is a vast body of evidence concerning the validity of PPP and the Fisher effect. Although much of the evidence is contradictory and subject to varied

TABLE 42.2   Alternative Cash Flow Estimates When Purchasing Power Parity Holds

Year	Option 1: Real Francs	Option 2: Nominal Francs	Option 3: Real Dollars	Option 4: Nominal Dollars
0	(FF5,000,000)	(FF5,000,000)	($1,000,000)	($1,000,000)
1	1,800,000	2,016,000	360,000	378,000
2	1,800,000	2,257,900	360,000	396,900
3	1,800,000	2,528,870	360,000	416,745
4	1,800,000	2,832,335	360,000	437,582
5	1,800,000	3,172,215	360,000	459,461
Discount rate	3%	15.36%	3%	8.15%
Net present value	FF3,244,000	FF3,244,000	$648,800	$648,800

interpretations, the general view is that over the long run the relationships are valid. This means, for example, that PPP does not hold month to month or even year to year but that over a 10- or 20-year period exchange rates do reflect inflation differentials. In addition, there is evidence that the deviations from PPP are not systematic but random. This implies that it is difficult if not impossible to accurately forecast the deviations, making the effort not worthwhile. Thus analysts use PPP as a working assumption about future rates. Since that's the case, why go to the trouble of using an option other than 1?

In fact, there are several reasons for doing so. First, PPP and the Fisher effect are macroeconomic relationships: For an economy as a whole they tend to be valid. At a more microeconomic level they are not as relevant, especially PPP.

PPP is based on some aggregate price performance measure such as the consumer price index, wholesale price index, or GNP deflator. Within that aggregate there is a great deal of variation. As a result, even if PPP holds for the economy as a whole, it is not going to be valid for every individual product or industry line. Moreover, it is unlikely that both revenues and costs will follow the same trend, as was assumed in the example. If that is not the case, then differences will arise between the value generated by each of the options.

A variety of factors can generate deviations in the growth paths of revenues and costs. The most general reason is that wages, which are a major component of costs, and prices are not perfectly correlated. More specifically, firms often contract long term for sales or labor. Those contracts generally are written in nominal terms with an expected inflation component built in. Deviations from the inflation expectations lead to windfall profits or losses depending on the direction of the forecast error. Along the same lines, other costs are generally not indexed for inflation. The most important of these is depreciation, which in most countries is based on historical costs. Inflation therefore dilutes the value of the tax shield that depreciation generates for the firm.

The Impact of Deviations from Parity

To demonstrate the impact of these factors, they can be introduced into the simple example given previously. Assume that the costs of 1.2 million current francs consist of 900,000 francs for labor and 300,000 depreciation expense. The depreciation cash flow is available for remittance to the U.S. parent but is not adjusted for inflation. Labor costs are determined by a contract which has two years remaining and calls for increases of 12 percent each year. After that time there will be a renegotiation and management anticipates a 15 percent annual increase. Taxes are levied at a rate of 25 percent. PPP and the Fisher effect are assumed to hold, so the exchange rates each period will be the same as those implicit in Table 42.2. The NPV for each of the options is given in Table 42.3.

A direct comparison between the results in the two tables is not appropriate because of the introduction of taxes in the calculations for Table 42.3. The appropriate contrast to make is in the relationship of the various options to one another within each table. In Table 42.2, all four options give essentially the same results. There is no difference introduced by the choice of nominal or real variables, nor is there a change in outcomes when the calculations are done in dollars as opposed to francs. The dollar values are exactly the franc values converted at the current spot rate of exchange. In Table 42.3, the nominal and real calculations differ. This result was brought about by the use of different inflation rates for revenues and costs, as well as the deviation of those rates from the expected rates implicit in the nominal discount rate. Across currencies, the two nominal NPVs and the two real NPVs are still equivalent. The first set are equal because PPP was assumed to be valid and the second set are equal because the required real return in each currency was the same. Altering those assumptions would lead to greater differences among the results under the four options.

Why then is option 4 the best choice? Because it does not rely on the empirical validity of the PPP and the Fisher effect propositions. If they hold, then the results provided by option 4 are still accurate, although more tedious to derive; if they do not hold, then option 4 takes the deviations into account. Deviations at the macroeconomic level might be hard to predict, but at the firm level many deviations are in fact very predictable. In the example, depreciation expense was known to have a zero inflation rate. Moreover, financial analysts within the firm have access to information that others do not have. They are more informed about the firm's intentions, cost structures, and sales patterns than anyone else. By using nominal rates they make use of that information. Moreover, the detailed development of pro forma financial statements forces the analyst to consider possible problem areas and to be aware of their potential impact on the profitability of a project.

Numerous examples could be given but one should be enough to demonstrate the point. For a particular project labor costs represent 60 percent of variable costs at current year's prices. During the last decade wages have not kept up with the general rate of inflation, so current real wages represent only 70 percent of the real wage rate of 10 years ago. This has been caused in part by wage controls deliberately set by the government to lag price increases. One result has been stepped up investment by labor intensive firms, but another has been labor unrest and union agitation. Consequently the analyst believes that

TABLE 42.3   Divergent Cash Flow Estimates

OPTION 1: Real Francs

	Year 0	Years 1–5
Investment	(FF5,000,000)	—
Revenue	—	FF3,000,000
Labor	—	(900,000)
Depreciation	—	(300,000)
Operating profits	—	FF1,800,000
Taxes	—	(450,000)
After tax profits	—	FF1,350,000
Depreciation	—	300,000
Cash flow	(FF5,000,000)	FF1,650,000

Net present value (at 3%) = FF2,556,505

OPTION 2: Nominal Francs

	Year 0	Year 1	Year 2	Year 3	Year 4	Year 5
Investment	(FF5,000,000)	—	—	—	—	—
Revenue	—	FF3,336,000	FF3,763,200	FF4,214,784	FF4,720,558	FF5,287,025
Labor	—	(1,008,000)	(1,128,960)	(1,298,304)	(1,493,049)	(1,717,007)
Depreciation	—	(300,000)	(300,000)	(300,000)	(300,000)	(300,000)
Operating profits	—	FF2,028,000	FF2,334,240	FF2,616,480	FF2,927,509	FF3,270,018
Taxes	—	(507,000)	(583,560)	(654,120)	(731,877)	(817,504)
After tax profits	—	FF1,521,000	FF1,750,680	FF1,962,360	FF2,195,632	FF2,452,514
Depreciation	—	300,000	300,000	300,000	300,000	300,000
Cash flow	(FF5,000,000)	FF1,821,000	FF2,050,680	FF2,262,360	FF2,495,632	FF2,752,514

Net present value (at 15.36%) = FF7,416,997

OPTION 3: Real Dollars

Investment	($1,000,000)
Annual cash inflow	330,000

Net present value (at 3%) = $511,301

OPTION 4: Nominal Dollars

	Year 0	Year 1	Year 2	Year 3	Year 4	Year 5
Investment	($1,000,000)	—	—	—	—	—
Annual cash inflows	—	$341,437	$360,474	$372,826	$385,563	$398,672

Net present value (at 8.15%) = $475,884

future wages will rise at a faster rate than prices thus squeezing the profitability of the project. Had the analyst relied on current real costs or past wage patterns, then the problem of rapidly rising future costs would have gone unnoticed.

The final point related to the choice of cash flows is that the use of real variables assumes there will not be any changes in competitive position brought about by exchange rate fluctuations. The traditional view is that a depreciation of a country's currency makes the country's goods more desirable due to price considerations, and that an appreciation makes those goods less desirable. According to this view, when a nation's currency devalues, its exports become cheaper and its imports more expensive. Consequently foreigners buy more of the nation's goods as do locals who reduce their volume of imports. A similar story with opposite results applies to the case of an appreciation.

The problem with the traditional story is that it ignores PPP and the individual firms' competitive position, both of which have an impact on whether or not revenues will change due to exchange rate fluctuations. Recall that if PPP holds perfectly, exchange rate changes are determined by and exactly reflect inflation differentials in the two countries. Since the relative cross-border price of a good is determined by the local currency price and the exchange rate, there is no change in the relative price if PPP holds. Any depreciation that lowers the value of the currency is precisely offset by the inflation effect that raises its local currency price. Therefore, currency fluctuations are neutral with respect to sales volumes and base currency revenues.

Other Relevant Factors

Once the PPP assumption is relaxed there is room for relative price changes and competitive adjustments. The net impact will be determined by the elasticities of supply and demand. They are affected in turn by a variety of factors, which should be taken into account when cash flows are estimated; even if the analyst cannot measure them exactly. Among the more important considerations are these:

1 The absolute and relative sizes of the domestic and export business of the firm
2 The extent of competition in domestic and foreign markets
3 Available capacity for expanding sales
4 The relative importance of local versus foreign content in manufacturing costs
5 Price restrictions and tariffs
6 Whether or not the product is priced for export in local currency or a single major currency

As indicated previously, each of the factors influences the elasticity of supply or demand either directly or indirectly. For example, if a firm competes solely in a domestic market against other local firms, then a devaluation will have little impact on sales. There will likely be some reduction in demand as consumers find themselves with lower purchasing power due to the devaluation, but the firm will not gain any price advantage from the change in exchange rates. If the firm is dependent on foreign sources of new materials or components, then the devaluation will increase its costs. Those increases might not be allowed to be passed on to consumers if local price controls are in effect, a fairly common situation in devaluing countries. The scenario described here would apply to many nations that are trying to encourage local manufacturing with protection from exports provided by prohibitive tariffs.

It is clear from the discussion that there are many factors to consider and a great many uncertainties. That makes the whole process more difficult but also highlights the importance of looking closely at the nominal foreign currency cash flows and the impact of deviations from parity relationships. It also suggests that sensitivity analysis should play an important role in the evaluation process. Literally, the question needs to be raised as to how sensitive investor's cash flows are to various perturbations that might take place. Not only does sensitivity analysis reveal interaction effects that might otherwise go unnoticed, but it also provides insights into the riskiness of the investment. More will be said about risk in the next section.

In summary of this section, a three-step process for the evaluation of foreign investment cash flows is advocated.

1 Look at the project cash flows as an independent freestanding local country investment. Those cash flows should be estimated in nominal foreign currency values.

2 Isolate those cash flows that would actually accrue to the investor. This step involves looking closely at available funds for dividend remittances, transfer payments, and other interdependencies.

3 Convert the investor's foreign currency flows to home currency values in order to produce a set of nominal dollar cash flows to be discounted with a nominal dollar rate of interest.

CAPITAL BUDGETING TECHNIQUES

Financial theory indicates clearly that a capital budgeting technique or decision rule should meet specific criteria. Most academics and practitioners agree that those criteria include the following:

1 The technique should be consistent with the notion of wealth maximization of the current shareholders.

2 It should reflect the time value of money.

3 It should provide a means of systematically dealing with risk.

4 It should yield consistent rankings of mutually exclusive alternatives.

5 It should utilize information available to the manager or decision maker.

It is generally agreed that a discounted cash flow approach is necessary for making capital budgeting decisions. The discount rate or required return hurdle is chosen in order to meet the first three criteria. To accomplish that, the discount rate must reflect the opportunity cost of funds to the shareholders and the riskiness of the investment. There are both theoretical and practical problems related to the choice of the discount rate; those problems are discussed in detail in earlier chapters dealing with capital budgeting for domestic projects. None of those problems disappears when the project involves cross-border investments and, in fact, several are compounded. The academic research tends to focus on the choice of the appropriate discount rate with the emphasis on its ability to measure risk. In general the methods developed for choosing the appropriate rate require information that is unavailable to managers. That problem is manifested in the number of firms that either do not use a discounted cash flow approach at all or make no attempt to adjust for risk utilizing one of the recommended theoretical techniques.

Because the purpose of this chapter is to provide guidance to practicing managers, the emphasis is on an approach that can be implemented with the information available to those individuals. This approach sometimes entails theoretical shortcuts, but it is better than the methods that surveys indicate are prevalent among firms.

This discussion focuses on two aspects of the capital budgeting problem: the choice of a discount rate and the method of risk adjustment. In theory the two issues are the same, because the theoretical models call for a discount rate that reflects the riskiness of an investment project as it relates to some measure of market risk. Here, they are separated in order to make implementation more tractable for the practicing manager.

Choosing a Discount Rate

The appropriate required rate of return is one that reflects the viewpoint of the parent and not that of the project. The cash flows that are generated by the project differ from those that accrue to the parent. Since the parent is concerned with cash flows that it receives, those cash flows should be discounted at a rate that reflects the cost of capital to the parent.

The correct cost of capital to use is the weighted average cost of capital (WACC) for the firm. WACC is calculated by looking at all the sources of funding for the corporation as a whole and weighing their cost according to their relative market values. The use of the WACC raises several questions in the international context. These questions are related to how the foreign investment is financed and whether or not the investment alters the financial structure of the corporation.

Frequently foreign investments are funded by an equity portion provided by the parent and long-term debt raised by the subsidiary. Some analysts mistakenly use only the equity as the parent's cash outflow in the calculations of present value. Their reasoning is that the parent has made an equity investment in exchange for future dividends, so the amount of the equity position and the dividend stream are the relevant cash flows. That argument overlooks two important points. First, the dividend stream is supported by all the assets of the foreign project regardless of how those assets are funded. Therefore, the total investment or cash outflow is the value of the assets, which is equal to both the debt and equity funding.

Second, it is unlikely that financial intermediaries and markets ignore the debt of the foreign subsidiary when evaluating the debt capacity of the parent. As a result, whether the debt is a direct obligation of the parent or an indirect one via the subsidiary, it represents a portion of the total pool of funds available to the corporation. If the debt of the subsidiary is viewed as increasing the financial risk of the firm, or if its operations are seen as increasing the operating risk of the parent, then some adjustment might be made in the cost of capital. The adjustment is no different from the adjustment suggested in the case of domestic projects involving financial leverage or systematic risk that differs from the corporation as a whole. The problem is that there is no easy way to measure the correct adjustment. One suggestion is to find independent companies with characteristics similar to those of the project whose cost of capital can be evaluated using market data. At best, this alternative is available for a smaller number of projects.

Another point raised in support of adjusting the cost of capital is the use of subsidized financing for a project. Countries eager to attract investment capital in order to create jobs often provide below market interest rate financing. Since these funds would not be available to the firm if the project were not undertaken, they are not part of the corporate pool. The argument is sound, although adjusting the discount rate is not the only way to account for the benefit of the subsidy. Another approach, and the one recommended here, is to include the value of the subsidy in the cash flows for the project and then discount the cash flows at the WACC. The major reason for doing this is that the NPV calculation assumes that cash flows will be reinvested at the discount rate. If the cash flows are returned to the present, then it is unlikely that they will be reinvested at the low subsidized rate; rather, they will be reinvested at a rate consistent with the firm's overall cost of capital.

To calculate the value of the subsidy it is necessary to compare the after-tax cost of the alternative borrowing. Assume the host country provides $3 million at 7 percent when the market rate is 12 percent and the firm's tax rate is 40 percent. The loan will be repaid in equal installments over three years. The net after-tax value of the subsidy is equal to 3 percent of the outstanding balance in each year. This is derived from the difference in the interest rates $(0.12-0.07)$ multiplied by a factor that accounts for the tax deductibility of interest $(1-0.4)$. The positive amount added to the cash flows in each of the three years of the loan should be $90,000, $60,000, and $30,000.

Adjusting for Project Risk

The discount rate might be adjusted if the project is in a different risk class than the firm as a whole. That adjustment is not related to the fact that the investment is foreign. Should there, however, be an adjustment just because the project is located overseas? And if there is an adjustment, does it necessarily increase the riskiness of the investment?

Portfolio theory indicates that shareholders are rewarded only for bearing systematic risk, that portion of variability which cannot be diversified away (see Chapter 14). In the earlier discussion of the motives for direct foreign investment, it is suggested that foreign investment might serve as a substitute for individual diversification. If that is the case, then investment in foreign projects could lead to a reduction in the systematic riskiness of the firm. This result comes about because the firm's operations are now affected by market conditions in more than one country. As long as the economic performances of those countries are not perfectly correlated, then foreign diversification leads to the reduction of systematic risk for the U.S. shareholder. Systematic risk is related to market movements. Because market movements in different countries are influenced by economic events in the individual countries, they are not perfectly correlated. Through international diversification, the systematic risk borne by the investor can be reduced as compared to a purely domestic portfolio. Thus, a strong theoretical argument can be made for *lowering* the required rate of return for foreign projects which have the affect of creating diversified positions.

Few managers would accept the conclusion just reached. Instead, they would cite a list of added risks related to foreign investments and assert the need to raise discount rates rather than lower them. There are enough intuitive reasons to support the pragmatic view as opposed to the theoretical one. The need to adjust for added risk is not disputed here. What is argued here is that having a higher hurdle rate for foreign projects is not the best way to proceed. The reasons are technical but not conceptually difficult.

Projects generally have uneven streams of cash flows. When the discount rate is raised to reflect additional risk, the effect is to lower the value of projects with long lives relatively more than those with short lives. In other words, near-term cash flows are not as greatly reduced as long-term ones. This might, but does not necessarily, reflect the timing of the added risk elements.

Another difficulty with using a discount rate adjustment is that different components of the cash stream might be subject to different risks. Some uncertainty is related to the operating cash flows and some to a tax break bestowed by the government. Adjusting the discount rate affects all the elements in the same way.

The alternative to adjusting the discount rate is to adjust the cash flows. Cash flows used in capital budgeting are estimates. These estimates can be adjusted by altering the probabilities of various events that will affect the cash flows. Sensitivity analysis can then reveal how dependent success is on either the mean or the most likely outcome being realized. Using sensitivity analysis is ad hoc; it does not provide a precise measure of a project's riskiness but it does give management a feel for the range of outcomes that are possible. Sensitivity analysis is also easy to perform and requires no additional information beyond that necessary for the basic cash flow analysis.

Adjusted Present Value

Several researchers have advocated a different approach to risk adjustment. It involves adjusting the discount rates, but it is done in a way that avoids the pitfalls associated with the blanket adjustment. This approach is called the adjusted present value (APV) method and has been applied to both domestic and international project evaluation.

The APV method begins with the premise that the project's cash flows can be decomposed into their constituent parts. Each is discounted at a different rate, reflecting the risk associated with it. With regard to an international project, the cash flow streams might consist of dividend remittances from operating income, royalties or other transfer payments, depreciation-related tax savings, and the benefits from a subsidized loan. An argument can be made that these

TABLE 42.4   Capital Budgeting Using APV

Investment	$4,000,000
After-tax operating cash flows	$800,000 per year
Depreciation tax shield	$350,000 per year
Subsidized borrowing benefit	$50,000 per year
Time horizon	5 years

Using a WACC of 12 percent:

$$NPV = -\$4,000,000 + \$1,200,000 \ (3.605)$$
$$= \$326,000$$

Using an all-equity rate of 14 percent for the operating cash flows and a risk-free rate of 8 percent for the other cash flows:

$$APV = \$4,000,000 + \$800,000 \ (3.433) + \$400,000 \ (3.993)$$
$$= \$343,600$$

cash flows, beginning with operating income, are subject to decreasing risk or uncertainty. Therefore, progressively lower discount rates would be used on each set.

It has been suggested that the operating flows be discounted using an all-equity rate which reflects the riskiness of a similar project if it were funded without financial leverage. The subsidy benefits should be discounted at the risk-free rate because they are not subject to operating uncertainty. The remaining flows would be discounted at rates somewhere between the two, reflecting their relative riskiness. Table 42.4 summarizes a very simple example of capital budgeting using APV and compares the outcome to that obtained using a WACC.

Although APV has considerable theoretical and intuitive appeal, it is much easier to describe than to implement. Choosing the various discount rates is not easy. Since most managers are uncomfortable with WACC calculations, it is unlikely that they will be willing to make the distinctions necessary to use APV.

Political and Operating Risk

Identifying, estimating, and adjusting for risk are major aspects of the evaluation process. Ignoring risk in making capital budgeting decisions would lead to suboptimal allocations of capital, so it is important that risk be taken into account. However, in planning the investment and in managing the operation many decisions can be made to reduce the risk to the investor or parent. A passive attitude toward risk likely increases the probability of just those events management would like to avoid. The keys to reducing risk are monitoring, anticipating, and adapting.

Monitoring Developments

Monitoring involves establishing an intelligence network that provides political, social, and economic information with which to understand events in the host country. For large firms with extensive worldwide investments, such as the major petroleum companies, the intelligence gathering process can be almost entirely in-house. The same is true for multinational banks with extensive branch systems. Area or divisional personnel can be assigned the primary responsibility for collecting information and forwarding it to headquarters for evaluation.

Many large companies now have staff economists and political scientists who provide country risk assessments. Although these staff people play an important role in the monitoring process, their analyses should be used in conjunction with evaluations of line personnel who are stationed in the country. Relying solely on either staff or line personnel can provide biased analysis. Staff evaluations tend to be more objective, but because they are done at a distance from a country they often ignore insights that can be gained only by extensive experience living in an area. Line personnel have that experience but are often unwilling to recognize or admit negative aspects about their own nation or the country for which they have managerial responsibility, in part because negative information might adversely affect their own activities. For example, bank calling officers or branch managers would be the appropriate line personnel to provide country information, but their personal interest is in expanding loans or the sale of other bank services. This basic conflict often introduces a bias into the information gathering process.

Smaller firms do not generally have the resources to develop their own information networks. Instead, they rely on information purchased from firms organized for that purpose. Even if the company's primary information sources are external, it should still establish an internal monitoring system as a secondary source. Area personnel should file informal country evaluations and headquarter's staff should visit the country on a regular basis. Their assessments should be matched against those of the external source to check for consistency and accuracy. A firm should not become too dependent on a single source nor too complacent to change to another advisory service if its current one is missing too many trends or changes.

Anticipating Policy

All information should be evaluated with the objective of anticipating policy changes of the government or in the attitudes of other stakeholders in the host country. Some changes affect the general operating environment of the firm whereas others have a direct impact on the operating or ownership structure of the firm.

Environmental changes can be both general and specific. Among the former are macroeconomic policies that attempt to stimulate or restrict economic activity. Countries with accelerating inflation or difficulty servicing external obligations are likely to pursue contractionary monetary or fiscal policies. For a firm with largely domestic sales, this would reduce revenues. Other changes related to macroeconomic policy are the imposition of price and wage controls or currency restrictions. From the earlier discussion of cash flow forecasts, it should be clear how these changes would affect the firm and the value of the investment. The point is that if management can anticipate the policies, it can take steps to reduce their impact: Prices might be raised prior to controls being enacted, foreign currency payments might be made before the local currency becomes inconvertible, or arrangements for parallel loans might be made to reduce the amount of local currency blocked in the country.

There are other longer-term policies that a firm might pursue to reduce risk. Labor unrest in the form of strikes varies in severity from country to country. In those nations where strikes are frequent, the firm might choose less labor intensive technology or adopt employment policies that reduce the threat of strikes.

A large U.S. electronics firm with major manufacturing facilities in Great Britain has a totally nonunion labor force in a highly unionized country. It has been able to maintain that status by having generous benefits and an open employee-management relationship. These policies entail some added costs but reduce the risk of labor strife. The company has not lost manufacturing time due to strikes and has added flexibility in establishing its seniority and compensation system.

More specific policies that arise from concerns about the economic environment can directly affect the operating structure of the firm. Requirements concerning local content in manufacturing and domestic nationals in management positions, pricing to subsidize local consumption, or requirements that firms provide investment in infrastructure are examples. In general, so are regulations that affect transfer pricing or establish restrictions on licensing arrangements and royalty payments.

The final type of political risk comes in the form of government interference with the ownership of the assets or investment. There are many ways in which governments can garner the wealth of foreign investors ranging from punitive taxes and fees to outright expropriation. In between are requirements for local participation in ownership and nationalization with some form of compensation. Regardless of the form it takes, it is unlikely that any involuntary change in ownership structure will benefit the original investors. If it would, then they would have brought it about without coercion. Generally, increased interference or changes in attitudes toward foreign investment are preceded by significant economic or political events. That is what makes the monitoring and anticipation activities worthwhile: They allow a firm to reduce its exposure while there is still room to manuever.

Adapting to Conditions

Adjustments and alterations in policies that firms make in response to changes are signs of their adaptability. Doing business overseas requires a willingness and ability to respond to different legal, political, social, and economic environments. Sometimes those adjustments are undesirable on other grounds but necessary in order to reduce risk related to investing overseas. Entering into a joint venture is an important example.

Joint ventures represent shared ownership and control of operating entities by two or more independent firms or groups of investors. A requirement of local joint ownership is often mandatory for foreign investors. It arises from a sense of nationalism and a desire that some of the returns on capital investment be retained in the host country. At other times firms voluntarily seek out joint venture relationships because of synergy. For example, one firm may have capital or an established distribution network and its partner may have special technological skills or a brand name. The joint venture activity in the U.S. automobile market represents one example of matching contributions: American Motors Corporation had a dealer network and Renault had a car design it wanted to introduce to the United States. In another case, Toyota is bringing its small car technology to a joint venture with General Motors Corporation, which has a dominant market position.

Despite some major exceptions, survey research has indicated that the majority of American firms are a priori opposed to joint ventures, especially those involving local partners. There seems to be a variety of grounds for the opposition, most focusing on the control aspects. The partner acquires access to technology and pricing information which might make him a formidable competitor at some future date. Differences in objectives might lead to disputes over dividend policies, transfer pricing, financial structure decisions, licensing agreements, and efforts by the foreign partner to rationalize production among its worldwide subsidiaries.

The trade-offs in favor of joint ventures include access to markets that might otherwise be unavailable and a reduction in the probability of government interference directed toward foreign investors. By having local nationals involved in ownership and management, the subsidiary loses some of its foreign character. That helps deflect criticisms related to exploitation, capital flight, and external control. The local partners have a stake in the company, which leads them to lobby on its behalf. Any restrictions imposed by the government might adversely affect local interests.

It is important to be careful in choosing a local partner. Under the best of circumstances the local partner brings to the enterprise skills or attributes other than a convenient nationality. If nationality is in fact the only contribution, then the foreign investor should try to find a partner that is reliable and in the mainstream of local politics. Having a local partner who is in the opposition party might lead to harsher treatment than would otherwise be the case.

A final course that might be followed to reduce risk exposure is the purchase of insurance. A number of developed nations including the United States have governmental or quasi-governmental programs for insuring foreign investment against the risk of war, expropriation, or currency inconvertibility. There is also a private insurance market organized through the auspices of Lloyd's. In the United States, the Overseas Private Investment Corporation (OPIC) provides insurance for U.S. private investments in less developed countries, as well as project financing. Its fees vary depending on the type of coverage and, to some extent, on the risk related to the investment. OPIC has been very successful at marketing its programs and the majority of nonpetroleum investments in less developed countries have some form of OPIC coverage.

The decision to buy OPIC insurance must be made along the lines of risk management decisions in general. Firms need to weigh the costs against expected losses and their willingness and ability to bear those losses. Buying OPIC coverage might create a moral hazard situation for firms. Having protection could lead firms to ignore other risk reduction policies and contribute to a higher incidence of loss. Ultimately this would show up in higher premiums or a lessened availability of insurance. Since settlements under OPIC are usually the result of a long negotiating process, firms should avoid the attitude of "why worry, we're insured."

As a final caveat, investors should not associate political risk only with investments in less developed countries. Each of the types of risk discussed in this section are or have been present in almost every nation. Certainly, the environmental factors are omnipresent, but even in western democracies nationalization and changing attitudes toward foreign investment are prevalent. The investor might have better recourse under the law in those nations, but the interference in business operations and the loss of wealth are real possibilities that must be considered in making investment decisions.

FINANCING FOREIGN SUBSIDIARIES

Establishing an overseas subsidiary entails making a variety of operating decisions, including selection of the best financing. Financial decisions for a MNC are influenced by the same considerations as those for a purely domestic firm with some added dimensions related to its international element. This section focuses solely on the international aspect. Therefore, the discussion begins with the assumption that the desired financial structure—debt/equity mix and maturity profile on debt—have been determined. What remains to be determined is the currency of denomination for the debt. Making that decision correctly requires an analytical framework that measures the expected cost and risk of the various alternatives. Once the framework is developed, the following factors influence the financing decision:

1 Willingness of the investor to bear risk
2 Validity of interest parity and the international Fisher effect
3 Availability of forward contracts
4 Tax policies and tax rates in the relevant countries
5 Political risk in the host country

To understand the approach developed here, the simplest case is explored first. In this situation taxes and forward rates are ignored. The parent must choose between using a local currency loan or a dollar loan provided by the parent in order to finance the subsidiary's working capital requirement for one year. The parent is interested in arranging for the lowest expected dollar cost.

Option 1: Local Currency Loan

The subsidiary requires one dollar of local currency (LC). A local currency loan is available at interest rate i_L. The amount that the subsidiary needs to borrow is

$1/SPT$, where SPT is the current exchange rate or spot rate of dollars per local currency unit. At the end of a year, the subsidiary will repay

$$\frac{1}{SPT}(1 + i_L) \tag{42.9}$$

worth of local currency. That local currency will have a dollar value of:

$$\frac{1}{SPT}(1 + i_L)\, FU\hat{T}SPT \tag{42.10}$$

where $FU\hat{T}SPT$ is the currently unknown exchange rate that will exist at the time of repayment (the future spot rate). The dollar cost in Equation 42.10 can be converted to an effective dollar interest rate by subtracting 1 from it.

$$\frac{FU\hat{T}SPT}{SPT}(1 + i_L) - 1 \tag{42.11}$$

A numerical example helps to clarify the formulation. Assume the following:

$SPT = 0.02$ or LC50 = \$1

$i_L = 30\%$

The expected dollar interest cost is

$$\frac{FU\hat{T}SPT(1.30)}{0.02} - 1 = 0.65\, FU\hat{T}SPT - 1$$

The higher the future spot rate is at the time of repayment, then the higher the dollar cost; the lower the future spot rate, the lower is the expected dollar cost. That follows because the firm has an obligation to pay local currency. The exchange rate will determine the dollar cost of obtaining the currency to clear the obligation. If the future spot rate is 0.03, then the effective interest rate will be 115 percent; if it is 0.01, then the cost will be -35 percent; and if it is 0.02, then the cost will be 30 percent. Equation 42.11 can be written in a slightly different form:

$$i_L(1 - d) - d \tag{42.12}$$

where d is the expected percentage change in the exchange rate. When d is known, Equation 42.12 can be used to calculate the actual cost of foreign currency borrowing.

Option 2: Parent Company Loan

When the parent provides funds, it incurs a cost, $i_\$$, which is its effective borrowing rate. There is also an interest rate transaction between the parent and the subsidiary in which the parent has income and the subsidiary an interest expense. Although in the current example the latter two are offsetting, once taxes are introduced that might no longer be the case. Therefore, income and interest expense are included in order to arrive at the dollar cost of providing a parent loan, which is

$$
\begin{array}{ccc}
\text{Interest cost} & \text{Interest income} & + & \text{Interest cost} \\
\text{to parent} & \text{of parent} & & \text{to subsidiary} \\
i_\$ & - & i_p & + & i_p
\end{array}
\tag{42.13}
$$

The interest rate charged by the parent is i_p.

The dollar cost of the parent loan is a certain value, since it is not affected by exchange rate considerations.

To determine which funding alternative is desirable, the firm solves for a breakeven value for d, the expected percentage change in the exchange rate. Continuing the example, assume that $i_\$$ equals 10 percent.

$$
i_\$ = 0.10 = 0.30(1 - d) - d
$$
$$
d = 0.154 \text{ or } 15.4\%
$$

If the firm expects d to be less than 15.4 percent, then it should borrow dollars and use a parent loan. On the other hand, if the devaluation is expected to be greater than 15.4 percent, it should allow the subsidiary to arrange a local currency loan.

The relationship between the expected change in exchange rates and relative interest rates is the international Fisher effect. It states that interest rates should reflect expected exchange rate changes in such a way as to make borrowers and lenders indifferent between denominating loans in one currency or another.

$$
i_\$ = i_L(1 - d) - d
$$

$$
d = \frac{i_L - i_\$}{1 + i_L}
\tag{42.14}
$$

What happens to the analysis if forward rates are introduced? Nothing changes with regard to the dollar cost of the parent loan, but the uncertainty related to the local currency loan can be eliminated. Recall from Equation 42.10 that the dollar cost of the local currency option was determined by the future spot rate. If a forward market exists, the rate at which the local currency will be acquired can be locked in at the time of the loan by buying a forward contract. The effective dollar cost is then

$$
\frac{FWD}{SPT} (1 + i_L) - 1
\tag{42.15}
$$

Comparing the known dollar costs of the two alternatives, the firm is indifferent if

$$
i_\$ = \frac{FWD}{SPT} (1 + i_L) - 1
\tag{42.16}
$$

Equation 42.16 can be shown to be the interest rate parity relationship. If parity holds then there is no cost advantage between a covered local currency loan and a parent company loan. Only if there are deviations will one option be better than the other. Using the numerical example started earlier, if the forward discount is less than 15. 4 percent, the parent loan is cheaper. At a forward discount greater than 15.4 percent, the local loan is cheaper. At 15.4 percent, the interest parity rate, the two options have the same cost.

It is important to be aware that the interest parity calculation determines the best way of taking a covered position. It does not provide a guide as to whether or not to cover. That decision must be based on the expected future spot rate and the risk preferences of the decision maker.

A second important point is that the political risk element might lead a firm to choose a higher cost financing option. By borrowing in the local market the firm reduces its net country exposure. If the subsidiary is nationalized or expropriated, the local liability acts as a partial offset for the lost assets. Some firms follow a rule of financing all subsidiaries with local debt, regardless of the cost, for just that reason. Such a rule is probably not desirable. It would be better to calculate the cost differential and then determine whether the risk reduction justifies the additional expense.

Tax Factors

The introduction of taxes into the analysis makes the formulations more complicated. It becomes necessary to distinguish between the impact of an exchange gain or loss itself and its tax implications. Of the two options under consideration here, the local currency loan carries exchange risk but no related tax affect. The parent loan involves no exchange risk but has a tax element related to exchange rate fluctuations.

The general formulation for the expected cost of the local currency loan is

Interest cost $-$ Exchange adjustment

$$i_L(1 - d)(1 - T_L) - d \tag{42.17}$$

where T_L is the effective tax rate paid by the subsidiary in the host country. The tax term enters into the formulation if interest expenses are tax deductible. If T_L is assumed to be 30 percent, then the expected dollar cost is

$$0.30(1 - d)(0.7) - d = 0.21 - 1.2d$$

The cost of the parent loan is affected by the tax rate that the parent pays on domestic income, T_D; the rate it pays on foreign source income, T_F; and the host country rate. The correct formula to utilize is:

Interest cost $-$ $\dfrac{\text{Interest income}}{\text{from subsidiary}}$ $+$ $\dfrac{\text{Subsidiary's}}{\text{income expense}}$ $-$ $\dfrac{\text{Tax gain}}{\text{or loss}}$

$$i_\${(1 - T_D)} - i_P(1 - T_F) + i_P(1 - T_L) - T_L d$$

The last term arises because the local subsidiary has a dollar exposure. If exchange gains or losses are tax deductible, then the subsidiary will realize a tax reduction or increase based on the exchange rate change that takes place. From

TABLE 42.5   Effective Dollar Cost of Financing

Percentage Change in Exchange-Rate	Local Currency Loan	Parent Loan
10 %	8.9%	3 %
16.5	1.4	1.4
23	−6.8	3

the standpoint of the corporation as a whole, there is no actual exchange gain or loss because the loan is intracorporate. The company holds both the asset and liability side of the transaction. Assuming that T_D is 50 percent and T_F is 40 percent, the expected cost of the parent loan is

$$0.10(1 - 0.5) - 0.10(1 - 0.4) + 0.10(1 - 0.3) - 0.3d = 0.06 - 0.3d$$

Note that the inclusion of the tax factor makes the cost of the parent loan uncertain. It now also depends on the percentage change in exchange rates. The same breakeven analysis as was applied before is used to select the best alternative:

$$0.06 - 0.3d = 0.21 - 1.21d$$
$$0.91d = 0.15$$
$$d = 0.165$$

The firm should choose the parent company loan if the expected percentage change in exchange rates is less than 16.5 percent and the local currency loan if it is greater.

Two additional points should be made in relation to the financing decision. First, there are clearly many more options than the two presented here. A firm needs to evaluate those options within the framework developed in this section. The second point is more technical but more important and less obvious: The analysis in this section looks strictly at expected financing costs. In addition the degree of uncertainty or variance should be considered. In other words, the manager should ask how sensitive these estimates are to error. For the two options analyzed here, the local currency loan is more sensitive. Therefore it generates a wider range of outcomes than the parent company loan. Table 42.5 gives an indication of that range by calculating the effective cost under different exchange rate scenarios. Choosing the best alternative now depends on estimates of the future spot rate, variances about that estimate, and the firm's willingness to bear risk.

SUGGESTED READING

Eiteman, David K., and Arthur I. Stonehill. *Multinational Business Finance*, 3rd ed. Reading, Mass.: Addison-Wesley, 1982.

Lessard, Donald R. *International Financial Management*. Boston: Warren, Gorham & Lamont, 1979.

Levi, Maurice. *International Finance*. New York: McGraw-Hill, 1983.

Shapiro, Alan C. *Multinational Financial Management*. Boston: Allyn and Bacon, 1982.

Zenoff, David B. *Management Principles for Finance in the Multinational*. London: Euromoney, 1980.

Index

[Chapter numbers are boldface and are followed by a bullet; lightface numbers after the bullet refer to pages within the chapter.]

[Chapter numbers are boldface and are followed by a bullet; lightface numbers after the bullet refer to pages within the chapter.]

[Chapter numbers are boldface and are followed by a bullet; lightface numbers after the bullet refer to pages within the chapter.]

[Chapter numbers are boldface and are followed by a bullet; lightface numbers after the bullet refer to pages within the chapter.]

[*Chapter numbers are boldface and are followed by a bullet; lightface
numbers after the bullet refer to pages within the chapter.*]

F

[Chapter numbers are boldface and are followed by a bullet; lightface numbers after the bullet refer to pages within the chapter.]

*[Chapter numbers are boldface and are followed by a bullet; lightface
numbers after the bullet refer to pages within the chapter.]*

[Chapter numbers are boldface and are followed by a bullet; lightface numbers after the bullet refer to pages within the chapter.]

[Chapter numbers are boldface and are followed by a bullet; lightface numbers after the bullet refer to pages within the chapter.]

[Chapter numbers are boldface and are followed by a bullet; lightface numbers after the bullet refer to pages within the chapter.]

[Chapter numbers are boldface and are followed by a bullet; lightface numbers after the bullet refer to pages within the chapter.]

[Chapter numbers are boldface and are followed by a bullet; lightface numbers after the bullet refer to pages within the chapter.]

*[Chapter numbers are boldface and are followed by a bullet; lightface
numbers after the bullet refer to pages within the chapter.]*

*[Chapter numbers are boldface and are followed by a bullet; lightface
numbers after the bullet refer to pages within the chapter.]*

[Chapter numbers are boldface and are followed by a bullet; lightface numbers after the bullet refer to pages within the chapter.]

[Chapter numbers are boldface and are followed by a bullet; lightface numbers after the bullet refer to pages within the chapter.]

*[Chapter numbers are boldface and are followed by a bullet; lightface
numbers after the bullet refer to pages within the chapter.]*

*[Chapter numbers are boldface and are followed by a bullet; lightface
numbers after the bullet refer to pages within the chapter.]*